Biological Psychology

10e

James W. Kalat
North Carolina State University

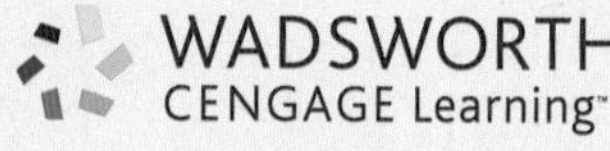

Australia • Brazil • Japan • Korea • Mexico • Singapore • Spain • United Kingdom • United States

Biological Psychology, Tenth Edition
James W. Kalat

Senior Sponsoring Editor: Jane Potter
Senior Development Editor: Renee Deljon
Senior Assistant Editor: Rebecca Rosenberg
Editorial Assistant: Nicolas Albert
Media Editor: Lauren Keyes
Executive Marketing Manager: Kim Russell
Marketing Manager: Tierra Morgan
Marketing Assistant: Molly Felz
Executive Marketing Communications Manager: Talia Wise
Senior Content Project Manager: Pat Waldo
Creative Director: Rob Hugel
Art Director: Vernon Boes
Print Buyer: Becky Cross
Image Permissions Manager: John Hill
Text Permissions Manager: Bob Kauser
Production Service: Nancy Shammas, New Leaf Publishing Services
Text Designer: Lisa Buckley
Art Editor: Lisa Torri
Photo Researcher: Martha Hall and Catherine Schnurr, Pre-PressPMG
Copy Editor: Frank Hubert
Illustrator: Precision Graphics
Cover Designer: Denise Davidson
Front Cover Image and Insets: © Argosy Publishing Inc.
Back Cover Image: © Getty Images
Compositor: Graphic World, Inc.

Library of Congress Control Number: 2008937644

Student Edition:
ISBN-13: 978-0-495-60300-9
ISBN-10: 0-495-60300-7

Wadsworth
10 Davis Drive
Belmont, CA 94002-3098
USA

Cengage Learning is a leading provider of customized learning solutions with office locations around the globe, including Singapore, the United Kingdom, Australia, Mexico, Brazil, and Japan. Locate your local office at **international.cengage.com/region.**

Cengage Learning products are represented in Canada by Nelson Education, Ltd.

For your course and learning solutions, visit **www.cengage.com.**

Purchase any of our products at your local college store or at our preferred online store **www.ichapters.com.**

Printed in Canada

2 3 4 5 6 7 12 11 10

About the Author

James W. Kalat (rhymes with ballot) is Professor of Psychology at North Carolina State University, where he teaches courses in introduction to psychology and biological psychology. Born in 1946, he received an AB degree summa cum laude from Duke University in 1968 and a PhD in psychology from the University of Pennsylvania in 1971. He is also the author of *Introduction to Psychology* (8th ed.) and coauthor with Michelle Shiota of *Emotion*. In addition to textbooks, he has written journal articles on taste-aversion learning, the teaching of psychology, and other topics. A remarried widower, he has three children, two stepchildren, and three grandchildren.

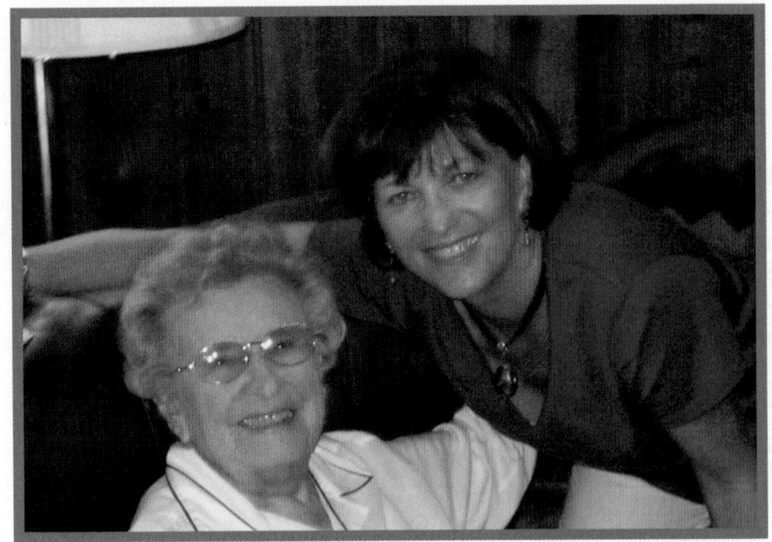

To my wife's aunt, Rochelle Pope, on the occasion of her 100th birthday.

Brief Contents

Contents

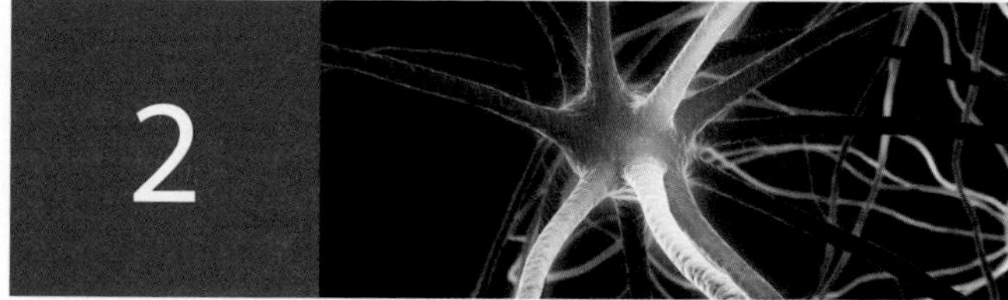

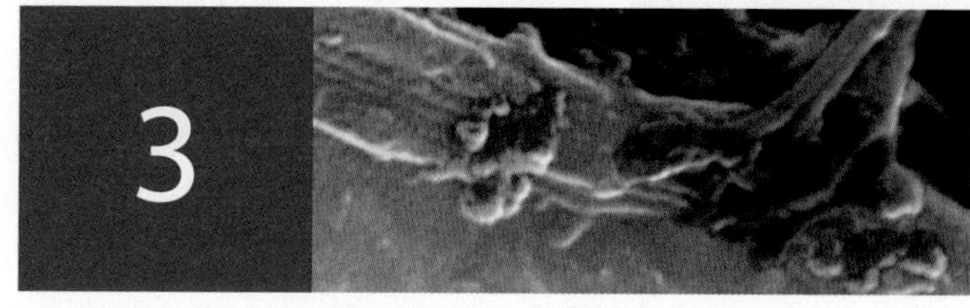

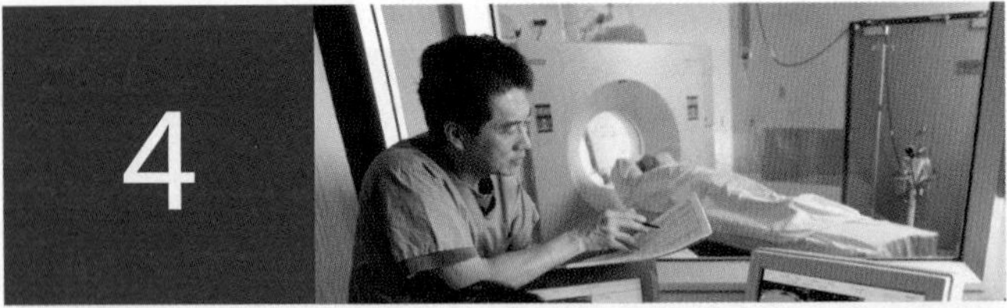

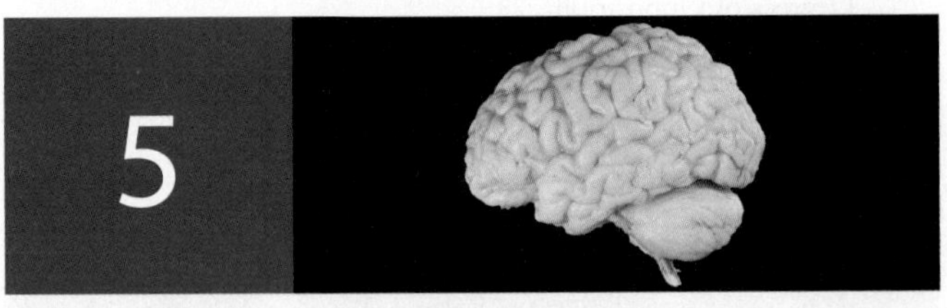

12
ATHENS 2004
1809
ATHENS 2004

13

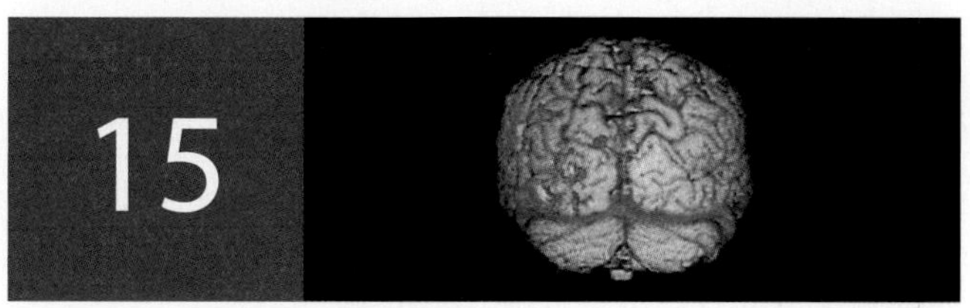

Preface

In the first edition of this text, published in 1981, I remarked, "I almost wish I could get parts of this text . . . printed in disappearing ink, programmed to fade within ten years of publication, so that I will not be embarrassed by statements that will look primitive from some future perspective." I would say the same thing today, except that I would like for the ink to fade faster. Biological psychology progresses rapidly, and many statements become out of date quickly.

The most challenging aspect of writing a text is selecting what to include and what to omit. My primary goal in writing this text through each edition has been to show the importance of neuroscience, genetics, and evolution for psychology and not just biology. I have focused on the biological mechanisms of such topics as language, learning, sexual behavior, anxiety, aggression, consciousness, attention, abnormal behavior, and the mind–body relationship. I hope that by the end of the book readers will clearly see what the study of the brain has to do with "real psychology" and that they will be interested in learning more.

Each chapter is divided into modules; each module begins with its own introduction and finishes with its own summary. This organization makes it easy for instructors to assign part of a chapter per day instead of a whole chapter per week. Modules can also be covered in a different order. Indeed, of course, whole chapters can be taken in different orders.

I assume that the reader has a basic background in psychology and biology and understands such basic terms as classical conditioning, reinforcement, vertebrate, mammal, gene, chromosome, cell, and mitochondrion. I also assume a high school chemistry course. Those with a weak background in chemistry or a fading memory of it may consult Appendix A.

Changes in This Edition

The main change is the availability of an electronic edition. For years, people have seen that electronic editions were coming, but the question has been, what shall we do with them? An electronic edition should be more than just a copy of the printed version, except on the screen. An electronic edition offers wonderful opportunities to enhance education, and we should take advantage of them. The electronic edition of this text includes animations and other demonstrations, videos, and interactive Try It Yourself activities. Many of these multimedia resources are new to this edition. In the electronic edition, the text's popular periodic Stop & Check concept review questions are in interactive, multiple-choice format. After selecting an answer, students receive feedback indicating whether their answer was right or wrong. If an answer is wrong, students are given the correct answer and, if necessary, told why one answer is right and another answer wrong. The electronic edition also offers the opportunity to directly access valuable Websites.

The 10th edition of the textbook also includes many changes in content to reflect the rapid progress in biological psychology. This text includes more than 500 new references, most of them from 2006 or later. Here are some other changes I would like to highlight:

Overall

- **New format for the end-of-module study resources.** Each module's study resources are now presented under the general heading In Closing. These new, easier-to-use sections begin with my concluding remarks, which are followed by the list of module summary points. Key Terms are now listed with page references in this section (previously they appeared at the end of chapters), immediately following the summary points and immediately before the Thought Questions that conclude each module's In Closing.
- **Many new and improved figures and photographs.** Appearing throughout the book, the new and improved figures and photos further strengthen this text's ability to help students learn visually. In addition to brand new photos and revised figures, this edition has the photos of well-known biological psychologists, and their quotes (previously on the book's last pages and the inside of its back cover), integrated in chapters so that they have greater context and visibility.
- **New location for the answers to the Stop & Check questions.** In the printed text, answers to Stop & Check questions now appear on the same page as the question (but upside down) instead of the end of each module. The new location should make it easier for students to find the answers and, therefore, make it likelier that they will try answering the Stop & Check questions.
- **All-new dynamic, more student-friendly interior design.** The new design is more colorful, dynamic, and student-friendly, and it helps readers navigate through the book more easily by setting off individual elements more clearly.

Chapter 1

- Shortened the discussion of genetics and moved most of the material on consciousness to Chapter 14.

Chapter 2

- Noted that action potentials in mammalian axons vary from one axon to another much more than researchers had previously seen in research with squid axons.
- Added a new animation that represents saltatory conduction.

Chapter 3

- Updated discussion of neuropeptides, which are released largely, perhaps mainly, by dendrites, from which they diffuse widely.
- Moved the discussion of substance abuse and addictions from Chapter 14 to Module 3.3 on Synapses, Drugs, and Addictions.
- Added three new animations that demonstrate EPSP, transmitter release, and metabotropic receptors.

Chapter 4

- Updated and revised the discussion of brain size and IQ, with a new section about differences between men's and women's brains.

Chapter 5

- Reorganized the order of topics' presentation, making a new section titled Differentiation of the Cortex, and moving the ferret experiment and other material to later in the first module.
- Updated the discussion of the formation of new neurons in the brain.

Chapter 6

- Added more emphasis on coding.
- Moved material on visual consciousness to Chapter 14.
- Updated material on suppressed visual consciousness during voluntary eye movements.
- Added a new animation demonstrating lateral inhibition.

Chapter 7

- Expanded discussion of tone deafness and absolute pitch.
- Added discussion of women tending to avoid romantic partners who smell too much like themselves, presumably as a way to reduce inbreeding.
- Integrated new research and droll photo showing ability of humans to track scent trails, if they get down on their hands and knees.
- Added new information on synesthesia, including people who experience a synesthetic taste for a word while the word itself is still "on the tip of the tongue."

Chapter 8

- Expanded discussion of the role of mirror neurons in behavior.
- Added discussion of new possibilities for treating Huntington's disease.
- Added two new animations titled Paths of Touch and Motor Control and Cells and Connections in the Cerebellum.

Chapter 9

- Added coverage of studies focused on how shifting to daylight savings time impairs performance for days.
- Added coverage of a study showing that people tend to awaken about half an hour earlier at the eastern end of Germany than at the western end, presumably because the sun rises earlier at the eastern end of the time zone.
- Clarified distinctions among sleep, coma, vegetative state, minimally conscious state, and brain death.
- Added a new animation titled Pathways Controlling Sleep and Waking.

Chapter 10

- Updated the material on obesity.
- Significantly revised section on weight loss techniques.

Chapter 11

- Added new section on the role of oxytocin in reproductive behavior.
- Revised and updated sections on intersexes and sexual orientation.
- Added discussion of new evidence about the biological influence of having an older brother on the probability of male homosexuality.

Chapter 12

- Restored the discussion of moral dilemmas that was in the eighth edition but not the ninth.
- Elaborated on Caspi's study of the interaction of genetics and environment in influencing aggressive behavior.
- Added new section on control of stress.

Chapter 13

- Added discussion of new hypothesis of how the prefrontal cortex stores temporary memory.
- Developed discussion of the importance of the hippocampus for contextual learning.
- Added a section on the importance of other areas besides the hippocampus in learning and memory.
- Added new animation representing localizing brain changes during classical conditioning.

Chapter 14

- Incorporated new sections on bilingualism and music.
- Revised discussion of dyslexia.
- Significantly revised the module on consciousness and attention, incorporating material previously in Chapters 1 and 6.
- Added two new animations that represent the capture of attention by a meaningful stimulus and "phi phenomenon."

Chapter 15

- Updated material on the genetics of depression.
- Added new section on the (low) effectiveness of antidepressant drugs.
- Significantly revised the section on genetics and schizophrenia, adding mention of a new hypothesis that many cases of schizophrenia arise from mutations in any of the hundreds of genes that control brain development.

A Comprehensive Teaching and Learning Package

***Biological Psychology,* 10th Edition,** is accompanied by an array of supplements developed to facilitate both instructors' and students' best experience inside as well as outside the classroom. All of the supplements continuing from the ninth edition have been thoroughly revised and updated; other supplements are new to this edition. Wadsworth invites you to take full advantage of the teaching and learning tools available to you and has prepared the following descriptions of each.

Instructor's Resource Manual

Prepared by John Agnew of the University of Colorado at Boulder, this manual, updated and expanded for the text's new edition, is designed to help streamline and maximize the effectiveness of your course preparation. It provides chapter outlines and learning objectives; class demonstrations and projects, including lecture tips and activities, with handouts; a list of video resources, additional suggested readings and related Websites, discussion questions designed to work both in class and on message boards for online classes; key terms from the text; suggested InfoTrac® College Edition search terms; and James Kalat's answers to the Thought Questions that conclude each module.

Test Bank for *Biological Psychology,* 10th Edition

By Ralf Greenwald of the University of Texas at Dallas. Simplify testing and assessment using this printed selection of more than 3,500 multiple choice, true/false, short answer, and essay questions, which have been thoroughly revised in this edition. All new questions are flagged as "New" to help instructors update their existing tests. This teaching resource includes separate questions for both a midterm and a comprehensive final exam.

PowerLecture with JoinIn™ and ExamView®

On CD or DVD, this one-stop class preparation tool contains ready-to-use Microsoft PowerPoint® slides, enabling you to assemble, edit, publish, and present custom lectures with ease. PowerLecture helps you bring together text-specific lecture outlines and art from Kalat's text along with videos and animations, as well as your own materials—culminating in powerful, personalized, media-enhanced presentations. The **JoinIn**™ content (for use with most "clicker" systems) available within PowerLecture delivers instant classroom assessment and active learning. Take polls and attendance, quiz, and invite students to actively participate while they learn. Featuring automatic grading, **ExamView**®, also available within PowerLecture, allows you to create, deliver, and customize tests and study guides (both print and online) in minutes. See assessments on screen exactly as they will print or display online. Build tests of up to 250 questions using up to 12 question types and enter an unlimited number of new questions or edit existing questions. PowerLecture also includes the text's Instructor's Resource Manual and Test Bank as Word documents.

WebTutor on Blackboard and WebCT

Jump-start your course with customizable, rich, text-specific content within your Course Management System. Simply load a content cartridge into your Course Management System to easily blend, add, edit, reorganize, or delete content, all of which is specific to Kalat's *Biological Psychology,* 10th edition, and includes media resources, quizzing, Web links, discussion topics, and interactive games and exercises.

CengageNOW With Cengage Learning Interactive, Media-Enhanced eBook and Infotrac College Edition

CengageNOW* is an online teaching and learning resource that gives you and your students more control in less time and delivers better outcomes—NOW. An online study system, CengageNOW gives students the option of taking a diagnostic pretest for each chapter. The system uses the results of each pretest to create personalized chapter study plans for students. The Personalized Study Plans

- help students save study time by identifying areas on which they should concentrate and gives them one-click access to corresponding pages of the interactive Cengage Learning eBook;
- provide interactive exercises and study tools to help students fully understand chapter concepts; and
- include a posttest for students to take to confirm that they are ready to move on to the next chapter.

The dynamic **interactive, media-enhanced eBook** available with CengageNOW contains numerous videos and animations and other demonstrations, as well as interactive Try It Yourself activities and Stop & Check concept reviews. The Cengage Learning eBook also includes highlighting and note-taking features, direct links to relevant Websites, and numerous hypertext navigation options, including hyperlinked key terms and glossary.

To help students get the most out of your course, along with CengageNOW's Personalized Study Plan and the Cengage Learning Interactive, Media-Enhanced eBook, students also receive access to **InfoTrac College Edition.** Ideal for selecting topics and gathering information for papers, this fully searchable database offers 20 years' worth of full-length articles (more than 20 million!) from nearly 6,000 diverse sources, such as academic journals, newsletters, and up-to-the-minute periodicals, including *The New York Times, Time, Newsweek, Science, Forbes,* and *USA Today.*

* CengageNOW may also be customized to work with your Blackboard, WebCT, or other eLearning platform.

Contact your Wadsworth sales representative for details. You may also wish to visit **www.cengage.com/tlc** for product demonstrations. To login to or to set up an instructor eResources account, go to **www.cengage.com/login.**

Study Guide for *Biological Psychology,* 10th Edition

Written by Elaine Hull of Florida State University and Juan Dominguez of the University of Texas at Austin, this guide helps students reinforce the concepts they have learned in class and in their reading. New for this edition, the Study Guide includes preprinted flashcards for all the key terms in the text, as well as coloring pages for many important illustrations. Additionally, the Study Guide contains chapter summaries; learning objectives; key terms and concepts; short answer, true/false, multiple choice, and fill-in-the-blank questions; and matching items.

eBook for *Biological Psychology,* 10th Edition

Available at **iChapters.com,** this PDF version of the book looks just like the printed text but also provides a convenient menu of links to each chapter's main headings so that students can easily navigate from section to section. Using Acrobat's search feature, students may also search for key terms or other specific information in this version of the text.

iChapters.com is the premier destination for purchasing textbooks, eBooks, and eChapters at a significant discount. There students can find new print textbooks at up to 40% off list price, sometimes costing less than a used book. iChapters also sells over 10,000 print and digital study tools, as well as online homework solutions such as CengageNOW.

Student Companion Website

http://www.cengage.com/psychology/kalat

The book's companion Website provides a wide range of study resources developed to encourage students' review of chapter material and preparation for tests, including an interactive glossary, flashcards, tutorial quizzes, updated Web links, and Try It Yourself activities, as well as a limited selection of the short videos and animated explanations of concepts available for each chapter.

These resources are available to qualified adopters, and ordering options for student supplements are flexible. Please consult your local Cengage Learning sales representative or visit us at **http://www.cengage.com** for more information, including ISBNs; to receive examination copies of any of these instructor or student resources; or for product demonstrations. Additional information is also accessible through the book's companion Website (**http://www.cengage.com/psychology/kalat**).

Acknowledgments

Let me tell you something about researchers in this field: As a rule, they are amazingly cooperative with textbook authors. Many of my colleagues sent me comments, ideas, articles, and photos. I thank especially the following:

- Allen Azizian, *University of California–Los Angeles*
- Danny Benbassat, *Ohio Northern University*
- Charles Evans, *LaGrange College*
- Jeannie Loeb, *University of North Carolina*

I have received an enormous number of letters and e-mail messages from students. Many included helpful suggestions; some managed to catch errors or inconsistencies that everyone else had overlooked. I thank especially Nathan Badera and Carol Johnson.

I appreciate the helpful comments provided by the following reviewers:

- John Agnew, *University of Colorado at Boulder*
- Susan Barron, *University of Kentucky*
- Bruce Bridgeman, *University of California–Santa Cruz*
- Nick Davenport, *University of Minnesota*
- Nakia Gordon, *University of North Carolina at Charlotte*
- Ralf Greenwald, *University of Texas at Dallas*
- Mary Ann Hooten, *Troy University*
- Skirmantas Janusonis, *University of California–Santa Barbara*
- Donald Katz, *Brandeis University*
- Mike Kisley, *University of Colorado at Colorado Springs*
- Inah Lee, *University of Iowa*
- Hoi-Chung Leung, *State University of New York–Stony Brook*
- Ben Newkirk, *Grossmont College*
- Katrina E. Nicholas, *University of Arizona*
- Claire Novosad, *Southern Connecticut State University*
- Jaime Olvarria, *University of Washington*
- Amy R. Pearce, *Arkansas State University*
- Christine M. Porter, *William and Mary*
- Amanda Price, *Elizabethtown College*
- Thomas Van Cantfort, *Fayetteville State University*
- Soni Verma, *Sierra College*
- Richard Wilmarth, *Central Alabama Community College*

In preparing this text, I have worked with three acquisitions editors, Erik Evans, Michele Sordi, and Jane Potter. My development editor, Renee Deljon, coordinated so many tasks, from the overall plan of the text to details of illustration and typeface. Nancy Shammas supervised the production, a major task for a book like this one. As art editor, Lisa Torri's considerable artistic abilities helped to compensate for my complete lack. Bob Kauser had charge of permissions, a major task for a book like this. John Hill was the photo manager and Martha Hall was the photo researcher; I hope you enjoy the new photos in this text as much as I do. Rebecca Rosenberg oversaw the development of supplements, such as the Instructor's Manual and test item file. I thank Lisa Buckley for the text design, and Do Mi Stauber for the indexes. I have been fortunate to have Frank Hubert again as my copy editor. He and I have worked through several editions together. All of these people have been splendid colleagues, and I thank them immensely.

I thank my wife, Jo Ellen, for keeping my spirits high, and my department head, Douglas Gillan, for his support and encouragement. I especially thank my son Sam for many discussions and many insightful ideas. Sam, coming from a background of biochemistry and computer science, has many original and insightful ideas about brain functioning.

I welcome correspondence from both students and faculty. Please write: James W. Kalat, Department of Psychology, Box 7650, North Carolina State University, Raleigh, NC 27695–7801, USA. E-mail: james_kalat@ncsu.edu

James W. Kalat

Renee Lynn/PhotoLibrary

The Major Issues

1

CHAPTER OUTLINE

OPPOSITE: It is tempting to try to "get inside the mind" of people and other animals, to imagine what they are thinking or feeling. In contrast, biological psychologists try to explain behavior in terms of its physiology, development, evolution, and function.

MAIN IDEAS

1. Biological explanations of behavior fall into several categories, including physiology, development, evolution, and function.
2. Nearly all current philosophers and neuroscientists reject the idea that the mind exists independently of the brain. Still, the question remains as to how and why brain activity is connected to consciousness.
3. The expression of a given gene depends on the environment and on interactions with other genes.
4. Research with nonhuman animals yields important information, but it sometimes inflicts distress or pain on the animals. Whether to proceed with a given experiment can be a difficult ethical issue.

> It is often said that Man is unique among animals. It is worth looking at this term "unique" before we discuss our subject proper. The word may in this context have two slightly different meanings. It may mean: Man is strikingly different—he is not identical with any animal. This is of course true. It is true also of all other animals: Each species, even each individual is unique in this sense. But the term is also often used in a more absolute sense: Man is so different, so "essentially different" (whatever that means) that the gap between him and animals cannot possibly be bridged—he is something altogether new. Used in this absolute sense the term is scientifically meaningless. Its use also reveals and may reinforce conceit, and it leads to complacency and defeatism because it assumes that it will be futile even to search for animal roots. It is prejudging the issue.
>
> *Niko Tinbergen (1973, p. 161)*

Biological psychologists study the "animal roots" of behavior, relating actions and experiences to genetics and physiology. In this chapter, we consider three major issues and themes: the relationship between mind and brain, the roles of nature and nurture, and the ethics of research. We also briefly consider prospects for further study.

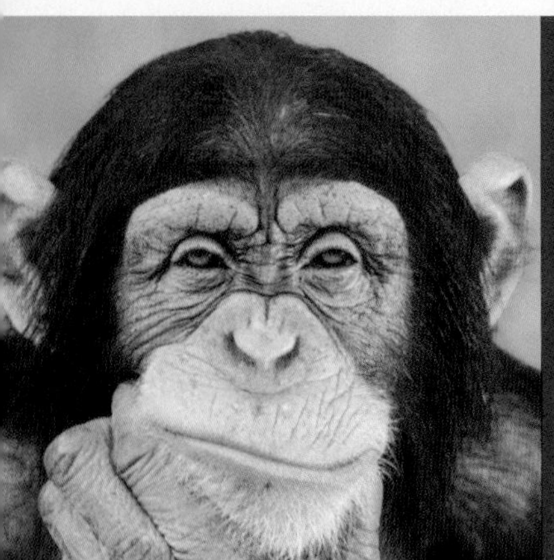

MODULE 1.1

The Mind–Brain Relationship

Biological psychology is the study of the physiological, evolutionary, and developmental mechanisms of behavior and experience. It is approximately synonymous with the terms biopsychology, psychobiology, physiological psychology, and behavioral neuroscience. The term *biological psychology* emphasizes that the goal is to relate biology to issues of psychology. *Neuroscience* includes much that is relevant to behavior but also includes more detail about anatomy and chemistry.

Biological psychology is not only a field of study. It is also a point of view. It holds that the proper way to understand behavior is in terms of how it evolved and how the functioning of the brain and other organs controls behavior. We think and act as we do because we have certain brain mechanisms, and we evolved those brain mechanisms because ancient animals with these mechanisms survived and reproduced better than animals with other mechanisms.

Much of biological psychology concerns brain functioning. Figure 1.1 offers a view of the human brain from the top (what anatomists call a *dorsal* view) and from the bottom (a *ventral* view). The labels point to a few important areas that will become more familiar as you proceed through this text. An inspection of brain areas reveals distinct subareas. At the microscopic level, we find two kinds of cells: the *neurons* (Figure 1.2) and the *glia*. Neurons, which convey messages to one another and to muscles and glands, vary enormously in size, shape, and functions. The glia, generally smaller than neurons, have many functions but do not convey information over great distances. The activities of neurons and glia *somehow* produce an enormous wealth of behavior and experience. This book is about researchers' attempts to elaborate on that word "somehow."

Biological psychology is the most interesting topic in the world. No doubt every professor or textbook author feels that way about his or her field. But the others are wrong. Biological psychology really *is* the most interesting topic.

When I make this statement to students, I get a laugh. But when I say it to biological psychologists or neuroscientists, they nod their heads in agreement, and I do mean it seriously. I do *not* mean that memorizing the names and functions of brain parts and chemicals is unusually interesting. I mean that biological psychology addresses fascinating issues that should excite anyone who is curious about nature.

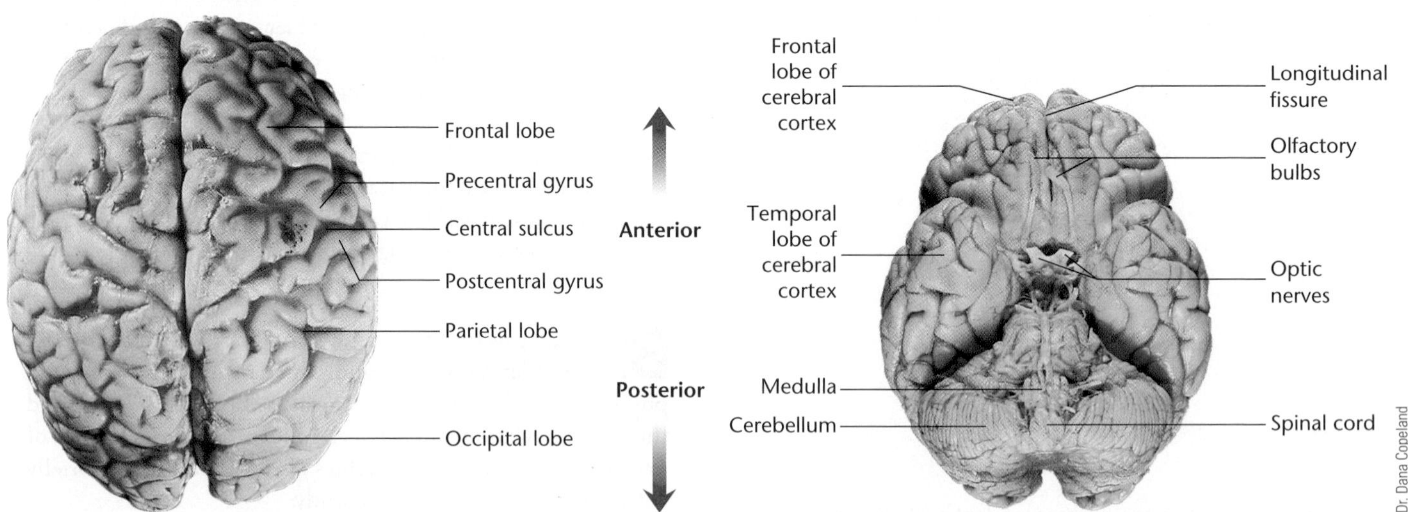

Figure 1.1 A dorsal view (from above) and a ventral view (from below) of the human brain
The brain has an enormous number of divisions and subareas; the labels point to a few of the main ones on the surface of the brain.

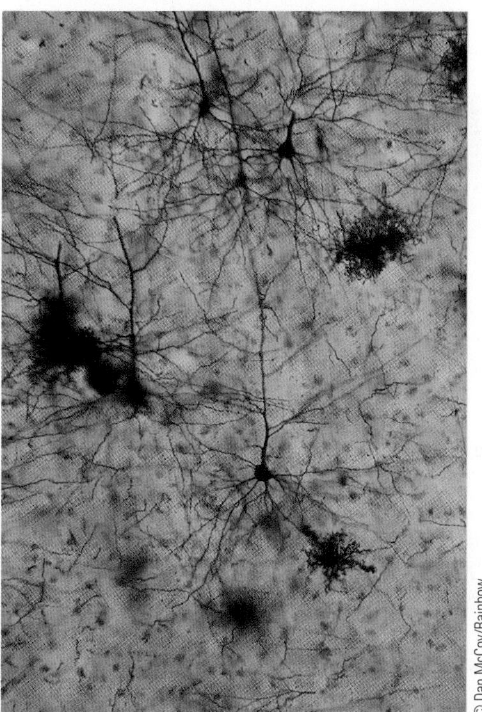
© Dan McCoy/Rainbow

Figure 1.2 Neurons, magnified
The brain is composed of individual cells called neurons and glia.

© Dorr/Premium Stock/Jupiter Images

Researchers continue to debate exactly what good yawning does. Yawning is a behavior that even people do without knowing its purpose.

Actually, I shall back off a bit and say that biological psychology is about tied with cosmology as the most interesting topic. Cosmology is the branch of physics that asks why the universe exists at all: Why is there *something* instead of *nothing*? And if there is something, why is it this particular kind of something? Biological psychologists ask: Given the existence of this universe composed of matter and energy, why is there consciousness? Is it a necessary function of the brain or an accident? Does it serve any useful function? How and why does some brain activity become conscious?

Researchers also ask more specific questions such as: What genes, prenatal environment, or other biological factors predispose people to psychological disorders? How can we promote recovery after brain damage? And what enables humans to learn language so easily?

© Steve Maslowski/Photo Researchers

Unlike other birds, doves and pigeons can drink with their heads down. (Others fill their mouths and then raise their heads.) A physiological explanation would describe these birds' unusual pattern of nerves and throat muscles. An evolutionary explanation states that all doves and pigeons share this behavioral capacity because they inherited their genes from a common ancestor.

Biological Explanations of Behavior

Common-sense explanations of behavior often refer to intentional goals such as, "He did this because he was trying to . . ." or "She did that because she wanted to . . . ." But often, we have no reason to assume intentions. A 4-month-old bird migrating south for the first time presumably does not know why. The next spring, when she lays an egg, sits on it, and defends it from predators, again she doesn't know why. Even humans don't always know the reasons for their own behaviors. Yawning and laughter are two examples. You do them, but can you explain what good they accomplish?

In contrast to common-sense explanations, biological explanations of behavior fall into four categories: physiological, ontogenetic, evolutionary, and functional (Tinbergen, 1951). A **physiological explanation** relates a behavior to the activity of the brain and other organs. It deals with the machinery of the body—for example, the chemical reactions that enable hormones to influence brain activity and the routes by which brain activity controls muscle contractions.

The term *ontogenetic* comes from Greek roots meaning the origin (or genesis) of being. An **ontogenetic explanation** describes how a structure or behavior develops, including the influences of genes, nutrition, experiences, and their interactions. For example, the ability to inhibit impulses develops gradually from infancy through the teenage years, reflecting gradual maturation of the frontal parts of the brain.

An **evolutionary explanation** reconstructs the evolutionary history of a structure or behavior. For example, frightened people get "goose bumps"—erections of the hairs, especially on their arms and shoulders. Goose bumps are useless to humans because our shoulder and arm hairs are so short. In most other mammals, however, hair erection makes a frightened animal look larger and more intimidating (Figure 1.3). An evolutionary explanation of human goose bumps is that the behavior evolved in our remote ancestors and we inherited the mechanism.

A **functional explanation** describes *why* a structure or behavior evolved as it did. Within a small, isolated population, a gene can spread by accident through a process called *genetic drift*. For example, a dominant male with many offspring spreads all his genes, including neutral and harmful ones. However, a gene that is prevalent in a large population presumably provided some advantage—at least in the past, though not necessarily today. A functional explanation identifies that advantage. For example, many species have an appearance that matches their background (Figure 1.4). A functional explanation is that camouflaged appearance makes the animal inconspicuous to predators. Some species use their behavior as part of the camouflage. For example, zone-tailed hawks, which live in Mexico and parts of the southwestern United States, fly among vultures and hold their wings in the same posture as vultures. Small mammals and birds run for cover when they see a hawk, but they learn to ignore vultures, which are no threat to a healthy animal. Because the zone-tailed hawks resemble vultures in both appearance and flight behavior, their prey disregard them, enabling the hawks to pick up easy meals (W. S. Clark, 2004).

Figure 1.3 A frightened cat with erect hairs
A functional explanation for the tendency for fear to erect the hairs is that it makes the animal look larger and more intimidating. An evolutionary explanation for human goose bumps is that we inherited the tendency from ancestors who had enough hair for the behavior to be useful.

ZITS **BY JERRY SCOTT AND JIM BORGMAN**

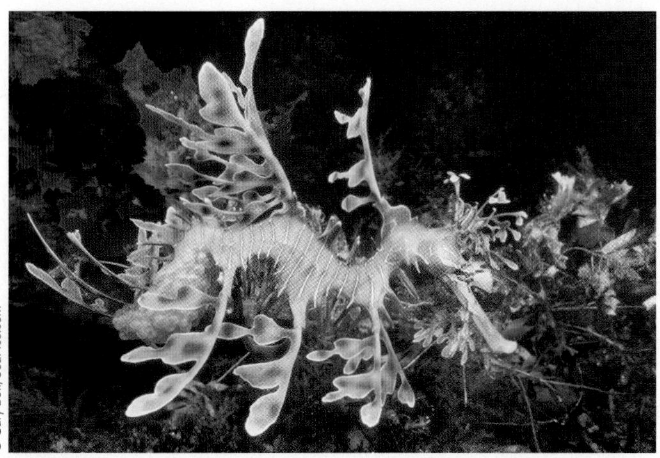

Figure 1.4 A seadragon, an Australian fish related to the seahorse, lives among kelp plants, looks like kelp, and usually drifts slowly and aimlessly, acting like kelp.
A functional explanation is that potential predators overlook a fish that resembles inedible plants. An evolutionary explanation is that genetic modifications expanded smaller appendages that were present in these fish's ancestors.

Functional explanations of human behavior are often controversial because many behaviors alleged to be part of our evolutionary heritage could have been learned instead. We examine one of these controversies in Chapter 11.

To contrast the four types of biological explanation, consider how they all apply to one example, birdsong (Catchpole & Slater, 1995):

Type of Explanation	Example From Birdsong
Physiological	A particular area of a songbird brain grows under the influence of testosterone; hence, it is larger in breeding males than in females or immature birds. That brain area enables a mature male to sing.
Ontogenetic	In many species, a young male bird learns its song by listening to adult males. Development of the song requires a certain set of genes and the opportunity to hear the appropriate song during a sensitive period early in life.
Evolutionary	Certain pairs of species have similar songs. For example, dunlins and Baird's sandpipers, two shorebird species, give their calls in distinct pulses, unlike other shorebirds. The similarity suggests that the two evolved from a single ancestor.
Functional	In most bird species, only the male sings. He sings only during the reproductive season and only in his territory. The functions of the song are to attract females and warn away other males. As a rule, a bird sings loudly enough to be heard only in the territory he can defend. In short, birds have evolved tendencies to sing in ways that improve their chances for mating.

We improve our understanding of behavior by combining these approaches whenever possible. For example, understanding the function of a behavior helps explain its evolution. Sometimes, understanding the development of a behavior sheds light on possible physiological mechanisms. Ideally, we want to understand behavior from as many aspects as possible.

STOP & CHECK

1. How does an evolutionary explanation differ from a functional explanation?

ANSWER

1. An evolutionary explanation states what evolved from what. For example, humans evolved from earlier primates and therefore have certain features that we inherited from those ancestors, even if the features are not useful to us today. A functional explanation states why something was advantageous and therefore evolutionarily selected.

The Brain and Conscious Experience

Explaining birdsong in terms of hormones, brain activity, and evolutionary selection presumably does not trouble you. But how do you feel about physical explanations applied to yourself? Suppose you say, "I became frightened because I saw a man with a gun," and a neuroscientist says, "You became frightened because of increased electrochemical activity in the central amygdala of your brain." Is one explanation right and the other wrong? Or if they are both right, what is the connection between them?

Biological explanations of behavior raise the **mind–body** or **mind–brain problem:** What is the relationship between the mind and the brain? The most widespread view among nonscientists is, no doubt, **dualism,** the belief that mind and body are different kinds of substance that exist independently. The French philosopher René Descartes defended dualism but recognized the vexing issue of how a mind that is not made of material could influence a physical brain. He proposed that mind and brain interact at a single point in space, which he suggested was the pineal gland, the smallest unpaired structure he could find in the brain (Figure 1.5).

Although we credit Descartes with the first explicit defense of dualism, he hardly originated the idea. Our experiences seem so different from the physical actions of the brain that most people take it for granted that mind and brain are different. However, nearly all current philosophers and neuroscientists reject dualism. The decisive objection is that dualism conflicts with one of the cornerstones of physics, known as the law of the conservation of matter and energy: So far as we can tell, the total amount of matter and energy in the universe has been fixed since the Big Bang that originated it all. Matter can transform into energy or energy into matter, but neither one appears out of nothing or disappears into nothing. Because matter alters its

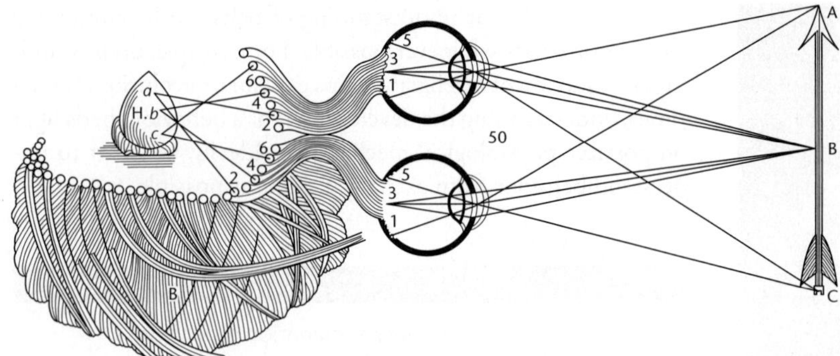

Figure 1.5 René Descartes's conception of brain and mind
Descartes understood how light from an object (the arrow) reached the retinas at the back of the eyes. The letters and numbers represent pathways that he imagined from the retinas to the pineal gland, a small unpaired organ in the brain. (His guesses about those pathways were wrong.) *(From Descartes' Treaties on Man.)*

course only when other matter or energy acts upon it, a mind that is not composed of matter or energy could not make anything happen, including muscle movements.

The alternative to dualism is **monism,** the belief that the universe consists of only one kind of substance. Various forms of monism are possible, grouped into the following categories:

- **materialism:** the view that everything that exists is material, or physical. According to one version of this view ("eliminative materialism"), mental events don't exist at all, and any folk psychology based on minds and mental activity is fundamentally mistaken. However, most of us find it difficult to believe that our minds are figments of our imagination! A more plausible version is that we will eventually find a way to explain all psychological experiences in purely physical terms.
- **mentalism:** the view that only the mind really exists and that the physical world could not exist unless some mind were aware of it. It is not easy to test this idea—go ahead and try!—but few philosophers or scientists take it seriously.
- **identity position:** the view that mental processes and certain kinds of brain processes are the same thing, described in different terms. In other words, the universe has only one kind of substance, which includes both material and mental aspects. By analogy, one could describe the *Mona Lisa* as an extraordinary painting, or one could list the exact color and brightness of each point on the painting. Although the two descriptions appear entirely different, they refer to the same object. According to the identity position, every mental experience *is* a brain activity, even though descriptions of thoughts sound so different from descriptions of brain activities.

Note how the definition of the identity position is worded. It does not say that the mind is the brain. Mind is brain *activity*. Just as fire is not a "thing," but what happens to something, mental activity is what happens in the brain.

Can we be sure that monism is correct? No. However, we adopt it as the most reasonable working hypothesis. That is, researchers see how much progress they can make on the assumption of monism. As you will find throughout this text, experiences and brain activities appear inseparable. Stimulation of any brain area provokes an experience, and any experience evokes brain activity. As far as we can tell, you cannot have mental activity without brain activity. You can still use terms like *mind* or *mental activity* if you make it clear that you regard these terms as descriptions of brain activity. However, if you lapse into using *mind* to mean a ghostlike something that is neither matter nor energy, don't underestimate the scientific and philosophical arguments that can be marshaled against you (Dennett, 1991).

(Does a belief in monism mean that we are lowering our evaluation of minds? Maybe not. Maybe we are elevating our concept of the material world.)

Even if we accept the monist position, however, we have done little more than restate the mind–brain problem. The questions remain: *Why* is consciousness a property of brain activity? Is it important or just an accident, like the noises a machine makes? *What kind* of brain activity produces consciousness? *How* does it produce consciousness? Occasional sections of this text touch on these questions, and we focus on particularly relevant research in Chapters 8 and 14.

Oh, and by the way . . . , what is consciousness, anyway? You may have noted the lack of a definition. A clear definition of consciousness is elusive. The same is true for many other terms that we feel comfortable using. For example, you know what *time* means, but can you define it?

STOP & CHECK

2. What is the main reason nearly all scientists and philosophers reject the idea of dualism?

ANSWER

2. Dualism contradicts the law of the conservation of matter and energy. According to that law, the only way to influence matter and energy, including that of your body, is to act on it with other matter and energy.

The function of consciousness is far from obvious. Several psychologists have argued that many nonhuman species are also conscious because their behavior is so complex that we cannot explain it without assuming consciousness (e.g., Griffin, 2001). Others have argued that even if other animals are conscious, their consciousness explains nothing. Consciousness may not be a useful scientific concept (Wynne, 2004).

Indeed, because we cannot observe consciousness, none of us knows for sure that other people, much less other species, are conscious. According to the position known as **solipsism** (SOL-ip-sizm, based on the Latin words *solus* and *ipse*, meaning "alone" and "self"), I alone exist, or I alone am conscious. Other people are either like robots or like the characters in a dream. (Solipsists don't form organizations because each is convinced that all other solipsists are wrong!) Although few people take solipsism seriously, it is hard to imagine evidence to refute it. The difficulty of knowing whether other people (or animals) have conscious experiences is known as the **problem of other minds.**

David Chalmers (1995) distinguished between what he calls the easy problems and the hard problem of consciousness. The easy problems pertain to such questions as the difference between wakefulness and sleep and the mechanisms that enable us to focus our attention. These issues are difficult scientifically but not philosophically. In contrast, the **hard problem** concerns why and how any kind of brain activity is associated with consciousness. As Chalmers (1995) put it, "Why doesn't all this information-processing go on 'in the dark,' free of any inner feel?" (p. 203). Why does brain activity *feel* like anything at all? Many scientists (Crick & Koch, 2004) and philosophers (Chalmers, 2004) agree that we cannot answer that question, at least at present. We don't even have a clear hypothesis to test. The best we can do is determine what brain activity is necessary or sufficient for consciousness. After we do so, maybe we will see a way to explain *why* that brain activity is associated with consciousness, or maybe we won't.

(Note the phrasing "is associated with consciousness" instead of "causes consciousness." According to the identity position, brain activity does not cause consciousness any more than consciousness causes brain activity. Each is the same as the other.)

Why are most of us not solipsists? That is, why do you—I assume—believe that other people have minds? We reason by analogy: "Other people look and act much like me, so they probably have internal experiences much like mine." How far do we extend this analogy? Chimpanzees look and act somewhat like humans. Most of us, but not all, assume that chimpanzees are conscious. If chimpanzees are conscious, how about dogs? Rats? Fish? Insects? Trees? Rocks? Where do we draw the line? A similar problem arises in human development: At what point between the fertilized egg and early childhood does someone become conscious? And how could we know?

What about computers and robots? Every year, they get more sophisticated. What if someone builds a robot that walks, talks, has intelligent conversations, laughs at jokes, describes its own fear about growing old and needing repairs, and so forth? At what point, if any, would we decide that the robot is conscious?

You might respond, "Never. A robot is just a machine that is programmed to do what it does." True, but the human brain is also a machine. (A machine is anything that converts one kind of energy into another.) We, too, are programmed—by our genes and past experiences. (We did not create ourselves.) Is consciousness a property of carbon compounds (like all known life), which would exclude silicon-based machines (Searle, 1992)? Or is it a property of any complex system organized in a particular way? Can you imagine any conceivable evidence that would persuade you that a robot is conscious? If you are curious about my answer, you'll find it at the end of this module. But think about your own answer first.

STOP & CHECK

3. What is meant by the "hard problem"?

ANSWER

3. The hard problem is why minds exist at all in a physical world. Why is there such a thing as consciousness, and how does it relate to brain activity?

Career Opportunities

If you want to consider a career related to biological psychology, you have a range of options. The relevant careers fall into two categories—research and therapy. Table 1.1 describes some of the major fields.

A research position ordinarily requires a PhD in psychology, biology, neuroscience, or other related field. People with a master's or bachelor's degree might work in a research laboratory but would not direct it. Many people with a PhD hold college or university positions, where they perform some combination of teaching and research. Other individuals have pure research positions in laboratories sponsored by the government, drug companies, or other industries.

Fields of therapy include clinical psychology, counseling psychology, school psychology, several specializations of medicine, and allied medical practice such as physical therapy. These fields range from neurologists (who deal exclusively with brain disorders) to social workers and clinical psychologists (who need to distinguish between adjustment problems and possible signs of brain disorder).

Anyone who pursues a career in research needs to stay up to date on new developments by attending conventions, consulting with colleagues, and reading research journals, such as *Journal of Neuroscience, Neurology, Behavioral Neuroscience, Brain Research, Nature Neuroscience,* and *Archives of General Psychiatry.* But what if you are entering a field on the outskirts of neuroscience, such as clinical psychology, school psychology, social work, or physical therapy? In that case, you probably don't want to wade through technical journal articles, but you do want to stay current on major developments, at least enough to converse intelligently with medical colleagues. You can find much information in the magazine *Scientific American Mind* or at Websites such as The Dana Foundation at http://www.dana.org

TABLE 1.1 Fields of Specialization

Specialization	Description
Research Fields	**Research positions ordinarily require a PhD. Researchers are employed by universities, hospitals, pharmaceutical firms, and research institutes.**
Neuroscientist	Studies the anatomy, biochemistry, or physiology of the nervous system. (This broad term includes any of the next five, as well as other specialties not listed.)
Behavioral neuroscientist (almost synonyms: psychobiologist, biopsychologist, or physiological psychologist).	Investigates how functioning of the brain and other organs influences behavior.
Cognitive neuroscientist	Uses brain research, such as scans of brain anatomy or activity, to analyze and explore people's knowledge, thinking, and problem solving.
Neuropsychologist	Conducts behavioral tests to determine the abilities and disabilities of people with various kinds of brain damage and changes in their condition over time. Most neuropsychologists have a mixture of psychological and medical training; they work in hospitals and clinics.
Psychophysiologist	Measures heart rate, breathing rate, brain waves, and other body processes and how they vary from one person to another or one situation to another.
Neurochemist	Investigates the chemical reactions in the brain.
Comparative psychologist (almost synonyms: ethologist, animal behaviorist)	Compares the behaviors of different species and tries to relate them to their habitats and ways of life.
Evolutionary psychologist (almost synonym: sociobiologist)	Relates behaviors, especially social behaviors, including those of humans, to the functions they have served and, therefore, the presumed selective pressures that caused them to evolve.
Practitioner Fields of Psychology	**In most cases, their work is not directly related to neuroscience. However, practitioners often need to understand it enough to communicate with a client's physician.**
Clinical psychologist	Requires PhD or PsyD. Employed by hospital, clinic, private practice, or college. Helps people with emotional problems.
Counseling psychologist	Requires PhD or PsyD. Employed by hospital, clinic, private practice, or college. Helps people make educational, vocational, and other decisions.
School psychologist	Requires master's degree or PhD. Most are employed by a school system. Identifies educational needs of schoolchildren, devises a plan to meet the needs, and then helps teachers implement it.
Medical Fields	**Practicing medicine requires an MD plus about 4 years of additional study and practice in a specialization. Physicians are employed by hospitals, clinics, medical schools and in private practice. Some conduct research in addition to seeing patients.**
Neurologist	Treats people with brain damage or diseases of the brain.
Neurosurgeon	Performs brain surgery.
Psychiatrist	Helps people with emotional distress or troublesome behaviors, sometimes using drugs or other medical procedures.
Allied Medical Field	**These fields ordinarily require a master's degree or more. Practitioners are employed by hospitals, clinics, private practice, and medical schools.**
Physical therapist	Provides exercise and other treatments to help people with muscle or nerve problems, pain, or anything else that impairs movement.
Occupational therapist	Helps people improve their ability to perform functions of daily life, for example, after a stroke.
Social worker	Helps people deal with personal and family problems. The activities of a clinical social worker overlap those of a clinical psychologist.

MODULE 1.1 IN CLOSING

Your Brain and Your Experience

The mind–brain issue is an exciting and challenging question, but we cannot go far with it until we discuss the elements of how the nervous system works. The goals in this module have been to preview the kinds of questions researchers hope to answer and to motivate the disciplined study you will need in the following chapters.

Biological psychologists are ambitious, hoping to explain as much as possible of psychology in terms of brain processes, genes, and the like. The guiding assumption is that the pattern of activity that occurs in your brain when you see a rabbit *is* your perception of a rabbit. The pattern that occurs when you feel fear *is* your fear. This is not to say, "your brain physiology controls you" any more than, "you control your brain." Rather, your brain *is* you! The rest of this book explores how far we can go with this guiding assumption.

SUMMARY

1. Biological psychologists try to answer four types of questions about any given behavior. Physiological: How does it relate to the physiology of the brain and other organs? Ontogenetic: How does it develop within the individual? Evolutionary: How did the capacity for the behavior evolve? Functional: Why did the capacity for this behavior evolve? (That is, what function does it serve?) 3
2. Biological explanations of behavior do not necessarily assume that the individual understands the purpose or function of the behavior. 4
3. Philosophers and scientists continue to address the mind–brain or mind–body relationship. Dualism, the view that the mind exists separately from the brain, is opposed by the principle that only matter and energy can affect other matter and energy. 5
4. Nearly all philosophers and scientists who have addressed the mind–brain problem favor some version of monism, the belief that the universe consists of only one kind of substance. 6
5. No one has found a way to answer the "hard problem" of why brain activity is related to mental experience at all. However, later chapters discuss studies of what types of brain activity are necessary for consciousness. 7

KEY TERMS

Terms are defined in the module on the page number indicated. They're also presented in alphabetical order with definitions in the book's Subject Index/Glossary. Interactive flashcards, audio reviews, and crossword puzzles are among the online resources available (www.cengage.com/psychology/kalat) to help you learn these terms and the concepts they represent.

biological psychology 2
dualism 5
evolutionary explanation 4
functional explanation 4
hard problem 7
identity position 6
materialism 6
mentalism 6
mind–body or mind–brain problem 5
monism 6
ontogenetic explanation 4
physiological explanation 4
problem of other minds 7
solipsism 7

THOUGHT QUESTIONS

Thought questions are intended to spark thought and discussion. The text does not answer them directly, although it might suggest some possibilities. In many cases, several answers are possible.

1. What would you say or do to try to convince a solipsist that you are conscious?
2. Now suppose a robot just said and did the same things you did in question 1. Will the robot convince you that it is conscious?

Continued

AUTHOR'S ANSWER ABOUT MACHINE CONSCIOUSNESS (P. 7)

(P. 7)

Here is a possibility similar to a proposal by J. R. Searle (1992): Suppose someone suffers damage to part of the visual cortex of the brain and becomes blind to part of the visual field. Engineers design artificial brain circuits to replace the damaged cells. Impulses from the eyes are routed to this device, which processes the information and sends electrical impulses to healthy portions of the brain that ordinarily get input from the damaged brain area. After this device is installed, the person remarks, "Ah! Now I can see it again! I see shapes, colors, movement—the whole thing, just as I used to!" Evidently, the machine has enabled conscious perception of vision. Then, the person suffers more brain damage, and engineers replace more of the visual cortex with artificial circuits. Once again, the person assures us that everything looks the same as before. Next, engineers install a machine to replace a damaged auditory cortex, and the person reports normal hearing. One by one, additional brain areas are damaged and replaced by machines. In each case, the behavior returns to normal and the person reports having normal experiences. Piece by piece, engineers replace the entire brain, and the person seems to be fully as before. At that point, I would say that the machine itself is conscious.

Note that all this discussion assumes that these artificial brain circuits and transplants are possible and that they could extend to all parts of the brain. That is an extremely ambitious assumption. The point is merely to show a kind of evidence that might persuade us of machine consciousness.

MODULE 1.2

The Genetics of Behavior

Everything you do depends on both your genes and your environment. Consider facial expressions. A contribution of the environment is obvious: You smile more when the world is treating you especially well and frown when things are going badly. Does heredity influence your facial expressions? Researchers examined facial expressions of people who were born blind and therefore could not have learned facial expressions by imitation. The facial expressions of the people born blind were remarkably similar to those of their sighted relatives, as shown in Figure 1.6 (Peleg et al., 2006). These results suggest a major role for genetics as well as environment in the control of facial expressions.

When we move beyond the generalization that both heredity and environment are important, controversies quickly arise. For example, do differences in human intelligence depend mostly on genetic differences, environmental influences, or both about equally? Similar disputes arise for sexual orientation, alcoholism, psychological disorders, weight gain, and so forth. This module does not address these controversies, but it should help you understand them as they arise later in this text or in other texts.

We begin with a review of elementary genetics. Readers already familiar with the concepts may skip or skim the first section.

Mendelian Genetics

Prior to the work of Gregor Mendel, a late-19th-century monk, scientists thought that inheritance was a blending process in which the properties of the sperm and the egg simply mixed, like two colors of paint.

Mendel demonstrated that inheritance occurs through **genes,** units of heredity that maintain their structural identity from one generation to another. As a rule, genes come in pairs because they are aligned along **chromosomes** (strands of genes), which also come in pairs. (As an exception to this rule, a male mammal has unpaired X and Y chromosomes with different genes.) Classically, a gene has been defined as a portion of a chromosome, which is composed of the double-stranded molecule **deoxyribonucleic acid (DNA).** As we learn more

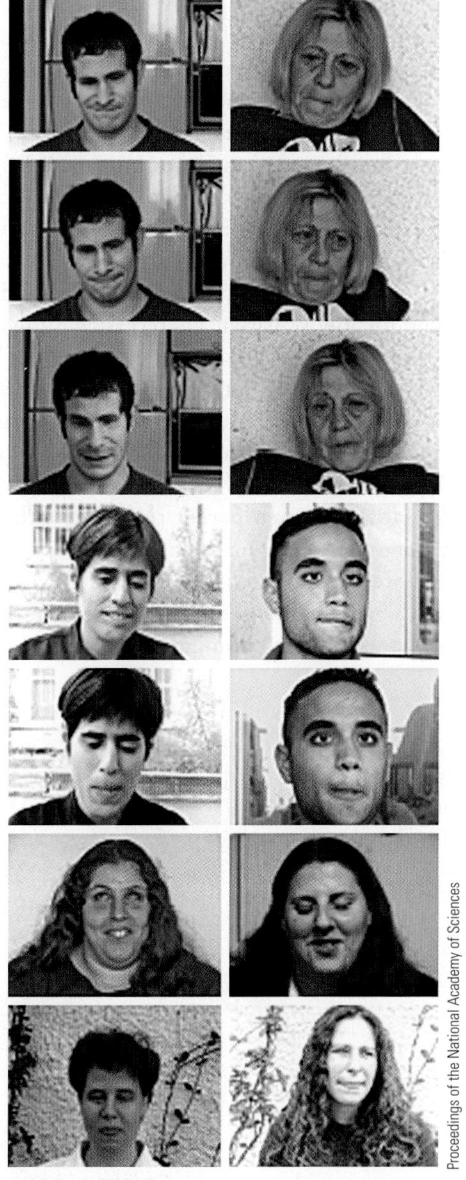

Figure 1.6 Facial expressions by people born blind (left) and their sighted relatives (right)
The marked similarities imply a genetic contribution to facial expressions.

about genetics, the concept gets fuzzier (Bird, 2007). Sometimes, several genes overlap on a stretch of chromosome. Sometimes, a genetic outcome depends on parts of two or more chromosomes. In many cases, part of a chromosome codes for no protein of its own, but it alters the expression of genes elsewhere.

A strand of DNA serves as a template (model) for the synthesis of **ribonucleic acid (RNA)** molecules. RNA is a single-strand chemical. One type of RNA molecule serves as a template for the synthesis of protein molecules. Figure 1.7 summarizes the main steps in translating information from DNA through RNA into proteins, which then determine the development of the organism. Some proteins form part of the structure of the body. Others serve as **enzymes,** biological catalysts that regulate chemical reactions in the body.

Anyone with an identical pair of genes on the two chromosomes is **homozygous** for that gene. An individual with an unmatched pair of genes is **heterozygous** for that gene. For example, you might have a gene for blue eyes on one chromosome and a gene for brown eyes on the other.

Genes are dominant, recessive, or intermediate. A **dominant** gene shows a strong effect in either the homozygous or heterozygous condition. A **recessive** gene shows its effects only in the homozygous condition. For example, the gene for ability to taste phenylthiocarbamide (PTC) is dominant, and the gene for low sensitivity is recessive. Only someone with two recessive genes has trouble tasting it (Wooding et al., 2004). Figure 1.8 illustrates the possible results of a mating between people who are both heterozygous for the PTC-tasting gene. Because each of them has one high-taste sensitivity gene—let's abbreviate it "T"—the parents can taste PTC. However, each parent transmits either a high-sensitivity gene (T) or a low-sensitivity gene (t) to a given child. Therefore, a child in this family has a 25% chance of two T genes, a 50% chance of the heterozygous Tt condition, and a 25% chance of being homozygous for the t gene.

STOP & CHECK

4. Suppose you have high sensitivity to tasting PTC. If your mother can also taste it easily, what (if anything) can you predict about your father's ability to taste it?

5. Suppose you have high sensitivity to the taste of PTC. If your mother has low sensitivity, what (if anything) can you predict about your father's taste sensitivity?

ANSWERS

4. If your mother has high sensitivity to the taste of PTC, we can make no predictions about your father. You may have inherited a high-sensitivity gene from your mother, and because the gene is dominant, you need only one copy of the gene to taste PTC. **5.** If your mother has low sensitivity, you must have inherited your high-sensitivity gene from your father, so he must have high sensitivity.

Sex-Linked and Sex-Limited Genes

The genes located on the sex chromosomes are known as **sex-linked genes.** All other chromosomes are autosomal chromosomes, and their genes are known as **autosomal genes.**

In mammals, the two sex chromosomes are designated **X** and **Y**: A female mammal has two X chromosomes; a male has an X and a Y. During reproduction, the female necessarily contributes an X chromosome, and the male contributes either an X or a Y. If he contributes an X, the offspring is female; if he contributes a Y, the offspring is male.

The Y chromosome is small. The human Y chromosome has genes for only 27 proteins, far fewer than other chromosomes. However, the Y chromosome has many sites that influence the functioning of genes on other chromosomes. As mentioned, the concept of a gene is not as simple as it once seemed. The X chromosome has genes for about 1,500 pro-

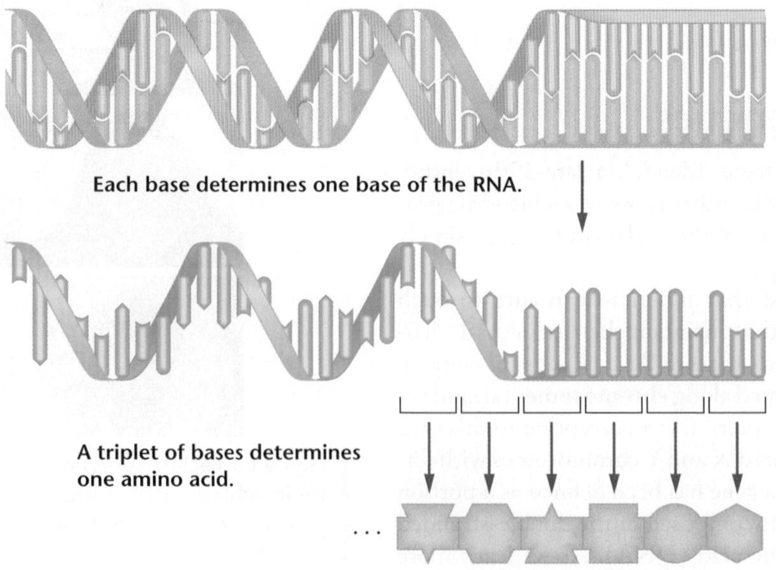
DNA
Self-replicating molecule
Each base determines one base of the RNA.
RNA
Copy of one strand of the DNA
A triplet of bases determines one amino acid.
Protein
Some proteins become part of the body's structure. Others are enzymes that control the rate of chemical reactions.

Figure 1.7 How DNA controls development of the organism
The sequence of bases along a strand of DNA determines the order of bases along a strand of RNA; RNA in turn controls the sequence of amino acids in a protein molecule.

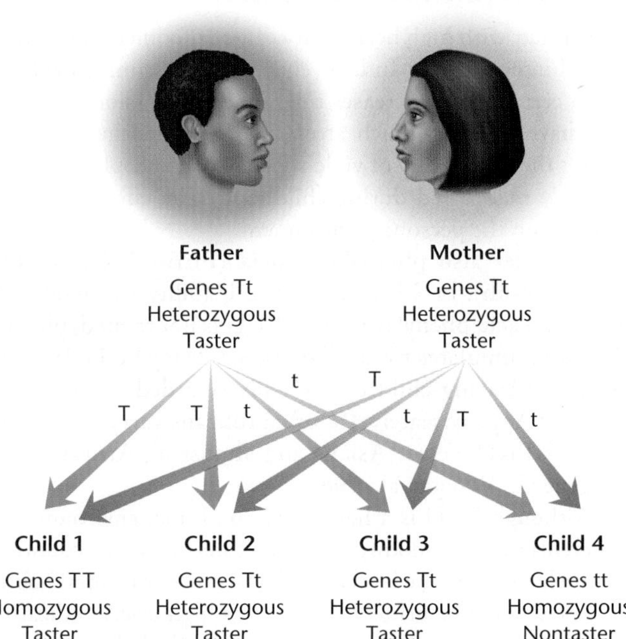

Figure 1.8 Four equally likely outcomes of a mating between parents who are heterozygous for a given gene (Tt)
A child in this family has a 25% chance of being homozygous for the dominant gene (TT), a 25% chance of being homozygous for the recessive gene (tt), and a 50% chance of being heterozygous (Tt).

teins (Arnold, 2004). Thus, when biologists speak of sex-linked genes, they usually mean X-linked genes.

An example of a human sex-linked gene is the recessive gene for red-green color vision deficiency. Any man with this gene on his X chromosome has red-green color deficiency because he has no other X chromosome. A woman is color deficient only if she has that recessive gene on both of her X chromosomes. So, for example, if 8% of human X chromosomes contain the gene for color vision deficiency, then 8% of men will be color deficient, but fewer than 1% of women will be (.08 × .08).

Distinct from sex-linked genes are the **sex-limited genes,** which are present in both sexes, generally on autosomal chromosomes, but active mainly in one sex. Examples include the genes that control the amount of chest hair in men, breast size in women, amount of crowing in roosters, and rate of egg production in hens. Both sexes have those genes, but sex hormones activate them primarily in one sex or the other.

STOP & CHECK

6. How does a sex-linked gene differ from a sex-limited gene?

ANSWER

6. A sex-linked gene is on a sex chromosome (usually the X chromosome). A sex-limited gene could be on any chromosome, but it is activated by sex hormones and therefore shows its effects only in one sex or the other.

Heredity and Environment

Unlike PTC sensitivity and color vision deficiency, most variations in behavior depend on the combined influence of many genes and environmental influences. You may occasionally hear someone ask about a behavior, "Which is more important, heredity or environment?" That question as stated is meaningless. Every behavior requires both heredity and environment. Take away either one, and nothing is possible.

However, we can rephrase the question meaningfully: Do the observed *differences* among individuals depend more on differences in heredity or differences in environment? For example, if you sing better than I do, the reason could be different genes, better training, or both.

To determine the contributions of heredity and environment, researchers rely mainly on two kinds of evidence. First, they compare **monozygotic** ("from one egg") twins and **dizygotic** ("from two eggs") twins. People usually call monozygotic twins "identical" twins, but that term is misleading, because identical twins can differ in important ways. (Some are mirror images of each other.) Still, they have the same genes. A stronger resemblance between monozygotic than dizygotic twins suggests a genetic contribution.

A second kind of evidence is studies of adopted children. Any tendency for adopted children to resemble their biological parents suggests a hereditary influence. If the variations in some characteristic depend largely on genetic differences, the characteristic has high **heritability.**

New biochemical methods make possible a third kind of evidence: In some cases, researchers have identified specific genes linked to a disorder. For example, certain genes are more common than average among people with depression. Identifying genes leads to further questions: *How much* is the gene associated with a condition? How does it produce its effect? Which environmental conditions moderate its effect? Can we find ways to undo the effects of a deleterious gene?

Researchers have found evidence for a significant heritability of almost every behavior they have tested (Bouchard & McGue, 2003). Examples include loneliness (McGuire & Clifford, 2000), neuroticism (Lake, Eaves, Maes, Heath, & Martin, 2000), television watching (Plomin, Corley, DeFries, & Fulker, 1990), and social attitudes (Posner, Baker, Heath, & Martin, 1996). About the only behavior anyone has tested that has *not* shown a significant heritability is religious affiliation—such as Jewish, Protestant, Catholic, or Buddhist (Eaves, Martin, & Heath, 1990).

Possible Complications

Humans are difficult research animals. Investigators cannot control people's heredity or environment, and even their best methods of estimating hereditary influences are subject to error (Bouchard & McGue, 2003; Rutter, Pickles, Murray, & Eaves, 2001).

For example, it is sometimes difficult to distinguish between hereditary and prenatal influences. Consider the studies showing that biological children of parents with criminal records are likely to have similar problems themselves, even if adopted by excellent parents. The parents with criminal records gave the children their genes, but they also gave them their prenatal environment. Many of the mothers had poor diets and poor medical care during pregnancy. Many of them smoked cigarettes, drank alcohol, and used other drugs that affect a fetus's brain development. Therefore, what looks like a genetic effect could reflect influences of the prenatal environment.

Another complication: Sometimes, a methyl group (CH_3) attaches to a gene and inactivates it (Tsankova, Renthal, Kumar, & Nestler, 2007). In some cases, an early experience such as malnutrition or severe stress inactivates a gene by attaching a methyl group, and then the individual passes on the inactivated gene to the next generation. Experiments have shown behavioral changes in rats based on experiences that happened to their mothers or grandmothers (Harper, 2005). Such results blur the distinction between hereditary and environmental effects.

Genes can also influence your behavior indirectly by changing your environment. For example, suppose your genes lead you to frequent temper tantrums. Other people—including your parents—react harshly, giving you still further reason to feel hostile. Dickens and Flynn (2001) call this tendency a **multiplier effect:** If genetic or prenatal influences produce even a small increase in some activity, the early tendency will change the environment in a way that magnifies that tendency, with a chain of effects like this:

Genes or prenatal influences → Increase of some tendency ⇄ Environment that facilitates

For a sports example, imagine a child born with genes promoting greater than average height, running speed, and coordination. The child shows early success at basketball, so parents and friends encourage the child to play basketball more and more. The increased practice improves skill, the skill leads to more success, and the success leads to more practice and coaching. What started as a small advantage becomes larger and larger. The same process could apply to schoolwork or any other endeavor. The outcome started with a genetic basis, but environmental reactions magnified it.

STOP & CHECK

7. Adopted children whose biological parents were alcoholics have an increased probability of becoming alcoholics themselves. One possible explanation is heredity. What is another?

ANSWER

7. If the mother drank much alcohol during pregnancy, the prenatal environment may have predisposed the child to later alcoholism.

Environmental Modification

Even a trait with high heritability can be modified by environmental interventions. In later chapters, we examine evidence that a certain gene increases the rate of depression in people who have endured much stress and that another gene increases the probability of violent behavior in people who were seriously maltreated during childhood. The effect of a gene depends on the person's environment.

Consider also **phenylketonuria** (FEE-nil-KEET-uhn-YOOR-ee-uh), or **PKU,** a genetic inability to metabolize the amino acid phenylalanine. If PKU is not treated, phenylalanine accumulates to toxic levels, impairing brain development and leaving children mentally retarded, restless, and irritable. Approximately 1% of Europeans carry a recessive gene for PKU. Fewer Asians and almost no Africans have the gene (T. Wang et al., 1989).

Although PKU is a hereditary condition, environmental interventions can modify it. Physicians in many countries routinely measure the level of phenylalanine or its metabolites in babies' blood or urine. If a baby has high levels, indicating PKU, physicians advise the parents to put the baby on a strict low-phenylalanine diet to minimize brain damage (Waisbren, Brown, de Sonneville, & Levy, 1994). Our ability to prevent PKU provides particularly strong evidence that *heritable* does not mean *unmodifiable.*

A couple of notes about PKU: The required diet is difficult. People have to avoid meats, eggs, dairy products, grains, and especially aspartame (NutraSweet), which is 50% phenylalanine. Instead, they eat an expensive formula containing all the other amino acids. Physicians long believed that children with PKU could quit the diet after a few years. Later experience has shown that high phenylalanine levels damage teenage and adult brains, too. A woman with PKU should be especially careful during pregnancy and when nursing. Even a genetically normal baby cannot handle the enormous amounts of phenylalanine that an affected mother might pass through the placenta.

STOP & CHECK

8. What example illustrates the point that even if some characteristic is highly heritable, a change in the environment can alter it?

ANSWER

8. Keeping a child with the PKU gene on a strict low-phenylalanine diet prevents the mental retardation that the gene ordinarily causes. The general point is that sometimes a highly heritable condition can be modified environmentally.

How Genes Affect Behavior

A biologist who speaks of a "gene for brown eyes" does not mean that the gene directly produces brown eyes. The gene produces a protein that makes the eyes brown, assuming normal health and nutrition. If we speak of a "gene for alcoholism," we should not imagine that the gene itself causes alcoholism. Rather, it produces a protein that under certain circumstances increases the probability of alcoholism. It is important to specify these circumstances as well as we can.

Exactly how a gene increases the probability of a given behavior is a complex issue. In later chapters, we encounter examples of genes that control brain chemicals. However, genes also affect behavior indirectly—for example, by changing the way other people treat you (Kendler, 2001). Suppose your genes make you unusually attractive. As a result, strangers smile at you and many people want to get to know you. Their reactions to your appearance may change your personality, and if so, the genes produced their behavioral effects by altering your environment!

Consequently, we should not be amazed by reports that nearly every human behavior has some heritability. A gene that affects almost anything in your body will influence your activities and the way other people respond.

The Evolution of Behavior

Evolution is a change over generations in the frequencies of various genes in a population. Note that, by this definition, evolution includes *any* change in gene frequencies, regardless of whether it helps or harms the species in the long run.

We distinguish two questions about evolution: How *did* some species evolve, and how *do* species evolve? To ask how a species did evolve is to ask what evolved from what, basing our answers on inferences from fossils and comparisons of living species. For example, biologists find that humans are more similar to chimpanzees than to other species, and they infer a common ancestor. Biologists have constructed "evolutionary trees" that show the relationships among various species (Figure 1.9). As new evidence becomes available, biologists change their opinions of how closely any two species are related.

The question of how species *do* evolve is a question of how the process works, and that process is, in its basic outlines, a logical necessity. That is, given what we know about reproduction, evolution *must* occur. The reasoning goes as follows:

- Offspring generally resemble their parents for genetic reasons.
- Mutations of genes occasionally introduce new heritable variations that help or harm an individual's chance of surviving and reproducing.
- Certain individuals successfully reproduce more than others do, thus passing on their genes to the next generation. Any gene that is consistently associated with reproductive success will become more prevalent in later generations. That is, the current generation of any species resembles the individuals that successfully reproduced in the past. You can witness and explore this principle with the interactive Try It Yourself activity "Genetic Generations."

Because plant and animal breeders have long known this principle, they choose individuals with a desired trait and make them the parents of the next generation. This process is called **artificial selection,** and over many generations, breeders have produced exceptional racehorses, hundreds of kinds of dogs, chickens that lay huge numbers of eggs, and so forth. Charles Darwin's (1859) insight was that nature also selects. If certain individuals are more successful than others in finding food, escaping enemies, attracting mates, or protecting their offspring, then their genes will become more prevalent in later generations.

Common Misunderstandings About Evolution

Let us clarify the principles of evolution by addressing a few misconceptions.

- *Does the use or disuse of some structure or behavior cause an evolutionary increase or decrease in that feature?* You may have heard people say something like, "Because we hardly ever use our little toes, they get smaller and smaller in each succeeding generation." This idea is a carryover of the biologist Jean Lamarck's theory of evolution through the inheritance of acquired characteristics, known as **Lamarckian evolution.** According to this idea, if you exercise your arm muscles, your children will be born with bigger arm muscles, and if you fail to use your little toes, your children's little toes will be smaller than yours. However, biologists have found no mechanism for Lamarckian evolution to occur and no evidence that it does. Using or failing to use some body structure does not change the genes.

  (It is possible that people's little toes might shrink in future evolution but only if people with genes for smaller little toes have an advantage over other people and manage to outreproduce them.)
- *Have humans stopped evolving?* Because modern medicine can keep almost anyone alive, and because welfare programs in prosperous countries provide the necessities of life for almost everyone, some people assert that humans are no longer subject to the principle of "survival of the fittest." Therefore, the argument goes, human evolution has slowed or stopped.

  The flaw in this argument is that the key to evolution is not survival but reproduction. If people with certain genes have more than the average number of children, their genes will spread in the population.
- *Does "evolution" mean "improvement"?* It depends on what you mean by "improvement." By definition, evolution improves the average **fitness** of the population, which is operationally defined as *the number of copies of one's genes that endure in later generations.* For example, if you have more children than average, you are evolutionarily fit, by definition, regardless of whether you are successful in any other way. You also increase your fitness by supporting your brother, sister, nieces and nephews, or anyone else

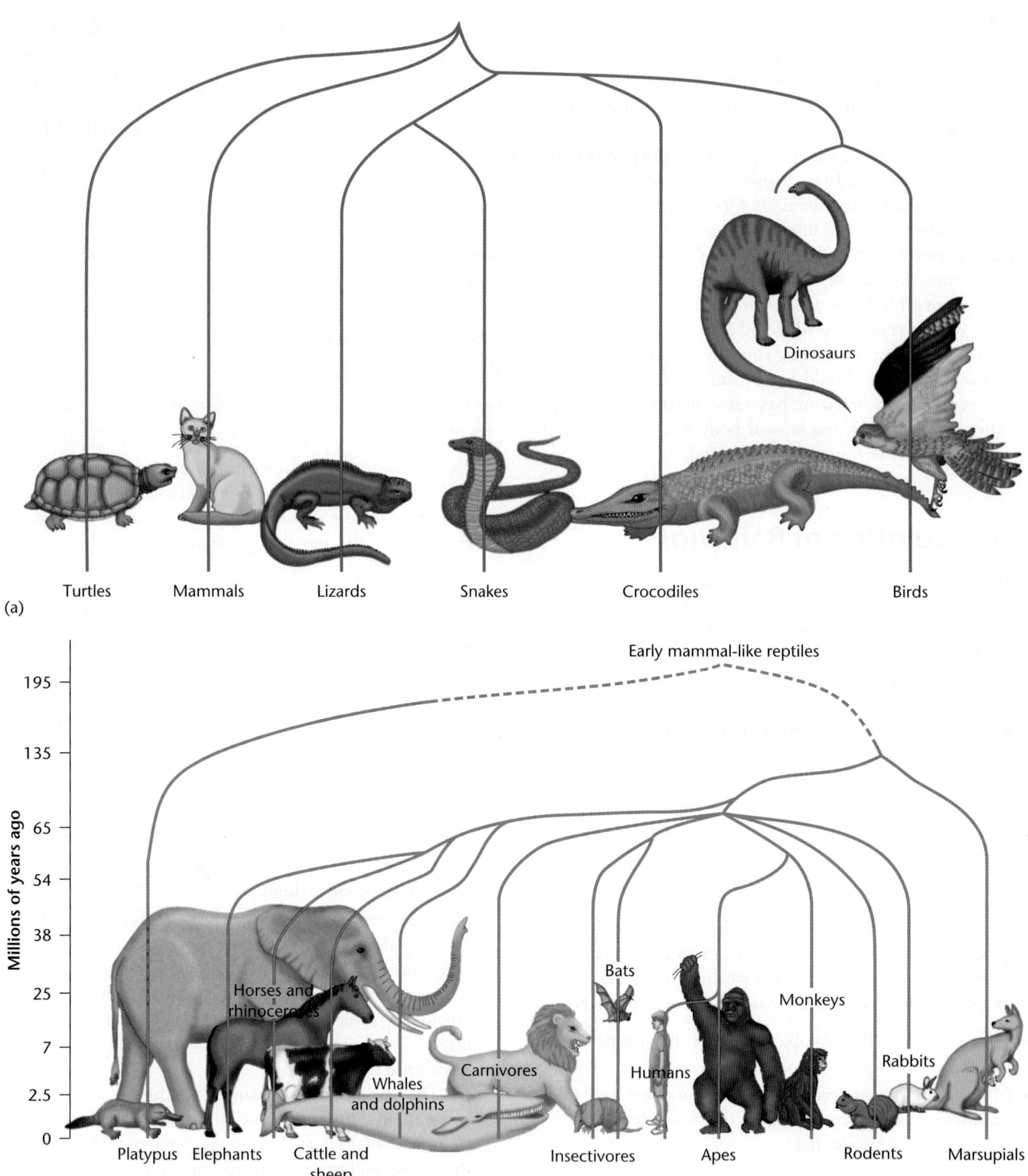

Figure 1.9 Evolutionary trees
(a) Evolutionary relationships among mammals, birds, and several kinds of reptiles. **(b)** Evolutionary relationships among various species of mammals.

who shares many of your genes. Any gene that spreads is, by definition, fit. However, genes that increase fitness at one time and place might be disadvantageous after a change in the environment. For example, the colorful tail feathers of the male peacock enable it to attract females but might become disadvantageous in the presence of a new predator that responds to bright colors. In other words, the genes of the current generation evolved because they were fit for *previous* generations. They may or may not be adaptive in the future.

Barry Lewis/Alamy Limited

It is possible to slow the rate of evolution but not just by keeping everyone alive. China has enacted a policy that attempts to limit each family to one child. Successful enforcement of this policy would certainly limit the possibility of genetic changes between generations.

© F. J. Hierschel/Okapia/Photo Researchers

Sometimes, a sexual display, such as a peacock's spread of its tail feathers, improves reproductive success and spreads the associated genes. In a changed environment, this gene could become maladaptive. For example, if an aggressive predator with good color vision enters the range of the peacock, the bird's colorful feathers could seal its doom.

- *Does evolution benefit the individual or the species?* Neither: It benefits the genes! In a sense, you don't use your genes to reproduce yourself. Rather, your genes use *you* to reproduce *themselves* (Dawkins, 1989). Imagine a gene that causes you to risk your life to protect your children. If that gene enables you to leave behind more surviving children than you would have otherwise, then that gene will increase in prevalence within your population.

STOP & CHECK

9. Many people believe the human appendix is useless. Will it become smaller and smaller with each generation?

ANSWER

9. No. Failure to use or need a structure does not make it become smaller in the next generation. The appendix will shrink only if people with a gene for a smaller appendix reproduce more successfully than other people do.

Evolutionary Psychology

Evolutionary psychology deals with how behaviors have evolved, especially social behaviors. The emphasis is on *evolutionary* and *functional* explanations, as defined earlier—that is, the presumed genes of our ancestors and why natural selection might have favored genes that promote certain behaviors. The assumption is that any behavior characteristic of a species must have arisen through natural selection and must have provided some advantage. Although exceptions to this assumption are possible, it is at least a helpful guide to research. Consider these examples:

- Some animal species have better color vision than others, and some have better peripheral vision. Presumably, species evolve the kind of vision they need for their way of life (see Chapter 7).
- Mammals and birds devote more energy to maintaining body temperature than to all other activities combined. We would not have evolved such an expensive mechanism unless it gave us major advantages (see Chapter 10).
- Bears eat all the food they can find, and small birds eat only enough to satisfy their immediate needs. Eating habits presumably relate to different needs by different species (see Chapter 11).

On the other hand, some characteristics of a species have a more debatable relationship to natural selection. Consider two examples:

- People grow old and die, with an average survival time of about 70 to 80 years under favorable circumstances. Do we deteriorate because of genes that cause us to get out of the way and stop competing with our children and grandchildren?
- More men than women enjoy the prospect of casual sex with multiple partners. Theorists have related this tendency to the fact that a man can spread his genes by impregnating many women, whereas a woman cannot multiply her children by having more sexual partners (Buss, 1994). Are men and women prewired to have different sexual behaviors? As we explore in Chapter 11, the answer is debatable.

To further illustrate evolutionary psychology, let's consider the theoretically interesting example of **altruistic behavior,** an action that benefits someone other than the actor. A gene that encourages altruistic behavior would help *other* individuals survive and spread their genes. How could a gene for altruism spread, if at all?

Let's begin with the question of how common altruism is. It certainly occurs in humans: We contribute to charities. We try to help people in distress. A student may explain something to a classmate who is competing for a good grade in a course. Among nonhumans, parents devote much effort and risk their lives to protect their young, but altruism toward nonrelatives is rare in most species. In one study, a chimpanzee could pull one rope to bring food into its own cage or a second rope that would bring food to itself and additional food to a familiar but unrelated chimpanzee in a neighboring cage. Most often, chimps pulled whichever rope happened to be on the right at the time, regardless of whether it brought food to only itself or to both chimpanzees. None of the tested chimps showed any preference for helping the other chimpanzee, even when the other made begging gestures (Silk et al., 2005).

Even when animals do appear altruistic, they often have a selfish motive. For example, when a crow finds food on the ground, it caws loudly, attracting other crows that will share the food. Altruism? Not really. A bird on the ground is vulnerable to attack by cats and other enemies. Having other crows around means more eyes to watch for danger.

Similarly, consider meerkats (a kind of mongoose). Periodically, one or another member of a meerkat colony stands and, if it sees danger, emits an alarm call that warns the others (Figure 1.10). Its alarm call helps the others (including its relatives), but the one who sees the danger first and emits the alarm call is the one most likely to escape (Clutton-Brock et al., 1999).

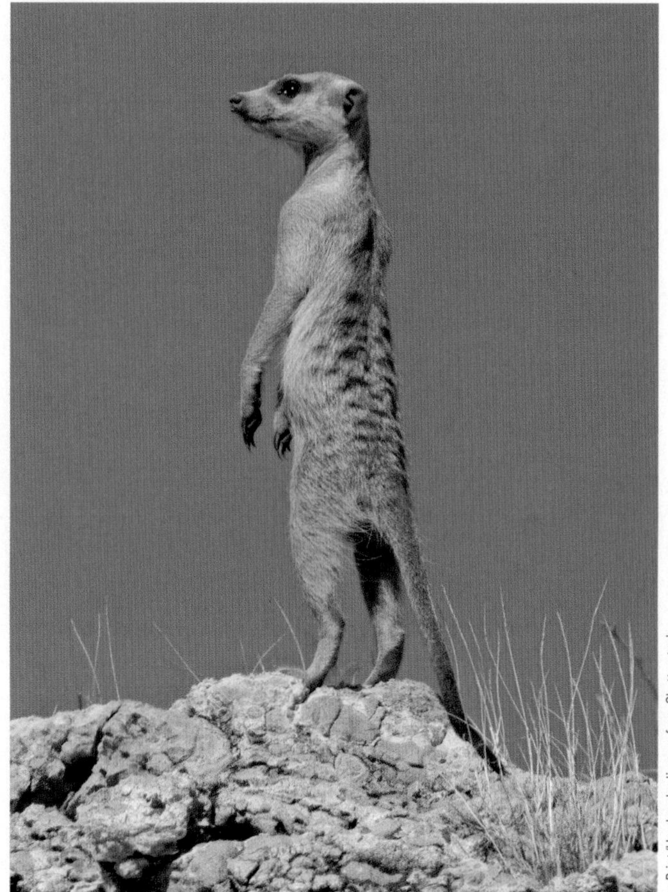

Figure 1.10 Sentinel behavior: altruistic or not?
As in many other prey species, meerkats sometimes show sentinel behavior in watching for danger and warning the others. However, the meerkat that emits the alarm is the one most likely to escape the danger.

For the sake of illustration, let's suppose—without evidence—that some gene increases altruistic behavior. Could it spread within a population? One common reply is that most altruistic behaviors cost very little. True, but being almost harmless is not good enough. A gene spreads only if the individuals with it reproduce more than those without it. Another common reply is that the altruistic behavior benefits the species. True again, but the rebuttal is the same. A gene that benefits the species but fails to help the individual dies out with that individual.

A more controversial hypothesis is *group selection*. According to this idea, altruistic groups survive better than less cooperative ones (Bowles, 2006). However, imagine that a cooperative group includes an individual with a mutated gene that leads to competitive, "cheating" behavior. If the uncooperative individual survives and reproduces more than others within this group, the uncooperative gene will spread. Group selection might work if the group has a way to punish or expel an uncooperative member.

A better explanation is **reciprocal altruism,** the idea that individuals help those who will return the favor. Researchers find that people are prone to help not only those who helped them but also people whom they observed helping someone else (Nowak & Sigmund, 2005). It's not just "you scratch my back, so I'll scratch yours," but "you scratched someone else's back, so I'll scratch yours." By helping others, you build a reputation for helpfulness, and others are willing to cooperate with you. However, this system works only if individuals recognize one another. Otherwise, it is easy for an uncooperative individual to accept favors, prosper, and never repay the favors. In other words, reciprocal altruism requires good sensory organs and excellent memory, especially excellent memory for faces or some other way of identifying individuals. Perhaps we now see why altruism is more common in humans than in most other species.

Another explanation is **kin selection,** selection for a gene that benefits the individual's relatives. A gene could spread if it caused you to risk your life to protect your children, who share many of your genes, including perhaps a gene for altruism. Natural selection can also favor altruism toward other relatives—such as cousins, nephews, or nieces—if the benefit to them outweighs the cost to you (Dawkins, 1989;

Hamilton, 1964; Trivers, 1985). In both humans and nonhumans, cooperative or altruistic behavior is more common toward relatives than toward unrelated individuals (Bowles & Posel, 2005; Krakauer, 2005).

At its best, evolutionary psychology leads to research that helps us understand a behavior. The search for a functional explanation directs researchers to explore species' different habitats and ways of life until we understand why they behave differently. However, this approach is criticized when its practitioners propose explanations without testing them (Schlinger, 1996).

STOP & CHECK

10. What are two plausible ways for possible altruistic genes to spread in a population?

ANSWER

10. Altruistic genes could spread because they facilitate care for one's kin or because they facilitate exchanges of favors with others (reciprocal altruism). Group selection may also work under some circumstances, especially if the cooperative group has some way to punish or expel an uncooperative individual.

MODULE 1.2 IN CLOSING

Genes and Behavior

In the control of behavior, genes are neither all important nor irrelevant. Certain behaviors have a high heritability, such as the ability to taste PTC. Many other behaviors are influenced by genes but also subject to strong influence by experience. Our genes and our evolution make it possible for humans to be what we are today, but they also give us the flexibility to change our behavior as circumstances warrant.

Understanding the genetics of human behavior is particularly important but also particularly difficult. Separating the roles of heredity and environment is always difficult, but especially so with humans, because researchers have such limited control over environmental influences. Inferring human evolution is also difficult, partly because we do not know enough about the lives of our ancient ancestors. Finally, we should remember that the way things *are* is not necessarily the same as the way they *should be*. For example, even if our genes predispose us to behave in a particular way, we can still decide to try to overcome those predispositions if they do not suit the needs of modern life.

SUMMARY

1. Genes are chemicals that maintain their integrity from one generation to the next and influence the development of the individual. A dominant gene affects development regardless of whether a person has pairs of that gene or only a single copy per cell. A recessive gene affects development only in the absence of the dominant gene. **11**
2. Most behavioral variations reflect the combined influences of many genes and many environmental factors. Heritability is an estimate of the amount of variation that is due to genetic variation as opposed to environmental variation. **13**
3. Researchers estimate heritability of a human condition by comparing monozygotic and dizygotic twins and by comparing adopted children to their biological and adoptive parents. In some cases, they identify specific genes that are more common in people with one type of behavior than another. **13**
4. The results sometimes overestimate human heritability. Most adoption studies do not distinguish between the effects of genes and those of prenatal environment. Also, after genes produce an early increase in some behavioral tendency, that behavior may lead to a change in the environment that magnifies the tendency. **13**
5. Even if some behavior shows high heritability for a given population, a change in the environment might significantly alter the behavioral outcome. **14**
6. Genes influence behavior directly by altering brain chemicals and indirectly by affecting other aspects of the body and therefore the way other people react to us. **15**
7. The process of evolution through natural selection is a logical necessity: Mutations sometimes occur in genes, and individuals with certain sets of genes reproduce more successfully than others do. **15**
8. Evolution spreads the genes of the individuals who have reproduced the most. Therefore, if some characteristic is widespread within a population, it is reasonable to look for ways in which that characteristic is or has been adaptive. However, we cannot take it for granted that all common behaviors are the product of our genes. We need to distinguish genetic influences from learning. **17**

Continued

KEY TERMS

Terms are defined in the module on the page number indicated. They're also presented in alphabetical order with definitions in the book's Subject Index/Glossary. Interactive flashcards, audio reviews, and crossword puzzles are among the online resources available to help you learn these terms and the concepts they represent.

altruistic behavior **18**
artificial selection **15**
autosomal genes **12**
chromosomes **11**
deoxyribonucleic acid (DNA) **11**
dizygotic **13**
dominant **12**
enzymes **12**
evolution **15**
evolutionary psychology **17**
fitness **15**
genes **11**
heritability **13**
heterozygous **12**
homozygous **12**
kin selection **18**
Lamarckian evolution **15**
monozygotic **13**
multiplier effect **14**
phenylketonuria (PKU) **14**
recessive **12**
reciprocal altruism **18**
ribonucleic acid (RNA) **12**
sex-limited genes **13**
sex-linked genes **12**
X chromosome **12**
Y chromosome **12**

THOUGHT QUESTIONS

1. For what human behaviors, if any, are you sure that heritability would be extremely low?
2. Genetic differences probably account for part of the difference between people who age slowly and gracefully and others who grow old more rapidly and die younger. Given that the genes controlling old age have their onset long after people have stopped having children, how could evolution have any effect on such genes?

MODULE 1.3

The Use of Animals in Research

Certain ethical disputes resist agreement. One is abortion. Another is the use of animals in research. In both cases, well-meaning people on each side of the issue insist that their position is proper and ethical. The dispute is not a matter of the good guys against the bad guys. It is between two views of what is good.

The animal welfare controversy is critical for biological psychology. As the knowledge and findings presented throughout this book show, research done on laboratory animals is responsible for a great deal of what we know about the brain and behavior. That research ranges from mere observation or painless experiments to studies in which it is clear that no animal would volunteer, if it had a choice. How shall we deal with the fact that, on the one hand, we want more knowledge, and on the other hand, we wish to minimize animal distress?

Reasons for Animal Research

Given that most biological psychologists and neuroscientists are primarily interested in the human brain and human behavior, why do they study nonhuman animals? Here are four reasons.

1. *The underlying mechanisms of behavior are similar across species and sometimes easier to study in a nonhuman species.* If you wanted to understand a complex machine, you might begin by examining a simpler machine. We also learn about brain–behavior relationships by starting with simpler cases. The brains and behavior of nonhuman vertebrates resemble those of humans in their chemistry and anatomy (Figure 1.11). Even invertebrate nerves follow the same basic principles as our own. Much research has been conducted on squid nerves, which are thicker than human nerves and therefore easier to study.
2. *We are interested in animals for their own sake.* Humans are naturally curious. We would love to know about life, if any, elsewhere in the universe, and we devote considerable money and effort to that search. Similarly, we would like to understand how bats chase insects in the dark, how migratory birds find their way over unfamiliar territory, and how schools of fish manage to swim in such unison.
3. *What we learn about animals sheds light on human evolution.* How did we come to be the way we are? What makes us different from chimpanzees and other primates? Why did primates evolve larger brains than other species? We approach such questions by studying other species.
4. *Certain experiments cannot use humans because of legal or ethical restrictions.* For example, investigators insert

Animals are used in many kinds of research studies, some dealing with behavior and others with the functions of the nervous system.

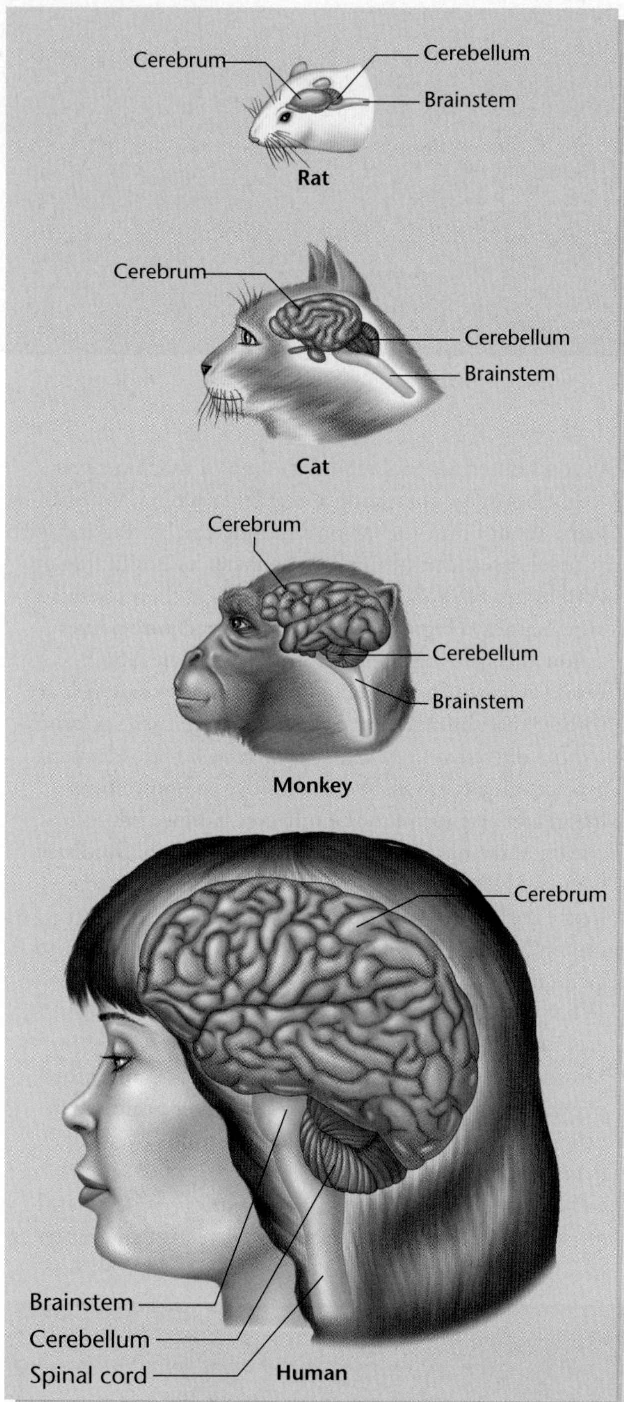

Figure 1.11 Brains of several species
The general plan and organization of the brain are similar for all mammals, even though the size varies from species to species.

electrodes into the brain cells of rats and other animals to determine the relationship between brain activity and behavior. Such experiments answer questions that investigators cannot address in any other way, including some that are critical for medical progress. They also raise an ethical issue: If the research is unacceptable with humans, shouldn't we also object to it with nonhumans?

STOP & CHECK

11. Describe reasons biological psychologists conduct much of their research on nonhuman animals.

ANSWER

11. Sometimes, the mechanisms of behavior are easier to study in a nonhuman species. We are curious about animals for their own sake. We study animals to understand human evolution. Certain procedures that might lead to important knowledge are illegal or unethical with humans.

The Ethical Debate

In some cases, researchers simply observe animals in nature as a function of different times of day, different seasons of the year, changes in diet, and so forth. These procedures do not even inconvenience the animals and raise no ethical problems. In other experiments, however, including many discussed in this book, animals have been subjected to brain damage, electrode implantation, injections of drugs or hormones, and so forth. Many people regard such experimentation as cruelty to animals and have reacted with tactics ranging from peaceful demonstrations to life-threatening violence. Examples include bombing a laboratory, placing a bomb under a professor's car, placing a bomb on a porch (intended for a researcher but accidentally placed on the neighbor's porch), banging on a researcher's children's windows at night, and inserting a garden hose through a window to flood the house (G. Miller, 2007a). Michael Conn and James Parker (2008, p. 186) quote a spokesperson for the Animal Defense League as follows: "I don't think you'd have to kill—assassinate—too many [doctors involved with animal testing] . . . I think for 5 lives, 10 lives, 15 human lives, we could save a million, 2 million, 10 million non-human lives."

On the one hand, many laboratory animals do undergo painful or debilitating procedures that are admittedly not for their own benefit. Anyone with a conscience (including scientists) is bothered by this fact. On the other hand, experimentation with animals has been critical to the medical research that led to methods for the prevention or treatment of polio, diabetes, measles, smallpox, massive burns, heart disease, and other serious conditions. Most Nobel prizes in physiology or medicine have been awarded for research conducted on nonhuman animals. The hope of finding methods to treat or prevent AIDS and various brain diseases (e.g., Alzheimer's disease) depends largely on animal research. Many kinds of research in biological psychology could not progress at all without animals, and many others would progress very slowly.

Degrees of Opposition

Opposition to animal research ranges considerably in degree. "Minimalists" tolerate animal research under certain conditions. They accept some kinds of research but wish to prohibit others depending on the probable value of the research, the amount of distress to the animal, and the type of animal. (Few people have serious qualms about hurting an insect, for example.) They favor firm regulations on research.

The "abolitionists" take a more extreme position and see no room for compromise. Abolitionists maintain that all animals have the same rights as humans. They regard killing an animal as murder, whether the intention is to eat it, use its fur, or gain scientific knowledge. Keeping an animal (presumably even a pet) in a cage is, in their view, slavery. Because animals cannot give informed consent to research, abolitionists insist it is wrong to use them in any way, regardless of the circumstances. According to one opponent of animal research, "We have no moral option but to bring this research to a halt. Completely. . . . We will not be satisfied until every cage is empty" (Regan, 1986, pp. 39–40). Advocates of this position sometimes claim that most animal research is painful and that it never leads to important results. However, for a true abolitionist, neither of those points really matters. Their moral imperative is that people have no right to use animals, even if the research is useful and even if it is painless.

The disagreement between abolitionists and animal researchers is a dispute between two ethical positions: "Never knowingly harm an innocent" and "Sometimes a little harm leads to a greater good." On the one hand, permitting research has the undeniable consequence of inflicting pain or distress. On the other hand, banning the use of animals for human purposes means a great setback in medical research as well as the end of animal-to-human transplants (e.g., using pig heart valves to help people with heart diseases) (Figure 1.12).

The often fervent and extreme nature of the argument makes it difficult for researchers to express intermediate or nuanced views, at least in public. Many frankly admit that not all research is worthwhile. Many remark that they really do care about animals, despite using them for research. Some neuroscientists are even vegetarians (Marris, 2006).

Practically everyone draws a line somewhere and says, "I will not do this experiment. The knowledge I might gain is not worth that much distress to the animals." To be sure, different researchers draw that line at different places.

Possible Compromise

Researchers believe strongly that at least some animal research is justified because of its potential to answer important questions. They nevertheless agree that they should use fewer animals and do as much as they can to minimize pain whenever possible. They also favor research to improve animal welfare (van Zutphen, 2001).

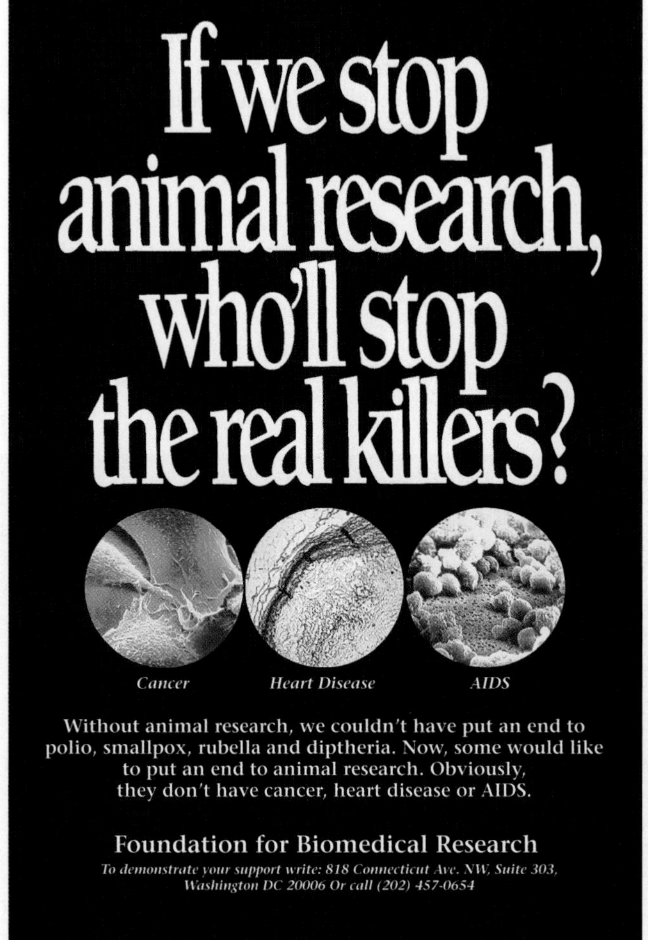

Figure 1.12 In defense of animal research
For many years, opponents of animal research have been protesting against experimentation with animals. This ad represents a reply by supporters of such research. *(Source: Courtesy of the Foundation for Biomedical Research)*

The legal standard emphasizes "the three Rs": *reduction* of animal numbers (using fewer animals), *replacement* (using computer models or other substitutes for animals, when possible), and *refinement* (modifying the procedures to reduce pain and discomfort). In the United States, every college or other institution that receives government research funds is required to have an Institutional Animal Care and Use Committee, composed of veterinarians, community representatives, and scientists, that evaluates proposed experiments, decides whether they are acceptable, and specifies procedures designed to minimize pain and discomfort. Similar regulations and committees govern research on human subjects. In addition, all research laboratories must abide by national laws requiring standards of cleanliness and animal care. Similar laws apply in other countries, and scientific journals require researchers to state that they followed all the laws and regulations in their research. Professional organizations such as the Society for Neuroscience publish guidelines for the use of animals in research (see Appendix B). The following Website by the National Institutes of Health's Office of Animal Care and Use describes U.S. regulations and advice on animal care: http://oacu.od.nih.gov/index.htm

STOP & CHECK

12. How does the "minimalist" position differ from the "abolitionist" position?

ANSWER

12. A "minimalist" wishes to limit animal research to studies with little discomfort and much potential value. An "abolitionist" wishes to eliminate all animal research regardless of how the animals are treated or how much value the research might produce.

MODULE 1.3 IN CLOSING

Humans and Animals

We began this chapter with a quote from the Nobel prize–winning biologist Niko Tinbergen, who argued that no fundamental gulf separates humans from other animal species. Because we are similar in many ways to other species, we learn much about ourselves from animal studies. Also because of that similarity, we identify with animals and we wish not to hurt them. Neuroscience researchers who decide to conduct animal research do not, as a rule, take this decision lightly. They want to minimize harm to animals, but they also want to increase knowledge. They believe it is better to inflict limited distress under controlled conditions than to permit ignorance and disease to inflict much greater distress. In some cases, however, it is a difficult decision.

SUMMARY

1. Researchers study animals because the mechanisms are sometimes easier to study in nonhumans, because they are interested in animal behavior for its own sake, because they want to understand the evolution of behavior, and because certain kinds of experiments are difficult or impossible with humans. **21**
2. The ethics of using animals in research is controversial. Some research does inflict stress or pain on animals; however, many research questions can be investigated only through animal research. **22**
3. Animal research today is conducted under legal and ethical controls that attempt to minimize animal distress. **23**

CHAPTER 1 Exploration and Study

In addition to the study materials provided at the end of each module, you may supplement your review of this chapter by using one or more of the book's electronic resources, which include its companion Website, interactive Cengage Learning eBook, Exploring Biological Psychology CD-ROM, and CengageNOW. Brief descriptions of these resources follow. For more information, visit **www.cengage.com/psychology/kalat.**

The book's companion Website, accessible through the author Web page indicated above, provides a wide range of study resources such as an interactive glossary, flashcards, tutorial quizzes, updated Web links, and Try It Yourself activities, as well as a limited selection of the short videos and animated explanations of concepts available for this chapter.

Exploring Biological Psychology

The Exploring Biological Psychology CD-ROM contains videos, animations, and Try-It-Yourself activities. These activities—as well as many that are new to this edition—are also available in the text's fully interactive, media-rich Cengage Learning eBook,* which gives you the opportunity to experience biological psychology in an even greater interactive and multimedia environment. The Cengage Learning eBook also includes highlighting and note-taking features and an audio glossary. For this chapter, the Cengage Learning eBook includes the following interactive explorations:

RNA, DNA, and Proteins
Genetic Generations
Evolutionary Studies
Offspring of Parents Homozygous and Heterozygous for Brown Eyes

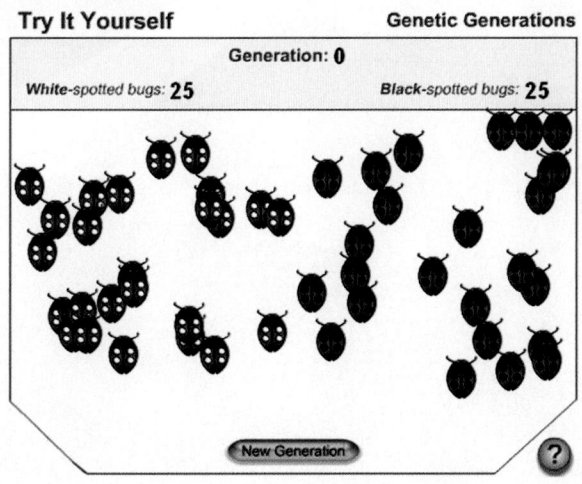

Try It Yourself **Genetic Generations**

Generation: 0
White-spotted bugs: 25
Black-spotted bugs: 25
New Generation
?

Genetic Generations is a Try It Yourself activity that demonstrates how reproductive success alters the prevalence of genes in later generations.

* Requires a Cengage Learning eResources account. Visit **www.cengage.com/login** to register or login.

CENGAGENOW™ is an easy-to-use resource that helps you study in less time to get the grade you want. An online study system, CengageNOW* gives you the option of taking a diagnostic pretest for each chapter. The system uses the results of each pretest to create personalized chapter study plans for you. The Personalized Study Plans

- help you save study time by identifying areas on which you should concentrate and give you one-click access to corresponding pages of the interactive Cengage Learning eBook;
- provide interactive exercises and study tools to help you fully understand chapter concepts; and
- include a posttest for you to take to confirm that you are ready to move on to the next chapter.

Suggestions for Further Exploration

The book's companion Website includes a list of suggested articles available through InfoTrac College Edition for this chapter. You may also want to explore some of the following books and Websites. The text's companion Website provides live, updated links to the sites listed below.

Books

Koch, C. (2004). *The quest for consciousness.* Englewood, CO: Roberts. A scientist's attempt to make sense of the mind–brain relationship.

Sunstein, C. R., & Nussbaum, M. C. (Eds.). (2004). *Animal rights: Current debates and new directions.* New York: Oxford University Press. A series of essays arguing both sides of the debate about animal rights and welfare.

Websites

National Society for Phenylketonuria Home Page
http://www.nspku.org

European Science Foundation: Statement on Use of Animals in Research
http://www.esf.org/ftp/pdf/SciencePolicy/ESPB9.pdf

U.S. government statement on animal care and use
http://oacu.od.nih.gov/index.htm

Timeline of Animal Research Progress
http://www.fbresearch.org/Education/Timeline/Timeline.htm

Dana Foundation for brain information**
http://www.dana.org

Biomedical terms**
http://medical.webends.com

University of Illinois at Chicago: Founders of Neurology**
http://www.uic.edu/depts/mcne/founders

** Sites that you may find helpful at many points throughout the text.

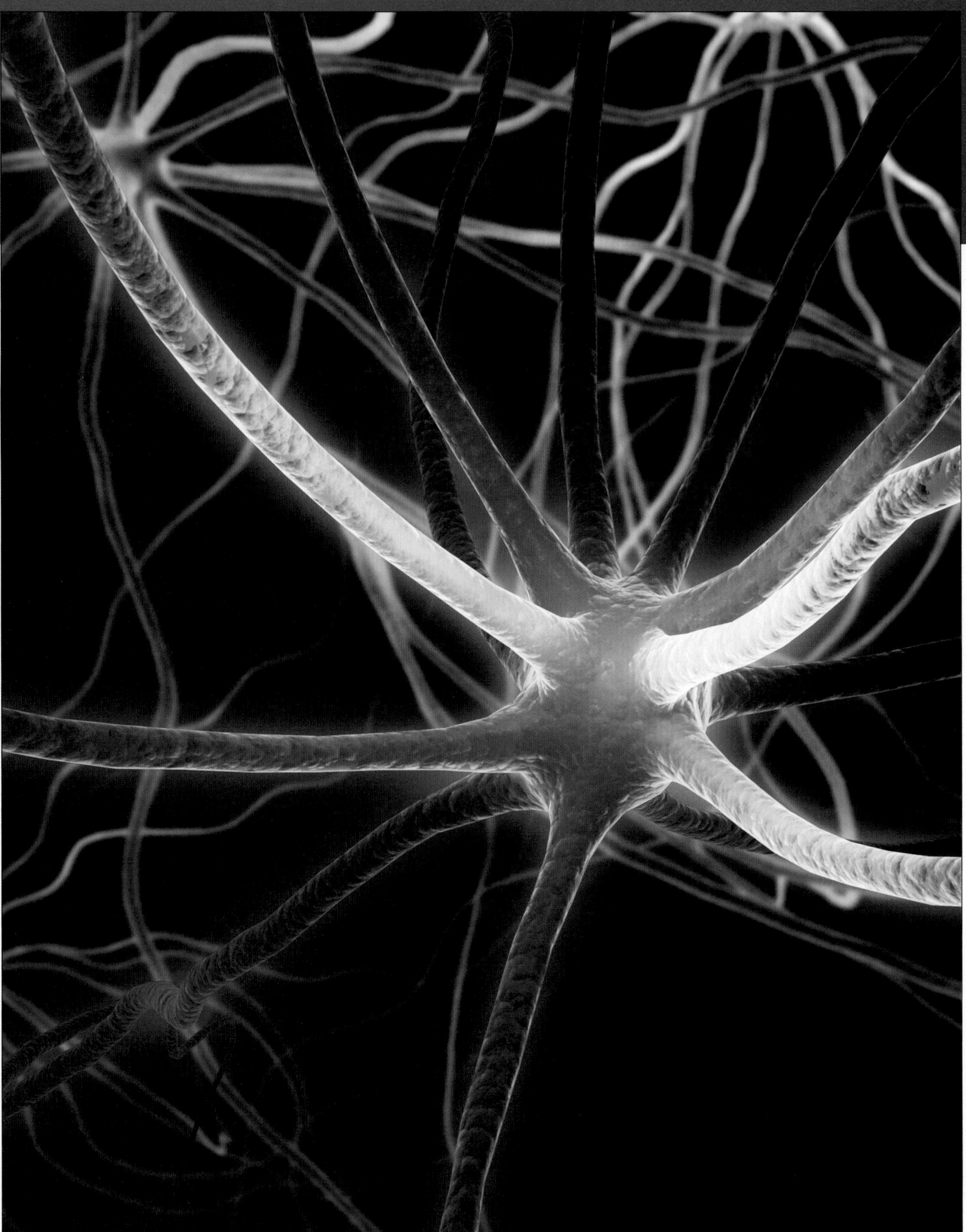

Nerve Cells and Nerve Impulses

2

CHAPTER OUTLINE

MAIN IDEAS

1. The nervous system is composed of two kinds of cells: neurons and glia. Only the neurons transmit impulses from one location to another.
2. The larger neurons have branches, known as axons and dendrites, which can change their branching pattern as a function of experience, age, and chemical influences.
3. Many molecules in the bloodstream that can enter other body organs cannot enter the brain.
4. The action potential, an all-or-none change in the electrical potential across the membrane of a neuron, is caused by the sudden flow of sodium ions into the neuron and is followed by a flow of potassium ions out of the neuron.
5. Local neurons are small and do not have axons or action potentials. Instead, they convey information to nearby neurons by graded potentials.

A nervous system, composed of many individual cells, is in some regards like a human society composed of many people: Each individual maintains an identity, and yet the whole can accomplish far more than any of the individuals could alone. We begin our study of the nervous system by examining single cells; later, we examine how cells act together.

Advice: Parts of this chapter and the next assume that you understand basic chemical concepts. If you need to refresh your memory, read Appendix A.

OPPOSITE: An electron micrograph of neurons, magnified tens of thousands of times. The color is added artificially. For objects this small, it is impossible to focus light to obtain an image. It is possible to focus an electron beam, but electrons do not show color.

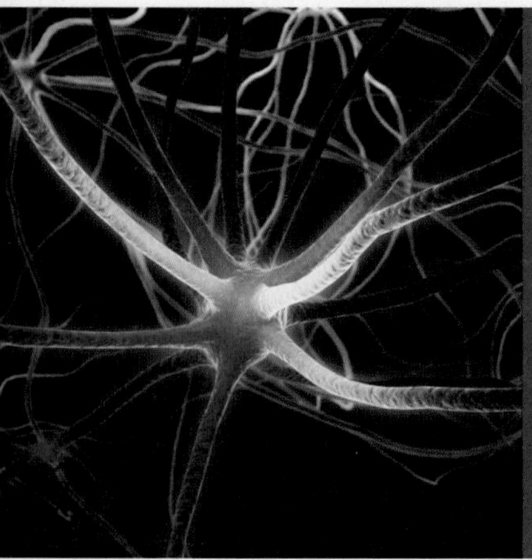

MODULE 2.1

The Cells of the Nervous System

Your nervous system controls everything you do, ranging from walking to changes in heart rate and breathing to the most complex kinds of problem solving. To understand how the nervous system works, we have to start with its microscopic units—the cells.

Anatomy of Neurons and Glia

The nervous system consists of two kinds of cells: neurons and glia. **Neurons** receive information and transmit it to other cells. Glia serve many functions that are difficult to summarize, and we shall defer that discussion until later in the chapter. According to one estimate, the adult human brain contains approximately 100 billion neurons (R. W. Williams & Herrup, 1988) (Figure 2.1). An accurate count would be more difficult than it is worth, and the actual number of neurons varies from person to person.

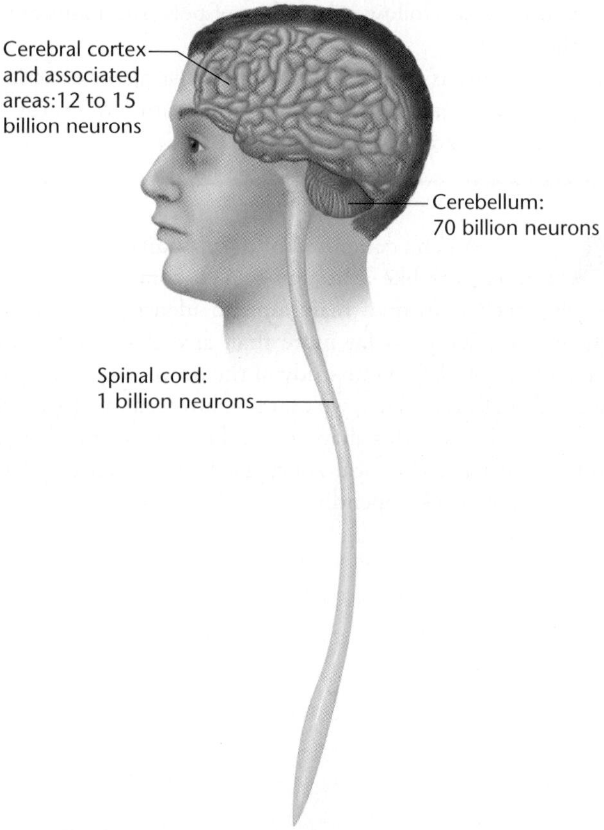

The idea that the brain is composed of individual cells is now so well established that we take it for granted. However, the idea was in doubt until the early 1900s. Until then, the best microscopic views revealed little detail about the organization of the brain. Observers noted long, thin fibers between one neuron's cell body and another, but they could not see whether each fiber merged into the next cell or stopped before it (Albright, Jessell, Kandel, & Posner, 2001). Then, in the late 1800s, Santiago Ramón y Cajal used newly developed staining techniques to show that a small gap separates the tips of one neuron's fibers from the surface of the next neuron. The brain, like the rest of the body, consists of individual cells.

Cerebral cortex and associated areas: 12 to 15 billion neurons

Cerebellum: 70 billion neurons

Spinal cord: 1 billion neurons

Figure 2.1 Estimated numbers of neurons in humans
Because of the small size of many neurons and the variation in cell density from one spot to another, obtaining an accurate count is difficult. *(Source: R. W. Williams & Herrup, 1988)*

APPLICATIONS AND EXTENSIONS

Santiago Ramón y Cajal, a Pioneer of Neuroscience

Two scientists are widely recognized as the main founders of neuroscience: Charles Sherrington, whom we shall discuss in Chapter 3, and the Spanish investigator Santiago Ramón y Cajal (1852–1934). Cajal's early career did not progress altogether smoothly. At one point, he was imprisoned in a solitary cell, limited to one meal a day, and taken out daily for public floggings—at the age of 10—for the crime of not paying attention during his Latin class (Cajal, 1901–1917/1937). (And *you* thought *your* teachers were strict!)

Cajal wanted to become an artist, but his father insisted that he study medicine as a safer way to make

Santiago Ramón y Cajal
(1852–1934)

How many interesting facts fail to be converted into fertile discoveries because their first observers regard them as natural and ordinary things! . . . It is strange to see how the populace, which nourishes its imagination with tales of witches or saints, mysterious events and extraordinary occurrences, disdains the world around it as commonplace, monotonous and prosaic, without suspecting that at bottom it is all secret, mystery, and marvel.

a living. He managed to combine the two fields, becoming an outstanding anatomical researcher and illustrator. His detailed drawings of the nervous system are still considered definitive today.

Before the late 1800s, microscopy could reveal few details about the nervous system. Then the Italian investigator Camillo Golgi found a way to stain nerve cells with silver salts. This method, which completely stained some cells without affecting others at all, enabled researchers to examine the structure of a single cell. Cajal used Golgi's methods but applied them to infant brains, in which the cells are smaller and therefore easier to examine on a single slide. Cajal's research demonstrated that nerve cells remain separate instead of merging into one another.

Philosophically, we can see the appeal of the old idea that neurons merge. We describe our experience as undivided, not the sum of separate parts, so it seems that all the cells in the brain should be joined together as one unit. How the separate cells combine their influences is a complex and still mysterious process.

The Structures of an Animal Cell

Figure 2.2 illustrates a neuron from the cerebellum of a mouse (magnified enormously, of course). Except for their distinctive shapes, neurons have much in common with the rest of the body's cells.

The surface of a cell is its **membrane** (or *plasma membrane*), a structure that separates the inside of the cell from the outside environment. It is composed of two layers of fat molecules that are free to flow around one another, as illustrated in Figure 2.3. Most chemicals cannot cross the membrane, but

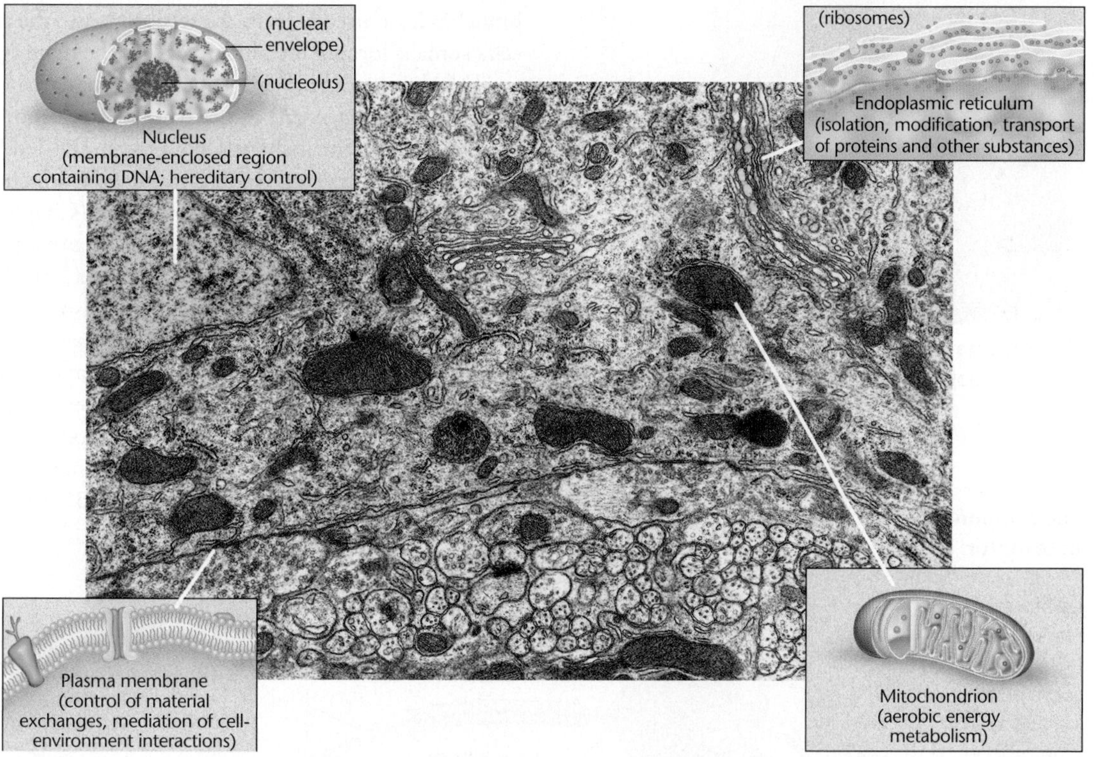

Figure 2.2 An electron micrograph of parts of a neuron from the cerebellum of a mouse
The nucleus, membrane, and other structures are characteristic of most animal cells. The plasma membrane is the border of the neuron. Magnification approximately x 20,000. *(Source: Micrograph courtesy of Dennis M. D. Landis)*

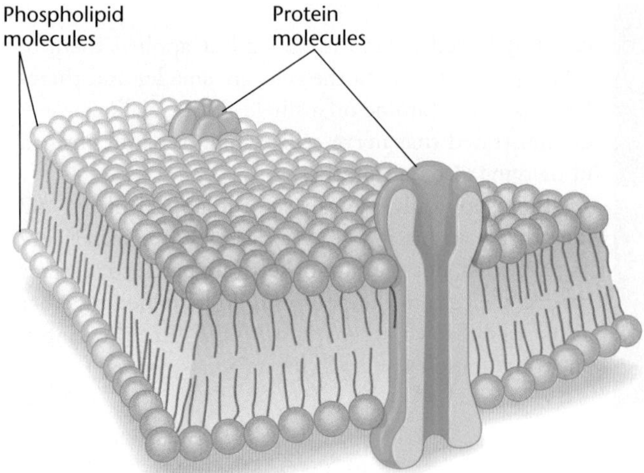

Figure 2.3 The membrane of a neuron
Embedded in the membrane are protein channels that permit certain ions to cross through the membrane at a controlled rate.

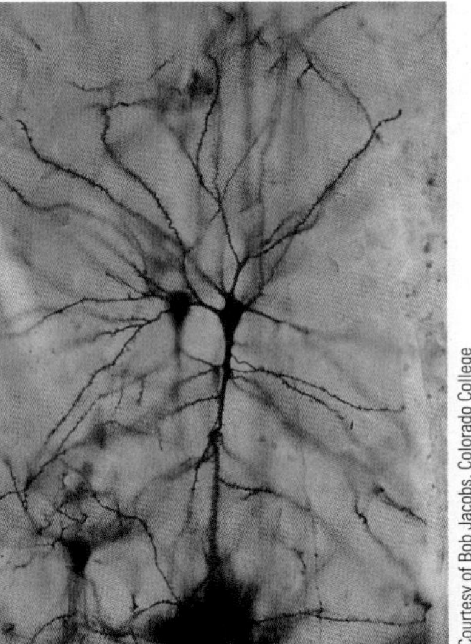

Figure 2.4 Neurons, stained to appear dark
Note the small fuzzy-looking spines on the dendrites.

specific protein channels in the membrane permit a controlled flow of water, oxygen, sodium, potassium, calcium, chloride, and other important chemicals.

Except for mammalian red blood cells, all animal cells have a **nucleus,** the structure that contains the chromosomes. A **mitochondrion** (pl.: mitochondria) is the structure that performs metabolic activities, providing the energy that the cell requires for all other activities. Mitochondria require fuel and oxygen to function. **Ribosomes** are the sites at which the cell synthesizes new protein molecules. Proteins provide building materials for the cell and facilitate various chemical reactions. Some ribosomes float freely within the cell. Others are attached to the **endoplasmic reticulum,** a network of thin tubes that transport newly synthesized proteins to other locations.

The Structure of a Neuron

Neurons are distinguished from other cells by their shape (Figure 2.4). The larger neurons have these components: dendrites, a soma (cell body), an axon, and presynaptic terminals. (The tiniest neurons lack axons, and some lack well-defined dendrites.) Contrast the motor neuron in Figure 2.5 and the sensory neuron in Figure 2.6. A **motor neuron** has its soma in the spinal cord. It receives excitation from other neurons through its dendrites and conducts impulses along its axon to a muscle. A **sensory neuron** is specialized at one end to be highly sensitive to a particular type of stimulation, such as light, sound, or touch. The sensory neuron shown in Figure 2.6 is a neuron conducting touch information from the skin to the spinal cord. Tiny branches lead directly from the receptors into the axon, and the cell's soma is located on a little stalk off the main trunk.

Dendrites are branching fibers that get narrower near their ends. (The term *dendrite* comes from a Greek root word meaning "tree"; a dendrite is shaped like a tree.) The dendrite's surface is lined with specialized *synaptic receptors,* at which the dendrite receives information from other neurons. (Chapter 3 concerns synapses.) The greater the surface area of a dendrite, the more information it can receive. Some dendrites branch widely and therefore have a large surface area. Some also contain **dendritic spines,** the short outgrowths that increase the surface area available for synapses (Figure 2.7). The shape of dendrites varies enormously from one neuron to another and can even vary from one time to another for a given neuron. The shape of the dendrite has much to do with how the dendrite combines different kinds of input (Häusser, Spruston, & Stuart, 2000).

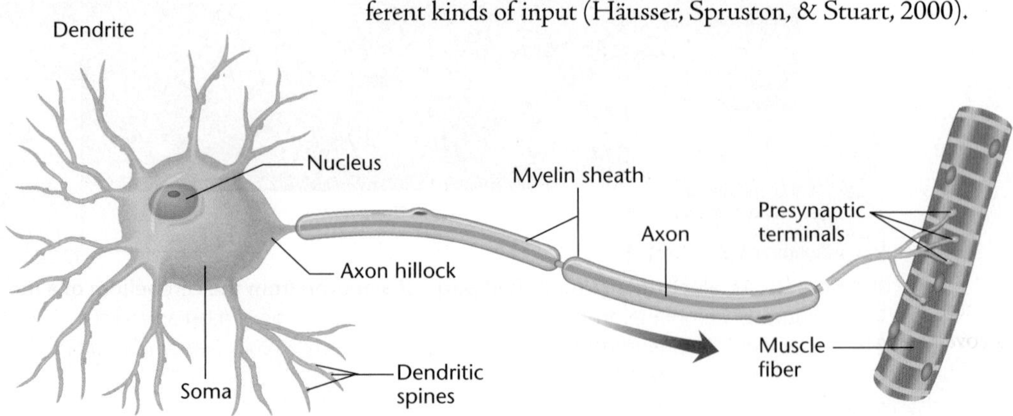

Figure 2.5 The components of a vertebrate motor neuron
The cell body of a motor neuron is located in the spinal cord. The various parts are not drawn to scale; in particular, a real axon is much longer in proportion to the soma.

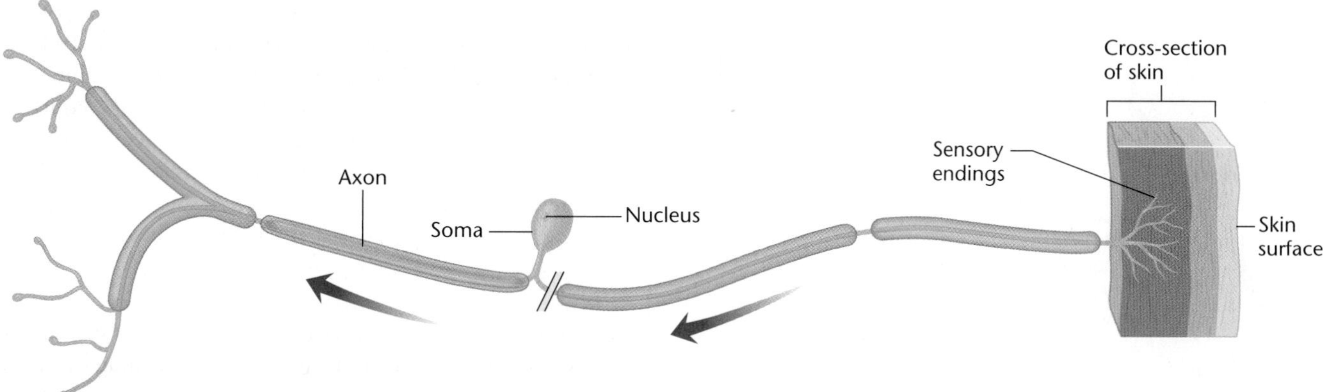

Figure 2.6 A vertebrate sensory neuron
Note that the soma is located on a stalk off the main trunk of the axon. (As in Figure 2.5, the various structures are not drawn to scale.)

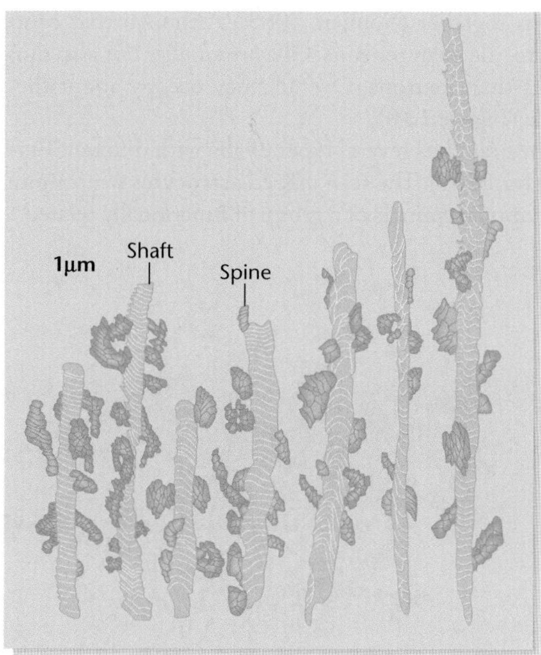

Figure 2.7 Dendritic spines
The dendrites of certain neurons are lined with spines, short outgrowths that receive specialized incoming information. That information apparently plays a key role in long-term changes in the neuron that mediate learning and memory. *(From K. M. Harris and J. K. Stevens, Society for Neuroscience, "Dendritic spines of CA1 pyramidal cells in the rat hippocampus: Serial electron microscopy with reference to their biophysical characteristics."* Journal of Neuroscience, 9, *1989, 2982–2997. Copyright © 1989 Society for Neuroscience. Reprinted by permission.)*

The **cell body,** or **soma** (Greek for "body"; pl.: somata), contains the nucleus, ribosomes, mitochondria, and other structures found in most cells. Much of the metabolic work of the neuron occurs here. Cell bodies of neurons range in diameter from 0.005 mm to 0.1 mm in mammals and up to a full millimeter in certain invertebrates. Like the dendrites, the cell body is covered with synapses on its surface in many neurons.

The **axon** is a thin fiber of constant diameter, in most cases longer than the dendrites. (The term *axon* comes from a Greek word meaning "axis.") The axon is the information sender of the neuron, conveying an impulse toward other neurons or an organ or muscle. Many vertebrate axons are covered with an insulating material called a **myelin sheath** with interruptions known as **nodes of Ranvier** (RAHN-vee-ay). Invertebrate axons do not have myelin sheaths. An axon has many branches, each of which swells at its tip, forming a **presynaptic terminal,** also known as an *end bulb* or *bouton* (French for "button"). This is the point from which the axon releases chemicals that cross through the junction between one neuron and the next.

A neuron can have any number of dendrites, but no more than one axon, which may have branches. Axons can range to a meter or more in length, as in the case of axons from your spinal cord to your feet. In most cases, branches of the axon depart from its trunk far from the cell body, near the terminals.

Other terms associated with neurons are *afferent, efferent,* and *intrinsic.* An **afferent axon** brings information into a structure; an **efferent axon** carries information away from a structure. Every sensory neuron is an afferent to the rest of the nervous system, and every motor neuron is an efferent from the nervous system. Within the nervous system, a given neuron is an efferent from one structure and an afferent to another. (You can remember that *efferent* starts with *e* as in *exit*; *afferent* starts with *a* as in *admission.*) For example, an axon that is efferent from the thalamus may be afferent to the cerebral cortex (Figure 2.8). If a cell's dendrites and axon are entirely contained within a single structure, the cell is an **interneuron** or **intrinsic neuron** of that structure. For example, an intrinsic neuron of the thalamus has its axon and all its dendrites within the thalamus.

STOP & CHECK

1. What are the widely branching structures of a neuron called? And what is the long thin structure that carries information to another cell called?

ANSWER

1. The widely branching structures of a neuron are called *dendrites*, and the long thin structure that carries information to another cell is called an *axon*.

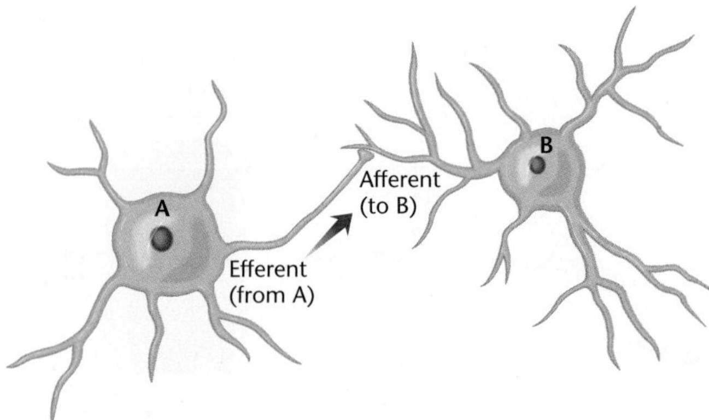

Figure 2.8 Cell structures and axons
It all depends on the point of view. An axon from A to B is an efferent axon from A and an afferent axon to B, just as a train from Washington to New York is exiting Washington and approaching New York.

Variations Among Neurons

Neurons vary enormously in size, shape, and function. The shape of a given neuron determines its connections with other neurons and thereby determines its contribution to the nervous system. Neurons with wider branching connect with more neurons.

The function of a neuron relates to its shape (Figure 2.9). For example, the widely branching dendrites of the Purkinje cell of the cerebellum (Figure 2.9a) enable it to receive input from a huge number of axons. By contrast, certain cells in the retina (Figure 2.9d) have only short branches on their dendrites and therefore pool input from only a few sources.

Glia

Glia (or neuroglia), the other major components of the nervous system, do not transmit information over long distances as neurons do, although they do exchange chemicals with adjacent neurons. In some cases, that exchange causes neurons to oscillate in their activity (Nadkarni & Jung, 2003). The term *glia,* derived from a Greek word meaning "glue," reflects early investigators' idea that glia were like glue that held the neurons together (Somjen, 1988). Although that concept is obsolete, the term remains. Glia are smaller but also more numerous than neurons. Overall, they occupy about the same volume (Figure 2.10).

The brain has several types of glia with different functions (Haydon, 2001). The star-shaped **astrocytes** wrap around the presynaptic terminals of a group of functionally related axons,

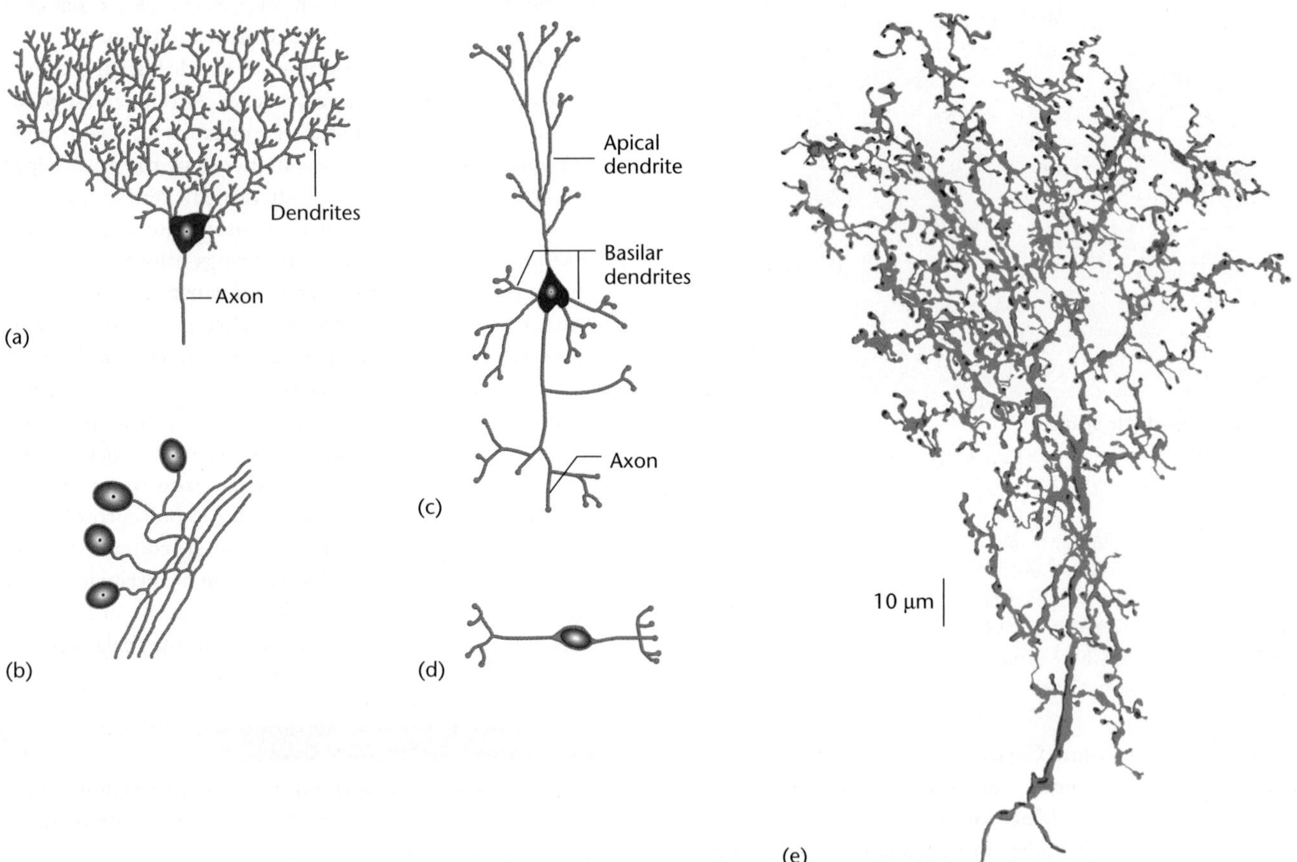

Figure 2.9 The diverse shapes of neurons
(a) Purkinje cell, a cell type found only in the cerebellum; **(b)** sensory neurons from skin to spinal cord; **(c)** pyramidal cell of the motor area of the cerebral cortex; **(d)** bipolar cell of retina of the eye; **(e)** Kenyon cell, from a honeybee. *(Part e, from R. G. Coss,* Brain Research, *October 1982. Reprinted by permission of R. G. Coss.)*

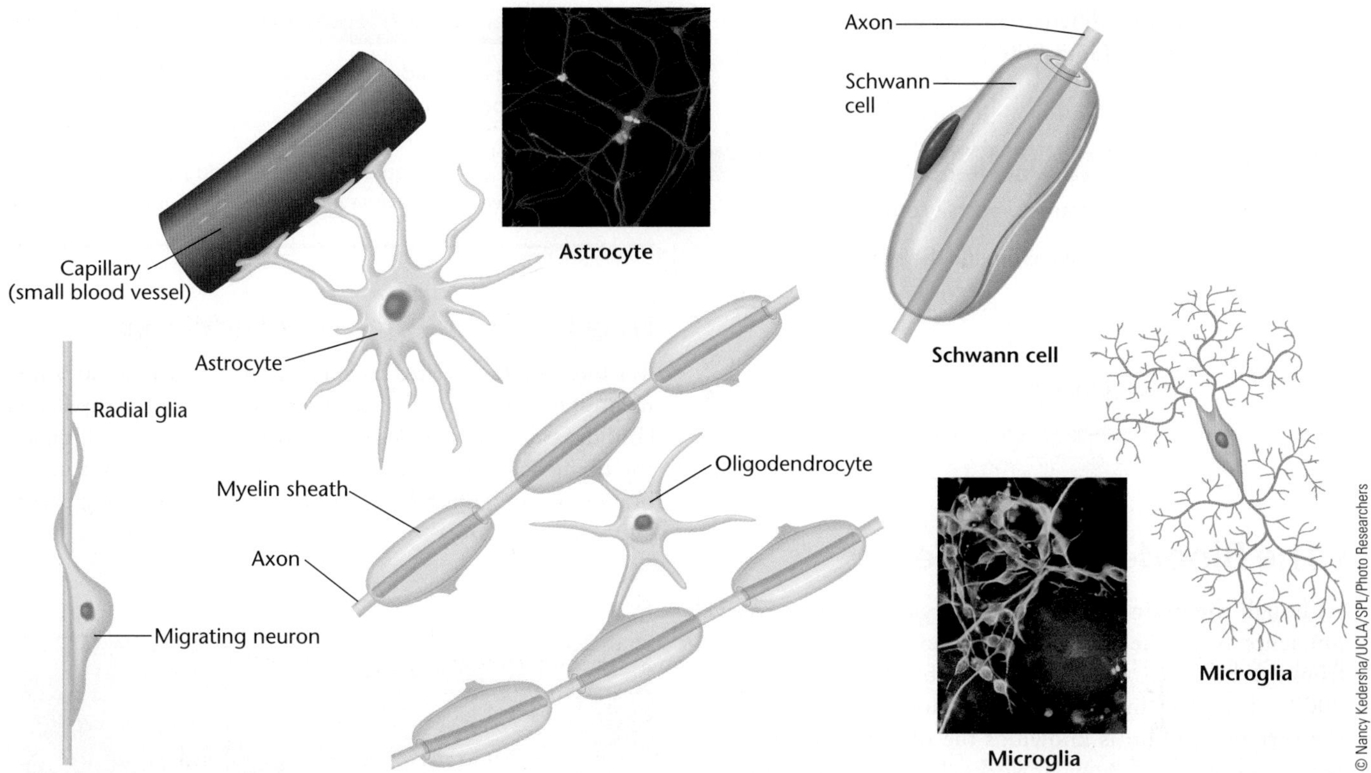

Figure 2.10 Shapes of some glia cells
Oligodendrocytes produce myelin sheaths that insulate certain vertebrate axons in the central nervous system; Schwann cells have a similar function in the periphery. The oligodendrocyte is shown here forming a segment of myelin sheath for two axons; in fact, each oligodendrocyte forms such segments for 30 to 50 axons. Astrocytes pass chemicals back and forth between neurons and blood and among neighboring neurons. Microglia proliferate in areas of brain damage and remove toxic materials. Radial glia (not shown here) guide the migration of neurons during embryological development. Glia have other functions as well.

as shown in Figure 2.11. By taking up chemicals released by axons and then releasing them back to axons, an astrocyte helps synchronize the activity of the axons, enabling them to send messages in waves (Angulo, Kozlov, Charpak, & Audinat, 2004; Antanitus, 1998). Astrocytes also remove waste material created when neurons die and control the amount of blood flow to each brain area (Mulligan & MacVicar, 2004). An additional function is that during periods of heightened activity in some brain area, astrocytes dilate the blood vessels to bring more nutrients into that area (Filosa et al., 2006; Takano et al., 2006). Furthermore, astrocytes release chemicals that modify the activity of neighboring neurons (Perea & Araque, 2007). Clearly, astrocytes do more than just support neurons. They are an important contributor to information processing.

Microglia, very small cells, also remove waste material as well as viruses, fungi, and other microorganisms. In effect, they function like part of the immune system (Davalos et al., 2005). **Oligodendrocytes** (OL-i-go-DEN-druh-sites) in the brain and spinal cord and **Schwann cells** in the periphery are specialized types of glia that build the myelin sheaths that surround and insulate certain vertebrate axons. **Radial glia** guide the migration of neurons and their axons and dendrites during embryonic development. When embryological development finishes, most radial glia differentiate into neurons,

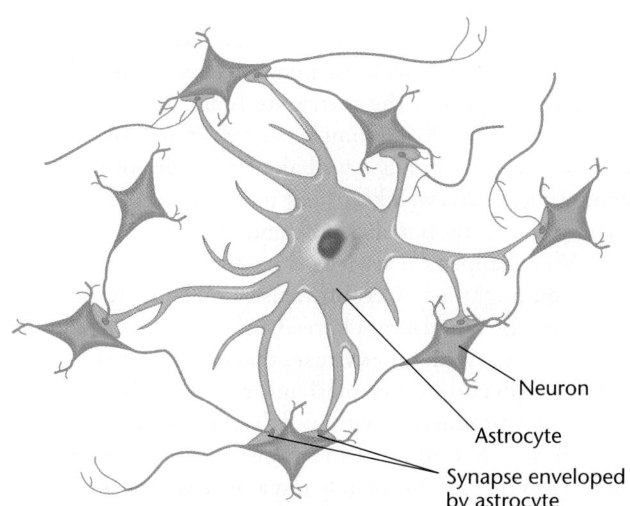

Figure 2.11 How an astrocyte synchronizes associated axons
Branches of the astrocyte (in the center) surround the presynaptic terminals of related axons. If a few of them are active at once, the astrocyte absorbs some of the chemicals they release. It then temporarily inhibits all the axons to which it is connected. When the inhibition ceases, all of the axons are primed to respond again in synchrony. *(Source: Based on Antanitus, 1998)*

and a smaller number differentiate into astrocytes and oligodendrocytes (Pinto & Götz, 2007).

STOP & CHECK

2. Identify the four major structures that compose a neuron.
3. Which kind of glia cell wraps around the synaptic terminals of axons?

ANSWERS

2. Dendrites, soma (cell body), axon, and presynaptic terminal. **3.** Astrocytes.

The Blood-Brain Barrier

Although the brain, like any other organ, needs to receive nutrients from the blood, many chemicals cannot cross from the blood to the brain (Hagenbuch, Gao, & Meier, 2002). The mechanism that keeps most chemicals out of the vertebrate brain is known as the **blood-brain barrier.** Before we examine how it works, let's consider why we need it.

Why We Need a Blood-Brain Barrier

When a virus invades a cell, mechanisms within the cell extrude virus particles through the membrane so that the immune system can find them. When the immune system cells identify a virus, they kill it and the cell that contains it. In effect, a cell exposing a virus through its membrane says, "Look, immune system, I'm infected with this virus. Kill me and save the others."

This plan works fine if the virus-infected cell is, say, a skin cell or a blood cell, which the body replaces easily. However, with few exceptions, the vertebrate brain does not replace damaged neurons. To minimize the risk of irreparable brain damage, the body builds a wall along the sides of the brain's blood vessels. This wall keeps out most viruses, bacteria, and harmful chemicals, but also most nutrients.

"What happens if a virus does enter the nervous system?" you might ask. Certain viruses, such as the rabies virus, evade the blood-brain barrier, infect the brain, and lead to death. For several other viruses that enter the nervous system, microglia and other mechanisms attack the viruses or slow their reproduction without killing the neurons they occupy (Binder & Griffin, 2001). However, a virus that enters your nervous system probably remains with you for life. For example, the virus responsible for chicken pox and shingles enters spinal cord cells. No matter how effectively the immune system attacks that virus outside the nervous system, virus particles remain in the spinal cord, from which they can emerge decades later. The same is true for the virus that causes genital herpes.

STOP & CHECK

4. Identify one major advantage and one disadvantage of having a blood-brain barrier.

ANSWER

4. The blood-brain barrier keeps out viruses (an advantage) and also most nutrients (a disadvantage).

How the Blood-Brain Barrier Works

The blood-brain barrier (Figure 2.12) depends on the arrangement of endothelial cells that form the walls of the capillaries (Bundgaard, 1986; Rapoport & Robinson, 1986). Outside the brain, such cells are separated by small gaps, but in the brain, they are joined so tightly that virtually nothing passes between them.

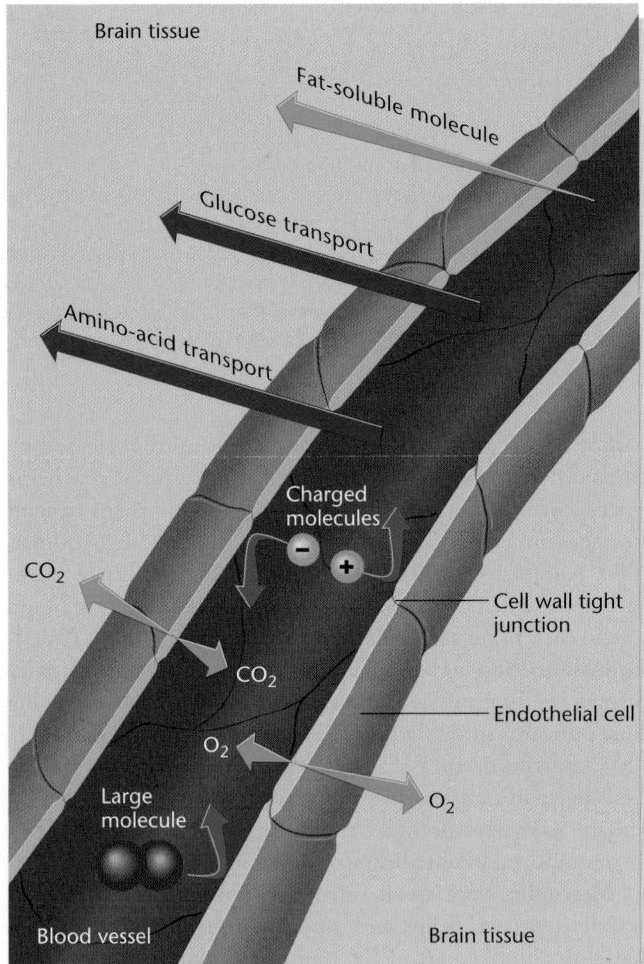

Figure 2.12 The blood-brain barrier
Most large molecules and electrically charged molecules cannot cross from the blood to the brain. A few small, uncharged molecules such as O_2 and CO_2 cross easily; so can certain fat-soluble molecules. Active transport systems pump glucose and certain amino acids across the membrane.

"If the blood-brain barrier is such a good defense," you might ask, "why don't we have similar walls around our other organs?" The answer is that the barrier that keeps out harmful chemicals also keeps out many useful ones.

The brain has several mechanisms to allow certain chemicals to cross through the endothelial cells. First, *small uncharged molecules,* including oxygen and carbon dioxide, cross freely. Water crosses through special protein channels in the wall of the endothelial cells (Amiry-Moghaddam & Ottersen, 2003). Second, *molecules that dissolve in the fats of the membrane* also cross passively. Examples include vitamins A and D.

For certain other essential chemicals, the brain uses **active transport,** a protein-mediated process that expends energy to pump chemicals from the blood into the brain. Chemicals that are actively transported into the brain include glucose (the brain's main fuel), amino acids (the building blocks of proteins), purines, choline, a few vitamins, iron, and certain hormones (Abbott, Rönnback, & Hansson, 2006; A. R. Jones & Shusta, 2007).

The blood-brain barrier is essential to health. In people with Alzheimer's disease or similar conditions, the endothelial cells lining the brain's blood vessels shrink, and harmful chemicals enter the brain (Zipser et al., 2006).

However, the barrier also poses a difficulty in medicine because it keeps out many medications. For example, brain cancers are difficult to treat because nearly all the drugs used for chemotherapy fail to cross the blood-brain barrier.

STOP & CHECK

5. Which chemicals cross the blood-brain barrier passively?

6. Which chemicals cross the blood-brain barrier by active transport?

ANSWERS

5. Small, uncharged molecules such as oxygen and carbon dioxide cross the blood-brain barrier passively. So do chemicals that dissolve in the fats of the membrane. **6.** Glucose, amino acids, purines, choline, certain vitamins, iron, and a few hormones.

The Nourishment of Vertebrate Neurons

Most cells use a variety of carbohydrates and fats for nutrition, but vertebrate neurons depend almost entirely on **glucose,** a simple sugar. (Cancer cells and the testis cells that make sperm also rely overwhelmingly on glucose.) The metabolic pathway that uses glucose requires oxygen; consequently, the neurons consume an enormous amount of oxygen compared with cells of other organs (Wong-Riley, 1989).

Why do neurons depend so heavily on glucose? Although neurons have the enzymes necessary to metabolize fats and several sugars, glucose is practically the only nutrient that crosses the blood-brain barrier in adults. The exceptions to this rule are *ketones* (a kind of fat), but ketones are seldom available in large amounts (Duelli & Kuschinsky, 2001), and large amounts of ketones cause medical complications.

Although neurons require glucose, glucose shortage is rarely a problem. The liver makes glucose from many kinds of carbohydrates and amino acids, as well as from glycerol, a breakdown product from fats. An inability to *use* glucose can be a problem, however. Many chronic alcoholics have a diet deficient in vitamin B_1, **thiamine,** a chemical that is necessary for the use of glucose. Prolonged thiamine deficiency can lead to death of neurons and a condition called *Korsakoff's syndrome,* marked by severe memory impairments (Chapter 13).

MODULE 2.1 IN CLOSING

Neurons

What does the study of individual neurons tell us about behavior? Perhaps the main lesson is that our experience and behavior *do not* follow from the properties of any one neuron. Just as a chemist must know about atoms to make sense of compounds, a biological psychologist or neuroscientist must know about cells to understand the nervous system. However, the nervous system is more than the sum of the individual cells, just as water is more than the sum of oxygen and hydrogen. Our behavior emerges from the communication among neurons.

SUMMARY

1. Neurons receive information and convey it to other cells. The nervous system also contains *glia*. **28**
2. In the late 1800s, Santiago Ramón y Cajal used newly discovered staining techniques to establish that the nervous system is composed of separate cells, now known as neurons. **29**
3. Neurons contain the same internal structures as other animal cells. **29**
4. Neurons have four major parts: a cell body, dendrites, an axon, and presynaptic terminals. Their shapes vary greatly depending on their functions and their connections with other cells. **30**
5. Glia do not convey information over great distances, but they aid the functioning of neurons in many ways. **32**
6. Because of the blood-brain barrier, many molecules cannot enter the brain. The barrier protects the nervous system from viruses and many dangerous chemicals. **34**
7. The blood-brain barrier consists of an unbroken wall of cells that surround the blood vessels of the brain and spinal cord. A few small uncharged molecules such as water, oxygen, and carbon dioxide cross the barrier freely. So do molecules that dissolve in fats. Active transport proteins pump glucose, amino acids, and possibly other chemicals into the brain and spinal cord. **34**
8. Adult neurons rely heavily on glucose, the only nutrient that can cross the blood-brain barrier. They need thiamine (vitamin B_1) to use glucose. **35**

KEY TERMS

Terms are defined in the module on the page number indicated. They're also presented in alphabetical order with definitions in the book's Subject Index/Glossary. Interactive flashcards, audio reviews, and crossword puzzles are among the online resources available (www.cengage.com/psychology/kalat) to help you learn these terms and the concepts they represent.

active transport **35**
afferent axon **31**
astrocytes **32**
axon **31**
blood-brain barrier **34**
cell body (soma) **31**
dendrites **30**
dendritic spines **30**
efferent axon **31**
endoplasmic reticulum **30**
glia **32**
glucose **35**
interneuron **31**
intrinsic neuron **31**
membrane **29**
microglia **33**
mitochondrion **30**
motor neuron **30**
myelin sheath **31**
neurons **28**
nodes of Ranvier **31**
nucleus **30**
oligodendrocytes **33**
presynaptic terminal **31**
radial glia **33**
ribosomes **30**
Schwann cells **33**
sensory neuron **30**
thiamine **35**

THOUGHT QUESTION

Drugs that affect behavior must somehow cross the blood-brain barrier. What can we infer about the nature of those drugs?

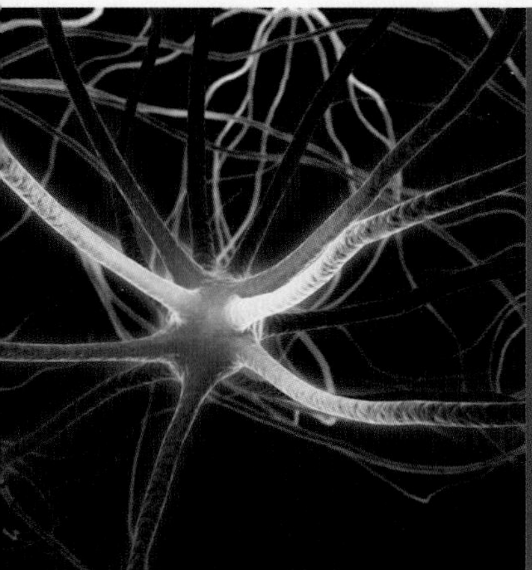

MODULE 2.2

The Nerve Impulse

Think about the axons that convey information from your feet's touch receptors toward your spinal cord and brain. If the axons used electrical conduction, they could transfer information at a velocity approaching the speed of light. However, given that your body is made of carbon compounds and not copper wire, the strength of the impulse would decay quickly on the way to your spinal cord and brain. A touch on your shoulder would feel much stronger than a touch on your abdomen. Short people would feel their toes more strongly than tall people could.

The way your axons actually function avoids these problems. Instead of simply conducting an electrical impulse, the axon regenerates an impulse at each point. Imagine a long line of people holding hands. The first person squeezes the second person's hand, who then squeezes the third person's hand, and so forth. The impulse travels along the line without weakening because each person generates it anew.

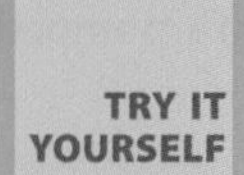

Although the axon's method of transmitting an impulse prevents a touch on your shoulder from feeling stronger than one on your toes, it introduces a different problem: Because axons transmit information at only moderate speeds (varying from less than 1 meter/second to about 100 m/s), a touch on your shoulder will reach your brain *sooner* than will a touch on your toes. If you get someone to touch you simultaneously on your shoulder and your toe, you will not notice that your brain received one stimulus before the other. In fact, if someone touches you on one hand and then the other, you won't be sure which hand you felt first, unless the delay between touches exceeds 70 milliseconds (ms) (S. Yamamoto & Kitazawa, 2001). Your brain is not set up to register small differences in the time of arrival of touch messages. After all, why should it be? You almost never need to know whether a touch on one part of your body occurred slightly before or after a touch somewhere else.

In vision, however, your brain *does* need to know whether one stimulus began slightly before or after another one. If two adjacent spots on your retina—let's call them A and B—send impulses at almost the same time, an extremely small difference in timing indicates whether a flash of light moved from A to B or from B to A. To detect movement as accurately as possible, your visual system compensates for the fact that some parts of the retina are slightly closer to your brain than other parts are. Without some sort of compensation, simultaneous flashes arriving at two spots on your retina would reach your brain at different times, and you might perceive a flash of light moving from one spot to the other. What prevents this illusion is the fact that axons from more distant parts of your retina transmit impulses slightly faster than those closer to the brain (Stanford, 1987)!

In short, the properties of impulse conduction in an axon are well adapted to the exact needs for information transfer in the nervous system. Let's examine the mechanics of impulse transmission.

The Resting Potential of the Neuron

The membrane of a neuron maintains an **electrical gradient,** a difference in electrical charge between the inside and outside of the cell. All parts of a neuron are covered by a membrane about 8 nanometers (nm) thick (just less than 0.00001 mm), composed of two layers (an inner layer and an outer layer) of phospholipid molecules (containing chains of fatty acids and a phosphate group). Embedded among the phospholipids are cylindrical protein molecules (see Figure 2.3). The structure of the membrane provides it with a good combination of flexibility and firmness and retards the flow of chemicals between the inside and the outside of the cell.

In the absence of any outside disturbance, the membrane maintains an electrical **polarization,** meaning a difference in electrical charge between two locations. The neuron inside the membrane has a slightly negative electrical potential with respect to the outside, primarily because of negatively charged proteins inside the cell. This difference in voltage in a resting neuron is called the **resting potential.** The resting potential is mainly the result of negatively charged proteins inside the cell.

Researchers can measure the resting potential by inserting a very thin *microelectrode* into the cell body, as Figure 2.13 shows. The diameter of the electrode must be as small as possible so that it can enter the cell without causing damage. By far the most common electrode is a fine glass tube filled with

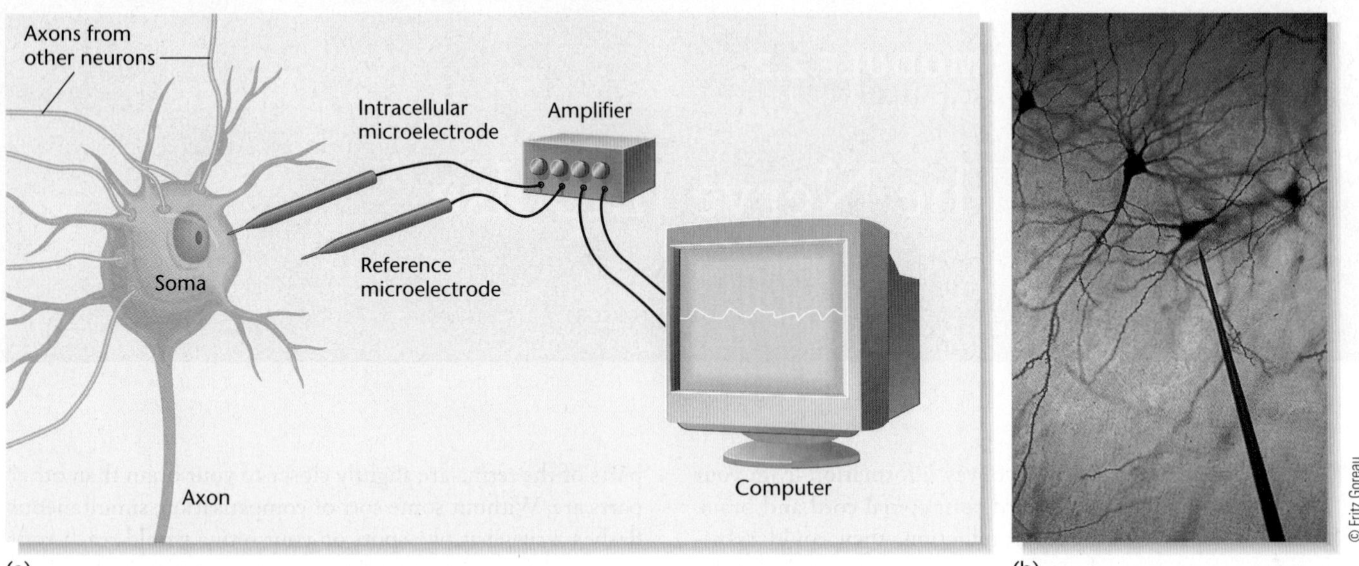

Figure 2.13 Methods for recording activity of a neuron
(a) Diagram of the apparatus and a sample recording. **(b)** A microelectrode and stained neurons magnified hundreds of times by a light microscope.

a concentrated salt solution and tapering to a tip diameter of 0.0005 mm or less. This electrode, inserted into the neuron, is connected to recording equipment. A reference electrode placed somewhere outside the cell completes the circuit. Connecting the electrodes to a voltmeter, we find that the neuron's interior has a negative potential relative to its exterior. A typical level is –70 millivolts (mV), but it varies from one neuron to another.

Forces Acting on Sodium and Potassium Ions

If charged ions could flow freely across the membrane, the membrane would depolarize at once. However, the membrane is **selectively permeable;** that is, some chemicals can pass through it more freely than others can. (This selectivity is *analogous* to the blood-brain barrier, but it is not the same thing.) Most large or electrically charged ions and molecules cannot cross the membrane at all. Oxygen, carbon dioxide, urea, and water cross freely through channels that are always open. A few biologically important ions, such as sodium, potassium, calcium, and chloride, cross through membrane channels (or gates) that are sometimes open and sometimes closed. When the membrane is at rest, the sodium channels are closed, preventing almost all sodium flow. These channels are shown in Figure 2.14. As we shall see in Chapter 3, certain kinds of stimulation can open the sodium channels. When the membrane is at rest, potassium channels are nearly but not entirely closed, so potassium flows slowly.

The **sodium-potassium pump,** a protein complex, repeatedly transports three sodium ions out of the cell while drawing two potassium ions into it. The sodium-potassium pump is an active transport requiring energy. Various poisons stop it, as does an interruption of blood flow. As a result of the sodium-potassium pump, sodium ions are more than 10 times more concentrated outside the membrane than inside, and potassium ions are similarly more concentrated inside than outside.

The sodium-potassium pump is effective only because of the selective permeability of the membrane, which prevents the sodium ions that were pumped out of the neuron from leaking right back in again. As it is, the sodium ions that are pumped out stay out. However, some of the potassium

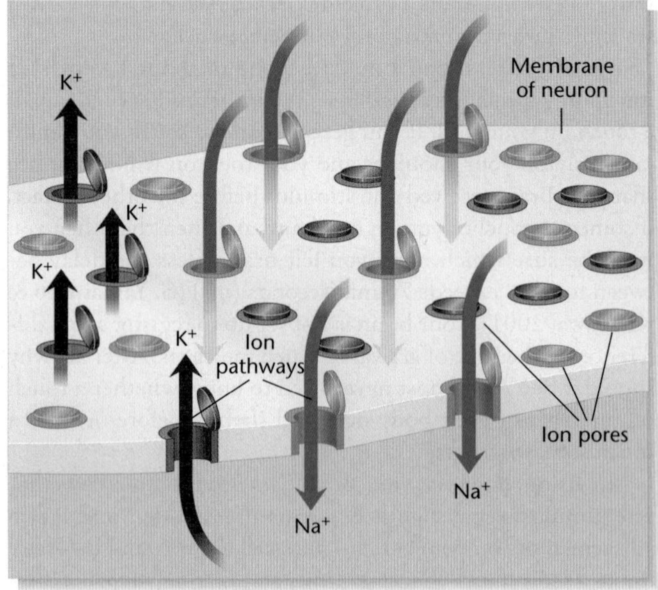

Figure 2.14 Ion channels in the membrane of a neuron
When a channel opens, it permits one kind of ion to cross the membrane. When it closes, it prevents passage of that ion.

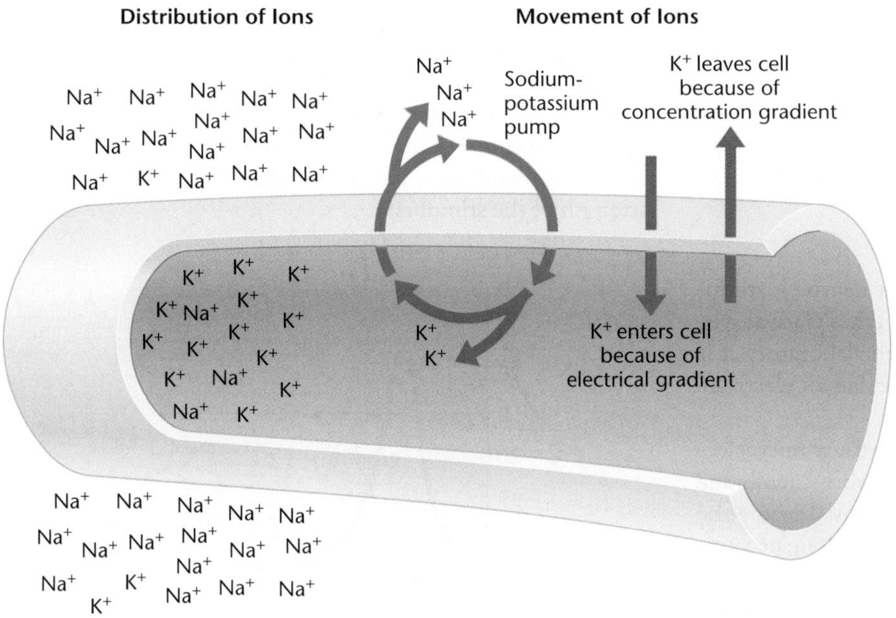

Figure 2.15 The sodium and potassium gradients for a resting membrane
Sodium ions are more concentrated outside the neuron; potassium ions are more concentrated inside. Protein and chloride ions (not shown) bear negative charges inside the cell. At rest, very few sodium ions cross the membrane except by the sodium-potassium pump. Potassium tends to flow into the cell because of an electrical gradient but tends to flow out because of the concentration gradient.

ions pumped into the neuron do leak out, carrying a positive charge with them. That leakage increases the electrical gradient across the membrane, as shown in Figure 2.15.

When the neuron is at rest, two forces act on sodium, both tending to push it into the cell. First, consider the **electrical gradient.** Sodium is positively charged and the inside of the cell is negatively charged. Opposite electrical charges attract, so the electrical gradient tends to pull sodium into the cell. Second, consider the **concentration gradient,** the difference in distribution of ions across the membrane. Sodium is more concentrated outside than inside, so just by the laws of probability, sodium is more likely to enter the cell than to leave it. (By analogy, imagine two rooms connected by a door. There are 100 cats are in room A and only 10 in room B. Cats are more likely to move from A to B than from B to A. The same principle applies to the movement of ions across a membrane.) Given that both the electrical gradient and the concentration gradient tend to move sodium ions into the cell, sodium would move rapidly if it could. However, the sodium channels are closed when the membrane is at rest, and almost no sodium flows except for the sodium pushed *out of* the cell by the sodium-potassium pump.

Potassium is subject to competing forces. Potassium is positively charged and the inside of the cell is negatively charged, so the electrical gradient tends to pull potassium in. However, potassium is more concentrated inside the cell than outside, so the concentration gradient tends to drive it out. If the potassium channels were wide open, potassium would have a moderate net flow out of the cell. That is, the electrical gradient and concentration gradient for potassium are almost in balance, but not quite. The sodium-potassium pump keeps pulling potassium in, so the two gradients cannot get completely in balance.

The cell has negative ions, too. Negatively charged proteins inside the cell are responsible for the membrane's polarization. Chloride ions, being negatively charged, are mainly outside the cell. In most neurons, the concentration gradient and electrical gradient balance, so opening chloride channels produces little effect when the membrane is at rest. However, chloride flow is important when the membrane's polarization changes, as we see later in this chapter and in Chapter 3.

STOP & CHECK

7. When the membrane is at rest, are the sodium ions more concentrated inside the cell or outside? Where are the potassium ions more concentrated?

8. When the membrane is at rest, what tends to drive the potassium ions out of the cell? What tends to draw them into the cell?

ANSWERS

7. Sodium ions are more concentrated outside the cell; potassium is more concentrated inside. **8.** When the membrane is at rest, the concentration gradient tends to drive potassium ions out of the cell; the electrical gradient draws them into the cell. The sodium-potassium pump also draws them into the cell.

Why a Resting Potential?

The body invests much energy to operate the sodium-potassium pump, which maintains the resting potential. Why is it worth so much energy? The resting potential prepares the neuron to respond rapidly. As we shall see in the next section, excitation of the neuron opens channels that let sodium enter the cell explosively. Because the membrane did its work in advance by maintaining the concentration gradient for sodium, the cell is prepared to respond strongly and rapidly to a stimulus.

The resting potential of a neuron can be compared to a poised bow and arrow: An archer who pulls the bow in advance and then waits is ready to fire as soon as the appropriate moment comes. Evolution has applied the same strategy to the neuron.

The Action Potential

The resting potential remains stable until the neuron is stimulated. Ordinarily, stimulation of the neuron takes place at synapses, which we consider in Chapter 3. In the laboratory, it is also possible to stimulate a neuron by inserting an electrode into it and applying current.

We can measure a neuron's potential with a microelectrode, as shown in Figure 2.13b. When an axon's membrane is at rest, the recordings show a negative potential inside the axon. If we now use another electrode to apply a negative charge, we can further increase the negative charge inside the neuron. The change is called **hyperpolarization,** which means increased polarization. As soon as the artificial stimulation ceases, the charge returns to its original resting level. The recording looks like this:

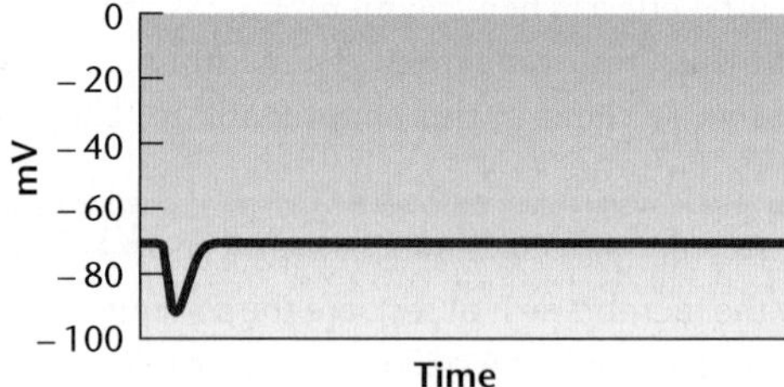

Now let's apply a current to **depolarize** the neuron—that is, reduce its polarization toward zero. If we apply a small depolarizing current, we get a result like this:

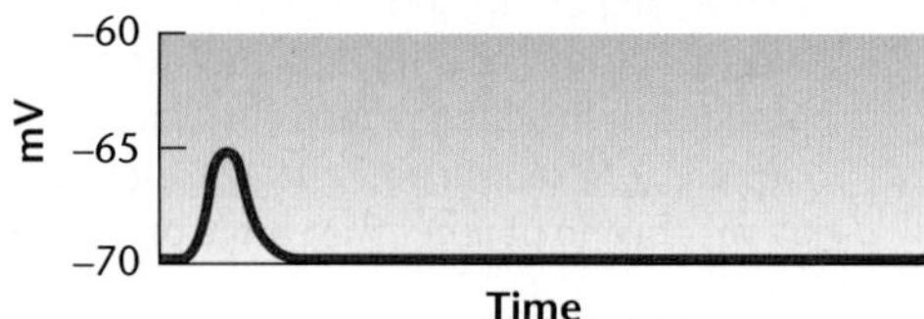

With a slightly stronger depolarizing current, the potential rises slightly higher but again returns to the resting level as soon as the stimulation ceases:

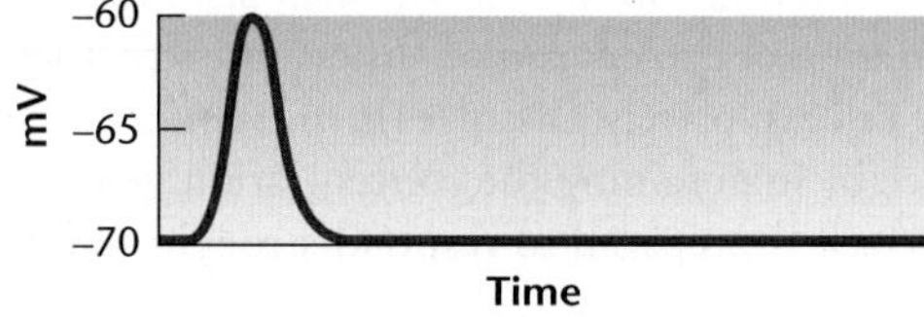

Now let's apply a still stronger current: Stimulation beyond a certain level called the **threshold of excitation** produces a massive depolarization of the membrane. When the potential reaches the threshold, the membrane suddenly opens its sodium channels and permits a rapid flow of ions across the membrane. The potential shoots up far beyond the strength of the stimulus:

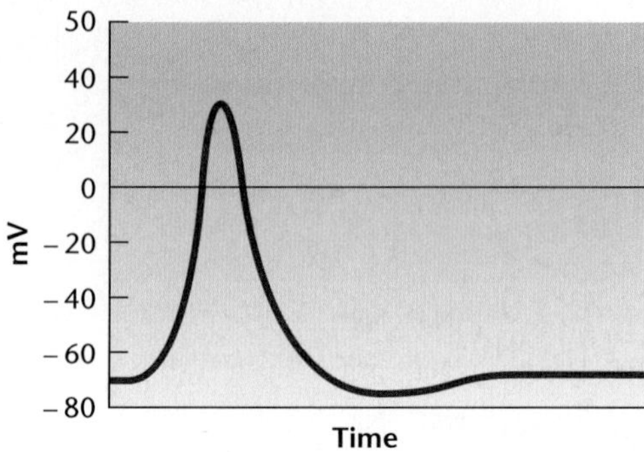

Any *subthreshold* stimulation produces a small response proportional to the amount of current. Any stimulation beyond the threshold, regardless of how far beyond, produces the same response, like the one just shown. That response, a rapid depolarization and slight reversal of the usual polarization, is referred to as an **action potential.** The peak of the action potential, shown as +30 mV in this illustration, varies from one axon to another, but it is consistent for a given axon.

STOP & CHECK

9. What is the difference between a hyperpolarization and a depolarization?

10. What is the relationship between the threshold and an action potential?

ANSWERS

9. A hyperpolarization is an exaggeration of the usual negative charge within a cell (to a more negative level than usual). A depolarization is a decrease in the amount of negative charge within the cell. **10.** A depolarization that passes the threshold produces an action potential. One that falls short of the threshold does not produce an action potential.

The Molecular Basis of the Action Potential

Remember that both the electrical gradient and the concentration gradient tend to drive sodium ions into the neuron. If sodium ions could flow freely across the membrane, they would enter rapidly.

The membrane proteins that control sodium entry are **voltage-gated channels,** membrane channels whose permeability depends on the voltage difference across the membrane. At the resting potential, the channels are closed. As the membrane becomes depolarized, the sodium channels begin to open and sodium flows more freely. If the depolarization is less than the threshold, sodium crosses the membrane only slightly more than usual. When the potential across the membrane reaches threshold, the sodium channels open wide. Sodium ions rush into the neuron explosively until the electrical potential across the membrane passes beyond zero to a reversed polarity, as shown in the following diagram:

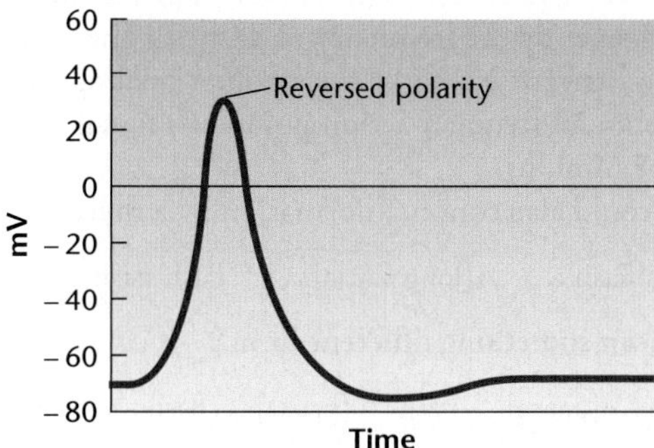

Compared to the total number of sodium ions in and around the axon, fewer than 1% of them cross the membrane during an action potential. Even at the peak of the action potential, sodium ions continue to be far more concentrated outside the neuron than inside. Because of the persisting concentration gradient, sodium ions should still tend to diffuse into the cell. However, at the peak of the action potential, the sodium gates quickly close and resist reopening for about the next millisecond.

After the peak of the action potential, what brings the membrane back to its original state of polarization? The answer is *not* the sodium-potassium pump, which is too slow for this purpose. After the action potential is underway, voltage-gated potassium channels open. Potassium ions flow out of the axon simply because they are much more concentrated inside than outside and they are no longer held inside by a negative charge. As they flow out of the axon, they carry with them a positive charge. Because the potassium channels open wider than usual and remain open after the sodium channels close, enough potassium ions leave to drive the membrane beyond the normal resting level to a temporary hyperpolarization. Meanwhile, negatively charged chloride ions, which are more concentrated outside the membrane, are no longer repelled by a negative charge within the cell, so they tend to flow inward. Figure 2.16 summarizes the key movements of ions during an action potential.

At the end of this process, the membrane has returned to its resting potential, but the inside of the neuron has slightly more sodium ions and slightly fewer potassium ions than

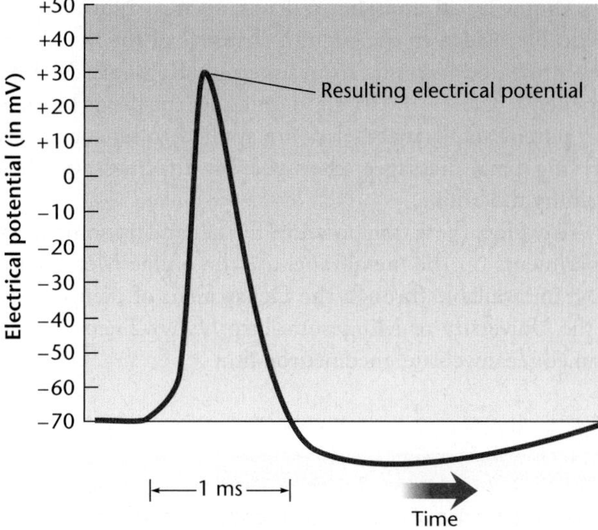

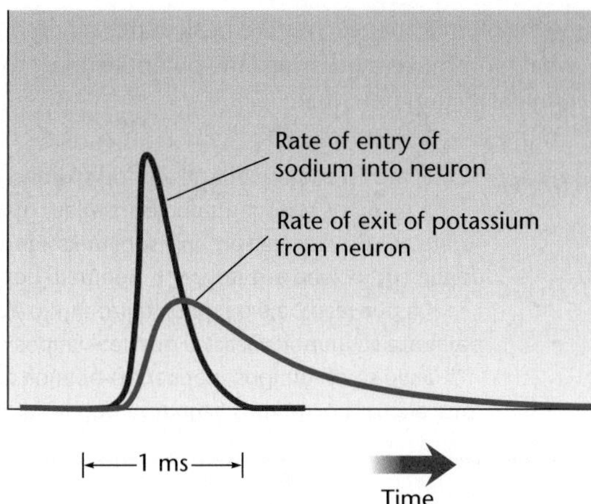

Figure 2.16 The movement of sodium and potassium ions during an action potential
Sodium ions cross during the peak of the action potential and potassium ions cross later in the opposite direction, returning the membrane to its original polarization.

before. Eventually, the sodium-potassium pump restores the original distribution of ions, but that process takes time. In fact, after an unusually rapid series of action potentials, the pump cannot keep up with the action, and sodium accumulates within the axon. Excessive buildup of sodium can be toxic to a cell. (Excessive stimulation occurs only under abnormal conditions, however, such as during a stroke or after the use of certain drugs. Don't worry that thinking too hard will explode your brain cells!)

For the neuron to function properly, sodium and potassium must flow across the membrane at just the right pace. Scorpion venom attacks the nervous system by keeping sodium channels open and closing potassium channels (Pappone & Cahalan, 1987; Strichartz, Rando, & Wang, 1987). As a result, the membrane goes into a prolonged depolarization and accumulates dangerously high amounts of sodium. **Local anesthetic** drugs, such as Novocain and Xylocaine, attach to the sodium channels of the membrane, preventing sodium ions from entering (Ragsdale, McPhee, Scheuer, & Catterall, 1994). In doing so, the drugs block action potentials. If anesthetics are applied to sensory nerves carrying pain messages, they prevent the messages from reaching the brain.

To explore the action potential further and try some virtual experiments on the membrane, use the online MetaNeuron program available through the Department of Neuroscience at the University of Minnesota: http://www2.neuroscience.umn.edu/eanwebsite/metaneuron.htm

STOP & CHECK

11. During the rise of the action potential, do sodium ions move into the cell or out of it? Why?

12. As the membrane reaches the peak of the action potential, what ionic movement brings the potential down to the original resting potential?

ANSWERS

11. During the action potential, sodium ions move into the cell. The voltage-dependent sodium gates have opened, so sodium can move freely. Sodium is attracted to the inside of the cell by both an electrical and a concentration gradient. **12.** After the peak of the action potential, potassium ions exit the cell, driving the membrane back to the resting potential. (The sodium-potassium pump is not the answer here; it is too slow.)

The All-or-None Law

Action potentials occur only in axons and cell bodies. When the voltage across an axon membrane reaches a certain level of depolarization (the threshold), voltage-gated sodium channels open wide to let sodium enter rapidly, and the incoming sodium depolarizes the membrane still further. Dendrites can depolarize also, but they don't have voltage-gated sodium channels, so opening the channels a little, letting in a little sodium, doesn't cause them to open even more and let in still more sodium. Thus, dendrites don't have action potentials. If the dendrites depolarize the cell enough, its axon produces an action potential.

For a given neuron, all action potentials are approximately equal in amplitude (intensity) and velocity under normal circumstances. This is the **all-or-none law:** The amplitude and velocity of an action potential are independent of the intensity of the stimulus that initiated it. By analogy, imagine flushing a toilet: You have to make a press of at least a certain strength (the threshold), but pressing harder does not make the toilet flush any faster or more vigorously.

Although the amplitude, velocity, and shape of action potentials are consistent over time for a given axon, they vary from one neuron to another. The earliest studies dealt with squid axons because squid have very thick axons that are easy to study. More recent studies of mammalian axons have found much variation in the types of protein channels and therefore in the dimensions of the action potentials (Bean, 2007).

The all-or-none law puts constraints on how an axon can send a message. To signal the difference between a weak stimulus and a strong stimulus, the axon can't send bigger or faster action potentials. All it can change is the timing. By analogy, suppose you agree to exchange coded messages with someone who can see your window when you flick the lights on and off. The two of you might agree, for example, to indicate some kind of danger by the frequency of flashes. (The more flashes, the more danger.) Much of the brain's signaling follows this principle; more frequent action potentials signal a greater intensity of stimulus.

You could also convey information by a rhythm.

Flash-flash . . . [long pause] . . . flash-flash

might mean something different from

Flash . . . [pause] . . . flash . . . [pause] . . . flash . . . [pause] . . . flash.

In some cases, the nervous system uses this kind of coding (Ikegaya et al., 2004; Oswald, Chacron, Doiron, Bastian, & Maler, 2004). For example, an axon might show one rhythm of responses for sweet tastes and a different rhythm for bitter tastes (Di Lorenzo, Hallock, & Kennedy, 2003).

The Refractory Period

While the electrical potential across the membrane is returning from its peak toward the resting point, it is still above the threshold. Why doesn't the cell produce another action potential during this period? Immediately after an action potential, the cell is in a **refractory period** during which it resists the production of further action potentials. In the first part of this period, the **absolute refractory period,** the membrane cannot produce an action potential, regardless of the stimulation. During the second part, the **relative refractory period,** a stronger than usual stimulus is necessary to initiate an action potential. The refractory period has two mechanisms: The sodium channels are closed, and potassium is flowing out of the cell at a faster than usual rate.

Most of the neurons that have been tested have an absolute refractory period of about 1 ms and a relative refractory period of another 2–4 ms. (To return to the toilet analogy, there is a short time right after you flush a toilet when you cannot make it flush again—an absolute refractory period. Then follows a period when it is possible but difficult to flush it again—a relative refractory period—before it returns to normal.)

STOP & CHECK

13. State the all-or-none law.

14. Does the all-or-none law apply to dendrites? Why or why not?

15. Suppose researchers find that axon A can produce up to 1,000 action potentials per second (at least briefly, with maximum stimulation), but axon B can never produce more than 100 per second (regardless of the strength of the stimulus). What could we conclude about the refractory periods of the two axons?

ANSWERS

13. According to the all-or-none law, the size and shape of the action potential are independent of the intensity of the stimulus that initiated it. That is, every depolarization beyond the threshold of excitation produces an action potential of about the same amplitude and velocity for a given axon. **14.** The all-or-none law does not apply to dendrites because they do not have action potentials. **15.** Axon A must have a shorter absolute refractory period, about 1 ms, whereas B has a longer absolute refractory period, about 10 ms.

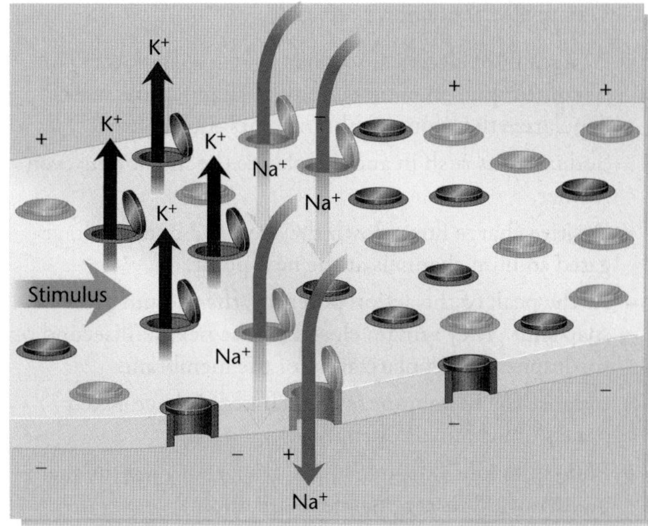

(a)

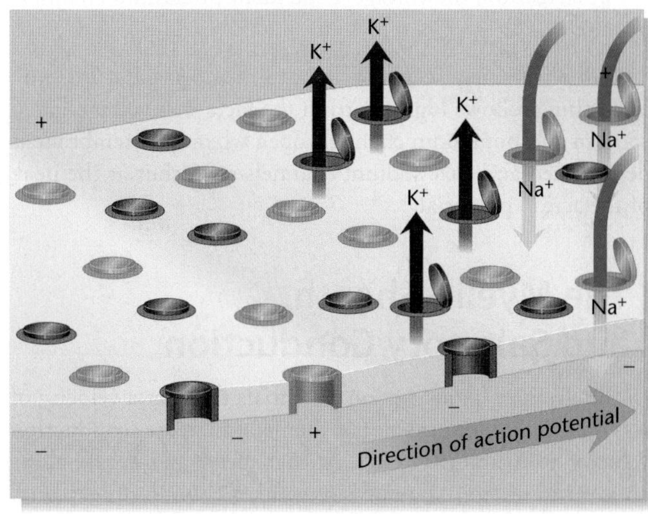

(b)

Figure 2.17 Propagation of an action potential
Current that enters an axon during the action potential flows down the axon, depolarizing adjacent areas of the membrane. The current flows more easily through thicker axons. Behind the area of sodium entry, potassium ions exit.

Propagation of the Action Potential

Up to this point, we have considered how the action potential occurs at one point on the axon. Now let us consider how it moves down the axon. Remember, it is important for axons to convey impulses without any loss of strength over distance.

In a motor neuron, an action potential begins on the **axon hillock,** a swelling where the axon exits the soma (see Figure 2.5, p. 30). Each point along the membrane regenerates the action potential in much the same way that it was generated initially. During the action potential, sodium ions enter a point on the axon. Temporarily, that location is positively charged in comparison with neighboring areas along the axon. The positive ions flow down the axon and across the membrane, as shown in Figure 2.17. Other things being equal, the greater the diameter of the axon, the faster the ions flow (because of decreased resistance). The positive charges now inside the membrane slightly depolarize the adjacent areas of the membrane, causing the next area to reach its threshold and open the voltage-gated sodium channels. Therefore, the membrane regenerates the action potential at that point. In this manner, the action potential travels like a wave along the axon.

The term **propagation of the action potential** describes the transmission of an action potential down an axon. The propagation of an animal species is the production of offspring; in a sense, the action potential gives birth to a new action potential at each point along the axon. In this manner, the action potential can be just as strong at the end of the axon as it was at the beginning. The action potential is much slower than electrical conduction because it requires the diffusion of sodium ions at successive points along the axon.

Let's reexamine Figure 2.17 for a moment. What is to prevent the electrical charge from flowing in the direction opposite that in which the action potential is traveling? Nothing. In fact, the electrical charge does flow in both directions. In that case, what prevents an action potential near the center of an axon from reinvading the areas that it has just passed? The answer is that the areas just passed are still in their refractory period.

Let's review the action potential:

- As a result of electrical stimulation (in a laboratory) or synaptic input (in nature), sodium channels open and depolarize the axon membrane to its threshold.
- Sodium ions rush in and depolarize the membrane even further.
- Positive charge flows down the axon and opens voltage-gated sodium channels at the next point.
- At the peak of the action potential, the sodium gates snap shut. They remain closed for the next millisecond or so, despite the depolarization of the membrane.
- Because the membrane is depolarized, voltage-gated potassium channels open.
- Potassium ions flow out of the axon, returning the membrane toward its original depolarization.
- After the membrane returns to its original level of polarization, the voltage-dependent potassium channels close.

All of this may seem like a lot to memorize, but it is not. Everything follows logically from the facts that voltage-gated sodium and potassium channels open when the membrane is depolarized and that sodium channels snap shut at the peak of the action potential.

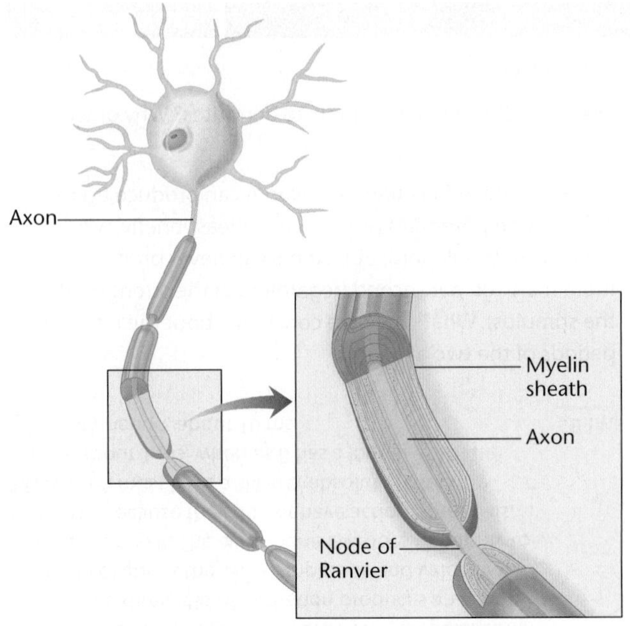

Figure 2.18 An axon surrounded by a myelin sheath and interrupted by nodes of Ranvier
The inset shows a cross-section through both the axon and the myelin sheath. Magnification approximately x 30,000. The anatomy is distorted here to show several nodes; in fact, the distance between nodes is generally at least 100 times as long as the nodes themselves.

The Myelin Sheath and Saltatory Conduction

In the thinnest axons, action potentials travel at a velocity of less than 1 m/s. Increasing the diameter increases conduction velocity up to about 10 m/s. At that speed, an impulse along an axon to or from a giraffe's foot takes about half a second. To increase the speed up to about 100 m/s, vertebrate axons evolved a special mechanism: sheaths of **myelin,** an insulating material composed of fats and proteins.

Consider the following analogy. Suppose my job is to take written messages over a distance of 3 kilometers (km) without using any mechanical device. Taking each message and running with it would be reliable but slow, like the propagation of an action potential along an unmyelinated axon. If I tied each message to a ball and threw it, I could increase the speed, but my throws would travel only a small fraction of the 3 km. The ideal compromise is to station people at moderate distances along the 3 km and throw the message-bearing ball from person to person until it reaches its destination.

The principle behind **myelinated axons,** those covered with a myelin sheath, is the same. Myelinated axons, found only in vertebrates, are covered with fats and proteins. The myelin sheath is interrupted periodically by short sections of axon called nodes of Ranvier, as shown in Figure 2.18. Each node is only about 1 micrometer wide. In most cases, the action potential starts at the axon hillock, but a few exceptions are known where it starts at the first node of Ranvier (Kuba, Ishii, & Ohmari, 2006).

Suppose an action potential starts at the axon hillock and propagates along the axon until it reaches the first myelin segment. The action potential cannot regenerate along the membrane between nodes because sodium channels are virtually absent between nodes (Catterall, 1984). After an action potential occurs at a node, sodium ions enter the axon and diffuse within the axon, repelling positive ions that were already present and pushing a chain of positive ions along the axon to the next node, where they regenerate the action potential (Figure 2.19). This flow of ions is considerably faster than the regeneration of an action potential at each point along the axon. The jumping of action potentials from node to node is referred to as **saltatory conduction,** from the Latin word *saltare,* meaning "to jump." (The same root shows up in the word *somersault.*) In addition to providing rapid conduction of impulses, saltatory conduction conserves energy: Instead of admitting sodium ions at every point along the axon and then having to pump them out via the sodium-potassium pump, a myelinated axon admits sodium only at its nodes.

Multiple sclerosis is one of several demyelinating diseases, in which the immune system attacks myelin sheaths. An axon that never had a myelin sheath conducts impulses, though at a relatively slow speed. An axon that has lost its myelin is not the same. When myelin forms along an axon, the axon loses its sodium channels under the myelin (Waxman & Ritchie, 1985). If the axon loses myelin, it still lacks sodium channels in the areas previously covered with myelin, and most action

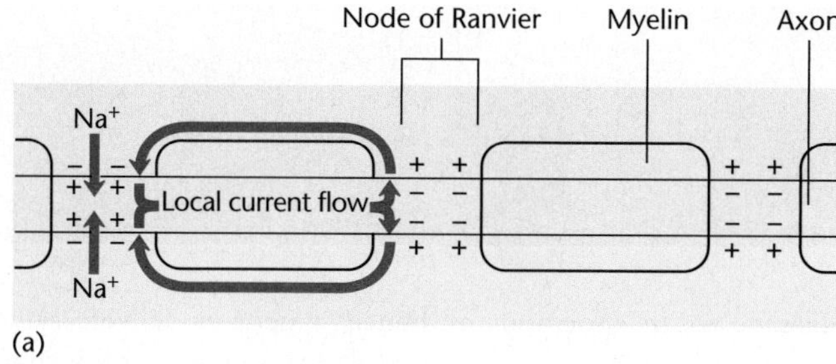

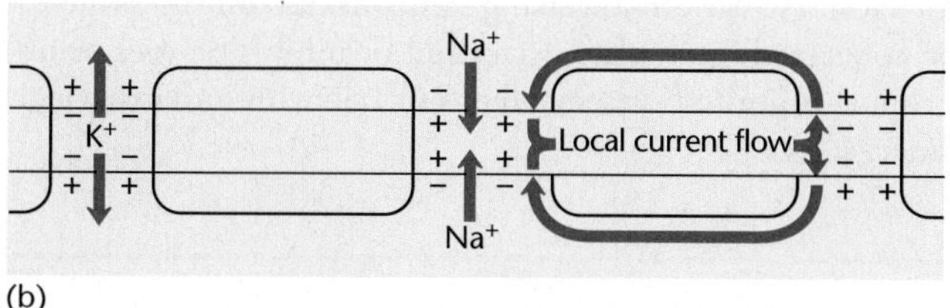

Figure 2.19 Saltatory conduction in a myelinated axon
An action potential at the node triggers flow of current to the next node, where the membrane regenerates the action potential.

potentials die out between one node and the next. People with multiple sclerosis suffer a variety of impairments, ranging from visual impairments to poor muscle coordination.

For an additional review of action potentials, visit the Website Neuroscience for Kids by Eric Chudler of the University of Washington, Seattle: http://faculty.washington.edu/chudler/ap.html

STOP & CHECK

16. In a myelinated axon, how would the action potential be affected if the nodes were much closer together? How might it be affected if the nodes were much farther apart?

ANSWER

16. If the nodes were closer, the action potential would travel more slowly. If they were much farther apart, the current might not be able to diffuse from one node to the next and still remain above threshold, so the action potentials might stop.

Local Neurons

Axons produce action potentials. However, some neurons do not have axons. These neurons are smaller but very important.

Graded Potentials

Neurons without axons exchange information only with their closest neighbors and are therefore known as **local neurons.** A local neuron receives information from other neurons and produces **graded potentials,** membrane potentials that vary in magnitude without following the all-or-none law. When a local neuron is stimulated, it depolarizes or hyperpolarizes in proportion to the intensity of the stimulus. The change in membrane potential is conducted to adjacent areas of the cell, in all directions, gradually decaying as it travels. Those various areas of the cell contact other neurons, which they excite or inhibit through synapses (which we consider in the next chapter). In Chapter 6, we discuss in some detail a particular local neuron, the *horizontal cell,* which is essential for local interactions within the retina of the eye.

In some ways, astrocytes, although they are glia cells, operate like local neurons (Volterra & Meldolesi, 2005). They have no action potentials, but they rapidly exchange chemicals back and forth with neighboring neurons.

APPLICATIONS AND EXTENSIONS

Small Neurons and Big Misconceptions

Local neurons are difficult to study because it is almost impossible to insert an electrode into a tiny cell without damaging it. A disproportionate amount of our knowledge, therefore, has come from large neurons, and that bias in our research methods may have led to an enduring misconception.

Many years ago, long before neuroscientists could investigate local neurons, all they knew about them was that they were small. Given that what they knew about the nervous system was based on large neurons, they considered the small neurons unimportant. Many scientists assumed that they were immature neurons. As one textbook author put it, "Many of these are small and apparently undeveloped, as if they constituted a reserve stock not yet utilized in the individual's cerebral activity" (Woodworth, 1934, p. 194). In other words, the small cells would contribute to behavior only if they grew.

Perhaps this misunderstanding was the origin of that widespread, nonsensical belief that "we use only 10% of our brain." It is difficult to imagine any reasonable justification for this belief. Surely, no one maintained that someone could lose 90% of the brain and still behave normally or that only 10% of neurons are active at any given moment. Whatever its source, the belief became popular, presumably because people wanted to believe it. Eventually, people were simply quoting one another long after everyone forgot what evidence they had (or didn't have) for it in the first place.

MODULE 2.2 IN CLOSING

Neural Messages

In this chapter, we have examined what happens within a single neuron, as if each neuron acted independently. It does not, of course; all of its functions depend on communication with other neurons, as we consider in the next chapter. We may as well admit from the start, however, that neural communication is amazing. Unlike human communication, in which a speaker sometimes presents a complicated message to an enormous audience, a neuron delivers only an action potential—a mere on/off message—to only that modest number of other neurons that receive branches of its axon. At various receiving neurons, an "on" message can be converted into either excitation or inhibition (yes or no). From this limited system, all of our behavior and experience emerge.

SUMMARY

1. The action potential transmits information without loss of intensity over distance. The cost is a delay between the stimulus and its arrival in the brain. **37**
2. The inside of a resting neuron has a negative charge with respect to the outside. Sodium ions are actively pumped out of the neuron, and potassium ions are pumped in. Potassium ions flow slowly across the membrane of the neuron, but sodium ions hardly cross it at all while the membrane is at rest. **37**
3. When the membrane is at rest, the electrical gradient and concentration gradient act in competing directions for potassium, almost balancing out. Both gradients tend to push sodium into the cell. **38**
4. When the charge across the membrane is reduced, sodium ions can flow more freely across the membrane. When the membrane potential reaches the threshold of the neuron, sodium ions enter explosively, suddenly reducing and reversing the charge across the membrane. This event is known as the action potential. **39**
5. After the peak of the action potential, the membrane returns to its original level of polarization because of the outflow of potassium ions. **41**
6. The all-or-none law: For any stimulus greater than the threshold, the amplitude and velocity of the action potential are independent of the size of the stimulus that initiated it. **42**
7. Immediately after an action potential, the membrane enters a refractory period during which it is resistant to starting another action potential. **42**
8. The action potential is regenerated at successive points along the axon by sodium ions flowing through the core of the axon and then across the membrane. The action potential maintains a constant magnitude as it passes along the axon. **43**
9. The principles of the action potential follow logically from these facts: Depolarization of the membrane opens voltage-gated sodium and potassium channels, and the sodium channels snap shut at the peak of the action potential. **44**
10. In axons that are covered with myelin, action potentials form only in the nodes that separate myelinated segments. Transmission in myelinated axons is much faster than in unmyelinated axons. **44**

KEY TERMS

Terms are defined in the module on the page number indicated. They're also presented in alphabetical order with definitions in the book's Subject Index/Glossary. Interactive flashcards, audio reviews, and crossword puzzles are among the online resources available to help you learn these terms and the concepts they represent.

absolute refractory period **42**
action potential **40**
all-or-none law **42**
axon hillock **43**
concentration gradient **39**
depolarize **40**
electrical gradient **39**
graded potentials **45**
hyperpolarization **40**
local anesthetic **42**
local neurons **45**
myelin **44**
myelinated axons **44**
polarization **37**
propagation of the action potential **43**
refractory period **42**
relative refractory period **42**
resting potential **37**
saltatory conduction **44**
selectively permeable **38**
sodium-potassium pump **38**
threshold of excitation **40**
voltage-gated channels **41**

THOUGHT QUESTIONS

1. Suppose the threshold of a neuron were the same as its resting potential. What would happen? At what frequency would the cell produce action potentials?
2. In the laboratory, researchers can apply an electrical stimulus at any point along the axon, making action potentials travel in both directions from the point of stimulation. An action potential moving in the usual direction, away from the axon hillock, is said to be traveling in the *orthodromic* direction. An action potential traveling toward the axon hillock is traveling in the *antidromic* direction. If we started an orthodromic action potential at the axon hillock and an antidromic action potential at the opposite end of the axon, what would happen when they met at the center? Why? What research might make use of antidromic impulses?
3. If a drug partly blocks a membrane's potassium channels, how does it affect the action potential?

CHAPTER 2 Exploration and Study

In addition to the study materials provided at the end of each module, you may supplement your review of this chapter by using one or more of the book's electronic resources, which include its companion Website, interactive Cengage Learning eBook, Exploring Biological Psychology CD-ROM, and CengageNOW. Brief descriptions of these resources follow. For more information, visit **www.cengage.com/psychology/kalat.**

The book's companion Website, accessible through the author Web page indicated above, provides a wide range of study resources such as an interactive glossary, flashcards, tutorial quizzes, updated Web links, and Try It Yourself activities, as well as a limited selection of the short videos and animated explanations of concepts available for this chapter.

Exploring Biological Psychology

The Exploring Biological Psychology CD-ROM contains videos, animations, and Try-It-Yourself activities. These activities—as well as many that are new to this edition—are also available in the text's fully interactive, media-rich Cengage Learning eBook,* which gives you the opportunity to experience biological psychology in an even greater interactive and multimedia environment. The Cengage Learning eBook also includes highlighting and note-taking features and an audio glossary. For this chapter, the Cengage Learning eBook includes the following interactive explorations:

The Parts of a Neuron
Neuron Membrane at Rest
Propagation of the Action Potential
Action Potential
Action Potential: Na^+ Ions
Salutatory Conduction
Neuron Puzzle
Resting Potential

CENGAGENOW™ is an easy-to-use resource that helps you study in less time to get the grade you want. An online study system, CengageNOW* gives you the option of taking a diagnostic pretest for each chapter. The system uses the results of each pretest to create personalized chapter study plans for you. The Personalized Study Plans

- help you save study time by identifying areas on which you should concentrate and give you one-click access to corresponding pages of the interactive Cengage Learning eBook;
- provide interactive exercises and study tools to help you fully understand chapter concepts; and
- include a posttest for you to take to confirm that you are ready to move on to the next chapter.

Suggestions for Further Exploration

The book's companion Website includes a list of suggested articles available through InfoTrac College Edition for this chapter. You may also want to explore some of the following books and Websites. The text's companion Website provides live, updated links to the sites listed below.

Books

Smith, C. U. M. (2002). *Elements of molecular neurobiology* (3rd ed.). Hoboken, NJ: Wiley. A detailed treatment of the molecular biology of neurons, including both action potentials and synaptic activity.

Websites

University of Minnesota: *MetaNeuron Program*
Here you can vary temperatures, ion concentrations, membrane permeability, and so forth to see the effects on action potentials.
http://www2.neuroscience.umn.edu/eanwebsite/metaneuron.htm

University of Washington, Seattle: *Lights, Camera, Action Potential*
From Eric Chudler's *Neuroscience for Kids.* (But don't assume that it's too childish for adults.)
http://faculty.washington.edu/chudler/ap.html

* Requires a Cengage Learning eResources account. Visit **www.cengage.com/login** to register or login.

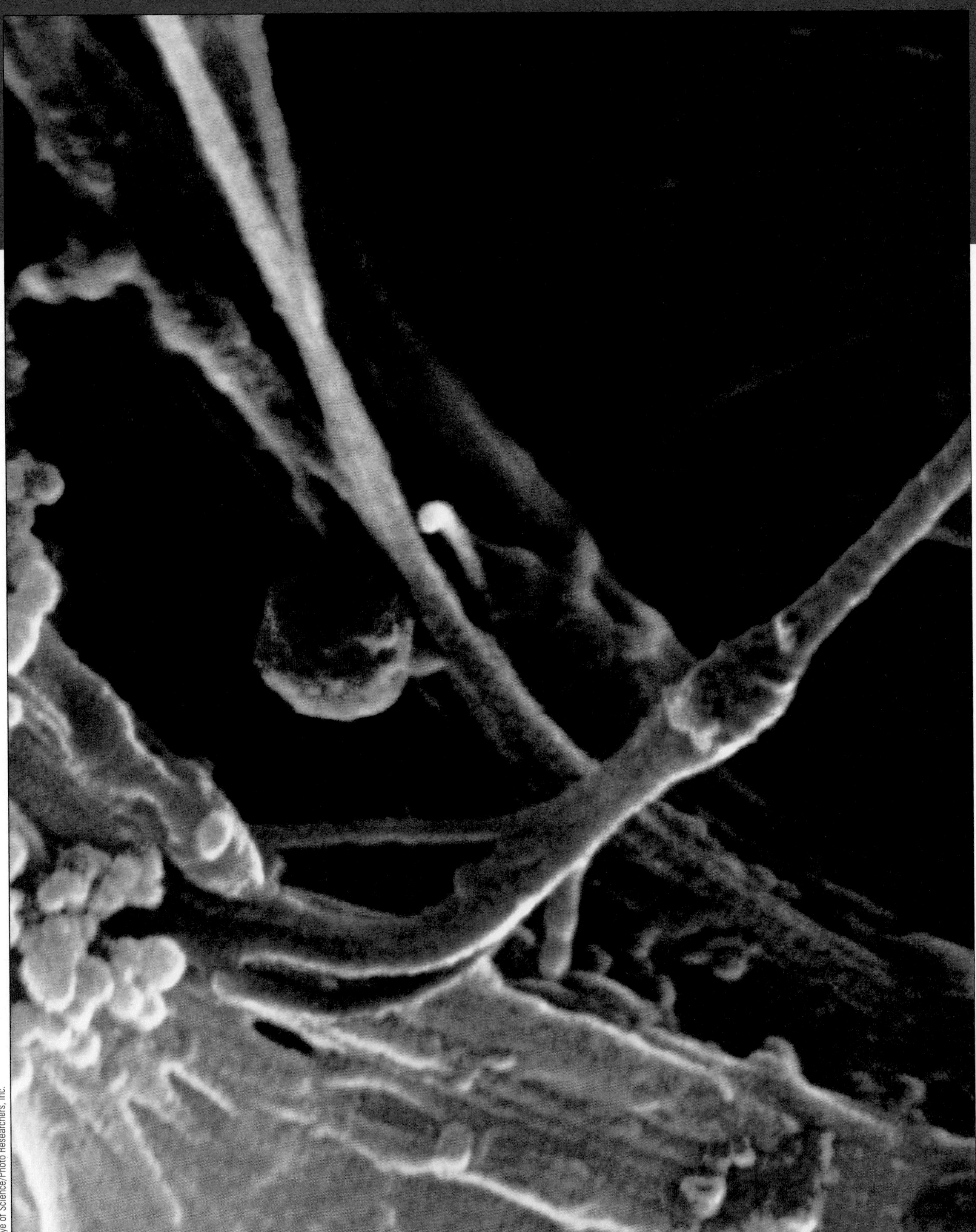

Synapses

3

CHAPTER OUTLINE

MAIN IDEAS

1. At a synapse, a neuron releases neurotransmitters (chemicals) that excite or inhibit another cell or alter its response to other input.
2. In most cases, a single release of neurotransmitter produces only a subthreshold response in the receiving cell. This response summates with other subthreshold responses to determine whether or not the cell produces an action potential.
3. Transmission at synapses goes through many steps, and interference at any of them can alter the outcome.
4. Nearly all drugs that affect behavior or experience do so by acting at synapses.
5. Nearly all abused drugs increase the release of dopamine in certain brain areas.
6. Addiction changes certain brain areas, increasing the tendency to seek the addictive substance and decreasing the response to other kinds of reinforcement.

If you had to communicate with someone without sound, what would you do? Chances are, your first choice would be a visual code, such as written words or sign language. Your second choice would probably be some sort of touch code or a system of electrical impulses. You might not even think of passing chemicals back and forth. Chemical communication is, however, the primary method of communication for your neurons. Neurons communicate by transmitting chemicals at specialized junctions called *synapses.*

OPPOSITE: This electron micrograph, with color added artificially, shows axons terminating onto another cell, forming connections called synapses.

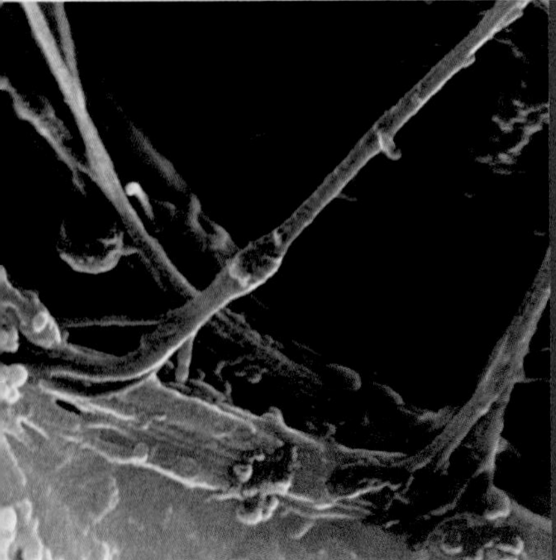

MODULE 3.1

The Concept of the Synapse

In the late 1800s, Ramón y Cajal anatomically demonstrated a narrow gap separating one neuron from another. In 1906, Charles Scott Sherrington physiologically demonstrated that communication between one neuron and the next differs from communication along a single axon. He inferred a specialized gap between neurons and introduced the term **synapse** to describe it. Cajal and Sherrington are regarded as the great pioneers of modern neuroscience, and their nearly simultaneous discoveries supported each other: If communication between one neuron and another was special in some way, then there could be no doubt that neurons were anatomically separate from one another. Sherrington's discovery was an amazing feat of scientific reasoning, as he used behavioral observations to infer the major properties of synapses about half a century before researchers had the technology to measure those properties directly.

Charles Scott Sherrington (1857–1952)

A rainbow every morning who would pause to look at? The wonderful which comes often or is plentifully about us is soon taken for granted. That is practical enough. It allows us to get on with life. But it may stultify if it cannot on occasion be thrown off. To recapture now and then childhood's wonder, is to secure a driving force for occasional grown-up thoughts.

The Properties of Synapses

Sherrington conducted his research on **reflexes,** automatic muscular responses to stimuli. In a leg flexion reflex, a sensory neuron excites a second neuron, which in turn excites a motor neuron, which excites a muscle, as in Figure 3.1. The circuit from sensory neuron to muscle response is called a **reflex arc.** If one neuron is separate from another, as Cajal had demonstrated, a reflex must require communication between neurons, and therefore, measurements of reflexes might reveal some of the special properties of that communication.

Sherrington strapped a dog into a harness above the ground and pinched one of the dog's feet. After a short delay—less than a second but long enough to measure—the dog *flexed* (raised) the pinched leg and *extended* the others. Sherrington found the same reflexive movements after he made a cut that disconnected the spinal cord from the brain; evidently, the spinal cord controlled the flexion and extension reflexes. In fact, the movements were more consistent after he separated the spinal cord from the brain. (In an intact animal, messages descending from the brain inhibit or modify the reflexes.)

Sherrington observed several properties of reflexes suggesting special processes at the junctions between neurons: (a) Reflexes are slower than conduction along an axon. (b) Several weak stimuli presented at slightly different times or slightly different locations produce a stronger reflex than

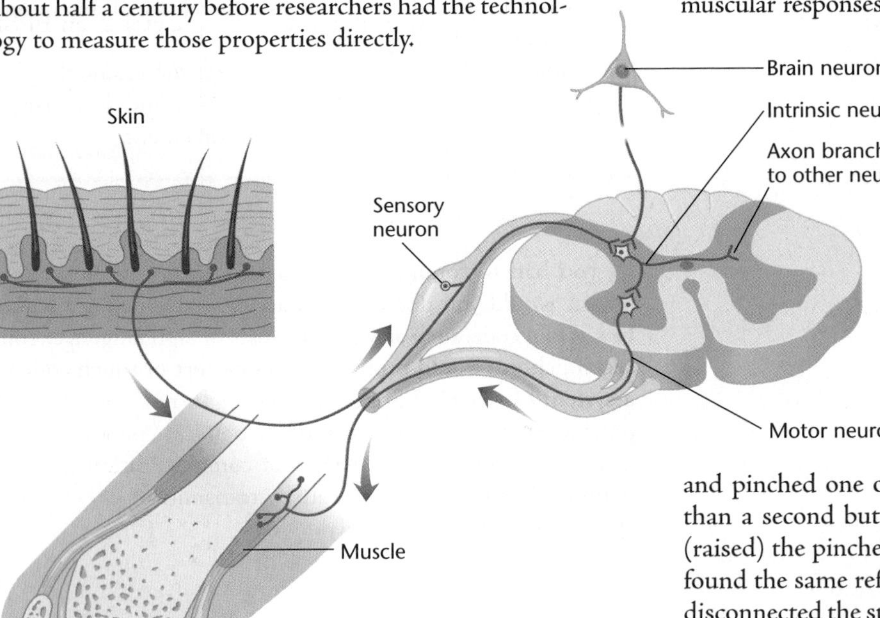

Figure 3.1 A reflex arc for leg flexion
The anatomy has been simplified to show the relationship among sensory neuron, intrinsic neuron, and motor neuron.

a single stimulus does. (c) When one set of muscles becomes excited, a different set becomes relaxed. Let's consider each of these points and their implications.

Speed of a Reflex and Delayed Transmission at the Synapse

When Sherrington pinched a dog's foot, the dog flexed that leg after a short delay. During that delay, an impulse had to travel up an axon from the skin receptor to the spinal cord, and then an impulse had to travel from the spinal cord back down the leg to a muscle. Sherrington measured the total distance that the impulse traveled from skin receptor to spinal cord to muscle and calculated the speed at which the impulse must have traveled to produce the response within the measured delay. He found that the speed of conduction through the reflex arc varied but was never more than about 15 meters per second (m/s). In contrast, previous research had measured action potential velocities along sensory or motor nerves at about 40 m/s. Sherrington concluded that some process was slowing conduction through the reflex, and he inferred that the delay must occur where one neuron communicates with another (Figure 3.2). This idea is critical, as it established the existence of synapses. Sherrington, in fact, introduced the term *synapse.*

STOP & CHECK

1. What evidence led Sherrington to conclude that transmission at a synapse is different from transmission along an axon?

ANSWER

1. Sherrington found that the velocity of conduction through a reflex arc was significantly slower than the velocity of an action potential along an axon. Therefore, some delay must occur at the junction between one neuron and the next.

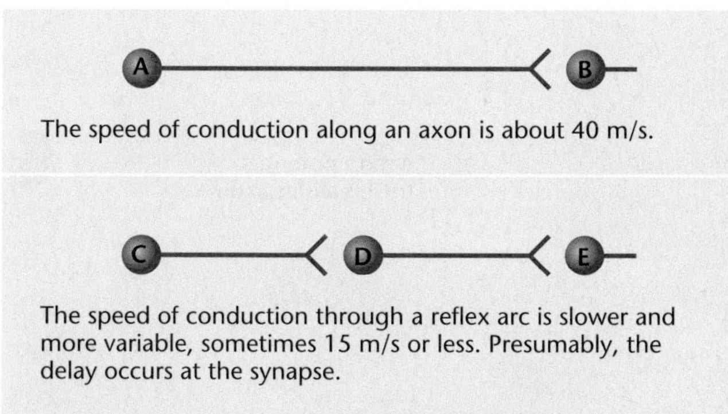

A
B
The speed of conduction along an axon is about 40 m/s.
C
D
E
The speed of conduction through a reflex arc is slower and more variable, sometimes 15 m/s or less. Presumably, the delay occurs at the synapse.

Figure 3.2 Sherrington's evidence for synaptic delay
An impulse traveling through a synapse in the spinal cord is slower than one traveling a similar distance along an uninterrupted axon.

Temporal Summation

Sherrington found that repeated stimuli within a brief time have a cumulative effect. He referred to this phenomenon as **temporal summation** (summation over time). A light pinch of the dog's foot did not evoke a reflex, but a few rapidly repeated pinches did. Sherrington surmised that a single pinch produced a synaptic transmission less than the threshold for the **postsynaptic neuron,** the cell that receives the message. (The neuron that delivers the synaptic transmission is the **presynaptic neuron.**) Sherrington proposed that this subthreshold excitation begins to decay shortly after it starts but can combine with a second excitation that quickly follows it. With a rapid succession of pinches, each adds its effect to what remained from the previous ones, until the combination exceeds the threshold of the postsynaptic neuron, producing an action potential.

Decades later, John Eccles (1964) attached microelectrodes to stimulate axons of presynaptic neurons while he recorded from the postsynaptic neuron. For example, after he had briefly stimulated an axon, Eccles recorded a slight depolarization of the membrane of the postsynaptic cell (point 1 in Figure 3.3).

Note that this partial depolarization is a graded potential. Unlike action potentials, which are always depolarizations, graded potentials may be either depolarizations (excitatory) or hyperpolarizations (inhibitory). A graded depolarization is known as an **excitatory postsynaptic potential (EPSP).** Like the action potentials discussed in Chapter 2, an EPSP occurs when sodium ions enter the cell. If an EPSP does not cause the cell to reach its threshold, the depolarization decays quickly.

When Eccles stimulated an axon twice in close succession, he recorded two consecutive EPSPs in the postsynaptic cell. If the delay between EPSPs was short enough, temporal summation occurred. That is, the second EPSP added to what was left of the first one (point 2 in Figure 3.3). At point 3 in Figure 3.3, three consecutive EPSPs combine to exceed the threshold and produce an action potential.

Spatial Summation

Sherrington's work with reflex arcs also suggested that synapses have the property of **spatial summation** (summation over space): Synaptic inputs from separate locations combine their effects on a neuron. Sherrington again began with a pinch too weak to elicit a reflex. This time, instead of pinching one point twice, he pinched two points at once. Although neither pinch alone produced a reflex, together they did. Sherrington concluded that pinching two points activated two sensory neurons, whose axons converged onto one neuron in the spinal cord. Excitation from either axon excited that neuron, but not enough to reach the threshold. A combination of excitations exceeded the threshold and produced an action potential (point 4 in Figure 3.3). Again, Eccles confirmed Sherrington's inference, demonstrating that EPSPs from several axons summate their effects on a postsynaptic cell (Figure 3.4).

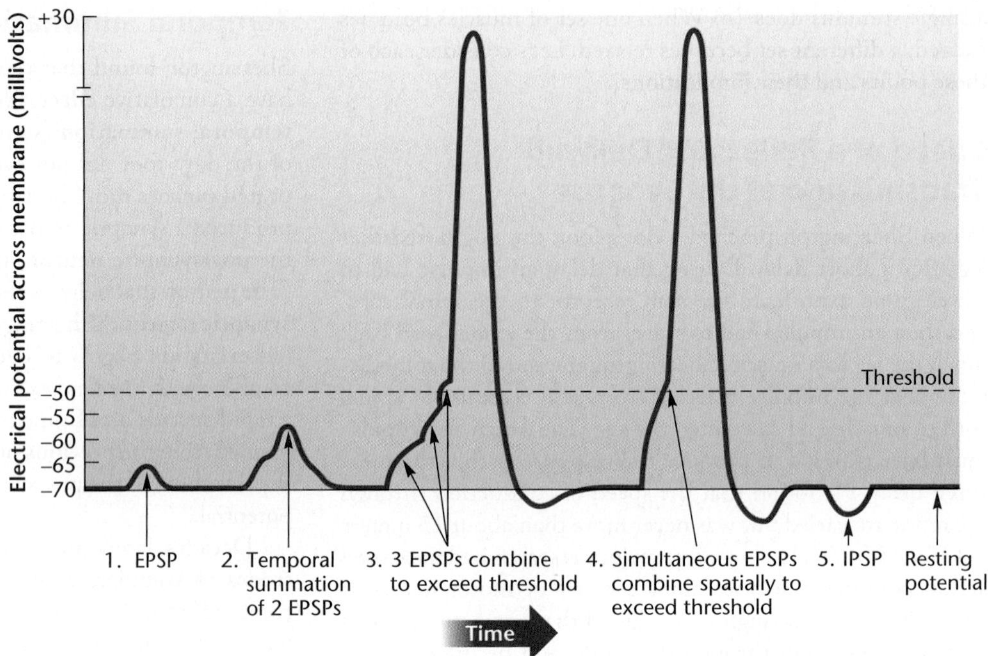

Figure 3.3 Recordings from a postsynaptic neuron during synaptic activation

Spatial summation is critical to brain functioning. Sensory input to the brain arrives at synapses that individually produce weak effects. However, each neuron receives many incoming axons, which are synchronized during sensory stimulation (Bruno & Sakmann, 2006). Spatial summation assures that a sensory stimulus will stimulate the cortical cells enough to activate them.

2. What is the difference between temporal summation and spatial summation?

ANSWER

2. Temporal summation is the combined effect of quickly repeated stimulation at a single synapse. Spatial summation is the combined effect of several nearly simultaneous stimulations at several synapses onto one neuron.

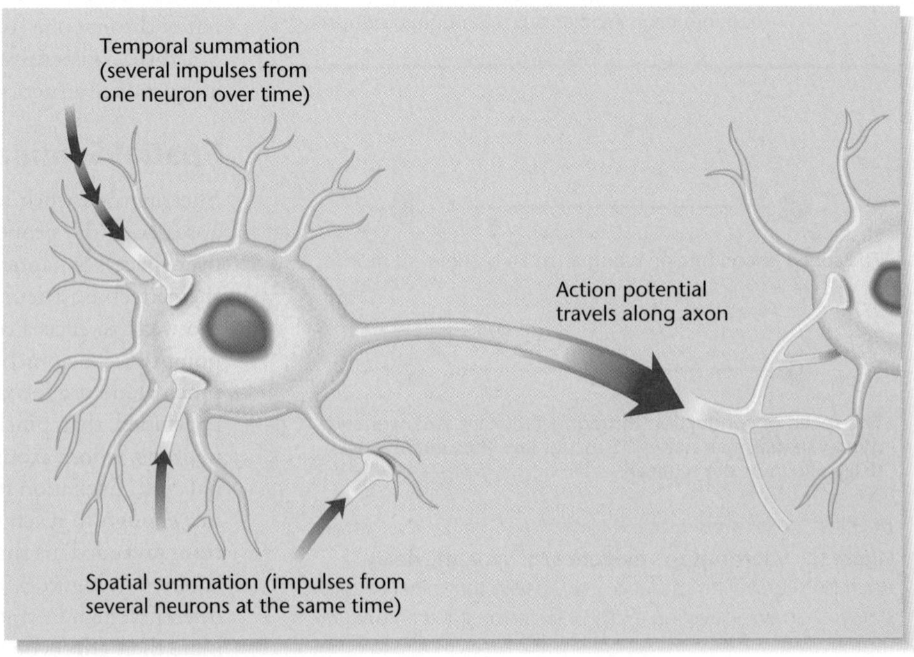

Figure 3.4 Temporal and spatial summation

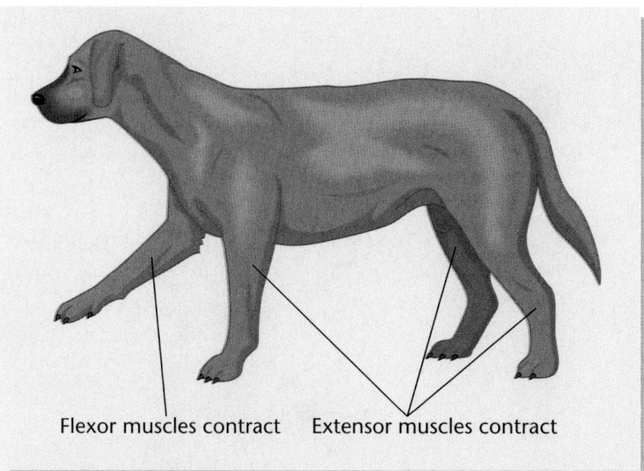

Figure 3.5 Antagonistic muscles
Flexor muscles draw an extremity toward the trunk of the body, whereas extensor muscles move an extremity away from the body.

Inhibitory Synapses

When Sherrington vigorously pinched a dog's foot, the flexor muscles of that leg contracted, and so did the extensor muscles of the other three legs (Figure 3.5). Also, the dog relaxed the extensor muscles of the stimulated leg and the flexor muscles of the other legs. Sherrington explained these results by assuming certain connections in the spinal cord: A pinch on the foot sends a message along a sensory neuron to an *interneuron* (an intermediate neuron) in the spinal cord, which in turn excites the motor neurons connected to the flexor muscles of that leg (Figure 3.6). Sherrington surmised that the interneuron also sends a message to block activity of motor neurons to the extensor muscles in the same leg and the flexor muscles of the three other legs.

Eccles and later researchers physiologically demonstrated the inhibitory synapses that Sherrington had inferred. At these synapses, input from an axon hyperpolarizes the postsynaptic cell. That is, it increases the negative charge within the cell, moving it further from the threshold and decreasing the probability of an action potential (point 5 in Figure 3.3). This temporary hyperpolarization of a membrane—called an **inhibitory postsynaptic potential,** or **IPSP**—resembles an EPSP. An IPSP occurs when synaptic input selectively opens the gates for potassium ions to leave the cell (carrying a positive charge with them) or for chloride ions to enter the cell (carrying a negative charge).

When we learn the basics of any scientific field, we sometimes take them for granted, as if people always knew them. For example, today, we take the concept of inhibition for granted, but at Sherrington's time, the idea was controversial, as no one could imagine a mechanism to accomplish it. Establishing the idea of inhibition was critical not just for neuroscience but for psychology as well.

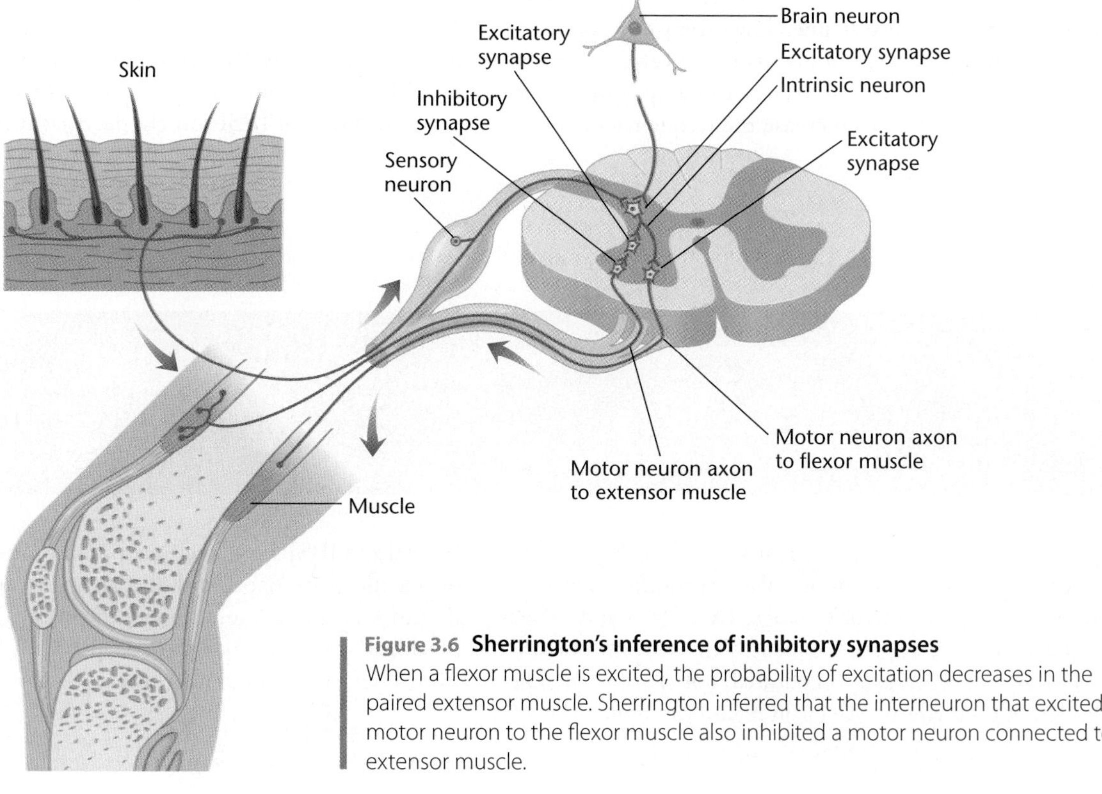

Figure 3.6 Sherrington's inference of inhibitory synapses
When a flexor muscle is excited, the probability of excitation decreases in the paired extensor muscle. Sherrington inferred that the interneuron that excited a motor neuron to the flexor muscle also inhibited a motor neuron connected to the extensor muscle.

STOP & CHECK

3. What was Sherrington's evidence for inhibition in the nervous system?

4. What ion gates in the membrane open during an EPSP? What gates open during an IPSP?

5. Can an inhibitory message propagate along an axon?

ANSWERS

3. Sherrington found that a reflex that stimulates a flexor muscle sends a simultaneous message that inhibits nerves to the extensor muscles of the same limb. **4.** During an EPSP, sodium gates open. During an IPSP, potassium or chloride gates open. **5.** No. Only action potentials propagate along an axon. Both EPSPs and IPSPs decay rapidly over time and distance. Their function is to determine whether the axon will send an action potential.

Relationship Among EPSP, IPSP, and Action Potentials

Sherrington's work opened the way to exploring the wiring diagram of the nervous system. For example, consider the neurons shown in Figure 3.7. When neuron 1 excites neuron 3, it also excites neuron 2, which inhibits neuron 3. The excitatory message reaches neuron 3 faster because it goes through just one synapse instead of two. The result is brief excitation (EPSP) in neuron 3, which stops quickly. You see how the inhibitory neurons, which are typically very small, can regulate the timing of activity. The nervous system is full of complex patterns of connections, which produce an unending variety of responses.

Most neurons have a **spontaneous firing rate,** a periodic production of action potentials even without synaptic input. In such neurons, the EPSPs increase the frequency of action potentials above the spontaneous rate, whereas IPSPs decrease it below that rate. For example, if the neuron's spontaneous firing rate is 10 action potentials per second, a stream of EPSPs might increase the rate to 15 or more, whereas a preponderance of IPSPs might decrease it to 5 or fewer.

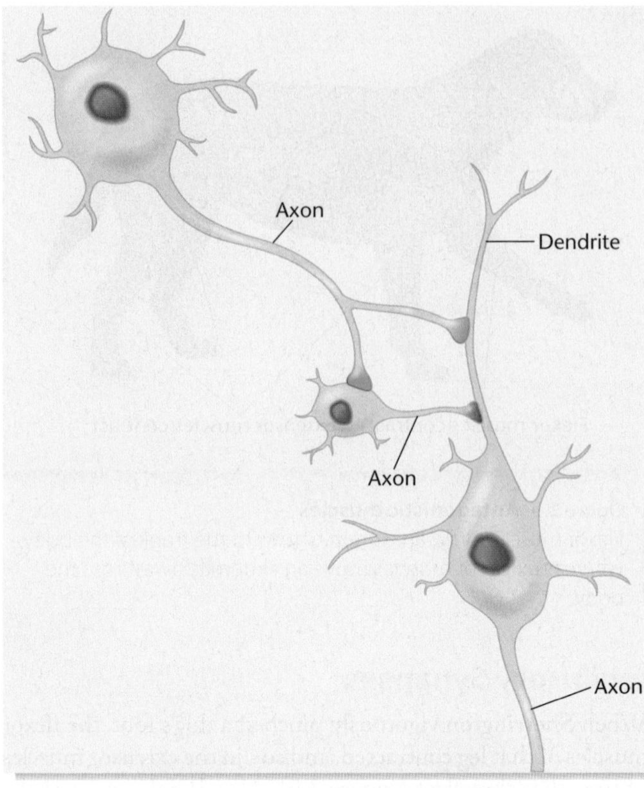

Figure 3.7 One of many possible wiring diagrams for synapses
Excitatory synapses are in green, and inhibitory synapses in red. Typically, neurons that produce inhibitory responses are small, as shown here. *(Based on Kullmann & Lamsa, 2007)*

MODULE 3.1 IN CLOSING

The Neuron as Decision Maker

Synapses are where the action is. Transmission along an axon merely sends information from one place to another. Synapses determine whether to send the message. The EPSPs and IPSPs reaching a neuron at a given moment compete with one another, and the net result is a complicated, not exactly algebraic summation of their effects. We could regard the summation of EPSPs and IPSPs as a "decision" because it determines whether or not the postsynaptic cell fires an action potential. However, do not imagine that any single neuron decides what to eat for breakfast. Complex behaviors depend on the contributions from a huge network of neurons.

SUMMARY

1. The synapse is the point of communication between two neurons. Charles S. Sherrington's observations of reflexes enabled him to infer the properties of synapses. **50**
2. Because transmission through a reflex arc is slower than transmission through an equivalent length of axon, Sherrington concluded that some process at the synapses delays transmission. **51**
3. Graded potentials (EPSPs and IPSPs) summate their effects. The summation of graded potentials from stimuli at different times is temporal summation. The summation of graded potentials from different locations is spatial summation. **51**
4. Inhibition is more than just the absence of excitation; it is an active "brake" that suppresses excitation. Within the nervous system, inhibition is just as important as excitation. Stimulation at a synapse produces a brief graded potential in the postsynaptic cell. An excitatory graded potential (depolarizing) is an EPSP. An inhibitory graded potential (hyperpolarizing) is an IPSP. An EPSP occurs when gates open to allow sodium to enter the neuron's membrane; an IPSP occurs when gates open to allow potassium to leave or chloride to enter. **53**
5. The EPSPs on a neuron compete with the IPSPs; the balance between the two increases or decreases the neuron's frequency of action potentials. **54**

KEY TERMS

Terms are defined in the module on the page number indicated. They're also presented in alphabetical order with definitions in the book's Subject Index/Glossary. Interactive flashcards, audio reviews, and crossword puzzles are among the online resources available to help you learn these terms and the concepts they represent.

excitatory postsynaptic potential (EPSP) **51**
inhibitory postsynaptic potential (IPSP) **53**
postsynaptic neuron **51**
presynaptic neuron **51**
reflex arc **50**
reflexes **50**
spatial summation **51**
spontaneous firing rate **54**
synapse **50**
temporal summation **51**

THOUGHT QUESTIONS

1. When Sherrington measured the reaction time of a reflex (i.e., the delay between stimulus and response), he found that the response occurred faster after a strong stimulus than after a weak one. Can you explain this finding? Remember that all action potentials—whether produced by strong or weak stimuli—travel at the same speed along a given axon.
2. A pinch on an animal's right hind foot excites a sensory neuron that excites an interneuron that excites the motor neurons to the flexor muscles of that leg. The interneuron also inhibits the motor neurons connected to the extensor muscles of the leg. In addition, this interneuron sends impulses that reach the motor neuron connected to the extensor muscles of the left hind leg. Would you expect the interneuron to excite or inhibit that motor neuron? (Hint: The connections are adaptive. When an animal lifts one leg, it must put additional weight on the other legs to maintain balance.)
3. Suppose neuron X has a synapse onto neuron Y, which has a synapse onto Z. Presume that no other neurons or synapses are present. An experimenter finds that stimulating neuron X causes an action potential in neuron Z after a short delay. However, she determines that the synapse of X onto Y is inhibitory. Explain how the stimulation of X might produce excitation of Z.

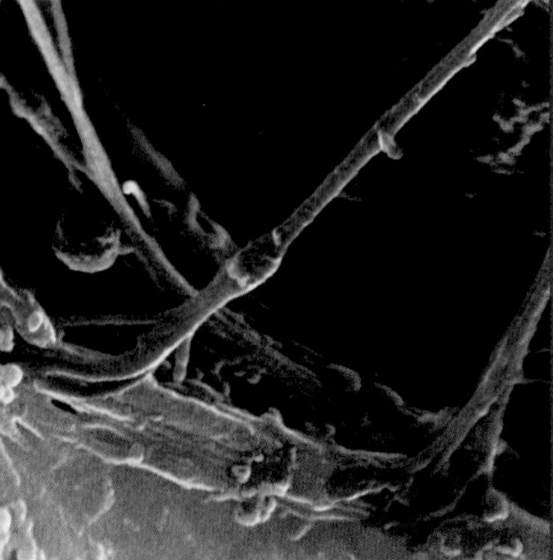

MODULE 3.2

Chemical Events at the Synapse

Although Charles Sherrington accurately inferred many properties of the synapse, he was wrong about one important point: Although he knew that synaptic transmission was slower than transmission along an axon, he thought it was still too fast to depend on a chemical process and therefore concluded that it must be electrical. We now know that the great majority of synapses rely on chemical processes, which are much faster and more versatile than Sherrington or anyone else of his era would have guessed.

The Discovery of Chemical Transmission at Synapses

A set of nerves called the sympathetic nervous system accelerates the heartbeat, relaxes the stomach muscles, dilates the pupils of the eyes, and regulates other organs. T. R. Elliott, a young British scientist, reported in 1905 that applying the hormone *adrenaline* directly to the surface of the heart, the stomach, and the pupils produces the same effects as those of the sympathetic nervous system. Elliott therefore suggested that the sympathetic nerves stimulate muscles by releasing adrenaline or a similar chemical.

However, Elliott's evidence was not decisive. Perhaps adrenaline merely mimicked effects that are ordinarily electrical in nature. At the time, Sherrington's prestige was so great that most scientists ignored Elliott's results and continued to assume that synapses transmitted electrical impulses. Otto Loewi, a German physiologist, liked the idea of chemical synapses but did not see how to demonstrate it more convincingly. Then in 1920, he awakened one night with a sudden idea. He wrote himself a note and went back to sleep. Unfortunately, the next morning he could not read his note. The following night he awoke at 3 A.M. with the same idea, rushed to the laboratory, and performed the experiment.

Loewi repeatedly stimulated the vagus nerve, thereby decreasing the frog's heart rate. He then collected fluid from that heart, transferred it to a second frog's heart, and found that the second heart also decreased its rate of beating. (Figure 3.8 illustrates this study.) Later, Loewi stimulated the accelerator nerve to the first frog's heart, increasing the heart rate. When he collected fluid from that heart and transferred it to the second heart, its heart rate increased. That is, stimulating one nerve released something that inhibited heart rate, and stimulating a different nerve released something that increased heart rate. He knew he was collecting and transferring chemicals, not loose electricity. Therefore, Loewi concluded, nerves send messages by releasing chemicals.

Loewi later remarked that if he had thought of this experiment in the light of day, he probably would not have tried it (Loewi, 1960). Even if synapses did release chemicals, his daytime reasoning went, they probably did not release much. Fortunately, by the time he realized that the experiment was unlikely to work, he had already completed it, for which he later won the Nobel prize.

Despite Loewi's work, most researchers over the next three decades continued to believe that most synapses were electrical and that chemical synapses were the exception. Finally, in the 1950s, researchers established that chemical transmission is the predominant type of communication throughout the nervous system. That discovery revolutionized our under-

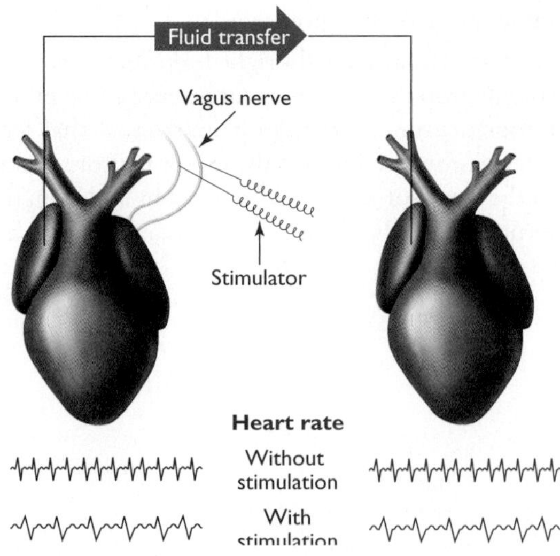

Figure 3.8 Loewi's experiment demonstrating that nerves send messages by releasing chemicals
Loewi stimulated the vagus nerve to one frog's heart, decreasing the heartbeat. When he transferred fluid from that heart to another frog's heart, he observed a decrease in its heartbeat.

standing and led to research developing new drugs for psychiatric uses (Carlsson, 2001).

STOP & CHECK

6. What was Loewi's evidence that neurotransmission depends on the release of chemicals?

ANSWER

6. When Loewi stimulated a nerve that increased or decreased a frog's heart rate, he could withdraw some fluid from the area around the heart, transfer it to another frog's heart, and thereby increase or decrease its rate also.

The Sequence of Chemical Events at a Synapse

Understanding the chemical events at a synapse is fundamental to biological psychology. Every year, researchers discover more and more details about synapses, their structure, and how those structures relate to function. Here are the major events:

1. The neuron synthesizes chemicals that serve as neurotransmitters. It synthesizes the smaller neurotransmitters in the axon terminals and neuropeptides in the cell body.
2. The neuron transports the neuropeptides that were formed in the cell body to the axon terminals or to the dendrites. (Neuropeptides are released from multiple sites in the cell.)
3. Action potentials travel down the axon. At the presynaptic terminal, an action potential enables calcium to enter the cell. Calcium releases neurotransmitters from the terminals and into the *synaptic cleft*, the space between the presynaptic and postsynaptic neurons.
4. The released molecules diffuse across the cleft, attach to receptors, and alter the activity of the postsynaptic neuron.
5. The neurotransmitter molecules separate from their receptors. Depending on the neurotransmitter, it may be converted into inactive chemicals.
6. The neurotransmitter molecules may be taken back into the presynaptic neuron for recycling or may diffuse away. In some cases, empty vesicles are returned to the cell body.
7. Some postsynaptic cells send reverse messages to control the further release of neurotransmitter by presynaptic cells.

Figure 3.9 summarizes these steps. Let's now consider each step in more detail.

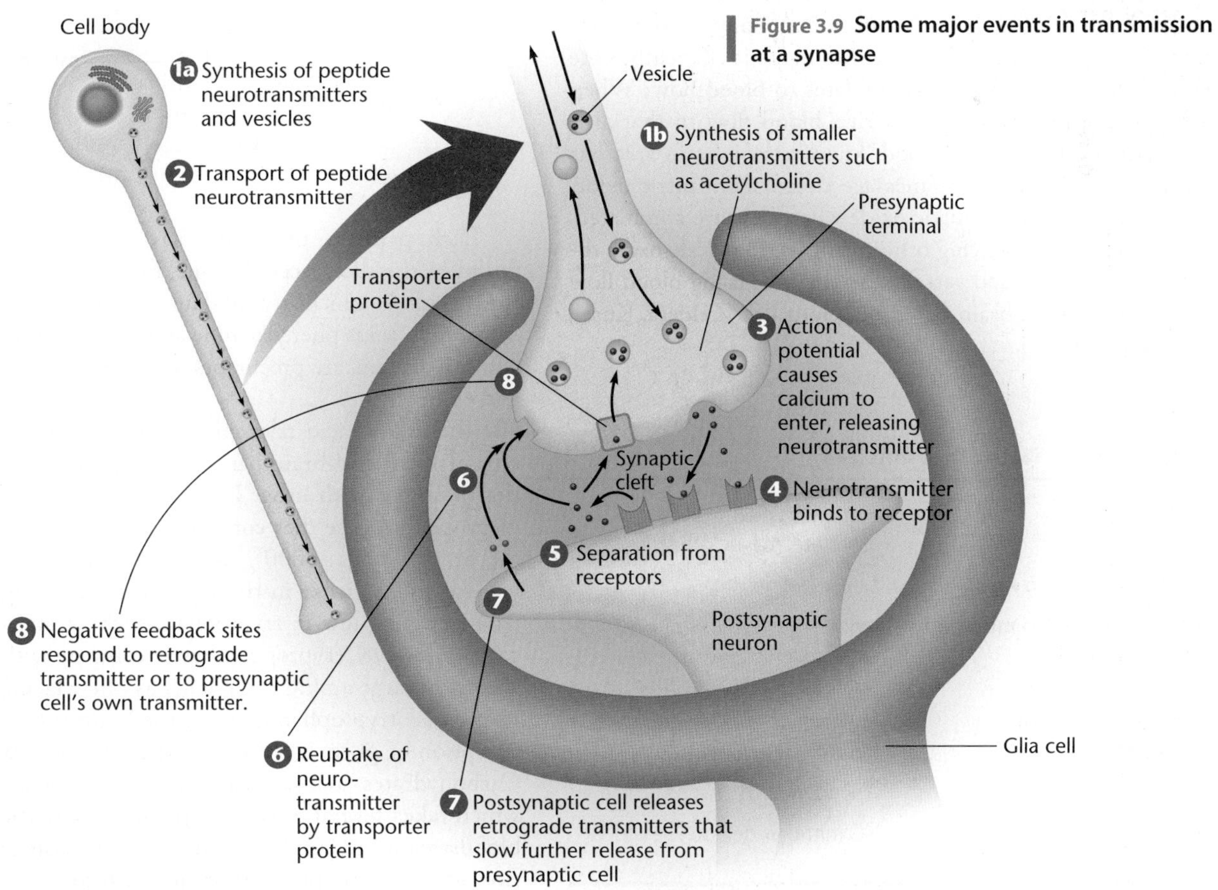

Figure 3.9 Some major events in transmission at a synapse

Types of Neurotransmitters

At a synapse, one neuron releases chemicals that affect a second neuron. Those chemicals are known as **neurotransmitters.** Research has gradually identified a hundred or more chemicals believed or suspected to be neurotransmitters, as shown in Table 3.1 (Borodinsky et al., 2004). Some major categories are:

amino acids acids containing an amine group (NH_2)

neuropeptides chains of amino acids

acetylcholine (a one-member "family") a chemical similar to an amino acid, except that the NH_2 group has been replaced by an $N(CH_3)_3$ group

monoamines neurotransmitters containing one amine group (NH_2), formed by a metabolic change in certain amino acids

purines a category of chemicals including adenosine and several of its derivatives

gases nitric oxide and possibly others

The neuropeptides and nitric oxide serve special functions, as we shall explore later in this module.

All but a few of the neurotransmitters are amino acids, derivatives of amino acids, or chains of amino acids. The most surprising exception is **nitric oxide** (chemical formula NO), a gas released by many small local neurons. (Do not confuse nitric oxide, NO, with nitrous oxide, N_2O, sometimes known as "laughing gas.") Nitric oxide is poisonous in large quantities and difficult to make in a laboratory. Yet, many neurons contain an enzyme that enables them to make it efficiently. One special function of nitric oxide relates to blood flow: When a brain area becomes highly active, blood flow to that area increases. How does the blood "know" that a brain area has become more active? The message comes from nitric oxide. Many neurons release nitric oxide when they are stimulated. In addition to influencing other neurons, the nitric oxide dilates the nearby blood vessels, thereby increasing blood flow to that area of the brain (Dawson, Gonzalez-Zulueta, Kusel, & Dawson, 1998).

TABLE 3.1 Neurotransmitters

Amino Acids	glutamate, GABA, glycine, aspartate, maybe others
A Modified Amino Acid	acetylcholine
Monoamines (also modified from amino acids)	indoleamines: serotonin catecholamines: dopamine, norepinephrine, epinephrine
Peptides (chains of amino acids)	endorphins, substance P, neuropeptide Y, many others
Purines	ATP, adenosine, maybe others
Gases	NO (nitric oxide), maybe others

STOP & CHECK

7. What does a highly active brain area do, in many cases, to increase its blood supply?

ANSWER

7. In a highly active brain area, many stimulated neurons release nitric oxide, which dilates the blood vessels in the area and thereby increases blood flow to the area.

Synthesis of Transmitters

Like any other cell in the body, a neuron synthesizes the chemicals it needs from substances in the diet. Figure 3.10 illustrates the chemical steps in the synthesis of acetylcholine, serotonin, dopamine, epinephrine, and norepinephrine. Note the relationship among epinephrine, norepinephrine, and dopamine—three closely related compounds known as **catecholamines** because they contain a catechol group and an amine group, as shown here:

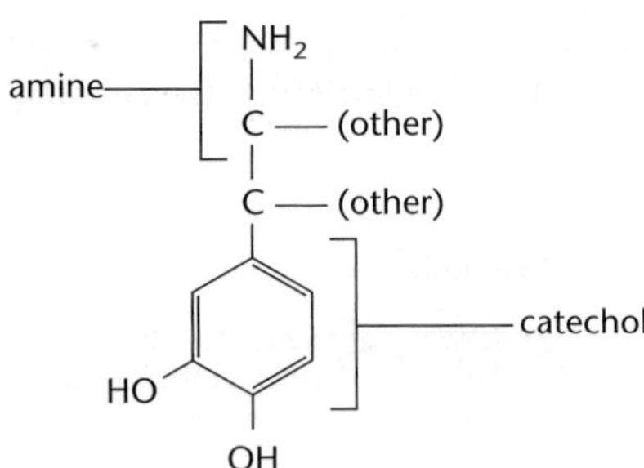

Each pathway in Figure 3.10 begins with substances found in the diet. Acetylcholine, for example, is synthesized from choline, which is abundant in milk, eggs, and peanuts. The amino acids phenylalanine and tyrosine, present in virtually any protein, are precursors of dopamine, norepinephrine, and epinephrine.

The amino acid *tryptophan*, the precursor to serotonin, crosses the blood-brain barrier by a special transport system that it shares with other large amino acids. The amount of tryptophan in the diet controls the amount of serotonin in the brain (Fadda, 2000), so your serotonin levels rise after you eat foods richer in tryptophan, such as soy, and fall after something low in tryptophan, such as maize (American corn). However, tryptophan has to compete with other, more abundant large amino acids, such as phenylalanine. One way to increase tryptophan entry to the brain is to decrease consumption of phenylalanine. Another is to eat carbohydrates. Carbohydrates increase the release of *insulin*, a hormone, which takes several of the competing amino acids out of the bloodstream and into body cells, thus decreasing the competition against tryptophan (Wurtman, 1985).

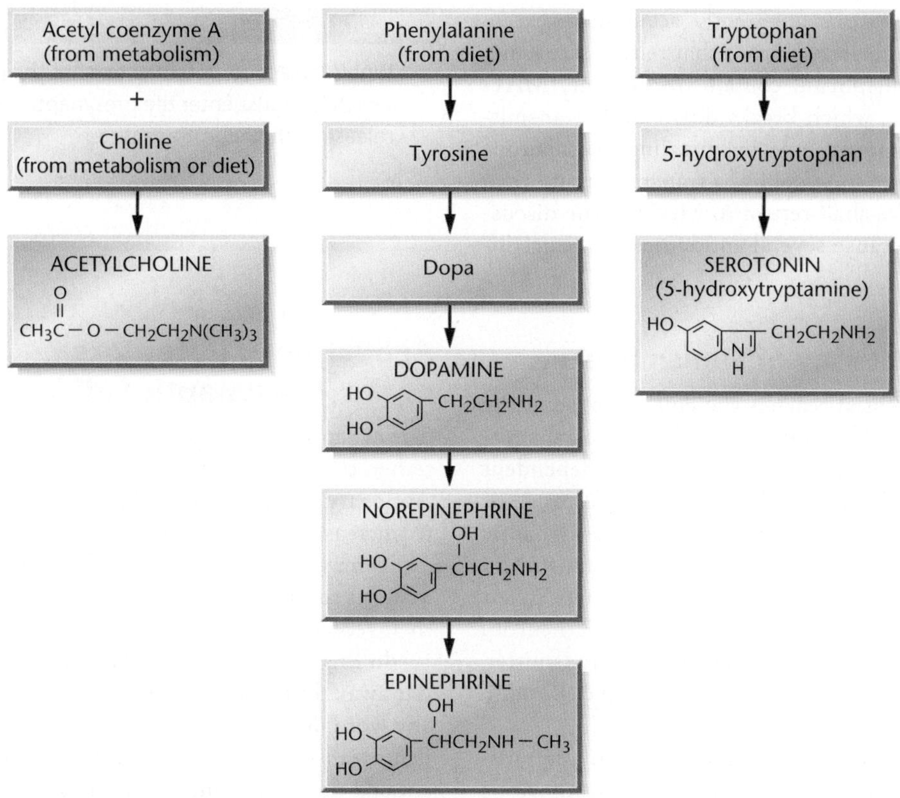

Figure 3.10 Pathways in the synthesis of acetylcholine, dopamine, norepinephrine, epinephrine, and serotonin
Arrows represent chemical reactions.

8. Name the three catecholamine neurotransmitters.

ANSWER

8. epinephrine, norepinephrine, and dopamine

Transport and Storage of Transmitters

The most abundant neurotransmitters are synthesized in the presynaptic terminal, near the point of release. However, the neuropeptides are synthesized in the cell body and then transported down the axon or into the dendrites. (Unlike other transmitters, neuropeptides are released from many sites in the cell.) The speed of transport varies from only 1 millimeter (mm) per day in thin axons to more than 100 mm per day in thicker ones.

The presynaptic terminal stores high concentrations of neurotransmitter molecules in **vesicles,** tiny nearly spherical packets (Figure 3.11). (Nitric oxide, the gaseous neurotransmitter mentioned earlier, is an exception to this rule. Neurons release nitric oxide as soon as they form it instead of storing it.) The presynaptic terminal also maintains much neurotransmitter outside the vesicles.

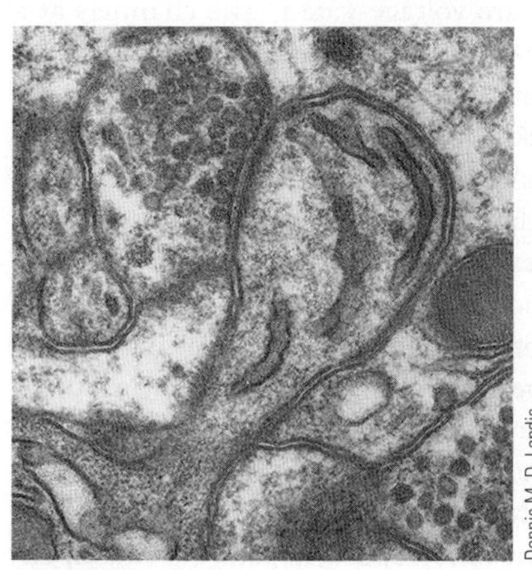

(a)

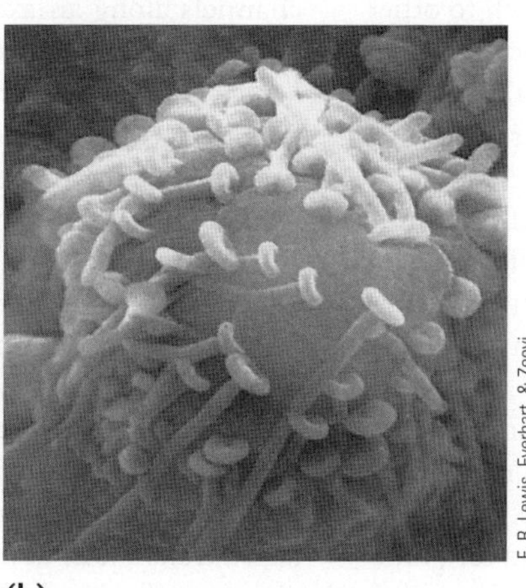

(b)

Figure 3.11 Anatomy of a synapse
(a) An electron micrograph showing a synapse from the cerebellum of a mouse. The small round structures are vesicles. *(From Landis, 1987)* **(b)** Electron micrograph showing axon terminals onto the soma of a neuron. *(From "Studying neural organization and aplysia with the scanning electron micrograph," by E. R. Lewis, et al.,* Science *1969, 165:1142. Copyright 1969 by the AAAS. Reprinted with permission of AAAS and E. R. Lewis.)*

In some cases, neurons apparently accumulate excess levels of a neurotransmitter. Neurons that release serotonin, dopamine, or norepinephrine contain an enzyme, **MAO** (monoamine oxidase), which breaks down these transmitters into inactive chemicals. It seems puzzling that neurons would sometimes make too much of a transmitter and then destroy the excess. We shall return to MAO in the discussion of depression because several antidepressant drugs inhibit MAO.

Release and Diffusion of Transmitters

When an action potential reaches the end of an axon, the action potential itself does not release the neurotransmitter. Rather, the depolarization opens voltage-dependent calcium gates in the presynaptic terminal. Within 1 or 2 milliseconds (ms) after calcium enters the presynaptic terminal, it causes **exocytosis**—release of neurotransmitter in bursts from the presynaptic neuron into the synaptic cleft that separates this neuron from the postsynaptic neuron. An action potential often fails to release any transmitter, and even when it does, the amount varies (Craig & Boudin, 2001).

After its release from the presynaptic cell, the neurotransmitter diffuses across the synaptic cleft to the postsynaptic membrane, where it attaches to a receptor. The neurotransmitter takes no more than 0.01 ms to diffuse across the cleft, which is only 20 to 30 nanometers (nm) wide. Remember, Sherrington did not believe chemical processes could be fast enough to account for the activity at synapses. Obviously, he did not imagine such a narrow gap through which chemicals could diffuse so quickly.

Although the brain as a whole uses many neurotransmitters, no single neuron releases them all. For many years, investigators believed that each neuron released just one neurotransmitter, but later researchers found that many, perhaps most, neurons release a combination of two or more transmitters (Hökfelt, Johansson, & Goldstein, 1984). Still later researchers found that at least one kind of neuron releases different transmitters from different branches of its axon: Motor neurons in the spinal cord have one branch to the muscles, where they release acetylcholine, and another branch to other spinal cord neurons, where they release both acetylcholine and glutamate (Nishimaru, Restrepo, Ryge, Yanagawa, & Kiehn, 2005). If one kind of neuron can release different transmitters at different branches, maybe others can, too.

Why does a neuron release a combination of transmitters instead of just one? Presumably, the combination makes the neuron's message more complex, such as brief excitation followed by slight but prolonged inhibition (P. Jonas, Bischofberger, & Sandkühler, 1998).

Although a neuron releases only a limited number of neurotransmitters, it may receive and respond to many neurotransmitters at different synapses. For example, at various locations on its membrane, it might have receptors for glutamate, serotonin, acetylcholine, and others.

STOP & CHECK

9. When the action potential reaches the presynaptic terminal, which ion must enter the presynaptic terminal to evoke release of the neurotransmitter?

ANSWER

9. calcium

Activation of Receptors of the Postsynaptic Cell

The synapse is a complicated place, with many proteins that tether the presynaptic neuron to the postsynaptic neuron. Abnormalities of these scaffolding proteins have been linked to increased anxiety, sleep disorders, and other behavioral problems (Welch et al., 2007). Their functions are to hold the neurons together and to guide neurotransmitter molecules to their receptors.

In English, a *fern* is a kind of plant. In German, *fern* means "far away." In French, the term is meaningless. The meaning of any word depends on the listener. Similarly, the meaning of a neurotransmitter depends on its receptor. Each of the well-studied neurotransmitters is known to interact with several different kinds of receptors, with different functions. Therefore, a drug or a genetic mutation that affects one receptor type may affect behavior in a specific way. For example, one type of serotonin receptor mediates nausea, and the drug *ondansetron* that blocks this receptor helps cancer patients undergo treatment without nausea.

A neurotransmitter receptor is a protein embedded in the membrane. When the neurotransmitter attaches to the active site of the receptor, the receptor can directly open a channel—exerting an *ionotropic* effect—or it can produce slower but longer effects—a *metabotropic* effect.

Ionotropic Effects. Certain neurotransmitters exert **ionotropic effects** on the postsynaptic neuron: When the neurotransmitter binds to a receptor on the membrane, it opens the channels for some type of ion. The sodium and potassium channels along an axon are voltage-gated. The channels at a synapse are **transmitter-gated** or **ligand-gated** channels. (A *ligand* is a chemical that binds to another chemical.) Ionotropic effects begin quickly, sometimes within less than a millisecond (Lisman, Raghavachari, & Tsien, 2007), and they last only about 20 ms (North, 1989; Westbrook & Jahr, 1989).

Most of the brain's excitatory ionotropic synapses use the neurotransmitter *glutamate*. Most of the inhibitory ionotropic synapses use the neurotransmitter GABA (gamma-aminobutyric acid), which opens chloride gates, enabling chloride ions, with their negative charge, to cross the membrane into the cell more rapidly than usual. Glycine is another common inhibitory transmitter (Moss & Smart, 2001). Acetylcholine, also a transmitter at many ionotropic synapses, has mostly excitatory effects, which have been extensively studied. Figure

3.12a shows a cross-section through an acetylcholine receptor as it might be seen from the synaptic cleft. Its outer portion (red) is embedded in the neuron's membrane; its inner portion (blue) surrounds the sodium channel. When at rest (unstimulated), the inner portion of the receptor coils together tightly enough to block sodium passage. When acetylcholine attaches, the receptor folds outward, widening the sodium channel. Figure 3.12b shows a side view of the receptor with acetylcholine attached (Miyazawa, Fujiyoshi, & Unwin, 2003).

Metabotropic Effects and Second Messenger Systems. At other synapses, neurotransmitters exert **metabotropic effects** by initiating a sequence of metabolic reactions that are slower and longer lasting than ionotropic effects (Greengard, 2001). Metabotropic effects emerge 30 ms or more after the release of the transmitter (North, 1989) and last seconds, minutes, or longer. Whereas most ionotropic effects depend on either glutamate or GABA, metabotropic synapses use a large variety of transmitters.

When the neurotransmitter attaches to a metabotropic receptor, it bends the receptor protein, enabling a portion of it inside the neuron to react with other molecules, as shown in Figure 3.13 (Levitzki, 1988; O'Dowd, Lefkowitz, & Caron, 1989). The portion inside the neuron activates a **G-protein**—one that is coupled to guanosine triphosphate (GTP), an energy-storing molecule. The activated G-protein in turn increases the concentration of a second messenger, such as cyclic adenosine monophosphate (cyclic AMP), inside the cell. Just as the "first messenger" (the neurotransmitter) carries information to the postsynaptic cell, the **second messenger** communicates to areas within the cell. The second messenger may open or close ion channels in the membrane or activate a portion of a chromosome. Note the contrast: An ionotropic synapse has effects localized to one point on the membrane, whereas a metabotropic synapse, by way of its second messenger, influences activity in much or all of the cell and over a longer time.

Ionotropic and metabotropic synapses contribute to different aspects of behavior. For vision and hearing, the brain needs rapid, quickly changing information, the kind that ionotropic synapses bring. In contrast, hunger, thirst, fear, and anger constitute long-term changes in the probabilities of many behaviors. Metabotropic synapses are better suited for that kind of function. Metabotropic synapses also mediate at least some of the input for taste (Huang et al., 2005) and pain (Levine, Fields, & Basbaum, 1993), which are slower and more enduring experiences than vision or hearing.

Researchers often describe the neuropeptides as **neuromodulators** because they have several properties that set

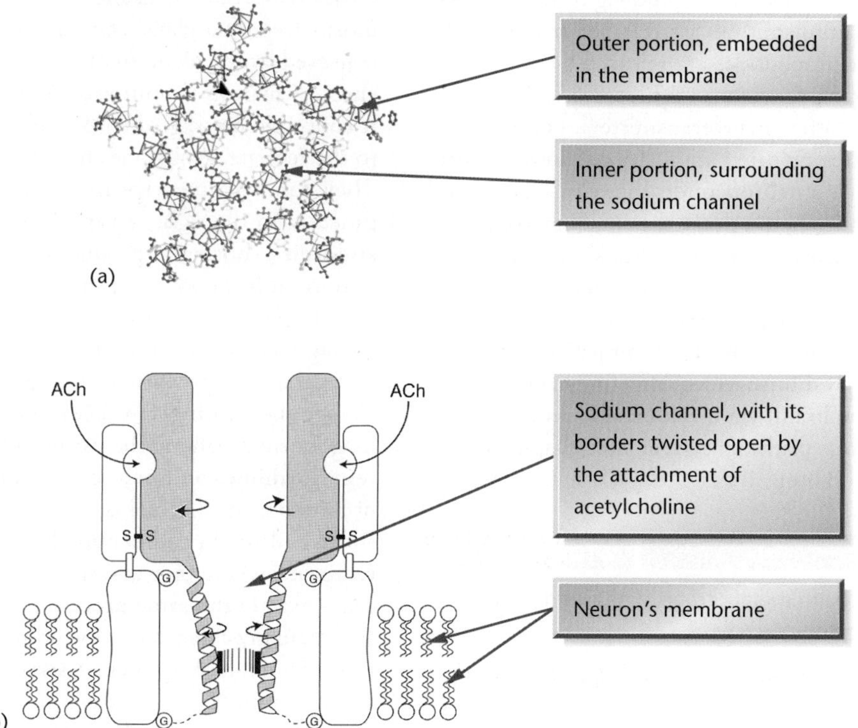

Figure 3.12 The acetylcholine receptor
(a) A cross-section, as viewed from the synaptic cleft. The membrane surrounds it. **(b)** A side view of the receptor, with the membrane to its left and right. Its outer portion is embedded in the neuron's membrane; its inner portion surrounds the sodium channel. When the receptor is at rest, the channel is too narrow to let sodium pass through it. When acetylcholine binds to the receptor, it unfolds the protein lining the channel and lets sodium ions pass. *(From A. Miyazawa, et al., "Structure and gating mechanism of the acetylcholine receptor pore,"* Nature, 423, *949–955. © 2003 Nature Publishing Group. Reprinted with permission of Macmillan Publishing Ltd.)*

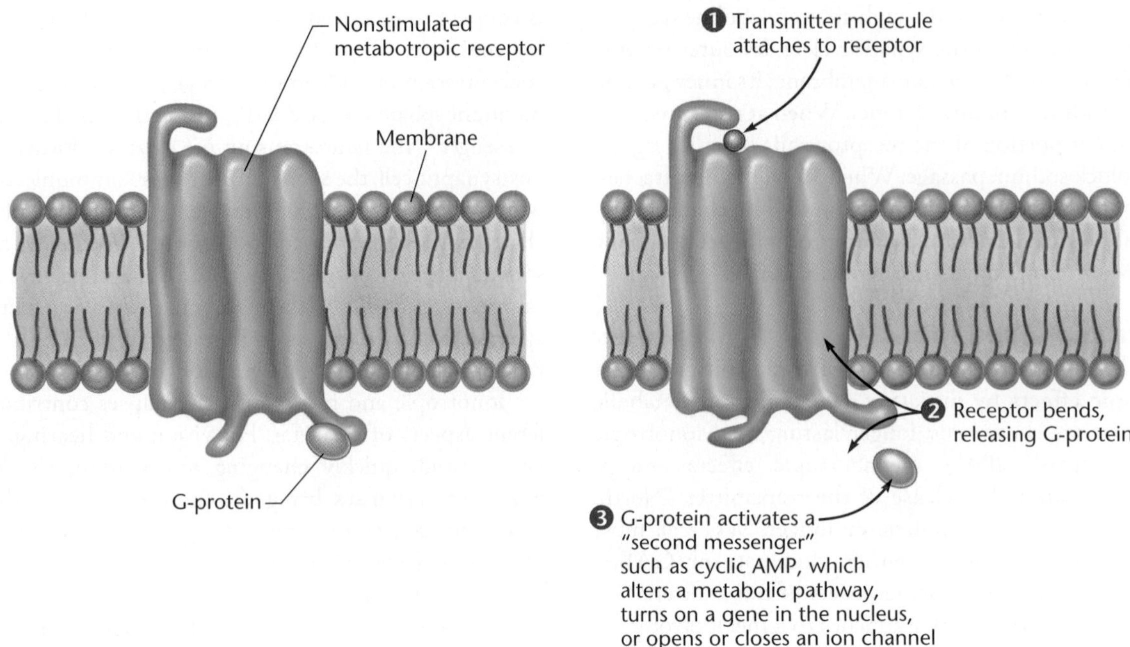

Nonstimulated metabotropic receptor
Membrane
G-protein
1 Transmitter molecule attaches to receptor
2 Receptor bends, releasing G-protein
3 G-protein activates a "second messenger" such as cyclic AMP, which alters a metabolic pathway, turns on a gene in the nucleus, or opens or closes an ion channel

Figure 3.13 Sequence of events at a metabotropic synapse, using a second messenger within the postsynaptic neuron

them apart from other transmitters (Ludwig & Leng, 2006). Whereas other neurotransmitters are released mainly at the axon terminal, the neuropeptides are released by cell bodies, dendrites, and sides of the axons. Whereas a single action potential can release other neurotransmitters, neuropeptide release usually requires repeated stimulation. However, after a few dendrites release a neuropeptide, the released chemical stimulates other dendrites to release the same neuropeptide, even without depolarization. That is, neurons containing neuropeptides do not release them often, but when they do, they release substantial amounts. Furthermore, unlike other transmitters, neuropeptides are not released immediately adjacent to their receptors. They diffuse widely, affecting many neurons in their region of the brain, via metabotropic receptors. We shall encounter neuropeptides in several later chapters, especially in the module on hunger.

STOP & CHECK

10. How do ionotropic and metabotropic synapses differ in speed and duration of effects?

11. What are second messengers, and which type of synapse relies on them?

ANSWERS

10. Ionotropic synapses act more quickly and more briefly. **11.** At metabotropic synapses, the neurotransmitter attaches to its receptor and thereby releases a chemical (the second messenger) within the postsynaptic cell, which alters metabolism or gene expression of the postsynaptic cell.

Hormones. A **hormone** is a chemical that is secreted, in most cases by a gland but also by other kinds of cells, and conveyed by the blood to other organs, whose activity it influences. A neurotransmitter is like a signal on a telephone line: It conveys a message directly and exclusively from the sender to the receiver. Hormones function more like a radio station: They convey a message to any receiver that happens to be tuned in to the right station. Figure 3.14 presents the major **endocrine** (hormone-producing) **glands.** Table 3.2 lists some important hormones and their principal effects.

Hormones are particularly useful for coordinating long-lasting changes in multiple parts of the body. For example, birds that are preparing to migrate secrete hormones that change their eating and digestion to store extra energy for a long journey. Among the various types of hormones are **protein hormones** and **peptide hormones,** composed of chains of amino acids. (Proteins are longer chains and peptides are shorter.) Protein and peptide hormones attach to membrane receptors, where they activate a second messenger within the cell—exactly the same process as at a metabotropic synapse. In fact, many chemicals—including epinephrine, norepinephrine, insulin, and oxytocin—serve as both neurotransmitters and hormones.

Just as circulating hormones modify brain activity, hormones secreted by the brain control the secretion of many other hormones. The **pituitary gland,** attached to the hypothalamus (Figure 3.15), consists of two distinct glands, the **anterior pituitary** and the **posterior pituitary,** which release different sets of hormones (see Table 3.2). The posterior pituitary, composed of neural tissue, can be considered an extension of the hypothalamus. Neurons in the hypothalamus syn-

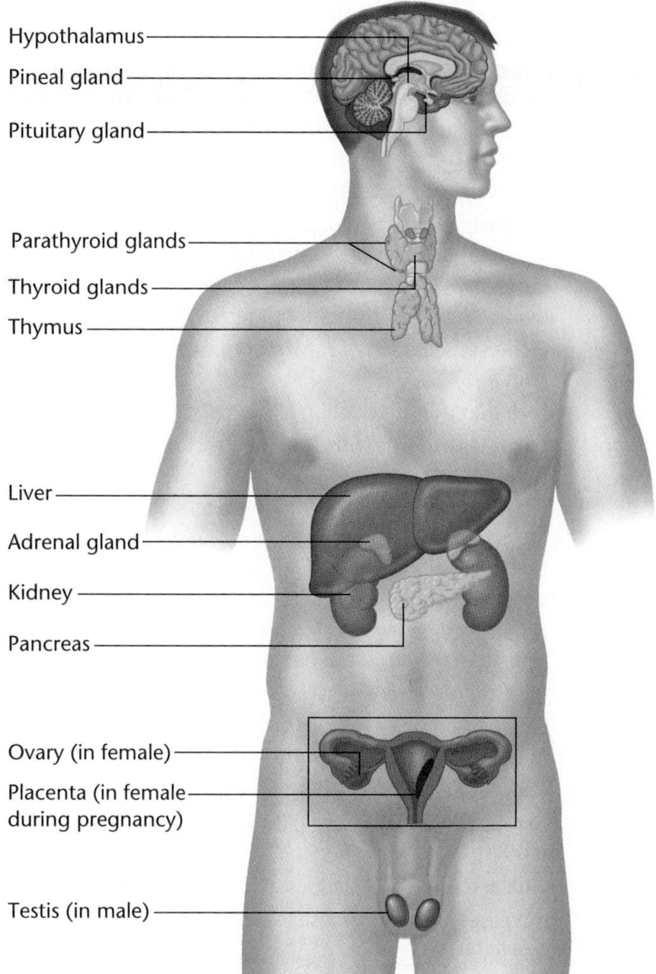

Figure 3.14 Location of some major endocrine glands
(Source: Starr & Taggart, 1989)

thesize the hormones **oxytocin** and **vasopressin** (also known as antidiuretic hormone), which migrate down axons to the posterior pituitary, as shown in Figure 3.16. Later, the posterior pituitary releases these hormones into the blood.

The anterior pituitary, composed of glandular tissue, synthesizes six hormones, although the hypothalamus controls their release (see Figure 3.16). The hypothalamus secretes **releasing hormones,** which flow through the blood to the anterior pituitary. There they stimulate or inhibit the release of the following hormones:

Adrenocorticotropic hormone (ACTH)	Controls secretions of the adrenal cortex
Thyroid-stimulating hormone (TSH)	Controls secretions of the thyroid gland
Prolactin	Controls secretions of the mammary glands
Somatotropin, also known as growth hormone (GH)	Promotes growth throughout the body
Gonadotropins Follicle-stimulating hormone (FSH) Luteinizing hormone (LH)	Control secretions of the gonads

The hypothalamus maintains fairly constant circulating levels of certain hormones through a negative feedback system. For example, when the level of thyroid hormone is low, the hypothalamus releases *TSH-releasing hormone,* which stimulates the anterior pituitary to release TSH, which in turn causes the thyroid gland to secrete more thyroid hormones (Figure 3.17). For more information about hormones in general, visit the Website of The Endocrine Society at http://www.endo-society.org/

STOP & CHECK

12. Which part of the pituitary—anterior or posterior—is neural tissue, similar to the hypothalamus? Which part is glandular tissue and produces hormones that control the secretions by other endocrine organs?

13. In what way is a neuropeptide intermediate between other neurotransmitters and hormones?

ANSWERS

12. The posterior pituitary is neural tissue, like the hypothalamus. The anterior pituitary is glandular tissue and produces hormones that control several other endocrine organs. **13.** Most neurotransmitters are released in small amounts close to their receptors. Neuropeptides are released into a brain area in larger amounts or not at all. When released, they diffuse more widely. Hormones are released into the blood for diffuse delivery throughout the body.

Inactivation and Reuptake of Neurotransmitters

A neurotransmitter does not linger at the postsynaptic membrane. If it did, it might continue exciting or inhibiting the receptor. Various neurotransmitters are inactivated in different ways.

After acetylcholine activates a receptor, it is broken down by the enzyme **acetylcholinesterase** (a-SEE-til-ko-lih-NES-teh-raze) into two fragments: acetate and choline. The choline diffuses back to the presynaptic neuron, which takes it up and reconnects it with acetate already in the cell to form acetylcholine again. Although this recycling process is highly efficient, it takes time, and the presynaptic neuron does not reabsorb every molecule it releases. A sufficiently rapid series of action potentials at any synapse can deplete the neurotransmitter faster than the presynaptic cell replenishes it, thus slowing or interrupting transmission (G. Liu & Tsien, 1995).

In the absence of acetylcholinesterase, acetylcholine remains and continues stimulating its receptor. Drugs that block acetylcholinesterase can be helpful for people with diseases that impair acetylcholine transmission, such as myasthenia gravis.

TABLE 3.2 Partial List of Hormone-Releasing Glands

Organ	Hormone	Hormone Functions
Hypothalamus	Various releasing hormones	Promote or inhibit release of various hormones by pituitary
Anterior pituitary	Thyroid-stimulating hormone (TSH)	Stimulates thyroid gland
	Luteinizing hormone (LH)	Increases production of progesterone (female), testosterone (male); stimulates ovulation
	Follicle-stimulating hormone (FSH)	Increases production of estrogen and maturation of ovum (female) and sperm production (male)
	ACTH	Increases secretion of steroid hormones by adrenal gland
	Prolactin	Increases milk production
	Growth hormone (GH), also known as somatotropin	Increases body growth, including the growth spurt during puberty
Posterior pituitary	Oxytocin	Controls uterine contractions, milk release, certain aspects of parental behavior, and sexual pleasure
	Vasopressin (also known as antidiuretic hormone)	Constricts blood vessels and raises blood pressure, decreases urine volume
Pineal	Melatonin	Increases sleepiness, influences sleep–wake cycle, also has role in onset of puberty
Thyroid	Thyroxine Triiodothyronine	Increase metabolic rate, growth, and maturation
Parathyroid	Parathyroid hormone	Increases blood calcium and decreases potassium
Adrenal cortex	Aldosterone	Reduces secretion of salts by the kidneys
	Cortisol, corticosterone	Stimulate liver to elevate blood sugar, increase metabolism of proteins and fats
Adrenal medulla	Epinephrine, norepinephrine	Similar to effects of sympathetic nervous system
Pancreas	Insulin	Increases entry of glucose to cells and increases storage as fats
	Glucagon	Increases conversion of stored fats to blood glucose
Ovary	Estrogens	Promote female sexual characteristics
	Progesterone	Maintains pregnancy
Testis	Androgens	Promote sperm production, growth of pubic hair, and male sexual characteristics
Liver	Somatomedins	Stimulate growth
Kidney	Renin	Converts a blood protein into angiotensin, which regulates blood pressure and contributes to hypovolemic thirst
Thymus	Thymosin (and others)	Support immune responses
Fat cells	Leptin	Decreases appetite, increases activity, necessary for onset of puberty

Serotonin and the catecholamines (dopamine, norepinephrine, and epinephrine) do not break down into inactive fragments at the postsynaptic membrane but simply detach from the receptor. At that point, the next step varies. In certain brain areas, the presynaptic neuron takes up most of the released neurotransmitter molecules intact and reuses them. This process, called **reuptake,** occurs through special membrane proteins called **transporters.** For example, in a brain area called the caudate nucleus, the dopamine transporters rapidly reuptake nearly all of the released dopamine. (As we explore in Chapter 15, many antidepressant drugs block reuptake and thereby prolong the effects of neurotransmitters on their receptors.) However, in other brain areas, fewer transporters are present, and reuptake is slower. If dopamine is released rapidly in those areas, large amounts begin to accumulate, and an enzyme called **COMT** (catechol-o-methyltransferase) breaks down the excess dopamine into inactive chemicals that cannot stimulate the dopamine receptors. Those breakdown products wash away and eventually show up in the blood and urine. In a brain area known as the prefrontal cortex, COMT breaks down about half of the released dopamine (Yavich, Forsberg, Karayiorgou, Gogos, & Männistö, 2007). A consequence is

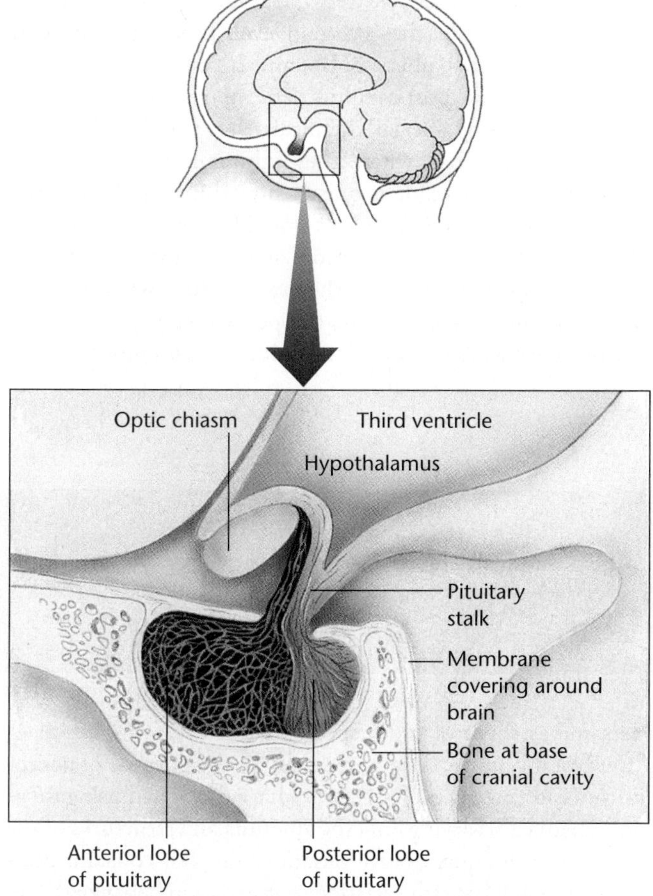

Figure 3.15 Location of the hypothalamus and pituitary gland in the human brain
(Source: Starr & Taggart, 1989)

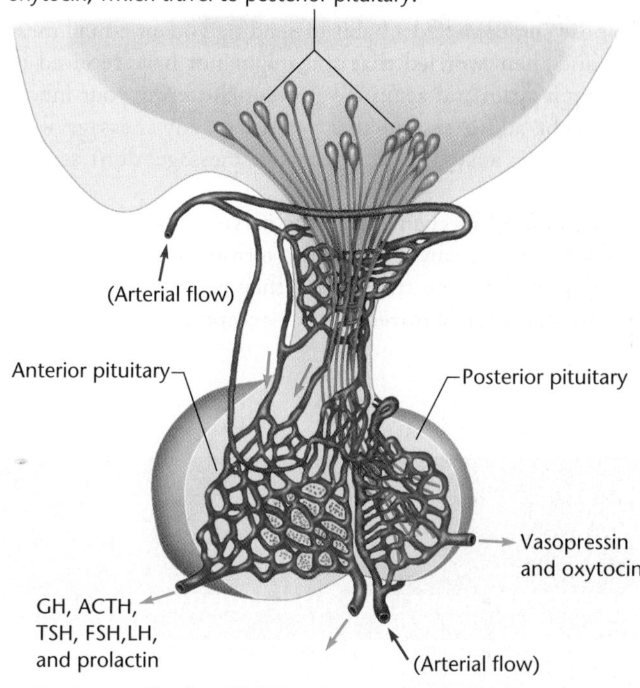

Figure 3.16 Pituitary hormones
The hypothalamus produces vasopressin and oxytocin, which travel to the posterior pituitary (really an extension of the hypothalamus). The posterior pituitary releases those hormones in response to neural signals. The hypothalamus also produces releasing hormones and inhibiting hormones, which travel to the anterior pituitary, where they control the release of six hormones synthesized there.

that neurons in that area diminish their supply of dopamine whenever they release much of it, and they cannot release dopamine rapidly for long.

The neuropeptides are neither inactivated nor reabsorbed. They simply diffuse away. Because these large molecules are resynthesized slowly, a neuron can temporarily exhaust its supply.

STOP & CHECK

14. What happens to acetylcholine molecules after they stimulate a postsynaptic receptor?

15. What happens to serotonin and catecholamine molecules after they stimulate a postsynaptic receptor?

ANSWERS

14. The enzyme acetylcholinesterase breaks acetylcholine molecules into two smaller molecules, acetate and choline, which are then reabsorbed by the presynaptic terminal. **15.** Most serotonin and catecholamine molecules are reabsorbed by the presynaptic terminal. Some of their molecules are broken down into inactive chemicals, which then float away.

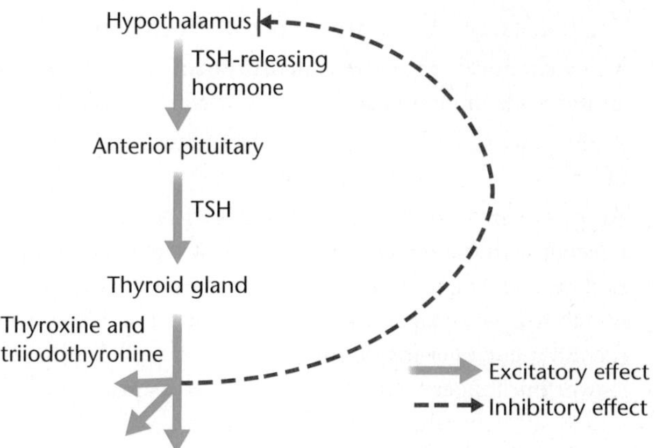

Figure 3.17 Negative feedback in the control of thyroid hormones
The hypothalamus secretes a releasing hormone that stimulates the anterior pituitary to release TSH, which stimulates the thyroid gland to release its hormones. Those hormones in turn act on the hypothalamus to decrease its secretion of the releasing hormone.

Negative Feedback From the Postsynaptic Cell

Suppose someone had a habit of sending you an e-mail message and then, worried that you might not have received it, sending it again and again. To prevent cluttering your inbox, you might add a system that replied to any message with an automatic answer, "Yes, I got your message; don't send it again."

A couple of mechanisms in the nervous system serve that function. First, many presynaptic terminals have receptors sensitive to the same transmitter they release. These receptors are known as **autoreceptors**—receptors that detect the amount of transmitter released and inhibit further synthesis and release after it reaches a certain level. That is, they provide negative feedback (Kubista & Boehm, 2006).

Second, some postsynaptic neurons respond to stimulation by releasing special chemicals that travel back to the presynaptic terminal, where they inhibit further release of transmitter. Nitric oxide is one such transmitter. Two others are *anandamide* and *2-AG* (*sn*-2 arachidonylglycerol), both of which bind to the same receptors as marijuana extracts. We shall discuss them further in the next module, when we consider drug mechanisms. Here, the point is that postsynaptic neurons have ways to control or limit their own input.

MODULE 3.2 IN CLOSING

Neurotransmitters and Behavior

In the first module of this chapter, you read how Charles Sherrington began the study of synapses with his observations of dogs. In this module, you read about cellular and molecular processes based on research with a wide variety of other species. The general principles of synapses are the same from one species to another. The neurotransmitters found in humans are the same as those of other species, with very few exceptions. After certain chemicals proved useful for the purpose of neurotransmission, newly evolved species have continued using those same chemicals, varying only the amounts and structures of the receptors. From quantitative variations in a few constant principles comes all the rich variation that we see in behavior.

SUMMARY

1. The great majority of synapses operate by transmitting a neurotransmitter from the presynaptic cell to the postsynaptic cell. Otto Loewi demonstrated this point by stimulating a frog's heart electrically and then transferring fluids from that heart to another frog's heart. **56**
2. Many chemicals are used as neurotransmitters. Most are amino acids or chemicals derived from amino acids. **58**
3. A given neuron releases one or a few neurotransmitters. **60**
4. At ionotropic synapses, a neurotransmitter attaches to a receptor that opens the gates to allow a particular ion, such as sodium, to cross the membrane more readily. At metabotropic synapses, a neurotransmitter activates a second messenger inside the postsynaptic cell, leading to slower but longer lasting changes. Neuropeptides diffuse widely, affecting many neurons. **60**
5. Hormones are released into the blood to affect receptors scattered throughout the body. Their mechanism of effect resembles that of a metabotropic synapse. **62**
6. After a neurotransmitter (other than a neuropeptide) has activated its receptor, many of the transmitter molecules reenter the presynaptic cell through transporter molecules in the membrane. This process, known as reuptake, enables the presynaptic cell to recycle its neurotransmitter. In some brain areas, much of the released dopamine breaks down into inactive chemicals instead of being reabsorbed. **63**
7. Postsynaptic neurons have mechanisms for slowing further release of neurotransmitter from the presynaptic neuron. **66**

KEY TERMS

Terms are defined in the module on the page number indicated. They're also presented in alphabetical order with definitions in the book's Subject Index/Glossary. Interactive flashcards, audio reviews, and crossword puzzles are among the online resources available to help you learn these terms and the concepts they represent.

acetylcholine **58**
acetylcholinesterase **63**
amino acids **58**
anterior pituitary **62**
autoreceptors **66**
catecholamines **58**
COMT **64**
endocrine glands **62**
exocytosis **60**
G-protein **61**
gases **58**
hormone **62**
ionotropic effects **60**
ligand-gated channels **60**
MAO **60**
metabotropic effects **61**
monoamines **58**
neuromodulators **61**
neuropeptides **58**
neurotransmitters **58**
nitric oxide **58**
oxytocin **63**
peptide hormones **62**
pituitary gland **62**
posterior pituitary **62**
protein hormones **62**
purines **58**
releasing hormones **63**
reuptake **64**
second messenger **61**
transmitter-gated channels **60**
transporters **64**
vasopressin **63**
vesicles **59**

THOUGHT QUESTION

1. Suppose axon A enters a ganglion (a cluster of neurons) and axon B leaves on the other side. An experimenter who stimulates A can shortly thereafter record an impulse traveling down B. We want to know whether B is just an extension of axon A or whether A formed an excitatory synapse on some neuron in the ganglion, whose axon is axon B. How could an experimenter determine the answer? You should be able to think of more than one good method. Presume that the anatomy within the ganglion is so complex that you cannot simply trace the course of an axon through it.

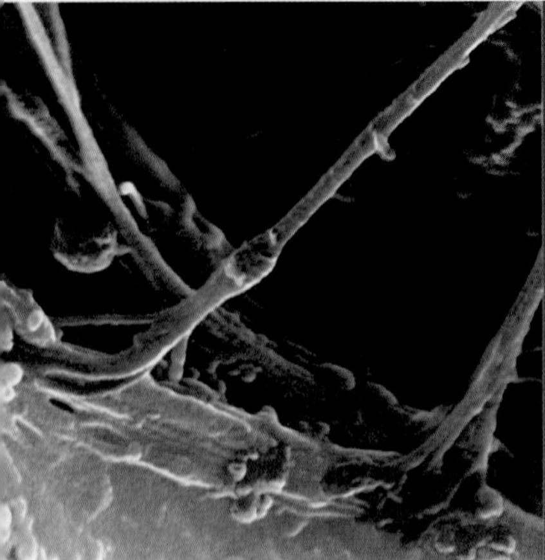

MODULE 3.3

Synapses, Drugs, and Addictions

Did you know that your brain is constantly making chemicals resembling opiates? It also makes its own marijuana-like chemicals, and it has receptors that respond to cocaine and LSD. Nearly every drug with psychological effects acts at the synapses. (The exceptions are Novocain and related anesthetic drugs that block sodium channels in the membrane instead of acting at synapses.) By studying the effects of drugs, we learn more about the drugs and also about synapses. This module deals mainly with abused drugs; later chapters will consider antidepressants, antipsychotic drugs, tranquilizers, and other psychiatric medications.

Most of the commonly abused drugs derive from plants. For example, nicotine comes from tobacco, opiates from poppies, and cocaine from coca. We might wonder why our brains respond to plant chemicals. An explanation is more apparent if we put it the other way: Why do plants produce chemicals that affect our brains? Nearly all neurotransmitters and hormones are the same in humans as in other species (Cravchik & Goldman, 2000). So if a plant evolves a chemical to attract bees or repel caterpillars, that chemical is likely to affect humans also.

Types of Mechanisms

Drugs can either facilitate or inhibit transmission at synapses. A drug that blocks the effects of a neurotransmitter is an **antagonist;** a drug that mimics or increases the effects is an **agonist.** (The term *agonist* is derived from a Greek word meaning "contestant." The term *agony* derives from the same root. An *antagonist* is an "anti-agonist," or member of the opposing team.) A *mixed agonist–antagonist* is an agonist for some effects of the neurotransmitter and an antagonist for others or an agonist at some doses and an antagonist at others.

Drugs influence synaptic activity in many ways. As in Figure 3.18, which illustrates a dopamine synapse, a drug can increase or decrease the synthesis of the neurotransmitter, cause it to leak from its vesicles, increase its release, decrease its reuptake, block its breakdown into inactive chemicals, or act on the postsynaptic receptors.

Investigators say that a drug has an **affinity** for a receptor if it binds to it, like a key into a lock. Affinities vary from strong to weak. A drug's **efficacy** is its tendency to activate the receptor. A drug that binds to a receptor but fails to stimulate it has a high affinity but low efficacy.

The effectiveness and side effects of drugs vary from one person to another. Why? Most drugs affect several kinds of receptors. People vary in their abundance of each kind of receptor. For example, one person might have a relatively large number of dopamine type D_4 receptors and relatively few D_1 or D_2 receptors, whereas someone else has the reverse (Cravchik & Goldman, 2000).

STOP & CHECK

16. Is a drug with high affinity and low efficacy an agonist or an antagonist?

ANSWER

16. Such a drug is an antagonist because, by occupying the receptor, it blocks out the neurotransmitter.

What Abused Drugs Have in Common

Abused drugs differ in many ways, but they share certain effects on dopamine and norepinephrine synapses. The story behind the discovery of the brain mechanisms begins with a pair of young psychologists who were trying to answer a different question.

James Olds and Peter Milner (1954) wanted to test whether stimulation of certain brain areas might influence which direction a rat turns. When they implanted the electrode, they missed their intended target and instead hit an area called the septum. To their surprise, when the rat received the brain stimulation, it sat up, looked around, and sniffed, as if reacting to a favorable stimulus. Olds and Milner later placed rats in boxes where they could press a lever to produce electrical **self-stimulation of the brain** (Figure 3.19). With electrodes in the septum and certain other places, rats sometimes pressed as often as 2,000 times per hour (Olds, 1958).

Later researchers found many brain areas that rats would work to stimulate. All those areas had axons that directly or

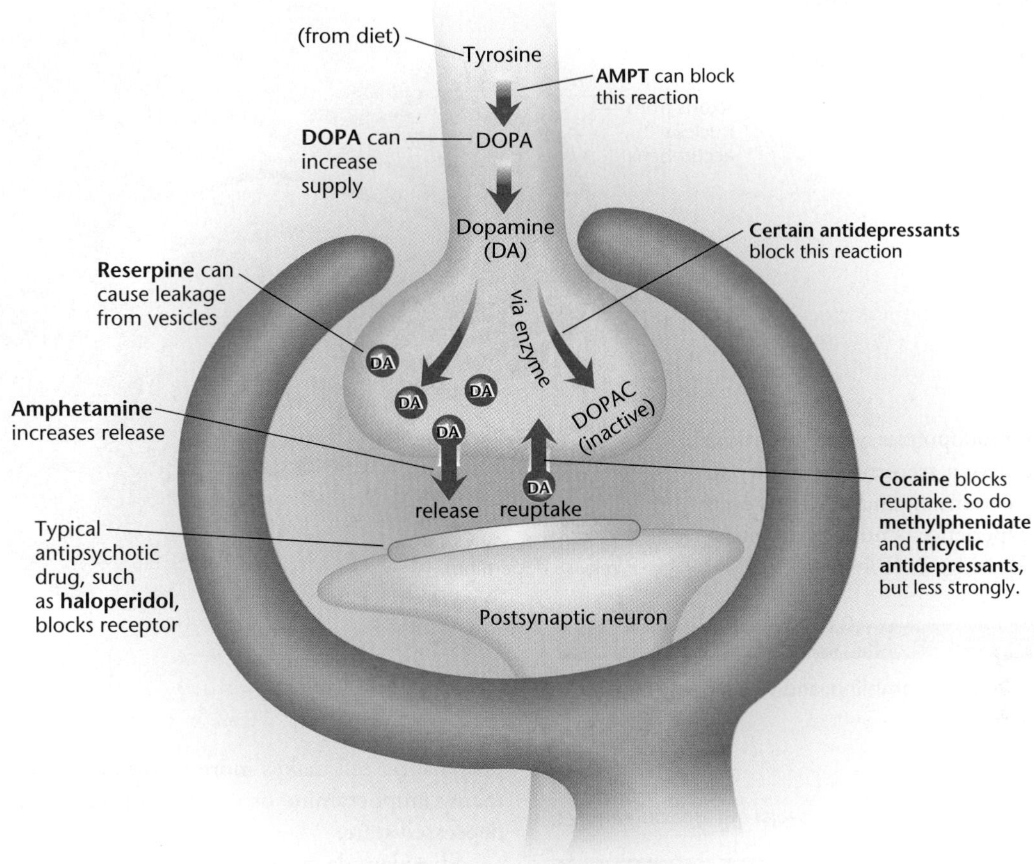

Figure 3.18 Effects of some drugs at dopamine synapses
Drugs can alter any stage of synaptic processing, from synthesis of the neurotransmitter through release and reuptake.

indirectly increase the release of dopamine in the **nucleus accumbens,** which is illustrated in Figure 3.20 (Wise, 1996). If prolonged, rapid brain stimulation depletes the dopamine supply, and brain stimulation becomes less reinforcing (Hernandez et al., 2006).

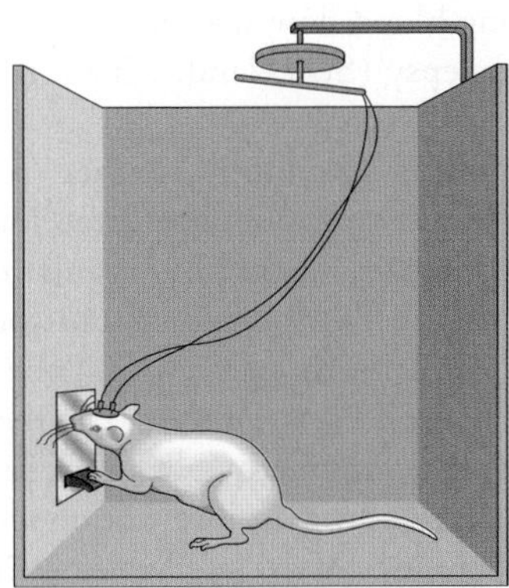

Figure 3.19 A rat pressing a lever for self-stimulation of its brain

Many other kinds of reinforcing experiences also stimulate dopamine release in that area, including sexual excitement (Damsma, Pfaus, Wenkstern, Phillips, & Fibiger, 1992; Lorrain, Riolo, Matuszewich, & Hull, 1999), gambling (Breiter, Aharon, Kahneman, Dale, & Shizgal, 2001), and video games, especially in habitual players (Koepp et al., 1998). Also, nearly all abused drugs increase the release of both dopamine and norepinephrine (Weinshenker & Schroeder, 2007). Although most mice will work to receive cocaine and similar drugs, mice deficient in dopamine receptors generally do not (Caine et al., 2007).

It might seem natural to assume that dopamine release in the nucleus accumbens brings pleasure. However, not everything that we work for provides joy. For example, you might work hard for a paycheck without feeling much happiness when you receive the paycheck. Many drug addicts say that the drug no longer provides much pleasure, even though their obsession with obtaining the drug continues.

According to Kent Berridge and Terry Robinson (1998), dopamine in the nucleus accumbens relates to how much you *want* something, not necessarily how much you *like* it. Some-

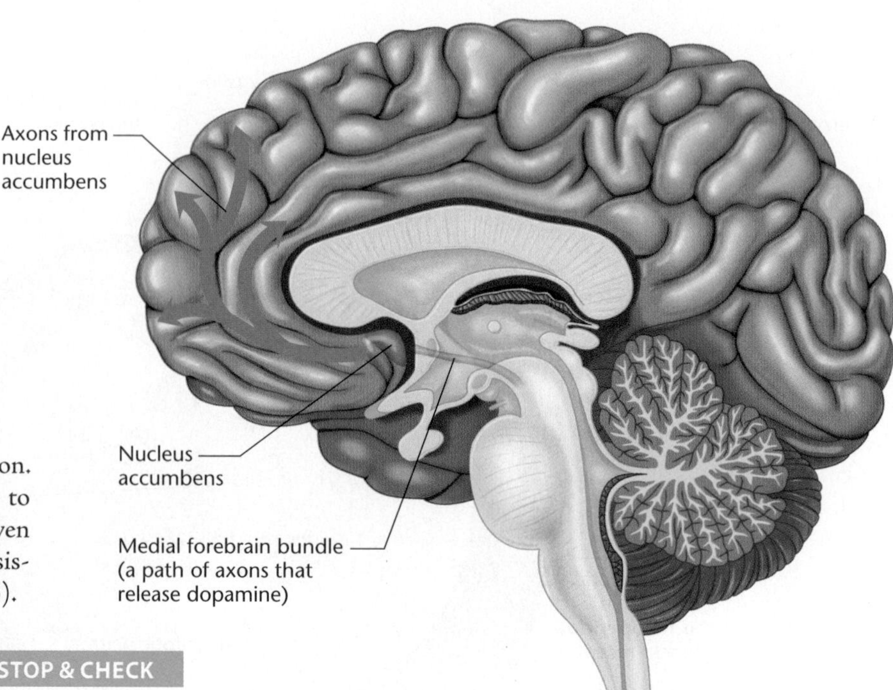

Figure 3.20 Location of the nucleus accumbens in the human brain
Nearly all abused drugs, as well as a variety of other highly reinforcing or addictive activities, increase dopamine release in the nucleus accumbens.

thing you want monopolizes your attention. Addictive drugs have a tremendous ability to dominate a user's attention and cravings, even when the drug experience is no longer consistently pleasant (Berridge & Robinson, 1995).

STOP & CHECK

17. What do drug use, sex, gambling, and video-game playing have in common?

ANSWER

17. They increase the release of dopamine in the nucleus accumbens.

A Survey of Abused Drugs

Let's consider some commonly abused drugs. In the process, we learn about synapses as well as drugs.

Stimulant Drugs

Stimulant drugs increase excitement, alertness, and activity, while elevating mood and decreasing fatigue. **Amphetamine** stimulates dopamine synapses by increasing the release of dopamine from the presynaptic terminal. The presynaptic terminal ordinarily reabsorbs released dopamine through a protein called the **dopamine transporter.** Amphetamine reverses the transporter, causing the cell to release dopamine instead of reabsorbing it (Giros, Jaber, Jones, Wightman, & Caron, 1996). Amphetamine's effects are nonspecific, as it also increases the release of serotonin, norepinephrine, and several other transmitters.

Cocaine blocks the reuptake of dopamine, norepinephrine, and serotonin, thus prolonging their effects. The behavioral effects depend mostly on dopamine and secondarily on serotonin (Rocha et al., 1998; Volkow, Wang, Fischman, et al., 1997). Many of the effects of cocaine resemble those of amphetamine.

By increasing the release of dopamine or decreasing its reuptake, cocaine and amphetamine increase the accumulation of dopamine in the synaptic cleft. However, the excess dopamine washes away from the synapse faster than the presynaptic cell makes more to replace it. A few hours after taking amphetamine or cocaine, a user "crashes" into a more depressed state.

Stimulant drugs produce many behavioral effects. In laboratory animals as well as humans, they impair attention and learning (Stalnaker et al., 2007). Stimulant use correlates with "impulsiveness," as measured by a tendency to choose a small, immediate reward instead of a larger but delayed reward. Rats with a genetic tendency toward impulsiveness, because of a deficiency of dopamine receptors, are more likely than others to self-administer large amounts of cocaine by lever pressing (Dalley et al., 2007). Also, repeatedly injecting any rat with cocaine gradually makes it more impulsive (N. W. Simon, Mendez, & Setlow, 2007).

A study of pairs of human twins, in which one twin abused cocaine or amphetamine and the other did not, found that the twin abusing stimulant drugs showed attentional problems that lingered for a year after quitting the drugs (Toomey et al., 2003). By altering blood flow, cocaine also increases the risk of stroke and epilepsy (Strickland, Miller, Kowell, & Stein, 1998).

Methylphenidate (Ritalin), another stimulant drug, is often prescribed for people with attention-deficit disorder (ADD), a condition marked by impulsiveness and poor control of attention. Methylphenidate and cocaine block the reuptake of dopamine in the same way at the same brain receptors. The differences between the drugs relate to dose and time course. People taking methylphenidate pills experience a gradual increase in the drug's concentration over an hour, followed by a slow decline. With timed-release capsules, the rise and fall are even slower. In contrast, sniffed or injected cocaine produces a rapid rise and fall of effects (Volkow, Wang, &

Fowler, 1997; Volkow, Wang, Fowler, et al., 1998). Therefore, methylphenidate does not produce the sudden rush of excitement, cravings, or addiction that are common with cocaine. In larger amounts or if taken by injection, methylphenidate's effects resemble cocaine's, including addiction.

Many people wonder whether prolonged use of methylphenidate in childhood makes people more likely to abuse drugs later. Although research on this topic has not been extensive, most studies have found that children who take methylphenidate are *less* likely than others to abuse drugs during adolescence or early adulthood (Katusic et al., 2005; Wilens, Faraone, Biederman, & Gunawardene, 2003). Experiments with rats point to the same conclusion. In one study, experimenters gave young rats moderate doses of methylphenidate and then, months later, gave them cocaine and tested their preference for the room where they received cocaine versus an adjoining room where they had not received it. Compared to other rats, those with early exposure to methylphenidate showed a lower preference for the stimuli associated with cocaine (Andersen, Arvanitogiannis, Pliakas, LeBlanc, & Carlezon, 2002; Carlezon, Mague, & Andersen, 2003; Mague, Andersen, & Carlezon, 2005). Although these studies contradict the worry that early methylphenidate treatment might lead to later drug abuse, prolonged use of methylphenidate does lead to other long-term disadvantages, including increased fearfulness (Bolaños, Barrot, Berton, Wallace-Black, & Nestler, 2003).

The drug methylenedioxymethamphetamine (MDMA, or "ecstasy") is a stimulant at low doses, increasing the release of dopamine. At higher doses (comparable to what people use recreationally), it also increases serotonin release, producing alterations in perception and cognition. Those alterations often include a decrease in depression and anxiety. Many people use MDMA at dance parties to increase their energy levels and pleasure. However, after the effects wear off, they experience lethargy and depression.

Many studies on rodents and monkeys have reported that repeated large injections of MDMA damage neurons that contain serotonin. One reason is that large doses of MDMA increase body temperature, and high temperature impairs neurons. Another mechanism is this: When excessive amounts of serotonin are released from vesicles, the cell's mitochondria oxidize the excess molecules, and one of the breakdown products is hydrogen peroxide (H_2O_2). The brain easily tolerates the small amounts that develop normally, but high doses of MDMA bombard the neurons with enough H_2O_2 to damage the mitochondria, thereby impairing and sometimes killing neurons (Alves et al., 2007).

The degree of risk to human users is not entirely clear. Most animal studies use larger doses than what most people take recreationally. Still, researchers tested 27 people at one dance party and found that 6 of them had blood MDMA levels in the range shown to produce damage in the laboratory (Irvine et al., 2006). Are the levels that produce damage in rats and mice equally toxic to humans? We cannot assume. Studies of humans using brain scan techniques (to be described in the next chapter) report that repeated heavy users show a loss of neurons containing serotonin, with gradual recovery over several months after quitting (Buchert et al., 2003; Cowan, 2006; Reneman, de Win, van den Brink, Booij, & den Heeten, 2006). However, the research on this point is limited, and most of the heaviest MDMA users abused other drugs also. An additional problem is that ecstasy, being an illegal drug, is usually not pure MDMA. Researchers are not yet certain how much damage MDMA causes in humans or how fully people recover afterward.

STOP & CHECK

18. How does amphetamine influence dopamine synapses?

19. How does cocaine influence dopamine synapses?

20. Why is methylphenidate generally less disruptive to behavior than cocaine is despite the drugs' similar mechanisms?

ANSWERS

18. Amphetamine causes the dopamine transporter to release dopamine instead of reabsorbing it. **19.** Cocaine interferes with reuptake of released dopamine. **20.** The effects of a methylphenidate pill develop and decline in the brain much more slowly than do those of cocaine.

Nicotine

Nicotine, a compound present in tobacco, has long been known to stimulate one type of acetylcholine receptor, conveniently known as the *nicotinic receptor*, which occurs both in the central nervous system and at the nerve–muscle junction of skeletal muscles. Nicotinic receptors are abundant on neurons that release dopamine in the nucleus accumbens, so nicotine increases dopamine release there (Levin & Rose, 1995; Pontieri, Tanda, Orzi, & DiChiara, 1996). In fact, nicotine increases dopamine release in mostly the same cells of the nucleus accumbens that cocaine does (Pich et al., 1997). Stimulation of the nicotinic receptor correlates with high activity in novel environments and high responsiveness to novel stimuli (Fagen, Mitchum, Vezina, & McGehee, 2007).

One consequence of repeated exposure to nicotine, as demonstrated in rat studies, is that after nicotine use, the nucleus accumbens cells responsible for reinforcement become less responsive than usual (Epping-Jordan, Watkins, Koob, & Markou, 1998). That is, many events, not just nicotine itself, become less reinforcing than they used to be.

STOP & CHECK

21. How does nicotine affect dopamine synapses?

ANSWER

21. Nicotine excites acetylcholine receptors on neurons that release dopamine and thereby increases dopamine release.

Opiates

Opiate drugs are derived from (or chemically similar to those derived from) the opium poppy. Familiar opiates include morphine, heroin, and methadone. Because heroin enters the brain faster than morphine, it produces a bigger "rush" of effects and is more strongly addictive. Opiates relax people, decrease their attention to real-world problems, and decrease their sensitivity to pain. Although opiates are frequently addictive, people who take them as painkillers under medical supervision almost never abuse them. Addiction depends on the person, the reasons for taking the drug, the dose, and the social setting.

People used morphine and other opiates for centuries without knowing how the drugs affected the brain. Then Candace Pert and Solomon Snyder found that opiates attach to specific receptors in the brain (Pert & Snyder, 1973). It was a safe guess that vertebrates had not evolved such receptors just to enable us to become drug addicts; the brain must produce its own chemical that attaches to these receptors. Soon investigators found that the brain produces neuropeptides now known as *endorphins*—a contraction of *endo*genous *morphines*. This discovery was important because it indicated that opiates relieve pain by acting on receptors in the brain, not in the skin or organs where people felt the pain. This finding also paved the way for the discovery of other neuropeptides that regulate emotions and motivations.

Endorphins indirectly activate dopamine release. Endorphin synapses inhibit ventral tegmental neurons (in the midbrain) that release GABA, a transmitter that inhibits the firing of dopamine neurons (North, 1992). By inhibiting an inhibitor, the net effect is to increase dopamine release. However, endorphins also have reinforcing effects independent of dopamine. Researchers managed to develop mice that had an almost complete lack of dopamine in the nucleus accumbens. These mice showed a preference for places in which they received morphine (Hnasko, Sotak, & Palmiter, 2005).

STOP & CHECK

22. How do opiates influence dopamine synapses?

ANSWER

22. Opiates stimulate endorphin synapses, which inhibit neurons that inhibit release of dopamine. By inhibiting an inhibitor, opiates increase the release of dopamine.

Marijuana

Marijuana leaves contain the chemical **Δ^9-tetrahydrocannabinol (Δ^9-THC)** and other **cannabinoids** (chemicals related to Δ^9-THC). Cannabinoids have been used medically to relieve pain or nausea, to combat glaucoma (an eye disorder), and to increase appetite. Purified THC (under the name *dronabinol*) has been approved for medical use in the United States, although marijuana itself has not—except in California, where state law and federal law conflict.

Common psychological effects of marijuana include an intensification of sensory experience and an illusion that time has slowed down. Studies have reported significant impairments of memory and cognition, especially in new users and heavy users. (Moderate users develop partial tolerance.) The observed memory impairments in heavy users could mean either that marijuana impairs memory or that people with memory impairments are more likely to use marijuana. However, former users recover normal memory after 4 weeks of abstention from the drug (Pope, Gruber, Hudson, Huestis, & Yurgelun-Todd, 2001). The recovery implies that marijuana impairs memory.

Investigators could not explain the effects of marijuana on the brain until 1988, when researchers finally found the brain's cannabinoid receptors (Devane, Dysarz, Johnson, Melvin, & Howlett, 1988). Cannabinoid receptors are among the most abundant receptors in the mammalian brain (Herkenham, 1992; Herkenham, Lynn, de Costa, & Richfield, 1991), except in the medulla, the area that controls breathing and heartbeat. Consequently, even large doses of marijuana do not stop breathing or heartbeat. In contrast, opiates have strong effects on the medulla, and opiate overdoses are life threatening.

Just as the discovery of opiate receptors in the brain led to finding the brain's endogenous opiates, investigators identified two brain chemicals that bind to cannabinoid receptors—**anandamide** (from the Sanskrit word *ananda*, meaning "bliss") (Calignano, LaRana, Giuffrida, & Piomelli, 1998; DiMarzo et al., 1994) and the more abundant *sn*-2 arachidonylglycerol, abbreviated **2-AG** (Stella, Schweitzer, & Piomelli, 1997).

Cannabinoid receptors are peculiar in being located on the *pre*synaptic neuron. When certain neurons are depolarized, they release anandamide or 2-AG as retrograde transmitters, which travel back to incoming axons and inhibit further transmitter release. In some cases, they inhibit the release of glutamate, an excitatory transmitter (Kreitzer & Regehr, 2001; R. I. Wilson & Nicoll, 2002). In other cases, they block the release of GABA, an inhibitory transmitter (Földy, Neu, Jones, & Soltesz, 2006; Oliet, Baimoukhametova, Piet, & Bains, 2007). In short, retrograde transmitters modify the input to many neurons.

Because marijuana mimics these retrograde transmitters, the effect is a complicated mixture of net increase in excitation at some synapses and net inhibition at others. As a further complication, a temporary decrease in inhibition sometimes leads to a greater effect of inhibitory input later (Oliet et al., 2007).

Why are marijuana's effects—at least some of them—pleasant or habit forming? Remember that virtually all abused drugs increase the release of dopamine in the nucleus accumbens. Cannabinoids do so indirectly. One place in which they inhibit GABA release is the ventral tegmental area of the midbrain, a major source of axons that release dopamine in the nucleus accumbens. When cannabinoids inhibit GABA there, they decrease inhibition (therefore increase activity) of the neurons that release dopamine in the nucleus accumbens (Cheer, Wassum, Heien, Phillips, & Wightman, 2004).

Researchers have tried to explain some of marijuana's other effects. Cannabinoids relieve nausea by inhibiting serotonin type 3 synapses ($5\text{-}HT_3$), which are known to be important for nausea (Fan, 1995). Cannabinoid receptors are abundant in areas of the hypothalamus that influence feeding, and mice lacking these receptors show decreased appetite under some circumstances (DiMarzo et al., 2001). Conversely, extra cannabinoid activity produces extra appetite, as many marijuana users report.

The report that "time passes more slowly" under marijuana's influences is harder to explain, but whatever the reason, we can demonstrate it in rats as well: Consider a rat that has learned to press a lever for food on a fixed-interval schedule, where only the first press of any 30-second period produces food. With practice, a rat learns to wait after each press before it starts pressing again. Under the influence of marijuana, rats press sooner after each reinforcer. For example, instead of waiting 20 seconds, a rat might wait only 10 or 15. Evidently, the 10 or 15 seconds *felt like* 20 seconds; time was passing more slowly (Han & Robinson, 2001).

STOP & CHECK

23. What are the effects of cannabinoids on neurons?

ANSWER

23. Cannabinoids released by the postsynaptic neuron attach to receptors on presynaptic neurons, where they inhibit further release of glutamate as well as GABA.

Hallucinogenic Drugs

Drugs that distort perception are called **hallucinogenic drugs.** Many hallucinogenic drugs, such as lysergic acid diethylamide (LSD), chemically resemble serotonin (Figure 3.21) and stimulate serotonin type 2A ($5\text{-}HT_{2A}$) receptors at inappropriate times or for longer than usual durations. Table 3.3 summarizes the effects of some commonly abused drugs.

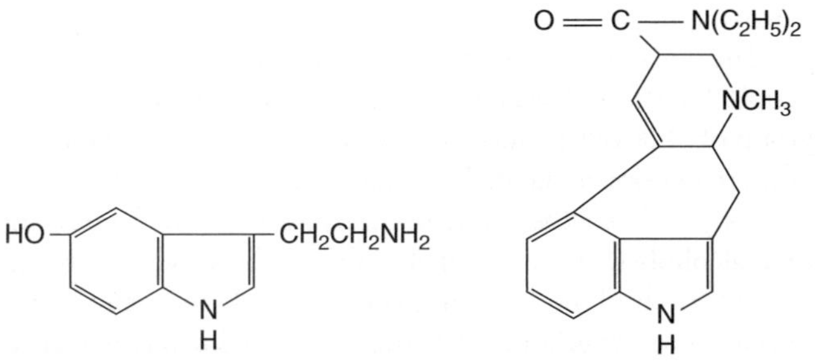

HO — $CH_2CH_2NH_2$ — N H — **Serotonin**

$O{=}C{-}N(C_2H_5)_2$ — NCH_3 — N H — **LSD**

Figure 3.21 Resemblance of the neurotransmitter serotonin to LSD, a hallucinogenic drug

STOP & CHECK

24. If incoming serotonin axons were destroyed, LSD would still have its full effects. However, if incoming dopamine axons were destroyed, amphetamine and cocaine would lose their effects. Explain the difference.

ANSWER

24. Amphetamine and cocaine act by releasing the net release of dopamine and other transmitters. If those neurons were damaged, amphetamine and cocaine would be ineffective. In contrast, LSD directly stimulates the receptor on the postsynaptic membrane.

Alcohol and Alcoholism

We treat alcohol separately because alcohol is the most common of the abused drugs and the research on it is the most extensive. Alcohol has been widely used in most of the world throughout history. In moderate amounts, it helps people relax, and certain kinds of wine apparently help prevent heart attacks in older people (Corder et al., 2006). In greater amounts, it damages the liver and other organs, impairs judgment, and ruins lives. **Alcoholism** or **alcohol dependence** is the continued use of alcohol despite medical or social harm, even after people have decided to quit or decrease their drinking.

Alcohol affects neurons in several ways. It facilitates response at the $GABA_A$ receptor, the brain's main inhibitory site, as we shall consider in more detail in Chapter 12. It doesn't directly stimulate that receptor, but it combines with GABA to produce longer effects than GABA would by itself. Alcohol also blocks activity at the glutamate receptors, the brain's main excitatory site (Tsai et al., 1998). Both the GABA effect and the glutamate effect lead to a decrease in brain activity. From a behavioral standpoint, people sometimes describe alcohol as a stimulant, but that is only because alcohol decreases activity in some brain areas that are responsible for inhibiting risky behaviors (Tu et al., 2007). Furthermore, alcohol increases stimulation at both dopamine and opiate receptors, including those in the nucleus accumbens (Gilman, Ramchandani, Davis, Bjork, & Hommer, 2008). With such diverse effects, no wonder it influences behavior in so many ways.

Genetics

Heredity has a stronger role in some cases of alcoholism than others. Researchers distinguish two types of alcoholism, although not everyone neatly fits one type or the other. People with **Type I** (or **Type A**) **alcoholism** develop alcohol problems gradually, usually after age 25, and do not always have relatives with alcohol abuse. Those with **Type II** (or **Type B**) **alcoholism** have more rapid onset, usually before age 25. Most are men, and most have close relatives with alcohol problems (J. Brown, Babor, Litt, & Kranzler, 1994; Devor, Abell, Hoffman, Tabakoff, & Cloninger, 1994).

TABLE 3.3 Summary of Some Drugs and Their Effects

Drugs	Main Behavioral Effects	Main Synaptic Effects
Amphetamine	Excitement, alertness, elevated mood, decreased fatigue	Increases release of dopamine and several other transmitters
Cocaine	Excitement, alertness, elevated mood, decreased fatigue	Blocks reuptake of dopamine and several other transmitters
Methylphenidate (Ritalin)	Increased concentration	Blocks reuptake of dopamine and others, but gradually
MDMA ("ecstasy")	Low dose: stimulant Higher dose: sensory distortions	Releases dopamine Releases serotonin, damages axons containing serotonin
Nicotine	Mostly stimulant effects	Stimulates nicotinic-type acetylcholine receptor, which (among other effects) increases dopamine release in nucleus accumbens
Opiates (e.g., heroin, morphine)	Relaxation, withdrawal, decreased pain	Stimulates endorphin receptors
Cannabinoids (marijuana)	Altered sensory experiences, decreased pain and nausea, increased appetite	Excites negative-feedback receptors on presynaptic cells; those receptors ordinarily respond to anandamide and 2AG
Hallucinogens (e.g., LSD)	Distorted sensations	Stimulates serotonin type 2A receptors (5-HT_{2A})

Genes influence the likelihood of alcoholism in various ways, most of which are not specific to alcohol. For example, many genes that affect alcohol have similar effects on nicotine intake (Lè et al., 2006). One identified gene controls the dopamine type 4 receptor, one of the five known types of dopamine receptor. People with the "longer" version of this gene report stronger cravings for additional alcohol after having one drink (Hutchison, McGeary, Smolen, & Bryan, 2002). The longer form of the gene leads to less sensitive receptors. Researchers believe that people with less sensitive receptors seek more alcohol to compensate for receiving less than normal reinforcement from other experiences.

Another key gene controls COMT, an enzyme that breaks down dopamine after its release. Some people have a gene that inserts the amino acid methionine at one point in the COMT protein, whereas others have the amino acid valine. The valine version of the gene, being more active, breaks down more dopamine and therefore tends to decrease reinforcements. People with the valine gene tend, on the average, to be more impulsive—to choose immediate rewards instead of bigger rewards later. This gene is common among people with the impulsive form of alcoholism (Boettiger et al., 2007). Other genes influence alcohol use by their effects on risk-taking behavior (Fils-Aime et al., 1996; Virkkunen et al., 1994) and responses to stress (Choi et al., 2004; Kreek, Nielsen, Butelman, & LaForge, 2005).

Prenatal environment also contributes to the risk for alcoholism. One study found that a person's probability of developing alcoholism correlated strongly with how much alcohol his or her mother drank during pregnancy, independently of how much she drank after the child was born (Baer, Sampson, Barr, Connor, & Streissguth, 2003).

STOP & CHECK

25. Which type of alcoholism has a stronger genetic basis? Which type has earlier onset?

26. Name at least two ways a gene could influence alcoholism.

ANSWERS

25. In both cases, Type II. **26.** Genes can influence alcoholism by producing less sensitive dopamine receptors, faster breakdown of dopamine by the enzyme COMT, greater risk-taking behavior, and altered responses to stress. Of course, other possibilities not mentioned in this section also exist.

Risk Factors

Are some people more likely than others to develop a severe alcohol problem? If so and if we can identify them, perhaps psychologists could intervene early to prevent alcoholism. We don't know whether early intervention would help, but it is worth a try.

The ideal research requires studying huge numbers of people for years: Measure as many factors as possible for a group of children or adolescents, years later determine which of them developed alcohol problems, and then see which early factors predicted the onset of alcoholism. Such studies find that alcoholism is more likely among those who were described in childhood as impulsive, risk-taking, easily bored, sensation-seeking, and outgoing (Dick, Johnson, Viken, & Rose, 2000; Legrand, Iacono, & McGue, 2005).

Other research follows this design: First, identify young men who are not yet problem drinkers. Compare those whose fathers were alcoholics to those who have no close relative with an alcohol problem. Because of the strong familial tendency toward alcoholism, researchers expect that many of the sons of alcoholics are future alcoholics themselves. (Researchers focus on men instead of women because almost all Type II alcoholics are men. They study sons of fathers with alcoholism instead of mothers to increase the chance of seeing genetic instead of prenatal influences.) The idea is that any behavior more common in the sons of alcoholics is probably a predictor of future alcoholism (Figure 3.22).

Here are the findings:

- Sons of alcoholics show *less* than average intoxication after drinking a moderate amount of alcohol. They report feeling less drunk, show less body sway, and register less change on an EEG (Schuckit & Smith, 1996; Volavka et al., 1996). Presumably, someone who begins to feel tipsy after a drink or two stops, and one who "holds his liquor well" continues drinking, perhaps enough to impair his judgment. A follow-up study found that sons of alcoholics who report low intoxication after moderate drinking have a probability greater than 60% of developing alcoholism (Schuckit & Smith, 1997).
- Alcohol decreases stress for most people, but it decreases it even more for sons of alcoholics (Levenson, Oyama, & Meek, 1987).
- Sons of alcoholics have some brain peculiarities, including a smaller than normal amygdala in the right hemisphere (Hill et al., 2001). These young men were not yet alcohol abusers, so the brain abnormality represents a predisposition to alcoholism, not a result of it.

STOP & CHECK

27. What are two ways sons of alcoholics differ, on average, from sons of nonalcoholics?

ANSWER

27. Sons of alcoholics show less intoxication, including less body sway, after drinking a moderate amount of alcohol. They also show greater relief from stress after drinking alcohol.

Addiction

As someone uses a substance more and more, the behavior becomes a compulsion or addiction. Consider a rat that presses a lever for an opportunity to receive cocaine. At first, it stops if the lever also produces a painful shock. However, after much use of cocaine, the rat continues pressing as rap-

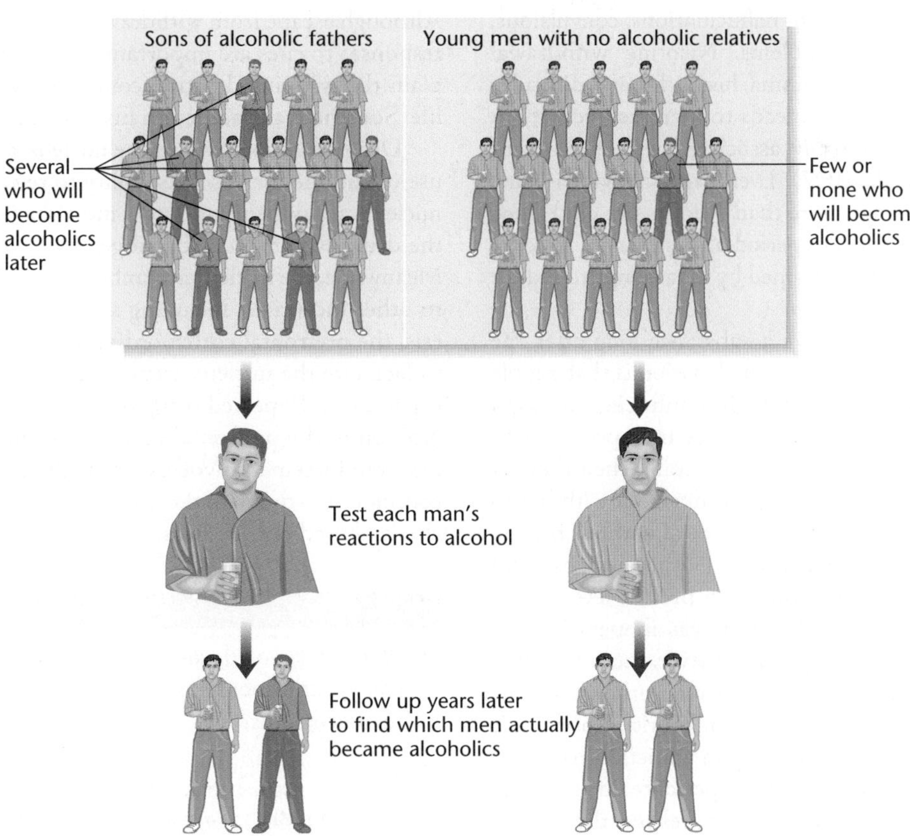

Figure 3.22 Design for studies of predisposition to alcoholism
Sons of alcoholic fathers are compared to other young men of the same age and same current drinking habits. Any behavior that is more common in the first group is presumably a predictor of later alcoholism.

idly with shocks as without them (Vanderschuren & Everitt, 2004). Similarly, many people continue using alcohol and other drugs despite obvious harm to their health, wealth, and relationships with others. Several explanations for addiction have been proposed.

Seeking Pleasure and Avoiding Displeasure

Substance use begins as an attempt to obtain a pleasant experience, but after repeated use, the pleasure declines and *tolerance* develops. As tolerance develops to the drug's effects, the individual also becomes less responsive to other types of reinforcement. In one study, rats had opportunities each day to press levers for heroin and for self-stimulation of the brain. Over 23 days, they took larger amounts of heroin. When self-stimulating the brain, they gradually became unresponsive to low amounts of electricity and would press levers only for higher amounts. Evidently, they were becoming less responsive to reinforcers in general (Kenny, Chen, Kitamura, Markou, & Koob, 2006).

Even after pleasure declines from drug use, the motivation to avoid displeasure remains. Someone who abstains from heroin or other opiates after frequent use experiences withdrawal symptoms, including anxiety, sweating, vomiting, and diarrhea. Symptoms of alcohol withdrawal include irritability, fatigue, shaking, sweating, and nausea. In more severe cases, alcohol withdrawal progresses to hallucinations, convulsions, fever, and cardiovascular problems. Nicotine withdrawal leads to irritability, fatigue, insomnia, headache, and difficulty concentrating. Drug abstinence leads to increased activity in several brain areas, presumably associated with feelings of distress (Z. Wang et al., 2007). Even excessive video-game players (those who average more than 4 hours per day) show withdrawal symptoms during a period of abstinence. To some extent, addictions can be maintained by an attempt to reduce withdrawal symptoms.

However, people often crave a substance long after the end of withdrawal symptoms. One explanation is that people learn that a substance can be strongly reinforcing during a time of severe stress. Researchers gave rats an opportunity to press a lever to inject themselves with heroin. Then they let some of the rats self-administer heroin during a withdrawal state, while others went through withdrawal without heroin. At a later time, when rats went through withdrawal a second time, all the rats had an opportunity to press a lever to try to get heroin, but this time, the lever was inoperative. Although both groups of rats pressed the lever, those that had self-administered heroin during the previous withdrawal state pressed far more frequently (Hutcheson, Everitt, Robbins, & Dickinson, 2001). Evidently, receiving an addictive drug during a withdrawal period is a powerful experience. In effect, the user—rat or human—learns that the drug relieves the distress caused by drug withdrawal and produces heightened effects at that time.

STOP & CHECK

28. Someone who has quit an addictive substance for the first time is strongly counseled not to try it again. Why?

ANSWER

28. Taking an addictive drug during the withdrawal period is strongly reinforcing and likely to lead to prolonged use.

Cravings in Response to Cues

Another hypothesis is that a drug user learns to associate various cues with a drug. Later, even after a long period of abstinence, exposure to those cues triggers a renewed craving. Both humans and rats that have abstained from a drug show heightened seeking of the drug (i.e., craving) during periods of stress or after any reminder of the drug (Ciccocioppo, Martin-Fardon, & Weiss, 2004; Ghitza, Fabbricatore, Prokopenko, Pawlak, & West, 2003; Kruzich, Congleton, & See, 2001). For example, seeing a lit cigarette triggers a craving in smokers (Hutchison, LaChance, Niaura, Bryan, & Smolen, 2002), a video of cocaine use triggers cravings in cocaine users (Volkow et al., 2006), and the sight of a popular video game triggers a craving in a habitual excessive video-game player (Thalemann et al., 2007).

Brain Reorganization

Although escape from withdrawal symptoms and conditioned responses to cues are important, they seem insufficient to explain the way an addiction completely dominates someone's life. Somehow, the addiction hijacks a person's motivations.

Drug addiction rewires the nucleus accumbens. Repeated use of cocaine increases its ability to release dopamine in the nucleus accumbens and the individual's tendency to seek the drug (Robinson & Berridge, 2001; Volkow et al., 2005). Meanwhile, the nucleus accumbens responds less than normal to other incentives, including sex. According to one hypothesis, the prefrontal cortex ordinarily sends stimulatory input to facilitate the nucleus accumbens's responses to reinforcing experiences. Repeated drug use increases the background inhibition in the prefrontal cortex such that it no longer facilitates reinforcement (Volkow et al., 2007). The addictive drug continues to stimulate the nucleus accumbens, but everything else is filtered out (Kalivas, Volkow, & Seamans, 2005).

STOP & CHECK

29. When addiction develops, how does the nucleus accumbens change its response to the addictive activity and to other reinforcements?

ANSWER

29. The nucleus accumbens becomes selectively sensitized, increasing its response to the addictive activity and decreasing its response to other reinforcing activities.

Medications to Combat Substance Abuse

Many people who are trying to overcome substance abuse join Alcoholics Anonymous, Narcotics Anonymous, or similar organizations, and others see psychotherapists. For those who do not respond well to those approaches, several medications are available.

Medications to Combat Alcohol Abuse

After someone drinks ethyl alcohol, enzymes in the liver metabolize it to *acetaldehyde***,** a poisonous substance. An enzyme, acetaldehyde dehydrogenase, then converts acetaldehyde to *acetic acid*, a chemical that the body uses for energy:

$$\text{Ethyl alcohol} \longrightarrow \text{Acetaldehyde} \xrightarrow{\text{Acetaldehyde dehydrogenase}} \text{Acetic acid}$$

People with a weaker gene for acetaldehyde dehydrogenase metabolize acetaldehyde more slowly. If they drink much alcohol, they accumulate acetaldehyde, which produces flushing of the face, increased heart rate, nausea, headache, abdominal pain, impaired breathing, and tissue damage. More than a third of the people in China and Japan have a gene that slows acetaldehyde metabolism. Probably for that reason, alcohol abuse has historically been uncommon in those countries (Luczak, Glatt, & Wall, 2006) (Figure 3.23).

The drug *disulfiram,* which goes by the trade name **Antabuse®,** antagonizes the effects of acetaldehyde dehydrogenase by binding to its copper ion. Its effects were discovered by accident. The workers in one rubber-manufacturing plant found that when they got disulfiram on their skin, they developed a rash (L. Schwartz & Tulipan, 1933). If they inhaled it, they couldn't drink alcohol without getting sick. Soon therapists tried using disulfiram as a drug, hoping that alcoholics would associate alcohol with illness and stop drinking.

Most studies find that Antabuse is moderately effective (Hughes & Cook, 1997). When it works, it supplements the alcoholic's own commitment to stop drinking. By taking a daily pill and imagining the illness that could follow a drink of alcohol, the person reaffirms a decision to abstain. In that case, it doesn't matter whether the pill really contains Antabuse or not because someone who never drinks does not experience the illness (Fuller & Roth, 1979). Those who drink in spite of taking the pill become ill, but often they quit taking the pill instead of quitting alcohol. Antabuse treatment is more effective if friends make sure the person takes the pill daily (Azrin, Sisson, Meyers, & Godley, 1982).

Another medication is naloxone (trade name Revia), which blocks opiate receptors. By decreasing the pleasure from alcohol, it decreases people's craving to use it. Like Antabuse, naloxone is moderately effective. It works best with people who are strongly motivated to quit and is more effective for Type II alcoholics (with a family history of alcoholism) than Type I alcoholics (Krishnan-Sarin, Krystal, Shi, Pittman, & O'Malley, 2007).

A third medication for alcohol abuse is acamprosate (trade name Campral). Acamprosate does not help people quit alcohol, but it helps those who have already quit cope with the withdrawal period. Alcohol withdrawal is a prolonged process characterized by excessive brain activation. Acamprosate antagonizes the receptors for glutamate, the brain's main excitatory transmitter. Again, this drug is moderately effective and best for those who have a strong motivation to quit alcohol (Mason, Goodman, Chabac, & Lehert, 2006; Scott, Figgitt, Keam, & Waugh, 2005). You will notice the pattern: Medications help people who want to quit alcohol, but they are no substitute for that desire.

James W. Kalat

Figure 3.23 Robin Kalat (the author's then-teenage daughter) finds an alcohol vending machine in Tokyo in 1998
Restrictions against buying alcohol were traditionally weak in a country where most people cannot quickly metabolize acetaldehyde and therefore drink alcohol only in moderation. However, in 2000, Japan banned public alcohol vending machines.

STOP & CHECK

30. Who would be likely to drink more alcohol—someone who metabolizes acetaldehyde to acetic acid rapidly or one who metabolizes it slowly?

31. How does Antabuse work?

ANSWERS

30. People who metabolize it rapidly would be more likely to drink alcohol because they suffer fewer unpleasant effects. **31.** Antabuse blocks the enzyme that converts acetaldehyde to acetic acid and therefore makes people sick if they drink alcohol. Potentially, it could teach people an aversion to alcohol, but more often, it works as a way for the person to make a daily recommitment to abstain from drinking.

Medications to Combat Opiate Abuse

Heroin is an artificial substance invented in the 1800s as a "safer" alternative for people who were trying to quit morphine (an opiate drug). Some physicians at the time recommended that people using alcohol switch to heroin (S. Siegel, 1987). They abandoned this idea when they discovered how addictive heroin is.

Still, the idea has persisted that people who can't quit opiates might switch to a less harmful drug. **Methadone** (METH-uh-don) is similar to heroin and morphine but has the advantage that it can be taken orally. (If heroin or morphine is taken orally, stomach acids break down most of it.) Methadone taken orally gradually enters the blood and then the brain, so its effects rise slowly, avoiding the "rush" experience. Because it is metabolized slowly, the withdrawal symptoms are also gradual. Furthermore, the user avoids the risk of an injection with an infected needle.

Buprenorphine and levomethadyl acetate (LAAM), additional drugs similar to methadone, are also used to treat opiate addiction. LAAM has the advantage of producing a long-lasting effect so that the person visits a clinic three times a week instead of daily. People using any of these drugs live longer and healthier, on the average, than heroin or morphine users and are far more likely to hold a job (Vocci, Acri, & Elkashef, 2005). However, these drugs have a variety of side effects, and they do not end the addiction. Anyone who quits the drugs experiences cravings again.

STOP & CHECK

32. Methadone users who try taking heroin experience little effect from it. Why?

ANSWER

32. Because methadone is already occupying the endorphin receptors, heroin cannot add much stimulation to them.

MODULE 3.3 IN CLOSING

Drugs and Behavior

In studying the effects of drugs, researchers have gained clues that may help combat drug abuse. They have also learned much about synapses. For example, the research on cocaine called attention to the importance of reuptake transporters, and the research on cannabinoids led to increased understanding of the retrograde signaling from postsynaptic cells to presynaptic cells.

However, from the standpoint of understanding the physiology of behavior, much remains to be learned. For example, research has identified dopamine activity in the nucleus accumbens as central to reinforcement and addiction, but . . . well, *why* is dopamine activity in that location reinforcing? Stimulation of 5-HT_{2A} receptors produces hallucinations, but again we ask, "Why?" In neuroscience or biological psychology, answering one question leads to new ones, and the deepest questions are usually the most difficult.

SUMMARY

1. A drug that increases activity at a synapse is an agonist; one that decreases activity is an antagonist. Drugs act in many ways, varying in their affinity (tendency to bind to a receptor) and efficacy (tendency to activate it). **68**
2. Reinforcing brain stimulation, reinforcing experiences, and self-administered drugs increase the activity of axons that release dopamine in the nucleus accumbens. **68**
3. Activity in the nucleus accumbens is not synonymous with pleasure or reward. According to one hypothesis, it relates more to "wanting" than "liking," and addiction represents an increase in wanting. **69**
4. Amphetamine increases the release of dopamine. Cocaine and methylphenidate act by blocking the reuptake transporters and therefore decreasing the reuptake of dopamine and serotonin after their release. **70**
5. Nicotine excites acetylcholine receptors, including the ones on axon terminals that release dopamine in the nucleus accumbens. **71**
6. Opiate drugs stimulate endorphin receptors, which inhibit the release of GABA, which would otherwise inhibit the release of dopamine. Thus, the net effect of opiates is increased dopamine release. **72**
7. At certain synapses in many brain areas, after glutamate excites the postsynaptic cell, the cell responds by releasing endocannabinoids, which inhibit further release of both glutamate and GABA by nearby neurons. Chemicals in marijuana mimic the effects of these endocannabinoids. **72**
8. Hallucinogens act by stimulating certain kinds of serotonin receptors. **73**

9. Compared to Type I alcoholism, Type II alcoholism starts faster and sooner, is usually more severe, and affects more men than women. Genes influence alcoholism in several ways, including effects on impulsiveness, and responses to stress. **73**
10. Risk factors for alcoholism, in addition to a family history, include feeling low intoxication after moderate drinking and experiencing much relief from stress after drinking. **74**
11. A key experience in the formation of addictive behavior is trying the substance during withdrawal. The user learns that this is a powerful experience and learns to use the substance as a way of coping with distress. **76**
12. Addiction is associated with sensitization of the nucleus accumbens so that it responds more strongly to the addictive activity and less to other kinds of reinforcement. **76**
13. Ethyl alcohol is metabolized to acetaldehyde, which is then metabolized to acetic acid. People who, for genetic reasons, are deficient in that second reaction tend to become ill after drinking and therefore are unlikely to drink heavily. **77**
14. Antabuse, a drug sometimes used to treat alcohol abuse, blocks the conversion of acetaldehyde to acetic acid. **77**
15. Methadone and similar drugs are sometimes offered as a substitute for opiate drugs. The substitutes have the advantage that if taken orally, they satisfy the cravings without severely interrupting the person's ability to carry on with life. **78**

KEY TERMS

Terms are defined in the module on the page number indicated. They're also presented in alphabetical order with definitions in the book's Subject Index/Glossary. Interactive flashcards, audio reviews, and crossword puzzles are among the online resources available to help you learn these terms and the concepts they represent.

affinity **68**
agonist **68**
alcoholism (alcohol dependence) **73**
amphetamine **70**
anandamide **72**
Antabuse **77**
antagonist **68**
cannabinoids **72**
cocaine **70**
Δ^9-tetrahydrocannabinol (Δ^9-THC) **72**
dopamine transporter **70**
efficacy **68**
hallucinogenic drugs **73**
methadone **78**
methylphenidate **70**
nicotine **71**
nucleus accumbens **69**
opiate drugs **72**
self-stimulation of the brain **68**
stimulant drugs **70**
2-AG **72**
Type I (Type A) alcoholism **73**
Type II (Type B) alcoholism **73**

THOUGHT QUESTIONS

1. People who take methylphenidate (Ritalin) for control of attention-deficit disorder often report that, although the drug increases their arousal for a while, they feel a decrease in alertness and arousal a few hours later. Explain.
2. The research on sensitization of the nucleus accumbens has dealt with addictive drugs, mainly cocaine. Would you expect a gambling addiction to have similar effects? How could someone test this possibility?

CHAPTER 3 Exploration and Study

In addition to the study materials provided at the end of each module, you may supplement your review of this chapter by using one or more of the book's electronic resources, which include its companion Website, interactive Cengage Learning eBook, Exploring Biological Psychology CD-ROM, and CengageNOW. Brief descriptions of these resources follow. For more information, visit **www.cengage.com/psychology/kalat.**

The book's companion Website, accessible through the author Web page indicated above, provides a wide range of study resources such as an interactive glossary, flashcards, tutorial quizzes, updated Web links, and Try It Yourself activities, as well as a limited selection of the short videos and animated explanations of concepts available for this chapter.

Exploring Biological Psychology

The Exploring Biological Psychology CD-ROM contains videos, animations, and Try It Yourself activities. These activities—as well as many that are new to this edition—are also available in the text's fully interactive, media-rich Cengage Learning eBook,* which gives you the opportunity to experience biological psychology in an even greater interactive and multimedia environment. The Cengage Learning eBook also includes highlighting and note-taking features and an audio glossary. For this chapter, the Cengage Learning eBook includes the following interactive explorations:

Post Synaptic Potentials
EPSP Demonstration
Transmitter Release
Release of Neurotransmitter
Cholinergic Synapse
Metabotropic Demonstration
Acetylcholinesterase Inhibits Acetylcholine
Understanding Addiction
Opiates

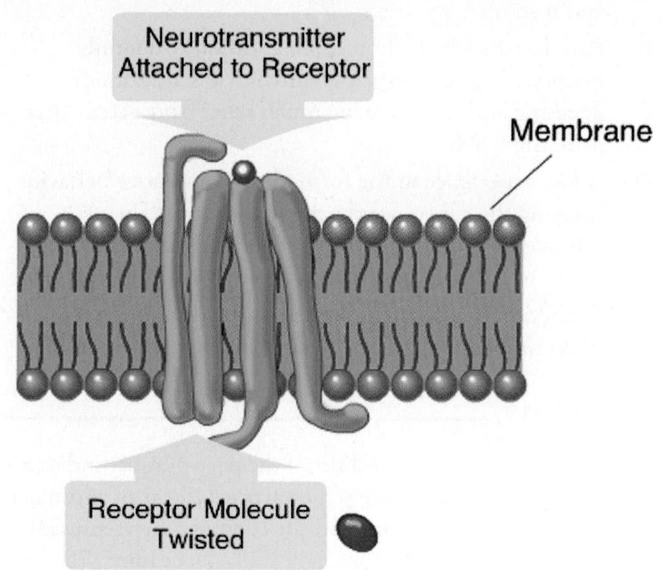

Metabotropic Demonstration is an animation that demonstrates how a neurotransmitter activates a metabotropic receptor, stimulating a second messenger within the cell.

CENGAGENOW™ is an easy-to-use resource that helps you study in less time to get the grade you want. An online study system, CengageNOW* gives you the option of taking a diagnostic pretest for each chapter. The system uses the results of each pretest to create personalized chapter study plans for you. The Personalized Study Plans

- help you save study time by identifying areas on which you should concentrate and give you one-click access to corresponding pages of the interactive Cengage Learning eBook;
- provide interactive exercises and study tools to help you fully understand chapter concepts; and
- include a posttest for you to take to confirm that you are ready to move on to the next chapter.

* Requires a Cengage Learning eResources account. Visit **www.cengage.com/login** to register or login.

Suggestions for Further Exploration

The book's companion Website includes a list of suggested articles available through InfoTrac College Edition for this chapter. You may also want to explore some of the following books and Websites. The text's companion Website provides live, updated links to the sites listed below.

Books

Cowan, W. M., Südhof, T. C., & Stevens, C. F. (2001). *Synapses.* Baltimore: Johns Hopkins University Press. If you are curious about some detailed aspect of synapses, this is a good reference book to check for an answer.

McKim, W. A. (2007). *Drugs and behavior* (6th ed.). Upper Saddle River, NJ: Prentice Hall. Concise, informative text on drugs and drug abuse.

Websites

The Endocrine Society
A source of much information about hormones.
http://www.endo-society.org/

Nucleus Accumbens
A brief description accompanied by links to many sites concerning addictions.
http://www.biopsychiatry.com/nucleus-accumbens.htm

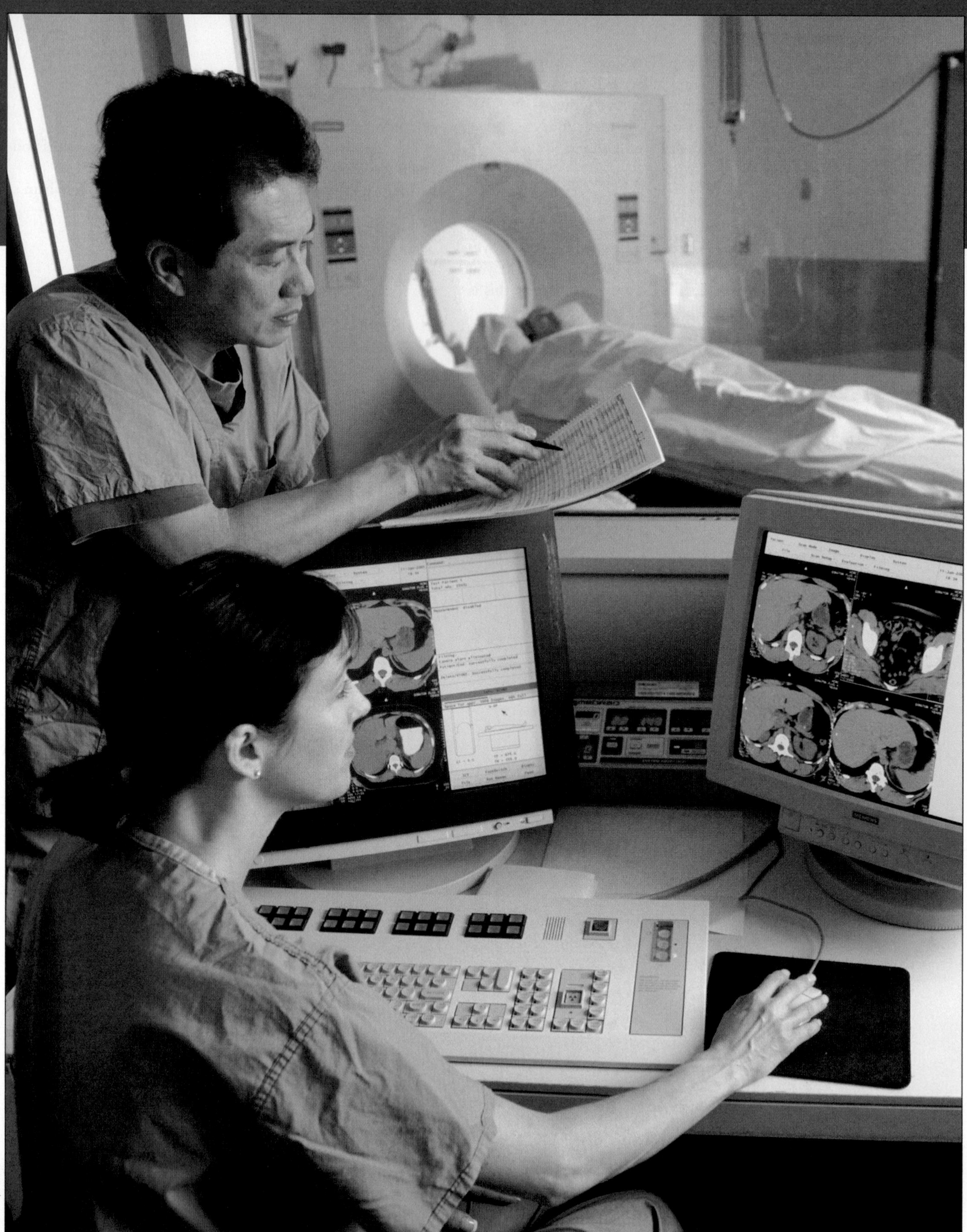

Peter Beck/CORBIS

Anatomy of the Nervous System

4

CHAPTER OUTLINE

OPPOSITE: New methods allow researchers to examine living brains.

MAIN IDEAS

1. Each part of the nervous system has specialized functions, and the parts work together to produce behavior. Damage to different areas results in different types of behavioral deficits.
2. The cerebral cortex, the largest structure in the mammalian brain, elaborately processes sensory information and provides for fine control of movement.
3. As research has identified the different functions of different brain areas, a new question has arisen: How do the areas work together to produce unified experience and behavior?
4. It is difficult to conduct research on the functions of the nervous system. Conclusions come from multiple methods and careful behavioral measurements.

Trying to learn **neuroanatomy** (the anatomy of the nervous system) from a book is like trying to learn geography from a road map. A map can tell you that Mystic, Georgia, is about 40 km north of Enigma, Georgia. Similarly, a book can tell you that the habenula is about 4.6 mm from the interpeduncular nucleus in a rat's brain (slightly farther in a human brain). But these little gems of information will seem both mysterious and enigmatic unless you are concerned with that part of Georgia or that area of the brain.

This chapter does not provide a detailed road map of the nervous system. It is more like a world globe, describing the large, basic structures (analogous to the continents) and some distinctive features of each.

The first module introduces key neuroanatomical terms and outlines overall structures of the nervous system. In the second module, we concentrate on the structures and functions of the cerebral cortex, the largest part of the mammalian central nervous system. The third module deals with the main methods that researchers use to discover the behavioral functions of different brain areas.

Be prepared: This chapter contains a huge number of new terms. You should not expect to memorize all of them at once, and it will pay to review this chapter repeatedly.

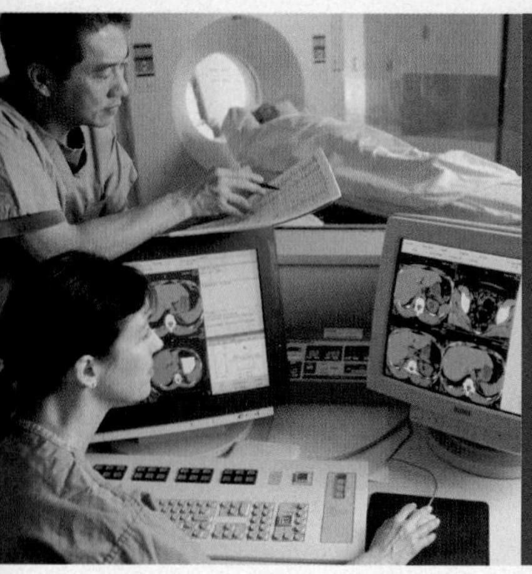

MODULE 4.1

Structure of the Vertebrate Nervous System

Your nervous system consists of many substructures, each of them including many neurons, each of which receives and makes many synapses. How do all those little parts work together to make one behaving unit? Does each neuron have an independent function so that, for example, one cell recognizes your grandmother, another controls your desire for pizzas, and another makes you smile at babies? Or does the brain operate as an undifferentiated whole, with each part doing the same thing as every other part?

The answer is, "something between those extremes." Individual neurons have specialized functions, but the activity of a single cell by itself has no more meaning than the letter *h* has out of context.

Terminology to Describe the Nervous System

For vertebrates, we distinguish the central nervous system from the peripheral nervous system (Figure 4.1). The distinction is artificial but useful for many purposes. The **central nervous system (CNS)** is the brain and the spinal cord. The **peripheral nervous system (PNS)** consists of the nerves outside the brain and spinal cord. Part of the PNS is the **somatic nervous system,** which consists of the axons conveying messages from the sense organs to the CNS and from the CNS to the muscles. The axons to the muscles are an extension from cell bodies in the spinal cord, so part of each cell is in the CNS

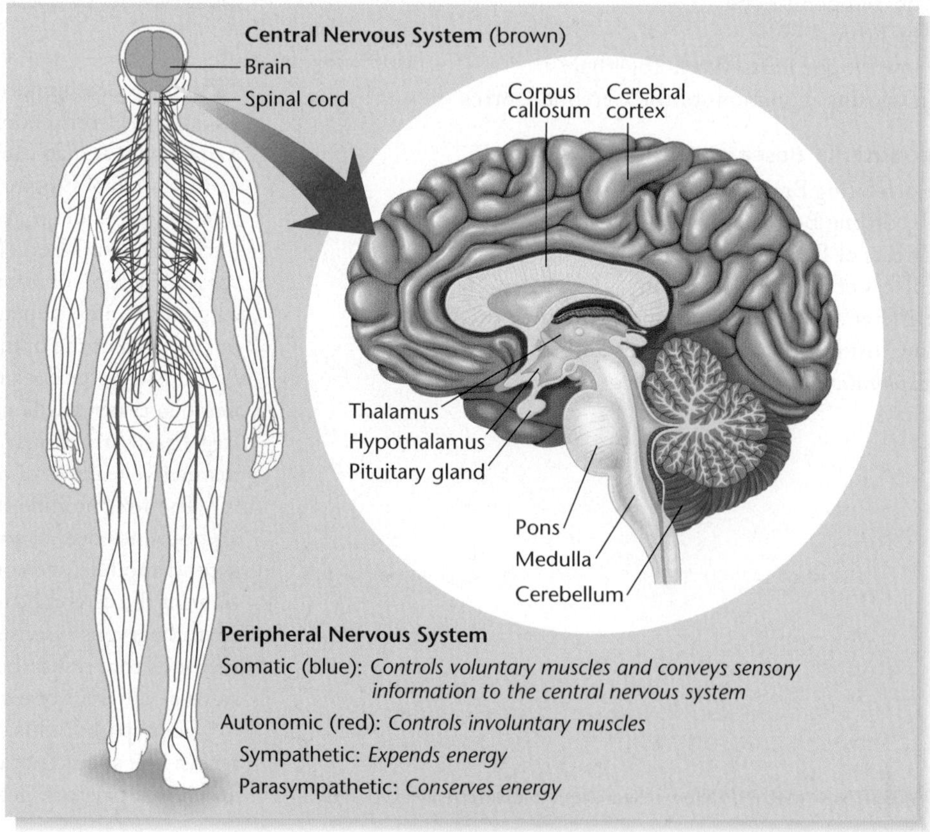

Figure 4.1 The human nervous system
Both the central nervous system and the peripheral nervous system have major subdivisions. The closeup of the brain shows the right hemisphere as seen from the midline. *(From Bruce F. Pennington, et al. "A Twin MRI Study of Size Variations in the Human Brain",* Journal of Cognitive Neuroscience, *12:1 (January, 2000), p. 223–232. © 2000 by the Massachusetts Institute of Technology. Reprinted by permission.)*

TABLE 4.1 Anatomical Terms Referring to Directions

Term	Definition	Term	Definition
Dorsal	Toward the back, away from the ventral (stomach) side. The top of the brain is considered dorsal because it has that position in four-legged animals.	**Proximal**	Located close (approximate) to the point of origin or attachment
		Distal	Located more distant from the point of origin or attachment
Ventral	Toward the stomach, away from the dorsal (back) side	**Ipsilateral**	On the same side of the body (e.g., two parts on the left or two on the right)
Anterior	Toward the front end	**Contralateral**	On the opposite side of the body (one on the left and one on the right)
Posterior	Toward the rear end	**Coronal plane**	A plane that shows brain structures as seen from the front (or frontal plane)
Superior	Above another part		
Inferior	Below another part	**Sagittal plane**	A plane that shows brain structures as seen from the side
Lateral	Toward the side, away from the midline	**Horizontal plane**	A plane that shows brain structures as seen from above (or transverse plane)
Medial	Toward the midline, away from the side		

and part in the PNS. That is a reason the CNS-PNS distinction is artificial. Another part of the PNS, the **autonomic nervous system,** controls the heart, the intestines, and other organs. The autonomic nervous system has some of its cell bodies within the brain or spinal cord and some in clusters along the sides of the spinal cord.

To follow a map, you must understand *north, south, east,* and *west.* Because the nervous system is three-dimensional, we need more terms to describe it. As Table 4.1 and Figure 4.2 indicate, **dorsal** means toward the back and **ventral** means toward the stomach. (One way to remember these terms is that a *ventri*loquist is literally a "stomach talker.") In a four-legged animal, the top of the brain is dorsal (on the same side as the animal's back), and the bottom of the brain is ventral (on the stomach side). When humans evolved upright posture, the position of our head changed relative to the spinal cord. For convenience, we still apply the terms *dorsal* and *ventral* to the same parts of

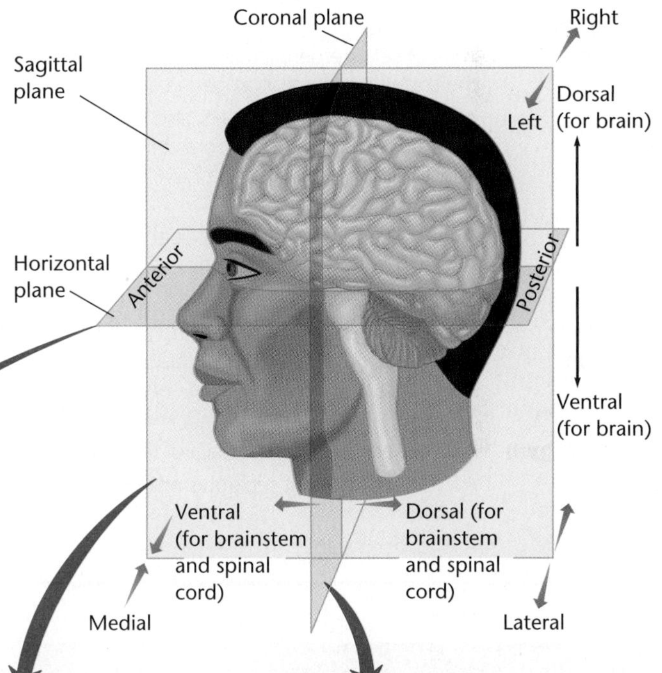

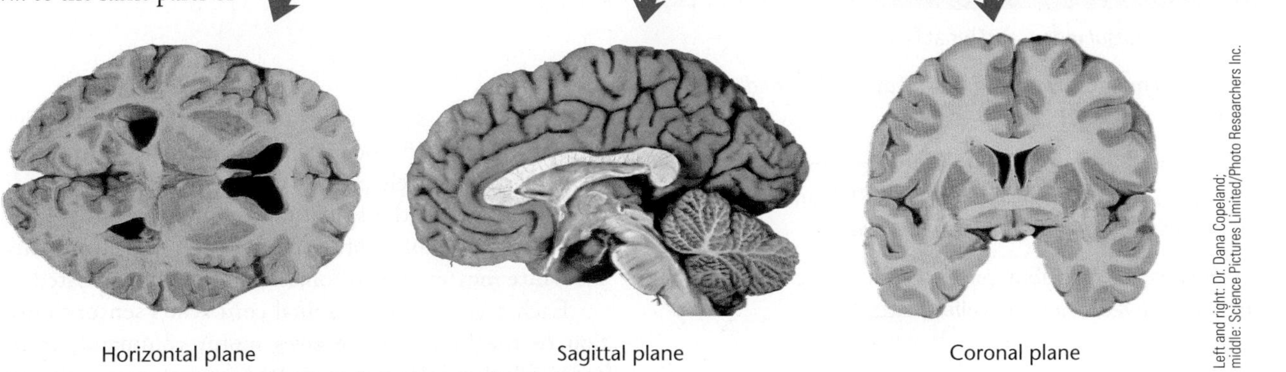

Figure 4.2 Terms for anatomical directions in the nervous system
In four-legged animals, dorsal and ventral point in the same direction for the head as they do for the rest of the body. However, humans' upright posture has tilted the head, so the dorsal and ventral directions of the head are not parallel to those of the spinal cord.

Left and right: Dr. Dana Copeland; middle: Science Pictures Limited/Photo Researchers Inc.

the human brain as other vertebrate brains. Consequently, the dorsal–ventral axis of the human brain is at a right angle to the dorsal–ventral axis of the spinal cord. If you picture a person in a crawling position with all four limbs on the ground but nose pointing forward, the dorsal and ventral positions of the brain become parallel to those of the spinal cord. Figure 4.2 also illustrates the three ways of taking a plane through the brain, known as horizontal, sagittal, and coronal (or frontal).

Table 4.2 introduces additional terms that are worth learning. Tables 4.1 and 4.2 require careful study and review. After you think you have mastered the terms, check yourself with the following.

TABLE 4.2 Terms Referring to Parts of the Nervous System

Term	Definition
Lamina	A row or layer of cell bodies separated from other cell bodies by a layer of axons and dendrites
Column	A set of cells perpendicular to the surface of the cortex, with similar properties
Tract	A set of axons within the CNS, also known as a *projection.* If axons extend from cell bodies in structure A to synapses onto B, we say that the fibers "project" from A onto B.
Nerve	A set of axons in the periphery, either from the CNS to a muscle or gland or from a sensory organ to the CNS
Nucleus	A cluster of neuron cell bodies within the CNS
Ganglion	A cluster of neuron cell bodies, usually outside the CNS (as in the sympathetic nervous system)
Gyrus (*pl.*: gyri)	A protuberance on the surface of the brain
Sulcus (*pl.*: sulci)	A fold or groove that separates one gyrus from another
Fissure	A long, deep sulcus

STOP & CHECK

1. What does *dorsal* mean, and what is its opposite?
2. What term means *toward the side, away from the midline,* and what is its opposite?
3. If two structures are both on the left side of the body, they are ______ to each other. If one is on the left and the other is on the right, they are ______ to each other.
4. The bulges in the cerebral cortex are called ______. The grooves between them are called ______.

ANSWERS

1. Dorsal means toward the back, away from the stomach side. Its opposite is ventral. **2.** lateral; medial **3.** ipsilateral; contralateral **4.** gyri; sulci. If you have trouble remembering sulcus, think of the word *sulk,* meaning "to pout" (and therefore lie low).

The Spinal Cord

The **spinal cord** is the part of the CNS within the spinal column. The spinal cord communicates with all the sense organs and muscles except those of the head. It is a segmented structure, and each segment has on each side a sensory nerve and a motor nerve, as Figure 4.3 shows. According to the **Bell-Magendie law,** which was one of the first discoveries about the functions of the nervous system, the entering dorsal roots (axon bundles) carry sensory information, and the exiting ventral roots carry motor information. The axons to and from the skin and muscles are the peripheral nervous system. The cell bodies of the sensory neurons are in clusters of neurons outside the spinal cord, called the **dorsal root ganglia.** (*Ganglia* is the plural of *ganglion,* a cluster of neurons. In most cases, a neuron cluster outside the CNS is called a ganglion, and a cluster inside the CNS is called a nucleus.) Cell bodies of the motor neurons are inside the spinal cord.

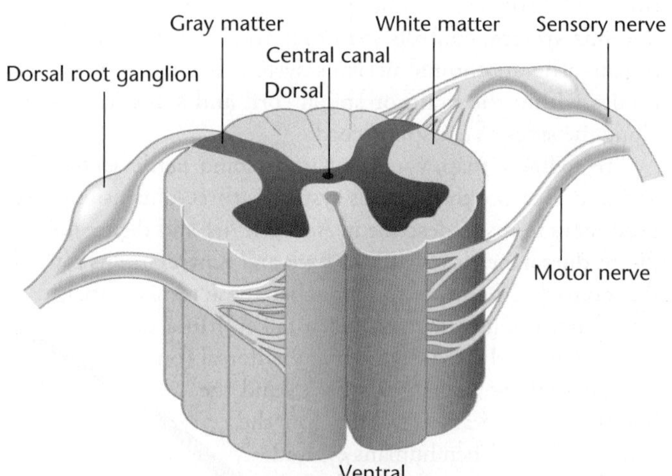

Figure 4.3 Diagram of a cross-section through the spinal cord
The dorsal root on each side conveys sensory information to the spinal cord; the ventral root conveys motor commands to the muscles.

In the cross-section through the spinal cord shown in Figures 4.4 and 4.5, the H-shaped **gray matter** in the center of the cord is densely packed with cell bodies and dendrites. Many neurons of the spinal cord send axons from the gray matter to the brain or other parts of the spinal cord through the **white matter,** which consists mostly of myelinated axons.

Each segment of the spinal cord sends sensory information to the brain and receives motor commands from the brain. All that information passes through tracts of axons in the spinal cord. If the spinal cord is cut at a given segment, the brain loses sensation from that segment and below. The brain also loses motor control over all parts of the body served by that segment and the lower ones.

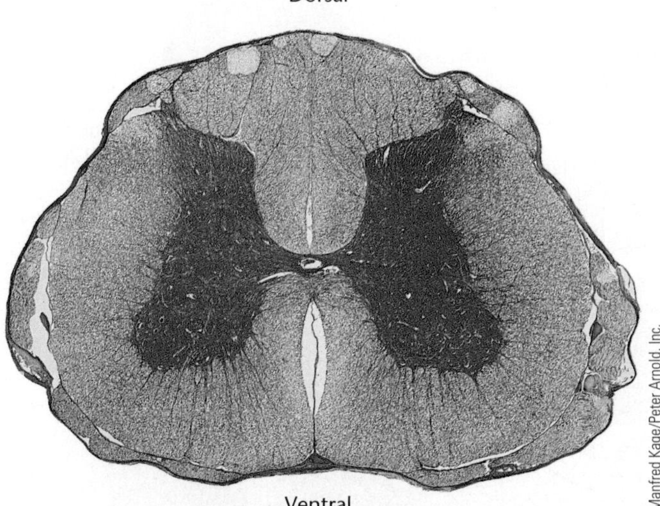

Figure 4.4 Photo of a cross-section through the spinal cord
The H-shaped structure in the center is gray matter, composed largely of cell bodies. The surrounding white matter consists of axons. The axons are organized in tracts; some carry information from the brain and higher levels of the spinal cord downward, while others carry information from lower levels upward.

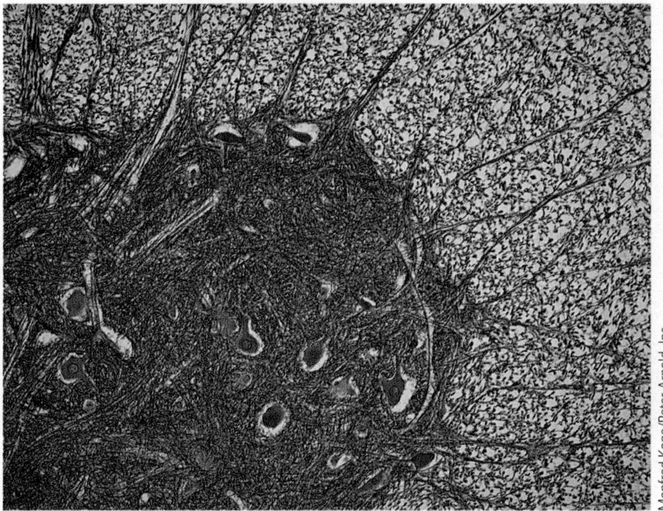

Figure 4.5 A section of gray matter of the spinal cord (lower left) and white matter surrounding it
Cell bodies and dendrites reside entirely in the gray matter. Axons travel from one area of gray matter to another in the white matter.

The Autonomic Nervous System

The autonomic nervous system consists of neurons that receive information from and send commands to the heart, intestines, and other organs. It has two parts: the sympathetic and parasympathetic nervous systems (Figure 4.6). The **sympathetic nervous system,** a network of nerves that prepare the organs for vigorous activity, consists of chains of ganglia just to the left and right of the spinal cord's central regions (the thoracic and lumbar areas). These ganglia are connected by axons to the spinal cord. Sympathetic axons prepare the organs for "fight or flight"—increasing breathing and heart rate and decreasing digestive activity. Because the sympathetic ganglia are closely linked, they often act as a single system "in sympathy" with one another, although various situations activate some parts more than others. The sweat glands, the adrenal glands, the muscles that constrict blood vessels, and the muscles that erect the hairs of the skin have only sympathetic, not parasympathetic, input.

APPLICATIONS AND EXTENSIONS

Goose Bumps

Erection of the hairs, known as "goose bumps" or "goose flesh," occurs when we are cold. What does it have to do with the fight-or-flight functions associated with the sympathetic nervous system? Part of the answer is that we also get goose bumps when we are frightened. You have heard the expression, "I was so frightened my hairs stood on end." You may also have seen a frightened cat erect its fur. Human body hairs are so short that erecting them accomplishes nothing, but a cat with erect fur looks bigger. A frightened porcupine erects its quills, which are just modified hairs (Richter & Langworthy, 1933). The behavior that makes the quills so useful, their erection in response to fear, evolved before the quills themselves did.

The **parasympathetic nervous system** facilitates vegetative, nonemergency responses. The term *para* means "beside" or "related to," and parasympathetic activities are related to, and generally the opposite of, sympathetic activities. For example, the sympathetic nervous system increases heart rate, but the parasympathetic nervous system decreases it. The parasympathetic nervous system increases digestive activity, whereas the sympathetic nervous system decreases it. Although the sympathetic and parasympathetic systems act in opposition, both are constantly active to varying degrees, and many stimuli arouse parts of both systems.

The parasympathetic nervous system is also known as the craniosacral system because it consists of the cranial nerves and nerves from the sacral spinal cord (see Figure 4.6). Unlike the ganglia in the sympathetic system, the parasympathetic ganglia are not arranged in a chain near the spinal cord. Rather, long *preganglionic* axons extend from the spinal cord to parasympathetic ganglia close to each internal organ; shorter *postganglionic* fibers then extend from the parasympathetic ganglia into the organs themselves. Because the parasympa-

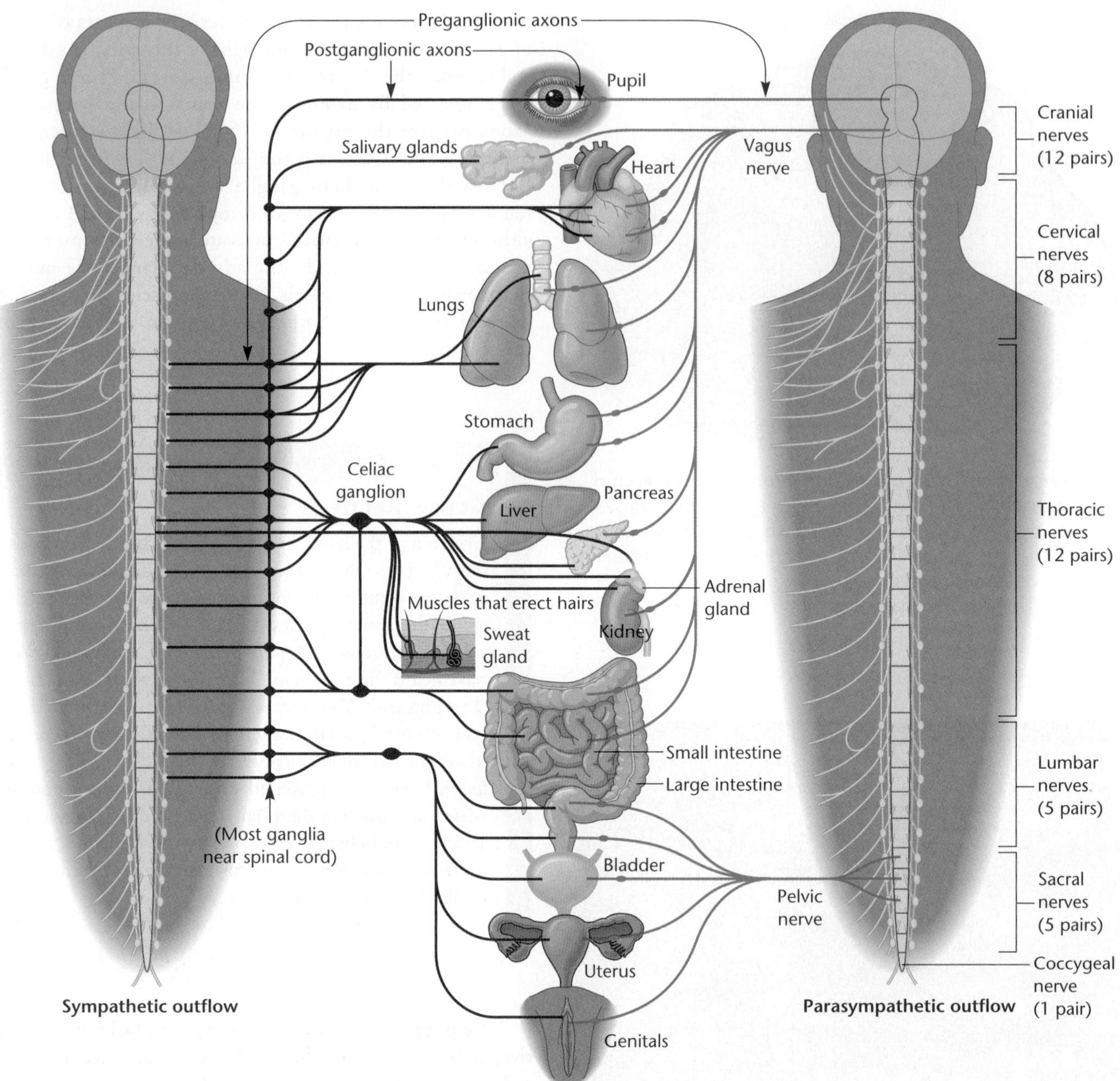

Figure 4.6 The sympathetic nervous system (red lines) and parasympathetic nervous system (blue lines)
Note that the adrenal glands and hair erector muscles receive sympathetic input only. *(Starr & Taggart, 1989)*

thetic ganglia are not linked to one another, they act more independently than the sympathetic ganglia do. Parasympathetic activity decreases heart rate, increases digestive rate, and in general, conserves energy.

The parasympathetic nervous system's postganglionic axons release the neurotransmitter acetylcholine. Most of the postganglionic synapses of the sympathetic nervous system use norepinephrine, although a few, including those that control the sweat glands, use acetylcholine. Because the two systems use different transmitters, certain drugs excite or inhibit one system or the other. For example, over-the-counter cold remedies exert most of their effects by blocking parasympathetic activity or increasing sympathetic activity. Because the flow of sinus fluids is a parasympathetic response, drugs that block the parasympathetic system inhibit sinus flow. The side effects of cold remedies stem from their sympathetic, antiparasympathetic activities: They inhibit salivation and digestion and increase heart rate.

STOP & CHECK

5. Sensory nerves enter which side of the spinal cord, dorsal or ventral?

6. Which functions are controlled by the sympathetic nervous system? Which are controlled by the parasympathetic nervous system?

ANSWERS

5. dorsal **6.** The sympathetic nervous system prepares the organs for vigorous fight-or-flight activity. The parasympathetic system increases vegetative responses such as digestion.

The Hindbrain

The brain has three major divisions: the hindbrain, the midbrain, and the forebrain (Figure 4.7 and Table 4.3). Brain investigators unfortunately use a variety of terms synonymously. For example, some people prefer words with Greek roots: rhombencephalon (hindbrain), mesencephalon (midbrain), and prosencephalon (forebrain). You may encounter these terms in other reading.

The **hindbrain,** the posterior part of the brain, consists of the medulla, the pons, and the cerebellum. The medulla and pons, the midbrain, and certain central structures of the forebrain constitute the **brainstem** (Figure 4.8).

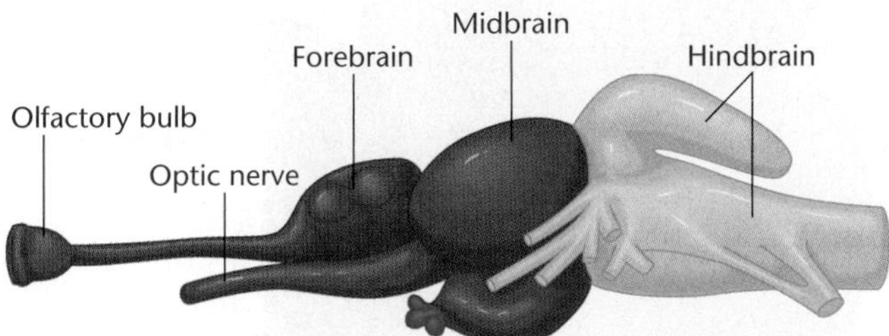

Figure 4.7 Three major divisions of the vertebrate brain
In a fish brain, as shown here, the forebrain, midbrain, and hindbrain are clearly visible as separate bulges. In adult mammals, the forebrain grows and surrounds the entire midbrain and part of the hindbrain.

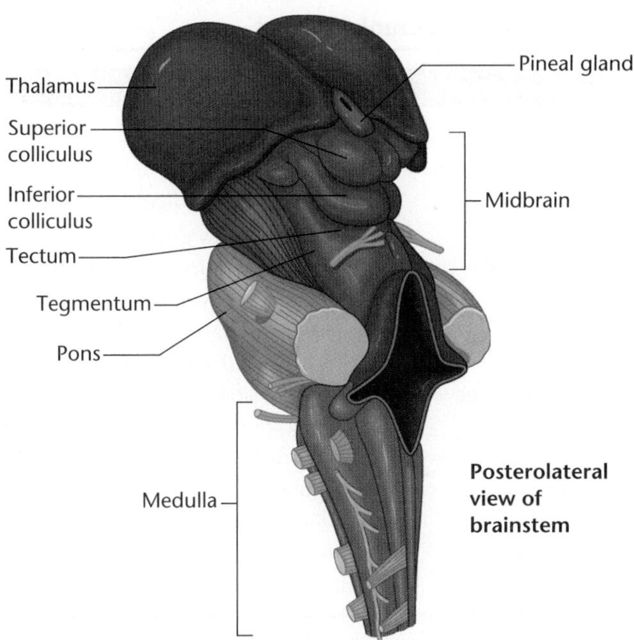

Figure 4.8 The human brainstem
This composite structure extends from the top of the spinal cord into the center of the forebrain. The pons, pineal gland, and colliculi are ordinarily surrounded by the cerebral cortex.

The **medulla,** or medulla oblongata, is just above the spinal cord and could be regarded as an enlarged extension of the spinal cord but located in the skull. The medulla controls some vital reflexes—including breathing, heart rate, vomiting, salivation, coughing, and sneezing—through the **cranial nerves,** which control sensations from the head, muscle movements in the head, and much of the parasympathetic output to the organs. Some of the cranial nerves include both sensory and motor components; others have just one or the other. Damage to the medulla is frequently fatal, and large doses of opiates are life-threatening because they suppress activity of the medulla.

Just as the lower parts of the body are connected to the spinal cord via sensory and motor nerves, the receptors and muscles of the head and organs connect to the brain by 12 pairs of cranial nerves (one of each pair on the right of the brain and one

TABLE 4.3 Major Divisions of the Vertebrate Brain

Area	Also Known as	Major Structures
Forebrain	Prosencephalon ("forward-brain")	
	Diencephalon ("between-brain")	Thalamus, hypothalamus
	Telencephalon ("end-brain")	Cerebral cortex, hippocampus, basal ganglia
Midbrain	Mesencephalon ("middle-brain")	Tectum, tegmentum, superior colliculus, inferior colliculus, substantia nigra
Hindbrain	Rhombencephalon (literally, "parallelogram-brain")	Medulla, pons, cerebellum
	Metencephalon ("afterbrain")	Pons, cerebellum
	Myelencephalon ("marrow-brain")	Medulla

TABLE 4.4 The Cranial Nerves

Number and Name	Major Functions
I. Olfactory	Smell
II. Optic	Vision
III. Oculomotor	Control of eye movements; pupil constriction
IV. Trochlear	Control of eye movements
V. Trigeminal	Skin sensations from most of the face; control of jaw muscles for chewing and swallowing
VI. Abducens	Control of eye movements
VII. Facial	Taste from the anterior two thirds of the tongue; control of facial expressions, crying, salivation, and dilation of the head's blood vessels
VIII. Statoacoustic	Hearing; equilibrium
IX. Glossopharyngeal	Taste and other sensations from throat and posterior third of the tongue; control of swallowing, salivation, throat movements during speech
X. Vagus	Sensations from neck and thorax; control of throat, esophagus, and larynx; parasympathetic nerves to stomach, intestines, and other organs
XI. Accessory	Control of neck and shoulder movements
XII. Hypoglossal	Control of muscles of the tongue

Cranial nerves III, IV, and VI are coded in red to highlight their similarity: control of eye movements. Cranial nerves VII, IX, and XII are coded in green to highlight their similarity: taste and control of tongue and throat movements. Cranial nerve VII has other important functions as well. Nerve X (not highlighted) also contributes to throat movements, although it is primarily known for other functions.

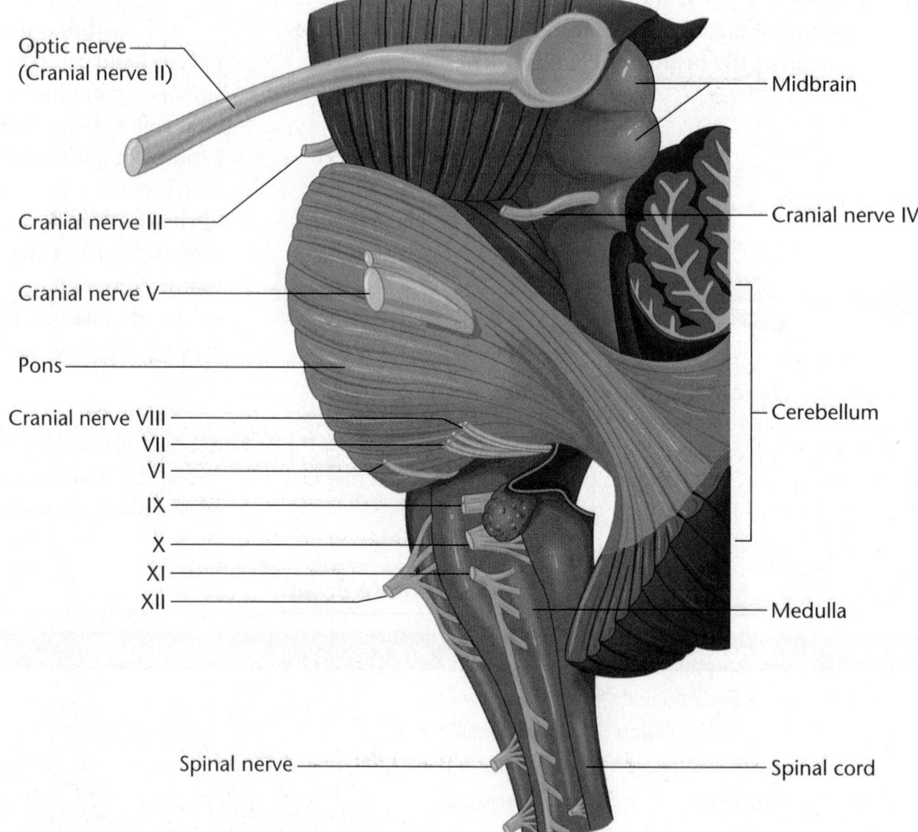

Figure 4.9 Cranial nerves II through XII
Cranial nerve I, the olfactory nerve, connects directly to the olfactory bulbs of the forebrain. *(Based on Braus, 1960)*

on the left), as shown in Table 4.4. Each cranial nerve originates in a *nucleus* (cluster of neurons) that integrates the sensory information, regulates the motor output, or both. The cranial nerve nuclei for nerves V through XII are in the medulla and pons. Those for cranial nerves I through IV are in the midbrain and forebrain (Figure 4.9).

The **pons** lies anterior and ventral to the medulla; like the medulla, it contains nuclei for several cranial nerves. The term *pons* is Latin for "bridge"; the name reflects the fact that many axons in the pons cross from one side of the brain to the other. This is in fact the location where axons from each half of the brain cross to the opposite side of the spinal cord so that the left hemisphere controls the muscles of the right side of the body and the right hemisphere controls the left side.

The medulla and pons also contain the reticular formation and the raphe system. The **reticular formation** has descending and ascending portions. The descending portion is one of several brain areas that controls the motor areas of the spinal cord. The ascending portion sends output to much of the cerebral cortex, selectively increasing arousal and attention in one area or another (Guillery, Feig, & Lozsádi, 1998). The **raphe system** also sends axons to much of the forebrain, modifying the brain's readiness to respond to stimuli (Mesulam, 1995).

The **cerebellum** is a large hindbrain structure with many deep folds. It has long been known for its contributions to the control of movement (see Chapter 8), and many older textbooks describe the cerebellum as important for "balance and coordination." True, people with cerebellar damage are clumsy and lose their balance, but the functions of the cerebellum extend far beyond balance and coordination. People with damage to the cerebellum have trouble shifting their attention back and forth between auditory and visual stimuli (Courchesne et al., 1994). They have much difficulty with timing, including sensory timing. For example, they are poor at judging whether one rhythm is faster than another.

The Midbrain

As the name implies, the **midbrain** is in the middle of the brain, although in adult mammals it is dwarfed and surrounded by the forebrain. In birds, reptiles, amphibians, and fish, the midbrain is a more prominent structure. The roof of the midbrain is called the **tectum.** (*Tectum* is the Latin word for "roof." The same root occurs in the geological term *plate tectonics.*) The swellings on each side of the tectum are the **superior colliculus** and the **inferior colliculus** (see Figures 4.8 and 4.10). Both are important for sensory processing—the inferior colliculus for hearing and the superior colliculus mainly for vision.

Under the tectum lies the **tegmentum,** the intermediate level of the midbrain. (In Latin, *tegmentum* means a "covering," such as a rug on the floor. The tegmentum covers several other midbrain structures, although it is covered by the tectum.) The tegmentum includes the nuclei for the third and fourth cranial nerves, parts of the reticular formation, and extensions

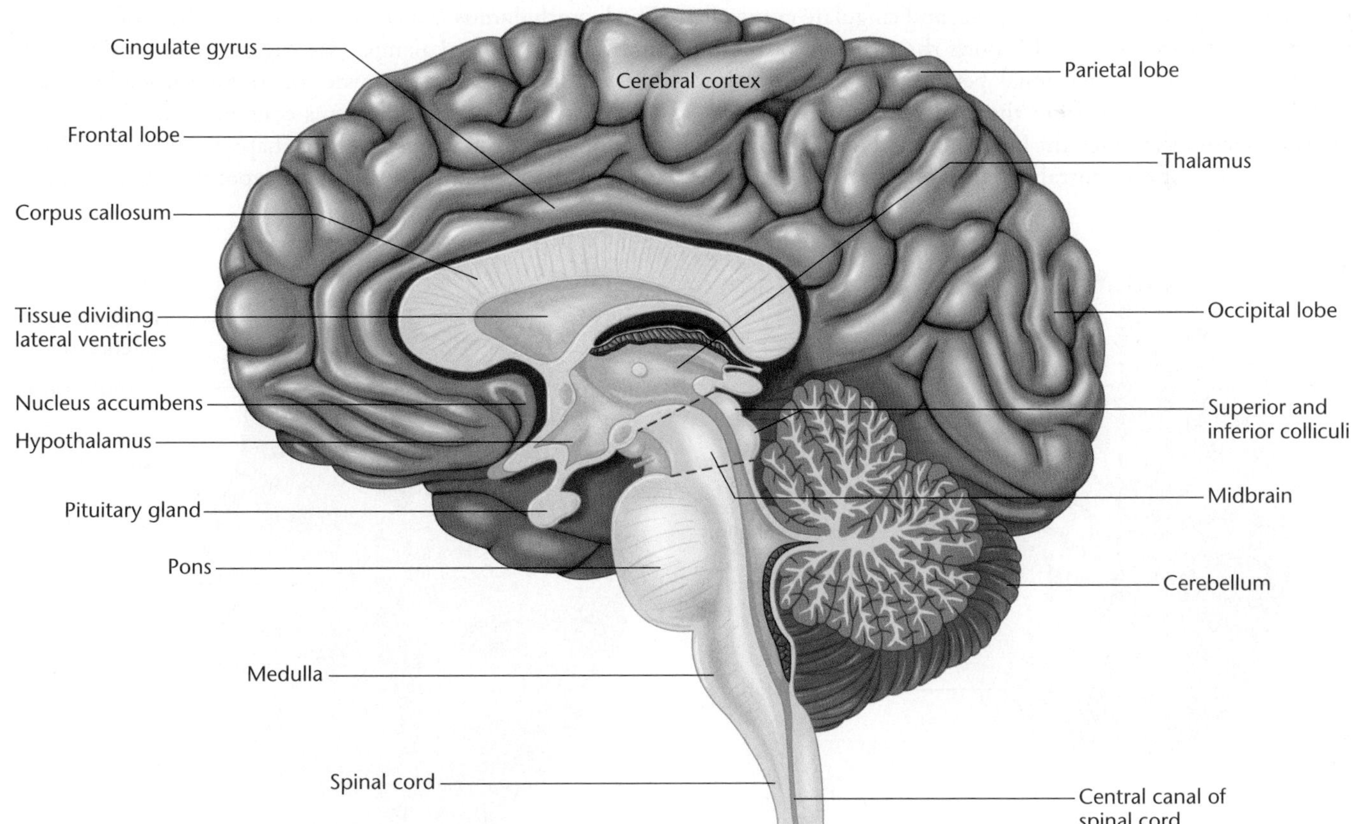

Figure 4.10 A sagittal section through the human brain
(After Nieuwenhuys, Voogd, & vanHuijzen, 1988)

of the pathways between the forebrain and the spinal cord or hindbrain. Another midbrain structure is the **substantia nigra,** which gives rise to the dopamine-containing pathway that facilitates readiness for movement (see Chapter 8).

The Forebrain

The **forebrain** is the most anterior and most prominent part of the mammalian brain. It consists of two cerebral hemispheres, one on the left and one on the right (Figure 4.11). Each hemisphere is organized to receive sensory information, mostly from the contralateral (opposite) side of the body, and to control muscles, mostly on the contralateral side, by way of axons to the spinal cord and the cranial nerve nuclei.

The outer portion is the cerebral cortex. (*Cerebrum* is a Latin word meaning "brain." *Cortex* is a Latin word for "bark" or "shell.") Under the cerebral cortex are other structures, including the thalamus, which is the main source of input to the cerebral cortex. A set of structures known as the basal ganglia plays a major role in certain aspects of movement. A number of other interlinked structures, known as the **limbic system,** form a border (or *limbus,* the Latin word for "border") around the brainstem. These structures are particularly important for motivations and emotions, such as eating, drinking, sexual activity, anxiety, and aggression. The structures of the limbic system are the olfactory bulb, hypothalamus, hippocampus, amygdala, and cingulate gyrus of the cerebral cortex. Figure 4.12 shows the positions of these structures in three-dimensional perspective. Figures 4.10 and 4.13 show coronal (from the front) and sagittal (from the side) sections through the human brain. Figure 4.13 also includes a view of the ventral surface of the brain.

In describing the forebrain, we begin with the subcortical areas; the next module focuses on the cerebral cortex. In later chapters, we return to each of these areas as they become relevant.

Thalamus

The thalamus and hypothalamus form the *diencephalon,* a section distinct from the *telencephalon,* which is the rest of the forebrain. The **thalamus** is a pair of structures (left and right) in the center of the forebrain. The term is derived from a Greek word meaning "anteroom," "inner chamber," or "bridal bed." It resembles two avocados joined side by side, one in the left hemisphere and one in the right. Most sensory information goes first to the thalamus, which processes it and sends output to the cerebral cortex. An exception to this rule is olfactory information, which progresses from the olfactory receptors to the olfactory bulbs and then directly to the cerebral cortex.

Many nuclei of the thalamus receive their input from a sensory system, such as vision, and transmit information to a single area of the cerebral cortex, as in Figure 4.14 on page 94. The cerebral cortex sends information back to the thalamus, prolonging and magnifying certain kinds of input at the expense of others, thereby focusing attention on particular stimuli (Komura et al., 2001).

Hypothalamus

The **hypothalamus** is a small area near the base of the brain just ventral to the thalamus (see Figures 4.10 and 4.12). It has widespread connections with the rest of the forebrain and the midbrain. The hypothalamus contains a number of distinct nuclei, which we examine in Chapters 10 and 11. Partly through nerves and partly through hypothalamic hormones,

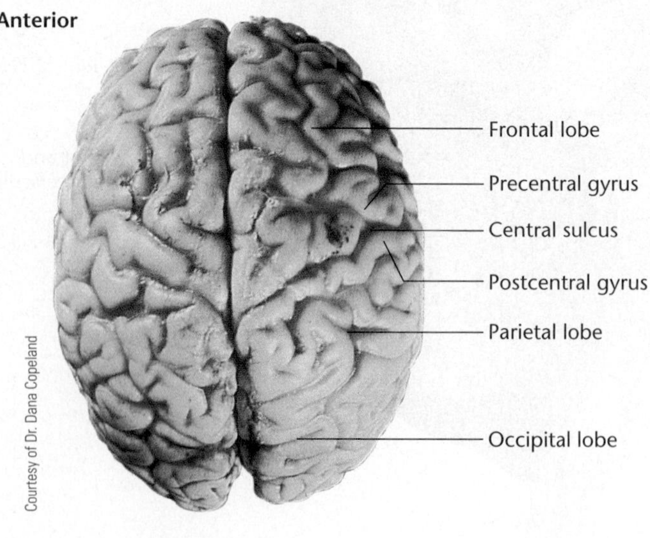

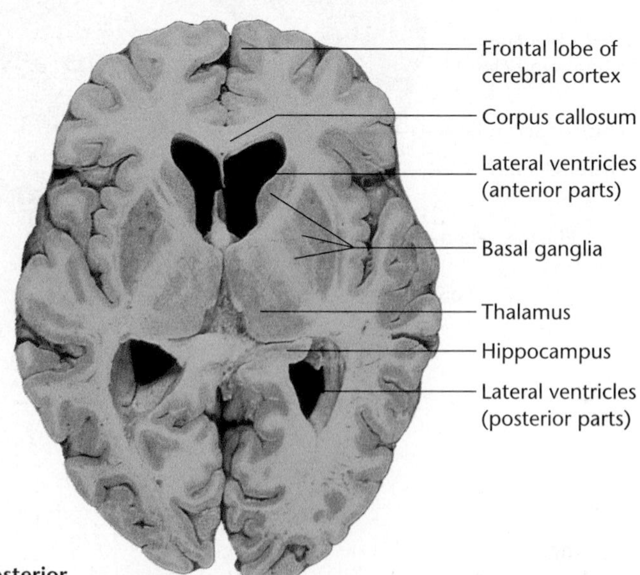

Figure 4.11 Dorsal view of the brain surface and a horizontal section through the brain

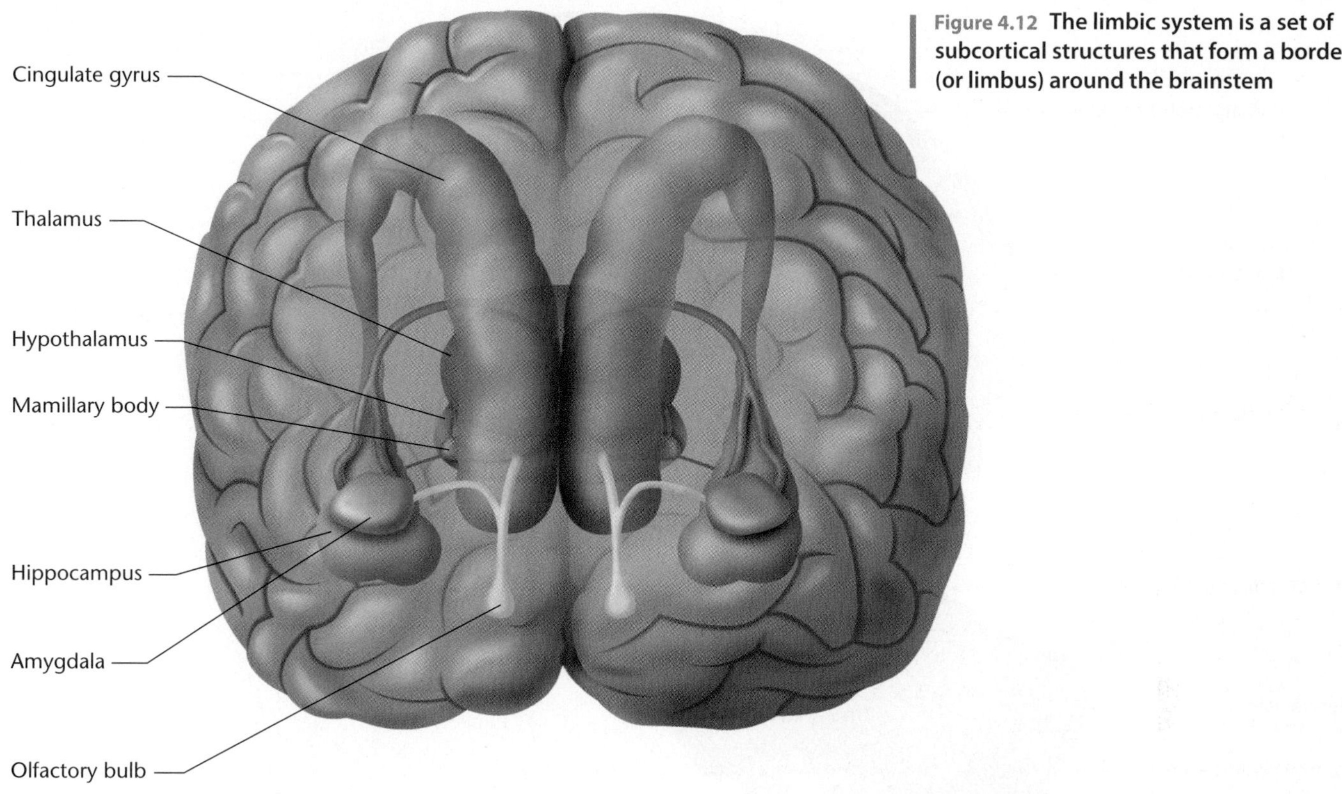

Figure 4.12 The limbic system is a set of subcortical structures that form a border (or limbus) around the brainstem

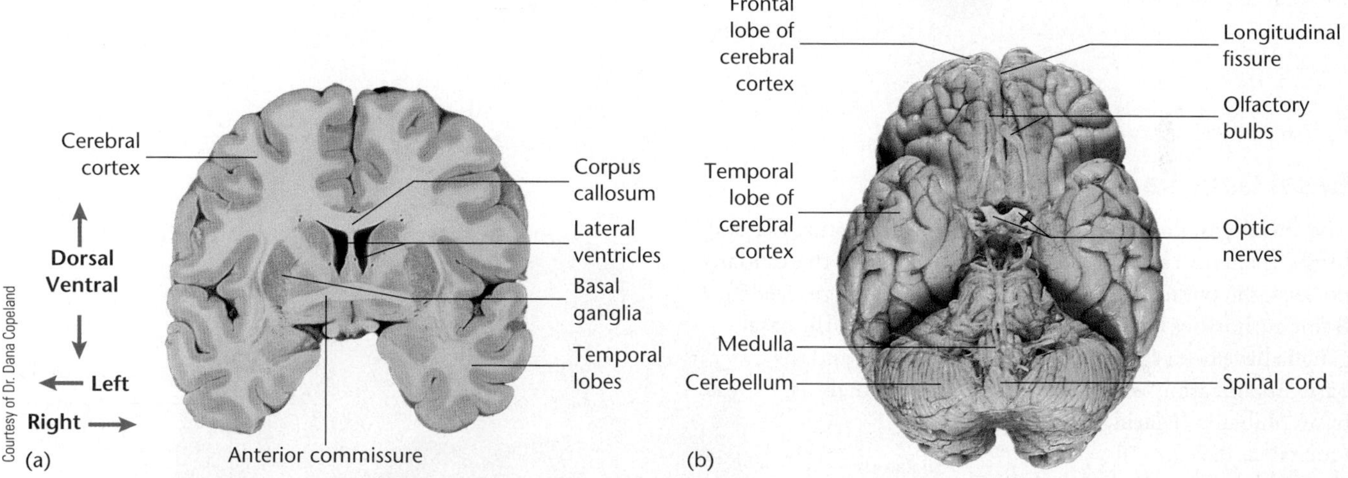

Figure 4.13 Two views of the human brain
(a) A coronal section. Note how the corpus callosum and anterior commissure provide communication between the left and right hemispheres. **(b)** The ventral surface. The optic nerves (cut here) extend from the eyes to the brain.

the hypothalamus conveys messages to the pituitary gland, altering its release of hormones. Damage to any hypothalamic nucleus leads to abnormalities in motivated behaviors, such as feeding, drinking, temperature regulation, sexual behavior, fighting, or activity level. Because of these important behavioral effects, the small hypothalamus attracts much research attention.

Pituitary Gland

The **pituitary gland** is an endocrine (hormone-producing) gland attached to the base of the hypothalamus by a stalk that contains neurons, blood vessels, and connective tissue (see Figure 4.10). In response to messages from the hypothalamus, the pituitary synthesizes and releases hormones into the bloodstream, which carries them to other organs.

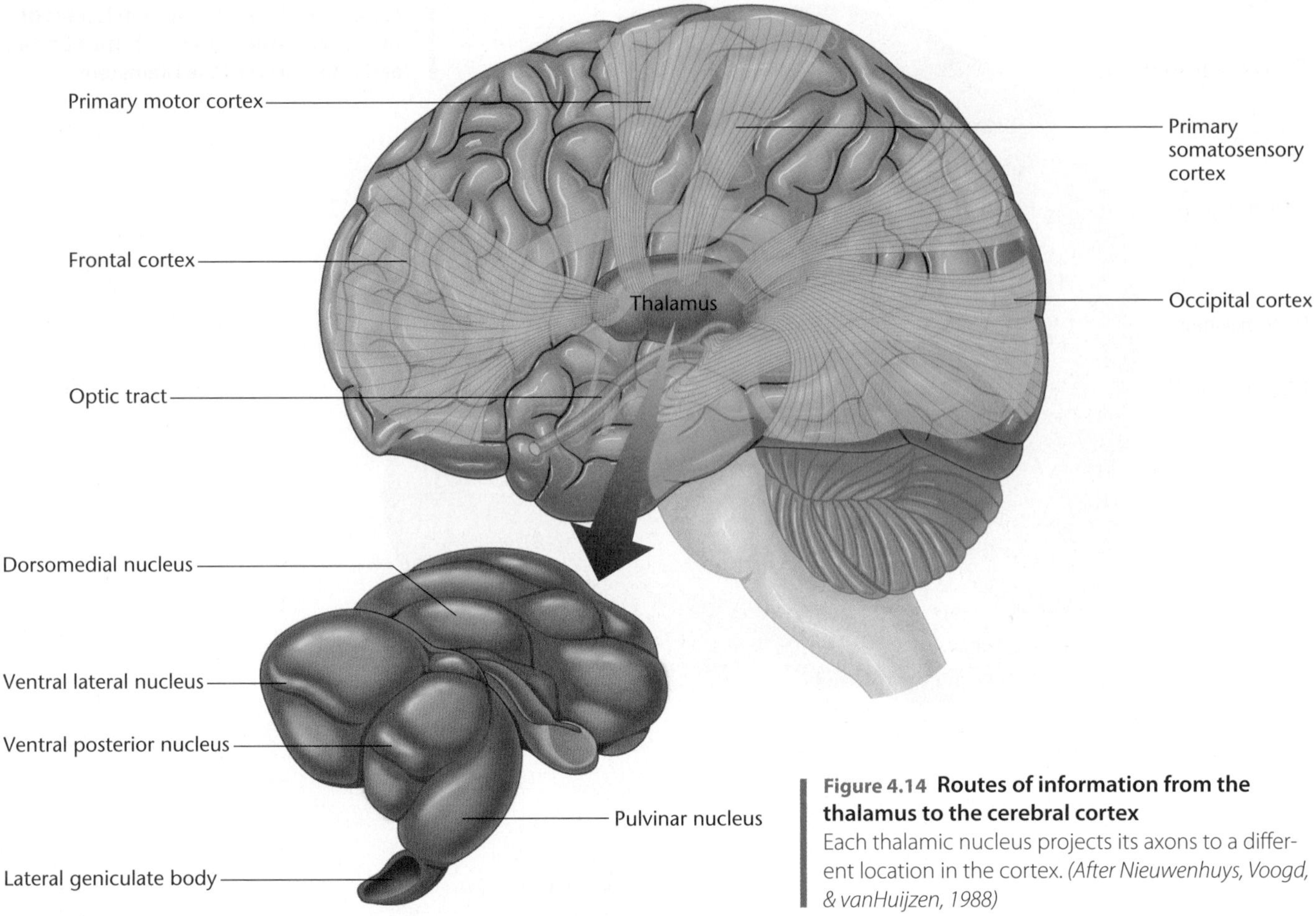

Primary motor cortex
Primary somatosensory cortex
Frontal cortex
Thalamus
Occipital cortex
Optic tract
Dorsomedial nucleus
Ventral lateral nucleus
Ventral posterior nucleus
Pulvinar nucleus
Lateral geniculate body

Figure 4.14 Routes of information from the thalamus to the cerebral cortex
Each thalamic nucleus projects its axons to a different location in the cortex. *(After Nieuwenhuys, Voogd, & vanHuijzen, 1988)*

Basal Ganglia

The **basal ganglia,** a group of subcortical structures lateral to the thalamus, include three major structures: the caudate nucleus, the putamen, and the globus pallidus (Figure 4.15). Some authorities include other structures as well. The basal ganglia have been conserved through evolution, and the basic organization is about the same in mammals as in amphibians (Marin, Smeets, & González, 1998).

The basal ganglia have subdivisions that exchange information with different parts of the cerebral cortex. The connections are most abundant with the frontal areas of the cortex, which are responsible for planning sequences of behavior and for certain aspects of memory and emotional expression (Graybiel, Aosaki, Flaherty, & Kimura, 1994). In conditions such as Parkinson's disease and Huntington's disease, in which the basal ganglia deteriorate, the most prominent symptom is impaired movement, but people also show depression and deficits of memory, reasoning, and attention.

Caudate nucleus
Thalamus
Globus pallidus (medial)
Putamen (lateral)
Amygdala

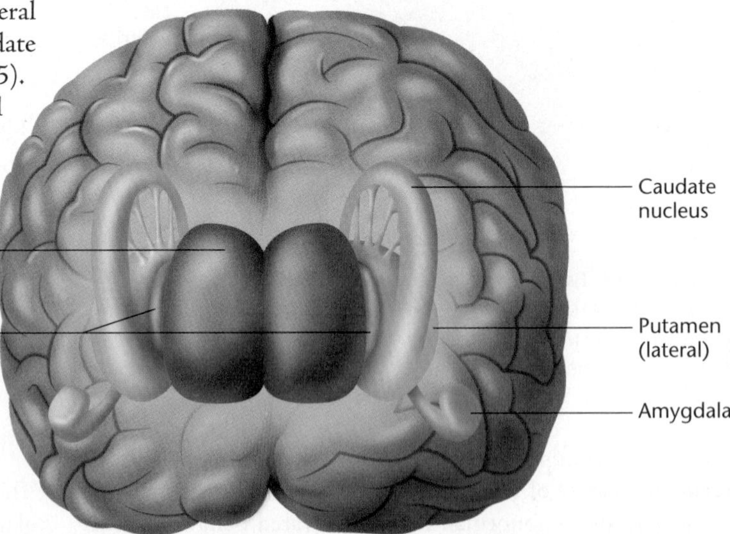

Figure 4.15 The basal ganglia
The thalamus is in the center, the basal ganglia are lateral to it, and the cerebral cortex is on the outside. *(After Nieuwenhuys, Voogd, & vanHuijzen, 1988)*

Basal Forebrain

Several structures lie on the ventral surface of the forebrain, including the **nucleus basalis,** which receives input from the hypothalamus and basal ganglia and sends axons that release acetylcholine to widespread areas in the cerebral cortex (Figure 4.16). The nucleus basalis is a key part of the brain's system for arousal, wakefulness, and attention, as we consider in Chapter 9. Patients with Parkinson's disease and Alzheimer's disease have impairments of attention and intellect because of inactivity or deterioration of their nucleus basalis.

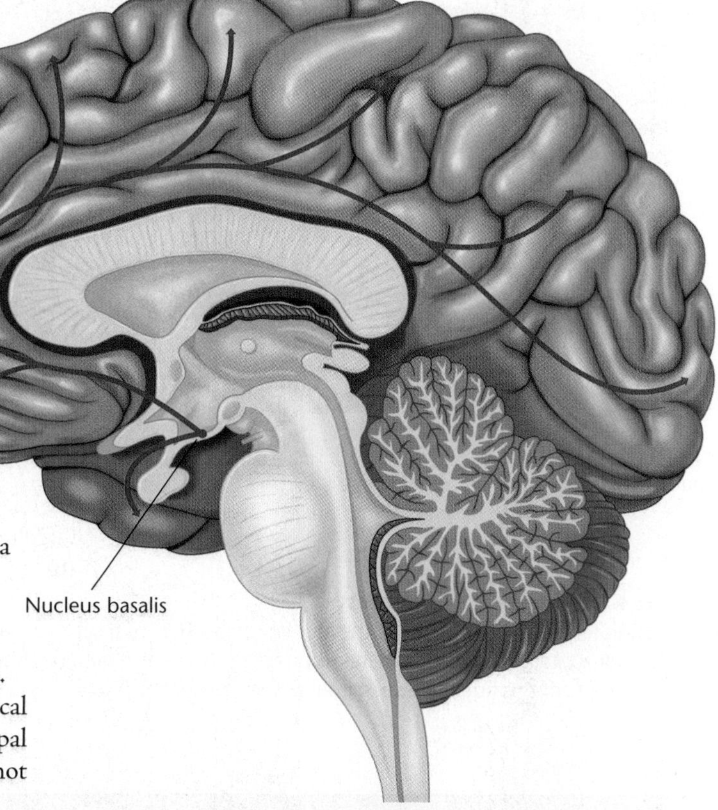

Figure 4.16 The basal forebrain
The nucleus basalis and other structures in this area send axons throughout the cortex, increasing its arousal and wakefulness through release of the neurotransmitter acetylcholine. *(After Woolf, 1991)*

Hippocampus

The **hippocampus** (from a Latin word meaning "seahorse," a shape suggested by the hippocampus) is a large structure between the thalamus and the cerebral cortex, mostly toward the posterior of the forebrain, as shown in Figure 4.12. We consider the hippocampus in more detail in Chapter 12. The gist of that discussion is that the hippocampus is critical for storing certain kinds of memories. People with hippocampal damage have trouble storing new memories, but they do not lose the memories they had before the damage occurred.

STOP & CHECK

7. Of the following, which are in the hindbrain, which in the midbrain, and which in the forebrain: basal ganglia, cerebellum, hippocampus, hypothalamus, medulla, pituitary gland, pons, substantia nigra, superior and inferior colliculi, tectum, tegmentum, thalamus?

8. Which area is the main source of input to the cerebral cortex?

ANSWERS

7. Hindbrain: cerebellum, medulla, and pons. Midbrain: substantia nigra, superior and inferior colliculi, tectum, and tegmentum. Forebrain: basal ganglia, hippocampus, hypothalamus, pituitary, and thalamus. **8.** thalamus

The Ventricles

The nervous system begins its development as a tube surrounding a fluid canal. The canal persists into adulthood as the **central canal,** a fluid-filled channel in the center of the spinal cord, and as the **ventricles,** four fluid-filled cavities within the brain. Each hemisphere contains one of the two large lateral ventricles (Figure 4.17). Toward their posterior, they connect to the third ventricle, positioned at the midline, separating the left thalamus from the right thalamus. The third ventricle connects to the fourth ventricle in the center of the medulla.

Cells called the *choroid plexus* inside the four ventricles produce **cerebrospinal fluid (CSF)**, a clear fluid similar to blood plasma. CSF fills the ventricles, flowing from the lateral ventricles to the third and fourth ventricles. From the fourth ventricle, some of it flows into the central canal of the spinal cord, but more goes into the narrow spaces between the brain and the thin **meninges,** membranes that surround the brain and spinal cord. In one of those narrow spaces, the subarachnoid space, the blood gradually reabsorbs the CSF. Although the brain has no pain receptors, the meninges do, and meningitis—inflammation of the meninges—is very painful. A swelling of blood vessels in the meninges is also responsible for the pain of a migraine headache (Hargreaves, 2007).

Cerebrospinal fluid cushions the brain against mechanical shock when the head moves. It also provides buoyancy. Just as a person weighs less in water than on land, cerebrospinal fluid helps support the weight of the brain. It also provides a reservoir of hormones and nutrition for the brain and spinal cord.

Sometimes, the flow of CSF is obstructed, and it accumulates within the ventricles or in the subarachnoid space, increasing pressure on the brain. When this occurs in infants, the skull bones may spread, causing an overgrown head. This condition, known as *hydrocephalus* (HI-dro-SEFF-ah-luss), is usually associated with mental retardation.

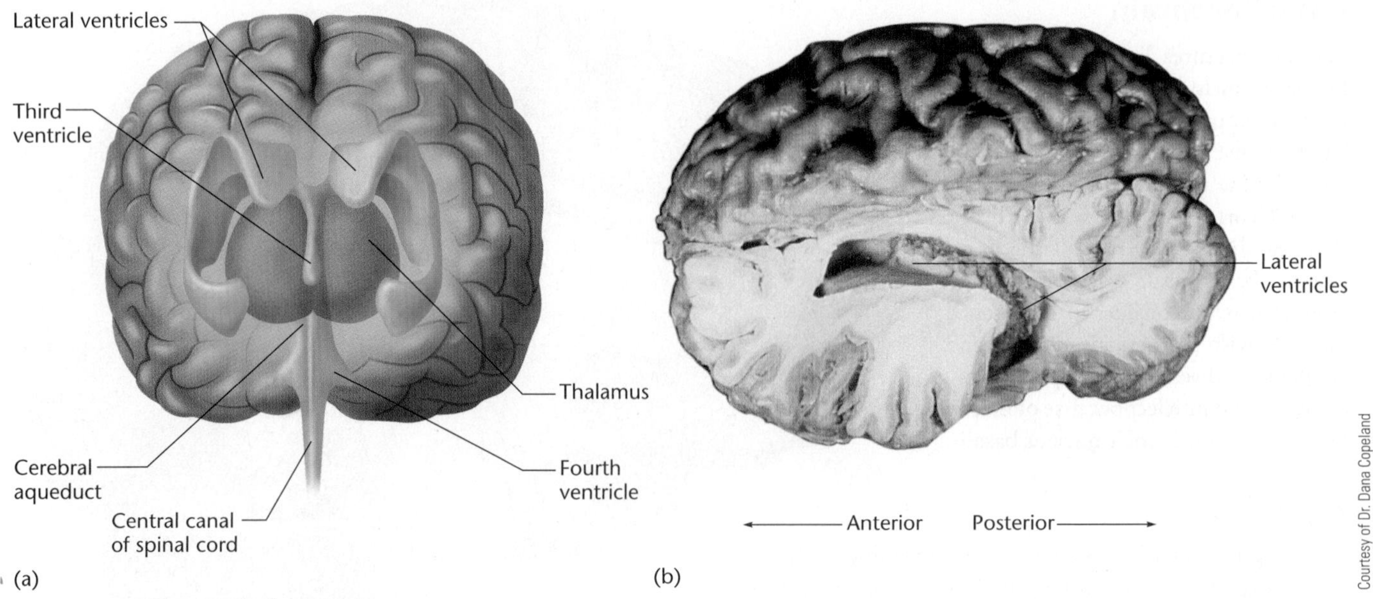

Figure 4.17 The cerebral ventricles
(a) Diagram showing positions of the four ventricles. **(b)** Photo of a human brain, viewed from above, with a horizontal cut through one hemisphere to show the position of the lateral ventricles. Note that the two parts of this figure are seen from different angles.

MODULE 4.1 IN CLOSING

Learning Neuroanatomy

The brain is a complex structure. This module has introduced a great many terms and facts; do not be discouraged if you have trouble remembering them. You didn't learn world geography all at once either. It will help to return to this module to review anatomy as you encounter structures again in later chapters. Gradually, the material will become more familiar.

It helps to see the brain from different angles and perspectives. Check this fantastic Website, The Whole Brain Atlas, which includes detailed photos of both normal and abnormal human brains: http://www.med.harvard.edu/AANLIB/home.html.

SUMMARY

1. The main divisions of the vertebrate nervous system are the central nervous system and the peripheral nervous system. **84**
2. Each segment of the spinal cord has a sensory nerve on each side and a motor nerve on each side. Spinal pathways convey information to the brain. **86**
3. The sympathetic nervous system (one of the two divisions of the autonomic nervous system) activates the body's internal organs for vigorous activities. The parasympathetic system (the other division) promotes digestion and other nonemergency processes. **87**
4. The central nervous system consists of the spinal cord, the hindbrain, the midbrain, and the forebrain. **89**
5. The hindbrain consists of the medulla, pons, and cerebellum. The medulla and pons control breathing, heart rate, and other vital functions through the cranial nerves. The cerebellum contributes to movement and timing short intervals. **89**
6. The cerebral cortex receives its sensory information (except for olfaction) from the thalamus. **92**
7. The subcortical areas of the forebrain include the thalamus, hypothalamus, pituitary gland, basal ganglia, and hippocampus. **92**

KEY TERMS

Terms are defined in the module on the page number indicated. They're also presented in alphabetical order with definitions in the book's Subject Index/Glossary. Interactive flashcards, audio reviews, and crossword puzzles are among the online resources available to help you learn these terms and the concepts they represent. Also, study the terms in Tables 4.1 and 4.2 (pages 85–86).

autonomic nervous system **85**
basal ganglia **94**
Bell-Magendie law **86**
brainstem **89**
central canal **95**
central nervous system (CNS) **84**
cerebellum **91**
cerebrospinal fluid (CSF) **95**
cranial nerves **89**
dorsal **85**
dorsal root ganglia **86**
forebrain **92**
gray matter **86**
hindbrain **89**
hippocampus **95**
hypothalamus **92**
inferior colliculus **91**
limbic system **92**
medulla **89**
meninges **95**
midbrain **91**
neuroanatomy **83**
nucleus basalis **95**
parasympathetic nervous system **87**
peripheral nervous system (PNS) **84**
pituitary gland **93**
pons **90**
raphe system **91**
reticular formation **91**
somatic nervous system **84**
spinal cord **86**
substantia nigra **92**
superior colliculus **91**
sympathetic nervous system **87**
tectum **91**
tegmentum **91**
thalamus **92**
ventral **85**
ventricles **95**
white matter **86**

THOUGHT QUESTION

The drug phenylephrine is sometimes prescribed for people suffering from a sudden loss of blood pressure or other medical disorders. It acts by stimulating norepinephrine synapses, including those that constrict blood vessels. One common side effect of this drug is goose bumps. Explain why. What other side effects might be likely?

MODULE 4.2

The Cerebral Cortex

The most prominent part of the mammalian brain is the **cerebral cortex**, consisting of the cellular layers on the outer surface of the cerebral hemispheres. The cells of the cerebral cortex are gray matter, and their axons extending inward are white matter (see Figure 4.13). Neurons in each hemisphere communicate with neurons in the corresponding part of the other hemisphere through two bundles of axons, the **corpus callosum** (see Figures 4.10, 4.11, and 4.13) and the smaller **anterior commissure** (see Figure 4.13). Several other commissures (pathways across the midline) link subcortical structures.

If we compare mammalian species, we see differences in the size of the cerebral cortex and the degree of folding (Figure 4.18). The cerebral cortex constitutes a higher percentage of the brain in **primates**—monkeys, apes, and humans—than in other species of comparable size. Figure 4.19 shows the size of the cerebral cortex in comparison to the rest of the brain for insectivores and two suborders of primates (Barton & Harvey, 2000). Figure 4.20 compares species in another way (D. A. Clark, Mitra, & Wang, 2001). The investigators arranged the insectivores and primates from left to right in terms of what percentage of their brain was devoted to the forebrain (telencephalon), which includes the cerebral cortex. They also inserted tree shrews, a species often considered intermediate. Note that as the proportion devoted to the forebrain increases, the relative sizes of the midbrain and medulla decrease. Curiously, the cerebellum occupies a remarkably constant percentage—approximately 13% of any mammalian brain (D. A. Clark et al., 2001). That is, the cerebellum maintains an almost constant proportion to the whole brain. (Why? No one knows.)

Organization of the Cerebral Cortex

The microscopic structure of the cells of the cerebral cortex varies substantially from one cortical area to another. The differences in appearance relate to differences in function. Much research has been directed toward understanding the relationship between structure and function.

In humans and most other mammals, the cerebral cortex contains up to six distinct **laminae,** layers of cell bodies that are parallel to the surface of the cortex and separated from each other by layers of fibers (Figure 4.21). The laminae vary in thickness and prominence from one part of the cortex to another, and a given lamina may be absent from certain areas. Lamina V, which sends long axons to the spinal cord and other distant areas, is thickest in the motor cortex, which has the greatest control of the muscles. Lamina IV, which receives axons from the various sensory nuclei of the thalamus, is prominent in all the primary sensory areas

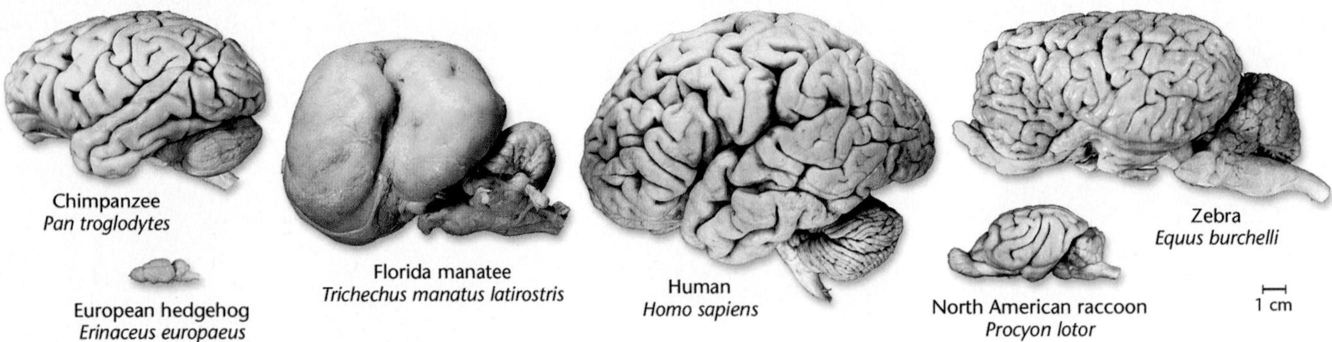

Figure 4.18 Comparison of mammalian brains
The human brain is the largest of those shown, although whales, dolphins, and elephants have still larger brains. All mammals have the same brain subareas in the same locations. *(From the University of Wisconsin—Madison Comparative Mammalian Brain Collection, Wally Welker, Curator. Project supported by the Natural Science Foundation.)*

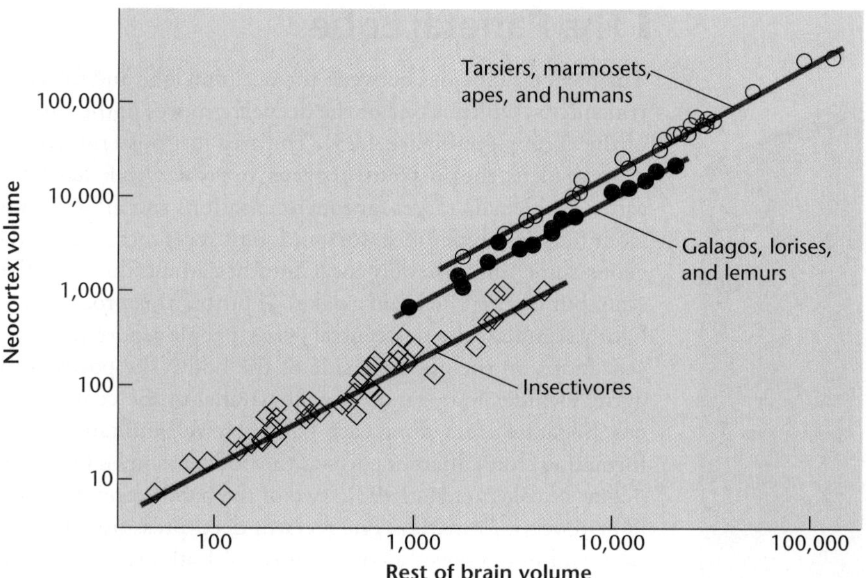

Figure 4.19 Relationship between volume of the cortex and volume of the rest of the brain
For each of the three groups, cortical volume increases quite predictably as a function of the volume of the rest of the brain. However, the lines for the two primate groups are displaced upward. *(Fig. 1, p. 1055 in R. A. Barton & R. H. Harvey, "Mosaic evolution of brain structure in mammals."* Nature, *405, p. 1055–1058. Reprinted with permission from Nature. Copyright © 2000 Macmillan Magazine Limited.)*

(visual, auditory, and somatosensory) but absent from the motor cortex.

The cells of the cortex are also organized into **columns** of cells perpendicular to the laminae. Figure 4.22 illustrates the idea of columns, although in nature they are not so straight.

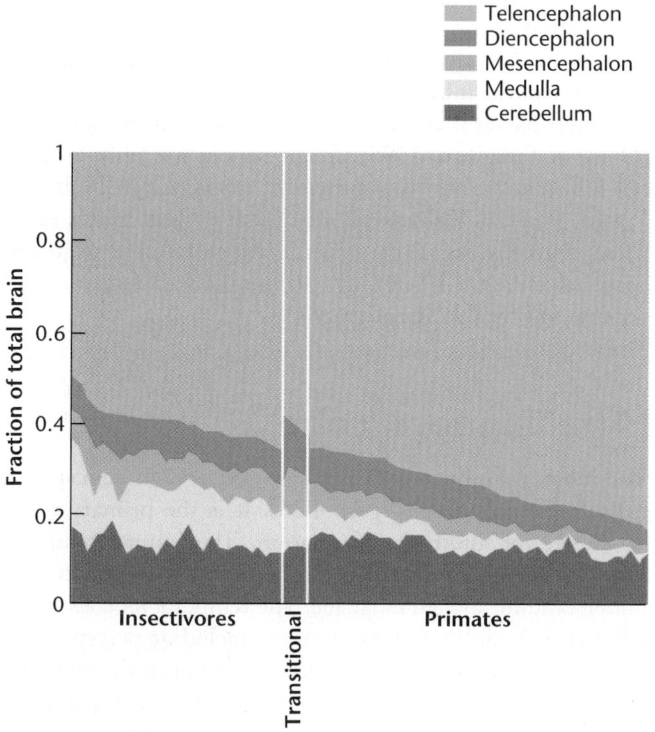

Telencephalon
Diencephalon
Mesencephalon
Medulla
Cerebellum

Fraction of total brain
1
0.8
0.6
0.4
0.2
0
Insectivores
Transitional
Primates

Figure 4.20 Relative sizes of five brain components in insectivores and primates
The forebrain composes a larger percentage of primate than insectivore brains. Note also the near constant fraction devoted to the cerebellum. *(Fig. 1, p. 189 in D. A. Clark, P. P. Mitra, & S. S-H. Wong, "Scalable architecture in mammalian brains."* Nature, 411, *pp. 189–193. Reprinted with permission from Nature. Copyright © 2001 Macmillan Magazine Limited.)*

The cells within a given column have similar properties to one another. For example, if one cell in a column responds to touch on the palm of the left hand, then the other cells in that column do, too. If one cell responds to a horizontal pattern of light at a particular location, then other cells in the column respond to the same pattern in nearby locations.

We now turn to some specific parts of the cortex. Researchers make ever finer distinctions among areas of the cerebral cortex based on the structure and function of cells. For convenience, we group these areas into four *lobes* named for the skull bones that lie over them: occipital, parietal, temporal, and frontal.

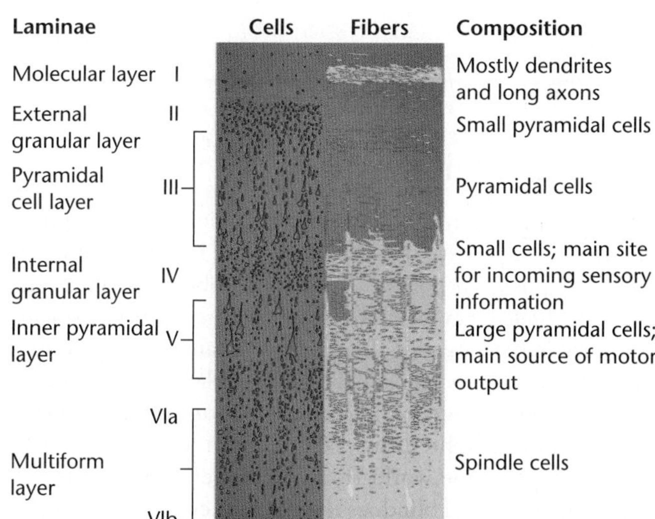

Figure 4.21 The six laminae of the human cerebral cortex
(From S. W. Ranson & S. L. Clark, The Anatomy of the Nervous System, *1959. Copyright © 1959 W. B. Saunders Co. Reprinted by permission.*

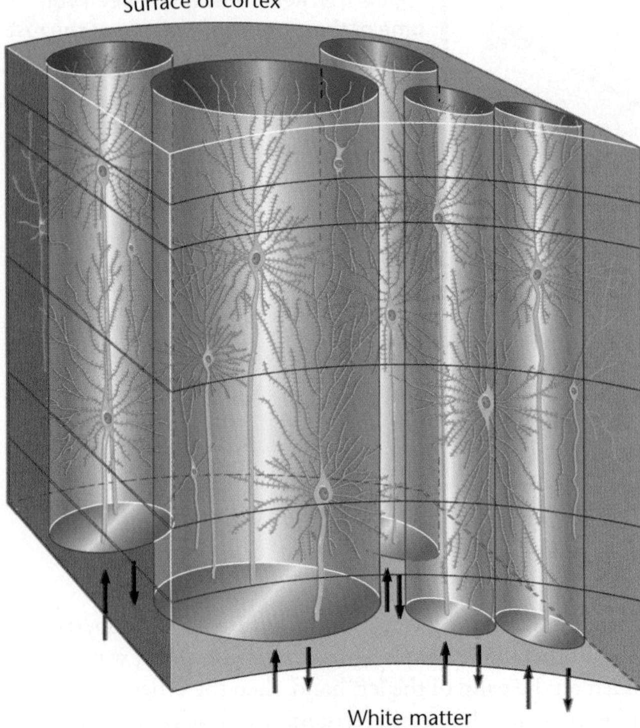

Figure 4.22 Columns in the cerebral cortex
Each column extends through several laminae. Neurons within a given column have similar properties. For example, in the somatosensory cortex, all the neurons within a given column respond to stimulation of the same area of skin.

STOP & CHECK

9. If several neurons of the visual cortex all respond best when the retina is exposed to horizontal lines of light, then those neurons are probably in the same _____.

ANSWER

9. column

The Occipital Lobe

The **occipital lobe,** located at the posterior (caudal) end of the cortex (Figure 4.23), is the main target for visual information. The posterior pole of the occipital lobe is known as the *primary visual cortex,* or *striate cortex,* because of its striped appearance in cross-section. Destruction of any part of the striate cortex causes *cortical blindness* in the related part of the visual field. For example, extensive damage to the striate cortex of the right hemisphere causes blindness in the left visual field (the left side of the world from the viewer's perspective). A person with cortical blindness has normal eyes, normal pupillary reflexes, and some eye movements but no pattern perception or visual imagery. People who suffer eye damage become blind, but if they have an intact occipital cortex and previous visual experience, they can still imagine visual scenes and can still have visual dreams (Sabo & Kirtley, 1982).

The Parietal Lobe

The **parietal lobe** lies between the occipital lobe and the **central sulcus,** which is one of the deepest grooves in the surface of the cortex (see Figure 4.23). The area just posterior to the central sulcus, the **postcentral gyrus,** or *primary somatosensory cortex,* is the main target for touch sensations and information from muscle-stretch receptors and joint receptors. Brain surgeons sometimes use only local anesthesia (anesthetizing the scalp but leaving the brain awake). If during this process they lightly stimulate the postcentral gyrus, people report "tingling" sensations on the opposite side of the body. The postcentral gyrus includes four bands of cells parallel to the central sulcus. Separate areas along each band receive simultaneous information from different parts of the body, as shown in Figure 4.24a (Nicolelis et al., 1998). Two of the bands receive mostly light-touch information, one receives deep-pressure information, and one receives a combination of both (Kaas, Nelson, Sur, Lin, & Merzenich, 1979). In effect, the postcentral gyrus represents the body four times.

Information about touch and body location is important not only for its own sake but also for interpreting visual and auditory information. For example, if you see something in the upper left portion of the visual field, your brain needs to know which direction your eyes are turned, the position of your head, and the tilt of your body before it can determine the location of the object that you see and therefore your direction if you want to approach or avoid it. The parietal lobe monitors all the information about eye, head, and body positions and passes it on to brain areas that control movement (Gross & Graziano, 1995). It is essential not only for spatial information but also numerical information (Hubbard, Piazza, Pinel, & Dehaene, 2005). That overlap makes sense when you consider all the ways in which number relates to space—from initially learning to count with our fingers, to geometry, and to all kinds of graphs.

The Temporal Lobe

The **temporal lobe** is the lateral portion of each hemisphere, near the temples (see Figure 4.23). It is the primary cortical target for auditory information. The human temporal lobe—in most cases, the left temporal lobe—is essential for understanding spoken language. The temporal lobe also contributes to complex aspects of vision, including perception of movement and recognition of faces. A tumor in the temporal lobe may give rise to elaborate auditory or visual hallucinations, whereas a tumor in the occipital lobe ordinarily evokes only simple sensations, such as flashes of light. In fact, when psychiatric patients report hallucinations, brain scans detect extensive activity in the temporal lobes (Dierks et al., 1999).

The temporal lobes also play a part in emotional and motivational behaviors. Temporal lobe damage can lead to a set of behaviors known as the **Klüver-Bucy syndrome** (named for the investigators who first described it). Previously wild and

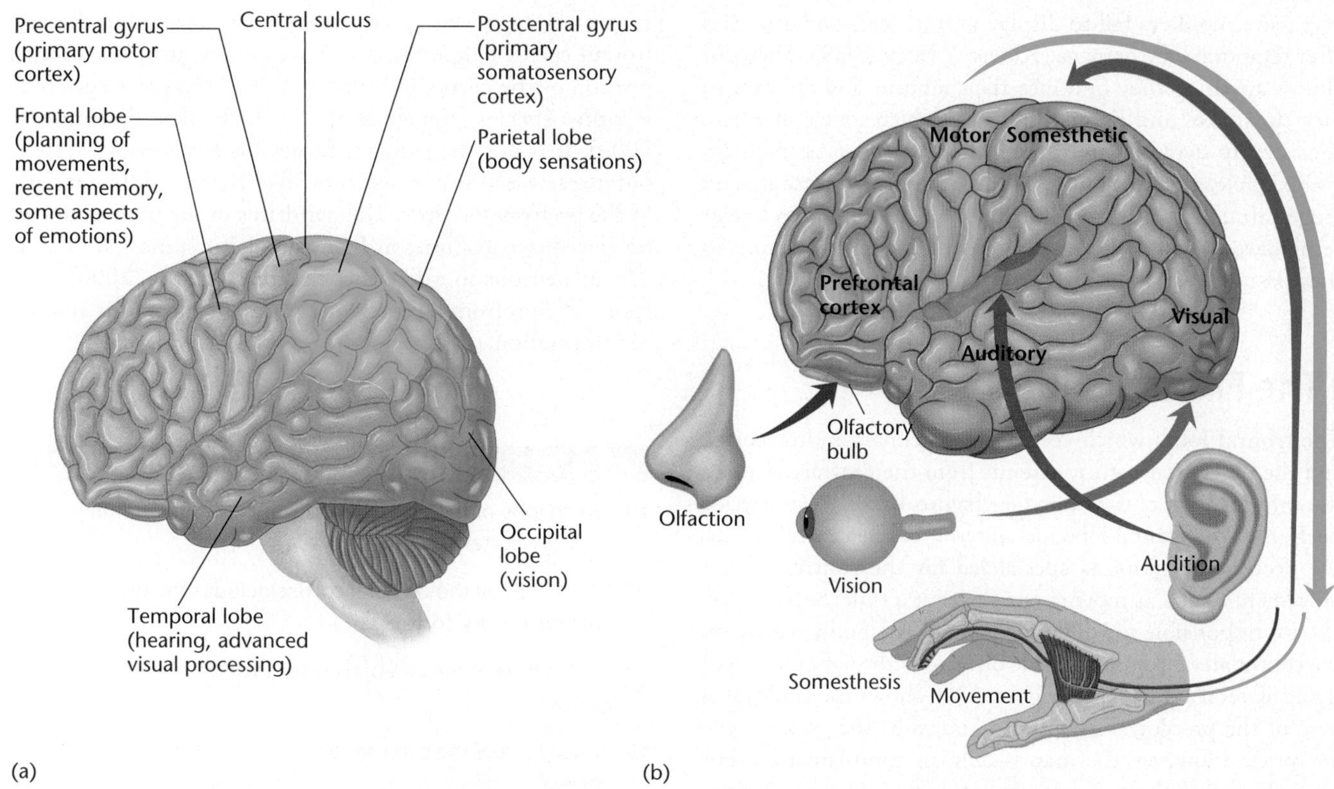

Figure 4.23 Areas of the human cerebral cortex
(a) The four lobes: occipital, parietal, temporal, and frontal. **(b)** The primary sensory cortex for vision, hearing, and body sensations; the primary motor cortex; and the olfactory bulb, a noncortical area responsible for the sense of smell. *(Part b: T. W. Deacon, 1990)*

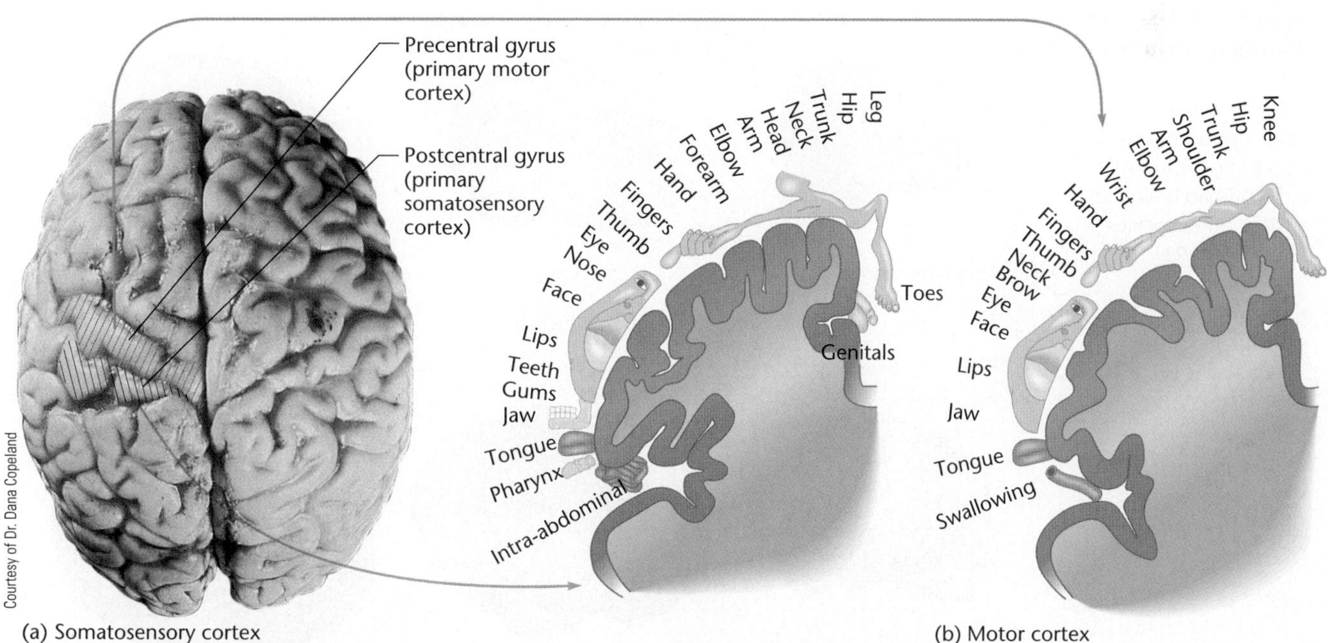

Figure 4.24 Approximate representation of sensory and motor information in the cortex
(a) Each location in the somatosensory cortex represents sensation from a different body part. **(b)** Each location in the motor cortex regulates movement of a different body part. *(After Penfield & Rasmussen, 1950)*

aggressive monkeys fail to display normal fears and anxieties after temporal lobe damage (Klüver & Bucy, 1939). They put almost anything they find into their mouths and attempt to pick up snakes and lighted matches (which intact monkeys consistently avoid). Interpreting this behavior is difficult. For example, a monkey might handle a snake because it is no longer afraid (an emotional change) or because it no longer recognizes what a snake is (a cognitive change). We return to these issues in Chapter 12.

The Frontal Lobe

The **frontal lobe,** which contains the primary motor cortex and the prefrontal cortex, extends from the central sulcus to the anterior limit of the brain (see Figure 4.23). The posterior portion of the frontal lobe just anterior to the central sulcus, the **precentral gyrus,** is specialized for the control of fine movements, such as moving one finger at a time. Separate areas are responsible for different parts of the body, mostly on the contralateral (opposite) side but also with slight control of the ipsilateral (same) side. Figure 4.24b shows the traditional map of the precentral gyrus, also known as the *primary motor cortex.* However, the map is only an approximation. For example, within the arm area, there is no one-to-one relationship between brain location and specific muscles (Graziano, Taylor, & Moore, 2002).

The most anterior portion of the frontal lobe is the **prefrontal cortex.** In general, the larger a species' cerebral cortex, the higher the percentage of it is devoted to the prefrontal cortex (Figure 4.25). For example, it forms a larger portion of the cortex in humans and all the great apes than in other species (Semendeferi, Lu, Schenker, & Damasio, 2002). It is not the primary target for any sensory system, but it receives information from all of them in different parts of the prefrontal cortex. The dendrites in the prefrontal cortex have up to 16 times as many dendritic spines (see Figure 2.7) as neurons in other cortical areas (Elston, 2000). As a result, the prefrontal cortex integrates an enormous amount of information.

STOP & CHECK

10. Which lobe of the cerebral cortex includes the primary auditory cortex?

11. Which lobe of the cerebral cortex includes the primary somatosensory cortex?

12. Which lobe of the cerebral cortex includes the primary visual cortex?

13. Which lobe of the cerebral cortex includes the primary motor cortex?

ANSWERS

10. temporal lobe **11.** parietal lobe **12.** occipital lobe **13.** frontal lobe

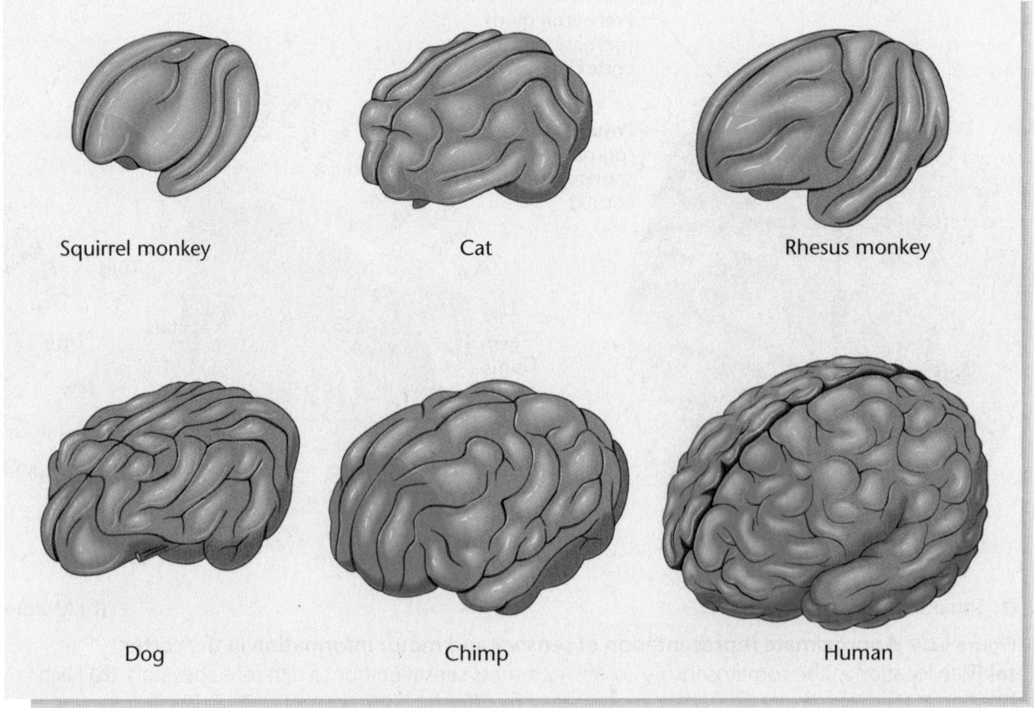

Figure 4.25 Species differences in prefrontal cortex
Note that the prefrontal cortex (blue area) constitutes a larger proportion of the human brain than of these other species. *(After Fuster, 1989)*

APPLICATIONS AND EXTENSIONS

The Rise and Fall of Prefrontal Lobotomies

You may have heard of the infamous procedure known as **prefrontal lobotomy**—surgical disconnection of the prefrontal cortex from the rest of the brain. The surgery consisted of damaging the prefrontal cortex or cutting its connections to the rest of the cortex. Lobotomy began with a report that damaging the prefrontal cortex of laboratory primates made them tamer without noticeably impairing their sensations or coordination. A few physicians reasoned (loosely) that the same operation might help people who suffered from severe, untreatable psychiatric disorders.

In the late 1940s and early 1950s, about 40,000 prefrontal lobotomies were performed in the United States (Shutts, 1982), many of them by Walter Freeman, a medical doctor untrained in surgery. His techniques were crude, even by the standards of the time, using such instruments as an electric drill and a metal pick. He performed many operations in his office or other nonhospital sites. (Freeman carried his equipment in his car, which he called his "lobotomobile.")

At first, Freeman and others limited the technique to people with severe schizophrenia, for which no effective treatment was available at the time. Lobotomy did calm some individuals, but the effects were often disappointing. Later, Freeman lobotomized people with less serious disorders, including some whom we would consider normal by today's standards. After drug therapies became available in the mid-1950s, lobotomies quickly dropped out of favor.

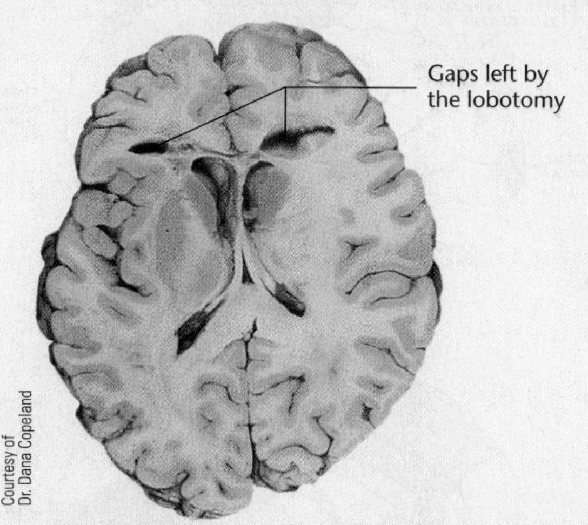

A horizontal section of the brain of a person who had a prefrontal lobotomy many years earlier. The two holes in the frontal cortex are the visible results of the operation.

Among the common consequences of prefrontal lobotomy were apathy, a loss of the ability to plan and take initiative, memory disorders, distractibility, and a loss of emotional expressions (Stuss & Benson, 1984). People with prefrontal damage lose their social inhibitions, ignoring the rules of polite, civilized conduct. They often act impulsively because they fail to calculate adequately the probable outcomes of their behaviors.

Modern View of the Prefrontal Cortex

Later researchers studying people and monkeys with brain damage found that the prefrontal cortex is important for *working memory,* the ability to remember recent stimuli and events, such as where you parked the car today or what you were talking about before being interrupted (Goldman-Rakic, 1988). The prefrontal cortex is especially important for the **delayed-response task,** in which a stimulus appears briefly, and the individual must respond to the remembered stimulus after a brief delay.

Neuroscientists have offered several other hypotheses about the function of the prefrontal cortex. One is that it is essential for behaviors that depend on the context (E. Miller, 2000). For example, if the phone rings, do you answer it? It depends: In your own home, yes, but at someone else's home, probably not. If you saw a good friend from a distance, would you shout out a greeting? Again, it depends: Yes in a public park, but not in a library. People with prefrontal cortex damage often fail to adjust to their context, so they behave inappropriately or impulsively.

STOP & CHECK

14. What are the functions of the prefrontal cortex?

ANSWER

14. The prefrontal cortex is especially important for working memory (memory for what is currently happening) and for planning actions based on the context.

How Do the Parts Work Together?

We have just considered a variety of brain areas, each with its own function. How do they combine to produce integrated behavior and the experience of a single self? In particular, consider the sensory areas of the cerebral cortex. The visual area, auditory area, and somatosensory area are in different locations, hardly even connected with one another. When you hold your radio or iPod, how does your brain know that the object you see is also what you feel and what you hear?

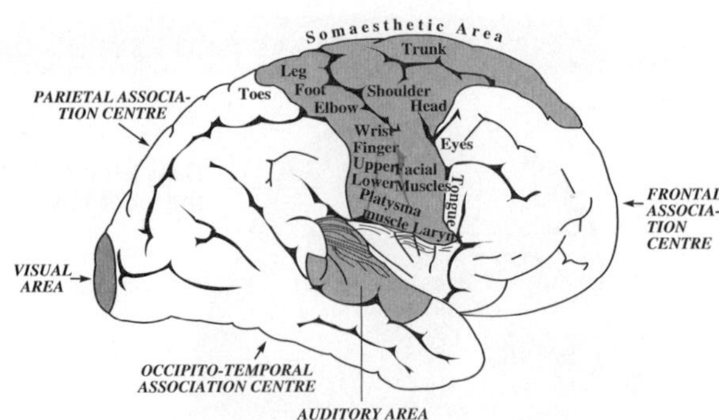

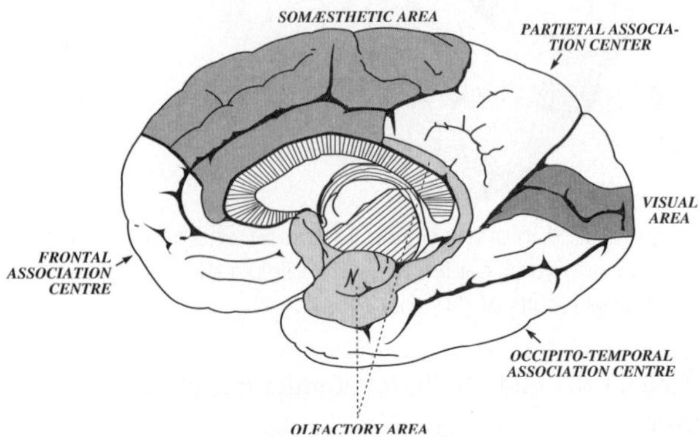

Figure 4.26 An old, somewhat misleading view of the cortex
Note the designation "association centre" in this illustration of the cortex from an old introductory psychology textbook (Hunter, 1923). Today's researchers are more likely to regard those areas as "additional sensory areas."

The question of how various brain areas produce a perception of a single object is known as the **binding problem,** or *large-scale integration* problem (Varela, Lachaux, Rodriguez, & Martinerie, 2001). In an earlier era, researchers thought that various kinds of sensory information converged onto what they called the association areas of the cortex (Figure 4.26). The guess was that those areas "associate" vision with hearing, hearing with touch, or current sensations with memories of previous experiences. However, later research found that the association areas perform advanced processing on a particular sensory system, such as vision or hearing, and few cells combine one sense with another. Discarding the idea that various senses converge in the association areas called attention to the binding problem. If they don't converge, then how do we know that something we see is also what we hear or feel?

Although we cannot fully explain binding, we know what is necessary for it to occur: Binding occurs if you perceive two sensations as happening at the same time and in the same place. For example, a skilled ventriloquist makes the dummy's mouth move at the same time as his or her own speech, in nearly the same place, so you perceive the sound as coming from the dummy. If you watch a foreign-language film that was poorly dubbed so that the lips do not move at the same time as the speech, you perceive that the words did *not* come from those lips.

Applying these principles, researchers arranged a camera to video someone's back and send the pictures to a three-dimensional display mounted to the person's head. The person saw his or her own back, apparently 2 meters in front. Then someone stroked the participant's back, and the person simultaneously felt the touch and saw the action, apparently 2 meters in front. After a while, the person had a true "out of body" experience, feeling that the body was actually 2 meters in front of its real position. When asked, "please return to your seat," the person walked to a spot displaced from the actual seat, as if he or she had actually been moved forward (Lenggenhager, Tadi, Metzinger, & Blanke, 2007).

Here is a demonstration for you to try: If you see a light flash once while you hear two beeps, you will sometimes think you saw the light flash twice. If the tone is soft, it is also possible to experience the opposite: The tone beeps twice during one flash of light, and you think you heard only one beep. If you saw three flashes of light, you might think you heard three beeps (Andersen, Tiippana, & Sams, 2004). The near simultaneity of lights and sounds causes you to bind them and perceive an illusion. You can experience this phenomenon with the Online Try It Yourself activity "Illustration of Binding."

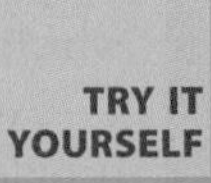

Here is another great demonstration to try (I. H. Robertson, 2005). Position yourself parallel to a large mirror, as in Figure 4.27, so that you see your right hand and its reflection in the mirror. Keep your left hand out of sight. Now repeatedly clench and unclench both hands in unison. You will feel your left hand clenching and unclenching at the same time you see the hand in the mirror doing the same thing. After 2 or 3 minutes, you may start to feel that the hand in the

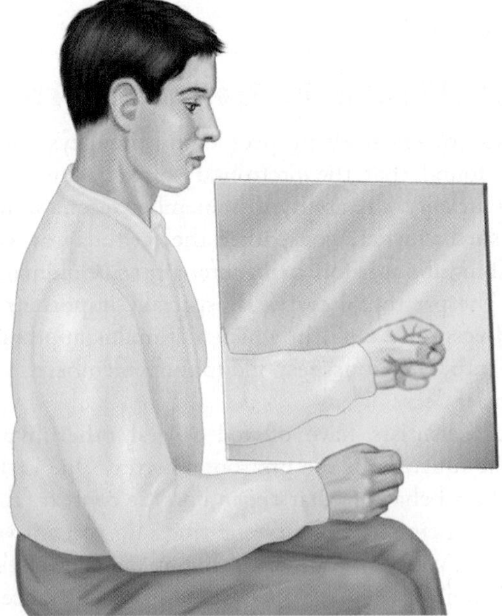

Figure 4.27 An illusion to demonstrate binding
Clench and unclench both hands while looking at your right hand and its reflection in the mirror. Keep your left hand out of sight. After a couple of minutes, you may start to experience the hand in the mirror as being your own left hand.

mirror is your own left hand. Some people even feel that they have three hands—the right hand, the real left hand, and the apparent left hand in the mirror.

So binding depends on perceiving two or more aspects of a stimulus as coming from approximately the same location. People with damage to the parietal cortex have trouble locating objects in space—that is, they are not sure where anything is—and they often fail to bind objects. For example, they have great trouble finding one red **X** among a group of green Xs and red **O**s (L. C. Robertson, 2003). Also, if they see a display such as

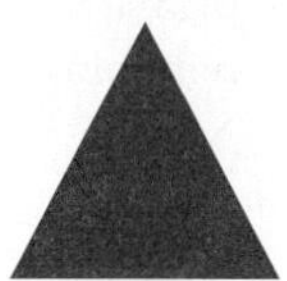

they could report seeing a green triangle and a red square instead of a red triangle and a green square (L. Robertson, Treisman, Friedman-Hill, & Grabowecky, 1997; Treisman, 1999; R. Ward, Danziger, Owen, & Rafal, 2002; Wheeler & Treisman, 2002).

Even people with intact brains sometimes make mistakes of this kind if the displays are flashed very briefly or while they are distracted (Holcombe & Cavanagh, 2001; Lehky, 2000). You can experience this failure of binding with the Online Try It Yourself activity "Failure of Binding."

STOP & CHECK

15. What is meant by the binding problem, and what is one hypothesis to explain it?

ANSWER

15. The binding problem is the question of how the brain combines activity in different brain areas to produce unified perception and coordinated behavior. One hypothesis is that binding requires identifying the location of an object. When the sight and sound appear to come from the same location, we bind them as a single experience.

MODULE 4.2 IN CLOSING

Functions of the Cerebral Cortex

The human cerebral cortex is so large that we easily slip into thinking of it as "the" brain. In fact, only mammals have a true cerebral cortex, and many animals produce impressive and complex behaviors without a cerebral cortex.

What, then, is the function of the cerebral cortex? The primary function seems to be one of elaborating sensory material. Even fish, which have no cerebral cortex, can see, hear, and so forth, but they do not recognize and remember all the complex aspects of sensory stimuli that mammals do. In a television advertisement, one company says that it doesn't make any products, but it makes lots of products better. The same could be said for the cerebral cortex.

SUMMARY

1. Although brain size varies among mammalian species, the overall organization is similar. **98**
2. The cerebral cortex has six laminae (layers) of neurons. A given lamina may be absent from certain parts of the cortex. The cortex is organized into columns of cells arranged perpendicular to the laminae. **98**
3. The occipital lobe of the cortex is primarily responsible for vision. Damage to part of the occipital lobe leads to blindness in part of the visual field. **99**
4. The parietal lobe processes body sensations. The postcentral gyrus contains four separate representations of the body. **99**
5. The temporal lobe contributes to hearing, complex aspects of vision, and processing of emotional information. **99**
6. The frontal lobe includes the precentral gyrus, which controls fine movements. It also includes the prefrontal cortex, which contributes to memories of current and recent stimuli, planning of movements, and regulation of emotional expressions. **102**
7. The prefrontal cortex is important for working memory and for planning actions that depend on the context. **103**
8. The binding problem is the question of how we connect activities in different brain areas, such as sights and sounds. The various brain areas do not all send their information to a single central processor. **104**
9. Binding requires locating an object in space. **104**

Continued

KEY TERMS

Terms are defined in the module on the page number indicated. They're also presented in alphabetical order with definitions in the book's Subject Index/Glossary. Interactive flashcards, audio reviews, and crossword puzzles are among the online resources available to help you learn these terms and the concepts they represent.

anterior commissure **98**
binding problem **104**
central sulcus **100**
cerebral cortex **98**
columns **99**
corpus callosum **98**
delayed-response task **103**
frontal lobe **102**
Klüver-Bucy syndrome **100**
laminae **98**
occipital lobe **100**
parietal lobe **100**
postcentral gyrus **100**
precentral gyrus **102**
prefrontal cortex **102**
prefrontal lobotomy **103**
primates **98**
temporal lobe **100**

THOUGHT QUESTION

When monkeys with Klüver-Bucy syndrome pick up lighted matches and snakes, we do not know whether they are displaying an emotional deficit or an inability to identify the object. What kind of research method might help answer this question?

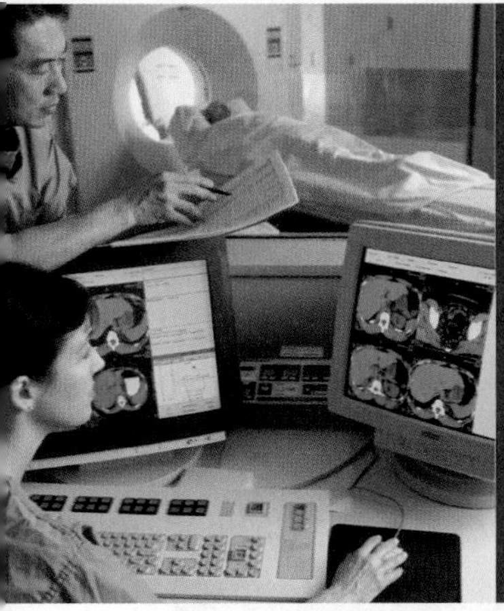

MODULE 4.3

Research Methods

Imagine yourself trying to understand a large, complex machine. You could begin by describing the appearance and location of the machine's parts. That task could be formidable, but it is easy compared to discovering what each part *does.*

Similarly, describing the structure of the brain is difficult enough, but the real challenge is to discover how it works. Throughout the text, we shall consider many research methods as they become relevant. However, most methods fall into a few categories. In this module, we consider those categories and the logic behind them. We also examine some common research techniques that will reappear in one chapter after another.

The main categories of methods for studying brain function are as follows:

1. *Correlate brain anatomy with behavior.* Do people with some unusual behavior also have unusual brains? If so, in what way?
2. *Record brain activity during behavior.* For example, we might record changes in brain activity during fighting, sleeping, finding food, or solving a problem.
3. *Examine the effects of brain damage.* After damage or temporary inactivation, what aspects of behavior are impaired?
4. *Examine the effects of stimulating some brain area.* Ideally, if damaging some area impairs a behavior, stimulating that area should enhance the behavior.

Correlating Brain Anatomy With Behavior

One of the first ways ever used for studying brain function sounds easy: Find someone with unusual behavior and then look for unusual features of the brain. In the 1800s, Franz Gall observed some people with excellent verbal memories who had protruding eyes. He inferred that verbal memory depended on brain areas behind the eyes that had pushed the eyes forward. Gall then examined the skulls of people with other talents or personalities. He assumed that bulges and depressions on their skull corresponded to the brain areas below them. His process of relating skull anatomy to behavior is known as **phrenology.** One of his followers made the phrenological map in Figure 4.28.

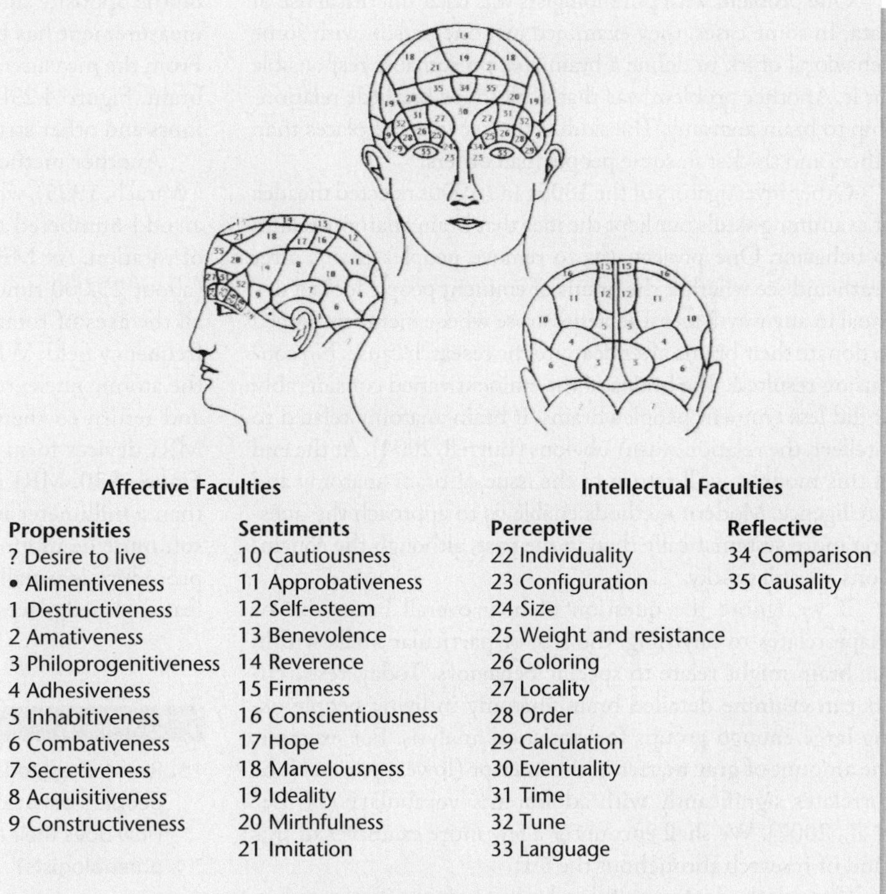

Figure 4.28 A phrenologist's map of the brain
Neuroscientists today also try to localize functions in the brain, but they use more careful methods and they study such functions as vision and hearing, not "secretiveness" and "marvelousness." *(From Spurzheim, 1908)*

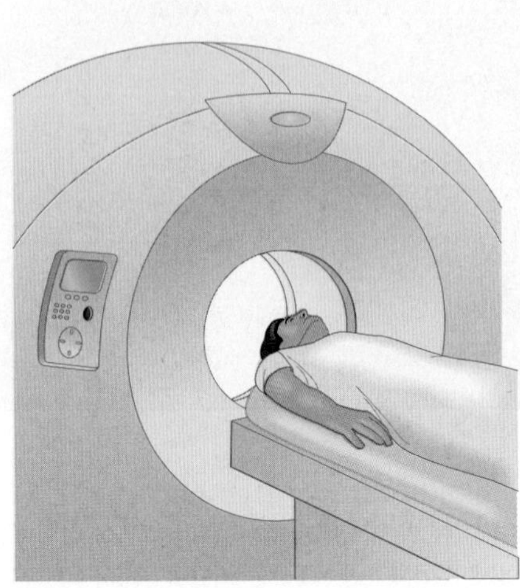

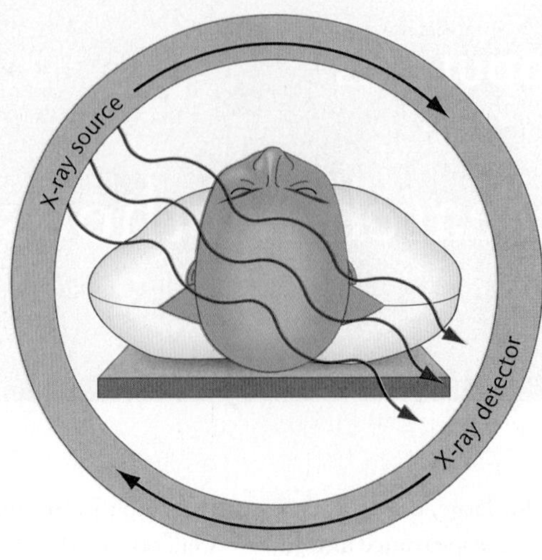

(a)

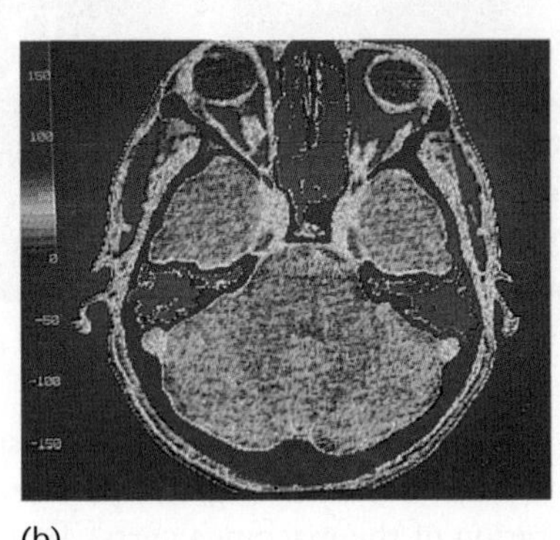

(b)

UpperCut Images/Getty Images

Figure 4.29 CT scanner
(a) A person's head is placed into the device and then a rapidly rotating source sends x-rays through the head while detectors on the opposite side make photographs. A computer then constructs an image of the brain. **(b)** A view of a normal human brain generated by computerized axial tomography (CT scanning).

One problem with phrenologists was their uncritical use of data. In some cases, they examined just one person with some behavioral quirk to define a brain area presumably responsible for it. Another problem was that skull shape has little relationship to brain anatomy. The skull is thicker in some places than others and thicker in some people than others.

Other investigators of the 1800s and 1900s rejected the idea of examining skulls but kept the idea that brain anatomy relates to behavior. One project was to remove people's brains after death and see whether the brains of eminent people looked unusual in any way. Several societies arose whose members agreed to donate their brains after death to the research cause. No conclusion resulted. The brains of the eminent varied considerably, as did less eminent people's brains. If brain anatomy related to intellect, the relation wasn't obvious (Burrell, 2004). At the end of this module, we'll return to the issue of brain anatomy and intelligence. Modern methods enable us to approach the question more systematically than in the past, although the conclusions are still murky.

If we ignore the question of how overall brain size or shape relates to anything, the size of particular areas within the brain might relate to specific behaviors. Today, researchers can examine detailed brain anatomy in living people using large enough groups for statistical analysis. For example, the amount of gray matter in the inferior (lower) parietal lobe correlates significantly with adolescents' vocabulary (H. Lee et al., 2007). We shall encounter a few more examples of this kind of research throughout the text.

One method of examining brain anatomy is **computerized axial tomography,** better known as a **CT** or **CAT scan** (Andreasen, 1988). A physician injects a dye into the blood (to increase contrast in the image) and then places the person's head into a CT scanner like the one shown in Figure 4.29a. X-rays are passed through the head and recorded by detectors on the opposite side. The CT scanner is rotated slowly until a measurement has been taken at each angle over 180 degrees. From the measurements, a computer constructs images of the brain. Figure 4.29b is an example. CT scans help detect tumors and other structural abnormalities.

Another method is **magnetic resonance imaging (MRI)** (Warach, 1995), which is based on the fact that any atom with an odd-numbered atomic weight, such as hydrogen, has an axis of rotation. An MRI device applies a powerful magnetic field (about 25,000 times the magnetic field of the earth) to align all the axes of rotation and then tilts them with a brief radio frequency field. When the radio frequency field is turned off, the atomic nuclei release electromagnetic energy as they relax and return to their original axis. By measuring that energy, MRI devices form an image of the brain, such as the one in Figure 4.30. MRI images anatomical details that are smaller than a millimeter in diameter. One drawback is that the person must lie motionless in a confining, noisy apparatus. The procedure is usually not suitable for children or people who fear enclosed places.

STOP & CHECK

16. Researchers today sometimes relate differences in people's behavior to differences in their brain anatomy. How does their approach differ from that of the phrenologists?

ANSWER

16. The phrenologists drew conclusions based on just one or a few people with some oddity of behavior. Today's researchers compare groups statistically. Also, today's researchers examine the brain itself, not the skull.

© Will and Demi McIntyre/Photo Researchers

Figure 4.30 A view of a living brain generated by magnetic resonance imaging
Any atom with an odd-numbered atomic weight, such as hydrogen, has an inherent rotation. An outside magnetic field can align the axes of rotation. A radio frequency field can then make all these atoms move like tiny gyros. When the radio frequency field is turned off, the atomic nuclei release electromagnetic energy as they relax. By measuring that energy, we can obtain an image of a structure such as the brain without damaging it.

Recording Brain Activity

When you watch a sunset, feel frightened, or solve a mathematical problem, which brain areas change their activity? With laboratory animals, researchers insert electrodes to record brain activity. They also use chemicals that stain certain proteins that form when neurons increase their activity. Studies of human brains use noninvasive methods—that is, methods that don't require inserting anything.

A device called the **electroencephalograph (EEG)** records electrical activity of the brain through electrodes—ranging from just a few to more than a hundred—attached to the scalp (Figure 4.31). Electrodes glued to the scalp measure the average activity at any moment for the population of cells under the electrode. The output is then amplified and recorded. This device can record spontaneous brain activity or activity in response to a stimulus, in which case we call the results **evoked potentials** or **evoked responses.** For one example of a study, researchers recorded evoked potentials from young adults as they watched pictures of nudes of both sexes. Men reported high arousal by the female nudes, while women reported neutral feelings to both the males and females, but both men's and women's brains showed strong evoked potentials to the opposite-sex nudes (Costa, Braun, & Birbaumer, 2003). That is, evoked potentials sometimes reveal information that self-reports do not.

A **magnetoencephalograph (MEG)** is similar, but instead of measuring electrical activity, it measures the faint magnetic fields generated by brain activity (Hari, 1994). Like EEG, an MEG recording identifies the approximate location of activity to within about a centimeter. However, an MEG has excellent temporal resolution, showing changes from 1 millisecond to the next.

Figure 4.32 shows an MEG record of brain responses to a brief tone heard in the right ear. The diagram represents a human head as viewed from above, with the nose at the top (Hari, 1994). Researchers using an MEG can identify the times at which various brain areas respond and thereby trace a wave of brain activity from its point of origin to all the other areas that process it (Salmelin, Hari, Lounasmaa, & Sams, 1994).

Another method, **positron-emission tomography (PET),** provides a high-resolution image of activity in a living brain by recording the emission of radioactivity from injected chemicals. First, the person receives an injection of glucose or some other chemical containing radioactive atoms. When a radioactive atom decays, it releases a positron that immediately collides with a nearby electron, emitting two gamma rays in exactly opposite directions. The person's head is surrounded by a set of gamma ray detectors (Figure 4.33). When two detectors record gamma rays at the same time, they identify a spot halfway between those detectors as the point of origin of the gamma rays. A computer uses this information to determine how many gamma rays are coming from each spot in the brain and therefore how much of the radioactive chemical is located in each area (Phelps &

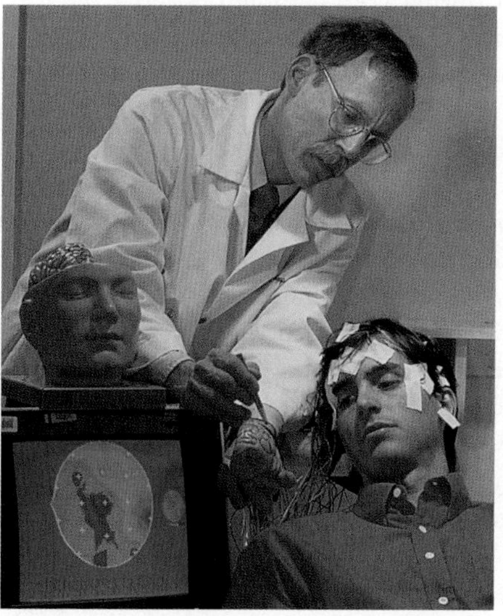
© Richard Nowitz/Photo Researchers

Figure 4.31 Electroencephalography
An electroencephalograph records the overall activity of neurons under various electrodes attached to the scalp.

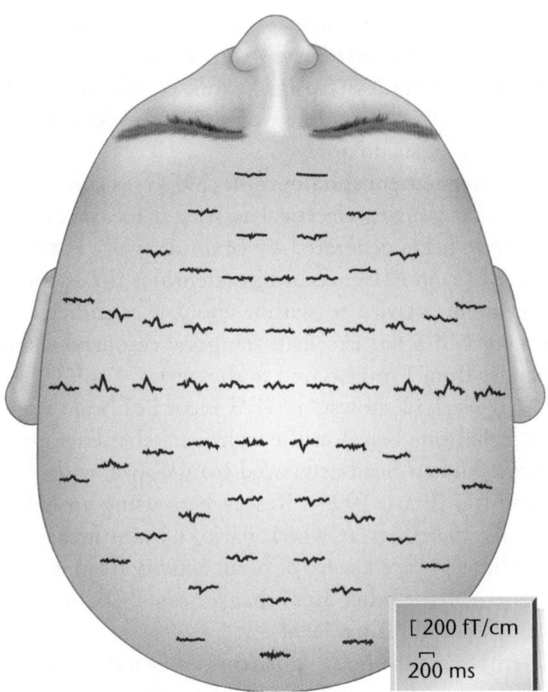

Figure 4.32 A result of magnetoencephalography, showing responses to a tone in the right ear
The nose is shown at the top. For each spot on the diagram, the display shows the changing response over a few hundred ms following the tone. (Note calibration at lower right.) The tone evoked responses in many areas, with the largest responses in the temporal cortex, especially on the left side. *(Reprinted from* Neuroscience: From the Molecular to the Cognitive, *by R. Hari, 1994, p. 165, with kind permission from Elsevier Science—NL, Sara Burgerhartstraat 25, 1055 KV Amsterdam, The Netherlands.)*

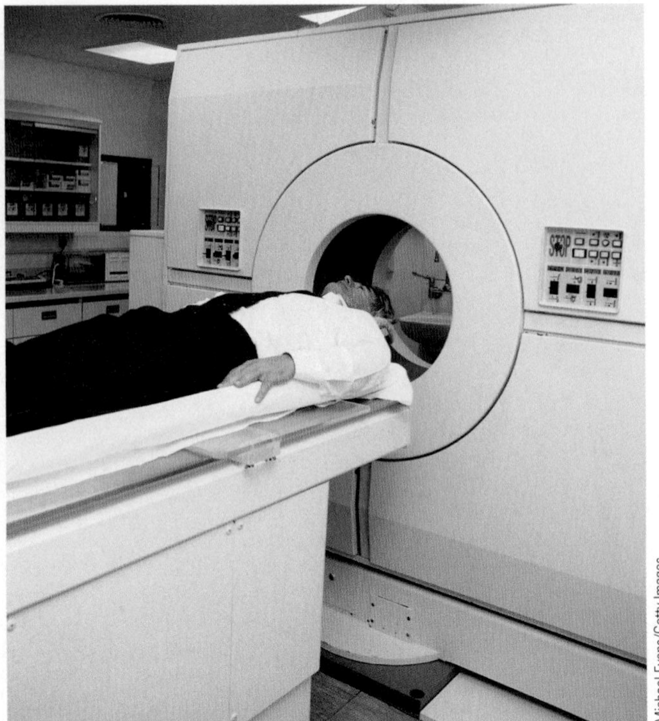

Figure 4.33 A PET scanner
A person engages in a cognitive task while attached to this apparatus that records which areas of the brain become more active and by how much.

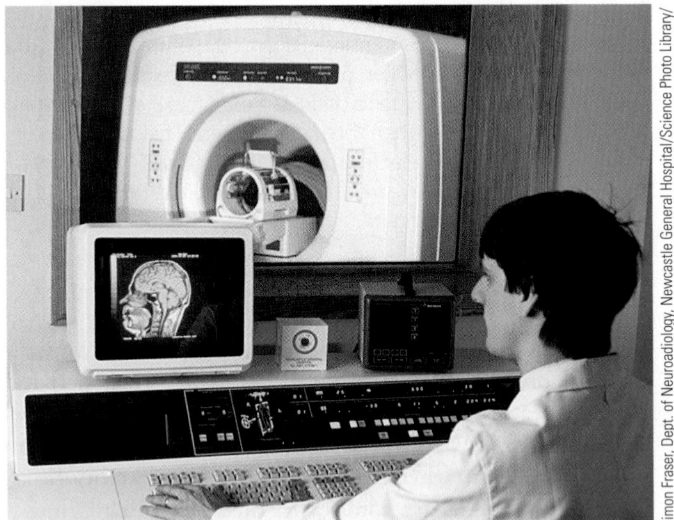

Figure 4.34 An fMRI scan of a human brain
An fMRI produces fairly detailed photos at rates up to about one per second. *(Wagner et al., 1998)*

Mazziotta, 1985). The areas showing the most radioactivity are the ones with the most blood flow and, therefore, presumably, the most brain activity. For an example of a PET study, we shall see in Chapter 9 how PET identified the brain areas that become active during a certain stage of sleep.

Ordinarily, PET scans use radioactive chemicals with a short half-life, made in a device called a cyclotron. Because cyclotrons are large and expensive, PET scans are available only at research hospitals. Furthermore, PET requires exposing the brain to radioactivity. For most purposes, PET scans have been replaced by functional magnetic resonance imaging (fMRI), which is less expensive and less risky. Standard MRI scans record the energy released by water molecules after removal of a magnetic field. The results show brain structure in good detail. **Functional magnetic resonance imaging (fMRI)** is a modified version of MRI based on hemoglobin (the blood protein that binds oxygen) (Detre & Floyd, 2001). Hemoglobin with oxygen reacts to a magnetic field differently from hemoglobin without oxygen. Because oxygen consumption increases when a brain area's activity increases (Mukamel et al., 2005), researchers set the fMRI scanner to detect changes in the oxygen content of the blood as it responds to the amount of synaptic input reaching each brain area (Viswanathan & Freeman, 2007). An fMRI image has a spatial resolution of 1 or 2 mm (almost as good as standard MRI) and temporal resolution of about a second (Figure 4.34). The fMRI method has been highly valuable in identifying brain areas that become activated during tests of memory and attention.

A measure of your brain activity while you were, for example, reading would mean nothing without a comparison to something else. So researchers would record your brain activity once while you were reading, and once during a comparison task and then subtract the brain activity during the comparison task to determine the excess activity that occurs during reading. As a comparison task, for example, researchers might ask you to look at a page written in a language you do not understand. That task would activate visual areas the same as the reading task did, but it presumably would not activate the language areas of your brain. Figure 4.35 illustrates the idea.

Still, reading requires attention, memory, language comprehension, and other skills, so further research would be needed to identify which brain areas do what. The task would be overwhelming for any single laboratory, but researchers share their results in an online library of fMRI results (Van Horn, Grafton, Rockmore, & Gazzaniga, 2004).

Interpreting the results is a complex task. Suppose someone collects fMRI data while you perform two tasks. If the results show greater brain activity during the task that you perform better, the interpretation is that you did better because you activated more of your brain. However, if you show more brain activity during the task you perform *worse*, the interpretation is that you needed to activate more of your brain to deal with the more difficult task (Gigi, Babai, Katzav, Atkins, & Hendler, 2007; Pexman, Hargreaves, Edwards, Henry, & Goodyear, 2007).

In spite of the complications, fMRI results sometimes provide valuable information. For example, researchers asked which brain areas become more active when your "mind wanders." Several brain areas, including the posterior cingulate cortex, consistently show increased activity during times when people have no particular task (M. F. Mason et al., 2007). Then, when researchers watched people's performance on a task requiring constant attention, they saw performance decline at the moments activity increased in the posterior cingulate and these other mind-wandering areas (Weissman, Roberts, Visscher, & Woldorff, 2006). Evidently, the non-task-related activity interferes with the brain processes necessary for vigilance.

In another study, researchers used fMRI to record activity in the visual cortex as people looked at 1,750 photographs. Then they showed 120 new photographs similar to one or more of the original ones and analyzed the fMRI results with a computer. In most cases, they were able to use the fMRI results to guess which of the new photographs the person was seeing. To a limited degree, they were able to "read people's mind" (Kay, Naselaris, Prenger, & Gallant, 2008).

Here is another fascinating example: Researchers used fMRI to record brain activity in one young woman who was in a persistent vegetative state following a brain injury in a traffic accident. She had neither spoken nor made any other purposive movements. However, when she was told to imagine playing tennis, the fMRI showed increased activity in motor areas of the cortex, similar to what healthy volunteers showed. When she was told to imagine walking through her house, a different set of brain areas became active, again similar to those of healthy volunteers (Owen et al., 2006). Follow-up studies found one other patient in a vegetative state whose brain showed these responses to instructions, although most others did not (K. Smith, 2007). Do these results mean that certain patients in a vegetative state are actually conscious? Do they mean at least that certain patients are more likely than others to become conscious at some later time? At present, neuroscientists are not agreed, but the possibilities are exciting.

Effects of Brain Damage

In 1861, the French neurologist Paul Broca found that a patient who had lost the ability to speak had damage in part of his left frontal cortex, an area now known as *Broca's area*. Fur-

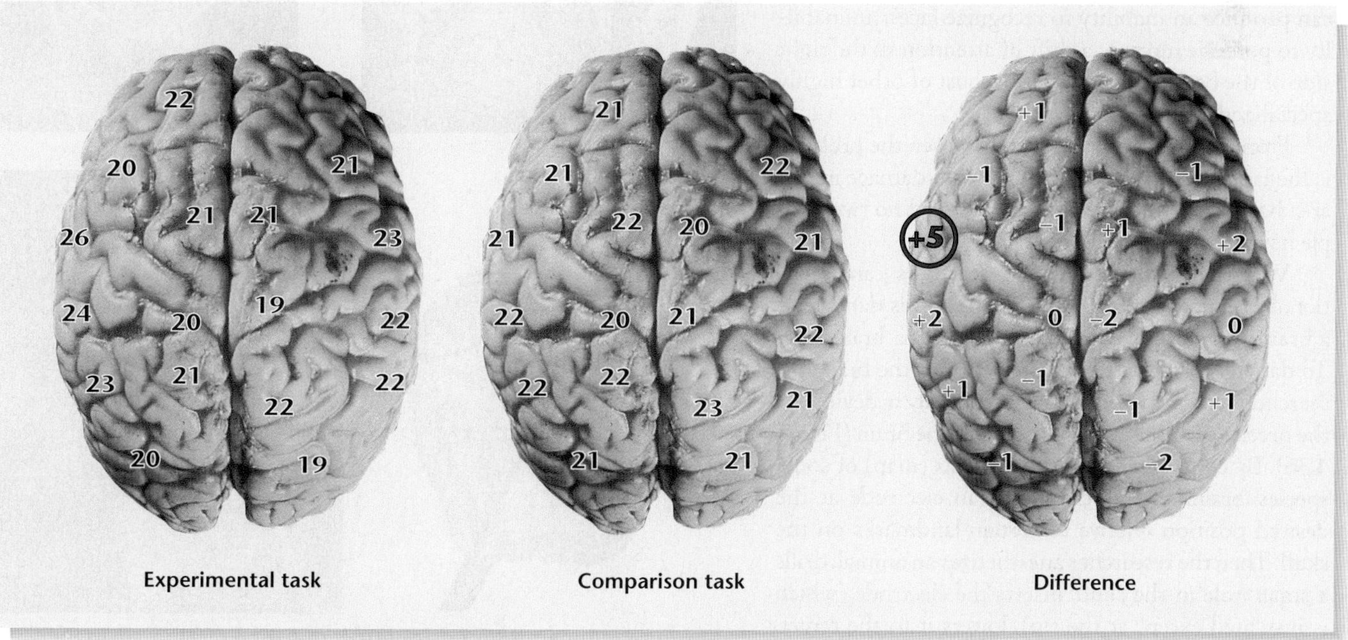

Figure 4.35 Subtraction for a brain scan procedure
Numbers on the brain at the left show hypothetical levels of arousal during some task, measured in arbitrary units. The brain at the center shows activity during the same brain areas during a comparison task. The brain at the right shows the differences. The highlighted area shows the largest difference. In actual data, the largest increases in activity would be one or two tenths of a percent.

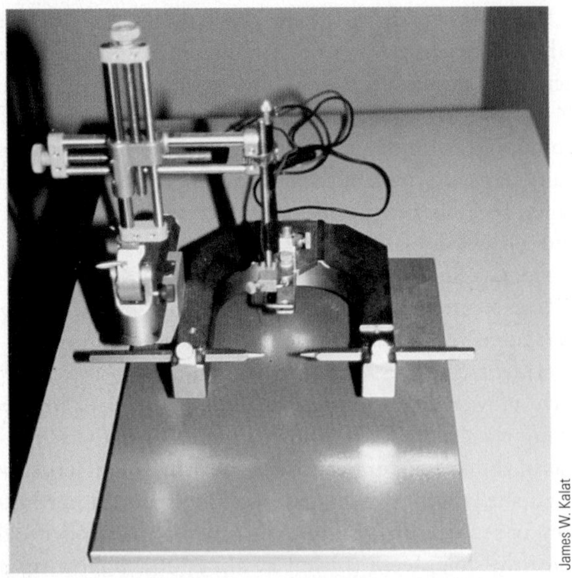

Figure 4.36 A stereotaxic instrument for locating brain areas in small animals
Using this device, researchers can insert an electrode to stimulate, record from, or damage any point in the brain.

ther patients with loss of speech also showed damage in and around that area. Previously, many neurologists had doubted that different brain areas had different functions at all, so Broca's discovery revolutionized the field.

Since then, researchers have made countless reports of behavioral impairments after brain damage, as we shall consider in later chapters. Brain damage can produce an inability to recognize faces, an inability to perceive motion, a shift of attention to the right side of the body and world, and a host of other highly specialized deficits.

From a research standpoint, however, the problem is the lack of control. Most people with damage in one area have damage to other areas, too, and no two people have exactly the same damage.

With laboratory animals, researchers can intentionally damage a selected area. A **lesion** is damage to a brain area; an **ablation** is a removal of a brain area. To damage a structure in the interior of the brain, researchers use a **stereotaxic instrument,** a device for the precise placement of electrodes in the brain (Figure 4.36). By consulting a stereotaxic atlas (map) of some species' brain, a researcher aims an electrode at the desired position relative to certain landmarks on the skull. Then the researcher anesthetizes an animal, drills a small hole in the skull, inserts the electrode (which is insulated except at the tip), lowers it to the target, and passes an electrical current sufficient to damage that area. For example, researchers have made lesions in parts of the hypothalamus to explore their contributions to eating and drinking. After the experiment, and after the death of the animal, someone takes slices of its brain, applies stains, and checks the actual location of the damage (which might be different from the intended location).

Suppose a researcher makes a lesion and reports some behavioral deficit. "Wait a minute," you might say. "How do we know the deficit wasn't caused by anesthetizing the animal, drilling a hole in its skull, and lowering an electrode to this target?" To test this possibility, an experimenter produces a **sham lesion** in a control group, performing all the same procedures except for passing the electrical current. Any behavioral difference between the two groups must result from the lesion and not the other procedures.

Besides lesions, several other procedures can inactivate various brain structures or systems. In the **gene-knockout approach,** researchers use biochemical methods to direct a mutation to a particular gene that is important for certain types of cells, transmitters, or receptors (Joyner & Guillemot, 1994). We already encountered one example of this approach in Chapter 3: Researchers demonstrated the importance of dopamine in drug abuse by showing that mice lacking the gene for dopamine type 1 receptors fail to respond to cocaine as a reinforcement (Caine et al., 2007).

Transcranial magnetic stimulation, the application of an intense magnetic field to a portion of the scalp, temporarily inactivates neurons below the magnet (Walsh & Cowey, 2000). This procedure enables researchers to study a given individu-

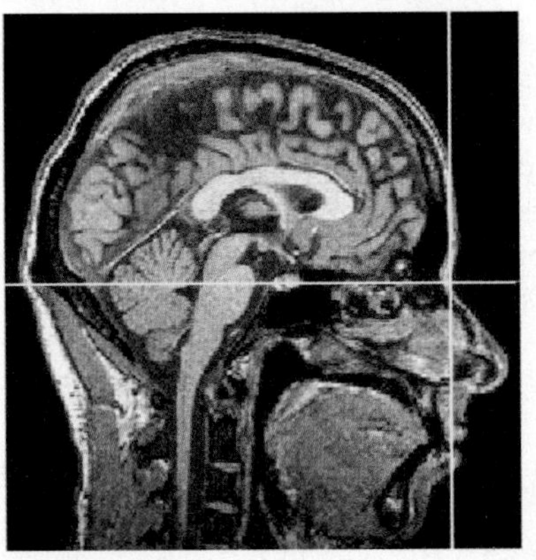

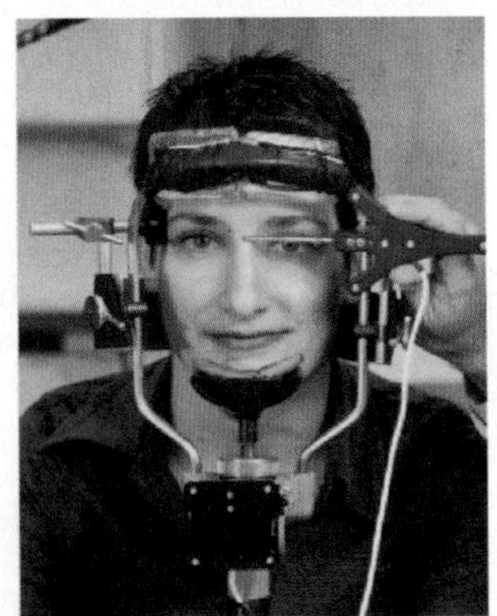

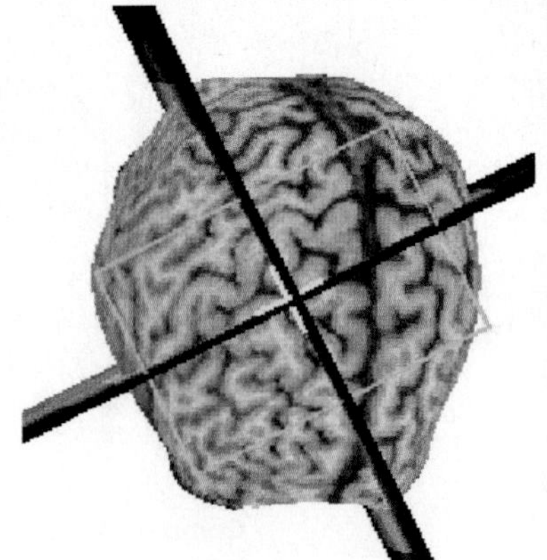

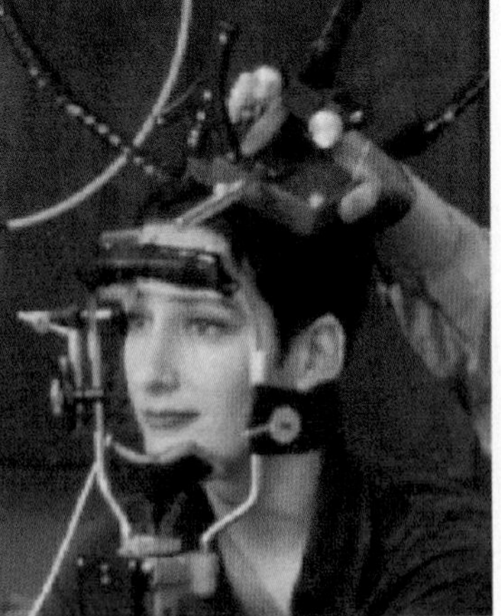

Figure 4.37 Apparatus for magnetic stimulation of a human brain
The procedure is known as transcranial magnetic stimulation, or TMS. *(Courtesy of Tomas Paus, McGill University. From Paus, T., "Combination of transcranial magnetic stimulation with brain imaging." In J. Mazziotta, A. Toga (Eds.)* Brain Mapping: The Methods, *Second Edition, Academic Press, pp. 691–705, 2002, Figure 1.)*

al's behavior with the brain area active, then inactive, and then active again. Figure 4.37 shows the apparatus for this procedure. For example, one study discussed in Chapter 6 found that people could direct their eye movements toward a light even when transcranial magnetic stimulation had temporarily silenced the visual cortex. This result suggests that other parts of the brain can produce motor responses to light, even though they do not produce conscious vision.

With any of these approaches, a big problem is to specify the exact behavioral deficit. By analogy, suppose you cut a wire in a television and the picture disappeared. You would know that this wire is necessary for the picture, but you would not know why. Similarly, if you damaged a brain area and the animal stopped eating, you wouldn't know how that area contributes to eating. A lesion study is a good start, but it is only a start.

Effects of Brain Stimulation

If brain damage impairs some behavior, stimulation should increase it. Researchers can insert electrodes to stimulate brain areas in laboratory animals. With humans, they use a less invasive (and less precise) method. Researchers apply a magnetic field to the scalp, thereby stimulating the brain areas beneath it (Fitzgerald, Brown, & Daskalakis, 2002). Whereas intense transcranial magnetic stimulation inactivates the underlying area, a brief, milder application stimulates it.

One limitation of any stimulation study is that complex behaviors and experiences depend on many brain areas, not just one, so an artificial stimulation produces artificial responses. For example, electrically or magnetically stimulating the primary visual areas of the brain produces reports of sparkling flashing points of light, not the sight of a face or other recognizable object. It is easier to discover which brain area is responsible for vision (or movement or whatever) than to discover how it produces a meaningful pattern.

Table 4.5 summarizes various methods of studying brain-behavior relationships.

STOP & CHECK

17. How do the effects of brief, mild magnetic stimulation differ from those of longer, more intense stimulation?

18. Why does electrical or magnetic stimulation of the brain seldom produce complex, meaningful sensations or movements?

ANSWERS

17. Brief, mild magnetic stimulation on the scalp increases activity in the underlying brain areas, whereas longer, more intense stimulation blocks it. **18.** Meaningful sensations and movements require a pattern of precisely timed activity in a great many cells, not just a burst of overall activity diffusely in one area.

TABLE 4.5 Brain-Behavior Research Methods

Correlate Brain Anatomy with Behavior	
Computerized axial tomography (CAT)	Maps brain areas, but requires exposure to x-rays
Magnetic resonance imaging (MRI)	Maps brain areas in detail, using magnetic fields
Record Brain Activity During Behavior	
Record from electrodes in brain	Invasive; used with laboratory animals, seldom humans
Electroencephalograph (EEG)	Records from scalp; measures changes by ms, with but low resolution of location of the signal
Evoked potentials	Similar to EEG but in response to stimuli
Magnetoencephalograph (MEG)	Similar to EEG but measures magnetic fields
Positron emission tomography (PET)	Measures changes over both time and location but requires exposing brain to radiation
Functional magnetic resonance imaging (fMRI)	Measures changes over about 1 second, identifies location within 1–2 mm, no use of radiation
Examine Effects of Brain Damage	
Study victims of stroke etc.	Used with humans; each person has different damage
Lesion	Controlled damage in laboratory animals
Ablation	Removal of a brain area
Gene-knockout	Effects wherever that gene is active (e.g., a receptor)
Transcranial magnetic stimulation	Intense application temporarily inactivates a brain area
Examine Effects of Stimulating a Brain Area	
Stimulating electrodes	Invasive; used with laboratory animals, seldom with humans
Transcranial magnetic stimulation	Brief, mild application activates underlying brain area

Differences in Brain Size and Structure

Although the organization of the brain is the same from one species to another, size varies, even within a species. For example, some people have two or three times as many axons from the eyes to the brain as others do. They also have more cells in their visual cortex (Andrews, Halpern, & Purves, 1997; Stevens, 2001; Sur & Leamey, 2001) and greater ability to detect brief, faint, or rapidly changing visual stimuli (Halpern, Andrews, & Purves, 1999).

People also differ in total brain size. Does brain size have anything to do with intelligence? This question, about which you might be curious, illustrates how new methods facilitate research.

As mentioned at the start of this module, many researchers compared the brains of eminent (presumably intelligent) people to those of less successful people but failed to find any obvious difference. Later neuroscientists examined the brain of the famous scientist Albert Einstein, again hoping to find something unusual. Einstein's total brain size was merely average. He did have a higher than average ratio of glia to neurons in one brain area (M. C. Diamond, Scheibel, Murphy, & Harvey, 1985). Another study found expansion of part of Einstein's parietal cortex, as shown in Figure 4.38 (Witelson, Kigar, & Harvey, 1999). However, when researchers examine many aspects of a particular brain and find a couple of unusual features, we don't know whether those features are significant or irrelevant.

Despite the lack of good evidence, the idea has lingered: Shouldn't brain size have *some* relationship to intelligence? Even if the idea isn't entirely right, is it completely wrong?

Comparisons Across Species

All mammalian brains have the same organization. That is, the visual cortex, auditory cortex, and other components are in the same relative locations. Also, the sizes of various areas within the brain are nearly proportional to one another, with the exception of the olfactory bulb, which is, for example, large in dogs and small in humans (Finlay & Darlington, 1995).

Mammalian brains differ enormously in size, however. The largest mammalian brains are 100,000 times as large as the smallest. In some orders, such as rodents, larger brains have larger neurons. However, among primates, brains become larger by adding more neurons of about the same size (Herculano-Houzel, Collins, Wong, & Kaas, 2007). You can examine a variety of mammalian brains at the Comparative Mammalian Brain Collections Website: http://www.brainmuseum.org/sections/index.html.

Do variations in brain size relate to animal intelligence? We humans like to think of ourselves as the most intelligent animals—after all, we get to define what intelligence means! However, humans do not have the largest brains. Sperm whales' brains are eight times larger than ours, and elephants' are four times larger. Perhaps, many people suggest, intelligence depends on brain-to-body ratio. Figure 4.39 illustrates

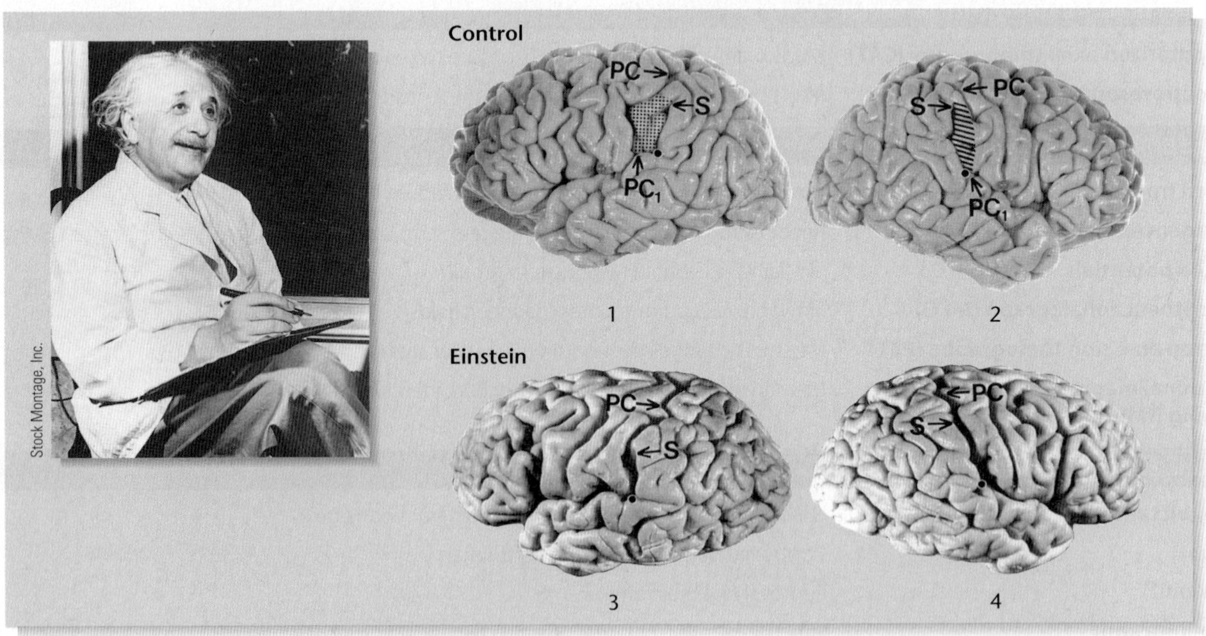

Figure 4.38 Einstein's brain
Parts 1 and 2 show the left and right hemispheres of an average brain; the stippled (left) and hatched (right) sections are a brain area called the parietal operculum. Parts 3 and 4 show Einstein's brain; the parietal operculum is absent because the inferior parietal lobe has expanded beyond its usual boundaries, occupying the area where one ordinarily finds the parietal operculum. *(Brain images reprinted from* The Lancet, 353/9170, *Witelson, S. R., Kigar, D. L., & Harvey, T., "The exceptional brain of Albert Einstein," p. 2151, 1999, with permission from Elsevier.)*

the relationship between logarithm of body mass and logarithm of brain mass for various vertebrates (Jerison, 1985). Note that the species we regard as most intelligent—such as, ahem, ourselves—have larger brains in proportion to body size than do the species we consider less impressive, such as frogs.

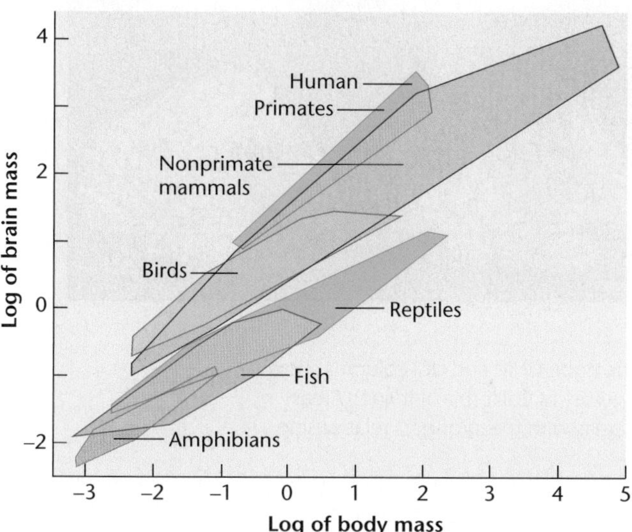

Figure 4.39 Relationship of brain mass to body mass across species
Each species is one point within one of the polygons. In general, log of body mass is a good predictor of log of brain mass. Note that primates in general and humans in particular have a large brain mass in proportion to body mass. *(Adapted from Jerison, 1985)*

However, brain-to-body ratio has problems also: Chihuahuas have the highest brain-to-body ratio of all dog breeds, not because they were bred for intelligence but because they were bred for small bodies (Deacon, 1997). Squirrel monkeys, which are also very thin, have a higher brain-to-body ratio than humans. (And with the increasing prevalence of human obesity, our brain-to-body ratio is declining!) The elephant-nose fish (Figure 4.40), which you might keep in an aquarium, has a 3% brain-to-body ratio compared to 2% for humans (Nilsson, 1999). So neither total brain mass nor brain-to-body ratio puts humans in first place.

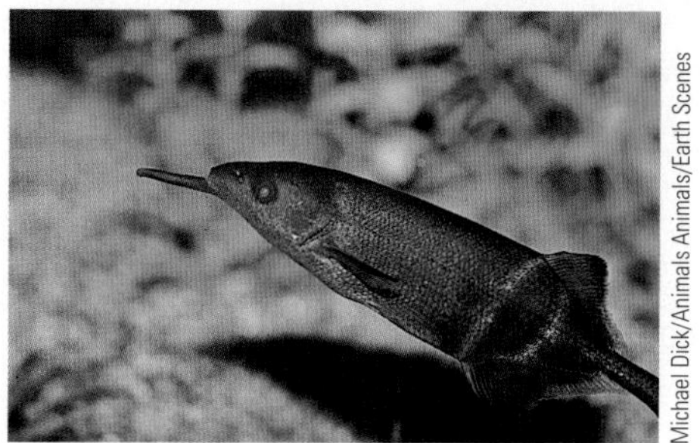

Figure 4.40 An elephant-nose fish
The brain of this odd-looking fish weighs 0.3 g (0.01 ounce), which is 3% of the weight of the whole fish—a vastly higher percentage than most other fish and higher even than humans. What this fish does with so much brain, we don't know, but it may relate to the fish's unusual ability to detect electrical fields.

We might look for some more complex measure that considers both total brain size and brain-to-body ratio. But before we can test various formulas, we need a clear definition of animal intelligence, and that has been an elusive concept, to say the least (Macphail, 1985). Furthermore, accurately weighing a brain is not as easy as it sounds (Healy & Rowe, 2007). (As soon as someone cuts into a skull to remove a brain, the moist brain begins drying out and losing weight.) Given that studies of brain and behavior in nonhumans are not helping, let's abandon that effort and turn to humans.

STOP & CHECK

19. Why are both brain size and brain-to-body ratio unsatisfactory ways of estimating animal intelligence?

ANSWER

19. If we consider ourselves to be the most intelligent species—and admittedly, that is just an assumption—we are confronted with the fact that we have neither the largest brains nor the highest brain-to-body ratios. Brain-to-body ratio depends on selection for thinness as well as selection for brain size. Furthermore, animal intelligence is undefined and poorly measured, so we cannot even determine what correlates with it.

Comparisons Among Humans

For many years, studies of human brain size and intelligence found correlations barely above zero. However, a low correlation between two variables can mean either that they are unrelated or that they were measured poorly. In this case, measurements of intelligence (by IQ tests) were of course imperfect, and the measurements of brain size were probably worse, relying on skull size instead of the brain itself. Today, however, MRI scans measure brain volume in healthy, living people. Most studies have found a moderate positive correlation between brain size and IQ, typically around .3 (McDaniel, 2005).

Another approach is to examine the correlation between IQ scores and specific brain areas. In one study, investigators used MRI to measure the size of gray matter and white matter areas throughout the brains of 23 young adults from one university campus and 24 middle-aged or older adults from another campus. In Figure 4.41, the areas highlighted in red showed a statistically significant correlation with IQ, and those highlighted in yellow showed an even stronger correlation. Note two points: First, IQ correlates with the size of many brain areas. Second, the results differed between the two samples (Haier, Jung, Yeo, Head, & Alkire, 2004). A later study suggested that general intelligence correlates with thickness of

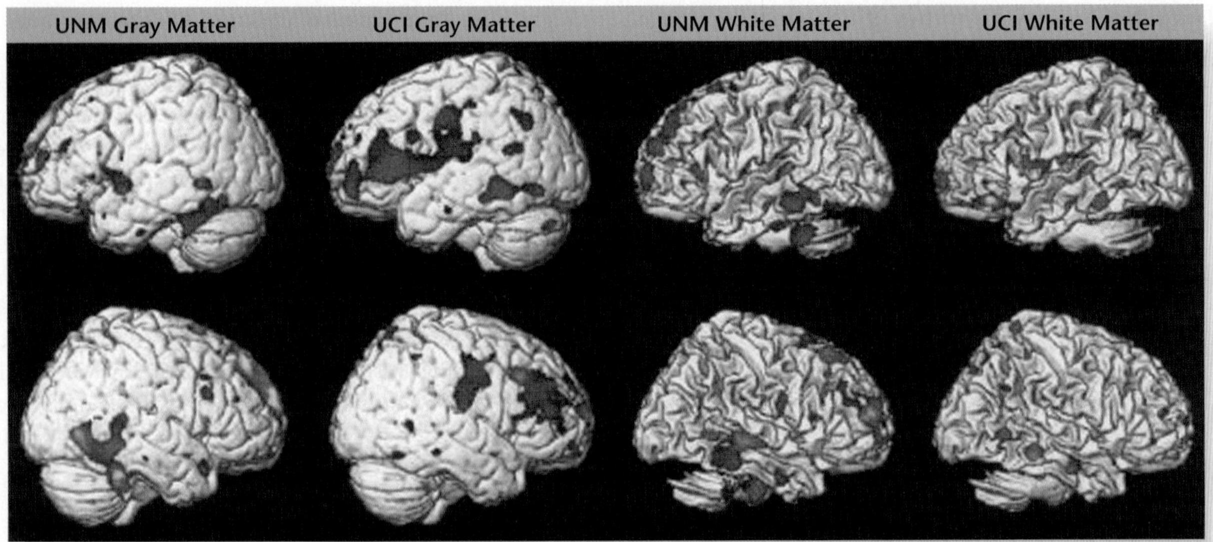

Figure 4.41 Cortical areas whose size correlated with IQ
The top row shows the left hemisphere; the bottom row shows the right. UNM and UCI columns show the results for two universities (University of New Mexico and University of California at Irvine). Areas whose size was significantly associated with IQ are shown in red; areas with the strongest relationship are shown in yellow. *(From Haier et al., 2004)*

gray matter throughout nearly the entire cortex (Colom, Jung, & Haier, 2006).

As always, correlation does not mean causation. For example, how many pencils someone can hold correlates with the size of the hand. But it also correlates with the size of the person's foot, just because most people with large hands also have large feet. Similarly, the size of one brain area correlates with the size of others, so even if intelligence depended on only one brain area, it still might correlate with the size of other areas.

Do the same genes that control brain size also influence IQ? Studies have found greater resemblance between monozygotic than dizygotic twins for both brain size and IQ scores (Pennington et al., 2000; Posthuma et al., 2002) (Figure 4.42). More important, two studies found a strong correlation between the brain volume of one monozygotic twin and the IQ score of the other twin (Pennington et al., 2000; Pol et al., 2006). This result implies that the genes controlling brain size also relate to IQ. Several genes have been identified that apparently influence both intellectual performance and the size of one or more brain areas (Peper, Brouwer, Boomsma, Kahn, & Hulshoff, 2007). However, so far, no one has identified any single gene with a large effect. Evidently, both brain size and IQ depend on contributions from many sources.

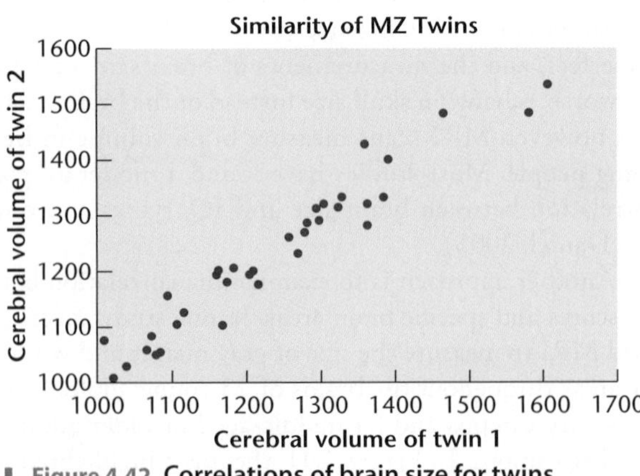

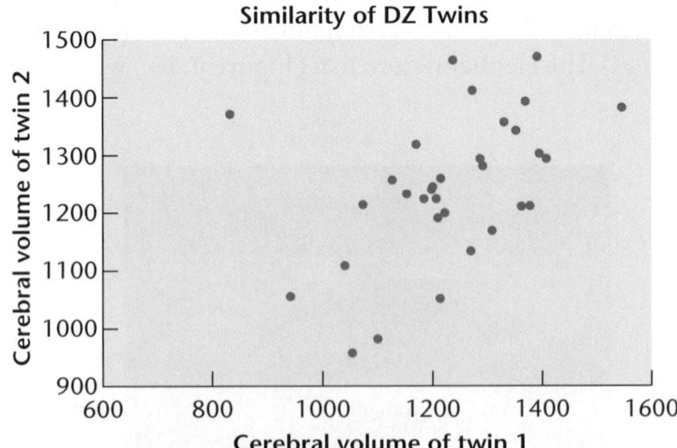

Figure 4.42 Correlations of brain size for twins
Each graph is a scatter plot, in which each dot represents one pair of twins. Brain size for one twin is shown along the *x* axis; brain size for the other twin is along the *y* axis. Note that both kinds of twins show similarities, but the correlation is stronger for the monozygotic twins. *(From B. F. Pennington et al., "A twin MRI study of size variations in the human brain,"* Journal of Cognitive Neuroscience, 12, *pp. 223–232., Figures 1, 2. © 2000 by the Massachusetts Institute of Technology. Reprinted with permission.)*

STOP & CHECK

20. Why do recent studies show a stronger relationship between brain size and IQ than older studies did?

21. What evidence indicates that the genes that control human brain size also influence IQ?

ANSWERS

20. The use of MRI greatly improves the measurement of brain size. **21.** For pairs of monozygotic twins, the size of one twin's brain correlates significantly with the other twin's IQ (as well as his or her own). Therefore, whatever genes increase the growth of the brain also increase IQ.

Comparisons of Men and Women

Now for the most confusing part: Although IQ correlates positively with brain size for men or women separately, men on the average have larger brains than women but equal IQs (Gilmore et al., 2007; Willerman, Schultz, Rutledge, & Bigler, 1991). Even if we take into account differences in height, men's brains remain larger (Ankney, 1992).

In fact, male and female brains differ, on the average, in more ways than you might expect, whereas behavioral differences, when carefully measured, are often smaller than most people expect. Certain brain areas are relatively larger in men, and others relatively larger in women, as Figure 4.43 shows (Cahill, 2006; J. M. Goldstein et al., 2001). For example, on the average, women have a greater density of neurons in part of the temporal lobe (Witelson, Glezer, & Kigar, 1995). The left temporal cortex exceeds the size of the right by a larger percentage in men than women (Good et al., 2001). The hippocampus tends to be larger in females; the amygdala is larger in males (Cahill, 2006). The shape of the visual cortex differs in several ways between males and females (Amunts et al., 2007). Because different brain areas mature at different times and rates, it is possible to have a "male-typical" brain in some ways and a "female-typical" brain in others (Woodson & Gorski, 2000).

Meanwhile, differences in many aspects of behavior are smaller than we might guess (Hyde, 2005). For example, most people believe that women talk much more than men. Perhaps they do in certain situations or in certain populations but not universally. In one study, male and female college students wore devices that recorded what they said at unpredictable times, without their knowing when the device was operating. Extrapolating from the samples to a full day, the investigators estimated that the average woman spoke 16,215 words per day compared to 15,669 for men—a statistically insignificant difference. Both groups showed much variation (Mehl, Vazire, Ramirez-Esparza, Slatcher, & Pennebaker, 2007). Another apparent difference pertains to chess. Vastly more men than women become grand masters in chess. However, a study of boys and girls starting chess found that they started at an equal level and progressed at equal rates. The main reason more men than women reached the highest level was that vastly more boys than girls *started* playing chess (Chabris & Glickman, 2006). The difference pertained to interests, not abilities.

A few cognitive differences do exist. When people give directions, more men than women answer in terms of north, south, east, and west, whereas more women describe landmarks, as shown in Figure 4.44 (Rahman, Andersson, & Govier, 2005). Also, on the average, girls get better grades than boys in most subjects, especially reading (Halpern, 2004). Boys tend to do better than girls at mental rotation tasks and tasks like the ones in Figure 4.45. However, playing 10 hours of action video games enables women to narrow this gap (Feng, Spence, & Pratt, 2007). Again, it appears that men and women differ more in interests than abilities.

How can we explain why intelligence tests show little or no difference between men and women, whereas men's and women's brains differ more substantially on the average? One potentially relevant factor pertains to relative amounts of gray and white matter. Women average more and deeper sulci on the surface of the cortex, especially in the frontal and parietal areas (Luders et al., 2004). Consequently, the surface area

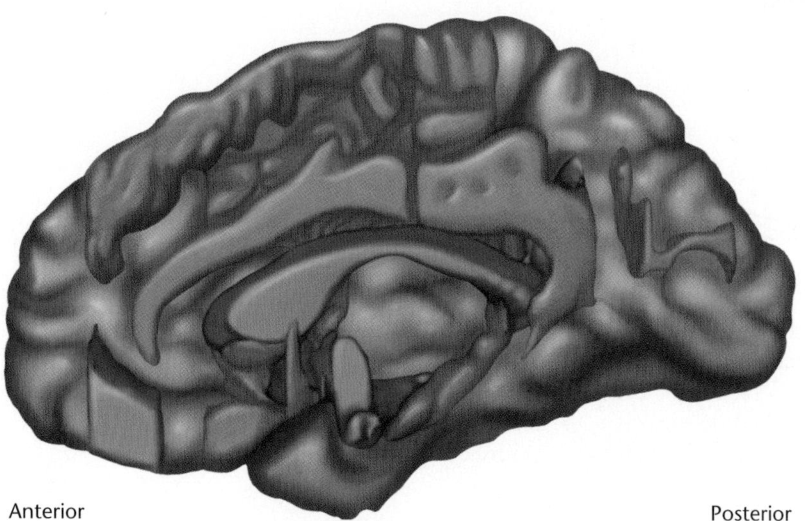

Figure 4.43 Men's and women's brains
Areas in pink are, on the average, larger in women relative to the total mass of the brain. Areas in blue are, on the average, larger in men relative to the total mass. *(Nature Reviews Neuroscience, 7, 477–484, from Cahill, L. (2006). Reprinted by permission of Macmillan Publishing Ltd.)*

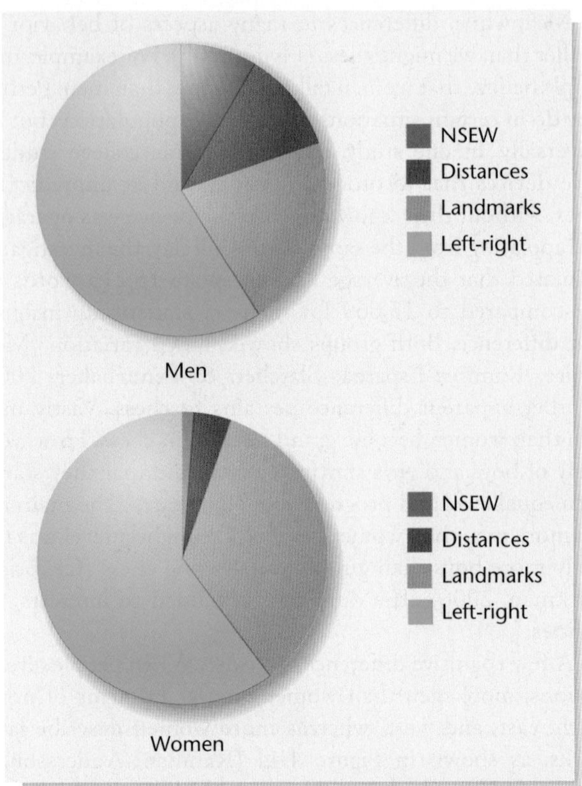

Figure 4.44 Relative use of different kinds of directions
Women used more landmark terms than men. Men were more likely than women to use terms relating to north-south-east-west or to distances. *(Based on data of Rahman, Andersson, & Govier, 2005)*

Can the set of blocks on the left be rotated to match the set at the right?

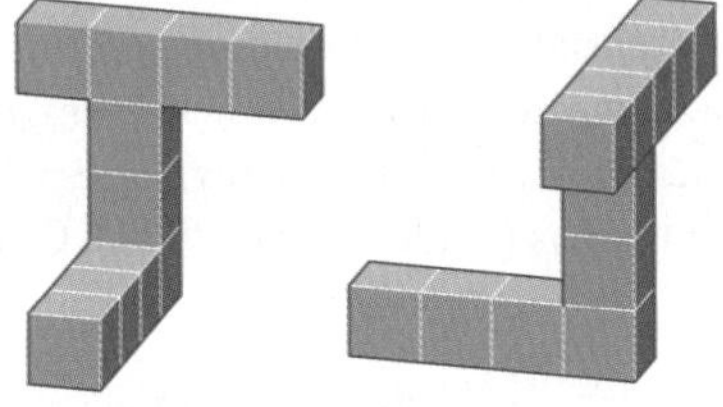

Which of the lines at the left has the same angle as the one at the right?

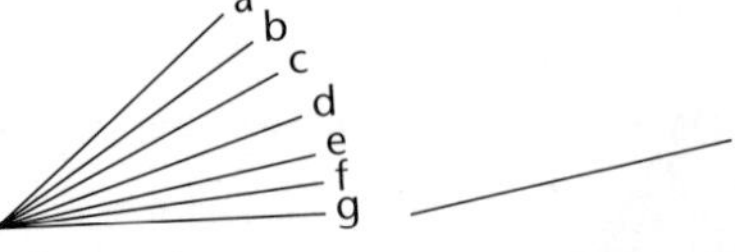

Figure 4.45 A spatial rotation task
People are presented with a series of pairs such as this one and asked whether the first figure could be rotated to match the second one. Here the answer is *no.* For the line-angle question, the correct answer is *e.*

of the cortex is almost the same in men and women. Because the surface is lined with neurons (gray matter), the sexes are nearly equal in number of neurons despite differences in brain volume (Allen, Damasio, Grabowski, Bruss, & Zhang, 2003). Because IQ appears to correlate more strongly with gray matter than with white matter (Narr et al., 2007), perhaps we can explain the equal IQs of men and women. Other differences in organization of male and female brains may be important also.

Although the relationship between brain size and intelligence certainly piques many people's curiosity, and although it does illustrate the way we can use modern technologies to approach difficult issues, the importance of the issue is questionable. Progress in psychology and neuroscience depends on making finer grained distinctions. How do the anatomy, chemistry, and other features of specific brain areas relate to specific aspects of behavior? In the rest of this text, we concentrate on those questions.

STOP & CHECK

22. On the average, although men have larger brains than women, men and women have equal IQ scores. What is a likely explanation?

ANSWER

22. Women have more and deeper sulci in the cortex and therefore about the same amount of surface area and neurons that men do.

MODULE 4.3 IN CLOSING

Research Methods and Their Limits

Descriptions of the history of science sometimes highlight a single study that "conclusively" established one theory or another. Such events are rare. Far more often, researchers gradually accumulate evidence that points in a particular direction, until eventually that view becomes dominant. Even in those rare cases when a single study appears to have been decisive, researchers often identify it as decisive only in retrospect, after several additional studies have confirmed the finding.

The reason we need so many studies is that almost any study has limitations. Sometimes, what seem like small differences in procedure produce very different outcomes. Even when several studies using the same method produce similar results, the possibility remains that the method itself has a hidden flaw. Therefore, scientists prefer whenever possible to compare results from widely different methods. The more types of evidence point to a given conclusion, the greater our confidence.

SUMMARY

1. People who differ with regard to some behavior sometimes also differ with regard to their brain anatomy. MRI is one modern method of imaging a living brain. However, correlations between behavior and anatomy should be evaluated cautiously. **107**
2. Researchers try to understand brain-behavior relationships by recording activity in various brain areas during a given behavior. Many methods are available, including EEG, MEG, and fMRI. **108**
3. Another way to study brain-behavior relationships is to examine the effects of brain damage. If someone loses an ability after some kind of brain damage, then that area contributes in some way, although we need more research to determine how. **111**
4. If stimulation of a brain area increases some behavior, presumably that area contributes to the behavior. **113**
5. Recent research using modern methods suggests a moderate positive relationship between brain size and intelligence, although many puzzles and uncertainties remain. **114**
6. Men's and women's brains differ fairly consistently in many regards, although the sexes do not differ much in any behavioral ability. Men and women are equal in IQ scores, on the average, despite men's having larger brains, on the average. Women's brains have more numerous and deeper sulci and therefore about the same surface area as men's. **117**

KEY TERMS

Terms are defined in the module on the page number indicated. They're also presented in alphabetical order with definitions in the book's Subject Index/Glossary. Interactive flashcards, audio reviews, and crossword puzzles are among the online resources available to help you learn these terms and the concepts they represent.

ablation **112**
computerized axial tomography (CT or CAT scan) **108**
electroencephalograph (EEG) **109**
evoked potentials or evoked responses **109**
functional magnetic resonance imaging (fMRI) **110**
gene-knockout approach **112**
lesion **112**
magnetic resonance imaging (MRI) **108**
magnetoencephalograph (MEG) **109**
phrenology **107**
positron-emission tomography (PET) **109**
sham lesion **112**
stereotaxic instrument **112**
transcranial magnetic stimulation **112**

THOUGHT QUESTION

Certain unusual aspects of brain structure were observed in the brain of Albert Einstein. One interpretation is that he was born with certain specialized brain features that encouraged his scientific and intellectual abilities. What is an alternative interpretation?

CHAPTER 4 Exploration and Study

In addition to the study materials provided at the end of each module, you may supplement your review of this chapter by using one or more of the book's electronic resources, which include its companion Website, interactive Cengage Learning eBook, Exploring Biological Psychology CD-ROM, and CengageNOW. Brief descriptions of these resources follow. For more information, visit **www.cengage.com/psychology/kalat**.

The book's companion Website, accessible through the author Web page indicated above, provides a wide range of study resources such as an interactive glossary, flashcards, tutorial quizzes, updated Web links, and Try It Yourself activities, as well as a limited selection of the short videos and animated explanations of concepts available for this chapter.

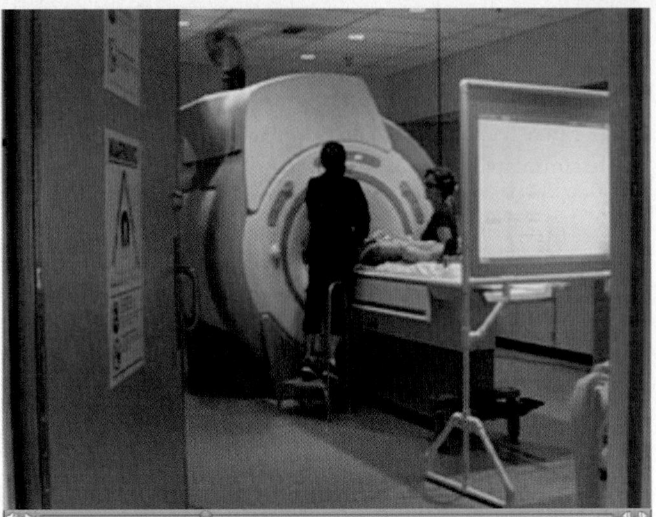

The video, *Research With Brain Scans*, shown here, explains how fMRI answers some important questions, and how these answers lead to new questions.

Exploring Biological Psychology

The Exploring Biological Psychology CD-ROM contains videos, animations, and Try It Yourself activities. These activities—as well as many that are new to this edition—are also available in the text's fully interactive, media-rich Cengage Learning eBook,* which gives you the opportunity to experience biological psychology in an even greater interactive and multimedia environment. The Cengage Learning eBook also includes highlighting and note-taking features and an audio glossary. For this chapter, the Cengage Learning eBook includes the following interactive explorations:

Virtual Reality Head Planes
3D Virtual Brain
Left Hemisphere Function #1
Sagittal Section: Right Hemisphere #1
Sagittal Section: Right Hemisphere #2
Sagittal Section: Right Hemisphere #3
Brain Puzzle
Cortex Puzzle
Sensory Cortex
Motor Cortex
Illustration of Binding
Possible Failure of Binding
Visual Mind Reading

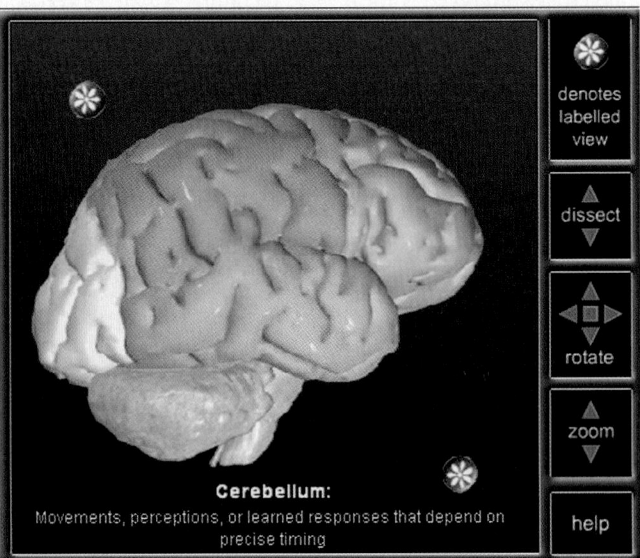

The interactive 3D Virtual Brain identifies the different parts of the brain and allows the user to rotate, zoom, and dissect the brain for a better look at each part.

CENGAGENOW™ is an easy-to-use resource that helps you study in less time to get the grade you want. An online study system, CengageNOW* gives you the option of taking a diagnostic pretest for each chapter. The system uses the results of each pretest to create personalized chapter study plans for you. The Personalized Study Plans

- help you save study time by identifying areas on which you should concentrate and give you one-click access to corresponding pages of the interactive Cengage Learning eBook;
- provide interactive exercises and study tools to help you fully understand chapter concepts; and
- include a posttest for you to take to confirm that you are ready to move on to the next chapter.

* Requires a Cengage Learning eResources account. Visit **www.cengage.com/login** to register or login.

Suggestions for Further Exploration

The book's companion Website includes a list of suggested articles available through InfoTrac College Edition for this chapter. You may also want to explore some of the following books and Websites. The text's companion Website provides live, updated links to the sites listed below.

Books

Burrell, B. (2004). *Postcards from the brain museum.* New York: Broadway Books. Fascinating history of the attempts to collect brains of successful people and try to relate their brain anatomy to their success.

Klawans, H. L. (1988). *Toscanini's fumble and other tales of clinical neurology.* Chicago: Contemporary Books. Description of illustrative cases of brain damage and their behavioral consequences.

Websites

Whole Brain Atlas
An amazing source of information about brain anatomy.
http://www.med.harvard.edu/AANLIB/home.html

Comparative Mammalian Brain Collections
Photographs of the brain, including internal structures, from a wide variety of mammalian species.
http://www.brainmuseum.org/sections/index.html

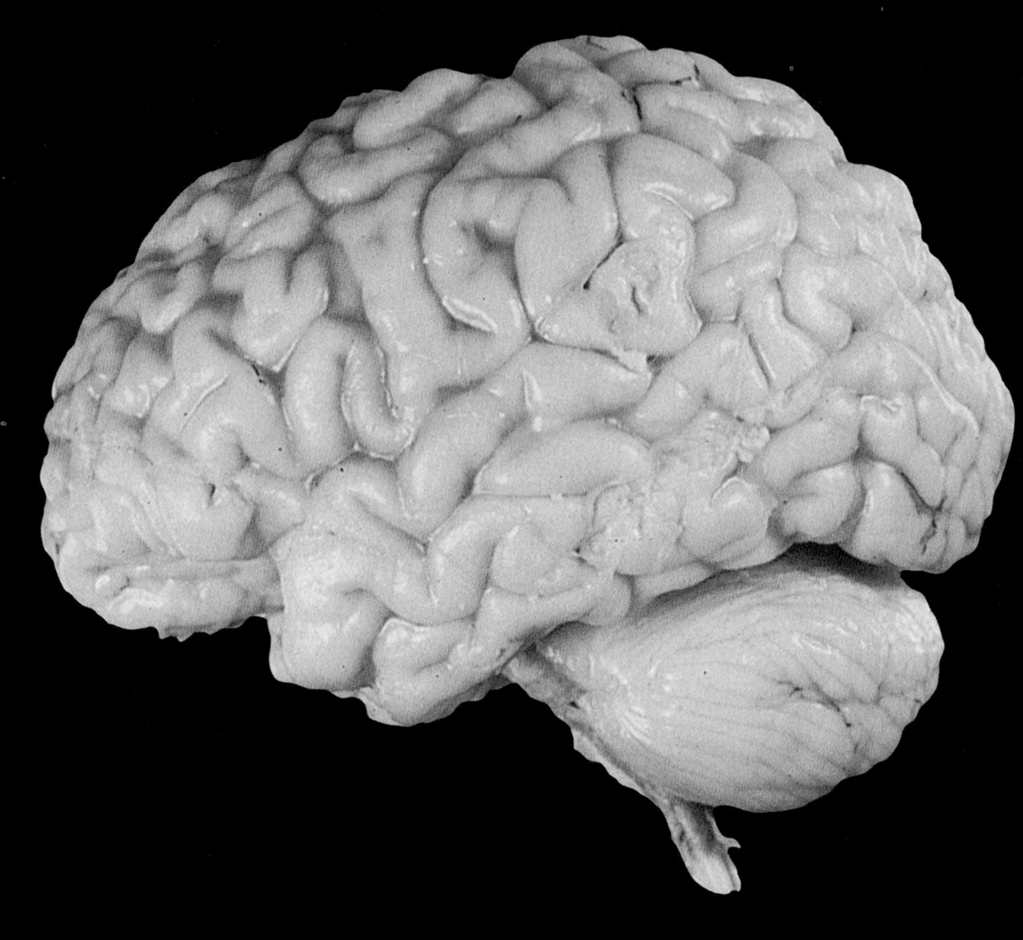

Dr. Dana Copeland

Development and Plasticity of the Brain

5

CHAPTER OUTLINE

OPPOSITE: An enormous amount of brain development has already occurred by the time a person is 1 year old.

MAIN IDEAS

1. Neurons begin by migrating to their proper locations and developing axons, which extend to their correct targets by following chemical pathways.
2. The nervous system at first forms far more neurons than it needs and then eliminates those that do not establish suitable connections or receive sufficient input. It also forms excess synapses and discards the less active ones.
3. Experiences, especially early in life, alter brain anatomy.
4. Many mechanisms contribute to recovery from brain damage, including restoration of undamaged neurons to full activity, regrowth of axons, readjustment of surviving synapses, and behavioral adjustments.

"Some assembly required." Have you ever bought a package with those ominous words? Sometimes, all you have to do is attach a few parts, but other times, you face page after page of barely comprehensible instructions. I remember putting together my daughter's bicycle and wondering how something that looked so simple could be so complicated.

The human nervous system requires an enormous amount of assembly, and the instructions are different from those for a bicycle. Instead of, "Put this piece here and that piece there," the instructions are, "Put these axons here and those dendrites there, and then wait to see what happens. Keep the connections that work the best and discard the others. Continue periodically making new connections and keeping only the successful ones."

Therefore, we say that the brain's anatomy is *plastic;* it is constantly changing, within limits. The brain changes rapidly in early development and continues changing throughout life.

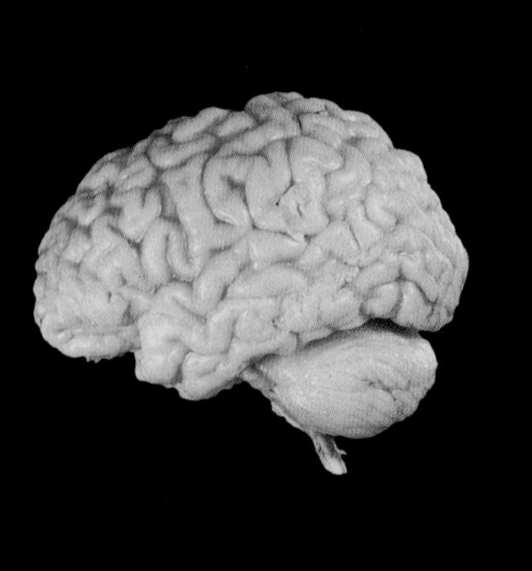

MODULE 5.1

Development of the Brain

Think of all the things you can do that you couldn't have done a few years ago—analyze statistics, read a foreign language, write brilliant critiques of complex issues, and so on. Have you developed these new skills because of brain growth? Many of your dendrites have grown new branches, but your brain as a whole has not grown.

Now think of all the things that 1-year-old children can do that they could not do at birth. Have *they* developed their new skills because of brain growth? To a large extent, yes, but the results depend on experiences as well as growth. As we shall see, many processes of brain development depend on experience in complex ways that blur the distinction between learning and maturation. In this module, we consider how neurons develop, how their axons connect, and how experience modifies development.

Maturation of the Vertebrate Brain

The human central nervous system begins to form when the embryo is about 2 weeks old. The dorsal surface thickens and then long thin lips rise, curl, and merge, forming a neural tube that surrounds a fluid-filled cavity (Figure 5.1). As the tube sinks under the surface of the skin, the forward end enlarges and differentiates into the hindbrain, midbrain, and forebrain (Figure 5.2). The rest becomes the spinal cord. The fluid-filled cavity within the neural tube becomes the central canal of the spinal cord and the four ventricles of the brain, containing the cerebrospinal fluid (CSF). At birth, the average human brain weighs about 350 grams. By the end of the first year, it weighs 1,000 g, close to the adult weight of 1,200 to 1,400 g.

Growth and Development of Neurons

Neuroscientists distinguish these processes in the development of neurons: proliferation, migration, differentiation, myelination, and synaptogenesis. **Proliferation** is the production of new cells. Early in development, the cells lining the ventricles of the brain divide. Some cells remain where they are (as *stem cells*), continuing to divide. Others become primitive neurons and glia that begin migrating to other locations. Neuron proliferation is similar among vertebrates, except for the number of cell divisions. For example, human brains differ from chimpanzee brains mainly because neurons continue proliferating longer in humans (Rakic, 1998; Vrba, 1998). It is possible that the difference between human and chimpanzee brains reflects a small number of genes.

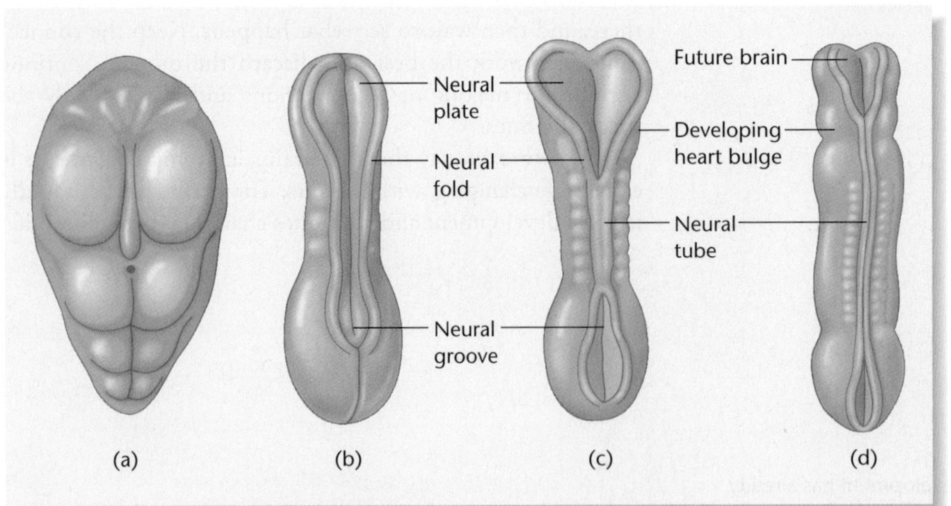

Figure 5.1 Early development of the human central nervous system
The brain and spinal cord begin as folding lips surrounding a fluid-filled canal. The stages shown occur at approximately age 2 to 3 weeks.

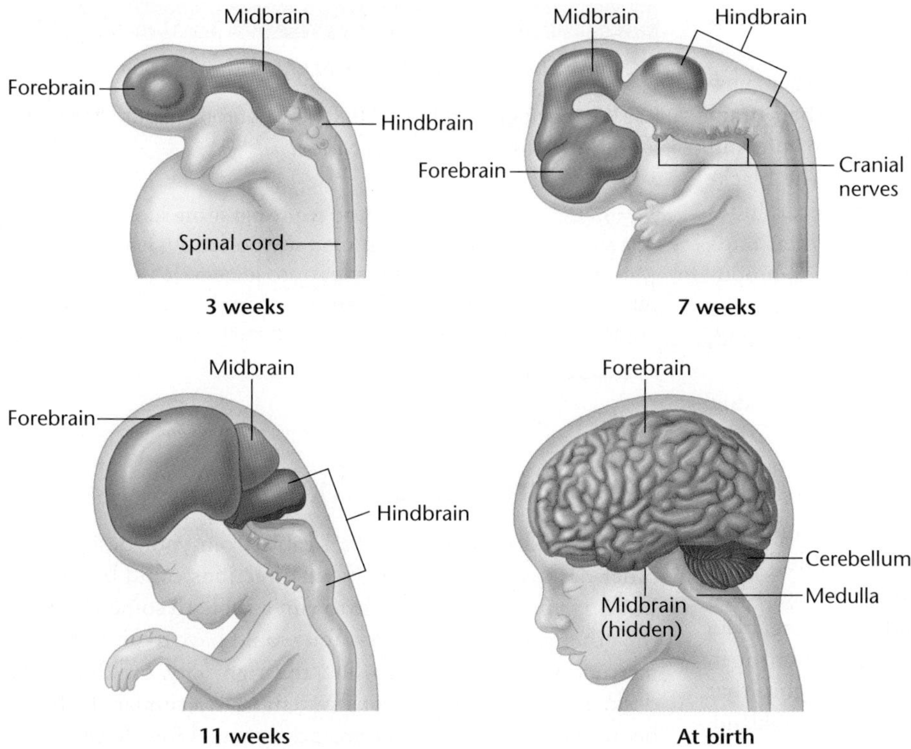

Figure 5.2 Human brain at four stages of development
Chemical processes develop the brain to an amazing degree even before the start of any experience with the world. Detailed changes in development continue to occur throughout life.

After cells have differentiated as neurons or glia, they **migrate** (move). Some neurons migrate much faster than others, and a few of the slowest don't reach their final destinations until adulthood (Ghashghaei, Lai, & Anton, 2007). Some neurons move radially from the inside of the brain to the outside; others move tangentially along the surface of the brain; and some move tangentially and then radially (Nadarajah & Parnavelas, 2002). Chemicals known as *immunoglobulins* and *chemokines* guide neuron migration. A deficit in these chemicals leads to impaired migration, decreased brain size, decreased axon growth, and mental retardation (Berger-Sweeney & Hohmann, 1997; Crossin & Krushel, 2000; Tran & Miller, 2003). On the other extreme, excesses of immunoglobulins have been linked to some cases of schizophrenia (Crossin & Krushel, 2000; Poltorak et al., 1997). The brain has many kinds of immunoglobulins and chemokines, presumably reflecting the complexity of brain development. The existence of so many chemicals implies that brain development can go wrong in many ways, but it also implies that if one chemical is lacking, another can compensate.

At first, a primitive neuron looks like any other cell. Gradually, the neuron **differentiates,** forming its axon and dendrites. The axon grows first. In many cases, a migrating neuron tows its growing axon along like a tail (Gilmour, Knaut, Maischein, & Nüsslein-Volhard, 2004), allowing its tip to remain at or near its target. In other cases, the axon needs to grow toward its target, finding its way through a jungle of other cells and fibers. After the migrating neuron reaches its destination, dendrites begin to form.

A later and slower stage of neuronal development is **myelination,** the process by which glia produce the insulating fatty sheaths that accelerate transmission in many vertebrate axons. Myelin forms first in the spinal cord and then in the hindbrain, midbrain, and forebrain. Unlike the rapid proliferation and migration of neurons, myelination continues gradually for decades (Benes, Turtle, Khan, & Farol, 1994).

The final stage is **synaptogenesis,** or the formation of synapses. Although this process begins before birth, it continues throughout life, as neurons form new synapses and discard old ones. However, the process slows in most older people, as does the formation of new dendritic branches (Buell & Coleman, 1981; Jacobs & Scheibel, 1993).

STOP & CHECK

1. Which develops first, a neuron's axon or its dendrites?

ANSWER

1. The axon forms first.

New Neurons Later in Life

Can the adult vertebrate brain generate new neurons? The traditional belief, dating back to Cajal's work in the late 1800s, was that vertebrate brains formed all their neurons in embryological development or early infancy at the latest. Beyond that point, neurons could modify their shape, but the brain could not develop new neurons. Gradually, researchers found exceptions.

The first were the olfactory receptors, which, because they are exposed to the outside world and its toxic chemicals, have a half-life of only 90 days. **Stem cells** in the nose remain immature throughout life. Periodically, they divide, with one cell remaining immature while the other differentiates to replace a dying olfactory receptor. It grows its axon back to the appropriate site in the brain (Gogos, Osborne, Nemes, Mendelsohn, & Axel, 2000; Graziadei & deHan, 1973). Later researchers also found a similar population of stem cells in the interior of the brain. They sometimes divide to form "daughter" cells that migrate to the olfactory bulb and transform into glia cells or neurons (Gage, 2000).

Still later researchers found evidence of other new neurons. For example, songbirds have an area in their brain necessary for singing, and in this area, old neurons die and new ones take their place (Nottebohm, 2002). The black-capped chickadee, a small North American bird, hides seeds during the late summer and early fall and then finds them during the winter. It grows new neurons in its hippocampus (a brain area important for spatial memory) during the late summer (Smulders, Shiflett, Sperling, & DeVoogd, 2000).

Stem cells also differentiate into new neurons in the adult hippocampus of mammals (Song, Stevens, & Gage, 2002; van Praag et al., 2002). Although these new neurons are not necessary for memory, they facilitate it (Meshi et al., 2006). In general, animals learn most easily when they are young. As they grow older, their neurons become less changeable. Newly formed neurons of the hippocampus go through a stage when they are highly changeable, like those of youth (Ge, Yang, Hsu, Ming, & Song, 2007; Schmidt-Hieber, Jonas, & Bischofberger, 2004). During this period, they integrate into new circuits that represent new memories (Kee, Teixeira, Wang, & Frankland, 2007; Ramirez-Amaya, Marrone, Gage, Worley, & Barnes, 2006). More of the newly formed neurons survive during times of new learning (Tashiro, Makino, & Gage, 2007). A supply of new neurons keeps the hippocampus "young" for learning new tasks. It is also possible that incorporating clusters of new neurons into a single new circuit may be a way of labeling memories that formed at a given time. It might lead to a recollection that certain events happened at the same time (Aimone, Wiles, & Gage, 2006).

New neurons probably do not form in the adult cerebral cortex. Researchers documented this point in a clever way, using a radioactive isotope of carbon, ^{14}C. The concentration of ^{14}C in the atmosphere, compared to other isotopes of carbon, was nearly constant until the era of nuclear bomb testing, which released much radioactivity. That era ended with the test ban treaty of 1963. The concentration of ^{14}C reached a peak in 1963 and has been declining since then. Researchers examined the carbon in the DNA of various cells. Every cell keeps its DNA molecules from its birth until death. When researchers examined people's skin cells, they found a concentration of ^{14}C corresponding to the year in which they did the test. That is, skin cells turn over rapidly, so all of your skin cells are less than a year old. When they examined skeletal muscle cells, they found a ^{14}C concentration corresponding to 15 years ago, indicating that skeletal muscles are replaced slowly, making the average cell 15 years old. When they examined neurons in the cerebral cortex, they found a ^{14}C concentration corresponding to the year of the person's birth. Evidently, the human brain forms few or no new neurons in the cerebral cortex after birth (Spalding, Bhardwaj, Buchholz, Druid, & Frisén, 2005).

STOP & CHECK

2. In which brain areas do new neurons form in adults?

3. What evidence indicated that new neurons seldom or never form in the adult cerebral cortex?

ANSWERS

2. olfactory receptors, neurons in the hippocampus, and neurons in the song-producing areas of some bird species **3.** The ^{14}C concentration in the DNA of cerebral cortex neurons corresponds to the level during the year the person was born, indicating that all or nearly all of those neurons are as old as the person is.

Pathfinding by Axons

If you asked someone to run a cable from your desk to another desk across the room, your directions could be simple. But imagine asking someone to run a cable to somewhere on the other side of the country. You would have to give detailed instructions about how to find the right city, building, and desk. The developing nervous system faces a similar challenge because it sends axons over great distances. How do they find their way?

Chemical Pathfinding by Axons

A famous biologist, Paul Weiss (1924), conducted an experiment in which he grafted an extra leg to a salamander and then waited for axons to grow into it. (Unlike mammals, salamanders and other amphibians accept transplants of extra limbs and generate new axon branches to the extra limbs. Research often requires finding the right species for a given study.) After the axons reached the muscles, the extra leg moved in synchrony with the normal leg next to it.

Weiss dismissed the idea that each axon found its way to exactly the correct muscle in the extra limb. He suggested instead that the nerves attached to muscles at random and then sent a variety of messages, each one tuned to a different muscle. The muscles were like radios tuned to different stations: Each muscle received many signals but responded to only one.

Specificity of Axon Connections

Weiss was wrong. Later evidence supported the interpretation he had rejected: The salamander's extra leg moved in synchrony with its neighbor because each axon found exactly the correct muscle.

Let's consider research on how sensory axons find their way to their correct targets. (The issues are the same as for axons finding their way to muscles.) In one study, Roger Sperry, a former student of Weiss, cut the optic nerves of some newts. The damaged optic nerve grew back and connected with the *tectum*, which is the main visual area of fish, amphibians, reptiles, and birds (Figure 5.3). When the new synapses formed, the newt regained normal vision.

Figure 5.3 Connections from eye to brain in a frog
The optic tectum is a large structure in fish, amphibians, reptiles, and birds. Its location corresponds to the midbrain of mammals, but its function is more elaborate, analogous to what the cerebral cortex does in mammals. Note: Connections from eye to brain are different in humans, as described in Chapter 14. *(After Romer, 1962)*

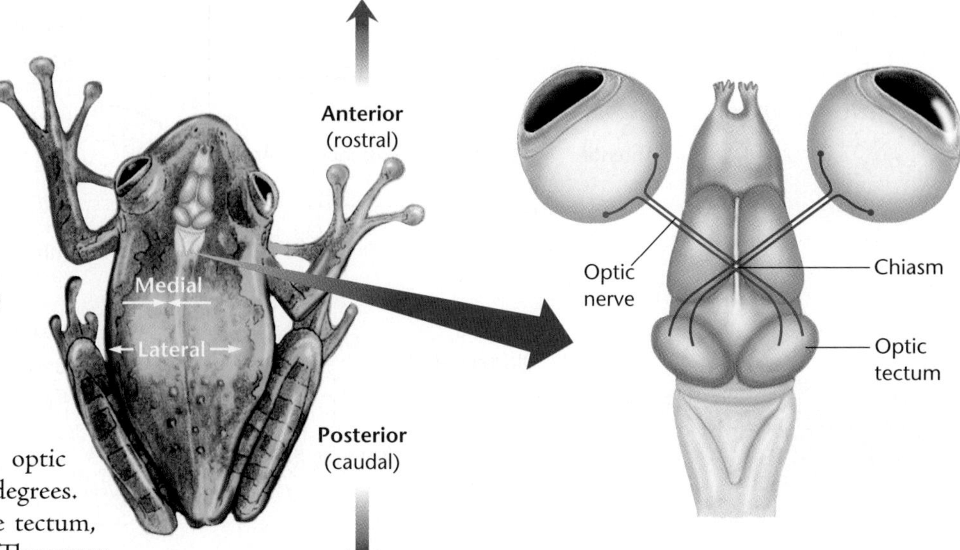

Then Sperry (1943) cut the optic nerve and rotated the eye by 180 degrees. When the axons grew back to the tectum, which targets would they contact? The axons from what had originally been the dorsal portion of the retina (which was now ventral) grew back to the area responsible for vision in the dorsal retina. Axons from what had once been the ventral retina (now dorsal) also grew back to their original targets. The newt now saw the world upside down and backward, responding to stimuli in the sky as if they were on the ground and to stimuli on the left as if they were on the right (Figure 5.4). Each axon regenerated to the area of the tectum where it had originally been, presumably by following a chemical trail.

Courtesy of the Archives, California Institute of Technology

Roger W. Sperry (1913–1994)

When subjective values have objective consequences . . . they become part of the content of science. . . . Science would become the final determinant of what is right and true, the best source and authority available to the human brain for finding ultimate axioms and guideline beliefs to live by, and for reaching an intimate understanding and rapport with the forces that control the universe and created man.

Chemical Gradients

The next question was: How specific is the axon's aim? The current estimate is that humans have only about 30,000 genes total—far too few to provide a specific target for each of the brain's billions of neurons. Nevertheless, axons find their correct targets with remarkable precision (Kozloski, Hamzei-Sichani, & Yuste, 2001). How do they do it?

A growing axon follows a path of cell-surface molecules, attracted by some chemicals and repelled by others, in a process that steers the axon in the correct direction (Yu & Bargmann, 2001). Some axons follow a trail based on one attractive chemical until they reach an intermediate location where they become insensitive to that chemical and start following a different attractant (Shirasaki, Katsumata, & Murakami, 1998; H. Wang & Tessier-Lavigne, 1999). Eventually, axons sort themselves over the surface of their target area by following a gradient of chemicals. For example, one chemical in the amphibian tectum is a protein known as TOP_{DV} (TOP for *top*ography; DV for *d*orso*v*entral). This protein is 30 times more concentrated in the axons of the dorsal retina than of the ventral retina and 10 times more concentrated in the ventral tectum than in the dorsal tectum. As axons from the retina grow toward the tectum, the retinal axons with the greatest concentration of TOP_{DV} connect to the tectal cells with the highest concentration of that chemical. The axons with the lowest concentration connect to the tectal cells with the lowest concentration. A similar gradient of another protein aligns the axons along the anterior–posterior axis (J. R. Sanes, 1993) (Figure 5.5). By analogy, you could think of men lining up from tallest to shortest, pairing up with women who lined up from tallest to shortest.

STOP & CHECK

4. What was Sperry's evidence that axons grow to a specific target instead of attaching at random?
5. If all cells in an amphibian's tectum produced the same amount of TOP_{DV}, what would be the effect on the attachment of axons?

ANSWERS

4. Sperry found that if he cut a newt's eye and inverted it, axons grew back to their original targets, even though they were inappropriate to their new position on the eye. **5.** Axons would attach haphazardly instead of arranging themselves according to their dorsoventral position on the retina.

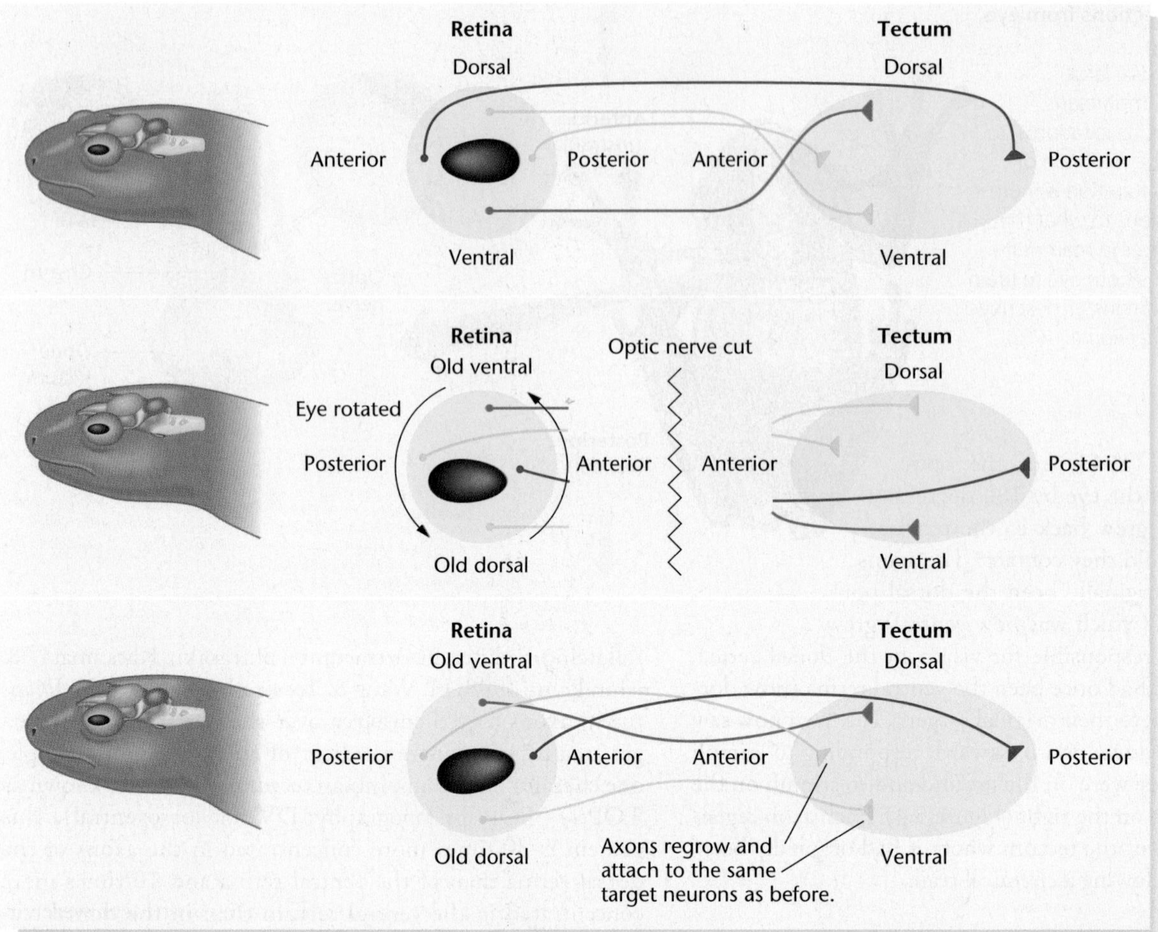

Figure 5.4 Summary of Sperry's experiment on nerve connections in newts
After he cut the optic nerve and inverted the eye, the optic nerve axons grew back to their original targets, not to the targets corresponding to the eye's current position.

Competition Among Axons as a General Principle

As you might guess from the experiments just described, when axons initially reach their targets, each one forms synapses onto many cells in approximately the correct location, and each target cell receives synapses from many axons. At first, axons make trial connections with many postsynaptic cells, and then each postsynaptic cell strengthens some synapses and eliminates others (Hua & Smith, 2004). Even at the earliest stages, this fine-tuning depends on the pattern of input from incoming axons (Catalano & Shatz, 1998). For example, one part of the thalamus receives input from many retinal axons. During embryological development, long before the first exposure to light, repeated waves of spontaneous activity sweep over the retina from one side to the other. Consequently, axons from adjacent areas of the retina send almost simultaneous messages to the thalamus. Each thalamic neuron selects a group of axons that are simultaneously active. In

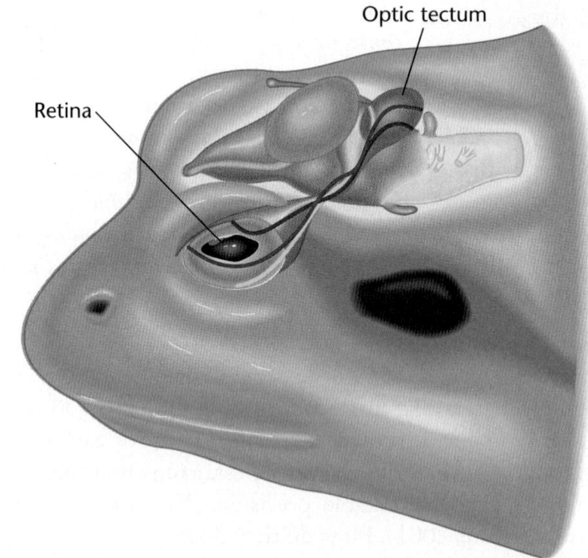

Figure 5.5 Retinal axons match up with neurons in the tectum by following two gradients
The protein TOP_{DV} is concentrated mostly in the dorsal retina and the ventral tectum. Axons rich in TOP_{DV} attach to tectal neurons that are also rich in that chemical. Similarly, a second protein directs axons from the posterior retina to the anterior portion of the tectum.

this way, it finds receptors from adjacent regions of the retina (Meister, Wong, Baylor, & Shatz, 1991). It then rejects synapses from other locations.

Carla J. Shatz
The functioning of the brain depends upon the precision and patterns of its neural circuits. How is this amazing computational machine assembled and wired during development? The biological answer is so much more wonderful than anticipated! The adult precision is sculpted from an early imprecise pattern by a process in which connections are verified by the functioning of the neurons themselves. Thus, the developing brain is not simply a miniature version of the adult. Moreover, the brain works to wire itself, rather than assembling itself first and then flipping a switch, as might happen in the assembly of a computer. This kind of surprise in scientific discovery opens up new vistas of understanding and possibility and makes the process of doing science infinitely exciting and fascinating.

To some theorists, these results suggest a general principle, called *neural Darwinism* (Edelman, 1987). In the development of the nervous system, we start with more neurons and synapses than we keep. Synapses form haphazardly, and then a selection process keeps some and rejects others. The most successful axons and combinations survive, and the others fail. The principle of competition among axons is an important one, although we should use the analogy with Darwinian evolution cautiously. Mutations in the genes are random events, but neurotrophins steer new axonal branches and synapses in the right direction.

STOP & CHECK

6. If axons from the retina were prevented from showing spontaneous activity during early development, what would be the probable effect on development of the lateral geniculate?

ANSWER

6. The axons would attach based on a chemical gradient but could not fine-tune their adjustment based on experience. Therefore, the connections would be less precise.

Determinants of Neuronal Survival

Getting just the right number of neurons for each area of the nervous system is more complicated than it might seem. Consider a specific example. The sympathetic nervous system sends axons to muscles and glands. Each ganglion has enough axons to supply the muscles and glands in its area, with no axons left over. How does the match come out so exact? Long ago, one explanation was that the muscles sent chemical messages to tell the sympathetic ganglion how many neurons to form. Rita Levi-Montalcini was largely responsible for disconfirming this hypothesis.

Erich Hartmann/Magnum Photos New York

Rita Levi-Montalcini
Many years later, I often asked myself how we could have dedicated ourselves with such enthusiasm to solving this small neuroembryological problem while German armies were advancing throughout Europe, spreading destruction and death wherever they went and threatening the very survival of Western civilization. The answer lies in the desperate and partially unconscious desire of human beings to ignore what is happening in situations where full awareness might lead one to self-destruction.

Levi-Montalcini's early life would seem most unfavorable for a scientific career. She was a young Italian Jewish woman during the Nazi era. World War II destroyed the Italian economy, and almost everyone at the time discouraged women from scientific or medical careers. She had to spend several years in hiding during the war. Furthermore, the research projects assigned to her as a young medical student were virtually impossible, as she described in her autobiography (Levi-Montalcini, 1988). Nevertheless, she developed a love for research and eventually discovered that the muscles do not determine how many axons *form;* they determine how many *survive.*

Initially, the sympathetic nervous system forms far more neurons than it needs. When one of its neurons forms a synapse onto a muscle, that muscle delivers a protein called **nerve growth factor (NGF)** that promotes the survival and growth of the axon (Levi-Montalcini, 1987). An axon that does not receive NGF degenerates, and its cell body dies. That is, each neuron starts life with a "suicide program": If its axon does not make contact with an appropriate postsynaptic cell by a certain age, the neuron kills itself through a process called **apoptosis,**[1] a programmed mechanism of cell death. (Apoptosis is distinct from *necrosis,* which is death caused by an injury or a toxic substance.) NGF cancels the program for apoptosis; it is the postsynaptic cell's way of telling the incoming axon, "I'll be your partner. Don't kill yourself."

The brain's system of overproducing neurons and then applying apoptosis enables the CNS to match the number of incoming axons to the number of receiving cells. For example, when the sympathetic nervous system begins sending axons

[1] Apoptosis is based on the Greek root *ptosis* (meaning "dropping"), which is pronounced TOE-sis. Therefore, most scholars insist that the second *p* in *apoptosis* should be silent, a-po-TOE-sis. Others argue that *helicopter* is also derived from a root with a silent *p (pteron),* but we pronounce the *p* in *helicopter,* so we should also pronounce the second *p* in *apoptosis.* Be prepared for either pronunciation.

toward the muscles and glands, it has no way to know the exact size of the muscles or glands. It makes more neurons than necessary and discards the excess.

Nerve growth factor is a **neurotrophin,** a chemical that promotes the survival and activity of neurons. (The word *trophin* derives from a Greek word for "nourishment.") In addition to NGF, the nervous system responds to *brain-derived neurotrophic factor* (BDNF) and several other neurotrophins (Airaksinen & Saarma, 2002). BDNF is the most abundant neurotrophin in the adult cerebral cortex. Remember it, because it becomes important again in Chapter 15 on depression and schizophrenia.

For an immature neuron to avoid apoptosis and survive, it needs to receive neurotrophins not only from its target cells but also from incoming axons. In one study, researchers examined mice with a genetic defect that prevented all release of neurotransmitters. The brains initially assembled normal anatomies, but then neurons started dying rapidly (Verhage et al., 2000). When neurons release neurotransmitters, they also release neurotrophins. Neurons that fail to receive neurotransmitters fail to receive neurotrophins, and so they die (Poo, 2001).

All areas of the developing nervous system initially make far more neurons than will survive into adulthood. Each brain area has a period of massive cell death, becoming littered with dead and dying cells (Figure 5.6). This loss of cells is a natural part of development (Finlay & Pallas, 1989). In fact, loss of cells in a particular brain area can indicate development and maturation. For example, teenagers lose cells in parts of the prefrontal cortex while showing increased neuronal activity in those areas (Sowell, Thompson, Holmes, Jernigan, & Toga, 1999) and sharp improvements in the kinds of memory that depend on those areas (D. A. Lewis, 1997). Evidently, maturation of appropriate cells is linked to simultaneous loss of less successful ones.

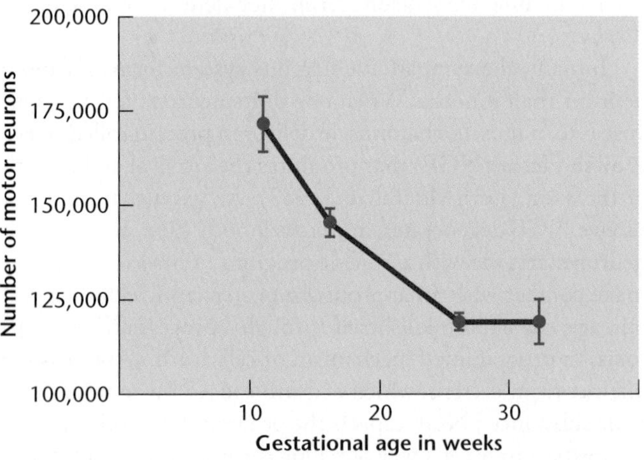

Figure 5.6 Cell loss during development of the nervous system
The graph shows the number of motor neurons in the ventral spinal cord of human fetuses. Note that the number of motor neurons is highest at 11 weeks and drops steadily until about 25 weeks, the age when motor neuron axons make synapses with muscles. Axons that fail to make synapses die. *(From N. G. Forger and S. M. Breedlove, Motoneuronal death in the human fetus.* Journal of Comparative Neurology, 264, *1987, 118–122. Copyright © 1987 Alan R. Liss, Inc. Reprinted by permission of N. G. Forger.)*

After maturity, the apoptotic mechanisms become dormant, except under traumatic conditions such as stroke (Benn & Woolf, 2004; G. S. Walsh, Orike, Kaplan, & Miller, 2004). Although adults no longer need neurotrophins for neuron survival, they do use them for other functions, especially for altering the branching of axons and dendrites (Baquet, Gorski, & Jones, 2004; Kesslak, So, Choi, Cotman, & Gomez-Pinilla, 1998; Kolb, Côté, Ribeiro-da-Silva, & Cuello, 1997). With a deficiency of neurotrophins, cortical neurons and their dendrites shrink (J. A. Gorski, Zeiler, Tamowski, & Jones, 2003).

STOP & CHECK

7. What process assures that the spinal cord has the right number of axons to innervate all the muscle cells?
8. What class of chemicals prevents apoptosis?
9. At what age does a person have the greatest number of neurons—before birth, during childhood, during adolescence, or during adulthood?

ANSWERS

7. The nervous system builds far more neurons than it needs and discards through apoptosis those that do not make lasting synapses. **8.** neurotrophins, such as nerve growth factor **9.** The neuron number is greatest before birth.

The Vulnerable Developing Brain

According to Lewis Wolpert (1991), "It is not birth, marriage, or death, but gastrulation, which is truly the most important time of your life." (Gastrulation is one of the early stages of embryological development.) Wolpert's point was that if you mess up in early development, you will have problems from then on. Actually, if you mess up badly during gastrulation, your life is over.

The early stages of brain development are critical. The developing brain is highly vulnerable to malnutrition, toxic chemicals, and infections that would produce only mild problems at later ages. For example, impaired thyroid function produces lethargy in adults but mental retardation in infants. (Thyroid deficiency was common in the past because of iodine deficiency. It is rare today because table salt is fortified with iodine.) A fever is a mere annoyance to an adult, but it impairs neuron proliferation in a fetus (Laburn, 1996). Low blood glucose decreases an adult's pep, but before birth, it impairs brain development (C. A. Nelson et al., 2000).

The infant brain is highly vulnerable to damage by alcohol. Children of mothers who drink heavily during pregnancy are born with **fetal alcohol syndrome,** a condition marked by

Bill Roth/AP Photo

Figure 5.7 Child with fetal alcohol syndrome
Note the facial pattern. Many children exposed to smaller amounts of alcohol before birth have behavioral deficits without facial signs.

hyperactivity, impulsiveness, difficulty maintaining attention, varying degrees of mental retardation, motor problems, heart defects, and facial abnormalities (Figure 5.7). Most dendrites are short with few branches.

When children with fetal alcohol syndrome reach adulthood, they have an increased risk of alcoholism, drug dependence, depression, and other psychiatric disorders (Famy, Streissguth, & Unis, 1998). Even in milder cases, those who were exposed to prenatal alcohol show impairments in learning, memory, language, and attention (Kodituwakku, 2007). The mechanism of fetal alcohol syndrome probably relates to apoptosis: Remember that to prevent apoptosis, a neuron must receive neurotrophins from the incoming axons as well as from its own axon's target cell. Alcohol suppresses the release of glutamate, the brain's main excitatory transmitter, and enhances activity of GABA, the main inhibitory transmitter. Consequently, many neurons receive less excitation and neurotrophins than normal, and they undergo apoptosis (Ikonomidou et al., 2000).

Prenatal exposure to other substances can be dangerous, too. On the average, children of mothers who use cocaine during pregnancy show a decrease in language skills compared to other children, a slight decrease in IQ scores, and impaired hearing (P. A. Fried, Watkinson, & Gray, 2003; Lester, LaGasse, & Seifer, 1998). Children of mothers who smoked during pregnancy are at increased risk of attention-deficit disorder, aggressive behavior, and impaired memory and intelligence (Huizink & Mulder, 2005). Because these are correlational studies, we cannot be sure of cause and effect. Mothers who smoke or use other substances tend to be of lower socioeconomic status, less educated, and so forth, so the effect of smoking is probably smaller than the results suggest (Thapar et al., 2003). However, controlled experiments with rats confirm that early exposure to nicotine produces long-term emotional effects (Huang, Liu, Griffith, & Winzer-Serhan, 2007).

Finally, the immature brain is highly responsive to influences from the mother. If a mother rat is exposed to stressful experiences, she becomes more fearful, she spends less than the usual amount of time licking and grooming her offspring, and her offspring become permanently more fearful in a variety of situations (Cameron et al., 2005). Analogously, the children of impoverished and abused women have, on the average, increased problems in both their academic and social lives. The mechanisms in humans are not exactly the same as those in rats, but the overall principles are similar: Stress to the mother changes her behavior in ways that change her offspring's behavior.

STOP & CHECK

10. Anesthetic drugs increase inhibition of neurons, blocking most action potentials. Why would we predict that exposure to anesthetics might be dangerous to the brain of a fetus?

ANSWER

10. Prolonged exposure to anesthetics might produce effects similar to fetal alcohol syndrome. Fetal alcohol syndrome occurs because alcohol increases inhibition and therefore increases apoptosis of developing neurons.

Differentiation of the Cortex

Neurons in different parts of the brain differ from one another in their shapes and chemical components. When and how does a neuron "decide" which kind of neuron it is going to be? It is not a sudden decision. Immature neurons experimentally transplanted from one part of the developing cortex to another develop the properties characteristic of their new location (S. K. McConnell, 1992). However, neurons transplanted at a slightly later stage develop some new properties while retaining some old ones (Cohen-Tannoudji, Babinet, & Wassef, 1994). The result resembles the speech of immigrant children: Those who enter a country when very young master the correct pronunciation, whereas older children retain an accent.

In one fascinating experiment, researchers explored what would happen to the immature auditory portions of the brain if they received input from the eyes instead of the ears. Ferrets—mammals in the weasel family—are born so immature that their optic nerves (from the eyes) have not yet reached the thalamus. On one side of the brain, researchers damaged the superior colliculus and the occipital cortex, the two main targets for the optic nerves. On that side, they also damaged the inferior colliculus, a major source of auditory input. Therefore, the optic nerve, unable to attach to its usual target, attached to the auditory area of the thalamus, which lacked its usual input. The result was that the parts of the thalamus and cortex that usually receive input from the ears now received input only from the eyes. Which would you guess happened? Did the visual input cause auditory sensations, or did the auditory cortex turn into a visual cortex?

The result, surprising to many, was this: What would have been auditory thalamus and cortex reorganized, developing some (but not all) of the characteristic appearance of a visual cortex (Sharma, Angelucci, & Sur, 2000). But how do we know whether the animals treated that activity as vision? Remember that the researchers performed these procedures on one side of the brain. They left the other side intact. The researchers presented stimuli to the normal side of the brain and trained the ferrets to turn one direction when they heard something and the other direction when they saw a light, as shown in Figure 5.8. After the ferrets learned this task well, the researchers presented a light that the rewired side could see. The result: The ferrets turned the way they had been taught to turn when they saw something. In short, the rewired temporal cortex, receiving input from the optic nerve, produced visual responses (von Melchner, Pallas, & Sur, 2000).

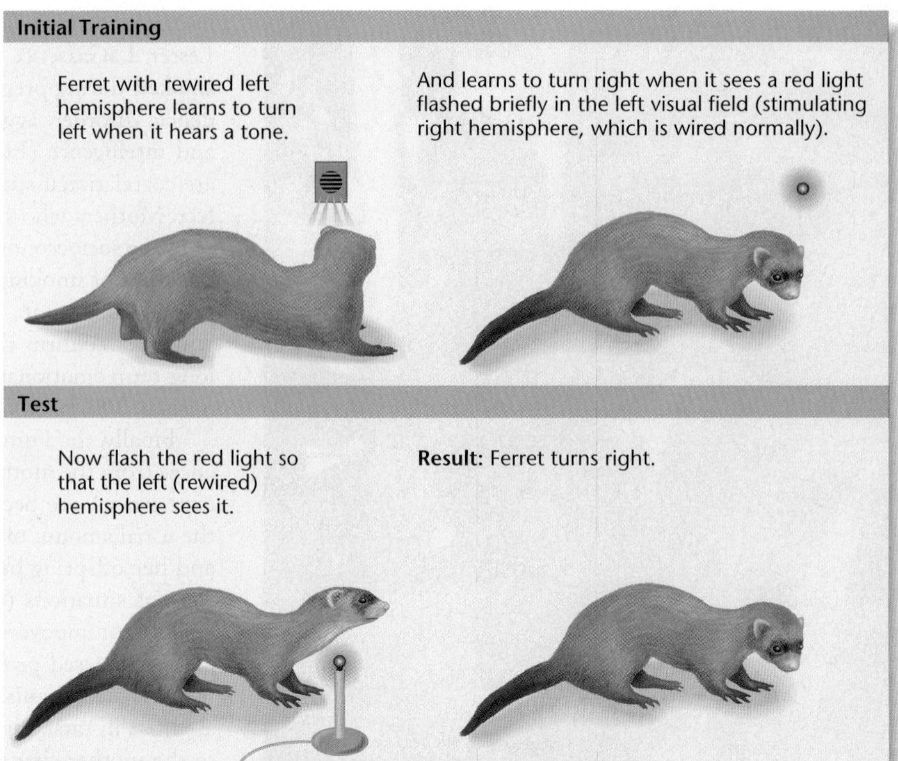

Initial Training
Ferret with rewired left hemisphere learns to turn left when it hears a tone.
And learns to turn right when it sees a red light flashed briefly in the left visual field (stimulating right hemisphere, which is wired normally).
Test
Now flash the red light so that the left (rewired) hemisphere sees it.
Result: Ferret turns right.

Figure 5.8 Behavior of a ferret with rewired temporal cortex
First, the normal (right) hemisphere is trained to respond to a red light by turning to the right. Then, the rewired (left) hemisphere is tested with a red light. The fact that the ferret turns to the right indicates that it regards the stimulus as light, not sound.

STOP & CHECK

11. In the ferret study, how did the experimenters determine that visual input to the auditory portions of the brain actually produced a visual sensation?

ANSWER

11. They trained the ferrets to respond to stimuli on the normal side, turning one direction in response to sounds and the other direction to lights. Then they presented light to the rewired side and saw that the ferret again turned in the direction it had associated with lights.

Fine-Tuning by Experience

The blueprints for a house determine its overall plan, but because architects can't anticipate every detail, construction workers sometimes have to improvise. The same is true, only more so, for your nervous system. Because of the unpredictability of life, our brains have evolved the ability to remodel themselves (within limits) in response to our experience (Shatz, 1992).

Experience and Dendritic Branching

Decades ago, researchers doubted that adult neurons substantially changed their shape. We now know that axons and dendrites continue to modify their structure throughout life. Dale Purves and R. D. Hadley (1985) developed a method of injecting a dye that enabled them to examine the structure of a living neuron at different times, days to weeks apart. They demonstrated that some dendritic branches extended between one viewing and another, whereas others retracted or disappeared (Figure 5.9). About 6% of dendritic spines appear or disappear within a month (Xu, Pan, Yang, & Gan, 2007). The gain or loss of spines means a turnover of synapses, which probably relates to learning. As animals grow older, they continue altering the anatomy of their neurons but more slowly (Gan, Kwon, Feng, Sanes, & Lichtman, 2003; Grutzendler, Kasthuri, & Gan, 2002).

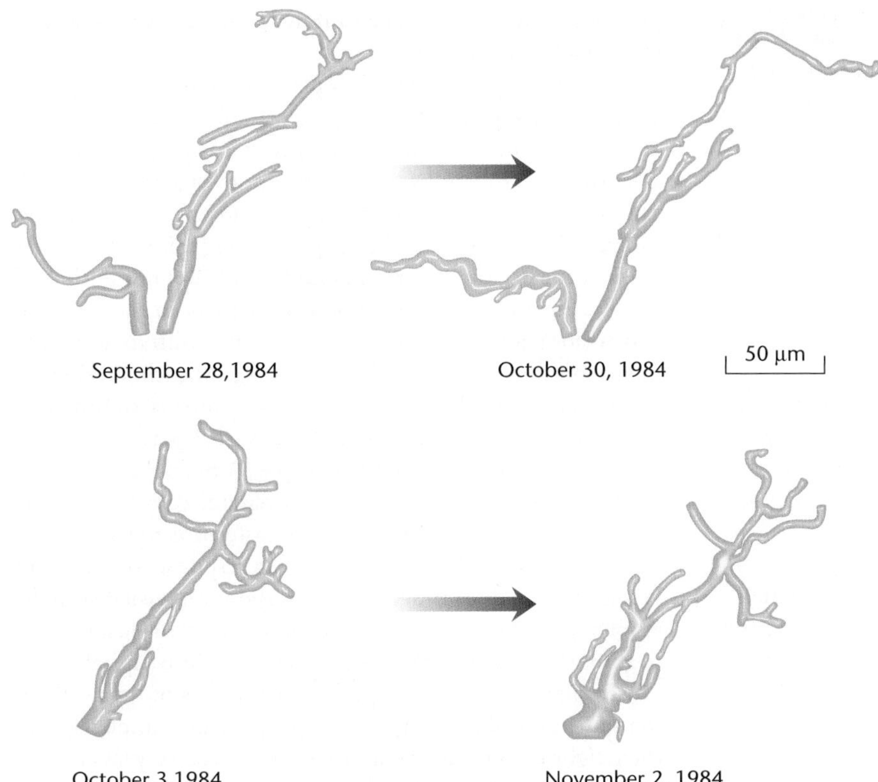

Figure 5.9 Changes over time in dendritic trees of two neurons
During a month, some branches elongated and others retracted. The shape of the neuron is in flux even during adulthood. *(Reprinted from "Changes in Dendritic Branching of Adult Mammalian Neurons Revealed by Repeated Imaging in Situ," by D. Purves and R. D. Hadley,* Nature, 315, *pp. 404–406. Copyright © 1985 Macmillan Magazines, Ltd. Reprinted by permission of D. Purves and Macmillan Magazines, Ltd.)*

Experiences guide the neuronal changes. Let's start with a simple example. Decades ago, it was typical for a laboratory rat to live alone in a small gray cage. Imagine by contrast 10 rats in a larger cage with a few pieces of junk to explore. Researchers called this an enriched environment, but it was enriched only in contrast to the deprived experience of a typical rat cage. A rat in the more stimulating environment developed a thicker cortex, more dendritic branching, and improved learning (Greenough, 1975; Rosenzweig & Bennett, 1996). Many of its neurons became more finely tuned, responding to a narrower range of stimuli (Polley, Kvasnák, & Frostig, 2004). An enriched environment enhances sprouting of axons and dendrites in a wide variety of other species also (Coss, Brandon, & Globus, 1980) (Figure 5.10). (As a result of this research, most rats today are kept in a more enriched environment than was typical in the past.)

We might suppose that the neuronal changes in an enriched environment depend on new and interesting experiences, and many of them do. For example, after practice of particular skills, the connections relevant to those skills proliferate, while other connections retract. Nevertheless, much—though not all—of the enhancement produced by the enriched environment is due to the fact that rats in a group cage are more active. Using a running wheel also enhances growth of axons and dendrites, even for rats in isolation (Pietropaolo, Feldon, Alleva, Cirulli, & Yee, 2006; Rhodes et al., 2003; van Praag, Kempermann, & Gage, 1999). In addition, activity improves learning and memory (Van der Borght, Havekes, Bos, Eggen, & Van der Zee, 2007). Neuronal changes have also been demonstrated in humans as a function of physical activity—such as daily practice of juggling balls, in one case (Draganski et al., 2004).

The advice to exercise for your brain's sake is particularly important for older people. On the average, the thickness of the cerebral cortex declines with advancing age, beginning at age 30 and accelerating in later years (Sowell et al., 2003). Neurons also become less active, partly because of decreased blood flow (Vaidya, Paradiso, Ponto, McCormick, & Robinson, 2007). However, brain volume and activity decline somewhat less in people who remain mentally active (Schooler, 2007) and much less in people who remain physically active (Colcombe et al., 2003). In one study, people older than 60 who were randomly assigned to participate in 6 months of aerobic exercise developed significantly greater thickness of the cortex, especially in the frontal lobes (Colcombe et al., 2006).

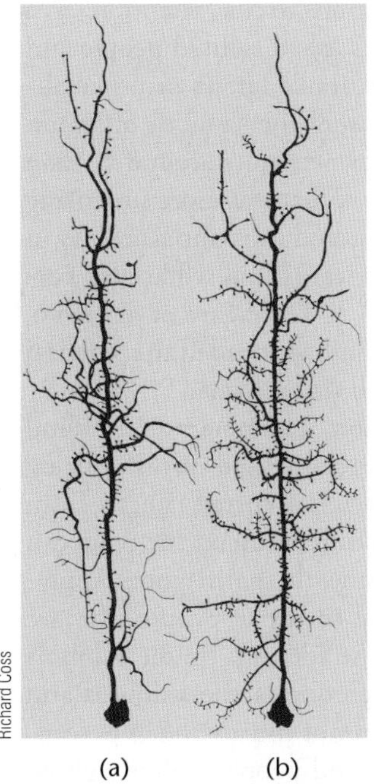

Figure 5.10 Effect of a stimulating environment on neuronal branching
(a) A jewel fish reared in isolation develops neurons with fewer branches. **(b)** A fish reared with others has more neuronal branches.

STOP & CHECK

12. An enriched environment promotes growth of axons and dendrites. What is known to be one important reason for this effect?

ANSWER

12. Animals in an enriched environment are more active, and their exercise enhances growth of axons and dendrites.

Effects of Special Experiences

Neurons become more responsive and more finely tuned to stimuli that have been important or meaningful in the past (e.g., Fritz, Shamma, Elhilali, & Klein, 2003; L. I. Zhang, Bao, & Merzenich, 2001). How much plasticity might occur after experiences that are far different from the average?

Brain Adaptations in People Blind Since Infancy

One way to ask this question is to consider what happens to the brain if one sensory system is impaired. Recall the experiment on ferrets, in which axons of the visual system, unable to contact their normal targets, attached instead to the brain areas usually devoted to hearing and managed to convert them into more or less satisfactory visual areas (p. 132). Might anything similar happen in the brains of people born deaf or blind?

People often say that blind people become better than usual at touch and hearing or that deaf people develop a finer sense of touch and vision. Those statements are true in a way, but we need to be more specific. Losing a sense does not affect the receptors of other sense organs. For example, being blind does not change the touch receptors in the fingers. However, losing a sense does increase attention to other senses, and eventually, the brain shows adaptations to that attention.

In several studies, investigators asked sighted people and people blind since infancy to feel Braille letters or other objects and say whether two items were the same or different. On the average, blind people performed more accurately than sighted people, to no one's surprise. What was more surprising was that PET and fMRI scans indicated substantial activity in the occipital cortex of people who were blind while they performed these tasks (Burton et al., 2002; Sadato et al., 1996, 1998). Evidently, touch information had invaded this cortical area, which is ordinarily devoted to vision alone.

To double-check this conclusion, researchers asked blind and sighted people to perform the same kind of task during temporary inactivation of the occipital cortex. Recall from Chapter 4 that intense magnetic stimulation on the scalp can temporarily inactivate neurons beneath the magnet. Applying this procedure to the occipital cortex of people who are blind interferes with their ability to identify Braille symbols or to notice the difference between one tactile stimulus and another. The same procedure does not impair touch perception in sighted people. In short, blind people, unlike sighted people, use the occipital cortex to help identify what they feel (L. G. Cohen et al., 1997).

On the average, blind people also outperform sighted people on many verbal skills. (If you can't see, you pay more attention to what you hear, including words.) One example is the task, "When you hear the name of an object (e.g., *apple*), say as quickly as possible the name of an appropriate action for that object (e.g., *eat*)." Again, performing this task activates parts of the occipital cortex in blind people but not in sighted people. Furthermore, the amount of activity in the occipital cortex (for people who are blind) correlates with their performance on the task (Amedi, Raz, Pianka, Malach, & Zohary, 2003). Inactivating the occipital cortex by intense transcranial magnetic stimulation interferes with verbal performance by blind people but not by sighted people (Amedi, Floel, Knecht, Zohary, & Cohen, 2004). So the occipital cortex of people who are blind serves verbal functions as well as touch.

As the occipital cortex increases its response to touch and verbal stimuli, does it decrease its response to visual stimuli? Applying brief transcranial magnetic stimulation (just enough to stimulate, not enough to inactivate) over the occipital cortex causes sighted people to report seeing flashes of light. When the same procedure is applied to people who completely lost their sight because of eye injuries more than 10 years earlier, most report seeing nothing or seeing flashes only rarely or in a few locations (Gothe et al., 2002). Note that this experiment used people who once had normal vision and then lost it, because researchers can ask them whether they see anything. Someone blind since birth presumably would not understand the question.

STOP & CHECK

13. Name two kinds of evidence indicating that touch information from the fingers invades the occipital cortex of people blind since birth.

ANSWER

13. First, brain scans indicate increased activity in the occipital cortex while blind people perform tasks such as feeling two objects and saying whether they are the same or different. Second, temporary inactivation of the occipital cortex blocks blind people's ability to perform that task, without affecting the ability of sighted people.

Effects of Music Training

Extensive practice of a skill, such as playing chess, makes someone more adept at that skill (Ericsson & Charness, 1994). In a few cases, researchers have begun to explore the relevant brain changes. The study of musicians has become especially popular. Professional musicians and serious music students practice 4 or more hours per day. The results include major changes in brain structure and function.

One study used magnetoencephalography (MEG, as described in Chapter 4) to record responses of the auditory cortex to pure tones. The responses in professional musicians were about twice as strong as those in nonmusicians. An examination of their brains, using MRI, found that one area of the temporal cortex in the right hemisphere was about 30% larger in the professional musicians (Schneider et al., 2002). Other studies found that subcortical brain structures also respond faster and more vigorously to music and speech sounds in musicians than in nonmusicians (Musacchia, Sams, Skoe, & Kraus, 2007). Subcortical changes help musicians attend to key sounds in tonal languages. For example, in Chinese, *nián* (with a rising tone) means year, and *niàn* (with a falling tone) means study. Musicians learn to attend to these differences faster than do other people (Wong, Skoe, Russo, Dees, & Kraus, 2007).

Another study used MRI to compare the entire brains of professional keyboard players, amateur keyboard players, and nonmusicians. Several areas showed that gray matter was thicker in the professionals than in the amateurs and thicker in the amateurs than in the nonmusicians, including the structures highlighted in Figure 5.11 (Gaser & Schlaug, 2003). The most strongly affected areas related to hand control and vision (which is important for reading music). A related study on stringed instrument players found that a larger than normal section of the postcentral gyrus in the right hemisphere was devoted to representing the fingers of the left hand, which they use to control the strings (Elbert, Pantev, Wienbruch, Rockstroh, & Taub, 1995). The area devoted to the left fingers was largest in those who began their music practice early (and therefore also continued for more years).

These results suggest that practicing a skill reorganizes the brain to maximize performance of that skill. However, an alternative hypothesis is that people who already had certain cognitive skills and brain features are more likely than others to become musicians. One way to address that question is with a longitudinal study. Researchers examined 39 five- to seven-year-olds who were beginning piano or string lessons and 31 other children not taking music lessons. At the time, neither brain scans nor cognitive tests showed any significant difference between the two groups (Norton et al., 2005). The researchers hope to study these individuals repeatedly in coming years to see whether any children who continue with their music lessons gradually develop the cognitive and brain features that are characteristic of musicians.

Another issue is whether music training produces bigger effects if it begins early in life, while the brain is more easily modified. Several studies have found major differences between young adults who started music training in childhood and those who began as teenagers. However, those studies do not separate the effects of age at starting from those of total years of practice. A later study compared young musicians who had started music training before age 7 with somewhat older musicians who had started later but continued for just as many years. The result was that those who started younger had the advantage on several tasks (Watanabe, Savion-Lemieux, & Penhune, 2007).

STOP & CHECK

14. Which brain area shows expanded representation of the left hand in people who began practicing stringed instruments in childhood and continued for many years?

ANSWER

14. postcentral gyrus of the right hemisphere

When Brain Reorganization Goes Too Far

Ordinarily, the expanded cortical representation of personally important information is beneficial. However, in extreme cases, the reorganization creates problems. As mentioned, when people play string instruments many hours a day for years, the representation of the left hand increases in the somatosensory cortex. Similar processes occur in people who play piano and other instruments.

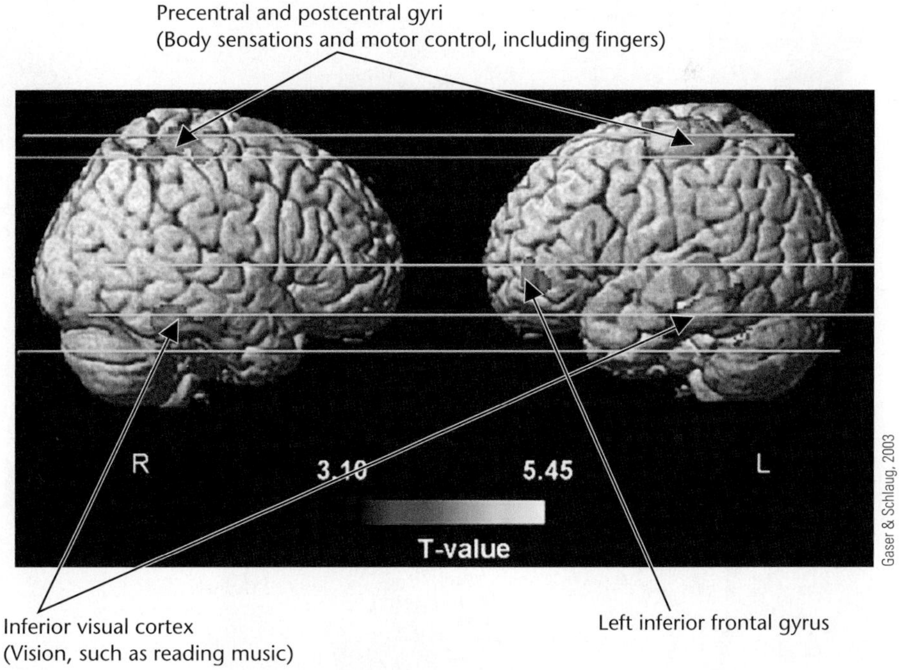

Figure 5.11 Brain correlates of extensive music practice
Areas marked in red showed thicker gray matter among professional keyboard players than in amateurs and thicker gray matter among amateurs than in nonmusicians. Areas marked in yellow showed even stronger differences in that same direction.

Imagine the normal representation of the fingers in the cortex:

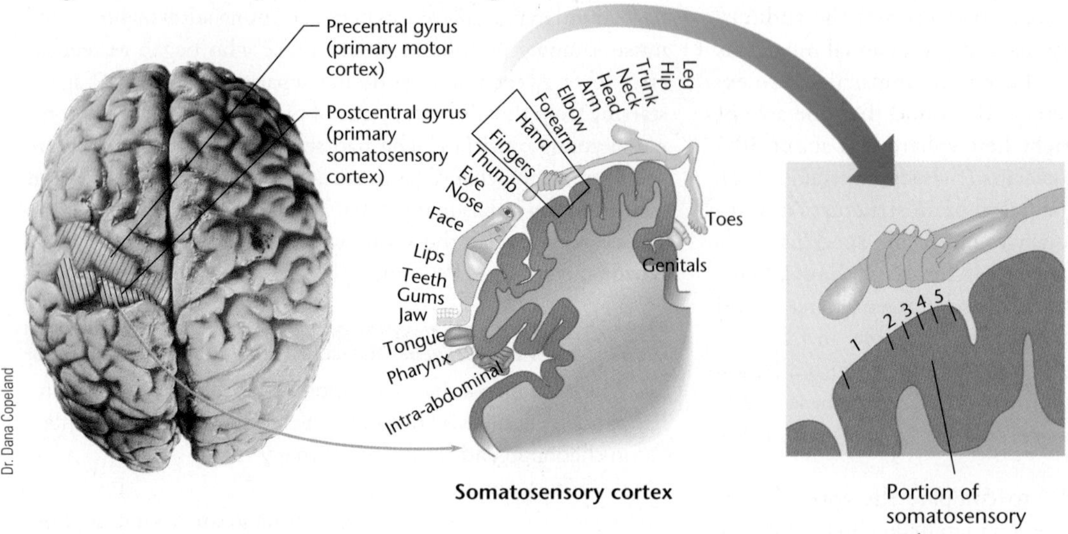

With extensive musical practice, the expanding representations of the fingers might spread out like this:

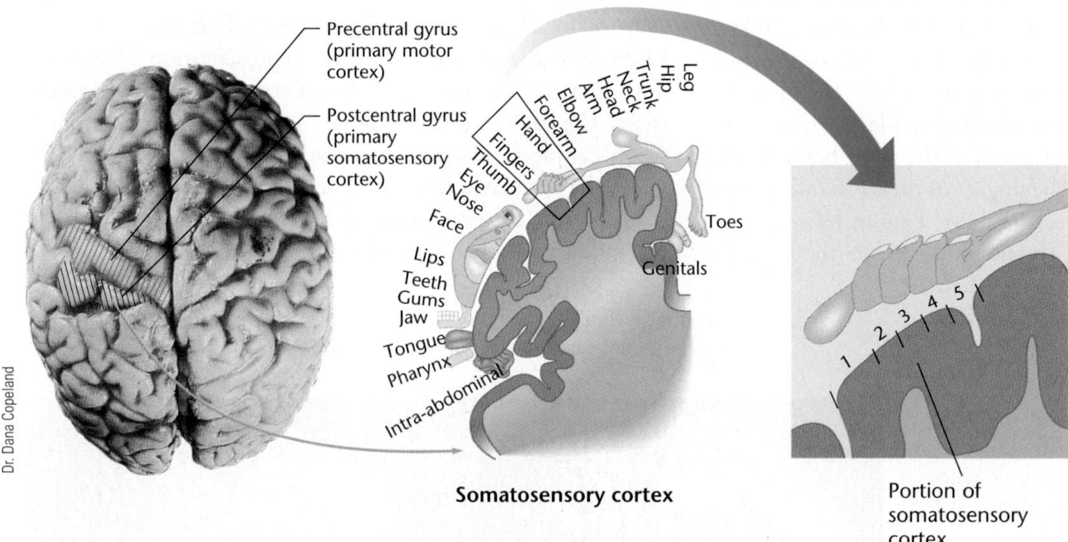

Or the representations of all fingers could grow from side to side without spreading out so that representation of each finger overlaps that of its neighbor:

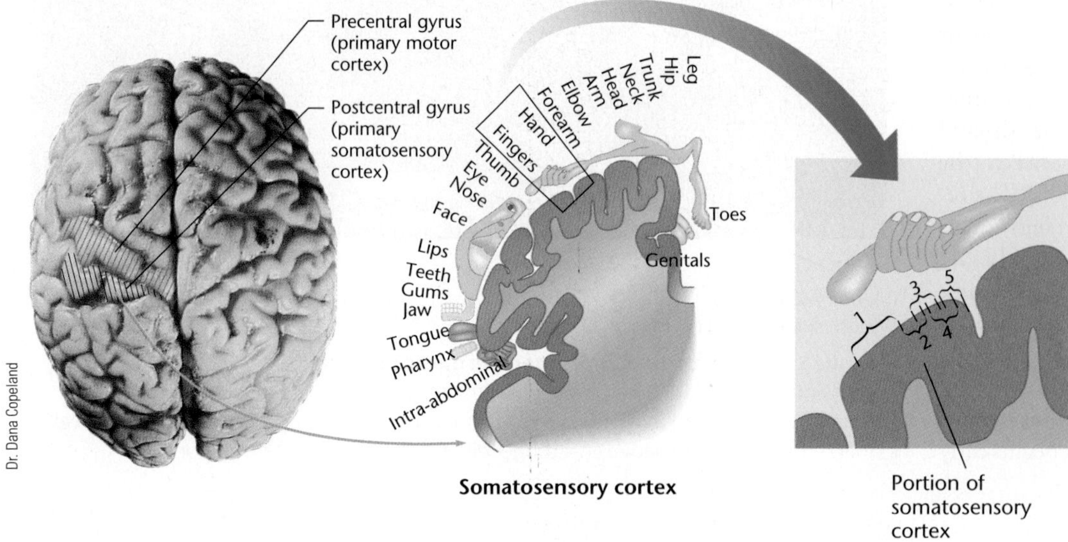

In some cases, the latter process does occur, such that stimulation on one finger excites mostly or entirely the same cortical areas as another finger. Consequently, the person has trouble distinguishing one finger from the other. Someone who can't clearly feel the difference between two fingers has trouble controlling them separately. This condition is "musician's cramp"—known more formally as **focal hand dystonia**—in which the fingers become clumsy, fatigue easily, and make involuntary movements that interfere with the task. This long-lasting condition is a potential career ender for a musician. Some people who spend all day writing develop the same problem, in which case it is known as "writer's cramp." Traditionally, physicians assumed that musician's cramp or writer's cramp was an impairment in the hands, but later research indicated that the cause is extensive reorganization of the sensory thalamus and cortex so that touch responses to one finger overlap those of another (Byl, McKenzie, & Nagarajan, 2000; Elbert et al., 1998; Lenz & Byl, 1999; Sanger, Pascual-Leone, Tarsy, & Schlaug, 2001; Sanger, Tarsy, & Pascual-Leone, 2001).

STOP & CHECK

15. What change in the brain is responsible for musician's cramp?

ANSWER

15. Extensive practice of violin, piano, or other instruments causes expanded representation of the fingers in the somatosensory cortex. In some cases, the representation of each finger invades the area representing other fingers. If the representation of two fingers overlaps too much, the person cannot feel them separately, and the result is musician's cramp.

MODULE 5.1 IN CLOSING

Brain Development

Considering the number of ways in which abnormal genes and chemicals can disrupt brain development, let alone the possible varieties of abnormal experience, it is a wonder that any of us develop normally. Evidently, the system has enough margin for error that we can function even if all of our connections do not develop quite perfectly. There are many ways for development to go wrong, but somehow, the system usually manages to work.

SUMMARY

1. In vertebrate embryos, the central nervous system begins as a tube surrounding a fluid-filled cavity. Developing neurons proliferate, migrate, differentiate, myelinate, and generate synapses. Neuron proliferation varies among species mainly by the number of cell divisions. Migration depends on a large number of chemicals that guide immature neurons to their destinations. **124**
2. Even in adults, new neurons can form in the olfactory system, the hippocampus, and the song-producing brain areas of some bird species. **125**
3. Growing axons manage to find their way close to the right locations by following chemicals. Then they array themselves over a target area by following chemical gradients. **126**
4. After axons reach their targets based on chemical gradients, the postsynaptic cell fine-tunes the connections based on experience, accepting certain combinations of axons and rejecting others. This kind of competition among axons continues throughout life. **128**
5. Initially, the nervous system develops far more neurons than will actually survive. Some axons make synaptic contacts with cells that release to them nerve growth factor or other neurotrophins. The neurons that receive neurotrophins survive; the others die in a process called apoptosis. **129**
6. The developing brain is vulnerable to chemical insult. Many chemicals that produce only mild, temporary problems for adults can permanently impair early brain development. **130**
7. At an early stage of development, the cortex is sufficiently plastic that visual input can cause what would have been the auditory cortex to develop different properties and now respond visually. **131**
8. Enriched experience leads to greater branching of axons and dendrites, partly because animals in enriched environments are more active than those in deprived environments. **133**
9. Specialized experiences can alter brain development, especially early in life. For example, in people who are born blind, representation of touch and language invades areas usually reserved for vision. **134**
10. Extensive practice of a skill expands the brain's representation of sensory and motor information relevant to that skill. For example, the representation of fingers expands in people who regularly practice musical instruments. **134**

Continued

KEY TERMS

Terms are defined in the module on the page number indicated. They're also presented in alphabetical order with definitions in the book's Subject Index/Glossary. Interactive flashcards, audio reviews, and crossword puzzles are among the online resources available to help you learn these terms and the concepts they represent.

apoptosis **129**
differentiates **125**
fetal alcohol syndrome **130**
focal hand dystonia **137**
migrate **125**
myelination **125**
nerve growth factor (NGF) **129**
neurotrophin **130**
proliferation **124**
stem cells **125**
synaptogenesis **125**

THOUGHT QUESTIONS

1. Biologists can develop antibodies against nerve growth factor (i.e., molecules that inactivate nerve growth factor). What would happen if someone injected such antibodies into a developing nervous system?
2. Decades ago, educators advocated teaching Latin and ancient Greek because the required mental discipline would promote overall intelligence and brain development in general. Occasionally, people today advance the same argument for studying calculus or other subjects. Do these arguments seem valid, considering modern research on expertise and brain development?

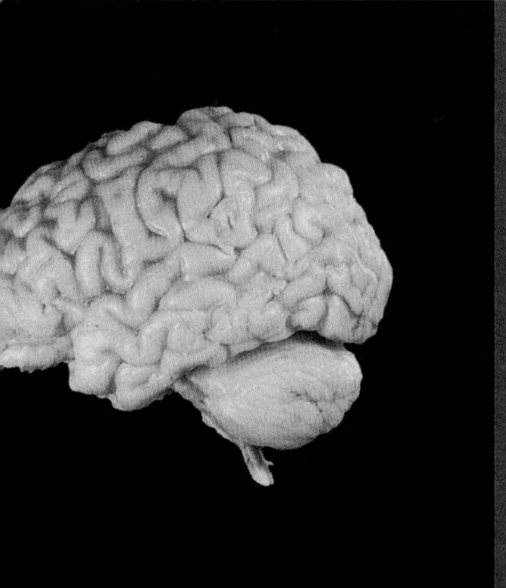

MODULE 5.2

Plasticity After Brain Damage

An American soldier who suffered a wound to the left hemisphere of his brain during the Korean War was at first unable to speak at all. Three months later, he could speak in short fragments. When he was asked to read the letterhead, "New York University College of Medicine," he replied, "Doctors—little doctors." Eight years later, when someone asked him again to read the letterhead, he replied, "Is there a catch? It says, 'New York University College of Medicine'" (Eidelberg & Stein, 1974).

Almost all survivors of brain damage show partial behavioral recovery, and in some cases, it is substantial. Some of the mechanisms rely on the growth of new branches of axons and dendrites, quite similar to the mechanisms of brain development discussed in the first module. Understanding the process may lead to better therapies for people with brain damage and to insights into the functioning of the healthy brain.

Brain Damage and Short-Term Recovery

The possible causes of brain damage include tumors, infections, exposure to radiation or toxic substances, and degenerative conditions such as Parkinson's disease and Alzheimer's disease. In young people, the most common cause is **closed head injury,** a sharp blow to the head resulting from an accident, assault, or other sudden trauma that does not actually puncture the brain. Closed head injuries are common, and mild ones produce little or no lasting damage. When damage does occur, one cause is the rotational forces that drive brain tissue against the inside of the skull. Another cause is blood clots that interrupt blood flow to the brain (Kirkpatrick, Smielewski, Czosnyka, Menon, & Pickard, 1995).

APPLICATIONS AND EXTENSIONS

How Woodpeckers Avoid Concussions

Speaking of blows to the head, have you ever wondered how woodpeckers manage to avoid giving themselves concussions? If you repeatedly banged your head into a tree at 6 or 7 meters per second (about 15 miles per hour), you would almost certainly harm yourself.

Using slow-motion photography, researchers found that woodpeckers usually start with a couple of quick preliminary taps against the wood, much like a carpenter lining up a nail with a hammer. Then the birds make a hard strike in a straight line, keeping a rigid neck. They almost completely avoid rotational forces and whiplash (May, Fuster, Haber, & Hirschman, 1979).

The researchers suggested that football helmets, racecar helmets, and so forth would give more protection if they extended down to the shoulders to prevent rotation and whiplash. They also suggest that if you see a crash about to happen, you should tuck your chin to your chest and tighten your neck muscles.

Reducing the Harm From a Stroke

A common cause of brain damage in older people (more rarely in the young) is temporary loss of blood flow to a brain area during a **stroke,** also known as a **cerebrovascular accident.** The more common type of stroke is **ischemia,** the result of a blood clot or other obstruction in an artery. The less common type is **hemorrhage,** the result of a ruptured artery. Strokes vary in severity from barely noticeable to immediately fatal. Figure 5.12 shows the brains of three people: one who died immediately after a stroke, one who survived

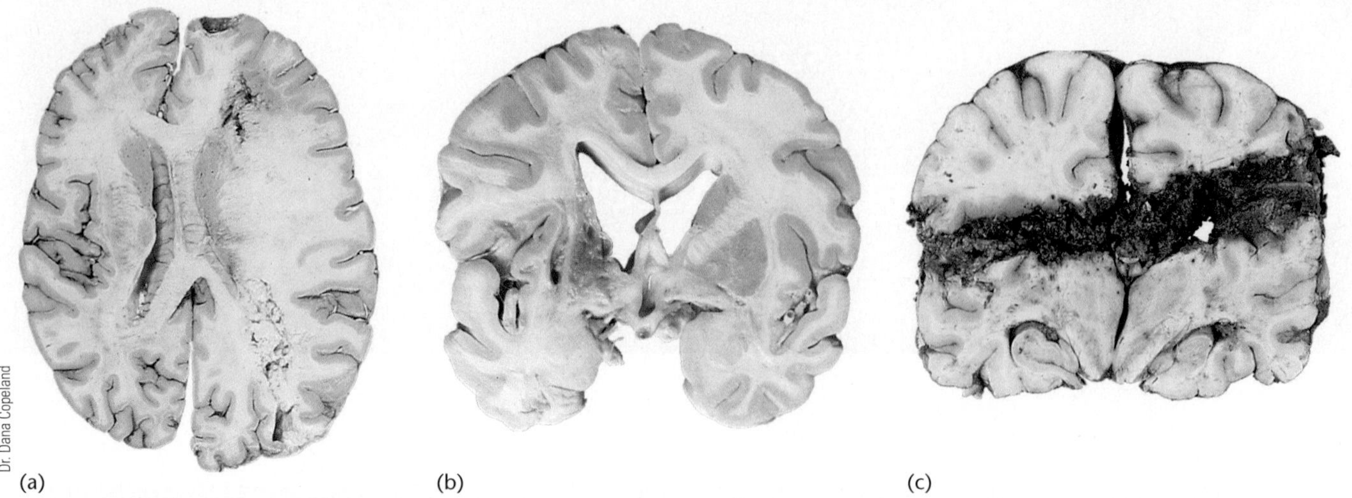

Dr. Dana Copeland

Figure 5.12 Three damaged human brains
(a) Brain of a person who died immediately after a stroke. Note the swelling on the right side. **(b)** Brain of a person who survived for a long time after a stroke. Note the cavities on the left side, where many cells were lost. **(c)** Brain of a person who suffered a gunshot wound and died immediately.

long after a stroke, and a bullet wound victim. For a good collection of information about stroke, visit the Web site of the National Stroke Association at http://www.stroke.org/

In ischemia, neurons are deprived of blood and therefore lose much of their oxygen and glucose supplies. In hemorrhage, they are flooded with blood and excess oxygen, calcium, and other chemicals. Both ischemia and hemorrhage lead to many of the same problems, including **edema** (the accumulation of fluid), which increases pressure on the brain and the probability of additional strokes (Unterberg, Stover, Kress, & Kiening, 2004). Both ischemia and hemorrhage also impair the sodium-potassium pump, leading to an accumulation of sodium inside neurons. The combination of edema and excess sodium provokes excess release of the transmitter glutamate (Rossi, Oshima, & Attwell, 2000), which overstimulates neurons: Sodium and other ions enter the neurons faster than the sodium-potassium pump can remove them. The excess positive ions block metabolism in the mitochondria and kill the neurons (Stout, Raphael, Kanterewicz, Klann, & Reynolds, 1998). As neurons die, microglia cells proliferate, removing the products of dead neurons and providing neurotrophins that promote survival of the remaining neurons (Lalancette-Hébert, Gowing, Simard, Weng, & Kriz, 2007).

Immediate Treatments

As recently as the 1980s, hospitals had little to offer to a stroke patient. Today, prospects are good for ischemia if physicians act quickly. (A hemorrhagic stroke is less common and less treatable.) A drug called **tissue plasminogen activator (tPA)** breaks up blood clots (Barinaga, 1996). To get significant benefit, a patient should receive tPA within 3 hours after a stroke, although slight benefits are possible during the next several hours. Unfortunately, by the time a patient's family gets the patient to the hospital, the delay is usually too long (Keskin, Kalemoglu, & Ulusoy, 2005; Stahl, Furie, Gleason, & Gazelle, 2003). A further problem is that tPA has serious side effects, including sometimes hemorrhage. Researchers are working on ways to reduce the side effects (Armstead et al., 2006).

It is often difficult to determine whether someone has had an ischemic or hemorrhagic stroke. Given that tPA is useful for ischemia but could only make matters worse in a hemorrhage, what is a physician to do? When in doubt, the usual decision is to give the tPA. Hemorrhage is less common and usually fatal anyway, so the risk of making a hemorrhage worse is small compared to the hope of alleviating ischemia.

After the First Hours

When it is too late for tPA to save cells from dying, hope remains for cells in the **penumbra** (Latin for "almost shadow"), the region surrounding the immediate damage (Hsu, Sik, Gallyas, Horváth, & Buzsáki, 1994; Jonas, 1995) (Figure 5.13). One idea is to prevent overstimulation by blocking glutamate synapses. However, the results have been disappointing (Hoyte, Barber, Buchan, & Hill, 2004). Physicians use only low levels of the drugs to avoid serious side effects, and usually, too little of the drugs reach the affected sites (Rossi, Brady, & Mohr, 2007).

So far, the most effective method of preventing brain damage after strokes in laboratory animals is to cool the brain, although the mechanism by which cooling prevents brain damage is not yet certain. Humans cannot be cooled safely to the same temperature that rats can, but cooling someone to about 33–36°C (91–97°F) for the first 3 days after a stroke is often beneficial (Steiner, Ringleb, & Hacke, 2001). Note that this approach goes contrary to most people's first impulse, which is to keep the patient warm and comfortable. However, prolonged cooling sometimes produces health problems of its own.

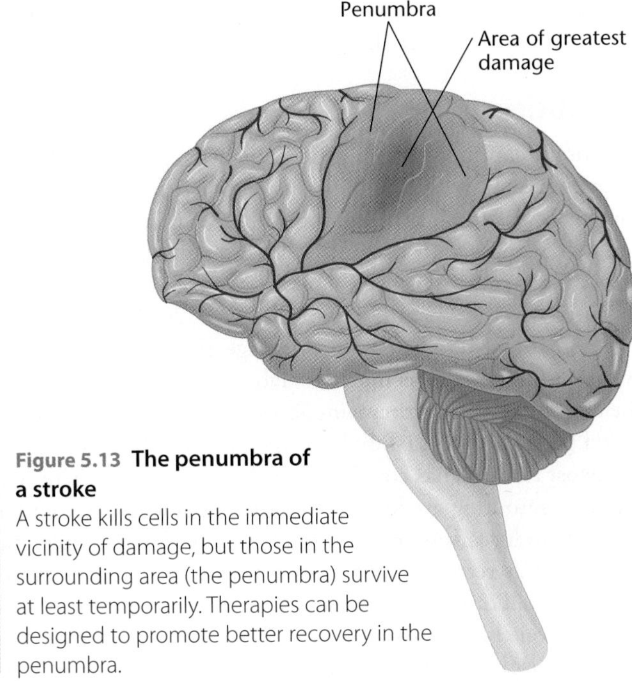

Figure 5.13 The penumbra of a stroke
A stroke kills cells in the immediate vicinity of damage, but those in the surrounding area (the penumbra) survive at least temporarily. Therapies can be designed to promote better recovery in the penumbra.

Among approaches that have minimized stroke damage in laboratory animals, one of the more interesting is to use cannabinoids—drugs related to marijuana (Nagayama et al., 1999). Cannabinoids reduce cell loss after stroke, closed head injury, and other kinds of brain damage (van der Stelt et al., 2002). The benefits are apparently due to cannabinoids' antioxidant or anti-inflammatory actions (Lastres-Becker, Molina-Holgado, Ramos, Mechoulam, & Fernández-Ruiz, 2005).

Still another possibility, which again has been tried with laboratory animals but not yet with humans, is injections of omega-3 fatty acids, like the ones found in fish oils. Omega-3 fatty acids, which are a major component of cell membranes, help to block apoptosis and other neural damage (V. R. King et al., 2006).

STOP & CHECK

16. What are the two kinds of stroke, and what causes each kind?

17. Why is tPA not helpful in cases of hemorrhage?

18. If one of your relatives has a stroke and a well-meaning person offers a blanket, what should you do?

ANSWERS

16. The more common form, ischemia, is the result of an occlusion of an artery. The other form, hemorrhage, is the result of a ruptured artery. **17.** The drug tPA breaks up blood clots, and the problem in hemorrhage is a ruptured blood vessel, not a blood clot. **18.** Refuse the blanket. Recovery will be best if the stroke victim remains cold for the first 3 days.

Later Mechanisms of Recovery

After the first days following brain damage, many of the surviving brain areas increase or reorganize their activity (Nishimura et al., 2007). They do not exactly take over the functions of the damaged area, but they compensate in several ways.

Increased Brain Stimulation

A behavioral deficit after brain damage reflects more than just the functions of the cells that were destroyed. Activity in any brain area stimulates many other areas, so damage to any area deprives other areas of their normal stimulation and thus interferes with their healthy functioning. For example, after damage to part of the left frontal cortex, activity decreases in the temporal cortex and several other areas (Price, Warburton, Moore, Frackowiak, & Friston, 2001). **Diaschisis** (di-AS-ki-sis, from a Greek term meaning "to shock throughout") refers to the decreased activity of surviving neurons after damage to other neurons.

If diaschisis contributes to behavioral deficits following brain damage, then increased stimulation should help. Researchers studied one man who had been in a "minimally conscious state" for 6 years, showing almost no activity or response to stimulation. Electrical stimulation of his central thalamus led to substantial improvements, including self-feeding and some intelligible speech (Schiff et al., 2007).

Stimulant drugs also promote recovery. In a series of experiments, D. M. Feeney and colleagues measured the behavioral effects of cortical damage in rats and cats. Depending on the location of the damage, the animals showed impairments in movement or depth perception. Injecting amphetamine significantly enhanced both behaviors, and animals that practiced the behaviors under the influence of amphetamine showed long-lasting benefits. Injecting a drug that blocks dopamine synapses impaired behavioral recovery (Feeney & Sutton, 1988; Feeney, Sutton, Boyeson, Hovda, & Dail, 1985; Hovda & Feeney, 1989; Sutton, Hovda, & Feeney, 1989).

Although amphetamine is too risky for use with human patients, other stimulant drugs are more promising (Whyte et al., 2005). Using stimulants violates many people's impulse to calm a stroke patient with tranquilizers. Tranquilizers decrease the release of dopamine and impair recovery after brain damage (L. B. Goldstein, 1993).

STOP & CHECK

19. After someone has had a stroke, would it be best (if possible) to direct stimulant drugs to the cells that were damaged or somewhere else?

ANSWER

19. It is best to direct the amphetamine to the cells that had been receiving input from the damaged cells. Presumably, the loss of input has produced diaschisis.

The Regrowth of Axons

Although a destroyed cell body cannot be replaced, damaged axons do grow back under certain circumstances. A neuron of the peripheral nervous system has its cell body in the spinal cord and an axon that extends into one of the limbs. If the axon is crushed, the degenerated portion grows back toward the periphery at a rate of about 1 mm per day, following its myelin sheath back to the original target. If the axon is cut instead of crushed, the myelin on the two sides of the cut may not line up correctly, and the regenerating axon may not have a sure path to follow. Sometimes, a motor nerve attaches to the wrong muscle, as Figure 5.14 illustrates.

Within a mature mammalian brain or spinal cord, damaged axons regenerate only a millimeter or two, if at all (Schwab, 1998). Therefore, paralysis caused by spinal cord injury is permanent. However, in many kinds of fish, axons do regenerate across a cut spinal cord far enough to restore nearly normal functioning (Bernstein & Gelderd, 1970; Rovainen, 1976; Scherer, 1986; Selzer, 1978). Why do damaged CNS axons regenerate so much better in fish than in mammals? Can we find ways to improve axon regeneration in mammals?

Several problems limit axon regeneration in mammals. First, a cut in the nervous system causes a scar to form (thicker in mammals than in fish), which creates a mechanical barrier. Second, neurons on the two sides of the cut pull apart. Third, when glia in the CNS react to brain damage, they release chemicals that inhibit axon growth (Yiu & He, 2006).

These problems are formidable, but hope remains. Researchers have developed a way to build a protein bridge, providing a path for axons to regenerate across a scar-filled gap. When they applied this technique to hamsters with a cut in the optic nerve, many axons from the eye grew back and established synapses, enabling most hamsters to regain partial vision (Ellis-Behnke et al., 2006).

Sprouting

The brain continually adds new branches of axons and dendrites while withdrawing old ones. Brain damage accelerates that process. After loss of a set of axons, the cells that lost their source of innervation react by secreting neurotrophins to induce other axons to form new branches, or **collateral sprouts,** that attach to the vacant synapses (Ramirez, 2001), as shown in Figure 5.15. In the area near the damage, the formation of new synapses increases to as much as eight times its usual rate over the next 2 weeks, and it remains above average 6 weeks after the lesion (C. E. Brown, Li, Boyd, Delaney, & Murphy, 2007).

Most research has concerned the hippocampus, where two types of sprouting are known to occur. First, damage to a set of axons induces sprouting by similar axons. For example, the hippocampus receives input from a nearby cortical area called the *entorhinal cortex,* and damage to axons from the entorhinal cortex of one hemisphere induces sprouting by axons from the other hemisphere. Those sprouts form gradually over weeks, simultaneous with improvements in memory task performance, and several kinds of evidence indicate that sprouting is essential for the improvement (Ramirez, Bulsara, Moore, Ruch, & Abrams, 1999; Ramirez, McQuilkin, Carrigan, MacDonald, & Kelley, 1996).

Second, damage sometimes induces sprouting by unrelated axons. For example, after damage to the entorhinal cortex of both hemispheres, axons from other areas form sprouts into the vacant synapses of the hippocampus. The information they bring is certainly not the same as what was lost. This kind of sprouting can be useful, neutral, or harmful (Ramirez, 2001).

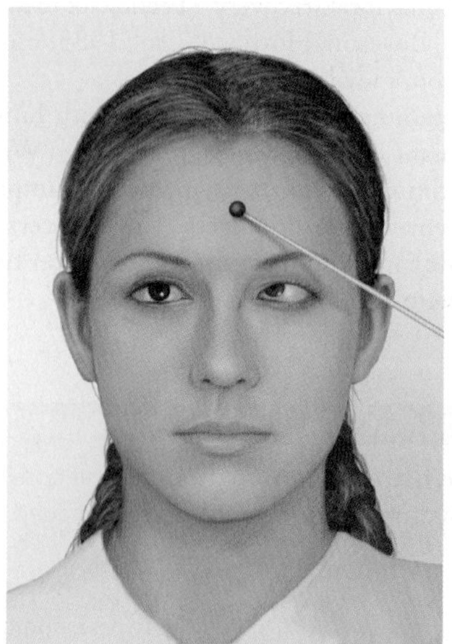

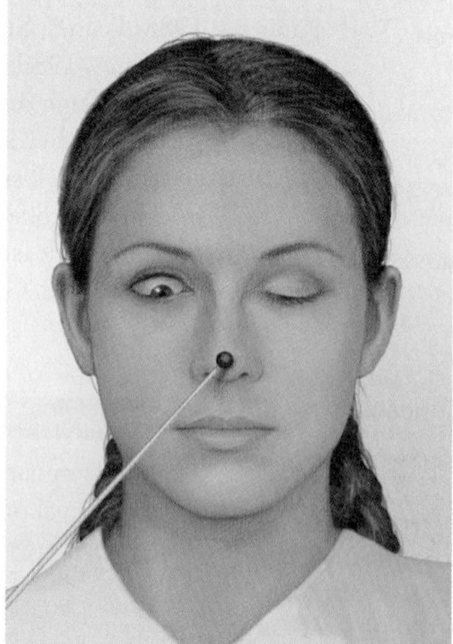

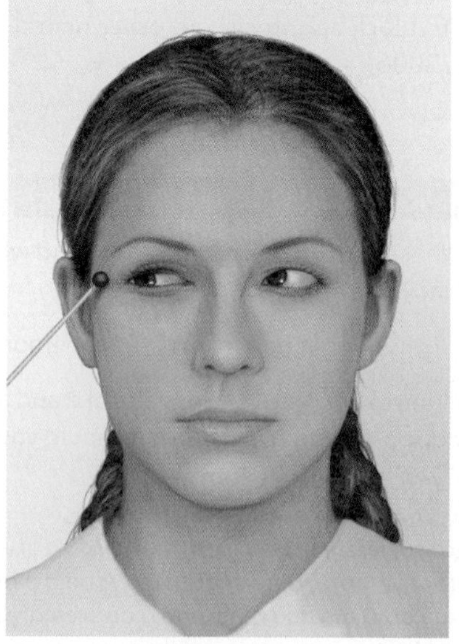

Figure 5.14 What can happen if damaged axons regenerate to incorrect muscles
Damaged axons to the muscles of the patient's right eye regenerated but attached incorrectly. When she looks down, her right eyelid opens wide instead of closing like the other eyelid. Her eye movements are frequently misaimed, and she has trouble moving her right eye upward or to the left.

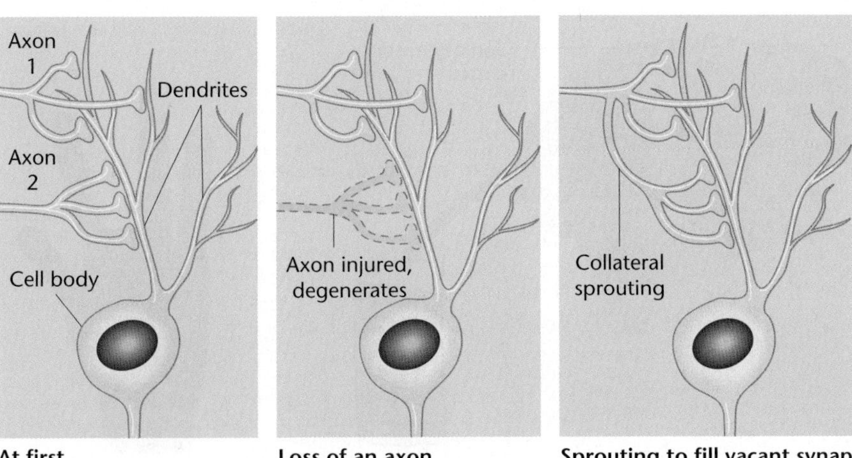

Figure 5.15 Collateral sprouting
A surviving axon grows a new branch to replace the synapses left vacant by a damaged axon.

Denervation Supersensitivity

A postsynaptic cell that is deprived of most of its synaptic inputs develops increased sensitivity to the neurotransmitters that it still receives. For example, a normal muscle cell responds to the neurotransmitter acetylcholine only at the neuromuscular junction. If the axon is cut or if it is inactive for days, the muscle cell builds additional receptors, becoming sensitive to acetylcholine over a wider area of its surface (Johns & Thesleff, 1961; Levitt-Gilmour & Salpeter, 1986). The same process occurs in neurons. Heightened sensitivity to a neurotransmitter after the destruction of an incoming axon is known as **denervation supersensitivity** (Glick, 1974). Heightened sensitivity as a result of inactivity by an incoming axon is called **disuse supersensitivity.** Supersensitivity results from an increased number of receptors (Kostrzewa, 1995) and increased effectiveness of receptors, perhaps by changes in second-messenger systems.

Denervation supersensitivity helps compensate for decreased input. In some cases, it enables people to maintain nearly normal behavior even after losing most of the axons in some pathway (Sabel, 1997). However, it can also have unpleasant consequences, such as chronic pain. Because spinal injury damages many axons, postsynaptic neurons develop increased sensitivity to the remaining ones. Therefore, even normal input produces enhanced responses (Hains, Everhart, Fullwood, & Hulsebosch, 2002).

STOP & CHECK

20. Is collateral sprouting a change in axons or dendritic receptors?

21. Is denervation supersensitivity a change in axons or dendritic receptors?

ANSWERS

20. axons **21.** dendritic receptors

Reorganized Sensory Representations and the Phantom Limb

As described in the first module of this chapter, experiences can modify the connections within the cerebral cortex to increase the representation of personally important information. Recall that after someone has played a string instrument for many years, the somatosensory cortex has an enlarged representation of the fingers of the left hand. Such changes represent either collateral sprouting of axons or increased receptor sensitivity by the postsynaptic neurons. Similar processes occur after nervous system damage.

For example, consider what happens after a stroke that damages the axons bringing information from the upper left visual field while leaving the visual cortex intact. The part of the visual cortex responding to the lower left visual field still gets its normal input. Gradually, axons representing the lower left field sprout into the vacated synapses representing the upper field. As that happens, a stimulus that should look as shown here on the left begins to look like the stimulus on the right (Dilks, Serences, Rosenau, Yantis, & McCloskey, 2007):

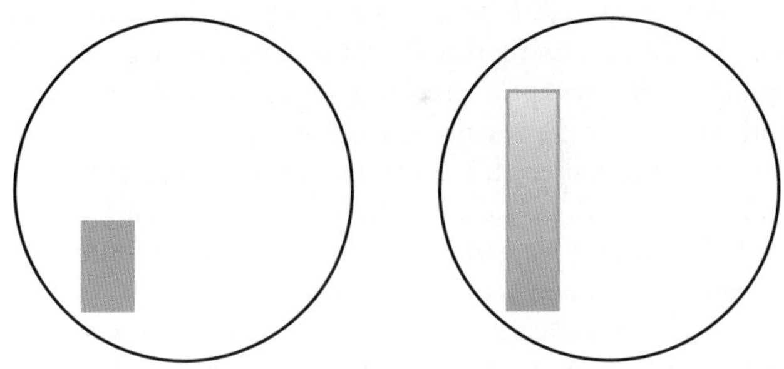

Also consider how the cortex reorganizes after an amputation. Reexamine Figure 4.24 on page 101: Each section along the somatosensory cortex receives input from a different part of the body. Within the area marked "fingers" in that figure, a closer examination reveals that each subarea responds more to one finger than to another. Figure 5.16 shows the arrangement for a monkey brain. In one study, experimenters amputated finger 3 of an owl monkey. The cortical cells that previously responded to information from that finger lost their input. Soon they became more responsive to finger 2, finger 4, or part of the palm, until the cortex developed the pattern of responsiveness shown in Figure 5.16b (Kaas, Merzenich, & Killackey, 1983; Merzenich et al., 1984).

What happens if an entire arm is amputated? For many years, neuroscientists assumed that the cortical area corresponding to that arm would remain permanently silent

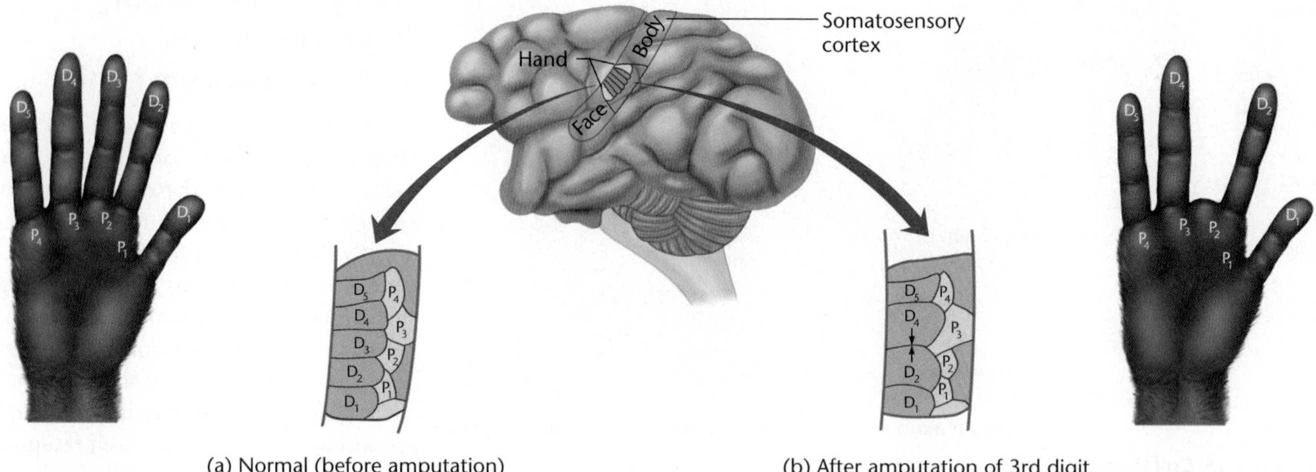

Figure 5.16 Somatosensory cortex of a monkey after a finger amputation
Note that the cortical area previously responsive to the third finger (D_3) becomes responsive to the second and fourth fingers (D_2 and D_4) and part of the palm (P_3). *(Redrawn from the* Annual Review of Neuroscience, *Vol. 6, © 1983, by Annual Reviews, Inc. Reprinted by permission of Annual Reviews, Inc. and Jon H. Kaas.)*

because axons from other cortical areas could not sprout far enough to reach the area representing the arm. Then came a surprise. Investigators recorded from the cerebral cortices of monkeys whose sensory nerves from one forelimb had been cut 12 years previously. They found that the stretch of cortex previously responsive to the limb was now responsive to the face (Pons et al., 1991). After loss of sensory input from the forelimb, the axons representing the forelimb degenerated, leaving vacant synaptic sites at several levels of the CNS. Evidently, axons representing the face sprouted into those sites in the spinal cord, brainstem, and thalamus (Florence & Kaas, 1995; E. G. Jones & Pons, 1998). (Or perhaps axons from the face were already present but became stronger through denervation supersensitivity.)

Brain scan studies confirm that the same processes occur with humans. Now consider what happens when cells in a reorganized cortex become activated. Previously, those neurons responded to arm stimulation, and now they receive information from the face. Does the response feel like stimulation on the face or on the arm?

The answer: It feels like the arm (K. D. Davis et al., 1998). Physicians have long noted that many people with amputations experience a **phantom limb,** a continuing sensation of an amputated body part. That experience can range from occasional tingling to intense pain. It is possible to have a phantom hand, foot, or anything else that has been amputated. The phantom sensation might fade within days or weeks, but sometimes, it lasts a lifetime (Ramachandran & Hirstein, 1998).

Until the 1990s, no one knew what caused phantom pains, and most believed that the sensations were coming from the stump of the amputated limb. Some physicians even performed additional amputations, removing more and more of the limb in a futile attempt to eliminate the phantom sensations. Modern methods have demonstrated that phantom limbs develop only if the relevant portion of the somatosensory cortex reorganizes and becomes responsive to alternative inputs (Flor et al., 1995). For example, axons representing the face may come to activate the cortical area previously devoted to an amputated hand. Whenever the face is touched, the person still feels the facial sensation but also feels a sensation in the phantom hand. It is possible to map out which part of the face stimulates sensation in which part of the phantom hand, as shown in Figure 5.17 (Aglioti, Smania, Atzei, & Berlucchi, 1997).

Note in Figure 4.24 on page 101 that the part of the cortex responsive to the feet is adjacent to the part responsive to the genitals. Two patients with foot amputations felt a phantom foot during sexual arousal! One reported feeling orgasm in the phantom foot as well as the genitals—and enjoyed it intensely (Ramachandran & Blakeslee, 1998). Evidently, the representation of the genitals had spread into the cortical area responsible for foot sensation.

Is there any way to relieve a painful phantom sensation? In some cases, yes. Amputees who learn to use an artificial arm report that their phantom sensations gradually disappear (Lotze et al., 1999). They start attributing sensations to the artificial arm, and in doing so, they displace abnormal connections from the face. Similarly, a study of one man found that after his hands were amputated, the area of his cortex that usually responds to the hands partly shifted to face sensitivity, but after he received hand transplants, his cortex gradually shifted back to hand sensitivity (Giraux, Sirigu, Schneider, & Dubernard, 2001).

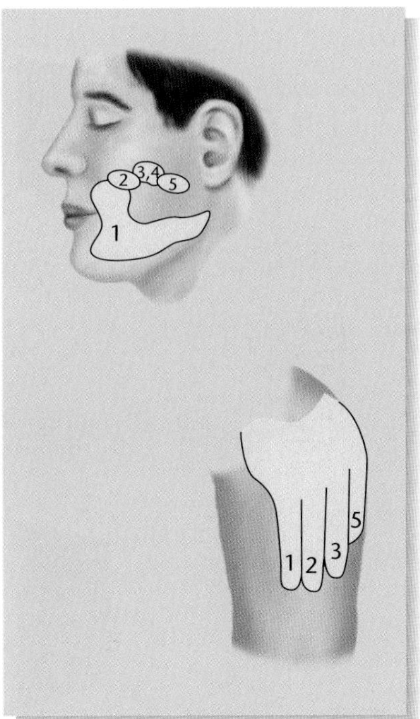

Figure 5.17 Sources of phantom sensation for one person
For this person, stimulation in the areas marked on the cheek produced phantom sensations of digits 1 (thumb), 2, 4, and 5. Stimulation on the shoulder also evoked phantom sensations of digits 1, 2, 3, and 5. *(Fig. 5.29 from* Phantoms in the Brain *by V. S. Ramachandran, M.D., Ph.D. and Sandra Blakeslee. Copyright © 1998 by V. S. Ramachandran and Sandra Blakeslee. Reprinted by permission of HarperCollins Publishers and authors.)*

Andy Manis/AP Photo

Amputees who feel a phantom limb are likely to lose those phantom sensations if they learn to use an artificial limb.

One important message from these studies is that connections in the brain remain plastic throughout life. There are limits on the plasticity, certainly, but they are less strict than neuroscientists once supposed.

STOP & CHECK

22. Cite an example in which reorganization of the brain is helpful and one in which it is harmful.

ANSWER

22. The small-scale reorganization that enables increased representation of a violinist's or Braille reader's fingers is helpful. The larger scale reorganization that occurs after amputation is harmful.

Learned Adjustments in Behavior

So far, the discussion has focused on anatomical changes. In fact, much recovery from brain damage is based on learning.

If you can't find your keys, perhaps you accidentally dropped them while hiking through the forest (so you will never find them), or perhaps you absentmindedly put them in an unusual place (where you will find them if you keep looking). Similarly, someone with brain damage who seems to have lost an ability may indeed have lost it or may be able to find it with enough effort. Much, probably most, recovery from brain damage depends on learning to make better use of the abilities that were spared. For example, if you lose your peripheral vision, you could learn to move your head from side to side to compensate (Marshall, 1985).

Sometimes, a person or animal with brain damage appears unable to do something but is in fact not trying. For example, consider an animal that incurred damage to the sensory nerves linking a forelimb to the spinal cord, as in Figure 5.18. The animal no longer feels the limb, although the motor nerves still connect to the muscles. We say the limb is **deafferented** because it has lost its afferent (sensory) input. A monkey with a deafferented limb does not spontaneously use it for walking, picking up objects, or any other voluntary behaviors (Taub & Berman, 1968).

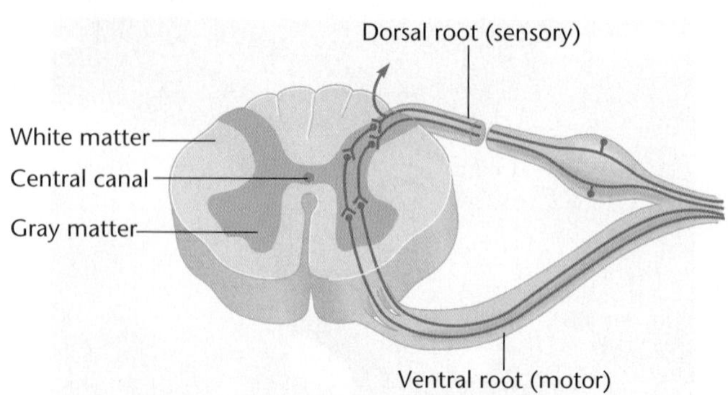

Figure 5.18 Cross-section through the spinal cord
A cut through the dorsal root (as shown) deprives the animal of touch sensations from part of the body but leaves the motor nerves intact.

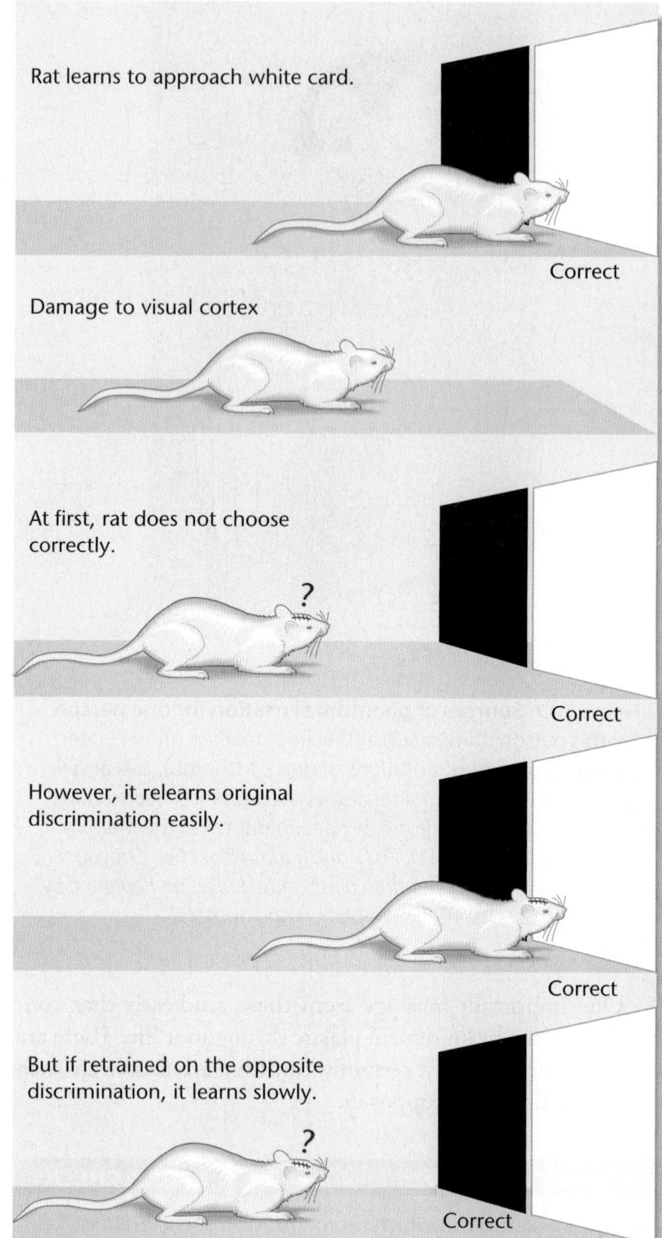

Figure 5.19 Memory impairment after cortical damage
Brain damage impairs retrieval of a memory but does not destroy it completely. *(Based on T. E. LeVere & Morlock, 1973)*

Investigators initially assumed that the monkey *could not* use a limb that it didn't feel. In a later experiment, however, they cut the afferent nerves of both forelimbs. Despite this more extensive damage, the monkey used its deafferented limbs to walk, climb the walls of metal cages, and pick up raisins. Apparently, a monkey fails to use a deafferented forelimb only because walking on three limbs is easier than using the impaired limb. When it has no choice but to use its deafferented limbs, it does.

For another example, consider a rat with damage to its visual cortex. Prior to the damage, it learned to approach a white card instead of a black card for food, but after the damage, it approaches one card or the other randomly. Has it completely forgotten the discrimination? Evidently not, because it can more easily relearn to approach the white card than learn to approach the black card (T. E. LeVere & Morlock, 1973) (Figure 5.19). Thomas LeVere (1975) proposed that a lesion to the visual cortex does not destroy the memory trace but merely impairs the rat's ability to find it. As the animal recovers, it regains access to misplaced memories.

Similarly, many people with brain damage find ways of getting through the tasks of their day without relying on their impaired skills. For example, someone with impaired language will rely on a spouse to do the talking, or someone with impaired face recognition will learn to recognize people by their voices. Therapy for people with brain damage focuses on encouraging them to practice skills that are impaired but not lost.

Treatment begins with careful evaluation of a patient's abilities and disabilities. Such evaluations are the specialty of neuropsychologists (see Table 1.1, p. 8), who develop tests to try to pinpoint the problems. For example, someone who has trouble carrying out spoken instructions might be impaired in hearing, memory, language, muscle control, or alertness. After identifying the problem, a neuropsychologist might refer a patient to a physical therapist or occupational therapist, who helps the patient practice the impaired skills. Therapists get their best results if they start soon after a patient's stroke, and animal researchers find the same pattern. In one study, rats with damage to the parietal cortex of one hemisphere showed poor coordination of the contralateral forepaw. Some of the rats received experiences designed to encourage them to use the impaired limb. Those who began practice 5 days after the damage recovered better than those who started after 14 days, who in turn recovered better than those who started after 30 days (Biernaskie, Chernenko, & Corbett, 2004). As other kinds of evidence have confirmed, the brain has increased plasticity during the first days after damage.

One important generalization is that behavior recovered after brain damage is effortful, and the recovery is precarious. A person with brain damage who appears to be functioning normally is working harder than usual. The recovered behavior deteriorates markedly after drinking alcohol, physical exhaustion, or other kinds of stress that would minimally affect most other people (Fleet & Heilman, 1986). It also deteriorates more than average in old age (Corkin, Rosen, Sullivan, & Clegg, 1989).

STOP & CHECK

23. Suppose someone has suffered a spinal cord injury that interrupts all sensation from the left arm. Now he or she uses only the right arm. Of the following, which is the most promising therapy: electrically stimulate the skin of the left arm, tie the right arm behind the person's back, or blindfold the person?

ANSWER

23. Tie the right arm behind the back to force the person to use the impaired arm instead of only the normal arm. Stimulating the skin of the left arm would accomplish nothing, as the sensory receptors have no input to the CNS. Blindfolding would be either irrelevant or harmful (by decreasing the visual feedback from left-hand movements).

MODULE 5.2 IN CLOSING

Brain Damage and Recovery

The mammalian body is well equipped to replace lost blood cells or skin cells but poorly prepared to deal with lost brain cells. Even the responses that do occur after brain damage, such as collateral sprouting of axons or reorganization of sensory representations, are not always helpful. It is tempting to speculate that we did not evolve many mechanisms of recovery from brain damage because, through most of our evolutionary history, an individual with brain damage was not likely to survive long enough to recover. Today, many people with brain and spinal cord damage survive for years, and we need continuing research on how to improve their lives.

SUMMARY

1. Brain damage has many causes, including blows to the head, obstruction of blood flow to the brain, or a ruptured blood vessel in the brain. Strokes kill neurons largely by overexcitation. **139**
2. During the first 3 hours after an ischemic stroke, tissue plasminogen activator (tPA) can reduce cell loss by breaking up the blood clot. Theoretically, it should also be possible to minimize cell loss by preventing overexcitation of neurons, but so far, procedures based on this idea have been ineffective. Cooling the brain or providing cannabinoids can reduce cell loss. **140**
3. When one brain area is damaged, other areas become less active than usual because of their loss of input. Stimulant drugs can help restore normal function of these undamaged areas. **141**
4. After an area of the CNS loses its usual input, other axons begin to excite it as a result of either sprouting or denervation supersensitivity. In some cases, this abnormal input produces odd sensations such as the phantom limb. **142**
5. Most recovery of function after brain damage relies on learning to make better use of spared functions. Many individuals with brain damage are capable of more than they show because they avoid using skills that have become impaired or difficult. **145**

Continued

KEY TERMS

Terms are defined in the module on the page number indicated. They're also presented in alphabetical order with definitions in the book's Subject Index/Glossary. Interactive flashcards, audio reviews, and crossword puzzles are among the online resources available to help you learn these terms and the concepts they represent.

cerebrovascular accident **139**
closed head injury **139**
collateral sprouts **142**
deafferented **145**
denervation supersensitivity **143**
diaschisis **141**
disuse supersensitivity **143**
edema **140**
hemorrhage **139**
ischemia **139**
penumbra **140**
phantom limb **144**
stroke **139**
tissue plasminogen activator (tPA) **140**

THOUGHT QUESTIONS

1. Ordinarily, patients with advanced Parkinson's disease (who have damage to dopamine-releasing axons) move very slowly if at all. However, during an emergency (e.g., a fire in the building), they may move rapidly and vigorously. Suggest a possible explanation.
2. Drugs that block dopamine synapses tend to impair or slow limb movements. However, after people have taken such drugs for a long time, some experience involuntary twitches or tremors in their muscles. Based on material in this chapter, propose a possible explanation.

CHAPTER 5 Exploration and Study

In addition to the study materials provided at the end of each module, you may supplement your review of this chapter by using one or more of the book's electronic resources, which include its companion Website, interactive Cengage Learning eBook, Exploring Biological Psychology CD-ROM, and CengageNOW. Brief descriptions of these resources follow. For more information, visit **www.cengage.com/psychology/kalat.**

The book's companion Website, accessible through the author Web page indicated above, provides a wide range of study resources such as an interactive glossary, flashcards, tutorial quizzes, updated Web links, and Try It Yourself activities, as well as a limited selection of the short videos and animated explanations of concepts available for this chapter.

Exploring Biological Psychology

The Exploring Biological Psychology CD-ROM contains videos, animations, and Try It Yourself activities. These activities—as well as many that are new to this edition—are also available in the text's fully interactive, media-rich Cengage Learning eBook,* which gives you the opportunity to experience biological psychology in an even greater interactive and multimedia environment. The Cengage Learning eBook also includes highlighting and note-taking features and an audio glossary. For this chapter, the Cengage Learning eBook includes the following interactive explorations:

Sperry Experiment
Brain Development
Phantom Limb
Stroke Robots

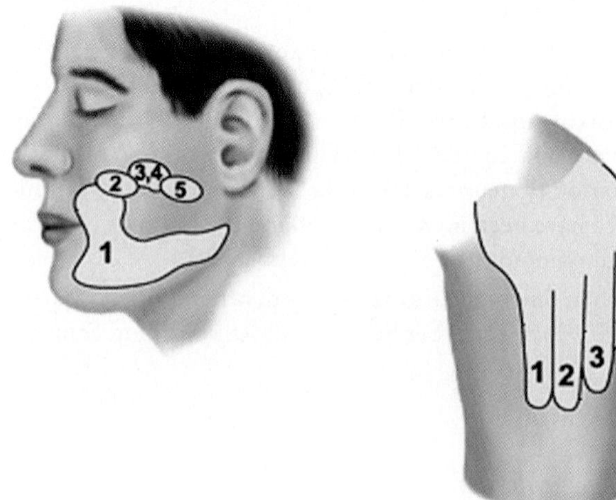

The animation *Phantom Limb* illustrates aspects of this experience.

CENGAGENOW™ is an easy-to-use resource that helps you study in less time to get the grade you want. An online study system, CengageNOW* gives you the option of taking a diagnostic pretest for each chapter. The system uses the results of each pretest to create personalized chapter study plans for you. The Personalized Study Plans

- help you save study time by identifying areas on which you should concentrate and give you one-click access to corresponding pages of the interactive Cengage Learning eBook;
- provide interactive exercises and study tools to help you fully understand chapter concepts; and
- include a posttest for you to take to confirm that you are ready to move on to the next chapter.

Suggestions for Further Exploration

The book's companion Website includes a list of suggested articles available through InfoTrac College Edition for this chapter. You may also want to explore some of the following books and Websites. The text's companion Website provides live, updated links to the sites listed below.

Books

Levi-Montalcini, R. (1988). *In praise of imperfection.* New York: Basic Books. Autobiography by the discoverer of nerve growth factor.

Ramachandran, V. S., & Blakeslee, S. (1998). *Phantoms in the brain.* New York: Morrow. One of the most thought-provoking books ever written about human brain damage, including the phantom limb phenomenon.

Websites

National Stroke Association
An excellent source about strokes, their causes, their symptoms, and their treatments.
http://www.stroke.org/

Mind Bluff: Create a Fake Phantom Limb
Would you like to experience (temporarily) an illusion similar to having a phantom limb? If you try this, note the relevance to the binding problem, as discussed in Chapter 4.
http://mindbluff.com/phantom.htm

* Requires a Cengage Learning eResources account. Visit **www.cengage.com/login** to register or login.

Vision

6

CHAPTER OUTLINE

OPPOSITE: Later in this chapter, you will understand why this prairie falcon has tilted its head.

MAIN IDEAS

1. Each sensory neuron conveys a particular type of experience. For example, anything that stimulates the optic nerve is perceived as light.
2. Vertebrate vision depends on two kinds of receptors: cones, which contribute to color vision, and rods, which do not.
3. Every cell in the visual system has a receptive field, an area of the visual world that can excite or inhibit it.
4. After visual information reaches the brain, concurrent pathways analyze different aspects, such as shape, color, and movement.
5. Neurons of the visual system establish approximately correct connections and properties through chemical gradients that are present before birth. However, visual experience can fine-tune or alter those properties, especially early in life.

Several decades ago, a graduate student taking his final oral exam for a PhD in psychology was asked, "How far can an ant see?" He turned pale. He did not know the answer, and evidently, he was supposed to. He tried to remember everything he knew about insect vision. Finally, he gave up and admitted he did not know.

With an impish grin, the professor told him, "Presumably, an ant can see 93 million miles—the distance to the sun." Yes, this was a trick question. However, it illustrates an important point: How far an ant sees, or how far you or I see, depends on how far the light travels. We see because light strikes our eyes. We do not send out "sight rays." That principle is far from intuitive. It was not known until the Arab philosopher Ibn al-Haythem (965–1040) demonstrated that light rays bounce off any object in all directions, but we see only those rays that strike the retina perpendicularly (Gross, 1999). Even today, a distressingly large number of college students believe that sight rays come out of their eyes when they see (Winer, Cottrell, Gregg, Fournier, & Bica, 2002). The sensory systems do not match our common-sense notions.

MODULE 6.1

Visual Coding

Imagine that you are a piece of iron. So there you are, sitting around doing nothing, as usual, when along comes a drop of water. What will be your perception of the water? Yes, I know, a bar of iron doesn't have a brain, and it wouldn't have any perception at all. But let's ignore the inconvenient facts and imagine what it would be like if a bar of iron could perceive the water.

From the standpoint of a piece of iron, water is above all *rustish*. Now return to your perspective as a human. You know that rustishness is not really a property of water itself but of how it reacts with iron.

The same is true of human perception. For example, you see grass as *green*. But green is no more a property of grass than rustish is a property of water. Green is the experience you have when the light bouncing off grass reacts with the neurons in your brain. Greenness is in us—just as rust is in the piece of iron.

General Principles of Perception

Every animal is surrounded by a world of objects that it needs to know about. You perceive objects by the energy that they transmit. They produce or reflect light and sound that strike your visual and auditory receptors. When you touch them, you feel the compression of receptors in your skin. Some objects have chemicals that you smell or taste.

After the information reaches your nervous system, you encode it. You don't store information about light by shining light waves in your brain or information about sound by echoing sound waves in your brain. You store the information in terms of responses by neurons in these ways: which neurons respond, their amount of response, and the timing of their responses.

One aspect of coding is *which* neurons are active. Impulses in one neuron indicate light, whereas impulses in another neuron indicate sound. In 1838, Johannes Müller described this insight as the **law of specific nerve energies.** Müller held that whatever excites a particular nerve establishes a special kind of energy unique to that nerve. In modern terms, activity by a particular nerve always conveys the same kind of information to the brain. The brain somehow interprets the action potentials from the auditory nerve as sounds, those from the olfactory nerve as odors, and so forth. Admittedly, that word "somehow" glosses over a deep mystery.

Here is a demonstration: If you rub your eyes, you may see spots or flashes of light even in a totally dark room. You applied mechanical pressure, which excited visual receptors in your eyes. Anything that excites those receptors is perceived as light. (If you try this demonstration, first remove any contact lenses. Shut your eyes and rub gently.)

TRY IT YOURSELF

STOP & CHECK

1. If someone electrically stimulated the auditory receptors in your ear, how would you perceive it?

ANSWER

1. Because of the law of specific nerve energies, you would perceive it as sound, not as shock. (Of course, if the shock were strong enough, it would spread far enough to excite some pain receptors also.)

Light stimulates one set of receptors, sound another, and so on. The strength of a stimulus determines the amount of a receptor cell's depolarization or hyperpolarization. The amplitude (amount) of the receptor's response determines how many action potentials the next set of neurons sends and their timing. Much of sensory coding depends on the frequency of firing. For example, when pain axons fire many action potentials per second, you feel intense pain. Fewer per second would produce less pain. Coding also depends on relative rates of firing. If one cell fires more than a second cell, you might see red. If the second fires more than the first, you might see green. We shall encounter many examples of coding throughout this and the next chapter.

From Neuronal Activity to Perception

Somehow, the brain makes sense of all this coded information. The challenge for researchers is to determine how the brain makes sense of it. Let us consider what is *not* an answer. The 17th-century philosopher René Descartes believed that the brain's representation of a stimulus resembled the stimulus. That is, the nerves from the eye would project a pattern of impulses arranged like a picture, right side up. In fact, the nerve impulses do not arrive in a pattern that looks anything like the original scene. Even if they did, the pattern would not help, unless we assume a little person in the head who looks at the picture. But then, how would the little person perceive the picture? (Maybe there is an even littler person inside the little person's head?) The early scientists and philosophers might have avoided this error if they had started by studying olfaction because we are less tempted to imagine that we create a little flower for a little person in the head to smell.

The point is that your brain's activity does not duplicate the objects that you see. When you see a table, the representation of the top of the table does not have to be on the top of your head, any more than a computer stores the top of a picture at the top of the computer's memory bank.

STOP & CHECK

2. If it were possible to flip your entire brain upside down, without breaking any of the connections to sense organs or muscles, what would happen to your perceptions of what you see, hear, and so forth?

ANSWER

2. Your perceptions would not change. The way visual or auditory information is coded in the brain does not depend on the physical location within the brain. Seeing something as "on top" or "to the left" depends on which neurons are active but does not depend on the physical location of those neurons.

The Eye and Its Connections to the Brain

Light enters the eye through an opening in the center of the iris called the **pupil** (Figure 6.1). It is focused by the lens (adjustable) and cornea (not adjustable) and projected onto the **retina,** the rear surface of the eye, which is lined with visual receptors. Light from the left side of the world strikes the right half of the retina, and vice versa. Light from above strikes the bottom half of the retina, and light from below strikes the top half. The inversion of the image poses no problem for the nervous system. Remember, the visual system does not duplicate the image. It codes it in various kinds of neuronal activity.

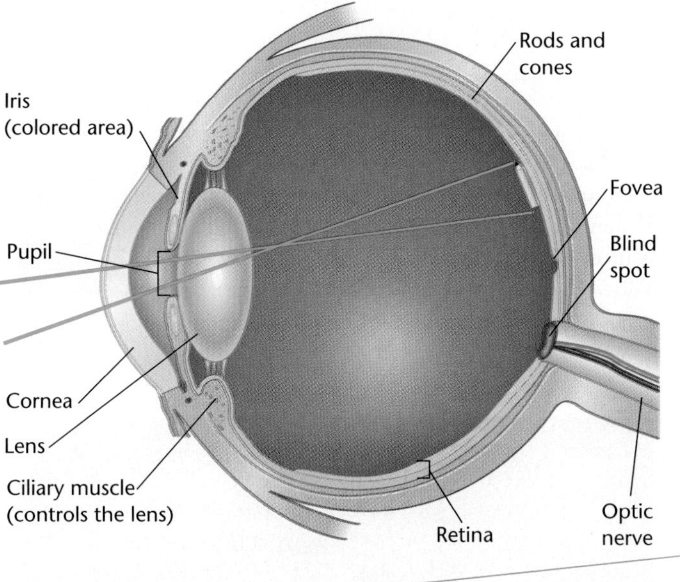

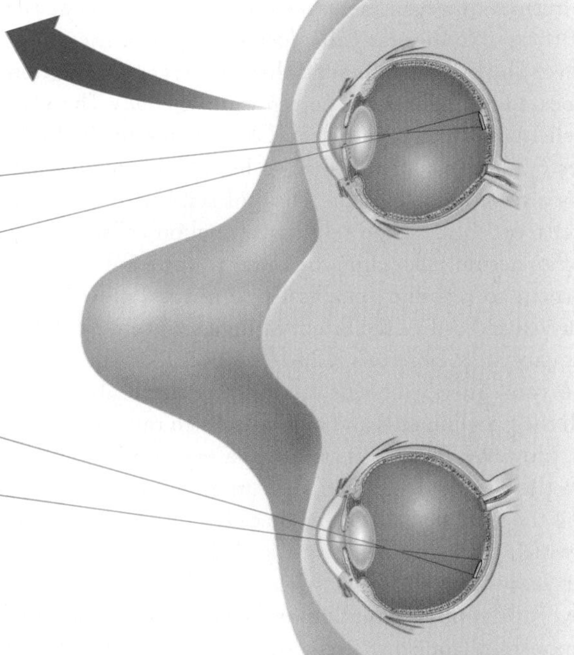

Figure 6.1 Cross-section of the vertebrate eye
An object in the visual field produces an inverted image on the retina. The optic nerve exits the eyeball on the nasal side (the side closer to the nose).

Figure 6.2 Visual path within the eye
The receptors send their messages to bipolar and horizontal cells, which in turn send messages to the amacrine and ganglion cells. The axons of the ganglion cells loop together to exit the eye at the blind spot. They form the optic nerve, which continues to the brain.

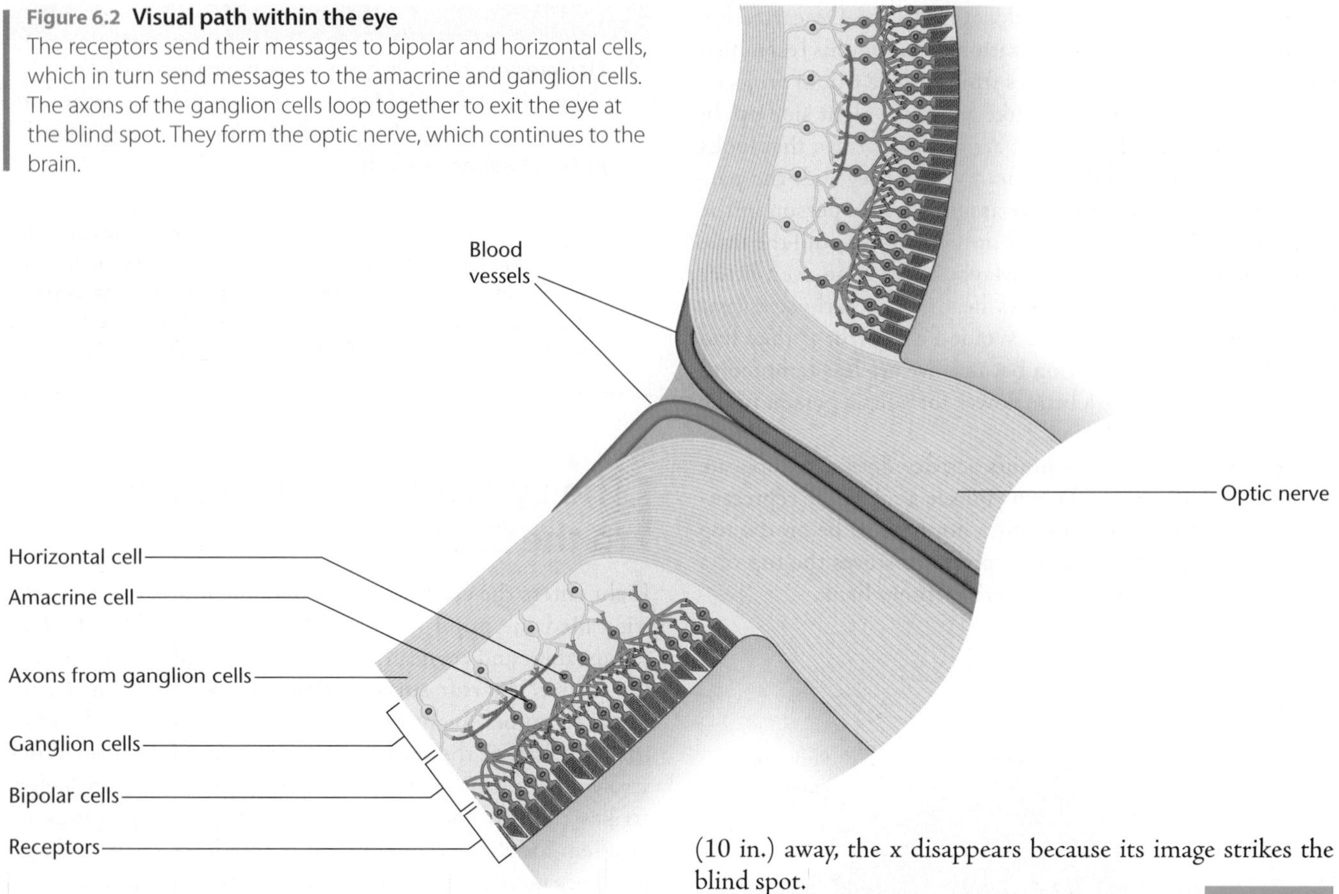

Route Within the Retina

If you or I were designing an eye, we would probably send the receptors' messages directly back to the brain. In the vertebrate retina, however, messages go from receptors at the back of the eye to **bipolar cells,** located closer to the center of the eye. The bipolar cells send their messages to **ganglion cells,** located still closer to the center of the eye. The ganglion cells' axons join together and travel back to the brain (Figures 6.2 and 6.3). Additional cells called *amacrine cells* get information from bipolar cells and send it to other bipolar cells, other amacrine cells, and ganglion cells. Various types of amacrine cells refine the input to ganglion cells, enabling them to respond specifically to shapes, movements, or other visual features (S. Fried, Münch, & Werblin, 2002; Sinclair, Jacobs, & Nirenberg, 2004; Wässle, 2004).

One consequence of this anatomy is that light passes through the ganglion cells and bipolar cells en route to the receptors. However, these cells are transparent, and light passes through them without distortion. A more important consequence is the *blind spot*. The ganglion cell axons form the **optic nerve,** which exits through the back of the eye. The point at which it leaves (which is also where the blood vessels enter and leave) is the **blind spot** because it has no receptors. You can demonstrate your own blind spot with Figure 6.4. Close your left eye and focus your right eye on the top o. Then move the page forward and back. When the page is about 25 cm (10 in.) away, the x disappears because its image strikes the blind spot.

Now repeat with the lower part of the figure. When the page is again about 25 cm away from your eyes, what do you see? The *gap* disappears! When the blind spot interrupts a straight line or other regular pattern, your brain fills in the gap.

TRY IT YOURSELF

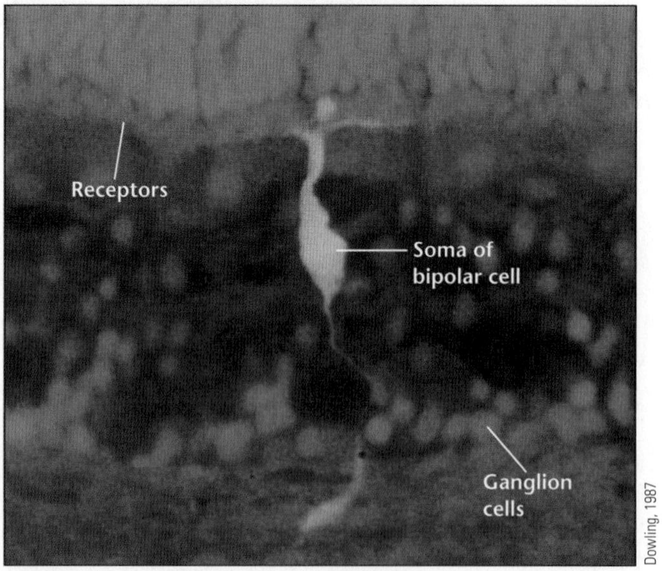

Figure 6.3 A bipolar cell from the retina of a carp, stained with Procion yellow
Bipolar cells get their name from the fact that a fibrous process is attached to each end (or pole) of the neuron.

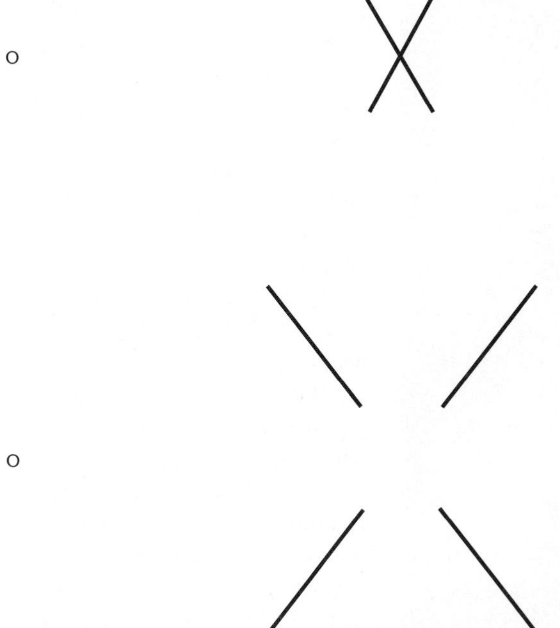

Figure 6.4 Two demonstrations of the blind spot of the retina
Close your left eye and focus your right eye on the o in the top part. Move the page toward you and away, noticing what happens to the x. At a distance of about 25 cm (10 in.), the x disappears. Now repeat this procedure with the bottom part. At that same distance, what do you see?

STOP & CHECK

3. What makes the blind spot of the retina blind?

ANSWER

3. The blind spot has no receptors because it is occupied by exiting axons and blood vessels.

Fovea and Periphery of the Retina

When you look at details such as letters on this page, you fixate them on the central portion of your retina, especially the **fovea** (meaning "pit"), a tiny area specialized for acute, detailed vision (see Figure 6.1). Because blood vessels and ganglion cell axons are almost absent near the fovea, it has nearly unimpeded vision. The tight packing of receptors also aids perception of detail.

More important, each receptor in the fovea connects to a single *bipolar cell,* which in turn connects to a single *ganglion cell,* which has an axon to the brain. The ganglion cells in the fovea of humans and other primates are called **midget ganglion cells** because each is small and responds to just a single cone. As a result, each cone in the fovea has a direct line to the brain, which registers the exact location of the input.

Toward the periphery, more and more receptors converge onto bipolar and ganglion cells. As a result, the brain cannot detect the exact location or shape of a peripheral light source. However, the summation enables perception of fainter lights in the periphery. In short, foveal vision has better *acuity* (sensitivity to detail), and peripheral vision has better sensitivity to dim light.

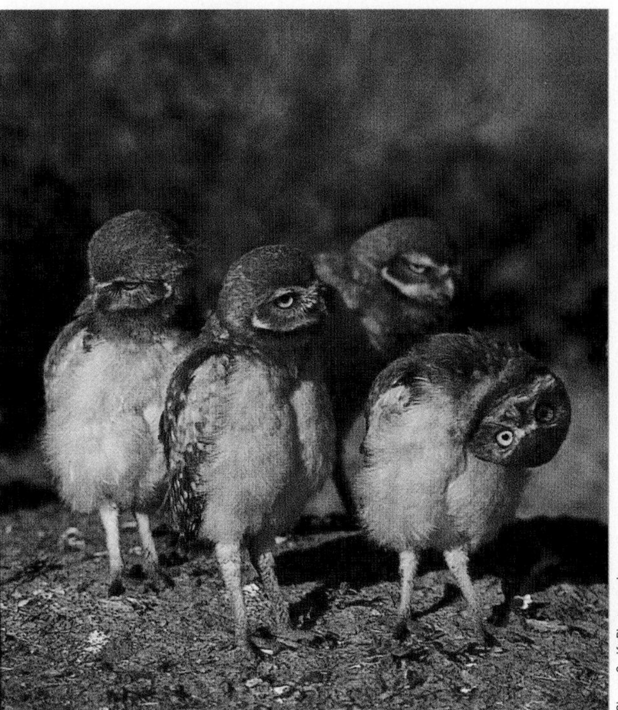

Chase Swift Photography

Figure 6.5 A behavioral consequence of how receptors are arranged on the retina
One owlet has turned its head almost upside down to see above itself. Birds of prey have a great density of receptors on the upper half of the retina, enabling them to see below them in great detail during flight. But they see objects above themselves poorly, unless they turn their heads. Take another look at the prairie falcon at the start of this chapter. It is not a one-eyed bird; it is a bird that has tilted its head. Do you now understand why?

You have heard the expression "eyes like a hawk." Many birds' eyes occupy most of the head, compared to only 5% of the head in humans. Furthermore, many bird species have two foveas per eye, one pointing ahead and one pointing to the side (Wallman & Pettigrew, 1985). The extra foveas enable perception of detail in the periphery.

Hawks and other predatory birds have a greater density of visual receptors on the top half of their retinas (looking down) than on the bottom half (looking up). That arrangement is adaptive because predatory birds spend most of their day soaring high in the air looking down. However, to look up, the bird must turn its head, as in Figure 6.5 (Waldvogel, 1990).

Conversely, many prey species such as rats have most of their receptors on the bottom half of the retina (Lund, Lund, & Wise, 1974). As a result, they see better above than below.

Visual Receptors: Rods and Cones

The vertebrate retina contains two types of receptors: rods and cones (Figure 6.6). The **rods,** which are abundant in the periphery of the human retina, respond to faint light but are not

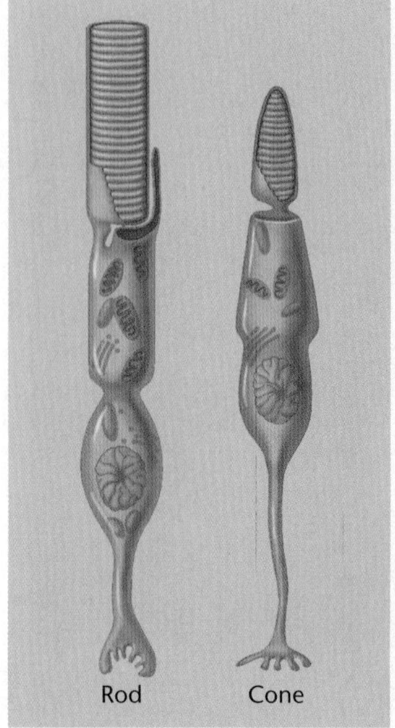

(a)

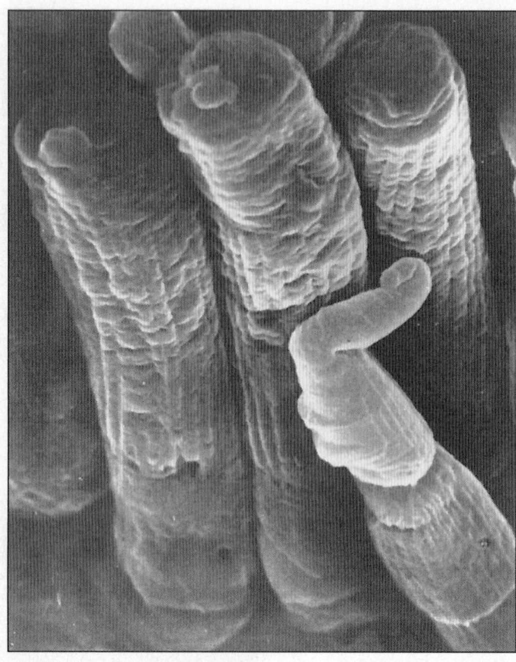

(b)

Figure 6.6 Structure of rod and cone
(a) Diagram of a rod and a cone. **(b)** Photo of rods and a cone, produced with a scanning electron microscope. Magnification x 7000. *(Reprinted from* Brain Research, 15(2), *E. R. Lewis, Y. Y. Zeevi and F. S. Werblin, "Scanning electron microscopy of vertebrate visual receptors," 1969, with permission from Elsevier.)*

useful in daylight because bright light bleaches them. **Cones,** which are abundant in and near the fovea, are less active in dim light, more useful in bright light, and essential for color vision. Because of the distribution of rods and cones, you have good color vision in the fovea but not in the periphery. Table 6.1 summarizes the differences between foveal and peripheral vision.

Although rods outnumber cones by about 20 to 1 in the human retina, cones provide about 90% of the brain's input (Masland, 2001). Remember the midget ganglion cells: In the fovea (all cones), each receptor has its own line to the brain. In the periphery (mostly rods), each receptor shares a line with tens or hundreds of others. Overall, 120 million rods and 6 million cones converge onto 1 million axons in the optic nerve, on the average.

A 20:1 ratio of rods to cones may sound high, but the ratio is much higher in species that are active at night. South American oilbirds, which live in caves and emerge only at night, have about 15,000 rods per cone. As a further adaptation to detect faint lights, their rods are packed three deep throughout the retina (G. Martin, Rojas, Ramírez, & McNeil, 2004).

Both rods and cones contain **photopigments,** chemicals that release energy when struck by light. Photopigments consist of 11-*cis*-retinal (a derivative of vitamin A) bound to proteins called *opsins,* which modify the photopigments' sensitivity to different wavelengths of light. Light converts 11-*cis*-retinal to all-*trans*-retinal, thus releasing energy that activates second messengers within the cell (Q. Wang, Schoenlein, Peteanu, Mathies, & Shank, 1994). (The light is absorbed in this process. It does not continue to bounce around the eye.)

STOP & CHECK

4. You sometimes find that you can see a faint star on a dark night better if you look slightly to the side of the star instead of straight at it. Why?

5. If you found a species with a high ratio of cones to rods in its retina, what would you predict about its way of life?

ANSWERS

4. If you look slightly to the side, the light falls on an area of the retina with more rods and more convergence of input. **5.** We should expect this species to be highly active during the day and seldom active at night.

TABLE 6.1 Human Foveal Vision and Peripheral Vision

Characteristic	Foveal Vision	Peripheral Vision
Receptors	Cones in the fovea itself; cones and rods mix in the surrounding area	Proportion of rods increases toward the periphery; the extreme periphery has only rods
Convergence of receptors	Just a few receptors send their input to each postsynaptic cell	Increasing numbers of receptors send input to each postsynaptic cell
Brightness sensitivity	Useful for distinguishing among bright lights; responds poorly to faint lights	Responds well to faint lights; less useful for making distinctions in bright light
Sensitivity to detail	Good detail vision because few receptors funnel their input to a postsynaptic cell	Poor detail vision because so many receptors send their input to the same postsynaptic cell
Color vision	Good (many cones)	Poor (few cones)

Color Vision

In the human visual system, the shortest visible wavelengths, about 350 nm (1 nm = nanometer, or 10^{-9} m), are perceived as violet; progressively longer wavelengths are perceived as blue, green, yellow, orange, and red, near 700 nm (Figure 6.7). The "visible" wavelengths depend on a species' receptors. For example, many species of birds, fish, and insects see ultraviolet wavelengths that we do not (Stevens & Cuthill, 2007). In some species of birds, the male and female look alike to us, but different to birds, because the male reflects more ultraviolet light.

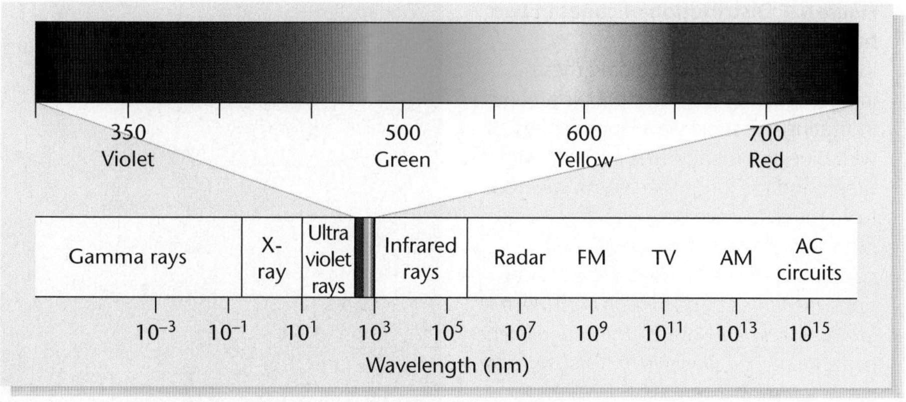

Figure 6.7 A beam of light separated into its wavelengths
Although the wavelengths vary over a continuum, we perceive them as several distinct colors.

The Trichromatic (Young-Helmholtz) Theory

People distinguish red, green, yellow, blue, orange, pink, purple, greenish-blue, and so forth. Presuming that we don't have a separate receptor for every possible color, how many types do we have?

The first person to approach this question fruitfully was an amazingly productive man named Thomas Young (1773–1829). Young was the first to start deciphering the Rosetta stone. He also founded the modern wave theory of light, defined energy in its modern form, founded the calculation of annuities, introduced the coefficient of elasticity, discovered much about the anatomy of the eye, and made major contributions to many other fields (Martindale, 2001). Previous scientists thought they could explain color by understanding the physics of light. Young recognized that color required a biological explanation. He proposed that we perceive color by comparing the responses across a few types of receptors, each of which was sensitive to a different range of wavelengths.

This theory, later modified by Hermann von Helmholtz, is now known as the **trichromatic theory** of color vision, or the **Young-Helmholtz theory.** According to this theory, we perceive color through the relative rates of response by three kinds of cones, each kind maximally sensitive to a different set of wavelengths. (*Trichromatic* means "three colors.") How did Helmholtz decide on the number three? He found that people could match any color by mixing appropriate amounts of just three wavelengths. Therefore, he concluded that three kinds of receptors—we now call them cones—are sufficient to account for human color vision.

Figure 6.8 shows wavelength-sensitivity functions for the *short-wavelength, medium-wavelength,* and *long-wavelength* cone types. Each cone responds to a broad range of wavelengths but to some more than others.

According to the trichromatic theory, we discriminate among wavelengths by the ratio of activity across the three types of cones. For example, light at 550 nm excites the medium-wavelength and long-wavelength receptors about equally and the short-wavelength receptor almost not at all. This ratio of responses among the three cones determines a perception of yellow-green. More intense light increases the activity of all three cones without much change in their ratio of responses. As a result, the light appears brighter but still the same color. When all three types of cones are equally active, we see white or gray. Think about this example of coding: The perception depends on frequency of firing, but it is the frequency of one cell relative to the frequency of another cell.

The response of any one cone is ambiguous. For example, a low response rate by a middle-wavelength cone might indicate low-intensity 540-nm light or brighter 500-nm light or still brighter 460-nm light. A high response rate could indicate

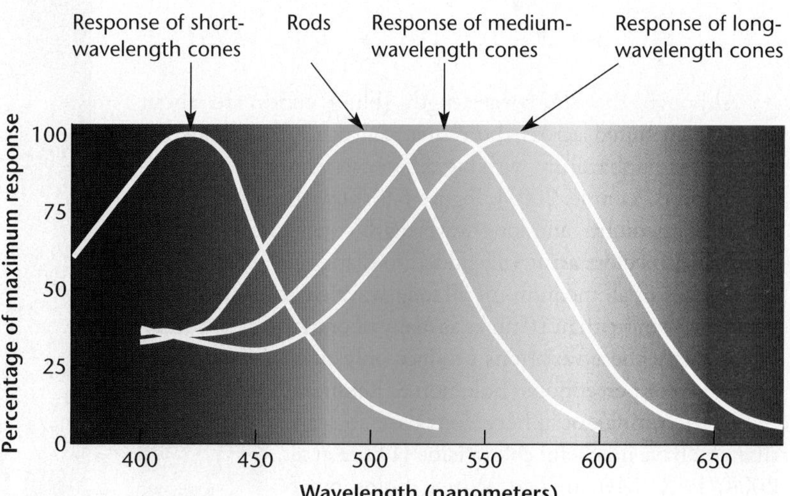

Figure 6.8 Response of rods and three kinds of cones to various wavelengths of light
Note that each kind responds somewhat to a wide range of wavelengths but best to wavelengths in a particular range. *(Adapted from Bowmaker & Dartnall, 1980)*

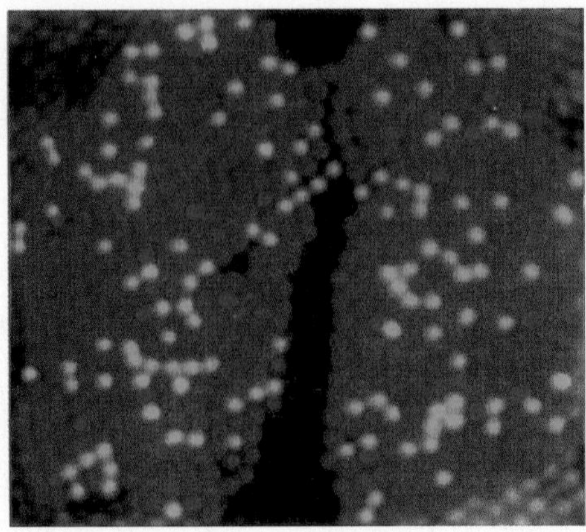
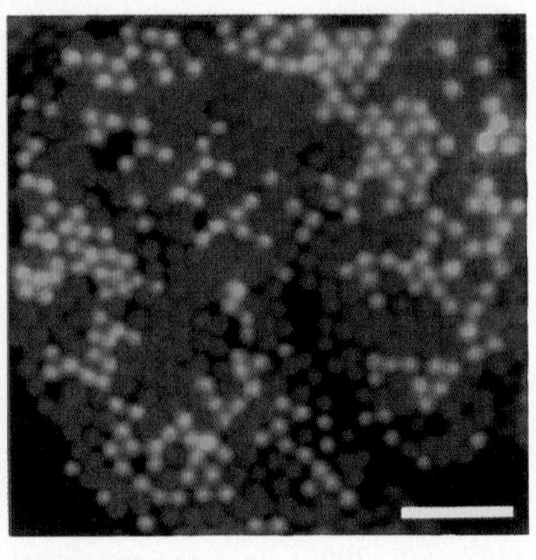

Roorda & Williams, 1999

Figure 6.9 Distribution of cones in two human retinas
Investigators artificially colored these images of cones from two people's retinas, indicating the short-wavelength cones with blue, the medium-wavelength with green, and the long-wavelength with red. Note the difference between the two people, the scarcity of short-wavelength cones, and the patchiness of the distributions. *(Reprinted by permission from Macmillan Publishers Ltd:* Nature, *"The arrangement of the three cone classes in the living human eye," Roorda & Williams, 1999.)*

bright light at just 540 nm, or bright white light, which includes 540 nm. The nervous system determines the color and brightness of the light by comparing the responses of different types of cones. (Consequently, animals such as mice, with only one kind of cone, are color blind.)

TRY IT YOURSELF

Given the desirability of seeing all colors in all locations, we might suppose that the three kinds of cones would be equally abundant and evenly distributed. In fact, they are not. Long- and medium-wavelength cones are far more abundant than short-wavelength (blue) cones, and consequently, it is easier to see tiny red, yellow, or green dots than blue dots (Roorda & Williams, 1999). Try this: Look at the dots in the following display, first from close and then from greater distances. You probably will notice that the blue dots look blue when close but appear black from a greater distance. The other colors are still visible when the blue is not.

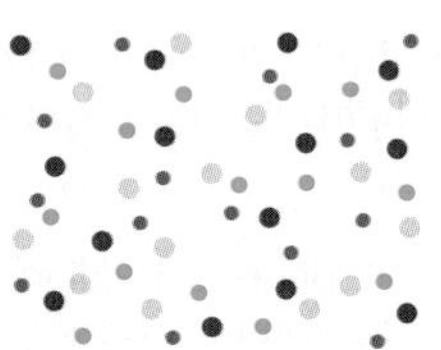

Although the short-wavelength (blue) cones are about evenly distributed across the retina, the other two kinds are distributed haphazardly, with big differences among individuals (Solomon & Lennie, 2007). Figure 6.9 shows the distribution of short-, medium-, and long-wavelength cones in two people's retinas, with colors artificially added to distinguish them. Note the patches of all medium- or all long-wavelength cones. Some people have more than 10 times as many of one kind as the other. Surprisingly, these variations produce only small differences in people's color perceptions (Solomon & Lennie, 2007).

In the retina's periphery, cones are so scarce that you have no useful color vision (Diller et al., 2004; P. R. Martin, Lee, White, Solomon, & Rütiger, 2001). Try this: Get someone to put a colored dot on the tip of your finger without telling you the color. A spot of colored ink will do. While keeping your eyes straight ahead, slowly move your finger from behind your head into your field of vision and gradually toward your fovea. At what point do you see the color? The smaller the dot, the farther you have to move it into your **visual field**—that is, the part of the world that you see—before you can identify the color.

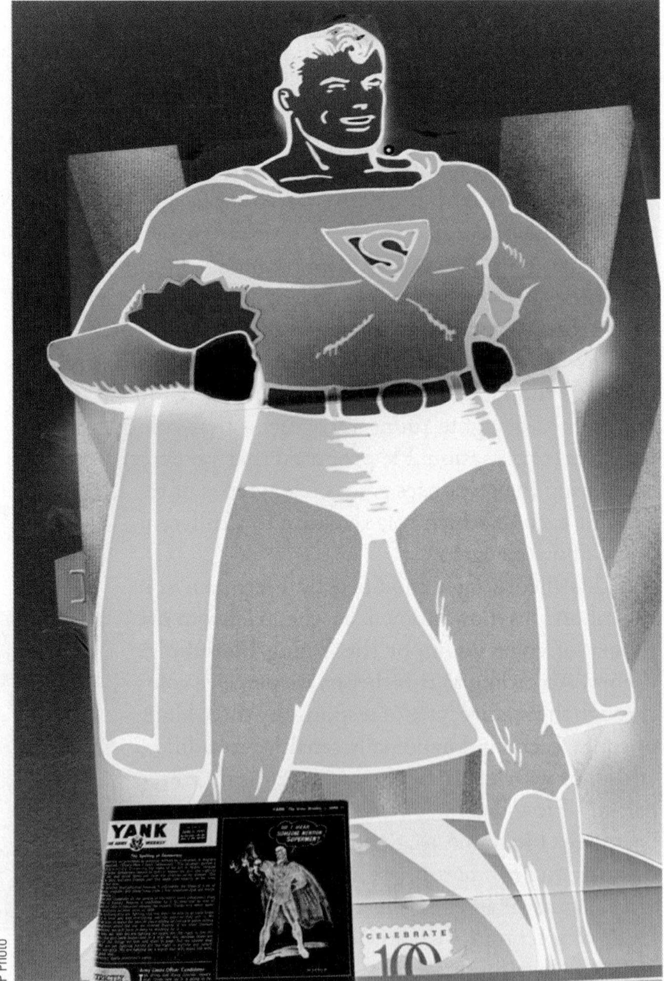

AP Photo

Figure 6.10 Stimulus for demonstrating negative color afterimages
Stare at any point on the face under bright light for about a minute and then look at a white field. You should see a negative afterimage.

The Opponent-Process Theory

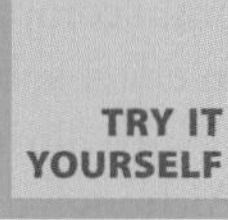

The trichromatic theory is incomplete as a theory of color vision. For example, try the following demonstration: Pick a point in the top portion of Figure 6.10—such as the tip of the nose—and stare at it under a bright light, without moving your eyes, for a minute. (The brighter the light and the longer you stare, the stronger the effect.) Then look at a plain white surface, such as a wall or a blank sheet of paper. Keep your eyes steady. You will see a **negative color afterimage,** a replacement of the red you had been staring at with green, green with red, yellow and blue with each other, and black and white with each other.

To explain this and related phenomena, Ewald Hering, a 19th-century physiologist, proposed the **opponent-process theory:** We perceive color in terms of opposites (Hurvich & Jameson, 1957). That is, the brain has a mechanism that perceives color on a continuum from red to green, another from yellow to blue, and another from white to black.

Here is a hypothetical mechanism: The bipolar cell diagrammed in Figure 6.11 is excited by short-wavelength (blue) light and inhibited by a mixture of long-wavelength and medium-wavelength light. An increase in this bipolar cell's activity produces the experience *blue,* and a decrease produces the experience *yellow.* If short-wavelength (blue) light stimulates this cell long enough, the cell becomes fatigued. If we now remove the short-wavelength light, the cell is more inhibited than excited, responds less than its baseline level, and therefore produces an experience of *yellow.* This example is a special kind of coding, in which an increase in response produces one perception, and a decrease produces a different perception.

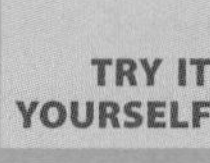

Although that explanation of negative color afterimages is appealingly simple, it cannot be the whole story. Try this: Stare at the x in the following diagram for a minute or more under the brightest light you can find and then look at a white page.

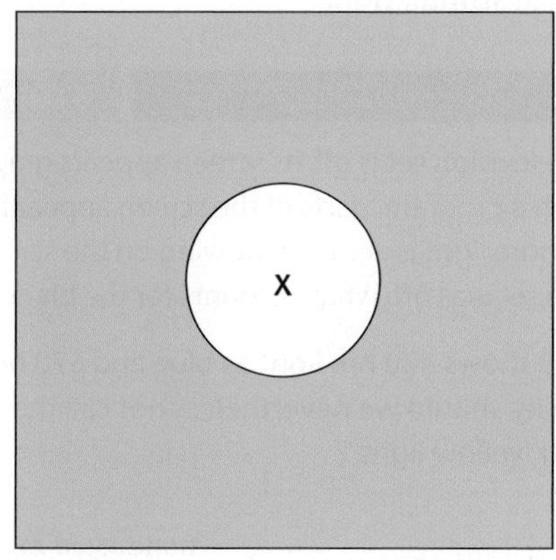

For the afterimage of the surrounding box, you saw red, as the theory predicts. But what about the circle inside? Theoretically, you should see a gray or black afterimage (the opposite of white), but in fact, if you used a bright enough light, you saw a green afterimage.

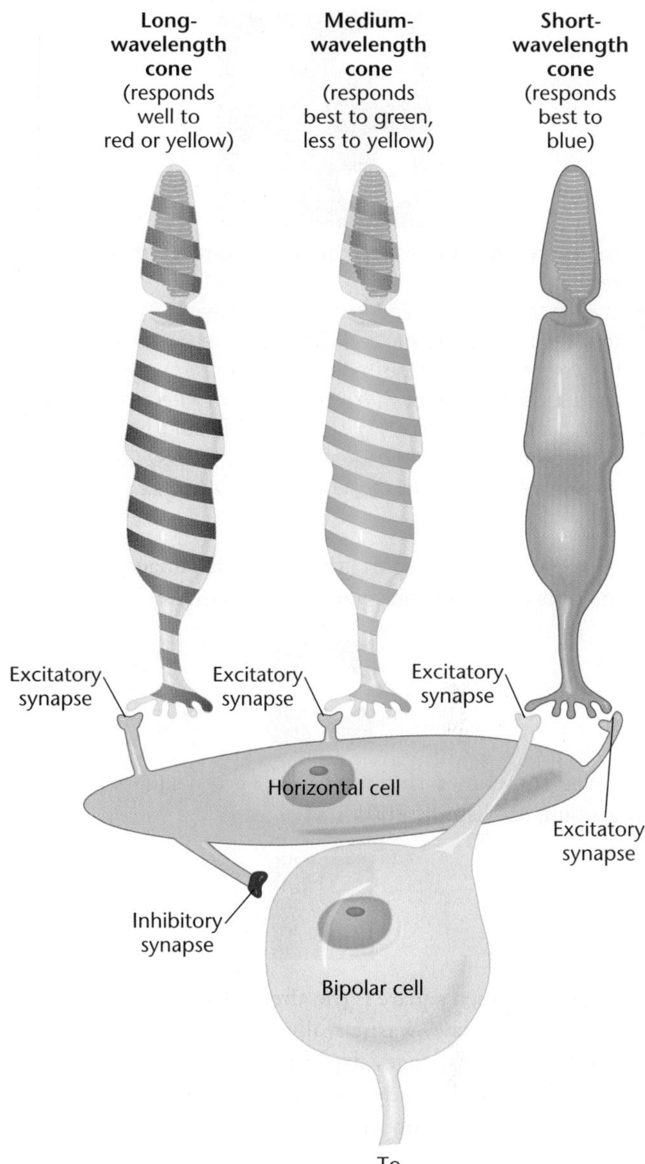

Figure 6.11 Possible wiring for one bipolar cell
Short-wavelength light (which we see as blue) excites the bipolar cell and (by way of the intermediate horizontal cell) also inhibits it. However, the excitation predominates, so blue light produces net excitation. Red, green, and yellow light inhibit this bipolar cell because they produce inhibition (through the horizontal cell). The strongest inhibition is from yellow light, which stimulates both the long- and medium-wavelength cones. Therefore, we can describe this bipolar cell as excited by blue and inhibited by yellow.

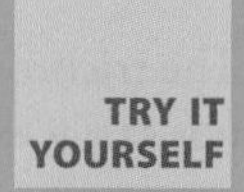

Here is another demonstration: First, look at Figure 6.12. Note that although it shows four red quarter circles, you have the illusion of a whole red square. (Look carefully to convince yourself that it is an illusion.) Now stare at the x in Figure 6.12 for at least a minute under bright lights. Then look at a white surface.

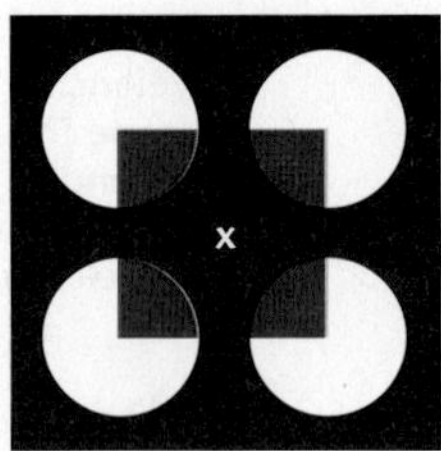

Figure 6.12 An afterimage hard to explain in terms of the retina

Stare at the tiny x under bright light for at least a minute and then look at a white surface. Many people report an alternation between two afterimages, one of them based on the illusion of a red square. *(Reprinted with permission from "Afterimage of perceptually filled-in surface," Fig. 1A, p. 1678 (left hand) by S. Shimojo, Y. Kamitani, and S. Nishida in* Science, *293, 1677–1680. Copyright 2001 American Association for the Advancement of Science.)*

People usually report that the afterimage fluctuates. Sometimes, they see four green quarter circles:

And sometimes, they see a whole green square (Shimojo, Kamitani, & Nishida, 2001):

A whole green square is the afterimage of an illusion! The red square you "saw" wasn't really there. This demonstration suggests that afterimages depend on the whole context, not just the light on individual receptors. Probably, the cerebral cortex is responsible, not the bipolar or ganglion cells.

STOP & CHECK

6. Suppose a bipolar cell receives excitatory input from medium-wavelength cones and inhibitory input from all three kinds of cones. When it is highly excited, what color would one see? When it is inhibited, what color perception would result?

ANSWER

6. Excitation of this cell should yield a perception of green under normal circumstances. Inhibition would produce the opposite sensation, red.

The Retinex Theory

The trichromatic theory and the opponent-process theory cannot easily explain **color constancy,** the ability to recognize colors despite changes in lighting (Kennard, Lawden, Morland, & Ruddock, 1995; Zeki, 1980, 1983). If you wear green-tinted glasses or replace your white light bulb with a green one, you still identify bananas as yellow, paper as white, and so forth. Your brain compares the color of one object with the color of another, in effect subtracting a fixed amount of green from each.

To illustrate, examine Figure 6.13a (Purves & Lotto, 2003). Although different colors of light illuminate the two scenes, you easily identify which of the little squares are red, yellow, blue, and so forth. Note the result of removing context. The bottom part shows the squares that looked red in the top part. Without the context that indicated yellow light or blue light, those on the left look orange and those on the right look purple. (For this reason, we should avoid talking about the "color" of a wavelength of light. A certain wavelength of light can appear as several different colors depending on the background.)

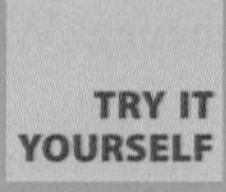

Similarly, our perception of the brightness of an object requires comparing it with other objects. Examine Figure 6.14 (Purves, Shimpi, & Lotto, 1999). You see what appears to have a gray top and a white bottom. Now cover the border between the top and the bottom with your fingers. You will notice that the top of the object has exactly the same brightness as the bottom! For additional examples like this, visit the Web site of Dale Purves, Center for Cognitive Neuroscience, Duke University, at http://www.purveslab.net

To account for color and brightness constancy, Edwin Land proposed the **retinex theory** (a combination of the words *retina* and *cortex*): The cortex compares information from various parts of the retina to determine the brightness and color for each area (Land, Hubel, Livingstone, Perry, & Burns, 1983).

Dale Purves and colleagues have expressed a similar idea in more general terms: Whenever we see anything, we make an inference. For example, when you look at the objects in Figures 6.13 and 6.14, you ask yourself, "On occasions when I have seen something that looked like this, what was it really?" You go through the same process for perceiving shapes, motion, or anything else (Lotto & Purves, 2002; Purves & Lotto, 2003). That is, visual perception requires a reasoning process, not just retinal stimulation.

STOP & CHECK

7. When a television set is off, its screen appears gray. When you watch a program, parts of the screen appear black, even though more light is actually showing on the screen than when the set was off. What accounts for the black perception?

8. Figure 6.8 shows 480 nm light as blue and 570 nm light as yellow. Why should we nevertheless not call them "blue light" and "yellow light"?

ANSWERS

7. The black experience arises by contrast with the other brighter areas. The contrast occurs by comparison within the cerebral cortex, as in the retinex theory of color vision. **8.** Color perception depends not just on the wavelength of light from a given spot but also the light from surrounding areas. As in Figure 6.13, the context can change the color perception.

(a)

(b)

(c)

Figure 6.13 Effects of context on color perception
In each block, we identify certain tiles as looking red. However, after removal of the context, those that appeared red on the left now look orange; those on the right appear purple. *(Why We See What We Do, by D. Purves and R. B. Lotto, figure 6.10, p. 134. Copyright 2003 Sinauer Associates, Inc. Reprinted by permission.)*

Figure 6.14 A powerful demonstration of brightness constancy
In the center of this figure, do you see a gray object above and a white object below? Place a finger over the border between them and then compare the objects. *(From "An Empirical Explanation of Cornsweet Effect," by D. Purves, A. Shimpi, & R. B. Lotto, in* Journal of Neuroscience, 19, *8542–8551. Copyright © 1999 by the Society for Neuroscience.)*

Color Vision Deficiency

Encyclopedias describe many examples of discoveries in astronomy, biology, chemistry, and physics, but what are psychologists' discoveries? One of the first was color blindness, better described as **color vision deficiency.** (Complete color blindness, perception of only black and white, is rare.) Before color vision deficiency was discovered in the 1600s, people assumed that vision copies the objects we see (Fletcher & Voke, 1985). By that theory, everyone should see objects the same way. Investigators *discovered* that it is possible to have otherwise satisfactory vision without seeing color. That is, color depends on what our brains do with incoming light. It is not a property of the light itself.

For genetic reasons, some people lack one or two of the types of cones. Some have three kinds of cones, but one kind is abnormal (Nathans et al., 1989). In the most common form of color vision deficiency, people have trouble distinguishing red from green because their long- and medium-wavelength cones have the same photopigment instead of different ones. The gene causing this deficiency is on the X chromosome. About 8% of men are red-green color deficient compared with less than 1% of women (Bowmaker, 1998).

APPLICATIONS AND EXTENSIONS

People with Four Cone Types

Does anyone have *more* than three kinds of cones? Some women do. The gene controlling the long-wavelength (LW) cone receptor varies, causing slight differences in which wavelength produces the maximum response (Stockman & Sharpe, 1998). The gene controlling this receptor is on the X chromosome, so—because men have only one X chromosome—men have only one type of LW receptor. For women, one X chromosome in each cell is activated and the other is inhibited, apparently at random. (There is a good reason for inactivating one X chromosome per cell. If both X chromosomes were active in women, then either women would be getting an overdose of the X-related proteins or men would be getting too little.) Women who have both kinds of long-wavelength genes produce slightly different long-wavelength (red) receptors in different cones (Neitz, Kraft, & Neitz, 1998).

If a brain gets this extra information, does it know what to do with it? Probably so. Ordinarily, mice have only one kind of cone, which helps them see differences of brightness but not color. Researchers genetically engineered some mice to have an additional kind of cone. These mice showed behavioral evidence of color vision (Jacobs, Williams, Cahill, & Nathans, 2007). Evidently, the brain adapts to use the information it receives.

Several studies have found that women with two kinds of long-wavelength receptors draw slightly finer color distinctions than other people do. That is, they see color differences between two objects that seem the same to other people (Jameson, Highnote, & Wasserman, 2001). This effect is small, however, and emerges only with careful testing.

For more information about the retina and vision, the Webvision site, John Moran Eye Center, University of Utah, provides an excellent treatment http://www.webvision.med.utah.edu

STOP & CHECK

9. Most people can use varying amounts of three colors to match any other color that they see. Who would be an exception to this rule, and how many colors would they need?

ANSWER

9. Red-green color-deficient people would need only two colors. Women with four kinds of cones might need four.

MODULE 6.1 IN CLOSING

Visual Receptors

I remember once explaining to my then-teenage son a newly discovered detail about the visual system, only to have him reply, "I didn't realize it would be so complicated. I thought the light strikes your eyes and then you see it." As you should now be starting to realize—and if not, the next module should convince you—vision requires complicated processing. If you tried to equip a robot with vision, you would quickly discover that shining light into its eyes accomplishes nothing, unless its visual detectors are connected to devices that identify the useful information and use it to select the proper action. We have such devices in our brains, although we are still far from fully understanding them.

SUMMARY

1. According to the law of specific nerve energies, the brain interprets any activity of a given sensory neuron as representing the sensory information to which that neuron is tuned **152**
2. Sensory information is coded so that the brain can process it. The coded information bears no physical similarity to the stimuli it describes. **153**
3. Light passes through the pupil of a vertebrate eye and stimulates the receptors lining the retina at the back of the eye. **153**
4. The axons from the retina loop around to form the optic nerve, which exits from the eye at a point called the blind spot. **154**
5. Visual acuity is greatest in the fovea, the central area of the retina. Because so many receptors in the periphery converge their messages to their bipolar cells, our peripheral vision is highly sensitive to faint light but poorly sensitive to detail. **155**
6. The retina has two kinds of receptors: rods and cones. Rods are more sensitive to faint light; cones are more useful in bright light. Rods are more numerous in the periphery of the eye. Cones are more numerous in the fovea. **155**
7. Light stimulates the receptors by triggering a molecular change in 11-*cis*-retinal, releasing energy, and thereby activating second messengers within the cell. **156**
8. According to the trichromatic (or Young-Helmholtz) theory of color vision, color perception begins with a given wavelength of light stimulating a distinctive ratio of responses by the three types of cones. **157**
9. According to the opponent-process theory of color vision, visual system neurons beyond the receptors themselves respond with an increase in activity to indicate one color of light and a decrease to indicate the opposite color. The three pairs of opposites are red-green, yellow-blue, and white-black. **158**
10. According to the retinex theory, the cortex compares the responses representing different parts of the retina to determine the brightness and color of each area. **160**
11. For genetic reasons, certain people are unable to distinguish one color from another. Red-green color deficiency is the most common type. **162**

KEY TERMS

Terms are defined in the module on the page number indicated. They're also presented in alphabetical order with definitions in the book's Subject Index/Glossary. Interactive flashcards, audio reviews, and crossword puzzles are among the online resources available to help you learn these terms and the concepts they represent.

bipolar cells **154**
blind spot **154**
color constancy **160**
color vision deficiency **162**
cones **156**
fovea **155**
ganglion cells **154**
law of specific nerve energies **152**
midget ganglion cells **155**
negative color afterimage **158**
opponent-process theory **158**
optic nerve **154**
photopigments **156**
pupil **153**
retina **153**
retinex theory **160**
rods **155**
trichromatic theory (or Young-Helmholtz theory) **157**
visual field **158**

Continued

THOUGHT QUESTION

How could you test for the presence of color vision in a bee? Examining the retina does not help because invertebrate receptors resemble neither rods nor cones. It is possible to train bees to approach one visual stimulus and not another. However, if you train bees to approach, say, a yellow card and not a green card, you do not know whether they solved the problem by color or by brightness. Because brightness is different from physical intensity, you cannot assume that two colors equally bright to humans are also equally bright to bees. How might you get around the problem of brightness to test color vision in bees?

MODULE 6.2

Neural Basis of Visual Perception

Long ago, people assumed that everyone who saw an object saw it the same way. The discovery of color blindness was a huge surprise in its time. Even today, you may be surprised—as were late 20th-century psychologists—by the phenomenon of *motion blindness*: Some people with otherwise satisfactory vision fail to see that an object is moving. "How could anyone see an object and not see that it is moving?" you might ask. Your question is not much different from the question raised in the 1600s: "How could anyone see something without seeing the color?"

The fundamental fact about vision takes a little getting used to: You have no central processor that sees every aspect of a visual stimulus at once. Different parts of your cortex process different aspects of vision, and you can lose one while sparing the others.

An Overview of the Mammalian Visual System

Let's begin with a general outline of the anatomy of the mammalian visual system and then examine certain stages in more detail. The rods and cones of the retina make synapses with **horizontal cells** and bipolar cells (see Figures 6.2 and 6.15). The horizontal cells make inhibitory contact onto bipolar cells, which in turn make synapses onto *amacrine cells* and ganglion cells. All these cells are within the eyeball.

The axons of the ganglion cells form the optic nerve, which leaves the retina and travels along the lower surface of the brain. The optic nerves from the two eyes meet at the optic chiasm (Figure 6.16a), where, in humans, half of the axons from each eye cross to the opposite side of the brain. As shown in Figure 6.16b, information from the nasal half of each eye crosses to the contralateral hemisphere. Information from the temporal half (the side toward the temporal cortex) goes to the ipsilateral hemisphere. The percentage of crossover varies from one species to another depending on the location of the eyes. In species with eyes far to the sides of the head, such as rabbits and guinea pigs, nearly all axons cross to the opposite side.

Most ganglion cell axons go to the **lateral geniculate nucleus,** part of the thalamus. (The term *geniculate* comes from the Latin root *genu*, meaning "knee." To *genuflect* is to bend the knee. The lateral geniculate looks a little like a knee, if you use some imagination.) A smaller number of axons go to the superior colliculus and other areas, including part of the hypothalamus that controls the waking–sleeping schedule (see Chapter 9). At any rate, most of the optic nerve goes to the lateral geniculate, which in turn sends axons to other parts of the thalamus and the occipital cortex. The cortex returns many axons to the thalamus, so the thalamus and cortex constantly feed information back and forth (Guillery, Feig, & van Lieshout, 2001).

STOP & CHECK

10. Where does the optic nerve start and where does it end?

ANSWER

10. It starts with the ganglion cells in the retina. Most of its axons go to the lateral geniculate nucleus of the thalamus; some go to the hypothalamus, superior colliculus, and elsewhere.

Processing in the Retina

At any instant, an enormous amount of information strikes your retina. You need to extract the meaningful patterns, such as the edges of objects. The wiring diagram enables cells in your eye and brain to identify the important patterns. To understand this idea, let's explore one example in detail: lateral inhibition, which occurs in the retina.

Lateral inhibition is the retina's way of sharpening contrasts to emphasize the borders of objects. We begin with the rods and cones. They have spontaneous levels of activity, and light striking them *decreases* their output. They have *inhibitory* synapses onto the bipolar cells, and therefore, light *decreases* their *inhibitory* output. To avoid double negatives, let's think of their output as excitation of the bipolar cells. In the fovea, each cone attaches to just one bipolar cell. Outside the fovea, larger numbers connect to each bipolar cell, as shown in Figure 6.2 on page 154. We'll consider the case of a cone in the fovea connected to just one bipolar.

Figure 6.15 The vertebrate retina
(a) Diagram of the neurons of the retina. The top of the figure is the back of the retina. All the optic nerve fibers group together and then turn around to exit through the back of the retina, in the "blind spot" of the eye. *(Based on "Organization of the Primate Retina," by J. E. Dowling and B. B. Boycott,* Proceedings of the Royal Society of London, B, 1966, 166, *pp. 80–111. Used by permission of the Royal Society of London and John Dowling.)*
(b) Photo of a cross-section through the retina. This section from the periphery of the retina has relatively few ganglion cells. A slice closer to the fovea would have a greater density.

Rod and cone receptors (R)
Horizontal cell (H)
Bipolar cells (B)
Amacrine cells (A)
Ganglion cells (G)
Light rays
(a)
Outer segment
Inner segment
Optic nerve fibers

In the next diagram, the green arrows represent excitation. Receptor 8, which is highlighted, produces increased excitation of bipolar cell 8, as indicated by the thicker green arrow. It also excites a horizontal cell, which *inhibits* the bipolar cells, as shown by red arrows. Because the horizontal cell spreads widely, excitation of any receptor inhibits many bipolar cells. Because the horizontal cell is a *local cell*, with no axon and no action potentials, its depolarization decays with distance. The horizontal cell inhibits bipolar cells 7 through 9 strongly, bipolars 6 and 10 a bit less, and so on. Bipolar cell 8 shows net excitation; the excitatory synapse outweighs the effect of the horizontal cell's inhibition. However, the bipolar cells to the sides (laterally) get no excitation but some inhibition by the horizontal cell. Bipolar cells 7 and 9 are strongly inhibited, so their activity falls below their spontaneous level. Bipolars 6 and 10 are inhibited less, so their activity decreases a bit less. In this diagram, the thickness of the arrow indicates the amount of excitation or inhibition.

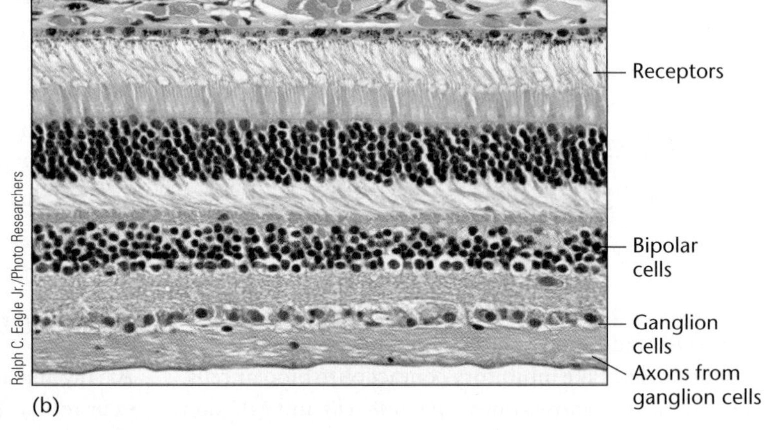

(b)

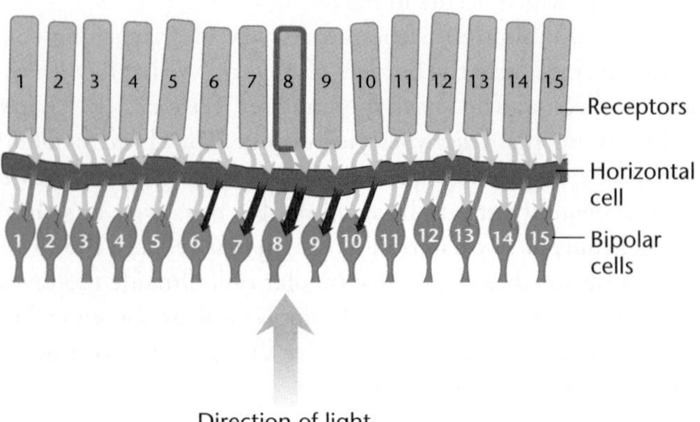

Now imagine that light excites receptors 6–10. These receptors excite bipolar cells 6–10 and the horizontal cell. Bipolar cells 6–10 all receive the same amount of excitation but not the same amount of inhibition. Remember, the response of the horizontal cell decays over distance. Bipolar cells 7, 8, and 9 are inhibited by input on both sides, but bipolar cells 6 and 10 are inhibited from one side and not the other. That is, the bipolar cells in the middle of the excited area are inhibited the most, and those on the edges are inhibited the least. Therefore, bipolar cells 6 and 10 respond *more* than bipolars 7–9.

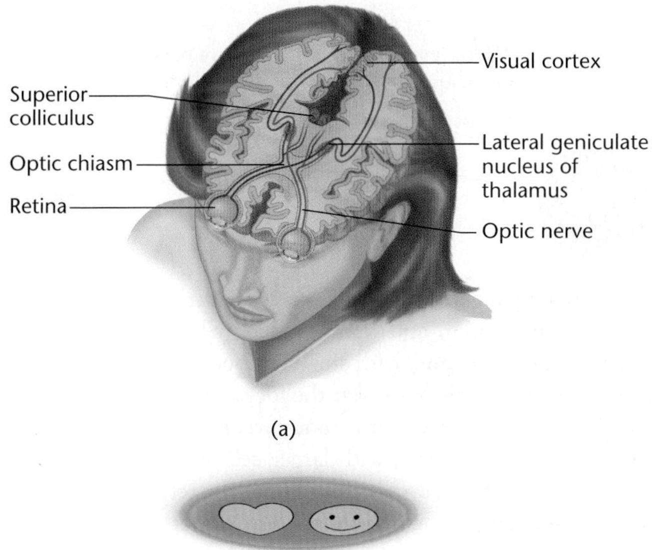

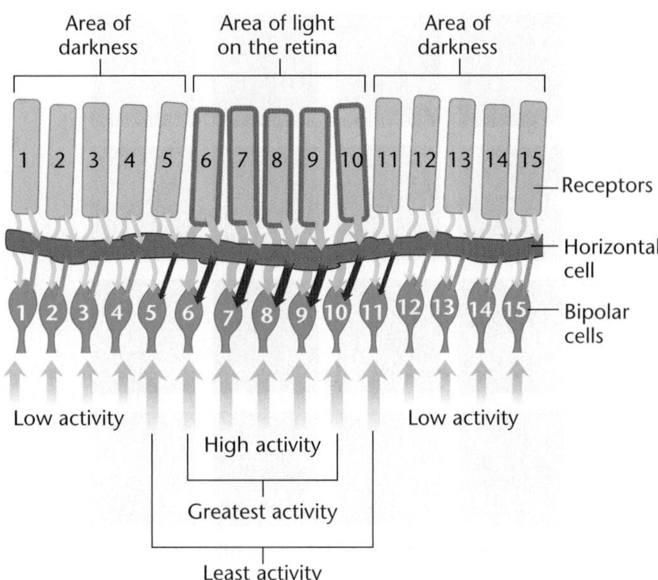

These results illustrate **lateral inhibition,** the reduction of activity in one neuron by activity in neighboring neurons (Hartline, 1949). The main function of lateral inhibition is to heighten the contrasts. When light falls on a surface, as shown here, the bipolars just inside the border are most excited, and those outside the border respond the least.

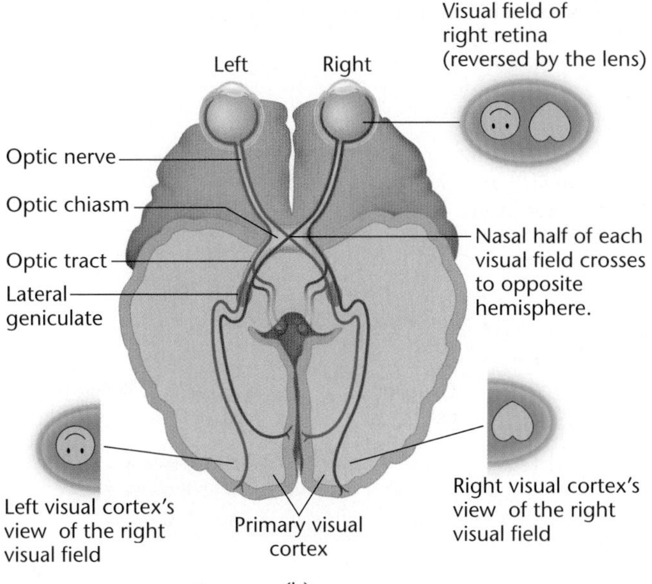

Figure 6.16 Major connections in the visual system of the brain
(a) Part of the visual input goes to the thalamus and from there to the visual cortex. Another part of the visual input goes to the superior colliculus. **(b)** Axons from the retina maintain their relationship to one another—what we call their *retinotopic organization*—throughout their journey from the retina to the lateral geniculate and then from the lateral geniculate to the cortex.

Now consider bipolar cells 5 and 11. What excitation do they receive? None. However, the horizontal cell inhibits them. Therefore, receiving inhibition but no excitation, they respond less than bipolar cells that are farther from the area of excitation.

STOP & CHECK

11. When light strikes a receptor, does the receptor excite or inhibit the bipolar cells? What effect does it have on horizontal cells? What effect does the horizontal cell have on bipolar cells?

12. If light strikes only one receptor, what is the net effect (excitatory or inhibitory) on the nearest bipolar cell that is directly connected to that receptor? What is the effect on bipolar cells off to the sides? What causes that effect?

13. Examine Figure 6.17. You should see grayish diamonds at the crossroads among the black squares. Explain why.

ANSWERS

11. The receptor excites both the bipolar cells and the horizontal cell. The horizontal cell inhibits the same bipolar cell that was excited plus additional bipolar cells in the surround. **12.** It produces more excitation than inhibition for the nearest bipolar cell. For surrounding bipolar cells, it produces only inhibition. The reason is that the receptor excites a horizontal cell, which inhibits all bipolar cells in the area. **13.** In the parts of your retina that look at the long white arms, each neuron is maximally inhibited by input on two of its sides (either above and below or left and right). In the crossroads, each neuron is maximally inhibited by input on all four sides. Therefore, the response in the crossroads is decreased compared to that in the arms.

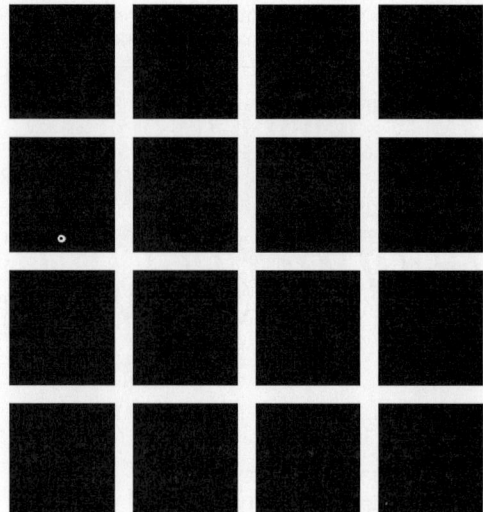

Figure 6.17 An illustration of lateral inhibition
Do you see dark diamonds at the "crossroads"?

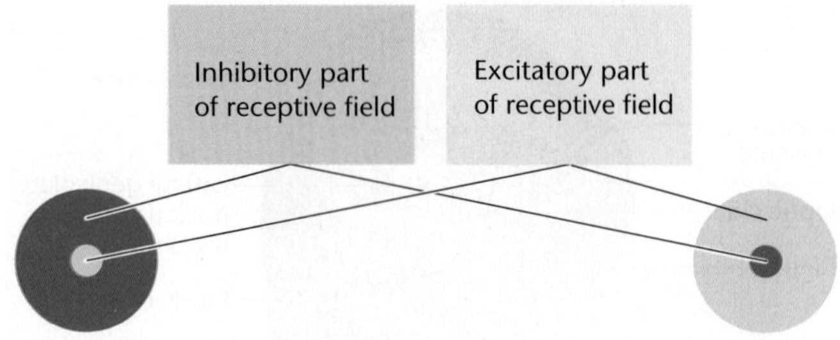

Primate ganglion cells fall into three categories: parvocellular, magnocellular, and koniocellular (Shapley, 1995). The **parvocellular neurons,** with small cell bodies and small receptive fields, are mostly in or near the fovea. (Parvocellular means "small celled," from the Latin root *parv*, meaning "small.") The **magnocellular neurons,** with larger cell bodies and receptive fields, are distributed evenly throughout the retina. (Magnocellular means "large celled," from the Latin root *magn*, meaning "large." The same root appears in *magnify*.) The **koniocellular neurons** have small cell bodies, similar to the parvocellular neurons, but they occur throughout the retina. (Koniocellular means "dust celled," from the Greek root meaning "dust." They got this name because of their granular appearance.)

Pathways to the Lateral Geniculate and Beyond

Perhaps you see someone walking by. Although your perception seems to be an integrated whole, different parts of your brain are analyzing different aspects. One set of neurons identifies the person's shape, another set concentrates on the colors, and another sees the speed and direction of movement (Livingstone, 1988; Livingstone & Hubel, 1988; Zeki & Shipp, 1988).

Each cell in the visual system of the brain has what we call a **receptive field,** which is the part of the visual field that excites or inhibits it. The receptive field of a receptor is simply the point in space from which light strikes the cell. Other visual cells derive their receptive fields from the pattern of excitatory and inhibitory connections to them. For example, a ganglion cell is connected to a group of bipolar cells, which in turn connect to receptors. The receptive field of the ganglion cell is the combined receptive fields of those receptors, as shown in Figure 6.18. The receptive fields of the ganglion cells converge to form the receptive fields of the next level of cells and so on.

To find a receptive field, an investigator shines light in various locations while recording from a neuron. If light from a particular spot excites the neuron, then that location is part of the neuron's excitatory receptive field. If it inhibits activity, the location is in the inhibitory receptive field.

The receptive field of a ganglion cell can be described as a circular center with an antagonistic doughnut-shaped surround. That is, light in the center of the receptive field might be excitatory, with the surround inhibitory, or the opposite.

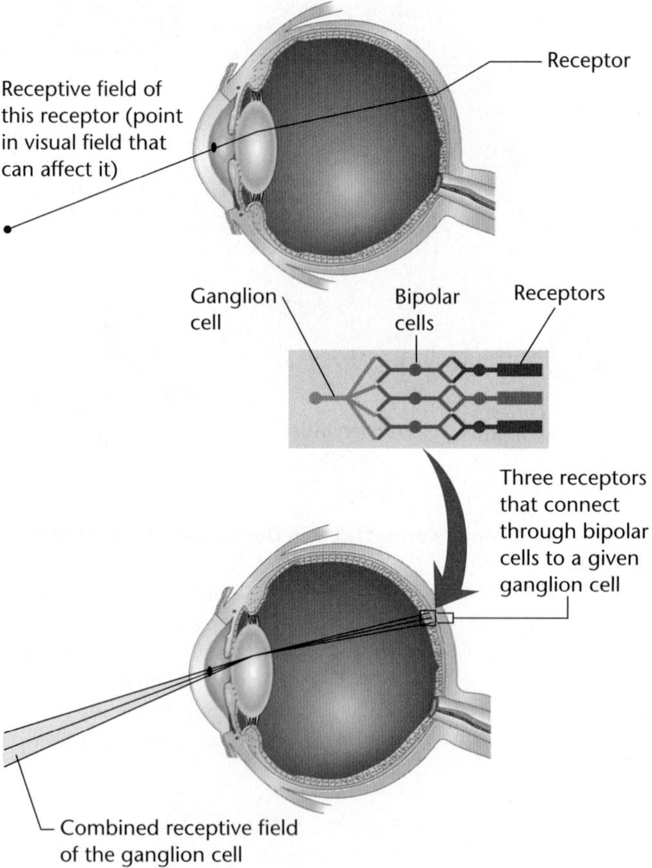

Figure 6.18 Receptive fields
The receptive field of a receptor is simply the area of the visual field from which light strikes that receptor. For any other cell in the visual system, the receptive field is determined by which receptors connect to the cell in question.

TABLE 6.2 Three Kinds of Primate Ganglion Cells

	Parvocellular Neurons	Magnocellular Neurons	Koniocellular Neurons
Cell bodies	Smaller	Larger	Small
Receptive fields	Smaller	Larger	Mostly small; variable
Retinal location	In and near fovea	Throughout the retina	Throughout the retina
Color sensitive	Yes	No	Some are
Respond to	Detailed analysis of stationary objects	Movement and broad outlines of shape	Varied and not yet fully described

The parvocellular neurons, with their small receptive fields, are well suited to detect visual details. They also respond to color, each neuron being excited by some wavelengths and inhibited by others. The high sensitivity to detail and color reflects the fact that parvocellular cells are located mostly in and near the fovea, which has many cones. The magnocellular neurons, in contrast, have larger receptive fields and are not color sensitive. They respond strongly to moving stimuli and large overall patterns but not details. Magnocellular neurons are found throughout the retina, including the periphery, where we are sensitive to movement but not color or details. Koniocellular neurons have several functions, and their axons terminate in several locations (Hendry & Reid, 2000). The existence of so many kinds of ganglion cells implies that the visual system analyzes information in several ways from the start. Table 6.2 summarizes the three kinds of primate ganglion cells.

Axons from the ganglion cells form the optic nerve, which proceeds to the optic chiasm, where half of the axons (in humans) cross to the opposite hemisphere. Most of the axons go to the lateral geniculate nucleus of the thalamus. Cells of the lateral geniculate have receptive fields that resemble those of the ganglion cells—an excitatory or inhibitory central portion and a surrounding ring with the opposite effect. After the information reaches the cerebral cortex, the receptive fields become more complicated.

STOP & CHECK

14. As we progress from bipolar cells to ganglion cells to later cells in the visual system, are receptive fields ordinarily larger, smaller, or the same size? Why?

15. What are the differences between the magnocellular and parvocellular systems?

ANSWERS

14. They become larger because each cell's receptive field is made by inputs converging at an earlier level. **15.** Neurons of the parvocellular system have small cell bodies with small receptive fields, are located mostly in and near the fovea, and are specialized for detailed and color vision. Neurons of the magnocellular system have large cell bodies with large receptive fields, are located in all parts of the retina, and are specialized for perception of large patterns and movement.

Pattern Recognition in the Cerebral Cortex

Most visual information from the lateral geniculate nucleus of the thalamus goes to the **primary visual cortex** in the occipital cortex, also known as **area V1** or the *striate cortex* because of its striped appearance. If you close your eyes and imagine a visual scene, activity increases in area V1 (Kosslyn & Thompson, 2003). Although we do not know whether conscious visual perception occurs *in* area V1, area V1 is apparently necessary for it. People with damage to area V1 report no conscious vision, no visual imagery, and no visual images in their dreams (Hurovitz, Dunn, Domhoff, & Fiss, 1999).

Nevertheless, some people with damage to area V1 show a surprising phenomenon called **blindsight,** an ability to respond to visual information that they report not seeing. If a light flashes within an area where they report no vision, they can nevertheless point to it or turn their eyes toward it, while insisting that they saw nothing and are only guessing (Bridgeman & Staggs, 1982; Weiskrantz, Warrington, Sanders, & Marshall, 1974).

The explanation remains controversial. After damage to area V1, other branches of the optic nerve deliver visual information to the superior colliculus and several other areas, including parts of the cerebral cortex (see Figure 6.16a). Perhaps those areas control the blindsight responses (Cowey & Stoerig, 1995; Moore, Rodman, Repp, & Gross, 1995). However, many people with area V1 damage do not show blindsight, or they show it only in certain parts of the visual field (Schärli, Harman, & Hogben, 1999; Wessinger, Fendrich, & Gazzaniga, 1997). An alternative explanation is that tiny islands of healthy tissue remain within an otherwise damaged visual cortex, not large enough to provide conscious perception but nevertheless enough for blindsight (Fendrich, Wessinger, & Gazzaniga, 1992).

Perhaps both hypotheses are correct. In some patients, a small amount of recordable activity in area V1 accompanies blindsight, supporting the "islands" explanation (Wüst, Kasten, & Sabel, 2002). In other patients, no activity in V1 is apparent (Morland, Lê, Carroll, Hoffmann, & Pambakian, 2004). In one study, experimenters temporarily suppressed the visual cortex of healthy, sighted people by transcranial magnetic stimulation (described in Chapter 4). Although people were not aware of a spot flashed on the screen during the period of suppression, the spot influenced their eye movements (Ro, Shelton, Lee, & Chang, 2004). That result also suggests that activity outside V1 can produce visually guided behavior.

All these blindsight responses occur without consciousness. The conclusion remains that conscious visual perception requires activity in area V1.

STOP & CHECK

16. If you were in a darkened room and researchers wanted to "read your mind" just enough to know whether you were having visual fantasies, what could they do?

17. What is an example of an "unconscious" visually guided behavior?

ANSWERS

16. Researchers could use fMRI, EEG, or other recording methods to see whether activity was high in your visual cortex. **17.** In blindsight, someone can point toward an object or move the eyes toward the object, despite insisting that he or she sees nothing.

Pathways in the Visual Cortex

The primary visual cortex sends information to the **secondary visual cortex** (area **V2**), which processes the information further and transmits it to additional areas, as shown in Figure 6.19. The connections in the visual cortex are reciprocal. For example, V1 sends information to V2, and V2 returns information to V1.

Within the cerebral cortex, a pathway with mainly parvocellular input, is sensitive to details of shape. Another pathway, with mostly magnocellular input, responds to movement. Still another, with mixed input, is sensitive mainly to brightness and color (E. N. Johnson, Hawken, & Shapley, 2001).

Note in Figure 6.19 that the shape, movement, and color/brightness pathways all lead to the temporal cortex. The path into the parietal cortex, with mostly magnocellular input, integrates vision with movement. Researchers refer collectively to the visual paths in the temporal cortex as the **ventral stream,** or the "what" pathway, because it is specialized for identifying and recognizing objects. The visual path in the parietal cortex is the **dorsal stream,** or the "where" or "how" pathway, because it helps the motor system find and use objects. Don't imagine a 100% division of labor. Cells in the two streams have overlapping properties (Denys et al., 2004).

People with damage to the ventral stream (temporal cortex) cannot fully describe what they see. They are also impaired in their visual imagination and memory—for example, trying to remember whether George Washington had a beard (Kosslyn, Ganis, & Thompson, 2001). However, they can still reach toward objects or walk around objects in their path (Fang & He, 2005). They see "where" but not "what."

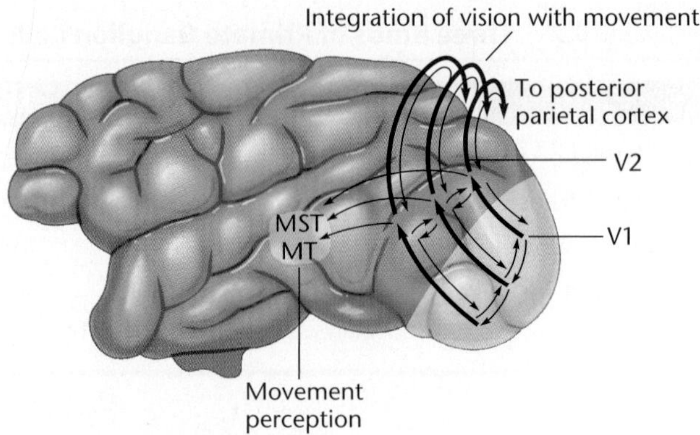

(a) Mostly magnocellular path

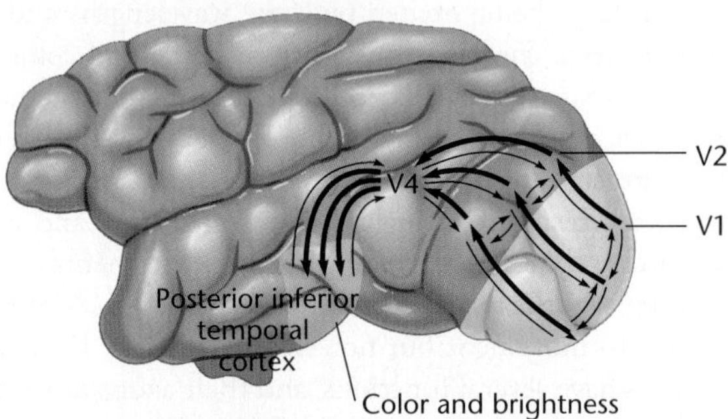

(b) Mixed magnocellular/parvocellular path

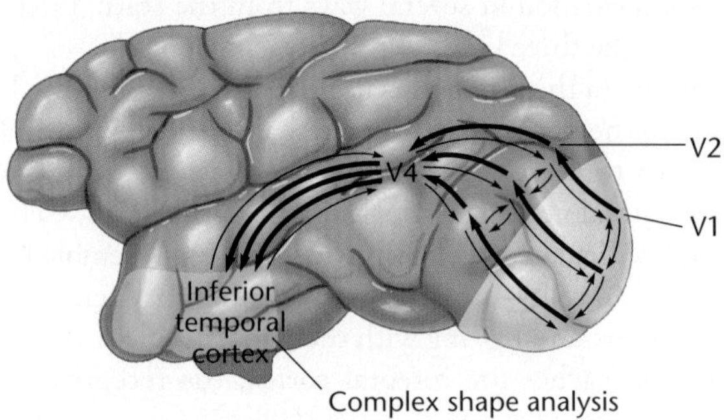

(c) Mostly parvocellular path

Figure 6.19 **Three visual pathways in the monkey cerebral cortex**
(a) A pathway originating mainly from magnocellular neurons. **(b)** A mixed magnocellular/parvocellular pathway. **(c)** A mainly parvocellular pathway. Neurons are only sparsely connected with neurons of other pathways. *(Based on DeYoe, Felleman, Van Essen, & McClendon, 1994; Ts'o & Roe, 1995; Van Essen & DeYoe, 1995)*

In contrast, people with damage to the dorsal stream (parietal cortex) cannot accurately reach out to grasp an object, even after describing its size, shape, and color (Goodale, 1996; Goodale, Milner, Jakobson, & Carey, 1991). Although they remember what their furniture looks like, they cannot remember how it is arranged in rooms of their house (Kosslyn et al., 2001). Furthermore, they are impaired at describing the position of unseen body parts, such as the location of a hand that is below the table (Schenk, 2006).

STOP & CHECK

18. Suppose someone can describe an object in detail but stumbles and fumbles when trying to walk toward it and pick it up. Which is probably damaged, the dorsal path or the ventral path?

ANSWER

18. The inability to guide movement based on vision implies damage to the dorsal path.

The Shape Pathway

In the 1950s, David Hubel and Torsten Wiesel (1959) recorded from cells in cats' and monkeys' brains while they shone light patterns on the retina (Methods 6.1). At first, they presented just dots of light, using a slide projector and a screen, and found little response by cortical cells. The first big response came when they were moving a slide into place. They quickly realized that the cell was responding to the edge of the slide and had a bar-shaped receptive field (Hubel & Wiesel, 1998). Their research, for which they received a Nobel prize, has often been called "the research that launched a thousand microelectrodes" because it inspired so much further research. By now, it has probably launched a million microelectrodes.

David Hubel

Brain science is difficult and tricky, for some reason; consequently one should not believe a result (one's own or anyone else's) until it is proven backwards and forwards or fits into a framework so highly evolved and systematic that it couldn't be wrong.

Torsten Wiesel

Neural connections can be modulated by environmental influences during a critical period of postnatal development. . . . Such sensitivity of the nervous system to the effects of experience may represent the fundamental mechanism by which the organism adapts to its environment during the period of growth and development.

Hubel and Wiesel distinguished several types of cells in the visual cortex. Figure 6.20 illustrates the receptive field of a **simple cell.** A simple cell has a receptive field with fixed excitatory and inhibitory zones. The more light shines in the excitatory zone, the more the cell responds. The more light shines in the inhibitory zone, the less the cell responds. In Figure 6.20, the receptive field is a vertical bar. Tilting the bar slightly decreases the cell's response because light then strikes inhibitory regions as well. Also, moving the bar left, right, up, or down reduces or eliminates the response. Most simple cells have bar-shaped or edge-shaped receptive fields. More of them respond to horizontal or vertical orientations than to diagonals. That disparity makes sense, considering the importance of horizontal and vertical objects in our world (Coppola, Purves, McCoy, & Purves, 1998).

Unlike simple cells, **complex cells,** located in areas V1 and V2, do not respond to the exact location of a stimulus. A complex cell responds to a pattern of light in a particular orientation (e.g., a vertical bar) anywhere within its large receptive field (Figure 6.21). It responds most strongly to a stimulus moving perpendicular to its axis—for example, a vertical bar moving horizontally. The best way to classify a cell as simple or complex is to move the stimulus. A cell that responds to a stimulus in only one location is a simple cell. One that responds equally throughout a large area is a complex cell.

End-stopped, or **hypercomplex,** cells resemble complex cells with one exception: An end-stopped cell has a strong inhibitory area at one end of its bar-shaped receptive field. The cell responds to a bar-shaped pattern of light anywhere in its broad receptive field, provided the bar does not extend beyond a certain point (Figure 6.22). Table 6.3 summarizes the properties of simple, complex, and end-stopped cells.

STOP & CHECK

19. How could a researcher determine whether a given neuron in the visual cortex is simple or complex?

ANSWER

19. First identify a stimulus, such as a horizontal line, that stimulates the cell. Then move the stimulus. If the cell responds only in one location, it is a simple cell. If it responds in several locations, it is a complex cell.

METHODS 6.1

Microelectrode Recordings

David Hubel and Torsten Wiesel pioneered the use of microelectrode recordings to study the properties of individual neurons in the cerebral cortex. With this method, investigators begin by anesthetizing an animal and drilling a small hole in the skull. Then they insert a thin electrode—either a fine metal wire insulated except at the tip or a narrow glass tube containing a salt solution and a metal wire. They direct the electrode either next to or into a single cell and then record its activity while they present various stimuli, such as patterns of light. Researchers use the results to determine what kinds of stimuli do and do not excite the cell.

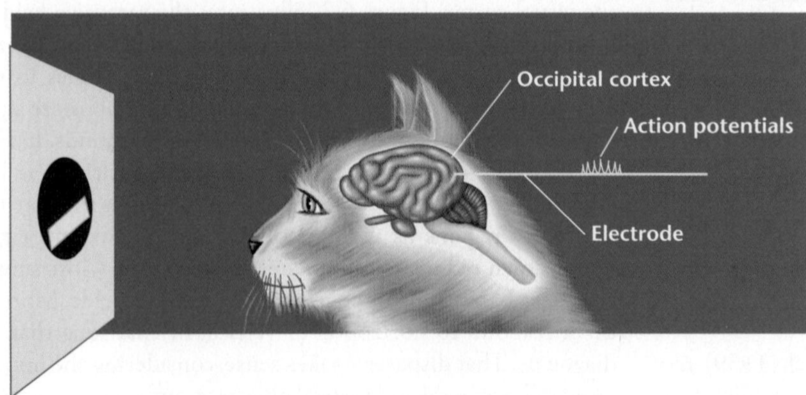

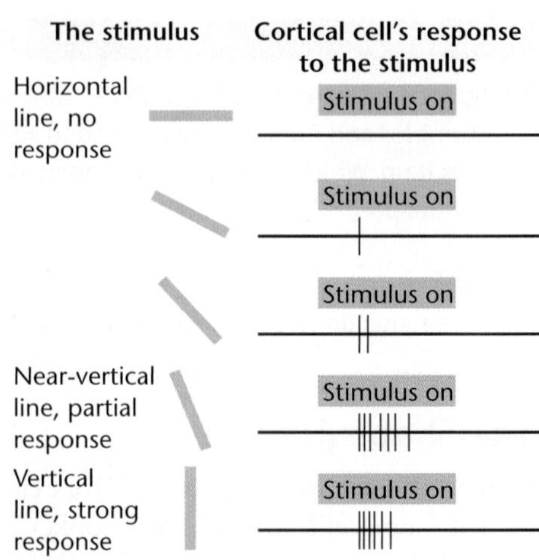

Figure 6.20 Responses of a cat's simple cell to a bar of light presented at varying angles
The short horizontal lines indicate when light is on. *(Right, from D. H. Hubel and T. N. Wiesel, "Receptive fields of single neurons in the cat's striate cortex,"* Journal of Physiology, 148, 1959, *574–591. Copyright © 1959 Cambridge University Press. Reprinted by permission.)*

The Columnar Organization of the Visual Cortex

Cells having various properties are grouped together in the visual cortex in columns perpendicular to the surface (Hubel & Wiesel, 1977) (see Figure 4.22 on page 100). For example, cells within a given column respond either to the left eye, the right eye, or both eyes about equally. Also, cells within a given column respond best to lines of a single orientation.

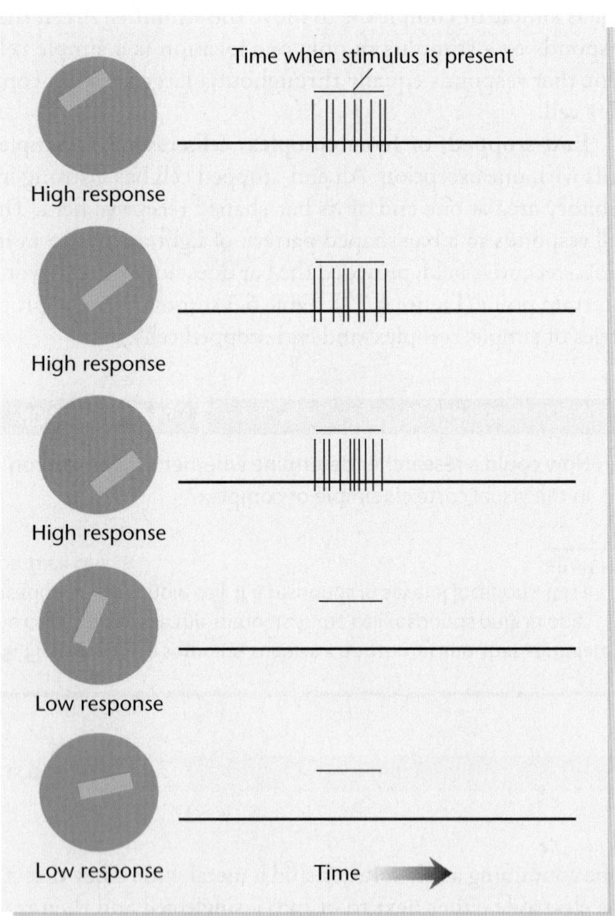

Figure 6.21 The receptive field of a complex cell in the visual cortex
Like a simple cell, its response depends on a bar of light's angle of orientation. However, a complex cell responds the same for a bar in any position within the receptive field.

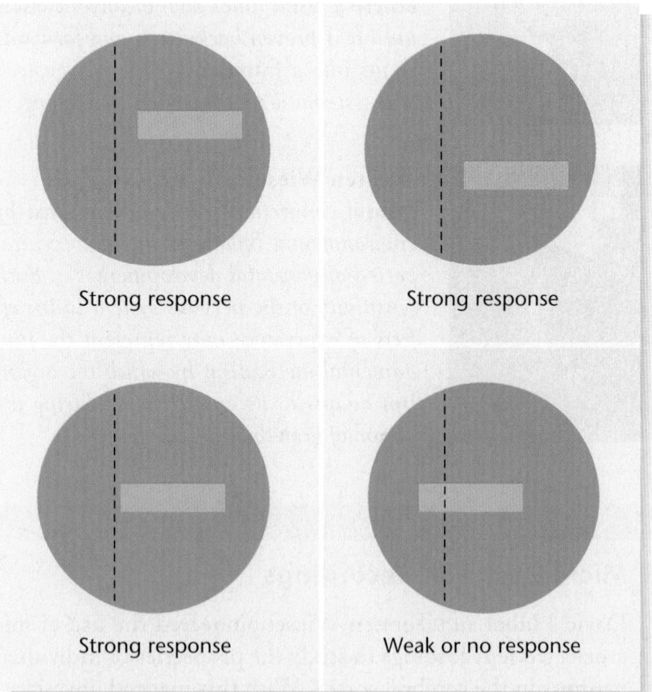

Figure 6.22 The receptive field of an end-stopped cell
The cell responds to a bar in a particular orientation (in this case, horizontal) anywhere in its receptive field, provided the bar does not extend into a strongly inhibitory area.

TABLE 6.3 Summary of Cells in the Primary Visual Cortex

Characteristic	Simple Cells	Complex Cells	End-Stopped Cells
Location	V1	V1 and V2	V1 and V2
Binocular input	Yes	Yes	Yes
Size of receptive field	Smallest	Medium	Largest
Receptive field	Bar- or edge-shaped, with fixed excitatory and inhibitory zones	Bar- or edge-shaped, without fixed excitatory or inhibitory zones; responds to stimulus anywhere in receptive field, especially if moving perpendicular to its axis	Same as complex cell but with strong inhibitory zone at one end

Figure 6.23 shows what happens when an investigator lowers an electrode into the visual cortex and records from each cell that it reaches. Each red line represents a neuron and shows the angle of orientation of its receptive field. In electrode path A, the first series of cells are all in one column and show the same orientation preferences. However, after passing through the white matter, the end of path A invades two columns with different preferred orientations. Electrode path B, which is not perpendicular to the surface of the cortex, crosses through three columns and encounters cells with different properties. In short, the cells within a given column process similar information.

Are Visual Cortex Cells Feature Detectors?

Given that neurons in area V1 respond strongly to bar- or edge-shaped patterns, it seems natural to suppose that the activity of such a cell *is* (or at least is necessary for) the perception of a bar, line, or edge. That is, such cells might be **feature detectors**—neurons whose responses indicate the presence of a particular feature. Cells in later areas of the cortex respond to more complex shapes, and perhaps they are square detectors, circle detectors, and so forth.

Supporting the concept of feature detectors is the fact that prolonged exposure to a given visual feature decreases sensitivity to that feature, as if one has fatigued the relevant detectors. For example, if you stare at a waterfall for a minute or more and then look away, the rocks and trees next to the waterfall appear to be flowing upward. This *waterfall illusion* suggests that you have fatigued the neurons that detect downward motion, leaving unopposed the detectors that detect the opposite motion.

However, later researchers found that a cortical cell that responds well to a single bar or line

also responds, generally even more strongly, to a sine wave grating of bars or lines:

Many cortical neurons respond best to a particular spatial frequency and hardly at all to other frequencies (DeValois, Albrecht, & Thorell, 1982). Most visual researchers therefore believe that neurons in area V1 detect spatial frequencies rather than bars or edges. How do we translate a series of spatial frequencies into perception? From a mathematical

Figure 6.23 Columns of neurons in the visual cortex
When an electrode passes perpendicular to the surface of the cortex (first part of A), it encounters a sequence of neurons responsive to the same orientation of a stimulus. (The colored lines show the preferred stimulus orientation for each cell.) When an electrode passes across columns (B, or second part of A), it encounters neurons responsive to different orientations. Column borders are drawn here to emphasize the point; no such borders are visible in the real cortex. *(Hubel, 1963)*

standpoint, sine wave frequencies are easy to work with. A branch of mathematics called Fourier analysis demonstrates that a combination of sine waves can produce an unlimited variety of other patterns. For example, the graph at the top of the following display is the sum of the five sine waves below it:

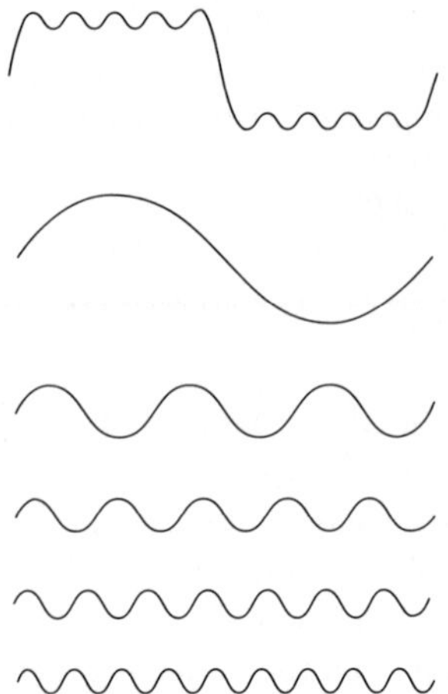

Therefore, a series of spatial frequency detectors, some sensitive to horizontal patterns and others to vertical patterns, could represent any possible display. Still, we perceive the world as objects, not sine waves. The activities of areas V1 and V2 are preliminary steps in visual perception (Lennie, 1998).

STOP & CHECK

20. What is a feature detector?

ANSWER

20. It is a neuron that detects the presence of a particular aspect of an object, such as a shape or a direction of movement.

Shape Analysis Beyond Area V1

As visual information goes from the simple cells to the complex cells and then to other brain areas, the receptive fields become more specialized. For example, in area V2 (next to V1), many cells still respond best to lines, edges, and sine wave gratings, but some cells respond selectively to circles, lines that meet at a right angle, or other complex patterns (Hegdé & Van Essen, 2000).

Response patterns are even more complex in the **inferior temporal cortex** (see Figure 6.19). For example, some cells respond about equally to a black square on a white background, a white square on a black background, and a square-shaped pattern of dots moving across a stationary pattern of dots (Sáry, Vogels, & Orban, 1993). On the other hand, a cell that responds about equally to and may hardly respond at all to (Vogels, Biederman, Bar, & Lorincz, 2001).

Examine Figure 6.24. Researchers measured responses in monkeys' inferior temporal cortex to several kinds of transformations. A cell that responded to a particular stimulus would respond almost equally to its negative image or mirror image but not to a physically similar stimulus in which the "figure" now appeared to be part of the "background" (Baylis & Driver, 2001). That is, cells in this area detect objects, not the amount of light or darkness on the retina. Cells in the inferior temporal neurons presumably contribute to our capacity for **shape constancy**—the ability to recognize an object's shape even as it changes position, angle, lighting, and so forth.

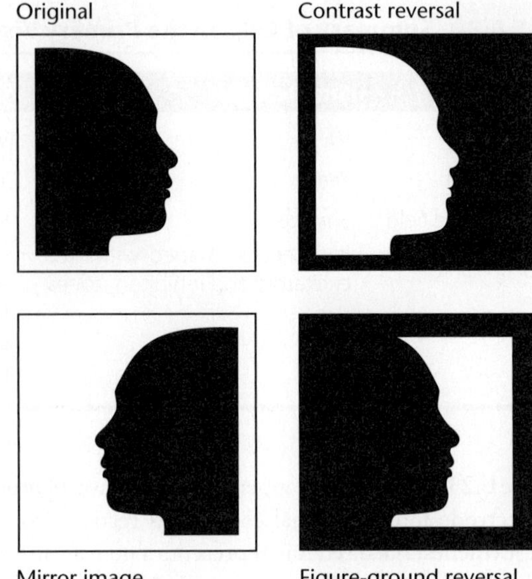

Figure 6.24 Three transformations of an original drawing
In the inferior temporal cortex, cells that respond strongly to the original respond about the same to the contrast reversal and mirror image but not to the figure–ground reversal. Note that the figure–ground reversal resembles the original in terms of the pattern of light and darkness; however, it is not perceived as the same object. *(Based on Baylis & Driver, 2001)*

Disorders of Object Recognition

Damage to the shape pathway of the cortex should lead to specialized deficits. An inability to recognize objects despite otherwise satisfactory vision is called **visual agnosia** (meaning "visual lack of knowledge"). It usually results from damage in the temporal cortex. Someone might be able to point to visual objects and slowly describe them but fail to recognize what they are or mean. For example, one patient, when shown a key, said, "I don't know what that is. Perhaps a file or a tool of some sort." When shown a stethoscope, he said that it was "a long cord with a round thing at the end." When he could not identify a smoker's pipe, the examiner told him what it was. He then replied, "Yes, I can see it now," and pointed out the stem and bowl of the pipe. Then the examiner asked, "Suppose I told you that the last object was not really a pipe?" The patient replied, "I would take your word for it. Perhaps it's not really a pipe" (Rubens & Benson, 1971).

A special type of agnosia—inability to recognize faces—is known as **prosopagnosia** (PROSS-oh-pag-NOH-see-ah). People with prosopagnosia can read, so visual acuity is not the problem. They recognize people's voices, so their problem is not memory (Farah, Wilson, Drain, & Tanaka, 1998). Furthermore, if they feel clay models of faces, they are worse than other people at determining whether two clay models are the same or different (Kilgour, de Gelder, & Lederman, 2004). Their problem relates specifically to faces.

When people with prosopagnosia look at a face, they can describe whether the person is old or young, male or female, but they cannot identify the person. (You would perform about the same if you viewed faces quickly, upside-down.) One patient was shown 34 photographs of famous people and had a choice of two identifications for each. By chance alone, he should have identified 17 correctly; in fact, he got 18. He remarked that he seldom enjoyed watching movies or television programs because he had trouble keeping track of the characters. Curiously, his favorite movie was *Batman*, in which the main characters wore masks much of the time (Laeng & Caviness, 2001).

Prosopagnosia occurs after damage to the *fusiform gyrus* of the inferior temporal cortex, especially in the right hemisphere (Figure 6.25). According to fMRI scans, recognizing a face depends on increased activity in the fusiform gyrus and part of the prefrontal cortex (McCarthy, Puce, Gore, & Allison, 1997; Ó Scalaidhe, Wilson, & Goldman-Rakic, 1997). The fusiform gyrus also increases activity when people look at the faces of dogs (Blonder et al., 2004) or a blurry area on a picture at the top of a body where a face *should* be (Cox, Meyers, & Sinha, 2004). That is, it responds to something about the *idea* of a face.

Is the fusiform gyrus a built-in module for recognizing faces? Given the importance of faces, the idea is plausible. An alternative is that the fusiform gyrus might relate to visual expertise of all types. When people develop enough expertise to recognize brands of cars at a glance, or species of birds or types of flowers, looking at those objects activates the fusiform gyrus, and people with greater expertise show greater activation (Tarr & Gauthier, 2000). People with damage to the fusiform gyrus have trouble recognizing cars, bird species, and so forth (Farah, 1990). However, even in people with extreme levels of expertise, many cells in the fusiform gyrus respond much more vigorously to faces than anything else (Grill-Spector, Knouf, & Kanwisher, 2004; Kanwisher, 2000). Also in monkeys, the corresponding brain area has many cells that respond vigorously to faces and only slightly to anything else (Tsao, Freiwald, Tootell, & Livingstone, 2006). So face recognition may indeed be special. Isn't it interesting that we have evolved a special brain mechanism for this purpose?

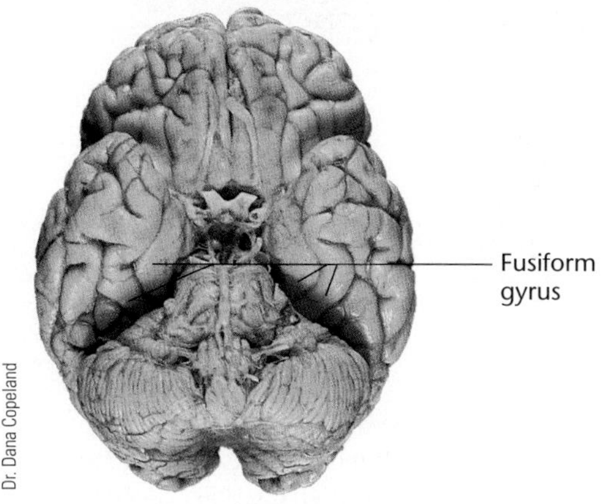

Figure 6.25 The fusiform gyrus
Many cells here are especially active during recognition of faces.

STOP & CHECK

21. What is prosopagnosia, and what does its existence tell us about separate shape recognition systems in the visual cortex?

ANSWER
21. Prosopagnosia is the inability to recognize faces. Its existence implies that the cortical mechanism for identifying faces is different from the mechanism for identifying other complex stimuli.

The Color, Motion, and Depth Pathways

Color perception depends on the parvocellular and koniocellular paths, as shown in Figure 6.19b. Area V4 is particularly important for color constancy (Hadjikhani, Liu, Dale, Cavanagh, & Tootell, 1998; Zeki, McKeefry, Bartels, & Frackowiak, 1998). Recall from the discussion of the retinex theory that color constancy is the ability to recognize the color of an object even if the lighting changes. Cells in area V4 respond to how the light in a particular area compares to the surrounding context (Kusunoki, Moutoussis, & Zeki, 2006). These cells identify that an object is still yellow (or green or whatever) even under different lighting. Monkeys and humans with damage to area V4 still have color vision, but they lose color constancy. For example, if they are trained to reach for a yellow object, they may not be able to find it if the overhead lighting is changed from white to blue (Rüttiger et al., 1999; Wild, Butler, Carden, & Kulikowski, 1985).

In addition to its role in color vision, area V4 has cells that contribute to visual attention (Leopold & Logothetis, 1996). Area V4 becomes active as people deliberately shift their attention from one part of a display to another (Hanson, Kay, & Gallant, 2007).

Motion Perception

Moving objects grab attention for good reasons. A moving object might be a possible mate, a possible prey, or a possible enemy. Several brain areas are specialized to detect motion.

Viewing a complex moving pattern activates many brain areas spread among all four lobes of the cerebral cortex (Sunaert, Van Hecke, Marchal, & Orban, 1999; Vanduffel et al., 2001).

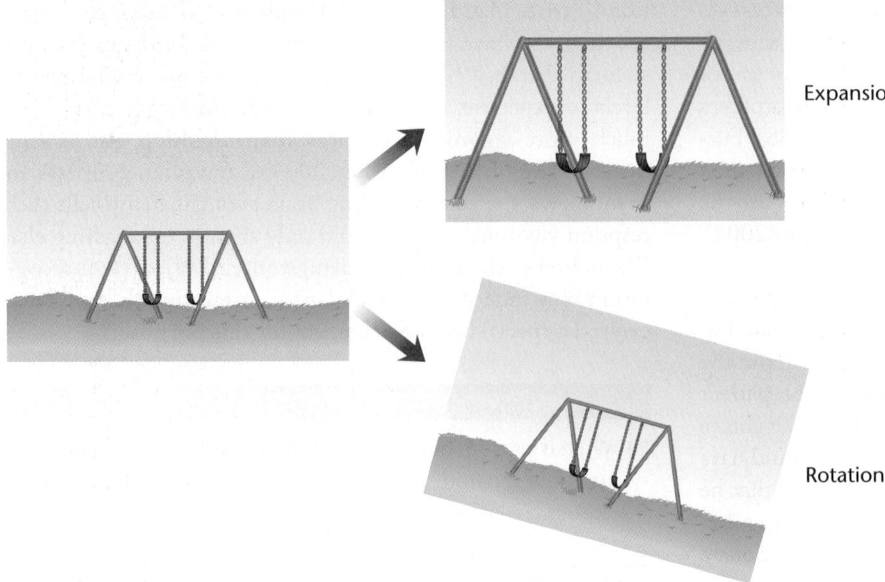

Figure 6.26 Stimuli that excite the dorsal part of area MST
Cells here respond if a whole scene expands, contracts, or rotates. That is, such cells respond if the observer moves forward or backward or tilts his or her head.

Two areas that are especially activated by motion are area **MT** (for middle-temporal cortex), also known as area **V5**, and an adjacent region, area **MST** (medial superior temporal cortex) (see Figure 6.19). Areas MT and MST receive input mostly from the magnocellular path (Nassi & Callaway, 2006), which detects overall patterns, including movement over large areas of the visual field. Most cells in area MT respond selectively when something moves at a particular speed in a particular direction (Perrone & Thiele, 2001). They detect the acceleration or deceleration as well as the absolute speed (Schlack, Krekelberg, & Albright, 2007). They evidently do some complex processing because they adjust for eye position and respond to where something has moved *in the world*, not where it has moved on the retina (d'Avossa et al., 2007). Area MT also responds to photographs that imply movement, such as a photo of people running (Kourtzi & Kanwisher, 2000).

Cells in the dorsal part of area MST respond best to more complex stimuli, such as the expansion, contraction, or rotation of a large visual scene, as illustrated in Figure 6.26. That kind of experience occurs when you move forward or backward or tilt your head. These two kinds of cells—the ones that record movement of single objects and the ones that record movement of the entire background—converge their messages onto neurons in the ventral part of area MST, where cells respond to an object that moves *relative to its background* (K. Tanaka, Sugita, Moriya, & Saito, 1993) (Figure 6.27).

Cells with such properties are critical for judging the motion of objects. When you move your head or eyes from left to right, everything in your visual field moves across your retina as if the world itself had moved right to left. (Go ahead and try it.) Yet the world seems stationary because nothing moved relative to anything else. Most neurons in area MST are silent during eye movements (Thiele, Henning, Kubischik, & Hoffmann, 2002). However, they respond briskly if something moves relative to the background. In short, MST neurons enable you to distinguish between the result of eye movements and the result of object movements.

Several other brain areas have specialized roles in motion perception. For example, the brain is particularly adept at detecting biological motion—the kinds of motion produced by people and animals. If you attach glow-in-the-dark dots to someone's elbows, knees, hips, shoulders, and a few other places, then when that person moves in an otherwise dark room, you perceive a moving person, even though you are actually watching only a few spots of light. Perceiving biological motion activates an area near area MT (Grossman & Blake, 2001; Grossman et al., 2000). You can view a wonderful demonstration at the Bio Motion Lab at http://www.biomotionlab.ca/Demos/BMLwalker.html

Figure 6.27 Stimuli that excite the ventral part of area MST
Cells here respond when an object moves relative to its background. They therefore react either when the object moves or when the object is steady and the background moves.

APPLICATIONS AND EXTENSIONS

Suppressed Vision During Eye Movements

If someone wiggles a movie camera rapidly from side to side, the picture is blurry. However, if you wiggle your eyes back and forth, you don't see a blur. Why not?

Try this demonstration: Look at yourself in a mirror and focus on your left eye. Then shift your focus to your right eye. *(Please do this now.)* Did you see your eyes move? No, you did not. *(I said to try this. I bet you didn't. None of this section will mean much unless you try the demonstration!)*

Why didn't you see your eyes move? Your first impulse is to say that the movement was too small or too fast. Wrong. Try looking at someone else's eyes while he or she focuses first on your left eye and then on your right. You *do* see the other person's eyes move. So an eye movement is neither too small nor too fast for you to see.

You do not see your own eyes move because several of the visual areas of your brain decrease their activity during voluntary eye movements, known as **saccades.** (They don't decrease activity while your eyes are following a moving object.) In effect, the brain areas that monitor saccades tell the visual cortex, "We're about to move the eye muscles, so take a rest for the next split second." Neural activity and blood flow in the visual cortex begin to decrease 75 milliseconds before the eye movement and remain suppressed during the movement (Burr, Morrone, & Ross, 1994; Paus, Marrett, Worsley, & Evans, 1995; Vallines & Greenlee, 2006). Suppression is particularly strong in the areas responsible for detecting visual movement (Kleiser, Seitz, & Krekelberg, 2004).

Although visual responsiveness drops to about one tenth of normal, it does not cease altogether, and so, for example, you would detect a sudden flash of light during a saccade (García-Pérez & Peli, 2001). Nevertheless, processing by the visual cortex decreases during a saccade (Irwin & Brockmole, 2004). If two stimuli flash on the screen during a saccade, 100 ms apart, the delay seems shorter than if the same stimuli flashed while no saccade was occurring (Morrone, Ross, & Burr, 2005). In short, visual consciousness declines during voluntary eye movements.

STOP & CHECK

22. When you wiggle your eyes back and forth, why don't you see a blur?

ANSWER

22. During your eye movements, responsiveness decreases sharply in much of your visual cortex.

Motion Blindness

People with damage to area MT become **motion blind,** able to see objects but impaired at seeing whether they are moving or, if so, which direction and how fast (Marcar, Zihl, & Cowey, 1997). They are not totally insensitive to movement. For example, one patient who could not say which direction something was moving could nevertheless reach out to grab a moving object—if it was moving slowly and if she had a fairly long opportunity to watch it (Schenk, Mai, Ditterich, & Zihl, 2000). It is interesting that she could act on the information without being able to describe it verbally.

Nevertheless, motion perception is a severe impairment. One patient with motion blindness reported that she felt uncomfortable when people walked around because they "were suddenly here or there but I have not seen them moving." She could not cross a street without help: "When I'm looking at the car first, it seems far away. But then, when I want to cross the road, suddenly the car is very near." Pouring coffee became difficult. The flowing liquid appeared to be frozen and unmoving, so she did not stop pouring until the cup overfilled (Zihl, von Cramon, & Mai, 1983). Many patients with Alzheimer's disease have a milder impairment of motion perception, which manifests itself in a difficulty finding their way around (Duffy, Tetewsky, & O'Brien, 2000).

You will wonder what it would be like to be motion blind. On a very small scale, you experienced motion blindness when you did the demonstration of trying to watch your eyes move in the mirror. (You *did* finally try that, didn't you? If not, do it now.) You saw your eyes in one position and then in another, but you weren't aware of any movement from one position to the other. For a split second, you, too, were motion blind.

The opposite of motion blindness also occurs: Some people are blind *except* for the ability to detect which direction something is moving. How could someone see movement without seeing the object that is moving? Area MT gets some input directly from the lateral geniculate nucleus of the thalamus. Therefore, even after extensive damage to area V1 (enough to produce blindness), area MT still has enough input to permit motion detection (Sincich, Park, Wohlgemuth, & Horton, 2004). Again, we wonder what kind of experience this person has. What would it be like to see motion without seeing the objects that are moving? The general point is that different areas of your brain process different kinds of visual information, and it is possible to develop many kinds of disability.

STOP & CHECK

23. What symptoms occur after damage limited to area MT? What may occur if MT is intact but area V1 is damaged?

ANSWER

23. Damage in area MT can produce motion blindness. If area MT is intact but area V1 is damaged, the person may be able to report motion direction despite no conscious identification of the moving object.

MODULE 6.2 IN CLOSING

From Single Cells to Vision

In this module, you have read about single cells that respond to shape, movement, and other aspects of vision. Does any single cell identify what you see?

Several decades ago, the early computers used to crash frequently. Some of the pioneers of computer science were puzzled. A single neuron in the brain, they realized, was surely no more reliable than a single computer chip. Individual neurons must make mistakes all the time, but your brain as a whole continues functioning well. It might make stupid decisions, but it doesn't "crash." Why not? The computer scientists surmised, correctly, that your brain has enough redundancy that the system as a whole works well even when individual units fail. The visual system offers many examples of this point. For example, in area MT, no one neuron consistently detects a moving dot within its receptive field, but a population of cells almost always detects the movement within a tenth of a second (Osborne, Bialek, & Lisberger, 2004). In short, each individual neuron contributes to vision, but no neuron is indispensable. Vision arises from the simultaneous activity of many cells.

SUMMARY

1. The optic nerves of the two eyes join at the optic chiasm, where half of the axons from each eye cross to the opposite side of the brain. Most of the axons then travel to the lateral geniculate nucleus of the thalamus, which communicates with the visual cortex. **165**
2. Lateral inhibition is a mechanism by which stimulation in any area of the retina suppresses the responses in neighboring areas, thereby enhancing the contrast at light–dark borders. Lateral inhibition in the vertebrate retina occurs because receptors stimulate bipolar cells and also stimulate the much wider horizontal cells, which inhibit both the stimulated bipolar cells and those to the sides. **166**
3. Each neuron in the visual system has a receptive field, an area of the visual field to which it is connected. Light in the receptive field excites or inhibits the neuron depending on the light's location, wavelength, movement, and so forth. **168**
4. The mammalian vertebrate visual system has a partial division of labor. In general, the parvocellular system is specialized for perception of color and fine details; the magnocellular system is specialized for perception of depth, movement, and overall patterns. **168**
5. After damage to area V1, people report no vision, even in dreams. However, some kinds of response to light (blindsight) can occur after damage to V1 despite the lack of conscious perception. **169**
6. The ventral stream in the cortex is important for shape perception ("what"), and the dorsal stream is specialized for localizing visual perceptions and integrating them with action ("where"). **170**
7. Within the primary visual cortex, neuroscientists distinguish simple cells, which have fixed excitatory and inhibitory fields, and complex cells, which respond to a light pattern of a particular shape regardless of its exact location. **171**
8. Neurons sensitive to shapes or other visual aspects may or may not act as feature detectors. In particular, cells of area V1 are highly responsive to spatial frequencies, even though we are not subjectively aware of spatial frequencies in our visual perception. **173**
9. Specialized kinds of visual loss can follow brain damage. For example, after damage to the fusiform gyrus of the temporal cortex, people have trouble recognizing faces **174**
10. The visual cortex is specialized to detect visual motion and to distinguish it from apparent changes due to head movement. The visual cortex becomes less responsive during quick eye movements. **175**

KEY TERMS

Terms are defined in the module on the page number indicated. They're also presented in alphabetical order with definitions in the book's Subject Index/Glossary. Interactive flashcards, audio reviews, and crossword puzzles are among the online resources available to help you learn these terms and the concepts they represent.

THOUGHT QUESTION

After a receptor cell is stimulated, the bipolar cell receiving input from it shows an immediate strong response. A fraction of a second later, the bipolar's response decreases, even though the stimulation from the receptor cell remains constant. How can you account for that decrease? (Hint: What does the horizontal cell do?)

MODULE 6.3

Visual Development

Suppose you had lived all your life in the dark. Then today, for the first time, you came out into the light and looked around. Would you understand anything?

Unless you were born blind, you did have this experience—on the day you were born! At first, presumably you had no idea what you were seeing. Within months, however, you began to recognize faces and crawl toward your favorite toys. How did you learn to make sense of what you saw?

Vision by Human Infants

When cartoonists show an infant character, they draw the eyes large in proportion to the head. Infant eyes approach full size sooner than the rest of the head does. Even a newborn has functional vision, although much remains to develop.

Attention to Faces and Face Recognition

Human newborns come into the world predisposed to pay more attention to some stimuli than to others. Even in the first 2 days, they spend more time looking at faces than at other stationary displays (Figure 6.28). That tendency supports the idea of a built-in face recognition module. However, the infant's concept of "face" is not like an adult's. Experimenters recorded infants' times of gazing at one face or the other, as shown in Figure 6.29. Newborns showed a strong preference for a right-side-up face over an upside-down face, regardless of whether the face was realistic (left pair) or distorted (central pair). When confronted with two right-side-up faces (right pair), they showed no significant preference between a realistic one and a distorted one (Cassia, Turati, & Simion, 2004). Evidently, a newborn's concept of "face" requires the eyes to be on top, but the face does not have to be realistic.

People's ability to recognize faces develops gradually, all the way into adolescence (Mondloch, Maurer, & Ahola, 2006). The precision is best for faces similar to what one has been seeing. For example, most adults are poor at recognizing monkey faces, but infants who get frequent exposure to monkey faces between ages 6 and 9 months develop much better ability to recognize them (Pascalis et al., 2005). The mechanism for this familiarity effect is that cells in the inferior temporal cortex develop a tuning to the "average" face. Then they detect small deviations from that average (Leopold, Bondar, & Giese, 2006).

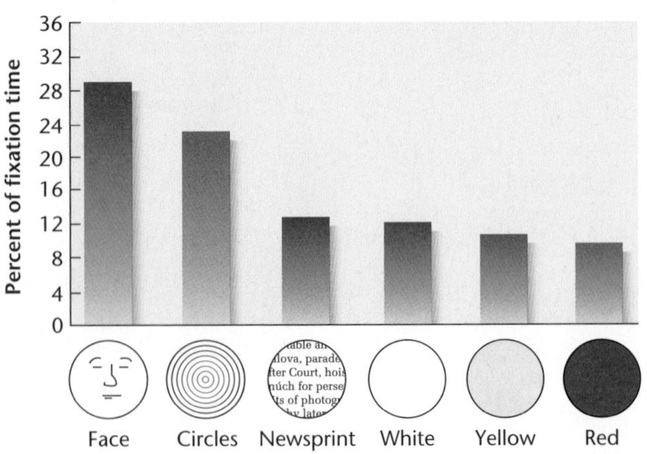

Figure 6.28 Amount of time infants spend looking at various patterns
Even in the first 2 days after birth, infants look more at faces than at most other stimuli. *(Based on Fantz, 1963)*

Early Experience and Visual Development

To examine visual development in more detail, investigators turn to laboratory animals. Research in this area has expanded our understanding of brain development and led to useful treatments for disorders. In a newborn mammal, many of the normal properties of the visual system develop normally at first, even for animals with retinal damage (Rakic & Lidow, 1995; Shatz, 1996) or those reared in complete darkness (Lein & Shatz, 2001; White, Coppola, & Fitzpatrick, 2001). However, the brain needs visual experience to maintain and fine-tune its connections.

Deprived Experience in One Eye

What would happen if a young animal could see with one eye but not the other? For cats and primates—which have both eyes pointed in the same direction—most neurons in the vi-

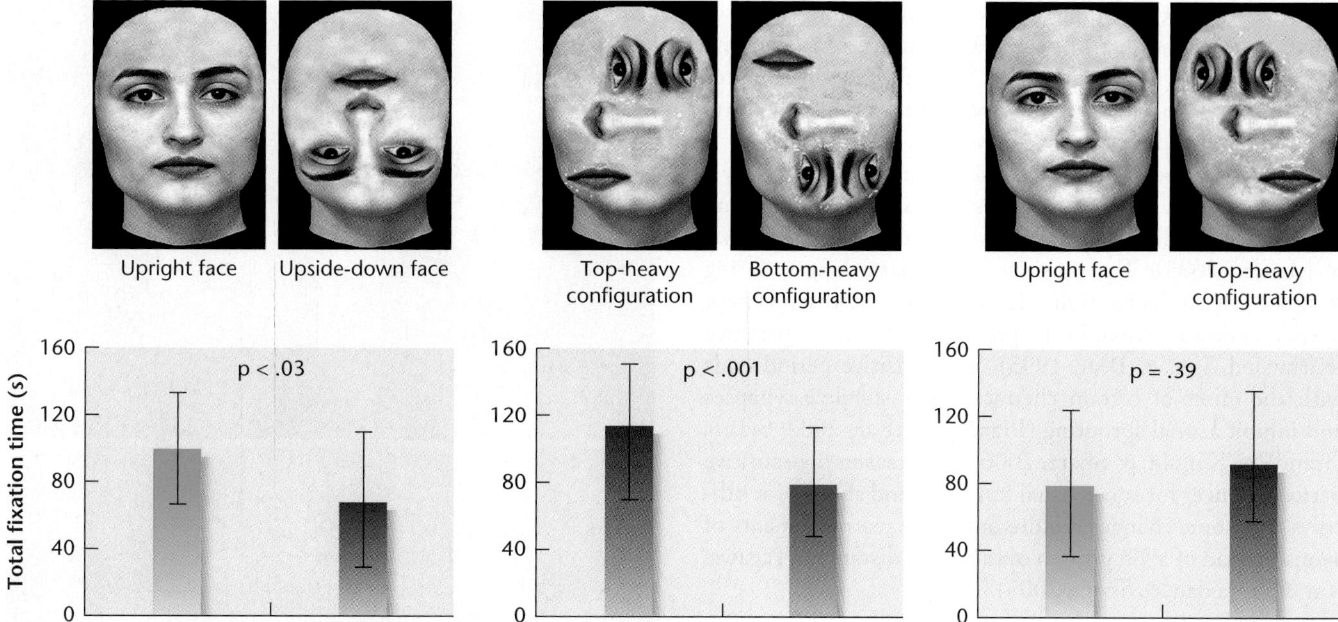

Figure 6.29 How infants divided their attention between two faces
A right-side-up face drew more attention than an upside-down one, regardless of whether the faces were realistic (left pair) or distorted (central pair). They divided their attention about equally between two right-side-up faces (right pair), even though one was realistic and the other was distorted. *(From "Can a nonspecific bias toward top-heavy patterns explain newborns' face preference?" by V. M. Cassia, C. Turati & F. Simon, 2004.* Psychological Science, 15, *379–383.)*

sual cortex receive **binocular input** (stimulation from both eyes). When a kitten opens its eyes, at about age 9 days, each neuron responds to areas in the two retinas that focus on approximately the same point in space (Figure 6.30). However, innate mechanisms cannot make the connections exactly right because the exact distance between the eyes varies from one kitten to another (and changes over age). Therefore, experience is necessary for fine-tuning.

If an experimenter sutures one eyelid shut for a kitten's first 4 to 6 weeks of life, synapses in the visual cortex gradually become unresponsive to input from the deprived eye (Rittenhouse, Shouval, Paradiso, & Bear, 1999). After the deprived eye is opened, the kitten does not respond to it (Wiesel, 1982; Wiesel & Hubel, 1963).

Deprived Experience in Both Eyes

If *both* eyes are kept shut for the first few weeks, we might expect the kitten to become blind in both, but it does not. Axons from the two eyes compete for responsiveness, beginning as soon as the eyes open (S. L. Smith & Trachtenberg, 2007). When just one eye is open, the synapses from the open eye inhibit the synapses from the closed eye (Maffei, Nataraj, Nelson, & Turrigiano, 2006). If neither eye is active, no axon outcompetes any other. For at least 3 weeks, the kitten's cortex remains responsive to both eyes. If the eyes remain shut still longer, the cortical responses start to become sluggish and lose their well-defined

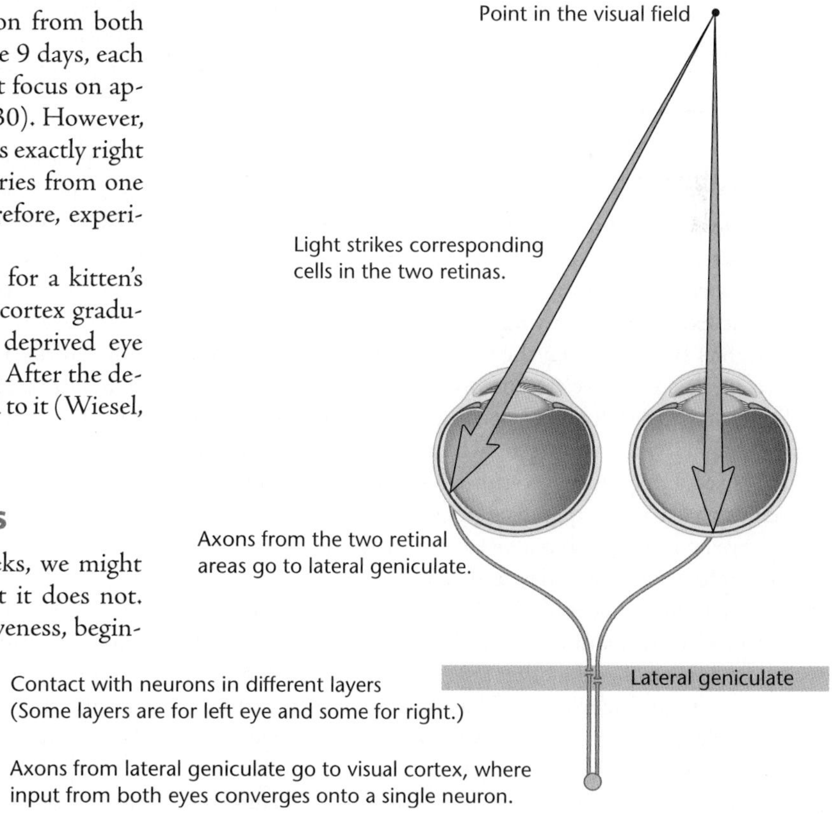

Point in the visual field
Light strikes corresponding cells in the two retinas.
Axons from the two retinal areas go to lateral geniculate.
Lateral geniculate
Contact with neurons in different layers (Some layers are for left eye and some for right.)
Axons from lateral geniculate go to visual cortex, where input from both eyes converges onto a single neuron.

Figure 6.30 The anatomical basis for binocular vision in cats and primates
Light from a point in the visual field strikes points in each retina. Those two retinal areas send their axons to separate layers of the lateral geniculate, which in turn send axons to a single cell in the visual cortex. That cell is connected (via the lateral geniculate) to corresponding areas of the two retinas.

receptive fields (Crair, Gillespie, & Stryker, 1998). They respond to visual stimuli but not much more strongly to one orientation than to another. Also, as mentioned in Chapter 5, if someone is born blind, the visual cortex eventually starts responding to auditory and touch stimuli.

For each aspect of visual experience, researchers identify a **sensitive period,** when experiences have a particularly strong and enduring influence (Crair & Malenka, 1995; T. L. Lewis & Maurer, 2005). The sensitive period lasts longer during complete visual deprivation—for example, if a kitten is kept in total darkness—than in the presence of limited experience (Kirkwood, Lee, & Bear, 1995). The sensitive period ends with the onset of certain chemicals that stabilize synapses and inhibit axonal sprouting (Pizzorusso et al., 2002; Syken, GrandPre, Kanold, & Shatz, 2006). One reason the sensitive period is longer for some visual functions and shorter for others is that some changes require only local rearrangements of axons instead of axon growth over greater distances (Tagawa, Kanold, Majdan, & Shatz, 2005).

STOP & CHECK

24. What is the effect of closing one eye early in life? What is the effect of closing both eyes?

ANSWER

24. If one eye is closed during early development, the cortex becomes unresponsive to it. If both eyes are closed, cortical cells remain somewhat responsive to both eyes for several weeks and then gradually become sluggish and unselective in their responses.

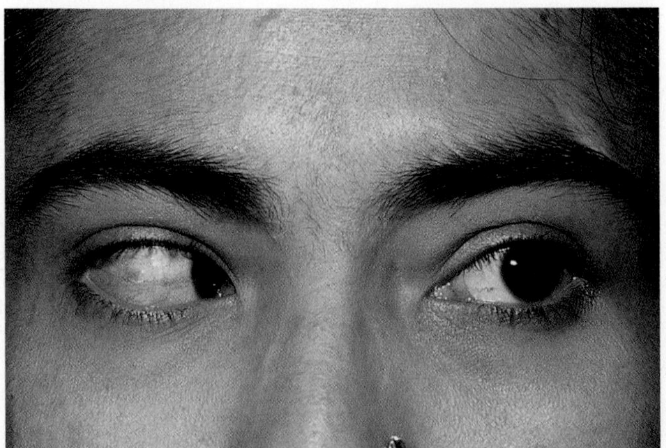

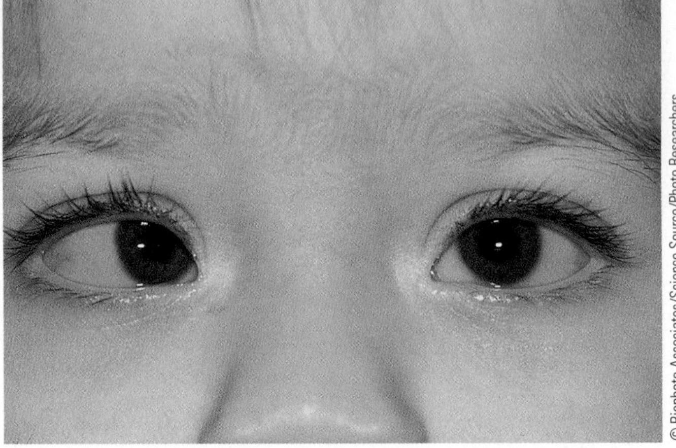

Two examples of "lazy eye."

Uncorrelated Stimulation in the Two Eyes

Almost every neuron in the human visual cortex responds to approximately corresponding areas of both eyes. (The exception: A few cortical neurons respond to only what the left eye sees at the extreme left or what the right eye sees at the extreme right.) By comparing the slightly different inputs from the two eyes, you achieve stereoscopic depth perception.

Stereoscopic depth perception requires the brain to detect **retinal disparity,** the discrepancy between what the left and right eyes see. Experience fine-tunes binocular vision, and abnormal experience disrupts it. Suppose an experimenter covers one eye at a time so that a kitten sees with the left eye one day, the right eye the next day, and so forth. Both eyes receive the same amount of stimulation but never at the same time. After several weeks, almost every neuron in the visual cortex responds to one eye or the other but not both. The kitten cannot detect retinal disparities and has poor depth perception.

Similarly, imagine a kitten with weak or damaged eye muscles so that its eyes do not point in the same direction. Both eyes are active, but no cortical neuron consistently receives messages from one eye that match messages from the other eye. Again, each neuron in the visual cortex becomes responsive to one eye or the other (Blake & Hirsch, 1975; Hubel & Wiesel, 1965).

A similar phenomenon occurs in humans. Certain children are born with **strabismus** (or strabismic amblyopia), also known as "lazy eye," a condition in which the eyes do not point in the same direction. Generally, they attend to one eye and not the other. The usual treatment is to put a patch over the active eye, forcing attention to the other one. That procedure works, to some extent, and early treatment works better than later treatment (T. L. Lewis & Maurer, 2005). However, the child still does not see with both eyes at the same time, does not develop stereoscopic depth perception, and perceives depth no better with two eyes than with one.

The reason is that each cortical cell increases its responsiveness to axons with synchronized activity (Singer, 1986). If part of the left retina usually focuses in the same direction as part of the right retina, then axons from those two areas carry synchronous messages, and a cortical cell strengthens its synapses with them. However, if the two eyes carry unrelated inputs, the cortical cell strengthens its synapses with axons from only one eye (usually the contralateral one).

A promising alternative to patching the active eye is to ask a child to play a video game that requires attention to a binocular three-dimensional display. Good performance requires increasing attention to exactly the kind of input we want to enhance. Preliminary results with this technique look encouraging (Eastgate et al., 2006).

Suppose someone with lazy eye in childhood shows impaired vision many years later. Patching one eye or practicing with a binocular video game produces no apparent effect. Is there any way to reopen the sensitive period? Researchers are exploring several possibilities. Animal research suggests that blocking GABA receptors in the visual cortex might help (Sale et al., 2007). Recall that inhibition by GABA is responsible for starting the sensitive period. Another animal study found that 10 days of complete darkness increased the plasticity of the visual cortex, enabling adult rats to gain responsiveness to an eye that had been covered throughout the sensitive period during infancy (He, Ray, Dennis, & Quinlan, 2007). A similar strategy might work with humans.

STOP & CHECK

25. What early experience is necessary to maintain binocular input to the neurons of the visual cortex?

ANSWER

25. To maintain binocular responsiveness, cortical cells must receive simultaneous activity from both eyes fixating on the same object at the same time.

Early Exposure to a Limited Array of Patterns

If a kitten spends its entire early sensitive period wearing goggles with horizontal lines painted on them (Figure 6.31), nearly all its visual cortex cells become responsive only to horizontal lines (Stryker & Sherk, 1975; Stryker, Sherk, Leventhal, & Hirsch, 1978). Even after months of later normal experience, the cat does not respond to vertical lines (D. E. Mitchell, 1980).

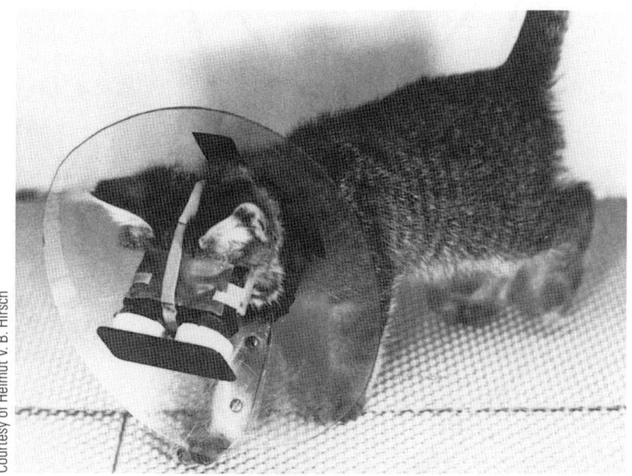

Courtesy of Helmut V. B. Hirsch

Figure 6.31 Procedure for restricting a kitten's visual experience during early development
For a few hours a day, the kitten wears goggles that show just one stimulus, such as horizontal stripes or diagonal stripes. For the rest of the day, the kitten stays with its mother in a dark room without the mask.

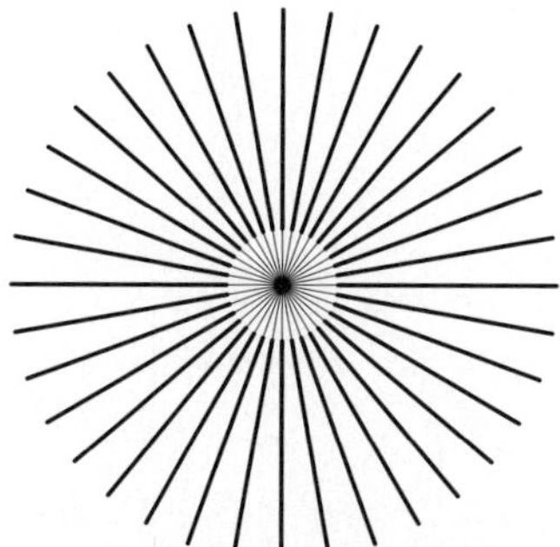

Figure 6.32 An informal test for astigmatism
Do the lines in one direction look darker or sharper than the other lines do? If so, notice what happens when you rotate the page. If you wear corrective lenses, try this demonstration both with and without your lenses.

What happens if human infants are exposed mainly to vertical or horizontal lines instead of both equally? They become more sensitive to the kind of line they have seen. You might wonder how such a bizarre thing could happen. No parents would let an experimenter subject their child to such a procedure, and it never happens in nature. Right?

Wrong. In fact, it probably happened to you! About 70% of all infants have **astigmatism,** a blurring of vision for lines in one direction (e.g., horizontal, vertical, or one of the diagonals), caused by an asymmetric curvature of the eyes. Normal growth reduces the prevalence of astigmatism to about 10% in 4-year-old children.

You can informally test yourself for astigmatism with Figure 6.32. Do the lines in some direction look faint? If so, rotate the page. You will notice that the appearance of the lines depends on their position. If you wear corrective lenses, try this demonstration with and without them. If you see a difference in the lines only without your lenses, then the lenses have corrected your astigmatism.

What happens if kittens grow up without seeing anything move? You can imagine the difficulty of arranging such a world; the kitten's head would move, even if nothing else did. Max Cynader and Garry Chernenko (1976) used an ingenious procedure: They raised kittens in an environment illuminated only by a strobe light that flashed eight times a second for 10 microseconds each. In effect, the kittens saw a series of still photographs. After 4 to 6 months, each neuron in the visual cortex responded normally to shapes but not to moving stimuli. The kittens had become motion blind.

Impaired Infant Vision and Long-Term Consequences

The existence of a sensitive period for the visual cortex means that after you pass that period, your visual cortex won't change much. If an infant has a problem early, we need to fix it early. For example, cataracts (cloudy spots) on one or both eyes during infancy cause visual deprivation, and a delay in surgically repairing the cataracts limits future vision.

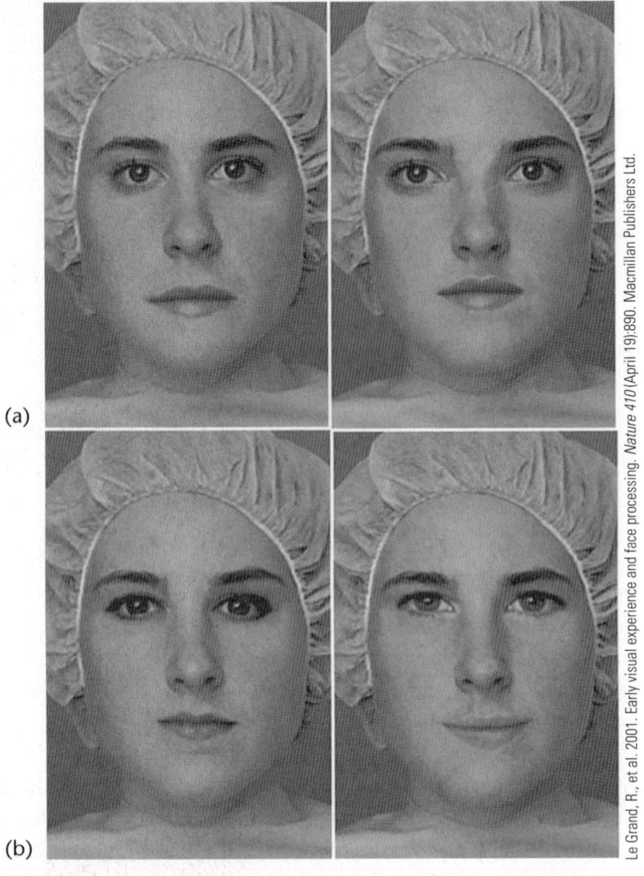

(a)
(b)
Le Grand, R., et al. 2001. Early visual experience and face processing. Nature 410 (April 19):890. Macmillan Publishers Ltd.

Figure 6.33 Faces that differ only in the eyes and mouth
The two upper faces **(a)** have the same eyes and mouth but in slightly different locations. The lower faces **(b)** have different eyes and mouth. People who had cataracts for the first few months of life detect the difference between the faces in **(b)** but have trouble detecting the difference in **(a).** Evidently, the early visual deprivation left deficits that could not be fully remedied by later experience.

In one study, investigators examined 14 people who had been born with cataracts in both eyes but had them repaired at ages 2–6 months. Although they developed nearly normal vision, they had subtle lingering problems. For example, for the faces shown in Figure 6.33, they detected the difference between the two lower faces, which have different eyes and mouth, but they saw no distinction between the two upper faces, which differ in the spacing between parts (Le Grand, Mondloch, Maurer, & Brent, 2001). Another study found that people who had cataracts in the first few months showed difficulties in linking sights with sounds. For example, for most people, seeing a word and hearing it at the same time make it easier to recognize. People who had early cataracts showed less facilitation (Putzar, Goerendt, Lange, Rösler, & Röder, 2007).

We might imagine that an early cataract on just one eye would not pose a problem, but it does if it is on the left eye. Remember that prosopagnosia is linked most strongly to damage to the fusiform gyrus in the right hemisphere. Apparently, the right hemisphere needs early experience to develop its particular expertise at face recognition.

In an adult, a cataract on just one eye affects both hemispheres equally because each hemisphere receives input from both eyes:

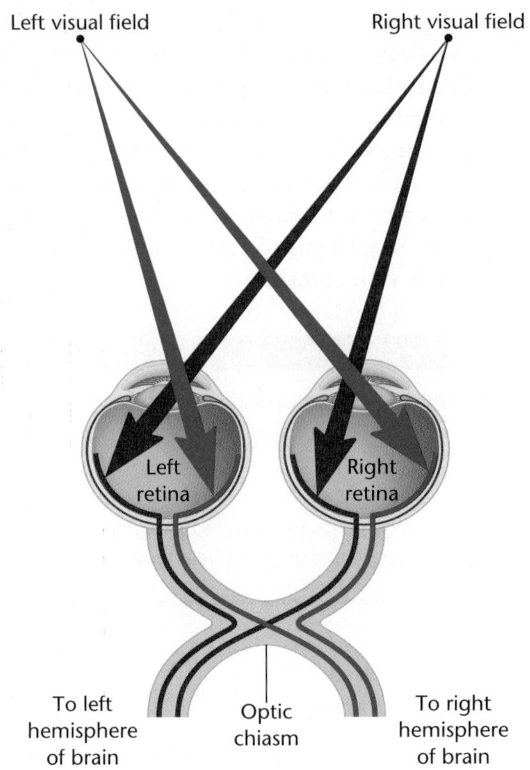

However, during early infancy, the crossed pathways from the two eyes develop faster than the uncrossed pathways:

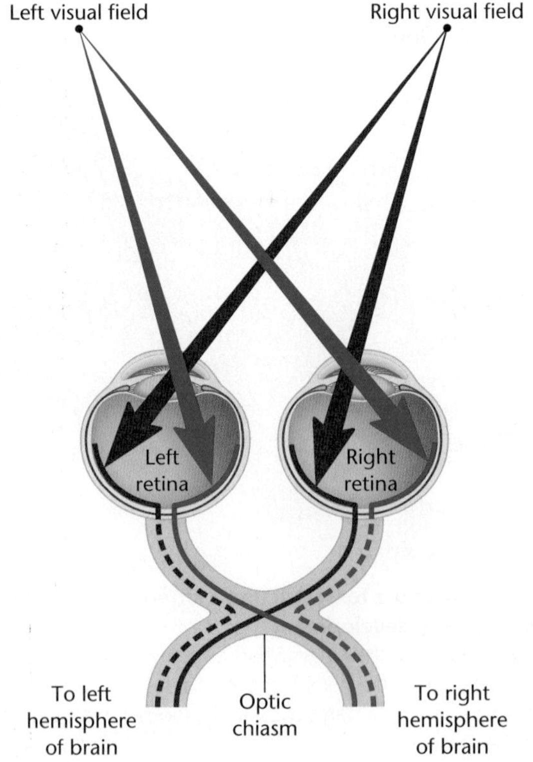

Consequently, each hemisphere gets its input almost entirely from the contralateral eye. Furthermore, the corpus callosum is immature in infancy, so information reaching one hemisphere does not cross to the other. In short, an infant with a left eye cataract has limited visual input to the right hemisphere. Years later, such people continue to show mild impairments in face recognition (Le Grand, Mondloch, Maurer, & Brent, 2003).

The impairment is more extreme if the cataracts remain until later in life. A girl in India had dense cataracts at birth, which were not surgically removed until she was 12. At first, she was nearly blind, but she gradually improved. Twenty years later, she performed normally on most visual tasks. However, even with glasses, her acuity was only 20/200, and she responded to all visual information slowly (Ostrovsky, Andalman, & Sinha, 2006).

Patient PD developed cataracts at approximately age $1^1/_2$ years. His physician treated him with eye drops to dilate the pupils wide enough to "see around" the cataracts, with limited success. After removal of his cataracts at age 43, his ability to perceive detail improved but never reached normal levels. Evidently, all those years without detailed pattern vision had made his cortical cells less able to respond sharply to patterns (Fine, Smallman, Doyle, & MacLeod, 2002). He remarked that the edges between one object and another were exaggerated. For example, where a white object met a dark one, the border of the white object looked extremely bright and the edge of the dark one looked extremely dark—suggesting lateral inhibition well beyond what most people experience. He was amazed by the strong emotional expressions on people's faces. He had seen faces before but not in much detail. He was also struck by the brightness of colors. "In fact, it made me kind of angry that people were walking around in this colorful world that I had never had access to" (Fine et al., 2002, p. 208).

A more extreme case is patient MM. When he was $3^1/_2$, hot corrosive chemicals splashed on his face, destroying one eye and obliterating the cornea of the other. For the next 40 years, he could see only light and dark blurs through the surviving eye. He had no visual memories or visual imagery. At age 43, he received a corneal transplant. Immediately, he could identify simple shapes such as a square, detect whether a bar was tilted or upright, state the direction of a moving object, and identify which of two objects is "in front." These aspects of vision were evidently well established by age $3^1/_2$ and capable of emerging again without practice (Fine et al., 2003). However, his perception of detail was poor and did not improve. Because his retina was normal, the failure to develop detail perception implied a limitation in his visual cortex. Over the next 2 years, he improved in his ability to understand what he was seeing but only to a limited extent. Prior to the operation, he had competed as a blind skier. (Blind contestants memorize the hills.) Immediately after the operation, he was frightened by what he saw as he skied, so he closed his eyes while skiing! After 2 years, he found vision somewhat helpful on the easy slopes, but he still closed his eyes on the difficult slopes, where vision was more frightening. He summarized his progress, "The difference between today and over two years ago is that I can guess better what I am seeing. What is the same is that I am still guessing" (Fine et al., 2003, p. 916).

What can we conclude? In humans as in other species, the visual cortex is more plastic early in life. Some degree of recovery is possible if vision is restored later in life, but perception of fine detail is still impaired. The visual expertise that most of us take for granted depends on years of practice.

STOP & CHECK

26. Why does a cataract on one eye produce greater visual impairments in infants than in adults?

ANSWER

26. First, infants' brains are more plastic; adults' brains are already fairly set and resist change in the event of distorted or deficient input. Furthermore, in the infant brain, each hemisphere gets nearly all its visual input from its contralateral eye. The crossed paths from the eyes to the hemispheres are more mature than the uncrossed paths, and the corpus callosum is immature.

MODULE 6.3 IN CLOSING

The Nature and Nurture of Vision

The nature–nurture issue arises in various ways throughout psychology. In vision, consider what happens when you look out your window. How do you know that what you see are trees, people, and buildings? In fact, how do you know they are objects? How do you know which objects are close and which are distant? Were you born knowing how to interpret what you see, or did you have to learn to understand it? The main message of this module is that vision requires a complex mixture of nature and nurture. We are indeed born with a certain amount of understanding, but we need experience to maintain, improve, and refine it. As usual, the influences of heredity and environment are not fully separable.

SUMMARY

1. Even newborn infants gaze longer at faces than at other stationary objects. However, they are as responsive to distorted as to realistic faces, provided the eyes are on top. Ability to recognize faces continues to improve for years. **180**
2. The cells in the visual cortex of infant kittens have nearly normal properties. However, experience is necessary to maintain and fine-tune vision. For example, if a kitten has sight in one eye and not in the other during the early sensitive period, its cortical neurons become responsive only to the open eye. **180**
3. Cortical neurons become unresponsive to axons from the inactive eye mainly because of competition with the active eye. If both eyes are closed, cortical cells remain somewhat responsive to axons from both eyes, although that response becomes sluggish and unselective as the weeks of deprivation continue. **181**
4. Abnormal visual experience has a stronger effect during an early sensitive period than later in life. **182**
5. To develop good stereoscopic depth perception, a kitten or human child must have experience seeing the same object with corresponding portions of the two eyes early in life. Otherwise, each neuron in the visual cortex becomes responsive to input from just one eye. **182**
6. If a kitten sees only horizontal or vertical lines during its sensitive period, most of the neurons in its visual cortex become responsive to such lines only. For the same reason, a young child with astigmatism may have decreased responsiveness to one kind of line or another. Those who do not see motion early in life lose their ability to see it. **183**
7. Some people have cataracts or other impediments to vision during infancy or childhood and then, after surgery, regain vision in adulthood. Visual impairment for the first few months leaves subtle visual deficits that evidently last throughout life. Someone who had vision, lost it in childhood, and then regained it decades later shows retention of some aspects of vision (e.g., motion perception) but loss of detail and many other aspects of vision. **184**

KEY TERMS

Terms are defined in the module on the page number indicated. They're also presented in alphabetical order with definitions in the book's Subject Index/Glossary. Interactive flashcards, audio reviews, and crossword puzzles are among the online resources available to help you learn these terms and the concepts they represent.

astigmatism **183**
binocular input **181**
retinal disparity **182**
sensitive period **182**
strabismus **182**

THOUGHT QUESTIONS

1. A rabbit's eyes are on the sides of its head instead of in front. Would you expect rabbits to have many cells with binocular receptive fields—that is, cells that respond to both eyes? Why or why not?
2. Would you expect the cortical cells of a rabbit to be just as sensitive to the effects of experience as are the cells of cats and primates? Why or why not?

CHAPTER 6 Exploration and Study

In addition to the study materials provided at the end of each module, you may supplement your review of this chapter by using one or more of the book's electronic resources, which include its companion Website, interactive Cengage Learning eBook, Exploring Biological Psychology CD-ROM, and CengageNOW. Brief descriptions of these resources follow. For more information, visit **www.cengage.com/psychology/kalat**.

The book's companion Website, accessible through the author Web page indicated above, provides a wide range of study resources such as an interactive glossary, flashcards, tutorial quizzes, updated Web links, and Try It Yourself activities, as well as a limited selection of the short videos and animated explanations of concepts available for this chapter.

Exploring Biological Psychology

The Exploring Biological Psychology CD-ROM contains videos, animations, and Try It Yourself activities. These activities—as well as many that are new to this edition—are also available in the text's fully interactive, media-rich Cengage Learning eBook,* which gives you the opportunity to experience biological psychology in an even greater interactive and multimedia environment. The Cengage Learning eBook also includes highlighting and note-taking features and an audio glossary. For this chapter, the Cengage Learning eBook includes the following interactive explorations:

The Retina
Virtual Reality Eye
Blind Spot
Color Blindness in Visual Periphery
Brightness Contrast
Lateral Inhibition
Motion Aftereffect

The Try It Yourself activity *Motion Aftereffect* produces an illusion that a face is expanding, as a result of fatiguing feature detectors for motion inward.

CENGAGENOW™ is an easy-to-use resource that helps you study in less time to get the grade you want. An online study system, CengageNOW* gives you the option of taking a diagnostic pretest for each chapter. The system uses the results of each pretest to create personalized chapter study plans for you. The Personalized Study Plans

- help you save study time by identifying areas on which you should concentrate and give you one-click access to corresponding pages of the interactive Cengage Learning eBook;
- provide interactive exercises and study tools to help you fully understand chapter concepts; and
- include a posttest for you to take to confirm that you are ready to move on to the next chapter.

Suggestions for Further Exploration

The book's companion Website includes a list of suggested articles available through InfoTrac College Edition for this chapter. You may also want to explore some of the following books and Websites. The text's companion Website provides live, updated links to the sites listed below.

Books

Purves, D., & Lotto, R. B. (2003). *Why we see what we do: An empirical theory of vision.* Sunderland, MA: Sinauer Associates. Discussion of how our perception of color, size, and other visual qualities depends on our previous experience with objects and not just on the light striking the retina.

Websites

Studies from the Dale Purves Lab
Fascinating demonstrations of how our perception of each item depends on its context.
http://www.purveslab.net

John Moran Eye Center
Detailed information about many aspects of the retina and vision.
http://www.webvision.med.utah.edu

Bio Motion Lab
Delightful demonstration of how highly prepared we are to detect biological motion, even from minimal stimuli.
http://www.biomotionlab.ca/Demos/BMLwalker.html

* Requires a Cengage Learning eResources account. Visit **www.cengage.com/login** to register or login.

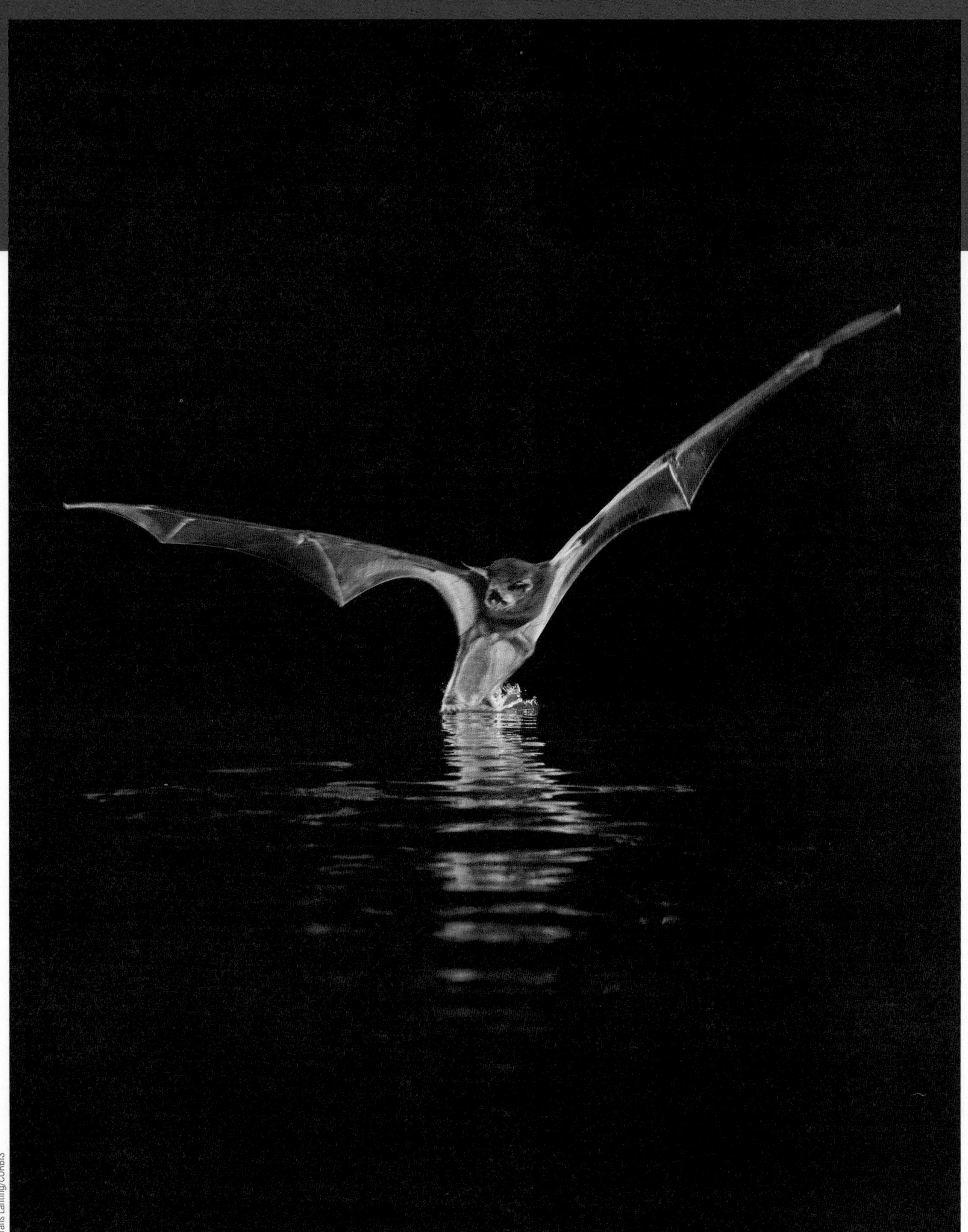

Frans Lanting/CORBIS

The Other Sensory Systems

7

CHAPTER OUTLINE

MAIN IDEAS

1. Our senses have evolved to give us information we can use rather than complete information about the world.
2. As a rule, the activity in a single sensory neuron is ambiguous by itself. The meaning depends on the pattern across a population of neurons.

According to a Native American saying, "A pine needle fell. The eagle saw it. The deer heard it. The bear smelled it" (Herrero, 1985). Different species are sensitive to different kinds of information. Bats locate insect prey by echoes from sonar waves that they emit at 20,000 to 100,000 hertz (Hz, cycles per second), well above the range of adult human hearing (Griffin, Webster, & Michael, 1960). The ears of the green tree frog, *Hyla cinerea*, are highly sensitive to sounds at two frequencies—900 and 3000 Hz—which are prominent in the adult male's mating call (Moss & Simmons, 1986). Mosquitoes have a specialized receptor that detects the odor of human sweat—and therefore helps them find us and bite us (Hallem, Fox, Zwiebel, & Carlson, 2004).

Humans, too, have important sensory specializations. For example, our sense of taste alerts us to the bitterness of poisons (Richter, 1950; Schiffman & Erickson, 1971) but does not respond to substances such as cellulose that neither help nor harm us. Our olfactory systems are unresponsive to gases that we don't need to detect (e.g., carbon dioxide) but highly responsive to the smell of rotting meat. This chapter concerns how our sensory systems process biologically useful information.

OPPOSITE: The sensory world of bats—which find insects by echolocation—must be very different from that of humans.

MODULE 7.1

Audition

Evolution has been described as "thrifty." After it has solved a particular problem, it modifies that solution for other problems instead of starting from scratch. For example, imagine a gene for visual receptors in an early vertebrate. Make a duplicate of that gene, modify it slightly, and presto: The new gene makes receptors that respond to different wavelengths of light, and the possibility emerges for color vision. In this chapter, you will see more examples of that principle. Various sensory systems have their specializations, but they also have much in common.

Sound and the Ear

The human auditory system enables us to hear not only falling trees but also the birds singing in the branches and the wind blowing through the leaves. Many people who are blind learn to click their heels as they walk and use the echoes to locate obstructions. Our auditory systems are amazingly well adapted for detecting and interpreting useful information.

Physical and Psychological Dimensions of Sound

Sound waves are periodic compressions of air, water, or other media. When a tree falls, the tree and the ground vibrate, setting up sound waves in the air that strike the ears. Sound waves vary in amplitude and frequency. The **amplitude** of a sound wave is its intensity. A bolt of lightning produces sound waves of great amplitude. **Loudness** is a sensation related to amplitude but not identical to it. For example, a rapidly talking person sounds louder than slow music of the same physical amplitude. If you complain that television advertisements are louder than the program, one reason is that the people in the advertisements talk faster.

The **frequency** of a sound is the number of compressions per second, measured in hertz (Hz, cycles per second). **Pitch** is the related aspect of perception. Higher frequency sounds are higher in pitch. Figure 7.1 illustrates the amplitude and frequency of sounds. The height of each wave corresponds to amplitude, and the number of waves per second corresponds to frequency.

Most adult humans hear sounds ranging from about 15 Hz to somewhat less than 20,000 Hz. Children hear higher frequencies because the ability to perceive high frequencies decreases with age and exposure to loud noises (B. A. Schneider, Trehub, Morrongiello, & Thorpe, 1986).

Structures of the Ear

Rube Goldberg (1883–1970) drew cartoons about complicated, far-fetched inventions. For example, a person's tread on the front doorstep would pull a string that raised a cat's tail, awakening the cat, which would then chase a bird that had been resting on a balance, which would swing up to strike a doorbell. The functioning of the ear may remind you of a Rube Goldberg device because sound waves are transduced into action potentials through a complex process. Unlike Goldberg's inventions, however, the ear actually works.

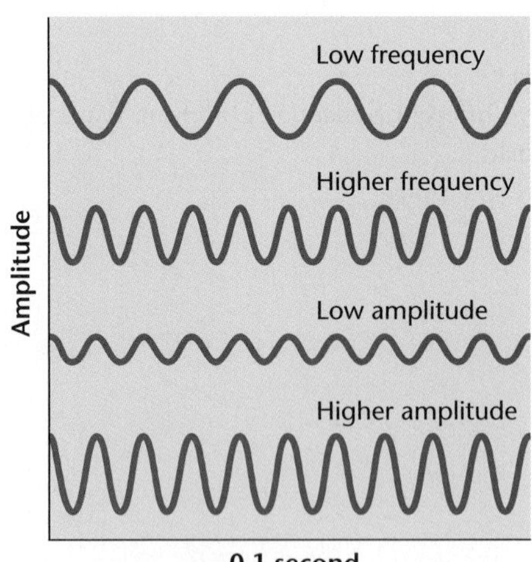

Figure 7.1 Four sound waves
The time between the peaks determines the frequency of the sound, which we experience as pitch. Here the top line represents five sound waves in 0.1 second, or 50 Hz—a very low-frequency sound that we experience as a very low pitch. The other three lines represent 100 Hz. The vertical extent of each line represents its amplitude or intensity, which we experience as loudness.

Anatomists distinguish the outer ear, the middle ear, and the inner ear (Figure 7.2). The outer ear includes the **pinna**, the familiar structure of flesh and cartilage attached to each side of the head. By altering the reflections of sound waves, the pinna helps us locate the source of a sound. We have to learn to use that information because each person's pinna is shaped differently from anyone else's (Van Wanrooij & Van Opstal, 2005). Rabbits' large movable pinnas enable them to localize sound sources even more precisely.

After sound waves pass through the auditory canal (see Figure 7.2), they strike the **tympanic membrane,** or eardrum, in the middle ear. The tympanic membrane vibrates at the same frequency as the sound waves that strike it. The tympanic membrane connects to three tiny bones that transmit the vibrations to the **oval window,** a membrane of the inner ear. These bones are sometimes known by their English names (hammer, anvil, and stirrup) and sometimes by their Latin names (malleus, incus, and stapes). The tympanic membrane is about 20 times larger than the footplate of the stirrup, which connects to the oval window. As in a hydraulic pump, the vibrations of the tympanic membrane transform into more forceful vibrations of the smaller stirrup. The net effect of the system converts the sound waves into waves of greater pressure on the small oval window. This transformation is important because more force is required to move the viscous fluid behind the oval window than to move the eardrum, which has air on both sides.

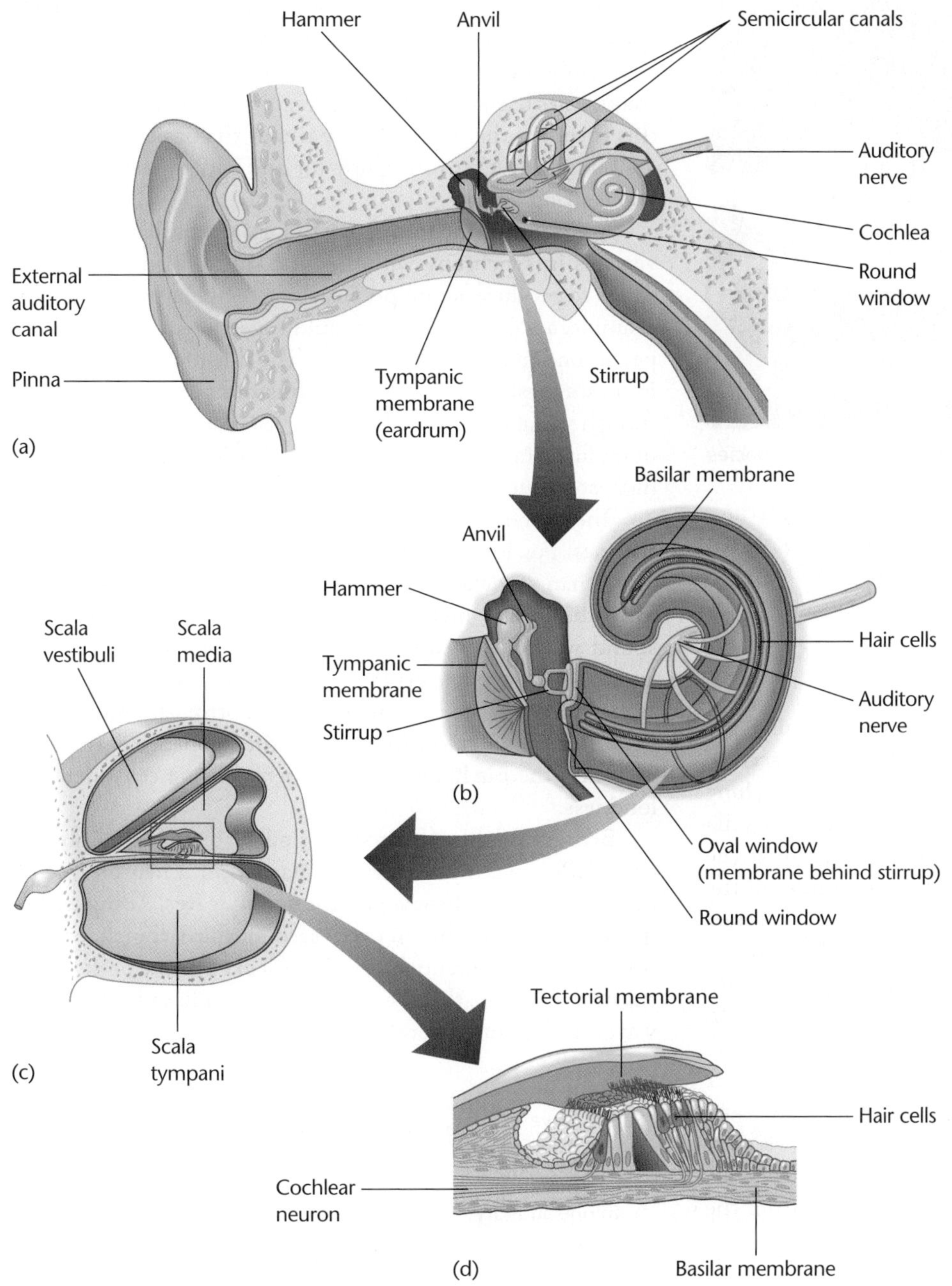

Figure 7.2 Structures of the ear
When sound waves strike the tympanic membrane in **(a),** they cause it to vibrate three tiny bones—the hammer, anvil, and stirrup—that convert the sound waves into stronger vibrations in the fluid-filled cochlea **(b).** Those vibrations displace the hair cells along the basilar membrane in the cochlea. **(c)** A cross-section through the cochlea. **(d)** A closeup of the hair cells.

Figure 7.3 Hair cells from the auditory systems of three species
(a, b) Hair cells from a frog sacculus, an organ that detects ground-borne vibrations. **(c)** Hair cells from the cochlea of a cat. **(d)** Hair cells from the cochlea of a fence lizard. Kc = kinocilium, one of the components of a hair bundle. *(From "The cellular basis of hearing: The biophysics of hair cells," by A. J. Hudspeth,* Science *1985, 230:4727, 745–752. Reprinted with permission from AAAS.)*

The inner ear contains a snail-shaped structure called the **cochlea** (KOCK-lee-uh, Latin for "snail"). A cross-section through the cochlea, as in Figure 7.2c, shows three long fluid-filled tunnels: the scala vestibuli, scala media, and scala tympani. The stirrup makes the oval window vibrate at the entrance to the scala vestibuli, thereby setting in motion the fluid in the cochlea. The auditory receptors, known as **hair cells,** lie between the basilar membrane of the cochlea on one side and the tectorial membrane on the other (Figure 7.2d). Vibrations in the fluid of the cochlea displace the hair cells. A hair cell responds within microseconds to displacements as small as 10^{-10} meter (0.1 nanometer, about the diameter of one atom), thereby opening ion channels in its membrane (Fettiplace, 1990; Hudspeth, 1985). Figure 7.3 shows electron micrographs of the hair cells of three species. The hair cells excite the cells of the auditory nerve, which is part of the eighth cranial nerve.

Pitch Perception

Our ability to understand speech or enjoy music depends on our ability to differentiate among sounds of different frequencies. How do we do it?

Frequency Theory and Place Theory

Recall from Chapter 6 that two of the main ways of coding sensory information are which cells are active and how frequently they fire. Those same principles apply to perception of pitch.

According to the **place theory,** the basilar membrane resembles the strings of a piano in that each area along the membrane is tuned to a specific frequency. (If you sound a note with a tuning fork near a piano, you vibrate the piano string tuned to that note.) According to this theory, each frequency activates the hair cells at only one place along the basilar membrane, and the nervous system distinguishes among frequencies based on which neurons respond. The downfall of this theory is that the various parts of the basilar membrane are bound together too tightly for any part to resonate like a piano string.

According to the **frequency theory,** the basilar membrane vibrates in synchrony with a sound, causing auditory nerve axons to produce action potentials at the same frequency. For example, a sound at 50 Hz would cause 50 action potentials per second in the auditory nerve. The downfall of this theory in its simplest form is that the refractory period of a neuron, though variable, is typically about $^{1}/_{1,000}$ second, so the maximum firing rate of a neuron is about 1000 Hz, far short of the highest frequencies we hear.

The current theory combines modified versions of both theories. For low-frequency sounds (up to about 100 Hz—more than an octave below middle C in music, which is 264 Hz), the basilar membrane vibrates in synchrony with the sound waves, in accordance with the frequency theory, and auditory nerve axons generate one action potential per wave. Soft sounds activate few neurons, and stronger sounds activate more. Thus, at low frequencies, the frequency of impulses identifies the pitch, and the number of firing cells identifies loudness.

Because of the refractory period of the axon, as sounds exceed 100 Hz, it is harder and harder for a neuron to continue firing in synchrony with the sound waves. At higher frequencies, it might fire on every second, third, fourth, or later wave. Its action potentials are phase-locked to the peaks of the sound waves (i.e., they occur at the same phase in the sound wave), as illustrated here:

Sound wave (about 1000 Hz)

Action potentials from one auditory neuron

Other auditory neurons also produce action potentials that are phase-locked with peaks of the sound wave, but they can be out of phase with one another:

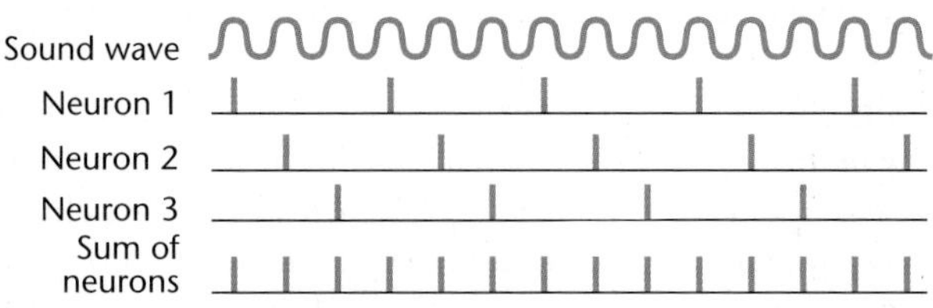

If we consider the auditory nerve as a whole, we find that with a tone of a few hundred Hz, each wave excites at least a few auditory neurons. According to the **volley principle** of pitch discrimination, the auditory nerve as a whole produces volleys of impulses for sounds up to about 4,000 per second, even though no individual axon approaches that frequency (Rose, Brugge, Anderson, & Hind, 1967). For this principle to work, auditory cells must time their responses quite precisely, and the evidence says that they do (Avissar, Furman, Saunders, & Parsons, 2007). However, beyond about 4000 Hz, even staggered volleys of impulses can't keep pace with the sound waves.

Most human hearing takes place below 4000 Hz, the approximate limit of the volley principle. For comparison, the highest key on a piano is 4224 Hz. When we hear very high frequencies, we use a mechanism similar to the place theory. The basilar membrane varies from stiff at its base, where the stirrup meets the cochlea, to floppy at the other end of the cochlea, the apex (von Békésy, 1956) (Figure 7.4). The hair cells along the basilar membrane have different properties based on their location, and they act as tuned resonators that vibrate only for sound waves of a particular frequency. The highest frequency sounds vibrate hair cells near the base, and lower frequency sounds vibrate hair cells farther along the membrane (Warren, 1999). Actually, the mechanisms of hearing at frequencies well over 4000 Hz are not entirely understood, as the ultrahigh frequencies alter several of the properties of neurons and their membranes (Fridberger et al., 2004).

People vary in their sensitivity to pitch. For almost any other aspect of behavior, people's performances follow a "normal curve," with continuous variation. However, for pitch perception, a fair number of people are not part of the normal distribution. An estimated 4% of people have *amusia*, impaired detection of frequency changes (commonly called "tone deafness") (Hyde & Peretz, 2004). They are not completely tone-deaf any more than "color-blind" people are completely insensitive to color, but they have trouble recognizing tunes, can't tell whether someone is singing off-key, and do not detect a "wrong" note in a melody. You can test your own ability at the Laboratoire Isabelle Peretz, Université de Montréal, Website: http://www.brams.umontreal.ca/amusia-demo/

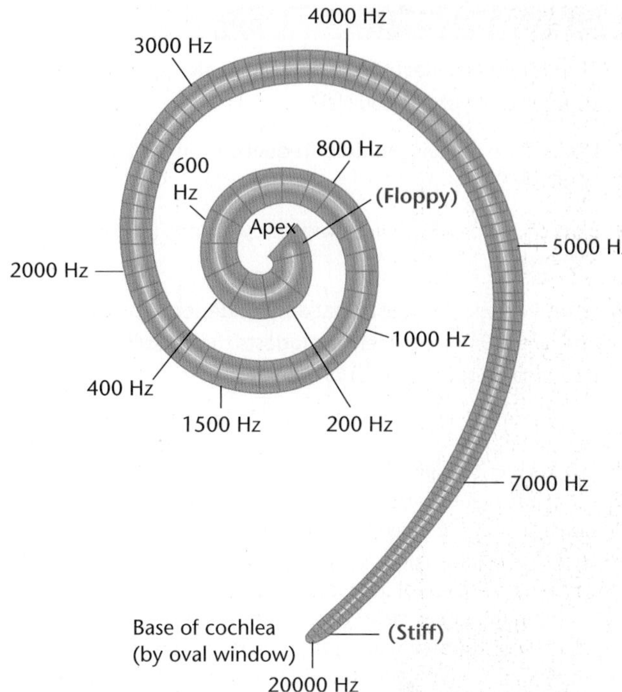

Figure 7.4 The basilar membrane of the human cochlea
High-frequency sounds excite hair cells near the base. Low-frequency sounds excite cells near the apex.

Many relatives of a person with amusia have the same condition, so it probably has a genetic basis (Peretz, Cummings, & Dube, 2007). Given that pitch perception depends on the auditory cortex, we might expect to find a thinner than average auditory cortex. In fact, amusia is associated with a thicker than average auditory cortex in the right hemisphere but less than average white matter—that is, axons (Hyde et al., 2007). Evidently, the condition relates to abnormal migration of auditory neurons during early development, paired with reduced connections between the auditory cortex and other areas.

Absolute pitch (or "perfect pitch") is the ability to hear a note and identify it—for example, "That's a C sharp." People have either high accuracy on this task or almost none. Intermediates are rare. Genetic predisposition may contribute to this condition, but the main determinant is early and extensive musical training. Not everyone with musical training develops absolute pitch, but almost everyone with absolute pitch had extensive musical training (Athos et al., 2007). Absolute pitch is more common among people who speak tonal languages, such as Vietnamese and Mandarin Chinese (Deutsch, Henthorn, Marvin, & Xu, 2006). In those languages, the meaning of a sound depends its pitch, and therefore, people learn from infancy to pay close attention to slight changes of pitch.

You can test yourself for absolute pitch at the University of California Absolute Pitch Study Website: http://perfectpitch.ucsf.edu/

STOP & CHECK

1. Through which mechanism do we perceive low-frequency sounds (up to about 100 Hz)?
2. How do we perceive middle-frequency sounds (100 to 4000 Hz)?
3. How do we perceive high-frequency sounds (above 4000 Hz)?
4. What evidence suggests that amusia depends on genetic differences? What evidence suggests that absolute pitch depends on special experiences?

ANSWERS

1. At low frequencies, the basilar membrane vibrates in synchrony with the sound waves, and each responding axon in the auditory nerve sends one action potential per sound wave. **2.** At intermediate frequencies, no single axon fires an action potential for each sound wave, but different axons fire for different waves, and so a volley (group) of axons fires for each wave. **3.** At high frequencies, the sound causes maximum vibration for the hair cells at one location along the basilar membrane. **4.** Many relatives of a person with amusia have the condition also. Absolute pitch occurs almost entirely among people who had early musical training and is much more common among people who speak tonal languages, which require greater attention to pitch.

Just as the visual cortex is active during visual imagery, area A1 is important for auditory imagery. In one study, people listened to several familiar and unfamiliar songs. At various points, parts of each song were replaced by 3- to 5-second gaps. When people were listening to familiar songs, they reported that they heard "in their heads" the notes or words that belonged in the gaps. That experience was accompanied by activity in area A1. During similar gaps in the unfamiliar songs, they did not hear anything in their heads, and area A1 showed no activation (Kraemer, Macrae, Green, & Kelley, 2005).

Also like the visual system, the auditory system requires experience for full development. Just as rearing an animal in the dark impairs visual development, rearing one in constant noise impairs auditory development (Chang & Merzenich, 2003). In people who are deaf from birth, the axons leading from the auditory cortex develop less than in other people (Emmorey, Allen, Bruss, Schenker, & Damasio, 2003).

However, the visual and auditory systems differ in this respect: Whereas damage to area V1 leaves someone blind, damage to area A1 does not produce deafness. People with damage to the primary auditory cortex hear simple sounds reasonably well, unless the damage extends into subcortical brain areas (Tanaka, Kamo, Yoshida, & Yamadori, 1991). Their main deficit is in the ability to recognize combinations or sequences of sounds, like music or speech. Evidently, the

The Auditory Cortex

As information from the auditory system passes through subcortical areas, axons cross over in the midbrain to enable each hemisphere of the forebrain to get most of its input from the opposite ear (Glendenning, Baker, Hutson, & Masterton, 1992). The information ultimately reaches the **primary auditory cortex (area A1)** in the superior temporal cortex, as shown in Figure 7.5.

The organization of the auditory cortex strongly parallels that of the visual cortex (Poremba et al., 2003). For example, just as the visual system has a "what" pathway and a "where" pathway, the auditory system has a "what" pathway sensitive to patterns of sound in the anterior temporal cortex and a "where" pathway sensitive to sound location in the posterior temporal cortex and the parietal cortex (Lomber & Malhotra, 2008). The superior temporal cortex includes areas important for detecting visual motion and the motion of sounds. Just as patients with damage in area MT become motion blind, patients with damage in parts of the superior temporal cortex become motion deaf. They hear sounds, but they do not detect that a source of a sound is moving (Ducommun et al., 2004).

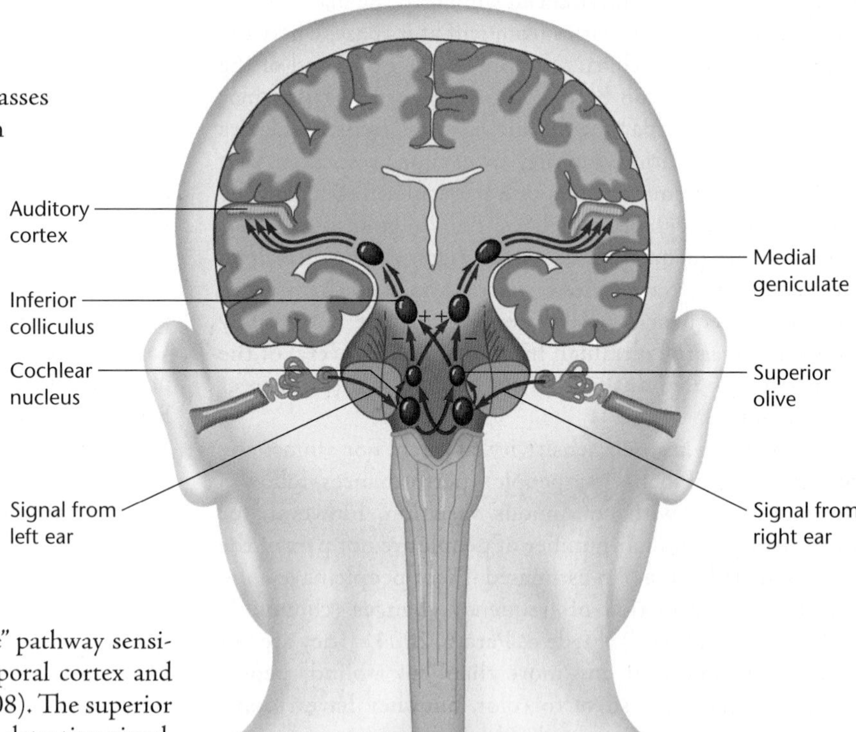

Figure 7.5 Route of auditory impulses from the receptors in the ear to the auditory cortex
The cochlear nucleus receives input from the ipsilateral ear only (the one on the same side of the head). All later stages have input originating from both ears.

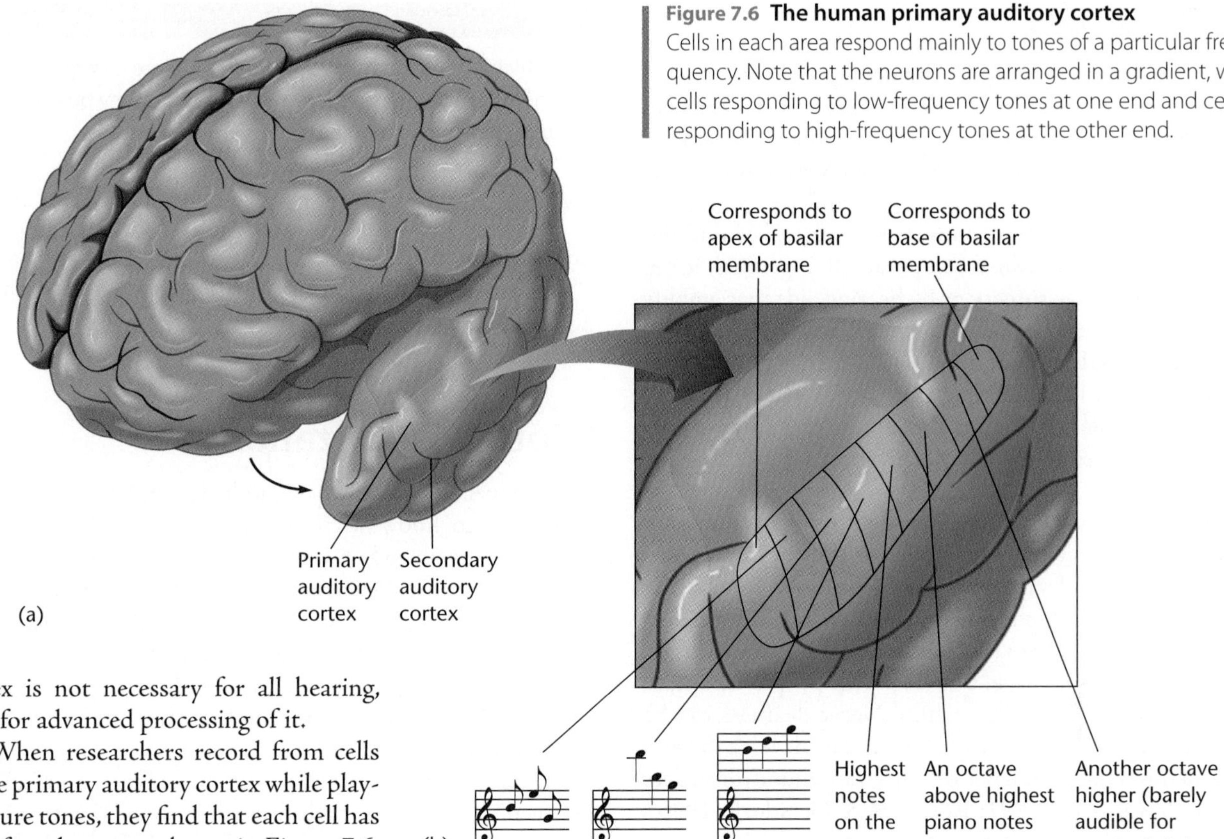

Figure 7.6 The human primary auditory cortex
Cells in each area respond mainly to tones of a particular frequency. Note that the neurons are arranged in a gradient, with cells responding to low-frequency tones at one end and cells responding to high-frequency tones at the other end.

cortex is not necessary for all hearing, only for advanced processing of it.

When researchers record from cells in the primary auditory cortex while playing pure tones, they find that each cell has a preferred tone, as shown in Figure 7.6. Note the gradient from one area of the cortex responsive to lower tones up to areas responsive to higher and higher tones. The auditory cortex provides a kind of map of the sounds—researchers call it a *tonotopic* map.

In alert, waking animals, each cell in area A1 gives a prolonged response to its preferred sound and little or no response to other sounds (X. Wang, Lu, Snider, & Liang, 2005). Most cells respond best to a complex sound, such as a dominant tone and several harmonics or other tones (Barbour & Wang, 2003; Griffiths, Uppenkamp, Johnsrude, Josephs, & Patterson, 2001; Penagos, Melcher, & Oxenham, 2004; Wessinger et al., 2001). For example, for a tone of 400 Hz, the harmonics are 800 Hz, 1200 Hz, and so forth. We experience a tone with harmonics as "richer" than one without them.

Surrounding the primary auditory cortex are additional auditory areas, in which cells respond more to changes in sounds than to any prolonged sound (Seifritz et al., 2002). Just as the visual system starts with cells that respond to simple lines and progresses to cells that detect faces and other complex stimuli, the same is true for the auditory system. Cells outside area A1 respond best to what we might call auditory "objects"—sounds such as animal cries, machinery noises, music, and so forth (Zatorre, Bouffard, & Belin, 2004). Many of these cells respond so slowly that they probably are not part of the initial perception of the sound itself. Rather, they interpret a sound's meaning (Gutschalk, Patterson, Scherg, Uppenkamp, & Rupp, 2004).

STOP & CHECK

5. How is the auditory cortex like the visual cortex?

6. What is one way in which the auditory and visual cortices differ?

7. What kinds of sounds most strongly activate the auditory cortex?

ANSWERS

5. Any of the following: (a) Both vision and hearing have "what" and "where" pathways. (b) Areas in the superior temporal cortex analyze movement of both visual and auditory stimuli. Damage there can cause motion blindness or motion deafness. (c) The visual cortex is essential for visual imagery, and the primary auditory cortex is essential for auditory imagery. (d) Both the visual and auditory cortices need normal experience early in life to develop normal sensitivities. **6.** Damage to the primary visual cortex leaves someone blind, but damage to the primary auditory cortex merely impairs perception of complex sounds without making the person deaf. **7.** Each cell in the primary auditory cortex has a preferred frequency. Many or most cells respond best to complex sounds that include harmonics. Outside the primary auditory cortex, most cells respond to "auditory objects" that mean something.

Hearing Loss

The great majority of hearing-impaired people respond at least slightly to loud noises. We distinguish two categories of hearing impairment: conductive deafness and nerve deafness.

Diseases, infections, or tumorous bone growth can prevent the middle ear from transmitting sound waves properly to the cochlea. The result is **conductive deafness,** or **middle-ear deafness.** It is sometimes temporary. If it persists, it can be corrected either by surgery or by hearing aids that amplify the stimulus. Because people with conductive deafness have a normal cochlea and auditory nerve, they hear their own voices, which can be conducted through the bones of the skull directly to the cochlea, bypassing the middle ear. Because they hear themselves clearly, they may blame others for talking too softly.

Nerve deafness, or **inner-ear deafness,** results from damage to the cochlea, the hair cells, or the auditory nerve. It can occur in any degree and may be confined to one part of the cochlea, in which case someone hears certain frequencies and not others. Hearing aids cannot compensate for extensive nerve damage, but they help people who have lost receptors in part of the cochlea. Nerve deafness can be inherited (A. Wang et al., 1998), or it can develop from a variety of prenatal problems or early childhood disorders (Cremers & van Rijn, 1991; Robillard & Gersdorff, 1986), including:

- Exposure of the mother to rubella (German measles), syphilis, or other diseases or toxins during pregnancy
- Inadequate oxygen to the brain during birth
- Deficient activity of the thyroid gland
- Certain diseases, including multiple sclerosis and meningitis
- Childhood reactions to certain drugs, including aspirin
- Repeated exposure to loud noises

Nerve deafness often produces **tinnitus** (tin-EYE-tus)—frequent or constant ringing in the ears. In some cases, tinnitus is due to a phenomenon like phantom limb, discussed in Chapter 5. Recall the example in which someone has an arm amputated, and then the axons reporting facial sensations invade the brain areas previously sensitive to the arm so that stimulation of the face produces a sensation of a phantom arm. Similarly, damage to part of the cochlea is like an amputation: If the brain no longer gets its normal input, axons representing other parts of the body may invade a brain area previously responsive to sounds, especially high-frequency sounds. Several patients have reported ringing in their ears whenever they move their jaws (Lockwood et al., 1998). Presumably, axons representing the lower face invaded their auditory cortex. Some people report a decrease in tinnitus after they start wearing hearing aids.

For practical information about coping with hearing loss, visit Mark Rejhon's Website at http://www.marky.com/hearing/

STOP & CHECK

8. Which type of hearing loss would be more common among members of rock bands and why? Would they be likely to benefit from hearing aids?

ANSWER

8. Nerve deafness is common among rock band members because their frequent exposure to loud noises causes damage to the cells of the ear. Hearing aids are usually not helpful in cases of nerve deafness.

Sound Localization

You are walking alone when suddenly you hear a loud noise. You want to know what produced it (friend or foe), but equally, you want to know where it came from (so you can approach or escape). Determining the direction and distance of a sound requires comparing the responses of the two ears. You can identify a sound's direction even if it occurs just briefly and while you are turning your head (Vliegen, Van Grootel, & Van Opstal, 2004), and owls can localize sound well enough to capture mice in the dark.

One cue for sound location is the difference in intensity between the ears. For high-frequency sounds, with a wavelength shorter than the width of the head, the head creates a *sound shadow* (Figure 7.7), making the sound louder for the closer ear. In adult humans, this mechanism produces accurate

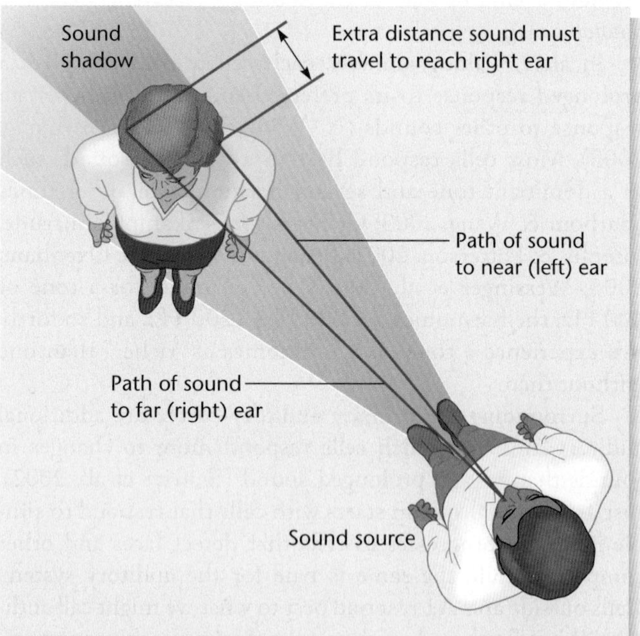

Figure 7.7 Differential loudness and arrival times as cues for sound localization
Sounds reaching the closer ear arrive sooner as well as louder because the head produces a "sound shadow." *(After Lindsay & Norman, 1972)*

sound localization for frequencies above 2000 to 3000 Hz and less accurate localizations for progressively lower frequencies. Another method is the difference in *time of arrival* at the two ears. A sound coming from directly in front of you reaches both ears at once. A sound coming directly from the side reaches the closer ear about 600 microseconds (μs) before the other. Sounds coming from intermediate locations reach the two ears at delays between 0 and 600 μs. Time of arrival is most useful for localizing sounds with a sudden onset. Most birds' alarm calls increase gradually in loudness, making them difficult for a predator to localize.

A third cue is the *phase difference* between the ears. Every sound wave has phases with two consecutive peaks 360 degrees apart. Figure 7.8 shows sound waves that are in phase and 45 degrees, 90 degrees, or 180 degrees out of phase. If a sound originates to the side of the head, the sound wave strikes the two ears out of phase, as shown in Figure 7.9. How much out of phase depends on the frequency of the sound, the size of the head, and the direction of the sound. Phase differences provide information that is useful for localizing sounds with frequencies up to about 1500 Hz in humans.

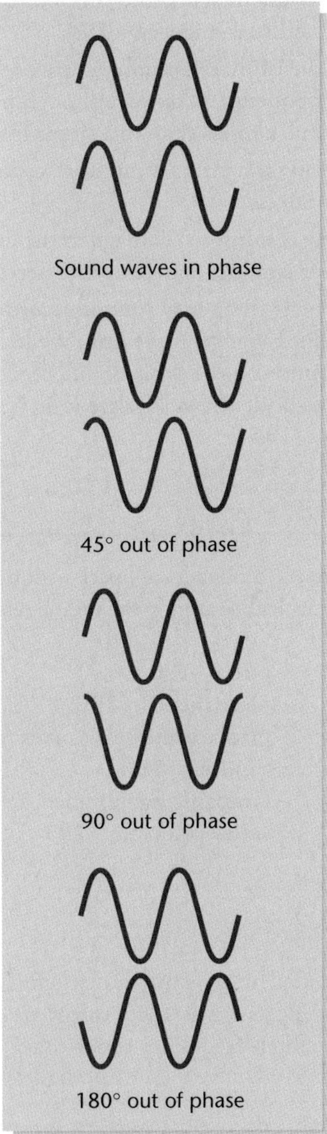

Figure 7.8 Sound waves can be in phase or out of phase
Sound waves that reach the two ears in phase are localized as coming from directly in front of (or behind) the hearer. The more out of phase the waves, the farther the sound source is from the body's midline.

Figure 7.9 Phase differences between the ears as a cue for sound localization
A sound coming from anywhere other than straight ahead or straight behind reaches the two ears at different phases of the sound wave. The difference in phase is a signal to the sound's direction. With high-frequency sounds, the phases can become ambiguous.

In short, humans localize low frequencies by phase differences and high frequencies by loudness differences. We localize a sound of any frequency by its time of onset if it occurs suddenly enough. We localize most speech sounds by their time of onset.

What would happen if someone became deaf in one ear? At first, as you would expect, all sounds seem to come directly from the side of the intact ear. (Obviously, that ear hears a sound louder and sooner than the other ear because the other ear doesn't hear it at all.) Eventually, however, people learn to interpret loudness cues when they hear familiar sounds in a familiar location. They infer that louder sounds come from the side of the intact ear and softer sounds come from the opposite side. Their accuracy does not match that of people with two ears, but it becomes accurate enough to be useful under some conditions (Van Wanrooij & Van Opstal, 2004).

STOP & CHECK

9. Which method of sound localization is more effective for an animal with a small head? Which is more effective for an animal with a large head? Why?

ANSWER

9. An animal with a small head localizes sounds mainly by differences in loudness because the ears are not far enough apart for differences in onset time to be very large. An animal with a large head localizes sounds mainly by differences in onset time because its ears are far apart and well suited to noting differences in phase or onset time.

MODULE 7.1 IN CLOSING

Functions of Hearing

We spend much of our day listening to language, and we sometimes forget that the original, primary function of hearing has to do with simpler but extremely important issues: What do I hear? Where is it? Is it coming closer? Is it a potential mate, a potential enemy, potential food, or something irrelevant? The organization of the auditory system is well suited to resolving these questions.

SUMMARY

1. Sound waves vibrate the tympanic membrane. Three tiny bones convert these vibrations into more forceful vibrations of the smaller oval window, setting in motion the fluid inside the cochlea. Waves of fluid inside the cochlea stimulate the hair cells that send messages to the brain. **191**
2. We detect the pitch of low-frequency sounds by the frequency of action potentials in the auditory system. At intermediate frequencies, we detect volleys of responses across many receptors. We detect the pitch of the highest frequency sounds by the area of greatest response along the basilar membrane. **192**
3. The auditory cortex resembles the visual cortex in many ways. Both have a "what" system and a "where" system. Both have specialized areas for detecting motion, and therefore, it is possible for a person with brain damage to be motion blind or motion deaf. The visual cortex is essential for visual imagery, and the auditory cortex is essential for auditory imagery. **194**
4. Each cell in the primary auditory cortex responds best to a particular frequency of tones, although many respond better to complex tones than to a single frequency. **195**
5. Areas bordering the primary auditory cortex analyze the meaning of sounds. **195**
6. Deafness may result from damage to the nerve cells or to the bones that conduct sounds to the nerve cells. **196**
7. We localize high-frequency sounds according to differences in loudness between the ears. We localize low-frequency sounds on the basis of differences in phase. If a sound occurs suddenly, we localize it by time of onset in the two ears. **196**

KEY TERMS

Terms are defined in the module on the page number indicated. They're also presented in alphabetical order with definitions in the book's Subject Index/Glossary. Interactive flashcards, audio reviews, and crossword puzzles are among the online resources available to help you learn these terms and the concepts they represent.

amplitude **190**
cochlea **192**
conductive deafness (middle-ear deafness) **196**
frequency **190**
frequency theory **192**
hair cells **192**
loudness **190**
nerve deafness (inner-ear deafness) **196**
oval window **191**
pinna **191**
pitch **190**
place theory **192**
primary auditory cortex (area A1) **194**
tinnitus **196**
tympanic membrane **191**
volley principle **193**

THOUGHT QUESTIONS

1. Why do you suppose that the human auditory system evolved sensitivity to sounds in the range of 20 to 20000 Hz instead of some other range of frequencies?
2. The text explains how we might distinguish loudness for low-frequency sounds. How might we distinguish loudness for a high-frequency tone?

MODULE 7.2

The Mechanical Senses

The next time you turn on your radio, place your hand on its surface. You feel the same vibrations that you hear. If you practiced enough, could you learn to "hear" the vibrations with your fingers? No, they would remain just vibrations. If an earless species had enough time, might its vibration detectors evolve into sound detectors? Yes! In fact, our ears evolved in just that way. Much of evolution consists of taking something that evolved for one purpose and modifying it for another purpose.

The *mechanical senses* respond to pressure, bending, or other distortions of a receptor. They include touch, pain, and other body sensations, as well as vestibular sensation, which detects the position and movement of the head. Audition is also a mechanical sense because the hair cells are modified touch receptors. We considered it separately because of its complexity and importance.

Vestibular Sensation

Try to read a page while you jiggle your head up and down or back and forth. You will find that you can read it fairly easily. Now hold your head steady and jiggle the page up and down, back and forth. Suddenly, you can hardly read it at all. Why?

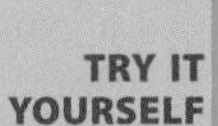

When you move your head, the vestibular organ adjacent to the cochlea monitors movements and directs compensatory movements of your eyes. When your head moves left, your eyes move right; when your head moves right, your eyes move left. Effortlessly, you keep your eyes focused on what you want to see (Brandt, 1991). When you move the page, however, the vestibular organ cannot keep your eyes on target.

Sensations from the vestibular organ detect the direction of tilt and the amount of acceleration of the head. We are seldom aware of our vestibular sensations except under unusual conditions, such as riding a roller coaster. They are nevertheless critical for guiding eye movements and maintaining balance. Astronauts, of course, become acutely aware of the *lack* of vestibular sensation while they are in orbit.

The vestibular organ, shown in Figure 7.10, consists of the *saccule, utricle,* and three semicircular canals. Like the hearing receptors, the vestibular receptors are modified touch receptors. Calcium carbonate particles called *otoliths* lie next to the hair cells. When the head tilts in different directions, the otoliths push against different sets of hair cells and excite them (Hess, 2001).

The three **semicircular canals,** oriented in perpendicular planes, are filled with a jellylike substance and lined with hair cells. Acceleration of the head at any angle causes the jellylike substance in one of these canals to push against the hair cells. Action potentials initiated by cells of the vestibular system travel through part of the eighth cranial nerve to the brainstem and cerebellum. (The eighth cranial nerve contains both an auditory component and a vestibular component.)

For the vestibular organ, as far as we can tell, the ideal size is nearly constant, regardless of the size of the animal. Whales are 10 million times as massive as mice, but their vestibular organ is only 5 times as large (Squires, 2004).

STOP & CHECK

10. People with damage to the vestibular system have trouble reading street signs while walking. Why?

ANSWER

10. The vestibular system enables the brain to shift eye movements to compensate for changes in head position. Without feedback about head position, a person would not be able to correct the eye movements, and the experience would be like watching a jiggling book page.

Somatosensation

The **somatosensory system,** the sensation of the body and its movements, is not one sense but many, including discriminative touch (which identifies the shape of an object), deep pressure, cold, warmth, pain, itch, tickle, and the position and movement of joints.

Somatosensory Receptors

The skin has many kinds of somatosensory receptors, including those listed in Figure 7.11. Table 7.1 lists the probable functions of these and other receptors (Iggo & Andres, 1982;

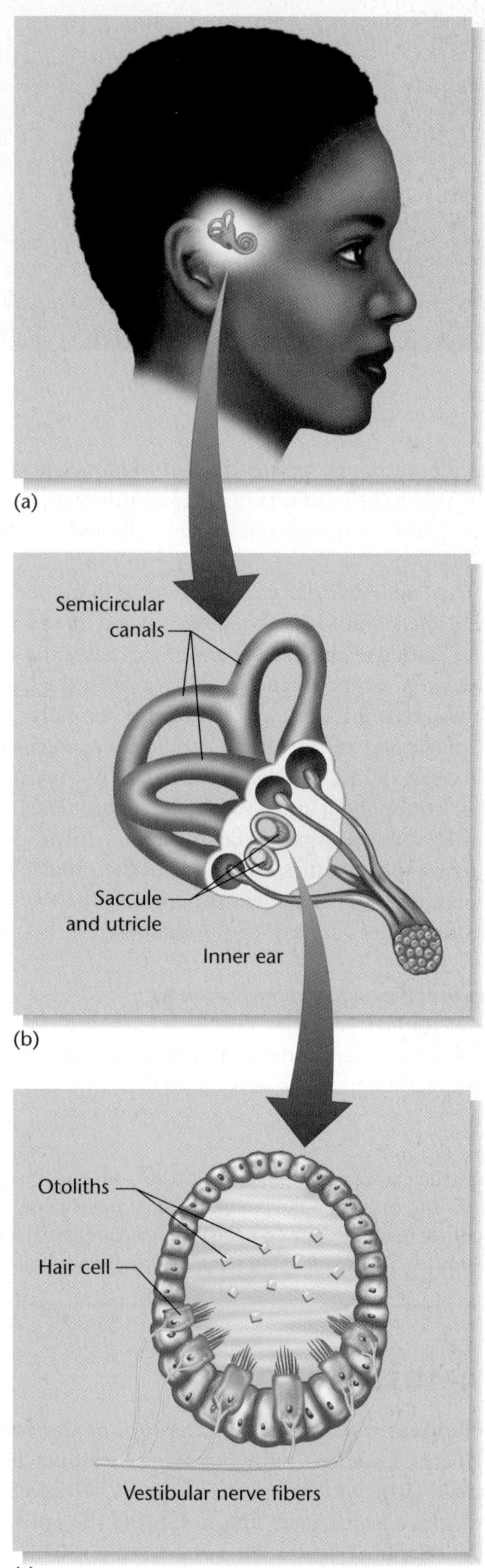

Figure 7.10 Structures for vestibular sensation
(a) Location of the vestibular organs. **(b)** Structures of the vestibular organs. **(c)** Cross-section through a utricle. Calcium carbonate particles, called otoliths, press against different hair cells depending on the direction of tilt and rate of acceleration of the head.

Paré, Smith, & Rice, 2002). Others (not in the table) respond to deep stimulation, joint movement, or muscle movements. However, most receptors respond to more than one kind of stimulus, such as touch and temperature.

A touch receptor may be a simple bare neuron ending (e.g., many pain receptors), an elaborated neuron ending (Ruffini endings and Meissner's corpuscles), or a bare ending surrounded by other cells that modify its function (Pacinian corpuscles). Stimulation of a touch receptor opens sodium channels in the axon, thereby starting an action potential (Price et al., 2000).

Let's consider the **Pacinian corpuscle,** which detects sudden displacements or high-frequency vibrations on the skin (Figure 7.12). Inside its outer structure is the neuron membrane. The onionlike outer structure provides mechanical support that resists gradual or constant pressure. It thereby insulates the neuron against most touch stimuli. However, a sudden or vibrating stimulus bends the membrane, enabling sodium ions to enter, depolarizing the membrane (Loewenstein, 1960).

Certain chemicals stimulate the receptors for heat and cold. The heat receptor responds to capsaicin, the chemical that makes jalapeños and similar peppers taste hot. The coolness receptor responds to menthol and less strongly to mint (McKemy, Neuhausser, & Julius, 2002). So advertisements mentioning "the cool taste of menthol" are literally correct. Mice deficient in this receptor show little response to cold and fail to seek a warmer place when they become cold (Bautista et al., 2007).

APPLICATIONS AND EXTENSIONS

Tickle

The sensation of tickle is interesting but poorly understood. Why does it exist at all? Why do you laugh if someone rapidly fingers your armpit, neck, or the soles of your feet? Chimpanzees respond to similar sensations with bursts of panting that resemble laughter. And yet tickling is unlike humor. Most people do not enjoy being tickled for long—if at all—and certainly not by a stranger. If a joke makes you laugh, you are more likely than usual to laugh at the next joke. But being tickled doesn't change your likelihood of laughing at a joke (C. R. Harris, 1999).

TRY IT YOURSELF

Why can't you tickle yourself? It is for the same reason that you can't surprise yourself. When you touch yourself, your brain compares the resulting stimulation to the "expected" stimulation and generates a weaker somatosensory response than you would experience from an unexpected touch (Blakemore, Wolpert, & Frith, 1998). Actually, some people can tickle themselves—a little—if they tickle the right side of the body with the left hand or the left side with the right hand. Try it. Also, you might be able to tickle yourself as soon as you wake up, before your brain is fully aroused. See whether you can remember to try that the next time you awaken.

TABLE 7.1 Somatosensory Receptors and Their Possible Functions

Receptor	Location	Responds to
Free nerve ending (unmyelinated or thinly myelinated axons)	Near base of hairs and elsewhere in skin	Pain, warmth, cold
Hair-follicle receptors	Hair-covered skin	Movement of hairs
Meissner's corpuscles	Hairless areas	Sudden displacement of skin; low-frequency vibration (flutter)
Pacinian corpuscles	Both hairy and hairless skin	Sudden displacement of skin; high-frequency vibration
Merkel's disks	Both hairy and hairless skin	Tangential forces across skin
Ruffini endings	Both hairy and hairless skin	Stretch of skin
Krause end bulbs	Mostly or entirely in hairless areas, perhaps including genitals	Uncertain

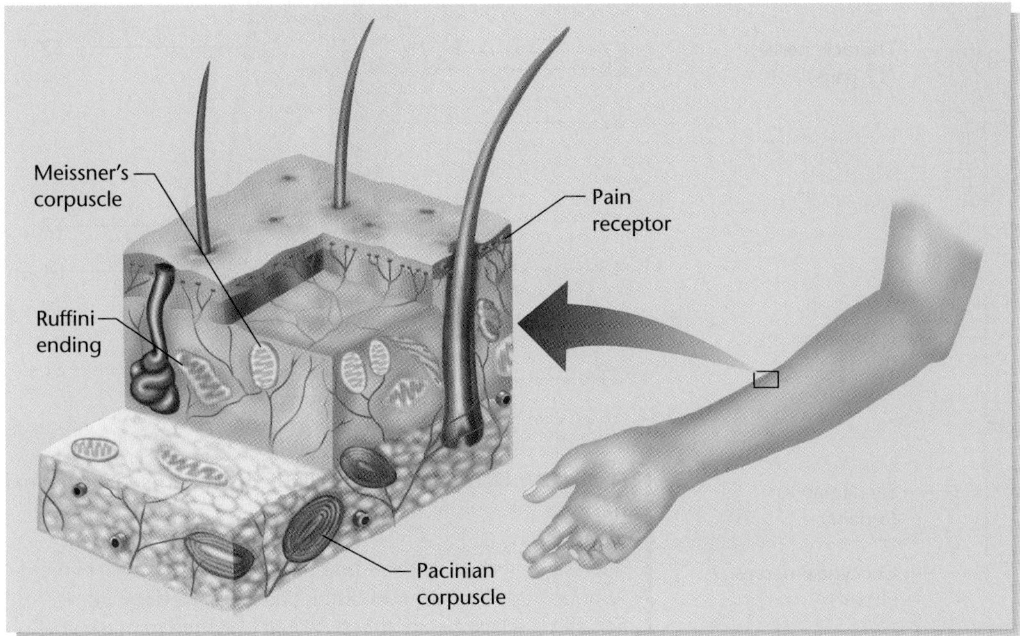

Figure 7.11 Some sensory receptors found in the skin, the human body's largest organ
Different receptor types respond to different stimuli, as described in Table 7.1.

Input to the Central Nervous System

Information from touch receptors in the head enters the central nervous system (CNS) through the cranial nerves. Information from receptors below the head enters the spinal cord and passes toward the brain through the 31 spinal nerves (Figure 7.13), including 8 cervical nerves, 12 thoracic nerves, 5 lumbar nerves, 5 sacral nerves, and 1 coccygeal nerve. Each spinal nerve has a sensory component and a motor component.

Each spinal nerve *innervates*, or connects to, a limited area of the body called a **dermatome** (Figure 7.14). For example, the third thoracic nerve (T3) innervates a strip of skin just above the nipples as well as the underarm area. But the borders between dermatomes are not so distinct as Figure 7.14 implies. Each dermatome overlaps one third to one half of the next dermatome.

The sensory information traveling through the spinal cord follows well-defined pathways toward the brain. For example, the touch pathway in the spinal cord is separate from the pain

Ed Reschke

Figure 7.12 A Pacinian corpuscle
Pacinian corpuscles are a type of receptor that responds best to sudden displacement of the skin or to high-frequency vibrations. They respond only briefly to steady pressure on the skin. The onionlike outer structure provides a mechanical support to the neuron inside it so that a sudden stimulus can bend it but a sustained stimulus cannot.

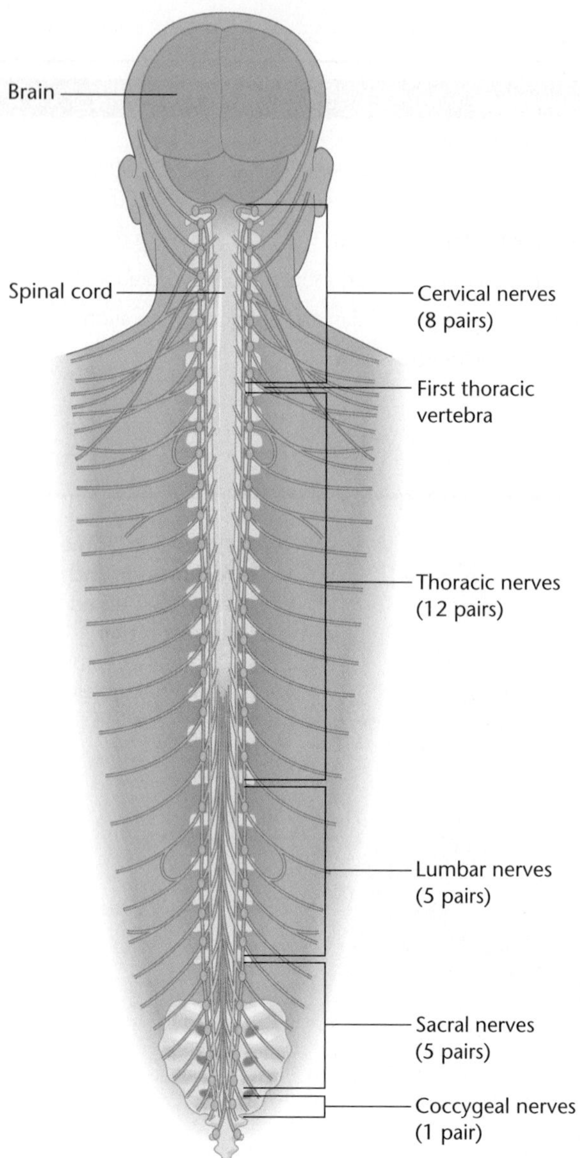

Figure 7.13 The human central nervous system (CNS)
Spinal nerves from each segment of the spinal cord exit through the correspondingly numbered opening between vertebrae. *(Starr & Taggart, 1989)*

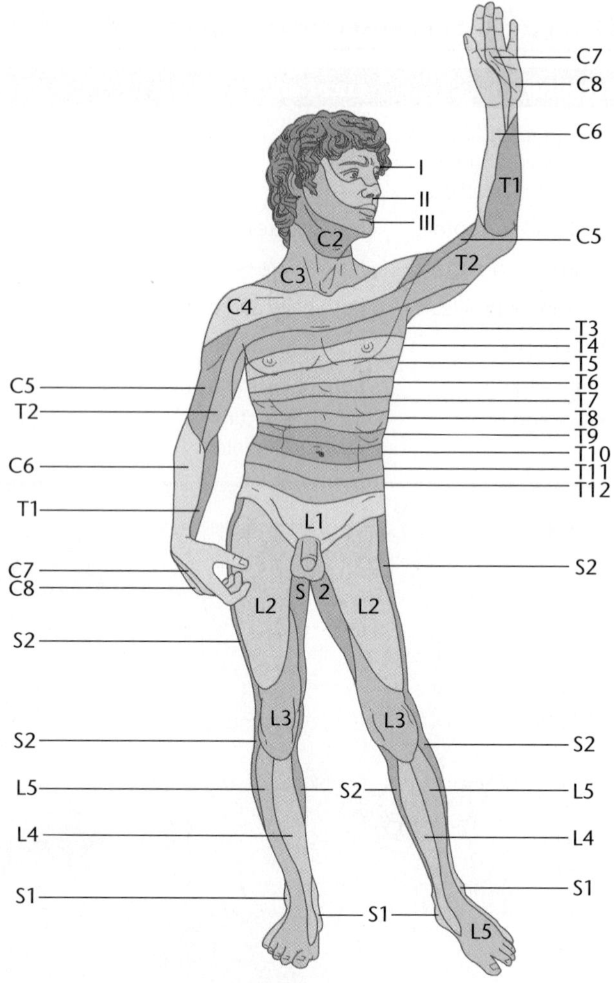

Figure 7.14 Dermatomes innervated by the 31 sensory spinal nerves
Areas I, II, and III of the face are not innervated by the spinal nerves but instead by three branches of the fifth cranial nerve. Although this figure shows distinct borders, the dermatomes actually overlap one another by about one third to one half of their width.

pathway, and the pain pathway itself has different populations of axons conveying sharp pain, slow burning pain, and painfully cold sensations (Craig, Krout, & Andrew, 2001). That is, the nervous system codes the differences among these sensations in terms of which cells are active. One patient had an illness that destroyed all the myelinated somatosensory axons from below his nose but spared his unmyelinated axons. He still felt temperature, pain, and itch, which depend on the unmyelinated axons. However, he had no sense of touch below the nose. Curiously, if someone lightly stroked his skin, all he experienced was a vague sense of pleasure. Recordings from his brain indicated no arousal of his primary somatosensory cortex but increased activity in the insular cortex, an area responsive to taste and to several kinds of emotional experience (Olausson et al., 2002). That is, he experienced the pleasurable, sensual aspects of touch even though he had no conscious detection of the touch itself.

The various areas of the somatosensory thalamus send their impulses to different areas of the primary somatosensory cortex, located in the parietal lobe. Two parallel strips in the somatosensory cortex respond mostly to touch on the skin. Two other parallel strips respond mostly to deep pressure and movement of the joints and muscles (Kaas, 1983). In short, various aspects of body sensation remain at least partly separate all the way to the cortex. Along each strip of somatosensory cortex, different subareas respond to different areas of the body. That is, the somatosensory cortex acts as a map of body location, as shown in Figure 4.22 (p. 100).

Just as conscious vision and hearing depend on the primary visual and auditory cortex, the primary somatosensory cortex is essential for conscious touch experiences. When weak, brief stimuli are applied to the fingers, people are consciously aware of only those that produce a certain minimum level of arousal in the primary somatosensory cortex (Palva, Linkenkaer-Hansen, Näätäen, & Palva, 2005). If someone touches you quickly on two nearby points on the hand, you will probably have an illusory experience of a single touch midway between those two points. When that happens, the activity in the primary somatosensory cortex corresponds to that midway point (Chen, Friedman, & Roe, 2003). In other words, the activity corresponds to what you experience, not what has actually stimulated your receptors.

Another demonstration of that principle is called the *cutaneous rabbit illusion*. If someone taps you very rapidly six times on the wrist and then three times near the elbow, you will have a sensation of something like a rabbit hopping from the wrist to the elbow, with an extra, illusionary, stop in between. The primary somatosensory cortex also responds as if you had been tapped in the intermediate location (Blankenburg, Ruff, Deichmann, Rees, & Driver, 2006). Unfortunately, you cannot easily try this yourself. For the illusion to work, you need all nine taps (six on the wrist and three near the elbow) within about four tenths of a second.

Damage to the somatosensory cortex impairs body perceptions. One patient with Alzheimer's disease, who had damage in the somatosensory cortex as well as elsewhere, had trouble putting her clothes on correctly, and she could not point correctly in response to such directions as "show me your elbow," although she pointed correctly to objects in the room. When told to touch her elbow, her most frequent response was to feel her wrist and arm and suggest that the elbow was probably around there, somewhere (Sirigu, Grafman, Bressler, & Sunderland, 1991).

STOP & CHECK

11. In what way is somatosensation several senses instead of one?

12. What evidence suggests that the somatosensory cortex is essential for the conscious perception of touch?

ANSWERS

11. We have several types of receptors, sensitive to touch, heat, and so forth, and different parts of the somatosensory cortex respond to different kinds of skin stimulation. **12.** People are consciously aware of only those touch stimuli that produce sufficient arousal in the primary somatosensory cortex.

Pain

Pain, the experience evoked by a harmful stimulus, directs our attention toward a danger and holds our attention. The prefrontal cortex, which is important for attention, typically responds only briefly to any new stimulus. With pain, it continues responding as long as the pain lasts (Downar, Mikulis, & Davis, 2003).

Have you ever wondered why morphine decreases pain after surgery but not during the surgery itself? Or why some people seem to tolerate pain so much better than others? Or why even the slightest touch on sunburned skin is so painful? Research on pain addresses these and other questions.

Pain Stimuli and Pain Pathways

Pain sensation begins with the least specialized of all receptors, a bare nerve ending (see Figure 7.11). Some pain receptors also respond to acids and heat. **Capsaicin**, a chemical found in hot peppers such as jalapeños, also stimulates those receptors. Capsaicin can produce burning or stinging sensations on many parts of your body, as you may have experienced if you ever touched the insides of hot peppers and then rubbed your eyes.

The axons carrying pain information have little or no myelin and therefore conduct impulses relatively slowly, in the range of 2 to 20 meters per second (m/s). The thicker and faster axons convey sharp pain; the thinner ones convey duller pain, such as postsurgical pain. Although pain messages reach the brain more slowly than most other sensations, the brain processes pain information rapidly. Motor responses to pain are faster than motor responses to touch stimuli (Ploner, Gross, Timmerman, & Schnitzler, 2006).

Pain axons release two neurotransmitters in the spinal cord. Mild pain releases the neurotransmitter glutamate, whereas stronger pain releases both glutamate and **substance P** (Cao et al., 1998). Mice that lack receptors for substance P react normally to mild pain but react to a severe injury as if it were a mild injury (DeFelipe et al., 1998). That is, without substance P, they do not detect the increased intensity.

The pain-sensitive cells in the spinal cord relay information to several sites in the brain. One pathway extends to the ventral posterior nucleus of the thalamus and from there to the somatosensory cortex, which responds to painful stimuli, memories of pain (Albanese, Duerden, Rainville, & Duncan, 2007), and signals that warn of impending pain (Babiloni et al., 2005). The spinal pathways for pain and touch are parallel, but with one important difference, as illustrated in Figure 7.15: The pain pathway crosses immediately from receptors on one side of the body to a tract ascending the contralateral side of the spinal cord. Touch information travels up the ipsilateral side of the spinal cord to the medulla, where it crosses to the contralateral side. So pain and touch reach nearby sites in the cerebral cortex. However, consider what happens to pain and touch if someone receives a cut that goes halfway through the spinal cord. You can reason out the answer for this Stop & Check question.

STOP & CHECK

13. Suppose someone suffers a cut through the spinal cord on the right side only. Will the person lose pain sensation on the left side or the right side? Will he or she lose touch sensation on the left side or the right side?

ANSWER

13. The person will lose pain sensation on the left side of the body because pain information crosses the spinal cord at once. He or she will lose touch sensation on the right side because touch pathways remain on the ipsilateral side until they reach the medulla.

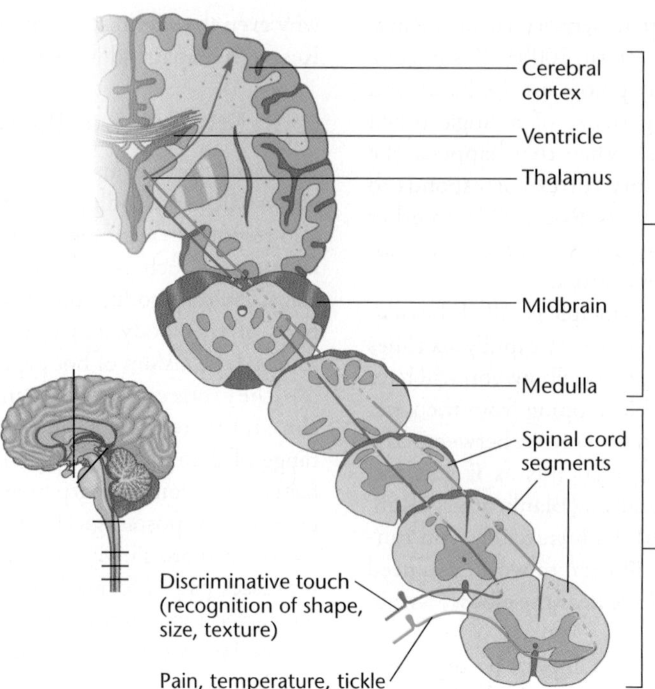
Cerebral cortex
Ventricle
Thalamus
From medulla to cerebral cortex, both touch and pain are represented on the contralateral side.
Midbrain
Medulla
Spinal cord segments
In spinal cord, information from one side of the body travels on ipsilateral side for touch and contralateral side for pain.
Discriminative touch (recognition of shape, size, texture)
Pain, temperature, tickle

Figure 7.15 Spinal pathways for touch and pain
Touch information and pain information both project to the cortex of the contralateral hemisphere, but the pain information crosses to the contralateral side of the spinal cord at once, whereas touch information does not cross until the medulla. Touch and pain sensations from the right side of the body (not shown in the figure) are the mirror image of what you see here. The inset at lower left shows the location of the slices.

Painful stimuli also activate a pathway through the reticular formation of the medulla and then to several of the central nuclei of the thalamus, the amygdala, hippocampus, prefrontal cortex, and cingulate cortex (Figure 7.16). These areas react not to the sensation but to its emotional associations (Hunt & Mantyh, 2001). If you watch someone—especially someone you care about—experiencing pain, you experience a "sympathetic pain" that shows up mainly as activity in your cingulate cortex (Singer et al., 2004). A hypnotic suggestion to feel no pain decreases the responses in the cingulate cortex without much effect on the somatosensory cortex (Rainville, Duncan, Price, Carrier, & Bushnell, 1997). That is, someone responding to a hypnotic sensation still feels the painful sensation but reacts with emotional indifference.

STOP & CHECK

14. How do jalapeños produce a hot sensation?

15. What would happen to a pain sensation if glutamate receptors in the spinal cord were blocked? What if substance P receptors were blocked?

ANSWERS

14. Jalapeños and other hot peppers contain capsaicin, which stimulates receptors that are sensitive to pain, acids, and heat. **15.** Blocking glutamate receptors would eliminate weak to moderate pain. (However, doing so would not be a good strategy for killing pain. Glutamate is the most abundant transmitter, and blocking it would disrupt practically everything the brain does.) Blocking substance P receptors makes intense pain feel mild.

Ways of Relieving Pain

Insensitivity to pain is dangerous. People with a gene that inactivates pain axons suffer repeated injuries and generally fail to learn to avoid dangers. One boy with this condition performed "street theater" in Pakistan by thrusting a knife through his arm or walking on burning coals. He died at age 14 by falling off a roof (Cox et al., 2006).

Opioids and Endorphins

After pain has alerted you to a danger, continuing pain messages are unnecessary. The brain puts the brakes on prolonged pain by **opioid mechanisms**—systems that respond to opiate drugs and similar chemicals. Candace Pert and Solomon Snyder (1973) discovered that opiates bind to receptors found mostly in the spinal cord and the **periaqueductal gray area** of the midbrain. Later researchers found that opiate receptors act by blocking the release of substance P (Kondo et al., 2005; Reichling, Kwiat, & Basbaum, 1988) (Figures 7.17 and 7.18).

The discovery of opiate receptors was exciting because it was the first evidence that opiates act on the nervous system rather than on the injured tissue. Furthermore, it implied that the nervous system must have its own opiate-type chemicals. The transmitters that attach to the same receptors as morphine are known as **endorphins**—a contraction of *endogenous morphines*. Most endorphins, such as β-endorphin, decrease pain, although one—dynorphin A—increases pain (Lai et al., 2006).

Inescapable pain is especially potent at stimulating endorphins and inhibiting further pain (Sutton et al., 1997). Presumably, the evolutionary function is that continued in-

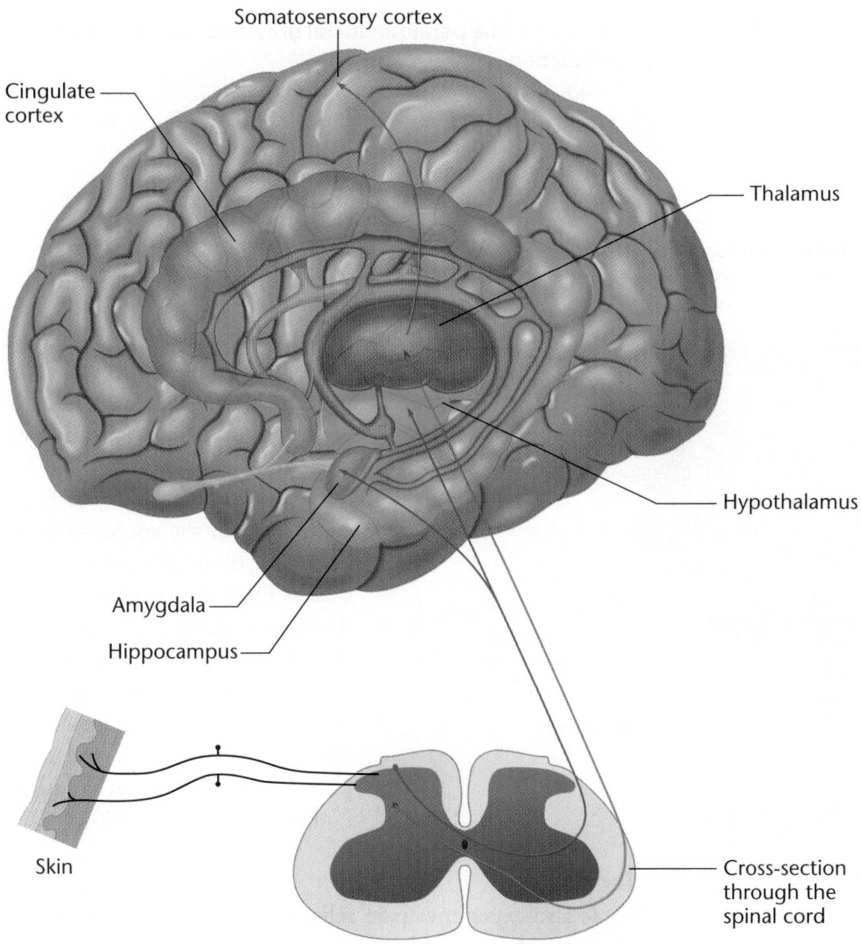

Somatosensory cortex
Cingulate cortex
Thalamus
Hypothalamus
Amygdala
Hippocampus
Skin
Cross-section through the spinal cord

Figure 7.16 Representation of pain in the human brain
A pathway to the thalamus, and from there to the somatosensory cortex, conveys the sensory aspects of pain. A separate pathway to the hypothalamus, amygdala, and other structures produces the emotional aspects. *(Hunt & Mantyh, 2001)*

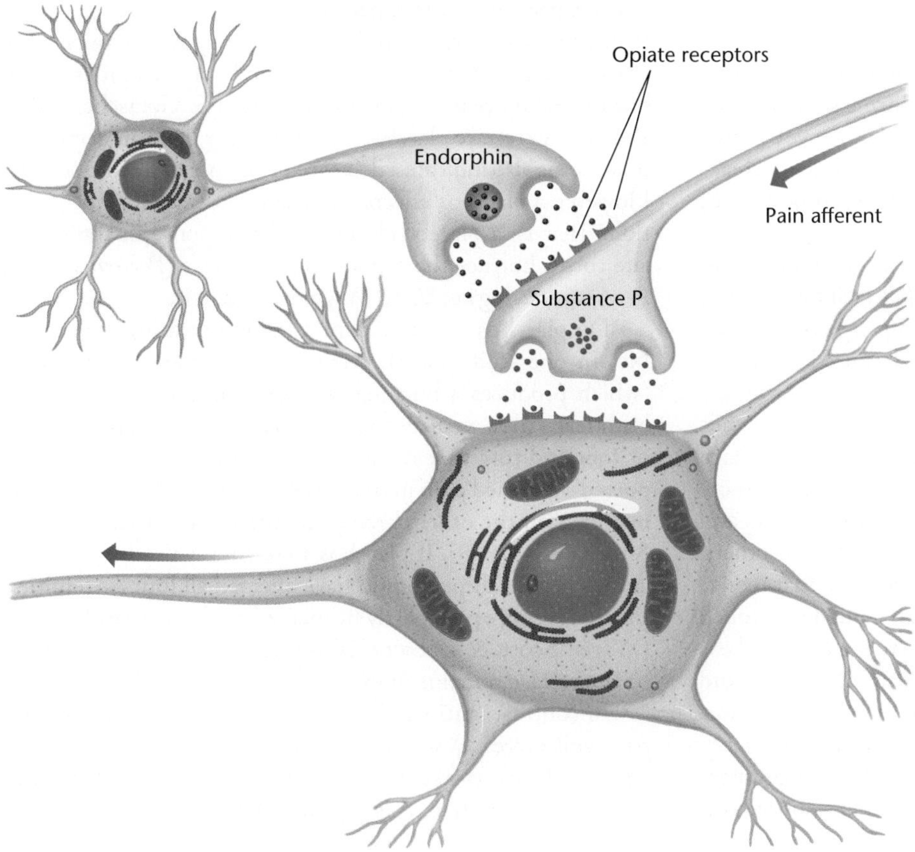

Opiate receptors
Endorphin
Pain afferent
Substance P

Figure 7.17 Synapses responsible for pain and its inhibition
The pain afferent neuron releases substance P as its neurotransmitter. Another neuron releases endorphin at presynaptic synapses; the endorphin inhibits the release of substance P and therefore alleviates pain.

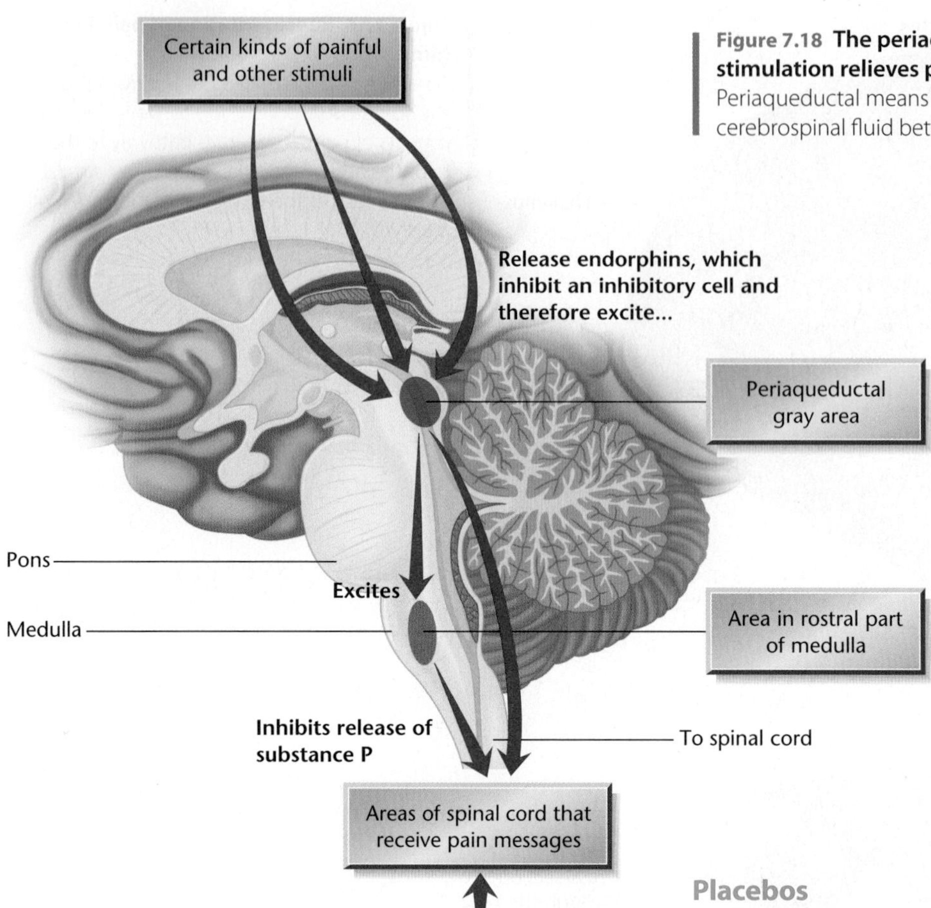

Figure 7.18 The periaqueductal gray area, where electrical stimulation relieves pain
Periaqueductal means "around the aqueduct," a passageway of cerebrospinal fluid between the third and fourth ventricles.

tense sensation of pain accomplishes nothing when escape is impossible. Endorphins are also released during sex and when you listen to thrilling music that sends a chill down your spine (A. Goldstein, 1980). Those experiences tend to decrease pain. You decrease your endorphin release if you brood about sad memories (Zubieta et al., 2003).

Many fluctuations in pain sensitivity relate to endorphins. For example, the female hormone *estradiol* facilitates opiate activity, and women tend to have lower pain sensitivity when their hormone levels are high than when they are low or rapidly changing (Y. R. Smith et al., 2006).

The discovery of endorphins provided physiological details for the gate theory, proposed decades earlier by Ronald Melzack and P. D. Wall (1965). The gate theory was an attempt to explain why some people withstand pain better than others and why the same injury hurts worse at some times than others. According to the **gate theory,** spinal cord neurons that receive messages from pain receptors also receive input from touch receptors and from axons descending from the brain. These other inputs can close the "gates" for the pain messages—and we now see that they do so at least partly by releasing endorphins. Although some details of Melzack and Wall's gate theory turned out wrong, the general principle is valid: Nonpain stimuli modify the intensity of pain. You have no doubt noticed this principle yourself. When you have an injury, you can decrease the pain by gently rubbing the skin around it or by concentrating on something else.

Morphine does not block the sharp pain of the surgeon's knife. For that, you need a general anesthetic. Instead, morphine blocks the slower, duller pain that lingers after surgery. Larger diameter axons, unaffected by morphine, carry sharp pain. Thinner axons convey dull postsurgical pain, and morphine does inhibit them (Taddese, Nah, & McCleskey, 1995).

Placebos

People also experience pain relief from placebos. A **placebo** is a drug or other procedure with no pharmacological effects. In many experiments, the experimental group receives the potentially active treatment, and the control group receives a placebo. Placebos have little effect in most kinds of medical research, but they often relieve pain (Hróbjartsson & Gøtzsche, 2001). People who receive placebos do not just *say* the pain decreased; brain scans also indicate a decreased response to painful stimuli. However, a placebo's effects are mainly on emotion, not sensation. That is, a placebo decreases the response in the cingulate cortex but not the somatosensory cortex (Petrovic, Kalso, Petersson, & Ingvar, 2002; Wager et al., 2004).

Do placebos decrease pain just by increasing relaxation? No. In one study, people were given injections of capsaicin (which produces a burning sensation) into both hands and both feet. They were also given a placebo cream on one hand or foot and told that it was a powerful painkiller. People reported decreased pain in the area that got the placebo but normal pain on the other three extremities (Benedetti, Arduino, & Amanzio, 1999). If placebos were simply producing relaxation, the relaxation should have affected all four extremities. Placebos relieve pain partly by increasing the release of opiates (Wager, Scott, & Zubieta, 2007). Exactly how they increase opiate release remains unknown.

In contrast, antiplacebos or *nocebos* (suggestions that the pain will increase) worsen pain by increasing anxiety. Antianxiety drugs weaken the effects of nocebos (Benedetti, Amanzio, Vighetti, & Asteggiano, 2006).

Cannabinoids and Capsaicin

Cannabinoids—chemicals related to marijuana—also block certain kinds of pain. Unlike opiates, cannabinoids act mainly in the periphery of the body rather than the CNS. Researchers found that if they deleted the cannabinoid receptors in the peripheral nervous system while leaving them intact in the CNS, cannabinoids lost most of their ability to decrease pain (Agarwal et al., 2007).

Another approach to relieving pain uses capsaicin. As mentioned, capsaicin produces a painful burning sensation by releasing substance P. However, it releases substance P faster than neurons resynthesize it, leaving the cells less able to send pain messages. Also, high doses of capsaicin damage pain receptors. Capsaicin rubbed onto a sore shoulder, an arthritic joint, or other painful area produces a temporary burning sensation followed by a longer period of decreased pain. However, do not try eating hot peppers to reduce pain in, say, your legs. The capsaicin you eat passes through the digestive system without entering the blood. Therefore, eating it will not relieve your pain—unless your tongue hurts (Karrer & Bartoshuk, 1991).

Electrical Stimulation of the Nervous System

If someone is in almost constant pain and no other treatment is effective, a final possibility is direct electrical stimulation in or near the pain pathways in the spinal cord or in the thalamus. Presumably, this procedure disrupts steady stimulation of pain synapses. However, the details remain uncertain. This procedure was pioneered in the 1970s, but was originally rejected, partly because of fears at the time that neurosurgeons would use stimulation to control people like puppets. That fear no longer seems realistic. However, although direct stimulation of the spinal cord or thalamus helps some people who had no other way of escaping chronic pain, most people do not experience long-lasting benefits (Hamani et al., 2006; Olsson, Meyerson, & Linderoth, 2008). A need for further research remains.

STOP & CHECK

16. Why do opiates relieve dull pain but not sharp pain?

17. How do the pain-relieving effects of cannabinoids differ from those of opiates?

ANSWERS

16. Endorphins block messages from the thinnest pain fibers, conveying dull pain, but not from thicker fibers, carrying sharp pain. **17.** Unlike opiates, cannabinoids exert most of their pain-relieving effects in the peripheral nervous system, not the CNS.

Sensitization of Pain

In addition to mechanisms for decreasing pain, the body has mechanisms that increase pain. For example, even a light touch on sunburned skin is painful. Damaged or inflamed tissue, such as sunburned skin, releases histamine, nerve growth factor, and other chemicals that help repair the damage but also magnify the responses in nearby heat and pain receptors (Chuang et al., 2001; Devor, 1996; Tominaga et al., 1998). Nonsteroidal anti-inflammatory drugs, such as ibuprofen, relieve pain by reducing the release of chemicals from damaged tissues (Hunt & Mantyh, 2001).

Some people suffer chronic pain long after an injury has healed. As we shall see in Chapter 13, a barrage of stimulation to a neuron can "potentiate" its synaptic receptors so that it responds more vigorously to the same input in the future. That mechanism is central to learning and memory, but unfortunately, pain activates the mechanism as well. A barrage of painful stimuli, even at a slow rate, potentiates the cells responsive to pain so that they respond more vigorously to similar stimulation in the future (Ikeda et al., 2006). In effect, the brain learns how to feel pain, and it gets better at it.

Therefore, to prevent chronic pain, it helps to limit pain from the start. Suppose you are about to undergo major surgery. Which approach is best?

A. Start taking morphine before the surgery.
B. Begin morphine soon after awakening from surgery.
C. Postpone the morphine as long as possible and take as little as possible.

Perhaps surprisingly, the research supports answer A: Start the morphine before the surgery (Coderre, Katz, Vaccarino, & Melzack, 1993). Allowing pain messages to bombard the brain during and after the surgery increases the sensitivity of the pain nerves and their receptors (Malmberg, Chen, Tonagawa, & Basbaum, 1997). People who begin taking morphine before surgery need less of it afterward.

For more information about pain, including links to research reports, visit the Website of the American Pain Society: http://www.ampainsoc.org/

STOP & CHECK

18. How do ibuprofen and other nonsteroidal anti-inflammatory drugs decrease pain?

19. Why is it preferable to start taking morphine before an operation instead of waiting until later?

ANSWERS

18. Anti-inflammatory drugs block the release of chemicals from damaged tissues, which would otherwise magnify the effects of pain receptors. **19.** The morphine will not decrease the sharp pain of the surgery itself. However, it will decrease the subsequent barrage of pain stimuli that can sensitize pain neurons.

Itch

Have you ever wondered, "What is itch, anyway? Is it a kind of pain? A kind of touch? Or something else altogether?" Researchers have not identified the receptors responsible for itch, but it appears to be a separate sensation, not a mild pain or a kind of touch.

You have at least two kinds of itch. They feel about the same, but the causes are different. First, when you have mild tissue damage—such as when your skin is healing after a cut—your skin releases histamines, which dilate blood vessels and produce an itching sensation. Second, contact with certain plants, especially cowhage (a tropical plant with barbed hairs), also produces itch. Antihistamines block the itch that histamines cause but not the itch that cowhage causes. Conversely, rubbing the skin with capsaicin relieves the itch that cowhage causes, but it has little effect on the itch that histamine causes (Johanek et al., 2007).

One spinal cord pathway conveys itch sensation (Andrew & Craig, 2001). Some of its axons respond to histamine itch and some to cowhage itch. Apparently, no axon responds to both kinds. However, these axons respond to heat as well, not just itch (S. Davidson et al., 2007). Itch axons activate certain neurons in the spinal cord that produce a chemical called *gastrin-releasing peptide*. Blocking that peptide has been shown to decrease scratching in mice without affecting their responses to pain (Sun & Chen, 2007).

TRY IT YOURSELF

The itch pathways are slow to respond, and when they do, the axons transmit impulses at the unusually slow velocity of only half a meter per second. At that rate, an action potential from your foot needs 3 or 4 seconds to reach your head. Imagine the delay for a giraffe or an elephant. You might try rubbing some sandpaper or very rough leaves against your ankle. Note how soon you feel the touch sensation and how much more slowly you notice the itch.

Itch is useful because it directs you to scratch the itchy area and presumably remove whatever is irritating your skin. Vigorous scratching produces mild pain, and pain inhibits itch. Opiates, which decrease pain, increase itch (Andrew & Craig, 2001). This inhibitory relationship between pain and itch is the strongest evidence that itch is not a type of pain.

This research helps explain an experience that you may have noticed. When a dentist gives you Novocain before drilling a tooth, part of your face becomes numb. An hour or more later, as the drug's effects start to wear off, you may feel an itchy sensation in the numb portion of your face. But when you try to scratch it, you feel nothing because the touch and pain sensations are still numb. Evidently, the effects of Novocain wear off faster for itch than for touch and pain axons. The fact that you can feel itch at this time is evidence that it is not just a form of touch or pain. It is interesting that scratching the partly numb skin does not relieve the itch. Evidently, scratching has to produce some pain to decrease the itch.

STOP & CHECK

20. Would opiates increase or decrease itch sensations?

21. Suppose someone suffers from constant itching. What kinds of drugs might help relieve it?

ANSWERS

20. Opiates increase itch by blocking pain sensations. (Pain decreases itch.) **21.** Two kinds of drugs might help—histamines or capsaicin—depending on the source of the itch. Also, drugs that block gastrin-releasing peptide might help.

MODULE 7.2 IN CLOSING

The Mechanical Senses

From the standpoint of the nervous system, what is the difference between touch, pain, temperature, and itch? The nervous system codes the different sensations in terms of which neurons are active. Their frequency of activity determines the intensity of sensation.

If the brain experiences input from one kind of neuron as touch and another as pain, how does it *know* which is which? At this point, we do not have a good answer. Evidently, processes early in embryological development set the meaning of different inputs. A few aspects of our experience have to be given, not learned.

SUMMARY

1. The vestibular system detects the position and acceleration of the head and adjusts body posture and eye movements accordingly. **199**
2. The somatosensory system depends on a variety of receptors that are sensitive to different kinds of stimulation of the skin and internal tissues. **199**

3. The brain maintains several parallel somatosensory representations of the body. **202**
4. Activity in the primary somatosensory cortex corresponds to what someone is experiencing, even if it is illusory and not the same as the actual stimulation. **203**
5. Injurious stimuli excite pain receptors, which are bare nerve endings. Some pain receptors also respond to acids, heat, and capsaicin. Axons conveying pain stimulation to the spinal cord and brainstem release glutamate in response to moderate pain and a combination of glutamate and substance P for stronger pain. **203**
6. Painful information takes two routes to the brain. A route leading to the somatosensory cortex conveys the sensory information, including location in the body. A route to the cingulate cortex conveys the unpleasant emotional aspect. **203**
7. Opiate drugs attach to the brain's endorphin receptors. Endorphins decrease pain by blocking release of substance P and other transmitters from pain neurons. Both pleasant and unpleasant experiences can release endorphins. **204**
8. A harmful stimulus may give rise to a greater or lesser degree of pain depending on other current and recent stimuli. According to the gate theory of pain, other stimuli can close certain gates and block the transmission of pain. Placebos increase opiate release and thereby decrease pain. **206**
9. Chronic pain bombards pain synapses with repetitive input, and increases their responsiveness to later stimuli, through a process like learning. Morphine is most effective as a painkiller if it is used promptly. Allowing the nervous system to be bombarded with prolonged pain messages increases the overall sensitivity to pain. **207**
10. Skin irritation releases histamine, which excites a spinal pathway responsible for itch. The axons of that pathway transmit impulses very slowly. They can be inhibited by pain messages. **207**

KEY TERMS

Terms are defined in the module on the page number indicated. They're also presented in alphabetical order with definitions in the book's Subject Index/Glossary. Interactive flashcards, audio reviews, and crossword puzzles are among the online resources available to help you learn these terms and the concepts they represent.

capsaicin **203**
dermatome **201**
endorphins **204**
gate theory **206**
opioid mechanisms **204**
Pacinian corpuscle **200**
periaqueductal gray area **204**
placebo **206**
semicircular canals **199**
somatosensory system **199**
substance P **203**

THOUGHT QUESTION

How could you determine whether hypnosis releases endorphins?

MODULE 7.3

The Chemical Senses

Suppose you had the godlike power to create a new species of animal, but you could equip it with only one sensory system. Which sense would you give it?

Your first impulse might be to choose vision or hearing because of their importance to humans. But an animal with only one sensory system is not going to be much like humans, is it? To have any chance of survival, it will have to be small, slow, and probably one-celled. What sense will be most useful to such an animal?

Most theorists believe that the first sensory system of the earliest animals was a chemical sensitivity (G. H. Parker, 1922). A chemical sense enables a small animal to find food, avoid certain kinds of danger, and even locate mates.

Now imagine that you have to choose one of your senses to lose. Which one will it be? Most of us would not choose to lose vision, hearing, or touch. Losing pain sensitivity can be dangerous. You might choose to sacrifice your smell or taste.

Curious, isn't it? If an animal is going to survive with only one sense, it almost has to be a chemical sense, and yet to humans, with many other well-developed senses, the chemical senses seem dispensable. Perhaps we underestimate their importance.

Chemical Coding

Suppose you run a bakery and need to send messages to your supplier down the street. Suppose further you can communicate only by ringing three large bells on the roof of your bakery. You would have to work out a code.

One possibility would be to label the three bells: The high-pitched bell means, "I need flour." The medium-pitched bell means, "I need sugar," and the low-pitched bell calls for eggs. The more you need something, the faster you ring the bell. We shall call this system the *labeled-line* code because each bell has a single unchanging label. Of course, you can use it for only flour, sugar, or eggs.

Another possibility would be to set up a code that depends on a relationship among the bells. Ringing the high and medium bells equally means that you need flour. The medium and low bells together call for sugar. The high and low bells together call for eggs. Ringing all three together means you need vanilla extract. Ringing mostly the high bell while ringing the other two bells slightly means you need hazelnuts. And so forth. We call this the *across-fiber pattern* code because the meaning depends on the pattern across bells.

A sensory system could theoretically use either type of coding. In a system relying on the **labeled-line principle,** each receptor would respond to a limited range of stimuli, and the meaning would depend entirely on which neurons are active. In a system relying on the **across-fiber pattern principle,** each receptor responds to a wider range of stimuli, and a given response by a given axon means little except in comparison to what other axons are doing (R. P. Erickson, 1982).

In color perception, we encountered a good example of an across-fiber pattern code. For example, the perception of green requires stronger response by the medium-wavelength cones than the long- and short-wavelength cones. In auditory pitch perception, a given receptor may respond best to a certain high-frequency tone, but it also responds in phase with a number of low-frequency tones (as do all the other receptors). Each receptor also responds to white noise (static) and to various mixtures of tones. Similarly, each taste and smell stimulus excites several kinds of neurons, and the meaning of a particular response by a particular neuron depends on the context of responses by other neurons. In short, all or nearly all perceptions depend on the pattern across an array of axons.

STOP & CHECK

22. Of the following, which use a labeled-line code and which use an across-fiber pattern code?
(a) a fire alarm
(b) a light switch
(c) typing a capital letter

ANSWER

22. Typing a capital letter is an example of an across-fiber pattern code. (The result depends on a combination of the letter key and the shift key.) A fire alarm and a light switch are labeled lines that convey only one message.

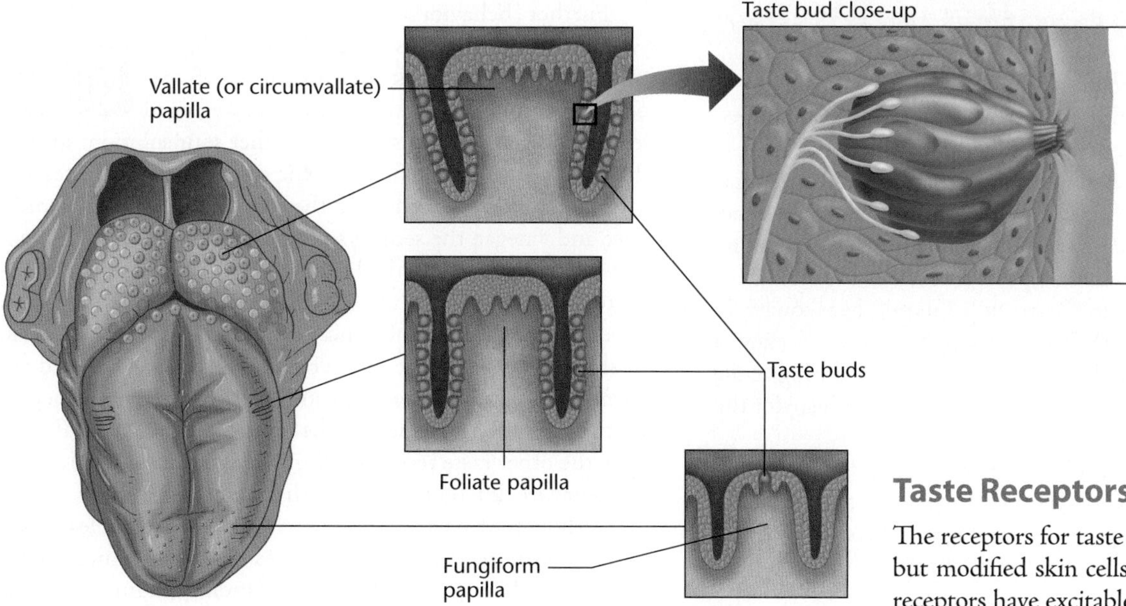

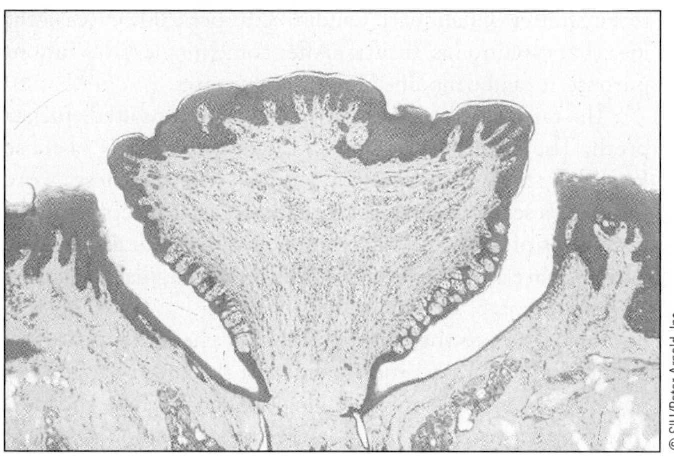

Figure 7.19 The organs of taste
(a) The tip, back, and sides of the tongue are covered with taste buds. Taste buds are located in papillae. **(b)** Photo showing cross-section of a taste bud. Each taste bud contains about 50 receptor cells.

Taste

Taste refers to the stimulation of the **taste buds,** the receptors on the tongue. When we talk about the taste of food, we generally mean flavor, which is a combination of taste and smell. Whereas other senses remain separate throughout the cortex, taste and smell axons converge onto many of the same cells in an area called the endopiriform cortex (W. Fu, Sugai, Yoshimura, & Onoda, 2004). That convergence enables taste and smell to combine their influences on food selection.

Taste Receptors

The receptors for taste are not true neurons but modified skin cells. Like neurons, taste receptors have excitable membranes and release neurotransmitters to excite neighboring neurons, which in turn transmit information to the brain. Like skin cells, however, taste receptors are gradually sloughed off and replaced, each one lasting about 10 to 14 days (Kinnamon, 1987).

Mammalian taste receptors are in taste buds located in **papillae** on the surface of the tongue (Figure 7.19). A given papilla may contain up to 10 or more taste buds (Arvidson & Friberg, 1980), and each taste bud contains about 50 receptor cells.

TRY IT YOURSELF

In adult humans, taste buds are located mainly along the outside edge of the tongue. You can demonstrate this principle as follows: Soak a small cotton swab in sugar water, saltwater, or vinegar. Then touch it lightly on the center of your tongue, not too far toward the back. If you get the position right, you will experience little or no taste. Then try it again on the edge of your tongue and notice how much stronger the taste is.

Now change the procedure a bit. Wash your mouth out with water and prepare a cotton swab as before. Touch the soaked portion to one edge of your tongue and then slowly stroke it to the center of your tongue. It will seem as if you are moving the taste to the center of your tongue. In fact, you are getting only a touch sensation from the center of your tongue. You attribute the taste you had on the side of your tongue to every other spot you stroke (Bartoshuk, 1991).

How Many Kinds of Taste Receptors?

Traditionally, people in Western society have described sweet, sour, salty, and bitter as the "primary" tastes. However, some tastes defy categorization in terms of these four labels (Schiffman & Erickson, 1980; Schiffman, McElroy, & Erickson, 1980). How could we determine how many kinds of taste we have?

APPLICATIONS AND EXTENSIONS

Chemicals That Alter the Taste Buds

One way to identify taste receptor types is to find procedures that alter one receptor but not others. For example, chewing a miracle berry (native to West Africa) gives little taste itself but temporarily changes sweet receptors. Miracle berries contain a protein, miraculin, that modifies sweet receptors in such a way that acids can stimulate them (Bartoshuk, Gentile, Moskowitz, & Meiselman, 1974). If you ever get a chance to chew a miracle berry (and I do recommend it), anything acidic will taste sweet in addition to its usual sour taste for the next half hour.

A colleague and I once spent an evening experimenting with miracle berries. We drank straight lemon juice, sauerkraut juice, even vinegar. All tasted extremely sweet, but we awoke the next day with mouths full of ulcers.

Miraculin was, for a time, commercially available in the United States as a diet aid. The idea was that dieters could coat their tongue with a miraculin pill and then enjoy unsweetened lemonade and so forth, which would taste sweet but provide almost no calories.

Have you ever drunk orange juice just after brushing your teeth? How could something so wonderful suddenly taste so bad? Most toothpastes contain sodium lauryl sulfate, a chemical that intensifies bitter tastes and weakens sweet ones, apparently by coating the sweet receptors and preventing anything from reaching them (DeSimone, Heck, & Bartoshuk, 1980; Schiffman, 1983).

TRY IT YOURSELF

Another taste-modifying substance is an extract from the plant *Gymnema sylvestre* (R. A. Frank, Mize, Kennedy, de los Santos, & Green, 1992). Some health-food and herbal-remedy stores, including online stores, sell dried leaves of *Gymnema sylvestre*, from which you can brew a tea. (*Gymnema sylvestre* pills won't work for this demonstration.) Soak your tongue in the tea for about 30 seconds and then try tasting various substances. Salty, sour, and bitter substances taste the same as usual, but sugar becomes tasteless. Candies now taste sour, bitter, or salty. (Those tastes were already present, but you barely noticed them because of the sweetness.) Curiously, the artificial sweetener aspartame (NutraSweet®) loses only some, not all, of its sweetness, implying that it stimulates an additional receptor besides the sugar receptor (Schroeder & Flannery-Schroeder, 2005). Note: Anyone with diabetes should refrain from this demonstration because *Gymnema sylvestre* also alters sugar absorption in the intestines.

TRY IT YOURSELF

Further behavioral evidence for separate types of taste receptors comes from studies of the following type: Soak your tongue for 15 seconds in a sour solution, such as unsweetened lemon juice. Then try tasting some other sour solution, such as dilute vinegar. You will find that the second solution tastes less sour than usual. Depending on the concentrations of the lemon juice and vinegar, the second solution may not taste sour at all. This phenomenon, called **adaptation,** reflects the fatigue of receptors sensitive to sour tastes. Now try tasting something salty, sweet, or bitter. These substances taste about the same as usual. In short, you experience little **cross-adaptation**—reduced response to one taste after exposure to another (McBurney & Bartoshuk, 1973). Evidently, the sour receptors are different from the other taste receptors. Similarly, you can show that salt receptors are different from the others and so forth.

Although we have long known that people have at least four kinds of taste receptors, several types of evidence suggested a fifth also, which is glutamate, as in monosodium glutamate (MSG). Researchers in fact located a glutamate taste receptor, which resembles the brain's receptors for glutamate as a neurotransmitter (Chaudhari, Landin, & Roper, 2000). Recall the idea that evolution is "thrifty": After something evolves for one purpose, it can be modified for other purposes.

The taste of glutamate resembles that of unsalted chicken broth. The English language had no word for this taste, so English-speaking researchers adopted the Japanese word *umami*. Researchers have also reported a fat receptor in the taste buds of mice and rats, although it is uncertain whether humans have a similar receptor (Laugerette, Gaillard, Passilly-Degrace, Niot, & Besnard, 2007).

In addition to the fact that different chemicals excite different receptors, they produce different rhythms of action potentials. For example, the following two records have the same total number of action potentials in the same amount of time but different temporal patterns:

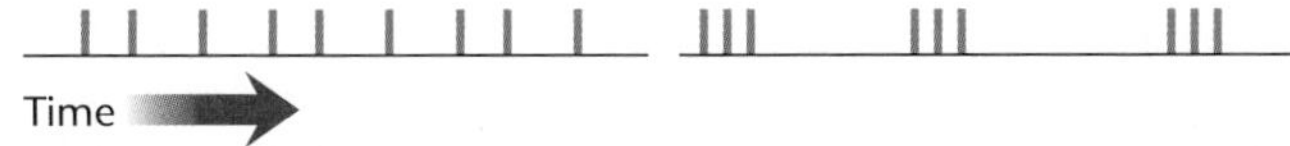

Researchers noticed that sweet, salty, and bitter chemicals produced different patterns of activity in the taste-sensitive area of the medulla. They recorded the pattern while rats were drinking quinine (a bitter substance) and later used an electrode to generate the same patterns while rats were drinking water. The rats then avoided the water, as if it tasted bad (Di Lorenzo, Hallock, & Kennedy, 2003). Evidently, the code to represent a taste includes the rhythm of activity and not just which cells are most active or their mean frequency of activity.

Mechanisms of Taste Receptors

The saltiness receptor is simple. Recall that a neuron produces an action potential when sodium ions cross its membrane. A saltiness receptor, which detects the presence of sodium, simply permits sodium ions on the tongue to cross its membrane.

Chemicals that prevent sodium from crossing the membrane weaken salty tastes (DeSimone, Heck, Mierson, & DeSimone, 1984; Schiffman, Lockhead, & Maes, 1983). Sour receptors detect the presence of acids (Huang et al., 2006).

Sweetness, bitterness, and umami receptors resemble one another chemically (He et al., 2004). After a molecule binds to one of these receptors, it activates a G-protein that releases a second messenger within the cell, as in the metabotropic synapses discussed in Chapter 3 (Lindemann, 1996). Although each receptor detects just one kind of taste, several receptors feed into the next set of cells in the taste system. So, beyond the receptors, each neuron responds to two or more kinds of taste, and taste depends on a pattern of responses across fibers, not a system of pure labeled lines (R. P. Erickson, DiLorenzo, & Woodbury, 1994; Tomchik, Berg, Kim, Chaudhari, & Roper, 2007).

Bitter taste has long been a puzzle because bitter substances include a long list of dissimilar chemicals. Their only common factor is that they are to some degree toxic. What receptor could identify such a diverse set of chemicals? The answer is that we have not one bitter receptor but a family of 25 or more (Adler et al., 2000; Behrens, Foerster, Staehler, Raguse, & Meyerhof, 2007; Matsunami, Montmayeur, & Buck, 2000).

One consequence of having so many bitter receptors is that we detect a great variety of dangerous chemicals. The other is that because each type of bitter receptor is present in small numbers, we can't detect very low concentrations of bitter substances.

STOP & CHECK

23. Suppose you find a new, unusual-tasting food. How could you determine whether we have a special receptor for that food or whether we taste it with a combination of the other known taste receptors?

24. Although the tongue has receptors for bitter tastes, researchers have not found neurons in the brain itself that respond more strongly to bitter than to other tastes. Explain, then, how it is possible for the brain to detect bitter tastes.

25. If someone injected into your tongue a chemical that blocks the release of second messengers, how would it affect your taste experiences?

ANSWERS

23. You could test for cross-adaptation. If the new taste cross-adapts with others, then it uses the same receptors. If it does not cross-adapt, it may have a receptor of its own. Another possibility would be to find some procedure that blocks this taste without blocking other tastes. **24.** Two possibilities: First, bitter tastes produce a distinctive temporal pattern of responses in cells sensitive to taste. Second, even if no one cell responds strongly to bitter tastes, the pattern of responses across many cells may be distinctive. Analogously, in vision, no cone responds primarily to purple, but we nevertheless recognize purple by its pattern of activity across a population of cones. **25.** The chemical would block your experiences of sweet, bitter, and umami but should not prevent you from tasting salty and sour.

Taste Coding in the Brain

Information from the receptors in the anterior two thirds of the tongue is carried to the brain along the chorda tympani, a branch of the seventh cranial nerve (the facial nerve). Taste information from the posterior tongue and the throat travels along branches of the ninth and tenth cranial nerves. What do you suppose would happen if someone anesthetized your chorda tympani? You would no longer taste anything in the anterior part of your tongue, but you probably would not notice because you would still taste with the posterior part. However, the probability is about 40% that you would experience taste "phantoms," analogous to the phantom limb experience discussed in Chapter 5 (Yanagisawa, Bartoshuk, Catalanotto, Karrer, & Kveton, 1998). That is, you might experience taste even when nothing was on your tongue. Evidently, the inputs from the anterior and posterior parts of your tongue interact in complex ways.

The taste nerves project to the **nucleus of the tractus solitarius (NTS),** a structure in the medulla (Travers, Pfaffmann, & Norgren, 1986). From the NTS, information branches out, reaching the pons, the lateral hypothalamus, the amygdala, the ventral-posterior thalamus, and two areas of the cerebral cortex (Pritchard, Hamilton, Morse, & Norgren, 1986; Yamamoto, 1984). One of these areas, the somatosensory cortex, responds to the touch aspects of tongue stimulation. The other area, known as the insula, is the primary taste cortex. Curiously, each hemisphere of the cortex receives input mostly from the ipsilateral side of the tongue (Aglioti, Tassinari, Corballis, & Berlucchi, 2000; Pritchard, Macaluso, & Eslinger, 1999). In contrast, each hemisphere receives mostly contralateral input for vision, hearing, and touch. A few of the major connections are illustrated in Figure 7.20. Within the cerebral cortex, cells mostly responsive to one kind of taste are intermingled with cells mostly responsive to other kinds (Accolla, Bathellier, Petersen, & Carleton, 2007).

Individual Differences in Taste

You may have had a biology instructor who asked you to taste phenythiocarbamide (PTC) and then take samples home for your relatives to try. Some people experience it as bitter, and others hardly taste it at all. Most of the variance is controlled by a dominant gene, which provides an interesting example for a genetics lab (Kim et al., 2003). (Did your instructor happen to mention that PTC is mildly toxic?)

Researchers have collected extensive data about the percentage of nontasters in different populations, as shown in Figure 7.21 (Guo & Reed, 2001). The figure shows no obvious relationship between tasting PTC and cuisine. For example, nontasters are common in India, where the food is spicy, and in Britain, where it is relatively bland.

In the 1990s, researchers discovered that people who are insensitive to PTC are also less sensitive than average to other tastes. People at the opposite extreme, known as **supertasters,** have the highest sensitivity to all tastes and mouth sensations (Drewnowski, Henderson, Shore, & Barratt-Fornell,

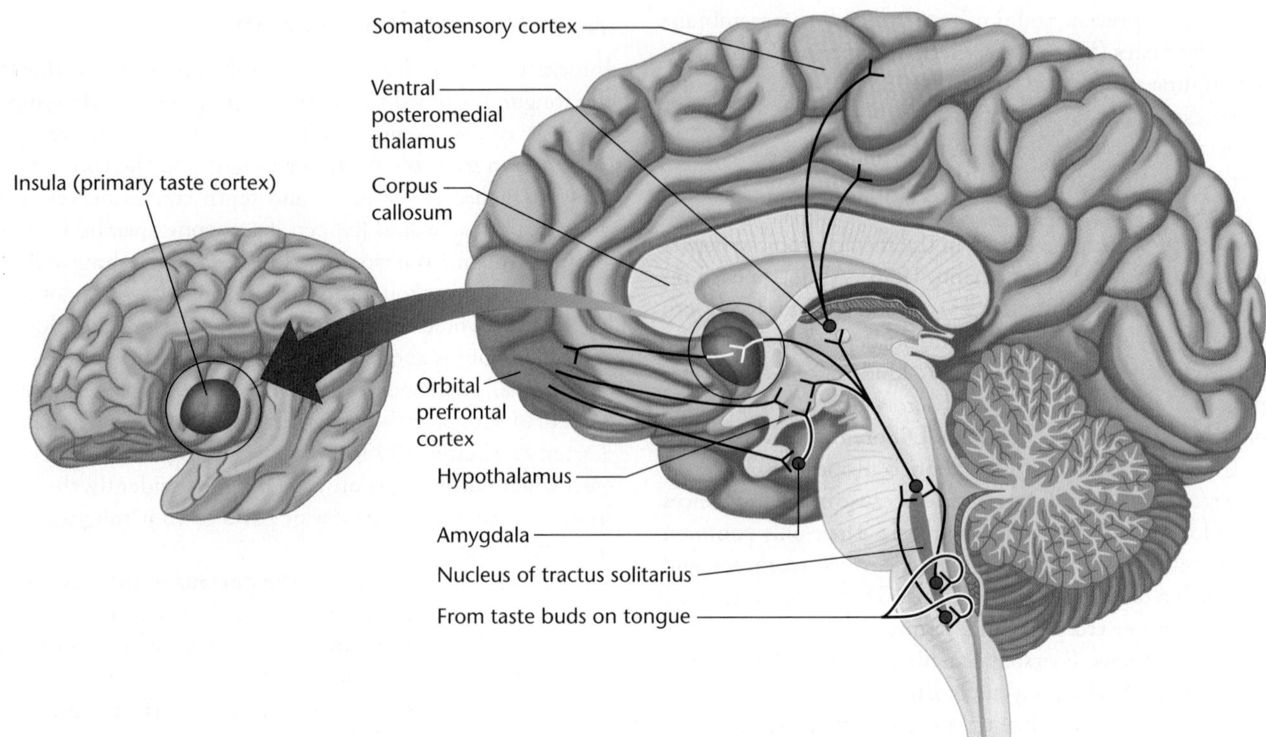

Figure 7.20 Major routes of impulses related to the sense of taste in the human brain
The thalamus and cerebral cortex receive impulses from both the left and the right sides of the tongue. *(Based on Rolls, 1995)*

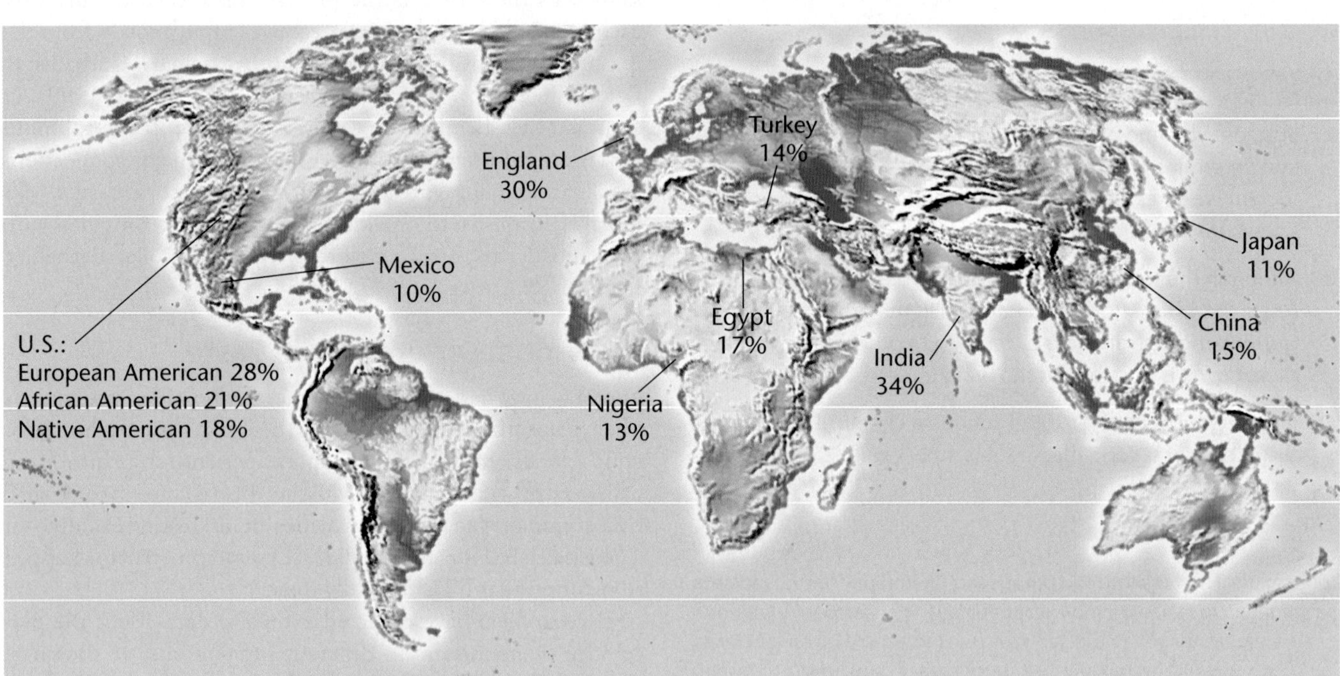

Figure 7.21 Percentage of nontasters in several human populations
Most of the percentages are based on large samples, including more than 31,000 in Japan and 35,000 in India. *(Based on Guo & Reed, 2001)*

1998). Supertasters tend to avoid strong-tasting or spicy foods. However, culture and familiarity exert larger effects on people's food preferences. Consequently, even after you think about how much you do or do not like strongly flavored foods, you cannot confidently identify yourself as a supertaster, taster, or nontaster.

The variations in taste sensitivity relate to the number of *fungiform papillae* near the tip of the tongue. Supertasters have the most, and nontasters have the fewest. That anatomical difference depends mostly on genetics but also on hormones and other influences. Women's taste sensitivity rises and falls with their monthly hormone cycles and reaches its maximum

TABLE 7.2 Are You a Supertaster, Taster, or Nontaster?

Equipment: $^{1}/_{4}$-inch hole punch, small piece of wax paper, cotton swab, blue food coloring, flashlight, and magnifying glass

Make a $^{1}/_{4}$-inch hole with a standard hole punch in a piece of wax paper. Dip the cotton swab in blue food coloring. Place the wax paper on the tip of your tongue, just right of the center. Rub the cotton swab over the hole in the wax paper to dye a small part of your tongue. With the flashlight and magnifying glass, have someone count the number of pink, unstained circles in the blue area. They are your fungiform papillae. Compare your results to the following averages:

Supertasters:	25 papillae
Tasters:	17 papillae
Nontasters:	10 papillae

during early pregnancy, when estradiol levels are very high (Prutkin et al., 2000). That tendency is probably adaptive: During pregnancy, a woman needs to be more careful than usual to avoid harmful foods.

If you would like to classify yourself as a taster, nontaster, or supertaster, follow the instructions in Table 7.2.

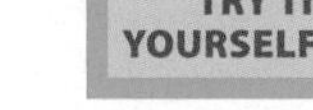

TRY IT YOURSELF

STOP & CHECK

26. How do genes and hormones influence taste sensitivity?

ANSWER

26. Genes and hormones influence the number of taste buds near the tip of the tongue.

Olfaction

Olfaction, the sense of smell, is the response to chemicals that contact the membranes inside the nose. For most mammals, olfaction is critical for finding food and mates and for avoiding dangers. For example, rats and mice show an immediate, unlearned avoidance of the smells of cats, foxes, and other predators. Mice that lack certain olfactory receptors fail to avoid, as illustrated in Figure 7.22.

Consider also the star-nosed mole and water shrew, two species that forage along the bottom of ponds and streams for worms, shellfish, and other edible invertebrates. We might assume that olfaction would be useless under water. These animals have to hold their breath, after all. However, they exhale tiny air bubbles onto the ground and then inhale them again. By doing so, they can follow an underwater trail well enough to track their prey (Catania, 2006).

Helmut Heintges/Photo Library

A water shrew

We marvel at feats like this or at the ability of a bloodhound to find someone by following an olfactory trail through a forest, and we assume that we could never do anything like that. We may be underestimating ourselves. Of course, we can't follow an olfactory trail while standing upright, with our noses far above the ground. But what might you be able to do if you

Photo by Ko & Reiko Kobayakawa/University of Tokyo

Figure 7.22 The result of losing one kind of olfactory receptors Normal mice innately avoid the smell of cats, foxes, and other predators. This cat had just finished a large meal. *(Kobayakawa et al., 2007)*

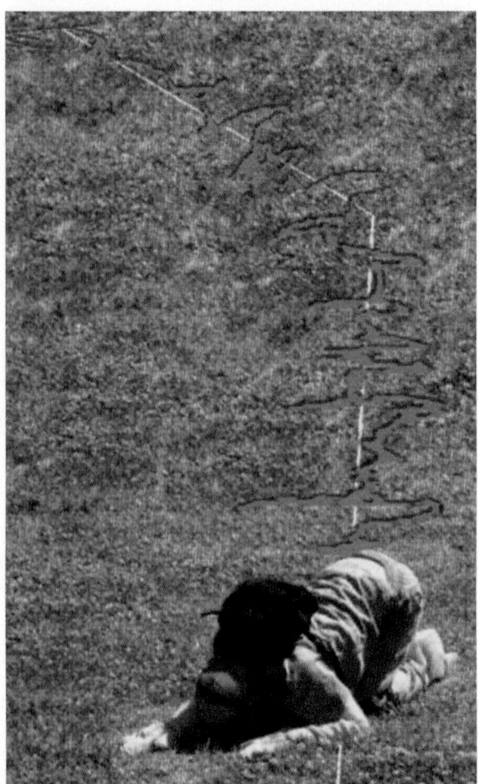

Figure 7.23 A person following a scent trail
Most people successfully followed a trail with only their nose to guide them. *(Reprinted by permission from Macmillan Publishers Ltd. From:* Nature Neuroscience, *10, 27–29, "Mechanisms of scent-tracking in humans," J. Porter et al., 2007.)*

got down on your hands and knees and put your nose to the ground? Researchers blindfolded 32 young adults, made them wear gloves, and then asked them to try to follow a scent trail across a field. The scent was chocolate oil. (I guess they might as well use something that people care about.) Most of the participants succeeded and improved their performance with practice. Figure 7.23 shows one example (Porter et al., 2007). So our olfaction can be surprisingly useful, if we give it a fair chance.

Olfaction is certainly important for food selection. It also plays a subtle role in social behavior. When people are offered several human smells and asked to identify the ones they would like or dislike in a potential romantic partner, they tend to prefer smells slightly similar to their own smell but not too similar (Jacob, McClintock, Zelano, & Ober, 2002; Pause et al., 2006). Avoiding someone who smells too much like yourself reduces the chance of mating with a close relative.

Olfactory Receptors

The neurons responsible for smell are the **olfactory cells,** which line the olfactory epithelium in the rear of the nasal air passages (Figure 7.24). In mammals, each olfactory cell has cilia (threadlike dendrites) that extend from the cell body into the mucous surface of the nasal passage. Olfactory receptors are located on the cilia.

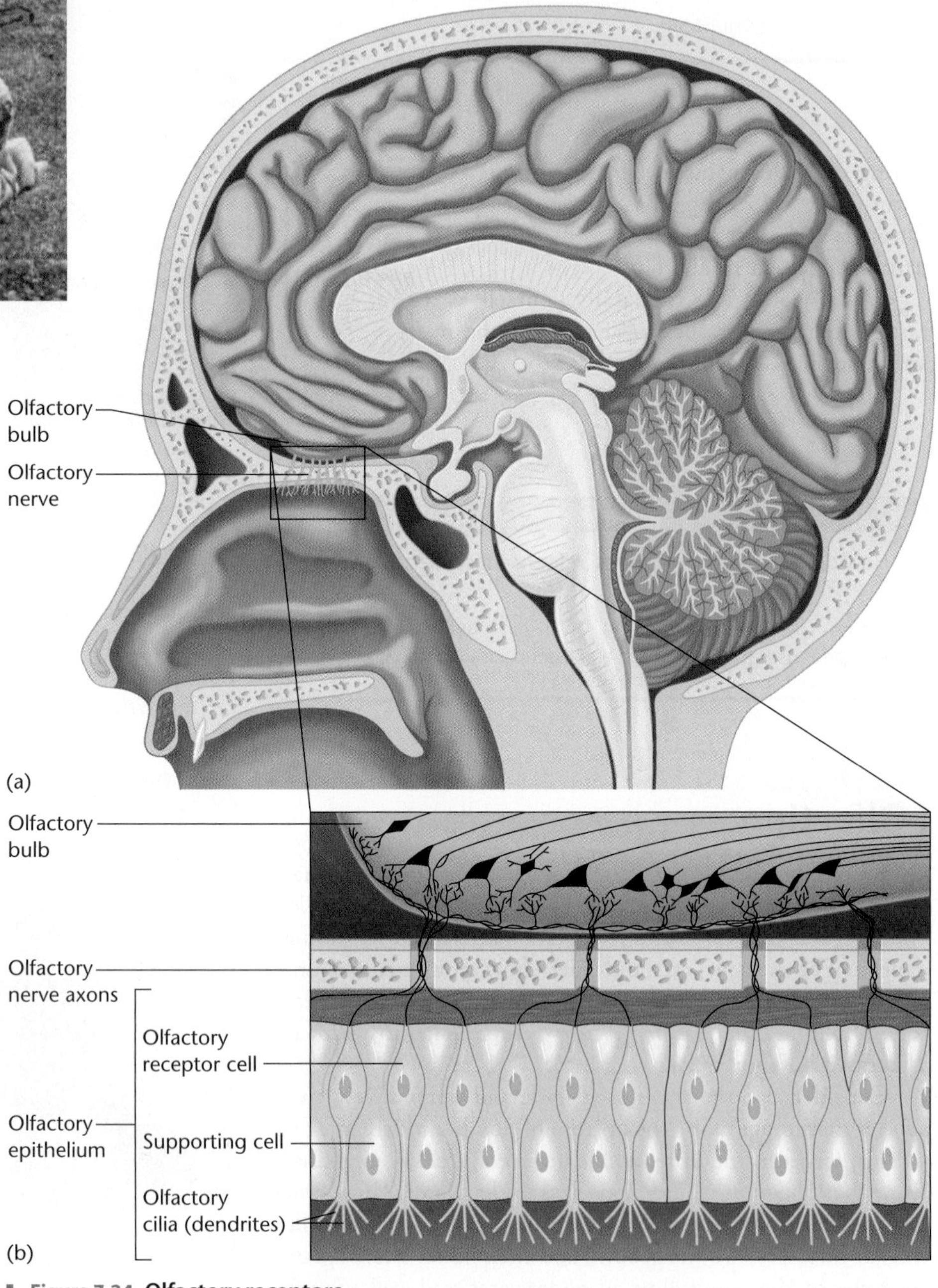

Figure 7.24 Olfactory receptors
(a) Location of receptors in nasal cavity. **(b)** Closeup of olfactory cells.

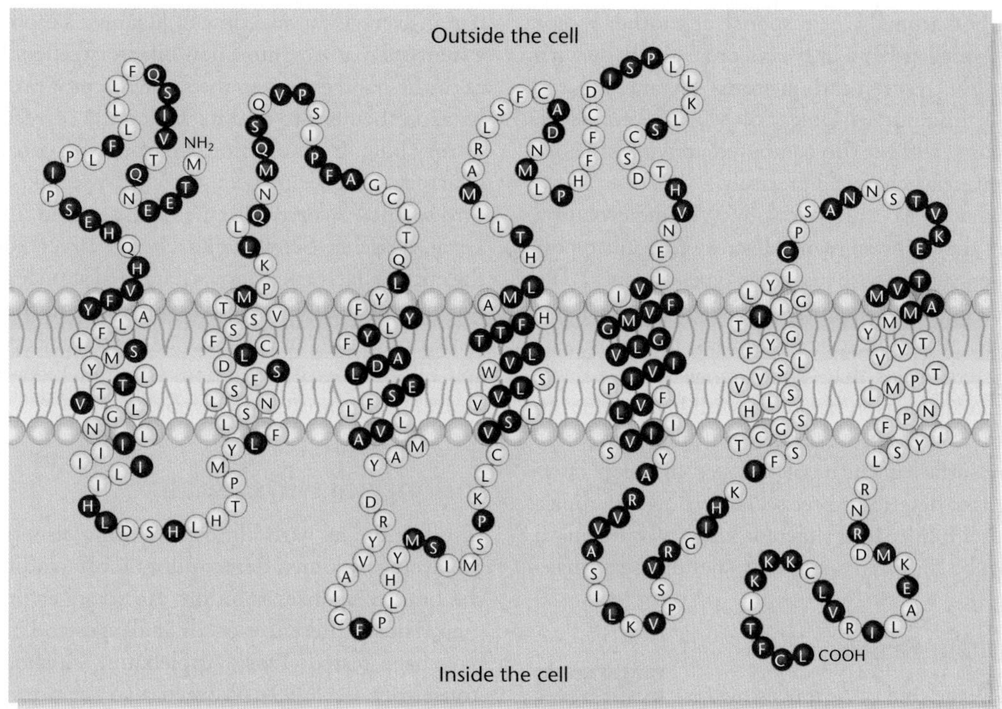

Figure 7.25 One of the olfactory receptor proteins
If you compare this protein with the synaptic receptor protein shown in Figure 3.13 on page 62, you will notice a great similarity. Each protein traverses the membrane seven times; each responds to a chemical outside the cell and triggers activity of a G-protein inside the cell. The protein shown is one of a family; different olfactory receptors contain different proteins, each with a slightly different structure. Each of the little circles in this diagram represents one amino acid of the protein. The white circles represent amino acids that are the same in most of the olfactory receptor proteins; the purple circles represent amino acids that vary from one protein to another. *(Based on Buck & Axel, 1991)*

How many kinds of olfactory receptors do we have? Researchers answered the analogous question for color vision in the 1800s but took much longer for olfaction. Linda Buck and Richard Axel (1991) identified a family of proteins in olfactory receptors, as shown in Figure 7.25. Like metabotropic neurotransmitter receptors, each of these proteins traverses the cell membrane seven times and responds to a chemical outside the cell (here an odorant molecule instead of a neurotransmitter) by triggering changes in a G-protein inside the cell. The G-protein then provokes chemical activities that lead to an action potential. The best estimate is that humans have several hundred olfactory receptor proteins, whereas rats and mice have about a thousand types (X. Zhang & Firestein, 2002). Correspondingly, rats can distinguish among odors that seem the same to humans (Rubin & Katz, 2001).

Although each chemical excites several types of receptors, the most strongly excited receptor inhibits the activity of other ones in a process analogous to lateral inhibition (Oka, Omura, Kataoka, & Touhara, 2004). The net result is that a given chemical produces a major response in one or two kinds of receptors and weaker responses in a few others.

STOP & CHECK

27. How do olfactory receptors resemble metabotropic neurotransmitter receptors?

ANSWER

27. Like metabotropic neurotransmitter receptors, an olfactory receptor acts through a G-protein that triggers further events within the cell.

Implications for Coding

We have only three kinds of cones and five kinds of taste receptors, so researchers were surprised to find hundreds of kinds of olfactory receptors. That diversity makes possible narrow specialization of functions. To illustrate, because we have only three kinds of cones, each cone contributes to almost every color perception. In olfaction, we have receptors that respond to few stimuli. The response of one olfactory receptor might mean, "I smell a fatty acid with a straight chain of three to five carbon atoms." The response of another receptor might mean, "I smell either a fatty acid or an aldehyde with a straight chain of five to seven carbon atoms" (Araneda, Kini, & Firestein, 2000; Imamura, Mataga, & Mori, 1992; Mori, Mataga, & Imamura, 1992). The combined activity of those two receptors identifies a chemical precisely.

The question may have occurred to you, "Why did evolution go to the bother of designing so many olfactory receptor types? After all, color vision gets by with just three types of cones." The main reason is that light energy can be arranged along a single dimension—wavelength. Olfaction processes an enormous variety of airborne chemicals that do not range along a single continuum. A secondary reason has to do with localization. In olfaction, space is no problem; we arrange our olfactory receptors over the entire surface of the nasal passages. In vision, however, the brain needs to determine precisely where on the retina a stimulus originates. Hundreds of different kinds of wavelength receptors could not be compacted into each spot on the retina.

Messages to the Brain

TRY IT YOURSELF

Researchers had considered olfaction a slow system, but later studies found that mice can respond to an odor within 200 ms of its presentation, comparable to reaction times for other senses (Abraham et al., 2004). However, olfaction is subject to more rapid adaptation than sight or hearing (Kurahashi, Lowe, & Gold, 1994). To demonstrate adaptation, take a bottle of an odorous chemical, such as lemon extract, and determine how far away you can hold the bottle and still smell it. Then hold it up to your nose and inhale deeply and repeatedly. Now test again: From how far away can you smell it?

When an olfactory receptor is stimulated, its axon carries an impulse to the olfactory bulb (see Figure 4.13 on page 93). Within the olfactory bulb, chemicals that smell similar excite neighboring areas, and chemicals that smell different excite more separated areas (Uchida, Takahashi, Tanifuji, & Mori, 2000). The olfactory bulb sends axons to the olfactory area of the cerebral cortex, where the response patterns are more complex but fairly consistent from one person to another (Zou, Horowitz, Montmayeru, Snapper, & Buck, 2001). Although a single chemical activates a limited population of cells, naturally occurring objects, such as foods, activate a larger and more scattered population of cells (Lin, Shea, & Katz, 2006; Rennaker, Chen, Ruyle, Sloan, & Wilson, 2007). Many cells give their greatest response to a particular kind of food, such as berries or melons (Yoshida & Mori, 2007). Repeated experience with a particular kind of smell increases the brain's ability to distinguish among similar smells (Li, Luxenberg, Parrish, & Gottfried, 2006). The same principle holds for other senses. For example, we gradually become more adept at distinguishing among faces similar to the ones we see most often. Musicians become more adept at distinguishing slight differences in familiar sounds.

Olfactory receptors are vulnerable to damage because they are exposed to the air. Unlike your receptors for vision and hearing, which remain with you for a lifetime, an olfactory receptor has an average survival time of just over a month. At that point, a stem cell matures into a new olfactory cell in the same location as the first and expresses the same receptor protein (Nef, 1998). Its axon then has to find its way to the correct target in the olfactory bulb. Each olfactory neuron axon contains copies of its olfactory receptor protein, which it uses like an identification card to find its correct partner (Barnea et al., 2004; Strotmann, Levai, Fleischer, Schwarzenbacher, & Breer, 2004). However, if the entire olfactory surface is damaged at once by a blast of toxic fumes so that the system has to replace all the receptors at the same time, many of them fail to make the correct connections, and olfactory experience does not fully recover (Iwema, Fang, Kurtz, Youngentob, & Schwob, 2004).

Individual Differences

In olfaction, as with almost anything else, people differ. On the average, women detect odors more readily than men, and the brain responses to odors are stronger in women than in men. Those differences occur at all ages and in all cultures that have been tested (Doty, Applebaum, Zusho, & Settle, 1985; Yousem et al., 1999). Women also seem to pay more attention to smells. Surveys have found that women are more likely than men to care about the smell of a potential romantic partner (Herz & Inzlicht, 2002).

In addition, if people repeatedly attend to some faint odor, young adult women gradually become more and more sensitive to it, until they can detect it in concentrations one ten-thousandth of what they could at the start (Dalton, Doolittle, & Breslin, 2002). Men, girls before puberty, and women after menopause do not show that effect, so it apparently depends on female hormones. We can only speculate on why we evolved a connection between female hormones and odor sensitization.

We know less about genetic variations in olfaction, with this exception: People with the more common form of the OR7D4 olfactory receptor describe the chemical *androstenone* as smelling like sweat or urine. Those with the less common form of the receptor describe the same chemical as sweet or like flowers (Keller, Zhuang, Chi, Vosshall, & Matsunami, 2007).

Finally, consider this surprising study: Through the wonders of bioengineering, researchers can examine the effects of deleting any particular gene. One gene controls a channel through which most potassium passes in the membranes of certain neurons of the olfactory bulb. Potassium, you will recall from Chapter 2, leaves a neuron after an action potential, thereby restoring the resting potential. With no particular hypothesis in mind, researchers tested what would happen if they deleted that potassium channel in mice.

Ordinarily, deleting any gene leads to deficits, and deleting an important gene is often fatal. Imagine the researchers' amazement when they found that the mice lacking this potassium channel had a greatly enhanced sense of smell. In fact, you could say they have a superpower: They detect faint smells, less than one-thousandth the minimum that other mice detect. Their olfactory bulb has an unusual anatomy, with more numerous but smaller clusters of neurons (Fadool et al., 2004). Exactly how the deletion of a gene led to this result remains uncertain, and presumably, the mice are deficient in some other way, or evolution would have deleted this gene long ago. Still, it is a remarkable example of how a single gene can make a huge difference.

For more information about olfaction, check the Website of Leffingwell & Associates: http://www.leffingwell.com/olfaction.htm

STOP & CHECK

28. What is the mean life span of an olfactory receptor?

29. What good does it do for an olfactory axon to have copies of the cell's olfactory receptor protein?

ANSWERS

28. Most olfactory receptors survive a little more than a month before dying and being replaced. **29.** The receptor molecule acts as a kind of identification to help the axon find its correct target cell in the brain.

Pheromones

An additional sense is important for most mammals, although less so for humans. The **vomeronasal organ (VNO)** is a set of receptors located near, but separate from, the olfactory receptors. Unlike the olfactory system, which identifies an enormous number of chemicals, the VNO's receptors are specialized to respond only to **pheromones,** which are chemicals released by an animal that affect the behavior of other members of the same species, especially sexually. For example, if you have ever had a female dog that wasn't neutered, whenever she was in her fertile (estrus) period, even though you kept her indoors, your yard attracted every male dog in the neighborhood that was free to roam.

Each VNO receptor responds to just one pheromone, such as the smell of a male or a female mouse. It responds to the preferred chemical in concentrations as low as one part in a hundred billion, but it hardly responds at all to other chemicals (Leinders-Zufall et al., 2000). Furthermore, the receptor does not adapt to a repeated stimulus. Have you ever been in a room that seems smelly at first but not a few minutes later? Your olfactory receptors respond to a new odor but not to a continuing one. VNO receptors, however, continue responding just as strongly even after prolonged stimulation (Holy, Dulac, & Meister, 2000).

In adult humans, the VNO is tiny and has no receptors (Keverne, 1999; Monti-Bloch, Jennings-White, Dolberg, & Berliner, 1994). It is vestigial—that is, a leftover from our evolutionary past. Nevertheless, part of the human olfactory mucosa contains receptors that resemble other species' pheromone receptors (Liberles & Buck, 2006; Rodriguez, Greer, Mok, & Mombaerts, 2000).

The behavioral effects of pheromones apparently occur unconsciously. That is, people respond behaviorally to certain chemicals in human skin even though they describe them as odorless. Exposure to these chemicals—especially chemicals from the opposite sex—alters skin temperature and other autonomic responses (Monti-Bloch, Jennings-White, & Berliner, 1998) and increases activity in the hypothalamus (Savic, Berglund, Gulyas, & Roland, 2001). The smell of male sweat causes women to increase their release of cortisol (Wyart et al., 2007). Cortisol is a stress hormone, so the implication is that women are not altogether charmed by the smell of a sweaty man.

The best-documented effect of a human pheromone relates to the timing of women's menstrual cycles. Women who spend much time together find that their menstrual cycles become more synchronized, unless they are taking birth-control pills (McClintock, 1971; Weller, Weller, Koresh-Kamin, & Ben-Shoshan, 1999; Weller, Weller, & Roizman, 1999). To test whether pheromones are responsible for the synchronization, researchers exposed young volunteer women to the underarm secretions of a donor woman. In two studies, most of the women exposed to the secretions became synchronized to the donor's menstrual cycle (Preti, Cutler, Garcia, Huggins, & Lawley, 1986; Russell, Switz, & Thompson, 1980).

Another study dealt with the phenomenon that a woman in an intimate relationship with a man tends to have more regular menstrual periods than women not in an intimate relationship. According to one hypothesis, the man's pheromones promote this regularity. In the study, young women who were not sexually active were exposed daily to a man's underarm secretions. (Getting women to volunteer for this study wasn't easy.) Gradually, over 14 weeks, most of these women's menstrual periods became more regular than before (Cutler et al., 1986). In short, human body secretions probably do act as pheromones, although the effects are more subtle than in most other mammals.

STOP & CHECK

30. What is one major difference between olfactory receptors and those of the vomeronasal organ?

ANSWER

30. Olfactory receptors adapt quickly to a continuous odor, whereas receptors of the vomeronasal organ continue to respond. Also, vomeronasal sensations are apparently capable of influencing behavior even without being consciously perceived.

Synesthesia

Finally, let's briefly consider something that is not one sense but a combination: **Synesthesia** is the experience of one sense in response to stimulation of a different sense. In the words of one person, "To me, the taste of beef is dark blue. The smell of almonds is pale orange. And when tenor saxophones play, the music looks like a floating, suspended coiling snake-ball of lit-up purple neon tubes" (Day, 2005, p. 11). For some people, the idea of a word triggers a synesthetic experience before they have thought of the word itself. One person unable to think of the word "castanets" said it was on the tip of the tongue . . . not sure what the word was, but it tasted like tuna (Simner & Ward, 2006). One man with color vision deficiency reports seeing synesthetic colors that he does not see in real life. He calls them "Martian colors" (Ramachandran, 2003). Evidently, his brain can see all the colors, even though his cones cannot send the messages.

No two people have quite the same synesthetic experience. It is estimated that about 1 person in 500 is synesthetic (Day, 2005), but that estimate probably overlooks people with a milder form of the condition, as well as many who hide their condition.

Various studies attest to the reality of synesthesia. For example, try to find the 2 among the 5s in each of the following displays:

```
555555555555   555555555555   555555555555
555555555555   555555555555   552555555555
555555525555   555555555555   555555555555
555555555555   555555555525   555555555555
```

One person with synesthesia was able to find the 2 consistently faster than other people, explaining that he just looked for a patch of orange! However, he was slower than other people to find an 8 among 6s because both 8 and 6 look bluish to him (Blake, Palmeri, Marois, & Kim, 2005). Another person had trouble finding an A among 4s because both look red but could easily find an A among 0s because 0 looks black (Laeng, Svartdal, & Oelmann, 2004). Oddly, however, someone who sees the letter P as yellow had no trouble finding it when it was printed (in black ink) on a yellow page. In some way, he sees the letter both in its real color (black) *and* its synesthetic color (Blake et al., 2005).

In another study, people were asked to identify as quickly as possible the shape formed by the less common character in a display like this:

Here, the correct answer is "rectangle," the shape formed by the Cs. People who perceive C and T as different colors find the rectangle faster than the average for other people. However, they do not find it as fast as other people would find the rectangle in this display, where the Cs really are in color:

In short, people with synesthesia see letters as if in color but not like real colors (Hubbard, Arman, Ramachandran, & Boynton, 2005). As further evidence, a study using fMRI found that viewing a black letter that produced a synesthetic color experience resulted in only slight activation of the brain areas responsible for color vision. Instead, it activated areas of the parietal cortex that are important for "binding" different aspects of a stimulus (Weiss, Zilles, & Fink, 2005).

One hypothesis is that some of the axons from one cortical area have branches into another cortical area. For people with number-color or letter-color synesthesia, the inferior temporal cortex has more than the average number of connections (Rouw & Scholte, 2007). However, surely this can't be the whole explanation. Obviously, no one is born with a connection between P and yellow or between 4 and red; we have to learn to recognize numbers and letters. Furthermore, when researchers find extra connections in the temporal lobe, we don't know whether that was the cause of synesthesia or the result of it. Exactly how synesthesia develops remains for further research.

STOP & CHECK

31. If someone reports seeing a particular letter in color, in what way is it different from a real color?

ANSWER

31. Someone who perceives a letter as yellow (when it is actually in black ink) can nevertheless see it on a yellow page.

MODULE 7.3 IN CLOSING

Different Senses as **Different Ways of Knowing the World**

Ask the average person to describe the current environment, and you will probably get a description of what he or she sees and hears. If nonhumans could talk, most species would start by describing what they smell. A human, a dog, and a snail may be in the same place, but the environments they perceive are very different.

We sometimes underestimate the importance of taste and smell. People who lose their sense of taste say they no longer enjoy eating and find it difficult to swallow (Cowart, 2005). A loss of smell can be a problem, too. Taste and smell can't compete with vision and hearing for telling us about what is happening in the distance, but they are essential for telling us about what is right next to us or about to enter our bodies.

SUMMARY

1. Sensory information can be coded in terms of either a labeled-line system or an across-fiber pattern system. **210**
2. Taste receptors are modified skin cells inside taste buds in papillae on the tongue. **211**
3. According to current evidence, we have five kinds of taste receptors, sensitive to sweet, sour, salty, bitter, and umami (glutamate) tastes. Taste is coded by the relative activity of different kinds of cells but also by the rhythm of responses within a given cell. **211**
4. Salty receptors respond simply to sodium ions crossing the membrane. Sour receptors respond to a stimulus by blocking potassium channels. Sweet, bitter, and umami receptors act by a second messenger within the cell, similar to the way a metabotropic neurotransmitter receptor operates. **212**
5. Mammals have about 25 kinds of bitter receptors, enabling them to detect a great variety of harmful substances that are chemically unrelated to one another. However, a consequence of so many bitter receptors is that we are not highly sensitive to low concentrations of any one bitter chemical. **213**
6. Part of the seventh cranial nerve conveys information from the anterior two thirds of the tongue. Parts of the ninth and tenth cranial nerves convey information from the posterior tongue and the throat. The two nerves interact in complex ways. **213**
7. Some people, known as supertasters, have more fungiform papillae than other people do and are more sensitive to a great variety of tastes. They tend to avoid strong-tasting foods. **213**
8. Olfactory receptors are proteins, each of them highly responsive to a few related chemicals and unresponsive to others. Vertebrates have hundreds of olfactory receptors, each contributing to the detection of a few related odors. **216**
9. Olfactory neurons in the cerebral cortex respond to complex patterns, such as those of a berry or melon. The cortex learns from experience and becomes more adept at distinguishing among closely related but familiar smells. **217**
10. Olfactory neurons survive only a month or so. When the brain generates new cells to replace them, the new ones become sensitive to the same chemicals as the ones they replace, and they send their axons to the same targets. **217**
11. In most mammals, each vomeronasal organ (VNO) receptor is sensitive to only one chemical, a pheromone. A pheromone is a social signal, usually for mating purposes. Unlike olfactory receptors, VNO receptors show little or no adaptation to a prolonged stimulus. Humans also respond somewhat to pheromones, although our receptors are in the olfactory mucosa, not the VNO. **219**
12. A small percentage of people experience synesthesia, a sensation in one modality after stimulation in another one. For example, someone might see purple neon tubes while listening to saxophones. The explanation is not known. **219**

Continued

KEY TERMS

Terms are defined in the module on the page number indicated. They're also presented in alphabetical order with definitions in the book's Subject Index/Glossary. Interactive flashcards, audio reviews, and crossword puzzles are among the online resources available to help you learn these terms and the concepts they represent.

across-fiber pattern principle **210**
adaptation **212**
cross-adaptation **212**
labeled-line principle **210**
nucleus of the tractus solitarius (NTS) **213**
olfaction **215**
olfactory cells **216**
papillae **211**
pheromones **219**
supertasters **213**
synesthesia **219**
taste bud **211**
vomeronasal organ (VNO) **219**

THOUGHT QUESTIONS

1. In the English language, the letter *t* has no meaning out of context. Its meaning depends on its relationship to other letters. Indeed, even a word, such as *to*, has little meaning except in its connection to other words. So is language a labeled-line system or an across-fiber pattern system?
2. Suppose a chemist synthesizes a new chemical that turns out to have an odor. Presumably, we do not have a specialized receptor for that chemical. Explain how our receptors detect it.

CHAPTER 7 Exploration and Study

In addition to the study materials provided at the end of each module, you may supplement your review of this chapter by using one or more of the book's electronic resources, which include its companion Website, interactive Cengage Learning eBook, Exploring Biological Psychology CD-ROM, and CengageNOW. Brief descriptions of these resources follow. For more information, visit **www.cengage.com/psychology/kalat**.

The book's companion Website, accessible through the author Web page indicated above, provides a wide range of study resources such as an interactive glossary, flashcards, tutorial quizzes, updated Web links, and Try It Yourself activities, as well as a limited selection of the short videos and animated explanations of concepts available for this chapter.

Exploring Biological Psychology

The Exploring Biological Psychology CD-ROM contains videos, animations, and Try It Yourself activities. These activities—as well as many that are new to this edition—are also available in the text's fully interactive, media-rich Cengage Learning eBook,* which gives you the opportunity to experience biological psychology in an even greater interactive and multimedia environment. The Cengage Learning eBook also includes highlighting and note-taking features and an audio glossary. For this chapter, the Cengage Learning eBook includes the following interactive explorations:

Sound Intensities
Ringtones and the Cochlea
Hearing Process Puzzle
Hearing

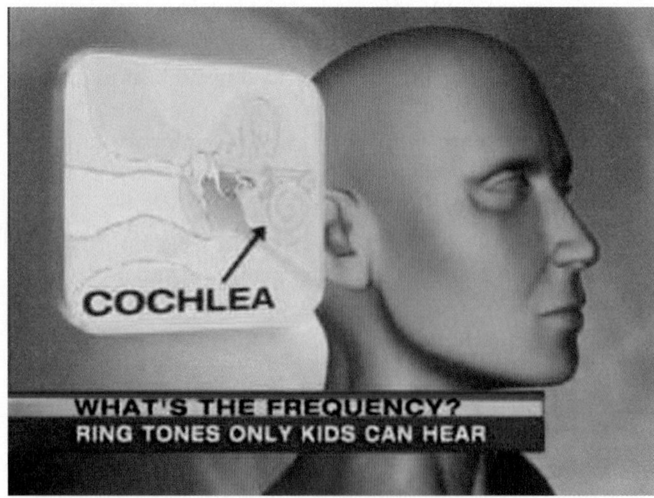

The video *Ringtones and the Cochlea* illustrates one consequence of the fact that younger people hear higher frequencies than older people.

* Requires a Cengage Learning eResources account. Visit **www.cengage.com/login** to register or login.

CENGAGENOW™ is an easy-to-use resource that helps you study in less time to get the grade you want. An online study system, CengageNOW* gives you the option of taking a diagnostic pretest for each chapter. The system uses the results of each pretest to create personalized chapter study plans for you. The Personalized Study Plans

- help you save study time by identifying areas on which you should concentrate and give you one-click access to corresponding pages of the interactive Cengage Learning eBook;
- provide interactive exercises and study tools to help you fully understand chapter concepts; and
- include a posttest for you to take to confirm that you are ready to move on to the next chapter.

Suggestions for Further Exploration

The book's companion Website includes a list of suggested articles available through InfoTrac College Edition for this chapter. You may also want to explore some of the following books and Websites. The text's companion Website provides live, updated links to the sites listed below.

Books

Pert, C. B. (1997). *Molecules of emotion.* New York: Simon & Schuster. Autobiographical statement by the woman who, as a graduate student, first demonstrated the opiate receptors.

Robertson, L. C., & Sagiv, N. (2005). *Synesthesia: Perspectives From cognitive neuroscience.* Oxford, England: Oxford University Press. A review of research on this fascinating phenomenon.

Websites

Laboratoire Isabelle Peretz, Université de Montréal
Test to yourself or others for tone-deafness.
http://www.brams.umontreal.ca/amusia-demo/

University of California Absolute Pitch Study
Now test yourself for the opposite extreme: Absolute pitch.
http://perfectpitch.ucsf.edu/

Mark Rejhon
A good source of information about hearing loss.
http://www.marky.com/hearing/

American Pain Society
Links to recent research reports about pain.
http://www.ampainsoc.org/

Leffingwell & Associates
An excellent source of information about olfaction.
http://www.leffingwell.com/olfaction.htm

Jim Rider/Zeis Images

Movement

8

CHAPTER OUTLINE

OPPOSITE: Ultimately, what brain activity accomplishes is the control of movement—a far more complex process than it might seem.

MAIN IDEAS

1. Movement depends on overall plans, not just connections between a stimulus and a muscle contraction.
2. Movements vary in sensitivity to feedback, skill, and variability in the face of obstacles.
3. Damage to different brain locations produces different kinds of movement impairment.
4. Brain damage that impairs movement also impairs cognitive processes. That is, control of movement is inseparably linked with cognition.

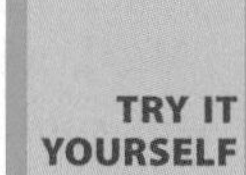

Before we get started, please try this: Get out a pencil and a sheet of paper, and put the pencil in your nonpreferred hand. For example, if you are right-handed, put it in your left hand. Now, with that hand, draw a face in profile—that is, facing one direction or the other but not straight ahead. *Please do this now before reading further.*

If you tried the demonstration, you probably notice that your drawing is more childlike than usual. It is as if some part of your brain stored the way you used to draw as a young child. Now, if you are right-handed and therefore drew the face with your left hand, why did you draw it facing to the right? At least I assume you did because more than two thirds of right-handers drawing with their left hand draw the profile facing right. Young children, age 5 or so, when drawing with the right hand, almost always draw people and animals facing left, but when using the left hand, they almost always draw them facing right. But *why?* The short answer is we don't know. We have much to learn about the control of movement and how it relates to perception, motivation, and other functions.

MODULE 8.1

The Control of Movement

Why do we have brains at all? Plants survive just fine without them. So do sponges, which are animals, even if they don't act like them. But plants don't move, and neither do sponges. A sea squirt (a marine invertebrate) swims and has a brain during its infant stage, but when it transforms into an adult, it attaches to a surface, becomes a stationary filter feeder, and digests its own brain, as if to say, "Now that I've stopped traveling, I won't need this brain thing anymore." Ultimately, the purpose of a brain is to control behaviors, and behaviors are movements.

"But wait," you might reply. "We need brains for other things, too, don't we? Like seeing, hearing, finding food, talking, understanding speech . . ."

Well, what would be the value of seeing and hearing if you couldn't do anything? Finding food or chewing it requires movement, and so does talking. Understanding speech wouldn't do you much good unless you could do something about it. A great brain without muscles would be like a computer without a monitor, printer, or other output. No matter how powerful the internal processing, it would be useless.

Gary Bell/Getty Images

Adult sea squirts attach to the surface, never move again, and digest their own brains.

Muscles and Their Movements

All animal movement depends on muscle contractions. Vertebrate muscles fall into three categories (Figure 8.1): **smooth muscles,** which control the digestive system and other organs; **skeletal,** or **striated, muscles,** which control movement of the body in relation to the environment; and **cardiac muscles** (the heart muscles), which have properties intermediate between those of smooth and skeletal muscles.

Each muscle is composed of many fibers, as Figure 8.2 illustrates. Although each muscle fiber receives information from only one axon, a given axon may innervate more than one muscle fiber. For example, the eye muscles have a ratio of about one axon per three muscle fibers, and the biceps muscles of the arm have a ratio of one axon to more than a hundred fibers (Evarts, 1979). This difference allows the eye to move more precisely than the biceps.

A **neuromuscular junction** is a synapse between a motor neuron axon and a muscle fiber. In skeletal muscles, every axon releases acetylcholine at the neuromuscular junction, and acetylcholine always excites the muscle to contract. Each muscle makes just one movement, contraction. It relaxes in the absence of excitation, but it never moves actively in the opposite direction. Moving a leg or arm back and forth requires opposing sets of muscles, called **antagonistic muscles.** At your elbow, for example, you have a **flexor** muscle that brings your hand toward your shoulder and an **extensor** muscle that straightens the arm (Figure 8.3).

A deficit of acetylcholine or its receptors in the muscles impairs movement. **Myasthenia gravis** (MY-us-THEE-nee-uh GRAHV-iss) is an *autoimmune disease,* in which the immune system forms antibodies that attack the acetylcholine receptors at neuromuscular junctions (Shah & Lisak, 1993), causing weakness and rapid fatigue of the skeletal muscles. Whenever anyone excites a given muscle fiber a few times in succession, later action potentials on the same motor neuron release less acetylcholine than before. For a healthy person, a slight decline in acetylcholine poses no problem. However, because people with myasthenia gravis have lost many of their receptors, even a slight decline in acetylcholine input produces clear deficits (Drachman, 1978).

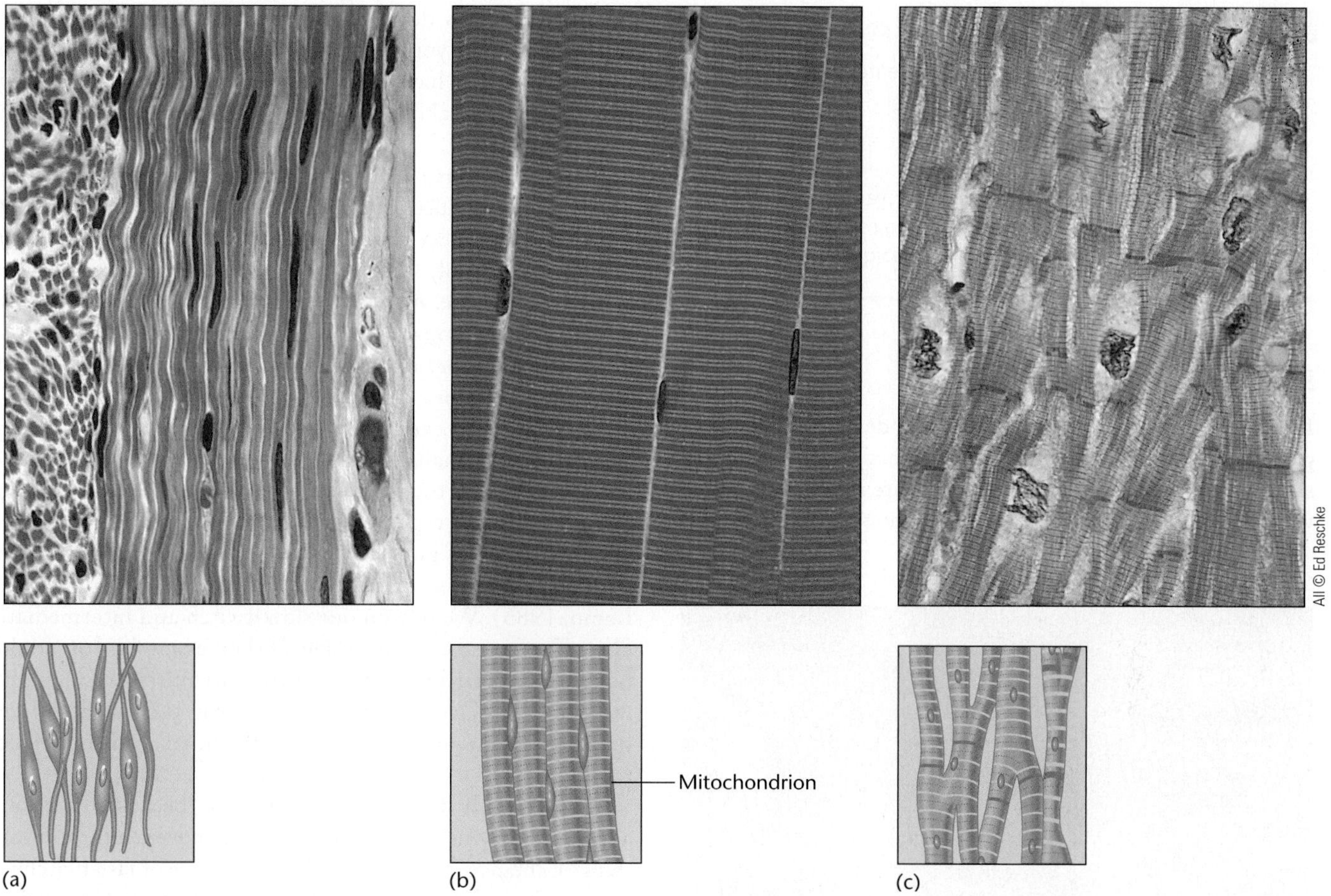

Mitochondrion

(a) (b) (c)

All © Ed Reschke

Figure 8.1 The three main types of vertebrate muscles
(a) Smooth muscle, found in the intestines and other organs, consists of long, thin cells. **(b)** Skeletal, or striated, muscle consists of long cylindrical fibers with stripes. **(c)** Cardiac muscle, found in the heart, consists of fibers that fuse together at various points. Because of these fusions, cardiac muscles contract together, not independently. *(Illustrations after Starr & Taggart, 1989)*

© Ed Reschke

Figure 8.2 An axon branching to innervate separate muscle fibers within a muscle
Movements can be much more precise where each axon innervates only a few fibers, as with eye muscles, than where it innervates many fibers, as with biceps muscles.

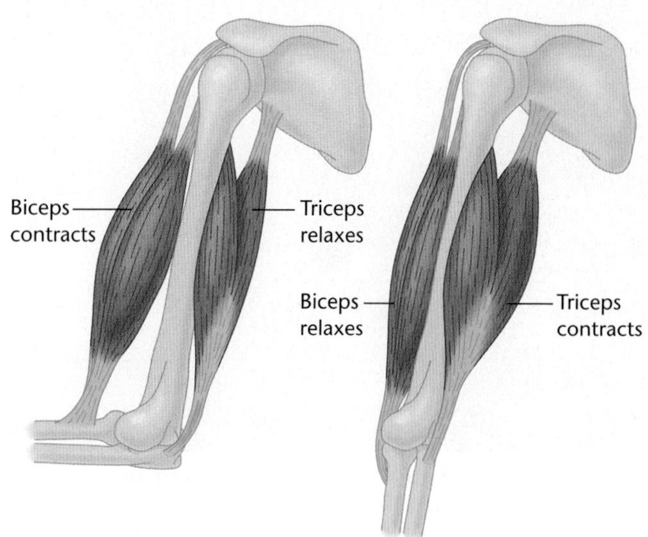

Figure 8.3 A pair of antagonistic muscles
The biceps of the arm is a flexor; the triceps is an extensor. *(Starr & Taggart, 1989)*

STOP & CHECK

1. Why can the eye muscles move with greater precision than the biceps muscles?

ANSWER

1. Each axon to the biceps muscles innervates about a hundred fibers; therefore, it is not possible to change the movement by just a few fibers. In contrast, an axon to the eye muscles innervates only about three fibers.

Fast and Slow Muscles

Imagine you are a small fish. Your only defense against bigger fish, diving birds, and other predators is your ability to swim away (Figure 8.4). Your temperature is the same as the water around you, and muscle contractions, being chemical processes, slow down in the cold. So when the water gets cold, presumably you will move slowly, right? Strangely, you will not. You will have to use more muscles than before, but you will swim at about the same speed (Rome, Loughna, & Goldspink, 1984).

Tui De Roy/Minden Pictures

Figure 8.4 Temperature regulation and movement
Fish are "cold blooded," but many of their predators (e.g., this pelican) are not. At cold temperatures, a fish must maintain its normal swimming speed, even though every muscle in its body contracts more slowly than usual. To do so, a fish calls upon white muscles that it otherwise uses only for brief bursts of speed.

A fish has three kinds of muscles: red, pink, and white. Red muscles produce the slowest movements, but they do not fatigue. White muscles produce the fastest movements, but they fatigue rapidly. Pink muscles are intermediate in speed and rate of fatigue. At high temperatures, a fish relies mostly on red and pink muscles. At colder temperatures, the fish relies more and more on white muscles, maintaining its speed but fatiguing faster.

All right, you can stop imagining you are a fish. Human and other mammalian muscles have various kinds of muscle fibers mixed together, not in separate bundles as in fish. Our muscle types range from **fast-twitch fibers** with fast contractions and rapid fatigue to **slow-twitch fibers** with less vigorous contractions and no fatigue (Hennig & Lømo, 1985). We rely on our slow-twitch and intermediate fibers for nonstrenuous activities. For example, you could talk for hours without fatiguing your lip muscles. You might walk for a long time, too. But if you run up a steep hill at full speed, you switch to fast-twitch fibers, which fatigue rapidly.

Slow-twitch fibers do not fatigue because they are **aerobic**—they use oxygen during their movements. You can think of them as "pay as you go." Vigorous use of fast-twitch fibers results in fatigue because the process is **anaerobic**—using reactions that do not require oxygen at the time, although they need oxygen for recovery. Using them builds up an "oxygen debt." Prolonged exercise can start with aerobic activity and shift to anaerobic. For example, imagine yourself bicycling. Your aerobic muscle activity uses glucose, but as the glucose supplies begin to dwindle, they activate a gene that inhibits the muscles from using glucose, thereby saving glucose for the brain's use (Booth & Neufer, 2005). You start relying more on fast-twitch muscles, which depend on anaerobic use of fatty acids. You continue bicycling, but your muscles gradually fatigue.

People have varying percentages of fast-twitch and slow-twitch fibers. The Swedish ultramarathon runner Bertil Järlaker built up so many slow-twitch fibers in his legs that he once ran 3,520 km (2,188 mi) in 50 days (an average of 1.7 marathons per day) with only minimal signs of pain or fatigue (Sjöström, Friden, & Ekblom, 1987). Contestants in the Primal Quest race have to walk or run 125 km, cycle 250 km, kayak 131 km, rappel 97 km up canyon walls, swim 13 km in rough water, ride horseback, and climb rocks over 6 days in summer heat. To endure this ordeal, contestants need many adaptations of their muscles and metabolism (Pearson, 2006). In contrast, competitive sprinters have a high percentage of fast-twitch fibers and other adaptations for speed instead of endurance (Andersen, Klitgaard, & Saltin, 1994; Canepari et al., 2005). Individual differences depend on both genetics and training.

STOP & CHECK

2. In what way are fish movements impaired in cold water?
3. Duck breast muscles are red ("dark meat"), whereas chicken breast muscles are white. Which species probably can fly for a longer time before fatiguing?
4. Why is an ultramarathoner like Bertil Järlaker probably not impressive at short-distance races?

ANSWERS

2. Although a fish can move rapidly in cold water, it fatigues easily. **3.** Ducks can fly enormous distances without evident fatigue, as they often do during migration. The white muscle of a chicken breast has the great power that is necessary to get a heavy body off the ground, but it fatigues rapidly. Chickens seldom fly far. **4.** An ultramarathoner builds up large numbers of slow-twitch fibers at the expense of fast-twitch fibers. Therefore, endurance is great, but maximum speed is not.

Muscle Control by Proprioceptors

You are walking along on a bumpy road. Occasionally, you set your foot down a little too hard or not quite hard enough. You adjust your posture and maintain your balance without even thinking about it. How do you do that?

A baby is lying on its back. You playfully tug its foot and then let go. At once, the leg bounces back to its original position. How and why?

In both cases, the mechanism is under the control of proprioceptors (Figure 8.5). A **proprioceptor** is a receptor that detects the position or movement of a part of the body—in these cases, a muscle. Muscle proprioceptors detect the stretch and tension of a muscle and send messages that enable the spinal cord to adjust its signals. When a muscle is stretched, the spinal cord sends a reflexive signal to contract it. This **stretch reflex** is *caused* by a stretch; it does not *produce* one.

One kind of proprioceptor is the **muscle spindle,** a receptor parallel to the muscle that responds to a stretch (Merton, 1972; Miles & Evarts, 1979). Whenever the muscle spindle is stretched, its sensory nerve sends a message to a motor neuron in the spinal cord, which in turn sends a message back to the muscles surrounding the spindle, causing a contraction. Note that this reflex provides for negative feedback: When a muscle and its spindle are stretched, the spindle sends a message that results in a muscle contraction that opposes the stretch.

When you set your foot down on a bump on the road, your knee bends a bit, stretching the extensor muscles of that leg. The sensory nerves of the spindles send action potentials to the motor neuron in the spinal cord, and the motor neuron sends action potentials to the extensor muscle. Contracting the extensor muscle straightens the leg, adjusting for the bump on the road.

A physician who asks you to cross your legs and then taps just below the knee is testing your stretch reflexes (Figure 8.6). The tap stretches the extensor muscles and their spindles, resulting in a message that jerks the lower leg upward. The same reflex contributes to walking; raising the upper leg reflexively moves the lower leg forward in readiness for the next step.

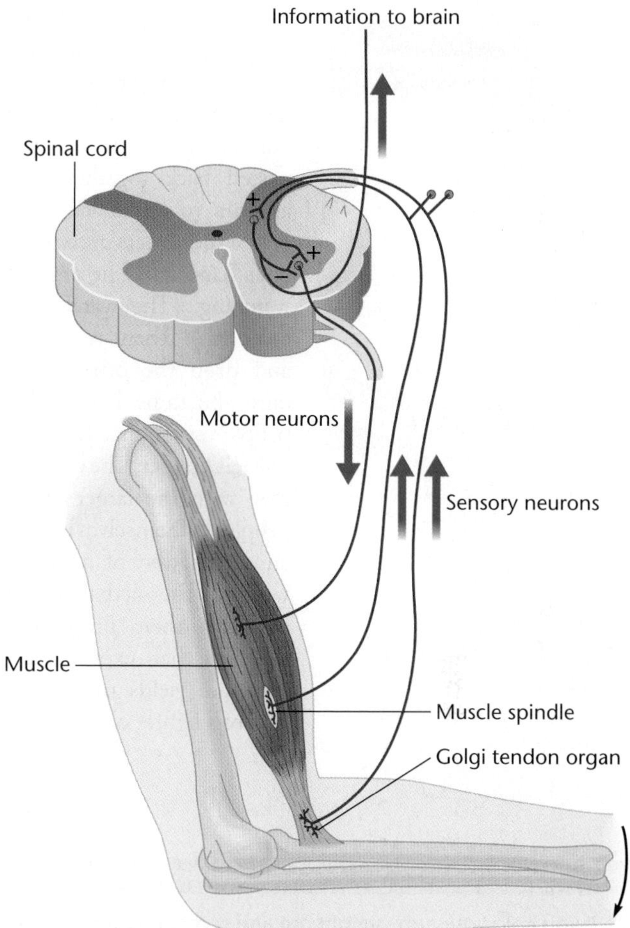

Figure 8.5 Two kinds of proprioceptors regulate the contraction of a muscle
When a muscle is stretched, the nerves from the muscle spindles transmit an increased frequency of impulses, resulting in a contraction of the surrounding muscle. Contraction of the muscle stimulates the Golgi tendon organ, which acts as a brake or shock absorber to prevent a contraction that is too quick or extreme.

Golgi tendon organs, also proprioceptors, respond to increases in muscle tension. Located in the tendons at opposite ends of a muscle, they act as a brake against an excessively vigorous contraction. Some muscles are so strong that they could damage themselves if too many fibers contracted at once. Golgi tendon organs detect the tension that results during a muscle contraction. Their impulses travel to the spinal cord, where they excite interneurons that inhibit the motor neurons. In short, a vigorous muscle contraction inhibits further contraction by activating the Golgi tendon organs.

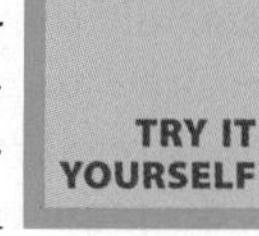

The proprioceptors not only control important reflexes but also provide the brain with information. Here is an illusion that you can demonstrate yourself: Find a small, dense object and a

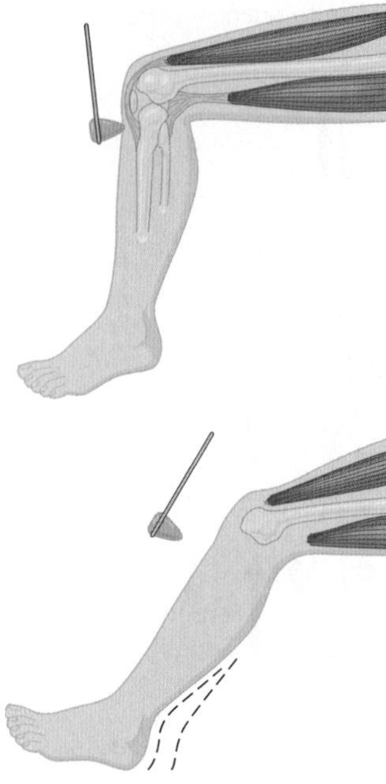

Figure 8.6 The knee-jerk reflex
This is one example of a stretch reflex.

larger, less dense object that weighs the same as the small one. For example, you might try a lemon and a hollowed-out orange, with the peel pasted back together so it appears to be intact. Drop one of the objects onto someone's hand while he or she is watching. (The watching is essential.) Then remove it and drop the other object onto the same hand. Most people report that the small one felt heavier. The reason is that with the larger object, people set themselves up with an expectation of a heavier weight. The actual weight displaces their proprioceptors less than expected and therefore yields the perception of a lighter object.

STOP & CHECK

5. If you hold your arm straight out and someone pulls it down slightly, it quickly bounces back. Which proprioceptor is responsible?
6. What is the function of Golgi tendon organs?

ANSWERS

5. the muscle spindle **6.** Golgi tendon organs respond to muscle tension and thereby prevent excessively strong muscle contractions.

Units of Movement

Movements include speaking, walking, threading a needle, and throwing a basketball while off balance and evading two defenders. Different kinds of movement depend on different kinds of control by the nervous system.

Voluntary and Involuntary Movements

Reflexes are consistent automatic responses to stimuli. We generally think of reflexes as *involuntary* because they are insensitive to reinforcements, punishments, and motivations. The stretch reflex is one example. Another is the constriction of the pupil in response to bright light.

APPLICATIONS AND EXTENSIONS

Infant Reflexes

Infants have several reflexes not seen in adults. For example, if you place an object firmly in an infant's hand, the infant grasps it (the **grasp reflex**). If you stroke the sole of the foot, the infant extends the big toe and fans the others (the **Babinski reflex**). If you touch an infant's cheek, the infant turns his or her head toward the stimulated cheek and begins to suck (the **rooting reflex**). The rooting reflex is not a pure reflex, as its intensity depends on the infant's arousal and hunger level.

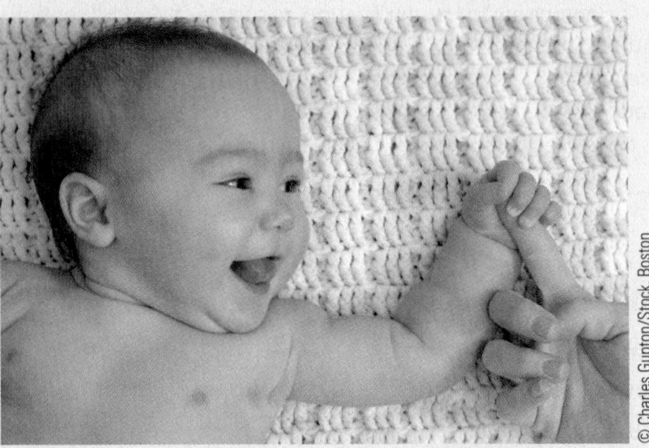

© Charles Gupton/Stock, Boston

(a)

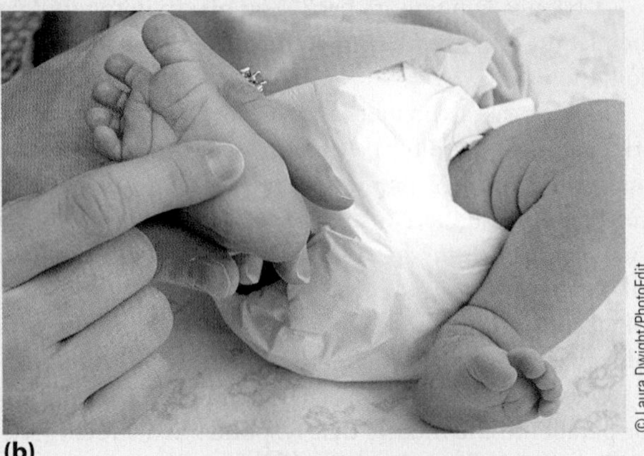

© Laura Dwight/PhotoEdit

(b)

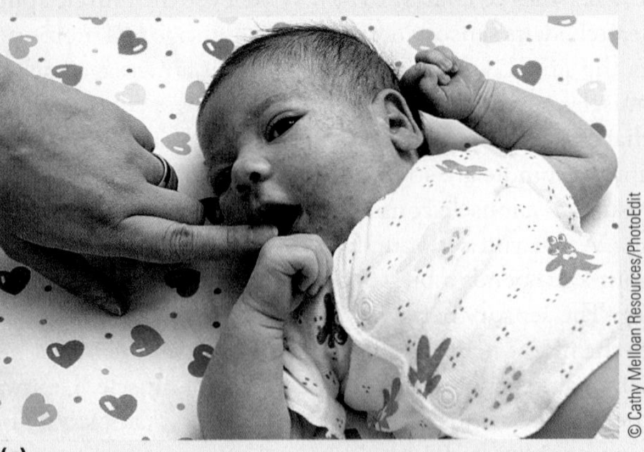

© Cathy Melloan Resources/PhotoEdit

(c)

Three reflexes in infants but ordinarily not in adults: **(a)** grasp reflex, **(b)** Babinski reflex, and **(c)** rooting reflex.

The grasp reflex enables an infant to cling to the mother while she travels.

Although such reflexes fade away with age, the connections remain intact, not lost but suppressed by axons from the maturing brain. If the cerebral cortex is damaged, the infant reflexes are released from inhibition. A physician who strokes the sole of your foot during a physical exam is looking for evidence of brain damage. This is hardly the most reliable test, but it is easy. If a stroke on the sole of your foot makes you fan your toes like a baby, the physician proceeds to further tests.

Infant reflexes sometimes return temporarily if alcohol, carbon dioxide, or other chemicals decrease the activity in the cerebral cortex. You might try testing for infant reflexes in a friend who has consumed too much alcohol.

TRY IT YOURSELF

Infants and children also show certain *allied reflexes* more strongly than adults. If dust blows in your face, you reflexively close your eyes and mouth and probably sneeze. These reflexes are *allied* in the sense that each of them tends to elicit the others. If you suddenly see a bright light—as when you emerge from a dark theater on a sunny afternoon—you reflexively close your eyes, and you may also close your mouth and perhaps sneeze. Many children and some adults react this way (Whitman & Packer, 1993).

Few behaviors can be classified as purely voluntary or involuntary, reflexive or nonreflexive. Even walking includes involuntary components. When you walk, you automatically compensate for the bumps and irregularities in the road. You also swing your arms automatically as an involuntary consequence of walking.

Try this: While sitting, raise your right foot and make clockwise circles. Keep your foot moving while you draw the number 6 in the air with your right hand. Or just move your right hand in counterclockwise circles. You will probably reverse the direction of your foot movement. It is difficult to make "voluntary" clockwise and counterclockwise movements on the same side of the body at the same time. Curiously, it is not at all difficult to move your left hand in one direction while moving the right foot in the opposite direction.

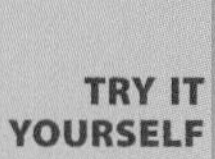

In some cases, voluntary behavior requires inhibiting an involuntary impulse. Here is a fascinating demonstration: Hold one hand to the left of a child's head and the other hand to the right. When you wiggle a finger, the child is instructed to look at the *other* hand. Before age 5 to 7 years, most children find it almost impossible to ignore the wiggling finger and look the other way. Ability to perform this task smoothly improves all the way to age 18, requiring areas of the prefrontal cortex that mature slowly. Even some adults—especially those with neurological or psychiatric disorders—have trouble on this task (Munoz & Everling, 2004).

TRY IT YOURSELF

Movements Varying in Sensitivity to Feedback

The military distinguishes between ballistic missiles and guided missiles. A ballistic missile is launched like a thrown ball, with no way to vary its aim. A guided missile detects the target and adjusts its trajectory to correct for any error.

Similarly, some movements are ballistic, and others are corrected by feedback. A **ballistic movement** is executed as a whole: Once initiated, it cannot be altered. Reflexes are ballistic, for example. However, most behaviors are subject to feedback correction. For example, when you thread a needle, you make a slight movement, check your aim, and then readjust. Similarly, a singer who holds a single note hears any wavering of the pitch and corrects it.

Sequences of Behaviors

Many of our behaviors consist of rapid sequences, as in speaking, writing, dancing, or playing a musical instrument. Some of these sequences depend on **central pattern generators,** neural mechanisms in the spinal cord that generate rhythmic patterns of motor output. Examples include the mechanisms that generate wing flapping in birds, fin movements in fish, and the "wet dog shake." Although a stimulus may activate a central pattern generator, it does not control the frequency of the alternating movements. For example, cats scratch themselves at a rate of three to four strokes per second. Cells in the lumbar segments of the spinal cord generate this rhythm, and they continue doing so even if they are isolated from the brain or if the muscles are paralyzed (Deliagina, Orlovsky, & Pavlova, 1983).

We refer to a fixed sequence of movements as a **motor program.** For an example of a built-in program, a mouse periodically grooms itself by sitting up, licking its paws, wiping them over its face, closing its eyes as the paws pass over them, licking the paws again, and so forth (Fentress, 1973). Once begun, the sequence is fixed from beginning to end. Many people develop learned but predictable motor sequences. An expert gymnast produces a smooth, coordinated sequence of movements. The same can be said for skilled typists, piano players, and so forth. The pattern is automatic in the sense that thinking or talking about it interferes with the action.

By comparing species, we begin to understand how a motor program can be gained or lost through evolution. For example, if you hold a chicken above the ground and drop it, its wings extend and flap. Even chickens with featherless wings make the same movements, though they fail to break their fall (Provine, 1979, 1981). Chickens, of course, still have the genetic programming to fly. On the other hand, ostriches, emus, and rheas, which have not used their wings for flight for millions of generations, have lost the genes for flight movements and do not flap their wings when dropped (Provine, 1984). (You might pause to think about the researcher who found a way to drop these huge birds to test the hypothesis.)

Do humans have any built-in motor programs? Yawning is one example (Provine, 1986). A yawn consists of a prolonged open-mouth inhalation, often accompanied by stretching, and a shorter exhalation. Yawns are consistent in duration, with a mean of just under 6 seconds. Certain facial expressions are also programmed, such as smiles, frowns, and the raised-eyebrow greeting.

Nearly all birds reflexively spread their wings when dropped. However, emus—which lost the ability to fly through evolutionary time—do not spread their wings.

MODULE 8.1 IN CLOSING

Categories of Movement

Charles Sherrington described a motor neuron in the spinal cord as "the final common path." He meant that regardless of what sensory and motivational processes occupy the brain, the final result is either a muscle contraction or the delay of a muscle contraction. A motor neuron and its associated muscle participate in a great many different kinds of movements, and we need many brain areas to control them.

SUMMARY

1. Vertebrates have smooth, skeletal, and cardiac muscles. **226**
2. All nerve-muscle junctions rely on acetylcholine as their neurotransmitter. **226**
3. Skeletal muscles range from slow muscles that do not fatigue to fast muscles that fatigue quickly. We rely on the slow muscles most of the time, but we recruit the fast muscles for brief periods of strenuous activity. **228**
4. Proprioceptors are receptors sensitive to the position and movement of a part of the body. Two kinds of proprioceptors, muscle spindles and Golgi tendon organs, help regulate muscle movements. **229**
5. Children and some adults have trouble shifting their attention away from a moving object toward an unmoving one. **231**
6. Some movements, especially reflexes, proceed as a unit, with little if any guidance from sensory feedback. Other movements, such as threading a needle, are guided and redirected by sensory feedback. **231**

KEY TERMS

Terms are defined in the module on the page number indicated. They're also presented in alphabetical order with definitions in the book's Subject Index/Glossary. Interactive flashcards, audio reviews, and crossword puzzles are among the online resources available to help you learn these terms and the concepts they represent.

THOUGHT QUESTION

Would you expect jaguars, cheetahs, and other great cats to have mostly slow-twitch, nonfatiguing muscles in their legs or mostly fast-twitch, quickly fatiguing muscles? What kinds of animals might have mostly the opposite kind of muscles?

MODULE 8.2

Brain Mechanisms of Movement

Why do we care how the brain controls movement? One goal is to help people with spinal cord damage or limb amputations. Suppose we could listen in on their brain messages and decode what movements they would like to make. Then biomedical engineers might route those messages to muscle stimulators or robotic limbs. Sound like science fiction? Not really. Researchers implanted an array of microelectrodes into the motor cortex of a man who was paralyzed from the neck down (Figure 8.7). They determined which neurons were most active when he intended various movements and then attached them so that, when the same pattern arose again, the movement would occur. He was then able, just by thinking, to turn on a television, control the channel and volume, move a robotic arm, open and close a robotic hand, and so forth (Hochberg et al., 2006). The hope is that refinements of the technology can increase and improve the possible movements. Another approach is to use evoked potential recordings from the surface of the scalp (Millán, Renkens, Mouriño, & Gerstner, 2004; Wolpaw & McFarland, 2004). That method avoids inserting anything into the brain but probably offers less precise control. In either case, progress will depend on both the technology and advances in understanding the brain mechanisms of movement.

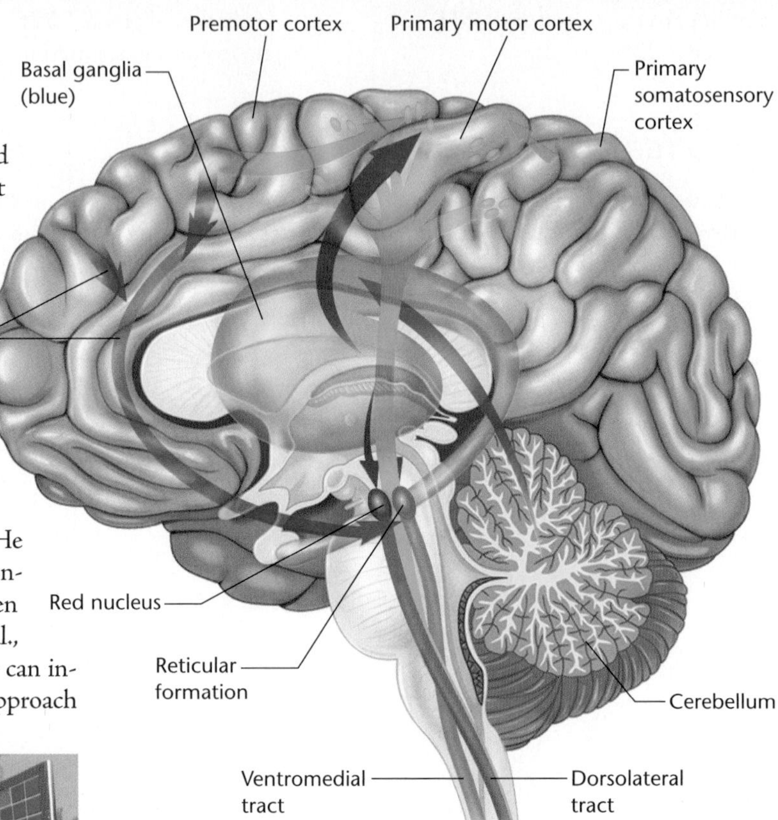

Figure 8.8 The major motor areas of the mammalian central nervous system

The cerebral cortex, especially the primary motor cortex, sends axons directly to the medulla and spinal cord. So do the red nucleus, reticular formation, and other brainstem areas. The medulla and spinal cord control muscle movements. The basal ganglia and cerebellum influence movement indirectly through their communication back and forth with the cerebral cortex and brainstem.

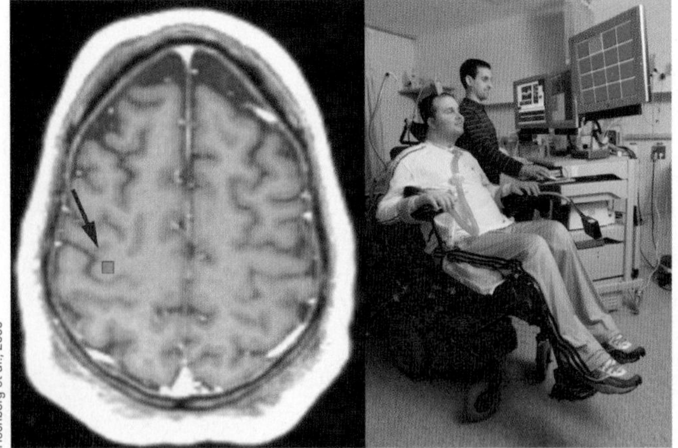

Figure 8.7 Paralyzed man with an electronic device implanted in his brain

Left: The arrow shows the location where the device was implanted. Right: Seated in a wheelchair, the man uses brain activity to move a cursor on the screen to the orange square. *(From Macmillan Publishing Ltd./Hochberg, Serruya, Friehs, Mukand, et al. (2006).* Nature, 442, *164–171)*

Controlling movement depends on many brain areas, as illustrated in Figure 8.8. Don't get too bogged down in details of the figure at this point. We shall attend to each area in due course.

The Cerebral Cortex

Since the pioneering work of Gustav Fritsch and Eduard Hitzig (1870), neuroscientists have known that direct electrical stimulation of the **primary motor cortex**—the precentral gyrus of the frontal cortex, just anterior to the central sulcus (Figure 8.9)—elicits movements. The motor cortex does not send messages directly to the muscles. Its axons extend to the brainstem and spinal cord, which generate the impulses that control the muscles. The cerebral cortex is particularly important for complex actions such as talking or writing. It is less important for coughing, sneezing, gagging, laughing, or crying (Rinn, 1984). Perhaps the lack of cerebral control explains why it is hard to perform such actions voluntarily.

Figure 8.10 (which repeats part of Figure 4.24 on page 101) indicates which area of the motor cortex controls which area of the body. For example, the brain area shown next to the hand is active during hand movements. In each case, the brain area controls a structure on the opposite side of the body. However, don't read this figure as implying that each spot in the motor cortex controls a single muscle. For example, the regions responsible for any finger overlap the regions responsible for other fingers, as shown in Figure 8.11 (Sanes, Donoghue, Thangaraj, Edelman, & Warach, 1995).

For many years, researchers studied the motor cortex in laboratory animals by stimulating neurons with brief electrical pulses, usually less than 50 milliseconds (ms) in duration. The results were brief, isolated muscle twitches. Later researchers found different results when they lengthened the pulses to half a second. Instead of twitches, they elicited complex movement patterns. For example, stimulation of one spot caused a monkey to make a grasping movement with its hand, move its hand to just in front of the mouth, and open its mouth (Graziano, Taylor, & Moore, 2002). Repeated stimulation of this same spot elicited the same result each time, regardless of what the monkey had been doing at the time and the position of its hand. That is, the stimulation produced a certain *outcome*. Depending on the position of the arm, the stimulation might activate biceps muscles, triceps, or whatever. In most cases, the motor cortex orders an outcome and leaves it to the spinal cord and other areas to find the right combination of muscles (S. H. Scott, 2004).

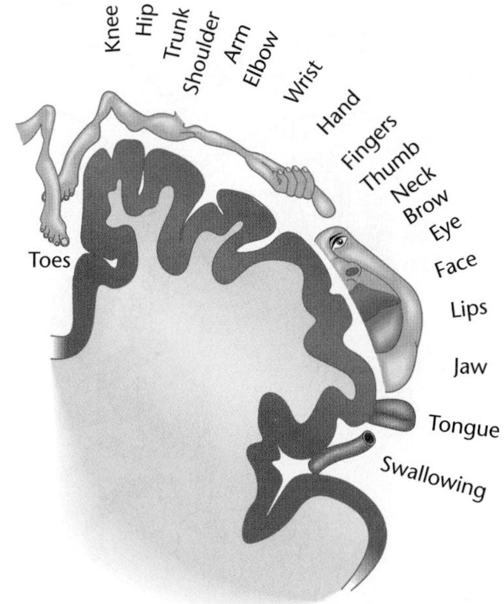

Figure 8.10 Coronal section through the primary motor cortex
Stimulation at any point in the primary motor cortex is most likely to evoke movements in the body area shown. However, actual results are usually messier than this figure implies: For example, individual cells controlling one finger may be intermingled with cells controlling another finger. *(Adapted from Penfield & Rasmussen, 1950)*

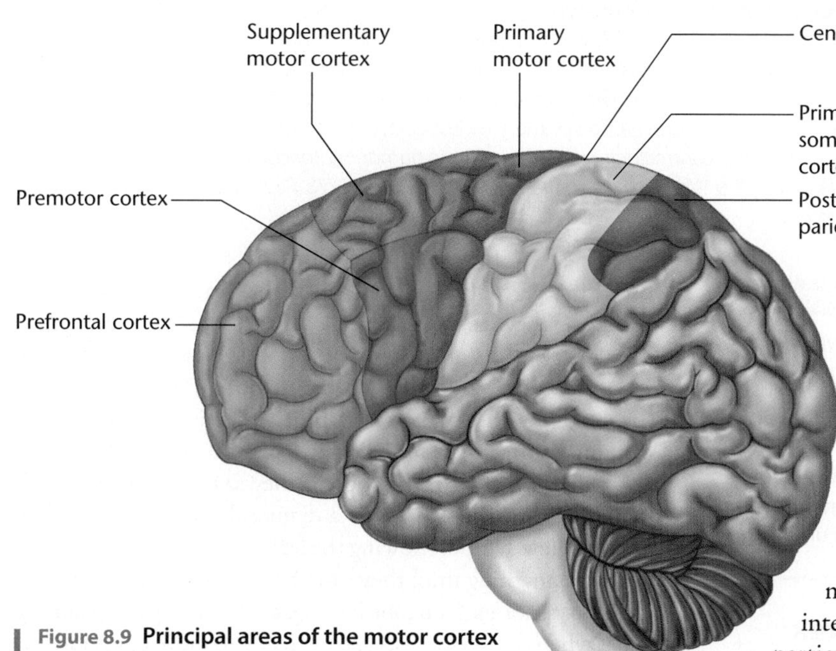

Figure 8.9 Principal areas of the motor cortex in the human brain
Cells in the premotor cortex and supplementary motor cortex are active during the planning of movements, even if the movements are never actually executed.

The primary motor cortex is active when people "intend" a movement. Researchers had an opportunity to examine brain activity in two patients who were paralyzed from the neck down. About 90% of neurons in the primary motor cortex became active when these patients intended movements of particular speeds toward particular locations. Different cells were specific to different speeds and locations. The motor cortex showed these properties even though the spinal cord damage made the movements impossible (Truccolo, Friehs, Donoghue, & Hochberg, 2008).

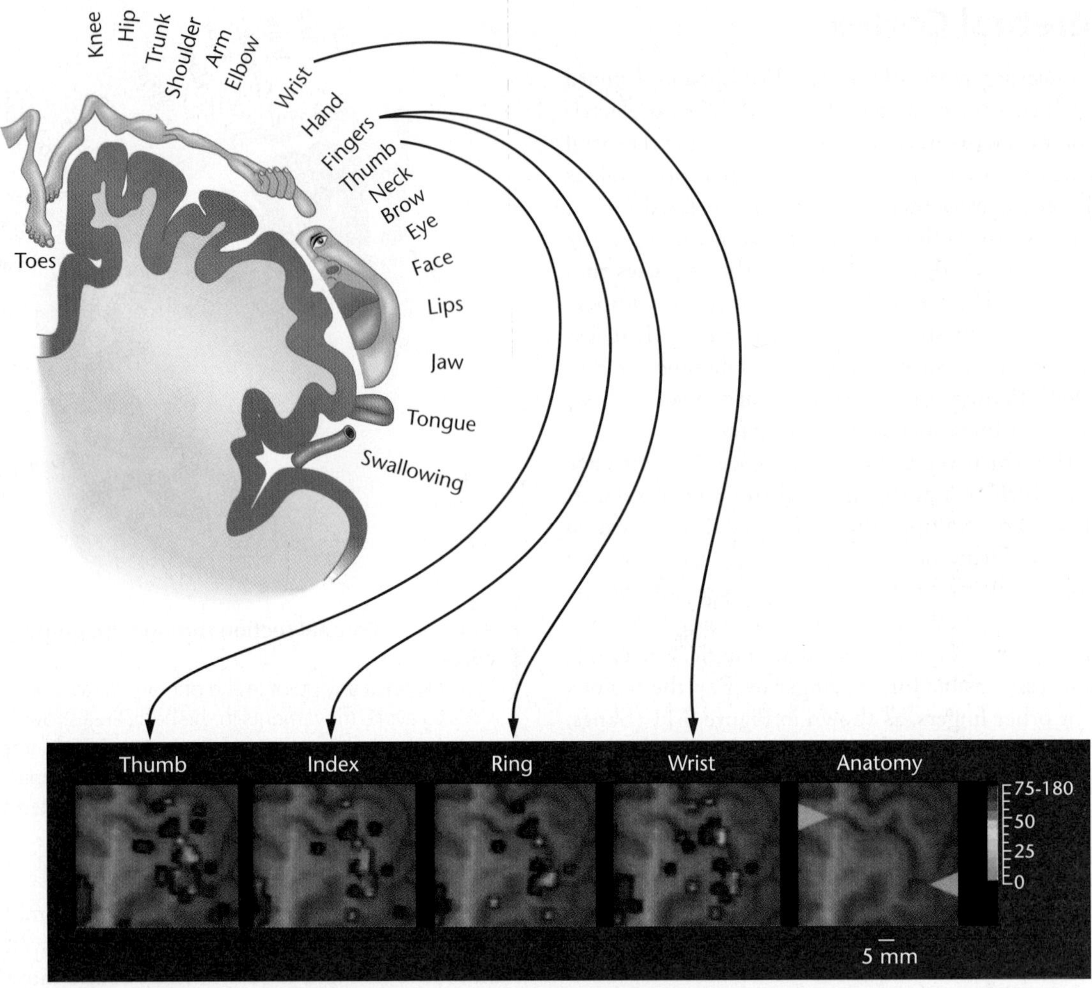

Figure 8.11 Motor cortex during movement of a finger or the wrist
In this functional MRI scan, red indicates the greatest activity, followed by yellow, green, and blue. Note that each movement activated a scattered population of cells and that the areas activated by any one part of the hand overlapped the areas activated by any other. The scan at the right (anatomy) shows a section of the central sulcus (between the two yellow arrows). The primary motor cortex is just anterior to the central sulcus. *(From "Shared neural substrates controlling hand movements in human motor cortex," by J. Sanes, J. Donoghue, V. Thangaraj, R. Edelman, & S. Warach,* Science *1995, 268:5218, 1774–1778. Reprinted with permission from AAAS/Science Magazine.)*

STOP & CHECK

7. What evidence indicates that cortical activity represents the "idea" of the movement and not just the muscle contractions?

ANSWER

7. Activity in the motor cortex leads to a particular outcome, such as movement of the hand to the mouth, regardless of what muscle contractions are necessary given the hand's current location.

Areas Near the Primary Motor Cortex

Areas near the primary motor cortex also contribute to movement (see Figure 8.9). The **posterior parietal cortex** keeps track of the position of the body relative to the world (Snyder, Grieve, Brotchie, & Andersen, 1998). People with posterior parietal damage accurately describe what they see, but they have trouble converting perceptions into action. They cannot walk toward something they see, walk around obstacles, or reach out to grasp something—even after describing its size, shape, and angle (Goodale, 1996; Goodale, Milner, Jakobson, & Carey, 1991). The posterior parietal cortex appears to be important also for planning movements. In one study, people were told to press a key with the left hand as soon as they saw a square and with the right hand when they saw a diamond. In some cases, they saw a preview symbol showing the left or right hand. They were not to do anything until they saw the square or diamond. Part of the posterior parietal lobe became active during the planning phase, when the person was getting ready to move one hand but not yet doing it (Hesse, Thiel, Stephan, & Fink, 2006).

The primary somatosensory cortex is the main receiving area for touch and other body information, as mentioned in Chapter 7. It provides the primary motor cortex with sensory information and also sends a substantial number of axons directly to the spinal cord. Neurons in this area are especially active when the hand grasps something, responding both to the shape of the object and the type of movement, such as grasping, lifting, or lowering (E. P. Gardner, Ro, Debowy, & Ghosh, 1999).

Cells in the prefrontal cortex, premotor cortex, and supplementary motor cortex (see Figure 8.9) prepare for a movement, sending messages to the primary motor cortex. The **prefrontal cortex** responds to lights, noises, and other signals for a movement. It also plans movements according to their probable outcomes (Tucker, Luu, & Pribram, 1995). If you had damage to this area, many of your movements would seem illogical or disorganized, such as showering with your clothes on or pouring water on the tube of toothpaste instead of the toothbrush (M. F. Schwartz, 1995). Interestingly, this area is inactive during dreams, and the actions we dream about doing are often as illogical as those of people with prefrontal cortex damage (Braun et al., 1998; Maquet et al., 1996).

The **premotor cortex** is active during preparations for a movement and less active during movement itself. It receives information about the target to which the body is directing its movement, as well as information about the body's current position and posture (Hoshi & Tanji, 2000). Both kinds of information are, of course, necessary to direct a movement toward a target.

Both the prefrontal cortex and the **supplementary motor cortex** are important for planning and organizing a rapid sequence of movements in a particular order (Shima, Isoda, Mushiake, & Tanji, 2007; Tanji & Shima, 1994). If you have a habitual action, such as turning left when you get to a certain corner, the supplementary motor cortex is essential for inhibiting that habit when you need to do something else (Isoda & Hikosaka, 2007).

The supplementary motor cortex becomes active during the second or two prior to a movement (Cunnington, Windischberger, & Moser, 2005). In one study, researchers electrically stimulated the supplementary motor cortex while people had their brains exposed in preparation for surgery. (Because the brain has no pain receptors, surgeons sometimes operate with only local anesthesia to the scalp.) Light stimulation of the supplementary motor cortex elicited reports of an "urge" to move some body part or an expectation that such a movement was about to start. Longer or stronger stimulation produced actual movements (I. Fried et al., 1991). Evidently, the difference between an urge to move and the start of a movement relates to the degree of activation.

STOP & CHECK

8. How does the posterior parietal cortex contribute to movement? The prefrontal cortex? The premotor cortex? The supplementary motor cortex?

ANSWER

8. The posterior parietal cortex is important for perceiving the location of objects and the position of the body relative to the environment, including those objects. The prefrontal cortex responds to sensory stimuli that call for some movement. The premotor cortex and supplementary motor cortex are active in preparing a movement immediately before it occurs.

Mirror Neurons

Of discoveries in neuroscience, one of the most exciting to psychologists has been **mirror neurons**, which are active both during preparation for a movement and while watching someone else perform the same or a similar movement (Iacoboni & Dapretto, 2006). Some cells respond to hearing an action (e.g., ripping a piece of paper) as well as seeing or doing it (Kohler et al., 2002). Cells in the insula (part of the cortex) become active when you see something disgusting, such as a filthy toilet, and when you see someone else show a facial expression of disgust (Wicker et al., 2003).

Mirror neurons were first reported in the premotor cortex of monkeys (Gallese, Fadiga, Fogassi, & Rizzolatti, 1996) and later in other areas and other species, including humans (Dinstein, Hasson, Rubin, & Heeger, 2007). These neurons are theoretically exciting because of the idea that they may be important for understanding other people, identifying with them, and imitating them. For example, children with autism seldom imitate other people, and they fail to form strong social bonds. Could their lack of socialization pertain to an absence of mirror neurons? Might the rise of mirror neurons have been the basis for forming human societies?

The possibilities are exciting, but before we speculate too far, important questions remain. Primarily, do mirror neurons *cause* imitation and social behavior, or do they *result from* them? Put another way, are we born with neurons that respond to the sight of a movement and also facilitate the same movement? If so, they could be important for social learning. However, another possibility is that we learn to identify with others and learn which visible movements correspond to movements of our own. In that case, mirror neurons do not cause imitation or socialization.

The answer may be different for different cells and different movements. Infants just a few days old do (in some cases) imitate a few facial movements, as shown in Figure 8.12. That result implies built-in mirror neurons that connect the sight of a movement to the movement itself (Meltzoff & Moore, 1977). Also, we so reliably laugh when others laugh that we are tempted (without evidence) to assume a built-in basis. However, consider another case. Researchers identified mirror neurons that responded both when people moved a certain finger, such as the index finger, and when they watched someone else move the same finger. Then they asked people to watch a display on the screen and move their index finger whenever the hand on the screen moved the little finger. They were to move their little finger whenever the hand on the screen moved the index finger. After some practice, these "mirror" neurons turned into "counter-mirror" neurons that responded to movements of one finger by that person and the sight of a different finger on the screen (Catmur, Walsh, & Heyes, 2007). In other words, at least some—probably many—mirror neurons develop their mirror quality by learning; they aren't born with it.

Furthermore, imitation is more complex than the idea of mirror neurons may suggest. Researchers examined people with brain damage who had difficulty imitating movements.

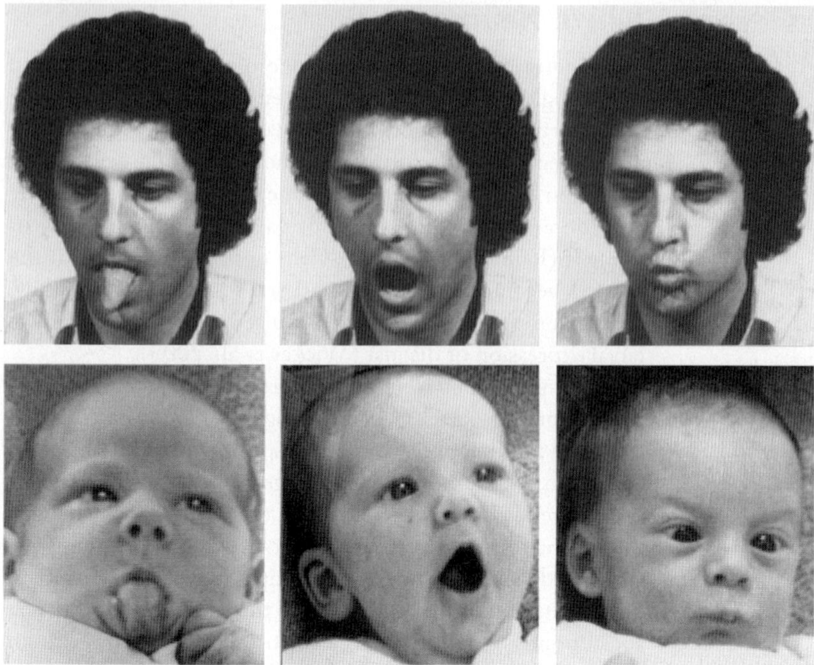

Figure 8.12 Infants in their first few days imitate certain facial expressions
These actions imply built-in mirror neurons. *(From: A.N. Meltzoff & M.K. Moore, "Imitation of facial and manual gestures by human neonates."* Science, 1977, 198, *75-78. Used by permission of Andrew N. Meltzoff, Ph.D.)*

The brain damage responsible for this difficulty varied depending on the body part. For example, the damage that impaired finger imitation was not the same as to the area that impaired hand imitation. The damage was centered in areas of the parietal and temporal cortex that are more important for perceptual processing than for motor control (Goldenberg & Karnath, 2006). Furthermore, studies of children with autism find that when they imitate, or try to imitate, other people's actions, they do show activity in the brain areas believed to contain mirror neurons (though the response is less extensive than in other people). Many other brain areas respond differently from average, however, so the problem is not a simple matter of lacking mirror neurons (J. H. G. Williams et al., 2006).

STOP & CHECK

9. When expert pianists listen to familiar, well-practiced music, they imagine the finger movements, and the finger area of their motor cortex becomes active, even if they are not moving their fingers (Haueisen & Knösche, 2001). If we regard those neurons as another kind of mirror neuron, what do these results tell us about the origin of mirror neurons?

ANSWER

9. These neurons must have acquired these properties through experience. That is, they did not enable pianists to copy what they hear; they developed after pianists learned to copy what they hear.

Conscious Decisions and Movements

Where does conscious decision come into all of this? Each of us has the feeling, "I consciously decide to do something, and then I do it." That sequence seems so obvious that we might not even question it, but research on the issue has found results that surprise most people.

Imagine yourself in the following study (Libet, Gleason, Wright, & Pearl, 1983). You are instructed to flex your wrist whenever you choose. That is, you don't choose which movement to make, but you can choose the time freely. You should not decide in advance when to move but let the urge occur as spontaneously as possible. The researchers take three measurements. First, they attach electrodes to your scalp to record evoked electrical activity over your motor cortex. Second, they attach a sensor to record when your hand starts to move. The third measurement is your self-report: You watch a clock-like device, as shown in Figure 8.13, in which a spot of light moves around the circle every 2.56 seconds. You are to watch that clock. Do not decide in advance that you will flex your wrist when the spot on the clock gets to a certain point. However, when you do decide to move, note where the spot of light is at that moment, and remember it so you can report it later.

The procedure starts. You think, "Not yet . . . not yet . . . not yet . . . NOW!" You note where the spot was at that critical instant and report, "I made my decision when the light was at the 25 position." The researchers compare your report to

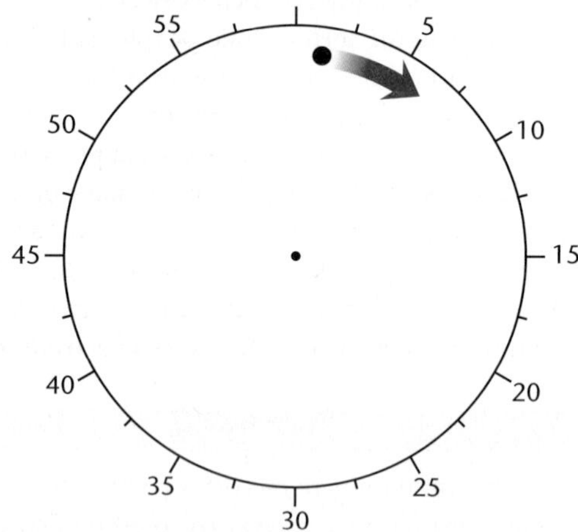

Figure 8.13 Procedure for a study of conscious decision and movement
As the light went rapidly around the circle, the participant was to make a spontaneous decision to move the wrist and remember where the light was at the time of that decision. *(From "Time of conscious intention to act in relation to onset of cerebral activities (readiness potential): The unconscious initiation of a freely voluntary act," by B. Libet et al., in* Brain, 106, 623–624 (12). *Reprinted by permission of Oxford University Press.)*

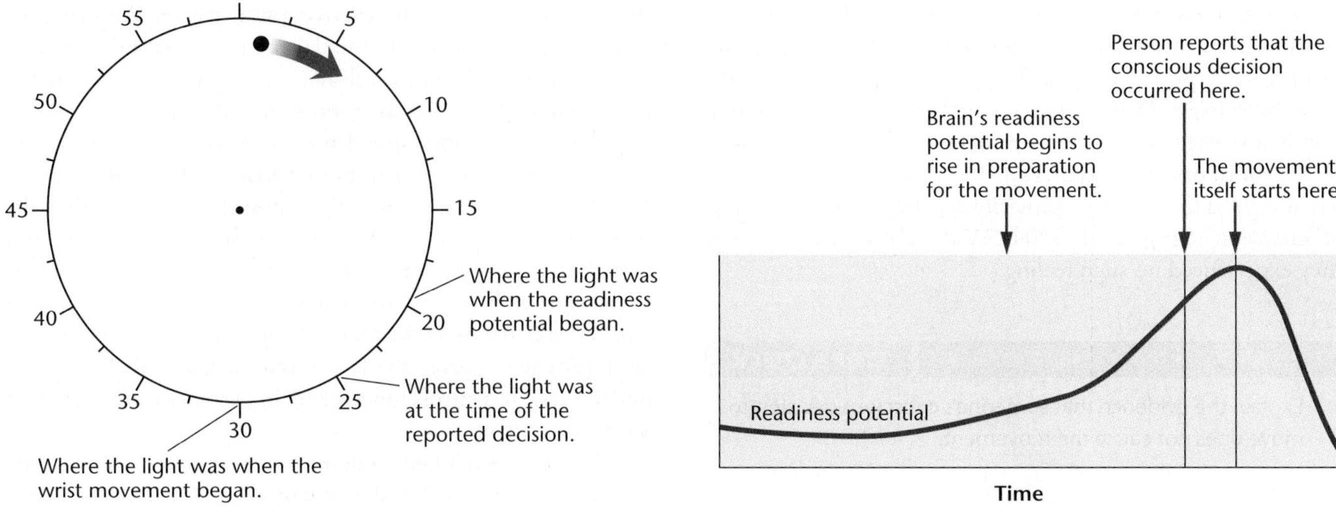

Figure 8.14 Results from study of conscious decision and movement
On the average, the brain's readiness potential began almost 300 ms before the reported decision, which occurred 200 ms before the movement.

their records of your brain activity and your wrist movement. On the average, people report that their decision to move occurred about 200 ms before the actual movement. (Note: It's the *decision* that occurred then. People make the *report* a few seconds later.) For example, if you reported that your decision to move occurred at position 25, your decision preceded the movement by 200 ms, so the movement itself began at position 30. (Remember, the light moves around the circle in 2.56 seconds.) However, your motor cortex produces a kind of activity called a **readiness potential** before any voluntary movement, and on the average, the readiness potential begins at least 500 ms before the movement. In this example, it would start when the light was at position 18, as illustrated in Figure 8.14.

The results varied among individuals, but most were similar. The key point is that the brain activity responsible for the movement apparently began *before* the person's conscious decision! The results seem to indicate that your conscious decision does not cause your action. Rather, you become conscious of the decision after the process leading to action has already been underway for about 300 milliseconds.

As you can imagine, this experiment has been controversial. The result itself has been replicated in several laboratories, so the facts are solid (e.g., Lau, Rogers, Haggard, & Passingham, 2004; Trevena & Miller, 2002). One challenge to the interpretation was that perhaps people cannot accurately report the time they become conscious of something. However, when people are asked to report the time of a sensory stimulus, or the time that they made a movement (instead of the decision to move), their estimates are usually within 30–50 ms of the correct time (Lau et al., 2004; Libet et al., 1983). That is, they cannot report the exact time when something happens, but they are close. In fact, their errors may be in the direction of estimating the time of an intention *earlier* than it was (Lau, Rogers, & Passingham, 2006).

A later study modified the procedure as follows: You watch a screen that displays letters of the alphabet, one at a time, changing every half-second. In this case, you choose not just when to act but which of two acts to do. The instruction is to decide at some point whether to press a button on the left or a button on the right, press it immediately, and remember what letter was on the screen at the moment when you *decided* which button to press. Meanwhile, the researchers record activity from several areas of your cortex. The result was that people usually reported a letter they saw within 1 second of making the response. Remember, the letters changed only twice a second, so it wasn't possible to determine the time of decision with great accuracy. However, it wasn't necessary, because parts of the frontal and parietal cortices showed activity specific to the left or right hand 7 to 10 seconds before the response (Soon, Brass, Heinze, & Haynes, 2008). That is, someone monitoring your cortex could, in this situation, predict which choice you were going to make a few seconds before you were aware of making the decision.

These studies imply that what we identify as a "conscious" decision is more the perception of an ongoing process than the cause of it. If so, we return to the issues raised in Chapter 1: What is the role of consciousness? Does it serve a useful function, and if so, what?

These results do not deny that you make a *voluntary* decision. The implication, however, is that your voluntary decision is, at first, unconscious. Just as a sensory stimulus has to reach a certain strength before it becomes conscious, your decision to do something has to reach a certain strength before it becomes conscious. Evidently, "voluntary" is not synonymous with "conscious."

Studies of patients with brain damage shed further light on the issue. Researchers used the spot-going-around-the-clock procedure with patients who had damage to the parietal cortex. These patients were just as accurate as other people in reporting when a tone occurred. However, if they tried to report when they formed an intention to make a hand movement, their report was virtually the same as the time of the movement itself. That is, they seemed unaware of any intention before they began the movement. Evidently, the parietal cortex monitors the preparation for a movement, including whatever it is that people ordinarily experience as their feeling of "intention" (Sirigu et al., 2004). Without the parietal cortex, they experienced no such feeling.

STOP & CHECK

10. Explain the evidence that someone's conscious decision to move does not cause the movement.

ANSWER

10. Researchers recorded responses in people's cortex that predicted the upcoming response, and those brain responses occurred earlier than the time people reported as "when they made the decision."

Connections From the Brain to the Spinal Cord

Messages from the brain must eventually reach the medulla and spinal cord, which control the muscles. Diseases of the spinal cord impair the control of movement in various ways, as listed in Table 8.1. Paths from the cerebral cortex to the spinal cord are called the **corticospinal tracts.** We have two such tracts, the lateral and medial corticospinal tracts. Nearly all movements rely on a combination of both tracts, but many movements rely on one tract more than the other.

The **lateral corticospinal tract** is a set of axons from the primary motor cortex, surrounding areas, and the **red nucleus,** a midbrain area that is primarily responsible for controlling the arm muscles (Figure 8.15). Axons of the lateral tract extend directly from the motor cortex to their target neurons in the spinal cord. In bulges of the medulla called *pyramids*, the lateral tract crosses to the contralateral (opposite) side of the spinal cord. (For that reason, the lateral tract is also called the pyramidal tract.) It controls movements in peripheral areas, such as the hands and feet.

Why does each hemisphere control the contralateral side instead of its own side? We do not know, but all vertebrates and many invertebrates have this pattern. In newborn humans, the immature primary motor cortex has partial control of both ipsilateral and contralateral muscles. As the contralateral control improves over the first year and a half of life, it displaces the ipsilateral control, which gradually becomes weaker. In some children with cerebral palsy, the contralateral path fails to mature, and the ipsilateral path remains relatively strong. The resulting competition causes clumsiness (Eyre, Taylor, Villagra, Smith, & Miller, 2001).

The **medial corticospinal tract** includes axons from many parts of the cerebral cortex, not just the primary motor cortex and surrounding areas. It also includes axons from the midbrain tectum, the reticular formation, and the **vestibular**

TABLE 8.1 Some Disorders of the Spinal Column

Disorder	Description	Cause
Paralysis	Lack of voluntary movement in part of the body.	Damage to spinal cord, motor neurons, or their axons.
Paraplegia	Loss of sensation and voluntary muscle control in both legs. Reflexes remain. Although no messages pass between the brain and the genitals, the genitals still respond reflexively to touch. Paraplegics have no genital sensations, but they can still experience orgasm (Money, 1967).	Cut through the spinal cord above the segments attached to the legs.
Quadriplegia	Loss of sensation and muscle control in all four extremities.	Cut through the spinal cord above the segments controlling the arms.
Hemiplegia	Loss of sensation and muscle control in the arm and leg on one side.	Cut halfway through the spinal cord or (more commonly) damage to one hemisphere of the cerebral cortex.
Tabes dorsalis	Impaired sensation in the legs and pelvic region, impaired leg reflexes and walking, loss of bladder and bowel control.	Late stage of syphilis. Dorsal roots of the spinal cord deteriorate.
Poliomyelitis	Paralysis.	Virus that damages cell bodies of motor neurons.
Amyotrophic lateral sclerosis	Gradual weakness and paralysis, starting with the arms and later spreading to the legs. Both motor neurons and axons from the brain to the motor neurons are destroyed.	Unknown.

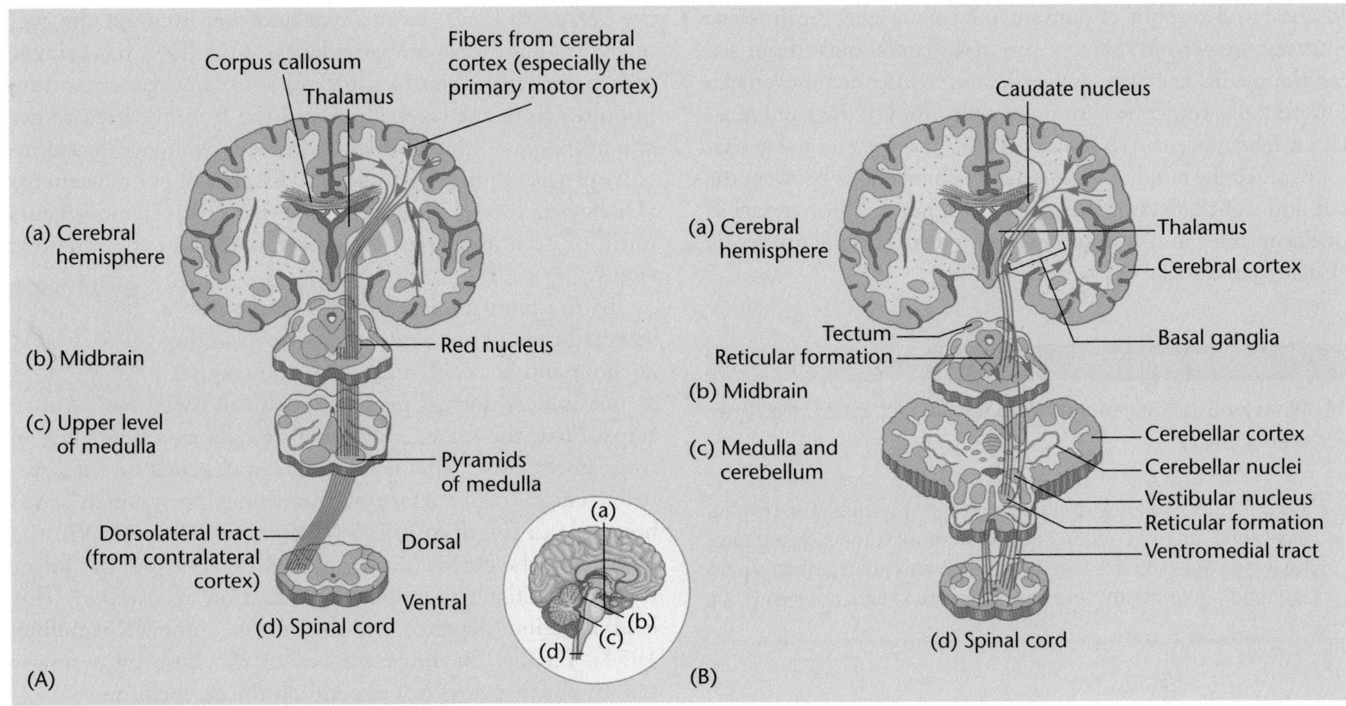

Figure 8.15 The lateral and medial corticospinal tracts
The lateral tract in part **(A)** crosses from one side of the brain to the opposite side of the spinal cord and controls precise and discrete movements of the extremities, such as hands, fingers, and feet. The medial tract in part **(B)** produces bilateral control of trunk muscles for postural adjustments and bilateral movements such as standing, bending, turning, and walking. The inset shows the locations of cuts a, b, c, and d.

nucleus, a brain area that receives input from the vestibular system (Figure 8.15). Axons of the medial tract go to *both* sides of the spinal cord, not just to the contralateral side. The medial tract controls mainly the muscles of the neck, shoulders, and trunk and therefore such movements as walking, turning, bending, standing up, and sitting down (Kuypers, 1989). Note that these movements are necessarily bilateral. You can move your fingers on just one side, but any movement of your neck or trunk must include both sides.

The functions of the lateral and medial tracts should be easy to remember: The lateral tract controls muscles in the lateral parts of the body, such as hands and feet. The medial tract controls muscles in the medial parts of the body, including trunk and neck.

Figure 8.15 compares the lateral and medial corticospinal tracts. Figure 8.16 compares the lateral tract to the spinal pathway bringing touch information to the cortex. Note that both paths cross in the medulla and that the touch information arrives at brain areas side by side with those areas responsible for motor control. Touch is obviously essential for movement. You have to know where your hands are and what they are feeling to control their next action.

Suppose someone suffers a stroke that damages the primary motor cortex of the left hemisphere. The result is a loss of the lateral tract from that hemisphere and a loss of movement control on the right side of the body. Eventually, depending on the

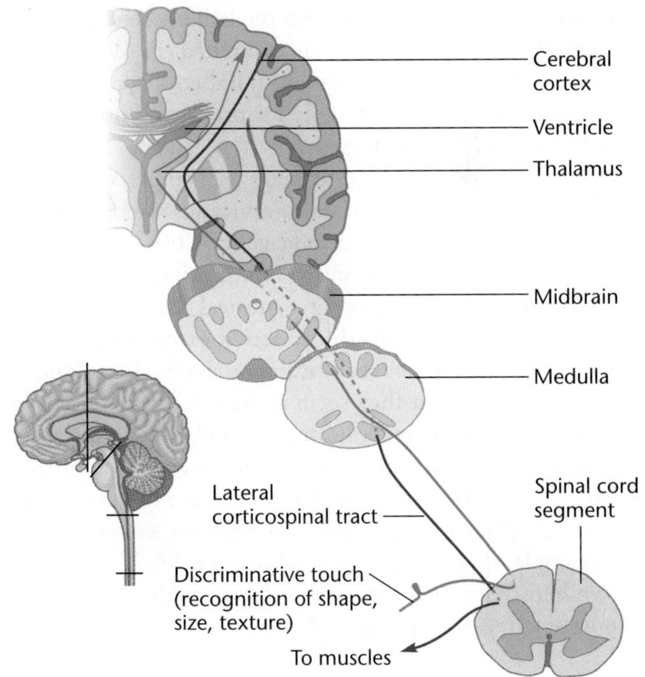

Figure 8.16 Comparison of touch path and lateral corticospinal tract
Both paths cross in the medulla so that each hemisphere has access to the opposite side of the body. The touch path goes from touch receptors toward the brain; the corticospinal path goes from the brain to the muscles.

location and amount of damage, the person may regain some muscle control from spared axons in the lateral tract. If not, using the medial tract can approximate the intended movement. For example, someone with no direct control of the hand muscles might move the shoulders, trunk, and hips in a way that repositions the hand. Also, because of connections between the left and right halves of the spinal cord, normal movements of one arm or leg induce associated movements on the other side (Edgley, Jankowska, & Hammar, 2004).

STOP & CHECK

11. What kinds of movements does the lateral tract control? The medial tract?

ANSWER

11. The lateral tract controls detailed movements in the periphery on the contralateral side of the body. (For example, the lateral tract from the left hemisphere controls the right side of the body.) The medial tract controls trunk movements bilaterally.

The Cerebellum

The term *cerebellum* is Latin for "little brain." Decades ago, the function of the cerebellum was described as "balance and coordination." Well, yes, people with cerebellar damage do lose balance and coordination, but that description understates the importance of this structure. The cerebellum contains more neurons than the rest of the brain combined (R. W. Williams & Herrup, 1988) and an enormous number of synapses. The cerebellum has far more capacity for processing information than its small size might suggest.

One effect of cerebellar damage is trouble with rapid movements that require accurate aim and timing. For example, people with cerebellar damage have trouble tapping a rhythm, clapping hands, pointing at a moving object, speaking, writing, typing, or playing a musical instrument. They are impaired at almost all athletic activities, except those like weightlifting that do not require aim or timing. Even long after the damage, when they seem to have recovered, they remain slow on sequences of movements and even on *imagining* sequences of movements (González, Rodríguez, Ramirez, & Sabate, 2005). They are normal, however, at a *continuous* motor activity (Spencer, Zelaznik, Diedrichsen, & Ivry, 2003). For example, they can draw continuous circles, like the ones shown here. Although the drawing has a rhythm, it does not require starting or stopping an action.

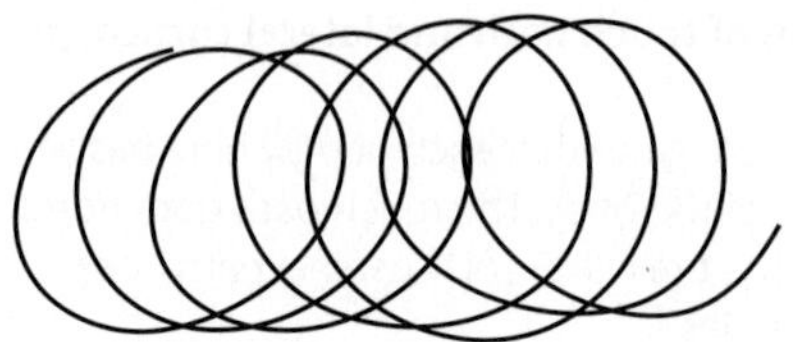

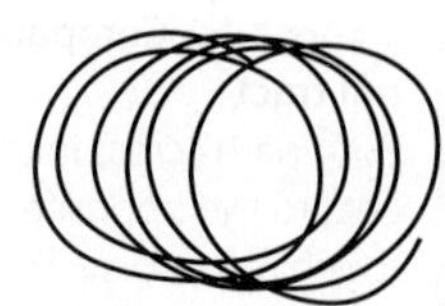

Here is a quick way to test someone's cerebellum: Ask the person to focus on one spot and then to move the eyes quickly to another spot. Saccades (sa-KAHDS), ballistic eye movements from one fixation point to another, depend on impulses from the cerebellum and the frontal cortex to the cranial nerves. Someone with cerebellar damage has difficulty programming the angle and distance of eye movements (Dichgans, 1984). The eyes make many short movements until, by trial and error, they eventually find the intended spot.

TRY IT YOURSELF

In the *finger-to-nose test,* the person is instructed to hold one arm straight out and then, at command, to touch his or her nose as quickly as possible. A normal person does so in three steps. First, the finger moves ballistically to a point just in front of the nose. This *move* function depends on the cerebellar cortex (the surface of the cerebellum), which sends messages to the deep nuclei (clusters of cell bodies) in the interior of the cerebellum (Figure 8.17). Second, the finger remains steady at that spot for a fraction of a second. This *hold* function depends on the nuclei alone (Kornhuber, 1974). Finally, the finger moves to the nose by a slower movement that does not depend on the cerebellum.

After damage to the cerebellar cortex, a person has trouble with the initial rapid movement. The finger stops too soon or goes too far, striking the face. If cerebellar nuclei have been damaged, the person may have difficulty with the hold segment: The finger reaches a point in front of the nose and then wavers.

The symptoms of cerebellar damage resemble those of alcohol intoxication: clumsiness, slurred speech, and inaccurate eye movements. A police officer testing someone for drunkenness may use the finger-to-nose test or similar tests because the cerebellum is one of the first brain areas that alcohol affects.

Role in Functions Other Than Movement

The cerebellum is not only a motor structure. In one study, functional MRI measured cerebellar activity while people performed several tasks (Gao et al., 1996). When they simply lifted objects, the cerebellum showed little activity. When they felt things with both hands to decide whether they were the same or different, the cerebellum was much more active. The cerebellum responded even when the experimenter rubbed an object across an unmoving hand. That is, the cerebellum responded to sensory stimuli even in the absence of movement.

What, then, is the role of the cerebellum? Masao Ito (1984) proposed that a key role is to establish new motor programs that enable one to execute a sequence of actions as a whole. Inspired by this idea, many researchers reported evidence that cerebellar damage impairs motor learning. Richard Ivry and his colleagues have emphasized the importance of the cerebellum for behaviors that depend on precise timing of short intervals (from about a millisecond to

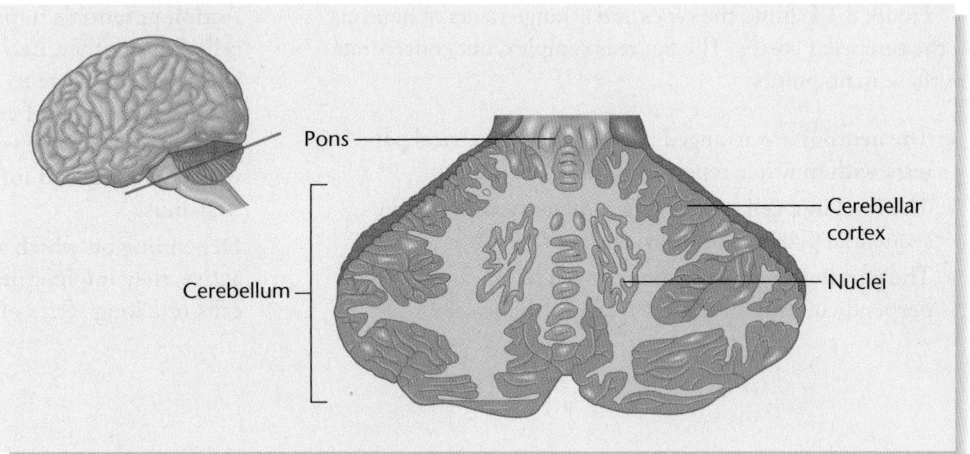

Figure 8.17 Location of the cerebellar nuclei relative to the cerebellar cortex
In the inset at the upper left, the line indicates the plane shown in detail at the lower right.

1.5 seconds). Any sequence of rapid movements obviously requires timing. Many perceptual and cognitive tasks also require timing—for example, judging which of two visual stimuli is moving faster or listening to two pairs of tones and judging whether the delay was longer between the first pair or the second pair.

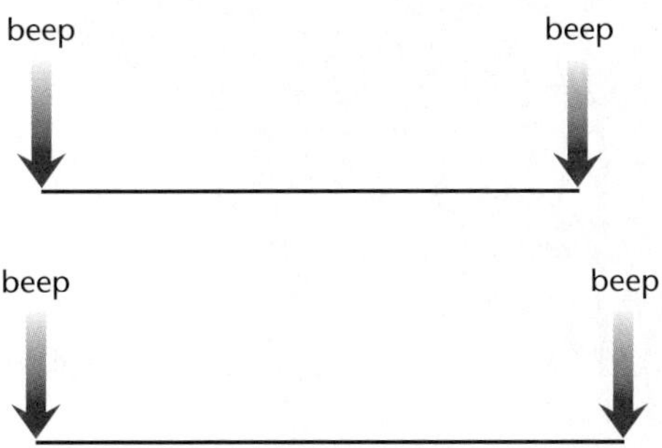

People who are accurate at one kind of timed movement, such as tapping a rhythm with a finger, tend also to be good at other timed movements, such as tapping a rhythm with a foot, and at judging which visual stimulus moved faster and which delay between tones was longer. People with cerebellar damage are impaired at all of these tasks but unimpaired at controlling the force of a movement or at judging which tone is louder (Ivry & Diener, 1991; Keele & Ivry, 1990). In short, the cerebellum is important mainly for tasks that require timing.

The cerebellum also appears critical for certain aspects of attention. For example, in one experiment, people were told to keep their eyes fixated on a central point. At various times, they would see the letter E on either the left or right half of the screen, and they were to indicate the direction in which it was oriented (E, Ǝ, Ш, or ᗰ) without moving their eyes. Sometimes, they saw a signal telling where the letter would be on the screen. For most people, that signal improved their performance even if it appeared just 100 ms before the letter. For people with cerebellar damage, the signal had to appear nearly a second before the letter to be helpful. Evidently, people with cerebellar damage need longer to shift their attention (Townsend et al., 1999).

Masao Ito

Brains seem to be built on several principles such that numerous neurons interact with each other through excitation and inhibition, that synaptic plasticity provides memory elements, that multi-layered neuronal networks bear a high computational power, and that combination of neuronal networks, sensors and effectors constitutes a neural system representing a brain function. Thus, Hebbian tradition has provided a very successful paradigm in modern neuroscience, but we may have to go beyond it in order to understand the entire functions of brains.

STOP & CHECK

12. What kind of perceptual task would be most impaired by damage to the cerebellum?

ANSWER

12. Damage to the cerebellum impairs perceptual tasks that depend on accurate timing.

Cellular Organization

The cerebellum receives input from the spinal cord, from each of the sensory systems by way of the cranial nerve nuclei, and from the cerebral cortex. That information eventually reaches the **cerebellar cortex,** the surface of the cerebellum (Figure 8.17).

Figure 8.18 shows the types and arrangements of neurons in the cerebellar cortex. The figure is complex, but concentrate on these main points:

- The neurons are arranged in a precise geometrical pattern, with multiple repetitions of the same units.
- The **Purkinje cells** are flat (two-dimensional) cells in sequential planes, parallel to one another.
- The **parallel fibers** are axons parallel to one another and perpendicular to the planes of the Purkinje cells.
- Action potentials in parallel fibers excite one Purkinje cell after another. Each Purkinje cell then transmits an inhibitory message to cells in the **nuclei of the cerebellum** (clusters of cell bodies in the interior of the cerebellum) and the vestibular nuclei in the brainstem, which in turn send information to the midbrain and the thalamus.
- Depending on which and how many parallel fibers are active, they might stimulate only the first few Purkinje cells or a long series of them. Because the parallel fibers'

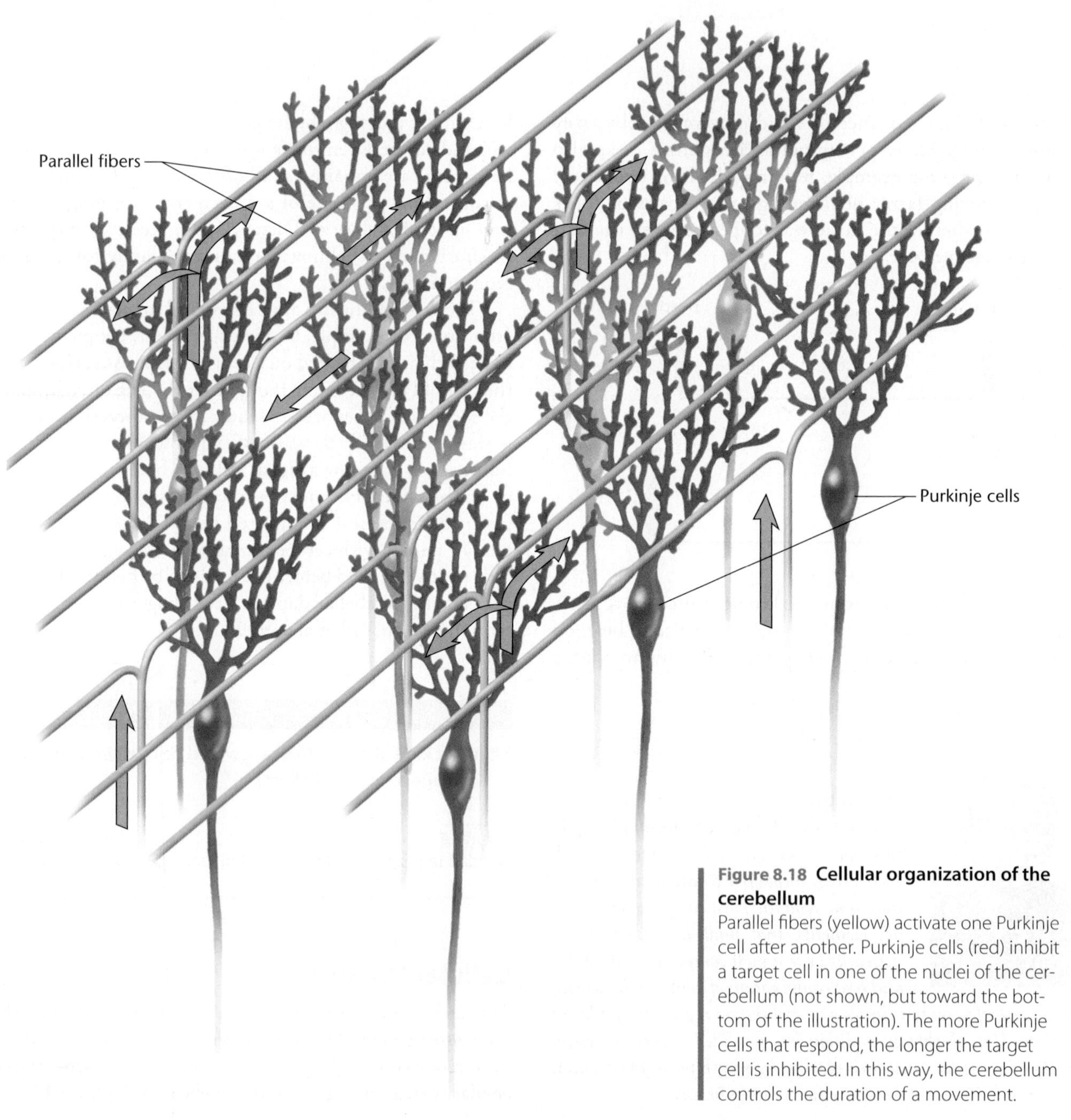

Figure 8.18 Cellular organization of the cerebellum
Parallel fibers (yellow) activate one Purkinje cell after another. Purkinje cells (red) inhibit a target cell in one of the nuclei of the cerebellum (not shown, but toward the bottom of the illustration). The more Purkinje cells that respond, the longer the target cell is inhibited. In this way, the cerebellum controls the duration of a movement.

messages reach different Purkinje cells one after another, the greater the number of excited Purkinje cells, the greater their collective *duration* of response. That is, if the parallel fibers stimulate only the first few Purkinje cells, the result is a brief message to the target cells; if they stimulate more Purkinje cells, the message lasts longer. The output of Purkinje cells controls the timing of a movement, including both its onset and offset (Thier, Dicke, Haas, & Barash, 2000).

STOP & CHECK

13. How are the parallel fibers arranged relative to one another and to the Purkinje cells?

14. If a larger number of parallel fibers are active, what is the effect on the collective output of the Purkinje cells?

ANSWERS

13. The parallel fibers are parallel to one another and perpendicular to the planes of the Purkinje cells. **14.** As a larger number of parallel fibers become active, the Purkinje cells increase their duration of response.

The Basal Ganglia

The term **basal ganglia** applies collectively to a group of large subcortical structures in the forebrain (Figure 8.19). (*Ganglia* is the plural of *ganglion*, so *ganglia* is a plural noun.) Various authorities differ in which structures they include as part of the basal ganglia, but everyone includes at least the **caudate nucleus,** the **putamen** (pyuh-TAY-men), and the **globus pallidus.** Input comes to the caudate nucleus and putamen, mostly from the cerebral cortex. Output from the caudate nucleus and putamen goes to the globus pallidus and from there mainly to the thalamus, which relays it to the cerebral cortex, especially its motor areas and the prefrontal cortex (Hoover & Strick, 1993).

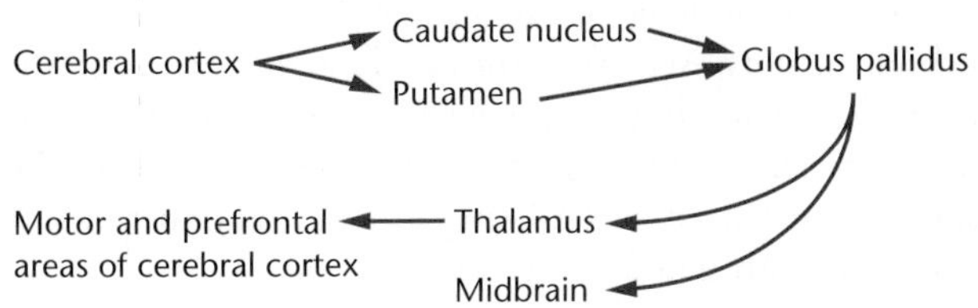

Most of the output from the globus pallidus to the thalamus releases GABA, an inhibitory transmitter, and neurons in the globus pallidus show much spontaneous activity. Thus, the globus pallidus is constantly inhibiting the thalamus. Input from the caudate nucleus and putamen tells the globus pallidus which movements to *stop inhibiting*. With extensive damage to the globus pallidus, as in people with Huntington's disease (which we shall consider later), the result is decreased inhibition and therefore many involuntary, jerky movements.

In effect, the basal ganglia select a movement by ceasing to inhibit it. This circuit is particularly important for self-initiated behaviors. For example, a monkey in one study was

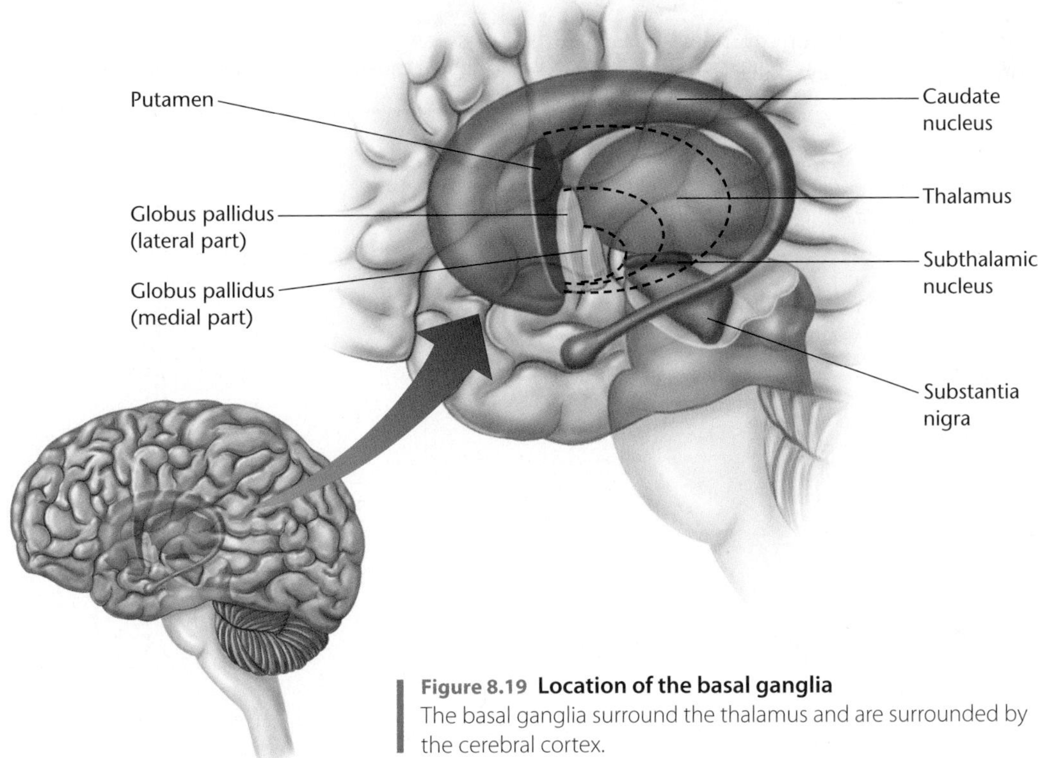

Figure 8.19 Location of the basal ganglia
The basal ganglia surround the thalamus and are surrounded by the cerebral cortex.

trained to move one hand to the left or right to receive food. On trials when it heard a signal indicating exactly when to move, the basal ganglia showed little activity. However, on other trials, the monkey saw a light indicating that it should start its movement in not less than 1.5 seconds and finish in not more than 3 seconds. Therefore, the monkey had to choose its own starting time. Under those conditions, the basal ganglia were highly active (Turner & Anderson, 2005).

In another study, people used a computer mouse to draw lines on a screen while researchers used PET scans to examine brain activity. Activity in the basal ganglia increased when people drew a new line but not when they traced a line already on the screen (Jueptner & Weiller, 1998). Again, the basal ganglia seem critical for initiating an action but not when the action is directly guided by a stimulus.

STOP & CHECK

15. Why does damage to the basal ganglia lead to involuntary movements?

ANSWER

15. Output from the basal ganglia to the thalamus releases the inhibitory transmitter GABA. Ordinarily, the basal ganglia produce steady output, inhibiting all movements or all except the ones selected at the time. After damage to the basal ganglia, the thalamus, and therefore the cortex, receive less inhibition. Thus, they produce unwanted actions.

Brain Areas and Motor Learning

Of all the brain areas responsible for control of movement, which are important for learning new skills? The apparent answer is all of them.

Neurons in the motor cortex adjust their responses as a person or animal learns a motor skill. At first, movements are slow and inconsistent. As movements become faster, relevant neurons in the motor cortex increase their firing rates (D. Cohen & Nicolelis, 2004). After prolonged training, the movement patterns become more consistent from trial to trial, and so do the patterns of activity in the motor cortex. In engineering terms, the motor cortex increases its signal-to-noise ratio (Kargo & Nitz, 2004).

TRY IT YOURSELF

The basal ganglia are critical for learning new habits (Yin & Knowlton, 2006). For example, when you are first learning to drive a car, you have to think about everything you do. Eventually, you learn to signal for a left turn, change gears, turn the wheel, and change speed all at once. If you try to explain exactly what you do, you will probably find it difficult. Similarly, if you know how to tie a man's necktie, try explaining it to someone who doesn't know—without any hand gestures. Or explain to someone how to draw a spiral without using the word *spiral* and without any gestures. People with basal ganglia damage are impaired at learning motor skills like these and at converting new movements into smooth, "automatic" responses (Poldrack et al., 2005; Willingham, Koroshetz, & Peterson, 1996).

STOP & CHECK

16. What kind of learning depends most heavily on the basal ganglia?

ANSWER

16. The basal ganglia are essential for learning motor habits that are difficult to describe in words.

MODULE 8.2 IN CLOSING

Movement Control and Cognition

It is tempting to describe behavior in three steps—first we perceive, then we think, and finally we act. The brain does not handle the process in such discrete steps. For example, the posterior parietal cortex monitors the position of the body relative to visual space and thereby helps guide movement. Thus, its functions are sensory, cognitive, and motor. The cerebellum has traditionally been considered a major part of the motor system, but it is now known to be important in timing sensory processes. People with basal ganglia damage are slow to start or select a movement. They are also often described as cognitively slow; that is, they hesitate to make any kind of choice. In short, organizing a movement is not something we tack on at the end of our thinking. It is intimately intertwined with all of our sensory and cognitive processes. The study of movement is not just the study of muscles. It is the study of how we decide what to do.

SUMMARY

1. The primary motor cortex is the main source of brain input to the spinal cord. The spinal cord contains central pattern generators that actually control the muscles. **235**
2. The primary motor cortex produces patterns representing the intended outcome, not just the muscle contractions. **235**
3. Areas near the primary motor cortex—including the prefrontal, premotor, and supplementary motor cortices—are active in detecting stimuli for movement and preparing for a movement. **236**
4. Mirror neurons in various brain areas respond to both a self-produced movement and an observation of a similar movement by another individual. Although some neurons may have built-in mirror properties, at least some of them acquire these properties by learning. Their role in imitation and social behavior is potentially important but as yet speculative. **237**
5. When people identify the instant when they formed a conscious intention to move, their time precedes the actual movement by about 200 ms but follows the start of motor cortex activity by about 300 ms. These results suggest that what we call a conscious decision is our perception of a process already underway, not really the cause of it. **238**
6. People with damage to part of the parietal cortex fail to perceive any intention prior to the start of their own movements. **239**
7. The lateral tract, which controls movements in the periphery of the body, has axons that cross from one side of the brain to the opposite side of the spinal cord. The medial tract controls bilateral movements near the midline of the body. **240**
8. The cerebellum is critical for rapid movements that require accurate aim and timing. **242**
9. The cerebellum has multiple roles in behavior, including sensory functions related to perception of the timing or rhythm of stimuli. **242**
10. The cells of the cerebellum are arranged in a regular pattern that enables them to produce outputs of precisely controlled duration. **244**
11. The basal ganglia are a group of large subcortical structures that are important for selecting and inhibiting particular movements. Damage to the output from the basal ganglia leads to jerky, involuntary movements. **245**
12. The learning of a motor skill depends on changes occurring in both the cerebral cortex and the basal ganglia. **246**

KEY TERMS

Terms are defined in the module on the page number indicated. They're also presented in alphabetical order with definitions in the book's Subject Index/Glossary. Interactive flashcards, audio reviews, and crossword puzzles are among the online resources available to help you learn these terms and the concepts they represent.

basal ganglia **245**
caudate nucleus **245**
cerebellar cortex **243**
corticospinal tracts **240**
globus pallidus **245**
lateral corticospinal tract **240**
medial corticospinal tract **240**
mirror neurons **237**
nuclei of the cerebellum **244**
parallel fibers **244**
posterior parietal cortex **236**
prefrontal cortex **237**
premotor cortex **237**
primary motor cortex **235**
Purkinje cells **244**
putamen **245**
readiness potential **239**
red nucleus **240**
supplementary motor cortex **237**
vestibular nucleus **240**

THOUGHT QUESTION

Human infants are at first limited to gross movements of the trunk, arms, and legs. The ability to move one finger at a time matures gradually over at least the first year. What hypothesis would you suggest about which brain areas controlling movement mature early and which areas mature later?

MODULE 8.3

Movement Disorders

If you have damage in your spinal cord, peripheral nerves, or muscles, you can't move, but cognitively, you are the same as ever. In contrast, brain disorders that impair movement also impair mood, memory, and cognition. We consider two examples: Parkinson's disease and Huntington's disease.

Parkinson's Disease

The symptoms of **Parkinson's disease** (also known as *Parkinson disease*) are rigidity, muscle tremors, slow movements, and difficulty initiating physical and mental activity (M. T. V. Johnson et al., 1996; Manfredi, Stocchi, & Vacca, 1995; Pillon et al., 1996). It strikes about 1% to 2% of people over age 65. In addition to the motor problems, patients are slow on cognitive tasks, such as imagining events or actions, even when they don't have to do anything (Sawamoto, Honda, Hanakawa, Fukuyama, & Shibasaki, 2002). Most patients also become depressed at an early stage, and many show deficits of memory and reasoning. These mental symptoms are probably part of the disease itself, not just a reaction to the muscle failures (Ouchi et al., 1999).

People with Parkinson's disease are not paralyzed or weak. They are impaired at initiating spontaneous movements in the absence of stimuli to guide their actions. Parkinsonian patients sometimes walk surprisingly well when following a parade, when walking up a flight of stairs, or when walking across lines drawn at one-step intervals (Teitelbaum, Pellis, & Pellis, 1991).

The slowness of movements by Parkonsonian patients enabled researchers to address a question that pertains to everyone's movement: What controls the speed of our movements? You might notice that almost everyone reaches for a coffee cup at almost exactly the same speed. Similarly, we have a typical speed for lighting a match, shaking hands, chewing food, and so on. Why? One hypothesis is that we choose a trade-off between speed and accuracy. For example, maybe if we reached faster for that cup of coffee, we would spill it. Observations of Parkinsonian patients contradict that idea. Although they are typically slow, they can speed up (temporarily) when instructed to do so, without any loss of accuracy. Therefore, their slower speed is not due to the relationship between speed and accuracy. They move slowly because their movements require more effort, as if their arms and legs were carrying heavy weights (Mazzoni, Hristrova, & Krakauer, 2007). Similarly, for all of us, we probably choose the speed of movement that requires the least effort and energy.

Possible Causes

The immediate cause of Parkinson's disease is the gradual progressive death of neurons, especially in the substantia nigra, which sends dopamine-releasing axons to the caudate nucleus and putamen. People with Parkinson's disease lose these axons and therefore dopamine. Dopamine excites the caudate nucleus and putamen, and a decrease in that excitation causes decreased inhibition of the globus pallidus. The result is *increased inhibition* of the thalamus and therefore *decreased excitation* of the cerebral cortex, as shown in Figure 8.20 (Wichmann, Vitek, & DeLong, 1995; Yin & Knowlton, 2006). In summary, a loss of dopamine activity leads to less stimulation of the motor cortex and slower onset of movements (Parr-Brownlie & Hyland, 2005).

Researchers estimate that the average person over age 45 loses substantia nigra neurons at a rate of almost 1% per year. Most people have enough to spare, but some people start with fewer or lose them faster. If the number of surviving substantia nigra neurons declines below 20%–30% of normal, Parkinsonian symptoms begin (Knoll, 1993). Symptoms become more severe as the cell loss continues.

In the late 1990s, the news media excitedly reported that researchers had located a gene that causes Parkinson's disease. That report was misleading. The research had found certain families in which people sharing a particular gene all developed Parkinson's disease with onset before age 50 (Shimura et al., 2001). Since then, several other genes have been found that lead to early-onset Parkinson's disease (Bonifati et al., 2003; Singleton et al., 2003; Valente et al., 2004). However, these genes are not linked to later-onset Parkinson's disease, which is far more common. Several other genes are linked to late-onset Parkinson's disease, including one gene that controls apoptosis (Maraganore et al., 2005; E. R. Martin et al., 2001; W. K. Scott et al., 2001). However, each of these genes has only a small impact. For example, one gene occurs in 82%

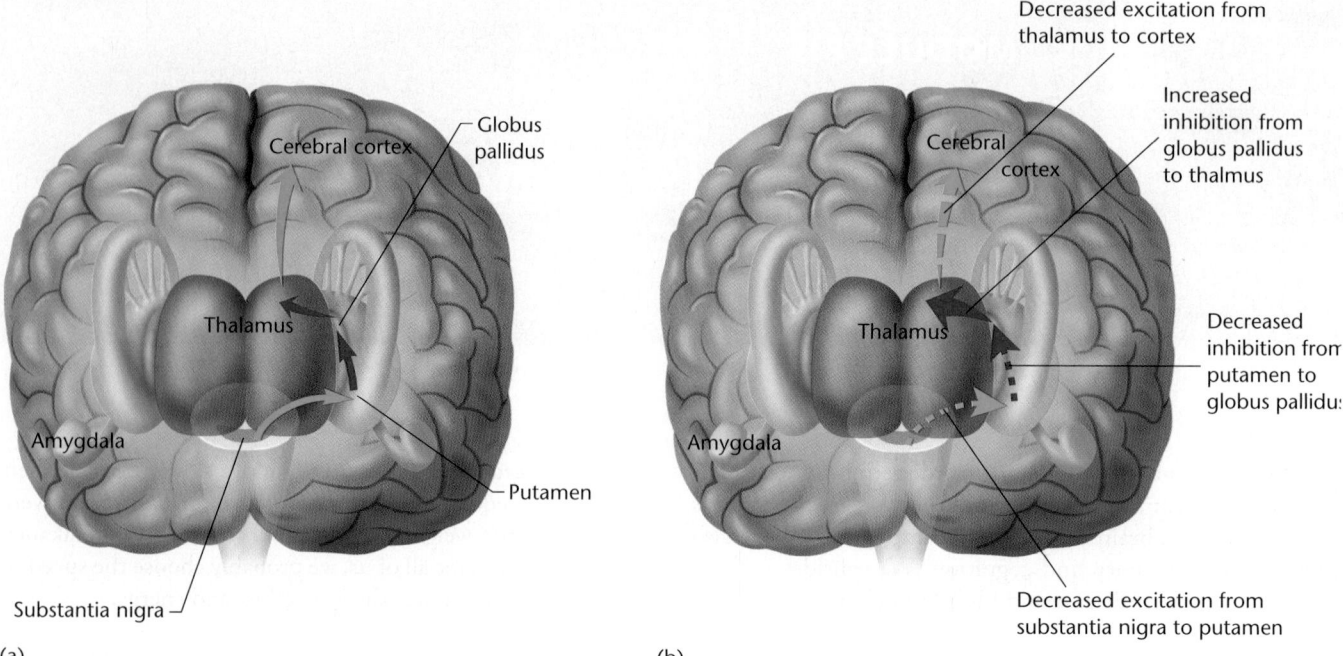

Figure 8.20 Connections from the substantia nigra: (a) normal and (b) in Parkinson's disease
Excitatory paths are shown in green; inhibitory are in red. Decreased excitation from the substantia nigra decreases inhibition from the putamen, leading to increased inhibition from the globus pallidus. The net result is decreased excitation from the thalamus to the cortex. *(Based on Yin & Knowlton, 2006)*

of the people with Parkinson's disease and in 79% of those without it.

One study examined Parkinson's patients who had twins. As shown in Figure 8.21, if you have a monozygotic (MZ) twin who develops early-onset Parkinson's disease, you are almost certain to get it, too. However, if your twin develops Parkinson's disease after age 50, your risk is the same *regardless* of whether your twin is monozygotic or dizygotic (Tanner et al., 1999). Equal concordance for both kinds of twins implies low heritability. However, this study had a small sample size. An additional

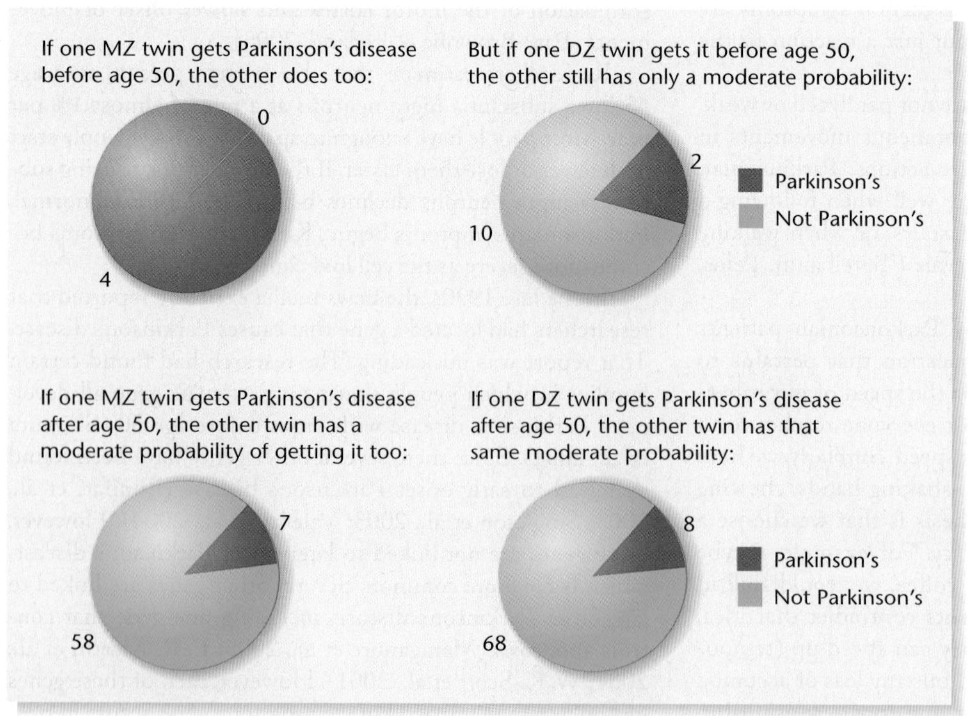

But if one DZ twin gets it before age 50, the other still has only a moderate probability:

Figure 8.21 Probability of developing Parkinson's disease if you have a twin who developed the disease before or after age 50
Having a monozygotic (MZ) twin develop Parkinson's disease before age 50 means that you are very likely to get it, too. A dizygotic (DZ) twin who gets it before age 50 does not pose the same risk. Therefore, early-onset Parkinson's disease shows a strong genetic component. However, if your twin develops Parkinson's disease later (as is more common), your risk is the same regardless of whether you are a monozygotic or dizygotic twin. Therefore, late-onset Parkinson's disease has low heritability. *(Based on data of Tanner et al., 1999)*

problem is that many twins who did not show symptoms at the time of the study might have developed them later. A study using brain scans found that many monozygotic twins without symptoms of Parkinson's disease did have indications of minor damage in the dopamine pathways (Piccini, Burn, Ceravolo, Maraganore, & Brooks, 1999). The consensus is that genes do influence the risk of late-onset Parkinson's disease, although not as strongly as they do the early-onset condition.

STOP & CHECK

17. Do monozygotic twins resemble each other more than dizygotic twins do for early-onset Parkinson's disease? For late-onset? What conclusion do these results imply?

ANSWER

17. Monozygotic twins resemble each other more than dizygotic twins do for early-onset Parkinson's disease, but not for late-onset. The conclusion is that early-onset Parkinson's disease has high heritability and late-onset does not.

What environmental influences might be relevant? An accidental discovery implicated exposure to toxins (Ballard, Tetrud, & Langston, 1985). In northern California in 1982, several young adults developed symptoms of Parkinson's disease after using a drug similar to heroin. Before the investigators could alert the community to the danger, many other users had developed symptoms ranging from mild to fatal (Tetrud, Langston, Garbe, & Ruttenber, 1989). The substance responsible for the symptoms was **MPTP,** a chemical that the body converts to **MPP$^+$**, which accumulates in, and then destroys, neurons that release dopamine[1] (Nicklas, Saporito, Basma, Geller, & Heikkila, 1992). Postsynaptic neurons react to the loss of input by increasing their number of dopamine receptors, as shown in Figure 8.22 (Chiueh, 1988).

No one supposes that Parkinson's disease is often the result of using illegal drugs. A more likely hypothesis is that people are sometimes exposed to MPTP or similar chemicals in herbicides and pesticides (Figure 8.23), many of which can damage cells of the substantia nigra. For example, rats exposed to the pesticide *rotenone* develop a condition closely resembling human Parkinson's disease (Betarbet et al., 2000). Parkinson's disease is more common than average among farmers and others who have had years of exposure to herbicides and pesticides (T. P. Brown, Rumsby, Capleton, Rushton, & Levy, 2006). Prenatal exposure to elevated levels of iron increases the later vulnerability if someone is exposed to herbicides and pesticides (Peng, Peng, Stevenson, Doctrow, & Andersen, 2007).

What else might influence the risk of Parkinson's disease? Researchers have compared the lifestyles of people who did and didn't develop the disease. One factor that stands out consistently is cigarette smoking and coffee drinking: People who smoke cigarettes or drink coffee have less chance of developing Parkinson's disease (Ritz et al., 2007). (Read that sentence again.) One study took questionnaire results from more than a thousand pairs of young adult twins and compared the results to medical records decades later. Of the twins who had never smoked, 18.4% developed Parkinson's disease. In contrast, 13.8% of the smokers developed the disease, and only 11.6% of the heaviest smokers developed it (Wirdefeldt, Gatz, Pawitan, & Pedersen, 2005). A study of U.S. adults compared coffee drinking in middle-aged adults to their medical histories later in life. Drinking coffee decreased the risk of Parkinson's disease, especially for men (Ascherio et al., 2004). Needless to say, smoking cigarettes increases the risk of lung cancer and other diseases more than it decreases the risk of Parkinson's disease. Coffee has less benefit for decreasing Parkinson's dis-

[1] The full names of these chemicals are 1-methyl-4 phenyl-1,2,3,6-tetrahydropyridine and 1-methyl-4-phenylpyridinium ion. (Let's hear it for abbreviations!)

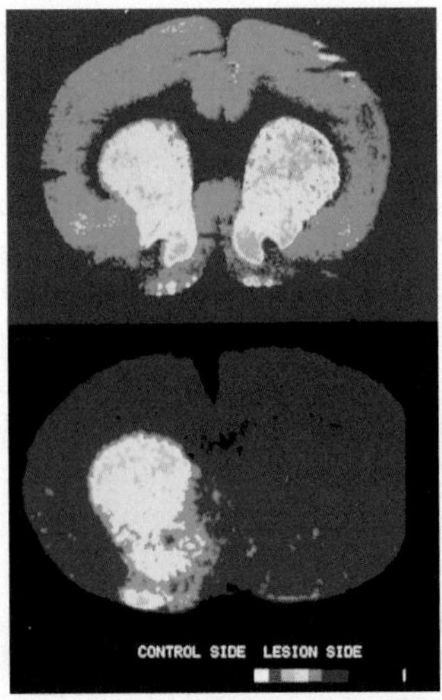

Figure 8.22 Results of injecting MPP into one hemisphere of the rat brain
The autoradiography above shows D_2 dopamine receptors; the one below shows axon terminals that contain dopamine. Red indicates the highest level of activity, followed by yellow, green, and blue. Note that the MPP$^+$ greatly depleted the number of dopamine axons and that the number of D_2 receptors increased in response to this lack of input. However, the net result is a great decrease in dopamine activity. *(From "Dopamine in the extrapyramidal motor function: A study based upon the MPTP-induced primate model of Parkinsonism," by C. C. Chiueh, 1988, Annals of the New York Academy of Sciences, 515, p. 223. Reprinted by permission.)*

CH_3 N $O_2CC_2H_5$ — MPPP
CH_3 N — MPTP
CH_3 ^+N — MPP$^+$
CH_3 ^+N ^+N CH_3 — Paraquat

Figure 8.23 The chemical structures of MPPP, MPTP, MPP$^+$, and paraquat
Exposure to paraquat and similar herbicides and pesticides may increase the risk of Parkinson's disease.

ease, but it's safer than smoking. In contrast to the effects of tobacco, marijuana increases the risk of Parkinson's disease (Glass, 2001). Researchers do not yet know how any of these drugs alters the risk of Parkinson's disease.

In short, Parkinson's disease probably results from a mixture of causes. What they have in common is damage to the mitochondria. When a neuron's mitochondria begin to fail—because of genes, toxins, infections, or whatever—a chemical called α-synuclein clots into clusters that damage neurons containing dopamine (Dawson & Dawson, 2003). Dopamine-containing neurons are especially vulnerable to damage from almost any metabolic problem (Zeevalk, Manzino, Hoppe, & Sonsalla, 1997).

STOP & CHECK

18. How does MPTP exposure influence the likelihood of Parkinson's disease? What are the effects of cigarette smoking?

ANSWER

18. Exposure to MPTP can induce symptoms of Parkinson's disease. Cigarette smoking is correlated with decreased prevalence of the disease.

L-Dopa Treatment

If Parkinson's disease results from a dopamine deficiency, then a logical goal is to restore the missing dopamine. A dopamine pill would be ineffective because dopamine does not cross the blood-brain barrier. **L-dopa,** a precursor to dopamine, does cross the barrier. Taken as a daily pill, L-dopa reaches the brain, where neurons convert it to dopamine. L-dopa is the main treatment for Parkinson's disease.

However, L-dopa is disappointing in several ways. First, it is ineffective for some patients, especially those in the late stages of the disease. Losing dopamine cells in one brain area and then supplying extra dopamine steadily throughout the brain does not bring someone back to normal. Abnormalities persist in the rate, pattern, and synchrony of neural activity in the basal ganglia (Heimer et al., 2006). Second, L-dopa does not prevent the continued loss of neurons. Third, L-dopa produces unpleasant side effects such as nausea, restlessness, sleep problems, low blood pressure, repetitive movements, hallucinations, and delusions.

STOP & CHECK

19. How does L-dopa relieve the symptoms of Parkinson's disease?

20. In what ways is L-dopa treatment disappointing?

ANSWERS

19. L-dopa enters the brain, where neurons convert it to dopamine, thus increasing the supply of a depleted neurotransmitter. **20.** L-dopa is ineffective for some people and has only limited benefits for most others. It does not stop the loss of neurons. It has unpleasant side effects.

Other Therapies

Given the limitations of L-dopa, researchers have sought alternatives and supplements. The following possibilities show promise (Chan et al., 2007; Kreitzer & Malenka, 2007; Siderowf & Stern, 2003; Wu & Frucht, 2005):

- Antioxidant drugs to decrease further damage
- Drugs that directly stimulate dopamine receptors
- Drugs that inhibit glutamate or adenosine receptors
- Drugs that block one type of calcium channel that becomes more abundant in old age (The drugs therefore force neurons to rely on the types of calcium channel that are more typical of youth.)
- Drugs that stimulate cannabinoid receptors
- Neurotrophins to promote survival and growth of the remaining neurons
- Drugs that decrease apoptosis (programmed cell death) of the remaining neurons
- High-frequency electrical stimulation of the globus pallidus or the subthalamic nucleus

High-frequency electrical stimulation is especially effective for blocking tremor and enhancing movement. However, it also leads to depressed mood by inhibiting serotonin release (Temel et al., 2007). By scrambling activity in the subthalamic nucleus, it leads to impulsive decision making (M. J. Frank, Samanta, Moustafa, & Sherman, 2007).

A potentially exciting strategy has been "in the experimental stage" since the 1980s. In a pioneering study, M. J. Perlow and colleagues (1979) injected the chemical 6-OHDA (a chemical modification of dopamine) into rats to damage the substantia nigra of one hemisphere, producing Parkinson's-type symptoms on the opposite side of the body. After the movement abnormalities stabilized, the experimenters removed the substantia nigra from rat fetuses and transplanted them into the damaged brains. Four weeks later, most recipients had recovered much of their normal movement. Control animals that suffered the same brain damage without receiving grafts showed little or no behavioral recovery. This is only a partial brain transplant, but still, the Frankensteinian implications are striking.

If such surgery works for rats, might it also for humans? The procedure itself is feasible. Perhaps because the blood-brain barrier protects the brain from foreign substances, the immune system is less active in the brain than elsewhere (Nicholas & Arnason, 1992), and physicians can give drugs to further suppress rejection of the transplanted tissue. However, only immature cells transplanted from a fetus can make connections, and simply making connections is not enough. In laboratory research, the recipient animal still has to relearn the behaviors dependent on those cells (Brasted, Watts, Robbins, & Dunnett, 1999). In effect, the animal has to practice using the transplanted cells.

Ordinarily, scientists test any experimental procedure extensively with laboratory animals before trying it on humans, but with Parkinson's disease, the temptation was too great. People in the late stages have little to lose and are willing to try almost anything. The obvious problem is where to get the donor tissue. Several early studies used tissue from the patient's own adrenal gland. Although that tissue is not composed of neurons, it produces and releases dopamine. Unfortunately, the adrenal gland transplants seldom produced much benefit (Backlund et al., 1985).

Another possibility is to transplant brain tissue from aborted fetuses. Fetal neurons transplanted into the brains of Parkinson's patients sometimes survive for years and make synapses with the patient's own cells. However, the operation is difficult and expensive, requiring brain tissue from four to eight aborted fetuses. One way to decrease the need for aborted fetuses is to grow cells in tissue culture, genetically alter them so that they produce large quantities of L-dopa, and then transplant them into the brain (Ljungberg, Stern, & Wilkin, 1999; Studer, Tabar, & McKay, 1998). That idea is particularly attractive if the cells grown in tissue culture are **stem cells**, immature cells that are capable of differentiating into a wide variety of other cell types. Researchers are developing methods to modify adult cells into stem cells so that they might take a patient's own cells and make them suitable for transplants into the brain (Park et al., 2008).

Unfortunately, the results so far with either fetal tissue or stem cells show only modest benefits at best (Freed et al., 2001; Lindvall, Kokaia, & Martinez-Serrano, 2004; Olanow et al., 2003). One limitation is that surgeons usually limit this procedure to aged patients in an advanced stage of the disease. Animal studies find that transplants work best if the damaged area is small and the surrounding cells are healthy (Breysse, Carlsson, Winkler, Björklund, & Kirik, 2007). By the time people reach the stage where surgery seems worth a try, it may be too late to do much good.

The research on brain transplants has suggested yet another possibility for treatment. In several experiments, the transplanted tissue failed to survive, or differentiated into cells other than dopamine cells, but the recipient showed behavioral recovery anyway (Redmond et al., 2007). In many cases, the transplanted tissue releases neurotrophins that stimulate axon and dendrite growth in the recipient's own brain. Providing neurotrophins may be a useful therapy if researchers can find a way to deliver them to the appropriate brain areas (Lindholm et al., 2007). (Neurotrophins do not cross the blood-brain barrier.)

For the latest information about Parkinson's disease, visit the Website of the World Parkinson Disease Association: http://www.wpda.org/

STOP & CHECK

21. What are some possible treatments for Parkinson's disease other than L-dopa?

ANSWER

21. Possible treatments include antioxidants, drugs that stimulate dopamine receptors, drugs that block glutamate or adenosine receptors, neurotrophins, drugs that decrease apoptosis, high-frequency electrical stimulation of the globus pallidus, and transplants of neurons or stem cells.

Huntington's Disease

Huntington's disease (also known as *Huntington disease* or *Huntington's chorea*) is a severe neurological disorder that strikes about 1 person in 10,000 in the United States (A. B. Young, 1995). Motor symptoms usually begin with arm jerks and facial twitches, and then tremors spread to other parts of the body and develop into writhing (M. A. Smith, Brandt, & Shadmehr, 2000). (*Chorea* comes from the same root as *choreography*. The rhythmic writhing of chorea resembles dancing.) Gradually, the tremors interfere more and more with walking, speech, and other voluntary movements. The ability to learn and improve new movements is especially limited (Willingham et al., 1996). The disorder is associated with gradual, extensive brain damage, especially in the caudate nucleus, putamen, and globus pallidus but also in the cerebral cortex (Tabrizi et al., 1999) (Figure 8.24).

People with Huntington's disease also suffer psychological disorders, including depression, sleep disorders, memory impairment, anxiety, hallucinations and delusions, poor judgment, alcoholism, drug abuse, and sexual disorders ranging from complete unresponsiveness to indiscriminate promiscuity (Shoulson, 1990). The psychological disorders often develop before the motor disorders, and some individuals in the early stages of Huntington's disease are misdiagnosed as having schizophrenia.

Huntington's disease most often appears between the ages of 30 and 50, although onset can occur at any time from early childhood to old age. Once the symptoms emerge, both the psychological and the motor symptoms grow progressively worse and culminate in death. People with earlier onset deteriorate more rapidly. At this point, no effective treatment is available.

Heredity and Presymptomatic Testing

Huntington's disease is controlled by an autosomal dominant gene (i.e., one not on the X or Y chromosome). As a rule, a mutant gene that causes the loss of a function is recessive. The

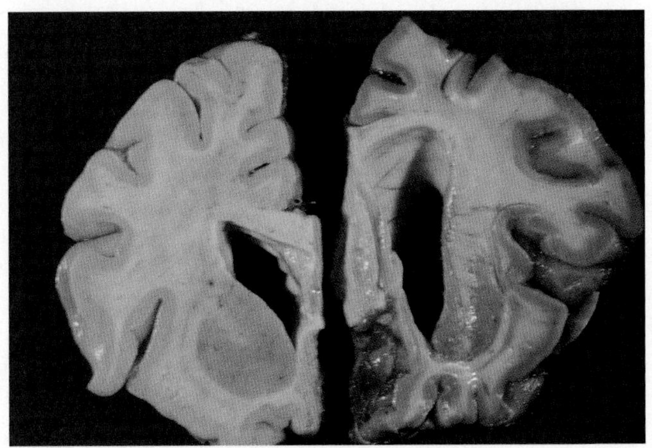

Robert E. Schmidt, Washington University

Figure 8.24 Brain of a normal person (left) and a person with Huntington's disease (right)
The angle of cut through the normal brain makes the lateral ventricle look larger in this photo than it actually is. Even so, note how much larger it is in the patient with Huntington's disease. The ventricles expand because of the loss of neurons.

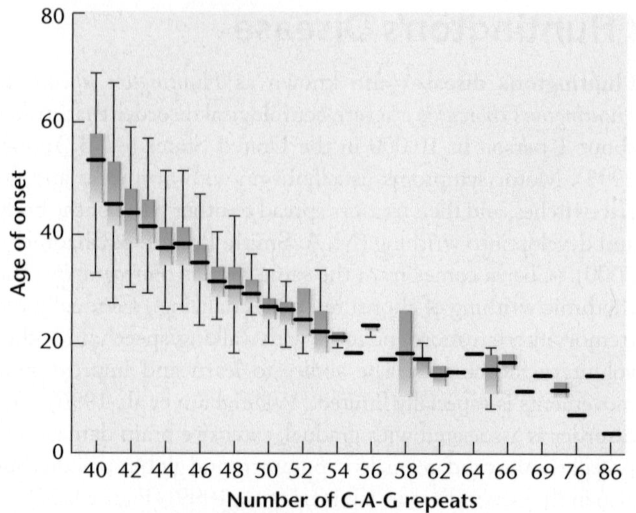

Figure 8.25 Relationship between C-A-G repeats and age of onset of Huntington's disease
For each number of C-A-G repeats, the graph shows the age of onset. The black bars show the range that includes the middle 50% of observations, from the 75th percentile to the 25th percentile. The vertical lines show the full range of observations. *(From the U.S.–Venezuela Collaborative Research Project [2004]. Proceedings of the National Academy of Sciences, USA, 101, 3498–3503.)*

fact that the Huntington's gene is dominant implies that it produces the gain of some undesirable function.

Imagine that as a young adult you learn that your mother or father has Huntington's disease. In addition to your grief about your parent, you know that you have a 50% chance of getting the disease yourself. Would you want to know in advance whether or not you were going to get the disease? Knowing the answer might help you decide whether to have children, whether to enter a career that required many years of education, and so forth. However, getting bad news might not be easy to handle.

In 1993, researchers located the gene for Huntington's disease on chromosome number 4, a spectacular accomplishment for the technology available at the time (Huntington's Disease Collaborative Research Group, 1993). Now an examination of your chromosomes can reveal with almost perfect accuracy whether or not you will get Huntington's disease.

The critical area of the gene includes a sequence of bases C-A-G (cytosine, adenine, guanine), which is repeated 11 to 24 times in most people. That repetition produces a string of 11 to 24 glutamines in the resulting protein. People with up to 35 C-A-G repetitions are considered safe from Huntington's disease. Those with 36 to 38 might get it, but probably not until old age. People with 39 or more repetitions are likely to get the disease, unless they die of other causes earlier. The more C-A-G repetitions someone has, the earlier the probable onset of the disease, as shown in Figure 8.25 (U.S.–Venezuela Collaborative Research Project, 2004). In short, a chromosomal examination can predict not only whether a person will get Huntington's disease but also approximately when.

The graph shows a considerable amount of variation in age of onset, especially for those with fewer C-A-G repeats. That variation probably depends partly on stressful experiences, diet, and other influences. It also depends on additional genes. Different forms of genes controlling glutamate receptors do not produce Huntington's disease by themselves, but they influence the age of onset of symptoms (Andresen et al., 2007).

Figure 8.26 shows comparable data for Huntington's disease and seven other neurological disorders. Each of them re-

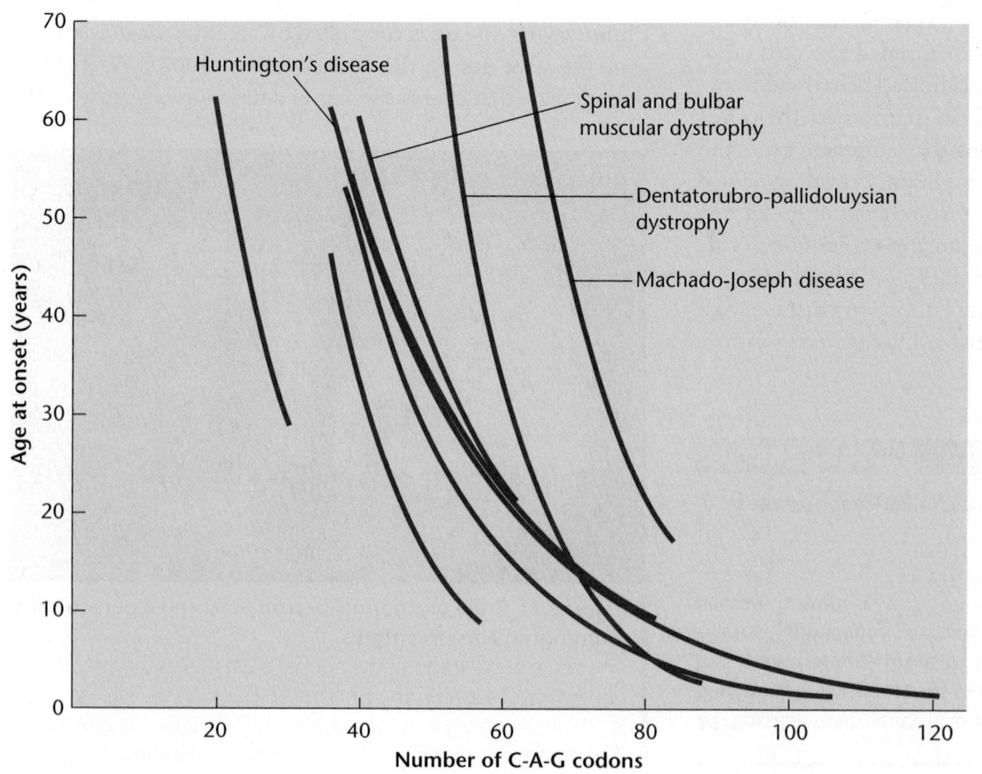

Figure 8.26 Relationship between C-A-G repeats and age of onset of eight diseases
The *x* axis shows the number of C-A-G repeats; the *y* axis shows the mean age at onset of disease. The various lines represent Huntington's disease and seven others. The four unlabeled lines are for four different types of spinocerebellar ataxia. The key point is that for each disease, the greater the number of repeats, the earlier the probable onset of symptoms. *(Reproduced with permission from "Molecular genetics: Unmasking polyglutamine triggers in neurogenerative disease," by J. F. Gusella and M. E. MacDonald, Fig. 1, p. 111 in* Neuroscience, 1, *pp. 109–115, copyright 2000 Macmillan Magazines, Ltd.)*

lates to an extended sequence of C-A-G repeats in a gene. In each case, people with more repeats have an earlier onset of disease (Gusella & MacDonald, 2000). Those with a smaller number will be older when they get the disease, if they get it at all. Recall a similar fact about Parkinson's disease: Several genes have been linked to early-onset Parkinson's disease, but the late-onset condition is less predictable and probably depends on environmental factors more than genes. As discussed elsewhere in this book, genetic factors are clearly important for early-onset Alzheimer's disease, alcoholism, depression, and schizophrenia. For people with later onset, the role of genetics is weaker or less certain.

Identification of the gene for Huntington's disease led to the discovery of the protein that it codes, which has been designated **huntingtin.** Huntingtin occurs throughout the human body, although its mutant form produces no known harm outside the brain. Within the brain, it occurs inside neurons, not on their membranes. The mutant form impairs neurons in several ways. In the early stages of the disease, it increases neurotransmitter release, sometimes causing overstimulation of the target cells (Romero et al., 2007). Later, the protein forms clusters that impair the neuron's mitochondria (Panov et al., 2002). Also, cells with the abnormal huntingtin protein fail to release the neurotrophin BDNF, which they ordinarily release along with their neurotransmitter (Zuccato et al., 2001). The result is impaired functioning of other cells.

Identifying the abnormal huntingtin protein and its cellular functions has enabled investigators to search for drugs that reduce the harm. Researchers have developed strains of mice with the same gene that causes Huntington's disease in humans. Research on these mice has found certain promising drugs. Several drugs block the glutamine chains from clustering (Sánchez, Mahlke, & Yuan, 2003; X. Zhang, Smith, et al., 2005). Another drug interferes with the RNA that enables expression of the huntingtin gene (Harper et al., 2005). Neurotrophins will probably be effective if researchers can find ways to get them into the brain (Bredesen, Rao, & Mehlen, 2006). The drug tetrabenazine decreases writhing movements by decreasing dopamine release. Another approach focuses on sleep. Mice with the Huntington's disease mutation, like people with the same mutation, show disrupted circadian patterns and poor sleep as well as impairments in learning and memory. Giving them a daily sleeping pill improved their sleep, learning, and memory (Pallier et al., 2007). Using the same approach with humans could improve the quality of life.

For the latest information, visit the Website of the Huntington's Disease Society of America: http://www.hdsa.org

STOP & CHECK

22. What procedure enables physicians to predict who will or will not get Huntington's disease and to estimate the age of onset?

ANSWER

22. Physicians can count the number of consecutive repeats of the combination C-A-G on one gene on chromosome 4. If the number is fewer than 36, the person will not develop Huntington's disease. For repeats of 36 or more, the larger the number, the more certain the person is to develop the disease and the earlier the probable age of onset.

MODULE 8.3 IN CLOSING

Heredity and Environment in Movement Disorders

Parkinson's disease and Huntington's disease show that genes influence behavior in different ways. Someone who examines the chromosomes can predict almost certainly who will and who will not develop Huntington's disease and with moderate accuracy predict when. A gene has also been identified for early-onset Parkinson's disease, but for the late-onset version, environmental influences appear to be more important. In later chapters, especially Chapter 15, we shall discuss other instances in which genes increase the risk of certain disorders, but we will not encounter anything with such a strong heritability as Huntington's disease.

SUMMARY

1. Parkinson's disease is characterized by impaired initiation of activity, slow and inaccurate movements, tremor, rigidity, depression, and cognitive deficits. **249**
2. Parkinson's disease is associated with the degeneration of dopamine-containing axons from the substantia nigra to the caudate nucleus and putamen. **249**
3. A gene has been identified that is responsible for early-onset Parkinson's disease. Heredity plays a smaller role in the more common form of Parkinson's disease, with onset after age 50. **249**
4. The chemical MPTP selectively damages neurons in the substantia nigra and leads to the symptoms of Parkinson's disease. Some cases of Parkinson's disease may result in part from exposure to toxins. **251**
5. The most common treatment for Parkinson's disease is L-dopa, which crosses the blood-brain barrier and enters neurons that convert it into dopamine. However, the effectiveness of L-dopa varies, and it produces unwelcome side effects. **252**
6. Many other treatments are in use or at least in the experimental stage. The transfer of immature neurons into a damaged brain area seems to offer great potential, but so far, it has provided little practical benefit. **252**
7. Huntington's disease is a hereditary condition marked by deterioration of motor control as well as depression, memory impairment, and other cognitive disorders. **253**
8. By examining chromosome 4, physicians can determine whether someone is likely to develop Huntington's disease later in life. The more C-A-G repeats in the gene, the earlier is the likely onset of symptoms. **254**
9. The gene responsible for Huntington's disease alters the structure of a protein, known as huntingtin. The altered protein interferes with functioning of the mitochondria. **255**

KEY TERMS

Terms are defined in the module on the page number indicated. They're also presented in alphabetical order with definitions in the book's Subject Index/Glossary. Interactive flashcards, audio reviews, and crossword puzzles are among the online resources available to help you learn these terms and the concepts they represent.

huntingtin **255**
Huntington's disease **253**
L-dopa **252**
MPP^+ **251**
MPTP **251**
Parkinson's disease **249**
stem cells **253**

THOUGHT QUESTIONS

1. Haloperidol is a drug that blocks dopamine synapses. What effect would it be likely to have in someone suffering from Parkinson's disease?
2. Neurologists assert that if people lived long enough, sooner or later everyone would develop Parkinson's disease. Why?

CHAPTER 8 Exploration and Study

In addition to the study materials provided at the end of each module, you may supplement your review of this chapter by using one or more of the book's electronic resources, which include its companion Website, interactive Cengage Learning eBook, Exploring Biological Psychology CD-ROM, and CengageNOW. Brief descriptions of these resources follow. For more information, visit **www.cengage.com/psychology/kalat**.

The book's companion Website, accessible through the author Web page indicated above, provides a wide range of study resources such as an interactive glossary, flashcards, tutorial quizzes, updated Web links, and Try It Yourself activities, as well as a limited selection of the short videos and animated explanations of concepts available for this chapter.

Exploring Biological Psychology

The Exploring Biological Psychology CD-ROM contains videos, animations, and Try It Yourself activities. These activities—as well as many that are new to this edition—are also available in the text's fully interactive, media-rich Cengage Learning eBook,* which gives you the opportunity to experience biological psychology in an even greater interactive and multimedia environment. The Cengage Learning eBook also includes highlighting and note-taking features and an audio glossary. For this chapter, the Cengage Learning eBook includes the following interactive explorations:

Withdrawal Reflex
Crossed Extensor Reflex
Visuo Motor Control
Somesthetic Experiment
Mirror Neurons
Paths of Touch and Motor Control
Major Motor Areas
Cells and Connections in the Cerebellum

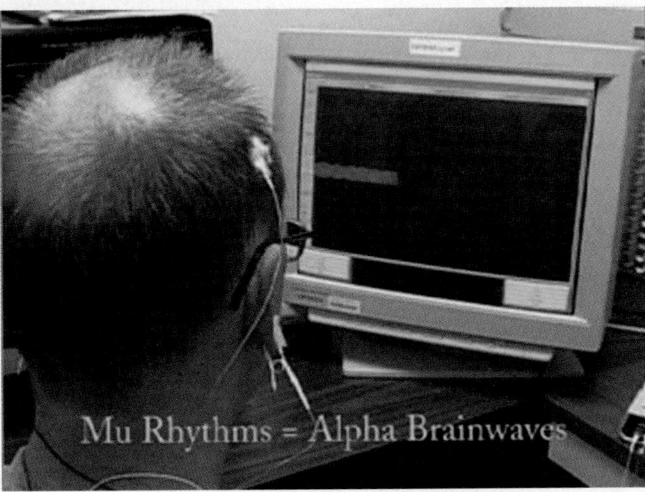

The video *Mirror Neurons* presents research on a newly discovered category of neurons.

CENGAGENOW™ is an easy-to-use resource that helps you study in less time to get the grade you want. An online study system, CengageNOW* gives you the option of taking a diagnostic pretest for each chapter. The system uses the results of each pretest to create personalized chapter study plans for you. The Personalized Study Plans

- help you save study time by identifying areas on which you should concentrate and give you one-click access to corresponding pages of the interactive Cengage Learning eBook;
- provide interactive exercises and study tools to help you fully understand chapter concepts; and
- include a posttest for you to take to confirm that you are ready to move on to the next chapter.

Suggestions for Further Exploration

The book's companion Website includes a list of suggested articles available through InfoTrac College Edition for this chapter. You may also want to explore some of the following books and Websites. The text's companion Website provides live, updated links to the sites listed below.

Books

Klawans, H. L. (1996). *Why Michael couldn't hit.* New York: Freeman. A collection of fascinating sports examples related to the brain and its disorders.

Lashley, K. S. (1951). The problem of serial order in behavior. In L. A. Jeffress (Ed.), *Cerebral mechanisms in behavior* (pp. 112–136). New York: Wiley. This classic article in psychology is a thought-provoking appraisal of what a theory of movement should explain.

Websites

Myasthenia Gravis Links
http://pages.prodigy.net/stanley.way/myasthenia/

Huntington's Disease Society of America
http://www.hdsa.org

World Parkinson Disease Association
http://www.wpda.org/

* Requires a Cengage Learning eResources account. Visit **www.cengage.com/login** to register or login.

Wakefulness and Sleep

9

CHAPTER OUTLINE

MAIN IDEAS

1. Wakefulness and sleep alternate on a cycle of approximately 24 hours. The brain itself generates this cycle.
2. Sleep progresses through various stages, which differ in brain activity, heart rate, and other aspects. A special type of sleep, known as paradoxical or REM sleep, is light in some ways and deep in others.
3. Areas in the brainstem and forebrain control arousal and sleep. Localized brain damage can produce prolonged sleep or wakefulness.
4. People have many reasons for failing to sleep well enough to feel rested the following day.
5. We need sleep and REM sleep, although much about their functions remains uncertain.

Every multicellular animal that we know about has daily rhythms of wakefulness and sleep, and if we are deprived of sleep, we suffer. But if life evolved on another planet with different conditions, could animals evolve life without a need for sleep? Imagine a planet that doesn't rotate on its axis. Some animals evolve adaptations to live in the light area, others in the dark area, and still others in the twilight zone separating light from dark. There would be no need for any animal to alternate active periods with inactive periods on any fixed schedule and perhaps no need at all for prolonged inactive periods. If you were the astronaut who discovered these nonsleeping animals, you might be surprised.

Now imagine that astronauts from that planet set out on their first voyage to Earth. Imagine *their* surprise to discover animals like us with long inactive periods resembling death. To someone who hadn't seen sleep before, it would seem strange and mysterious indeed. For the purposes of this chapter, let's adopt their perspective and ask why animals as active as we are spend one third of our lives doing so little.

OPPOSITE: Rock hyraxes at a national park in Kenya.

MODULE 9.1

Rhythms of Waking and Sleeping

You are, I assume, not particularly surprised to learn that your body spontaneously generates its own rhythm of wakefulness and sleep. Psychologists of an earlier era strongly resisted that idea. When behaviorism dominated experimental psychology during the mid-1900s, many psychologists believed that every behavior could be traced to external stimuli. For example, alternation between wakefulness and sleep must depend on something in the outside world, such as changes in light or temperature. The research of Curt Richter (1922) and others implied that the body generates its own cycles of activity and inactivity. Gradually, the evidence became stronger that animals generate approximately 24-hour cycles of waking and sleeping even in unchanging environments. The idea of self-generated rhythms was a major step toward viewing animals as active producers of behaviors.

Endogenous Cycles

An animal that produced its behavior entirely in response to current stimuli would be at a serious disadvantage. Animals often need to prepare for changes in sunlight and temperature before they occur. For example, migratory birds start flying toward their winter homes before their summer territory becomes too cold. A bird that waited for the first frost would be in serious trouble. Similarly, squirrels begin storing nuts and putting on extra layers of fat in preparation for winter long before food becomes scarce.

Animals' readiness for a change in seasons comes partly from internal mechanisms. For example, several cues tell a migratory bird when to fly south for the winter, but after it reaches the tropics, what tells it when to fly back north? In the tropics, the temperature and amount of daylight are nearly the same throughout the year. Nevertheless, a migratory bird flies north at the right time. Even if it is kept in a cage with no clues to the season, it becomes restless in the spring, and if it is released, it flies north (Gwinner, 1986). Evidently, the bird generates a rhythm that prepares it for seasonal changes. We refer to that rhythm as an **endogenous circannual rhythm.** (*Endogenous* means "generated from within." *Circannual* comes from the Latin words *circum*, for "about," and *annum*, for "year.")

Similarly, animals produce **endogenous circadian rhythms** that last about a day. (*Circadian* comes from *circum*, for "about," and *dies*, for "day.") If you go without sleep all night—as most college students do, sooner or later—you feel sleepier and sleepier as the night goes on, but as morning arrives, you feel less sleepy. For one reason, the light from the sun helps you feel less sleepy. Furthermore, your urge to sleep depends partly on the time of day, not just how many hours you have been awake (Babkoff, Caspy, Mikulincer, & Sing, 1991).

Figure 9.1 represents the activity of a flying squirrel kept in total darkness for 25 days. Each horizontal line represents one 24-hour day. A thickening in the line represents a period of activity by the animal. Even in this unchanging environment, the animal generates a regular rhythm of activity and sleep. Depending on the individual and the details of the procedure, the self-generated cycle may be slightly shorter than 24 hours, as in Figure 9.1, or slightly longer (Carpenter & Grossberg, 1984).

Humans also generate wake–sleep rhythms. Naval personnel on U.S. nuclear powered submarines are cut off from sunlight for months at a time, living under faint artificial light. In many cases, they have been asked to live on a schedule of 6 hours of work alternating with 12 hours of rest. Even though they sleep (or *try* to sleep) on this 18-hour schedule, their bodies generate rhythms of alertness and body chemistry that average about 24.3 to 24.4 hours (Kelly et al., 1999). Researchers using properly timed bright lights have found it possible to train people to produce a 25-hour rhythm, but no one has succeeded in producing a rhythm far from the 24-hour norm (Gronfier, Wright, Kronauer, & Czeisler, 2007).

Mammals, including humans, have circadian rhythms in their waking and sleeping, eating and drinking, urination, secretion of hormones, sensitivity to drugs, and other variables. For example, although we ordinarily think of human body temperature as 37°C, normal temperature fluctuates over the course of a day from a low near 36.7°C during the night to almost 37.2°C in late afternoon (Figure 9.2).

Circadian rhythms differ among individuals. Some people ("morning people," or "larks") awaken early, quickly become productive, and become less alert as the day progresses.

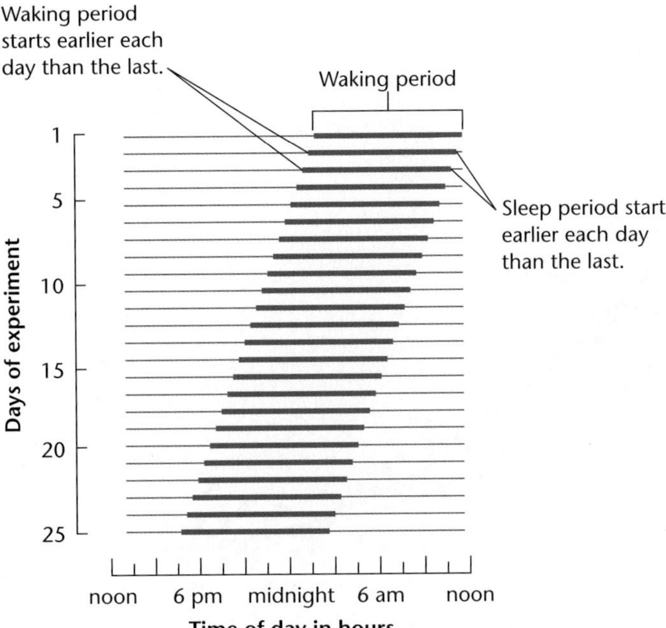

Figure 9.1 Activity record of a flying squirrel kept in constant darkness
The thickened segments indicate periods of activity as measured by a running wheel. Note that the free-running activity cycle lasts slightly less than 24 hours. *(From "Phase Control of Activity in a Rodent," by P. J. DeCoursey,* Cold Spring Harbor Symposia on Quantitative Biology, *1960, 25:49–55. Reprinted by permission of Cold Spring Harbor and P. J. DeCoursey.)*

Others ("evening people," or "owls") warm up more slowly, both literally and figuratively, reaching their peak in the late afternoon or evening. They tolerate staying up all night better than morning people do (Taillard, Philip, Coste, Sagaspe, & Bioulac, 2003).

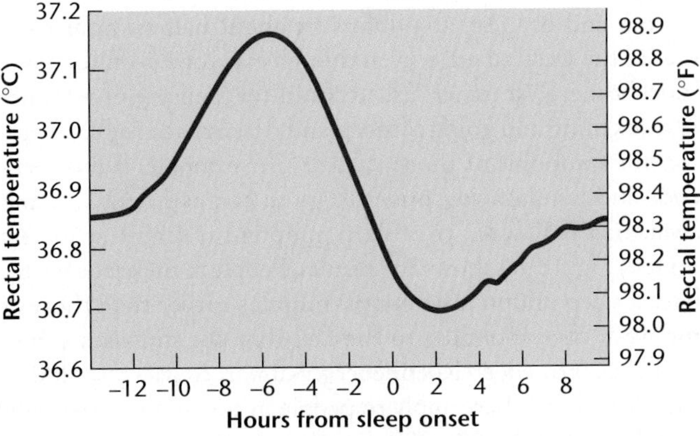

Figure 9.2 Mean rectal temperatures for nine adults
Body temperature reaches its low for the day about 2 hours after sleep onset; it reaches its peak about 6 hours before sleep onset. *(From "Sleep-Onset Insomniacs Have Delayed Temperature Rhythms," by M. Morris, L. Lack, and D. Dawson,* Sleep, *1990,* 13, 1–14. Reprinted by permission.)

Not everyone falls neatly into one extreme or the other, of course. A convenient way to compare people is to ask, "On holidays and vacations when you have no obligations, what time is the middle of your sleep?" For example, if you slept from 1 A.M. until 9 A.M. on those days, your middle would be 5 A.M. As Figure 9.3 shows, people differ by age. As a child, you almost certainly went to bed early and woke up early. As you entered adolescence, you started staying up later and waking up later, when you had the opportunity. The mean preferred time of going to sleep gets later and later until about age 20 and then starts a gradual reversal (Roenneberg et al., 2004).

Do people older than 20 learn to go to bed earlier because they have jobs that require them to get up early? Maybe, but two facts point instead to a biological explanation. First, in Figure 9.3, note how the shift continues gradually over decades. If people were simply adjusting to their jobs, we might expect a sudden shift in the early 20s and a reversal at retirement. Second, a similar trend occurs in rats: Older rats reach their best performance shortly after awakening, whereas younger rats tend to improve performance as the day progresses (Winocur & Hasher, 1999, 2004).

STOP & CHECK

1. What evidence indicates that humans have an internal biological clock?

ANSWER

1. People who have lived in an environment with a light–dark schedule much different from 24 hours fail to follow that schedule and instead become wakeful and sleepy on about a 24-hour basis.

Setting and Resetting the Biological Clock

Our circadian rhythms generate a period close to 24 hours, but they are not perfect. We readjust our internal workings daily to stay in phase with the outside world. Sometimes, we misadjust them. On weekends, when most of us are freer to set our own schedules, we expose ourselves to lights, noises, and activity at night and then awaken late the next morning. By Monday morning, when the clock indicates 7 A.M., the biological clock within us says about 5 A.M., and we stagger off to work or school without much pep (Moore-Ede, Czeisler, & Richardson, 1983).

Although circadian rhythms persist without light, light is critical for resetting them. I used to have a windup wristwatch that lost about 2 minutes per day, which would accumulate to an hour per month if I didn't reset it. It had a **free-running rhythm** of 24 hours and 2 minutes—that is, a rhythm that occurs when no stimuli reset or alter it. The circadian rhythm of the body is similar. Without something to reset it, it would drift further and further. The stimulus that resets the circadian

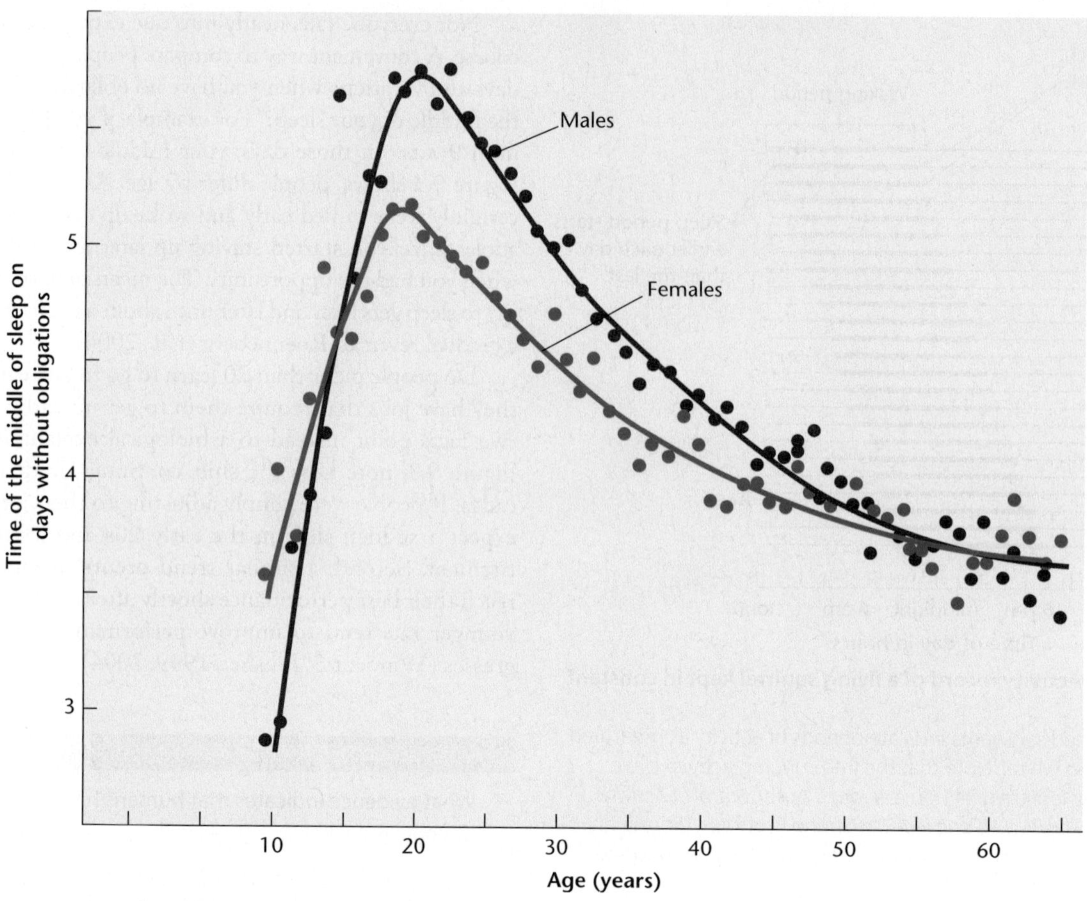

Figure 9.3 Age differences in circadian rhythms
People of various ages identified the time of the middle of their sleep, such as 3 A.M. or 5 A.M., on days when they had no obligations. People around age 20 were the most likely to go to bed late and wake up late. *(Reprinted from T. Roenneberg et al., "A marker for the end of adolescence,"* Current Biology, 14, *R1038–R1039, Figure 1, Copyright 2004, with permission from Elsevier.)*

rhythm is referred to by the German term **zeitgeber** (TSITE-gay-ber), meaning "time-giver." Light is the dominant zeitgeber for land animals (Rusak & Zucker, 1979). (The tides are important for many marine animals.) In addition to light, other zeitgebers include exercise (Eastman, Hoese, Youngstedt, & Liu, 1995), noise, meals, and the temperature of the environment (Refinetti, 2000). However, these additional zeitgebers merely supplement or alter the effects of light. On their own, their effects are generally weak. For example, people who are working in Antarctica during the Antarctic winter, with no sunlight, try to maintain a 24-hour rhythm, but different people generate different free-running rhythms, until they find it more and more difficult to work together (Kennaway & Van Dorp, 1991).

Even when we try to set our wake–sleep cycles by the clock, the sun has its influence. Consider what happens when we shift to daylight savings time in spring. You set your clock to an hour later, and when it shows your usual bedtime, you dutifully go to bed, even though it seems an hour too early. The next morning, when the clock says it is 7 A.M. and time to get ready for work, your brain still registers 6 A.M. Most people are inefficient and ill-rested for days after the shift to daylight savings time. The adjustment is especially difficult for evening people and those who were already sleep-deprived, including most college students (Lahti et al., 2006; Monk & Aplin, 1980).

Particularly impressive evidence for the importance of sunlight comes from a study in Germany. The "sun" time at the eastern end of Germany differs by about half an hour from that at the western edge, even though everyone is on the same "clock" time. Researchers asked adults for their preferred times of awakening and going to sleep and determined for each person the midpoint of those values. (For example, if on weekends and holidays you prefer to go to bed at 12:30 A.M. and awaken at 8:30 A.M., your sleep midpoint is 4:30 A.M., or 4.5 hours.) Figure 9.4 shows the results. People at the eastern edge have a sleep midpoint about 30 minutes earlier than those at the west, corresponding to the fact that the sun rises earlier at the eastern edge (Roenneberg, Kumar, & Merrow, 2007). The data shown here apply to people in towns and cities with populations under 300,000. People in larger cities show a less consistent trend, presumably because they spend more time indoors and have less exposure to the sun.

What about blind people, who need to set their circadian rhythms by zeitgebers other than light? The results vary. Some do set their circadian rhythms by noise, temperature,

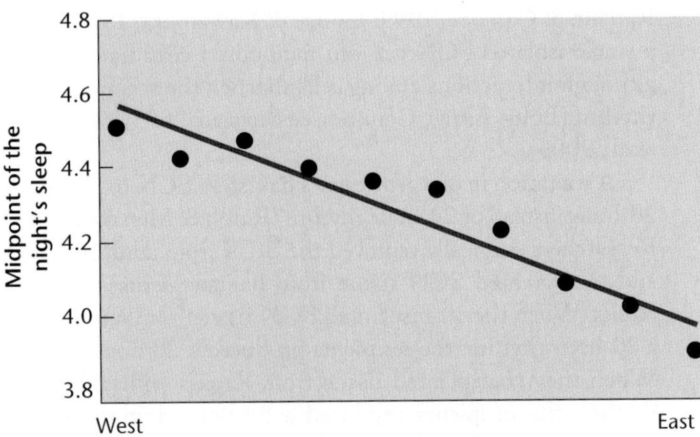

Figure 9.4 Sun time competes with social time
On days when people have no obligation to awaken at a particular time, they awaken about half an hour earlier at the eastern edge of Germany than at the western edge and at intermediate times for intermediate longitudes. Points along the *y* axis represent the midpoint between the preferred bedtime and the preferred waking time. Data are for people living in towns and cities with populations less than 300,000. *(From Roenneberg, T., et al. [2007], "The human circadian clock entrains to sun time."* Current Biology, 17, *R44-R45. Reprinted by permission of the Copyright Clearance Center.)*

meals, and activity. However, others who are not sufficiently sensitive to these secondary zeitgebers produce free-running circadian rhythms that are a little longer than 24 hours. When their cycles are in phase with the clock, all is well, but when they drift out of phase, they experience insomnia at night and sleepiness during the day (Sack & Lewy, 2001).

STOP & CHECK

2. Why do people at the eastern edge of Germany awaken earlier than those at the western edge on their weekends and holidays?

ANSWER

2. The sun rises about half an hour earlier at the eastern edge than at the western edge. Evidently, the sun controls waking–sleeping schedules even when people follow the same clock time for their work schedule.

Jet Lag

A disruption of circadian rhythms due to crossing time zones is known as **jet lag.** Travelers complain of sleepiness during the day, sleeplessness at night, depression, and impaired concentration. All these problems stem from the mismatch between internal circadian clock and external time (Haimov & Arendt, 1999). Most of us find it easier to adjust to crossing time zones going west than east. Going west, we stay awake later at night and then awaken late the next morning, already partly adjusted to the new schedule. We *phase-delay* our circadian rhythms. Going east, we *phase-advance* to sleep earlier and awaken earlier (Figure 9.5). Most people find it difficult to go to sleep before their body's usual time.

Adjusting to jet lag is more stressful for some people than for others. Stress elevates blood levels of the adrenal hormone *cortisol,* and many studies have shown that prolonged elevations of cortisol damage neurons in the hippocampus, a brain area important for memory. One study examined flight attendants who had spent the previous 5 years making flights across seven or more time zones—such as Chicago to Italy—with mostly short breaks (fewer than 6 days) between trips. On the average, they showed smaller than average volumes of the hippocampus and surrounding structures, and they showed some memory impairments (Cho, 2001). These results suggest a danger from repeated adjustments of the circadian rhythm, although the problem here could be just air travel itself. (A good control group would have been flight attendants who flew long north–south routes.)

Shift Work

People who sleep irregularly—such as pilots, medical interns, and shift workers in factories—find that their duration of sleep depends on when they go to sleep. When they have to sleep in the morning or early afternoon, they sleep only briefly, even if they have been awake for many hours (Frese & Harwich, 1984; Winfree, 1983).

People who work on a night shift, such as midnight to 8 A.M., sleep during the day. At least they try to. Even after months or years on such a schedule, many workers adjust incompletely. They continue to feel groggy on the job, they do

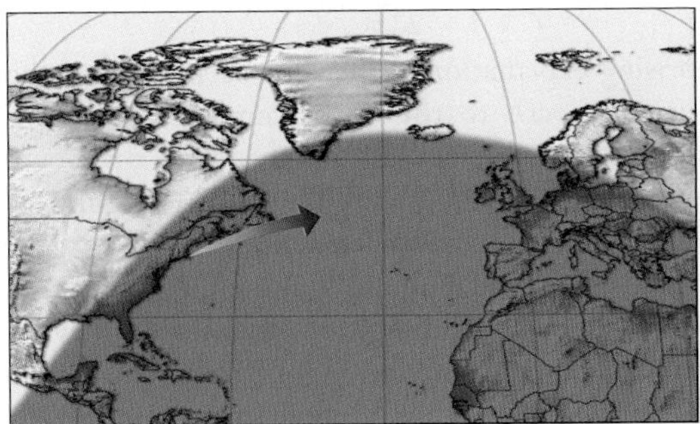

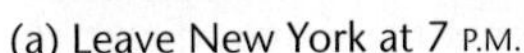
(a) Leave New York at 7 P.M.

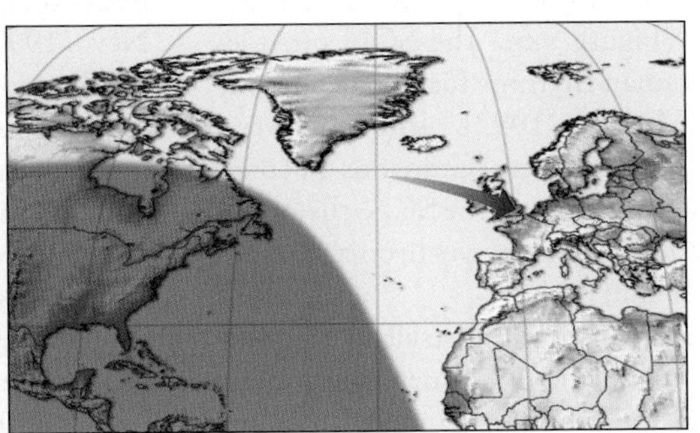
(b) Arrive in London at 7 A.M., which is 2 A.M. in New York

Figure 9.5 Jet lag
Eastern time is later than western time. People who travel six time zones east fall asleep on the plane and then must awaken when it is morning at their destination but still night back home.

not sleep soundly during the day, and their body temperature continues to peak when they are trying to sleep in the day instead of while they are working at night. In general, night-shift workers have more accidents than day-shift workers.

Working at night does not reliably change the circadian rhythm because most buildings use artificial lighting in the range of 150–180 lux, which is only moderately effective in resetting the rhythm (Boivin, Duffy, Kronauer, & Czeisler, 1996). People adjust best to night work if they sleep in a very dark room during the day and work under very bright lights at night, comparable to the noonday sun (Czeisler et al., 1990).

Mechanisms of the Biological Clock

How does the body generate a circadian rhythm? Curt Richter (1967) introduced the concept that the brain generates its own rhythms—a biological clock—and he reported that the biological clock is insensitive to most forms of interference. Blind or deaf animals generate circadian rhythms, although they slowly drift out of phase with the external world. The circadian rhythm is surprisingly steady despite food or water deprivation, x-rays, tranquilizers, alcohol, anesthesia, lack of oxygen, most kinds of brain damage, or the removal of hormonal organs. Even an hour or more of induced hibernation often fails to reset the biological clock (Gibbs, 1983; Richter, 1975). Evidently, the biological clock is a hardy, robust mechanism.

Curt P. Richter (1894–1988)
I enjoy research more than eating.

The Suprachiasmatic Nucleus (SCN)

The biological clock depends on part of the hypothalamus, called the **suprachiasmatic** (soo-pruh-kie-as-MAT-ik) **nucleus,** or **SCN.** It gets its name from its location just above ("supra") the optic chiasm (Figure 9.6). The SCN provides the main control of the circadian rhythms for sleep and body temperature (Refinetti & Menaker, 1992), although several other brain areas generate local rhythms (Granados-Fuentes, Tseng, & Herzog, 2006). After damage to the SCN, the body's rhythms are less consistent and no longer synchronized to environmental patterns of light and dark.

The SCN generates circadian rhythms itself in a genetically controlled, unlearned manner. If SCN neurons are disconnected from the rest of the brain or removed from the body and maintained in tissue culture, they continue to produce a circadian rhythm of action potentials (Earnest, Liang, Ratcliff, & Cassone, 1999; Inouye & Kawamura, 1979). Even a single isolated SCN cell can maintain a circadian rhythm, although interactions among cells sharpen the accuracy of the rhythm (Long, Jutras, Connors, & Burwell, 2005; Yamaguchi et al., 2003).

A mutation in one gene causes hamsters' SCN to produce a 20-hour instead of 24-hour rhythm (Ralph & Menaker, 1988). Researchers surgically removed the SCN from adult hamsters and transplanted SCN tissue from hamster fetuses into the adults. When they transplanted SCN tissue from fetuses with a 20-hour rhythm, the recipients produced a 20-hour rhythm. When they transplanted tissue from fetuses with a 24-hour rhythm, the recipients produced a 24-hour rhythm (Ralph, Foster, Davis, & Menaker, 1990). That is, the rhythm followed the pace of the donors, not the recipients. Again, the results show that the rhythms come from the SCN itself.

STOP & CHECK

3. What evidence strongly indicates that the SCN produces the circadian rhythm itself?

ANSWER

3. SCN cells produce a circadian rhythm of activity even if they are kept in cell culture isolated from the rest of the body.

How Light Resets the SCN

The SCN is located just above the optic chiasm. (Figure 9.6 shows the position in the human brain. The relationship is similar in other mammals.) A small branch of the optic nerve, known as the *retinohypothalamic path,* extends directly from the retina to the SCN. Axons of that path alter the SCN's settings.

Most of the input to that path, however, does not come from normal retinal receptors. Mice with genetic defects that destroy nearly all their rods and cones nevertheless reset their biological clocks in synchrony with the light (Freedman et al., 1999; Lucas, Freedman, Muñoz, Garcia-Fernández, & Foster, 1999). Also, consider blind mole rats (Figure 9.7). Their eyes are covered with folds of skin and fur; they have neither eye muscles nor a lens with which to focus an image. They have fewer than 900 optic nerve axons compared with 100,000 in hamsters. Even a bright flash of light evokes no startle response and no measurable change in brain activity. Nevertheless, light resets their circadian rhythms (de Jong, Hendriks, Sanyal, & Nevo, 1990).

The surprising explanation is that, for all mammals, the retinohypothalamic path to the SCN comes from a special population of retinal ganglion cells that have their own photopigment, called *melanopsin,* unlike the ones found in rods and cones (Hannibal, Hindersson, Knudsen, Georg, & Fahrenkrug, 2001; Lucas, Douglas, & Foster, 2001). These special ganglion cells respond directly to light even if they do not receive any input from rods or cones (Berson, Dunn, & Takao, 2002). They do, nevertheless, receive some input from the rods and cones, which supplements their own direct response to light (Güler et al., 2008). The special ganglion cells

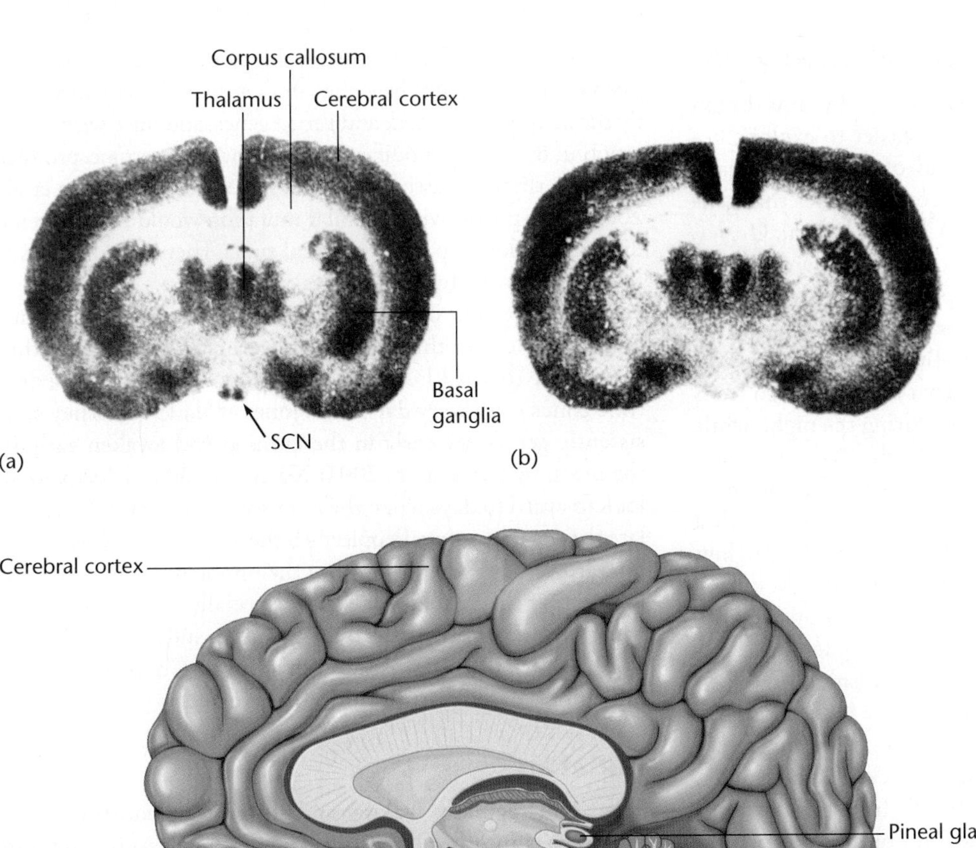

Figure 9.6 The suprachiasmatic nucleus (SCN) of rats and humans
The SCN is located at the base of the brain, just above the optic chiasm, which has torn off in these coronal sections through the plane of the anterior hypothalamus. Each rat was injected with radioactive 2-deoxyglucose, which is absorbed by the most active neurons. A high level of absorption of this chemical produces a dark appearance on the slide. Note that the level of activity in SCN neurons is much higher in section **(a),** in which the rat was injected during the day, than it is in section **(b),** in which the rat received the injection at night. *(From "Suprachiasmatic nucleus: Use of 14C-labeled deoxyglucose uptake as a functional marker," by W. J. Schwartz and H. Gainer,* Science 1977, *197:1089–1091. Reprinted with permission from AAAS/American Association for the Advancement of Science.)* **(c)** A sagittal section through a human brain showing the location of the SCN and the pineal gland.

Figure 9.7 A blind mole rat
Although blind mole rats are indeed blind in all other regards, they reset their circadian rhythms in response to light.

are located mainly near the nose, not evenly throughout the retina (Visser, Beersma, & Daan, 1999). (That is, they see toward the periphery.) These cells respond to light slowly and turn off slowly when the light ceases (Berson et al., 2002). Therefore, they respond to the overall average amount of light, not to instantaneous changes in light. The average intensity over a period of minutes or hours is, of course, exactly the information the SCN needs to gauge the time of day. Because they do not contribute to vision, the cells do not need to respond to momentary changes in light.

STOP & CHECK

4. How does light reset the biological clock?

ANSWER

4. A branch of the optic nerve, the retinohypothalamic path, conveys information about light to the SCN. The axons comprising that path originate from special ganglion cells that respond to light by themselves, even if they do not receive input from rods or cones.

The Biochemistry of the Circadian Rhythm

Research on the mechanism of circadian rhythms began with insects, where the genetic basis is easier to explore, because they reproduce in weeks instead of months or years. Studies on the fruit fly *Drosophila* discovered genes that generate a circadian rhythm (X. Liu et al., 1992; Sehgal, Ousley, Yang, Chen, & Schotland, 1999). Two genes, known as *period* (abbreviated *per*) and *timeless* (*tim*), produce the proteins Per and Tim. Those proteins start in small amounts early in the morning and increase during the day. By evening, they reach a high level that makes the fly sleepy. That high level also feeds back to the genes to shut them down. During the night, while the genes no longer produce Per or Tim, their concentration declines until the next morning, when the cycle begins anew. When the Per and Tim levels are high, they interact with a protein called Clock to induce sleepiness. When they are low, the result is wakefulness. Furthermore, a pulse of light during the night inactivates the Tim protein, so extra light during the evening decreases sleepiness and resets the biological clock. Figure 9.8 summarizes this feedback mechanism.

Why do we care about flies? The answer is that after researchers understood the mechanism in flies, they found very similar genes and proteins in mammals (Reick, Garcia, Dudley, & McKnight, 2001; Zheng et al., 1999). In mammals, light alters the production of the Per and Tim proteins, which increase the activity of certain neurons in the SCN (Kuhlman, Silver, LeSauter, Bult-Ito, & McMahon, 2003).

Understanding these mechanisms helps make sense of some unusual sleep disorders. Mice with damage to their *clock* gene, which interacts with the *per* and *tim* genes, sleep less than normal (Naylor et al., 2000), and presumably, some cases of decreased sleep in humans might have the same cause. Various genes modify the activity of the *clock* and *period* genes, and mice with a mutation in one of the modifier genes, known as *overtime*, produce circadian rhythms lasting 26 hours instead of 24 (Siepka et al., 2007). Any people with a similar mutation would have extreme difficulty waking up at the normal time. They would feel as if they were moving two time zones east every day.

One mutation of the *period* gene has been found in humans. People with this mutation have a circadian rhythm that runs faster than 24 hours, as if they were moving one or two time zones west every day (C. R. Jones et al., 1999). They consistently get sleepy early in the evening and awaken early in the morning (Toh et al., 2001; Xu et al., 2005). Most people look forward to days when they can stay up late and then sleep late the next morning. People with the altered *period* gene look forward to days when they have the opportunity to go to bed even earlier than usual and waken especially early the next day. Most people with this sleep abnormality suffer from depression (Xu et al., 2005). As we see again in Chapter 15, sleep difficulties and depression are closely linked.

Melatonin

The SCN regulates waking and sleeping by controlling activity levels in other brain areas, including the **pineal gland** (PIN-ee-al; see Figure 9.6), an endocrine gland located just posterior to the thalamus (Aston-Jones, Chen, Zhu, & Oshinsky, 2001; von Gall et al., 2002). The pineal gland releases the hormone **melatonin,** which influences both circadian and circannual rhythms (Lincoln, Clarke, Hut, &

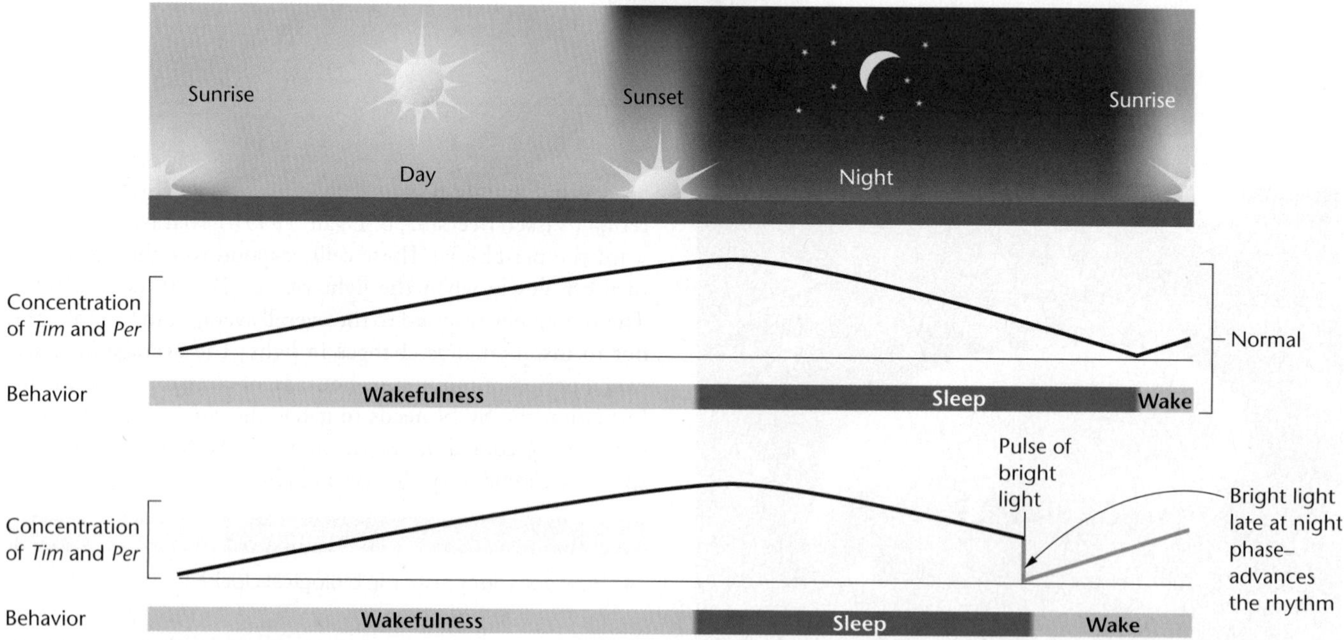

Figure 9.8 Feedback between proteins and genes to control sleepiness
In fruit flies (*Drosophila*), the Tim and Per proteins accumulate during the day. When they reach a high level, they induce sleepiness and shut off the genes that produce them. When their levels decline sufficiently, wakefulness returns and so does the gene activity. A pulse of light during the night breaks down the Tim protein, thus increasing wakefulness and resetting the circadian rhythm.

Hazlerigg, 2006). The human pineal gland secretes melatonin mostly at night, making us sleepy at that time. When people shift to a new time zone and start following a new schedule, they continue to feel sleepy at their old times until the melatonin rhythm shifts (Dijk & Cajochen, 1997). People who have pineal gland tumors sometimes stay awake for days at a time (Haimov & Lavie, 1996).

Melatonin secretion starts to increase about 2 or 3 hours before bedtime. Taking a melatonin pill in the evening has little effect on sleepiness because the pineal gland produces melatonin at that time anyway. However, people who take melatonin at other times become sleepy within 2 hours (Haimov & Lavie, 1996). Melatonin pills are sometimes helpful when people travel across time zones or for any other reason need to sleep at an unaccustomed time.

Melatonin also feeds back to reset the biological clock through its effects on receptors in the SCN (Gillette & McArthur, 1996). A moderate dose of melatonin (0.5 mg) in the afternoon phase-advances the clock. That is, it makes the person get sleepy earlier in the evening and wake up earlier the next morning. A single dose of melatonin in the morning has little effect (Wirz-Justice, Werth, Renz, Müller, & Kräuchi, 2002), although repeated morning doses can phase-delay the clock, causing the person to get sleepy later than usual at night and awaken later the next morning.

Taking melatonin has become something of a fad. Melatonin is an antioxidant, so it has some health benefits (Reiter, 2000). However, in laboratory animals, it has been shown to impair learning, presumably as a result of increasing drowsiness (Rawashdeh, Hernandez de Borsetti, & Cahill, 2007). Also, long-term use impairs animals' reproductive fertility and, if taken during pregnancy, harms the development of the fetus (J. Arendt, 1997; Weaver, 1997). The long-term effects on humans are not known, but the cautious advice is, as with any medication, don't take it unless you need it.

STOP & CHECK

5. How do the proteins Tim and Per relate to sleepiness in *Drosophila*?

ANSWER

5. The proteins Tim and Per accumulate during the wakeful period. When they reach a high enough level, they trigger sleepiness and turn off the genes that produced them. Therefore, their levels decline until they reach a low enough level for wakefulness to begin anew.

MODULE 9.1 **IN CLOSING**

Sleep–Wake Cycles

Unlike an electric appliance that stays on until someone turns it off, the brain periodically turns itself on and off. Sleepiness is not a voluntary or optional act. We have biological mechanisms that prepare us to wake at certain times and sleep at other times, even if we would prefer different schedules.

SUMMARY

1. Animals, including humans, have internally generated rhythms of activity lasting about 24 hours. **260**
2. Most older people tend to awaken early and go to bed early. Young adults are variable, but on the average, they awaken later and go to bed later. **260**
3. Although the biological clock can continue to operate in constant light or constant darkness, the onset of light resets the clock. **261**
4. It is easier for people to follow a cycle longer than 24 hours (as when traveling west) than to follow a cycle shorter than 24 hours (as when traveling east). **263**
5. If people wish to work at night and sleep during the day, the best way to shift the circadian rhythm is to have bright lights at night and darkness during the day. **263**
6. The suprachiasmatic nucleus (SCN), a part of the hypothalamus, generates the body's circadian rhythms for sleep and temperature. **264**
7. Light resets the biological clock partly by a branch of the optic nerve that extends to the SCN. Those axons originate from a special population of ganglion cells that respond directly to light in addition to receiving some input from rods and cones. **264**
8. The genes controlling the circadian rhythm are almost the same in mammals as in insects. Across species, certain proteins increase in abundance during the day and then decrease during the night. **266**
9. The SCN controls the body's rhythm partly by directing the release of melatonin by the pineal gland. The hormone melatonin increases sleepiness; if given at certain times of the day, it can also reset the circadian rhythm. **266**

Continued

KEY TERMS

Terms are defined in the module on the page number indicated. They're also presented in alphabetical order with definitions in the book's Subject Index/Glossary. Interactive flashcards, audio reviews, and crossword puzzles are among the online resources available to help you learn these terms and the concepts they represent.

endogenous circadian rhythms **260**
endogenous circannual rhythm **260**
free-running rhythm **261**
jet lag **263**
melatonin **266**
pineal gland **266**
suprachiasmatic nucleus (SCN) **264**
zeitgeber **262**

THOUGHT QUESTIONS

1. Is it possible for the onset of light to reset the circadian rhythms of a person who is blind? Explain.
2. Why would evolution have enabled blind mole rats to synchronize their SCN activity to light, even though they cannot see well enough to make any use of the light?
3. If you travel across several time zones to the east and want to use melatonin to help reset your circadian rhythm, at what time of day should you take it? What if you travel west?

MODULE 9.2

Stages of Sleep and Brain Mechanisms

Suppose I buy a new radio. After I play it for 4 hours, it suddenly stops. I wonder whether the batteries are dead or whether the radio needs repair. Later, I discover that this radio always stops after playing for 4 hours but operates again a few hours later even without repairs or a battery change. I begin to suspect that the manufacturer designed it this way, perhaps to prevent me from listening to the radio all day. Now I want to find the device that turns it off whenever I play it for 4 hours. Notice that I am asking a new question. When I thought that the radio stopped because it needed repairs or new batteries, I did not ask which device turned it off.

Similarly, if we think of sleep as something like wearing out a machine, we do not ask which part of the brain produces it. But if we think of sleep as a specialized state evolved to serve particular functions, we look for the mechanisms that regulate it.

Sleep and Other Interruptions of Consciousness

Let's start with some distinctions. Sleep is a state that the brain actively produces, characterized by a moderate decrease in brain activity and decreased response to stimuli. In contrast, **coma** (KOH-muh) is an extended period of unconsciousness caused by head trauma, stroke, or disease. It is possible to awaken a sleeping person but not someone in a coma. A person in a coma has a low level of brain activity that remains fairly steady throughout the day. The person shows little or no response to stimuli, including those that would ordinarily be painful. If any movements occur, they are purposeless and not directed toward anything in the environment. A typical coma lasts weeks, after which the person dies or begins to show some recovery.

During a **vegetative state**, a person alternates between periods of sleep and moderate arousal, although even during the more aroused state, the person shows no awareness of surroundings. Breathing is more regular, and a painful stimulus produces at least the autonomic responses of increased heart rate, breathing, and sweating. The person does not speak, respond to speech, or show any purposeful activity. However, variations do occur, and some patients in this state probably have some cognitive activity (Guérit, 2005). A **minimally conscious state** is one stage higher, with occasional, brief periods of purposeful actions and a limited amount of speech comprehension. A vegetative or minimally conscious state can last for months or years.

Brain death is a condition with no sign of brain activity and no response to any stimulus. Physicians usually wait until someone has shown no sign of brain activity for 24 hours before pronouncing brain death, at which point most people consider it ethical to remove life support.

The Stages of Sleep

Nearly every scientific advance comes from new or improved measurements. Researchers did not even suspect that sleep has different stages until they accidentally measured them. The electroencephalograph (EEG), as described in Chapter 4, records an average of the electrical potentials of the cells and fibers in the brain areas nearest each electrode on the scalp (Figure 9.9). That is, if half the cells in some area increase their electrical potentials while the other half decrease, they cancel out. The EEG record rises or falls when cells act in synchrony—do the same thing at the same time. You might compare it to a record of the noise in a crowded sports stadium: It shows only slight fluctuations until some event gets everyone yelling at once. The EEG enables brain researchers to compare brain activity at different times during sleep.

Figure 9.10 shows data from a **polysomnograph,** a combination of EEG and eye-movement records, for a college student during various stages of sleep. Figure 9.10a presents a period of relaxed wakefulness for comparison. Note the steady series of **alpha waves** at a frequency of 8 to 12 per second. Alpha waves are characteristic of relaxation, not of all wakefulness.

In Figure 9.10b, sleep has just begun. During this period, called stage 1 sleep, the EEG is dominated by irregular, jagged, low-voltage waves. Overall brain activity is less than in relaxed wakefulness but higher than other sleep stages. As Figure 9.10c shows, the most prominent characteristics of stage 2 are sleep spindles and K-complexes. A **sleep spindle** consists of 12- to 14-Hz waves during a burst that lasts at

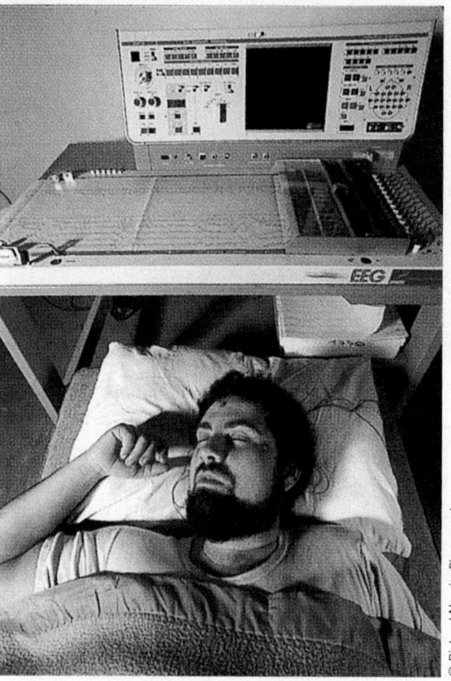

© Richard Nowitz Photography

Figure 9.9 Sleeping person with electrodes in place on the scalp for recording brain activity
The printout above his head shows the readings from each electrode.

least half a second. Sleep spindles result from oscillating interactions between cells in the thalamus and the cortex. A **K-complex** is a sharp high-amplitude wave. Sudden stimuli can evoke K-complexes during other stages of sleep (Bastien & Campbell, 1992), but they are most common in stage 2.

In the succeeding stages of sleep, heart rate, breathing rate, and brain activity decrease, while slow, large-amplitude waves become more common (see Figures 9.10d and e). By stage 4, more than half the record includes large waves of at least a half-second duration. Stages 3 and 4 together constitute **slow-wave sleep (SWS).**

Slow waves indicate that neuronal activity is highly synchronized. In stage 1 and in wakefulness, the cortex receives a great deal of input, much of it at high frequencies. Nearly all neurons are active, but different populations of neurons are active at different times. Thus, the EEG is full of short, rapid, choppy waves. By stage 4, however, sensory input to the cerebral cortex is greatly reduced, and the few remaining sources of input can synchronize many cells.

STOP & CHECK

6. What do long, slow waves on an EEG indicate?

ANSWER

6. Long, slow waves indicate a low level of activity, with much synchrony of response among neurons.

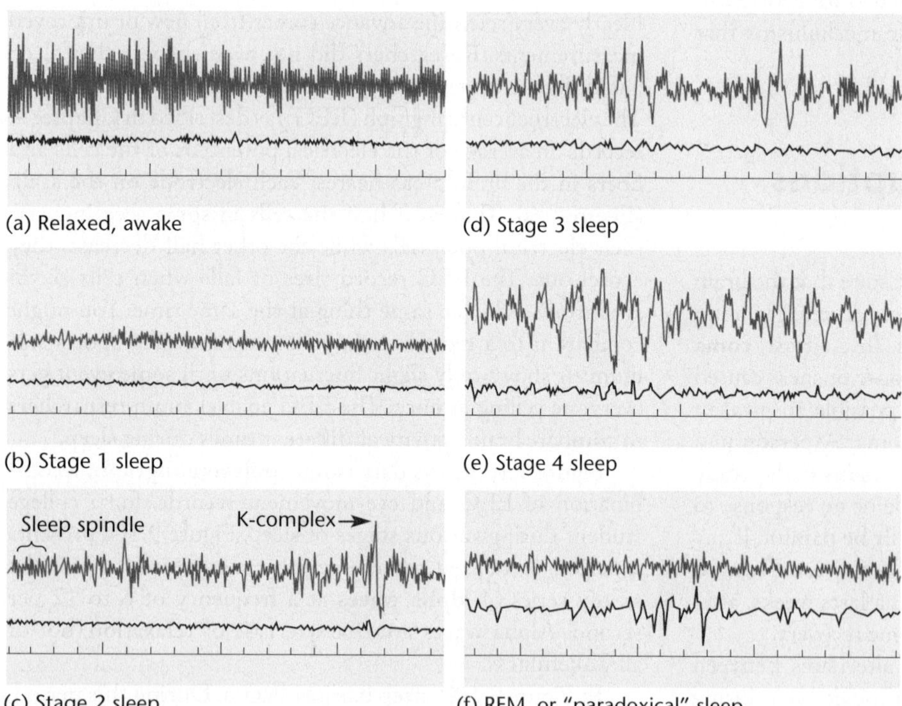

Figure 9.10 Polysomnograph records from a male college student
A polysomnograph includes records of EEG, eye movements, and sometimes other data, such as muscle tension or head movements. For each of these records, the top line is the EEG from one electrode on the scalp; the middle line is a record of eye movements; and the bottom line is a time marker, indicating 1-second units. Note the abundance of slow waves in stages 3 and 4. *(Records provided by T. E. LeVere)*

Paradoxical or REM Sleep

Many discoveries occur when researchers stumble upon something by accident and then notice that it might be important. In the 1950s, the French scientist Michel Jouvet was trying to test the learning abilities of cats after removal of the cerebral cortex. Because decorticate mammals don't do much, Jouvet recorded slight movements of the muscles and EEGs from the hindbrain. During certain periods of apparent sleep, the cats' brain activity was relatively high, but their neck muscles were completely relaxed. Jouvet (1960) then recorded the same phenomenon in normal, intact cats and named it **paradoxical sleep** because it is deep sleep in some ways and light in others. (The term *paradoxical* means "apparently self-contradictory.")

Meanwhile, in the United States, Nathaniel Kleitman and Eugene Aserinsky were observing eye movements of sleeping people as a means of measuring depth of sleep, assuming that

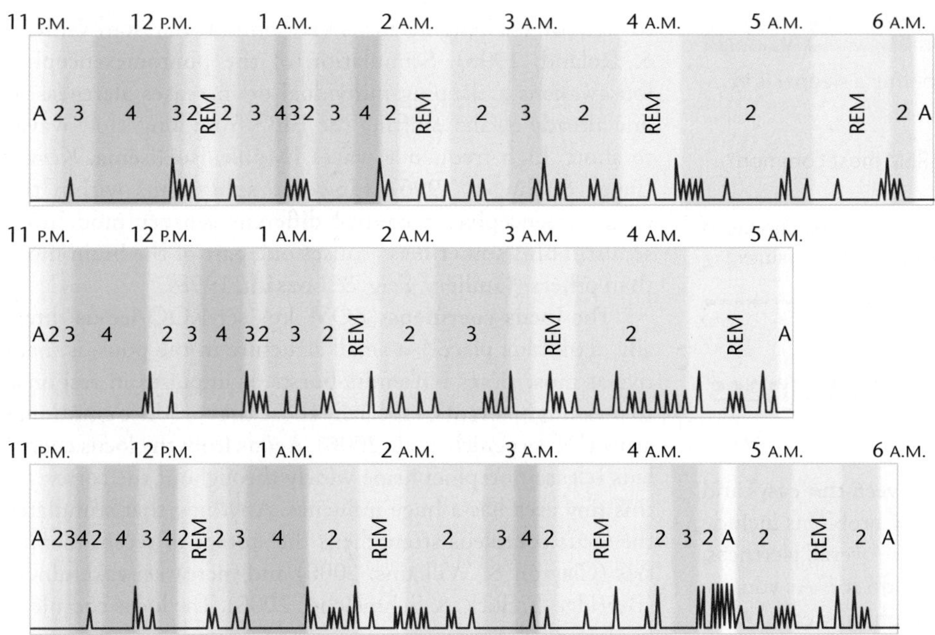

Figure 9.11 Sequence of sleep stages on three representative nights
Columns indicate awake (A) and sleep stages 2, 3, 4, and REM. Deflections in the line at the bottom of each chart indicate shifts in body position. Note that stage 4 sleep occurs mostly in the early part of the night's sleep, whereas REM sleep becomes more prevalent toward the end. *(Based on Dement & Kleitman, 1957a)*

eye movements would stop during sleep. At first, they recorded only a few minutes of eye movements per hour because the recording paper was expensive and they did not expect to see anything interesting in the middle of the night anyway. When they occasionally found periods of eye movements in people who had been asleep for hours, the investigators assumed that something was wrong with their machines. Only after repeated careful measurements did they conclude that periods of rapid eye movements do exist during sleep (Dement, 1990). They called these periods **rapid eye movement (REM) sleep** (Aserinsky & Kleitman, 1955; Dement & Kleitman, 1957a) and soon realized that REM sleep was synonymous with what Jouvet called *paradoxical sleep*. Researchers use the term *REM sleep* when referring to humans but often prefer the term *paradoxical sleep* for nonhumans because many species lack eye movements.

During paradoxical or REM sleep, the EEG shows irregular, low-voltage fast waves that indicate increased neuronal activity. In this regard, REM sleep is light. However, the postural muscles of the body, such as those that support the head, are more relaxed during REM than in other stages. In this regard, REM is deep sleep. REM is also associated with erections in males and vaginal moistening in females. Heart rate, blood pressure, and breathing rate are more variable in REM than in stages 2 through 4. In short, REM sleep combines deep sleep, light sleep, and features that are difficult to classify as deep or light. Consequently, it is best to avoid the terms *deep* and *light* sleep.

In addition to its steady characteristics, REM sleep has intermittent characteristics such as facial twitches and eye movements, as shown in Figure 9.10f. The EEG record is similar to that for stage 1 sleep, but notice the difference in eye movements. The stages other than REM are known as **non-REM (NREM) sleep.**

Anyone who falls asleep starts in stage 1 and slowly progresses through stages 2, 3, and 4 in order, although loud noises or other intrusions can interrupt the sequence. After about an hour of sleep, the person begins to cycle back from stage 4 through stages 3, 2, and then REM. The sequence repeats, with each cycle lasting about 90 minutes. Early in the night, stages 3 and 4 predominate. Toward morning, the duration of stage 4 grows shorter and the duration of REM increases. Figure 9.11 shows typical sequences. The amount of REM depends on time of day more than how long you have been asleep. That is, if you go to sleep later than usual, you still increase your REM at about the same time that you would have ordinarily (Czeisler, Weitzman, Moore-Ede, Zimmerman, & Knauer, 1980). Most people with depression enter REM quickly after falling asleep, even when sleeping at their normal time, suggesting that their circadian rhythm is out of synchrony with clock time.

Initially after the discovery of REM, researchers believed it was almost synonymous with dreaming. William Dement and Nathaniel Kleitman (1957b) found that people who were awakened during REM reported dreams 80% to 90% of the time. Later researchers, however, found that people also sometimes reported dreams when they were awakened from NREM sleep. REM dreams are more likely than NREM dreams to include striking visual imagery and complicated plots, but not always. Some people continue to report dreams despite no evidence of REM sleep (Solms, 1997). In short, REM and dreams usually overlap, but they are not the same thing.

William C. Dement
The average person would not, at first blush, pick watching people sleep as the most apparent theme for a spine-tingling scientific adventure thriller. However, there is a subtle sense of awe and mystery surrounding the "short death" we call sleep.

STOP & CHECK

7. How can an investigator determine whether a sleeper is in REM sleep?

8. During which part of a night's sleep is REM most common?

ANSWERS

7. Examine EEG pattern and eye movements. **8.** REM becomes more common toward the end of the night's sleep.

Brain Mechanisms of Wakefulness and Arousal

Recall from Chapter 1 the distinction between the "easy" and "hard" problems of consciousness. The easy problems include such matters as, "Which brain areas increase overall alertness, and by what kinds of transmitters do they do so?" As you are about to see, that question may be philosophically easy, but it is scientifically complex.

Brain Structures of Arousal and Attention

After a cut through the midbrain separates the forebrain and part of the midbrain from all the lower structures, an animal enters a prolonged state of sleep for the next few days. Even after weeks of recovery, the wakeful periods are brief. We might suppose a simple explanation: The cut isolated the brain from the sensory stimuli that come up from the medulla and spinal cord. However, if a researcher cuts each individual tract that enters the medulla and spinal cord, thus depriving the brain of the sensory input, the animal still has normal periods of wakefulness and sleep. Evidently, the midbrain does more than just relay sensory information; it has its own mechanisms to promote wakefulness.

A cut through the midbrain decreases arousal by damaging the **reticular formation,** a structure that extends from the medulla into the forebrain. Some neurons of the reticular formation have axons ascending into the brain, and some have axons descending into the spinal cord. Those with axons descending into the spinal cord form part of the medial tract of motor control, as discussed in Chapter 8. In 1949, Giuseppe Moruzzi and H. W. Magoun proposed that those with ascending axons are well suited to regulate arousal. The term *reticular* (based on the Latin word *rete,* meaning "net") describes the widespread connections among neurons in this system. One part of the reticular formation that contributes to cortical arousal is known as the **pontomesencephalon** (Woolf, 1996). (The term derives from *pons* and *mesencephalon,* or "midbrain.") These neurons receive input from many sensory systems and generate spontaneous activity of their own. Their axons extend into the forebrain, as shown in Figure 9.12, releasing acetylcholine and glutamate, which excite cells in the hypothalamus, thalamus, and basal forebrain. Consequently, the pontomesencephalon maintains arousal during wakefulness and increases it in response to new or challenging tasks (Kinomura, Larsson, Gulyás, & Roland, 1996). Stimulation of the pontomesencephalon awakens a sleeping individual or increases alertness in one already awake, shifting the EEG from long, slow waves to short, high-frequency waves (Munk, Roelfsema, König, Engel, & Singer, 1996). However, subsystems within the pontomesencephalon control different sensory modalities, so a stimulus sometimes arouses one part of the brain more than others (Guillery, Feig, & Lozsádi, 1998).

The **locus coeruleus** (LOW-kus ser-ROO-lee-us; literally, "dark blue place"), a small structure in the pons, is inactive at most times but emits bursts of impulses in response to meaningful events, especially those that produce emotional arousal (Sterpenich et al., 2006). Axons from the locus coeruleus release norepinephrine widely throughout the cortex, so this tiny area has a huge influence. Anything that stimulates the locus coeruleus strengthens the storage of recent memories (Clayton & Williams, 2000) and increases wakefulness (Berridge, Stellick, & Schmeichel, 2005). The locus coeruleus is silent during sleep.

The hypothalamus has several axon pathways that influence arousal. One pathway releases the neurotransmitter *histamine* (J.-S. Lin, Hou, Sakai, & Jouvet, 1996), which produces excitatory effects throughout the brain (Haas & Panula, 2003). Cells releasing histamine are active during arousal and alertness. As you might guess, they are less active when you are getting ready for sleep and when you have just awakened in the morning (K. Takahashi, Lin, & Sakai, 2006). Antihistamine drugs, often used for allergies, counteract this transmitter and produce drowsiness. Antihistamines that do not cross the blood-brain barrier avoid that side effect.

Another pathway from the hypothalamus, mainly from the lateral and posterior nuclei of the hypothalamus, releases a peptide neurotransmitter called either **orexin** or **hypocretin.** For simplicity, this text will stick to one term, orexin, but if you find the term hypocretin in other reading, it means the same thing. The axons releasing orexin extend to the basal forebrain and other areas, where they stimulate neurons responsible for wakefulness (Sakurai, 2007). Orexin is not necessary for waking up, but it is for *staying* awake. That is, most adult humans stay awake for roughly 16–17 hours at a time, even when nothing much is happening. Staying awake depends on orexin, especially toward the end of the day (Lee, Hassani, & Jones, 2005). A study of squirrel monkeys found that orexin levels rose throughout the day and remained high when the monkeys were kept awake beyond their usual sleep time. As soon as the monkeys went to sleep, the orexin levels dropped (Zeitzer et al., 2003). Drugs that block orexin receptors increase sleep (Brisbare-Roch et al., 2007), and procedures that increase orexin (e.g., a nasal spray of orexin itself) lead to increased wakefulness and alertness (Deadwyler, Porrino, Siegel, & Hampson, 2007; Prober, Rihel, Onah, Sung, & Schier, 2006). Perhaps drugs based on orexin will become available for people with sleep disorders.

Other pathways from the lateral hypothalamus regulate cells in the **basal forebrain** (an area just anterior and dorsal

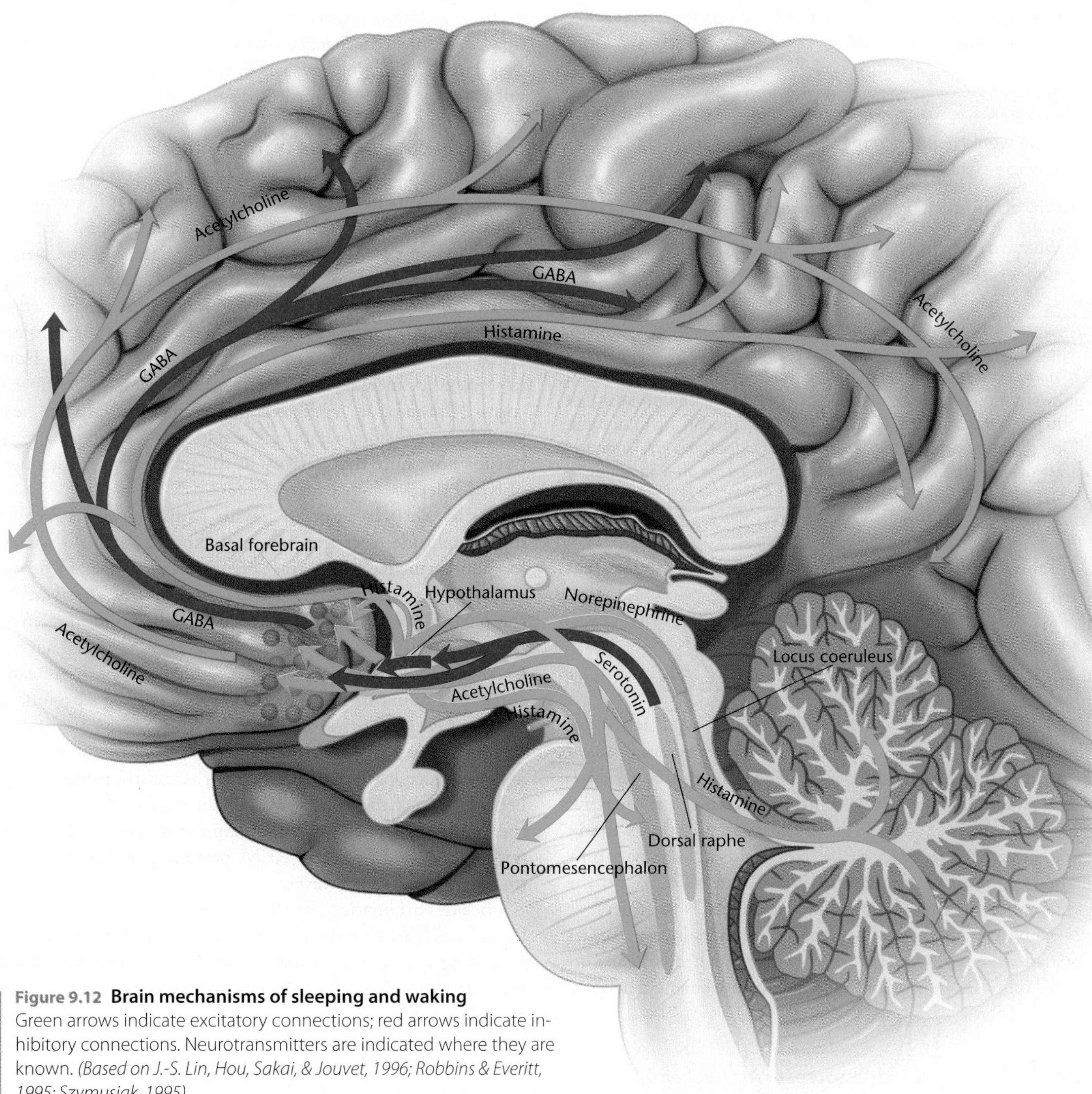

Figure 9.12 Brain mechanisms of sleeping and waking
Green arrows indicate excitatory connections; red arrows indicate inhibitory connections. Neurotransmitters are indicated where they are known. *(Based on J.-S. Lin, Hou, Sakai, & Jouvet, 1996; Robbins & Everitt, 1995; Szymusiak, 1995)*

to the hypothalamus). Basal forebrain cells provide axons that extend throughout the thalamus and cerebral cortex (see Figure 9.12). Some of these axons release acetylcholine, which is excitatory and tends to increase arousal (Mesulam, 1995; Szymusiak, 1995). People with Alzheimer's disease (Chapter 13) lose many of these acetylcholine-releasing cells.

Figure 9.12 labels some other axons (shown in red) as GABA axons, but in fact, these are axons that stimulate other neurons to release GABA. Almost always, it is small local cells that release GABA, the brain's main inhibitory transmitter. Without the inhibition provided by GABA, sleep would not occur (Gottesmann, 2004). The functions of GABA help explain what we experience during sleep: During sleep, body temperature and metabolic rate decrease slightly, and so does the activity of neurons, but by less than we might expect. Spontaneously active neurons continue to fire at almost their usual rate, and neurons in the brain's sensory areas continue to respond to sounds and other stimuli. Nevertheless, we are unconscious. The explanation is that GABA inhibits synaptic activity. A neuron may be active, either spontaneously or in response to a stimulus, but the increased GABA levels prevent its axons from spreading the stimulation to other areas. Researchers demonstrated that a stimulus could excite a brain area as strongly during sleep as during wakefulness, but the excitation was briefer than usual and did not spread to other areas (Massimini et al., 2005).

STOP & CHECK

9. What would happen to the sleep–wake schedule of someone who took a drug that blocked GABA?

10. Why do most antihistamines make people drowsy?

11. What would happen to the sleep–wake schedule of someone who lacked orexin?

ANSWERS

9. Someone who took a drug that blocks GABA would remain awake. (Tranquilizers put people to sleep by facilitating GABA.) **10.** Two paths from the hypothalamus—one to the basal forebrain and one to the pontomesencephalon—use histamine as their neurotransmitter to increase arousal. Antihistamines that cross the blood-brain barrier block those synapses. **11.** Someone without orexin would alternate between brief periods of waking and sleeping.

Table 9.1 summarizes the effects of some key brain areas on arousal and sleep.

Brain Function in REM Sleep

Researchers interested in the brain mechanisms of REM decided to use a PET scan to determine which areas increased or decreased in activity during REM. Although that research might sound simple, PET requires injecting a radioactive chemical. Imagine trying to give sleepers an injection without awakening them. Further, a PET scan yields a clear image only if the head remains motionless during data collection. If the person tosses or turns even slightly, the image is worthless.

To overcome these difficulties, researchers in two studies persuaded young people to sleep with their heads firmly attached to masks that did not permit any movement. They also inserted a cannula (plastic tube) into each person's arm so that they could inject radioactive chemicals at various times during the night. So imagine yourself in that setup. You have a cannula in your arm and your head is locked into position. Now try to sleep.

Because the researchers foresaw the difficulty of sleeping under these conditions (!), they had their participants stay awake the entire previous night. Someone who is tired enough can sleep even under trying circumstances. (Maybe.)

Now that you appreciate the heroic nature of the procedures, here are the results. During REM sleep, activity increased in the pons and the limbic system (which is important for emotional responses). Activity decreased in the primary visual cortex, the motor cortex, and the dorsolateral prefrontal cortex but increased in parts of the parietal and temporal cortex (Braun et al., 1998; Maquet et al., 1996). In the next module, we consider what these results imply about dreaming, but for now, note that activity in the pons triggers the onset of REM sleep.

REM sleep is associated with a distinctive pattern of high-amplitude electrical potentials known as **PGO waves,** for pons-geniculate-occipital (Figure 9.13). Waves of neural activity are detected first in the pons, shortly afterward in the lateral geniculate nucleus of the thalamus, and then in the occipital cortex (D. C. Brooks & Bizzi, 1963; Laurent, Cespuglio, & Jouvet, 1974). Each animal maintains a nearly constant amount of PGO waves per day. During a prolonged period of REM deprivation, PGO waves begin to emerge during sleep stages 2 to 4—when they do not normally occur—and even during wakefulness, often in association with strange behaviors, as if the animal were hallucinating. At the end of the deprivation period, when an animal is permitted to sleep without interruption, the REM periods have an unusually high density of PGO waves.

Besides originating the PGO waves, cells in the pons contribute to REM sleep by sending messages to the spinal cord, inhibiting the motor neurons that control the body's large muscles. After damage to the floor of the pons, a cat still has

TABLE 9.1 Brain Structures for Arousal and Sleep

Structure	Neurotransmitter(s) It Releases	Effects on Behavior
Pontomesencephalon	Acetylcholine, glutamate	Increases cortical arousal
Locus coeruleus	Norepinephrine	Increases information storage during wakefulness; suppresses REM sleep
Basal forebrain		
Excitatory cells	Acetylcholine	Excites thalamus and cortex; increases learning, attention; shifts sleep from NREM to REM
Inhibitory cells	GABA	Inhibits thalamus and cortex
Hypothalamus (parts)	Histamine	Increases arousal
(parts)	Orexin	Maintains wakefulness
Dorsal raphe and pons	Serotonin	Interrupts REM sleep

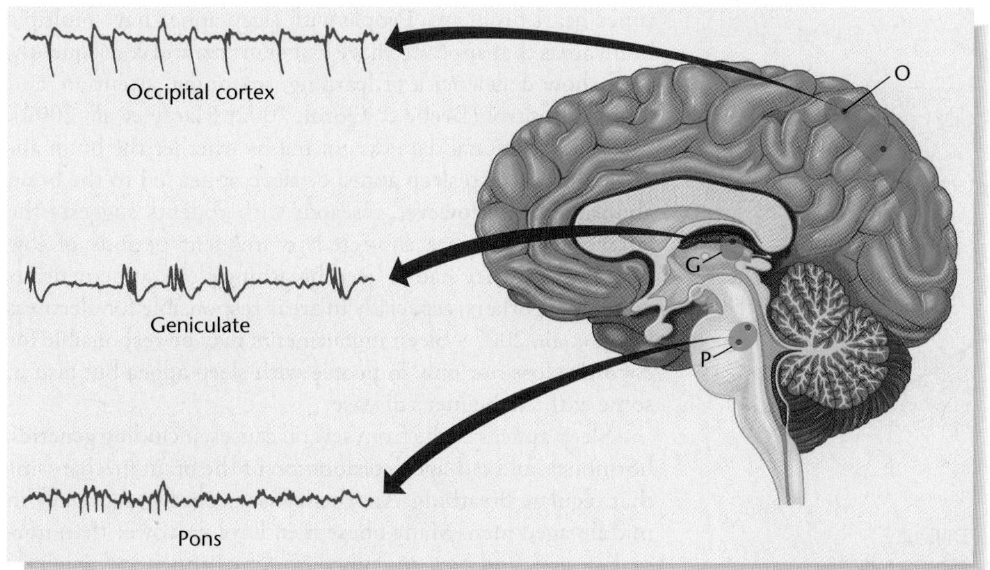

Figure 9.13 PGO waves
PGO waves start in the pons (P) and then show up in the lateral geniculate (G) and the occipital cortex (O). Each PGO wave is synchronized with an eye movement in REM sleep.

REM sleep periods, but its muscles are not relaxed. It walks around awkwardly during REM periods, behaves as if it were chasing an imagined prey, jumps as if startled, and so forth (Morrison, Sanford, Ball, Mann, & Ross, 1995) (Figure 9.14). Is the cat acting out dreams? We do not know; the cat cannot tell us. Evidently, one function of the messages from the pons to the spinal cord is to prevent action during REM sleep.

REM sleep apparently depends on a relationship between the neurotransmitters serotonin and acetylcholine. Injections of the drug *carbachol,* which stimulates acetylcholine synapses, quickly move a sleeper into REM sleep (Baghdoyan, Spotts, & Snyder, 1993). Note that acetylcholine is important for both wakefulness and REM sleep, states of brain arousal. Serotonin and norepinephrine interrupt REM sleep (Boutrel, Franc, Hen, Hamon, & Adrien, 1999; Singh & Mallick, 1996).

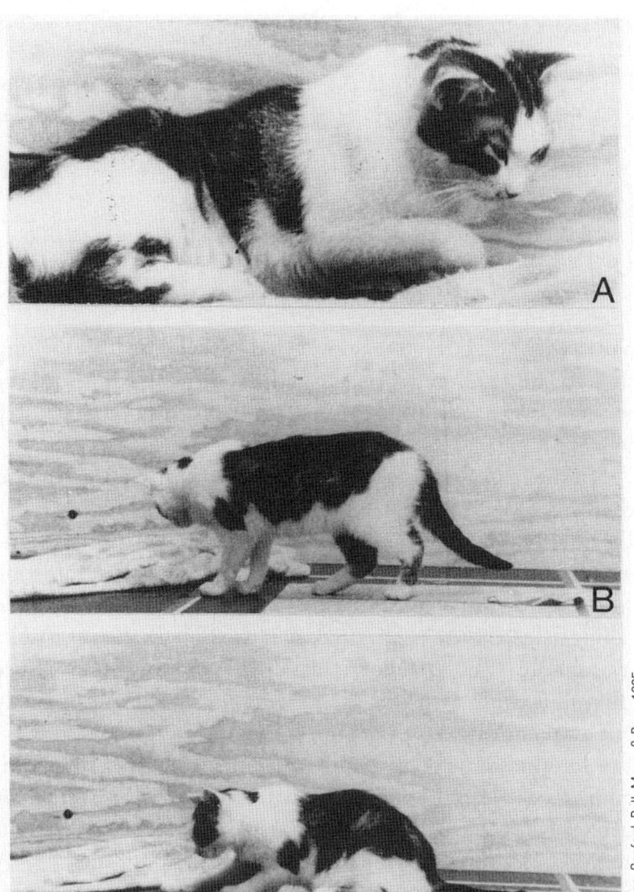

Figure 9.14 A cat with a lesion in the pons, wobbling about during REM sleep
Cells of an intact pons send inhibitory messages to the spinal cord neurons that control the large muscles. *(From Morrison, A. R., Sanford, L. D., Ball, W. A., Mann, G. L., & Ross, R. J., "Stimulus-elicited behavior in rapid eye movement sleep without atonia,"* Behavioral Neuroscience, 109, *972–979, 1995. Published by APA and reprinted with permission.)*

Sleep Disorders

How much sleep is enough? Different people need different amounts. Most adults need about 7 $^1/_2$ to 8 hours of sleep per night, but some have been known to get by with less than 3 hours per night, without unpleasant consequences (H. S. Jones & Oswald, 1968; Meddis, Pearson, & Langford, 1973).

The best gauge of **insomnia**—inadequate sleep—is how someone feels the following day. If you feel tired during the day, you are not sleeping enough at night. Causes of insomnia include noise, uncomfortable temperatures, stress, pain, diet, and medications. Insomnia can also be the result of epilepsy, Parkinson's disease, brain tumors, depression, anxiety, or other neurological or psychiatric conditions. Some children suffer insomnia because they are milk-intolerant, and their parents, not realizing the intolerance, give them milk to drink right before bedtime (Horne, 1992). One man suffered insomnia until he realized that he dreaded going to sleep because he

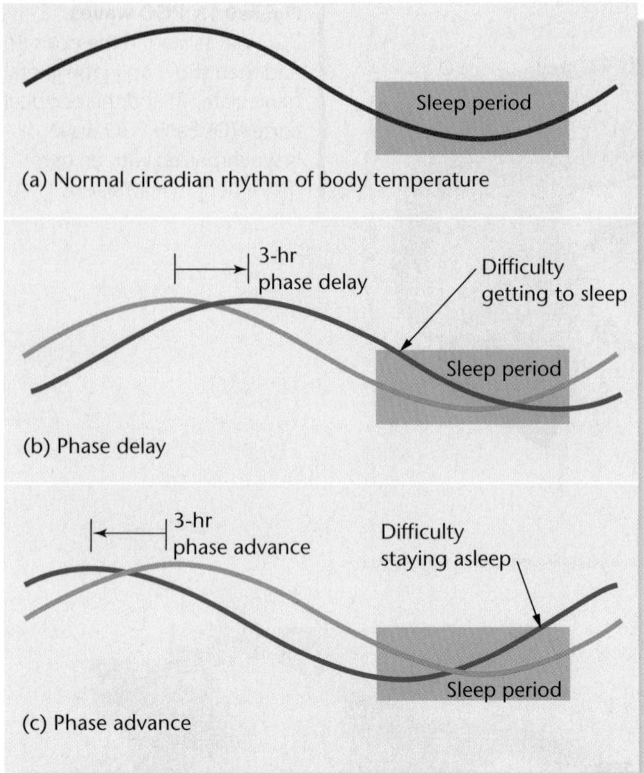

Figure 9.15 Insomnia and circadian rhythms
A delay in the circadian rhythm of body temperature is associated with onset insomnia; an advance, with termination insomnia.

hated waking up to go jogging. After he switched his jogging time to late afternoon, he slept without difficulty. In short, try to identify the reasons for your sleep problems before you try to solve them.

Some cases of insomnia relate to shifts in circadian rhythms (MacFarlane, Cleghorn, & Brown, 1985a, 1985b). Ordinarily, people fall asleep while their temperature is declining and awaken while it is rising, as in Figure 9.15a. Someone whose rhythm is *phase delayed,* as in Figure 9.15b, has trouble falling asleep at the usual time, as if the hypothalamus thinks it isn't late enough (Morris et al., 1990). Someone whose rhythm is *phase advanced,* as in Figure 9.15c, falls asleep easily but awakens early.

Another cause of insomnia is, paradoxically, the use of tranquilizers as sleeping pills. Although tranquilizers may help a person fall asleep, repeated use causes dependence and an inability to sleep without the pills (Kales, Scharf, & Kales, 1978). Similar problems arise when people use alcohol to get to sleep.

Sleep Apnea

One type of insomnia is **sleep apnea,** impaired ability to breathe while sleeping. People with sleep apnea have breathless periods of about a minute from which they awaken gasping for breath. They may not remember all their awakenings, although they certainly notice the consequences—sleepiness during the day, impaired attention, depression, and sometimes heart problems. People with sleep apnea have multiple brain areas that appear to have lost neurons, and consequently, they show deficiencies of learning, reasoning, attention, and impulse control (Beebe & Gozal, 2002; Macey et al., 2002). These correlational data do not tell us whether the brain abnormalities led to sleep apnea or sleep apnea led to the brain abnormalities. However, research with rodents suggests the latter: Mice that are subjected to frequent periods of low oxygen (as if they hadn't been breathing) lose some neurons and impair others, especially in areas responsible for alertness (Zhu et al., 2007). Sleep impairments may be responsible for cognitive loss not only in people with sleep apnea but also in some with Alzheimer's disease.

Sleep apnea results from several causes, including genetics, hormones, and old-age deterioration of the brain mechanisms that regulate breathing. Another cause is obesity, especially in middle-aged men. Many obese men have narrower than normal airways and have to compensate by breathing frequently or vigorously. During sleep, they cannot keep up that rate of breathing. Furthermore, their airways become even narrower than usual when they adopt a sleeping posture (Mezzanotte, Tangel, & White, 1992).

People with sleep apnea are advised to lose weight and avoid alcohol and tranquilizers (which impair the breathing muscles). Medical options include surgery to remove tissue that obstructs the trachea (the breathing passage) or a mask that covers the nose and delivers air under enough pressure to keep the breathing passages open (Figure 9.16).

STOP & CHECK

12. What kinds of people are most likely to develop sleep apnea?

ANSWER

12. Sleep apnea is most common among people with a genetic predisposition, old people, and overweight middle-aged men.

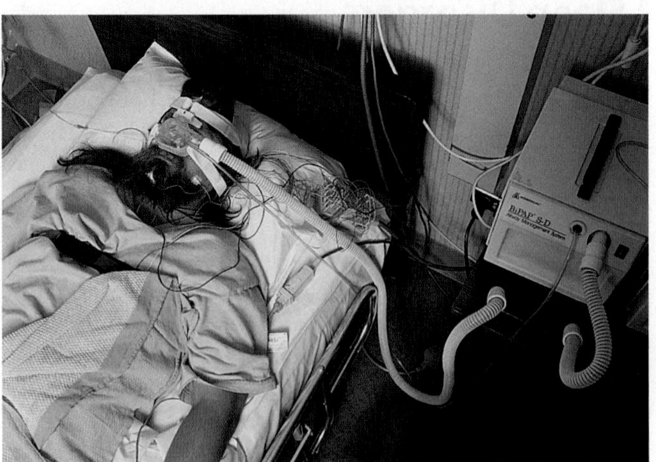

Figure 9.16 A Continuous Positive Airway Pressure (CPAP) mask
The mask fits snugly over the nose and delivers air at a fixed pressure, strong enough to keep the breathing passages open.

Narcolepsy

Narcolepsy, a condition characterized by frequent periods of sleepiness during the day (Aldrich, 1998), strikes about 1 person in 1,000. It sometimes runs in families, although no gene for narcolepsy has been identified, and many people with narcolepsy have no close relatives with the disease. Narcolepsy has four main symptoms, although not every patient has all four. Each of these symptoms can be interpreted as an intrusion of a REM-like state into wakefulness:

1. Gradual or sudden attacks of sleepiness during the day.
2. Occasional **cataplexy**—an attack of muscle weakness while the person remains awake. Cataplexy is often triggered by strong emotions, such as anger or great excitement. (One man suddenly collapsed during his own wedding ceremony.)
3. Sleep paralysis—an inability to move while falling asleep or waking up. Other people may experience sleep paralysis occasionally, but people with narcolepsy experience it more frequently.
4. *Hypnagogic hallucinations*—dreamlike experiences that the person has trouble distinguishing from reality, often occurring at the onset of sleep.

The cause relates to the neurotransmitter orexin. People with narcolepsy lack the hypothalamic cells that produce and release orexin (Thanickal et al., 2000). Why they lack them is unknown, but heredity does not appear to be a major factor. Recall that orexin is important for maintaining wakefulness. Consequently, people lacking orexin alternate between short waking periods and short sleepy periods, instead of staying awake throughout the day. Dogs that lack the gene for orexin receptors have symptoms much like human narcolepsy, with frequent alternations between wakefulness and sleep (L. Lin et al., 1999). The same is true for mice that lack orexin (Hara, 2001; Mochizuki et al., 2004).

As discussed in Chapter 8, people with Huntington's disease have widespread damage in the basal ganglia. In addition, most lose neurons in the hypothalamus, including the neurons that make orexin. As a result, they have problems staying awake during the day and difficulty staying asleep at night (Morton et al., 2005).

Theoretically, we might imagine combating narcolepsy with drugs that restore orexin. Perhaps eventually, such drugs will become available. Currently, the most common treatment is stimulant drugs, such as methylphenidate (Ritalin), which enhance dopamine and norepinephrine activity.

STOP & CHECK

13. What is the relationship between orexin and narcolepsy?

ANSWER

13. Orexin is important for staying awake. Therefore, people or animals lacking either orexin or the receptors for orexin develop narcolepsy, characterized by bouts of sleepiness during the day.

Periodic Limb Movement Disorder

Another sleep disorder is **periodic limb movement disorder,** characterized by repeated involuntary movement of the legs and sometimes the arms (Edinger et al., 1992). Many people, perhaps most, experience an occasional involuntary kick, especially when starting to fall asleep. Leg movements are not a problem unless they become persistent. In some people, mostly middle-aged and older, the legs kick once every 20 to 30 seconds for minutes or hours, mostly during NREM sleep. Frequent or especially vigorous leg movements may awaken the person or his or her partner. In some cases, tranquilizers help suppress the movements (Schenck & Mahowald, 1996).

REM Behavior Disorder

For most people, the major postural muscles are relaxed and inactive during REM sleep. However, people with **REM behavior disorder** move around vigorously during their REM periods, apparently acting out their dreams. They frequently dream about defending themselves against attack, and they may punch, kick, and leap about. Most of them injure themselves or other people and damage property (Olson, Boeve, & Silber, 2000).

REM behavior disorder occurs mostly in older people, especially older men with brain diseases such as Parkinson's disease (Olson et al., 2000). Presumably, the damage includes the cells in the pons that send messages to inhibit the spinal neurons that control large muscle movements.

Night Terrors, Sleep Talking, and Sleepwalking

Night terrors are experiences of intense anxiety from which a person awakens screaming in terror. A night terror is different from a nightmare, which is simply an unpleasant dream. Night terrors occur during NREM sleep and are far more common in children than in adults. Dream content, if any, is usually simple, such as a single image.

Sleep talking is common and harmless. Many people, probably most, talk in their sleep occasionally. Unless someone hears you talking in your sleep and later tells you about it, you could talk in your sleep for years and never realize it. Sleep talking occurs during both REM and non-REM sleep (Arkin, Toth, Baker, & Hastey, 1970).

Sleepwalking runs in families and occurs mostly in children, although 1% to 2% of adults have sleepwalked at least once. The causes are not well understood, but sleepwalking is more common when people are sleep deprived or after they take alcohol or various other drugs or medications. It is most common during stage 3 or stage 4 sleep early in the night and usually not accompanied by dreaming. (It does not occur during REM sleep, when the large muscles are completely relaxed.) Sleepwalking is usually harmless but not always. One teenage girl walked out of her house, climbed a crane, and went back to sleep on a support beam. Fortunately, a pedestrian saw her and called the police. Sleepwalkers have been known to eat, rearrange furniture, fall off balconies, and drive cars—while disregarding lanes and traffic lights. Unlike wakeful actions, the deeds of sleepwalkers are poorly planned and not remembered. Evidently, parts of the brain are awake and other parts are asleep (Gunn & Gunn, 2007). Incidentally, contrary to common sayings, it is not dangerous to awaken a sleepwalker.

An analogous condition is sleep sex or sexsomnia, in which people engage in sexual behavior, either with a partner or by masturbation, during a sleeplike state, and do not remember it afterward. In some cases, they injure themselves or others, and even in physically harmless cases, sexsomnia poses a threat to romances and marriages. As one woman said, "After getting married a few years ago, my husband told me I was masturbating in my sleep. I was mortified, thinking back to all the slumber parties as a girl, and then when I was older and my little sister stayed the night at my house! How many others might have witnessed and not said anything? My new marriage is on the rocks, since I'm having such good sex in my sleep, I have NO desire while I'm awake. This is killing my relationship with my husband" (Mangan, 2004, p. 290).

For more information about a variety of sleep disorders, check The Sleep Site at The Columbus Community Health Regional Sleep Disorders Center: **http://www.thesleepsite.com/**

MODULE 9.2 IN CLOSING

Stages of Sleep

In many cases, scientific progress depends on drawing useful distinctions. Chemists divide the world into different elements, biologists divide life into different species, and physicians distinguish one disease from another. Similarly, psychologists try to recognize the most natural or useful distinctions among types of behavior or experience. The discovery of different stages of sleep was a major landmark in psychology because researchers found a previously unrecognized distinction that is both biologically and psychologically important. It also demonstrated that external measurements—in this case, EEG recordings—can be used to identify internal experiences. We now take it largely for granted that an electrical or magnetic recording from the brain can tell us something about a person's experience, but it is worth pausing to note what a surprising discovery that was in its time.

SUMMARY

1. During sleep, brain activity decreases, but a stimulus can awaken the person. Someone in a coma cannot be awakened. A vegetative state or minimally conscious state can last months or years, during which the person shows only limited responses. Brain death is a condition without brain activity or responsiveness of any kind. 269
2. Over the course of about 90 minutes, a sleeper goes through stages 1, 2, 3, and 4 and then returns through stages 3 and 2 to a stage called REM. REM is characterized by rapid eye movements, more brain activity than other sleep stages, complete relaxation of the trunk muscles, irregular breathing and heart rate, penile erection or vaginal lubrication, and an increased probability of vivid dreams. 269
3. The brain has multiple systems for arousal. The pontomesencephalon and parts of the hypothalamus control various cell clusters in the basal forebrain that send axons releasing acetylcholine throughout much of the forebrain. 272
4. The locus coeruleus is active in response to meaningful events. It facilitates attention and new learning; it also blocks the onset of REM sleep. 272
5. Orexin is a peptide that maintains wakefulness. Cells in the lateral and posterior nuclei of the hypothalamus release this peptide. 272
6. Other cells in the basal forebrain have axons that release GABA, which is essential for sleep. 273
7. REM sleep is associated with increased activity in a number of brain areas, including the pons, limbic system, and parts of the parietal and temporal cortex. Activity decreases in the prefrontal cortex, the motor cortex, and the primary visual cortex. 274
8. REM sleep begins with PGO waves, which are waves of brain activity transmitted from the pons to the lateral geniculate to the occipital lobe. 274
9. People with sleep apnea have long periods without breathing while they sleep. Many have indications of neuronal loss, probably as a result of decreased oxygen while they sleep. 276
10. People with narcolepsy have attacks of sleepiness during the day. Narcolepsy is associated with a deficiency of the peptide neurotransmitter orexin. 277

KEY TERMS

Terms are defined in the module on the page number indicated. They're also presented in alphabetical order with definitions in the book's Subject Index/Glossary. Interactive flashcards, audio reviews, and crossword puzzles are among the online resources available to help you learn these terms and the concepts they represent.

alpha waves **269**
basal forebrain **272**
brain death **269**
cataplexy **277**
coma **269**
insomnia **274**
K-complex **270**
locus coeruleus **272**
minimally conscious state **269**
narcolepsy **277**
night terrors **277**
non-REM (NREM) sleep **271**
orexin (or hypocretin) **272**
paradoxical sleep **270**
periodic limb movement disorder **277**
PGO waves **274**
polysomnograph **269**
pontomesencephalon **272**
rapid eye movement (REM) sleep **271**
REM behavior disorder **277**
reticular formation **272**
sleep apnea **276**
sleep spindle **269**
slow-wave sleep (SWS) **270**
vegetative state **269**

THOUGHT QUESTION

When cats are deprived of REM sleep and then permitted uninterrupted sleep, the longer the period of deprivation—up to about 25 days—the greater the rebound of REM when they can sleep uninterrupted. However, REM deprivation for more than 25 days produces no additional rebound. Speculate on a possible explanation. (Hint: Consider what happens to PGO waves during REM deprivation.)

MODULE 9.3

Why Sleep? Why REM? Why Dreams?

Why do you sleep? "That's easy," you reply. "I sleep because I get tired." Well, yes, but you are not tired in the sense of muscle fatigue. You need almost as much sleep after a day of sitting around the house as after a day of intense physical or mental activity (Horne & Minard, 1985; Shapiro, Bortz, Mitchell, Bartel, & Jooste, 1981). Furthermore, you could rest your muscles just as well while awake as while asleep. (In fact, if your muscles ache after strenuous exercise, you probably find it difficult to sleep.)

You feel tired at the end of the day because inhibitory processes in your brain force you to become less aroused and less alert. That is, we evolved mechanisms to force us to sleep. Why?

Functions of Sleep

Sleep serves many functions. During sleep, we rest our muscles, decrease metabolism, rebuild proteins in the brain (Kong et al., 2002), reorganize synapses, and strengthen memories (Sejnowski & Destexhe, 2000). People deprived of sleep have trouble concentrating and become more vulnerable to illness. Clearly, we need to sleep for many reasons. Is there one primary reason?

Sleep and Energy Conservation

Even if we could agree on the most important function of sleep for humans today, it might not be the function for which sleep originally evolved. By analogy, consider computers: People use computers today to write papers, send e-mail, search the Internet, play video games, store and display photographs, play music, and find a date. Someone who didn't know the history might not guess that computers were built originally for mathematical calculations.

Similarly, sleep probably started with a simple function to which evolution added others later. All species sleep, not just vertebrates with big brains and complex memories. Even bacteria have circadian rhythms (Mihalcescu, Hsing, & Leibler, 2004). What benefit of sleep applies to all species?

A likely hypothesis is that sleep's original function was to save energy (Kleitman, 1963; Webb, 1974). Virtually every species is more efficient at some times of day than at others. Those with good vision are more efficient in the day. Those that rely on olfaction instead of vision are more efficient at night, when their predators cannot see them. Sleep conserves energy during the inefficient times, when activity would do more harm than good. NASA's Rover spacecraft, built to explore Mars, had a mechanism to make it "sleep" at night to conserve its batteries. During sleep, a mammal's body temperature decreases by 1 or 2 Celsius degrees, enough to save a significant amount of energy. Muscle activity decreases, saving more energy. Animals increase their sleep duration during food shortages, when energy conservation is especially important (Berger & Phillips, 1995).

Sleep is therefore in some ways analogous to hibernation. Hibernation is a true need. A ground squirrel that is prevented from hibernating can become as disturbed as a person who is prevented from sleeping. However, the function of hibernation is simply to conserve energy while food is scarce.

APPLICATIONS AND EXTENSIONS

Hibernation

Hibernating animals decrease their body temperature to only slightly above that of the environment (but they don't let it go low enough for their blood to freeze). Brain activity declines to almost nothing, neuron cell bodies shrink, and dendrites lose almost one fourth of their branches, replacing them when body temperature increases (von der Ohe, Darian-Smith, Garner, & Heller, 2006). A few curious facts about hibernation:

1. Hibernation occurs in certain small mammals such as ground squirrels and bats. Whether or not bears hibernate is a matter of definition. Bears sleep most of the winter, but they do not lower their body temperatures as much as smaller animals do.
2. Hamsters also hibernate. If you keep your pet hamster in a cool, dimly lit place during the winter, and it appears to have died, make sure that it is not just hibernating before you bury it!

3. Hibernating animals come out of hibernation for a few hours every few days, raising their body temperature to about normal. However, they spend most of this nonhibernating time asleep (B. M. Barnes, 1996).
4. Hibernation retards the aging process. Hamsters that spend longer times hibernating have proportionately longer life expectancies than other hamsters do (Lyman, O'Brien, Greene, & Papafrangos, 1981). Hibernation is also a period of relative invulnerability to infection and trauma. Procedures that would ordinarily damage the brain, such as inserting a needle into it, produce little if any harm during hibernation (F. Zhou et al., 2001).

Animal species vary in their sleep habits in accordance with how many hours per day they devote to finding food, how safe they are from predators while they sleep, and other aspects of their way of life (Allison & Cicchetti, 1976; Campbell & Tobler, 1984). For example, grazing animals that need to eat for many hours per day get less sleep than carnivores (meat eaters), which can satisfy their nutritional needs quickly. Animals that need to be on the alert for predators get little sleep, whereas the predators themselves can sleep easily (Figure 9.17).

Several other species show interesting specializations in their sleep. For example, consider dolphins and other aquatic mammals. At night, they need to be alert enough to surface for a breath of air. Dolphins and several other species have evolved the ability to sleep on one side of the brain at a time. That is, the two hemispheres take turns sleeping while the other is awake enough to control swimming and breathing (Rattenborg, Amlaner, & Lima, 2000). (Evidently, sleep serves functions for dolphins other than energy conservation because a sleeping dolphin is still expending a fair amount of energy.)

Migratory birds face a different kind of problem. During a week or two in fall and spring, many species forage for food during the day and do their migratory flying at night. That schedule leaves little or no time for sleep. The birds apparently decrease their *need* for sleep during migration. If a migratory bird is kept in a cage, it flutters around restlessly at night during the migration season, sleeping only one third its usual amount. It compensates to some extent with many brief (less than 30 second) periods of drowsiness or closing one eyelid during the day (Fuchs, Haney, Jechura, Moore, & Bingman, 2006). Still, it is not getting a normal amount of sleep. Nevertheless, the bird remains alert and performs normally on learning tasks. If the same bird is deprived of its normal sleep during other seasons of the year, its performance suffers (Rattenborg et al., 2004). Exactly how a bird decreases its sleep need is unknown.

Swifts are small, dark birds that chase insects. They get all the nutrition and water they need from the insects. Here is a trivia question for you: When a baby European swift first takes off from its nest, how long would you guess its first flight lasts, until it comes to land again?

A European swift.

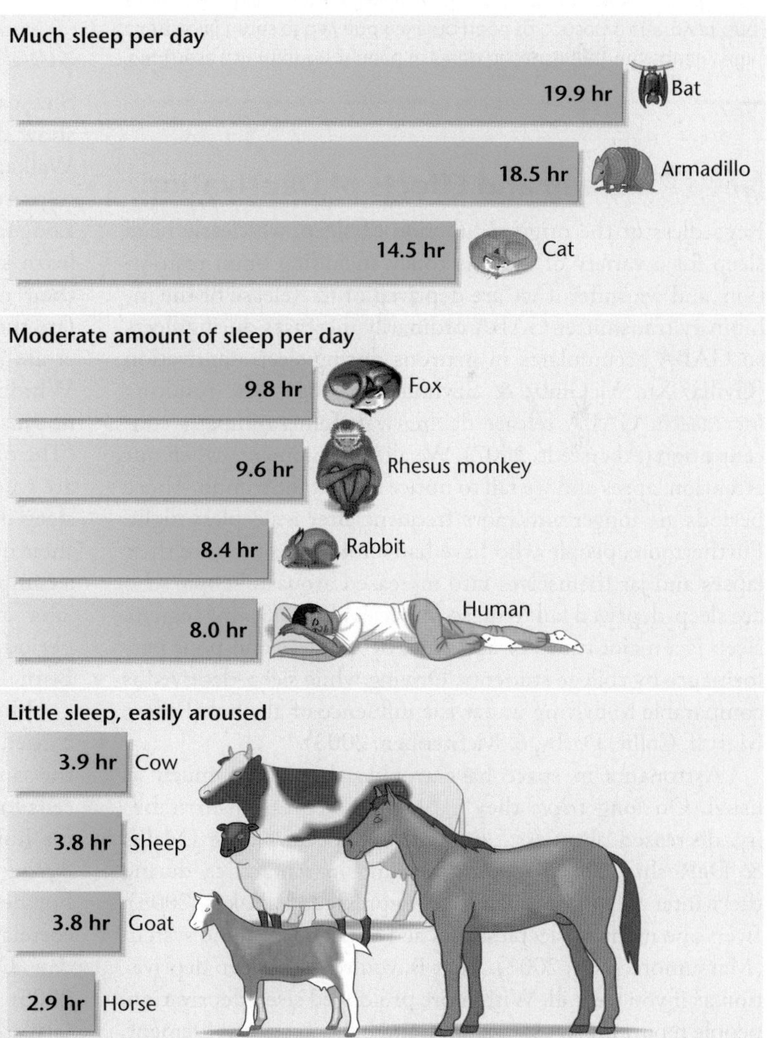

Figure 9.17 Hours of sleep per day for various animal species
Generally, predators and others that are safe when they sleep tend to sleep a great deal; animals in danger of being attacked while they sleep spend less time asleep.

The answer: up to 2 years. Except during huge storms, it doesn't come down until it is old enough to mate and build a nest. In the meantime, it spends both days and nights in the air. A swift at night heads into the wind, sticks out its wings, and glides. It picks an altitude where the air is not too cold, accepts the risk of being blown a great distance, and awakens the next morning to resume its chase of flying insects (Bäckman & Alerstam, 2001). Perhaps it, like dolphins, sleeps on one side of its brain at a time, but we won't know until someone figures out how to measure the EEG of a bird in flight.

STOP & CHECK

14. Some fish live in caves or the deep ocean with no light. What might one predict about their sleep?

ANSWER

14. These fish might not need to sleep because they are equally efficient at all times of day and have no need to conserve energy at one time more than another. The fish might sleep, however, as a relic left over from ancestors that lived in the light—just as humans still erect our arm hairs in response to cold, a response that was useful for our hairier ancestors but not for us.

Need for Sleep and Effects of Deprivation

Regardless of the original function of sleep, we clearly need sleep for a variety of reasons today, including brain restoration, and we suffer if we are deprived of it. Release of the inhibitory transmitter GABA ordinarily increases during sleep, so GABA accumulates in neurons during sleep deprivation (Gvilia, Xu, McGinty, & Szymusiak, 2006). The resulting increase in GABA release during wakefulness impairs concentration (Åkerstedt, 2007). We all have moments when our attention lapses and we fail to notice important stimuli. Those periods are longer and more frequent after a sleepless night. Furthermore, people who have had enough sleep notice their lapses and jar themselves into increased arousal. People who are sleep-deprived fail to do so (Chee et al., 2008). Inadequate sleep is a major cause of accidents by workers and poor performance by college students. Driving while sleep-deprived is comparable to driving under the influence of alcohol (Falleti, Maruff, Collie, Darby, & McStephen, 2003).

Astronauts in space have trouble sleeping as much as usual. On long trips, they experience depression, irritability, decreased alertness, and impaired performance (Mallis & DeRoshia, 2005). People working in Antarctica during the winter sleep poorly and feel depressed (Palinkas, 2003). Even one night of sleeplessness activates the immune system (Matsumoto et al., 2001). That is, you react to sleep deprivation as if you were ill. With more prolonged sleep deprivation, people report dizziness, tremors, and hallucinations (Dement, 1972; L. C. Johnson, 1969).

However, individuals vary in their need for sleep. People who tolerate sleep deprivation relatively well differ from others in several regards. They are usually "evening people," who like to waken late and stay up late. They tend to show greater than average levels of brain arousal, as indicated by fMRI (Caldwell et al., 2005). The people who are least able to tolerate sleep deprivation generally report greater than average arousal benefits from caffeine (Rétey et al., 2006). **Caffeine,** a drug found in coffee, tea, and many soft drinks, increases arousal by blocking the receptors for adenosine (ah-DENN-o-seen), a chemical that accumulates during wakefulness and increases drowsiness (Rainnie, Grunze, McCarley, & Greene, 1994).

STOP & CHECK

15. If we want to choose people for a job that requires sometimes working without sleep, how could we quickly determine which ones were probably best able to tolerate sleep deprivation?

ANSWER

15. Use fMRI to measure brain arousal. Those with strongest responses tend to tolerate sleeplessness better than others.

Sleep and Memory

Sleep aids memory. Young adults deprived of a night's sleep show deficits on memory tasks (Yoo, Hu, Gujar, Jolesz, & Walker, 2007). Mice deprived of sleep for even 4 hours show impairments in their ability to alter synaptic activity (Kopp, Longordo, Nicholson, & Lüthi, 2006). In contrast, if people learn something and then go to sleep, or even take a nap, their memory usually improves to greater than it was *before* the sleep (Hu, Stylos-Allan, & Walker, 2006; Korman et al., 2007; Stickgold, James, & Hobson, 2000; Stickgold, Whidbee, Schirmer, Patel, & Hobson, 2000). That is, we see not just an absence of forgetting but also a gain of memory. (The obvious message to students: Feel well rested when you are studying. And reviewing something right before you go to sleep is an excellent idea.) Sleep also helps people reanalyze their memories: In one study, people who had just practiced a complex task were more likely to perceive a hidden rule (an "aha" experience) after a period of sleep than after a similar period of wakefulness (Wagner, Gais, Haider, Verleger, & Born, 2004).

How does sleep enhance memory? Researchers have recorded brain activity during learning, and then recorded from the same locations during sleep, using microelectrodes within cells for laboratory animals and gross electrodes on the scalp for humans. The results: The same patterns that occurred during learning occurred again, except faster, during sleep. Furthermore, the amount of activity in those areas during sleep correlated highly with the improvement in skill seen the next day (Derégnaucourt, Mitra, Fehér, Pytte, & Tchernichovski, 2005; Euston, Tatsuno, & McNaughton, 2007; Huber, Ghilardi, Massimini, & Tononi, 2004; Ji & Wilson, 2007; Maquet et al., 2000; Peigneux et al., 2004). Apparently, the brain replays the experience repeatedly during sleep.

In one experiment, people had the task of memorizing the locations of various objects. Some of them did the task in the presence of rose odor. That night, the experimenters presented rose odor to half of the people in each group during their sleep. The people who learned in the presence of rose odor and again smelled roses during their sleep showed the greatest enhancement of memory. Presenting rose odor later in the day during wakefulness had less effect (Rasch, Büchel, Gais, & Born, 2007). These results suggest that replaying an experience during sleep helps enhance the memory.

One way for sleep to strengthen memory is by weeding out the less successful connections. In Chapter 13, we shall examine the phenomenon of long-term potentiation, which is the ability of certain kinds of experiences to strengthen synaptic connections and therefore memories. But suppose every time you learned something, your brain strengthened certain synapses without making adjustments elsewhere. As a result, as you grew older and learned more, you would have increasingly active synapses and ever more brain activity. By middle age, your brain might be burning with constant activity. To prevent runaway overactivity, your brain compensates for strengthening some synapses by weakening others. That weakening process occurs mostly during sleep (Vyazovskiy, Cirelli, Pfister-Genskow, Faraguna, & Tononi, 2008). Weakening synapses during sleep emphasizes the effect of strengthening others during wakefulness, and this process could be a major explanation for sleep's benefits on memory.

Another aspect of sleep's contribution to memory relates to sleep spindles. Recall that sleep spindles are waves of activity, about 12–14 Hz, that are particularly common during stage 2 sleep. They indicate an exchange of information between the thalamus and cerebral cortex. In both rats and humans, sleep spindles increase in number after new learning (Eschenko, Mölle, Born, & Sara, 2006). Most people are fairly consistent in their amount of spindle activity from one night to another, and the amount of spindle activity correlates more than .7 with nonverbal tests of IQ (Fogel, Nader, Cote, & Smith, 2007). Who would have guessed that brain waves during sleep could predict IQ?

STOP & CHECK

16. Do memories become improved during sleep by strengthening or weakening synapses?

ANSWER

16. The evidence so far points to weakening the synapses that were not strengthened during the day. Weakening these less relevant synapses enables the strengthened ones to stand out by contrast.

Functions of REM Sleep

An average person spends about one third of his or her life asleep and about one fifth of sleep in REM, totaling about 600 hours of REM per year. Presumably, REM serves a biological function. But what is it?

One way to approach this question is to compare the people or animals with more REM to those with less. REM sleep is widespread in mammals and birds, indicating that the capacity for it is part of our ancient evolutionary heritage. Some species, however, have more than others. As a rule, the species with the most total sleep hours also have the highest percentage of REM sleep (J. M. Siegel, 1995). Cats spend up to 16 hours a day sleeping, much or most of it in REM sleep. Rabbits, guinea pigs, and sheep sleep less and spend little time in REM.

Figure 9.18 illustrates the relationship between age and REM sleep for humans. The trend is the same for other mammalian species. Infants get more REM and more total sleep than adults do, confirming the pattern that more total sleep predicts a higher percentage of REM sleep. Among adult humans, those who sleep 9 or more hours per night have the highest percentage of REM sleep, and those who sleep 5 or fewer hours have the lowest percentage. This pattern implies that although REM is no doubt important, NREM is more tightly regulated. That is, the amount of NREM varies less among individuals and among species.

One hypothesis is that REM is important for memory storage, especially for weakening the inappropriate connections (Crick & Mitchison, 1983). REM and non-REM sleep may be important for consolidating different types of memories. Depriving people of sleep early in the night (mostly non-REM sleep) impairs verbal learning, such as memorizing a list of words, whereas depriving people of sleep during the second half of the night (more REM) impairs consolidation of learned motor skills (Gais, Plihal, Wagner, & Born, 2000; Plihal & Born, 1997).

However, many people take MAO inhibitors, antidepressant drugs that severely decrease REM sleep, without incurring noticeable memory problems. Research on laboratory animals indicates that MAO inhibitors sometimes even enhance memory (Parent, Habib, & Baker, 1999).

Another hypothesis sounds odd because we tend to imagine a glamorous role for REM sleep: David Maurice (1998) proposed that REM just shakes the eyeballs back and forth enough to get sufficient oxygen to the corneas of the eyes. The corneas, unlike the rest of the body, get oxygen directly from the surrounding air. During sleep, because they are shielded from the air, they deteriorate slightly (Hoffmann & Curio, 2003). They do get some oxygen from the fluid behind them (see Figure 6.1 on page 153), but when the eyes are motionless, that fluid becomes stagnant. Moving the eyes increases the oxygen supply to the corneas. According to this view, REM is a way of arousing a sleeper just enough to shake the eyes back and forth, and the other manifestations of REM—including dreams—are just by-products. This idea makes sense of the fact that REM occurs mostly toward the end of the night's sleep, when the fluid behind the eyes would be the most stagnant. It also makes sense of the fact that individuals who spend more hours asleep devote a greater percentage of sleep to REM. (If you don't sleep long, you have less need to shake up the stagnant fluid.) However, as mentioned, many people take MAO inhibitors, which greatly restrict REM sleep. They are not known to suffer damage to the cornea. In short, the evidence does not convincingly support any current hypothesis about the function of REM.

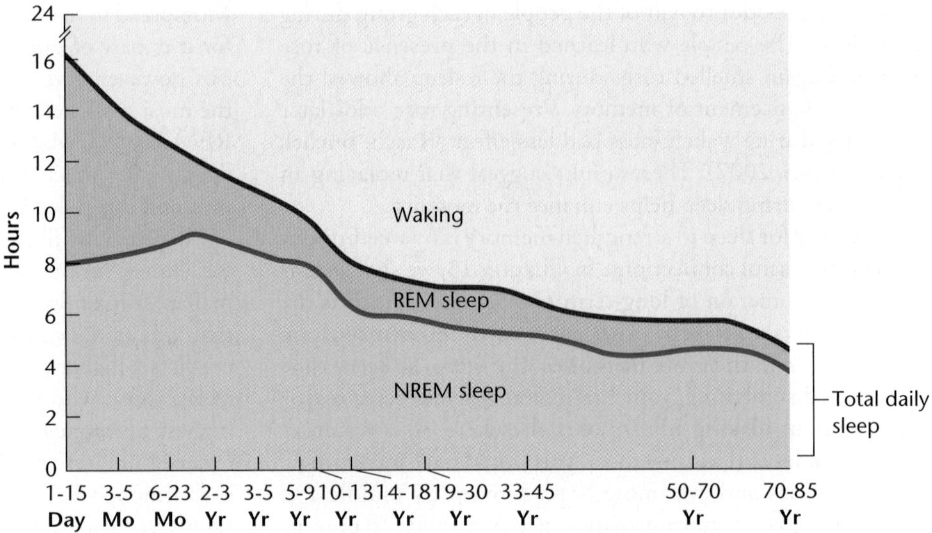

Figure 9.18 Time spent by people of different ages in waking, REM sleep, and NREM sleep
REM sleep occupies about 8 hours a day in newborns but less than 2 hours in most adults. The sleep of infants is not quite like that of adults, however, and the criteria for identifying REM sleep are not the same. *(From "Ontogenetic Development of Human Sleep-Dream Cycle," by H. P. Roffwarg, J. N. Muzio, and W. C. Dement,* Science, 152, *1966, 604–609. Copyright 1966 AAAS. Reprinted by permission.)*

STOP & CHECK

17. What kinds of individuals get more REM sleep than others? (Think in terms of age, species, and long versus short sleepers.)

ANSWER

17. Much REM sleep is more typical of the young than the old, of those who get much sleep than those who get little, and of species that sleep much of the day and are unlikely to be attacked during their sleep.

Biological Perspectives on Dreaming

Dream research faces a special problem: All we know about dreams comes from people's self-reports, and researchers have no way to check the accuracy of those reports. In fact, we forget most dreams quickly, and even when we do remember them, most of the details fade quickly. Thus, any discussion of dream content is fraught with difficulty.

The Activation-Synthesis Hypothesis

According to the **activation-synthesis hypothesis,** a dream represents the brain's effort to make sense of sparse and distorted information. Dreams begin with periodic bursts of spontaneous activity in the pons—the PGO waves previously described—which activate some parts of the cortex but not others. The cortex combines this haphazard input with whatever other activity was already occurring and does its best to synthesize a story that makes sense of the information (Hobson & McCarley, 1977; Hobson, Pace-Schott, & Stickgold, 2000; McCarley & Hoffman, 1981). The input from the pons usually activates the amygdala, a portion of the temporal lobe highly important for emotional processing, and therefore, most dreams have strong emotional content.

Consider how this theory handles a couple of common dreams. Most people have had occasional dreams of falling or flying. Well, while you are asleep, you lie flat, unlike your posture for the rest of the day. Your brain in its partly aroused condition feels the vestibular sensation of your position and interprets it as flying or falling. Have you ever dreamed that you were trying to move but couldn't? Most people have. An interpretation based on the activation-synthesis theory is that during REM sleep (which accompanies most dreams), your motor cortex is inactive and your major postural muscles are virtually paralyzed. That is, when you are dreaming, you really *can't* move, you feel your lack of movement, and thus, you dream of failing to move.

One criticism is that the theory's predictions are vague. If we dream about falling because of the vestibular sensations from lying down, why don't we *always* dream of falling? If we dream we can't move because our muscles are paralyzed during REM sleep, why don't we *always* dream of being paralyzed?

The Clinico-Anatomical Hypothesis

An alternative view of dreams has been labeled the **clinico-anatomical hypothesis** because it was derived from clinical studies of patients with various kinds of brain damage (Solms, 1997, 2000). Like the activation-synthesis theory, this theory emphasizes that dreams begin with arousing stimuli that are generated within the brain combined with recent memories and any information the brain is receiving from the senses. However, the clinico-anatomical hypothesis puts less emphasis on the pons, PGO waves, or REM sleep. It regards dreams as thinking that takes place under unusual conditions.

One of those conditions is that the brain is getting little information from the sense organs, and the primary visual and auditory areas of the cortex have lower than usual activity, so other brain areas are free to generate images without constraints or interference. Also, the primary motor cortex is suppressed, as are the motor neurons of the spinal cord, so arousal cannot lead to action. Activity is suppressed in the prefrontal cortex, which is important for working memory (memory of very recent events). Consequently, we not only forget most dreams after we awaken, but we also lose track of what has been happening within a dream, so sudden scene changes are common.

Meanwhile, activity is relatively high in the inferior (lower) part of the parietal cortex, an area important for visuospatial perception. Patients with damage here have problems binding body sensations with vision. They also report no dreams. Fairly high activity is also found in the areas of visual cortex outside V1. Those areas are presumably important for the visual imagery that accompanies most dreams. Finally, activity is high in the hypothalamus, amygdala, and other areas important for emotions and motivations (Gvilia, Turner, McGinty, & Szymusiak, 2006).

So the idea is that either internal or external stimulation activates parts of the parietal, occipital, and temporal cortex. No sensory input from V1 overrides the stimulation, so it develops into hallucinatory perceptions. This idea, like the activation-synthesis hypothesis, is hard to test because it does not make specific predictions about who will have what dream and when.

For more information about the content of dreams, visit Adam Schneider and G. William Domhoff's Website for The Quantitative Study of Dreams: **http://www.dreamresearch.net**

STOP & CHECK

18. What is a key point of disagreement between the activation-synthesis hypothesis and the clinico-anatomical hypothesis?

ANSWER

18. The activation-synthesis hypothesis puts much more emphasis on the importance of the pons.

MODULE 9.3 IN CLOSING

Our Limited Self-Understanding

Without minimizing how much we do understand about sleep, it is noteworthy how many basic questions remain. What is the function of REM sleep? Does dreaming have a function, or is it just an accident? Our lack of knowledge about activities that occupy so much of our time underscores a point about the biology of behavior: We evolved tendencies to behave in certain ways that lead to survival and reproduction. The behavior can serve its function even when we do not fully understand that function.

SUMMARY

1. Animal species vary in their sleep per day depending on their feeding habits and how much danger they face while asleep. Some species modify their sleep needs to stay on the move. **281**
2. In addition to saving energy, sleep serves other functions, including enhancement of memory. **282**
3. REM sleep occupies the greatest percentage of sleep in individuals and species that sleep the most total hours. **283**
4. According to the activation-synthesis hypothesis, dreams are the brain's attempts to make sense of the information reaching it, based mostly on haphazard input originating in the pons. **284**
5. According to the clinico-anatomical hypothesis, dreams originate partly with external stimuli but mostly from the brain's own motivations, memories, and arousal. The stimulation often produces peculiar results because it does not have to compete with normal visual input and does not get censored by the prefrontal cortex. **284**

Continued

KEY TERMS

Terms are defined in the module on the page number indicated. They're also presented in alphabetical order with definitions in the book's Subject Index/Glossary. Interactive flashcards, audio reviews, and crossword puzzles are among the online resources available to help you learn these terms and the concepts they represent.

activation-synthesis hypothesis **284**
caffeine **282**
clinico-anatomical hypothesis **284**

THOUGHT QUESTION

Why would it be harder to deprive someone of just NREM sleep than just REM sleep?

CHAPTER 9 Exploration and Study

In addition to the study materials provided at the end of each module, you may supplement your review of this chapter by using one or more of the book's electronic resources, which include its companion Website, interactive Cengage Learning eBook, Exploring Biological Psychology CD-ROM, and CengageNOW. Brief descriptions of these resources follow. For more information, visit **www.cengage.com/psychology/kalat**.

The book's companion Website, accessible through the author Web page indicated above, provides a wide range of study resources such as an interactive glossary, flashcards, tutorial quizzes, updated Web links, and Try It Yourself activities, as well as a limited selection of the short videos and animated explanations of concepts available for this chapter.

Exploring Biological Psychology

The Exploring Biological Psychology CD-ROM contains videos, animations, and Try It Yourself activities. These activities—as well as many that are new to this edition—are also available in the text's fully interactive, media-rich Cengage Learning eBook,* which gives you the opportunity to experience biological psychology in an even greater interactive and multimedia environment. The Cengage Learning eBook also includes highlighting and note-taking features and an audio glossary. For this chapter, the Cengage Learning eBook includes the following interactive explorations:

Sleep Patterns
Brain Re-growth
Sleep Rhythms
Pathways Controlling Sleep and Waking

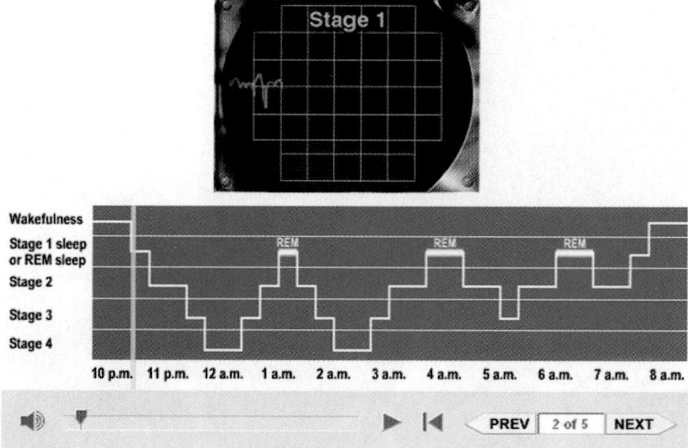

Sleep Rhythms presents a step-by-step view of the stages of sleep.

CENGAGENOW™ is an easy-to-use resource that helps you study in less time to get the grade you want. An online study system, CengageNOW* gives you the option of taking a diagnostic pretest for each chapter. The system uses the results of each pretest to create personalized chapter study plans for you. The Personalized Study Plans

- help you save study time by identifying areas on which you should concentrate and give you one-click access to corresponding pages of the interactive Cengage Learning eBook;
- provide interactive exercises and study tools to help you fully understand chapter concepts; and
- include a posttest for you to take to confirm that you are ready to move on to the next chapter.

Suggestions for Further Exploration

The book's companion Website includes a list of suggested articles available through InfoTrac College Edition for this chapter. You may also want to explore some of the following books and Websites. The text's companion Website provides live, updated links to the sites listed below.

Books

Dement, W. C. (1992). *The sleepwatchers.* Stanford, CA: Stanford Alumni Association. Fascinating, entertaining account of sleep research by one of its leading pioneers.

Foster, R. G., & Kreitzman, L. (2004). *Rhythms of life.* New Haven, CT: Yale University Press. Nontechnical discussion of research on circadian rhythms.

Moorcroft, W. H. (2003). *Understanding sleep and dreaming.* New York: Kluwer. Excellent review of the psychology and neurology of sleep and dreams.

Refinetti, R. (2005). *Circadian physiology* (2nd ed.). Boca Raton, FL: CRC Press. Marvelous summary of research on circadian rhythms and the relevance to human behavior.

Websites

The Sleep Site, specializing in sleep disorders
http://www.thesleepsite.com/

The Quantitative Study of Dreams, by Adam Schneider and G. William Domhoff
http://www.dreamresearch.net

* Requires a Cengage Learning eResources account. Visit **www.cengage.com/login** to register or login.

BOIL
WATER
BEFORE
DRINKING

Gail R. Hill/Bimbimbie Ornithological Services

Internal Regulation

10

CHAPTER OUTLINE

OPPOSITE: All life on Earth requires water, and animals drink it wherever they can find it.

MAIN IDEAS

1. Many physiological and behavioral processes maintain a near constancy of certain body variables, and they anticipate as well as react to needs.
2. Mammals and birds maintain constant body temperature as a way of staying ready for rapid muscle activity at any temperature of the environment. They use both behavioral and physiological processes to maintain temperature.
3. Thirst mechanisms respond to the osmotic pressure and total volume of the blood.
4. Hunger and satiety are regulated by many factors, including taste, stomach distension, the availability of glucose to the cells, and chemicals released by the fat cells. Many brain peptides help regulate feeding and satiety.

What is life? We could define life in many ways depending on whether the purpose is medical, legal, philosophical, or poetic. Biologically, what is necessary for life is *a coordinated set of chemical reactions.* Not all chemical reactions are alive, but all life has well-regulated chemical reactions.

Every chemical reaction in a living body takes place in a water solution at a rate that depends on the identity and concentration of molecules in the water, the temperature of the solution, and the presence of contaminants. Our behavior is organized to keep the right chemicals in the right proportions and at the right temperature.

MODULE 10.1

Temperature Regulation

Here's an observation that puzzled biologists for years: When a small male garter snake emerges from hibernation in early spring, it emits female pheromones for the first day or two. The pheromones attract larger males that swarm all over him, trying to copulate. Presumably, the tendency to release female pheromones must have evolved to provide the small male some advantage. But what? Biologists speculated about ways in which this pseudo-mating experience might help the small male attract real females. The truth is simpler: A male that has just emerged from hibernation is so cold that it has trouble slithering out of its burrow. The larger males emerged from hibernation earlier and already had a chance to warm themselves in a sunny place. When the larger males swarm all over the smaller male, they warm him and increase his activity level (Shine, Phillips, Waye, LeMaster, & Mason, 2001).

Here are some more examples of otherwise puzzling behaviors that make sense in terms of temperature regulation:

- Have you ever noticed gulls, ducks, or other large birds standing on one leg (Figure 10.1)? Why do they do that, when balancing on two legs would seem easier? The answer is they stand this way when their legs are getting cold. Tucking a leg under the body keeps it warm (Ehrlich, Dobkin, & Wheye, 1988).
- Vultures sometimes defecate onto their own legs. Are they just careless slobs? No. They defecate onto their legs on hot days so that the evaporating excretions will cool their legs (Ehrlich et al., 1988).
- Most lizards live solitary lives, but Australian thick-tailed geckos frequently get together into tight huddles. Why? These geckos live in an environment with rapid temperature fluctuations. They huddle only when the environmental temperature is falling rapidly. By huddling, they gain insulation and prevent a rapid drop in body temperature (Shah, Shine, Hudson, & Kearney, 2003).
- Decades ago, psychologists found that infant rats appeared deficient in certain aspects of learning, eating, and drinking. Later results showed that the real problem was temperature control. Researchers generally test animals at normal room temperature, about 20°–23°C (68–73°F), which is comfortable for adult humans but dangerously cold for an isolated baby rat (Figure 10.2). In a warmer room, infant rats show abilities that we once assumed required more brain maturity (Satinoff, 1991).
- Certain studies found that female rats learned best during their fertile period (estrus). In other studies, they learned best a day or two before their fertile period (proestrus). The difference depends on temperature. Rats in estrus do better in a cooler environment, presumably because they are generating so much heat on their own. Rats in proestrus do better in a warmer environment (Rubinow, Arseneau, Beverly, & Juraska, 2004).

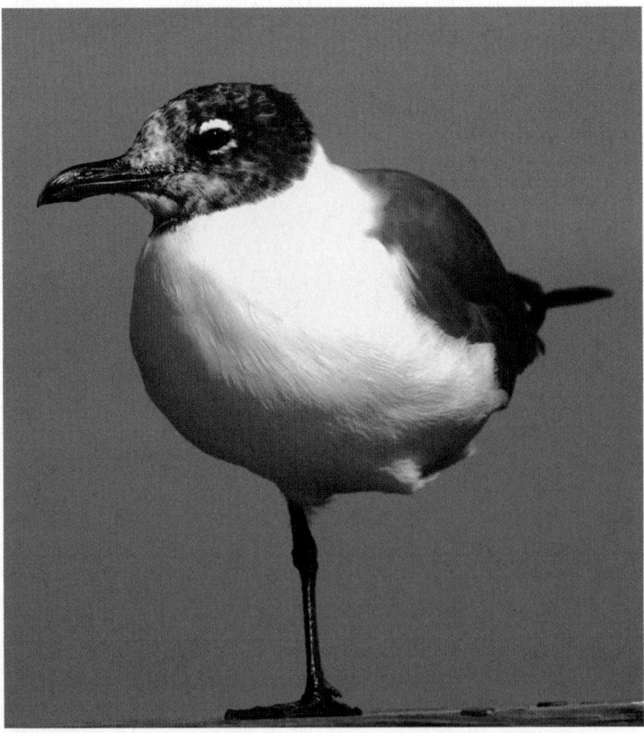

f1 online/Alamy Limited

Figure 10.1 Why do birds sometimes stand on one foot? Like many other puzzling behaviors, this one makes sense in terms of temperature regulation. The bird keeps one leg warm by holding it next to the body.

Figure 10.2 The special difficulties of temperature regulation for a newborn rodent
A newborn rat has no hair, thin skin, and little body fat. If left exposed to the cold, it becomes inactive.

The point is that temperature affects behavior in many ways that we might overlook. Temperature regulation is more important and more interesting than many psychologists realize.

Homeostasis and Allostasis

Physiologist Walter B. Cannon (1929) introduced the term **homeostasis** (HO-mee-oh-STAY-sis) to refer to temperature regulation and other biological processes that keep body variables within a fixed range. The process is like the thermostat in a house with heating and cooling systems. Someone sets the minimum and maximum temperatures on the thermostat. When the temperature in the house drops below the minimum, the thermostat triggers the furnace to provide heat. When the temperature rises above the maximum, the thermostat turns on the air conditioner.

Similarly, homeostatic processes in animals trigger physiological and behavioral activities that keep certain variables within a set range. In many cases, the range is so narrow that we refer to it as a **set point,** a single value that the body works to maintain. For example, if calcium is deficient in your diet and its concentration in the blood begins to fall below the set point of 0.16 g/L (grams per liter), storage deposits in your bones release additional calcium into the blood. If the calcium level in the blood rises above 0.16 g/L, you store part of the excess in your bones and excrete the rest. Similar mechanisms maintain constant blood levels of water, oxygen, glucose, sodium chloride, protein, fat, and acidity (Cannon, 1929). Processes that reduce discrepancies from the set point are known as **negative feedback.** Much of motivated behavior can be described as negative feedback: Something happens to cause a disturbance, and behavior varies until it relieves the disturbance.

The body's set points change from time to time (Mrosovsky, 1990). For example, many animals (including most humans) increase their body fat in fall and decrease it in spring. Your body maintains a higher temperature during the day than at night, even if room temperature is the same. To describe these dynamic changes in set points, researchers use the term **allostasis** (from the Greek roots meaning "variable" and "standing"), which means the adaptive way in which the body changes its set points depending on the situation (McEwen, 2000). As you will see throughout this chapter, much of the control depends on cells in the hypothalamus.

STOP & CHECK

1. How does the idea of allostasis differ from homeostasis?

ANSWER

1. Homeostasis is a set of processes that keep certain body variables within a fixed range. Allostasis is an adjustment of that range, increasing it or decreasing it as circumstances change.

Controlling Body Temperature

If you were to list your strongest motivations in life, you might not think to include temperature regulation, but it is a high priority biologically. An average young adult expends about 2,600 kilocalories (kcal) per day. Where do you suppose all that energy goes? It is not to muscle movements or mental activity. You use about two thirds of your energy for **basal metabolism,** the energy used to maintain a constant body temperature while at rest (Burton, 1994).

Amphibians, reptiles, and most fish are **poikilothermic** (POY-kih-lo-THER-mik)—that is, their body temperature matches the temperature of their environment. They lack physiological mechanisms of temperature regulation such as shivering and sweating. People often apply the term "cold-blooded," but that term is misleading because poikilothermic animals can remain warm most of the day by choosing an appropriate location. A desert lizard moves between sunny areas, shady areas, and burrows to maintain a nearly steady, fairly high body temperature at most times.

With few exceptions, mammals and birds are **homeothermic.** (One exception is that animals become poikilothermic when they hibernate.) They use physiological mechanisms to maintain a nearly constant body temperature despite changes in the temperature of the environment. Homeothermy is costly, especially for small animals. An animal *generates* heat in proportion to its total mass; it *radiates* heat in proportion to its surface area. A small mammal or bird, such as a mouse or a hummingbird, has a high surface-to-volume ratio and therefore radiates heat rapidly. Such animals need a great deal of fuel each day to maintain their body temperature.

Homeothermic animals use both behavioral and physiological mechanisms to control body temperature. To cool ourselves when the air is warmer than body temperature, we have only one physiological mechanism, which is sweating. Species that don't sweat will instead pant or lick themselves. Sweating, panting, or licking exposes water, which cools the body as it evaporates. This mechanism is limited, however: If the air is humid as well as hot, the moisture will not evaporate. Furthermore, you incur health problems if you cannot drink enough to replace the water you lose by sweating.

You have several physiological mechanisms to increase body heat in a cold environment. One is shivering. Any muscle contractions, such as those of shivering, generate heat. Second, decreased blood flow to the skin prevents the blood from cooling before it reaches the brain, heart, other organs, and muscles. A third mechanism works well for most mammals, though not humans: They fluff out their fur to increase insulation. (We humans also fluff out our "fur" by erecting the tiny hairs on our skin—"goose bumps." Back when our remote ancestors had a fuller coat of fur, that mechanism did some good.)

We also use behavioral mechanisms, just as poikilothermic animals do. In fact, we prefer to rely on behavioral mechanisms when we can. The more we regulate our temperature behaviorally, the less we need to rely on energetically costly physiological efforts (Refinetti & Carlisle, 1986). Finding a cool place on a hot day is much better than sweating (Figure 10.3).

Bryan & Cherry Alexander Photography/Alamy Limited

Figure 10.4 Behavioral regulation of body temperature
A 1-month-old emperor penguin chick is poorly insulated against Antarctic temperatures that often drop below −30°C (−22°F). However, when many chicks huddle together tightly, they act like one large well-insulated organism. The cold ones on the outside push their way inward, and the warm ones on the inside passively drift outward. The process is so effective that a cluster of penguin chicks has to move frequently to prevent melting a hole in the ice.

Sun-Journal, Ken Love/AP Photos

Figure 10.3 One way to cope with the heat
Overheated animals, like overheated people, look for the coolest spot they can find.

Finding a warm place on a cold day is much smarter than shivering. Here are a few other behavioral mechanisms of temperature regulation:

- Put on more clothing or take it off. This human strategy accomplishes what other mammals accomplish by fluffing out or sleeking their fur.
- Become more active to get warmer or less active to avoid overheating.
- To get warm, huddle or cuddle with others. You might be shy about hugging strangers to keep warm, but many other species are not (Figure 10.4). For example, spectacled eiders (in the duck family) spend their winters in the Arctic Ocean, which is mostly covered with ice. With more than 150,000 eiders crowded together, they not only keep one another warm but also maintain a 20-mile hole in the ice so they can dive for fish throughout the winter (Weidensaul, 1999).

APPLICATIONS AND EXTENSIONS

Surviving in Extreme Cold

If the atmospheric temperature drops below 0°C (32°F), you and I maintain our normal body temperature by shivering, shifting blood flow away from the skin, and so forth. However, a poikilothermic animal, which by definition takes the temperature of its environment, is vulnerable. If its body temperature drops below the freezing point of water, ice crystals form. Because water expands when it freezes, ice crystals would tear apart blood vessels and cell membranes, killing the animal.

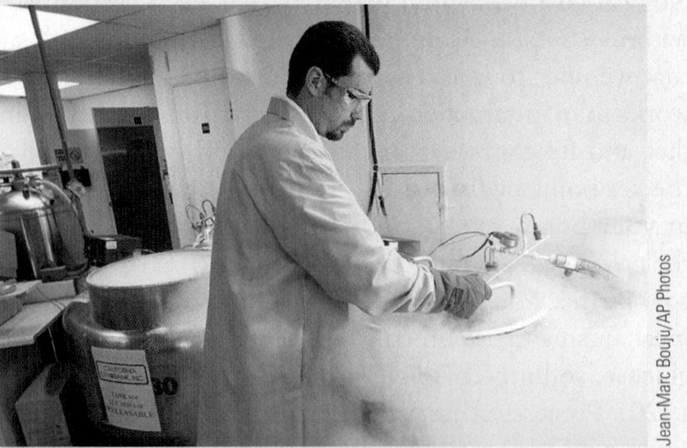
Jean-Marc Bouju/AP Photos

Companies will freeze a dead body with the prospect that future technologies can restore the person to life.

Ordinarily, amphibians and reptiles avoid that risk by burrowing underground or finding other sheltered locations. However, some frogs, fish, and insects survive through winters in northern Canada where even the underground temperature approaches –40° C (which is also –40° F). How do they do it? Some insects and fish stock their blood with glycerol and other antifreeze chemicals at the start of the winter (Liou, Tocilj, Davies, & Jia, 2000). Wood frogs actually do freeze, but they have several mechanisms to reduce the damage. They start by withdrawing most fluid from their organs and blood vessels and storing it in extracellular spaces. Therefore, ice crystals have room to expand when they do form, without tearing the blood vessels and cells. Also, they have chemicals that cause ice crystals to form gradually, not in chunks. Finally, they have such extraordinary blood-clotting capacity that they can quickly repair any blood vessels that do rupture (Storey & Storey, 1999).

As you may have heard, some people have had their bodies frozen after death in hopes that scientists will discover a cure for their disease *and* a way to bring a frozen body back to life. If you had enough money, would you choose this route to possible life after death?

I would advise against it. The wood frogs that survive after freezing begin by dehydrating their organs and blood vessels. Unless you underwent similar dehydration—before dying!—ice crystals are sure to tear up blood vessels and cell membranes throughout your body. Repairing all those membranes sounds pretty close to impossible.

The Advantages of Constant High Body Temperature

As mentioned, we spend about two thirds of our total energy maintaining body temperature (basal metabolism). A poikilothermic animal, such as a frog, has a lower level of basal metabolism and consequently needs far less fuel. If we didn't maintain a constant, high body temperature, we could eat much less and therefore spend less effort finding food. Furthermore, research suggests that, other things being equal, laboratory animals with a lower body temperature live longer than those with a higher temperature (Conti et al., 2006). Given the substantial costs of maintaining our body temperature, it must provide an important advantage, or we would not have evolved these mechanisms. What is that advantage?

For the answer, think back to Chapter 8: As the water gets colder, a fish has to recruit more and more fast-twitch muscle fibers to remain active, at the risk of rapid fatigue. Birds and mammals keep their muscles warm at all times, regardless of air temperature, and therefore stay constantly ready for vigorous activity. In other words, we eat a great deal to support our high metabolism so that even when the weather is cold, we can still run as fast and far as possible.

Why did mammals evolve a body temperature of 37°C (98°F) instead of some other value? From the standpoint of muscle activity, we gain an advantage by being as warm as possible. A warmer animal has warmer muscles and therefore runs faster and with less fatigue than a cooler animal. When a reptile has a choice of environments at different temperatures, it usually chooses to warm itself to 37°–38°C (Wagner & Gleeson, 1997).

If warmer is better, why not heat ourselves to an even higher temperature? Beyond about 40° or 41°C, proteins begin to break their bonds and lose their useful properties. Birds' body temperatures are in fact about 41°C (105°F).

It is possible to evolve proteins that are stable at higher temperatures; indeed, odd microscopic animals called thermophiles survive in water close to boiling (Hoffman, 2001). However, to do so, they need many extra bonds to stabilize their proteins. The enzymatic properties of proteins depend on the proteins' flexible structure, so making them rigid enough to withstand high temperatures decreases their versatility and usefulness (Somero, 1996). In short, our body temperature of 37°C is a trade-off between the advantages of high temperature for rapid movement and the disadvantages of high temperature for protein stability.

Reproductive cells require a somewhat cooler environment than the rest of the body (Rommel, Pabst, & McLellan, 1998). Birds lay eggs and sit on them, instead of developing them internally, because the birds' internal temperature is too hot for an embryo. Similarly, in most male mammals, the scrotum hangs outside the body because sperm production requires a cooler temperature than the rest of the body. (A man who wears his undershorts too tight keeps his testes too close to the body, overheats them, and therefore produces fewer healthy sperm cells.) Pregnant women are advised to avoid hot baths and anything else that might overheat a developing fetus.

STOP & CHECK

2. What is the primary advantage of maintaining a constant high body temperature?

3. Why did we evolve a temperature of 37°C (98°F) instead of some other temperature?

ANSWERS

2. The primary advantage of a constant high body temperature is that it keeps the animal ready for rapid, prolonged muscle activity even if the air is cold. **3.** Animals gain an advantage in being as warm as possible and therefore as fast as possible. However, proteins lose stability at temperatures much above 37°C (98°F).

Brain Mechanisms

The physiological changes that defend body temperature—such as shivering, sweating, and changes in blood flow to the skin—depend on areas in and near the hypothalamus (Figure 10.5), especially the anterior hypothalamus and the preoptic area, which is just anterior to the anterior hypothalamus. (It is called *preoptic* because it is near the optic chiasm, where the optic nerves cross.) Because of the close relationship between the preoptic area and the anterior hypothalamus, they are often treated as a single area, the **preoptic area/anterior hypothalamus,** or **POA/AH.**

The POA/AH monitors body temperature partly by monitoring its own temperature (D. O. Nelson & Prosser, 1981). If an experimenter heats the POA/AH, an animal pants or sweats,

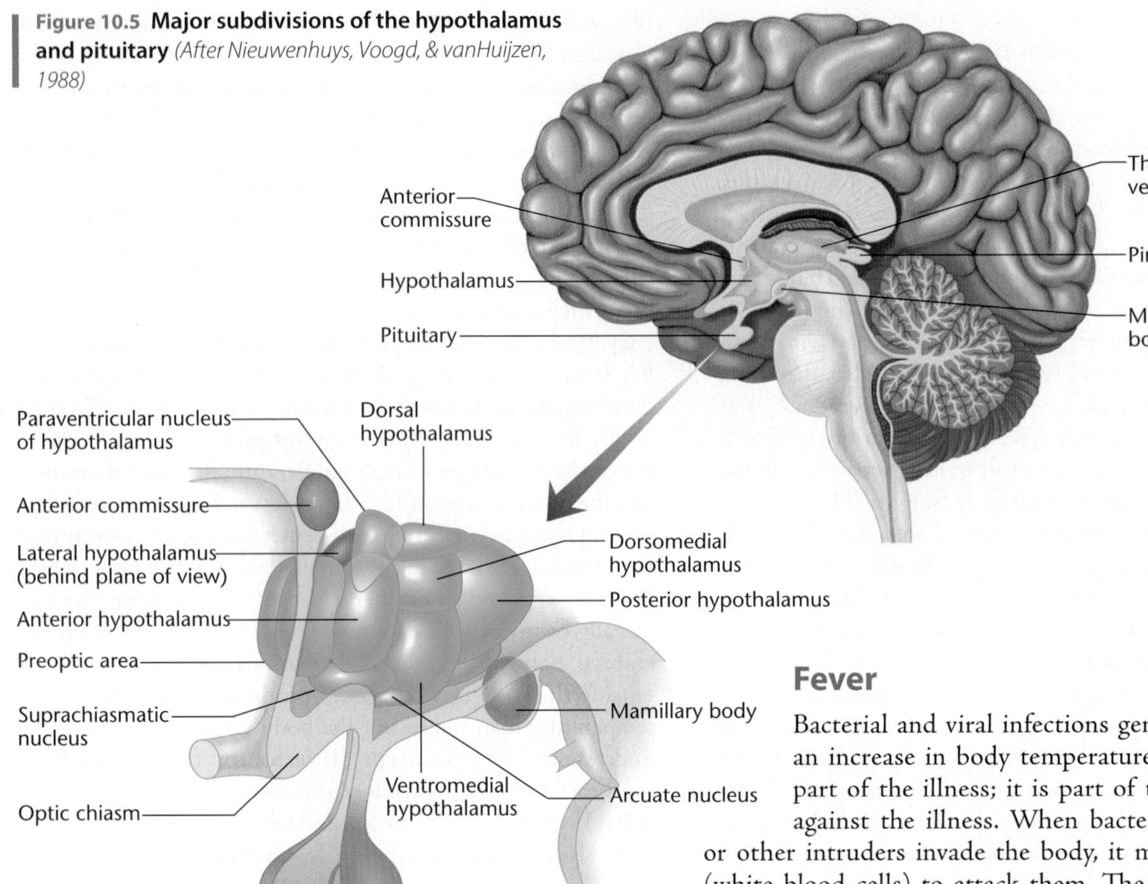

Figure 10.5 Major subdivisions of the hypothalamus and pituitary *(After Nieuwenhuys, Voogd, & vanHuijzen, 1988)*

even in a cool environment. If the same area is cooled, the animal shivers, even in a warm room. An animal also reacts to a heated or cooled POA/AH by pressing a lever or doing other work for cold air or hot air reinforcements (Satinoff, 1964). That is, the animal acts as if it feels hot when its hypothalamus is hot. It acts as if it feels cold when its hypothalamus is cold.

Cells of the POA/AH also receive input from temperature receptors in the skin and spinal cord. The animal shivers most vigorously when both the POA/AH and the other receptors are cold. It sweats or pants most vigorously when both are hot. After damage to the POA/AH, mammals are reduced to using just behavioral mechanisms such as seeking a warmer or colder location (Satinoff & Rutstein, 1970; Van Zoeren & Stricker, 1977).

STOP & CHECK

4. What evidence do we have that the POA/AH controls body temperature?

5. How can an animal regulate body temperature after damage to the POA/AH?

ANSWERS

4. Direct cooling or heating of the POA/AH leads to shivering or sweating. Also, damage there impairs physiological control of temperature. 5. It can regulate temperature through behavior, such as by finding a warmer or cooler place.

Fever

Bacterial and viral infections generally cause fever, an increase in body temperature. The fever is not part of the illness; it is part of the body's defense against the illness. When bacteria, viruses, fungi, or other intruders invade the body, it mobilizes *leukocytes* (white blood cells) to attack them. The leukocytes release small proteins called **cytokines** that attack the intruders. Cytokines also stimulate the vagus nerve, which sends signals to the hypothalamus (Ek et al., 2001; Leon, 2002), increasing the release of chemicals called prostaglandins. Stimulation of a particular kind of prostaglandin receptor in one nucleus of the hypothalamus is necessary for fever. If you didn't have those receptors, illnesses would not give you a fever (Lazarus et al., 2007).

A fever represents an increased set point for body temperature. Just as you shiver or sweat when your body temperature goes below or above its usual 37°C, when you have a fever of, say, 39°C, you shiver or sweat whenever your temperature deviates from that level. Moving to a cooler room does not lower your fever. It just makes your body work harder to keep its temperature at the feverish level.

Because newborn rabbits have an immature hypothalamus, they do not shiver in response to infections. If they are given a choice of environments, however, they select a spot warm enough to raise their body temperature (Satinoff, McEwen, & Williams, 1976). That is, they develop a fever by behavioral means. Fish and reptiles with an infection also choose a warm enough environment, if they can find one, to produce a feverish body temperature (Kluger, 1991). Again, the point is that fever is something the animal does to fight an infection.

Does fever do any good? Certain types of bacteria grow less vigorously at high temperatures than at normal mammalian body temperatures. Also, fever enhances activity of the immune system (Skitzki, Chen, Wang, & Evans, 2007).

Other things being equal, developing a moderate fever probably increases an individual's chance of surviving a bacterial infection (Kluger, 1991). However, a fever above about 39°C (103°F) in humans does more harm than good, and a fever above 41°C (109°F) is life-threatening (Rommel et al., 1998).

STOP & CHECK

6. What evidence indicates that fever is an adaptation to fight illness?

ANSWER

6. The body will shiver or sweat to maintain its elevated temperature. Also, fish, reptiles, and immature mammals with infections use behavioral means to raise their temperature to a feverish level. Furthermore, a moderate fever inhibits bacterial growth and increases the probability of surviving a bacterial infection.

MODULE 10.1 IN CLOSING

Combining Physiological and Behavioral Mechanisms

One of the key themes of this module has been the redundancy of mechanisms. Your body has various physiological mechanisms to maintain constant body temperature, including shivering, sweating, and changes in blood flow. You also rely on behavioral mechanisms, such as finding a cooler or warmer place, adding or removing clothing, and so forth. Redundancy reduces your risk: If one mechanism fails, another mechanism comes to your rescue. It is not, however, a true redundancy in the sense of two mechanisms doing exactly the same thing. Each of your mechanisms of temperature regulation solves a different aspect of the problem in a different way. We shall see this theme again in the discussions of thirst and hunger.

SUMMARY

1. It is easy to overlook the importance of temperature regulation. Many seemingly odd animal behaviors make sense as ways to heat or cool the body. **290**
2. Homeostasis is a tendency to maintain a body variable near a set point. Temperature, hunger, and thirst are almost homeostatic, but the set point changes in varying circumstances. **291**
3. A high body temperature enables a mammal or bird to move rapidly and without fatigue even in a cold environment. **293**
4. From the standpoint of muscle activity, the higher the body temperature, the better. However, as temperatures exceed 41°C, protein stability decreases, and more energy is needed to maintain body temperature. Mammalian body temperature of 37°C is a compromise between these competing considerations. **293**
5. The preoptic area and anterior hypothalamus (POA/AH) are critical for temperature control. Cells there monitor both their own temperature and that of the skin and spinal cord. **293**
6. Even homeothermic animals rely partly on behavioral mechanisms for temperature regulation, especially in infancy and after damage to the POA/AH. **294**
7. A moderate fever helps an animal combat an infection. **294**

KEY TERMS

Terms are defined in the module on the page number indicated. They're also presented in alphabetical order with definitions in the book's Subject Index/Glossary. Interactive flashcards, audio reviews, and crossword puzzles are among the online resources available to help you learn these terms and the concepts they represent.

allostasis **291**
basal metabolism **291**
cytokines **294**
homeostasis **291**
homeothermic **291**
negative feedback **291**
poikilothermic **291**
preoptic area/anterior hypothalamus (POA/AH) **293**
set point **291**

THOUGHT QUESTION

Speculate on why birds have higher body temperatures than mammals.

MODULE 10.2

Thirst

Water constitutes about 70% of the mammalian body. Because the concentration of chemicals in water determines the rate of all chemical reactions in the body, the water must be regulated within narrow limits. The body also needs enough fluid in the circulatory system to maintain normal blood pressure. People sometimes survive for weeks without food, but not without water.

Mechanisms of Water Regulation

Different species have different strategies for maintaining the water they need. Beavers and other species that live in rivers or lakes drink plenty of water, eat moist foods, and excrete dilute urine. In contrast, gerbils and other desert animals may go through their entire lives without drinking. They gain enough water from their food, and they have many adaptations to avoid losing water, including the ability to excrete very dry feces and very concentrated urine. Unable to sweat, they avoid the heat of the day by burrowing under the ground. Their highly convoluted nasal passages minimize water loss when they exhale.

We humans vary our strategy depending on circumstances. If you cannot find enough to drink or if the water tastes bad, you conserve water by excreting more concentrated urine, decreasing your sweat, and other autonomic responses. Your posterior pituitary (see Figure 10.5) releases a hormone called **vasopressin,** which raises blood pressure by constricting the blood vessels. (The term *vasopressin* comes from *vas*cular *press*ure.) The increased pressure helps compensate for the decreased volume. Vasopressin is also known as **antidiuretic hormone (ADH)** because it enables the kidneys to reabsorb water from urine and therefore make the urine more concentrated. (*Diuresis* means "urination.") You cannot succeed as well as gerbils, however. Gerbils can drink ocean water, and we cannot.

In most cases, our strategy is closer to that of beavers: We drink more than we need and excrete the excess. (However, if you drink extensively without eating, as many alcoholics do, you may excrete enough body salts to harm yourself.) Most of our drinking is with meals or in social situations, and most people seldom experience intense thirst.

STOP & CHECK

7. If you lacked vasopressin, would you drink like a beaver or like a gerbil? Why?

ANSWER

7. If you lacked vasopressin, you would have to drink more like a beaver. You would excrete much fluid, so you would need to drink an equal amount to replace it.

Osmotic Thirst

We distinguish two types of thirst. Eating salty foods causes *osmotic* thirst, and losing fluid, such as by bleeding or sweating, induces *hypovolemic* thirst.

The combined concentration of all *solutes* (molecules in solution) in mammalian body fluids remains at a nearly constant level of 0.15 M (molar). (Molarity is a measure of the number of particles per unit of solution, regardless of the size of each particle. A 1.0 M solution of sugar and a 1.0 M solution of sodium chloride have the same number of molecules per liter.) This fixed concentration of solutes can be regarded as a set point, similar to the set point for temperature. Any deviation activates mechanisms that restore the concentration of solutes to the set point.

The solutes inside and outside a cell produce an **osmotic pressure,** the tendency of water to flow across a semipermeable membrane from the area of low solute concentration to the area of higher concentration. A semipermeable membrane is one through which water can pass but solutes cannot. The membrane surrounding a cell is almost a semipermeable membrane because water flows across it freely and various solutes flow either slowly or not at all between the *intracellular fluid* inside the cell and the *extracellular fluid* outside it. Osmotic pressure occurs when solutes are more concentrated on one side of the membrane than on the other.

If you eat something salty, sodium ions spread through the blood and the extracellular fluid but do not cross the membranes into cells. The result is a higher concentration of

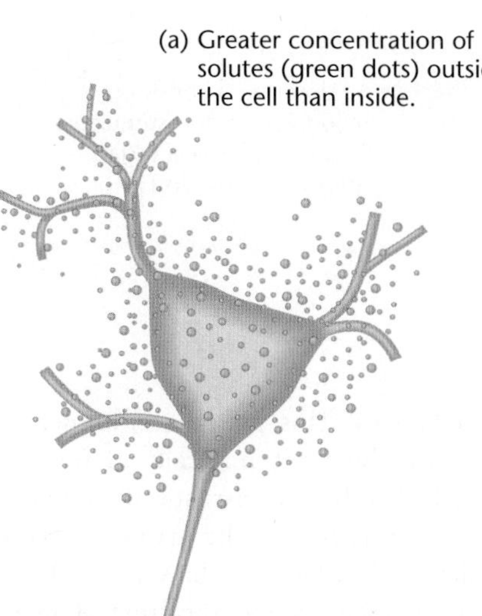

(a) Greater concentration of solutes (green dots) outside the cell than inside.

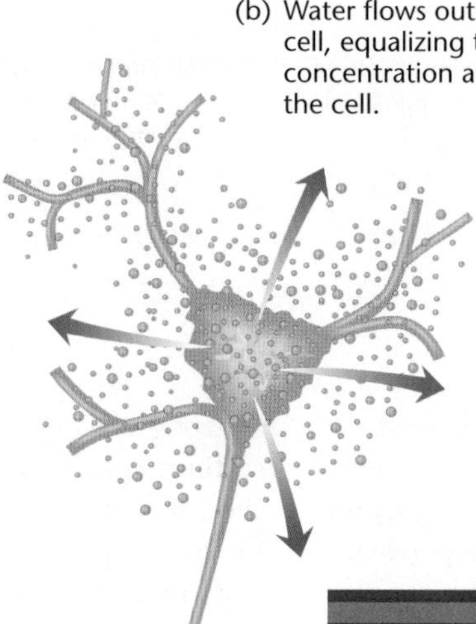

(b) Water flows out of the cell, equalizing the solute concentration and shrinking the cell.

Figure 10.6 The consequence of a difference in osmotic pressure
(a) A solute such as NaCl is more concentrated outside the cell than inside. **(b)** Water flows by osmosis out of the cell until the concentrations are equal. Neurons in certain brain areas detect their own dehydration and trigger thirst.

solutes outside the cells than inside, and the resulting osmotic pressure draws water from the cells into the extracellular fluid. Certain neurons detect their own loss of water and then trigger **osmotic thirst,** which helps restore the normal state (Figure 10.6). The kidneys also excrete more concentrated urine to rid the body of excess sodium and maintain as much water as possible.

How does the brain detect osmotic pressure? It gets part of the information from receptors around the third ventricle (Figure 10.7). Of all brain areas, those around the third ventricle have the leakiest blood-brain barrier (Simon, 2000). A weak blood-brain barrier would be harmful for most neurons, but it helps cells monitor the contents of the blood. The areas important for detecting osmotic pressure and the salt content of the blood include the **OVLT** (organum vasculosum laminae terminalis) and the **subfornical organ (SFO)** (Hiyama, Watanabe, Okado, & Noda, 2004). The brain also gets information from receptors in the stomach that detect high levels of sodium (Kraly, Kim, Dunham, & Tribuzio, 1995), enabling the brain to anticipate an osmotic need before the rest of the body actually experiences it.

Receptors in the OVLT, the subfornical organ, the stomach, and elsewhere relay their information to several parts of the hypothalamus, including the **supraoptic nucleus** and the **paraventricular nucleus (PVN),** which control the rate at which the posterior pituitary releases vasopressin. Receptors also relay information to the **lateral preoptic area** and surrounding parts of the hypothalamus, which control drinking (Saad, Luiz, Camargo, Renzi, & Manani, 1996).

After osmotic pressure triggers thirst, how do you know when to stop drinking? You do *not* wait until water has restored normal osmotic pressure for the receptors in the brain. The water you drink has to be absorbed through the digestive system and then pumped through the blood to the brain. That process takes 15 minutes or so, and if you continued drinking for that long, you would drink far more than you need. The body monitors swallowing and detects the distension of the stomach and upper part of the small intestine. Those messages limit drinking to not much more than you need at a given time (Stricker & Hoffmann, 2007).

STOP & CHECK

8. Would adding salt to the body's extracellular fluids increase or decrease osmotic thirst?

ANSWER

8. Adding salt to the extracellular fluids would increase osmotic thirst because it would draw water from the cells into the extracellular spaces.

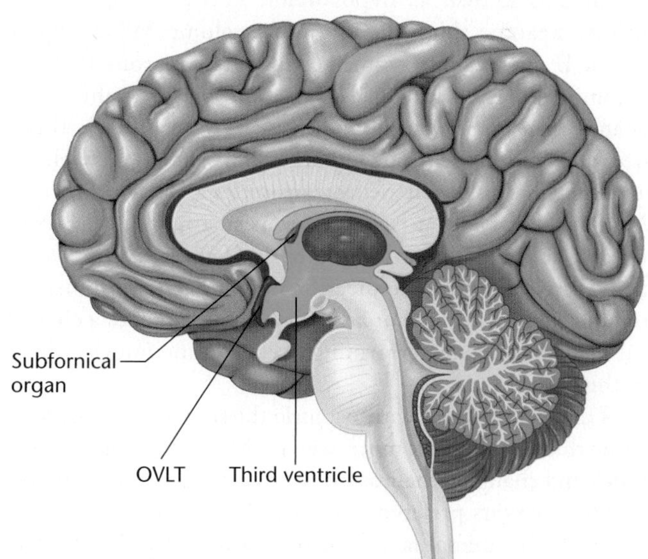

Figure 10.7 The brain's receptors for osmotic pressure and blood volume
These neurons are in areas surrounding the third ventricle of the brain, where no blood-brain barrier prevents blood-borne chemicals from entering the brain. *(Based in part on DeArmond, Fusco, & Dewey, 1974; Weindl, 1973)*

Hypovolemic Thirst and Sodium-Specific Hunger

Suppose you lose a significant amount of body fluid by bleeding, diarrhea, or sweating. Although osmotic pressure has not changed anywhere in your body, you need fluid. Your heart

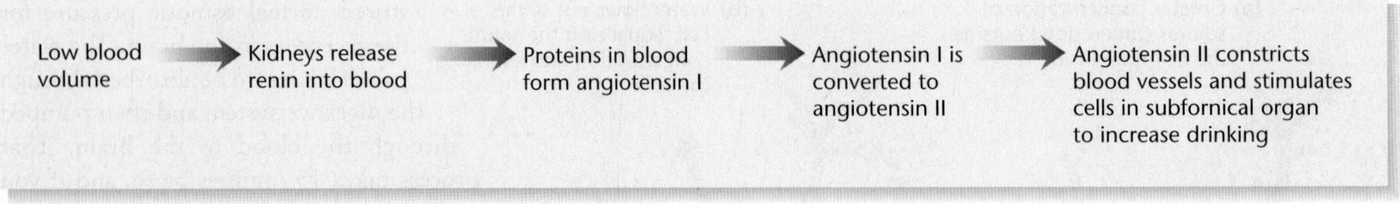

Low blood volume → Kidneys release renin into blood → Proteins in blood form angiotensin I → Angiotensin I is converted to angiotensin II → Angiotensin II constricts blood vessels and stimulates cells in subfornical organ to increase drinking

Figure 10.8 Hormonal response to hypovolemia

has trouble pumping blood up to the head, and nutrients do not flow as easily as usual into your cells. Your body will react with hormones that constrict blood vessels—vasopressin and *angiotensin II*. When blood volume drops, the kidneys release the enzyme *renin*, which splits a portion off angiotensinogen, a large protein in the blood, to form angiotensin I, which other enzymes convert to **angiotensin II.** Like vasopressin, angiotensin II constricts the blood vessels, compensating for the drop in blood pressure (Figure 10.8).

Angiotensin II also helps trigger thirst in conjunction with receptors that detect blood pressure in the large veins. However, this thirst is different from osmotic thirst because you need to restore lost salts and not just water. This kind of thirst is known as **hypovolemic** (HI-po-vo-LEE-mik) **thirst,** meaning thirst based on low volume. When angiotensin II reaches the brain, it stimulates neurons in areas adjoining the third ventricle (Fitts, Starbuck, & Ruhf, 2000; Mangiapane & Simpson, 1980; Tanaka et al., 2001). Those neurons send axons to the hypothalamus, where they release angiotensin II as their neurotransmitter (Tanaka, Hori, & Nomura, 2001). That is, the neurons surrounding the third ventricle both respond to angiotensin II and release it. As in many other cases, the connection between a neurotransmitter and its function is not arbitrary. The brain uses a chemical that was already performing a related function elsewhere in the body.

Unlike an animal with osmotic thirst, one with hypovolemic thirst can't drink much water without diluting its body fluids and changing their osmotic pressure. The animal therefore increases its preference for slightly salty water (Stricker, 1969). If the animal is offered both water and salt, it alternates between them to yield an appropriate mixture. It shows a strong craving for salty tastes. This preference, known as **sodium-specific hunger,** develops automatically as soon as the need exists (Richter, 1936). In contrast, specific hungers for other vitamins and minerals have to be learned by trial and error (Rozin & Kalat, 1971). You may have noticed this phenomenon yourself. A woman around the time of menstruation, or anyone who has sweated heavily, finds that salty snacks taste especially good.

Sodium-specific hunger depends partly on hormones (Schulkin, 1991). When the body's sodium reserves are low, the adrenal glands produce the hormone **aldosterone** (al-DOSS-ter-one), which causes the kidneys, salivary glands, and sweat glands to retain salt (Verrey & Beron, 1996). Aldosterone and angiotensin II together change the properties of taste receptors on the tongue, neurons in the nucleus of the tractus solitarius (part of the taste system), and neurons elsewhere in the brain to increase salt intake (Krause & Sakal, 2007). Figure 7.20 on page 214 illustrates part of the pathway. Table 10.1 summarizes the differences between osmotic thirst and hypovolemic thirst.

STOP & CHECK

9. Who would drink more pure water—someone with osmotic thirst or someone with hypovolemic thirst?

ANSWER

9. The person with osmotic thirst would have a stronger preference for pure water. The one with hypovolemic thirst would drink more if the solution contained salts.

TABLE 10.1 Comparison of Osmotic and Hypovolemic Thirst

Type of Thirst	Stimulus	Best Relieved by Drinking	Receptor Location	Hormone Influences
Osmotic	High solute concentration outside cells causes loss of water from cells	Water	OVLT, a brain area adjoining the third ventricle	Accompanied by vasopressin secretion to conserve water
Hypovolemic	Low blood volume	Water containing solutes	1. Receptors, measuring blood pressure in the veins 2. Subfornical organ, a brain area adjoining the third ventricle	Increased by angiotensin II

MODULE 10.2 IN CLOSING

The Psychology and Biology of Thirst

You may have thought that temperature regulation happens automatically and that water regulation depends on your behavior. You can see now that the distinction is not entirely correct. You control your body temperature partly by automatic means, such as sweating or shivering, but also partly by behavioral means, such as choosing a warm or a cool place. You control your body water partly by the behavior of drinking but also by hormones that alter kidney activity. If your kidneys cannot regulate your water and sodium adequately, your brain gets signals to change your drinking or sodium intake. In short, keeping your body's chemical reactions going depends on both skeletal and autonomic controls.

SUMMARY

1. Different mammalian species have evolved different ways of maintaining body water, ranging from frequent drinking (beavers) to extreme conservation of fluids (gerbils). Humans alter their strategy depending on the availability of acceptable fluids. **296**
2. An increase in the osmotic pressure of the blood draws water out of cells, causing osmotic thirst. Neurons in the OVLT, an area adjoining the third ventricle, detect changes in osmotic pressure and send information to hypothalamic areas responsible for vasopressin secretion and for drinking. **296**
3. Loss of blood volume causes hypovolemic thirst. Animals with hypovolemic thirst drink more water containing solutes than pure water. **297**
4. Hypovolemic thirst is triggered by the hormone angiotensin II, which increases when blood pressure falls. **298**
5. Loss of sodium salts from the body triggers sodium-specific cravings. **298**

KEY TERMS

Terms are defined in the module on the page number indicated. They're also presented in alphabetical order with definitions in the book's Subject Index/Glossary. Interactive flashcards, audio reviews, and crossword puzzles are among the online resources available to help you learn these terms and the concepts they represent.

aldosterone **298**
angiotensin II **298**
antidiuretic hormone (ADH) **296**
hypovolemic thirst **298**
lateral preoptic area **297**
osmotic pressure **296**
osmotic thirst **297**
OVLT **297**
paraventricular nucleus (PVN) **297**
sodium-specific hunger **298**
subfornical organ (SFO) **297**
supraoptic nucleus **297**
vasopressin **296**

THOUGHT QUESTIONS

1. An injection of concentrated sodium chloride triggers osmotic thirst, but an injection of equally concentrated glucose does not. Why not?
2. If all the water you drank leaked out through a tube connected to the stomach, how would your drinking change?
3. Many women crave salt during menstruation or pregnancy. Why?

MODULE 10.3

Hunger

Different species use different eating strategies. A snake or crocodile might have a huge meal and then eat nothing more for months (Figure 10.9). Bears eat as much as they can whenever they can. It is a sensible strategy because bears' main foods—fruits and nuts—are available in large quantities for only short times. Bears' occasional feasts tide them over through times of starvation. You might think of it as survival of the fattest. (Sorry about that one.)

Small birds, at the other extreme, eat only what they need at the time. They store a little, but not much. The advantage of restraint is that its low weight helps it fly away from predators (Figure 10.10). However, in some climates, a bird needs to store a substantial amount to get through the night. Tiny chickadees manage to survive through Alaska winters. Every night, a chickadee finds a hollowed tree or other nesting site that provides as much insulation as possible, and it lowers its body temperature into a state almost like hibernation. Still, it has to shiver throughout the night to prevent its body from freezing, and that much shivering requires much energy. During Alaskan winters, a chickadee eats enough to increase its body weight by 10% during the day and then loses it all at night (Harrison, 2008; Sharbaugh, 2001). For comparison, imagine a 50 kg (110 lb) person gaining 5 kg (11 lb) during the day and then shivering it off at night.

Arco Images GmbH/Alamy

Figure 10.10 A great tit, a small European bird
Ordinarily, when food is abundant, tits eat just what they need each day and maintain very low fat reserves. When food is harder to find, they eat all they can and live off fat reserves between meals. During one era when their predators were scarce, tits started putting on more fat regardless of the food supplies.

© Gunter Ziesler/Bruce Coleman Inc.

Figure 10.9 A python swallowing a gazelle
The gazelle weighs about 50% more than the snake. Many reptiles eat huge but infrequent meals, and their total intake over a year is far less than that of a mammal. We mammals need far more fuel because we use so much more energy, mainly for maintaining basal metabolism.

Humans eat more than we need for today, unlike small birds, but we do not stuff ourselves like bears—not as a rule, anyway. Choosing which food to eat and how much is an important decision. We use a wide array of learned and unlearned mechanisms to help in the process.

How the Digestive System Influences Food Selection

To start, examine the digestive system, as diagramed in Figure 10.11. Its function is to break food into smaller molecules that the cells can use. Digestion begins in the mouth, where enzymes in the saliva break down carbohydrates. Swallowed food travels down the esophagus to the stomach, where it mixes with hydrochloric acid and enzymes that digest proteins. The stomach stores food for a time, and then a round

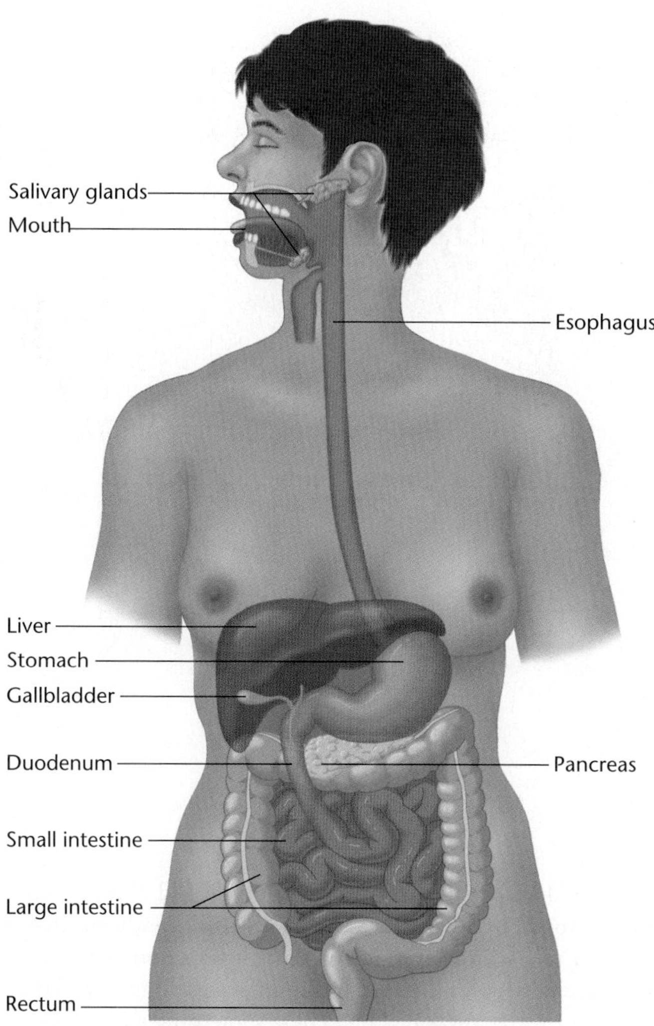

Figure 10.11 The human digestive system

sphincter muscle opens at the end of the stomach to release food to the small intestine.

The small intestine has enzymes that digest proteins, fats, and carbohydrates. It is also the site for absorbing digested materials into the bloodstream. The blood carries those chemicals to body cells that either use them or store them for later use. The large intestine absorbs water and minerals and lubricates the remaining materials to pass as feces.

Enzymes and Consumption of Dairy Products

Newborn mammals survive at first on mother's milk. As they grow older, they stop nursing for several reasons: The milk dries up, the mother pushes them away, and they begin to try other foods. Also, most mammals at about the age of weaning lose the intestinal enzyme **lactase,** which is necessary for metabolizing **lactose,** the sugar in milk. From then on, milk consumption causes stomach cramps and gas (Rozin & Pelchat, 1988). Adult mammals can drink a little milk, as you may have noticed with a pet dog, but generally not much. The declining level of lactase may be an evolved mechanism to encourage weaning at the appropriate time.

Humans are a partial exception to this rule. Many adults have enough lactase levels to consume milk and other dairy products throughout life. Worldwide, however, most adults cannot comfortably tolerate large amounts of milk products. Most human beings, after all, are Asians, and nearly all the people in China and surrounding countries lack the gene that enables adults to metabolize lactose (Flatz, 1987). They eat cheese and yogurt, which are easier to digest than milk, and moderate quantities of other dairy products, but they develop cramps or gas pains if they consume too much. Consequently, they generally limit their intake of dairy products. Figure 10.12 shows the worldwide distribution of lactose tolerance.

Within Africa, the distribution of ability to digest lactose varies in a patchy way from place to place. Whereas Europeans who can digest lactose in adulthood all have variants of the same gene, people in different parts of Africa have genes different from one another and different from Europeans, indicating that the genes for lactose digestion evolved independently in different places, probably within the last few thousand years, in response to the domestication of cattle (Tishkoff et al., 2006). When cow's milk became available, the selective pressure was strong in favor of genes enabling people to digest it.

STOP & CHECK

10. What genetic difference is most important for variants in likelihood of drinking milk in adulthood?

ANSWER

10. Likelihood of drinking milk in adulthood depends largely on a gene that controls the ability to digest lactose, the main sugar in milk.

Other Influences on Food Selection

For a **carnivore** (meat eater), selecting a satisfactory diet is relatively simple. A lion won't get vitamin deficient unless it eats vitamin-deficient zebras. However, **herbivores** (plant eaters) and **omnivores** (those that eat both meat and plants) must distinguish between edible and inedible substances and find enough vitamins and minerals. One way to do so is to learn from the experiences of others. For example, juvenile rats tend to imitate the food selections of their elders (Galef, 1992). Similarly, children acquire their culture's food preferences, especially the spices, even if they do not like every food their parents enjoy (Rozin, 1990).

But how did their parents, grandparents, or whoever learn what to eat? If you parachuted onto an uninhabited island covered with unfamiliar plants, you would use many strategies to select edible foods (Rozin & Vollmecke, 1986). First, you would select sweet foods, avoid bitter ones, and eat salty or sour foods in moderation. Most sweets are nutritious, and bitter substances are harmful (T. R. Scott & Verhagen, 2000). Second, you would prefer anything that tasted familiar. After

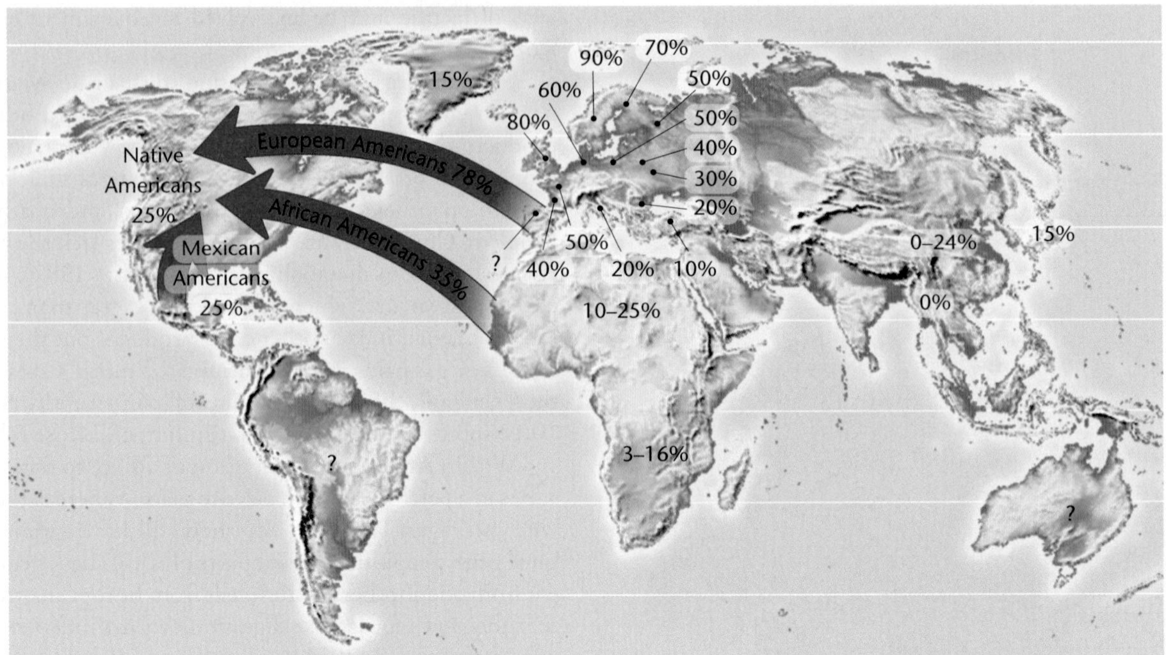

Figure 10.12 Percentage of adults who are lactose tolerant
People in areas with high lactose tolerance (e.g., Scandinavia) are likely to enjoy milk and other dairy products throughout their lives. Adults in areas with low tolerance (including much of Southeast Asia) drink less milk, if any. *(Based on Flatz, 1987; Rozin & Pelchat, 1988)*

all, familiar foods are safe, and new foods may not be. What did you think of coffee the first time you tried it? Hot peppers? Most people like any flavor better after it becomes familiar.

Third, you would learn the consequences of eating each food you try. If you try something new and then become ill, even hours later, your brain blames the illness on the food, and it won't taste good to you the next time (Rozin & Kalat, 1971; Rozin & Zellner, 1985). This phenomenon is known as **conditioned taste aversion.** It is a robust phenomenon that occurs reliably after just a single pairing of food with illness, even if the illness came hours after the food. In fact, you will come to dislike a food that is followed by intestinal discomfort even if you know that the nausea came from a thrill ride at the amusement park.

Short- and Long-Term Regulation of Feeding

Eating is far too important to be entrusted to just one mechanism. Your brain gets messages from your mouth, stomach, intestines, fat cells, and elsewhere to regulate your eating.

Oral Factors

You're a busy person, right? If you could get all the nutrition you needed by swallowing a pill, would you do it? Once in a while you might, but not often. People *like* to eat. In fact, many people like to taste and chew even when they are not hungry. Figure 10.13 shows a piece of 6,500-year-old chewing gum made from birch-bark tar. The tooth marks indicate that a child or teenager chewed it. Anthropologists don't know how the ancient people removed the sap to make the gum, and they aren't sure why anyone would chew something that tasted as bad as this gum probably did (Battersby, 1997). Clearly, the urge to chew is strong.

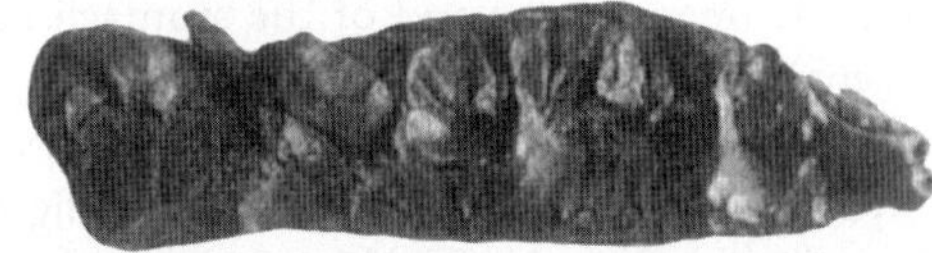

Figure 10.13 Chewing gum from about 4500 B.C.
The gum, made from birch-bark tar, has small tooth marks indicating that a child or adolescent chewed it. *(Reprinted by permission from Macmillan Publishers Ltd:* Nature, *Plus c'est le même chews, Stephen Battersby, 1997.)*

If necessary, could you become satiated without tasting your food? In one experiment, college students consumed lunch five days a week by swallowing one end of a rubber tube and then pushing a button to pump a liquid diet into the stomach (Jordan, 1969; Spiegel, 1973). (They were paid for participating.) After a few days of practice, each person established a consistent pattern of pumping in a constant volume of the liquid each day and maintaining a constant body weight. Most found the untasted meals unsatisfying, however, and reported a desire to taste or chew something (Jordan, 1969).

Could you be satisfied if you tasted something without ingesting it? In **sham-feeding** experiments, everything an animal swallows leaks out of a tube connected to the esophagus or stomach. Sham-feeding animals eat and swallow almost continually without becoming satiated (G. P. Smith, 1998). In short, taste and other mouth sensations contribute to satiety, but they are not enough by themselves.

STOP & CHECK

11. What is the evidence that taste is not sufficient for satiety?

ANSWER

11. When animals sham-feed (and the food leaks out of their digestive system), they chew and taste their food but do not become satiated.

The Stomach and Intestines

Ordinarily, we end a meal before the food reaches the blood, much less the muscles and other cells. Usually, the main signal to end a meal is distension of the stomach. In one experiment, researchers attached an inflatable cuff at the connection between the stomach and the small intestine (Deutsch, Young, & Kalogeris, 1978). When they inflated the cuff, food could not pass from the stomach to the duodenum. They carefully ensured that the cuff was not traumatic to the animal and did not interfere with feeding. The key result was that, with the cuff inflated, an animal ate a normal-size meal and then stopped. Evidently, stomach distension is sufficient to produce satiety.

The stomach conveys satiety messages to the brain via the vagus nerve and the splanchnic nerves. The **vagus nerve** (cranial nerve X) conveys information about the stretching of the stomach walls, providing a major basis for satiety. The **splanchnic** (SPLANK-nik) **nerves** convey information about the nutrient contents of the stomach (Deutsch & Ahn, 1986).

However, people who have had their stomach surgically removed (because of stomach cancer or other disease) still report satiety, so stomach distension can't be necessary for satiety. Later researchers found that meals end after distension of either the stomach or the duodenum (Seeley, Kaplan, & Grill, 1995). The **duodenum** (DYOU-oh-DEE-num or dyuh-ODD-ehn-uhm) is the part of the small intestine adjoining the stomach. It is the first digestive site that absorbs a significant amount of nutrients.

STOP & CHECK

12. What is the evidence that stomach distension is sufficient for satiety?

ANSWER

12. If a cuff is attached to the junction between the stomach and duodenum so that food cannot leave the stomach, an animal becomes satiated when the stomach is full.

Food in the duodenum releases the hormone **cholecystokinin** (ko-leh-SIS-teh-KI-nehn) **(CCK),** which limits meal size in two ways (Gibbs, Young, & Smith, 1973). First, CCK closes the sphincter muscle between the stomach and the duodenum, causing the stomach to hold its contents and fill more quickly than usual (McHugh & Moran, 1985; G. P. Smith & Gibbs, 1998). Second, CCK stimulates the vagus nerve, which sends a message to the hypothalamus, causing cells there to release a neurotransmitter that is a shorter version of the CCK molecule itself (Kobett et al., 2006; G. J. Schwartz, 2000). The process is something like sending a fax: The CCK in the intestines can't cross the blood-brain barrier, but it stimulates cells to release something almost like it. As in the case of angiotensin and thirst, the body uses the same chemical in the periphery and in the brain for closely related functions.

Given that CCK helps to end a meal, could we use it to help people who are trying to lose weight? Unfortunately, no. CCK produces short-term effects only. It limits the size of the meal, but an animal that has eaten a smaller than usual meal compensates by overeating at the next meal (Cummings & Overduin, 2007).

STOP & CHECK

13. What are two mechanisms by which CCK increases satiety?

ANSWER

13. When the duodenum is distended, it releases CCK, which closes the sphincter muscle between the stomach and duodenum. CCK therefore increases the rate at which the stomach distends. Also, neural signals from the intestines cause certain cells in the hypothalamus to release CCK as a neurotransmitter, and at its receptors, it triggers decreased feeding.

Glucose, Insulin, and Glucagon

Much digested food enters the bloodstream as glucose, an important source of energy throughout the body and nearly the only fuel used by the brain. When the blood's glucose level is high, liver cells convert some of the excess into glycogen, and fat cells convert some of it into fat. When the blood's glucose level starts to fall, the liver converts some of its glycogen back into glucose. So blood glucose levels stay fairly steady for most people most of the time.

However, the glucose in the blood is not equally available to the cells at all times. Two pancreatic hormones, insulin and glucagons, regulate the flow of glucose. **Insulin** enables glucose to enter the cells, except for brain cells, where glucose does not need insulin to enter. When insulin levels are high, cells receive glucose easily. When someone is getting ready for a meal, insulin levels rise, letting some of the blood glucose enter the cells in preparation for the rush of additional glucose about to enter the blood. Insulin increases even more during and after a meal. As you might guess, high levels of insulin tend to decrease appetite. When much glucose is already entering the cells, you don't need to eat more.

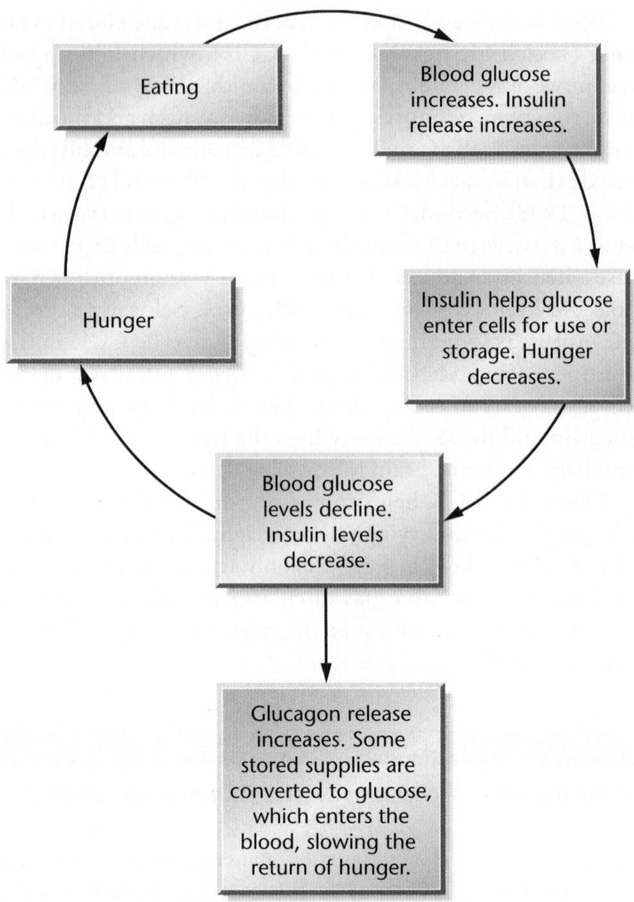

Figure 10.14 Insulin and glucagon feedback system
When glucose levels rise, the pancreas releases the hormone insulin, which causes cells to store the excess glucose as fats and glycogen. The entry of glucose into cells suppresses hunger and decreases eating, thereby lowering the glucose level.

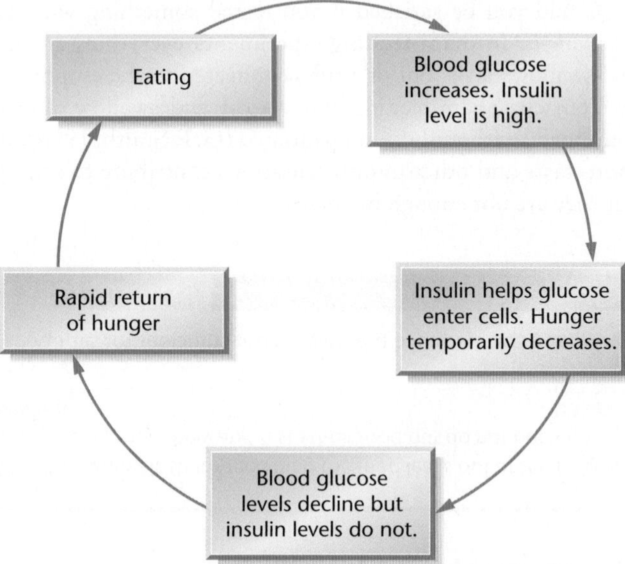

Figure 10.15 Effects of steadily high insulin levels on feeding
Constantly high insulin causes blood glucose to be stored as fats and glycogen. Because it becomes difficult to mobilize the stored nutrients, hunger returns soon after each meal.

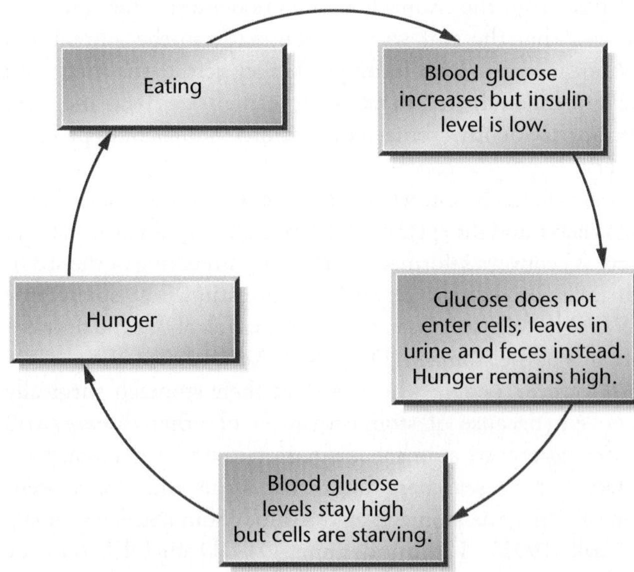

Figure 10.16 People with untreated diabetes eat much but lose weight
Because of their low insulin levels, the glucose in their blood cannot enter the cells, either to be stored or to be used. Consequently, they excrete glucose in their urine while their cells are starving.

As time passes after a meal, the blood glucose level falls. Therefore, insulin levels drop, glucose enters the cells more slowly, and hunger increases (Pardal & López-Barneo, 2002) (Figure 10.14). **Glucagon** stimulates the liver to convert some of its stored glycogen to glucose to replenish low supplies in the blood.

If the insulin level stays constantly high, the body continues rapidly moving blood glucose into the cells, including the liver cells and fat cells, long after a meal. Consequently, blood glucose drops and hunger increases in spite of the high insulin level. In late autumn, animals that are preparing for hibernation have constantly high insulin levels. They rapidly deposit much of each meal as fat and glycogen, grow hungry again, and continue gaining weight (Figure 10.15). At that time, weight gain is a valuable preparation for a season when the animal will have to survive off its fat reserves.

If the insulin level remains constantly low, as in people with diabetes, blood glucose levels may be three or more times the normal level, but little of it enters the cells (Figure 10.16). People and animals with diabetes eat more food than normal because their cells are starving (Lindberg, Coburn, & Stricker, 1984), but they excrete most of their glucose, and they lose weight. Note that either prolonged high or prolonged low insulin levels increase eating, although for different reasons and with different effects on body weight.

STOP & CHECK

14. Why do people with very low insulin levels eat so much? Why do people with constantly high levels eat so much?

15. What would happen to someone's appetite if insulin levels and glucagon levels were both high?

ANSWERS

14. Those with very low levels, as in diabetes, cannot get glucose to enter their cells, and therefore, they are constantly hungry. They pass much of their nutrition in the urine and feces. Those with constantly high levels deposit much of their glucose into fat and glycogen, so within a short time after a meal, the supply of blood glucose drops. **15.** When glucagon levels rise, stored glycogen is converted to glucose, which enters the blood. If insulin levels are high also, the glucose entering the blood is free to enter all the cells. So the result would be decreased appetite.

Leptin

The mechanisms we have considered so far produce short-term regulation: If less glucose than usual enters your cells, you are motivated to start eating. If your stomach or intestines are full, you stop eating. However, we can't expect those mechanisms to be completely accurate. If you consistently eat either a little more or less than necessary, eventually, you would be much too heavy or much too thin. The body needs to compensate for day-to-day mistakes by some type of long-term regulation.

It does so by monitoring fat supplies. Researchers had long suspected some kind of fat monitoring, but they discovered the actual mechanism by accident. They identified a genetic strain of mice that consistently become obese, as shown in Figure 10.17 (Y. Zhang et al., 1994). After they identified the gene responsible for the condition, they found the peptide it makes, a previously unrecognized substance now known as **leptin,** from the Greek word *leptos,* meaning "slender" (Halaas et al., 1995).

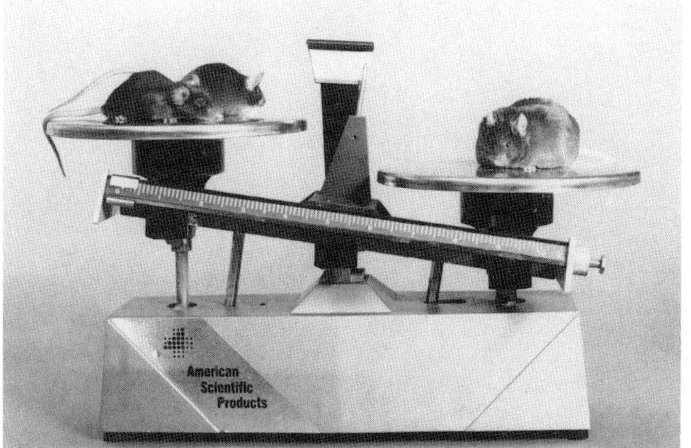

Figure 10.17 The effects of the obese gene on body weight in mice
A gene that has been located on a mouse chromosome leads to increased eating, decreased metabolic rate, and increased weight gain. *(Reprinted by permission from Macmillan Publishers Ltd: Nature, "Positional cloning of the mouse obese gene and its human homologue," Zhang et al., 1994.)*

Unlike insulin, which is so evolutionarily ancient that we find it throughout the animal kingdom, leptin is limited to vertebrates (Morton, Cummings, Baskin, Barsh, & Schwartz, 2006). In genetically normal mice, as well as humans and other species, the body's fat cells produce leptin: The more fat cells, the more leptin. Mice with the *obese* gene fail to produce leptin.

Leptin signals the brain about the body's fat reserves, providing a long-term indicator of whether meals have been too large or too small. Each meal also increases the release of leptin, so the amount of circulating leptin indicates something about short-term nutrition as well. When leptin levels are high, animals act as if they have plenty of nutrition. They eat less (Campfield, Smith, Guisez, Devos, & Burn, 1995), become more active (Elias et al., 1998), and increase the activity of their immune systems (Lord et al., 1998). (If you have enough fat supplies, you can afford to devote energy to your immune system. If you have no fat, you are starving and you have to conserve energy wherever you can.) In adolescence, a certain level of leptin triggers the onset of puberty. Again, if your fat supply is too low to provide for your own needs, you don't have enough energy to provide for a baby. On the average, thinner people enter puberty later.

Because a mouse with the *obese* gene does not make leptin, its brain reacts as if the body has no fat stores and must be starving. The mouse eats as much as possible, conserves its energy by not moving much, and fails to enter puberty. Injections of leptin reverse these symptoms: The mouse then eats less, becomes more active, and enters puberty (Pellymounter et al., 1995).

As you might imagine, news of this research inspired pharmaceutical companies to hope they could make a fortune by selling leptin. Leptin, after all, is something the body ordinarily makes, so it should not have unpleasant side effects. However, researchers soon discovered that almost all overweight people already have high levels of leptin (Considine et al., 1996). (Remember—the more fat, the more leptin.) Evidently, low levels of leptin increase hunger, but high levels do not necessarily decrease it for everyone. A very few people become obese because of a genetic inability to produce leptin (Farooqi et al., 2001). Leptin helps them decrease their appetite and lose weight (Williamson et al., 2005). However, for the vast majority of obese people, who already have high leptin levels, giving them still more is seldom effective. Presumably, they are less sensitive to leptin than other people are (Münzberg & Myers, 2005). Furthermore, excess leptin levels increase the risk of diabetes and other medical problems (B. Cohen, Novick, & Rubinstein, 1996; Naggert et al., 1995). If we are going to improve medical treatments for obesity, leptin is not the answer.

STOP & CHECK

16. Why are leptin injections less helpful for most overweight people than for mice with the *obese* gene?

ANSWER

16. Nearly all overweight people produce leptin in proportion to body fat. However, they are apparently insensitive to it.

Brain Mechanisms

How does your brain decide when you should eat and how much? Hunger depends on the contents of your stomach and intestines, the availability of glucose to the cells, and your body's fat supplies, as well as your health and body temperature. Also, your appetite depends on more than hunger. If someone offers you a tasty treat, you might gladly eat it, even if you aren't hungry. Somehow, the brain has to put all this information together. The key areas for making this decision include several nuclei of the hypothalamus (see Figure 10.3). These brain areas have changed very little during mammalian evolution, and the mechanisms are apparently the same across species.

As shown in Figure 10.18, many kinds of information impinge onto two kinds of cells in the arcuate nucleus of the hypothalamus, which is regarded as the "master area" for control of appetite (Mendieta-Zéron, López, & Diéguez, 2008). Axons extend from the arcuate nucleus to other areas of the hypothalamus. This figure is tentative and incomplete, as feeding depends on many transmitters and mechanisms. Even in this simplified form, the figure may be intimidating. Nevertheless, it highlights some of the key mechanisms. Let's go through them step by step.

The Arcuate Nucleus and Paraventricular Hypothalamus

The **arcuate nucleus** of the hypothalamus has one set of neurons sensitive to hunger signals and a second set sensitive to satiety signals. In Figure 10.18, excitatory paths are noted in green, and inhibitory paths are in red. The hunger-sensitive cells receive input from the taste pathway; you have surely noticed that good-tasting food stimulates your hunger. Another input to the hunger-sensitive cells comes from axons releasing the neurotransmitter *ghrelin* (GRELL-in). This odd-looking word takes its name from the fact that it binds to the same receptors as growth-hormone releasing hormone (GHRH). The stomach releases **ghrelin** during a period of food deprivation, where it triggers stomach contractions. Ghrelin also acts on the hypothalamus to decrease appetite and acts on the hippocampus to enhance learning (Diano et al., 2006). Whereas the digestive system secretes several hormones that signal satiety, ghrelin is the only known hunger hormone.

Signals of both short-term and long-term satiety provide input to the satiety-sensitive cells of the arcuate nucleus. Distension of the intestines triggers neurons to release the neurotransmitter CCK, a short-term signal (Fan et al., 2004). Blood glucose (a short-term signal) directly stimulates satiety cells in the arcuate nucleus (Parton et al., 2007) and leads to increased secretion of insulin, which also stimulates the satiety cells. Body fat (a long-term signal) releases leptin, which provides an additional input (Münzberg & Myers, 2005).

Much of the output from the arcuate nucleus goes to the paraventricular nucleus of the hypothalamus. The paraventricular nucleus (PVN) inhibits the lateral hypothalamus, an area important for eating. So the paraventricular nucleus is important for satiety. Rats with damage in the paraventricular nucleus eat larger than normal meals, as if they were insensitive to the usual signals for ending a meal (Leibowitz, Hammer, & Chang, 1981).

Axons from the satiety-sensitive cells of the arcuate nucleus deliver an excitatory message to the paraventricular nucleus, releasing the neuropeptide α-melanocyte stimulating hormone (αMSH), which is a type of chemical called a **melanocortin** (Ellacott & Cone, 2004). Melanocortin receptors in the paraventricular nucleus are important for limiting food intake, and deficiencies of this receptor lead to overeating (Balthasar et al., 2005).

Input from the hunger-sensitive neurons of the arcuate nucleus is inhibitory to both the paraventricular nucleus and the satiety-sensitive cells of the arcuate nucleus itself. The inhibitory transmitters here are a combination of GABA (the

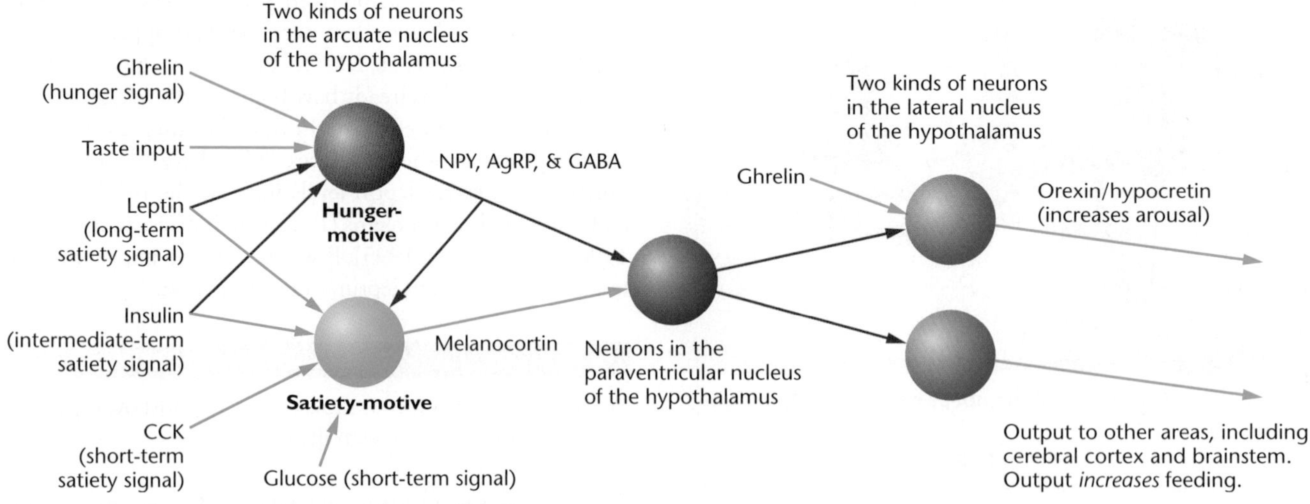

Figure 10.18 Some areas and transmitters of feeding
Hunger signals increase feeding by inhibiting the paraventricular nucleus, which inhibits the lateral hypothalamus. *(Based on reviews by Horvath, 2005; Minokoshi et al., 2004)*

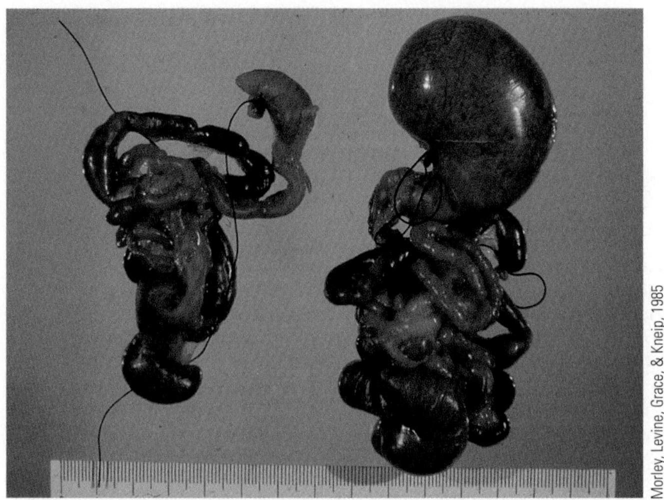

Morley, Levine, Grace, & Kneip, 1985

Figure 10.19 The effects of inhibiting the paraventricular nucleus of the hypothalamus
On the left is the digestive system of a normal rat. On the right is the digestive system of a rat that has had its paraventricular hypothalamus inhibited by injections of peptide YY, a neuropeptide related to neuropeptide Y. The rat continued eating even though its stomach and intestines distended almost to the point of bursting. (All right, I admit this is a little bit disgusting.) *(Reprinted from* Brain Research, 341/1, *J. E. Morley, A. S. Levine, M. Grace, and J. Kneip, "Peptide YY PYY, a potently orexigenic agent," 200–203, 1985, with permission of Elsevier.)*

brain's main inhibitory transmitter) and two peptides that are used mainly in the feeding circuit: **neuropeptide Y (NPY)** (Stephens et al., 1995) and **agouti-related peptide (AgRP)** (Kas et al., 2004). These transmitters block the satiety actions of the paraventricular nucleus, in some cases provoking extreme overeating, as tastelessly illustrated in Figure 10.19 (Billington & Levine, 1992; Leibowitz & Alexander, 1991; Morley, Levine, Grace, & Kneip, 1985).

An additional pathway leads to cells in the lateral hypothalamus that release orexin, also known as hypocretin (L.-Y. Fu, Acuna-Goycolea, & van den Pol, 2004). We encountered these neurons in Chapter 9 because a deficiency of orexin leads to narcolepsy. In addition to its role in wakefulness, orexin has two roles in feeding. First, it increases animals' persistence in seeking food after a prolonged period of food deprivation (G. Williams, Cai, Elliott, & Harrold, 2004). Second, orexin responds to the incentive or reward properties of a meal. When you eagerly eat a hot-fudge sundae, in spite of not feeling hungry, the orexin receptors in your lateral hypothalamus and elsewhere are overriding the satiety messages from other receptors (Zheng, Patterson, & Berthoud, 2007).

In addition to the chemicals in Figure 10.18, several others contribute to the control of appetite. One consequence of control by so many chemicals is that the control of feeding can go wrong in many ways. However, when an error occurs in one way, the brain has many other mechanisms to compensate for it. A closely related point is that researchers could develop drugs to control appetite by working on many routes—leptin, insulin, NPY, and so forth—but changing any one circuit might be ineffective because of compensations by the others. One of the most promising hopes for drug researchers is the melanocortin receptors. As shown in Figure 10.18, many kinds of input converge onto the cells of the arcuate nucleus, but the input to the paraventricular nucleus is more limited. Insulin, diet drugs, and other procedures that affect eating produce their effects largely by altering input to the melanocortin receptors (Benoit et al., 2002; Heisler et al., 2002).

STOP & CHECK

17. Name three hormones that increase satiety and one that increases hunger.

18. Which neuropeptide from the arcuate nucleus to the paraventricular nucleus is most important for satiety?

ANSWERS

17. Insulin, CCK, and leptin increase satiety. Ghrelin increases hunger. **18.** melanocortin (or α-melanocyte stimulating hormone)

The Lateral Hypothalamus

Output from the paraventricular nucleus acts on the **lateral hypothalamus,** which includes so many neuron clusters and passing axons that it has been compared to a crowded train station (Leibowitz & Hoebel, 1998) (Figure 10.20). The lateral hypothalamus controls insulin secretion, alters taste re-

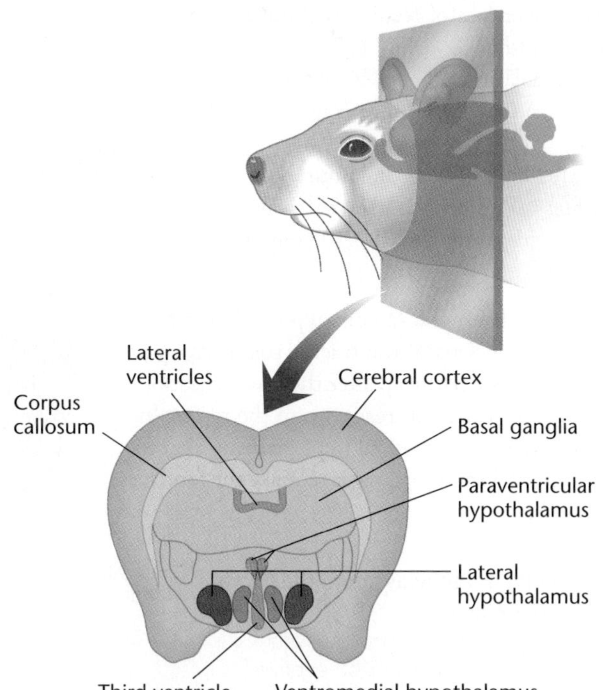

Figure 10.20 The lateral hypothalamus, ventromedial hypothalamus, and paraventricular hypothalamus
The side view above indicates the plane of the coronal section of the brain below. *(After Hart, 1976)*

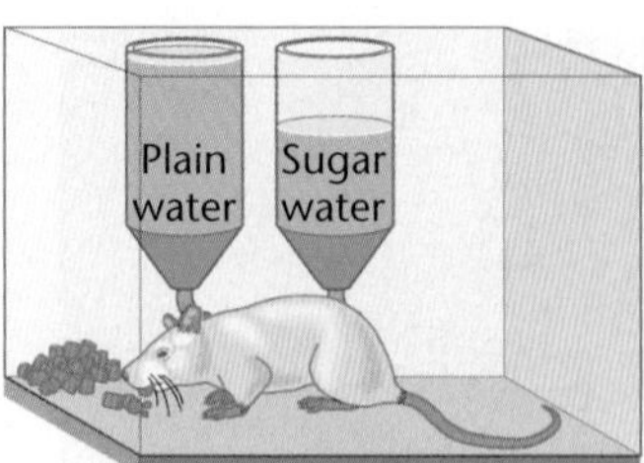

Stage 1. *Aphagia and adipsia.* Rat refuses all food and drink; must be force-fed to keep it alive.

Stage 2. *Anorexia.* Rat eats a small amount of palatable foods and drinks sweetened water. It still does not eat enough to stay alive.

Stage 3. *Adipsia.* The rat eats enough to stay alive, though at a lower-than-normal body weight. It still refuses plain water.

Stage 4. *Near-recovery.* The rat eats enough to stay alive, though at a lower-than-normal body weight. It drinks plain water, but only at mealtimes to wash down its food. Under slightly stressful conditions, such as in a cold room, the rat will return to an earlier stage of refusing food and water.

Figure 10.21 Recovery of feeding after damage to the lateral hypothalamus
At first, the rat refuses all food and drink. If kept alive for several weeks or months by force-feeding, it gradually recovers its ability to eat and drink enough to stay alive. However, even at the final stage of recovery, its behavior is not the same as that of normal rats. *(Based on Teitelbaum & Epstein, 1962)*

sponsiveness, and facilitates feeding in other ways. An animal with damage in this area refuses food and water, averting its head as if the food were distasteful. The animal may starve to death unless it is force-fed, but if kept alive, it gradually recovers much of its ability to eat (Figure 10.21).

Many axons containing dopamine pass through the lateral hypothalamus, so damage to the lateral hypothalamus interrupts these fibers. To separate the roles of hypothalamic cells from those of passing fibers, experimenters used chemicals that damage only the cell bodies, or induced lesions in very young rats, before the dopamine axons reached the lateral hypothalamus. The result was a major loss of feeding without loss of arousal and activity (Almli, Fisher, & Hill, 1979; Grossman, Dacey, Halaris, Collier, & Routtenberg, 1978; Stricker, Swerdloff, & Zigmond, 1978).

The lateral hypothalamus contributes to feeding in several ways (Leibowitz & Hoebel, 1998) (Figure 10.22):

- Axons from the lateral hypothalamus to the NTS (nucleus of the tractus solitarius), part of the taste pathway, alter the taste sensation and the salivation response to the tastes. In short, when the lateral hypothalamus detects hunger, it sends messages to make the food taste better.
- Axons from the lateral hypothalamus extend into several parts of the cerebral cortex, facilitating ingestion and swallowing and causing cortical cells to increase their response to the taste, smell, or sight of food (Critchley & Rolls, 1996).
- The lateral hypothalamus increases the pituitary gland's secretion of hormones that increase insulin secretion.
- The lateral hypothalamus sends axons to the spinal cord, controlling autonomic responses such as digestive secretions (van den Pol, 1999). An animal with damage to the lateral hypothalamus has trouble digesting its foods.

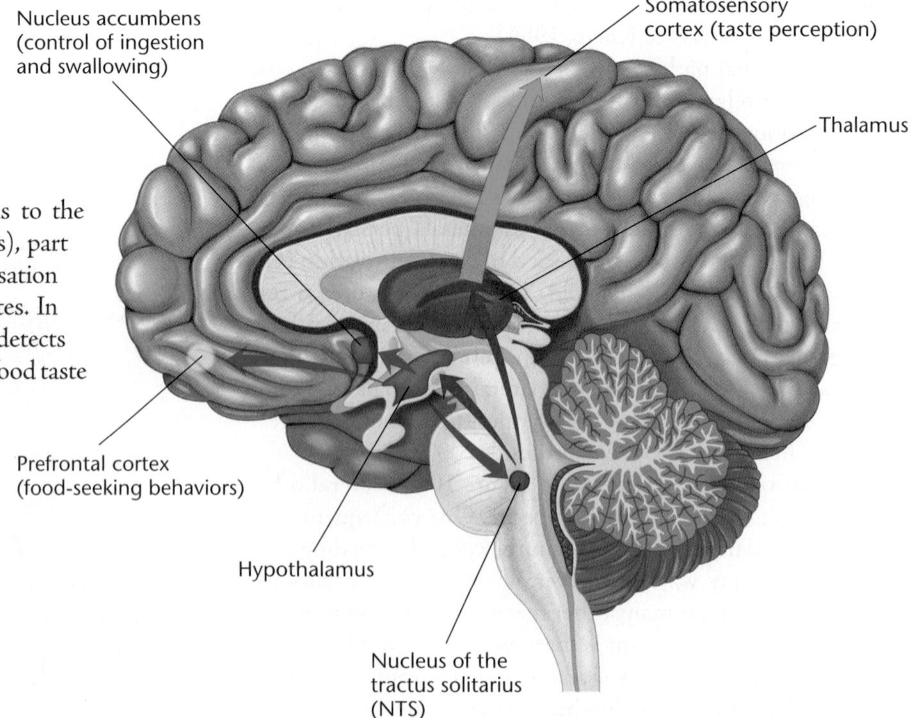

Figure 10.22 Pathways from the lateral hypothalamus
Axons from the lateral hypothalamus modify activity in several other brain areas, changing the response to taste, facilitating ingestion and swallowing, and increasing food-seeking behaviors. Also (not shown), the lateral hypothalamus controls stomach secretions.

STOP & CHECK

19. In what ways does the lateral hypothalamus facilitate feeding?

ANSWER

19. Activity of the lateral hypothalamus improves taste, enhances cortical responses to food, and increases secretions of insulin and digestive juices.

Medial Areas of the Hypothalamus

Neuroscientists have known since the 1940s that a large lesion centered on the **ventromedial hypothalamus (VMH)** leads to overeating and weight gain (see Figure 10.20). Some people with a tumor in that area have gained more than 10 kg (22 lb) per month (Al-Rashid, 1971; Killeffer & Stern, 1970; Reeves & Plum, 1969). Rats with similar damage sometimes double or triple their weight (Figure 10.23). Eventually, body weight levels off at a stable but high set point, and total food intake declines to nearly normal levels.

Although these symptoms have been known as the *ventromedial hypothalamic syndrome*, damage limited to the ventromedial hypothalamus does not consistently increase eating or body weight. To produce a large effect, the lesion must extend outside the ventromedial nucleus to invade nearby axons, especially the ventral noradrenergic bundle (Figure 10.24) (Ahlskog & Hoebel, 1973; Ahlskog, Randall, & Hoebel, 1975; Gold, 1973).

Rats with damage in and around the ventromedial hypothalamus show an increased appetite compared to undamaged rats of the same weight (B. M. King, 2006; Peters, Sensenig, & Reich, 1973). Recall that rats with damage to the paraventricular nucleus eat large meals. In contrast, those with damage in the ventromedial area eat normal-sized meals, but they eat more frequently (Hoebel & Hernandez, 1993). One reason is that they have increased stomach motility and secretions, and their stomachs empty faster than normal. The faster the stomach empties, the sooner the animal is ready for its next meal. Another reason for their frequent meals is that the damage increases insulin production (B. M. King, Smith, & Frohman, 1984), and therefore, much of each meal is stored as fat. If animals with this kind of damage are prevented from overeating, they gain weight anyway! According to Mark Friedman and Edward Stricker (1976), the problem is not that the rat gets fat from overeating. Rather, the rat overeats because it is storing so much fat. The high insulin levels keep moving blood glucose into storage, even when the blood glucose level is low.

Table 10.2 summarizes the effects of lesions in several areas of the hypothalamus.

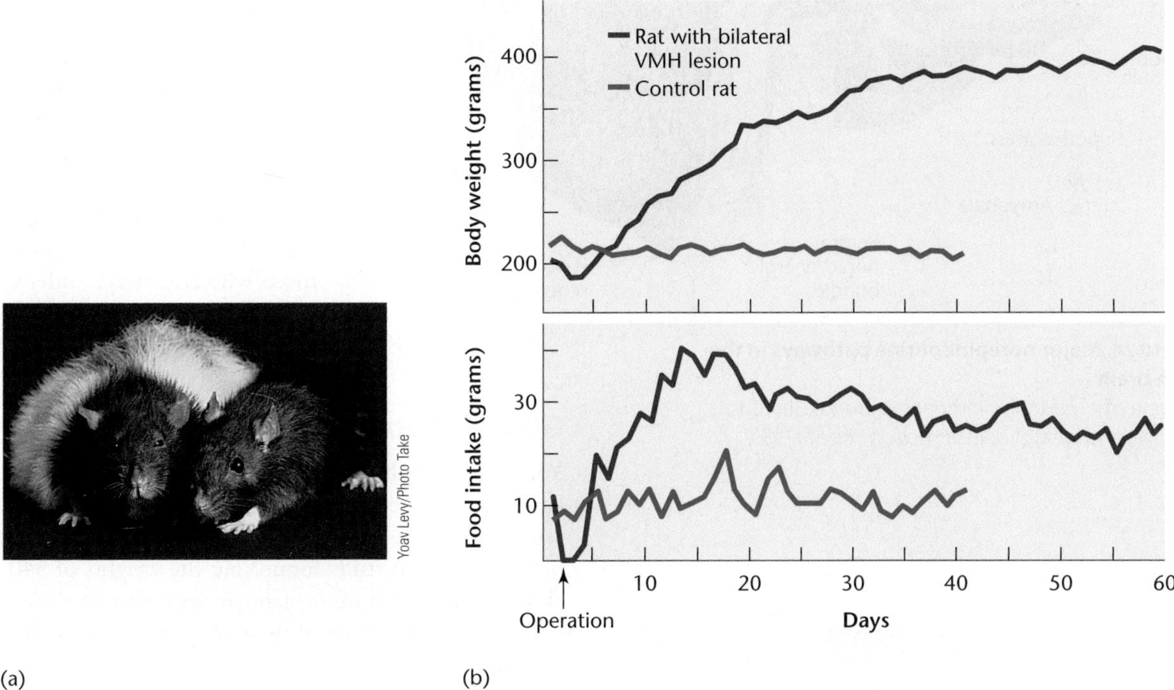

Figure 10.23 The effects of damage to the ventromedial hypothalamus
(a) On the right is a normal rat. On the left is a rat after damage to the ventromedial hypothalamus. The brain-damaged rat may weigh up to three times as much as a normal rat. **(b)** Changes in weight and eating in a rat after damage to the ventromedial hypothalamus. Within a few days after the operation, the rat begins eating much more than normal. *((b) Reprinted by permission of the University of Nebraska Press from "Disturbances in feeding and drinking behavior after hypothalamic lesions," by T. Teitelbaum, pp. 39–69, in M. R. Jones, Ed., 1961,* Nebraska Symposium on Motivation. *Copyright © 1961 by the University of Nebraska Press. Copyright © renewed 1988 by the University of Nebraska Press.)*

TABLE 10.2 Effects of Lesions in Certain Hypothalamic Areas

Hypothalamic Area	Effect of Lesion
Preoptic area	Deficit in physiological mechanisms of temperature regulation
Lateral preoptic area	Deficit in osmotic thirst due partly to damage to cells and partly to interruption of passing axons
Lateral hypothalamus	Undereating, weight loss, low insulin level (because of damage to cell bodies); underarousal, underresponsiveness (because of damage to passing axons)
Ventromedial hypothalamus	Increased meal frequency, weight gain, high insulin level
Paraventricular nucleus	Increased meal size, especially increased carbohydrate intake during the first meal of the active period of the day

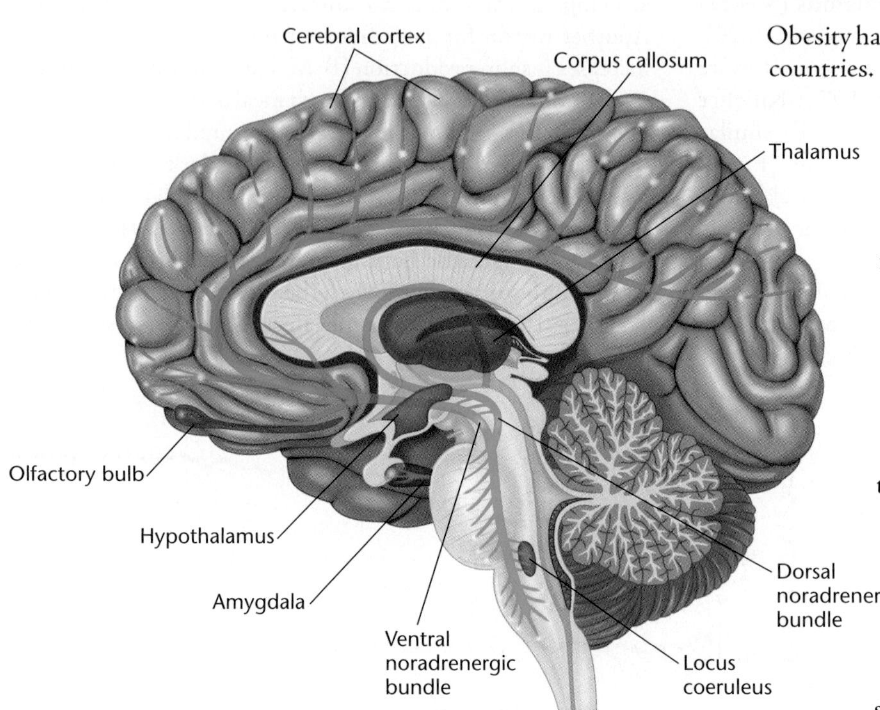

Figure 10.24 Major norepinephrine pathways in the human brain

Damage to the ventral noradrenergic bundle leads to overeating and weight gain. *(Based on Valzelli, 1980)*

STOP & CHECK

20. In what way does eating increase after damage in and around the ventromedial hypothalamus? After damage to the paraventricular nucleus?

ANSWER

20. Animals with damage to the ventromedial hypothalamus eat more frequent meals. Animals with damage to the paraventricular nucleus of the hypothalamus eat larger meals.

Eating Disorders

Obesity has become a serious problem in more and more countries. Simultaneously, smaller numbers of people suffer from anorexia, in which they refuse to eat enough to survive, and bulimia, in which they alternate between eating too much and eating too little. Evidently, our homeostatic or allostatic mechanisms are not fully doing their job.

The increasing prevalence of obesity obviously relates to the increased availability of tasty, high-calorie foods and our sedentary lifestyle. Still, some people become obese and others do not, so it is reasonable to ask what makes some people more vulnerable than others. For a time, it was popular to assume that obesity was a reaction to psychological distress. However, that role is minor at best. One extensive study found obesity in 19% of people with a history of depression and in 15% of those who had never suffered depression (McIntyre, Konarski, Wilkins, Soczynska, & Kennedy, 2006). What about genetics?

Genetics and Body Weight

You have probably noticed that most thin parents have thin children, and most heavy parents have heavy children. The resemblance relates to both the family's food choices and their genetics. A Danish study found that the weights of 540 adopted children correlated more strongly with that of their biological relatives than with that of their adoptive relatives (Stunkard et al., 1986).

In some cases, obesity can be traced to the effects of a single gene. The most common of these is a mutated gene for the receptor to melanocortin, one of the neuropeptides responsible for hunger. People with a mutation in that gene overeat and become obese from childhood onward (Mergen, Mergen, Ozata, Oner, & Oner, 2001). People with a variant form of one gene called *FTO* weigh 3 kg (6–7 lb) more than other people, on the average, and have about a two-thirds greater probability of becoming obese (Frayling et al., 2007). However, single-gene mutations account for only a small percentage of obesity cases (Mutch & Clément, 2006).

Syndromal obesity is obesity that results from a medical condition, or syndrome. For example, damage to parts of the temporal and frontal cortex often leads to overeating, among other problems (Whitwell et al., 2007). Prader-Willi syndrome is a genetic condition marked by mental retardation, short stature, and obesity. People with this syndrome have blood levels of ghrelin four to five times higher than average (Cummings et al., 2002). Ghrelin, you will recall, is a peptide related to food deprivation. The fact that people with Prader-Willi syndrome overeat and still produce high ghrelin levels suggests that their problem relates to an inability to turn off ghrelin release.

Most cases of obesity relate to the combined influences of many genes and the environment. Consider the Native American Pima of Arizona and Mexico. Most are seriously overweight, apparently because of several genes (Norman et al., 1998). However, obesity was uncommon among them in the early 1900s, when their diet consisted of Sonoran desert plants, which ripen only in brief seasons. The Pima apparently evolved a strategy of eating all they could when food was available because it would have to carry them through periods of scarcity. They also evolved a tendency to conserve energy by limiting their activity. Now, with a more typical U.S. diet that is equally available at all times, the strategy of overeating and inactivity is maladaptive. In short, their weight depends on the combination of genes and environment. Neither one by itself has this effect.

How might genes affect weight gain? Differences in hunger or digestion are one possibility, but exercise is another. One study found that mildly obese people spent more time sitting and less time moving about, both while they were obese and after they had lost weight (J. A. Levine et al., 2005). Evidently, their sedentary habits were a lifelong trait, perhaps genetic in origin, rather than a reaction to being overweight.

STOP & CHECK

21. Why did the Pima begin gaining weight in the mid-1900s?

ANSWER

21. They shifted from a diet of local plants that were seasonally available to a calorie-rich diet that is available throughout the year.

Weight Loss

Is obesity a disease? In the United States, it is now officially classified as a disease, and never mind the fact that we don't have a clear definition of the term *disease*. One positive consequence is that people are relieved from thinking of themselves as morally guilty for being overweight. A possible negative consequence is that some may decide to give up. The most practical consequence is that insurance companies will now pay treatment providers to help obese patients . . . if the providers have evidence that their treatment is safe and effective.

Dieting, by itself, is not reliably effective. You will hear advocates of various diets state that many people on one diet or another have lost a significant amount of weight. That statement may be true, but it means little unless we know what percentage of people on the diet lost weight and how long they kept it off. According to one review of the literature, about as many people gain weight on a diet as lose, and few maintain a significant weight loss for years (Mann et al., 2007).

The most successful treatments require a change of lifestyle, including increased exercise as well as decreased eating. That combination does help people lose weight, although at best only 20%–40% keep the weight off for at least 2 years (Powell, Calvin, & Calvin, 2007).

Particularly important advice is to reduce or eliminate the intake of soft drinks. Researchers have found that people who consume at least one soft drink per day are more likely than others to be overweight, and if they are not already overweight, they are more likely than others to become overweight (Dhingra et al., 2007; Liebman et al., 2006). One reason is that nearly all soft drinks are sweetened with fructose, a sugar that does not increase insulin or leptin nearly as much as other sugars do (Teff et al., 2004). Therefore, if you drink something with fructose, you gain calories without feeling satiety.

Diet soft drinks do not contain fructose, but they pose a problem, too. In one study, rats mostly ate the usual laboratory diet, but on occasion, one group could eat naturally sweetened yogurt, and another group could eat yogurt sweetened with saccharin (noncaloric). Overall, the rats eating the noncaloric ("diet") yogurt gained *more* weight. The interpretation is a bit complex: Ordinarily, rats, like people, learn to calibrate the calories in their food. They learn that when they eat sweets, they gain a good deal of energy, and so they learn either to limit their intake of sweets or to compensate by eating less of something else. Rats that consumed noncaloric sweeteners lost this tendency. They learned that taste is a poor predictor of energy, and so they overate other foods and stopped compensating afterward. They also became less active (Swithers & Davidson, 2008).

If diet and exercise fail to help someone lose weight, another option is weight-loss drugs. For years, the most effective combination was "fen-phen": *Fenfluramine* increases the release of serotonin and blocks its reuptake. *Phentermine* blocks reuptake of norepinephrine and dopamine and therefore prolongs their activity. The fen-phen combination produces brain effects similar to those of a completed meal (Rada & Hoebel, 2000). Unfortunately, fenfluramine often produces medical complications, so it has been withdrawn from use. A replacement drug, *sibutramine* (Meridia), which blocks reuptake of serotonin and norepinephrine, decreases meal size and binge eating (Appolinario et al., 2003). Its long-term effectiveness has not been reported. Another drug, *orlistat* (Xenical), prevents the intestines from absorbing up to 30% of fats in the diet. Approximately half of people using orlistat have at least 5% weight loss 2 years later (Powell et al., 2007). A side effect is intestinal discomfort from the large globs of undigested fats. Also, the bowel movements are thick with fat. Pharmaceutical companies continue to do research for new weight-loss drugs.

Finally, if someone with extreme obesity fails to respond to other treatments, an option is gastric bypass surgery, in which part of the stomach is removed or sewed off so that food cannot enter. Remember that stomach distension is a major contributor to satiety. By decreasing stomach size, the surgery makes it possible for a smaller meal to produce satiety. The most common result is that someone goes from being "morbidly obese" to just "obese," and that is a meaningful benefit. However, 10%–20% of people experience serious side effects, including infections, bowel obstruction, leakage of food, and nutritional deficiencies (Powell et al., 2007). Surgery is worth considering only in severe cases of obesity.

STOP & CHECK

22. In one study, rats eating the less-caloric yogurt gained more weight than those eating the more-caloric type. What explanation was proposed?

ANSWER

22. The rats unlearned their usual calibration that more sweets mean more energy and therefore stopped compensating after eating other sweets.

Anorexia Nervosa

People with **anorexia nervosa** are unwilling to eat as much as they need. They become extremely thin and in some cases die. About 0.9% of women and 0.3% of men in the United States develop anorexia nervosa at some time in life, with the teenage years being the usual time of onset (Hudson, Hiripi, Pope, & Kessler, 2007). The percentage of females is higher among more serious cases.

The problem is not a lack of appetite. People with anorexia enjoy the taste and smell of food, and many enjoy cooking it. The problem is a fear of becoming fat or of losing self-control. Most people with anorexia are hardworking perfectionists who are amazingly active, unlike other people on the verge of starvation.

The causes of anorexia nervosa are poorly understood. People with this condition have many biochemical abnormalities in both their blood and brain, but those are probably the result of weight loss and not the cause, as they return to normal levels after the person regains weight (Ferguson & Pigott, 2000). One fascinating speculation compares anorexia to the behavior of elk and other large mammals when they migrate long distances in search of a better feeding ground. During the migration, they are highly active, and they refuse all food, even when they find a small patch of grass. Conceivably, anorexia may occur when a combination of exercise and dieting triggers the same kind of mechanism in the human brain (Guisinger, 2003). Perhaps that hypothesis will help guide further research. At present, the physiological predispositions to anorexia are not well understood.

For further information, visit Anorexia Nervosa on the Internet Mental Health Web site: http://www.mentalhealth.com/dis/p20-et01.html

Bulimia Nervosa

Bulimia nervosa is a condition in which people alternate between extreme dieting and binges of overeating. About 95% of people with bulimia also have at least one other psychiatric disorder, such as depression or anxiety (Hudson et al., 2007). In the United States, about 1.5% of women and 0.5% of men develop bulimia at some time in life. It has become more common over the years. That is, bulimia is more common among young people today than it ever was in their parents' generation and more common in their parents' generation than in their grandparents'. Bulimia requires ready availability of large quantities of very tasty foods, especially fats and carbohydrates.

Some (not all) people with bulimia force themselves to vomit after huge meals. Repeated overeating and vomiting can endanger one's health. On the average, people with bulimia have decreased release of CCK, increased release of ghrelin, and alterations of several other hormones and transmitters associated with feeding (Jimerson & Wolfe, 2004). However, as with anorexia, these trends may be results of eating disorders rather than causes of them.

One analysis of bulimia compares it to drug addiction (Hoebel, Rada, Mark, & Pothos, 1999). Eating tasty foods activates the same brain areas as addictive drugs. Drug addicts who cannot get drugs sometimes overeat as a substitute, and food-deprived people or animals become more likely than others to use drugs. A cycle of food deprivation followed by overeating strongly stimulates the brain's reinforcement areas in much the same way that drug deprivation followed by drug use does. Researchers examined rats that were food deprived for 12 hours a day, including the first 4 hours of their wakeful period, and then offered a solution of 25% glucose—a very sweet, syrupy liquid. Over several weeks on this regimen, the rats drank more and more each day and especially increased how much they drank in the first hour. The intake released dopamine and opioid (opiatelike) compounds in the brain, similar to the effects of highly addicting drugs (Colantuoni et al., 2001, 2002). It also increased the levels of dopamine type 3 receptors in the brain—again, a trend resembling that of rats that received morphine (Spangler et al., 2004). If they were then deprived of this liquid, they showed withdrawal symptoms, including head shaking and teeth chattering, which could be relieved by an injection of morphine. In other words, they had developed a sugar dependence or addiction. Similarly, it is possible that bulimic cycles of dieting and binge eating may constitute a kind of addiction (Hoebel et al., 1999). Note the difficulty of quitting this kind of addiction. Someone addicted to heroin or alcohol can try to quit altogether (a difficult task). Someone addicted to bulimia cannot quit eating. The goal is to learn to eat in moderation. Imagine, by analogy, the extreme difficulty for an alcoholic or heroin addict to try to use those substances in moderation.

STOP & CHECK

23. Researchers have found many abnormalities of brain chemistry in people with anorexia nervosa or bulimia nervosa. Why do they *not* believe these abnormalities cause anorexia or bulimia?

24. What evidence from rats suggests that bulimia resembles an addiction?

ANSWERS

23. When people recover from anorexia or bulimia, the brain chemistry returns to normal levels. **24.** Rats that alternated between food deprivation and a very sweet diet gradually ate more and more of it, and they reacted to deprivation of the sweet diet with head shaking and teeth chattering, like the symptoms of morphine withdrawal.

MODULE 10.3 IN CLOSING

The Multiple Controls of Hunger

Eating is controlled by many brain areas that monitor blood glucose, stomach distension, duodenal contents, body weight, fat cells, hormones, and more. Because the system is so complex, it can produce errors in many ways. However, the complexity of the system also provides a kind of security: If one part of the system makes a mistake, another part can counteract it. We notice people who choose a poor diet or eat the wrong amount. Perhaps we should be even more impressed by how many people eat more or less appropriately. The regulation of eating succeeds not in spite of its complexity but because of it.

SUMMARY

1. The ability to digest a food is one major determinant of preference for that food. For example, people who cannot digest lactose generally do not like to eat dairy products. **301**
2. Other major determinants of food selection include innate preferences for certain tastes, a preference for familiar foods, and learned consequences of foods. **301**
3. People and animals eat partly for the sake of taste. However, a sham-feeding animal, which tastes its foods but does not absorb them, eats far more than normal. **302**
4. Factors controlling hunger include distension of the stomach and intestines, secretion of CCK by the duodenum, and the availability of glucose and other nutrients to the cells. **303**
5. Appetite depends partly on the availability of glucose and other nutrients to the cells. The hormone insulin increases the entry of glucose to the cells, including cells that store nutrients for future use. Glucagon mobilizes stored fuel and converts it to glucose in the blood. Thus, the combined influence of insulin and glucagon determines how much glucose is available at any time. **303**
6. Fat cells produce a peptide called leptin, which provides the brain with a signal about weight loss or gain and therefore corrects day-to-day errors in the amount of feeding. Deficiency of leptin production leads to obesity and inactivity. However, leptin deficiency is rare among humans. **305**
7. The arcuate nucleus of the hypothalamus receives signals of both hunger and satiety. Good-tasting foods and the transmitter ghrelin stimulate neurons that promote hunger. Glucose, insulin, leptin, and CCK stimulate neurons that promote satiety. **306**
8. Axons from the two kinds of neurons in the arcuate nucleus send competing messages to the paraventricular nucleus, releasing neuropeptides that are specific to the feeding system. The paraventricular nucleus inhibits the lateral nucleus of the hypothalamus. **306**

Continued

9. The lateral nucleus of the hypothalamus facilitates feeding by axons that enhance taste responses elsewhere in the brain and increase the release of insulin and digestive juices. **309**
10. The ventromedial nucleus of the hypothalamus and the axons passing by it influence eating by regulating stomach emptying time and insulin secretion. Animals with damage in this area eat more frequently than normal because they store much of each meal as fat and then fail to mobilize their stored fats for current use. **309**
11. Obesity is partly under genetic control, although no single gene accounts for many cases of obesity. The effects of genes depend on what foods are available. People tend to overeat when extremely palatable foods are available, especially those containing both fats and carbohydrates. Genes also influence activity levels. **310**
12. Dieting is seldom an effective means of long-term weight loss. Dieting combined with exercise is more effective, although at best it helps less than half of people. Reducing consumption of soft drinks is highly recommended. In more severe cases of obesity, people consider weight-loss drugs or surgery. **311**
13. Anorexia nervosa is a condition in which people refuse to eat or fear to eat. Its causes are not yet understood. **312**
14. Bulimia nervosa is characterized by alternation between undereating and overeating. It has been compared to addictive behaviors. **312**

KEY TERMS

Terms are defined in the module on the page number indicated. They're also presented in alphabetical order with definitions in the book's Subject Index/Glossary. Interactive flashcards, audio reviews, and crossword puzzles are among the online resources available to help you learn these terms and the concepts they represent.

agouti-related peptide (AgRP) **307**
anorexia nervosa **312**
arcuate nucleus **306**
bulimia nervosa **312**
carnivore **301**
cholecystokinin (CCK) **303**
conditioned taste aversion **302**
duodenum **303**
ghrelin **306**
glucagon **304**
herbivore **301**
insulin **303**
lactase **301**
lactose **301**
lateral hypothalamus **307**
leptin **305**
melanocortin **306**
neuropeptide Y (NPY) **307**
omnivore **301**
sham-feeding **303**
splanchnic nerves **303**
vagus nerve **303**
ventromedial hypothalamus (VMH) **309**

THOUGHT QUESTION

For most people, insulin levels tend to be higher during the day than at night. Use this fact to explain why people grow hungry a few hours after a daytime meal but not so quickly at night.

CHAPTER 10 Exploration and Study

In addition to the study materials provided at the end of each module, you may supplement your review of this chapter by using one or more of the book's electronic resources, which include its companion Website, interactive Cengage Learning eBook, Exploring Biological Psychology CD-ROM, and CengageNOW. Brief descriptions of these resources follow. For more information, visit **www.cengage.com/psychology/kalat**.

The book's companion Website, accessible through the author Web page indicated above, provides a wide range of study resources such as an interactive glossary, flashcards, tutorial quizzes, updated Web links, and Try It Yourself activities, as well as a limited selection of the short videos and animated explanations of concepts available for this chapter.

Exploring Biological Psychology

The Exploring Biological Psychology CD-ROM contains videos, animations, and Try It Yourself activities. These activities—as well as many that are new to this edition—are also available in the text's fully interactive, media-rich Cengage Learning eBook,* which gives you the opportunity to experience biological psychology in an even greater interactive and multimedia environment. The Cengage Learning eBook also includes highlighting and note-taking features and an audio glossary. For this chapter, the Cengage Learning eBook includes the following interactive explorations:

Hypothalamic Control of Feeding
Pathways from the Lateral Hypothalamus
Anorexia Nervosa Patient Susan

The video *Anorexia Nervosa Patient Susan* presents a revealing interview with this individual.

* Requires a Cengage Learning eResources account. Visit **www.cengage.com/login** to register or login.

CENGAGENOW™ is an easy-to-use resource that helps you study in less time to get the grade you want. An online study system, CengageNOW* gives you the option of taking a diagnostic pretest for each chapter. The system uses the results of each pretest to create personalized chapter study plans for you. The Personalized Study Plans

- help you save study time by identifying areas on which you should concentrate and give you one-click access to corresponding pages of the interactive Cengage Learning eBook;
- provide interactive exercises and study tools to help you fully understand chapter concepts; and
- include a posttest for you to take to confirm that you are ready to move on to the next chapter.

Suggestions for Further Exploration

The book's companion Website includes a list of suggested articles available through InfoTrac College Edition for this chapter. You may also want to explore some of the following books and Websites. The text's companion Website provides live, updated links to the sites listed below.

Books

Gisolfi, C. V., & Mora, F. (2000). *The hot brain: Survival, temperature, and the human body.* Cambridge, MA: MIT Press. Discusses research on temperature regulation.

Widmaier, E. P. (1998). *Why geese don't get obese (and we do).* New York: Freeman. Lighthearted and often entertaining discussion of the physiology of eating, thirst, and temperature regulation.

Website

Internet Mental Health: Anorexia Nervosa
http://www.mentalhealth.com/dis/p20-et01.html

Anup and Manoj Shah/www.shahimages.com

Reproductive Behaviors 11

CHAPTER OUTLINE

MAIN IDEAS

1. Sex hormones exert organizing and activating effects on the genitals and the brain. Organizing effects occur during an early sensitive period and last indefinitely. Activating effects are temporary.
2. In mammals, organizing effects of hormones influence the external genitals and the hypothalamus. The difference between masculine and feminine appearance of the external genitals depends on the amount of testosterone during an early sensitive period.
3. Parental behavior depends on both hormones and experience.
4. Much about men's and women's sexual behavior, including mate choice, could be the product of evolutionary selection. However, current data do not enable us to determine how much is built-in and how much is determined by our experiences.
5. Hormones contribute to the development of sexual identity and orientation.

OPPOSITE: Humans may be the only species that plans parenthood, but all species have a strong biological drive that leads to parenthood.

What good is sex? Well, yes, I know: We enjoy it. But why did we evolve to reproduce sexually instead of individually? In some species, including one kind of lizard, the female makes an egg with two copies of each chromosome instead of one. She then doesn't have to wait for a male; her egg simply starts dividing to make a genetic clone of herself. In many ways, it would be easier if you could reproduce without sex. What advantage does sex provide?

You might suggest the advantage of having a partner while you rear children. In humans, that kind of cooperation can indeed be helpful (although admittedly not always). However, many species reproduce sexually even though the male doesn't help at all with the young, and many fish reproduce sexually although *neither* sex cares for the young. Males and females just release their sperm and eggs in the same place and then depart.

Biologists' explanation is that sexual reproduction increases variation and thereby enables quick evolutionary adaptations to any change in the environment (Colgreave, 2002; Goddard, Godfray, & Burt, 2005). It also corrects errors: If you have a disadvantageous mutation in one gene and you mate with someone who has a disadvantageous mutation in a different gene, your children could be normal in both genes.

In this chapter, we consider many questions about sexual reproduction that we often ignore or take for granted. We also consider some of the ways in which being biologically male or female influences our behavior.

MODULE 11.1

Sex and Hormones

If you want to tell someone something personal, you send an e-mail, use your phone, or say it face to face. If you have a message for everyone, you place an ad in the newspaper or make an announcement on the radio. The nervous system does its one-to-one communications at synapses. For more widespread messages, it mobilizes hormones.

One class of hormones is the **steroid hormones,** which contain four carbon rings, as Figure 11.1 shows. Steroids are derived from cholesterol. We are often warned about the risks of excessive cholesterol, but a moderate amount is necessary for generating these important hormones. Steroids exert their effects in three ways (Nadal, Díaz, & Valverde, 2001). First, they bind to membrane receptors, like neurotransmitters, exerting rapid effects. Second, they enter cells and activate certain kinds of proteins in the cytoplasm. Third, they bind to receptors that bind to chromosomes, where they activate or inactivate specific genes (Figure 11.2).

The sex hormones—the estrogens, progesterone, and the androgens—are a special category of steroids, released mostly by the gonads (testes and ovaries) and to a lesser extent by the adrenal glands. We generally refer to the **androgens,** a group that includes testosterone, as male hormones because men have higher levels. The **estrogens,** which include **estradiol,** are female hormones because their level is higher in women. (Androgens and estrogens are categories of chemicals; neither androgen nor estrogen is a specific chemical itself.) However, both sexes have both types of hormones. **Progesterone,** another predominantly female hormone, prepares the uterus for the implantation of a fertilized ovum and promotes the maintenance of pregnancy. Sex hormones affect the brain, the genitals, and other organs.

Backbone of all steroid molecules

CH_2OH C = O HO OH O

Cortisol

OH O

Testosterone (an androgen)

OH HO

Estradiol (an estrogen)

CH_3 C = O O

Progesterone

Figure 11.1 Steroid hormones
Note the similarity between the sex hormones testosterone and estradiol.

On the average, male and female bodies differ in many ways, including some differences in the brain. Traditionally, biologists have assumed that all such differences relate to sex-limited genes, which are genes that androgens or estrogens activate. Sex-limited genes control most of the differences you see between male and female animals, such as the antlers of male deer. In humans, estrogen activates the genes responsible for breast development in women, and androgen activates the genes responsible for the growth of facial hair in men. Within the brain, sex hormones increase or decrease the rate of apoptosis (cell death) in various regions, causing certain areas to be slightly larger in males and others slightly larger in females (Forger et al., 2004; Morris, Jordan, & Breedlove, 2004). However, other mechanisms account for some of the sex differences. At least three genes on the Y chromosome (found only in men) are active in specific brain areas, and at

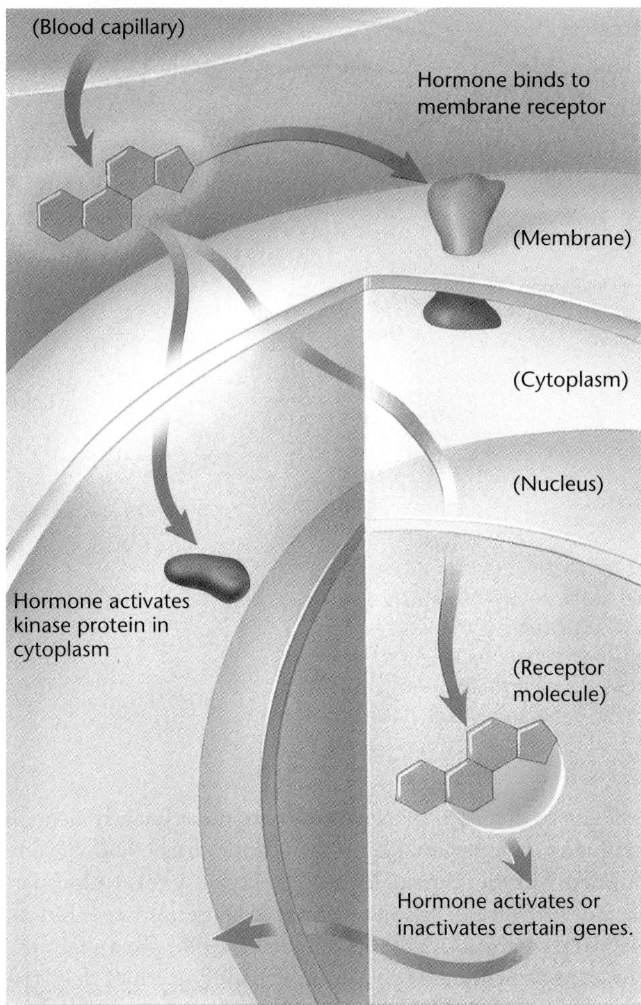

Figure 11.2 Three routes of action for steroid hormones
Steroid hormones such as estrogens and androgens bind to membrane receptors, activate proteins in the cytoplasm, and activate or inactivate specific genes. *(Revised from Starr & Taggart, 1989)*

least one gene on the X chromosome is active only in the female brain (Arnold, 2004; Carruth, Reisert, & Arnold, 2002; Vawter et al., 2004). In both humans and nonhumans, the Y chromosome has many sites that do not code for proteins but alter the expression of genes on other chromosomes (Lemos, Araripe, & Hartl, 2008).

STOP & CHECK

1. How do sex hormones affect neurons?

ANSWER

1. Sex hormones, which are steroids, bind to receptors on the membrane, activate certain proteins in the cell's cytoplasm, and activate or inactivate particular genes.

Organizing Effects of Sex Hormones

If we injected estrogens into adult males and androgens into adult females, could we make males act like females and females act like males? Researchers of the 1950s and 1960s, working with a variety of mammals and birds, were surprised to find that the answer was almost always *no*. But the same hormones injected early in life have much stronger effects.

We distinguish between the organizing and activating effects of sex hormones. The **organizing effects** of sex hormones occur mostly at a sensitive stage of development—shortly before and after birth in rats and well before birth in humans. They determine whether the brain and body will develop female or male characteristics. **Activating effects** can occur at any time in life, when a hormone temporarily activates a particular response. Activating effects on an organ last longer than the hormone remains in an organ, but they do not last indefinitely. The distinction between the two kinds of effects is not absolute. Hormones early in life exert temporary effects while they are organizing body development, and during puberty, hormones induce long-lasting structural changes as well as activating effects (Arnold & Breedlove, 1985; C. L. Williams, 1986).

Sex Differences in the Gonads

Sexual differentiation begins with the chromosomes. In addition to the autosomal (nonsex) chromosomes, a female mammal has two X chromosomes. A male has an X and a Y. During an early stage of prenatal development in mammals, both male and female have a set of Müllerian ducts and a set of Wolffian ducts, as well as primitive gonads (testes or ovaries). The male's Y chromosome includes the **SRY** (sex-determining region on the Y chromosome) **gene,** which causes the primitive gonads to develop into **testes,** the sperm-producing organs. The developing testes produce the hormone **testosterone** (an androgen), which increases the growth of the testes, causing them to produce more testosterone and so forth. That positive feedback cannot go on forever, but it lasts for a period of early development. Testosterone also causes the primitive **Wolffian ducts,** which are precursors for other male reproductive structures, to develop into *seminal vesicles* (saclike structures that store semen) and the *vas deferens* (a duct from the testis into the penis). A peptide hormone, *Müllerian inhibiting hormone (MIH),* causes degeneration of the **Müllerian ducts,** precursors to the female's oviducts, uterus, and upper vagina (Graves, 1994). The result of all the testosterone-induced changes is the development of a penis and scrotum. Because typical females do not have the SRY gene, their gonads develop into ovaries, the egg-producing organs. The Wolffian ducts degenerate, and the primitive Müllerian ducts develop and mature. Figure 11.3 shows how the primitive unisex structures develop into male or female external genitals.

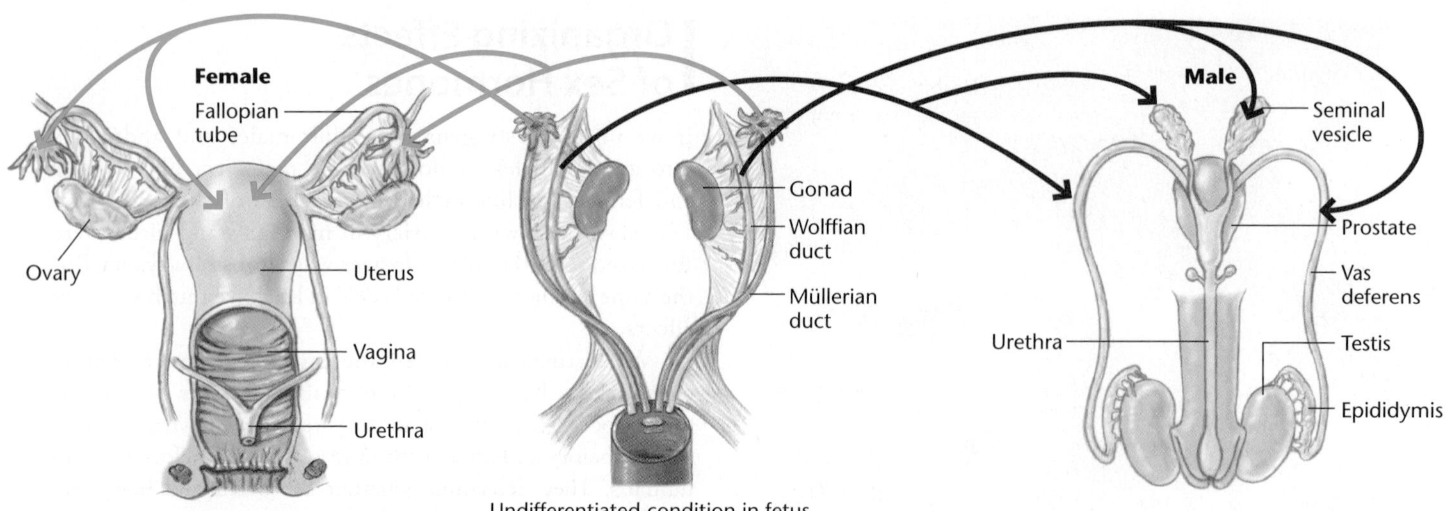

Figure 11.3 Differentiation of human genitals
We all begin life with undifferentiated structures, as shown here in the center, greatly magnified. The structure shown in blue for the fetus in the center develops into either the ovaries of the female, as shown on the left, or the testes of the male, as shown on the right. The Müllerian ducts of the fetus develop into a female's uterus, oviducts, and the upper part of the vagina. The Wolffian ducts of the fetus develop into a male's seminal vesicles (which store semen) and vas deferens, a duct from the testis into the penis. The Müllerian ducts degenerate in males, and the Wolffian ducts degenerate in females. *(Based on Netter, 1983)*

You might imagine that testosterone produces male genitals and estradiol produces female genitals. No. Differentiation of the external genitals and some aspects of brain development depend mainly on the level of testosterone during a **sensitive period,** an early period when hormones have long-lasting effects. A high level of testosterone causes the external genitals to develop the male pattern, and a low level leads to the female pattern. Estrogens produce important effects on the internal organs, but they have little effect on the external genitals.

The human sensitive period for genital formation is about the 3rd and 4th months of pregnancy (Money & Ehrhardt, 1972). In rats, testosterone begins masculinizing the external genitals during the last several days of pregnancy and first few days after birth and then continues at a declining rate for the next month (Bloch & Mills, 1995; Bloch, Mills, & Gale, 1995; E. C. Davis, Shryne, & Gorski, 1995; Rhees, Shryne, & Gorski, 1990). A female rat that is injected with testosterone shortly before or after birth is partly masculinized, just as if her own body had produced the testosterone (I. L. Ward & Ward, 1985). Her clitoris grows larger than normal, and her behavior is partly masculinized. She approaches sexually receptive females (Woodson & Balleine, 2002), mounts them, and makes copulatory thrusting movements rather than arching her back and allowing males to mount her. In short, early testosterone promotes the male pattern and inhibits the female pattern (Gorski, 1985; J. D. Wilson, George, & Griffin, 1981).

A genetic male develops the female-typical pattern of anatomy and behavior if he lacks androgen receptors, if he is castrated (deprived of his testes), or if he is exposed to substances that block testosterone effects. Drugs that tend to feminize or demasculinize early development include alcohol, marijuana, haloperidol (an antipsychotic drug), and cocaine (Ahmed, Shryne, Gorski, Branch, & Taylor, 1991; Dalterio & Bartke, 1979; Hull, Nishita, Bitran, & Dalterio, 1984; Raum, McGivern, Peterson, Shryne, & Gorski, 1990). To a slight extent, even aspirin interferes with the male pattern of development (Amateau & McCarthy, 2004). Although estradiol does not feminize a male to the same degree that testosterone masculinizes a female, estradiol and several related compounds do produce abnormalities and malformations of the prostate gland—the gland that stores sperm and releases it during intercourse. Some of those estradiol-like compounds are now prevalent in the linings of plastic bottles and cans, so almost everyone is exposed to them (Timms, Howdeshell, Barton, Richter, & vom Saal, 2005). In short, male development is a fragile, vulnerable process.

The overall mechanism of early sexual differentiation has been described by saying that nature's "default setting" is to make every mammal a female. Add early testosterone and the individual becomes a male; without testosterone, it develops as a female, regardless of the amount of estradiol or other estrogens. That generalization, however, is an overstatement. A genetic female that lacks estradiol during the early sensitive period develops approximately normal female external anatomy but does not develop normal sexual behavior. Even if she is given estradiol injections as an adult, she shows little sexual response toward either male or female partners (Bakker, Honda, Harada, & Balthazart, 2002). So estradiol contributes to female development, including some aspects of brain differentiation, even if it is not important for external anatomy.

STOP & CHECK

2. What would be the genital appearance of a mammal exposed to high levels of both androgens and estrogens during early development? What if it were exposed to low levels of both?

3. From the standpoint of protecting a male fetus's sexual development, what are some drugs that a pregnant woman should avoid?

ANSWERS

2. A mammal exposed to high levels of both male and female hormones will appear male. One exposed to low levels of both will appear female. Genital development depends mostly on the presence or absence of androgens. **3.** Pregnant women should avoid alcohol, marijuana, haloperidol, and cocaine because these drugs interfere with male sexual development. Even aspirin and the chemicals lining bottles and cans produce mild abnormalities. Obviously, the results depend on both quantities and timing of these chemicals.

Sex Differences in the Hypothalamus

In addition to controlling differences in the external genitals, sex hormones early in life bind to receptors in specific areas of the hypothalamus, amygdala, and other brain areas (Shah et al., 2004). The hormones thereby induce anatomical and physiological differences between the sexes. For example, one area in the anterior hypothalamus, known as the **sexually dimorphic nucleus,** is larger in the male than in the female and contributes to control of male sexual behavior. Parts of the female hypothalamus can generate a cyclic pattern of hormone release, as in the human menstrual cycle. The male hypothalamus cannot, and neither can the hypothalamus of a female who was exposed to extra testosterone early in life. Typical female rats have a characteristic way of holding food and dodging from other rats that might try to take it away. A female rat that was either deprived of estrogens or exposed to extra testosterone in infancy pivots around the midpoint of her trunk, like males, instead of around her pelvis, like other females (Field, Whishaw, Forgie, & Pellis, 2004).

In humans, testosterone produces its organizing effects on the hypothalamus by itself. In rodents, testosterone exerts much of its organizing effect through a surprising route: After it enters a neuron in early development, it is converted to estradiol! Testosterone and estradiol are chemically very similar, as you can see in Figure 11.1. In organic chemistry, a ring of six carbon atoms containing three double bonds is an *aromatic* compound. An enzyme found in the brain can *aromatize* testosterone into estradiol. Other androgens that cannot be aromatized into estrogens are less effective in masculinizing the hypothalamus. Drugs that prevent testosterone from being aromatized to estradiol block some of the organizing effects of testosterone on sexual development and thereby impair male sexual behavior and fertility (Gerardin & Pereira, 2002; Rochira et al., 2001).

Why, then, is the female rodent not masculinized by her own estradiol? During the early sensitive period, immature mammals have a protein called **alpha-fetoprotein,** which is not present in adults (Gorski, 1980; MacLusky & Naftolin, 1981). Alpha-fetoprotein in rodents binds with estradiol and prevents it from affecting the fetus. Because testosterone does not bind to alpha-fetoprotein, enzymes at strategic points within a cell can convert it into estradiol. That is, testosterone is a way of getting estradiol to its receptors when estradiol circulating in the blood is inactivated.

This explanation of testosterone's effects makes sense of an otherwise puzzling fact: Injecting a large amount of estradiol actually masculinizes a female rodent's development. The reason is that normal amounts are bound to alpha-fetoprotein, but a larger amount exceeds the capacity of alpha-fetoprotein and therefore enters the cells and masculinizes them.

STOP & CHECK

4. How would the external genitals appear on a genetic female rat that lacked alpha-fetoprotein?

ANSWER

4. A female that lacked alpha-fetoprotein would be masculinized by her own estrogens, as researchers have in fact demonstrated (Bakker et al., 2006).

Activating Effects of Sex Hormones

At any time in life, not just during an early sensitive period, current levels of testosterone or estradiol exert activating effects, temporarily modifying behavior. Changes in hormonal secretions influence sexual behavior within 15 minutes (Taziaux, Keller, Bakker, & Balthazart, 2007). Behaviors can also influence hormonal secretions. For example, when doves court each other, each stage of their behavior initiates hormonal changes that alter the birds' readiness for the next sequence of behaviors (C. Erickson & Lehrman, 1964; Lehrman, 1964; Martinez-Vargas & Erickson, 1973).

Hormones do not *cause* sexual behavior. They alter the activity in various brain areas to change the way the brain responds to various stimuli. They also change sensitivity in the penis, vagina, and cervix (Etgen, Chu, Fiber, Karkanias, & Morales, 1999).

Rodents

For rodents, as for other mammals, sex hormones facilitate sexual activity. Arousal also depends on previous experience. Sexually experienced rats are aroused more easily because the effects of previous experience sensitize the response to future stimuli (Dominguez, Brann, Gil, & Hull, 2006).

After removal of the testes from a male rodent or the ovaries from a female, sexual behavior declines as the sex hormones decline. It may not disappear altogether, partly because the adrenal glands also produce steroid hormones. Testosterone injections to a castrated male restore sexual behavior, as do injections of testosterone's two major metabolites, dihydrotestosterone and estradiol (M. J. Baum & Vreeburg, 1973). A combination of estradiol and progesterone is the most effective combination for females (Matuszewich, Lorrain, & Hull, 2000).

Sex hormones activate sexual behavior partly by enhancing sensations. Estrogens increase the sensitivity of the *pudendal nerve,* which transmits tactile stimulation from the pubic area to the brain (Komisaruk, Adler, & Hutchison, 1972). Sex hormones also bind to receptors that increase responses of certain areas of the hypothalamus, including the ventromedial nucleus, the medial preoptic area (MPOA), and the anterior hypothalamus. Part of the anterior hypothalamic area, known as the *sexually dimorphic nucleus (SDN),* is distinctly larger in males than in females. The exact importance of the SDN is still unclear. Stimulating this area increases male sexual behavior in many species (G. J. Bloch, Butler, & Kohlert, 1996), but lesions produce only mild deficits in sexual behavior (de Jonge et al., 1989).

Testosterone and estradiol prime the MPOA and several other brain areas to release dopamine. MPOA neurons release dopamine strongly during sexual activity, and the more dopamine they release, the more likely the male is to copulate (Putnam, Du, Sato, & Hull, 2001). Castrated male rats produce normal amounts of dopamine in the MPOA, but they do not release it in the presence of a receptive female, and they do not attempt to copulate (Hull, Du, Lorrain, & Matuszewich, 1997).

In moderate concentrations, dopamine stimulates mostly type D_1 and D_5 receptors, which facilitate erection of the penis in the male (Hull et al., 1992) and sexually receptive postures in the female (Apostolakis et al., 1996). In higher concentrations, dopamine stimulates type D_2 receptors, which lead to orgasm (Giuliani & Ferrari, 1996; Hull et al., 1992). The sudden burst of dopamine in several brain areas at the time of orgasm resembles the "rush" that addictive drugs produce (Holstege et al., 2003). Whereas dopamine stimulates sexual activity, the neurotransmitter serotonin inhibits it, in part by blocking dopamine release (Hull et al., 1999). Many popular antidepressant drugs increase serotonin activity, and one of their side effects is to decrease sexual arousal and orgasm.

Researchers found what appeared to be a major difference between male and female rats in their sexual motivation: If a pair of rats have had sexual relations in a particular cage, the opportunity to return to that cage is strongly reinforcing for males but not for females. Then the researchers varied the procedure. The male rat was confined to that cage, but the female was free to enter or leave at any time. She could therefore control the timing of when their sexual activity started, stopped, and started again. Under these conditions, females developed a clear preference for that cage (Paredes & Vazquez, 1999). Evidently, female rats find sex reinforcing only if they control the timing. (The rumor is that the same trend may be true for other species as well.)

STOP & CHECK

5. By what mechanism do testosterone and estradiol affect the hypothalamic areas responsible for sexual behavior?

ANSWER

5. Testosterone and estradiol prime hypothalamic cells to be ready to release dopamine.

Humans

Although humans are less dependent on current sex hormone levels than other species are, hormones alter people's sexual arousal. They also affect several brain systems with functions not immediately related to sex. For example, testosterone decreases pain and anxiety, and estrogens probably do, too (Edinger & Frye, 2004). Decreases of sex hormones—for example, in men being treated for prostate cancer—lead to impairments of memory (Bussiere, Beer, Neiss, & Janowsky, 2005). Estrogen stimulates growth of dendritic spines in the hippocampus (Behl, 2002; McEwen, 2001) and increased production of dopamine type D_2 receptors and serotonin type 5-HT_{2A} receptors in the nucleus accumbens, the prefrontal cortex, the olfactory cortex, and several other cortical areas (Fink, Sumner, Rosie, Grace, & Quinn, 1996).

Men. Among males, levels of testosterone correlate positively with sexual arousal and the drive to seek sexual partners. Researchers found that, on the average, married men and men living with a woman in a committed relationship have lower testosterone levels than single, unpaired men of the same age (M. McIntyre et al., 2006). The apparently obvious interpretation was that once a man established a lasting relationship, he no longer needed to work so hard to seek a sexual partner, and his testosterone levels would drop. However, another study found that men's testosterone levels did not change when they married. Instead, men with lower testosterone levels were more likely to marry than were men with high testosterone levels (van Anders & Watson, 2006). The idea stands that testosterone is related to seeking partners. When men with high testosterone levels do marry, they tend to continue seeking additional sex partners outside marriage (M. McIntyre et al., 2006).

Decreases in testosterone levels generally decrease male sexual activity. For example, castration (removal of the testes) generally decreases a man's sexual interest and activity (Carter, 1992). However, low testosterone is not the usual basis for **impotence,** the inability to have an erection. The most common cause is impaired blood circulation, especially in older men. Other common causes include neurological problems, reactions to drugs, and psychological tension (Andersson, 2001). Erection depends partly on the fact that testosterone increases the release of nitric oxide (NO). Nitric oxide facilitates the hypothalamic neurons important for sexual behavior (Lagoda, Muschamp, Vigdorchik, & Hull, 2004) and increases blood flow to the penis. The drug sildenafil (Viagra) increases male sexual ability by prolonging the effects of nitric oxide (Rowland & Burnett, 2000).

Testosterone reduction has sometimes been tried as a means of controlling sex offenders, including exhibitionists, rapists, child molesters, and those who commit incest. Sex offenders are a diverse group. Most have about average testosterone levels (Lang, Flor-Henry, & Frenzel, 1990), but one study found elevated levels among child molesters (Rösler & Witztum, 1998). (They reported masturbating about four or five times a day, on average.) Even for sex offenders with high testosterone levels, the hormones do not explain their behaviors. (Many other men with high levels do not engage in offensive behaviors.) Nevertheless, reducing the testosterone levels of sex offenders does reduce their sexual activities. Some sex offenders have been treated with drugs that reduce testosterone levels. Results have often been favorable in men who continue taking the drugs, but dropping out is a frequent problem (Hughes, 2007).

STOP & CHECK

6. What is the explanation for why married men tend to have lower testosterone levels than single men of the same age?

ANSWER

6. Men with lower testosterone levels are more likely to get married than are men with higher testosterone levels.

Women. A woman's hypothalamus and pituitary interact with the ovaries to produce the **menstrual cycle,** a periodic variation in hormones and fertility over the course of about 28 days (Figure 11.4). After the end of a menstrual period, the anterior pituitary releases **follicle-stimulating hormone (FSH),** which promotes the growth of a follicle in the ovary. The follicle nurtures the *ovum* (egg cell) and produces several types of estrogen, including estradiol. Toward the middle of the menstrual cycle, the follicle builds up more and more receptors to FSH, so even though the actual concentration of FSH in the blood is decreasing, its effects on the follicle increase. As a result, the follicle produces increasing amounts of estradiol. The increased release of estradiol causes an increased release of FSH as well as a sudden surge in the release of **luteinizing hormone (LH)** from the anterior pituitary (see the top graph in Figure 11.6). FSH and LH combine to cause the follicle to release an ovum.

The remnant of the follicle (now called the *corpus luteum*) releases the hormone progesterone, which prepares the uterus for the implantation of a fertilized ovum. Progesterone also inhibits the further release of LH. Toward the end of the menstrual cycle, the levels of LH, FSH, estradiol, and progesterone all decline. If the ovum is not fertilized, the lining of the uterus is cast off (menstruation), and the cycle begins again. If the ovum is fertilized, the levels of estradiol and progesterone increase gradually throughout pregnancy. One consequence of high estradiol and progesterone levels is fluctuating activ-

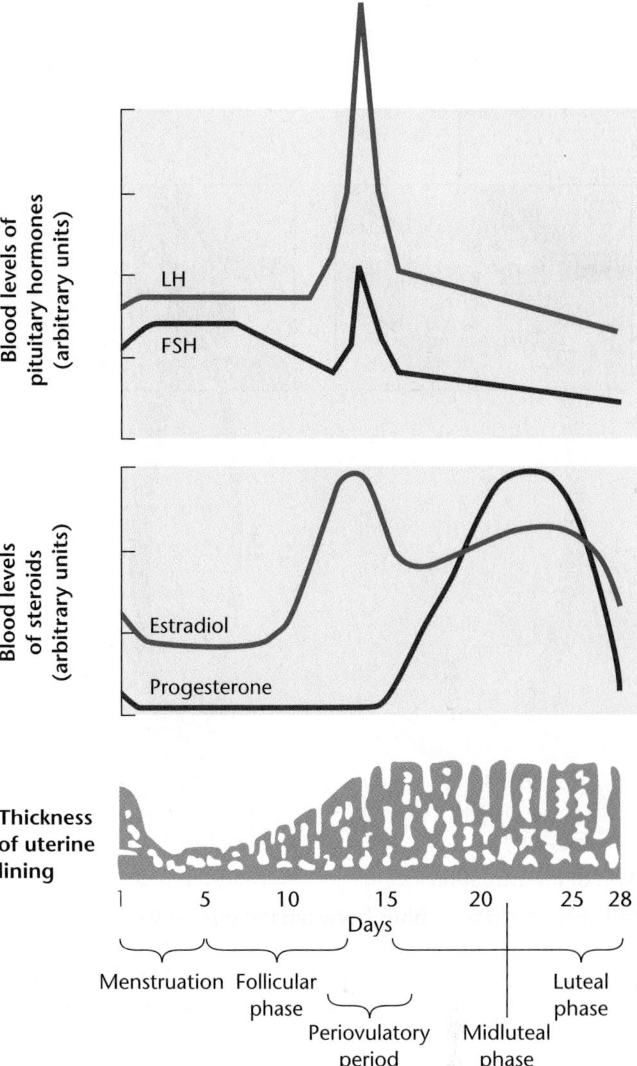

Figure 11.4 Blood levels of four hormones during the human menstrual cycle
Note that estrogen and progesterone are both at high levels during the midluteal phase but drop sharply at menstruation.

ity at the serotonin 3 ($5HT_3$) receptor, which is responsible for nausea (Rupprecht et al., 2001). Pregnant women often experience nausea because of the heightened activity of that receptor. Figure 11.5 summarizes the interactions between the pituitary and the ovary.

Birth-control pills prevent pregnancy by interfering with the usual feedback cycle between the ovaries and the pituitary. The most widely used birth-control pill, the *combination pill,* containing both estrogen and progesterone, prevents the surge of FSH and LH that would otherwise release an ovum. The estrogen–progesterone combination also thickens the mucus of the cervix, making it harder for a sperm to reach the egg, and prevents an ovum, if released, from implanting in the uterus. Thus, the pill prevents pregnancy in many ways. Note, however, that it does not protect against sexually transmitted diseases such as AIDS or syphilis. "Safe sex" must go beyond the prevention of pregnancy.

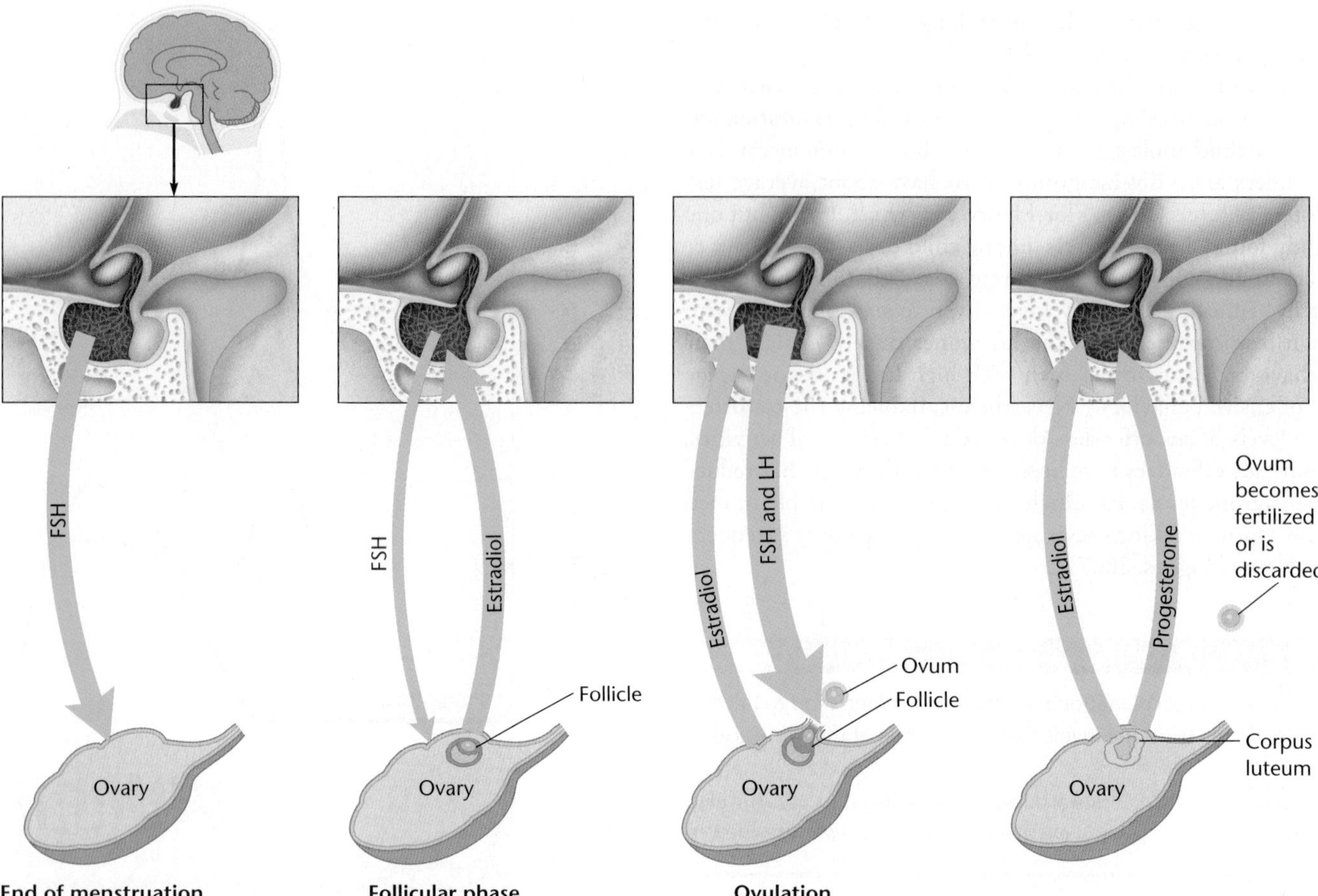

Figure 11.5 Interactions between the pituitary and the ovary
FSH from the pituitary stimulates a follicle of the ovary to develop and produce estradiol, triggering a release of a burst of FSH and LH from the pituitary. Those hormones cause the follicle to release its ovum and become a corpus luteum. The corpus luteum releases progesterone while the ovary releases estradiol.

Changes in hormones over the menstrual cycle also alter women's sexual interest. The **periovulatory period,** consisting of the days around the middle of the menstrual cycle, is the time of maximum fertility and high estrogen levels. According to two studies, women not taking birth-control pills initiate more sexual activity (either with a partner or by masturbation) during the periovulatory period than at other times of the month (D. B. Adams, Gold, & Burt, 1978; Udry & Morris, 1968) (Figure 11.6). According to another study, women rate an erotic video as more pleasant and arousing if they watch it during the periovulatory period than if they watch it at other times (Slob, Bax, Hop, Rowland, & van der Werff ten Bosch, 1996).

Another study used a method that is, shall we say, not standard with laboratory researchers. The researchers studied erotic lap dancers, who earn tips by dancing between a man's legs, rubbing up against his groin, while wearing, in most cases, just a bikini bottom. Lap dancers recorded the dates of their menstrual periods and the amount of tip income they received each night. Lap dancers who were taking contraceptive pills (which keep hormone levels about constant through the month) earned about the same amount from one day to another. Those not taking contraceptive pills received the most tips on 9 to 15 days after menstruation, which is a time of increasing estrogen levels (G. Miller, Tybur, & Jordan, 2007). A likely hypothesis is that the women felt and acted sexier at this time.

Sex hormones also influence women's attention to sex-related stimuli. Women in one study were asked to look at facial photos on a screen and classify each as male or female as quickly as possible. They made the classifications more quickly when they were in their periovulatory period than at other times of the cycle (Macrae, Alnwick, Milne, & Schloerscheidt, 2002). In another study, women were presented with a computer that enabled them to modify pictures of men's faces to make each one look more feminine or more masculine. When they were asked specifically to show the face of the man they would prefer for a "short-term sexual relationship," women who were in their periovulatory period preferred more masculine-looking faces than did women in other phases of the menstrual cycle (Penton-Voak et al., 1999). When women were asked to view videotapes of two men and choose one for a short-term relationship, women in the periovulatory period were more likely to choose a man who seemed athletic, competitive, and assertive and who did *not* describe himself as having a "nice personality"

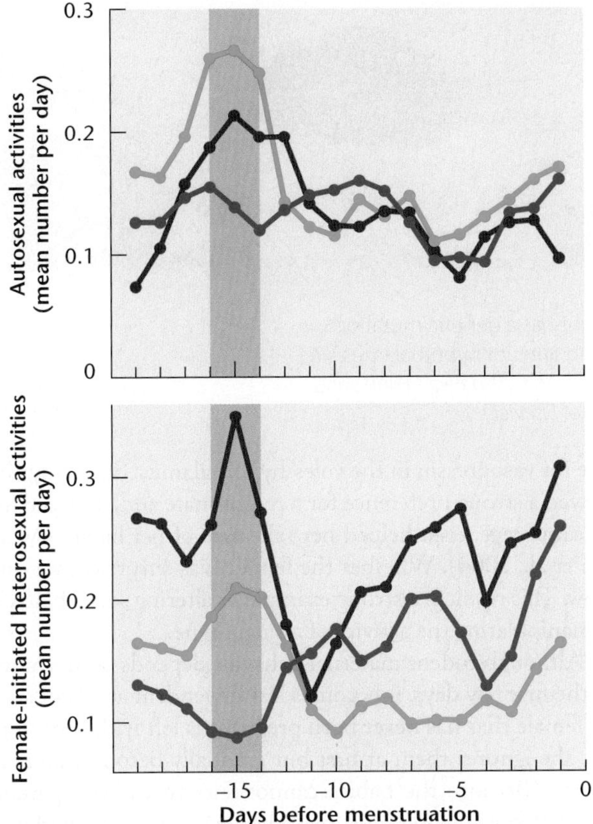

Figure 11.6 Female-initiated sexual activities during the monthly cycle
The top graph shows autosexual activities (masturbation and sexual fantasies); the bottom graph shows female-initiated activities with a male partner. "Intrusive" birth-control methods are diaphragm, foam, and condom; "nonintrusive" methods are IUD and vasectomy. Note that women other than pill users increase self-initiated sex activities when their estrogen levels peak. *(From "Rise in female-initiated sexual activity at ovulation and its suppression by oral contraceptives," by D. B. Adams, A. R. Gold, and A. D. Burt, 1978,* New England Journal of Medicine, 299, *pp. 1145–1150. Reprinted by permission of The New England Journal of Medicine.)*

(Gangestad, Simpson, Cousins, Garver-Apgar, & Christensen, 2004). In short, the hormones associated with fertility move women's mate preferences toward men who look and act more masculine.

STOP & CHECK

7. At what time in a woman's menstrual cycle do her estradiol levels increase? When are they lowest?

ANSWER

7. Estrogen levels increase during the days leading up to the middle of the menstrual cycle. They are lowest during and just after menstruation.

Oxytocin. In addition to the sex hormones, the pituitary hormone **oxytocin** is also important for reproductive behavior. Oxytocin stimulates contractions of the uterus during delivery of a baby, and it stimulates the mammary gland to release milk.

Sexual pleasure also releases oxytocin, especially at orgasm (M. R. Murphy, Checkley, Seckl, & Lightman, 1990). People typically experience a state of complete relaxation shortly after orgasm as a result of the release of oxytocin. In animal studies, rats show increased exploration of potentially dangerous places—and therefore, decreased anxiety—after orgasm. Blocking the release of oxytocin prevents that effect, so oxytocin is apparently responsible for the calmness and lack of anxiety after orgasm (Waldherr & Neumann, 2007). Strong release of oxytocin facilitates formation of pair bonds between the mating partners (Kosfeld, Heinrichs, Zak, Fischbacher, & Fehr, 2005). It is also apparently related to the formation of a pair bond between mother and infant. A study found that the women who had the highest oxytocin levels during pregnancy spent the most time gazing at, vocalizing to, touching, and pleasurably interacting with their infants after delivery (Feldman, Welle, Zagoory-Sharon, & Levine, 2007).

STOP & CHECK

8. What behavioral change occurs after orgasm, and which hormone is responsible?

ANSWER

8. Anxiety decreases after orgasm because of release of the pituitary hormone oxytocin.

Parental Behavior

In birds and mammals, hormonal changes prepare the mother for parenthood. Late in pregnancy (or egg incubation for birds), the female secretes large amounts of estradiol, prolactin, and oxytocin (Pedersen, Caldwell, Walker, Ayers, & Mason, 1994). Prolactin is necessary for milk production and also for aspects of maternal behavior such as retrieving any wandering young back to the nest (Lucas, Ormandy, Binart, Bridges, & Kelly, 1998). In those species in which fathers contribute to parental care, hormones alter several aspects of their brain functioning (Kozorovitskiy, Hughes, Lee, & Gould, 2006).

In addition to secreting hormones, the female changes her pattern of hormone receptors. For example, late in pregnancy, her brain increases its sensitivity to estradiol in the areas responsible for maternal behavior (Rosenblatt, Olufowobi, & Siegel, 1998). The hormonal changes increase the mothers' attention to their young after delivery. Hormones increase activity in the medial preoptic area and anterior hypothalamus (Featherstone, Fleming, & Ivy, 2000), areas that are necessary for rats' maternal behavior (J. R. Brown, Ye, Bronson, Dikkes, & Greenberg, 1996) (Figure 11.7). (We have already encountered the preoptic area/anterior hypothalamus, or POA/AH,

Figure 11.7 Brain development and maternal behavior in mice
The mouse on the left shows normal maternal behavior. The one on the right has a genetic mutation that, among other effects, impairs the development of the preoptic area and anterior hypothalamus. *(Reprinted from* Cell, *86/2, Brown, J. R., Ye, H., Bronson, R. T., Dikkes, P., and Greenberg, M. E., "A defect in nurturing in mice lacking the immediate early gene fosB," 297–309, 1996, with permission of Elsevier.)*

because of its importance for temperature regulation, thirst, and sexual behavior. It's a busy little area.)

Another key hormone is vasopressin, synthesized by the hypothalamus and secreted by the posterior pituitary gland. Male prairie voles, which secrete much vasopressin, establish long-term pair bonds with females and help rear their young. A male meadow vole, with much lower vasopressin levels, mates with a female and then virtually ignores her (Figure 11.8). Imagine a male meadow vole in a long, narrow cage. At one end, he can sit next to a female with which he has just mated. (She is confined there.) At the other end, he can sit next to a different female. Will he choose his recent mate (loyalty) or the new female (variety)? The answer: neither. In most cases, he sits right in the middle, by himself, as far away as he can get from both females. However, these little social isolates changed their behavior after researchers found a way to increase activity of the genes responsible for vasopressin in the voles' hypothalamus. Suddenly, they showed a strong preference for a recent mate and, if placed into the same cage, even helped her take care of her babies (M. M. Lim et al., 2004). Whether the female was surprised, we don't know. This result is a strong example of altering social behavior by manipulating the activity of a single gene.

Although rodent maternal behavior depends on hormones for the first few days, it becomes less dependent at a later stage. If a female that has never been pregnant is left with some baby rats, she ignores them at first but gradually becomes more attentive. (Because the babies cannot survive without parental care, the experimenter must periodically replace them with new, healthy babies.) After about 6 days, the adoptive mother builds a nest, assembles the babies in the nest, licks them, and does everything else that normal mothers do, except nurse them. This experience-dependent behavior does not require hormonal

(a)

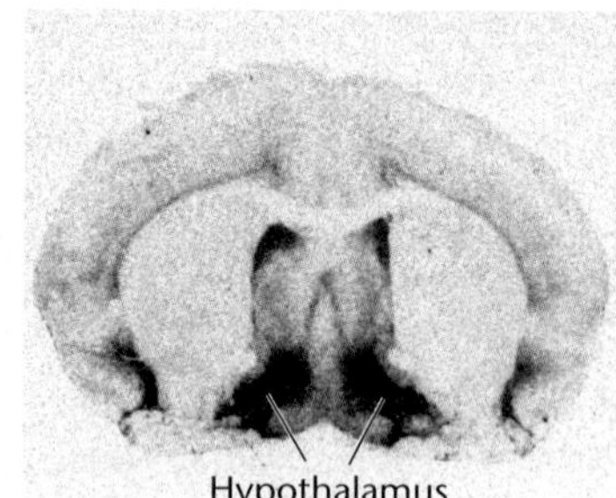

(b)

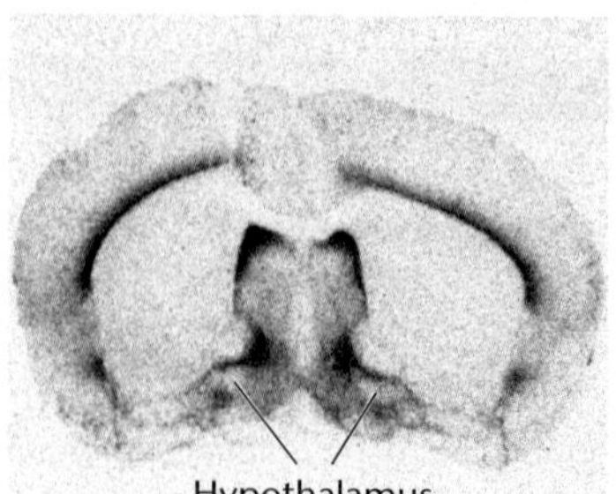

Figure 11.8 Effects of vasopressin on social and mating behaviors
(a) Prairie voles form long-term pair bonds. Staining of their brain shows much expression of the hormone vasopressin in the hypothalamus. **(b)** A closely related species, meadow voles, mate but then separate and show no social attachments. Their brains have much lower vasopressin levels, as indicated by less staining in the hypothalamus. *(Reprinted with permission from "Enhanced partner preference in a promiscuous species by manipulating the expression of a single gene," by Lim, M. M., Wang, Z., Olazabal, D. E., Ren, X., Terwillinger, E. F., & Young, L. J.,* Nature, *429, 754–757. Copyright 2004 Nature Publishing Group/Macmillan Magazines Ltd.)*

changes and occurs even in rats that have had their ovaries removed (Mayer & Rosenblatt, 1979; Rosenblatt, 1967). That is, humans are not the only species in which a mother can adopt young without first going through pregnancy.

An important influence from being with babies is that the mother becomes accustomed to their odors. Infant rats release chemicals that stimulate the mother's vomeronasal organ, which responds to pheromones (see Chapter 7). We might imagine that evolution would have equipped infants with pheromones that elicit maternal behavior, but actually, their pheromones stimulate aggressive behaviors that *interfere* with maternal behavior (Sheehan, Cirrito, Numan, & Numan, 2000). For a mother that has just gone through pregnancy, this interference does not matter because her hormones primed her medial preoptic area so strongly that it overrides competing impulses. A female without hormonal priming, however, rejects the young until she has become familiar with their smell (Del Cerro et al., 1995).

Why do mammals need two mechanisms for maternal behavior—one hormone-dependent and one not? In the early phase, hormones compensate for the mother's lack of familiarity with the young. In the later phase, experience maintains the maternal behavior even though the hormones start to decline (Rosenblatt, 1970).

Are hormones important for human parental behavior? Hormonal changes are necessary for a woman to nurse a baby, and as mentioned, oxytocin levels correlate with several aspects of motherly attention to an infant. However, hormonal changes are not necessary to prime human parental behavior. After all, many people adopt children and become excellent parents.

9. What factors are responsible for maternal behavior shortly after rats give birth? What factors become more important in later days?

ANSWER

9. The early stage of rats' maternal behavior depends on a surge in the release of the hormones prolactin and oxytocin. A few days later, her experience with the young decreases the vomeronasal responses that would tend to make her reject them. Experience with the young maintains maternal behavior after the hormone levels begin to drop.

MODULE 11.1 IN CLOSING

Reproductive Behaviors and Motivations

A mother rat licks her babies all over shortly after their birth, and that stimulation is essential for their survival. Why does she do it? Presumably, she does not understand that licking will help them. She licks because they are covered with a salty fluid that tastes good to her. If she has access to other salty fluids, she stops licking her young (Gubernick & Alberts, 1983). Analogously, sexual behavior in general serves the function of passing on our genes, but we engage in sexual behavior just because it feels good. We evolved a tendency to enjoy the sex act. The same principle holds for hunger, thirst, and other motivations: We evolved tendencies to enjoy acts that have, in general, increased our ancestors' probability of surviving and reproducing.

SUMMARY

1. Male and female behaviors differ because of sex hormones that activate particular genes. Also, certain genes on the X and Y chromosomes exert direct effects on brain development. **318**
2. Organizing effects of a hormone, exerted during an early sensitive period, produce relatively permanent alterations in anatomy and physiology. **319**
3. In the absence of sex hormones, an infant mammal develops female-looking external genitals. The addition of testosterone shifts development toward the male pattern. Extra estradiol, within normal limits, does not determine whether the individual looks male or female. However, estradiol and other estrogens modify development of the brain and the internal sexual organs. **319**
4. During early development in rodents, testosterone is converted within certain brain cells to estradiol, which actually masculinizes their development. Estradiol in the blood does not masculinize development because it is bound to proteins in the blood. **321**
5. In adulthood, sex hormones activate sex behaviors, partly by facilitating activity in the medial preoptic area and anterior hypothalamus. The hormones prime cells to release dopamine in response to sexual arousal. **321**
6. A woman's menstrual cycle depends on a feedback cycle that increases and then decreases the release of several hormones. In many species, females are sexually responsive only when they are fertile. Women can respond sexually at any time in their cycle, although, on the average, they show increased sexual interest when estrogen levels are increasing. **323**

Continued

7. The pituitary hormone oxytocin is important for sexual pleasure, delivery of a baby, and milk production. Its release after orgasm decreases anxiety. **325**

8. Hormones released around the time of giving birth facilitate maternal behavior in females of many mammalian species. Prolonged exposure to young also induces parental behavior. Hormonal facilitation is not necessary for human parental behavior. **325**

KEY TERMS

Terms are defined in the module on the page number indicated. They're also presented in alphabetical order with definitions in the book's Subject Index/Glossary. Interactive flashcards, audio reviews, and crossword puzzles are among the online resources available to help you learn these terms and the concepts they represent.

activating effects **319**
alpha-fetoprotein **321**
androgens **318**
estradiol **318**
estrogens **318**
follicle-stimulating hormone (FSH) **323**
impotence **322**
luteinizing hormone (LH) **323**
menstrual cycle **323**
Müllerian ducts **319**
organizing effects **319**
ovaries **319**
oxytocin **325**
periovulatory period **324**
progesterone **318**
sensitive period **320**
sexually dimorphic nucleus **321**
SRY gene **319**
steroid hormones **318**
testes **319**
testosterone **319**
Wolffian ducts **319**

THOUGHT QUESTIONS

1. The pill RU-486 produces abortions by blocking the effects of progesterone. Why would blocking progesterone interfere with pregnancy?
2. The presence or absence of testosterone determines whether a mammal will differentiate as a male or a female. In birds, the story is the opposite: The presence or absence of estrogen is critical (Adkins & Adler, 1972). What problems would sex determination by estrogen create if that were the mechanism for mammals? Why do those problems not arise in birds? (Hint: Think about the difference between live birth and hatching from an egg.)
3. Antipsychotic drugs, such as haloperidol and chlorpromazine, block activity at dopamine synapses. What side effects might they have on sexual behavior?

MODULE 11.2

Variations in Sexual Behavior

People vary considerably in their frequency of sexual activity, preferred types of sexual activity, and sexual orientation. Because sexual activity occurs mostly in private, most of us are not aware of how much diversity exists. In this module, we explore some of that diversity, but first we consider a few differences between men and women in general. Do men's and women's mating behaviors make biological sense? If so, should we interpret these behaviors as products of evolution? These questions have proved to be difficult and controversial.

Evolutionary Interpretations of Mating Behavior

Many aspects of sexual differences in animals make sense in terms of evolution. For example, in many bird species, such as pigeons, male and female look alike, and in others, such as cardinals and peacocks, the male is more brilliantly colored. Why? In species where the sexes look alike, both take turns sitting on the nest. Bright colors would be a problem because they would attract predators' attention. In species where the male is more brilliantly colored, only the female sits on the nest. In those species, females tend to prefer to mate with brightly colored males, presumably because they tend to be healthier than those with duller feathers. (It takes more energy to make brightly colored feathers.) In a few species, such as phalaropes, the female is more brightly colored. The pattern holds: In those species, the female lays the egg and deserts it, leaving the dull-colored male to sit on the nest and tend the young.

A great reed warbler is a European bird species. Males share nesting duties with females and also guard the territory. If a male has a particularly good territory, one or more extra females may build nests nearby. He fertilizes their eggs but otherwise does not help. However, if the eggs of the primary female are ever left unattended, the extra females attack and destroy them. Why? At that point, the male abandons the nest with destroyed eggs and helps one of the extra females (Hansson, Bensch, & Hasselquist, 1997).

Do human mating behaviors also make sense in terms of evolutionary advantages? Evolutionary psychologists cite several possible examples, but each has been controversial (Buss, 2000). Let's examine the evidence and reasoning.

A. Morris/Vireo: The Academy of Natural Sciences

Phalaropes are shore birds, in which the female is brilliantly colored and the male is drabber. The female lays eggs and deserts the nest, leaving the male to attend to it.

Interest in Multiple Mates

More men than women seek opportunities for casual sexual relationships with many partners. Why? From the evolutionary standpoint of spreading one's genes, men can succeed by either of two strategies (Gangestad & Simpson, 2000): Be loyal to one woman and devote your energies to helping her and her babies, or mate with many women and hope that some of them can raise your babies without your help. No one needs to be conscious of these strategies, of course. The idea is that men who acted these ways in the past propagated their genes, and today's men, their descendants, might have genes that promote the same behaviors. In contrast, a woman can have no more than one pregnancy per 9 months, regardless of her number of sex partners. So evolution may have predisposed men, or at least some men, to be more interested in multiple mates than women are.

One objection is that a woman does sometimes gain from having multiple sex partners (Hrdy, 2000). If her husband is infertile, mating with another man could be her only way of reproducing. Also, another sexual partner may provide aid of various sorts to her and her children. In addition, she has the possibility of "trading up," abandoning her first mate for a better one. So the prospect of multiple mates may be more appealing to men, but it has advantages for women, too.

Another objection is that researchers have no direct evidence that genes influence people's preferences for one mate or many. We shall return to this issue later.

What Men and Women Seek in a Mate

Many of the priorities of men and women are the same, but some are different. Men and women both prefer a healthy, intelligent, honest, physically attractive mate. Women have some additional interests. For example, most women prefer mates who are likely to be good providers. As you might guess, that tendency is strongest in societies where women have no income of their own. However, in all known societies, women are more interested in men's wealth and success than men care about women's wealth and success (Buss, 2000). According to evolutionary theorists, the reason is this: While a woman is pregnant or taking care of a small child, she needs help getting food and other requirements. Evolution would have favored any gene that caused women to seek good providers. Related to this tendency, most women tend to be cautious during courtship. Even if a man seems interested in her, a woman waits before concluding that he has a strong commitment to her (Buss, 2001). She would not want a man who acts interested temporarily and then leaves when she needs him.

A woman is also much more likely to reject a man because of his smell than a man is to reject a woman because of her smell (Herz & Inzlicht, 2002). One possible reason is that more men smell bad than women do, but another reason is more interesting, theoretically: Body odor relates to some of the same genes that control the immune system, known as the *major histocompatibility complex*. Research has found that a woman tends to be less sexually responsive to a man whose immune genes, and therefore body odor, are too similar to her own (Garver-Apgar, Gangestad, Thornhill, Miller, & Olp, 2006). Avoiding a man of similar odor may be a mechanism to avoid inbreeding.

Men tend to have a stronger preference for a young partner. An evolutionary explanation is that young women are likely to remain fertile longer than older women are, so a man can have more children by pairing with a young woman. Curiously, male chimpanzees show no preference for young females, perhaps because chimpanzee mating does not entail a long-term commitment to stay with one mate and no other. In fact, they usually prefer older (but still fertile) females, who tend to have higher social rank than younger females do (Muller, Thompson, & Wrangham, 2006).

Men remain fertile into old age, so a woman has less need to insist on youth. Women do prefer young partners when possible, but in many societies, only older men have enough financial resources to get married.

Differences in Jealousy

Traditionally, men have been more jealous of women's infidelities than women have been of men's infidelities. Passages in the Old Testament and the Koran call for death by stoning for a wife caught in infidelity, but they do not institute any punishment for a man. From an evolutionary standpoint, why might men be more jealous than women? If a man is to pass on his genes—the key point in evolution—he needs to be sure that the children he supports are his own. An unfaithful wife threatens that certainty. A woman knows that any children she bears are her own, so she does not have the same worry. However, her husband's sexual infidelity threatens her interests to the extent that he directs his attention and resources to another woman. (It also threatens her if he contracts a sexually transmitted disease.)

One way to test this interpretation of jealousy is to compare cultures. Some cultures consider sexual infidelity acceptable for both husband and wife; some prohibit it completely for both; and some consider it more acceptable for the husband than for the wife. However, no known society considers it more acceptable for the wife. Should we be more impressed that jealousy is always at least as strong for men as for women, and usually more, or should we be more impressed that jealousy varies among cultures? The answer is not obvious.

Which would upset you more: if your partner had a brief sexual affair with someone else, or if he or she became emotionally close to someone else? According to several studies, men say they would be more upset by the sexual infidelity, whereas women would be more upset by the emotional infidelity (Shakelford, Buss, & Bennett, 2002). However, those studies dealt with hypothetical situations. Most men and women who have actually dealt with an unfaithful partner say they were more upset by their partner's becoming emotionally close to someone else than by the sexual affair (C. H. Harris, 2002).

Evolved or Learned?

If a behavior has clear advantages for survival or reproduction and is similar across cultures, can we conclude that it developed by evolution? Not necessarily. Of course, the brain evolved, just like any other organ, and of course, our behavioral tendencies are a product of evolution. But the key question is whether evolution has micromanaged our behavior down to such details as whether to look for a mate with high earning potential or how jealous to be of an unfaithful mate.

Cross-cultural similarity is not strong evidence for an evolved tendency. For example, people throughout the world agree that $2 + 2 = 4$, but we don't assume that they have a gene for that belief. To establish that we evolved a tendency to act in some way, the most decisive evidence would be to demonstrate genes that affect the relevant behaviors. For example, if most men have genes influencing them to prefer young women, then presumably, we should be able to find some men with a mutation in that gene causing them to lose that preference. Although this example may not be the best, the point is that we need to be cautious about inferring what is a product of our evolution and what is learned.

Conclusions

Discussing these issues is difficult. Ideally, we would like to consider the evidence and logical arguments entirely on their scientific merits. However, when someone describes how evolutionary selection may have led men to be interested in multiple sex partners or to be more jealous than women are, it sometimes sounds like a justification for men to act that way. No gene forces men or women to behave in any particular way.

Even leaving aside the social implications as far as we can, no firm scientific consensus emerges. We need more data, especially about the effects of particular genes, before we can draw a conclusion.

STOP & CHECK

10. What evolutionary advantage is suggested for why women are more interested in men's wealth and success than men are interested in women's wealth?

ANSWER

10. During pregnancy and early child care, a female is limited in her ability to get food and therefore prefers a male partner who can provide for her. A healthy male is not similarly dependent on a female.

Gender Identity and Gender-Differentiated Behaviors

The coral goby is a species of fish in which the male and female tend their eggs and young together. If one of them dies, the survivor looks for a new partner. But it does not look far. This is a very stay-at-home kind of fish. If it cannot easily find a partner of the opposite sex but does find an unmated member of its own sex—oh, well—it simply changes sex and mates with the neighbor. Male-to-female and female-to-male switches are equally common (Nakashima, Kuwamura, & Yogo, 1995).

People cannot switch sexes and remain fertile, but we do have variations in sexual development. Sexual development is a sensitive issue, so let us specify from the start: "Different" does not mean "wrong." People differ naturally in their sexual development just as they do in their height, weight, emotions, and memory.

Gender identity is how we identify sexually and what we call ourselves. The biological differences between males and females are *sex differences*, whereas the differences that result from people's thinking about themselves as male or female are *gender differences*. To maintain this useful distinction, we should resist the trend to speak of the "gender" of dogs, fruit flies, and so forth. Gender identity is a human characteristic.

Most people accept the gender identity that matches their external appearance, which is ordinarily also the way they were reared. However, some are dissatisfied with their assigned gender, and many would describe themselves as being more masculine in some ways and more feminine in others. Psychologists have long assumed that gender depends mainly or entirely on the way people rear their children. However, several kinds of evidence suggest that biological factors, especially prenatal hormones, are important also.

Intersexes

Some people have anatomies intermediate between male and female (Haqq & Donahoe, 1998). For example, some XY males with a mutation in the SRY gene have poorly developed genitals. Some people are born with an XX chromosome pattern but an SRY gene that translocated from the father's Y chromosome onto another chromosome. Despite their XX chromosomes, they have either an ovary and a testis, or two testes, or a mixture of testis and ovary tissue on each side.

Accord Alliance

This group of adult intersexed people have gathered to provide mutual support and to protest against the early surgical treatments they received. They requested that their names be used to emphasize their openness about their condition and to emphasize that intersexuality should not be considered shameful. They are from left to right: Martha Coventry, Max Beck, David Vandertie, Kristi Bruce, and Angela Moreno.

Others develop an intermediate appearance because of an atypical hormone pattern. Recall that testosterone masculinizes the genitals and the hypothalamus during early development. A genetic male who has low levels of testosterone or a mutation of the testosterone receptors may develop a female or intermediate appearance (Misrahi et al., 1997). A genetic female who is exposed to more testosterone than the average female can be partly masculinized.

The most common cause of this condition is **congenital adrenal hyperplasia (CAH)**, meaning overdevelopment of the adrenal glands from birth. Ordinarily, the adrenal gland has a negative feedback relationship with the pituitary gland. The pituitary secretes adrenocorticotropic hormone (ACTH), which stimulates the adrenal gland. Cortisol, one of the hormones from the adrenal gland, feeds back to decrease the release of ACTH. Some people have a genetic limitation in their ability to produce cortisol. Because the pituitary fails to receive much cortisol as a feedback signal, it continues secreting more

ACTH, causing the adrenal gland to secrete larger amounts of its other hormones, including testosterone. In a genetic male, the extra testosterone causes no apparent problems. However, genetic females with this condition develop various degrees of masculinization of their external genitals. (The ovaries and other internal organs are less affected.) Figure 11.9 shows a structure that appears intermediate between clitoris and penis and swellings that appear intermediate between labia and scrotum. After birth, these children are given medical treatments to bring their adrenal hormones within normal levels. Some are also given surgery to alter their external genital appearance, as we shall discuss later.

Individuals who appear to be a mixture of male and female are referred to as **hermaphrodites** (from Hermes and Aphrodite in Greek mythology). The *true hermaphrodite*, a rarity, has a testis on one side of the body and an ovary on the other or a mixture of testis tissue and ovary tissue on each side. People whose sexual development is intermediate or ambiguous, such as the one in Figure 11.9, are called **intersexes.**

How common are intersexes? An estimated 1 child in 100 in the United States is born with some degree of genital ambiguity, and 1 in 2,000 has enough ambiguity to make its male or female status uncertain (Blackless et al., 2000). However, the accuracy of these estimates is doubtful, as hospitals and families keep the information private. Maintaining confidentiality is of course important, but an unfortunate consequence of secrecy is that intersexed people have trouble finding others like themselves. For more information, consult the Web site of the Intersex Society of North America (ISNA): http://www.isna.org/

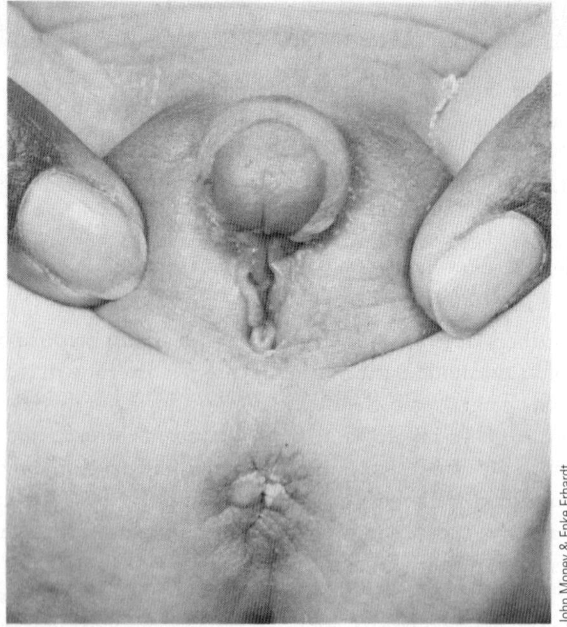

Figure 11.9 External genitals of a genetic female, age 3 months
Masculinized by excess androgens from the adrenal gland before birth, the infant shows the effects of the adrenogenital syndrome. *(From Money, John and Ehrhardt, Anke A.,* Man and Woman, Boy and Girl: Differentiation and Dimorphism of Gender Identity from Conception to Maturity, *p. 115, figure 6.2. © 1973 The Johns Hopkins University Press. Reprinted with permission of The Johns Hopkins University Press.)*

STOP & CHECK

11. What is a common cause for a genetic female (XX) to develop a partly masculinized anatomy?

ANSWER **11.** If a genetic female is genetically deficient in her ability to produce cortisol, the pituitary gland does not receive negative feedback signals and therefore continues stimulating the adrenal gland. The adrenal gland then produces large amounts of other hormones, including testosterone, which masculinizes development.

Interests and Preferences of CAH Girls

Genetic females with CAH or similar conditions are in most cases reared as girls. However, their brains were exposed to higher than normal testosterone levels during prenatal and early postnatal life compared to other girls. Is their behavior masculinized? In several studies, girls with CAH were observed in a room full of toys—including some that were girl typical (dolls, plates and dishes, cosmetics kits), some that were boy typical (toy car, tool set, gun), and some that were neutral (puzzles, crayons, board games). Figure 11.10 shows the results from one such study (Pasterski et al., 2005). Note how girls with CAH were intermediate between the preferences of boys and girls without CAH. When the children tested with a parent present, again the girls with CAH were intermediate between the other two groups.

Other studies have reported similar results and have found that the girls exposed to the largest amount of testosterone in early development showed the largest preference for boys' toys (Berenbaum, Duck, & Bryk, 2000; Nordenström, Servin, Bohlin, Larsson,{ & Wedell, 2002). You might wonder whether the parents, knowing that these girls had been partly masculinized in appearance, might have encouraged "tomboyish" activities. The observations suggest the opposite: The parents encouraged the girls with CAH any time they played with girl-typical toys (Pasterski et al., 2005). A study of some CAH girls in adolescence found that, on the average, their interests were intermediate between those of typical male and female adolescents. For example, they read more sports magazines and fewer teen and glamour magazines than the average for other teenage girls (Berenbaum, 1999). Another study found an influence of prenatal hormones on the toy preferences even for girls without CAH. The researchers took blood samples from pregnant women, measuring their testosterone levels (some of which would enter the fetus). When the daughters reached age 3½, researchers observed their toy play. Those who had been exposed to higher testosterone levels in prenatal life showed slightly elevated preferences for boys' toys (Hines et al., 2002).

Among girls with a history of CAH, those who had the highest degree of testosterone exposure before birth tend to have the highest interest in boys' toys in childhood and the lowest romantic interest in men during adolescence and

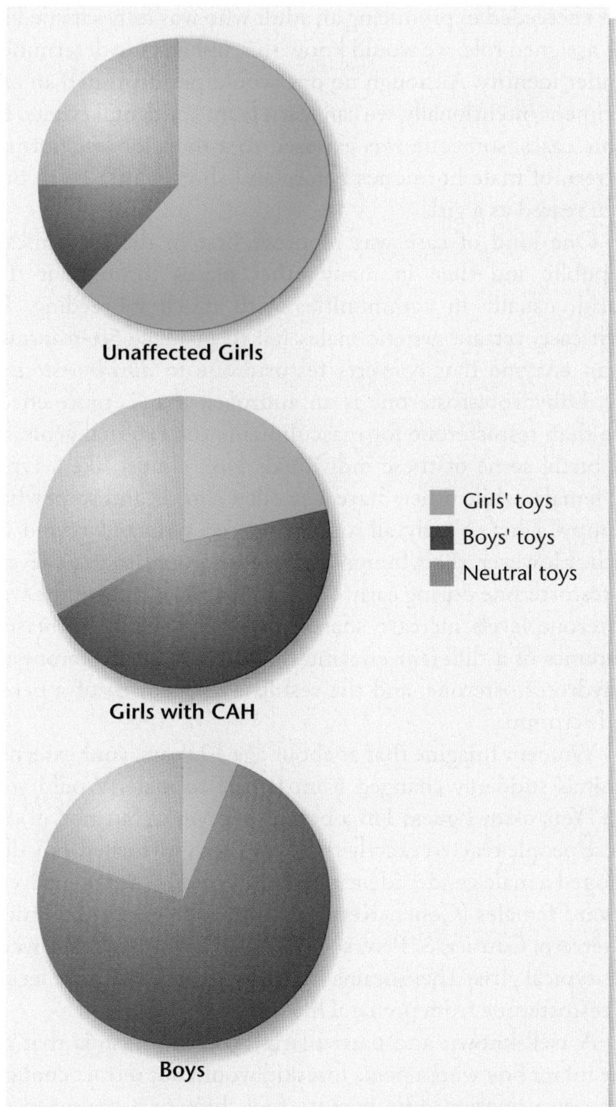

Figure 11.10 Toy preferences by CAH girls, unaffected girls, and unaffected boys
CAH girls were intermediate between unaffected girls and boys. These data show results when the children played alone. Results changed slightly when the mother or father was present, but in each case, the CAH girls were intermediate between the other groups. *(Based on data of Byne et al., 2001)*

adulthood (Meyer-Bahlburg, Dolezal, Baker, & New, 2008). A moderate number report homosexual or bisexual activity, and a larger than average number report low interest in sexual activity of any type (Zucker et al., 1996).

STOP & CHECK

12. If a genetic female is exposed to extra testosterone during prenatal development, what behavioral effect is likely?

ANSWER

12. A girl who is exposed to extra testosterone during prenatal development is more likely than most other girls to prefer boy-typical toys.

Testicular Feminization

Certain individuals with an XY chromosome pattern have the genital appearance of a female. This condition is known as **androgen insensitivity,** or **testicular feminization.** Although such individuals produce normal amounts of androgens (including testosterone), they lack the androgen receptor that enables it to activate genes in a cell's nucleus. Consequently, the cells are insensitive to androgens, and development proceeds as if the level of testosterone and related hormones was very low. This condition occurs in various degrees, resulting in anatomy that ranges from a smaller than average penis to genitals like those of a normal female. In some cases, no one has any reason to suspect the person is anything other than a normal female, until puberty. Then, in spite of breast development and broadening of the hips, menstruation does not begin because the body has internal testes instead of ovaries and a uterus. (The vagina is short and leads to nothing but skin.) Also, pubic hair is sparse or absent because it depends on androgens in females as well as males.

STOP & CHECK

13. What would cause a genetic male (XY) to develop a partly feminized external anatomy?

ANSWER

13. A genetic male with a gene that prevents testosterone from binding to its receptors will develop an appearance that partly or completely resembles a female.

Issues of Gender Assignment and Rearing

Many girls with CAH and related conditions are born with a normal or near normal appearance, but some look as much male as female and presumably have been exposed to elevated levels of prenatal testosterone. Some genetic males are born with a very small penis because of a condition called *cloacal exstrophy*, a defect of pelvis development (Reiner & Gearhart, 2004). Despite their genital anatomy, they had typical male levels of testosterone in prenatal development.

How should children with either of these conditions be reared? Beginning in the 1950s, medical doctors began recommending that all intersexed people be reared as girls, using surgery if necessary to make their genitals look more feminine (Dreger, 1998). The reason was that it is easier to reduce an enlarged clitoris to normal size than expand it to penis size. If necessary, surgeons can build an artificial vagina or lengthen a short one. After the surgery, the child looks female. Physicians and psychologists assumed that any child who was consistently reared as a girl would fully accept that identity.

And she lives happily ever after, right? Not necessarily. Of those with cloacal exstrophy who are reared as girls, all develop typical male interests, many or most eventually demand reassignment as males, and nearly all develop sexual attraction toward women, not men (Reiner & Gearhart, 2004).

Girls with the CAH history also have a difficult adjustment, especially if they were subjected to clitoris-reduction surgery. A surgically created or lengthened vagina may be satisfactory to a male partner, but it provides no sensation to the woman and requires almost daily attention to prevent it from scarring over. A study of 18 women who had clitoris-reduction surgery in childhood found that 10 of them had no sexual activity, 7 others never experienced orgasm, and all had significant sexual difficulties (Minto, Liao, Woodhouse, Ransley, & Creighton, 2003). Many intersexes wish they had their original "abnormal" enlarged clitoris instead of the mutilated, insensitive structure left to them by a surgeon. Moreover, intersexes resent being deceived. Historian Alice Dreger (1998) describes the case of one intersex:

> As a young person, was told she had "twisted ovaries" that had to be removed; in fact, her testes were removed. At the age of twenty, "alone and scared in the stacks of a [medical] library," she discovered the truth of her condition. Then "the pieces finally fit together. But what fell apart was my relationship with both my family and physicians. It was not learning about chromosomes or testes that caused enduring trauma, it was discovering that I had been told lies. I avoided all medical care for the next 18 years.... [The] greatest source of anxiety is not our gonads or karyotype. It is shame and fear resulting from an environment in which our condition is so unacceptable that caretakers lie." (p. 192)

So how *should* such a child be reared? On that question, specialists do not agree. A growing number, however, follow these recommendations (Diamond & Sigmundson, 1997):

- Be completely honest with the intersexed person and the family, and do nothing without their informed consent.
- Identify the child as male or female based mainly on the predominant external appearance. That is, there should be no bias toward calling every intersex a female.
- Rear the child as consistently as possible, but be prepared that the person might later be sexually oriented toward males, females, both, or neither.
- Do *not* perform surgery to reduce the ambiguous penis/clitoris to the size of a normal clitoris. Such surgery impairs the person's erotic sensation and is at best premature, as no one knows how the child's sexual orientation will develop. If the intersexed person makes an informed request for such surgery in adulthood, then it is appropriate, but otherwise it should be avoided.

Discrepancies of Sexual Appearance

The evidence from intersexes does not indisputably resolve the roles of rearing and hormones in determining gender identity. From a scientific viewpoint, the most decisive way to settle the issue would be to raise a normal male baby as a female or to raise a normal female baby as a male. If the process succeeded in producing an adult who was fully satisfied in the assigned role, we would know that upbringing determines gender identity. Although no one would perform such an experiment intentionally, we can learn from accidental events. In some cases, someone was exposed to a more-or-less normal pattern of male hormones before and shortly after birth but then reared as a girl.

One kind of case was reported first in the Dominican Republic and then in many other places throughout the world, usually in communities with much inbreeding. In each case, certain genetic males fail to produce *5α-reductase 2*, an enzyme that converts testosterone to *dihydrotestosterone*. Dihydrotestosterone is an androgen that is more effective than testosterone for masculinizing the external genitals. At birth, some of these individuals look almost like a typical female, while others have a swollen clitoris and somewhat "lumpy" labia. Nearly all are considered girls and reared as such. However, their brains had been exposed to male levels of testosterone during early development. At puberty, the testosterone levels increase sharply, the body makes increased amounts of a different enzyme that converts testosterone to dihydrotestosterone, and the result is the growth of a penis and scrotum.

Women: Imagine that at about age 12 years, your external genitals suddenly changed from female to male. Would you say, "Yep, okay, I guess I'm a boy now"? Most (but not all) of these people reacted exactly that way. The girl-turned-boy developed a male gender identity and directed his sexual interest toward females (Cohen-Kettenis, 2005; Imperato-McGinley, Guerrero, Gautier, & Peterson, 1974). Remember, these were not typical girls. Their brains had been exposed to male levels of testosterone from prenatal life onward.

A well-known and particularly upsetting case is that of one infant boy whose penis foreskin would not retract enough for easy urination. His parents took him to a physician to circumcise the foreskin, but the physician, using an electrical procedure, set the current too high and accidentally burned off the entire penis. On the advice of respected and well-meaning authorities, the parents elected to rear the child as a female, with the appropriate surgery. What makes this a particularly interesting case is that the child had a twin brother (whom the parents did not let the physician try to circumcise). If both twins developed satisfactory gender identities, one as a girl and the other as a boy, the results would imply that rearing was decisive in gender identity.

Initial reports claimed that the child reared as a girl had a female gender identity, though she also had strong tomboyish tendencies (Money & Schwartz, 1978). However, by about age 10, she had figured out that something was wrong and that "she" was really a boy. She had preferred boys' activities and played only with boys' toys. She even tried urinating in a standing position, despite always making a mess. By age 14, she insisted that she wanted to live as a boy. At that time, her (now his) father tearfully explained the earlier events. The child changed names and became known as a boy. At age 25, he married a somewhat older woman and adopted her children. Clearly, a biological predisposition had won out over the family's attempts to rear the child as a girl (Colapinto, 1997; Diamond & Sigmundson, 1997). Some years later, the story ended tragically with this man's suicide.

We should not draw universal conclusions from a single case. However, the point is that it was a mistake to impose surgery and hormonal treatments to try to force this child to become female. When the prenatal hormone pattern of the brain is in conflict with a child's appearance, no one can be sure how that child will develop psychologically. Hormones don't have complete control, but rearing patterns don't, either.

STOP & CHECK

14. What does the enzyme 5α-reductase 2 do?

ANSWER

14. The enzyme 5α-reductase 2 catalyzes the conversion of testosterone to dihydrotestosterone, which is more effective in masculinizing the genitals.

Sexual Orientation

Homosexual or bisexual behavior occurs in both humans and nonhumans. Contrary to what biologists previously assumed, homosexual behavior is not limited to captive animals, those that cannot find a member of the opposite sex, or those with hormonal abnormalities (Bagemihl, 1999). Sexual orientation, like almost any other aspect of behavior, shows natural variation.

What accounts for differences in sexual orientation? We are not going to find a single answer. Researchers have identified several predisposing factors in genetics and prenatal environment for male homosexuality, as we shall see. They have also identified several anatomical and behavioral correlates of sexual orientation in men. For women, the story appears to be different. A genetic predisposition is demonstrable, but it appears weaker than in men. Whereas most men discover their sexual orientation early, many women are slower. Feminine-type behaviors in childhood and adolescence correlate strongly with homosexual orientation in adulthood for men, but early masculine-type behaviors are poorer predictors of sexual orientation in women (Udry & Chantala, 2006). Furthermore, a higher percentage of women than men acknowledge at least some physical attraction to both males and females (Chivers, Rieger, Latty, & Bailey, 2004; Lippa, 2006), and a moderate percentage of women switch one time or more between homosexual and heterosexual orientations (Diamond, 2007). Such switches are rare for men. Although we shall note certain biological correlates of female homosexuality, the case for a biological predisposition seems stronger for men.

Behavioral and Anatomical Differences

On the average, homosexual and heterosexual people differ anatomically in many subtle ways. On the average, the bones of the arms, legs, and hands are longer in heterosexual men than in homosexual men and longer in homosexual women than in heterosexual women (J. T. Martin & Nguyen, 2004). The length of those bones begins to differ before puberty. These differences represent averages, and they do not apply to all cases.

On the average, the left and right hemispheres of the cerebral cortex are of nearly equal size in heterosexual females, whereas the right hemisphere is a few percent larger in heterosexual males. Homosexual males resemble heterosexual females in this regard, and homosexual females are intermediate between heterosexual females and males. Also, in heterosexual females, the left amygdala has more widespread connections than the right amygdala, whereas in heterosexual males, the right amygdala has more widespread connections. Again, homosexual males resemble heterosexual females in this regard, and homosexual females are intermediate (Savic & Lindström, 2008).

On the average, people who differ in sexual orientation also differ in several behaviors that are not directly related to sex. As discussed in Chapter 4, more men than women give directions in terms of distances and north, south, east, or west. Women are more likely to describe landmarks. Gay men also tend to use landmarks and are better than heterosexual men at remembering landmarks (Hassan & Rahman, 2007). Also consider this task: Experimenters repeatedly present a loud noise and measure the startle response. On some trials, they present a weaker noise just before the loud noise; the first noise decreases the startle response to the louder one. The decrease is called "prepulse inhibition." Prepulse inhibition is ordinarily stronger in men than in women. In this regard, homosexual men do not differ significantly from heterosexual men, but homosexual women are slightly shifted in the male direction compared to heterosexual women (Rahman, Kumari, & Wilson, 2003).

Overall, what do these results indicate? The differences in anatomy and behavior show that sexual orientation is not an arbitrary decision. It is an integral part of the person. The results also indicate that the situation is complex. Homosexual men are shifted toward the female direction in some aspects and not others. Homosexual women are shifted toward the male direction in some ways and not others. Furthermore, the differences apply only on the average. Homosexual people are not all alike any more than heterosexual people are.

STOP & CHECK

15. Name a physical or behavioral difference between homosexual and heterosexual men other than sexual activities.

ANSWER

15. Homosexual men are more likely to have smaller bones in the arms and legs, equal size of left and right cerebral hemispheres, more widespread connections of the left than right amygdala, and better memory for landmarks.

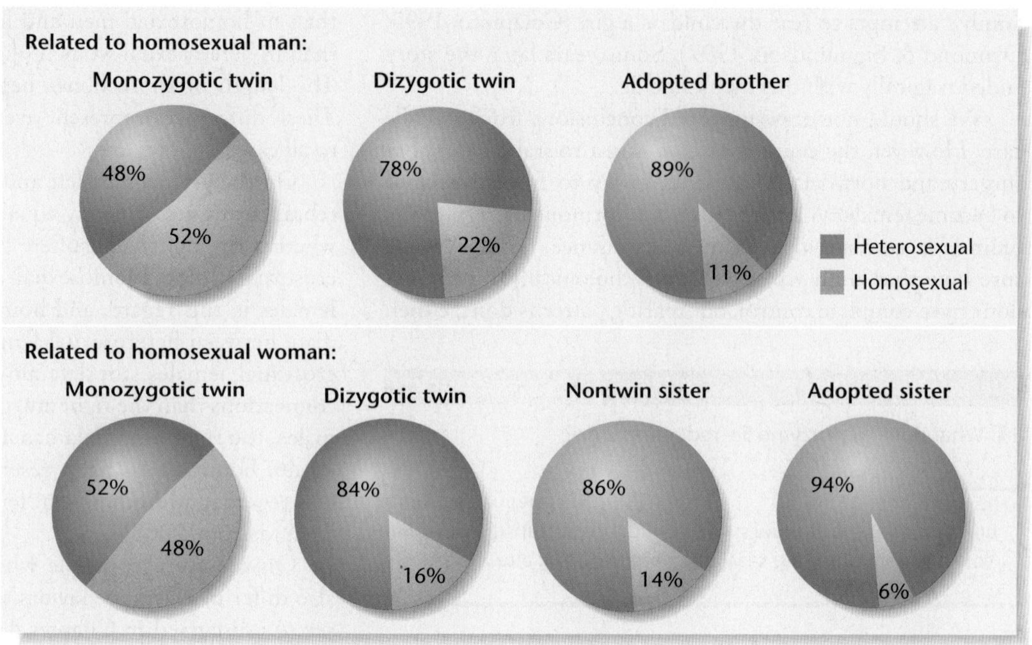

Figure 11.11 Sexual orientations in adult relatives of a homosexual man or woman The probability of a homosexual orientation is highest among monozygotic twins of a homosexual individual, lower among dizygotic twins, and still lower among adopted brothers or sisters. These data suggest a genetic contribution to sexual orientation. *(Based on the data of Bailey & Pillard, 1991; Bailey, Pillard, Neale, & Agyei, 1993)*

Genetics

Studies of the genetics of sexual orientation have focused mainly on twins. Several studies of the genetics of human sexual orientation have advertised in gay or lesbian publications for homosexual men or women with twins. Then they contacted the other twin to fill out a questionnaire. The questionnaire included diverse items to conceal the fact that the real interest was sexual orientation. As shown in Figure 11.11, two such studies found a higher probability of homosexuality in a monozygotic (identical) twin of a homosexual person than in a dizygotic twin and a still lower probability in adopted brothers or sisters (Bailey & Pillard, 1991; Bailey, Pillard, Neale, & Agyei, 1993). Still, the probability in adopted siblings is higher than for the population at large, which is between 2% and 6% for men, depending on which study one examines, and about half that much for women. The results imply significant contributions by both hereditary and environmental influences.

One concern is that the people who answer ads in gay publications may not be typical. To deal with this concern, another study examined the data from 794 pairs of twins who had responded to a national (U.S.) survey not related to sex. Of those 794 pairs, only 43 included at least one homosexual person, so the sample size was small. When one twin (either male or female) had a homosexual orientation, the other did also in 31% of monozygotic pairs and 8% of dizygotic pairs (Kendler, Thornton, Gilman, & Kessler, 2000). So far, researchers have not identified a particular gene associated with sexual orientation. However, a search of the entire human genome identified a few genes that occur more commonly in homosexual than heterosexual males (Mustanski et al., 2005). It may be that each of several genes influences sexual orientation to a moderate degree in combination with other genes and the environment.

Several studies have reported a higher incidence of homosexuality among the maternal than paternal relatives of homosexual men (Camperio-Ciani, Corna, & Capiluppi, 2004; Hamer, Hu, Magnuson, Hu, & Pattatucci, 1993). For example, uncles and cousins on the mother's side were more likely to be homosexual than uncles and cousins on the father's side. These results suggest a gene on the X chromosome, which a man necessarily receives from his mother. However, other studies have not replicated these results, and the current status is inconclusive (Bailey et al., 1999; Rice, Anderson, Risch, & Ebers, 1999).

An Evolutionary Question

If certain genes promote a homosexual orientation, why hasn't evolution selected strongly against those genes, which decrease the probability of reproduction? Several possibilities are worth considering (Gavrilets & Rice, 2006). One is that genes for homosexuality are maintained by kin selection, as discussed in Chapter 1. That is, even if homosexual people do not have children themselves, they might do a wonderful job of helping their brothers and sisters rear children. However, survey data indicate that homosexual men are no more likely than heterosexuals to help their nephews or nieces (Bobrow & Bailey, 2001). Indeed, many are estranged from their families.

According to a second hypothesis, genes that produce homosexuality in males produce advantageous effects in their sisters and other female relatives, increasing their probability of reproducing and spreading the genes. The results of one study support this hypothesis. Homosexual men's mothers and aunts had a greater than average number of children (Camperio-Ciani et al., 2004). However, a common estimate is that the average homosexual man has one fifth as many children as the average heterosexual man. Could his female relatives have enough children to compensate for this decrease? It seems unlikely.

A third hypothesis is that certain genes lead to homosexuality in men homozygous for the gene but produce reproductive advantages in men heterozygous for the gene (Rahman & Wilson, 2003). A closely related idea is that several genes produce advantages for survival or reproduction, but a combination of them leads to homosexuality. It will be difficult to test these ideas until someone identifies specific genes linked to sexual orientation.

A fourth idea is that homosexuality relates to the activation or inactivation of genes (Bocklandt, Horvath, Vilain, & Hamer, 2006). As mentioned in Chapter 1, it is possible for environmental events to attach a methyl group (CH_3) to a gene and inactivate it. A parent can pass the inactivation of a gene to the next generation. Conceivably, this mechanism might produce a significant amount of heritable homosexuality without relying on the spread of a gene that promotes homosexuality.

STOP & CHECK

16. It seems difficult to explain how a gene could remain at a moderately high frequency in the population if most men with the gene do not reproduce. How would the hypothesis about inactivation by a methyl group help with the explanation?

ANSWER

16. According to this hypothesis, some unknown event in the environment can attach a methyl group to some unidentified gene, inactivating the gene. That gene could be passed to the next generation, producing evidence for a hereditary effect, even though there is no "gene for homosexuality." If this event of attaching a methyl group to that gene happens often enough, the result could be a moderately high prevalence of homosexuality, even if men with the inactivated gene seldom reproduce.

Prenatal Influences

Sexual orientation is *not* related to adult hormone levels. On the average, the adult testosterone and estrogen levels of homosexual men are about the same as those of heterosexual men, and most lesbian women have about the same hormone levels as heterosexual women. However, it is possible that sexual orientation depends on testosterone levels during a sensitive period of brain development (Ellis & Ames, 1987). Animal studies have shown that prenatal or early postnatal hormones can produce organizing effects on both anatomy and sexual behavior.

The mother's immune system may also exert prenatal effects. The probability of a homosexual orientation is higher among men who have older brothers. Younger brothers make no difference, nor do younger or older sisters (Bogaert, 2003b; Purcell, Blanchard, & Zucker, 2000). Furthermore, what matters is the number of *biological* older brothers. Growing up with older stepbrothers or adopted brothers has no apparent influence. Having a biological older brother has an influence, even if the brothers were reared separately (Bogaert, 2006). In short, the influence does not stem from social experiences. The key is how many previous times the mother gave birth to a son. The most prominent hypothesis is that a mother's immune system sometimes reacts against a protein in a son and then attacks subsequent sons enough to alter their development. That hypothesis fits with the observation that later-born homosexual men tend to be shorter than average (Bogaert, 2003a). A further piece of the puzzle: Having an older brother specifically increases the probability of homosexuality among right-handed younger brothers but not among left-handed younger brothers (Bogaert, Blanchard, & Crosthwait, 2007). Researchers have hypotheses about what that pattern means, but at this point, there is not enough information to decide among those hypotheses.

Another aspect of prenatal environment relates to stress on the mother during pregnancy. Research has shown that prenatal stress alters sexual development in laboratory animals. In several experiments, rats in the final week of pregnancy had the stressful experience of confinement in tight Plexiglas tubes for more than 2 hours each day under bright lights. In some cases, they were given alcohol as well. These rats' daughters looked and acted approximately normal. The sons, however, had normal male anatomy but, in adulthood, often responded to the presence of another male by arching their backs in the typical rat female posture for sex (I. L. Ward, Ward, Winn, & Bielawski, 1994). Most males that were subjected to either prenatal stress or alcohol developed male sexual behavior in addition to these female sexual behaviors, but those that were subjected to both stress and alcohol had decreased male sexual behaviors (I. L. Ward, Bennett, Ward, Hendricks, & French, 1999).

Prenatal stress and alcohol may alter brain development through several routes. Stress releases endorphins, which can antagonize the effects of testosterone on the hypothalamus (O. B. Ward, Monaghan, & Ward, 1986). Stress also elevates levels of the adrenal hormone corticosterone, which decreases testosterone release (O. B. Ward, Ward, Denning, French, & Hendricks, 2002; M. T. Williams, Davis, McCrea, Long, & Hennessy, 1999). The long-term effects of either prenatal stress or alcohol include several changes in the structure of the nervous system, making the affected males' anatomy closer to that of females (Nosenko & Reznikov, 2001; I. L. Ward, Romeo, Denning, & Ward, 1999).

Although the relevance of these results to humans is uncertain, they prompted investigators to examine possible effects of prenatal stress on humans. One approach is to ask the mothers of homosexual men whether they experienced any unusual stress during pregnancy. Three surveys compared mothers of homosexual sons to mothers of heterosexual sons. In two of the three, the mothers of homosexual sons recalled more than average stressful experiences during their pregnancies (Bailey, Willerman, & Parks, 1991; Ellis, Ames, Peckham,

& Burke, 1988; Ellis & Cole-Harding, 2001). However, these studies relied on women's memories of pregnancies more than 20 years earlier. A better but more difficult procedure would be to measure stress during pregnancy and examine the sexual orientation of the sons many years later.

STOP & CHECK

17. By what route does having an older brother probably increase the probability of male homosexuality?

18. How might stress to a pregnant rat alter the sexual orientation of her male offspring?

ANSWERS

17. Having an older brother evidently increases the probability of male homosexuality by altering the mother's immune system in the prenatal environment. The effect of the older brother does not depend on growing up in the same home. **18.** Evidently, the stress increases the release of endorphins in the hypothalamus, and very high endorphin levels can block the effects of testosterone.

Brain Anatomy

Do brains also differ as a function of sexual orientation? The results are complex. On the average, homosexual men are shifted partly in the female-typical direction for some brain structures but not others. Similarly, on the average, homosexual women's brains are slightly shifted in the male direction in some ways but not others (Rahman & Wilson, 2003). The anterior commissure (see Figures 4.13 on page 93 and 14.4 on page 408) is, on the average, larger in heterosexual women than in heterosexual men. In homosexual men, it is at least as large as in women, perhaps even slightly larger (Gorski & Allen, 1992). The behavioral implications of this difference are unclear. The suprachiasmatic nucleus (SCN) is also larger in homosexual men than in heterosexual men (Swaab & Hofman, 1990). As discussed in Chapter 9, the SCN controls circadian rhythms. How might a difference in the SCN relate to sexual orientation? The answer is not clear, but male rats that are deprived of testosterone during early development also show abnormalities in the SCN, and their preference for male or female sexual partners varies with time of day. They make sexual advances toward both male and female partners early in their active period of the day but mostly toward females as the day goes on (Swaab, Slob, Houtsmuller, Brand, & Zhou, 1995). Does human sexual orientation fluctuate depending on time of day? No research has been reported.

The most widely cited research concerns the third interstitial nucleus of the anterior hypothalamus (INAH-3), which is generally more than twice as large in heterosexual men as in women. This area has more cells with androgen receptors in men than in women (Shah et al., 2004) and probably plays a role in sexual behavior, although the exact role is uncertain. Simon LeVay (1991) examined INAH-3 in 41 people who had died between the ages of 26 and 59. Of these, 16 were heterosexual men, 6 were heterosexual women, and 19 were homosexual men. All of the homosexual men, 6 of the 16 heterosexual men, and 1 of the 6 women had died of AIDS. LeVay found that the mean volume of INAH-3 was larger in heterosexual men than in heterosexual women or homosexual men, who were about equal in this regard. Figure 11.12 shows typical cross-sections for a heterosexual man and a homosexual man. Figure 11.13 shows the distribution of volumes for the three groups. Note that the difference between heterosexual men and the other two groups is fairly large, on the average, and that the cause of death (AIDS versus other) has no clear relationship to the results. LeVay (1993) later examined the hypothalamus of a homosexual man who died of lung cancer; he had a small INAH-3, like the homosexual men who died of AIDS. In Figure 11.13, note also the substantial amount of difference among individuals. If you could examine some man's INAH-3, you could make a reasonable guess about sexual orientation, but you could not be confident.

A later study partly replicated these trends. Researchers found that the INAH-3 nucleus was slightly larger in heterosexual than homosexual men, although in this study the homosexual men's INAH-3 nucleus was larger than that of heterosexual women (Byne et al., 2001). Among heterosexual men or women, the INAH-3 nucleus was larger in those who were HIV negative than those who were HIV positive, but even if we look only at HIV+ men, we still find a difference in the hypothalamus between heterosexual and homosexual men. Figure 11.14 displays the means for the five groups. On microscopic examination of the INAH-3, researchers found that heterosexual men had larger neurons than homosexual

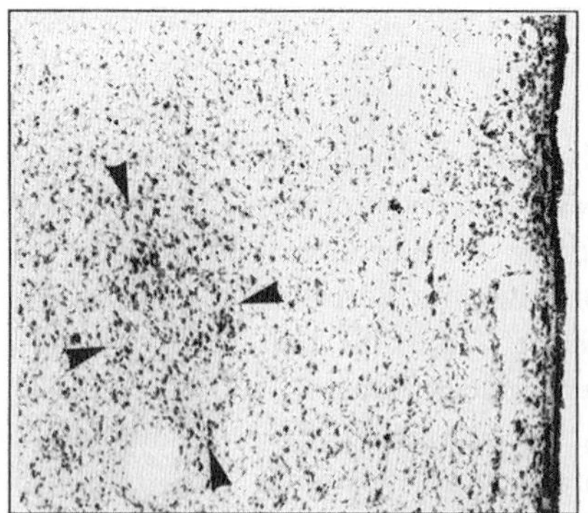

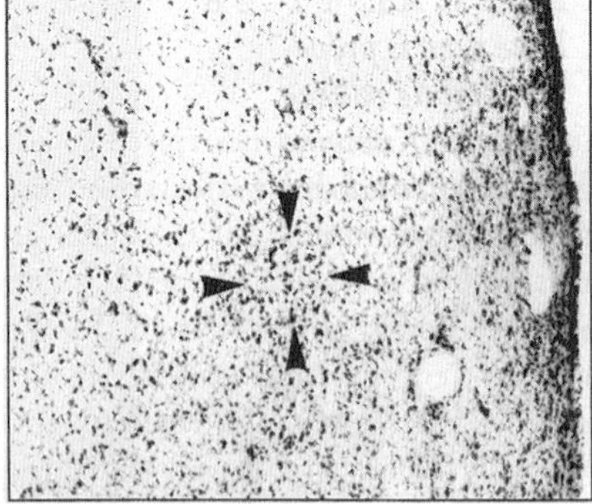

Figure 11.12 Typical sizes of interstitial nucleus 3 of the anterior hypothalamus On the average, the volume of this structure was more than twice as large in a sample of heterosexual men (left) than in a sample of homosexual men (right), for whom it was about the same size as that in women. Animal studies have implicated this structure as important for male sexual activities. *(From "A difference in hypothalamic structure between heterosexual and homosexual men," S. LeVay,* Science, *253, pp. 1034–1037. Copyright 1991. Reprinted with permission from AAAS.)*

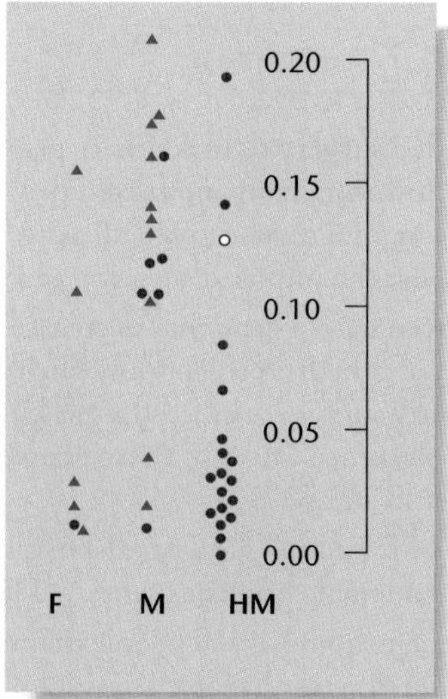

Figure 11.13 Volumes of the interstitial nucleus 3 of the anterior hypothalamus (INAH-3)
Samples are females (F), heterosexual males (M), and homosexual males (HM). Each filled circle represents a person who died of AIDS, and each triangle represents a person who died from other causes. The one open circle represents a bisexual man who died of AIDS. *(Reprinted with permission from "A difference in hypothalamic structure between heterosexual and homosexual men," by S. LeVay,* Science, 253, *pp. 1034–1037. Copyright © 1991 American Association for the Advancement of Science.)*

men but about the same number. (Neither this study nor LeVay's earlier study included homosexual females.)

The meaning of these results is not clear. Do differences in the hypothalamus influence sexual orientation, or does sexual activity influence the size of hypothalamic neurons? Some brain areas do grow or shrink in adults because of hormones or behavioral activities (Cooke, Tabibnia, & Breedlove, 1999). Studies of nonhumans offer suggestive results. About 8% of rams (male sheep) direct their sexual behavior toward other males. One area of the anterior hypothalamus was larger in female-oriented rams than in male-oriented rams and larger

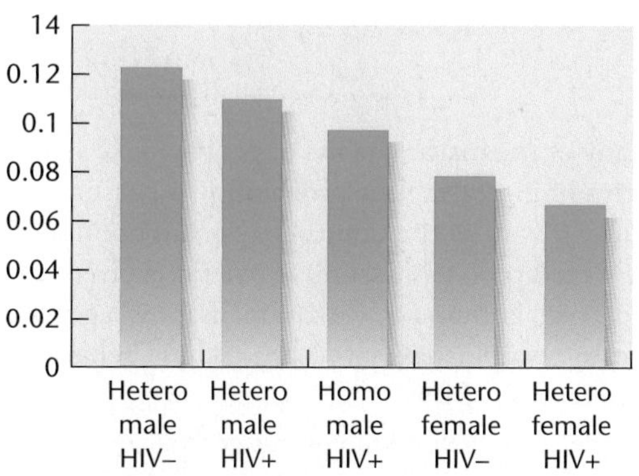

Figure 11.14 Another comparison of INAH-3
In this study, the mean volume for homosexual men was larger than that of women but smaller than that of men. *(Based on data of Byne et al., 2001)*

in them than in females (Roselli, Larkin, Resko, Stellflug, & Stormshak, 2004). (Whether this area corresponds to human INAH-3 is unknown.) This area becomes larger in male than female sheep before birth as a result of prenatal testosterone levels (Roselli, Stadelman, Reeve, Bishop, & Stormshak, 2007). In sheep, at least, an anatomical difference appears before any sexual behavior, and so it is more likely a cause than a result. The same may or may not be true in humans.

STOP & CHECK

19. In LeVay's study, what evidence argues against the idea that INAH-3 volume depends on AIDS rather than sexual orientation?

ANSWER

19. The average size of INAH-3 was about the same for heterosexual men who died of AIDS and those who died of other causes. One homosexual man who died of other causes had about the same size INAH-3 as heterosexual men who died of AIDS.

MODULE 11.2 IN CLOSING

We Are Not All the Same

When Alfred Kinsey conducted the first massive surveys of human sexual behavior, he found that most of the people he interviewed considered their own behavior "normal," whatever it was. Many believed that sexual activity much more frequent than their own was excessive and abnormal and might even lead to insanity (Kinsey, Pomeroy, & Martin, 1948; Kinsey, Pomeroy, Martin, & Gebhard, 1953).

How far have we come since then? People today are more aware of sexual diversity than they were in Kinsey's time and generally more accepting. Still, intolerance remains common. Biological research will not tell us how to treat one another, but it can help us understand how we come to be so different.

Continued

SUMMARY

1. Many of the mating habits of people make sense in terms of increasing the probability of passing on our genes. If we saw the same behaviors in nonhumans, we would probably assume a genetic, evolved basis. However, in humans, we cannot assume a genetic basis because people may have learned these behaviors and preferences. **329**
2. People can develop ambiguous genitals or genitals that don't match their chromosomal sex for several reasons. One is congenital adrenal hyperplasia, in which a genetic defect in cortisol production leads to overstimulation of the adrenal gland and therefore extra testosterone production. When that condition occurs in a female fetus, she becomes partly masculinized. **331**
3. On the average, girls with a history of congenital adrenal hyperplasia show more interest in boy-typical toys than other girls do, and during adolescence and young adulthood, they continue to show partly masculinized interests. These trends apparently relate to the influence of prenatal hormones. **332**
4. Testicular feminization, or androgen insensitivity, is a condition in which someone with an XY chromosome pattern is partly or fully insensitive to androgens and therefore develops a female external appearance. **333**
5. People born with intermediate or ambiguous genitals are called intersexes. Traditionally, physicians have recommended surgery to make these people look more feminine. However, many intersexed people do not develop an unambiguous female identity, and many protest against the imposed surgery. **333**
6. Some children have a gene that decreases their early production of dihydrotestosterone. Such a child looks female at birth and is considered a girl but develops a penis at adolescence. Most of these people then accept a male gender identity. **334**
7. The evidence for a biological predisposition is stronger for male than female homosexuality. **335**
8. On the average, homosexual people differ from heterosexual people in several anatomical and physiological regards. However, the data do not fit a hypothesis of anyone's being masculinized or feminized *in general.* Different aspects of anatomy and behavior are affected in different ways. **335**
9. Plausible biological explanations for homosexual orientation include genetics, prenatal hormones, and (in males) reactions to the mother's immune system. Hormone levels in adulthood are within the normal range. **336**
10. Several hypotheses have been offered for how genes promoting homosexuality could remain at moderate frequencies in the population when most homosexual people do not have children. **336**

KEY TERMS

Terms are defined in the module on the page number indicated. They're also presented in alphabetical order with definitions in the book's Subject Index/Glossary. Interactive flashcards, audio reviews, and crossword puzzles are among the online resources available to help you learn these terms and the concepts they represent.

androgen insensitivity **333**
congenital adrenal hyperplasia (CAH) **331**
gender identity **331**
hermaphrodite **332**
intersex **332**
testicular feminization **333**

THOUGHT QUESTIONS

1. On the average, intersexes have IQ scores in the 110 to 125 range, well above the mean for the population (Dalton, 1968; Ehrhardt & Money, 1967; Lewis, Money, & Epstein, 1968). One possible interpretation is that a hormonal pattern intermediate between male and female promotes great intellectual development. Another possibility is that intersexuality may be more common in intelligent families than in less intelligent ones or that the more intelligent families are more likely to bring their intersexed children to an investigator's attention. What kind of study would be best for deciding among these hypotheses? (For one answer, see Money & Lewis, 1966.)
2. Recall LeVay's study of brain anatomy in heterosexual and homosexual men. Certain critics have suggested that one or more of the men classified as "heterosexual" might actually have been homosexual or bisexual. If so, would that fact strengthen or weaken the overall conclusions?

CHAPTER 11 Exploration and Study

In addition to the study materials provided at the end of each module, you may supplement your review of this chapter by using one or more of the book's electronic resources, which include its companion Website, interactive Cengage Learning eBook, Exploring Biological Psychology CD-ROM, and CengageNOW. Brief descriptions of these resources follow. For more information, visit **www.cengage.com/psychology/kalat**.

The book's companion Website, accessible through the author Web page indicated above, provides a wide range of study resources such as an interactive glossary, flashcards, tutorial quizzes, updated Web links, and Try It Yourself activities, as well as a limited selection of the short videos and animated explanations of concepts available for this chapter.

Exploring Biological Psychology

The Exploring Biological Psychology CD-ROM contains videos, animations, and Try It Yourself activities. These activities—as well as many that are new to this edition—are also available in the text's fully interactive, media-rich Cengage Learning eBook,* which gives you the opportunity to experience biological psychology in an even greater interactive and multimedia environment. The Cengage Learning eBook also includes highlighting and note-taking features and an audio glossary. For this chapter, the Cengage Learning eBook includes the following interactive explorations:

Menstruation Cycle
Erectile Dysfunction

The video *Erectile Dysfunction* describes a common complaint related to sexual behavior.

* Requires a Cengage Learning eResources account. Visit **www.cengage.com/login** to register or login.

CENGAGENOW™ is an easy-to-use resource that helps you study in less time to get the grade you want. An online study system, CengageNOW* gives you the option of taking a diagnostic pretest for each chapter. The system uses the results of each pretest to create personalized chapter study plans for you. The Personalized Study Plans

- help you save study time by identifying areas on which you should concentrate and give you one-click access to corresponding pages of the interactive Cengage Learning eBook;
- provide interactive exercises and study tools to help you fully understand chapter concepts; and
- include a posttest for you to take to confirm that you are ready to move on to the next chapter.

Suggestions for Further Exploration

The book's companion Website includes a list of suggested articles available through InfoTrac College Edition for this chapter. You may also want to explore some of the following books and Websites. The text's companion Website provides live, updated links to the sites listed below.

Books

Colapinto, J. (2000). *As nature made him: The boy who was raised as a girl.* New York: HarperCollins. Describes the boy whose penis was accidentally removed, as presented on page •••.

Diamond, J. (1997). *Why is sex fun?* New York: Basic Books. Human sexual behavior differs from that of other species in many ways and therefore raises many evolutionary issues, which this book addresses. For example, why do humans have sex at times when the woman cannot become pregnant? Why do women have menopause? Why don't men breast-feed their babies? And what good are men, anyway? If you haven't thought about such questions before, you should read this book.

Dreger, A. D. (1998). *Hermaphrodites and the medical invention of sex.* Cambridge, MA: Harvard University Press. A fascinating history of how the medical profession has treated and mistreated hermaphrodites.

Website

The Endocrine Society
http://www.endo-society.org/

Intersex Society of North America
http://www.isna.org/

Michael Steele/Getty Images

Emotional Behaviors

12

CHAPTER OUTLINE

MAIN IDEAS

1. Emotions include cognitions, actions, and feelings. Several kinds of evidence support the theory that emotional feelings result from actions of the muscles or organs.
2. Many brain areas contribute to emotions. It is not clear that different emotions are localized differently in the brain.
3. Aggressive and fearful behaviors represent the combined outcome of many biological and environmental influences.
4. The amygdala responds quickly to emotional stimuli. Damage to the amygdala interferes with attention to information that is relevant to emotions.
5. Stressful events arouse the sympathetic nervous system and later the adrenal cortex. Prolonged or severe stress produces many of the same bodily responses that illness does.

OPPOSITE: People express emotion by facial expressions, gestures, and postures.

> [W]e know the meaning so long as no one asks us to define it.
>
> William James (1892/1961, p. 19)

> Unfortunately, one of the most significant things ever said about emotion may be that everyone knows what it is until they are asked to define it.
>
> Joseph LeDoux (1996, p. 23)

Suppose researchers have discovered a new species—let's call it species X—and psychologists begin testing its abilities. They place food behind a green card and nothing behind a red card and find that after a few trials, X always goes to the green card. So we conclude that X shows learning, memory, and hunger. Then researchers offer X a green card and a variety of gray cards; X still goes to the green, so it must have color vision and not just brightness discrimination. Next they let X touch a blue triangle that is extremely hot. X makes a loud sound and backs away. Someone picks up the blue triangle (with padded gloves) and starts moving with it rapidly toward X. As soon as X sees this happening, it makes the same sound, turns, and starts moving rapidly away. Shall we conclude that it feels the emotion of fear?

If you said yes, now let me add: I said this was a new species, and so it is, but it's a new species of robot, not animal. Do you still think X feels emotions? Most people are willing to talk about artificial learning, memory, intelligence, and motivation, but not emotion. "The robot was just programmed to make that sound and move away from hot objects," we say. "It doesn't really feel an emotion."

If such behavior isn't adequate evidence for emotion in a robot, is it adequate evidence for an animal? Emotion is a difficult topic because it implies conscious feelings that we cannot observe. Biological researchers therefore concentrate mostly on emotional *behaviors*, which are observable, even if the emotional feelings are not. Still, most of us hope eventually to learn something about the emotional experiences themselves.

MODULE 12.1

What Is Emotion?

Psychologists typically define emotion in terms of three components—cognitions ("This is a dangerous situation"), feelings ("I feel frightened"), and actions ("Run for the nearest exit"). Of these, the feelings are the most central to our concept of emotion. If someone reports feeling frightened, we attribute emotion to that person at once. However, if someone calculates, "This is a dangerous situation," and takes action to escape it, but doesn't feel any tenseness or arousal, we would be less inclined to attribute emotion. What are emotional feelings, what causes them, and what function do they serve?

Emotions, Autonomic Arousal, and the James-Lange Theory

Emotional situations arouse the autonomic nervous system, which has two branches—the sympathetic and the parasympathetic. Figure 12.1 reviews the anatomy of the autonomic nervous system. The sympathetic nervous system prepares the body for brief, vigorous "fight-or-flight" responses. The parasympathetic nervous system increases digestion and other processes that save energy and prepare for later events. However, each situation evokes its own special mixture of sympathetic and parasympathetic arousal (Wolf, 1995). For example, nausea is associated with sympathetic stimulation of the stomach (decreasing its contractions and secretions) and parasympathetic stimulation of the intestines and salivary glands.

Walter B. Cannon (1871–1945)

As a matter of routine I have long trusted unconscious processes to serve me. . . . [One] example I may cite was the interpretation of the significance of bodily changes which occur in great emotional excitement, such as fear and rage. These changes—the more rapid pulse, the deeper breathing, the increase of sugar in the blood, the secretion from the adrenal glands—were very diverse and seemed unrelated. Then, one wakeful night, after a considerable collection of these changes had been disclosed, the idea flashed through my mind that they could be nicely integrated if conceived as bodily preparations for supreme effort in flight or in fighting.

How does the autonomic nervous system relate to emotions? Common sense holds that first we feel an emotion, which then changes our heart rate and prompts other responses. In contrast, according to the **James-Lange theory** (James, 1884), the autonomic arousal and skeletal actions come first. What we experience as an emotion is the label we give to our responses: I am afraid *because* I run away; I am angry *because* I attack.

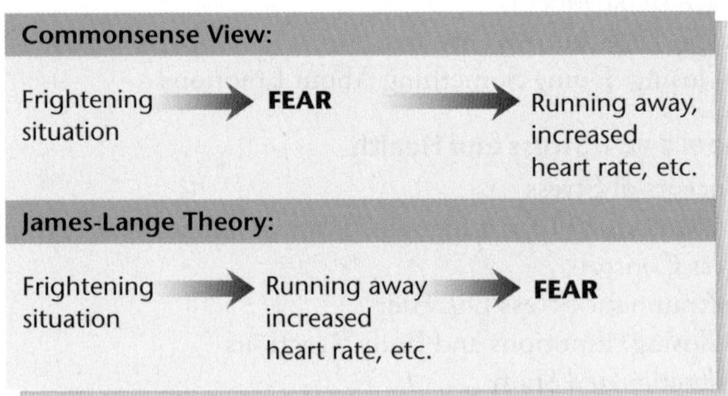

You might object, "How would I know that I should run away before I was scared?" In a later paper, William James (1894) clarified his position. An emotion has three components: cognitions, actions, and feelings. The cognitive aspect comes first. You appraise something as good, bad, frightening, or whatever. Ordinarily, you make that appraisal within a split second (Kawasaki et al., 2001). Your appraisal of the situation leads to an appropriate action, such as running away, attacking, or sitting motionless with your heart racing. When William James had said that arousal and actions lead to emotions, what he meant was the *feeling* aspect of an emotion. That is,

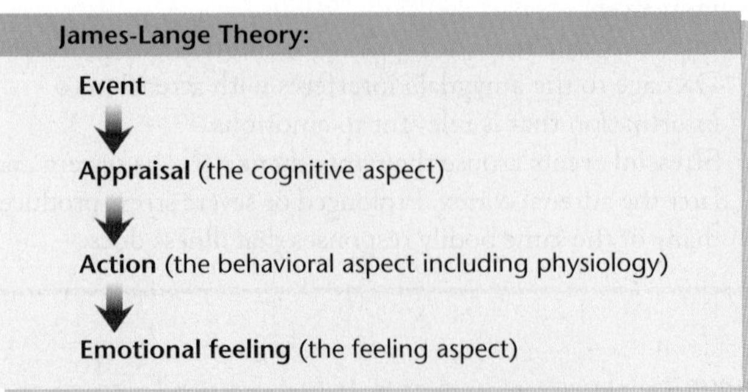

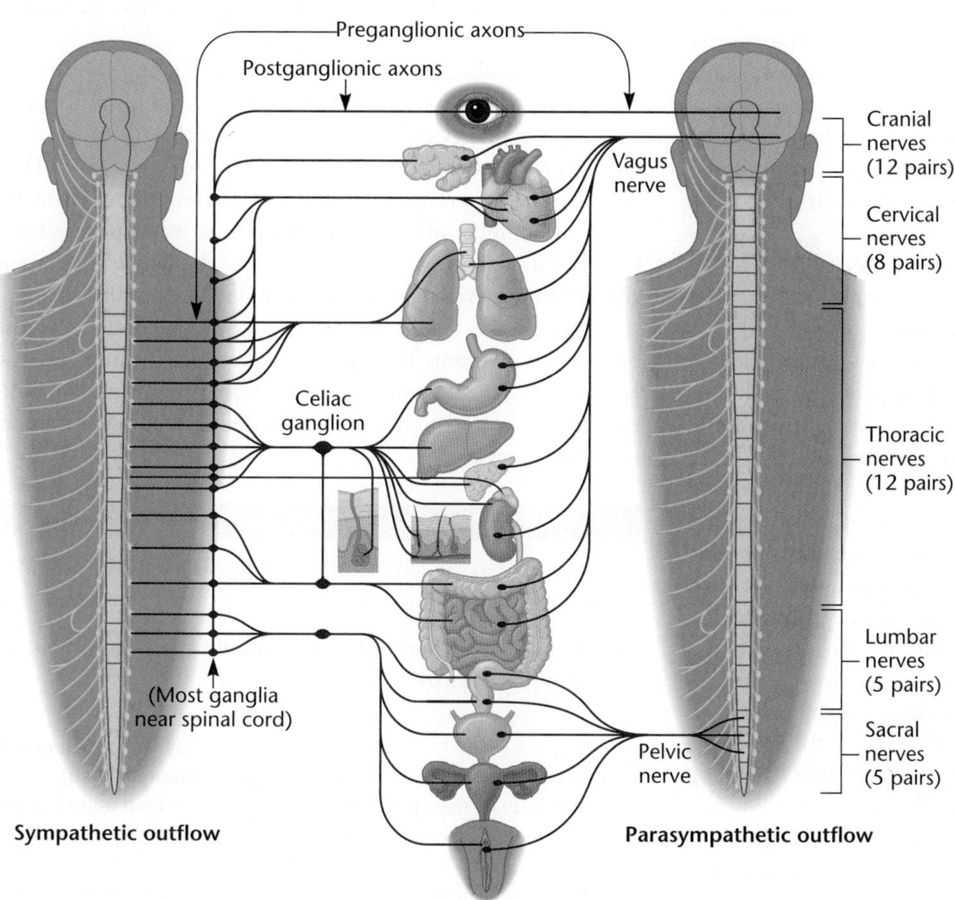

Figure 12.1 The sympathetic and parasympathetic nervous systems
Review Chapter 4 for more information.

The James-Lange theory leads to two predictions: People with weak autonomic or skeletal responses should feel less emotion, and causing or increasing someone's responses should enhance an emotion. Let's consider the evidence.

Is Physiological Arousal *Necessary* for Emotions?

People with damage to the spinal cord are paralyzed from the level of the damage downward. People who cannot move their arms and legs certainly cannot attack or run away. Most of them report that they feel emotions about the same as before their injury (Cobos, Sánchez, Pérez, & Vila, 2004). This finding indicates that emotions do not require feedback from muscle movements. However, paralysis does not affect the autonomic nervous system, so it remains possible that emotional feelings depend on feedback from autonomic responses.

In people with an uncommon condition called **pure autonomic failure,** output from the autonomic nervous system to the body fails either completely or almost completely. Heart beat and other organ activities continue, but the nervous system no longer regulates them. One effect occurs when people stand up. When you suddenly stand, gravity and inertia would pull the blood from your head toward the ground, except that your autonomic nervous system increases your heart rate and constricts the veins in your head. Someone with pure autonomic failure lacks those reflexes and must stand up slowly to avoid fainting. Also, someone with this condition does not react to stressful experiences with changes in heart rate, blood pressure, or sweating. According to the James-Lange theory, we would expect such people to report no emotions. In fact, they report the same emotions as anyone else and have little difficulty identifying what emotion a character in a story would probably experience (Heims, Critchley, Dolan, Mathias, & Cipolotti, 2004). However, they report that they feel their emotions much less intensely than previously (Critchley, Mathias, & Dolan, 2001). Presumably, when they report emotions, they refer to the cognitive aspect: "Yes, I'm angry, because this is a situation that calls for anger." But they do not *feel* the anger, or if they do, they feel it weakly. Their decreased emotional feeling is consistent with predictions from the James-Lange theory.

Is Physiological Arousal *Sufficient* for Emotions?

According to the James-Lange theory, emotional feelings result from the body's actions. If your heart started racing and you started breathing rapidly and sweating, would you suddenly feel an emotion? Well, it depends. If you had those responses because you ran a mile, you would attribute your feelings to the exercise, not emotion. However, if they occurred spontaneously, you might indeed interpret your increased sympathetic nervous system arousal as fear. Rapid breathing in particular makes people worry that they are suffocating, and they experience a **panic attack,** marked by extreme sympathetic nervous system arousal (Klein, 1993). If someone has repeated panic attacks and starts to worry about them, the result is a condition called panic disorder.

TRY IT YOURSELF

What about other emotions? For example, if you find yourself smiling, would you become happier? If we want to test this hypothesis, how could we get people to smile? Yes, of course, we could tell them to smile. However, if we tell people to smile and then ask whether they are happy, people guess what the experiment is about and say what they think we want to hear. Clever researchers found a way to get people to smile while concealing the purpose of the study. It is a method you could easily try yourself: Hold a pen in your mouth, either with your teeth or with your lips, as shown in Figure 12.2. Now examine a page of comic strips in your newspaper. Mark each one + for very funny, ✓ for somewhat funny, or − for not funny. Most people rate cartoons funnier when holding a pen with their teeth—which forces a smile—than when holding it with their lips—which prevents a smile (Strack, Martin, & Stepper, 1988). That is, the sensation of smiling increases happiness, although only slightly. (Telling a depressed person to cheer up and smile does not help.)

Researchers also found a clever way to ask people to frown without saying so. They said they wanted to test people's ability to do a cognitive task and a motor task at the same time. The cognitive task was to examine photographs and rate their pleasantness or unpleasantness. For the motor task, researchers attached golf tees to each of the person's eyebrows and said to try to keep the tips of the golf tees touching each other. The only way to do that was to frown. People given this instruction rated the photographs as more unpleasant than the average for people who were not induced to frown (Larsen, Kasimatis, & Frey, 1992).

However, although smiles and frowns slightly alter happiness, smiles are not *necessary* for happiness. People with a rare condition called *Möbius syndrome* are unable to move their facial muscles to make a smile, as shown in Figure 12.3. They nevertheless experience happiness and amusement, although they have trouble making friends because other people react to the lack of smiling. The girl shown in the figure underwent surgery to give her an artificial smile (G. Miller, 2007b).

Overall, the results suggest that our perceptions of the body's actions contribute to our emotional feelings, as the James-Lange theory proposed. The more important contribution comes from the effects of the autonomic nervous system, not muscle activity.

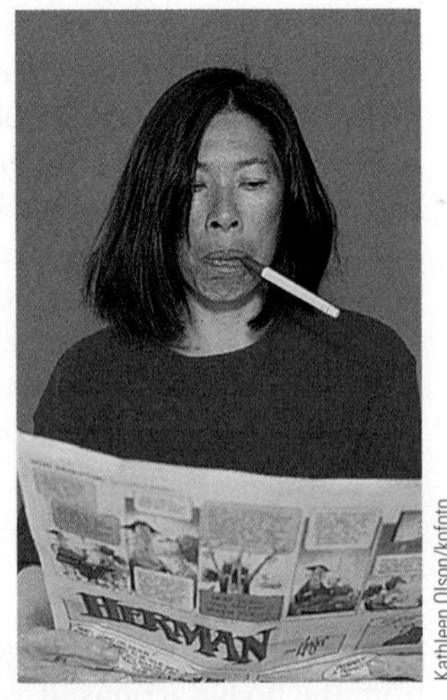

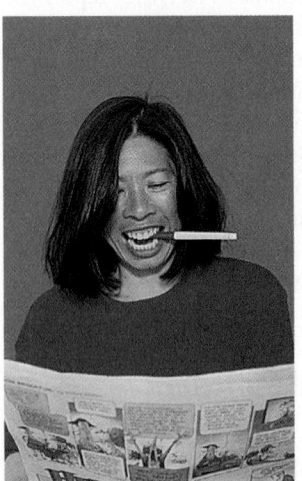

Kathleen Olson/kofoto

Figure 12.2 Effect of facial expression on emotion
People who hold a pen in their teeth, and who are therefore forced to smile, are more likely to report amusement or humor than are people who hold a pen in their lips, who are therefore not smiling.

STOP & CHECK

1. According to the James-Lange theory, what kind of person should feel no emotions?
2. How did researchers get people to smile or frown without using those words?

ANSWERS

1. Someone who had no muscle movements and no perceivable changes in any organ should feel no emotions. However, such a person might still recognize the cognitive aspects of emotion. ("This is a sad situation.") **2.** They got people to smile by telling them to hold a pen between their teeth. They got people to frown by attaching golf tees to their eyebrows and then telling them to keep the two tees touching each other.

Brain Areas Associated With Emotion

Do different emotions activate different brain areas? Moreover, which brain areas react most strongly to emotions?

Attempts to Localize Specific Emotions

Traditionally, the **limbic system**—the forebrain areas surrounding the thalamus—has been regarded as critical for emotion (see Figure 12.4). We consider one part of it, the amygdala, in more detail later in this chapter. Much of the cerebral cortex also reacts to emotional situations.

To induce emotions and examine their effects on the brain, researchers ask participants to look at photographs, listen to stories, or recall personal emotional experiences. One approach is to measure evoked responses (Chapter 4), a method that is very sensitive to rapid changes in the brain's electrical activity. Researchers find that the brain responds very quickly (within 120–180 ms) to a photo of a face showing an emotional expression, indicating that the human brain is specialized to attend strongly to faces. However, different emotions evoked activity in the same brain areas (Eimer & Holmes, 2007).

Another approach is to use PET or fMRI techniques to identify the cortical areas more active during an emotion than

Courtesy of Lori Thomas

Figure 12.3 Möbius syndrome
People with this condition are unable to move the facial muscles to smile. This girl went through surgery to give her an artificial smile, as shown in the bottom right photo. The lack of a smile, before surgery, did not rob her of happiness or a sense of humor, although it did interfere with her ability to make friends.

during a neutral period. Figure 12.5 summarizes the results of many studies. Each dot represents one study that found significant activation of a particular cortical area associated with an emotion. The color of the dot labels the emotion (Phan, Wager, Taylor, & Liberzon, 2002). The frontal and temporal cortices have many dots, and other kinds of research also point to these areas as important for emotions (Kringelbach, 2005). However, the most salient point of this figure is the variability of location for each emotion. The results apparently depend more on the details of procedure than which emotion was targeted.

Sometimes, physicians insert electrodes directly into the brains of patients with epilepsy to monitor their responses over time. In one study, researchers used these implanted electrodes to record responses to emotional pictures. They did find particular cells that responded mainly to pleasant pictures and others that responded mainly to unpleasant pictures (Kawasaki et al., 2005). However, no one has demonstrated cells that respond only to a particular unpleasant emotion, such as sadness or fear.

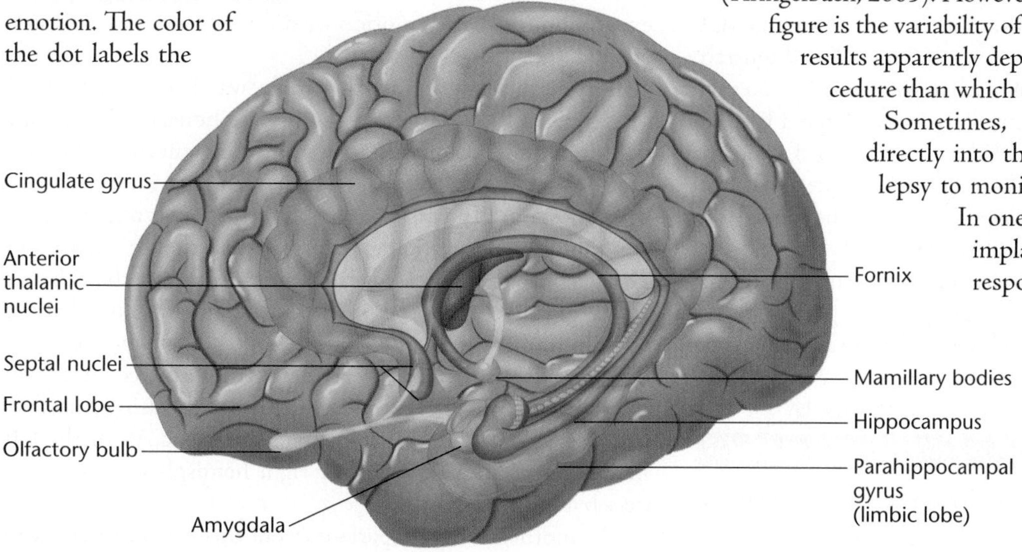

Cingulate gyrus
Anterior thalamic nuclei
Septal nuclei
Frontal lobe
Olfactory bulb
Amygdala
Fornix
Mamillary bodies
Hippocampus
Parahippocampal gyrus (limbic lobe)

Figure 12.4 The limbic system
The limbic system is a group of structures in the interior of the brain. Here you see them as if you could look through a transparent exterior of the brain. *(Based on MacLean, 1949)*

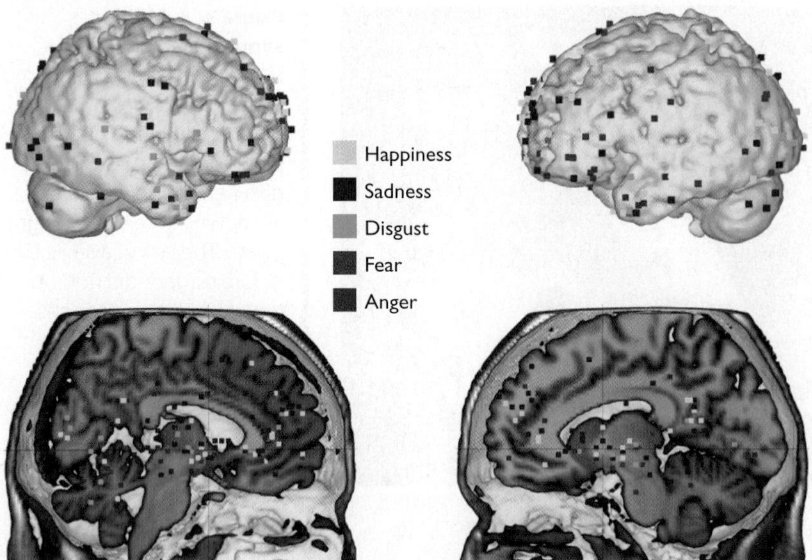

Figure 12.5 Brain areas associated with particular emotions
Each dot represents one study that found increased activity in a given brain area associated with the emotion designated by the color of the dot. *(Reprinted from* NeuroImage, 16, *Phan, K. L., Wagner, T., Taylor, S. F., & Liberzon, I., "Functional neuroanatomy of emotion: A meta-analysis of emotion activation studies in PET and fMRI," pages 331–348, Copyright 2002, with permission from Elsevier.)*

Of all emotions, the only one for which the evidence suggests brain localization is disgust. The *insular cortex,* or *insula,* is strongly activated if you see a disgusting picture (F. C. Murphy, Nimmo-Smith, & Lawrence, 2003; M. L. Phillips et al., 1997) or the facial expression of someone else who is feeling disgusted (Wicker et al., 2003). That is, if you see someone who looks disgusted, you feel disgusted, too.

Locating disgust in the insula is interesting because that is the primary taste cortex (see Figure 7.20 on page 214). *Disgust* is literally *dis-gust,* or bad taste. To react with disgust is to react as if something tasted bad; we want to spit it out. One man with damage to his insular cortex not only failed to experience disgust in daily life but also had trouble recognizing other people's disgust expressions. When he heard a retching sound, he did not recognize that it meant nausea or vomiting. How disgusted would you be if you found a cockroach in your soup? If you saw someone whose intestines were spilling out through a hole in the abdomen, how disgusted would you be? What if you saw people with feces on their hands and faces? To questions like these, this patient gave much lower ratings than other people do (Calder, Keane, Manes, Antoun, & Young, 2000).

However, the insula reacts to frightening pictures as well as to disgusting ones (Schienle et al., 2002), and disgusting experiences activate brain areas in addition to the insula (Benuzzi, Lui, Duzzi, Nichelli, & Porro, 2008). Therefore, we should not too closely associate disgust with activity of the insula.

STOP & CHECK

3. Which kind of emotion, and which kind of sensation, depend most heavily on the insula?

ANSWER **3.** The insula is important for disgust and taste.

Contributions of the Left and Right Hemispheres

Another hypothesis relates the two hemispheres of the brain to different categories of emotion. Activity of the left hemisphere, especially its frontal and temporal lobes, relates to what Jeffrey Gray (1970) called the **Behavioral Activation System (BAS),** marked by low to moderate autonomic arousal and a tendency to approach, which could characterize either happiness or anger. Increased activity of the frontal and temporal lobes of the right hemisphere is associated with the **Behavioral Inhibition System (BIS),** which increases attention and arousal, inhibits action, and stimulates emotions such as fear and disgust (Davidson & Fox, 1982; Davidson & Henriques, 2000; F. C. Murphy et al., 2003; Reuter-Lorenz & Davidson, 1981).

The difference between the hemispheres relates to personality: On the average, people with greater activity in the frontal cortex of the left hemisphere tend to be happier, more outgoing, and more fun-loving. People with greater right-hemisphere activity tend to be socially withdrawn, less satisfied with life, and prone to unpleasant emotions (Knyazev, Slobodskaya, & Wilson, 2002; Schmidt, 1999; Urry et al., 2004). We return to this point in Module 15.2.

The right hemisphere appears to be more responsive to emotional stimuli than the left. For example, listening to either laughter or crying activates the right amygdala more than the left (Sander & Scheich, 2001). When people look at faces, drawing their attention to the emotional expression increases the activity in the right temporal cortex (Narumoto, Okada, Sadato, Fukui, & Yonekura, 2001). People with damage to the right temporal cortex have trouble identifying other people's emotional expressions or even saying whether two people are expressing the same emotion or different ones (H. J. Rosen et al., 2002).

In one fascinating study, people watched videotapes of 10 people. All 10 described themselves honestly during one speech and completely dishonestly during another. The task of the observers was to guess which of the two interviews was the honest one. The task is more difficult than it might sound, and most people are no more correct than chance (about 5 of 10). The only group tested that performed better than chance was a group of people with left-hemisphere brain damage (Etcoff, Ekman, Magee, & Frank, 2000). They got only 60% correct—not great, but at least better than chance. Evidently, the right hemisphere is better not only at expressing emotions but also at detecting other people's emotions. With the left hemisphere out of the way, the right hemisphere was free to do what it does best.

In another study, 11 patients went through a procedure in which one hemisphere at a time was anesthetized by drug injection into one of the carotid arteries, which provide blood to the head. (This procedure, called the Wada procedure, is used before certain kinds of brain surgery.) All 11 patients had left-hemisphere language, so they could not be interviewed with the left hemisphere inactivated. When they were tested with the right hemisphere inactivated, something fascinating happened: They could still describe any of the sad, frightening, or irritating events they had experienced in life, but they remembered only the facts, not the emotion. For example, one patient remembered a car wreck, another remembered visiting his mother while she was dying, and another remembered a time his wife threatened to kill him. But they denied they had felt any significant fear, sadness, or anger. When they described the same events with both hemispheres active, they remembered strong emotions. So evidently, when the right hemisphere is inactive, people do not experience strong emotions and do not even remember feeling them (Ross, Homan, & Buck, 1994).

STOP & CHECK

4. What are the contributions of the right hemisphere to emotional behaviors and interpreting other people's emotions?

ANSWER

4. Activation of the right hemisphere is associated with withdrawal from events and social contact. The right hemisphere is also more specialized than the left for interpreting other people's expressions of emotions.

The Functions of Emotions

If we evolved the capacity to experience and express emotions, emotions must have been adaptive to our ancestors, and they probably are to us as well. What good do emotions do?

For certain emotions, the answer is clear. Fear alerts us to escape from danger. Anger directs us to attack an intruder. Disgust tells us to avoid something that might cause illness. The adaptive value of happiness, sadness, embarrassment, and other emotions is less obvious, although researchers have suggested some plausible possibilities.

Also, emotions provide a useful guide when we need to make a quick decision. Sometimes, your "gut feeling" is useful. In one study, college students viewed a series of slides of snakes and spiders, each presented for just 10 ms, followed by a masking stimulus—a random array of unrecognizable patterns. Under these conditions, people cannot identify whether they saw a snake or a spider. For each participant, one kind of stimulus—either the snakes or the spiders—was always followed by a mild shock 5.6 seconds later. Most of those shocked after spider pictures developed a bigger heart rate increase after spider pictures, and people shocked after snake pictures learned an increased heart rate after snake pictures, even though neither group could consciously identify the pictures. On certain trials, participants were asked to report any perceived changes in their heart rate, which were compared to measurements of their actual heart rate. On other trials, after the stimulus, they guessed whether a shock was forthcoming. In general, those who were most accurate at reporting their heart rate increases were the most accurate at predicting whether they were about to get a shock (Katkin, Wiens, & Öhman, 2001). The interpretation is that people who are good at detecting their autonomic responses may have valid gut feelings about dangers that they cannot identify consciously.

Emotions and Moral Decisions

We base many important decisions partly on emotional considerations—how we think one outcome or another will make us feel. Consider the following moral dilemmas, of which Figure 12.6 illustrates three.

The Trolley Dilemma. A runaway trolley is headed toward five people on a track. The only way you can prevent their death is to switch the trolley onto another track, where it will kill one person. Would it be right to pull the switch?

The Footbridge Dilemma. You are standing on a footbridge overlooking a trolley track. A runaway trolley is headed toward five people on a track. The only way you can prevent their death is to push a heavy-set stranger off the footbridge and onto the track so that he will block the trolley. Would it be right to push him?

The Lifeboat Dilemma. You and six other people are on a lifeboat in icy waters, but it is overcrowded and starting to sink. If you push one of the people off the boat, the boat will stop sinking and the rest of you will survive. Would it be right to push someone off?

The Hospital Dilemma. You are a surgeon, and five of your patients will die soon unless they get organ transplants. Each needs the transplant of a different organ. You haven't been able to find organ donors for any of them. Then a nurse bursts into your office: "Good news! A visitor to the hospital has just arrived, who has exactly the same tissue type as all five of your patients! We can kill this visitor and use the organs to save the five others!" Would it be right to do so?

In each of these dilemmas, you can save five people (including yourself in the lifeboat case) by killing one person. However, although that may be true logically, the decisions do not feel the same. Most people (though not all) say yes to pulling the switch in the trolley dilemma. Fewer say yes in the footbridge and lifeboat dilemmas. Almost no one endorses killing one person to save five others in the hospital dilemma. Brain scans show that contemplating the footbridge or lifeboat dilemma activates brain areas known to respond to emotions, including parts of the prefrontal cortex and cingulate gyrus (Greene, Sommerville, Nystrom, Darley, & Cohen, 2001). Responses in the amygdala are also important. We don't want to act to harm someone else because we identify with that other person and begin to feel the pain that our actions might cause that other person (Pfaff, 2007). In short, when we are making a decision about right and wrong, we seldom work it out rationally. One decision or the other immediately "feels" right. After we have already decided, we try to think of a logical justification (Haidt, 2001).

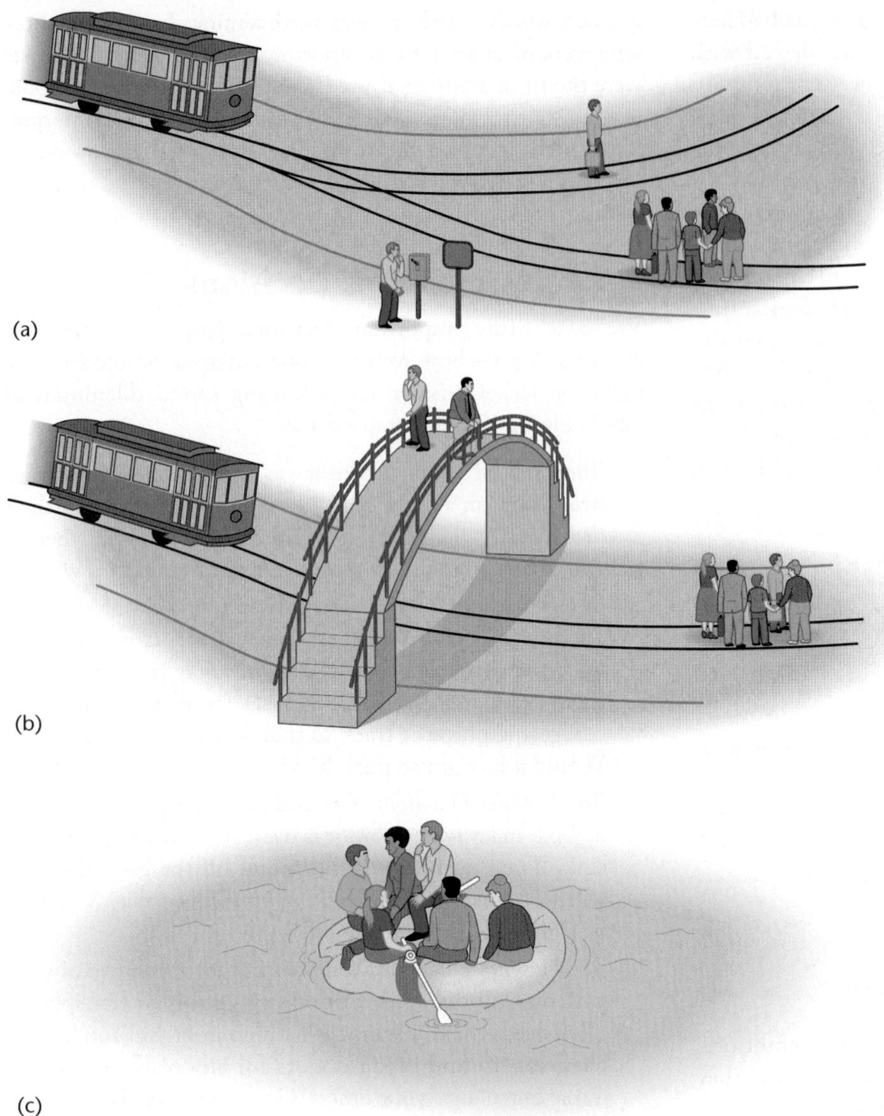

Figure 12.6 Three moral dilemmas
(a) Would you divert a runaway train so it kills one person instead of five? **(b)** Would you push someone off a footbridge so a runaway train kills him instead of five others? **(c)** Would you push someone off a sinking lifeboat to save yourself and four others?

Decision Making After Brain Damage That Impairs Emotions

Damage to parts of the prefrontal cortex blunts people's emotions in most regards, except for occasional outburst of anger. It also impairs decision making. People with such damage often make impulsive decisions without pausing to consider the consequences, including how they will feel after a possible mistake. When given a choice, they frequently make a quick decision and then immediately sigh or wince, knowing that they have made the wrong choice (Berlin, Rolls, & Kischka, 2004). You might think of impulsive decisions as emotional, but these people's decisions often seem unemotional. For example, if confronted with the trolley car dilemma or the other dilemmas we just discussed, people with prefrontal damage are more likely than average to choose the utilitarian option of killing one to save five, even in situations where most people find the choice emotionally unacceptable (Koenigs et al., 2007).

Historically, the most famous case of a person with prefrontal damage is that of Phineas Gage. In 1848, an explosion sent an iron rod through Gage's prefrontal cortex. Amazingly, he survived. During the next few months, his behavior was impulsive and he made poor decisions. These are common symptoms of prefrontal damage. However, the reports about his behavior provide little detail. Over the years, with multiple retellings, people elaborated on the original. If you have read about this case, you probably read an exaggerated account (Kotowicz, 2007).

We know more about a modern case. Antonio Damasio (1994) examined a man with prefrontal cortex damage who expressed almost no emotions. Nothing angered him. He was never very sad, even about his own brain damage. Nothing gave him much pleasure, not even music. Far from being purely rational, he frequently made bad decisions that cost him his job, his marriage, and his savings. When tested in the laboratory, he successfully predicted the probable outcomes of various decisions. For example, when asked what would happen if he cashed a check and the bank teller handed him too much money, he knew the probable consequences of returning it or walking away with it. But he admitted, "I still wouldn't know what to do" (A. R. Damasio, 1994, p. 49). He knew that one action would win him approval and another would get him in trouble, but he apparently did not anticipate that approval would feel good and trouble would feel bad. In a sense, any choice requires consideration of values and emotions—how we think one outcome or another will make us feel. In Damasio's words, "Inevitably, emotions are inseparable from the idea of good and evil" (A. Damasio, 1999, p. 55).

Investigators also studied two young adults who had suffered prefrontal cortex damage in infancy (S. W. Anderson, Bechara, Damasio, Tranel, & Damasio, 1999). Apparently, they never learned moral behavior. From childhood onward, they frequently stole, lied, physically and verbally abused others, and failed to show any guilt. Neither had any friends and neither could keep a job.

Here is an experiment to explore further the role of emotions in making decisions. In the Iowa Gambling Task, people can draw one card at a time from four piles. They always win $100 in play money from decks A and B, $50 from C and D. However, some of the cards also have penalties:

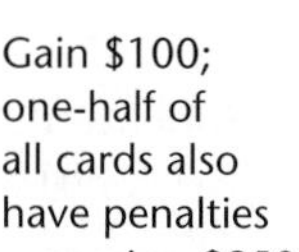

A	B	C	D
Gain $100; one-half of all cards also have penalties averaging $250	Gain $100; one-tenth of all cards also have penalties of $1250	Gain $50; one-half of all cards also have penalties averaging $50	Gain $50; one-tenth of all cards also have penalties of $250

When you see all the payoffs laid out, you can easily determine that the best strategy is to pick cards from decks C and D. In the experiment, however, people have to discover the payoffs by trial and error. Ordinarily, as people sample from all four decks, they gradually start showing signs of nervous tension whenever they draw a card from A or B, and they start shifting their preference toward C and D. People with damage to either the prefrontal cortex or the amygdala (part of the temporal lobe) show difficulties processing emotional information. In this experiment, they do not show any nervous tension associated with decks A and B, and they continue drawing from those decks (Bechara, Damasio, Damasio, & Lee, 1999). In short, failure to anticipate the unpleasantness of likely outcomes leads to bad decisions.

To be fair, it is also true that emotions sometimes interfere with good decisions. If you were driving and suddenly started skidding on a patch of ice, what would you do? A patient with damage to his prefrontal cortex who happened to face this situation calmly followed the advice he had always heard: Take your foot off the accelerator and steer in the direction of the skid (Shiv, Loewenstein, Bechara, Damasio, & Damasio, 2005). Most people in this situation panic, hit the brakes, and steer away from the skid, making a bad situation worse.

STOP & CHECK

5. If brain damage impairs someone's emotions, what happens to the person's decision making?

ANSWER

5. After brain damage that impairs emotion, people make impulsive decisions, evidently because they do not quickly imagine how bad a poor decision might make them feel.

MODULE 12.1 IN CLOSING

Emotions and the Nervous System

Although we regard emotions as nebulous internal states, they are fundamentally biological. As William James observed well over a century ago, emotions are "embodied"—an emotional feeling requires some action of the body and perception of that action.

Biological research sheds light on many of the central questions about the psychology of emotions. For example, one issue is whether people have a few "basic" emotions or continuous dimensions along which emotions vary. If researchers found that different emotions depended on different brain areas or different neurotransmitters, the evidence would strongly support the idea of basic emotions. However, so far, the researchers have found no evidence that each emotion has a specific physiology, with the possible exception of disgust.

Studies of people with brain damage also shed light on the functions of emotion, particularly with relation to moral behavior and decision making. Far from being an impediment to intelligent behavior, emotional reactions are often a useful quick guide to appropriate actions. In short, understanding emotions and understanding their biology go hand in hand.

SUMMARY

1. According to the James-Lange theory, the feeling aspect of an emotion results from feedback from actions of the muscles and organs. 344
2. Consistent with the James-Lange theory, people who have impaired autonomic responses have weaker emotional feelings, although they continue to identify the cognitive aspects of emotion. 345
3. Feedback from facial movements or other actions can strengthen an emotional feeling, but they are not necessary for such feelings. 345
4. Emotional experiences arouse many brain areas, as measured by fMRI scans or EEG recordings. So far, the research does not convincingly assign different emotions to different brain areas, with the possible exception of disgust. 346

Continued

5. Activation of the frontal and temporal areas of the left hemisphere is associated with approach and the Behavioral Activation System. The corresponding areas of the right hemisphere are associated with withdrawal, decreased activity, and the Behavioral Inhibition System. The right hemisphere is more effective than the left for recognizing emotional expressions. **348**

6. Brain damage that impairs emotional feelings and responses also impairs decision making. One interpretation is that people decide badly because they do not quickly imagine their emotional reactions to possible consequences. **350**

KEY TERMS

Terms are defined in the module on the page number indicated. They're also presented in alphabetical order with definitions in the book's Subject Index/Glossary. Interactive flashcards, audio reviews, and crossword puzzles are among the online resources available to help you learn these terms and the concepts they represent.

Behavioral Activation System (BAS) **348**
Behavioral Inhibition System (BIS) **348**
James-Lange theory **344**
limbic system **346**
panic attack **346**
pure autonomic failure **345**

THOUGHT QUESTION

According to the James-Lange theory, we should expect people with pure autonomic failure to experience weaker than average emotions. What kind of people might experience stronger than average emotions?

MODULE 12.2

Attack and Escape Behaviors

Have you ever watched a cat play with a rat or mouse before killing it? It might kick, bat, toss, pick up, shake, and carry the rodent. Is the cat sadistically tormenting its prey? No. Most of what we call its "play" behaviors are a compromise between attack and escape: When the rodent is facing away, the cat approaches; if the rodent turns around to face the cat, and especially if it bares its teeth, the cat bats it or kicks it defensively (Pellis et al., 1988). A cat usually goes for a quick kill if the rodent is small and inactive or if the cat has been given drugs that lower its anxiety. The same cat withdraws altogether if confronted with a large, menacing rodent. "Play" occurs in intermediate situations (Adamec, Stark-Adamec, & Livingston, 1980; Biben, 1979; Pellis et al., 1988).

Most of the vigorous emotional behaviors we observe in animals fall into the categories of attack and escape, and it is no coincidence that we describe the sympathetic nervous system as the fight-or-flight system. These behaviors and their corresponding emotions—anger and fear—are closely related both behaviorally and physiologically.

Attack Behaviors

Attack behavior may be passionate or calm and detached. For example, a soldier in battle may feel no anger toward the enemy, and people sometimes make "cold-blooded" attacks for financial gain. We can hardly expect to find a single explanation for all aggressive behaviors.

Attack behavior depends on the individual as well as the situation. Consider hamsters. If one intrudes into another's territory, the home hamster sniffs the intruder and eventually attacks, but usually not at once. Suppose the intruder leaves, and a little later, another hamster intrudes. The home hamster attacks faster and more vigorously than before. The first attack increases the probability of a second attack against any intruder for the next 30 minutes or more (Potegal, 1994). It is as if the first attack gets the hamster in the mood to attack again. During that period, activity increases in the corticomedial area of the amygdala, a structure in the temporal lobe (Potegal, Ferris, Hebert, Meyerhoff, & Skaredoff, 1996) (Figure 12.7). If we directly stimulate the corticomedial amygdala, a hamster is primed to attack, even without the previous experience of fighting (Potegal, Hebert, DeCoster, & Meyerhoff, 1996).

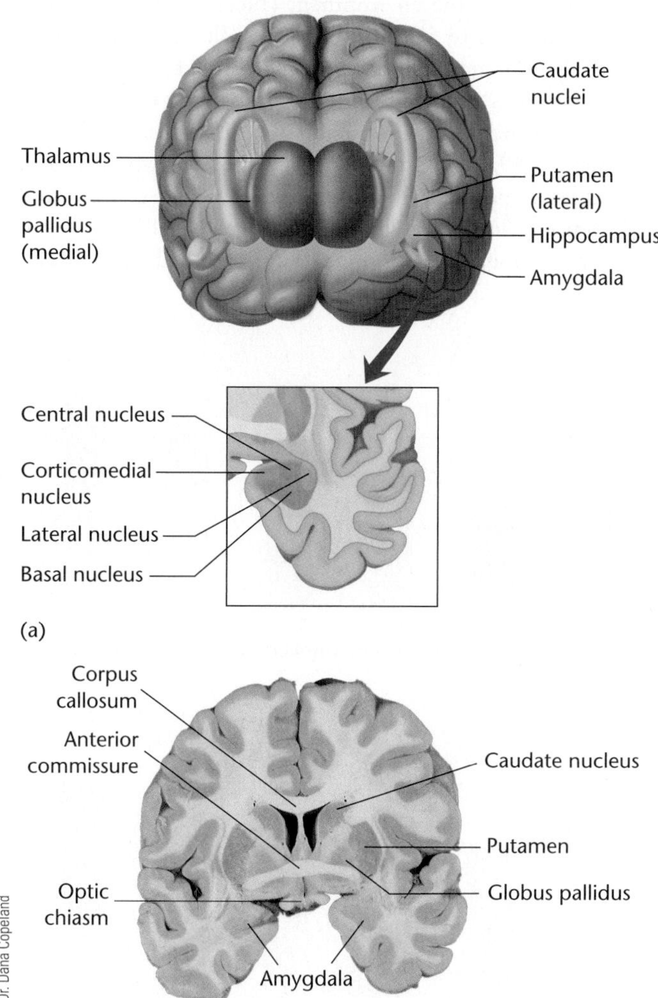

Figure 12.7 Location of amygdala in the human brain
The amygdala, located in the interior of the temporal lobe, receives input from many cortical and subcortical areas. Part **(a)** shows a blowup of separate nuclei of the amygdala. *([a] After Hanaway, Woolsey, Gado, & Roberts, 1998; Nieuwenhuys, Voogd, & vanHuijzen, 1988)*

Human behaviors are similar in this regard: After someone has insulted you, you become more aggressive, and that mood can last. Even though one person has irritated you, you might yell at someone else (Potegal, 1994). You have probably been told, "If you become angry, count to 10 before you act." Counting to a few thousand would work better, but the idea is correct.

Heredity and Environment in Violence

Why do some people turn to violence more readily than others do? One likely environmental factor is exposure to lead, which is harmful to developing brains. Since the banning of lead-based paints and the rise of unleaded gasoline, the prevalence of violent crime has declined, possibly as a result of the decreased lead in the environment (Nevin, 2007). Another possible contributor is the mother's smoking habits during pregnancy. The amount that a woman smokes during pregnancy correlates positively with the probability of adolescent and adult criminal activity by her sons (Brennan, Grekin, & Mednick, 1999; Fergusson, Woodward, & Horwood, 1998). This effect is particularly strong if the woman smoked *and* had complications during delivery (Figure 12.8). However, these correlations do not demonstrate cause and effect. Many women who smoke also use other drugs and differ, on the average, from other women in genetics, diet, child-rearing practices, and so forth. Nevertheless, animal studies show that prenatal exposure to nicotine does impair brain development. If we could control for all the other ways in which mothers who smoke differ from those who do not, smoking would probably remain as a predictor, but only a small predictor, of later aggressive behavior (Button, Maughan, & McGuffin, 2007).

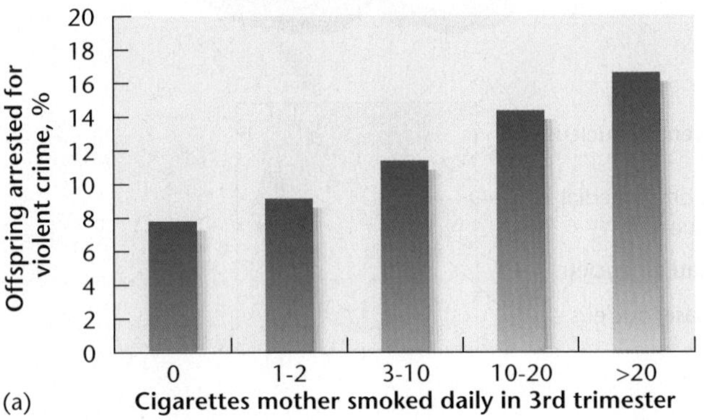

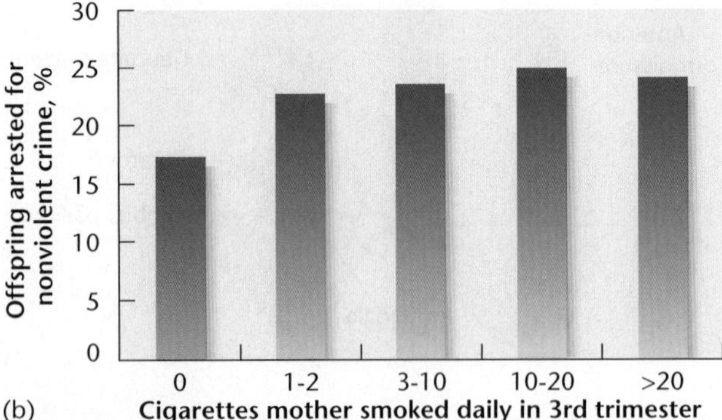

Figure 12.8 Effects of maternal smoking on later criminal behavior by her sons

(a) The greater the number of cigarettes the mother smoked during the third trimester of pregnancy, the greater the percentage of her sons eventually arrested for violent crimes. **(b)** Cigarette use did not correlate with nonviolent crimes. *(From "Maternal smoking during pregnancy and adult male criminal outcomes," by P. A. Brennan, E. R. Grekin, and S. A. Mednick,* Archives of General Psychiatry, *56, pp. 215–219. Copyright ©1999 American Medical Association. Reprinted by permission.)*

Heredity is important also. Monozygotic twins resemble each other more closely than dizygotic twins do with regard to violent and criminal behaviors, and adopted children resemble their biological parents more closely than their adoptive parents. The results imply a significant genetic contribution (Rhee & Waldman, 2002).

However, many attempts to identify a specific gene linked to aggressive behavior found only weak effects. Researchers therefore began to explore the possibility of interactions between heredity and environment. Several studies have found that violence is particularly enhanced in people with both a genetic predisposition *and* a troubled early environment (Cadoret, Yates, Troughton, Woodworth, & Stewart, 1995; Caspi et al., 2002; Widom & Brzustowicz, 2006). Figure 12.9 illustrates the results of one study, in which investigators compared people who had genetic differences in production of the enzyme *monoamine oxidase A* (MAO_A). This enzyme breaks down the neurotransmitters dopamine, norepinephrine, and serotonin, thus lowering the available amounts. Researchers find little difference in aggressive or other antisocial behavior, on the average, between people with high or low amounts of MAO_A. However, the effects of this gene apparently interact with childhood experience. As the figure shows, the rate of antisocial behavior was low among people who were treated well in childhood, regardless of their MAO_A levels. In those who endured a small amount of mistreatment in childhood, the rate of antisocial behavior was increased, but again, their MAO_A levels did not make much difference. However, among those who were seriously maltreated in childhood, the rate of antisocial behavior was significantly higher for those with low MAO_A activity (Caspi et al., 2002). This result is fascinating because of its apparent demonstration of an interaction between genetics and environment, although not all other investigators have replicated this finding (Prichard, Mackinnon, Jorm, & Easteal, 2008). The interaction between MAO_A levels and childhood maltreatment may depend on other circumstances that researchers have not yet identified. In any case, from a theoretical standpoint, it is not clear why decreased MAO_A should be linked to increased aggression.

STOP & CHECK

6. What relationship did Caspi et al. (2002) report between the enzyme MAO_A and antisocial behavior?

ANSWER

6. Overall, people with genes for high or low production of MAO_A do not differ significantly in their probability of antisocial behavior. However, among those who suffered serious maltreatment during childhood, people with lower levels of the enzyme showed higher rates of antisocial behavior.

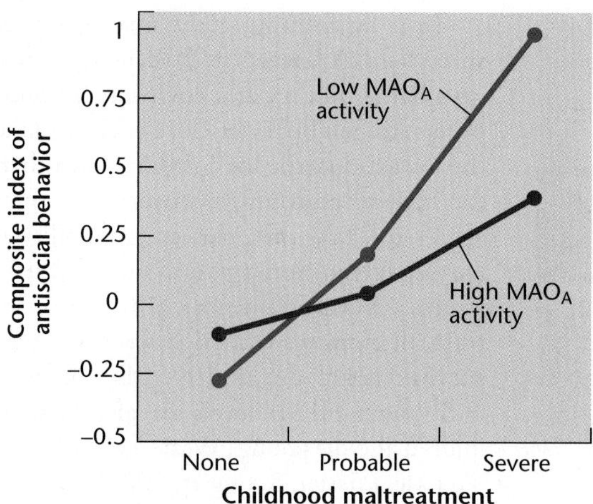

Figure 12.9 Genes, environment, and antisocial behavior in men
The *y* axis represents a complex score combining several types of measurement. The key point is that higher scores indicate more aggressive behaviors. *(From "Role of genotype in the cycle of violence in maltreated children," from Caspi, A., et al.,* Science, 297, *851–854. © 2002 AAAS.)*

Hormones

Most fighting throughout the animal kingdom is by males competing for mates or females defending their young. Male aggressive behavior depends heavily on testosterone, which is highest for adult males in the reproductive season.

Similarly, throughout the world, men fight more often than women, get arrested for violent crimes more often, shout insults at each other more often, and so forth. Moreover, young adult men, who have the highest testosterone levels, also have the highest rate of aggressive behaviors and violent crimes. Women commit violent acts also, but they are usually more minor attacks (Archer, 2000).

Do the men with higher testosterone levels also commit more violent behavior? Yes, if we take the average over enough men, although the effects are usually smaller than most people expect (Archer, Birring, & Wu, 1998; Archer, Graham-Kevan, & Davies, 2005). Figure 12.10 shows one set of results. Note that high testosterone levels were more common among men imprisoned for rape or murder than among those imprisoned for nonviolent crimes. Note also that the differences are not huge. They are also hard to interpret because environmental stressors could affect hormone levels and violent behavior independently.

Testosterone exerts its effects partly by modifying the way people react to various stimuli. In one study, instead of comparing men who had different testosterone levels (and who might differ in other ways also), researchers manipulated testosterone levels by giving testosterone injections to young women, temporarily raising their levels to those typical of men. The women's task was to examine photos of faces and try to identify the emotion, among six choices: anger, disgust, fear, happiness, sadness, and surprise. The photos were morphed from 0% (neutral expression) to 100% expression of an emotion. Figure 12.11 shows the example for anger.

The result was that after women received testosterone, most became less accurate at recognizing facial expressions of anger (van Honk & Schutter, 2007). Meanwhile, other research shows that testosterone *increases* responses of the amygdala to photos showing angry expressions (Hermans, Ramsey, & van Honk, 2008). Evidently, testosterone affects different brain areas differently, increasing the responses of emotion-related areas, while decreasing the ability of the cerebral cortex to identify the emotion consciously. We can speculate that the result could be increased emotional arousal and decreased ability to regulate that emotion deliberately.

STOP & CHECK

7. How does testosterone influence emotional and cognitive responses to a facial expression of anger?

ANSWER

7. It decreases ability to recognize the expression consciously but increases the responses in emotion-related areas of the brain.

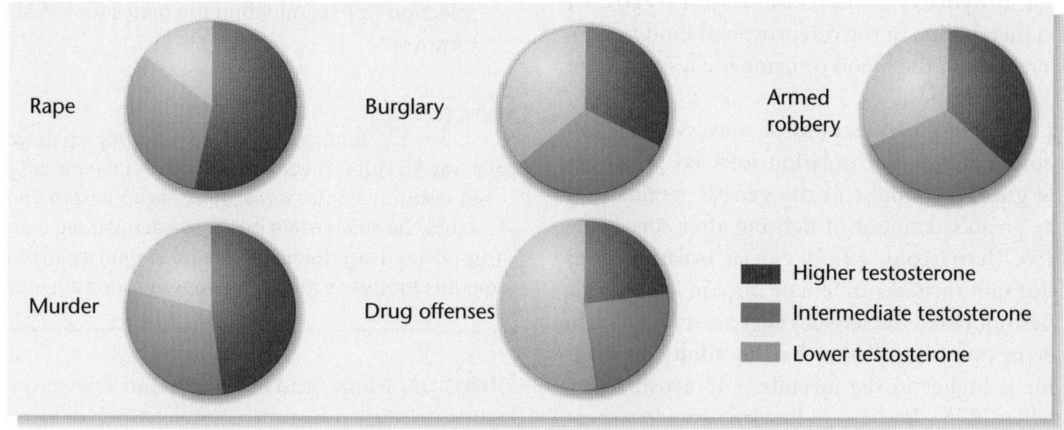

Figure 12.10 Testosterone levels for men convicted of various crimes
Men convicted of rape and murder have higher testosterone levels, on the average, than men convicted of burglary or drug offenses. *(Based on Dabbs, Carr, Frady, & Riad, 1995)*

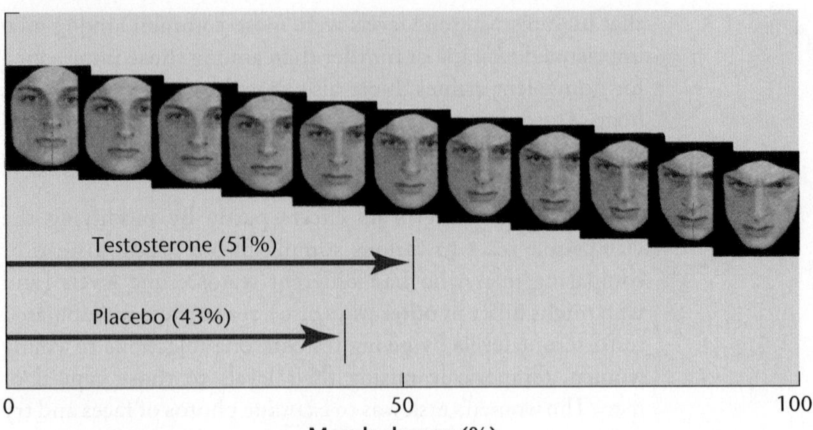

Figure 12.11 Stimuli to measure people's ability to identify emotion
For each of six emotions, researchers prepared views ranging from 0% to 100% expression of the emotion. In this case, the emotion is anger. Women identified the expression more quickly, on the average, after a placebo injection than after a testosterone injection. *(From van Honk, J., & Schutter, D. J. L. G. (2007), "Testosterone reduces conscious detection of signals serving social correction,"* Psychological Science, *18, 663–667. Used by permission of Blackwell Publishing.)*

Serotonin Synapses and Aggressive Behavior

Several lines of evidence link aggressive behavior to low serotonin release. We first examine some of this evidence and then consider the complexity of serotonin's role in aggression.

Nonhuman Animals. Much of the earliest evidence came from studies on mice. Luigi Valzelli (1973) found that isolating male mice for 4 weeks increased their aggressive behavior and decreased their serotonin *turnover*. When neurons release a neurotransmitter such as serotonin, they reabsorb most of it and synthesize enough to replace the amount that washed away. Thus, the amount present in neurons remains fairly constant, and if we examine that amount, we have little idea how much the neurons have been releasing. However, if we measure the serotonin metabolites in body fluids, we gauge the **turnover,** which is the amount that neurons released and replaced. Researchers estimate serotonin turnover from the concentration of **5-hydroxyindoleacetic acid (5-HIAA),** serotonin's main metabolite, in the cerebrospinal fluid (CSF). Measuring the amount in the blood or urine is a less accurate alternative.

Comparing different genetic strains of mice, Valzelli and his colleagues found that social isolation lowered serotonin turnover by the greatest amount in the genetic strains that reacted with the greatest amount of fighting after social isolation (Valzelli & Bernasconi, 1979). Social isolation does not decrease serotonin turnover in female mice in any genetic strain, and it does not make the females aggressive. Serotonin activity is lower in juvenile rodents than in adults, and aggressive behavior is higher in the juveniles (Taravosh-Lahn, Bastida, & Delville, 2006). Perhaps in humans, too, low serotonin activity may be a reason for increased aggressiveness in adolescent males.

In a fascinating study, investigators measured 5-HIAA levels in 2-year-old male monkeys living in a natural environment and then observed their behavior closely. The monkeys in the lowest quartile for 5-HIAA, and therefore the lowest serotonin turnover, were the most aggressive, had the greatest probability of attacking larger monkeys, and incurred the most injuries. Most of them died by age 6. In contrast, all monkeys with high serotonin turnover survived (Higley et al., 1996). Female monkeys with low 5-HIAA levels are also likely to get injured and die young (Westergaard, Cleveland, Trenkle, Lussier, & Higley, 2003).

If most monkeys with low turnover die young, why hasn't natural selection eliminated the genes for low serotonin turnover? One possibility is that evolution selects for an intermediate amount of aggression and anxiety (Trefilov, Berard, Krawczak, & Schmidtke, 2000). The most fearless animals get into fights and die young, but those with excessive fears have other problems. We could say the same about humans: People with too little fear take excessive risks—wrestling alligators, bungee jumping with a frayed cord, things like that. Those with too much fear are withdrawn and unlikely to succeed (Nettle, 2006).

We can also see aggressiveness as a high-risk, high-payoff strategy: A monkey with low 5-HIAA starts many fights and probably dies young. However, a monkey who wins enough of those fights survives and achieves a dominant status within the group (Howell et al., 2007). Under some circumstances, risking death to achieve a dominant status might be a reasonable gamble.

STOP & CHECK

8. If we want to know how much serotonin the brain has been releasing, what should we measure?

9. Given that monkeys with low serotonin turnover pick many fights and in most cases die young, what keeps natural selection from eliminating the genes for low serotonin turnover?

ANSWERS

8. We can measure the concentration of 5-HIAA, a serotonin metabolite, in the cerebrospinal fluid or other body fluids. The more 5-HIAA, the more serotonin has been released and presumably resynthesized. **9.** Although most monkeys with low serotonin turnover die young, many of the survivors achieve a dominant status that enables them to get more of the food and to reproduce more frequently.

Humans. Many studies have found low serotonin turnover in people with a history of violent behavior, including people convicted of arson and other violent crimes (Virkkunen, Nuutila, Goodwin, & Linnoila, 1987) and people who at-

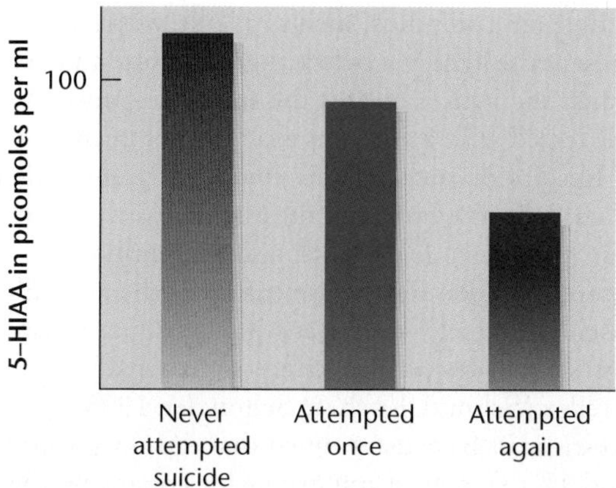

Figure 12.12 Levels of 5-HIAA in the CSF of depressed people Measurements for the two suicide-attempting groups were taken after the first attempt. Low levels of 5-HIAA indicate low serotonin turnover. *(Based on results of Roy, DeJong, & Linnoila, 1989)*

tempt suicide by violent means, as illustrated in Figure 12.12 (G. L. Brown et al., 1982; Edman, Åsberg, Levander, & Schalling, 1986; Mann, Arango, & Underwood, 1990; Pandey et al., 1995; Roy, DeJong, & Linnoila, 1989; Sher et al., 2006; Spreux-Varoquaux et al., 2001). Follow-up studies on people released from prison have found that those with lower serotonin turnover had a greater probability of further convictions for violent crimes (Virkkunen, DeJong, Bartko, Goodwin, & Linnoila, 1989; Virkkunen, Eggert, Rawlings, & Linnoila, 1996). However, although each of these relationships is statistically reliable, the effects are not sufficiently powerful that we could use blood tests to make important decisions about individuals, such as which prisoners should be eligible for parole.

It is possible to alter serotonin synthesis by changes in diet. Neurons synthesize serotonin from tryptophan, an amino acid found in small amounts in proteins. Tryptophan crosses the blood-brain barrier by an active transport channel that it shares with phenylalanine and other large amino acids. Thus, a diet high in other amino acids impairs the brain's ability to synthesize serotonin. One study found that many young men on such a diet showed an increase in aggressive behavior a few hours after eating (Moeller et al., 1996). Under the circumstances, it would seem prudent for anyone with aggressive or suicidal tendencies to reduce consumption of aspartame (NutraSweet), which is 50% phenylalanine, and maize (American corn), which is high in phenylalanine and low in tryptophan (Lytle, Messing, Fisher, & Phebus, 1975).

Much of the variation in serotonin activity, and therefore violence, relates to genetics. People vary in the gene that controls *tryptophan hydroxylase*, the enzyme that converts tryptophan into serotonin. People with less active forms of this enzyme are more likely than average to report frequent anger and aggression (Hennig, Reuter, Netter, Burk, & Landt, 2005; Rujescu et al., 2002) and more likely to make violent suicide attempts (Abbar et al., 2001).

These results showing a consistent relationship between low serotonin and increased violence seem to suggest the simple idea that serotonin decreases violence. However, the story is more complicated: The brain releases serotonin during aggressive behavior (van der Vegt et al., 2003). Apparently, a low level of serotonin activity prior to aggravation magnifies the response when serotonin is suddenly released at the start of an aggressive encounter (Nelson & Trainor, 2007).

Furthermore, clinical depression is linked to low serotonin activity, but most people with depression are not violent. If some treatment suddenly lowered your serotonin level, would you at once become violent, depressed, or what? When researchers use drugs or diet to suppress serotonin levels, some people feel depressed, others become more aggressive or impulsive, and those with previous drug problems report a craving for drugs (Kaplan, Muldoon, Manuck, & Mann, 1997; Van der Does, 2001; S. N. Young & Leyton, 2002). In short, serotonin's role is not specific to aggression. A better hypothesis is that high levels of serotonin inhibit a variety of impulses.

STOP & CHECK

10. What change in diet can alter the production of serotonin?

ANSWER

10. To raise production of serotonin, increase consumption of tryptophan or decrease consumption of proteins high in phenylalanine and other large amino acids that compete with tryptophan for entry to the brain.

Escape, Fear, and Anxiety

Chapter 3 discussed the nucleus accumbens, a brain area important for reinforcement. Within that area, cells toward one end are more important for approach responses, and cells toward the other end are tuned for avoidance. When rats are in a quiet, dark, familiar (safe) place, the border between the "approach" and "avoid" areas shifts so that most of the cells respond to stimuli for approach. To make rats feel as threatened as possible, without actually harming them, researchers put them in cages with bright lights and unpredictable loud bursts of punk-rock music (!). In that environment, the border shifted in the opposite direction, and most of the nucleus accumbens cells signaled avoidance (Reynolds & Berridge, 2008). That is, proneness to approach, avoidance, and anxiety varies with the situation.

Anxiety also varies among individuals for genetic reasons (Chen et al., 2006; Weisstaub et al., 2006). The amygdala is one of the main areas for integrating both environmental and genetic influences and then regulating the current level of anxiety.

Fear, Anxiety, and the Amygdala

Do we have any built-in, unlearned fears? Yes, at least one: Even newborns are frightened by loud noises. The response to an unexpected loud noise, known as the **startle reflex,** is extremely fast: Auditory information goes first to the cochlear nucleus in the medulla and from there directly to an area in the pons that commands the tensing of the muscles, especially the neck muscles. Tensing the neck muscles is important because the neck is so vulnerable to injury. (Chapter 5 discussed how woodpeckers protect their necks while pecking a tree.) Information reaches the pons within 3 to 8 ms after a loud noise, and the full startle reflex occurs in less than two tenths of a second (Yeomans & Frankland, 1996).

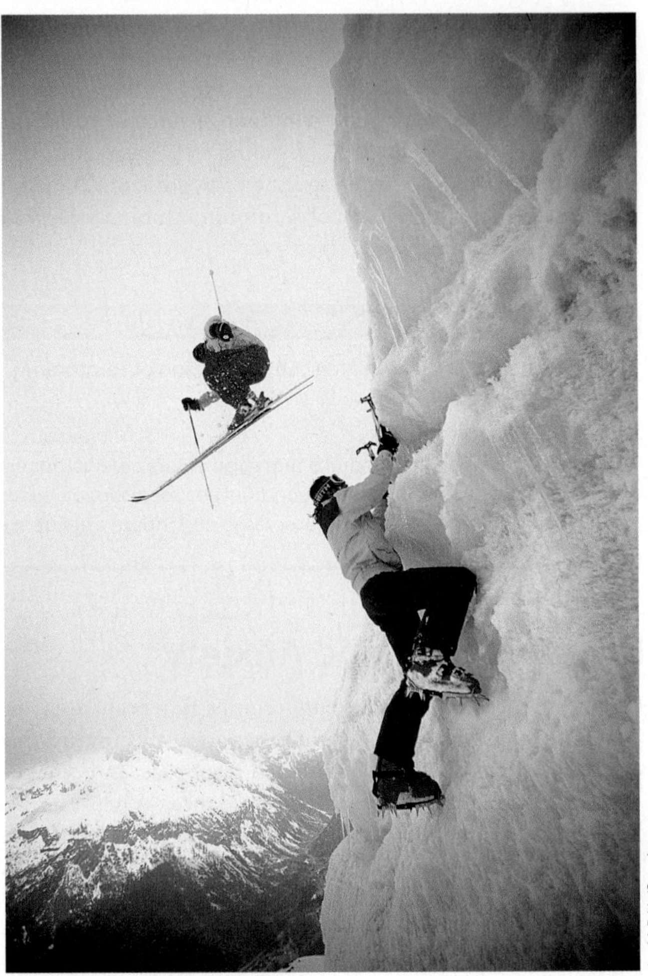
Joe McBride/Getty Images

People's choices of activities depend in part on how easily they develop anxiety.

Although you don't learn your fear of loud noises, your current mood or situation modifies your reaction. Your startle reflex is more vigorous if you are already tense. People with posttraumatic stress disorder, who are certainly known for their intense anxiety, show a much enhanced startle reflex (Grillon, Morgan, Davis, & Southwick, 1998).

Studies of Rodents

Psychologists measure variations in the startle reflex as a gauge of fear or anxiety. In research with nonhumans, psychologists first measure the normal response to a loud noise. Then they repeatedly pair a stimulus, such as a light, with shock. Finally, they present the light just before the loud noise and determine how much the light increases the startle response. A control group is tested with a stimulus that has not been paired with shock. Results of such studies consistently show that after animals have learned to associate a stimulus with shock, that stimulus becomes a fear signal, and presenting the stimulus just before a sudden loud noise enhances the animal's startle response. Conversely, a stimulus previously associated with pleasant stimuli becomes a safety signal that decreases the startle reflex (Schmid, Koch, & Schnitzler, 1995).

Investigators have determined that the amygdala (Figures 12.7 and 12.13) is most important for enhancing the startle reflex. Many cells in the amygdala, especially in the basolateral and central nuclei, get input from pain fibers as well as vision or hearing, so the circuitry is well suited to establishing conditioned fears (Uwano, Nishijo, Ono, & Tamura, 1995). Some cells in the amygdala respond strongly to rewards, others to punishments, and still others to surprises in either direction (Belova, Paton, Morrison, & Salzman, 2007).

Output from the amygdala to the hypothalamus controls autonomic fear responses, such as increased blood pressure. The amygdala also has axons to areas of the prefrontal cortex that control approach and avoidance responses (Garcia, Vouimba, Baudry, & Thompson, 1999; Lacroix, Spinelli, Heidbreder, & Feldon, 2000). Additional axons extend to areas in the midbrain that relay information to the pons to control the startle reflex (LeDoux, Iwata, Cicchetti, & Reis, 1988; Zhao & Davis, 2004). Figure 12.13 shows the connections.

Although a rat with damage to the amygdala still shows a normal startle reflex, signals before the loud noise do not modify the reflex. In one study, rats were repeatedly exposed to a light followed by shock and then tested for their responses to a loud noise. Intact rats showed a moderate startle reflex to the loud noise and an enhanced response if the light preceded the noise. In contrast, rats with damage in the path from the amygdala to the hindbrain showed the same startle reflex with or without the light (Hitchcock & Davis, 1991). Damage to the amygdala interferes with the learning of fear responses more than the retention of fear responses learned previously (Antoniadis, Winslow, Davis, & Amaral, 2007; Wilensky, Schafe, Kristensen, & LeDoux, 2006).

Do these results indicate that amygdala damage destroys fear? No. An alternative explanation is that the rats have trouble interpreting or understanding stimuli with emotional consequences. The same issue arises with humans, as we shall see.

An odd parasite has evolved a way to exploit the consequences of amygdala damage (Berdoy, Webster, & Macdonald, 2000). *Toxoplasma gondii* is a protozoan that infects many mammals but reproduces only in cats. Cats excrete the parasite's eggs in their feces, thereby releasing them into the ground. Rats that burrow in the ground can become infected with the parasite. When the parasite enters a rat, it migrates to the brain where it apparently damages the amygdala. The rat then fearlessly approaches a cat, guaranteeing that the cat will eat the rat and that the parasite will find its way back into a cat!

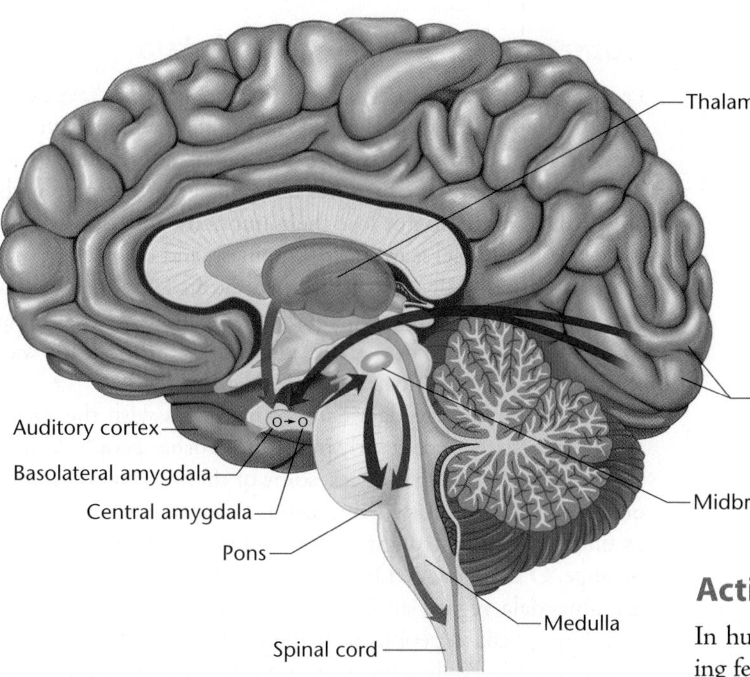

Figure 12.13 Amygdala and connections relevant to learned fears
Cells in the lateral and basolateral parts of the amygdala receive visual and auditory information and then send messages to the central amygdala, which then sends its output to the central gray area of the midbrain, which relays the information to a nucleus in the pons responsible for the startle reflex. Damage at any point along the route from amygdala to pons interferes with learned fears, although only damage to the pons would block the startle reflex itself.

STOP & CHECK

11. What brain mechanism enables the startle reflex to be so fast?

12. How could a researcher use the startle reflex to determine whether some stimulus causes fear?

ANSWERS

11. Loud noises activate a path from the cochlea to cells in the pons that directly trigger a tensing of neck muscles. **12.** Present the stimulus before giving a loud noise. If the stimulus increases the startle reflex beyond its usual level, then the stimulus produced fear.

Studies of Monkeys

The effect of amygdala damage in monkeys was described in classic studies early in the 1900s and is known as the *Klüver-Bucy syndrome,* from the names of the primary investigators. Monkeys showing this syndrome are tame and placid. They attempt to pick up lighted matches and other objects that they ordinarily avoid. They display less than the normal fear of snakes or of larger, more dominant monkeys (Kalin, Shelton, Davidson, & Kelley, 2001).

However, not all monkeys with amygdala damage react with the full Klüver-Bucy syndrome. The most prominent effect is an alteration of monkeys' social behaviors, although the exact results vary depending on the age of the monkeys, the social situation, and the exact location of the damage. Some monkeys with damage to the amygdala are withdrawn and fearful, but others are friendly and fearless (Bauman, Toscano, Mason, Lavenex, & Amaral, 2006; Emery et al., 2001; Kalin, Shelton, & Davidson, 2004; Machado et al., 2008; Rosvold, Mirsky, & Pribram, 1954). Friendliness and fearlessness are closely related. Most monkeys, like most humans, are shy about approaching unfamiliar individuals. A fearless monkey has no such inhibitions.

Activation of the Human Amygdala

In humans as in other species, the amygdala is activated during fear conditioning, where people learn that a signal predicts shock (Cheng, Knight, Smith, & Helmstetter, 2006). It is also activated when people look at photos of frightening stimuli or people who are expressing fear. The amygdala's responses are not limited to fear, however. For example, in one study, participants read names of famous people under varying instructions. Sometimes, they were to evaluate how good each person was; at other times, they evaluated how bad. Regardless of instructions, names of widely disliked people, like Adolf Hitler, consistently stimulated the amygdala. Names of highly admired people, such as Mother Teresa, also activated the amygdala if people were instructed to rate how good each person was (Cunningham, Van Bavel & Johnsen, 2008). That is, attention to any type of emotion heightens the amygdala's responses to the relevant stimuli.

Ordinarily, people experience strong emotions when they see other people expressing emotions, especially anger and fear, and the amygdala responds strongly as well. Your experienced emotion depends on where the other person appears to be gazing. An angry face directed at you is threatening, whereas a fearful face directed toward you is usually puzzling. ("Why would someone look at me with fear? I'm not scary.") In contrast, an angry face directed to the side is less upsetting. ("That person is angry with someone else.") A fearful face directed to the side is more upsetting. ("Something over there is dangerous! I need to find out what, and why!") Consequently, you ordinarily recognize an angry expression faster if it is directed toward you and a fearful expression faster if it is directed to the side (Adams & Kleck, 2005).

The response of the amygdala to angry and fearful expressions also depends on gaze direction but not in the simple way we might guess. For angry expressions, one study found greater amygdala response to faces directed toward the viewer (Sato, Yoshikawa, Kochiyama, & Matsumura, 2004), and another study found greater response to faces directed to the side (Adams, Gordon, Baird, Ambady, & Kleck, 2003). The one study that compared gaze directions for fearful expressions

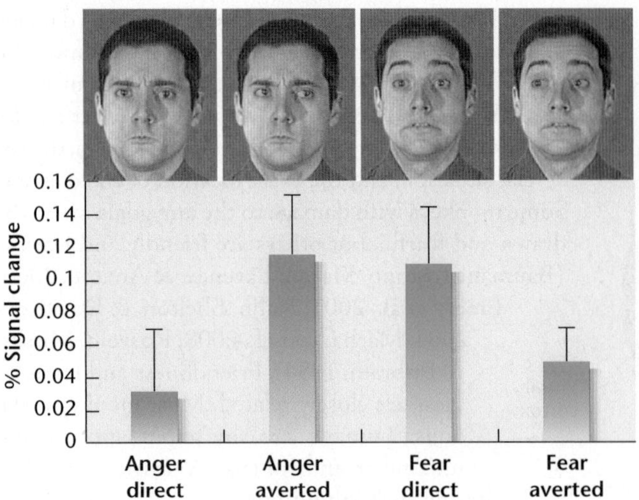

Figure 12.14 Amygdala response and direction of gaze People respond more strongly to an angry face directed toward the viewer and to a frightened face directed toward something else. The amygdala shows the reverse, because it works harder to interpret ambiguous stimuli. *(From "Effects of gaze on amygdala sensitivity to anger and fear faces," by R. B. Adams et al.,* Science *2003, 300:1536. Reprinted with permission from AAAS/Science Magazine.)*

found greater amygdala response for faces directed toward the viewer (Adams et al., 2003) (Figure 12.14). That is, a fearful face directed toward the viewer is *less* emotionally arousing, but it stimulates the amygdala more strongly. The researchers suggested that the amygdala responds strongly when the emotional interpretation is not obvious—when emotional processing is somewhat difficult.

The amygdala responds even to emotional stimuli that people do not identify consciously. For example, if an angry or frightened face is flashed on a screen briefly, while the person is attending to something else, the person may not detect it. The amygdala nevertheless responds and stimulates sweating and other autonomic responses (Kubota et al., 2000; Vuilleumier, Armony, Driver, & Dolan, 2001). (Recall the earlier discussion about "gut feelings." Sometimes, the body reacts emotionally when we do not consciously understand why.) Flashing similar pictures does not affect the autonomic responses of people with damage to the amygdala (Gläscher & Adolphs, 2003).

Further evidence that the amygdala can react to emotional information without conscious identification comes from studies of cortical blindness. One patient lost all conscious vision after strokes damaged his visual cortex in both hemispheres. Although he could not detect the presence of light, colors, or other visual information, when a face was displayed on a screen, he could guess whether it was happy or sad, or happy or fearful, with about 60% accuracy. Looking at emotional expressions activated his right amygdala and no cortical areas (Pegna, Khateb, Lazeyrus, & Seghier, 2004).

Damage to the Human Amygdala

People with the rare genetic disorder *Urbach-Wiethe disease* suffer skin lesions; many of them also accumulate calcium in the amygdala until it wastes away. Other people incur damage to the amygdala because of strokes or brain surgery. People with amygdala damage do not lose their emotions; they report that they continue to feel fear, anger, happiness, and other emotions more or less normally as a result of life events (A. K. Anderson & Phelps, 2002). However, they are impaired at processing emotional information when the signals are subtle or in any way ambiguous (Baxter & Murray, 2002; Whalen, 1998).

For example, amygdala damage interferes with the social judgments that we constantly make about other people. When we look at other people's faces, some of them strike us, rightly or wrongly, as "untrustworthy," and looking at a face we regard as untrustworthy strongly activates the amygdala (Winston, Strange, O'Doherty, & Dolan, 2002). People with damage to the amygdala regard all faces as about equally trustworthy, and they approach people for help indiscriminately, instead of trying to find people who seem friendly (Adolphs, Tranel, & Damasio, 1998).

People with amygdala damage also fail to focus their attention on emotional stimuli the way other people do. For example, when most people with an intact brain look at a picture of something highly emotional, such as one person attacking another, they remember the emotional part and forget most of the background details (Adolphs, Denburg, & Tranel, 2001). When they hear a highly emotional story, such as one about children who died in a plane crash, they remember the emotional gist and forget the details. When they see a series of words flashed briefly on the screen under distracting conditions, they notice more of the emotionally charged words like *kill* than unemotional words like *pear*. In all these regards, people with amygdala damage are different. They remember the irrelevant details of a story as much as the emotional part (Adolphs, Tranel, & Buchanan, 2005), and they notice a flashed word like *pear* about as much as one like *kill* (A. K. Anderson & Phelps, 2001).

Such people also often fail to recognize the emotions that people in photographs express, especially when they express fear or disgust (Boucsein, Weniger, Mursch, Steinhoff, & Irle, 2001). They also have some trouble recognizing anger, surprise, arrogance, guilt, admiration, and flirtation (Adolphs, Baron-Cohen, & Tranel, 2002; Adolphs, Tranel, Damasio, & Damasio, 1994). When one woman was asked to rate the apparent intensity of emotional expressions, she rated the intensity in the frightened, angry, or surprised faces much lower than any other observer did. Finally, when she was asked to draw faces showing certain emotions (Figure 12.15), she made good drawings of most expressions but had trouble drawing a fearful expression, saying that she did not know what such a face would look like. When the researcher urged her to try, she drew someone crawling away with hair on end, as cartoonists often indicate fear (Adolphs, Tranel, Damasio, & Damasio, 1995).

Why do people with amygdala damage fail to identify fearful expressions in photographs? They are not incapable of rec-

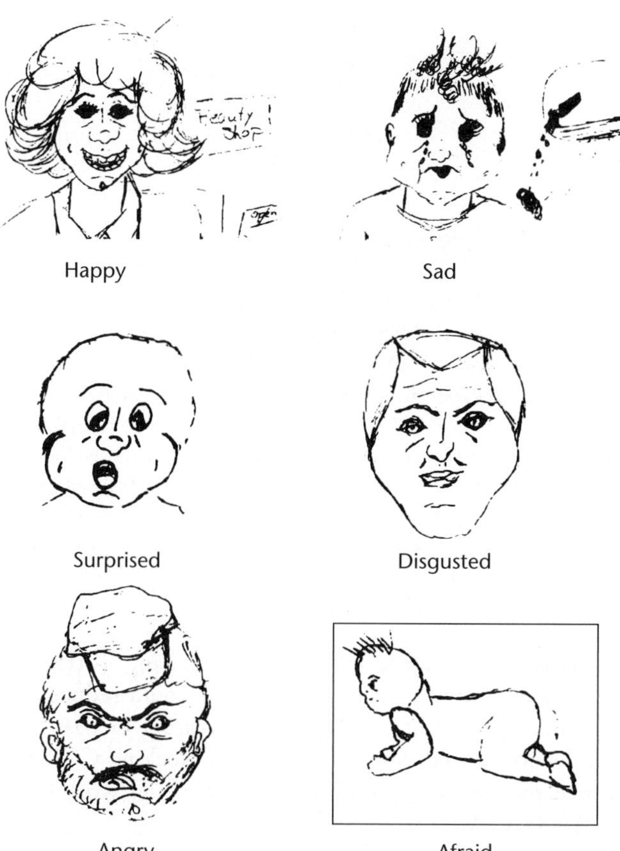

Figure 12.15 Drawings by a woman with a damaged amygdala
Note that her drawings of emotional expressions are fairly realistic and convincing except for fear. She at first declined to draw a fearful expression because, she said, she could not imagine it. When urged to try, she used the fact that frightened people try to escape, and she remembered that frightened people are often depicted with their hair on end, at least in cartoons. *(From "Fear and the human amygdala," by R. Adolphs, D. Tranel, H. Damasio, and A. Damasio,* Journal of Neuroscience, *15, pp. 5879–5891. Copyright © 1995 Oxford University Press. Reprinted by permission.)*

ognizing fear. Ralph Adolphs and his colleagues observed that a woman with amygdala damage focused almost entirely on the nose and mouth of each photograph. Also in everyday life, she almost never made eye contact, looking at the mouth instead (Spezio, Huang, Castelli, & Adolphs, 2007). When they asked her to look at the eyes, she easily recognized fearful expressions (Adolphs et al., 2005). Focusing on the nose and mouth impairs fear recognition much more than that of other emotions. People express happiness mainly with the mouth, but fear almost entirely with the eyes (Morris, deBonis, & Dolan, 2002; Vuilleumier, 2005). Examine Figure 12.16, which shows only the whites of the eyes of people who were expressing two emotions. Most people react to the face on the left as showing fear (Whalen et al., 2004). A happy expression depends on the mouth, and people cannot recognize happiness from the eyes alone.

Might differences in the amygdala relate to differences in personality and anxiety disorders? Most people's tendency toward anxiety generally remains fairly consistent over years and decades. Most infants with an "inhibited" temperament

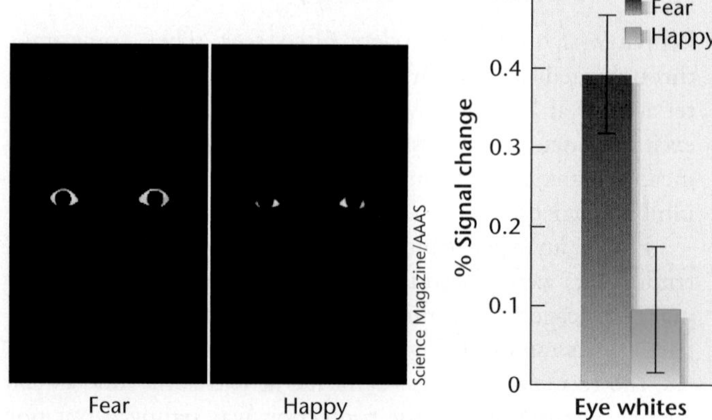

Figure 12.16 Eye whites for two facial expressions
The eye whites alone enable most people to guess that the person on the left was feeling afraid. Eye whites do not enable us to identify happiness (right). The amygdala responds more strongly to the fearful eye whites than to happy eye whites. *(From "Human amygdala responsivity to mask fearful eye whites," by P. J. Whalen et al.,* Science, *2004, 306:2061. Reprinted with permission from AAAS/Science Magazine.)*

develop into shy, fearful children and then into adults who show an enhanced amygdala response to the sight of any unfamiliar face (Schwartz, Wright, Shin, Kagan, & Rauch, 2003). Arousal of the amygdala, and therefore the tendency to experience strong negative emotions, relates strongly to genes that regulate serotonin reuptake in the amygdala (Hariri et al., 2002; Rhodes et al., 2007). In short, genetic variations in amygdala arousal probably underlie some of the variation in anxiety and its disorders.

Ralph Adolphs

Will a better understanding of the social brain lead to a better understanding of social behavior? And can such knowledge ultimately be used to help our species negotiate and survive in the vastly complex social world it has helped create? To approach such questions, social neuroscientists will need to establish dialogues with other disciplines in the social and behavioral sciences, and to be highly sensitive to the public consequences of the data they generate.

STOP & CHECK

13. Why do people with amygdala damage have trouble recognizing expressions of fear?

ANSWER

13. They focus their vision on the nose and mouth. Expressions of fear depend almost entirely on the eyes.

Anxiety-Reducing Drugs

People with excessive anxiety often seek relief, sometimes through medications. Drugs intended to control anxiety alter activity at amygdala synapses. One of the amygdala's main excitatory neuromodulators is CCK (cholecystokinin), which increases anxiety. The main inhibitory transmitter, GABA, inhibits anxiety.

Here is an experiment showing the role of CCK: Male "intruder" rats were placed in a protected area within a resident male rat's cage for 30 minutes, at which point the protective barrier was removed (Figure 12.17). For some of the intruders, the resident male was removed at the same time as the barrier. For the others, the protection was removed but not the resident. The resident always attacked and defeated the intruder. (The "home field advantage" is enormous for rats.) After four repetitions of this experience, the researchers implanted a cannula into the intruder male's brain and used microdialysis (see Methods 12.1) to measure brain chemistry. The result was that an intruder male that had been defeated four times by the resident male showed clear signs of anxiety when again placed into that male's cage (motionlessness, defensive postures, and squeals); his prefrontal cortex showed an enormous increase in release of CCK. However, if he was given a drug that blocked his CCK type B receptors, he showed no anxiety, even when placed in the dangerous cage (C. Becker et al., 2001).

Injections of CCK-stimulating drugs into the amygdala enhance the startle reflex (Frankland, Josselyn, Bradwejn, Vaccarino, & Yeomans, 1997), and drugs that block GABA type B receptors can induce an outright panic (Strzelczuk & Romaniuk, 1996). In principle, drugs could reduce anxiety either by blocking CCK or by increasing GABA activity. However, so far, no drugs based on blocking CCK have reached the market, and all the available drugs work by enhancing GABA.

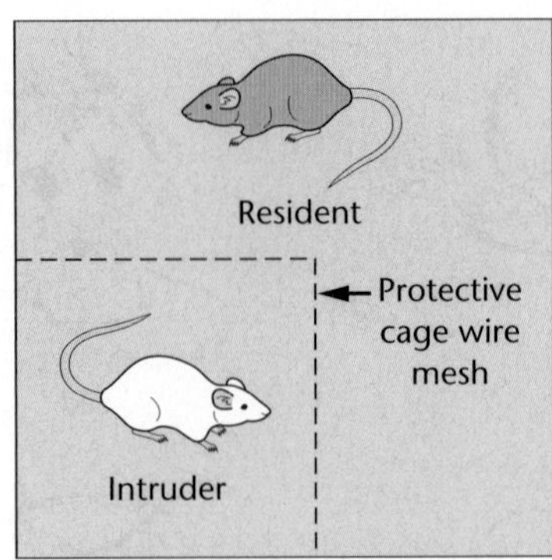

Figure 12.17 Procedure for giving male rats anxiety
Male rats were placed in a cage, protected from the resident male. Later, the protection was removed. For some, the resident male was removed at the same time, so the intruder was safe. For others, the protection was removed but the resident male was left to attack the intruder. Those who were attacked (and inevitably defeated) developed great anxiety when again placed in the same location.

Benzodiazepines. The most commonly used anti-anxiety drugs are the **benzodiazepines** (BEN-zo-die-AZ-uh-peens), such as diazepam (trade name Valium), chlordiazepoxide

METHODS 12.1

Microdialysis

In microdialysis, an investigator implants into the brain a double fluid-filled tube with a thin membrane tip across which chemicals can diffuse. The experimenter slowly delivers some fluid through one tube, while an equal amount of fluid exits through the other tube and brings with it some of the brain chemicals that have diffused across the membrane. In this manner, researchers discover which neurotransmitters are released during particular behaviors (e.g., Stanley, Schwartz, Hernandez, & Hoebel, 1989). This procedure is used with laboratory animals, not humans. *(Reprinted with permission from Dr. Juan Dominguez.)*

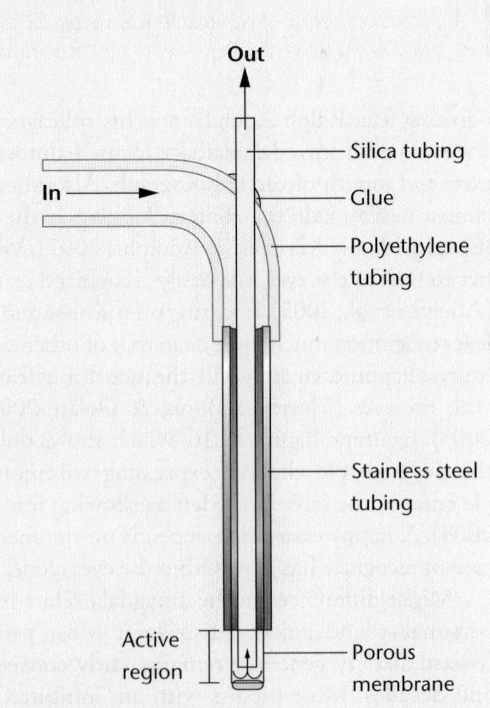

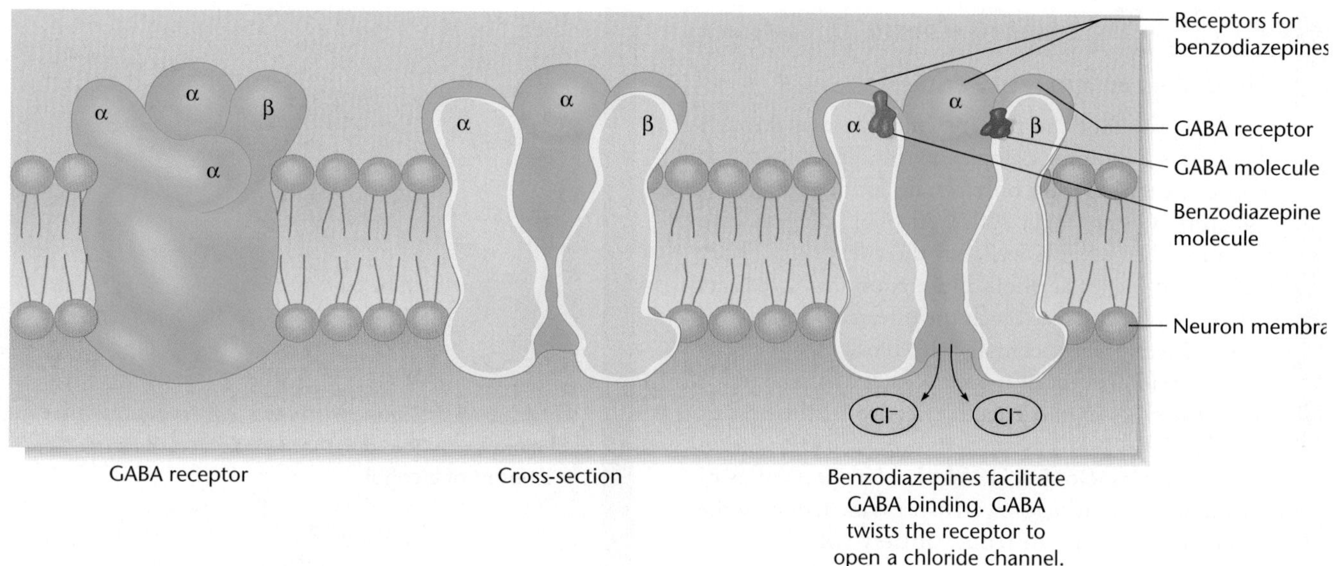

Figure 12.18 The GABA$_A$ receptor complex
Of its four receptor sites sensitive to GABA, the three α sites are also sensitive to benzodiazepines. *(Based on Guidotti, Ferrero, Fujimoto, Santi, & Costa, 1986)*

(Librium), and alprazolam (Xanax). Benzodiazepines bind to the **GABA$_A$ receptor,** which includes a site that binds GABA as well as sites that modify the sensitivity of the GABA site (Figure 12.18). (The brain also has other kinds of GABA receptors, such as GABA$_B$, with different behavioral effects.)

At the center of the GABA$_A$ receptor is a chloride channel. When open, it permits chloride ions (Cl^-) to cross the membrane into the neuron, hyperpolarizing the cell. (That is, the synapse is inhibitory.) Surrounding the chloride channel are four units, each containing one or more sites sensitive to GABA. Benzodiazepines bind to additional sites on three of those four units (labeled α in Figure 12.18). When a benzodiazepine molecule attaches, it neither opens nor closes the chloride channel but twists the receptor so that the GABA binds more easily (Macdonald, Weddle, & Gross, 1986). Benzodiazepines thus facilitate the effects of GABA.

Benzodiazepines exert their anti-anxiety effects in the amygdala, hypothalamus, midbrain, and several other areas. A minute amount of benzodiazepines injected directly to a rat's amygdala decreases learned shock-avoidance behaviors (Pesold & Treit, 1995), relaxes the muscles, and increases social approaches to other rats (S. K. Sanders & Shekhar, 1995). Benzodiazepines also decrease the responses in a rat's brain to the smell of a cat. Ordinarily, that smell triggers an apparently built-in fear (McGregor, Hargreaves, Apfelbach, & Hunt, 2004).

Given that benzodiazepines decrease anxiety, we should expect a strong effect on the startle reflex. Research results vary on whether the drugs decrease the startle reflex. However, the results are more consistent that benzodiazepines suppress influences that would otherwise increase the startle reflex. For example, ordinarily, the startle reflex is enhanced in the presence of a signal previously paired with shock. Benzodiazepines decrease that effect (Gifkins, Greba, & Kokkinidis, 2002).

Benzodiazepines produce a variety of additional effects. When they reach the thalamus and cerebral cortex, they induce sleepiness, block epileptic convulsions, and impair memory (Rudolph et al., 1999). The mixture of effects is a problem. For example, you might want to reduce your anxiety without becoming sleepy, and presumably, you don't want to impair your memory. Researchers hope to develop drugs with more specific and limited effects (Korpi & Sinkkonen, 2006).

The brain produces chemicals that bind to the same sites as benzodiazepines. One such chemical is the protein **diazepam-binding inhibitor (DBI),** which blocks the behavioral effects of diazepam and other benzodiazepines (Guidotti et al., 1983). This and several related proteins are also known as **endozepines,** a contraction of "*endo*genous benzodia*zepine*," although their effects are actually the opposite to those of benzodiazepines. So really, an endozepine is an endogenous *anti*-benzodiazepine. Preliminary results suggest that variations in genes controlling endozepines may relate to people's probability of developing panic disorder and other anxiety disorders (Thoeringer et al., 2007).

Endozepines are an odd kind of neuromodulator. Glia cells release them, and neurons do not (Patte et al., 1999). Why do our brains secrete endozepines and thereby increase our level of fears and anxieties? Presumably, the "right" level of fear varies from time to time, and these chemicals help regulate that level.

APPLICATIONS AND EXTENSIONS

Alcohol as an Anxiety Reducer

Alcohol promotes the flow of chloride ions through the $GABA_A$ receptor complex by binding strongly at a special site found on only certain kinds of $GABA_A$ receptors (Glykys et al., 2007). Alcohol influences the brain in other ways as well, but the effects on GABA are responsible for alcohol's anti-anxiety and intoxicating effects. Drugs that block the effects of alcohol on the $GABA_A$ receptor complex also block most of alcohol's behavioral effects. One experimental drug, known as Ro15-4513, is particularly effective in this regard (Suzdak et al., 1986). Besides affecting the $GABA_A$ receptor complex, Ro15-4513 blocks the effects of alcohol on motor coordination, its depressant action on the brain, and its ability to reduce anxiety (H. C. Becker, 1988; Hoffman, Tabakoff, Szabó, Suzdak, & Paul, 1987; Ticku & Kulkarni, 1988) (Figure 12.19).

Could Ro15-4513 be useful as a "sobering-up" pill or as a treatment to help people who want to stop drinking alcohol? Hoffman-LaRoche, the company that discovered it, eventually concluded that the drug would be too risky. People who relied on the pill might think they were sober and try to drive home when they were still somewhat impaired. Furthermore, giving such a pill to alcoholics would probably backfire. Because alcoholics generally drink to get drunk, a pill that decreased their feeling of intoxication would probably increase their drinking. Ro15-4513 reverses the behavioral effects of moderate alcohol doses, but a large dose can still be a health hazard (Poling, Schlinger, & Blakely, 1988). For these reasons, Ro15-4513 is used only in experimental laboratories.

Science Magazine/AAAS

Figure 12.19 Two rats that were given the same amount of alcohol
The rat on the right was later given the experimental drug Ro15-4513. Within 2 minutes, its performance on motor tasks improved significantly. *(Courtesy of Jules Asher. From "New Drug Counters Alcohol Intoxication" by G. Kolata, 1986,* Science, *231, p. 1199. Copyright 1986 by the AAAS. Used by permission AAAS/Science Magazine.)*

STOP & CHECK

14. What would be the effect of benzodiazepines on someone who had no GABA?

ANSWER

14. Benzodiazepines facilitate the effects of GABA, so a person without GABA would have no response to benzodiazepines.

MODULE 12.2 IN CLOSING

Doing Something About Emotions

It is hard to foresee future developments, but suppose researchers make sudden advances in linking emotional behaviors to physiological measurements. Imagine if we could take a blood sample—measuring 5-HIAA or whatever—plus an fMRI scan and a few other measurements and then predict which people will commit violent crime. What would we want to do with that information, if anything?

And what about anxiety? Suppose research enables us to modulate people's anxiety precisely without undesirable side effects. Would it be a good idea to use these methods to assure that everyone had the "right" anxiety level—not too much, not too little? Future research will give us new options and opportunities. Deciding what to do with them is another matter.

SUMMARY

1. Either a provoking experience, such as fighting, or the direct stimulation of the corticomedial area of the amygdala temporarily heightens the readiness to attack. **353**
2. Aggressive behavior relates to both genetic and environmental influences. Some, but not all, studies indicate that one gene increases aggressive behavior only among people who had abusive experiences in childhood. **354**
3. Differences in testosterone levels correlate weakly with variations in aggressive behavior. However, testosterone has an interesting mixed effect of increasing emotional responses to an angry face while decreasing conscious recognition of the angry expression. **355**
4. Low serotonin turnover is associated with an increased likelihood of impulsive behavior, sometimes including violence. Monkeys with low serotonin turnover get into many fights and in most cases die young. However, those who survive have a high probability of achieving a dominant status. **356**
5. The role of serotonin is complex, as it is released during aggressive behavior. Apparently, the release of serotonin during a hostile encounter produces bigger effects if the usual level of serotonin release is low. **357**
6. Researchers measure enhancement of the startle reflex as an indication of anxiety or learned fears. **357**
7. The amygdala is critical for increasing or decreasing the startle reflex on the basis of learned information. Animals with damage to the amygdala often act fearless, apparently because they are slow to process emotional information. **358**
8. According to studies using fMRI, the human amygdala responds strongly to fear stimuli and any other stimuli that evoke strong emotional processing. The amygdala responds to emotional stimuli even when they are presented under conditions that prevent people from recognizing them consciously. **359**
9. People with damage to the amygdala fail to focus their attention on stimuli with important emotional content. **360**
10. Damage to the amygdala impairs recognition of fear expressions mainly because people with such damage focus on the nose and mouth instead of the eyes. **360**
11. Anti-anxiety drugs decrease fear by facilitating the binding of the neurotransmitter GABA to the $GABA_A$ receptors, especially in the amygdala. **361**

KEY TERMS

Terms are defined in the module on the page number indicated. They're also presented in alphabetical order with definitions in the book's Subject Index/Glossary. Interactive flashcards, audio reviews, and crossword puzzles are among the online resources available to help you learn these terms and the concepts they represent.

benzodiazepines **362**
diazepam-binding inhibitor (DBI) **363**
endozepines **363**
$GABA_A$ receptor **363**
5-hydroxyindoleacetic acid (5-HIAA) **356**
startle reflex **357**
turnover **356**

THOUGHT QUESTIONS

1. Much of the play behavior of a cat can be analyzed into attack and escape components. Is the same true for children's play?
2. People with amygdala damage approach other people indiscriminately instead of trying to choose people who look friendly and trustworthy. What might be a possible explanation?

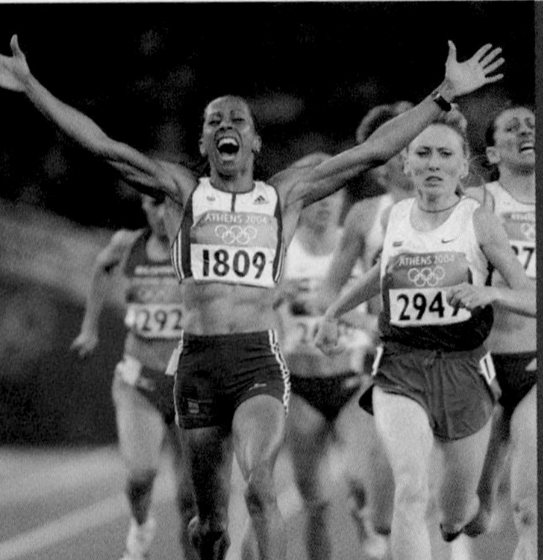

MODULE 12.3

Stress and Health

In the early days of scientific medicine, physicians made little allowance for the relation of personality or emotions to health and disease. If someone became ill, the cause had to be structural, like a virus or bacterium. Today, **behavioral medicine** emphasizes the effects on health of diet, smoking, exercise, stressful experiences, and other behaviors. We accept the idea that emotions and other experiences influence people's illnesses and patterns of recovery. This view does not imply mind-body dualism. Stress and emotions are brain activities, after all.

Concepts of Stress

The term *stress,* like the term *emotion,* is hard to define or quantify. Hans Selye (1979) defined **stress** as the nonspecific response of the body to any demand made upon it. When Selye was in medical school, he noticed that patients with a wide variety of illnesses had much in common: They develop a fever, they lose their appetite, they become inactive, they are sleepy most of the day, and their immune systems become more active. Later, when doing laboratory research, he found that rats exposed to heat, cold, pain, confinement, or the sight of a cat responded to these dissimilar stimuli in similar ways, including increased heart rate, breathing rate, and adrenal secretions. Selye inferred that any threat to the body, in addition to its specific effects, activated a generalized response to stress, which he called the **general adaptation syndrome.** The initial stage, which he called *alarm,* is characterized by increased activity of the sympathetic nervous system, readying the body for brief emergency activity. During the second stage, *resistance,* the sympathetic response declines, but the adrenal cortex secretes **cortisol** and other hormones that enable the body to maintain prolonged alertness, fight infections, and heal wounds. After intense, prolonged stress, the body enters the third stage, *exhaustion.* During this stage, the individual is tired, inactive, and vulnerable because the nervous system and immune systems no longer have the energy to sustain their heightened responses (Sapolsky, 1998).

Stress-related illnesses and psychiatric problems are widespread in industrial societies, possibly because of changes in the type of stresses that we face. As Robert Sapolsky (1998) has argued, many of our crises are prolonged, such as advancing in a career, paying a mortgage, or caring for a relative with a chronic health problem. If a long-term, almost inescapable issue activates the general adaptation syndrome, the result can be exhaustion.

Selye's concept of stress included any *change* in one's life, such as either getting fired from your job or getting promoted. Bruce McEwen (2000, p. 173) proposed an alternative definition that is better for most purposes: "events that are interpreted as threatening to an individual and which elicit physiological and behavioral responses." Although this definition differs from Selye's, the idea remains that many kinds of events can be stressful, and the body reacts to all kinds of stress in similar ways.

For access to many Web sites dealing with stress, visit the Stress Less site: **http://www.stressless.com/AboutSL/StressLinks.cfm**

Stress and the Hypothalamus-Pituitary-Adrenal Cortex Axis

Stress activates two body systems. One is the sympathetic nervous system, which prepares the body for brief emergency responses—"fight or flight." The other is the **HPA axis**—the hypothalamus, pituitary gland, and adrenal cortex. Activation of the hypothalamus induces the anterior pituitary gland to secrete **adrenocorticotropic hormone (ACTH),** which in turn stimulates the human adrenal cortex to secrete cortisol, which enhances metabolic activity and elevates blood levels of sugar and other nutrients (Figure 12.20). Many researchers refer to cortisol as a "stress hormone" and use measurements of cortisol level as an indication of someone's recent stress level. Compared to the autonomic nervous system, the HPA axis reacts more slowly, but it becomes the dominant response to prolonged stressors, such as living with an abusive parent or spouse.

Cortisol helps the body mobilize its energies to fight a difficult situation, but the effects depend on amount. Brief or moderate release of cortisol improves attention and memory formation (Abercrombie, Kalin, Thurow, Rosenkranz, &

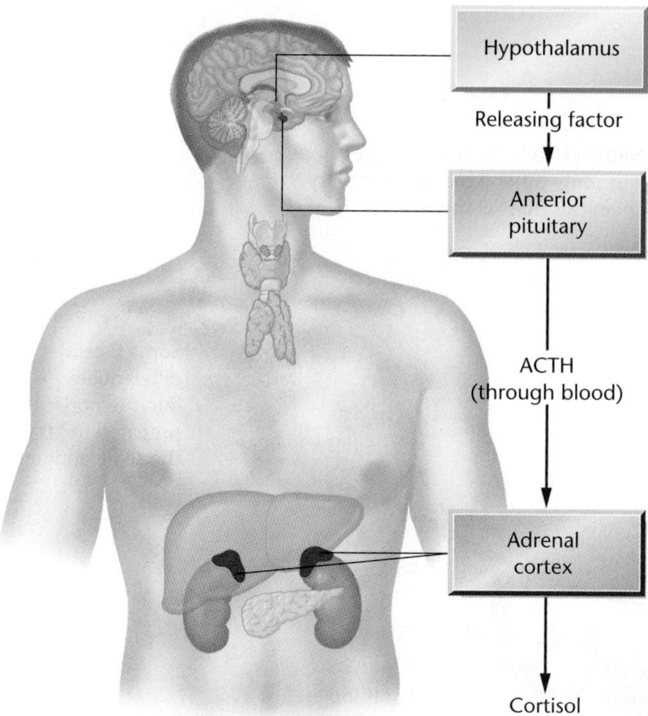

Figure 12.20 The hypothalamus-pituitary-adrenal cortex axis Prolonged stress leads to the secretion of the adrenal hormone cortisol, which elevates blood sugar and increases metabolism. These changes help the body sustain prolonged activity but at the expense of decreased immune system activity.

Davidson, 2003; Beckner, Tucker, Delville, & Mohr, 2006). It also enhances activity of the immune system, helping it fight illnesses (Benschop et al., 1995). However, prolonged increases in cortisol impair memory and immune activity. To see why, we start with an overview of the immune system.

The Immune System

The **immune system** consists of cells that protect the body against viruses, bacteria, and other intruders. The immune system is like a police force: If it is too weak, the "criminals" (viruses and bacteria) run wild and create damage. If it becomes too strong and unselective, it starts attacking "law-abiding citizens" (the body's own cells). When the immune system attacks normal cells, we call the result an *autoimmune disease*. Myasthenia gravis, mentioned in Chapter 8, is one example of an autoimmune disease. Rheumatoid arthritis is another.

Leukocytes. The most important elements of the immune system are the **leukocytes,** commonly known as white blood cells (Kiecolt-Glaser & Glaser, 1993; O'Leary, 1990).

We distinguish several types of leukocytes, including B cells, T cells, and natural killer cells (Figure 12.21):

- *B cells,* which mature mostly in the bone marrow, secrete **antibodies,** which are Y-shaped proteins that attach to particular kinds of antigens, just as a key fits a lock. Every cell has surface proteins called **antigens** (antibody-generator molecules), and your body's antigens are as unique as your fingerprints. The B cells recognize the "self" antigens, but when they find an unfamiliar antigen, they attack the cell. This kind of attack defends the body against viruses and bacteria. It also causes rejection of organ transplants, unless physicians take special steps to minimize the attack. After the body has made antibodies against a particular intruder, it "remembers" the intruder and quickly builds more of the same kind of antibody if it encounters that intruder again.
- *T cells* mature in the thymus gland. Several kinds of T cells attack intruders directly (without secreting antibodies), and some help other T cells or B cells to multiply.
- *Natural killer cells,* another kind of leukocytes, attack tumor cells and cells that are infected with viruses. Whereas each B or T cell attacks a particular kind of foreign antigen, natural killer cells attack all intruders.

In response to an infection, leukocytes and other cells produce small proteins called **cytokines** (e.g., interleukin-1, or IL-1), which combat infections and also communicate with the brain to elicit appropriate behaviors (Maier & Watkins, 1998). Cytokines are the immune system's way of telling the brain that the body is ill. Cytokines in the brain trigger the hypothalamus to produce fever, sleepiness, lack of energy, lack of appetite, and loss of sex drive. The immune system also reacts to infection by increased production of *prostaglandins,* additional chemicals that promote sleepiness. In other words, cytokines and prostaglandins are responsible for what Selye called the general adaptation syndrome.

Note also that what we usually consider symptoms are actually part of the body's way of fighting the illness. Most people think of fever and sleepiness as something the illness did to them, but in fact, fever and sleepiness are strategies we have evolved for fighting the illness. As discussed in Chapter 10, a moderate fever helps fight many infections. Sleep and inactivity are ways of conserving energy so that the body can devote more energy to its immune attack against the intruders.

STOP & CHECK

15. What kind of cell releases cytokines?

16. What behavioral changes do cytokines stimulate?

ANSWERS

15. Leukocytes, which are part of the immune system, release cytokines. **16.** Cytokines stimulate neurons to produce fever, decreased hunger, decreased sex drive, and increased sleepiness.

Effects of Stress on the Immune System

The nervous system has more control than we might have guessed over the immune system. The study of this relationship, called **psychoneuroimmunology,** deals with the ways experiences alter the immune system and how the immune

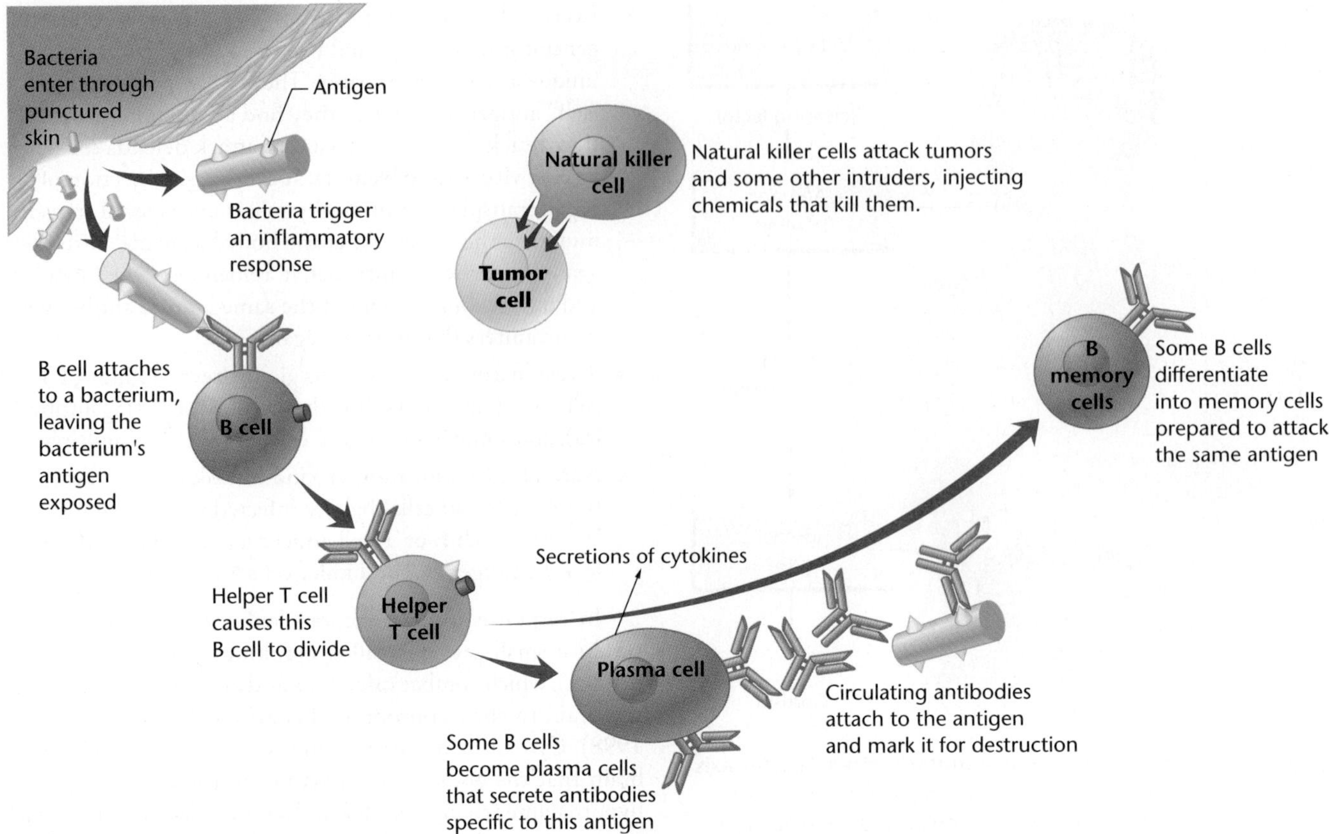
Bacteria enter through punctured skin
Antigen
Bacteria trigger an inflammatory response
Natural killer cell
Natural killer cells attack tumors and some other intruders, injecting chemicals that kill them.
Tumor cell
B cell attaches to a bacterium, leaving the bacterium's antigen exposed
B cell
B memory cells
Some B cells differentiate into memory cells prepared to attack the same antigen
Secretions of cytokines
Helper T cell causes this B cell to divide
Helper T cell
Plasma cell
Circulating antibodies attach to the antigen and mark it for destruction
Some B cells become plasma cells that secrete antibodies specific to this antigen

Figure 12.21 Immune system responses to a bacterial infection
B cells bind to bacteria and produce antibodies against the bacteria. A helper T cell attaches to the B cell; it stimulates the B cell to generate copies of itself, called B memory cells, which immunize the body against future invasions by the same kind of bacteria.

system in turn influences the central nervous system (Ader, 2001).

Stress affects the immune system in several ways. In response to a stressful experience, the nervous system activates the immune system to increase its production of natural killer cells and the secretion of cytokines (Segerstrom & Miller, 2004). Even fear or anger enhances the immune system response, temporarily (Mayne, 1999). During the stressful period of final exams, many college students have increased immune system activity (L. Y. Liu et al., 2002). The elevated cytokine levels help combat infections, but they also trigger the brain to produce the same symptoms as if one were ill. Rats subjected to inescapable shocks show symptoms resembling illness, including fever, sleepiness, and decreased appetite. The same is true for people who are under great stress, such as those who are dreading some public speech they have to give (Maier & Watkins, 1998). Many of the symptoms of depression, such as loss of interest and loss of appetite, are similar to those of illness and are probably related to the increased cytokines found in depressed people (Dantzer, O'Connor, Freund, Johnson, & Kelley, 2008). In short, if you have been under much stress and start to feel ill, one possibility is that your symptoms are reactions to the stress itself.

A prolonged stress response is as draining on the body as a prolonged illness would be (Segerstrom & Miller, 2004; Zorrilla et al., 2001). A likely hypothesis is that prolonged increase of cortisol directs energy toward increasing metabolism and therefore detracts energy from synthesizing proteins, including the proteins of the immune system. For example, in 1979 at the Three Mile Island nuclear power plant, a major accident was barely contained. The people who continued to live in the vicinity during the next year had lower than normal levels of B cells, T cells, and natural killer cells. They also complained of emotional distress and showed impaired performance on a proofreading task (A. Baum, Gatchel, & Schaeffer, 1983; McKinnon, Weisse, Reynolds, Bowles, & Baum, 1989). A study of research scientists in Antarctica found that a 9-month period of cold, darkness, and social isolation reduced T cell functioning to about half of normal levels (Tingate, Lugg, Muller, Stowe, & Pierson, 1997).

In one study, 276 volunteers filled out an extensive questionnaire about stressful life events before being injected with a moderate dose of common cold virus. (The idea was that those with the strongest immune responses could fight off the cold, but others would succumb.) People who reported brief stressful experiences were at no more risk for catching a cold than were people who reported no stress. However, for people who reported stress lasting longer than a month, the longer it lasted, the greater the risk of illness (S. Cohen et al., 1998).

Prolonged stress can also harm the hippocampus. Stress releases cortisol, and cortisol enhances metabolic activity throughout the body. When metabolic activity is high in the hippocampus, its cells become more vulnerable. Toxins or overstimulation are then more likely than usual to damage or kill neurons in the hippocampus (Sapolsky, 1992). Rats exposed to high stress—which in this case consisted of being restrained in a mesh wire retainer for 6 hours a day for 3 weeks—show shrinkage of dendrites in the hippocampus and impairments in the kinds of memory that depend on the hippocampus (Kleen, Sitomer, Killeen, & Conrad, 2006). High cortisol levels may also be responsible for the deterioration of the hippocampus and decline of memory that occur in many older people (Cameron & McKay, 1999). Older people with the highest cortisol levels tend to be those with the smallest hippocampi and the greatest memory problems (Lupien et al., 1998).

Stress also impairs the adaptability of hippocampal neurons. In several studies, researchers exposed pregnant rats or newborn rats to stress. The methods were restraint of the mother during pregnancy, providing the mother with inadequate nesting material after giving birth, or separating infant rats from their mothers for 3 hours a day. In each case, the rats were reared normally and tested in adulthood. In each case, they showed decreased plasticity in the hippocampus and impairments of spatial learning (Brunson et al., 2005; Mirescu, Peters, & Gould, 2004; Son et al., 2005). That is, early stressful experiences led to lifelong deficits.

STOP & CHECK

17. True or false: Fear and anger are consistently harmful to health.

18. How does prolonged stress damage the hippocampus?

ANSWERS

17. False. Fear, anger, or any other stressor impairs health if continued for a long time, but brief experiences arouse the sympathetic nervous system and enhance the activity of the immune system. **18.** Stress increases the release of cortisol, which enhances metabolic activity throughout the body. When neurons in the hippocampus have high metabolic activity, they become more vulnerable to damage by toxins or overstimulation.

Stress Control

People have found many ways to reduce stress or control their responses to it. Possibilities include special breathing routines, exercise, meditation, and distraction, as well as, of course, trying to deal with the problem that caused the stress. Social support is one of the most powerful methods of coping with stress, and researchers have demonstrated its effectiveness by brain measurements as well as people's self-reports. In one study, happily married women were given moderately painful shocks to their ankles. On various trials, they held the hand of their husband, a man they did not know, or no one. Holding the husband's hand reduced the response indicated by fMRI in several brain areas, including the prefrontal cortex. Holding the hand of an unknown man reduced the response a little, on the average, but not as much as holding the husband's hand (Coan, Schaefer, & Davidson, 2006). In short, as expected, brain responses correspond to people's self-reports that social support from a loved one helps reduce stress.

Posttraumatic Stress Disorder

People have long recognized that many soldiers returning from battle are prone to continuing anxieties and distress. In the past, people called this condition *battle fatigue* or *shell shock*. Today, they call it **posttraumatic stress disorder (PTSD).** PTSD occurs in some people who have endured terrifying experiences such as a life-threatening attack or watching someone get killed. The symptoms, lasting at least a month after the event, include frequent distressing recollections (flashbacks) and nightmares about the traumatic event, avoidance of reminders of it, and exaggerated arousal in response to noises and other stimuli (Yehuda, 2002).

However, not all people who endure traumas develop PTSD. For example, investigators in one study examined 218 people admitted to a hospital emergency ward after severe automobile accidents. All showed about similar stress responses at the time and 1 week later, but the responses declined over time in some and increased in others so that about one sixth of them met the criteria for PTSD 4 months after the accident (Shalev et al., 2000). The ones developing PTSD had not been in consistently worse wrecks than the others. Evidently, they were more vulnerable to PTSD. Other studies have confirmed that the people showing the greatest distress shortly after a traumatic event are not necessarily the ones who later develop PTSD (Harvey & Bryant, 2002).

What accounts for differences in vulnerability? Most PTSD victims have a smaller than average hippocampus (Stein, Hanna, Koverola, Torchia, & McClarty, 1997). It might seem natural to assume that severe stress elevated the cortisol secretion and that the high cortisol levels damaged the hippocampus. However, PTSD victims show *lower* than normal cortisol levels both immediately after the traumatic event and weeks later (Delahanty, Raimonde, & Spoonster, 2000; Yehuda, 1997). The low levels suggest another hypothesis: Perhaps people with low cortisol levels are ill-equipped to combat stress and therefore more vulnerable to the damaging effects of stress and more prone than other people to PTSD.

To determine whether certain people are predisposed to PTSD, investigators examined men who developed PTSD during a war. First, they confirmed earlier reports that most PTSD victims had a smaller than average hippocampus. Then they found cases in which the PTSD victim had an identical twin

STOP & CHECK

19. How do the cortisol levels of PTSD victims compare to those of other people?

20. What evidence indicates that a smaller than average hippocampus makes people more vulnerable to PTSD?

ANSWERS

19. People with PTSD have lower than normal cortisol levels in contrast to most people, who show elevated cortisol levels in response to stress. **20.** On the average, PTSD victims have a smaller than average hippocampus. For those who have an identical twin, the twin also has a smaller than average hippocampus, even if he or she does not have PTSD.

who had not been in battle and who did not have PTSD. The results showed that the twin without PTSD *also* had a smaller than average hippocampus (Gilbertson et al., 2002). Presumably, both twins had a smaller than average hippocampus from the start, which increased the susceptibility to PTSD.

One further point about PTSD: A study compared Vietnam War veterans who suffered injuries that produced various kinds of brain damage. Of those whose damage included the amygdala, *none* suffered PTSD. Of those with damage elsewhere in the brain, 40% suffered PTSD (Koenigs et al., 2008). Apparently, the amygdala, which is so important for emotional processing, is essential for the extreme emotional impact that produces PTSD.

MODULE 12.3 IN CLOSING

Emotions and Body Reactions

Research on stress and health provides an interesting kind of closure. Decades ago, Hans Selye argued that any stressful event leads to the general adaptation syndrome, marked by fever and other signs of illness. We now see why: The body reacts to prolonged stress by activating the adrenal cortex and the immune system, and the resulting increase in cytokines produces the same reactions that an infection would. Research has also improved our understanding of the predispositions behind posttraumatic stress disorder and makes it possible to foresee a new era of advances in psychosomatic medicine. Emotional states, which once seemed too ephemeral for scientific study, are now part of mainstream biology.

SUMMARY

1. Hans Selye introduced the idea of the general adaptation syndrome, which is the way the body responds to all kinds of illness and stress. **366**
2. Brief stress activates the sympathetic nervous system. More prolonged stress activates the hypothalamus-pituitary-adrenal cortex axis. The adrenal cortex releases cortisol, which increases metabolism. **366**
3. Although brief stress enhances the immune response and facilitates memory formation, prolonged stress drains the body of the resources it needs for other purposes. **367**
4. Stress activates the immune system, helping to fight viruses and bacteria. The immune system releases cytokines, which stimulate the hypothalamus to initiate activities to combat illness. **367**
5. Because stress causes release of cytokines, it can lead to fever, sleepiness, and other symptoms that resemble those of illness. **368**
6. The high cortisol levels associated with prolonged stress damages cells in the hippocampus, thereby impairing memory. Stress also impairs production of new neurons. **369**
7. Successful methods of coping with stress, such as social support, produce measurable effects in brain responses as well as in people's self-reports. **369**
8. After a severely trying event, some people but not others develop posttraumatic stress disorder (PTSD). Evidently, people with a smaller than average hippocampus and lower than average cortisol levels are predisposed to PTSD. **369**

KEY TERMS

Terms are defined in the module on the page number indicated. They're also presented in alphabetical order with definitions in the book's Subject Index/Glossary. Interactive flashcards, audio reviews, and crossword puzzles are among the online resources available to help you learn these terms and the concepts they represent.

adrenocorticotropic hormone (ACTH) **366**
antibody **367**
antigen **367**
behavioral medicine **366**
cortisol **366**
cytokine **367**
general adaptation syndrome **366**
HPA axis **366**
immune system **367**
leukocyte **367**
posttraumatic stress disorder (PTSD) **369**
psychoneuroimmunology **367**
stress **366**

THOUGHT QUESTION

If someone were unable to produce cytokines, what would be the consequences?

CHAPTER 12 Exploration and Study

In addition to the study materials provided at the end of each module, you may supplement your review of this chapter by using one or more of the book's electronic resources, which include its companion Website, interactive Cengage Learning eBook, Exploring Biological Psychology CD-ROM, and CengageNOW. Brief descriptions of these resources follow. For more information, visit **www.cengage.com/psychology/kalat**.

The book's companion Website, accessible through the author Web page indicated above, provides a wide range of study resources such as an interactive glossary, flashcards, tutorial quizzes, updated Web links, and Try It Yourself activities, as well as a limited selection of the short videos and animated explanations of concepts available for this chapter.

Exploring Biological Psychology

The Exploring Biological Psychology CD-ROM contains videos, animations, and Try It Yourself activities. These activities—as well as many that are new to this edition—are also available in the text's fully interactive, media-rich Cengage Learning eBook,* which gives you the opportunity to experience biological psychology in an even greater interactive and multimedia environment. The Cengage Learning eBook also includes highlighting and note-taking features and an audio glossary. For this chapter, the Cengage Learning eBook includes the following interactive explorations:

Amygdala and Fear Conditioning
Facial Analysis
GABA Receptors
CNS Depressants
The Immune System
Health and Stress

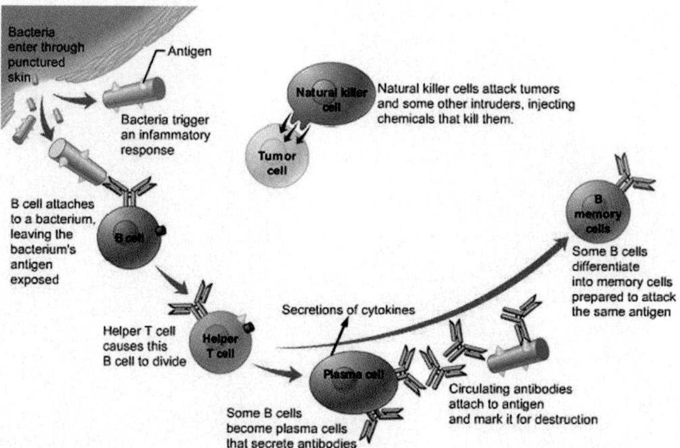
Bacteria enter through punctured skin
Antigen
Bacteria trigger an infammatory response
Natural killer cell
Natural killer cells attack tumors and some other intruders, injecting chemicals that kill them.
Tumor cell
B cell attaches to a bacterium, leaving the bacterium's antigen exposed
B cell
B memory cells
Some B cells differentiate into memory cells prepared to attack the same antigen
Secretions of cytokines
Helper T cell causes this B cell to divide
Helper T cell
Plasma cell
Circulating antibodies attach to antigen and mark it for destruction
Some B cells become plasma cells that secrete antibodies

The video *The Immune System* introduces research on how stress modifies the immune response, and therefore overall health.

* Requires a Cengage Learning eResources account. Visit **www.cengage.com/login** to register or login.

CENGAGENOW™ is an easy-to-use resource that helps you study in less time to get the grade you want. An online study system, CengageNOW* gives you the option of taking a diagnostic pretest for each chapter. The system uses the results of each pretest to create personalized chapter study plans for you. The Personalized Study Plans

- help you save study time by identifying areas on which you should concentrate and give you one-click access to corresponding pages of the interactive Cengage Learning eBook;
- provide interactive exercises and study tools to help you fully understand chapter concepts; and
- include a posttest for you to take to confirm that you are ready to move on to the next chapter.

Suggestions for Further Exploration

The book's companion Website includes a list of suggested articles available through InfoTrac College Edition for this chapter. You may also want to explore some of the following books and Websites. The text's companion Website provides live, updated links to the sites listed below.

Books

Damasio, A. (1999). *The feeling of what happens.* New York: Harcourt Brace. A neurologist's account of the connection between emotion and consciousness, full of interesting examples.

McEwen, B. S., with Lasley, E. N. (2002). *The end of stress as we know it.* Washington, DC: Joseph Henry Press. Readable review by one of the leading researchers.

Pfaff, D. W. (2007). *The neuroscience of fair play.* New York: Dana Press. Exploration of how the physiology of emotions, especially the amygdala, relates to moral behavior.

Websites

Stress-Related Links
http://www.stressless.com/AboutSL/StressLinks.cfm

Tim Davis/CORBIS

The Biology of Learning and Memory

13

CHAPTER OUTLINE

MAIN IDEAS

1. To understand the physiology of learning, we must answer two questions: What changes occur in a single cell during learning, and how do changed cells work together to produce adaptive behavior?
2. Psychologists distinguish among several types of memory, each of which can be impaired by a different kind of brain damage.
3. During learning, changes occur that facilitate or decrease the activity at particular synapses.

Suppose you type something on your computer and then save it. A year later, you come back, click the correct filename, and retrieve what you wrote. How did the computer remember what to do?

That question is really two questions. First, how do the physical properties of silicon chips enable them to alter their properties when you type certain keys? Second, how does the wiring diagram take the changes in individual silicon chips and convert them into some useful display or activity?

Similarly, when we try to explain how you remember some experience, we deal with two questions. First, how does a pattern of sensory information alter the properties of certain neurons? Second, after neurons change their properties, how does the nervous system produce the behavioral changes that we call learning or memory? What happens in a single cell does not explain learned behaviors.

We begin this chapter by considering how the various brain areas interact to produce learning and memory. In the second module, we turn to the detailed physiology of how experience changes neurons and synapses.

OPPOSITE: Learning produces amazingly complex behaviors.

MODULE 13.1

Learning, Memory, Amnesia, and Brain Functioning

Suppose you lost your ability to form long-lasting memories. You remember what just happened but nothing earlier. It's as if you awakened from a long sleep only a second ago. So you write on a sheet of paper, "Just now, for the first time, I have suddenly become conscious!" A little later, you forget this experience, too. As far as you can tell, you have just now emerged into consciousness after a long sleeplike period. You look at this sheet of paper on which you wrote about becoming conscious, but you don't remember writing it. How odd! You must have written it when in fact you were not conscious! Irritated, you cross off that statement and write anew, "*NOW* I am for the first time conscious!" And a minute later, you cross that one off and write it again. Eventually, someone finds this sheet of paper on which you have repeatedly written and crossed out statements about suddenly feeling conscious for the first time.

Sound far-fetched? It really happened to a patient who developed severe memory impairments after encephalitis damaged his temporal cortex (B. A. Wilson, Baddeley, & Kapur, 1995). Life without memory means no sense of existing across time. Your memory is almost synonymous with your sense of "self."

Localized Representations of Memory

What happens in the brain during learning and memory? One early idea was that a connection grew between two brain areas. The Russian physiologist Ivan Pavlov pioneered the investigation of what we now call **classical conditioning** (Figure 13.1a), in which pairing two stimuli changes the response to one of them (Pavlov, 1927). The experimenter starts by presenting a **conditioned stimulus (CS),** which initially elicits no response of note, and then presents the **unconditioned stimulus (UCS),** which automatically elicits the **unconditioned response (UCR).** After some pairings of the CS and the UCS (perhaps just one or two, perhaps many), the individual begins making a new, learned response to the CS, called a **conditioned response (CR).** In his original experiments, Pavlov presented a dog with a sound (CS) followed by meat (UCS), which stimulated the dog to salivate (UCR). After many such pairings, the sound alone (CS) stimulated the dog to salivate (CR). In that case and many others, the CR resembles the UCR, but in some cases, it does not. For example, if a rat experiences a CS paired with shock, the shock elicits screaming and jumping, but the CS elicits a freezing response.

In **operant conditioning,** an individual's response leads to a reinforcer or punishment (Figure 13.1b). A **reinforcer** is any event that increases the future probability of the response. A **punishment** is an event that suppresses the frequency of the response. For example, when a rat enters one arm of a maze and finds Froot Loops cereal (a potent reinforcer for a rat), its probability of entering that arm again increases. If it receives a shock instead, the probability decreases. The primary difference between classical and operant conditioning is that in operant conditioning the individual's response determines the outcome (reinforcer or punishment), whereas in classical conditioning the CS and UCS occur at certain times regardless of the individual's behavior. (The behavior is useful, however, in anticipating the effects of the UCS.)

Some cases of learning are difficult to label as classical or operant. For example, after a male songbird hears the song of his own species during his first few months, he imitates it the following year. The song that he heard was not paired with any other stimulus, as in classical conditioning. He learned the song without reinforcers or punishments, so we can't call it operant conditioning either. That is, animals have specialized methods of learning other than classical and operant conditioning. Also, the way animals (including people) learn varies from one situation to another. For example, in most situations, learning occurs only if the CS and UCS, or response and reinforcer, occur close together in time. But if you eat something, especially something unfamiliar, and get sick later, you learn a strong aversion to the taste of that food, even if taste and illness are separated by hours (Rozin & Kalat, 1971; Rozin & Schull, 1988).

Lashley's Search for the Engram

Pavlov proposed that classical conditioning reflects a strengthened connection between a CS center and a UCS center in the brain. That strengthened connection lets any excitation of the CS center flow to the UCS center, evoking the uncon-

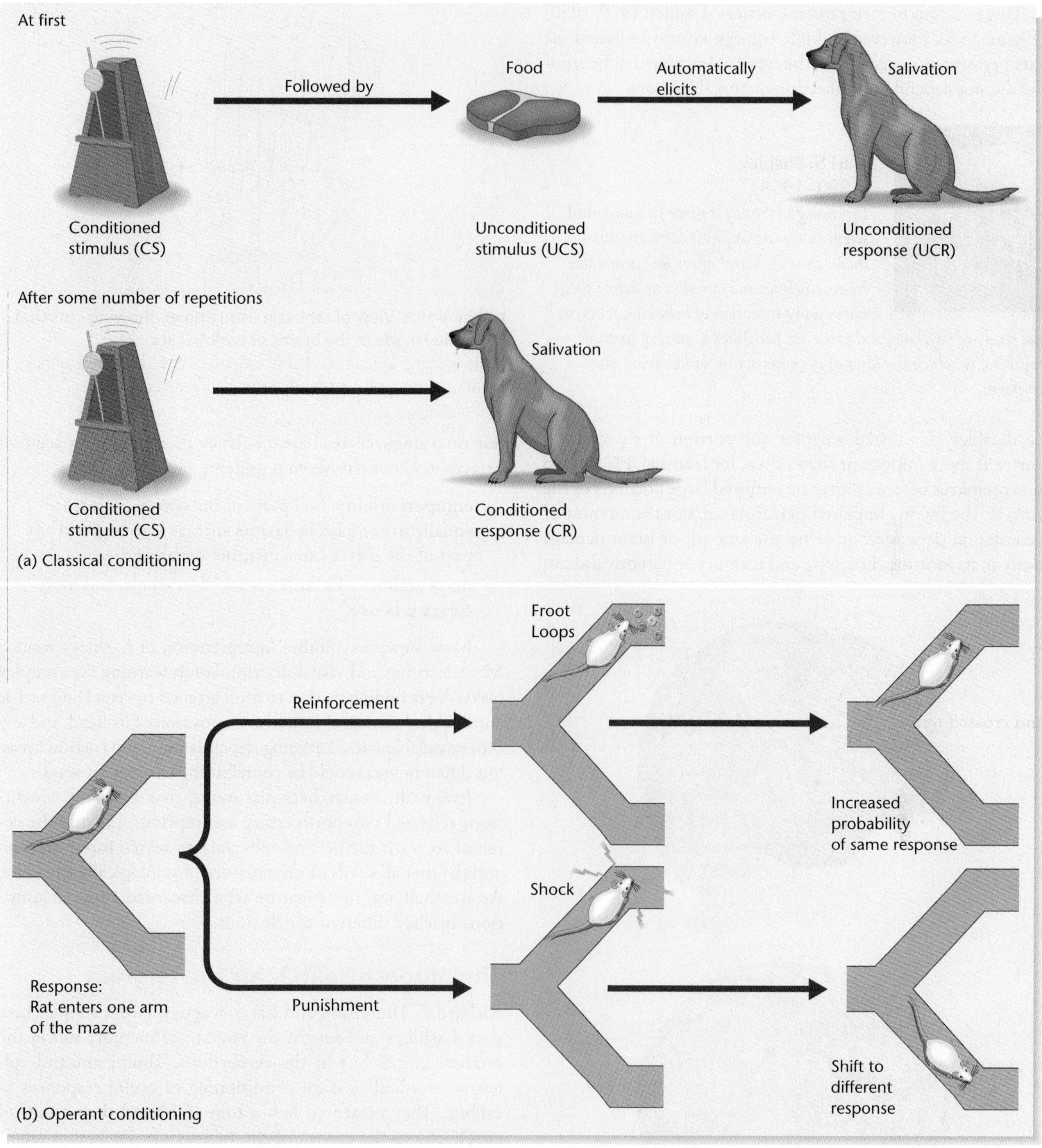

Figure 13.1 Procedures for classical conditioning and operant conditioning
(a) In classical conditioning, two stimuli (CS and UCS) are presented at certain times regardless of what the learner does. **(b)** In operant conditioning, the learner's behavior controls the presentation of reinforcer or punishment.

ditioned response (Figure 13.2). Karl Lashley set out to test this hypothesis. Lashley was searching for the **engram**—the physical representation of what has been learned. (A connection between two brain areas would be a possible example of an engram.)

Lashley reasoned that if learning depends on new or strengthened connections between two brain areas, a knife cut somewhere in the brain should interrupt that connection and abolish the learned response. He trained rats on mazes and a brightness discrimination task and then made deep cuts in varying locations in their cerebral cortices (Lashley, 1929, 1950) (Figure 13.3). However, no knife cut significantly impaired the rats' performances. Evidently, the types of learning that he studied did not depend on connections across the cortex.

McGraw-Hill Education

Karl S. Lashley (1890–1958)

Psychology is today a more fundamental science than neurophysiology. By this I mean that the latter offers few principles from which we may predict or define the normal organization of behavior, whereas the study of psychological processes furnishes a mass of factual material to which the laws of nervous action in behavior must conform.

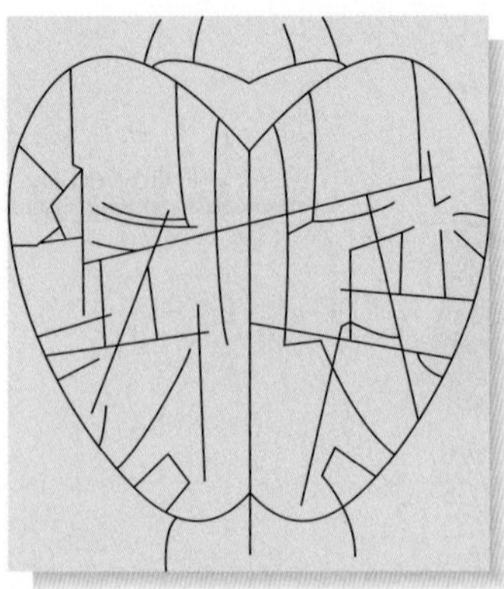

Figure 13.3 View of rat brain from above, showing cuts that Lashley made in the brains of various rats
He found that no cut or combination of cuts interfered with a rat's memory of a maze. *(Adapted from Lashley, 1950)*

Lashley also tested whether any portion of the cerebral cortex is more important than others for learning. He trained rats on mazes before or after he removed large portions of the cortex. The lesions impaired performance, but the amount of retardation depended more on the amount of brain damage than on its location. Learning and memory apparently did not rely on a single cortical area. Lashley therefore proposed two principles about the nervous system:

- **equipotentiality**—all parts of the cortex contribute equally to complex behaviors such as learning, and any part of the cortex can substitute for any other.
- **mass action**—the cortex works as a whole, and more cortex is better.

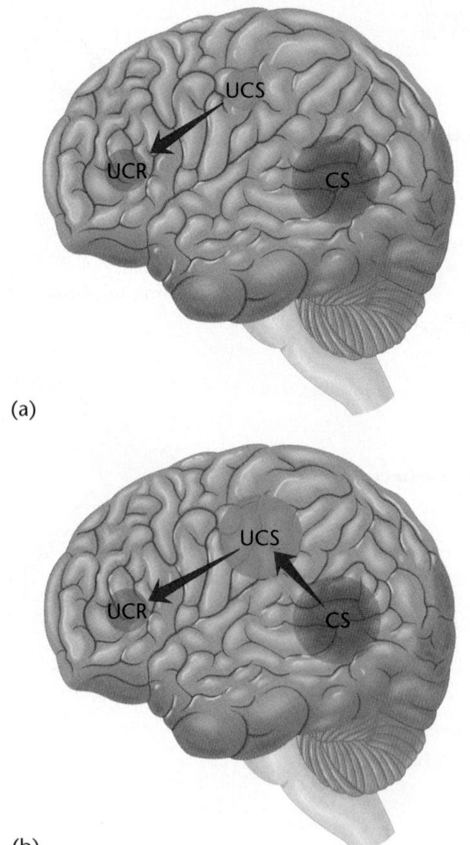

Figure 13.2 Pavlov's view of the physiology of learning
(a) Initially, the UCS excites the UCS center, which then excites the UCR center. The CS excites the CS center, which elicits no response of interest. **(b)** After training, excitation in the CS center flows to the UCS center, thus eliciting the same response as the UCS.

Note, however, another interpretation of Lashley's results: Maze learning and visual discrimination learning are complex tasks. A rat finding its way to food attends to visual and tactile stimuli, the location of its body, the position of its head, and any other available cues. Learning depends on many cortical areas, but different areas could be contributing in different ways.

Eventually, researchers discovered that Lashley's conclusions reflected two unnecessary assumptions: (a) that the cerebral cortex is the best or only place to search for an engram and (b) that all kinds of memory are physiologically the same. As we shall see, investigators who discarded these assumptions reached different conclusions.

The Modern Search for the Engram

Richard F. Thompson and his colleagues used a simpler task than Lashley's and sought the engram of memory not in the cerebral cortex but in the cerebellum. Thompson and colleagues studied classical conditioning of eyelid responses in rabbits. They presented first a tone (CS) and then a puff of air (UCS) to the cornea of the rabbit's eye. At first, a rabbit blinked at the airpuff but not at the tone. After repeated pairings, classical conditioning occurred and the rabbit blinked at the tone also. Investigators recorded the activity in various brain cells to determine which ones changed their responses during learning.

Thompson set out to determine the location of learning. Imagine a sequence of brain areas from the sensory receptors to the motor neurons controlling the muscles:

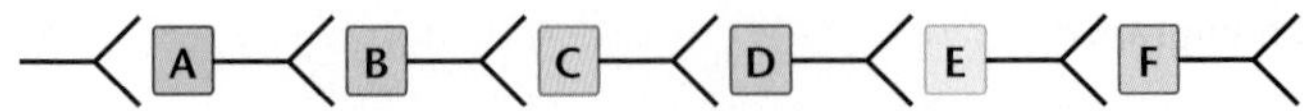

If we damage any one of those areas, learning will be impaired, but we can't be sure that learning occurred in the damaged area. For example, if the learning occurs in area D, damage in C will prevent learning by blocking the input to D. Damage in E will prevent learning by blocking the output from D. However, Thompson and colleagues reasoned as follows: Suppose the learning occurs in D. If so, then D has to be active at the time of the learning, and so do all the areas leading up to D (A, B, and C). However, learning would not require areas E and beyond. If area E were blocked, nothing would relay information to the muscles, so we would see no response, but learning could occur nevertheless.

Thompson identified one nucleus of the cerebellum, the **lateral interpositus nucleus (LIP),** as essential for learning. At the start of training, those cells showed little response to the tone, but as learning proceeded, their responses increased (R. F. Thompson, 1986). If the investigators temporarily suppressed that nucleus of an untrained rabbit, either by cooling the nucleus or by injecting a drug into it, and then presented the CSs and UCSs, the rabbit showed no responses during the training. Then they waited for the LIP to recover and continued training. At that point, the rabbit began to learn, but it learned *at the same speed as animals that had received no previous training.* Evidently, while the LIP was suppressed, the training had no effect.

But does learning actually occur *in* the LIP, or does this area just relay the information to a later area where learning occurs? In the next experiments, investigators suppressed activity in the red nucleus, a midbrain motor area that receives input from the cerebellum. When the red nucleus was suppressed, the rabbits again showed no responses during training. However, as soon as the red nucleus had recovered from the cooling or drugs, the rabbits showed strong learned responses to the tone (R. E. Clark & Lavond, 1993; Krupa, Thompson, & Thompson, 1993). In other words, suppressing the red nucleus temporarily prevented the response but did not prevent learning. That is, learning did not depend on the red nucleus or any area after it. The researchers concluded, therefore, that the learning occurred in the LIP. Figure 13.4 summarizes these experiments.

How did they know that learning didn't depend on some area *before* the LIP? If it did, then suppressing the LIP would not have prevented learning.

Later experiments demonstrated that the LIP has to be intact not only during learning but also during any later test. That is, the structure is necessary both for learning and for retention (Christian & Thompson, 2005). It is also essential for extinction of the learned response (Robleto & Thompson, 2008).

The mechanisms for this type of conditioning are probably the same in humans. According to PET scans on young adults, when pairing a stimulus with an airpuff produces a conditioned eye blink, activity increases in the cerebellum, red nucleus, and several other areas (Logan & Grafton, 1995). People who have damage in the cerebellum have weaker conditioned eye blinks, and the blinks are less accurately timed relative to the onset of the airpuff (Gerwig et al., 2005).

STOP & CHECK

1. Thompson found a localized engram, whereas Lashley did not. What key differences in procedures or assumptions were probably responsible for their different results?

2. What evidence indicates that the red nucleus is necessary for performance of a conditioned response but not for learning the response?

ANSWERS

1. Thompson studied a different, probably simpler type of learning. Also, he looked in the cerebellum instead of the cerebral cortex. **2.** If the red nucleus is inactivated during training, the animal makes no conditioned responses during the training, so the red nucleus is necessary for the response. However, as soon as the red nucleus recovers, the animal can show conditioned responses at once, without any further training, so learning occurred while the red nucleus was inactivated.

Types of Memory

Psychologists distinguish between learning and memory. If nothing else, learning researchers and memory researchers use different methods. Most learning researchers focus on classical or operant conditioning, using laboratory animals. Memory researchers ask people to describe events in words. In reality, the distinction is arbitrary, as you can't learn something without remembering it, and you can't remember something without learning it.

Nevertheless, regardless of whether we use the term *learning* or *memory,* we need to draw distinctions among various types. Decades ago, psychologists expected to find laws of learning or laws of memory that would apply to all situations. Gradually, they became aware of important differences among different types of learning and memory. Researchers continue to explore exactly what are the best distinctions to draw, and studies of brain damage make an important contribution to this pursuit.

Short-Term and Long-Term Memory

Donald Hebb (1949) reasoned that no one mechanism could account for all the phenomena of learning. We form memories quickly, and some memories last a lifetime. Hebb could not imagine a chemical process that occurs fast enough to account for immediate memory yet remains stable enough to provide permanent memory. He therefore distinguished between **short-term memory** of events that have just occurred and **long-term memory** of events from further back. Several types of evidence supported this distinction:

- Short-term memory and long-term memory differ in their capacity. If you hear a series of numbers or letters, such as DZLAUV, you can probably repeat no more than about seven of them, and with other kinds of material, your maximum is even less. Long-term memory has a vast, difficult-to-estimate capacity.

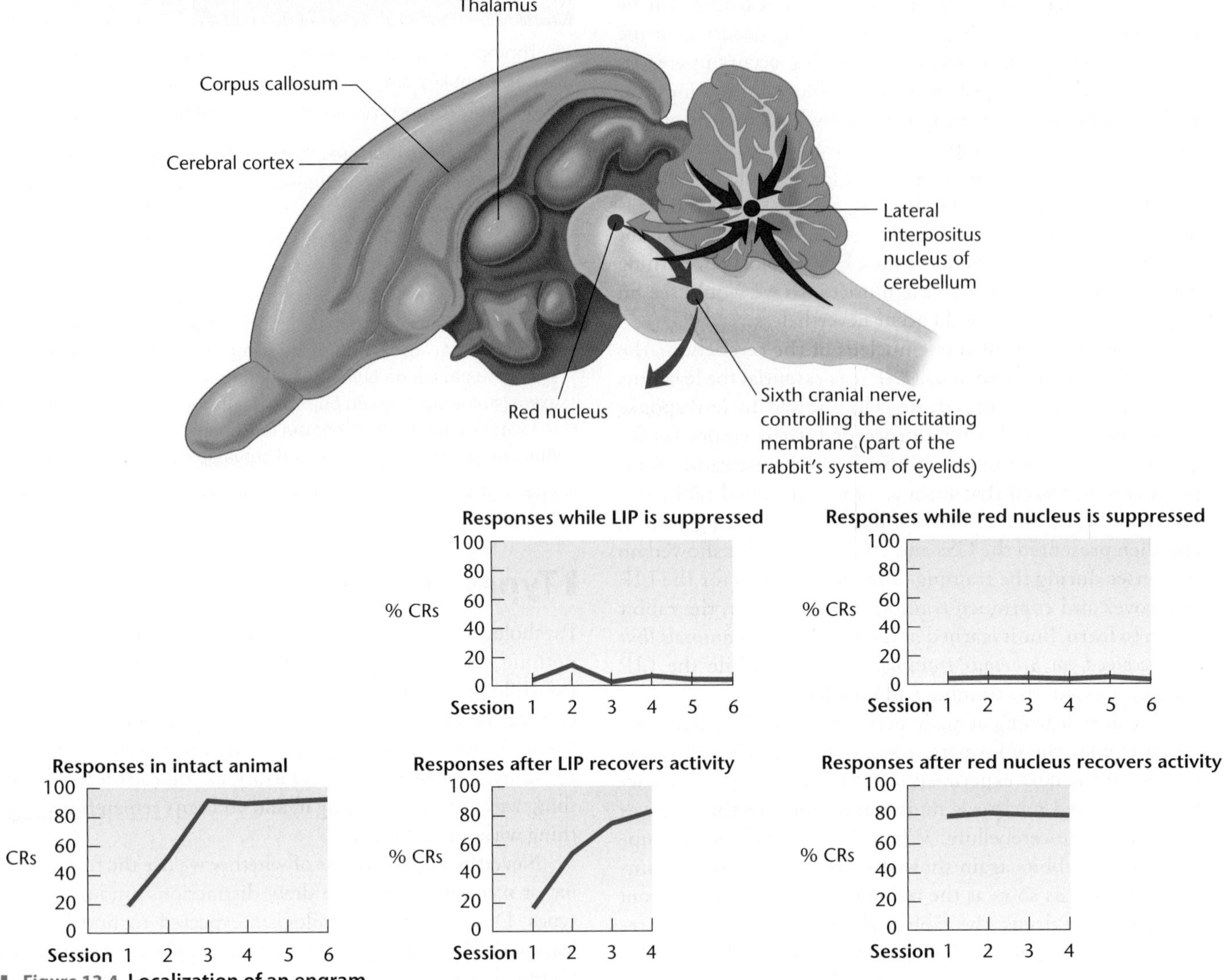

Figure 13.4 Localization of an engram
Temporary inactivation of the lateral interpositus nucleus of a rabbit blocked all indications of learning. After the inactivation wore off, the rabbits learned as slowly as rabbits with no previous training. Temporary inactivation of the red nucleus blocked the response during the period of inactivation, but the learned response appeared as soon as the red nucleus recovered. (Source: Based on the experiments of Clark & Lavond, 1993; Krupa, Thompson, & Thompson, 1993)

- Short-term memories fade quickly unless you rehearse them. For example, if you read the letter sequence DZLAUV and then something distracts you, your chance of repeating the letters declines rapidly over about 20 seconds (Peterson & Peterson, 1959). You can recall long-term memories that you haven't thought about in years.
- With short-term memory, once you have forgotten something, it is lost. With long-term memory, a hint might help you reconstruct something you thought you had forgotten. For example, try naming all your high school teachers. After you have named all you can, you can name still more if someone shows you photos and tells you the teachers' initials.

Based on these distinctions, researchers proposed that all information initially entered a short-term storage, where it stayed until the brain had time to **consolidate** it into long-term memory. If anything interrupted the rehearsal before consolidation took place, the information was simply lost.

Working Memory

Later studies weakened the distinction between short-term and long-term memory. For example, most of the research demonstrating rapid loss of unrehearsed short-term memories dealt with meaningless materials, such as a series of letters or numbers. You hold onto many memories for hours or days without constant rehearsal—such as where you plan to meet someone for lunch, where you parked your car, or when is your next dentist's appointment. Furthermore, the time needed for consolidation varies enormously. You know this from your own experience. If someone tells you something you consider interesting, about a topic you already know well, you learn it quickly and remember it well. If you hear something about a topic unfamiliar to you, remembering it is much more difficult. The same is true for laboratory animals: If they have had much training of a particular type, remembering new material of the same type is easy and requires little practice (Tse et al., 2007).

As an alternative to the concept of short-term memory, A. D. Baddeley and G. J. Hitch (1974, 1994) introduced the term **working memory** to emphasize that temporary storage is not a station on the route to long-term memory but the way we store information while we are working with it. A common test of working memory is the **delayed response task,** which requires responding to something that you saw or heard a short while ago. For example, imagine that a light shines above one of several doors. The light goes off, you wait a few seconds, and now you have to go to the door where you saw the light. The delay can be increased or decreased to test your limits. This task can be modified for use with nonhumans as well as humans. During the delay, the learner has to store a representation of the stimulus, and much research points to the prefrontal cortex as the primary location for this storage (Kikuchi-Yorioka & Sawaguchi, 2000; Klingberg, Forssberg, & Westerberg, 2002; Leung, Gore, & Goldman-Rakic, 2002; Sakai, Rowe, & Passingham, 2002). Initially, researchers assumed that the cells stored the information by repetitive action potentials. However, action potentials consume much energy. The brain may use some more economical way of representing temporary information, such as elevated levels of calcium, which would potentiate later responses, when the time comes (Mongillo, Barak, & Tsodyks, 2008).

Many older people have impairments of working memory, probably because of changes in the prefrontal cortex. Studies on aged monkeys find decreases in the number of neurons and the amount of input in certain parts of the prefrontal cortex (D. E. Smith, Rapp, McKay, Roberts, & Tuszynski, 2004). Older humans who show declining memory show declining activity in the prefrontal cortex, whereas those with intact memory show *greater* activity than young adults (A. C. Rosen et al., 2002; Rossi et al., 2004). Presumably, the increased activity means that the prefrontal cortex is working harder in these older adults to compensate for impairments elsewhere in the brain. Furthermore, stimulant drugs that enhance activity in the prefrontal cortex produce a long-lasting improvement in the memory of aged monkeys (Castner & Goldman-Rakic, 2004). Such treatments may have potential for treating people with failing memory.

STOP & CHECK

3. What is the primary brain location for working memory, and what is one hypothesis for how it stores temporary information?

ANSWER

3. The prefrontal cortex is the primary location. According to one hypothesis, it stores temporary information by elevated calcium levels, which potentiate later responses.

The Hippocampus and Amnesia

Amnesia is memory loss. One patient ate lunch and, 20 minutes later, ate a second lunch, apparently having forgotten the first meal. Another 20 minutes later, he started on a third lunch and ate most of it. A few minutes later, he said he would like to "go for a walk and get a good meal" (Rozin, Dow, Moscovitch, & Rajaram, 1998). However, even in severe cases like this, no one loses all kinds of memory equally. This patient still remembered how to eat with a knife and fork, for example, even though he could not remember what he had eaten or when. Studies on amnesia help clarify the distinctions among different kinds of memory and enable us to explore the mechanisms of memory.

People With Hippocampal Damage

In 1953, a man known as H. M. suffered about 10 minor epileptic seizures per day and a major seizure about once a week, despite trying every available antiepileptic drug. Eventually, he and his neurosurgeon considered a desperate measure. Because of evidence suggesting that epilepsy sometimes originates in the hippocampus, the neurosurgeon removed it from both hemispheres, as well as much of the amygdala and other nearby structures in the temporal cortex. Researchers knew almost nothing about the hippocampus at the time, and no one knew what to expect after the surgery. We now know that various parts of the hippocampus are active during both the formation of memories and later recall (Eldridge, Engel, Zeineh, Bookheimer, & Knowlton, 2005). Although the operation reduced H. M.'s epilepsy to no more than two major seizures per year, he almost certainly would have preferred to remain epileptic (Milner, 1959; Penfield & Milner, 1958; Scoville & Milner, 1957). Figure 13.5 shows the normal anatomy of the hippocampus and the damage in H. M. For more about the hippocampus, explore the University of Washington's BrainInfo Web site: http://braininfo.rprc.washington.edu/menumain.html

Anterograde and Retrograde Amnesia. After the surgery, H. M.'s intellect and language abilities remained intact, and his personality remained the same except for emotional placidity, probably related to the amygdala damage (Eichenbaum, 2002). For example, he rarely complained (even about pain) or requested anything (even food). However, he suffered massive **anterograde amnesia** (inability to form memories for events that happened after brain damage). He also suffered a **retrograde amnesia** (loss of memory for events that occurred before the brain damage). Initially, researchers said his retrograde amnesia was confined to 1 to 3 years before the surgery. Later, they found it was more extensive. H. M. is representative of many people who have suffered amnesia after damage to the hippocampus and surrounding structures, which together constitute the medial temporal lobe. All show both anterograde and retrograde amnesia, with the retrograde amnesia being most severe for the last few years before the damage. For example, amnesic patients can usually tell where they lived as a child and where they lived as a teenager but

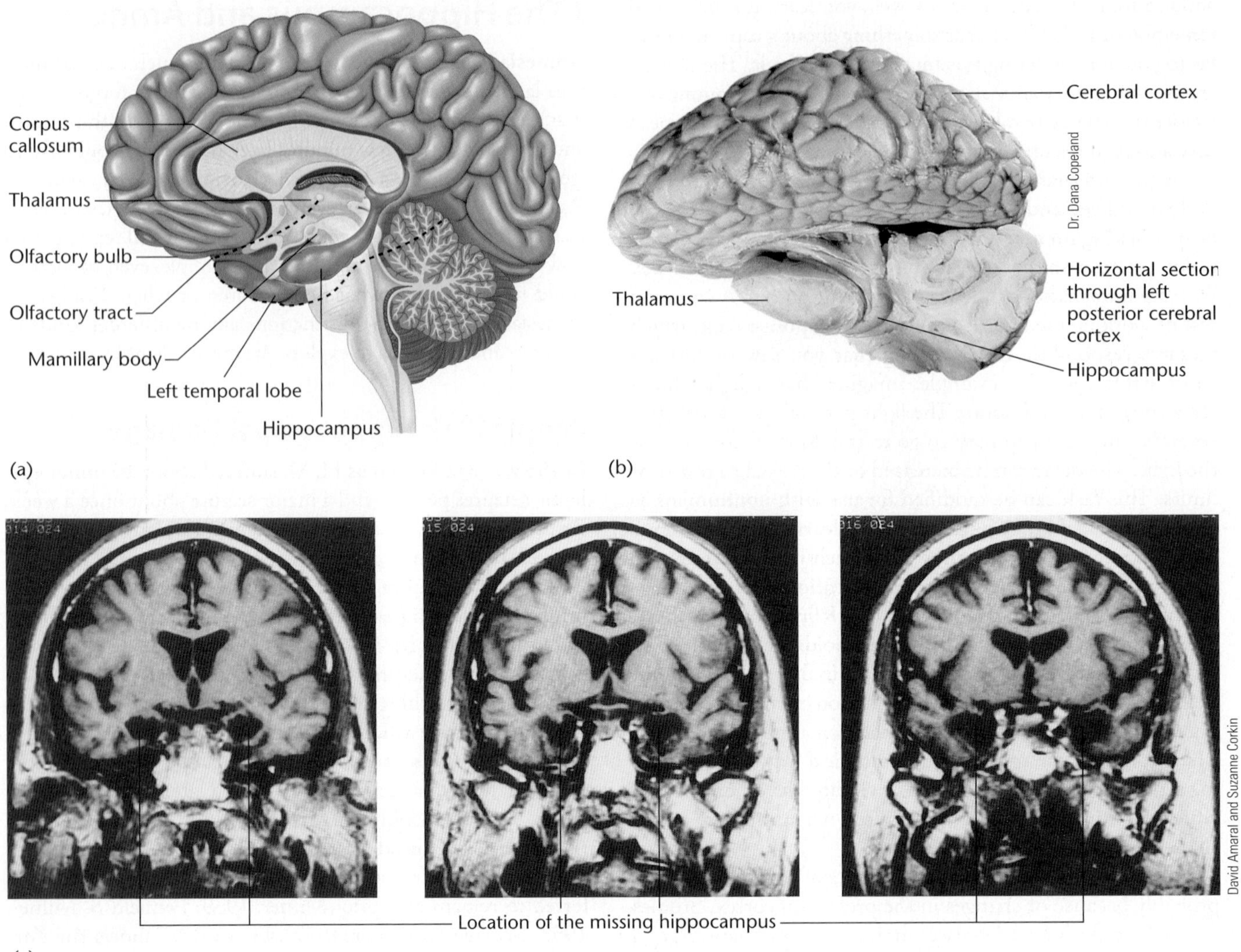

Figure 13.5 The hippocampus
(a) Location of the hippocampus in the human brain. The hippocampus is in the interior of the temporal lobe, so the left hippocampus is closer to the viewer than the rest of this plane; the right hippocampus is behind the plane. The dashed line marks the location of the temporal lobe, which is not visible in the midline. **(b)** Photo of a human brain from above. The right hemisphere is intact. The top part of the left hemisphere has been cut away to show how the hippocampus loops over (dorsal to) the thalamus, posterior to it, and then below (ventral to) it. **(c)** MRI scan of the brain of H. M., showing absence of the hippocampus. Note the large size of this lesion. The three views show coronal planes at successive locations, anterior to posterior.

might not be able to say where they lived 3 years ago (Bayley, Hopkins, & Squire, 2006).

Intact Short-term Memory. Despite H. M.'s huge deficits in forming long-term memories, his short-term or working memory remained intact. In one test, Brenda Milner (1959) asked him to remember the number 584. After a 15-minute delay without distractions, he recalled it correctly, explaining, "It's easy. You just remember 8. You see, 5, 8, and 4 add to 17. You remember 8, subtract it from 17, and it leaves 9. Divide 9 in half and you get 5 and 4, and there you are, 584. Easy." A moment later, after his attention had shifted to another subject, he had forgotten both the number and the complicated line of thought he had associated with it. Most other patients with severe amnesia also show normal short-term or working memory (Shrager, Levy, Hopkins, & Squire, 2008).

Impaired Storage of Long-term Memory. H. M. can read a magazine repeatedly without losing interest. Sometimes, he tells someone about a childhood incident and then, a minute or two later, tells the same person the same story again (Eichenbaum, 2002). In 1980, he moved to a nursing home. Four years later, he could not say where he lived or who cared for him. Although he watches the news on television every night, he recalls only a few fragments of events since 1953. Over the years, many new words have entered the English language, such as *jacuzzi* and *granola*. H. M. cannot define them and treats them as nonsense (Corkin, 2002). For several years after the operation, whenever he was asked his age and the date, he answered "27" and "1953." After a few years, he started guessing wildly, generally underestimating his age by 10 years or more and missing the date by as many as 43 years (Corkin, 1984).

You might wonder whether he is surprised at his own appearance in a mirror or photo. Yes and no. When asked his age or whether his hair has turned gray, he replies that he does not know. When shown a photo of himself with his mother, taken long after his surgery, he recognizes his mother but not himself. However, when he sees himself in the mirror, he shows no surprise (Corkin, 2002). He has, of course, seen himself daily in the mirror over all these years. He also has the context of knowing that the person in the mirror must be himself, whereas the person in the photo could be anyone.

H. M. has formed a few weak semantic (factual) memories for information he encountered repeatedly (Corkin, 2002). For example, although he does not recognize the faces of people who became famous after 1953, he has learned the names of people who were in the news repeatedly, but only if he is given a substantial hint (O'Kane, Kensinger, & Corkin, 2004). When he was given first names and asked to fill in appropriate last names, his replies included some who became famous after 1953, such as these:

	H. M.'s Answer
Elvis	Presley
Martin Luther	King
Billy	Graham
Fidel	Castro
Lyndon	Johnson

He provided even more names when he was given additional information:

	H. M.'s Answer
Famous artist, born in Spain . . . Pablo	Picasso

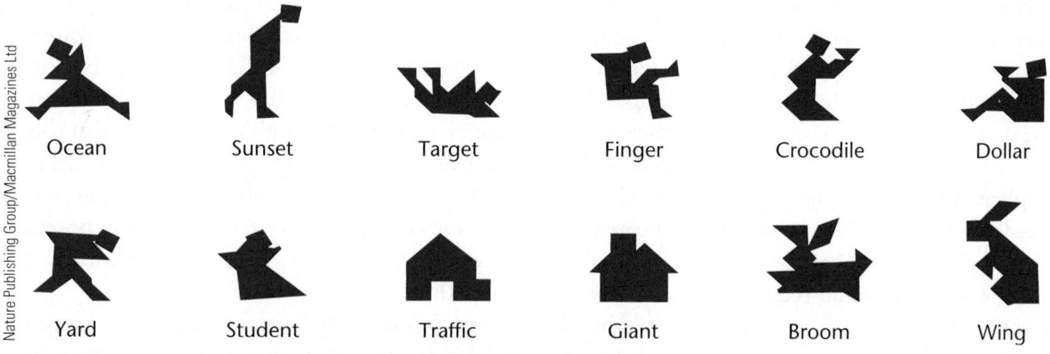

One study found an interesting qualification to the usual rule that patients with amnesia cannot learn new information. The investigators showed a series of shapes with unrelated labels, as shown in Figure 13.6. As expected, amnesic patients made no progress toward learning the labels for each shape. Then the researchers let the patients devise their own labels. Each patient had to look at one shape at a time and describe it so that another person, who was looking at the 12 shapes unlabeled, would know which one the patient was looking at. At first, the descriptions were slow and uninformative. For the shape at the upper right of Figure 13.6, one patient said, "The next one looks almost . . . the opposite of somebody kind uh . . . slumped down, on the ground, with the same type of . . ." Eventually, he said it looked like someone sleeping with his knees bent. By the fourth trial, he quickly labeled that shape as "the siesta guy," and he continued saying the same thing from then on, even in later sessions on later days (Duff, Hengst, Tranel, & Cohen, 2006).

Severe Impairment of Episodic Memory. H. M. has particularly severe impairment of **episodic memories,** memories of single events. He cannot describe any experience that he has had since 1953. His retrograde amnesia is also greatest for episodic memories. He can describe facts that he learned before his operation but very few personal experiences. Another patient, K. C., suffered widespread brain damage after a motorcycle accident, with scattered damage in the hippocampus and other locations. Like H. M., he is very limited in learning any new factual information. In addition, he has an apparently complete loss of episodic memories. He cannot describe a single event from any time of his life, although he remembers many facts that he had known before the damage. When he looks at old family pictures in a photo album, he can identify the people and sometimes the places, but he cannot remember anything about the events that happened in the photos (Rosenbaum et al., 2005). Although his brain damage is so diffuse that we cannot be sure which part of the damage is responsible for his memory loss, the observations do tell us that the brain treats episodic memories differently from other memories.

How would memory loss affect people's ability to imagine the future? If you try to imagine a future event, you call upon your memory of similar experiences and modify them. Studies using fMRI show that describing past events and imagining future events activate mostly the same areas, including the hippocampus (Addis, Wong, & Schacter, 2007). People with amnesia are just as impaired at imagining the future as they are at describing the past. For example, here is part of one patient's attempt to imagine a visit to a museum, with prompts by

Figure 13.6 Displays for a memory test of amnesic patients
Although they could not remember the arbitrary labels that an experimenter gave to each object (as shown), they did remember the descriptions that they devised themselves. *(From Duff, M. C., Hengst, J., Tranel, D., & Cohen, N. J. (2006). Development of shared information in communication despite hippocampal amnesia.* Nature Neuroscience, 9, *140–146. Used by permission, Macmillan Publishing Ltd.)*

a psychologist (Hassabis, Kumaran, Vann, & Maguire, 2007, p. 1727):

Patient: [pause] There's not a lot, as it happens.
Psychologist: So what does it look like in your imagined scene?
Patient: Well, there's big doors. The openings would be high, so the doors would be very big with brass handles, the ceiling would be made of glass, so there's plenty of light coming through. Huge room, exit on either side of the room, there's a pathway and map through the center and on either side there'd be the exhibits. [pause] I don't know what they are. There'd be people. [pause] To be honest there's not a lot coming. . . . My imagination isn't . . . well, I'm not imagining it, let's put it that way. . . . I'm not picturing anything at the moment.

Better Implicit Than Explicit Memory.

H. M. and nearly all other patients with amnesia show better *implicit* than *explicit* memory. **Explicit memory** is deliberate recall of information that one recognizes as a memory. It is tested by such questions as: "What was the last novel you read?" and "What did you eat for dinner last night?" **Implicit memory** is an influence of recent experience on behavior, even if one does not recognize that influence. For example, you might be talking to someone about sports while other people nearby are carrying on a conversation about the latest movies. If asked, you could not say what the others were talking about, but suddenly, you comment for no apparent reason, "I wonder what's on at the movies?" To experience implicit memory, try the Online Try It Yourself exercise "Implicit Memories."

Here is another example of implicit memory: Have you ever played the video game Tetris? In Tetris, geometrical forms such as and fall from the top, and the player must move and rotate them to fill available spaces at the bottom of the screen. Normal people improve their skill over a few hours and can describe the game and its strategy. After playing the same number of hours, patients with amnesia cannot describe the game and say they don't remember playing it. Nevertheless, they improve—a little. Moreover, when they are about to fall asleep, they report seeing images of little piles of blocks falling and rotating (Stickgold, Malia, Maguire, Roddenberry, & O'Connor, 2000). They are puzzled and wonder what these images mean!

Still another example of implicit memory: As an experiment, three hospital workers agreed to act in special ways toward a patient with amnesia. One was as pleasant as possible. The second was neutral. The third was stern, refused all requests, and made the patient perform boring tasks. After 5 days, the patient was asked to look at photos of the three workers and try to identify them or say anything he knew about them. He said he did not recognize any of them. Then he was asked which one he would approach as a possible friend or which one he would ask for help. He was asked this question repeatedly—it was possible to ask repeatedly because he never remembered being asked before—and he usually chose the photo of the "friendly" person and never chose the "unfriendly" person in spite of the fact that the unfriendly person was a beautiful woman, smiling in the photograph (Tranel & Damasio, 1993). He could not say why he did not prefer her.

In summary, H. M. and similar patients with amnesia have:

- Normal short-term or working memory
- Severe anterograde amnesia for declarative memory—that is, difficulty forming new declarative memories
- In many cases, a severe loss of episodic memories
- Better implicit than explicit memory

STOP & CHECK

4. What is the difference between anterograde and retrograde amnesia?
5. Which types of memory are least impaired in H. M.?

ANSWERS

4. Retrograde amnesia is forgetting events before brain damage; anterograde amnesia is failing to store memories of events after brain damage. 5. H. M. is least impaired on short-term memory and implicit memory.

Theories of the Function of the Hippocampus

Exactly how does the hippocampus contribute to memory? Some of the research comes from H. M. and other patients with damage to the hippocampus, but to get better control over both the anatomy and the environment, researchers also conduct research on laboratory animals.

The Hippocampus and Declarative Memory. Although patients with hippocampal damage have enormous trouble learning new facts, they acquire new skills without apparent difficulty. They have impaired **declarative memory,** the ability to state a memory in words, but intact **procedural memory,** the development of motor skills and habits. For example, H. M. has learned to read words written backward, as they would be seen in a mirror, although he is surprised at this skill, as he does not remember having tried it before (Corkin, 2002). Patient K. C. has a part-time job at a library and has learned to use the Dewey decimal system in sorting books, although he does not remember when or where he learned it (Rosenbaum et al., 2005).

Therefore, Larry Squire (1992) proposed that the hippocampus is critical for declarative memory, especially episodic memory. How could we test this hypothesis with nonhumans, who cannot "declare" anything? What could they do that would be the equivalent of declarative or episodic memory?

Larry R. Squire

Memory is personal and evocative, intertwined with emotion, and it provides us with a sense of who we are. During the past two decades there has been a revolution in our understanding of what memory is and what happens in the brain when we learn and remember. At the beginning of the 21st century, one has the sense that memory may be the first mental faculty that will be understandable in terms of molecules, cells, brain systems, and behavior. Yet, even with all the progress, there can be no doubt that the study of the brain is still a young science, rich with opportunity for the student and beginning scientist. This is a good time to hear about the promise and excitement of neuroscience. The best is yet to come.

Here is one attempt: A rat digs food out of five piles of sand, each with a different odor. Then it gets a choice between two of the odors and is rewarded if it goes toward the one it smelled first. Intact rats learn to respond correctly, apparently demonstrating memory of not only what they smelled but also when they smelled it. Memory of a specific event qualifies as episodic, at least by a broad definition. Rats with hippocampal damage do poorly on this task (Fortin, Agster, & Eichenbaum, 2002; Kesner, Gilbert, & Barua, 2002).

In the **delayed matching-to-sample task,** an animal sees an object (the sample) and then, after a delay, gets a choice between two objects, from which it must choose the one that matches the sample. In the **delayed nonmatching-to-sample task,** the procedure is the same except that the animal must choose the object that is different from the sample (Figure 13.7). In both cases, the animal must remember which object was present on this occasion, thereby showing what we might call a declarative memory, perhaps an episodic memory. Hippocampal damage strongly impairs performance in most cases (Zola et al., 2000).

At one time, researchers expected to find that one set of memory tasks (declarative) depends on the hippocampus, and another set (procedural) depends on other areas, probably the basal ganglia. The results turned out to be more complex. With what seem like minor variations in procedure, the delayed matching- and nonmatching-to-sample tasks might require an intact hippocampus or might not (Aggleton, Blindt, & Rawlins, 1989). Many tasks ordinarily call upon both the hippocampus and the basal ganglia (Albouy et al., 2008). Furthermore, one system can substitute for the other. For example, imagine that you have to learn to choose ✂ instead of ⌘, ✈ instead of ✳, and so forth through a series of eight pairs. Most normal adults learn all the pairs quickly and can describe the correct and incorrect patterns. People with damage to the temporal lobes, including the hippocampus, seem at first incapable of learning, but they make slow progress. After they have learned, their results are different from other people's learning. They report that they do not recognize the task, and they cannot describe what they have learned. From all indications, they are learning motor habits or procedures, rather than declarative memories, the way other people do (Bayley, Frascino, & Squire, 2005).

It is possible to mimic these results with people who have an intact brain. Suppose you have this task: You will see a series of displays, each containing a set of shapes that provide clues about tomorrow's weather in some city. You are to examine the clues and guess whether it will rain. At first, you are just guessing, but the experimenter tells you whether you guessed correctly, and you gradually learn which shapes predict rain and which ones don't. Your guesses become more accurate. Furthermore, you can explain how you made your decision: One shape means a little more than three-fourths chance of rain, another shape means a little more than one-half chance of rain, and so forth. If two or three symbols are present at once, you combine the clues, paying the most attention to the ones with highest accuracy. Studies with fMRI confirm that this task activates your hippocampus.

Now imagine you had done the same task, except with a major distraction: While trying to guess the weather, you listen to a series of high and low tones, and you have to count the high-pitched tones. You will still be able to learn to make reasonable predictions, but you won't be able to say (declarative memory) how you did it. With this procedure, fMRI results say that you are relying on your basal ganglia, not your hippocampus (Foerde, Knowlton, & Poldrack, 2006).

Together, these results do suggest that the hippocampus is more important for declarative memory and the basal ganglia more important for procedural memory. However, they argue strongly against dividing tasks into procedural and declarative tasks. Most tasks tap both kinds of memory, and it is possible to shift from one type of memory to the other, even on the same task.

Monkey lifts sample object to get food. Food is under the new object.

Figure 13.7 Procedure for delayed nonmatching-to-sample task

STOP & CHECK

6. If you learn a skill (e.g., predicting the weather) as a declarative memory, instead of learning the same skill as a procedural habit, how will the outcome differ?

ANSWER

6. If you learn it as a declarative memory, you will be able to describe what you have learned and probably apply the skill in a greater variety of situations. Also, the memory will depend more on the hippocampus instead of the basal ganglia.

The Hippocampus and Spatial Memory. A second hypothesis is that the hippocampus is especially important for spatial memories. Electrical recordings indicate that many neurons in a rat's hippocampus are tuned to particular spatial locations, responding best when an animal is in a particular place (O'Keefe & Burgess, 1996) or looking in a particular direction (Dudchenko & Taube, 1997; Rolls, 1996a). In one study, rats ran down a runway to get food. Various cells of the hippocampus were active at different locations along the way. When a rat stopped, the same cells were active again in reverse order, as if rewinding a tape recording. Researchers speculate that this process may help store memories of where the rat was (Foster & Wilson, 2006).

Ordinarily, a given hippocampal cell responds in the same way whenever the rat is in a particular environment. If we move the rat to a new environment or change the current environment—for example, widening the cage—the various cells "remap" their new environment (Leutgeb et al., 2005; Moita, Rosis, Zhou, LeDoux, & Blair, 2004). Younger rats readjust their hippocampal maps faster than older rats and more quickly learn to find their way to important places (Rosenzweig, Redish, McNaughton, & Barnes, 2003). When people perform spatial tasks, such as imagining the best route between one friend's house and another, fMRI results show enhanced activity in the hippocampus (Kumaran & Maguire, 2005). All of these results suggest that the hippocampus is particularly important for spatial memory.

Researchers conducted PET scans on the brains of London taxi drivers as they answered questions such as, "What's the shortest legal route from the Carlton Tower Hotel to the Sherlock Holmes Museum?" (London taxi drivers are well trained and answer with impressive accuracy.) Answering these route questions activated their hippocampus much more than did answering nonspatial questions. MRI scans also revealed that the taxi drivers have a larger than average posterior hippocampus and that the longer they had been taxi drivers, the larger their posterior hippocampus (Maguire et al., 2000). This surprising result suggests actual growth of the adult human hippocampus in response to spatial learning experiences.

Consider a couple of nonhuman examples of spatial memory. A **radial maze** has eight or more arms, some of which have a bit of food or other reinforcer at the end (Figure 13.8).

Robert Folz/Visuals Unlimited

Figure 13.8 A radial maze
A rat that reenters one arm before trying other arms has made an error of spatial working memory.

A rat placed in the center can find food by exploring each arm once and only once. In a variation of the task, a rat might have to learn that the arms with a rough floor never have food or that the arms pointing toward the window never have food. So a rat can make a mistake either by entering a never-correct arm or by entering a correct arm twice.

Rats with damage to the hippocampus seldom enter the never-correct arms, but they often enter a correct arm twice. That is, they forget which arms they have already tried (Jarrard, Okaichi, Steward, & Goldschmidt, 1984; Olton & Papas, 1979; Olton, Walker, & Gage, 1978). Rats show similar impairments after damage to the areas of thalamus and cortex that send information to the hippocampus (Mair, Burk, & Porter, 2003).

Hippocampal damage also impairs performance on another test of spatial memory, the **Morris water maze task,** in which a rat must swim through murky water to find a rest platform that is just under the surface (Figure 13.9). (Rats swim as little as they can. Humans are among the very few land mammals that swim recreationally. Polar bears and some dog breeds do, also.) A rat with hippocampal damage slowly learns to find the platform if it always starts from the same place and the rest platform is always in the same place. However, if it has to start from a different location or if the rest platform occasionally moves from one location to another, the rat is disoriented (Eichenbaum, 2000; P. Liu & Bilkey, 2001).

If a rat has already learned to find the platform before damage to the hippocampus, the damage leaves the rat exploring the water haphazardly, like a rat that had never been in the water maze before. It ignores landmarks, including a beacon of light pointing to the platform. Researchers observed that the rat acts as if it not only forgot where the platform was but also forgot that there even was a platform (R. E. Clark, Broadbent, & Squire, 2007).

Interesting evidence for the role of the hippocampus in spatial memory comes from comparisons of closely related species that differ in their spatial memory. Clark's nutcracker,

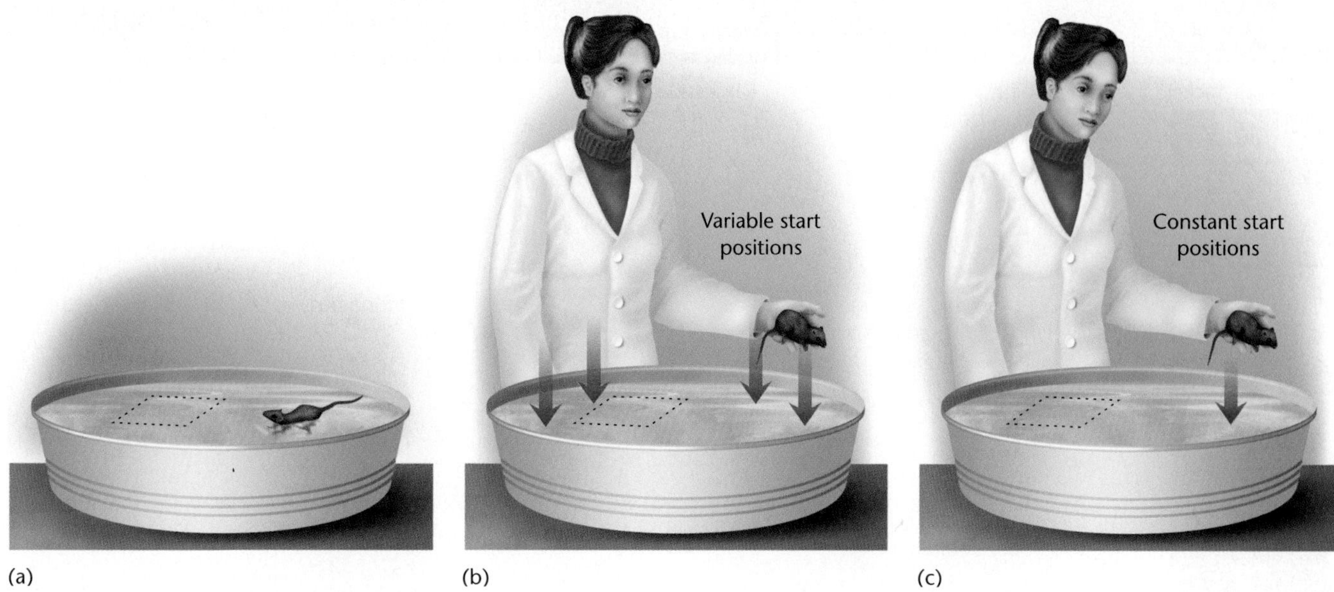

Figure 13.9 The Morris water maze task
A rat is placed in murky water. A platform that would provide support is submerged so the rat cannot see it. Rats with hippocampal damage have trouble remembering the location of the platform.

a member of the jay family, lives at high altitudes in western North America. During the summer and fall, it buries seeds in thousands of locations and then digs them up to survive the winter, when other food is unavailable. Pinyon jays, which live at lower elevations, bury less food and depend on it less to survive the winter. Scrub jays and Mexican jays, living at still lower altitudes, depend even less on stored food. Researchers have found that of these four species, the Clark's nutcrackers have the largest hippocampus and perform best on tests of spatial memory. Pinyon jays are second best in both respects. On nonspatial tasks, such as color memory, size of hippocampus does not correlate with success (Basil, Kamil, Balda, & Fite, 1996; Olson, Kamil, Balda, & Nims, 1995) (Figure 13.10). In short, the species comparisons support a link between the hippocampus and spatial memory.

The Hippocampus and Context. A third hypothesis relates to learning about context. You could try this yourself: Recall something that you learned in class within the last day or two, and describe what was going on when you learned it. Then similarly describe something you learned in class several months or years ago. How do your two narratives differ? Your recent narrative almost certainly includes more detail. You might remember where you were, who else was there, where people were sitting, perhaps what some of them were wearing, exactly what the professor said, maybe the weather outside, and other important and not so important details. When you describe something you learned in class long ago, you have lost most of those details. You remember the highlights or "gist" of what you learned but little about the context of learning it.

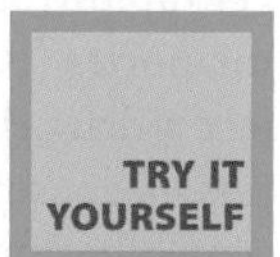

The hippocampus may be particularly important for remembering the details and context of an event. A recent memory, which generally depends on the hippocampus, includes much detail. As time passes, memory becomes less detailed and less dependent on the hippocampus. The same is true of rats: When rats are trained to do something, and then tested again after a short delay, they remember the response best if they are tested in the same location. That is, their memory depends on the context. As time passes, the context matters less and less, and to the extent that rats remember the response, they remember it equally well in a different location. If we do the same research on rats with damage to the hippocampus, they never show a difference between testing in the place where they were trained and some other place. Their memory doesn't depend on context at all, presumably because they do not remember the context (Winocur, Moscovitch, & Sekeres, 2007).

In humans, recalling a recent memory (which usually includes details and context) activates the hippocampus. Recalling an older memory may or may not activate the hippocampus, except for episodic memories, which necessarily include at least some context details. This hypothesis is well suited to dealing with the observation that people with hippocampal damage have particular trouble with episodic memories.

We have considered three hypotheses of the role of the hippocampus and found evidence to support each. The views are not necessarily in conflict. It is possible for the hippocampus to be contributing in more than one way. It is also possible that researchers will find some way to combine all three hypotheses into one.

	Habitat	Size of Hippocampus Relative to Rest of Brain	Spatial Memory	Color Memory
Clark's nutcracker	Lives high in mountains; stores food in summer and relies on finding it to survive the winter.	Largest	Best	Slightly worse
Pinyon jay	Lives at fairly high altitude; depends on stored food to survive the winter.	Second largest	Second best	Slightly better
Scrub jay	Stores some food but less dependent on it.	Smaller	Less good	Slightly worse
Mexican jay	Stores some food but less dependent on it.	Smaller	Less good	Slightly better

Figure 13.10 Hippocampus and spatial memory in jays
Of four western North American birds in the jay family, the species that rely most heavily on stored food to get through the winter have the largest hippocampus and perform best on laboratory tests of spatial memory. They have no consistent advantage on nonspatial memory. *(Based on results of Basil, Kamil, Balda, & Fite, 1996; Olson, Kamil, Balda, & Nims, 1995)*

STOP & CHECK

7. Suppose a rat is in a radial maze in which six arms have food once per day, and two other arms never have food. What kind of mistake does a rat with hippocampal damage make?

8. According to the context hypothesis, why does hippocampal damage impair episodic memory?

ANSWERS

7. Although it learns not to enter the arms that are never correct, it seems to forget which arms it has entered today, and it enters a single arm repeatedly. **8.** The hippocampus is especially important for remembering context, and episodic memory necessarily includes some context and detail.

The Hippocampus and Consolidation

As mentioned, Donald Hebb's original concept specified that short-term memories are gradually consolidated, or strengthened, into long-term memories. One way of describing amnesia after hippocampal damage is that people form short-term but not long-term memories. That is, they fail to consolidate. Rats with damage to the hippocampus, or the input from other structures to the hippocampus, learn responses but forget rapidly, suggesting that they do not consolidate long-term memories (Remondes & Schuman, 2004). Similarly, if we inject a drug that blocks protein synthesis in a rat's hippocampus, it does not prevent learning, but it prevents the rat from remembering the correct response 2 days later. Injecting the drug shortly *after* the training has the same effect. Evidently, the drug does not block learning but does block consolidation (Canal & Gold, 2007).

Consolidating a long-term memory clearly depends on more than the passage of time. Think about your high school experiences. You may have spent hours memorizing historical names and dates that you then quickly forgot. Yet you clearly remember the first time a special person smiled at you, the time you said something foolish in class and people laughed at you, the time you won a major honor, or the frightening moment when you heard that a friend was hurt in a car accident. Emotionally stirring memories consolidate quickly.

How does the emotional response enhance consolidation? Remember from Chapter 12 that stressful or emotionally exciting experiences increase the secretion of epinephrine (adrenaline) and cortisol. Small to moderate amounts of cortisol activate the amygdala and hippocampus, where they enhance the storage and consolidation of recent experiences (Cahill & McGaugh, 1998). The amygdala in turn stimulates the hippocampus and cerebral cortex, which are both important for memory storage. However, prolonged stress, which releases even more cortisol, impairs memory (deQuervain, Roozendaal, & McGaugh, 1998; Newcomer et al., 1999).

James L. McGaugh

Memory is perhaps the most critical capacity that we have as humans. Memory is not simply a record of experiences; it is the basis of our knowledge of the world, our skills, our hopes and dreams and our ability to interact with others and thus influence our destinies. Investigation of how the brain enables us to bridge our present existence with our past and future is thus essential for understanding human nature. Clearly, the most exciting challenge of science is to determine how brain cells and systems create our memories.

Even if time is not the only or main influence in consolidation, memories do sometimes grow stronger over time. In one study, eight people aged 60 to 70 years examined photos of people who were famous at various times in the past. According to fMRI scans, several brain areas responded most strongly to recently famous people and least to those famous long ago, even though the participants easily recognized all of the faces (Haist, Gore, & Mao, 2001). In two other studies, fMRI showed stronger responses while people recalled recent events from their own lives than when they recalled autobiographical events from longer ago, despite equal accuracy (Maguire & Frith, 2003; Niki & Luo, 2002). One interpretation is that the brain works harder to identify the recent items, whereas the older ones are stored more firmly. However, the interpretation is uncertain: Did early memories consolidate over the decades, or did they form more strongly in the first place? People generally remember music, movies, politicians, and almost anything else from their adolescence and young adulthood better than they remember similar items from later in life; events from ages 10 to 30 are sometimes called the "autobiographical memory bump" (Berntsen & Rubin, 2002).

STOP & CHECK

9. How do epinephrine and cortisol enhance memory storage?

ANSWER

9. Epinephrine and cortisol both enhance emotional memories by stimulating the amygdala and hippocampus.

Other Types of Amnesia

Different kinds of brain damage produce different types of amnesia. Here we briefly consider two more examples: Korsakoff's syndrome and Alzheimer's disease.

Korsakoff's Syndrome and Other Prefrontal Damage

Korsakoff's syndrome, also known as *Wernicke-Korsakoff syndrome,* is brain damage caused by prolonged thiamine deficiency. Severe thiamine deficiency occurs mostly in chronic alcoholics who go for weeks at a time on a diet of nothing but alcoholic beverages, which are lacking in vitamins. The brain needs thiamine (vitamin B_1) to metabolize glucose, its primary fuel. Prolonged thiamine deficiency leads to a loss or shrinkage of neurons throughout the brain, and one of the areas most affected is the dorsomedial thalamus, which is the main source of input to the prefrontal cortex (Squire, Amaral, & Press, 1990; Victor, Adams, & Collins, 1971). The symptoms of Korsakoff's syndrome are similar to those of people with damage to the prefrontal cortex, including apathy, confusion, and memory loss. One patient was in a fencing duel when the opponent's foil went through his nostril and into his dorsomedial thalamus. The injury left him with a severe memory loss (Squire, Amaral, Zola-Morgan, Kritchevsky, & Press, 1989).

Korsakoff's patients and other patients with frontal lobe damage have difficulties in reasoning about their memories (Moscovitch, 1992). Suppose I ask, "Which happened to you most recently—graduation from high school, getting your first driver's license, or reading Chapter 2 of *Biological Psychology?*" You reason it out: "I started driving during my junior year of high school, so that came before graduation. *Biological Psychology* is one of my college texts, so I started reading it after high school." Someone with frontal lobe damage has trouble with even this simple kind of reasoning.

A distinctive symptom of Korsakoff's syndrome is **confabulation,** in which patients guess to fill in memory gaps. They confabulate only on questions for which they would expect to know the answer. For example, to a nonsense question like "Who is Princess Lolita?" they reply, "I don't know." They confabulate mainly on questions about themselves, their family, and other familiar topics (Schnider, 2003). Usually, the confabulated answer was true in the past but not now, such as, "I went dancing last night," or "I need to go home and take care of my children." Most of the confabulated answers are more pleasant than the currently true answers (Fotopoulou, Solms, & Turnbull, 2004). That tendency may reflect the patient's attempt to maintain pleasant emotions or merely the fact that for a patient in a hospital, life in the past was, on the whole, more pleasant than the present.

The tendency to confabulate produces a fascinating influence on the strategies for studying. Suppose you had to learn a long list of three-word sentences such as: "Medicine cured hiccups" and "Tourist desired snapshot." Would you simply reread the list many times? Or would you alternate between reading the list and testing yourself?

Medicine cured ______________________.

Tourist desired ______________________.

Almost everyone learns better the second way. Completing the sentences forces you to be more active and calls your attention to the items you have not yet learned. Korsakoff's patients, however, learn much better the first way, by reading the list over and over. The reason is, when they test themselves, they confabulate. ("*Medicine cured headache. Tourist desired passport.*") Then they remember their confabulation instead of the correct answer (Hamann & Squire, 1995).

STOP & CHECK

10. On what kind of question is someone with Korsakoff's syndrome most likely to confabulate?

ANSWER

10. Patients with Korsakoff's syndrome confabulate on questions for which they would expect to know the answer, such as questions about themselves. Their confabulations are usually statements that were true at one time.

Alzheimer's Disease

Another cause of memory loss is **Alzheimer's** (AHLTZ-hime-ers) **disease.** Daniel Schacter (1983) reported playing golf with an Alzheimer's patient who remembered the rules and jargon of the game correctly but could not remember how many strokes he took on any hole. On five occasions, he teed off, waited for the other player to tee off, and then teed off again, having forgotten his first shot. As with H. M. and Korsakoff's patients, Alzheimer's patients have better procedural than declarative memory. They learn new skills but then surprise themselves with their good performance because they don't remember doing it before (Gabrieli, Corkin, Mickel, & Growdon, 1993). Their memory and alertness vary substantially from one day to another and from one time to another within a day, suggesting that many of their problems result from malfunctioning neurons, not just the death of neurons (Palop, Chin, & Mucke, 2006).

Alzheimer's disease gradually progresses to more serious memory loss, confusion, depression, restlessness, hallucinations, delusions, sleeplessness, and loss of appetite. It occasionally strikes people younger than age 40 but becomes more common with age, affecting almost 5% of people between ages 65 and 74 and almost 50% of people over 85 (Evans et al., 1989).

The first major clue to the cause of Alzheimer's was the fact that people with *Down syndrome* (a type of mental retardation) almost invariably get Alzheimer's disease if they survive into middle age (Lott, 1982). People with Down syndrome have three copies of chromosome 21 rather than the usual two. That fact led investigators to examine chromosome 21, where they found a gene linked to many cases of early-onset Alzheimer's disease (Goate et al., 1991; Murrell, Farlow, Ghetti, & Benson, 1991). Later researchers found genes on other chromosomes that also lead to early-onset Alzheimer's disease (Levy-Lahad et al., 1995; Schellenberg et al., 1992; Sherrington et al., 1995). However, more than 99% of cases have onset after age 60 to 65. Genes have less control for late-onset Alzheimer's disease, and about half of all patients have no known relatives with the disease (St George-Hyslop, 2000).

Although genes do not completely control Alzheimer's disease, understanding their mode of action has shed light on the underlying causes. The genes controlling early-onset Alzheimer's disease cause a protein called **amyloid-β** or **β-amyloid** to accumulate both inside and outside neurons (LaFerla, Green, & Oddo, 2007). High levels of amyloid damage axons and dendrites. Those damaged structures cluster into structures called *plaques***,** which begin to form before the behavioral symptoms appear (Selkoe, 2000). As the plaques accumulate, the cerebral cortex, hippocampus, and other areas atrophy (waste away), as Figures 13.11 and 13.12 show.

In addition to amyloid-β, Alzheimer's patients also accumulate an abnormal form of the **tau protein** that is part of the intracellular support structure of neurons (Davies, 2000). Tau

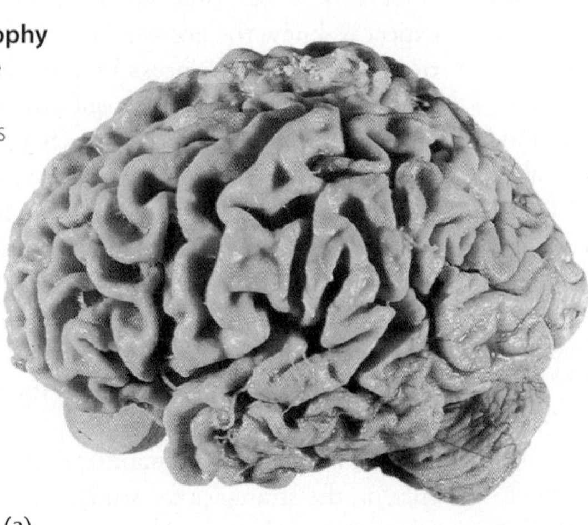

(a)

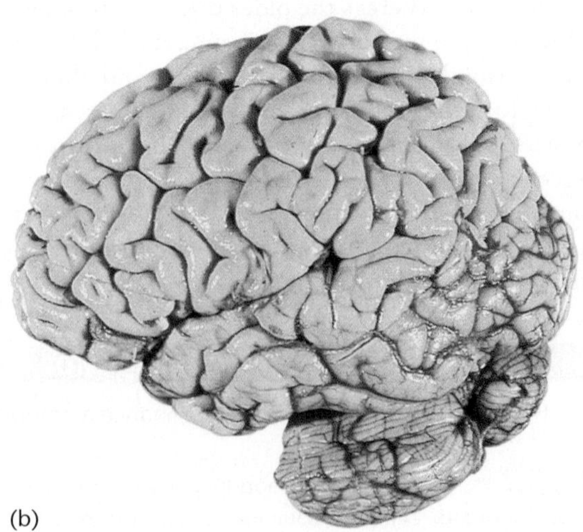

(b)

Figure 13.11 Brain atrophy in Alzheimer's disease
The cerebral cortex of a patient with Alzheimer's **(a)** has gyri that are clearly shrunken in comparison with those of a normal person **(b).**

Dr. Robert D. Terry, Department of Neurosciences, School of Medicine, University of California at San Diego.

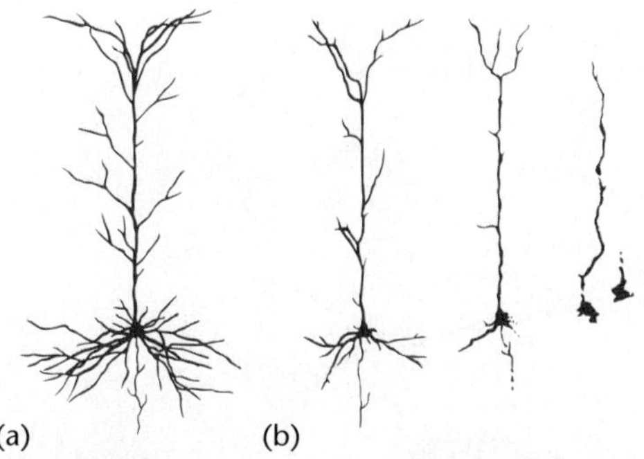

Figure 13.12 Neuronal degeneration in Alzheimer's disease
(a) A cell in the prefrontal cortex of a normal human; **(b)** cells from the same area of cortex in Alzheimer's disease patients at various stages of deterioration. Note the shrinkage of the dendritic tree. *(After "Dendritic changes," by A. B. Scheibel, p. 70. In B. Reisberg, Ed.,* Alzheimer's Disease, *1983. Free Press.)*

produces *tangles*, structures formed from degenerating structures within neuronal cell bodies (Figure 13.13).

Most researchers are convinced that amyloid deposits are the origin of Alzheimer's disease, but the combination of amyloid and tau produces the behavioral deficits. Treatments that reduce tau levels decrease the memory impairments of mice with a condition resembling Alzheimer's disease (Roberson et al., 2007; SantaCruz et al., 2005).

At this point, no drug is highly effective for Alzheimer's disease, although many new possibilities are under investigation (Roberson & Mucke, 2006). The most common treatment is to give drugs that stimulate acetylcholine receptors or prolong acetylcholine release. The result is increased arousal. A promising approach for preventing Alzheimer's is to decrease amyloid-β production by increased consumption of antioxidants, such as those found in dark fruits and vegetables (Joseph et al., 1998). A particularly promising possibility is *curcumin*, a component of turmeric, a spice in Indian curries. Research with aged mice found that curcumin reduced amyloid levels and plaques (Yang et al., 2005). For links to more information about Alzheimer's disease, check the Alzheimer Research Forum Web site: http://www.alzforum.org/default.asp

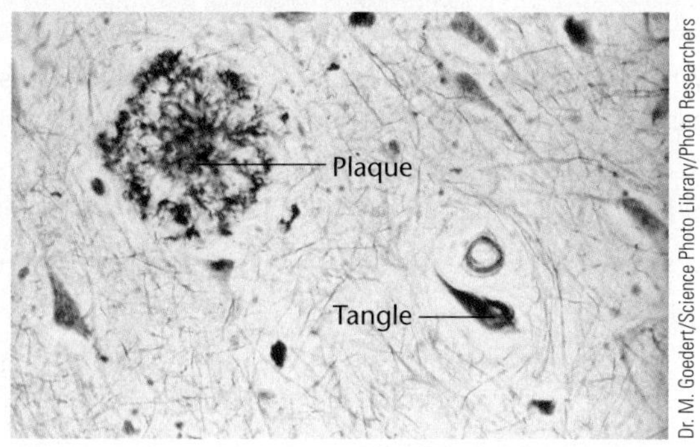

Figure 13.13 Cerebral cortex of an Alzheimer's patient
Amyloid plaque is composed of the protein $A\beta_{42}$. *(From Taylor, Hardy, & Fischbeck, 2002)*

What Patients With Amnesia Teach Us

The study of patients with amnesia reveals that people do not lose all aspects of memory equally. A patient with great difficulty establishing new memories may be able to remember events from long ago, and someone with greatly impaired factual memory may be able to learn new skills reasonably well. Evidently, people have several somewhat independent kinds of memory that depend on different brain areas.

STOP & CHECK

11. What is amyloid-β and how does it relate to Alzheimer's disease?

ANSWER

11. The protein amyloid-β accumulates in the brains of patients with Alzheimer's disease and is probably the cause of the disease.

The Role of Other Brain Areas in Memory

So far, we have focused on the hippocampus (important for storing certain kinds of memories), the basal ganglia (important for procedural memories), and the prefrontal cortex (important for working memory and reasoning). Other brain areas are important for learning and memory, too. In fact, nearly the entire cortex and many subcortical areas contribute in one way or another.

Much research shows that the amygdala is particularly important for fear learning, such as when a stimulus is paired with shock (Reijmers, Perkins, Matsuo, & Mayford, 2007). This result is what we would expect, considering what Chapter 12 reported about the importance of the amygdala in fear.

Investigators asked two patients with parietal lobe damage to describe various events from their past. When tested this way, their episodic memory appeared sparse, almost devoid of details. However, the investigators asked follow-up questions, such as, "Where were you?" and "Who else was there at the time?" These patients had no trouble answering these questions, indicating that their episodic memories were intact, as well as their speech and their willingness to cooperate. What was lacking was their ability to elaborate on a memory spontaneously (Berryhill, Phuong, Picasso, Cabeza, & Olson, 2007). Ordinarily, when most of us recall an event, one thing reminds us of another, and we start adding one detail after another, until we have said all that we know. In people with parietal lobe damage, that process of associating one piece with another is impaired.

People with damage in the anterior and inferior regions of the temporal lobe suffer **semantic dementia,** which is a loss of semantic memory. For example, one patient while riding down

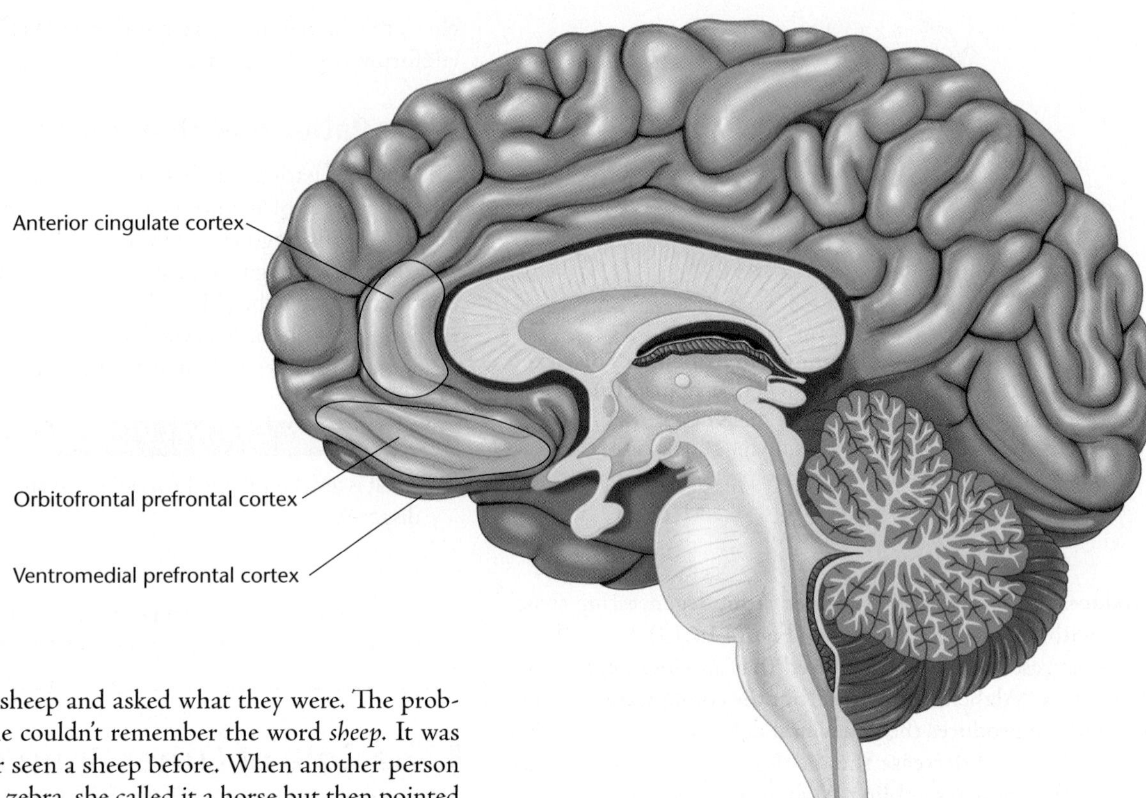

Figure 13.14 Three areas important for making decisions
These areas respond to the expected outcome of a decision relative to other possible outcomes and to discrepancies between actual and expected outcomes. The orbitofrontal cortex gets its name because it is close to the orbit of the eye.

a road saw some sheep and asked what they were. The problem wasn't that he couldn't remember the word *sheep*. It was as if he had never seen a sheep before. When another person saw a picture of a zebra, she called it a horse but then pointed at the stripes and asked what "those funny things" were. She hadn't merely lost the word *zebra* but had lost the concept of zebra. Such patients cannot remember the typical color of common fruits and vegetables or the appearance of various animals. Don't think of the anterior and inferior temporal lobe as the sole point of storage for semantic memory. These areas store some of the information and serve as a "hub" for communicating with other brain areas to bring together a full concept (Patterson, Nestor, & Rogers, 2007).

Parts of the prefrontal cortex, shown in Figure 13.14, are important for learning about rewards and punishments. The basal ganglia also learn about the reward values of various actions, but they learn slowly, based on the average reward over a long period of time. The prefrontal cortex responds more quickly, based on the most recent events. If you are confronted with an opportunity to make a response, cells in the ventromedial prefrontal cortex respond based on the reward to be expected, based on past experience. Cells in the orbitofrontal cortex respond based on how that reward compares to other possible choices. For example, a \$2 reward might be good or bad depending on whether other choices offer a \$1 or \$5 reward. Within the anterior cingulate cortex, some cells respond when the reward is more than expected, and others when it is less than expected (Plassman, O'Doherty, & Rangel, 2007; Roesch & Olson, 2004; Rushworth & Behrens, 2008). According to fMRI data, some people show greater prefrontal cortex reactions than others do when they incur disappointments or losses. Curiously, those people tend to be more willing than others to take big risks—that is, to gamble (Tom, Fox, Trepel, & Poldrack, 2007). Research on the prefrontal cortex shows the possibility of relating decision making to brain functioning.

STOP & CHECK

12. Which brain area records the expected gains and losses associated with possible actions?

ANSWER

12. the prefrontal cortex

MODULE 13.1 IN CLOSING

Different Types of Memory

"Overall intelligence," as measured by an IQ test, is a convenient fiction. It is convenient because, under most circumstances, people who are good at one kind of intellectual task are also good at other kinds, so an overall test score makes useful predictions. However, it is a fiction because different kinds of abilities rely on different brain processes, and it is possible to damage one but not another. Even memory is composed of separate abilities, and it is possible to lose one type or aspect of memory without impairing others. The study of amnesia shows how the brain operates as a series of partly independent mechanisms serving specific purposes.

SUMMARY

1. Ivan Pavlov suggested that learning depends on the growth of a connection between two brain areas. Karl Lashley showed that learning does *not* depend on new connections across the cerebral cortex. **374**
2. Richard Thompson found that some instances of classical conditioning take place in small areas of the cerebellum. **376**
3. Psychologists distinguish between short-term memory and long-term memory. Short-term memory holds only a small amount of information and retains it only briefly unless it is constantly rehearsed. **377**
4. Working memory, a modern alternative to the concept of short-term memory, stores information that one is currently using. **378**
5. People with damage to the hippocampus have great trouble forming new long-term declarative memories, although they still show implicit memory, they still store short-term memories, and they still form new procedural memories. **379**
6. The hippocampus is important for some kinds of learning and memory but not all. The hippocampus is critical for declarative memory, spatial memory, and memory for details and context. **382**
7. The hippocampus is important for consolidation of some kinds of memories. Emotional arousal enhances consolidation. Arousing events increase the release of epinephrine and cortisol, which stimulate the amygdala. The amygdala enhances activity in the hippocampus and cerebral cortex. **386**
8. Patients with Korsakoff's syndrome or other types of prefrontal damage have impairments of memory, including difficulty in reasoning about memories. They often fill in their memory gaps with confabulations, which they then remember as if they were true. **387**
9. Alzheimer's disease is a progressive disease, most common in old age, characterized by impaired memory and attention. It is related to deposition of amyloid-β protein in the brain. **388**
10. Other brain areas are important for elaborating episodic memories, for semantic memories, and for memories of the reward or punishment values of various possible actions. **389**

Continued

KEY TERMS

Terms are defined in the module on the page number indicated. They're also presented in alphabetical order with definitions in the book's Subject Index/Glossary. Interactive flashcards, audio reviews, and crossword puzzles are among the online resources available to help you learn these terms and the concepts they represent.

Alzheimer's disease **388**
amnesia **379**
amyloid-β (or β-amyloid) **388**
anterograde amnesia **379**
classical conditioning **374**
conditioned response (CR) **374**
conditioned stimulus (CS) **374**
confabulation **387**
consolidation **378**
declarative memory **382**
delayed matching-to-sample task **383**
delayed nonmatching-to-sample task **383**
delayed response task **379**
engram **375**
episodic memory **381**
equipotentiality **376**
explicit memory **382**
implicit memory **382**
Korsakoff's syndrome **387**
lateral interpositus nucleus (LIP) **377**
long-term memory **377**
mass action **376**
Morris water maze task **384**
operant conditioning **374**
procedural memory **382**
punishment **374**
radial maze **384**
reinforcer **374**
retrograde amnesia **379**
semantic dementia **389**
short-term memory **377**
tau protein **388**
unconditioned response (UCR) **374**
unconditioned stimulus (UCS) **374**
working memory **379**

THOUGHT QUESTION

Lashley sought to find the engram, the physiological representation of learning. In general terms, how would you recognize an engram if you saw one? That is, what would someone have to demonstrate before you could conclude that a particular change in the nervous system was really an engram?

MODULE 13.2

Storing Information in the Nervous System

If you walk through a field, are the footprints that you leave "memories"? How about the mud that you pick up on your shoes? If the police wanted to know who walked across that field, a forensics expert could check your shoes to answer the question. And yet we would not call these physical traces memories in the usual sense.

Similarly, when a pattern of activity passes through the brain, it leaves a path of physical changes, but not every change is a memory. The task of finding how the brain stores memories is a little like searching for the proverbial needle in a haystack, and researchers have explored many avenues that seemed promising for a while but now seem fruitless.

APPLICATIONS AND EXTENSIONS

Blind Alleys and Abandoned Mines

Textbooks, this one included, concentrate mostly on successful research that led to our current understanding of a field. You may get the impression that science progresses smoothly, with each investigator contributing to the body of knowledge. However, if you look at old journals or textbooks, you will find discussions of many "promising" or "exciting" findings that we disregard today. Scientific research does not progress straight from ignorance to enlightenment. It explores one direction after another, a little like a rat in a complex maze, abandoning the dead ends and pursuing arms that lead further.

The problem with the maze analogy is that an investigator seldom runs into a wall that clearly identifies the end of a route. A better analogy is a prospector digging for gold, never certain whether to abandon an unprofitable spot or to keep digging just a little longer. Many once-exciting lines of research in the physiology of learning are now of little more than historical interest. Here are three examples.

1. Wilder Penfield sometimes performed brain surgery for severe epilepsy on conscious patients who had only scalp anesthesia. When he applied a brief, weak electrical stimulus to part of the brain, the patient could describe the experience that the stimulation evoked. Stimulation of the temporal cortex sometimes evoked vivid descriptions such as:

   I feel as though I were in the bathroom at school.
   I see myself at the corner of Jacob and Washington in South Bend, Indiana.
   I remember myself at the railroad station in Vanceburg, Kentucky; it is winter and the wind is blowing outside, and I am waiting for a train.

   Penfield (1955; Penfield & Perot, 1963) suggested that each neuron stores a particular memory, like a videotape of one's life. However, brain stimulation rarely elicited a memory of a specific event. Usually, it evoked vague sights and sounds, or recollections of repeated experiences such as "seeing a bed" or "hearing a choir sing 'White Christmas.'" Stimulation almost never elicited memories of doing anything—just of seeing and hearing. Also, some patients reported events that they had never actually experienced, such as being chased by a robber or seeing Christ descend from the sky. In short, the stimulation produced something more like a dream than a memory.
2. G. A. Horridge (1962) apparently demonstrated that decapitated cockroaches can learn. First he cut the connections between a cockroach's head and the rest of its body. Then he suspended the cockroach so that its legs dangled just above a surface of water. An electrical circuit was arranged as in Figure 13.15 so that the roach's leg received a shock whenever it touched the water. Each experimental roach was paired with a control roach that got a leg shock whenever the first roach did. Only the experimental roach had any control over the shock, however. This kind of experiment is known as a "yoked-control" design.

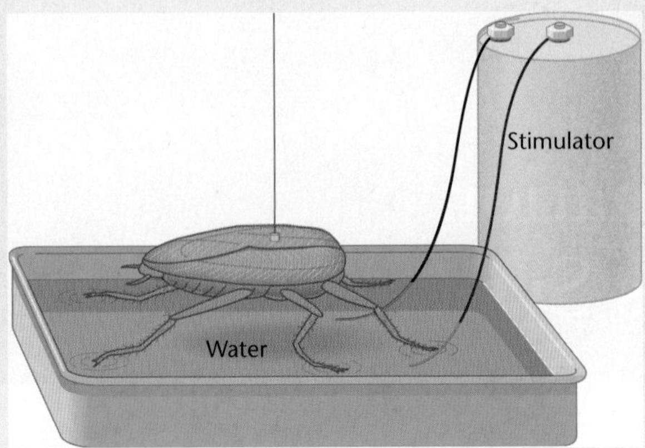

Figure 13.15 Learning in a headless cockroach?
The decapitated cockroach is suspended just above the water; it receives a shock whenever its hind leg touches the water. A cockroach in the control group gets a shock whenever the first roach does regardless of its own behavior. According to some reports, the experimental roach learned to keep its leg out of the water. *(From G. A. Horridge, "Learning of Leg Position by the Ventral Nerve Cord in Headless Insects."* Proceedings of the Royal Society of London, B, 157, *1962, 33–52. Copyright © 1962 The Royal Society of London. Reprinted by permission of the Royal Society of London and G. A. Horridge.)*

Over 5 to 10 minutes, roaches in the experimental group increased a response of tucking the leg under the body to avoid shocks. Roaches in the control group did not, on the average, change their leg position as a result of the shocks. Thus, the changed response apparently qualifies as learning and not as an accidental by-product of the shocks.

These experiments initially seemed a promising way to study learning in a simple nervous system (Eisenstein & Cohen, 1965). Unfortunately, decapitated cockroaches learn slowly, and the results vary sharply from one individual to another, limiting the usefulness of the results. After a handful of studies, interest in this line of research faded.

3. In the 1960s and early 1970s, several investigators proposed that each memory is coded as a specific molecule, probably RNA or protein. The boldest test of that hypothesis was an attempt to transfer memories chemically from one individual to another. James McConnell (1962) reported that, when planaria (flatworms) cannibalized other planaria that had been classically conditioned to respond to a light, they apparently "remembered" what the cannibalized planaria had learned. At least they learned the response faster than planaria generally do.

   Inspired by that report, other investigators trained rats to approach a clicking sound for food (Babich, Jacobson, Bubash, & Jacobson, 1965). After the rats were well trained, the experimenters ground up their brains, extracted RNA, and injected it into untrained rats. The recipient rats learned to approach the clicking sound faster than rats in the control group did.

   That report led to a wealth of studies on the transfer of training by brain extracts. In *some* of these experiments, rats that received brain extracts from a trained group showed apparent memory of the task, whereas those that received extracts from an untrained group did not (Dyal, 1971; Fjerdingstad, 1973). The results were inconsistent and unreplicable, however, even within a single laboratory (L. T. Smith, 1975). Many laboratories failed to find any hint of a transfer effect. By the mid-1970s, most biological psychologists saw no point in continuing this research.

Learning and the Hebbian Synapse

Research on the physiology of learning began with Ivan Pavlov's concept of classical conditioning. Although, as we considered earlier, that theory led Karl Lashley to an unsuccessful search for connections in the cerebral cortex, it also stimulated Donald Hebb to propose a mechanism for change at a synapse.

Donald O. Hebb (1904–1985)
Modern psychology takes completely for granted that behavior and neural function are perfectly correlated. . . . There is no separate soul or life force to stick a finger into the brain now and then and make neural cells do what they would not otherwise. . . . It is quite conceivable that some day the assumption will have to be rejected. But it is important also to see that we have not reached that day yet. . . . One cannot logically be a determinist in physics and chemistry and biology, and a mystic in psychology.

Hebb suggested that when the axon of neuron A "repeatedly or persistently takes part in firing , some growth process or metabolic change takes place in one or both cells" that increases the subsequent ability of axon A to excite cell B (Hebb, 1949, p. 62). In other words, an axon that has successfully stimulated cell B in the past becomes even more successful in the future.

Consider how this process relates to classical conditioning. Suppose axon A initially excites cell B slightly, and axon C excites B more strongly. If A and C fire together, their combined effect on B may produce an action potential. You might think of axon A as the CS and axon C as the UCS. Pairing activity in axons A and C increases the future effect of A on B.

A synapse that increases in effectiveness because of simultaneous activity in the presynaptic and postsynaptic neurons is called a **Hebbian synapse.** In Chapter 6, we encountered examples of this type of synapse. In the development of the visual system, if an axon from the left eye consistently fires at the same time as one from the right eye, a neuron in the visual cortex increases its response to both of them. Such synapses may also be critical for many kinds of associative learning. Neuroscientists have discovered much about the mechanisms of Hebbian (or almost Hebbian) synapses.

STOP & CHECK

13. How can a Hebbian synapse account for the basic phenomena of classical conditioning?

ANSWER

13. In a Hebbian synapse, pairing the activity of a weaker (CS) axon with a stronger (UCS) axon produces an action potential and in the process strengthens the response of the cell to the CS axon. On later trials, it will produce a bigger depolarization of the postsynaptic cell, which we can regard as a conditioned response.

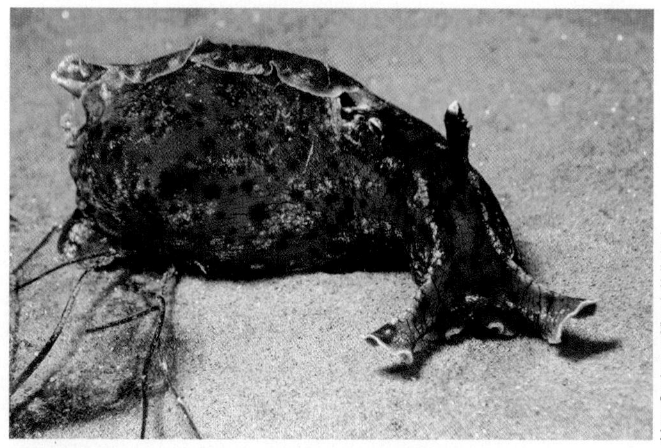

Marty Snyderman/Visuals Unlimited

Figure 13.16 ***Aplysia*, a marine mollusk**
A full-grown animal is a little larger than the average human hand.

Eric R. Kandel
The questions posed by higher cognitive processes such as learning and memory are formidable, and we have only begun to explore them. Although elementary aspects of simple forms of learning have been accessible to molecular analysis in invertebrates, we are only now beginning to know a bit about the genes and proteins involved in more complex, hippocampus based, learning processes of mammals.

Single-Cell Mechanisms of Invertebrate Behavior Change

If we are going to look for a needle in a haystack, a good strategy is to look in a small haystack. Therefore, many researchers have turned to studies of invertebrates. Vertebrate and invertebrate nervous systems are organized differently, but the chemistry of the neuron, the principles of the action potential, and even the neurotransmitters are the same. If we identify the physical basis of learning and memory in an invertebrate, we have at least a hypothesis of what *might* work in vertebrates. (Biologists have long used this strategy for studying genetics, embryology, and other biological processes.)

Aplysia as an Experimental Animal

Aplysia, a marine invertebrate related to the common slug, has been a popular animal for studies of the physiology of learning (Figure 13.16). Compared to vertebrates, it has fewer neurons, many of which are large and easy to study. Moreover, unlike vertebrates, *Aplysia* neurons are virtually identical from one individual to another so that different investigators can study the properties of the same neuron.

One commonly studied behavior is the withdrawal response: If someone touches the siphon, mantle, or gill of an *Aplysia* (Figure 13.17), the animal vigorously withdraws the irritated structure. Investigators have traced the neural path from the touch receptors through other neurons to the motor neurons that direct the response. Using this neural pathway, investigators have studied changes in behavior as a result of experience. In 2000, Eric Kandel won a Nobel prize for this work.

Habituation in *Aplysia*

Habituation is a decrease in response to a stimulus that is presented repeatedly and accompanied by no change in other stimuli. For example, if your clock chimes every hour, you gradually respond less and less. If we repeatedly stimulate an *Aplysia*'s gills with a brief jet of seawater, at first, it withdraws,

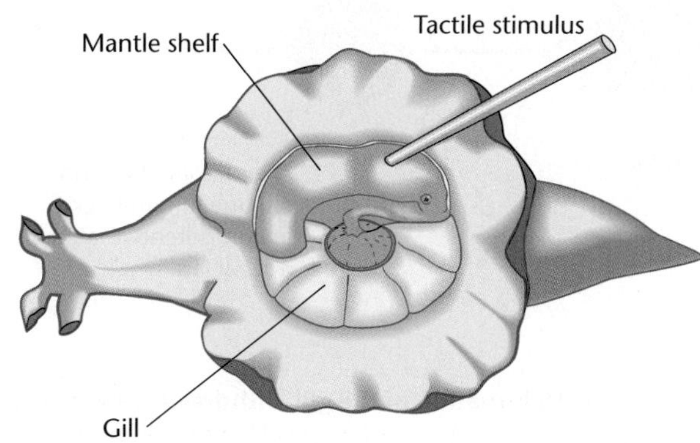

Figure 13.17 Touching an *Aplysia* causes a withdrawal response
The sensory and motor neurons controlling this reaction have been identified and studied.

but after many repetitions, it stops responding. The decline in response is not due to muscle fatigue because, even after habituation has occurred, direct stimulation of the motor neuron produces a full-sized muscle contraction (Kupfermann, Castellucci, Pinsker, & Kandel, 1970). We can also rule out changes in the sensory neuron. The sensory neuron still gives a full, normal response to stimulation; it merely fails to excite the motor neuron as much as before (Kupfermann et al., 1970). We are therefore left with the conclusion that habituation in *Aplysia* depends on a change in the synapse between the sensory neuron and the motor neuron (Figure 13.18).

Sensitization in *Aplysia*

If you experience an unexpected, intense pain, you temporarily react more strongly than usual to other strong, sudden stimuli. This phenomenon is **sensitization,** an increase in response to mild stimuli as a result of exposure to more intense stimuli. Similarly, a strong stimulus almost anywhere on *Aplysia's* skin can intensify later withdrawal responses to a touch.

Researchers traced sensitization to changes at identified synapses (Cleary, Hammer, & Byrne, 1989; Dale, Schacher, & Kandel, 1988; Kandel & Schwartz, 1982). Strong stimulation on the skin excites a *facilitating interneuron,* which releases serotonin (5-HT) onto the presynaptic terminals of many sensory neurons. The serotonin blocks potassium channels in these membranes. The result is that after later action potentials, the membrane takes longer than usual to repolarize (because potassium is slow to flow into the cell). Therefore, the presynaptic neuron continues releasing its neurotransmitter for longer than usual. Repeating this process causes the sensory neuron to synthesize new proteins that produce long-term sensitization (C. H. Bailey, Giustetto, Huang, Hawkins, & Kandel, 2000). This research shows how it is possible to explain one example of behavioral plasticity in terms of molecular events. Later studies explored mechanisms of classical and operant conditioning in *Aplysia*.

STOP & CHECK

14. When serotonin blocks potassium channels on the presynaptic terminal, what is the effect on transmission?

ANSWER

14. Blocking potassium channels prolongs the action potential and therefore prolongs the release of neurotransmitters, producing an increased response.

Long-Term Potentiation in Vertebrates

Since the work of Sherrington and Cajal, most neuroscientists have assumed that learning depends on changes at synapses, and the work on *Aplysia* confirms that synaptic changes *can* produce behavioral changes. The first evidence for a similar process among vertebrates came from studies of neurons in the rat hippocampus (Bliss & Lømo, 1973). The phenomenon, known as **long-term potentiation (LTP),** is this: One or more axons connected to a dendrite bombard it with a brief but rapid series of stimuli—such as 100 per second for 1 to 4 seconds. The burst of intense stimulation leaves some of the synapses potentiated (more responsive to new input of the same type) for minutes, days, or weeks.

LTP shows three properties that make it an attractive candidate for a cellular basis of learning and memory:

- **specificity**—If some of the synapses onto a cell have been highly active and others have not, only the active ones become strengthened. However, establishing LTP

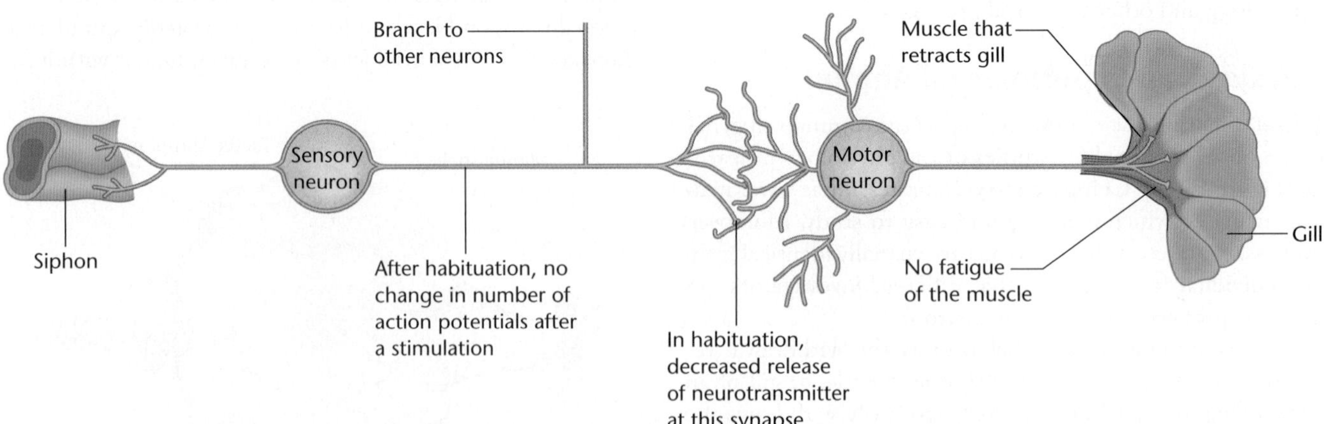

Figure 13.18 Habituation of the gill-withdrawal reflex in *Aplysia*
Touching the siphon causes a withdrawal of the gill. After many repetitions, the response habituates (declines) because of decreased transmission at the synapse between the sensory neuron and the motor neuron. *(Redrawn from "Neuronal Mechanisms of Habituation and Dishabituation of the Gill-Withdrawal Reflex in* Aplysia,*" by V. Castellucci, H. Pinsker, I. Kupfermann, and E. Kandel,* Science, *1970, 167, pp. 1745–1748. Copyright © 1970 by AAAS. Used by permission of AAAS and V. Castellucci.)*

at one synapse does briefly facilitate the formation of LTP at nearby synapses on the same dendrite (Harvey & Svoboda, 2007).

- **cooperativity**—Nearly simultaneous stimulation by two or more axons produces LTP much more strongly than does repeated stimulation by just one axon.
- **associativity**—Pairing a weak input with a strong input enhances later response to the weak input. In this regard, LTP matches what we would expect of Hebbian synapses.

The opposite change, long-term depression, occurs in both the hippocampus (Kerr & Abraham, 1995) and the cerebellum (Ito, 1989, 2002). **Long-term depression (LTD),** a prolonged decrease in response at a synapse, occurs when axons have been less active than others. You can think of this as a compensatory process. As one synapse strengthens, another weakens (Royer & Paré, 2003). If learning produces only a strengthening of synapses, then every time you learned something, your brain would get more and more active, burning more and more fuel!

Biochemical Mechanisms

Determining how LTP or LTD occurs has been a huge research challenge because each neuron has many tiny synapses, sometimes in the tens of thousands. Isolating the chemical changes at any one synapse takes an enormous amount of creative research. The mechanisms vary among brain areas (Li, Chen, Xing, Wei, & Rogawski, 2001; Mellor & Nicoll, 2001). We shall discuss LTP in the hippocampus, where it is easiest to demonstrate and where its mechanisms have been most extensively studied.

AMPA and NMDA Synapses. In a few cases, LTP depends on changes at GABA synapses (Nugent, Penick, & Kauer, 2007), but in most cases, it depends on changes at glutamate synapses. The brain has several types of receptors for glutamate, its most abundant transmitter. In past chapters, you have seen that neuroscientists identify different dopamine receptors by number, such as D_1 and D_2, and different GABA receptors by letter, such as $GABA_A$. For glutamate, they named the different receptors after drugs that stimulate them. Here we are interested in two types of glutamate receptors, called AMPA and NMDA. The **AMPA receptor** is excited by the neurotransmitter glutamate, but it can also respond to a drug called α-amino-3-hydroxy-5-methyl-4-isoxazolepropionic acid (abbreviated AMPA). The **NMDA receptor** is also ordinarily excited only by glutamate, but it can respond to a drug called N-methyl-D-aspartate (abbreviated NMDA).

Both are ionotropic receptors. That is, when they are stimulated, they open a channel to let ions enter the postsynaptic cell. The AMPA receptor is a typical ionotropic receptor that opens sodium channels. The NMDA receptor, however, is different: Its response to the transmitter glutamate *depends on the degree of polarization across the membrane.* When glutamate attaches to an NMDA receptor while the membrane is at its resting potential, the ion channel is usually blocked by magnesium ions. (Magnesium ions, positively charged, are attracted to the negative charge inside the cells but do not fit through the NMDA channel.) The NMDA channel opens only if the magnesium leaves, and the surest way to detach the magnesium is to depolarize the membrane, decreasing the negative charge that attracts it (Figure 13.19).

Suppose an axon releases glutamate repeatedly. Better yet, let's activate two axons repeatedly, side by side on the same dendrite. So many sodium ions enter through the AMPA channels that the dendrite becomes significantly depolarized, though it does not produce an action potential. (Remember, dendrites do not produce action potentials.) The depolarization displaces the magnesium molecules, enabling glutamate to open the NMDA channel. At that point, both sodium and calcium enter through the NMDA channel (Figure 13.20).

The entry of calcium is the key to the later changes. When calcium enters through the NMDA channel, it activates a protein called CaMKII (α-calcium-calmodulin-dependent protein kinase II), which migrates to the synapse (Otmakhov et al., 2004). CaMKII is both necessary and sufficient for LTP (Lisman, Schulman, & Cline,

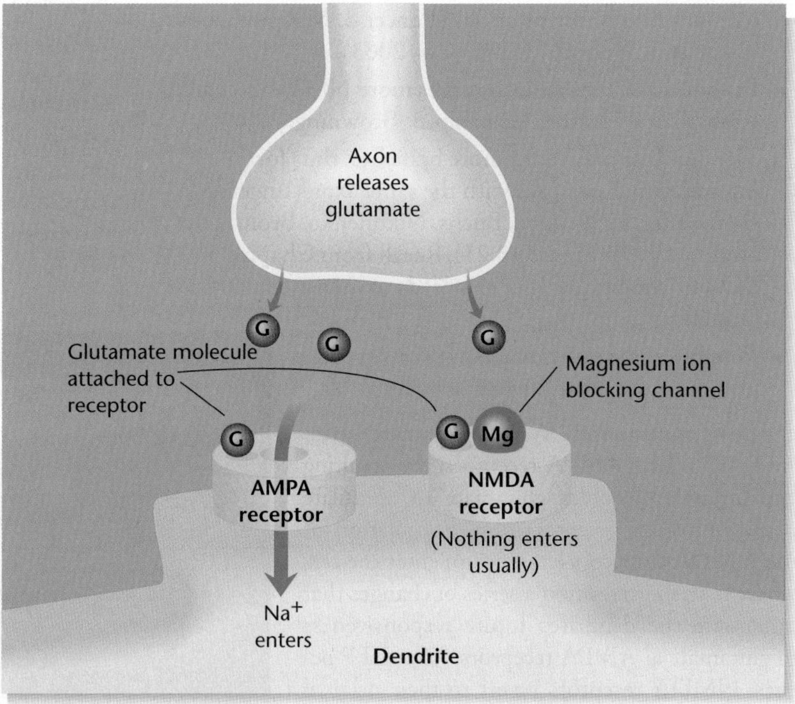

Figure 13.19 The AMPA and NMDA receptors before LTP
Glutamate attaches to both receptors. At the AMPA receptor, it opens a channel to let sodium ions enter. At the NMDA receptor, it binds but usually fails to open the channel, which is blocked by magnesium ions.

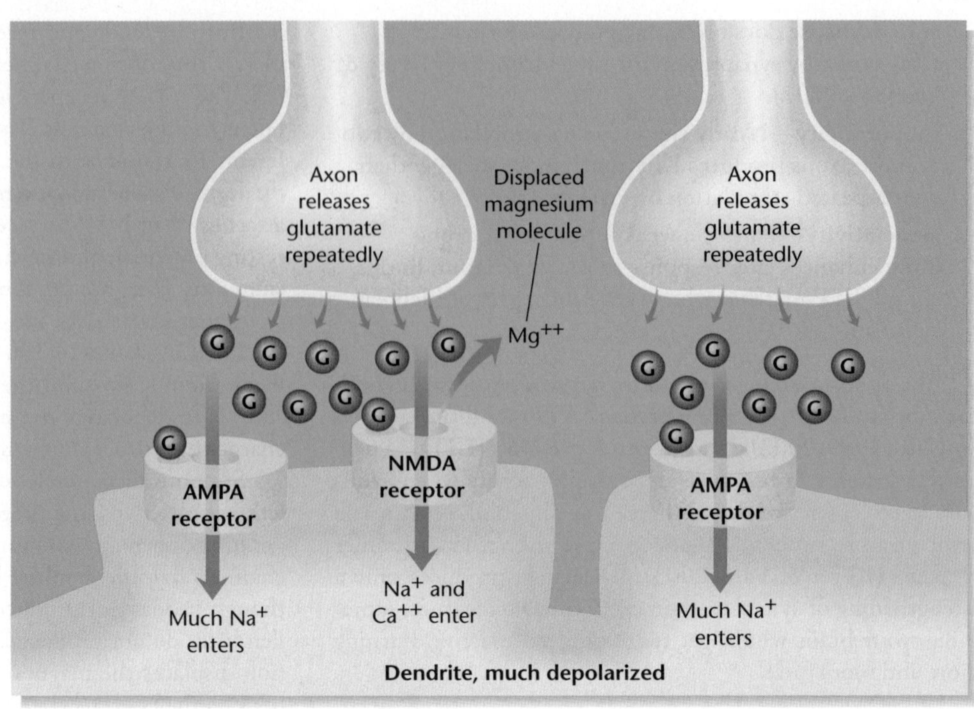

Figure 13.20 The AMPA and NMDA receptors during LTP
If one or more AMPA receptors have been repeatedly stimulated, enough sodium enters to largely depolarize the dendrite's membrane. Doing so displaces the magnesium ions and enables glutamate to open the NMDA receptor, through which sodium and calcium enter.

2002). Variations in the genes controlling CaMKII correlate with variations in memory among humans (de Quervain & Papassotiropoulos, 2006).

The protein CaMKII sets in motion many processes, varying from one neuron to another. In fact, a great deal varies from one neuron to another. When a large number of neurons are highly activated, fewer than half of them undergo LTP, while the others do not (Han et al., 2007). Researchers do not know what determines which ones do and which ones do not. Perhaps it is a competition of some sort. At any rate, when LTP occurs, here are some of the mechanisms by which it happens:

- The dendrite builds more AMPA receptors or moves old ones into better positions (Poncer & Malinow, 2001; Takahashi, Svoboda, & Malinow, 2003).
- In some cases, the neuron makes more NMDA receptors (Grosshans, Clayton, Coultrap, & Browning, 2002).
- The dendrite may make more branches, thus forming additional synapses with the same axon (Engert & Bonhoeffer, 1999; Toni, Buchs, Nikonenko, Bron, & Muller, 1999) (Figure 13.21). Recall from Chapter 5 that enriched experience also leads to increased dendritic branching.
- Possibly, some individual AMPA receptors become more responsive than before.

Let's summarize: When glutamate massively stimulates AMPA receptors, the resulting depolarization enables glutamate to stimulate nearby NMDA receptors also. Stimulation of the NMDA receptors lets calcium enter the cell, where it sets into motion a series of changes that potentiate the dendrite's future responsiveness to glutamate at AMPA receptors. After LTP occurs, NMDA receptors revert to their original condition.

The mechanisms of LTD are virtually the opposite of LTP. For example, where LTP leads to expanded dendrites and more synapses, LTD is associated with shrinkage of dendrites and decreased numbers of synaptic receptors (Zhou, Homma, & Poo, 2004).

Once LTP has been established, it no longer depends on NMDA synapses. Drugs that block NMDA synapses prevent the *establishment* of LTP, but they do not interfere with the *maintenance* of LTP that was already established (Gustafsson & Wigström, 1990; Uekita & Okaichi, 2005). In other words, once LTP occurs, the AMPA receptors stay potentiated, regardless of what happens to the NMDAs.

Presynaptic Changes. The changes just described occur in the postsynaptic neuron. In many cases, LTP depends on changes in the presynaptic neuron instead or in addition. Extensive stimulation of a postsynaptic cell causes it to release a **retrograde transmitter** that travels back to the presynaptic cell to modify it. In many cases, that retrograde transmitter

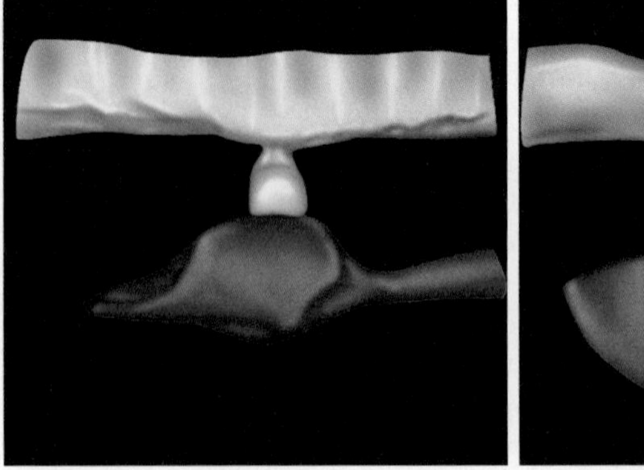
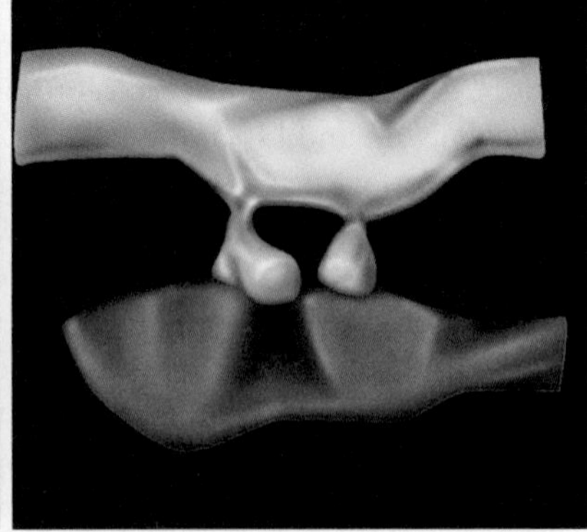

Figure 13.21 One way in which LTP occurs
In some cases, the dendrite makes new branches, which attach to branches of the same axon, thus increasing the overall stimulation. *(Based on Toni, Buchs, Nikonenko, Bron, & Muller, 1999)*

is nitric oxide (NO). As a result, a presynaptic neuron decreases its threshold for producing action potentials (Ganguly, Kiss, & Poo, 2000), increases its release of neurotransmitter (Zakharenko, Zablow, & Siegelbaum, 2001), expands its axon (Routtenberg, Cantallops, Zaffuto, Serrano, & Namgung, 2000), and releases its transmitter from additional sites along its axon (Reid, Dixon, Takahashi, Bliss, & Fine, 2004). In short, LTP reflects increased activity by the presynaptic neuron as well as increased responsiveness by the postsynaptic neuron.

STOP & CHECK

15. Before LTP: In the normal state, what is the effect of glutamate at the AMPA receptors? At the NMDA receptors?

16. During the formation of LTP: When a burst of intense stimulation releases much more glutamate than usual at two or more incoming axons, what is the effect of the glutamate at the AMPA receptors? At the NMDA receptors? Which ions enter at the NMDA receptors?

17. After the neuron has gone through LTP: What is now the effect of glutamate at the AMPA receptors? At the NMDA receptors?

ANSWERS

15. Before LTP, glutamate stimulates AMPA receptors but usually has little effect at the NMDA receptors because magnesium blocks them. **16.** During the formation of LTP, the massive glutamate input strongly stimulates the AMPA receptors, thus depolarizing the dendrite. This depolarization enables glutamate to excite the NMDA receptors also. Both calcium and sodium enter there. **17.** After LTP has been established, glutamate stimulates the AMPA receptors more than before, mainly because of an increased number of AMPA receptors. At the NMDA receptors, it is again usually ineffective.

LTP and Behavior

LTP occurs not just in the situations we ordinarily think of as learning but also when animals explore a new environment, develop a drug addiction, or receive repetitive sensory stimulation (Clem, Celikel, & Barth, 2008; Fedulov et al., 2007; Kauer & Malenko, 2007). Evidence suggests that LTP is necessary for long-term learning and memory. Drugs that block NMDA receptors do not prevent immediate learning, but they greatly impair retention 24 hours later (Holahan et al., 2005).

Understanding the mechanisms of LTP may enable researchers to understand what could impair or improve memory. LTP increases production of several proteins. Enhancing production of these proteins enhances memory in rodents (Routtenberg et al., 2000), and drugs that inhibit their production weakens memory, even if the drugs are given days after the training (Shema, Sacktor, & Dudai, 2007). Several pharmaceutical companies are investigating drugs that might improve learning by enhancing LTP (Farah et al., 2004).

Drugs and Memory

While we are on the topic of drugs, let's consider some others. Several drugs do enhance learning or memory. To take the simplest example, caffeine enhances learning and memory by increasing arousal. Many patients with Alzheimer's disease take drugs that facilitate acetylcholine by blocking the enzyme that degrades it (Farah et al., 2004). Other drugs under investigation act on glutamate or dopamine synapses or proteins that alter synaptic receptors.

You may have heard claims that memory can be improved by taking the herb *Ginkgo biloba* or several other chemicals. Drug companies face stiff regulation by the Food and Drug Administration before they can market a new drug, but a company marketing a naturally occurring supplement does not have to do any research at all, provided that the label does not claim medical benefits. Unfortunately, not all supplements are either safe or effective. Research on ginkgo biloba has not been extensive, but so far, it suggests that the herb offers mild benefits to a limited number of people. Ginkgo biloba dilates blood vessels and therefore increases blood flow to the brain. When given to Alzheimer's patients or other people with memory problems, ginkgo biloba sometimes produces small but measurable benefits (Gold, Cahill, & Wenk, 2002). Similarly, a number of other "memory-boosting" supplements increase blood flow to the brain or increase metabolism. Some studies have shown small memory benefits for these drugs in laboratory animals or aged people (McDaniel, Maier, & Einstein, 2002). It is worth noting that the only demonstrated benefits have been for people with circulatory problems and other disorders, not for young people with normal brains. Little is known about the side effects and risks of these drugs.

Researchers have also been developing drugs that might block memory. Why would anyone want to do that, you might ask. The idea is to block painful memories, such as traumatic experiences that might lead to posttraumatic stress disorder. Whether that would be a good idea or not is uncertain, but researchers have found several drugs, including propanolol, that weaken memories of recent events (Altemus & Debiec, 2007).

MODULE 13.2 IN CLOSING

The Physiology of Memory

In this module, we examined biochemical changes at synapses. After we understand these mechanisms more completely, what can we do with the information? Presumably, we will help people overcome or prevent memory deterioration. We can expect much better therapies for Alzheimer's disease and so forth. Should we also look forward to improving memory for normal people? Would you like to have a supermemory?

Maybe, but let's be cautious. Even though I could add memory chips to my computer to store ever-larger quantities of information, I don't want to keep everything I write or every e-mail message I receive. Similarly, I'm not sure I would want my brain to retain every experience, even if it had unlimited storage capacity. The ideal memory would not just record more information. It would faithfully record the important information and discard the rest. If we can improve memory in any way, we will still want to maintain that selectivity.

SUMMARY

1. A Hebbian synapse is one that is strengthened by being repeatedly active when the postsynaptic neuron produces action potentials. **394**
2. Habituation of the gill-withdrawal reflex in *Aplysia* depends on a mechanism that decreases the release of transmitter from a particular presynaptic neuron. **395**
3. Sensitization of the gill-withdrawal reflex in *Aplysia* occurs when serotonin blocks potassium channels in a presynaptic neuron and thereby prolongs the release of transmitter from that neuron. **396**
4. Long-term potentiation (LTP) is an enhancement of response at certain synapses because of a brief but intense series of stimuli delivered to a neuron, generally by two or more axons delivering simultaneous inputs. **396**
5. If axons are active at a very slow rate, their synapses may decrease in responsiveness—a process known as long-term depression (LTD). **397**
6. LTP in hippocampal neurons occurs as follows: Repeated glutamate excitation of AMPA receptors depolarizes the membrane. The depolarization removes magnesium ions that had been blocking NMDA receptors. Glutamate is then able to excite the NMDA receptors, opening a channel for calcium ions to enter the neuron. **397**
7. When calcium enters through the NMDA-controlled channels, it activates a protein that sets in motion a series of events that build more AMPA receptors and increase the growth of dendritic branches. These changes increase the later responsiveness of the dendrite to incoming glutamate at AMPA receptors. **397**
8. At many synapses, LTP relates to increased release of transmitter from the presynaptic neuron, in addition to or instead of changes in the postsynaptic neuron. **398**
9. Procedures that enhance or impair LTP have similar effects on certain kinds of learning. Research on LTP may lead to drugs that help improve memory. **399**

KEY TERMS

Terms are defined in the module on the page number indicated. They're also presented in alphabetical order with definitions in the book's Subject Index/Glossary. Interactive flashcards, audio reviews, and crossword puzzles are among the online resources available to help you learn these terms and the concepts they represent.

AMPA receptor **397**
associativity **397**
cooperativity **397**
habituation **395**
Hebbian synapse **395**
long-term depression (LTD) **397**
long-term potentiation (LTP) **396**
NMDA receptor **397**
retrograde transmitter **398**
sensitization **396**
specificity **396**

THOUGHT QUESTION

If a synapse has already developed LTP once, should it be easier or more difficult to get it to develop LTP again? Why?

CHAPTER 13 Exploration and Study

In addition to the study materials provided at the end of each module, you may supplement your review of this chapter by using one or more of the book's electronic resources, which include its companion Website, interactive Cengage Learning eBook, Exploring Biological Psychology CD-ROM, and CengageNOW. Brief descriptions of these resources follow. For more information, visit **www.cengage.com/psychology/kalat**.

The book's companion Website, accessible through the author Web page indicated above, provides a wide range of study resources such as an interactive glossary, flashcards, tutorial quizzes, updated Web links, and Try It Yourself activities, as well as a limited selection of the short videos and animated explanations of concepts available for this chapter.

Exploring Biological Psychology

The Exploring Biological Psychology CD-ROM contains videos, animations, and Try It Yourself activities. These activities—as well as many that are new to this edition—are also available in the text's fully interactive, media-rich Cengage Learning eBook,* which gives you the opportunity to experience biological psychology in an even greater interactive and multimedia environment. The Cengage Learning eBook also includes highlighting and note-taking features and an audio glossary. For this chapter, the Cengage Learning eBook includes the following interactive explorations:

Classical Conditioning
Localizing Brain Changes during Classical Conditioning
Mike, an Amnesic Patient
Implicit Memories
Amnesia and Different Types of Memory
Tom, a Patient with Alzheimer's
Brain Food
Neural Networks and Memory
Long-term Potentiation
Boosting Your Memory

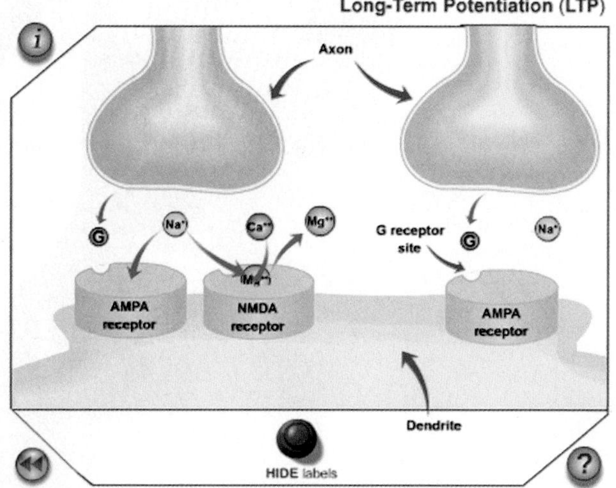

The Try-It-Yourself exercise *Long-Term Potentiation* enables the student to do a simple mock experiment to produce long-term potentiation.

* Requires a Cengage Learning eResources account. Visit **www.cengage.com/login** to register or login.

CENGAGENOW™ is an easy-to-use resource that helps you study in less time to get the grade you want. An online study system, CengageNOW* gives you the option of taking a diagnostic pretest for each chapter. The system uses the results of each pretest to create personalized chapter study plans for you. The Personalized Study Plans

- help you save study time by identifying areas on which you should concentrate and give you one-click access to corresponding pages of the interactive Cengage Learning eBook;
- provide interactive exercises and study tools to help you fully understand chapter concepts; and
- include a posttest for you to take to confirm that you are ready to move on to the next chapter.

Suggestions for Further Exploration

The book's companion Website includes a list of suggested articles available through InfoTrac College Edition for this chapter. You may also want to explore some of the following books and Websites. The text's companion Website provides live, updated links to the sites listed below.

Book

Eichenbaum, H. (2002). *The cognitive neuroscience of memory.* New York: Oxford University Press. Thoughtful treatment of both the behavioral and physiological aspects of memory.

Websites

Alzheimer Research Forum
http://www.alzforum.org/default.asp

U.S. Food and Drug Administration: Coping With Memory Loss
http://www.fda.gov/consumer/features/memoryloss0507.html

University of Washington: BrainInfo
http://braininfo.rprc.washington.edu/menumain.html

Daly & Newton/Getty Images

Cognitive Functions

14

CHAPTER OUTLINE

OPPOSITE: Language may have evolved from our tendency to make gestures.

MAIN IDEAS

1. The left and right hemispheres of the brain communicate primarily through the corpus callosum, although other smaller commissures also exchange some information between the hemispheres. After damage to the corpus callosum, each hemisphere has access to information only from the opposite half of the body and from the opposite visual field.
2. For most people, the left hemisphere is specialized for language and analytical processing. The right hemisphere is specialized for certain complex visuospatial tasks and synthetic processing.
3. The language specializations of the human brain are enormous elaborations of features that are present in other primates.
4. Abnormalities of the left hemisphere can lead to a great variety of specific language impairments.
5. Stimuli become conscious when corresponding brain activity reaches a high enough level, spreading through much of the cerebral cortex.

Biological explanations of vision, hearing, and movement are fairly detailed. Explanations of motivations, emotions, and memory are less precise, mainly because researchers can less precisely measure the behaviors. Language, thought, and attention are difficult to measure, much less explain physiologically. Nevertheless, they have been integral topics for neuroscience since its earliest days, beginning with Paul Broca's report in the 1860s that speech depends on part of the left frontal cortex.

Although research on the biology of cognition is difficult, many of the results are fascinating. After damage to the corpus callosum, which connects the two hemispheres, people act as if they have two fields of awareness—separate "minds," you might say. With damage to certain areas of the left hemisphere, people lose their language abilities, while remaining unimpaired in other ways. People with damage to parts of the right hemisphere ignore the left side of their body and the left side of the world. Studies of such people offer clues about how the brain operates and raise stimulating questions.

MODULE 14.1

Lateralization of Function

Symmetry is common in nature. The sun, stars, and planets are nearly symmetrical, as are most animals and plants. When an atom undergoes radioactive decay, it emits identical rays in exactly opposite directions. However, a few kinds of asymmetry in nature are noteworthy:

- At the "Big Bang," the universe had slightly more matter than antimatter. If equal amounts of matter and antimatter had formed, they would have canceled each other out, and no stars or planets could have formed.
- Proteins are made of amino acids, nearly all of which come in mirror-image forms, called D and L. Although both kinds of amino acid form equally easily in a chemistry laboratory, animals and plants use the L forms almost exclusively.
- In the human brain, the left hemisphere has somewhat different functions from the right hemisphere.

This module addresses only the last example. (Sorry, I can't explain the asymmetry of the Big Bang.) Presumably, assigning different functions to the two hemispheres provides some advantage.

The Left and Right Hemispheres

The left hemisphere of the cerebral cortex is connected to skin receptors and muscles mainly on the right side of the body. The right hemisphere is connected to skin receptors and muscles mainly on the left side. As an exception to this rule, both hemispheres control the trunk muscles and facial muscles. The left hemisphere sees only the right half of the world. The right hemisphere sees only the left half of the world. Each hemisphere gets auditory information from both ears but slightly stronger information from the contralateral ear. Taste and smell, however, are uncrossed. Each hemisphere gets taste information from its own side of the tongue (Aglioti, Tassinari, Corballis, & Berlucchi, 2000; Pritchard, Macaluso, & Eslinger, 1999) and smell information from the nostril on its own side (Herz, McCall, & Cahill, 1999; Homewood & Stevenson, 2001).

Why all vertebrates (and many invertebrates) evolved so that each hemisphere controls the contralateral (opposite) side of the body, no one knows. At any rate, the left and right hemispheres of the cerebral cortex exchange information through a set of axons called the **corpus callosum** (Figure 14.1; see also Figures 4.10 on page 93 and 4.13 on page 91) and through the anterior commissure, the hippocampal commissure, and a couple of other small commissures. Information that initially enters one hemisphere crosses quickly so that both hemispheres have access to the information.

The two hemispheres are not mirror images of each other. In most humans, the left hemisphere is specialized for language. The functions of the right hemisphere are more difficult to summarize, as we shall see later. Such division of labor between the two hemispheres is known as **lateralization.** If you had no corpus callosum, your left hemisphere could react only to information from the right side of your body, and your right hemisphere could react only to information from the left. Because of the corpus callosum, however, each hemisphere receives information from both sides. Only after damage to the corpus callosum (or to one hemisphere) do we see clear evidence of lateralization.

Visual and Auditory Connections to the Hemispheres

Before we can discuss lateralization in any detail, we must consider how the eyes connect to the brain. The hemispheres are connected to the eyes such that each hemisphere gets input from the opposite half of the visual world. That is, the left hemisphere sees the right side of the world, and the right hemisphere sees the left side. In rabbits and other species with eyes far to the side of the head, the left eye connects to the right hemisphere, and the right eye connects to the left. *Human eyes are not connected to the brain in this way.* Both of your eyes face forward. You see the left side of the world almost as well with your right eye as with your left eye.

Figure 14.2 illustrates the connections from the eyes to the brain in humans. Light from the right half of the **visual field**—what is visible at any moment—shines onto the left half of *both* retinas, and light from the left visual field shines onto the right half of both retinas. The left half of *each* retina connects to the left hemisphere, which therefore sees the right visual field. Similarly, the right half of each retina con-

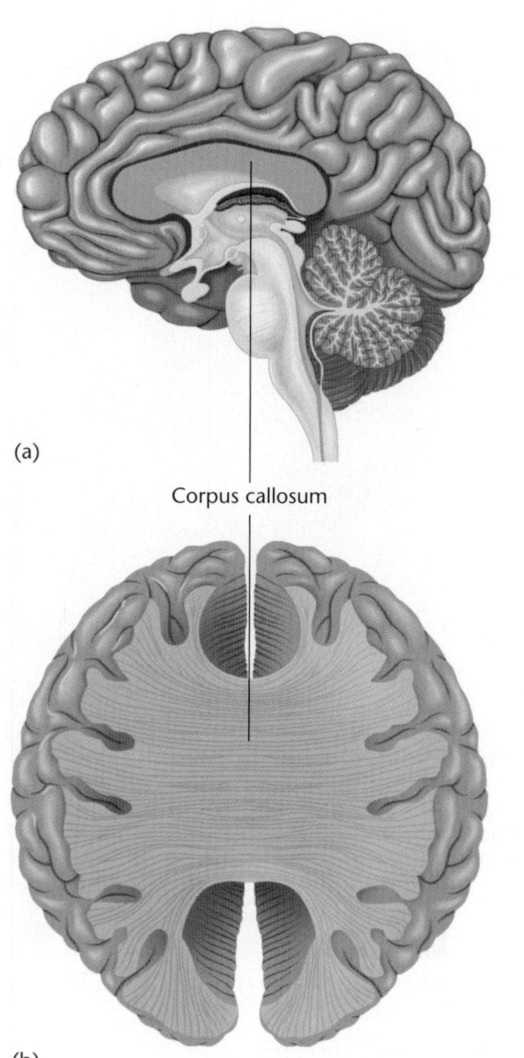

Figure 14.1 Two views of the corpus callosum
The corpus callosum is a large set of axons conveying information between the two hemispheres. **(a)** A sagittal section through the human brain. **(b)** A dissection (viewed from above) in which gray matter has been removed to expose the corpus callosum.

nects to the right hemisphere, which sees the left visual field. A small vertical strip down the center of each retina, covering about 5 degrees of visual arc, connects to both hemispheres (Innocenti, 1980; Lavidor & Walsh, 2004). In Figure 14.2, note how half of the axons from each eye cross to the opposite side of the brain at the **optic chiasm** (literally, the "optic cross").

Right visual field ⇒ left half of each retina ⇒ left hemisphere

Left visual field ⇒ right half of each retina ⇒ right hemisphere

The auditory system is organized differently. Each ear sends the information to both sides of the brain because any part of the brain that contributes to localizing sounds must receive input from both ears. However, when the two ears receive different information, each hemisphere does pay more attention to the ear on the opposite side (Hugdahl, 1996).

STOP & CHECK

1. The left hemisphere of the brain is connected to the right eye in guinea pigs. In humans, the left hemisphere is connected to the left half of each retina. Explain the reason for this species difference.

2. In humans, light from the right visual field shines on the _____ half of each retina, which sends its axons to the _____ hemisphere of the brain.

ANSWERS

1. In guinea pigs, the right eye is far to the side of the head and sees only the right visual field. In humans, the eyes point straight ahead and half of each eye sees the right visual field. **2.** left . . . left

Cutting the Corpus Callosum

Damage to the corpus callosum prevents the two hemispheres from exchanging information. Occasionally, surgeons sever the corpus callosum as a treatment for severe **epilepsy**, a condition characterized by repeated episodes of excessive synchronized neural activity, mainly because of decreased release of the inhibitory neurotransmitter GABA (During, Ryder, & Spencer, 1995). It can result from a mutation in a gene controlling the GABA receptor (Baulac et al., 2001), from trauma or infection in the brain, brain tumors, or exposure to toxic substances. Often, the cause is not known. About 1% to 2% of all people have epilepsy. The symptoms vary depending on the location and type of brain abnormality.

Antiepileptic drugs block sodium flow across the membrane or enhance the effects of GABA. More than 90% of epileptic patients respond well enough to live a normal life. However, if someone continues having frequent seizures despite medication, physicians consider surgically removing the **focus**, or point in the brain where the seizures begin. The location of the focus varies from one person to another.

Removing the focus is not an option if someone has several foci. Therefore, the idea arose to cut the corpus callosum to prevent epileptic seizures from crossing from one hemisphere to the other. One benefit is that, as predicted, the person's epileptic seizures affect only half the body. (The abnormal activity cannot cross the corpus callosum, so it remains within one hemisphere.) A surprising bonus is that the seizures become less frequent. Evidently, epileptic activity rebounds back and forth between the hemispheres and prolongs seizures. If it can't bounce back and forth across the corpus callosum, a seizure may not develop at all.

How does severing the corpus callosum affect other aspects of behavior? People who have undergone surgery to the corpus callosum, referred to as **split-brain people**, maintain their intel-

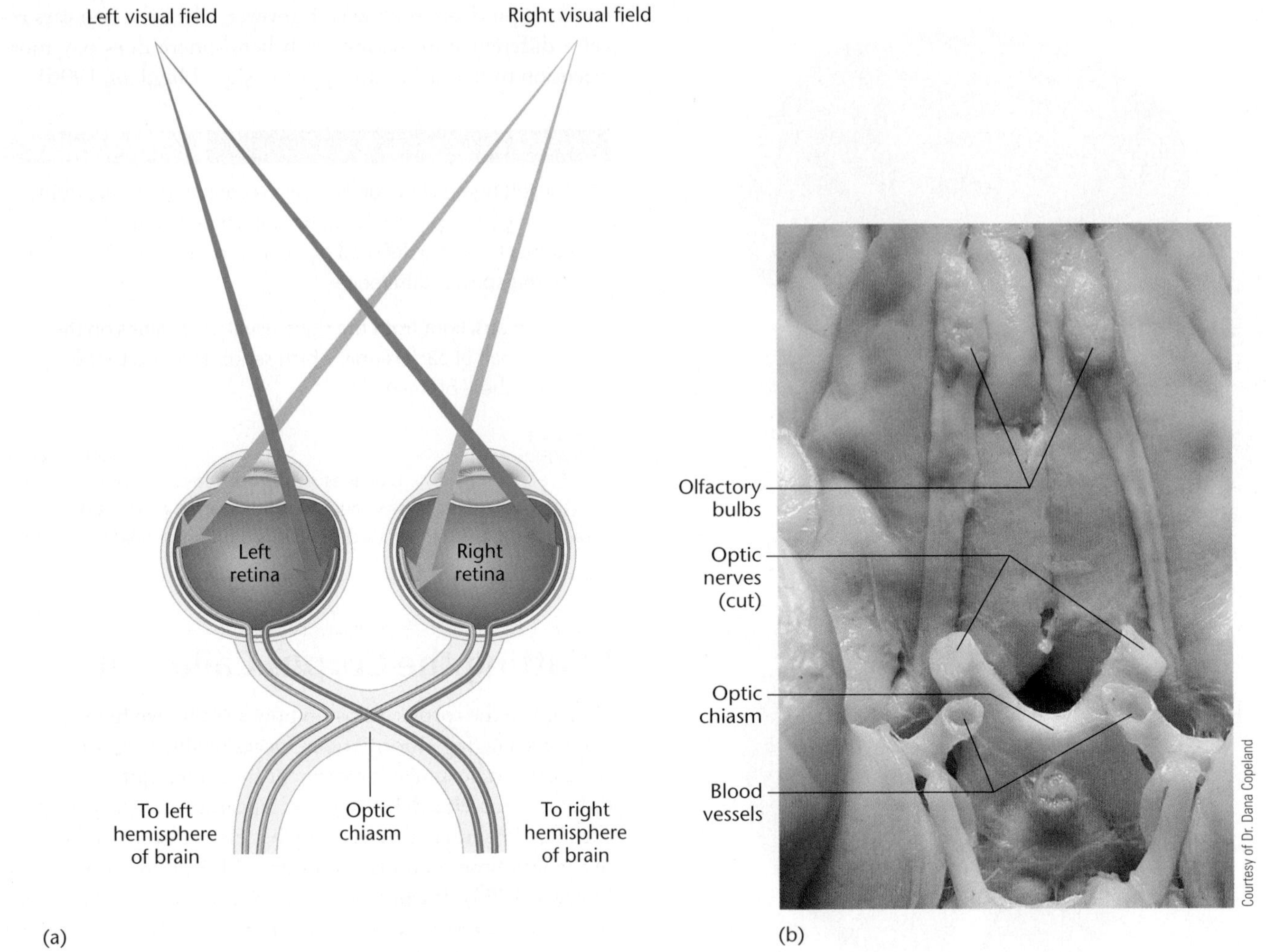

Courtesy of Dr. Dana Copeland

Figure 14.2 Connections from the eyes to the human brain
(a) Route of visual input to the two hemispheres of the brain. Note that the left hemisphere is connected to the left half of each retina and thus gets visual input from the right half of the world; the opposite is true of the right hemisphere. **(b)** Closeup of olfactory bulbs and the optic chiasm. At the optic chiasm, axons from the right half of the left retina cross to the right hemisphere, and axons from the left half of the right retina cross to the left hemisphere.

lect and motivation, and they still walk without difficulty. They also use the two hands together on familiar tasks such as tying shoes. However, if they are asked to pretend they are hitting a golf ball, threading a needle, or attaching a fishhook to a line, they struggle with the less familiar tasks, which have not become automatic for them (Franz, Waldie, & Smith, 2000).

Split-brain people can use their two hands independently in a way that other people cannot. For example, try drawing ∪ with your left hand while simultaneously drawing ⊃ with your right hand. Most people find this task difficult, but split-brain people do it with ease. Or try drawing circles with both hands simultaneously, but one of them just a little faster than the other (not twice as fast).

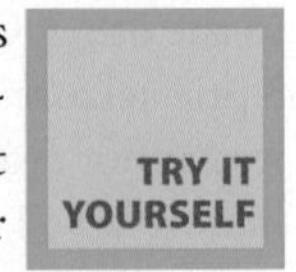

Most people find this task difficult; split-brain people spontaneously draw the circles at different speeds (Kennerley, Diedrichsen, Hazeltine, Semjen, & Ivry, 2002).

The difficulty of simultaneously moving your left hand one way and your right hand a different way reflects a cognitive difficulty more than a motor limitation. It is hard to draw a ∪ with one hand and a ⊃ with the other, but if you carefully draw both of them and then try to *trace over* the ∪ with one hand and a ⊃ with the other, you will find it easier.

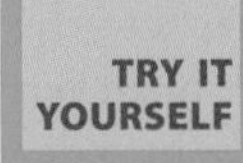

Evidently, it is difficult to plan two actions at once unless you have clear targets to direct your movements. Split-brain people have no trouble planning two actions at once.

Research by Roger Sperry and his students (Nebes, 1974) revealed subtle behavioral effects when stimuli were limited to one side of the body. In a typical experiment, a split-brain person stared straight ahead as the experimenter flashed words or pictures on either side of a screen (Figure 14.3). Information that went to one hemisphere could not cross to the other because of the damage to the corpus callosum. The information stayed on the screen long enough to be visible but not long enough for the person to move his or her eyes. The person could then point with the left hand to what the right hemisphere had seen and could point with the right hand to what the left hemisphere had seen. It was as if each side had only half of the answers. The two halves of the brain had different information, and they could not communicate with each other.

Courtesy of the Archives, CA Inst. of Technology

Roger W. Sperry (1913–1994)

When subjective values have objective consequences . . . they become part of the content of science. . . . Science would become the final determinant of what is right and true, the best source and authority available to the human brain for finding ultimate axioms and guideline beliefs to live by, and for reaching an intimate understanding and rapport with the forces that control the universe and created man.

According to fMRI data and other methods, the left hemisphere is dominant for speech production in more than 95% of right-handers and nearly 80% of left-handers (McKeever, Seitz, Krutsch, & Van Eys, 1995). Not many left-handers have complete right-hemisphere dominance for speech. A more common pattern is mixed left- and right-hemisphere dominance.

In contrast to speech production, speech comprehension is more equally divided. The left hemisphere understands speech better than the right hemisphere, but for most people, the right hemisphere understands speech reasonably well, except with complex grammar (Beeman & Chiarello, 1998).

The left and right hemispheres respond about equally to nonlanguage sounds. Shepherds on one of the Canary Islands developed a simplified version of Spanish that they whistle, using just four consonants and two vowels, to communicate over long distances. When they listen to these sounds, language areas of their left temporal cortex respond strongly. People who don't understand the language react to it as music, without activating the language areas (Carreiras, Lopez, Rivero, & Corina, 2005).

A split-brain person can name an object after viewing it briefly in the right visual field, seeing it with the left hemisphere. But the same person viewing a display in the left visual field (right hemisphere) usually cannot name or describe it. I say "usually" because a small amount of information travels between the hemispheres through several smaller commissures, as shown in Figure 14.4, and some split-brain people get enough information to describe some objects in part (Berlucchi, Mangun, & Gazzaniga, 1997; Forster & Corballis, 2000). A patient who cannot name something points to it correctly with the left hand, even while saying, "I don't know what it was." (Of course, a split-brain person who watches the left hand point out an object can then name it.)

Is there any advantage in having just one hemisphere control speech? Possibly. Many people who have bilateral control of speech stutter (Fox et al., 2000), although not all people who stutter have bilateral control of speech. Perhaps having two speech centers produces competing messages to the speech muscles.

STOP & CHECK

3. Can a split-brain person name an object after feeling it with the left hand? With the right hand? Explain.

4. After a split-brain person sees something in the left visual field, how can he or she describe or identify the object?

ANSWERS

3. A split-brain person cannot describe something after feeling it with the left hand but can with the right. The right hand sends its information to the left hemisphere, which is dominant for language in most people. The left hand sends its information to the right hemisphere, which cannot speak. **4.** After seeing something in the left visual field, a split-brain person could point to the correct answer with the left hand.

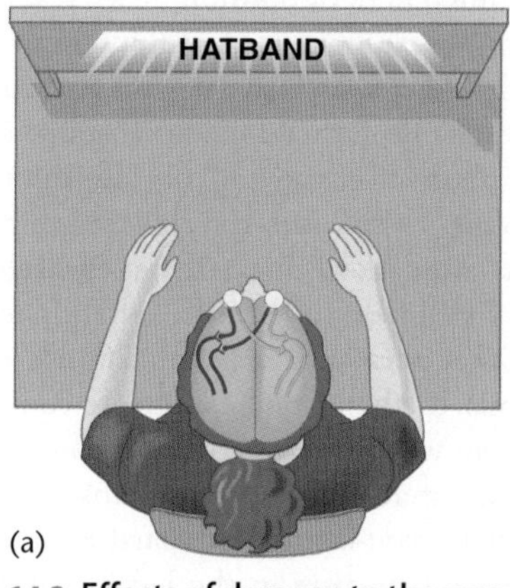

(a)

(b)

(c)

Figure 14.3 Effects of damage to the corpus callosum
(a) When the word *hatband* is flashed on a screen, **(b)** a woman with a split brain can report only what her left hemisphere saw, "band." **(c)** However, with her left hand, she can point to a hat, which is what the right hemisphere saw.

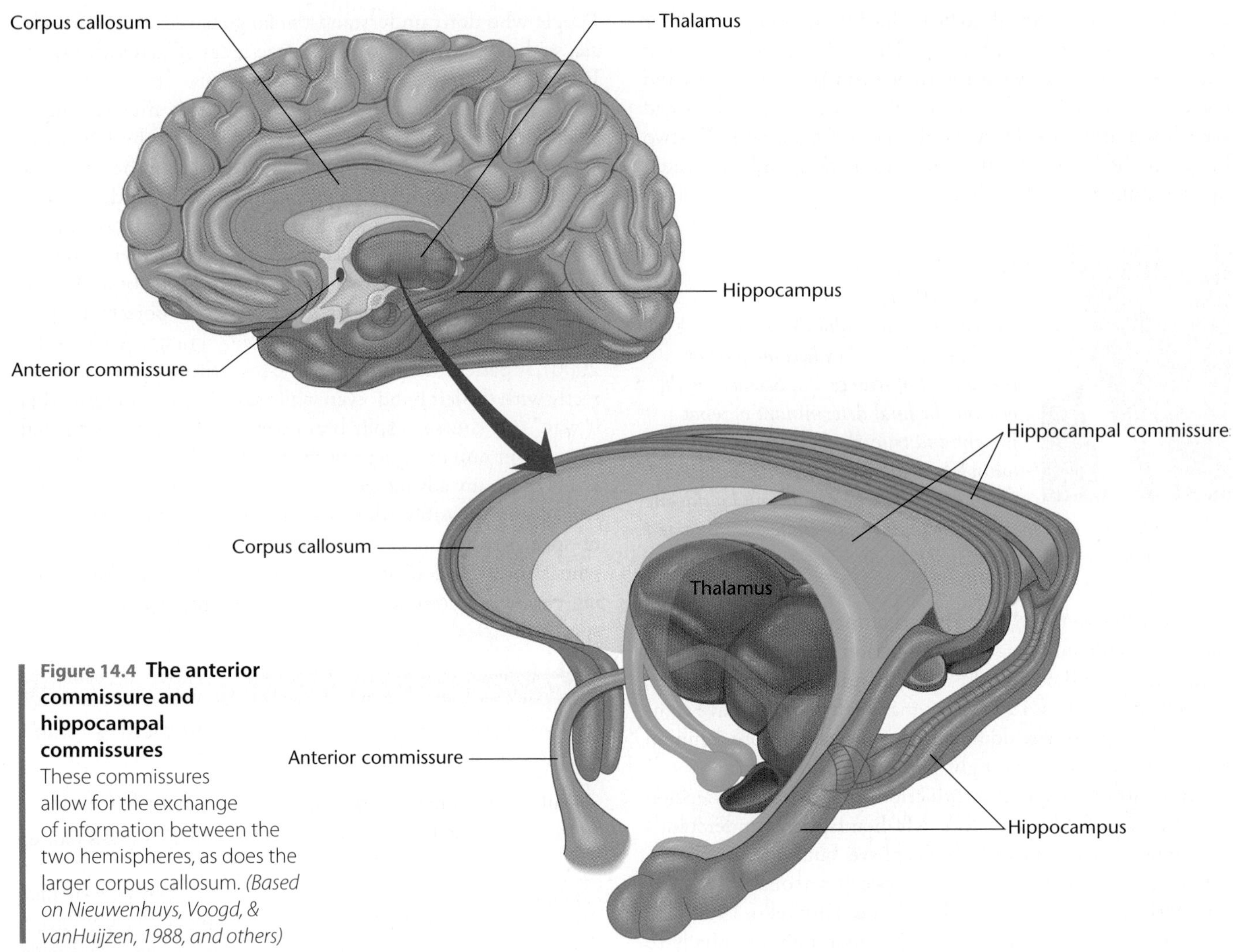

Figure 14.4 The anterior commissure and hippocampal commissures
These commissures allow for the exchange of information between the two hemispheres, as does the larger corpus callosum. *(Based on Nieuwenhuys, Voogd, & vanHuijzen, 1988, and others)*

Split Hemispheres: Competition and Cooperation

Each hemisphere of a split-brain person processes information independently of the other. In the first weeks after surgery, the hemispheres act like separate people sharing one body. One split-brain person repeatedly took items from the grocery shelf with one hand and returned them with the other (Reuter-Lorenz & Miller, 1998).

Another person—specifically, his left hemisphere—described his experience as follows (Dimond, 1979):

> If I'm reading, I can hold the book in my right hand; it's a lot easier to sit on my left hand, than to hold it with both hands. . . . You tell your hand—I'm going to turn so many pages in a book—turn three pages—then somehow the left hand will pick up two pages and you're at page 5, or whatever. It's better to let it go, pick it up with the right hand, and then turn to the right page. With your right hand, you correct what the left has done. (p. 211)

Such conflicts are more common soon after surgery than later. The corpus callosum does not heal, but the brain learns to use the smaller connections between the left and right hemispheres (Myers & Sperry, 1985). The left hemisphere somehow suppresses the right hemisphere's interference and takes control in some situations. However, even then, the hemispheres show "differences of opinion" if we test carefully enough. In one study, researchers used computers to "morph" photos to look partly like a split-brain person and partly like another familiar person. Then they asked this split-brain person to identify each photo after viewing it briefly in one visual field or the other. When he saw it in the right visual field (left hemisphere), he was more likely to say it was himself. When he saw it in the left visual field (right hemisphere), he usually thought it was the other person (Turk et al., 2002).

In other situations, the hemispheres learn to cooperate. A split-brain person who was tested with the apparatus shown in Figure 14.3 used an interesting strategy to answer a yes–no question about what he saw in the left visual field. Suppose an experimenter flashes a picture in the left visual field and asks, "Was it green?" The left (speaking) hemisphere takes a guess: "Yes." That guess might be correct. If not, the right hemisphere, which knows the correct answer, makes the face frown. (Both hemispheres control facial muscles on both sides of the face.) The left hemisphere, feeling the frown, says, "Oh, I'm sorry, I meant 'no.'"

In another experiment, a split-brain person saw two words flashed at once, one on each side. He was then asked to draw a picture of what he had read. Each hemisphere saw a full word, but the two words could combine to make a different word. For example,

Left Visual Field	**Right Visual Field**
(Right Hemisphere)	(Left Hemisphere)
hot	dog
honey	moon
sky	scraper
rain	bow

With the right hand, he almost always drew what he had seen in the right visual field (left hemisphere), such as *dog* or *moon*. However, with the left hand, he sometimes drew a literal combination of the two words. For example, after seeing *hot* and *dog*, he drew an overheated dog, not a wiener on a bun, and after seeing *sky* and *scraper*, he drew a sky and a scraper (Figure 14.5). The right hemisphere, which predominantly controls the left hand, drew what it saw in the left visual field (*hot* or *sky*). Ordinarily, the left hemisphere doesn't control the left hand, but through the bilateral mechanisms of the medial corticospinal pathway (described in Chapter 8), it can move the left hand clumsily and, evidently, enough to add what it saw in the right visual field (*dog* or *scraper*). However, neither hemisphere could combine the words into one concept (Kingstone & Gazzaniga, 1995).

SCRAPER-SKY

Figure 14.5 Left-hand drawing by a split-brain person
He saw the word *sky* in the left visual field and *scraper* in the right visual field. His left hemisphere controlled the left hand enough to draw a scraper, and his right hemisphere controlled it enough to draw a sky. Neither hemisphere could combine the two words to make the emergent concept *skyscraper. (From "Subcortical Transfer of Higher Order Information: More Illusory Than Real?" by A. Kingstone and M. S. Gazzaniga, 1995.* Neuropsychology, *9, pp. 321–328. Copyright © 1995 American Psychological Association. Reprinted with permission.)*

The Right Hemisphere

Suppose you watch a series of videotapes of people talking about themselves. Each person speaks twice, once telling the truth and the other time saying nothing but lies. Could you guess which version was the truth? The average score for MIT undergraduates was 47% correct, a bit worse than the 50% they should have had by random guessing. Most other groups did equally badly, except for one group of people who got 60% correct—still not a great score, but at least better than random (Etcoff, Ekman, Magee, & Frank, 2000). Who do you suppose they were? They were people with left-hemisphere brain damage! They could not understand the speech very well, but they were adept at reading gestures and facial expressions. As mentioned in Chapter 12, the right hemisphere is better than the left at perceiving the emotions in people's gestures and tone of voice, such as happiness or sadness (Adolphs, Damasio, & Tranel, 2002). If the left hemisphere is damaged (and therefore prevented from interfering with the right hemisphere), the right hemisphere is free to make reliable judgments (Buck & Duffy, 1980). In contrast, people with damage in parts of the right hemisphere speak in a monotone voice, do not understand other people's emotional expressions, and usually fail to understand humor and sarcasm (Beeman & Chiarello, 1998).

TRY IT YOURSELF

The right hemisphere is dominant for recognizing emotions in others, including both pleasant and unpleasant emotions (Narumoto, Okada, Sadato, Fukui, & Yonekura, 2001). In a split-brain person, the right hemisphere does better than the left at recognizing whether two photographs show the same or different emotions (Stone, Nisenson, Eliassen, & Gazzaniga, 1996). Moreover, according to Jerre Levy and her colleagues' studies of brain-intact people, when the left and right hemispheres perceive different emotions in someone's face, the response of the right hemisphere dominates. For example, examine the faces in Figure 14.6. Each of these combines half of a smiling face with half of a neutral face. Which looks happier to you: face (a) or face (b)? Most people choose face (a), with the smile on the viewer's left (Heller & Levy, 1981; Hoptman & Levy, 1988; Levy, Heller, Banich, & Burton, 1983). Similarly, a frown on the viewer's left looks sadder than a frown on the viewer's right (Sackeim, Putz, Vingiano, Coleman, & McElhiney, 1988). Remember, what you see in your left visual field stimulates your right hemisphere first.

Jerre Levy
Despite the quite amazing progress of the last half century in neuroscientific understanding, we are still, in my view, as distant now as ever in knowing what questions to ask about how and why brains make minds. It is simply evading the issue to say, as some philosophers do, that our mental experiences are just the inside view of the stuff we measure on the outside. Why is the inside view so utterly different from our external measurements? Even if we specified all the critical spatiotemporal neural dynamics that were necessary and sufficient for a given mental experience, this would not tell us why those dynamics give rise to any experience at all. . . . Nature will answer if we ask the right questions.

The right hemisphere also appears more adept than the left at comprehending spatial relationships. For example, one

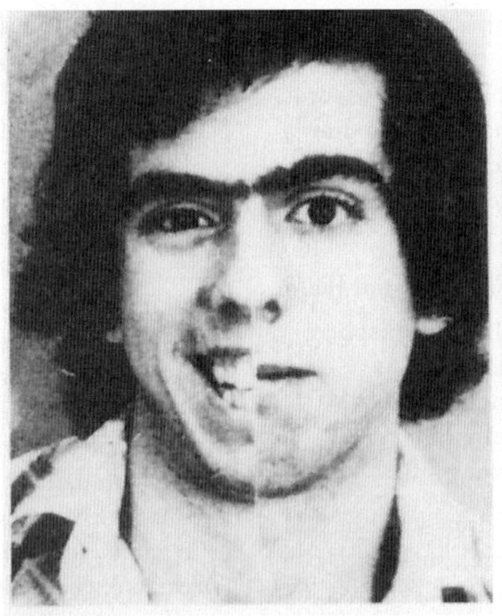
(a)

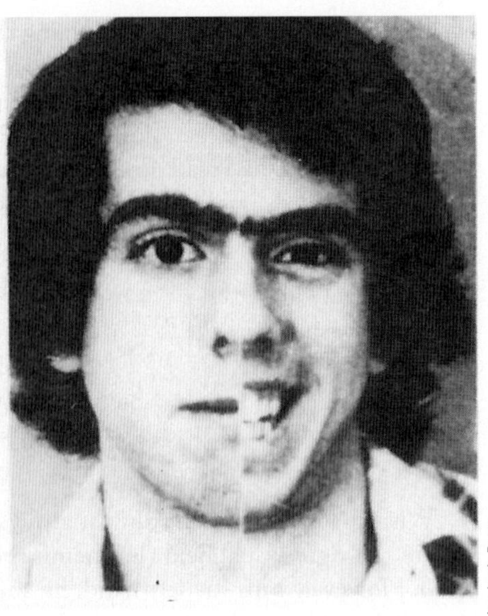
(b)

Academic Press

Figure 14.6 Half of a smiling face combined with half of a neutral face
Which looks happier to you—**(a)** the one with a smile on your left or **(b)** the one with a smile on your right? Your answer may suggest which hemisphere of your brain is dominant for interpreting emotional expressions. *(Reprinted from* Brain and Cognition, *2/4, Levy, J., Heller, W., Banich, M. T., Burton, L. A., "Asymmetry of perception in free viewing of chimeric faces," 404-419, 1983, with permission from Elsevier.)*

young woman with damage to her posterior right hemisphere had trouble finding her way around, even in familiar areas. To reach a destination, she needed directions with specific visual details, such as, "Walk to the corner where you see a building with a statue in front of it. Then turn left and go to the corner that has a flagpole and turn right. . . ." Each of these directions had to include an unmistakable feature; if the instruction was "go to the city government building—that's the one with a tower," she might go to a different building that happened to have a tower (Clarke, Assal, & deTribolet, 1993). Later studies found that damage to part of the right temporal cortex impaired people's ability to remember the visual features of objects. For example, when one woman was asked to describe various objects, she was far below normal in her descriptions of their shape, color, and parts (Vandenbulcke, Peeters, Fannes, & Vandenberghe, 2006).

How can we best describe the difference in functions between the hemispheres? According to Robert Ornstein (1997), the left hemisphere focuses more on details and the right hemisphere more on overall patterns. For example, in one study, people with intact brains examined visual stimuli such as the one in Figure 14.7, in which many repetitions of a small letter compose a different large letter. When they were asked to identify the small letters (in this case, B), activity increased in the left hemisphere, but when they were asked to identify the large overall letter (H), activity was greater in the right hemisphere (Fink et al., 1996).

```
B           B
B           B
B           B
B           B
B B B B B B B
B           B
B           B
B           B
B           B
```

Figure 14.7 Stimulus to test analytical and holistic perception
When people were told to name the large composite letter, they had more activity in the right hemisphere. When told to name the small component letters, they had more activity in the left hemisphere. *(Based on Fink, Halligan, et al., 1996)*

Hemispheric Specializations in Intact Brains

Even in people without brain damage, we can demonstrate differences between the two hemispheres, although the effects are small. Here is something you can try yourself: Tap with your right hand as many times as you can in a short period of time. Rest and repeat with your left hand. Then repeat with each hand while talking. The Online Try It Yourself activity "Hemisphere Control" will keep track of your totals. For most right-handers and many left-handers, talking decreases the tapping rate with the right hand more than with the left hand (Kinsbourne & McMurray, 1975). Evidently, it is more difficult to do two things at once when both activities depend on the same hemisphere.

STOP & CHECK

5. Which hemisphere is dominant for each of the following in most people: speech, emotional inflection of speech, interpreting other people's emotional expressions, spatial relationships, perceiving overall patterns?

ANSWER

5. The left hemisphere is dominant for speech; the right hemisphere is dominant for all the other items listed.

Development of Lateralization and Handedness

Because most people's language depends primarily on the left hemisphere, it is natural to ask whether the hemispheres differ anatomically. If so, is the difference present before speech develops, or does it develop later? What is the relationship between handedness and hemispheric dominance for speech?

Anatomical Differences Between the Hemispheres

The human brain is specialized to attend to language sounds. If you listen to a repeated syllable ("*pack pack pack pack . . .*") and then suddenly the vowel sound changes ("*. . . pack pack pack peck . . .*"), the change will catch your attention and will evoke larger electrical responses measured on your scalp. Changing from *pack* to *peck* also increases the evoked response from a baby, even a premature infant (Cheour-Luhtanen et al., 1996). Evidently, humans attend to language sounds from the start.

Do the hemispheres differ from the start? Norman Geschwind and Walter Levitsky (1968) found that one section of the temporal cortex, called the **planum temporale** (PLAY-num tem-poh-RAH-lee), is larger in the left hemisphere for 65% of people (Figure 14.8). The difference in its size between the left and right hemispheres is slightly greater, on the average, for people who are strongly right-handed (Foundas, Leonard, & Hanna-Pladdy, 2002). Smaller but still significant differences are found between left and right hemispheres of chimpanzees, bonobos, and gorillas (Hopkins, 2006). Chimpanzees with a larger left than right planum temporale generally show a preference for using their right hand, as most humans do (Hopkins, Russell, & Cantalupo, 2007). Evidently, the specialization we see in the human brain built upon lesser specializations already present in our apelike ancestors of long ago.

Sandra Witelson and Wazir Pallie (1973) examined the brains of infants who died before age 3 months and found that the left planum temporale was larger in 12 of 14. Later studies using MRI scans found that healthy 5- to 12-year-old children with the biggest ratio of left to right planum temporale performed best on language tests, whereas children with nearly equal hemispheres were better on certain nonverbal tasks (Leonard et al., 1996). People who suffer damage to the left hemisphere in infancy eventually develop less language than those with equal damage to the right hemisphere (Stark & McGregor, 1997). In short, the left hemisphere is specialized for language from the start in most people.

Maturation of the Corpus Callosum

The corpus callosum matures gradually over the first 5 to 10 years of human life (Trevarthen, 1974). The developmental process is not a matter of growing new axons but of selecting certain axons and discarding others. At an early stage, the brain generates far more axons in the corpus callosum than it will have at maturity (Ivy & Killackey, 1981; Killackey & Chalupa, 1986). The reason is that any two neurons connected by the corpus callosum need to have corresponding functions. For example, a neuron in the left hemisphere that responds to light in the center of the fovea should be connected to a right-hemisphere neuron that responds to light in the same location. During early embryonic development, the genes cannot specify exactly where those two neurons will be. Therefore, many connections are made across the corpus callosum, but only those axons that happen to connect very similar cells survive (Innocenti & Caminiti, 1980).

Because the connections take years to develop their mature adult pattern, certain behaviors of young children resemble those of split-brain adults. In one study, 3- and 5-year-old children were asked to feel two fabrics, either with one hand at two times or with two hands at the same time, and say whether the materials felt the same or different. The 5-year-olds did equally well with one hand or with two. The 3-year-olds made 90% more errors with two hands than with one (Galin, Johnstone, Nakell, & Herron, 1979). The likely interpretation is that the corpus callosum matures sufficiently between ages 3 and 5 to facilitate the comparison of stimuli between the two hands.

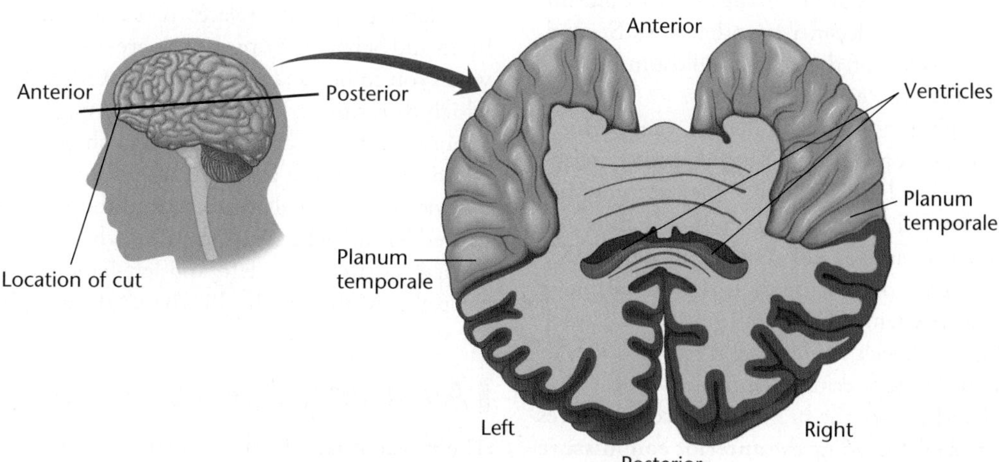

Figure 14.8 Horizontal section through a human brain
This cut, taken just above the surface of the temporal lobe, shows the planum temporale, an area that is critical for speech comprehension. Note that it is substantially larger in the left hemisphere than in the right hemisphere. *(From "Human Brain: Left-Right Asymmetries in Temporal Speech Region," by N. Geschwind and W. Levitsky, 1968,* Science, 161, *pp. 186–187. Copyright © 1968 by AAAS and N. Geschwind. Reprinted with permission.)*

Other kinds of tasks show continuing maturation of the corpus callosum in 5- and 6-year-olds. Did you ever play with an Etch-A-Sketch toy? You can rotate two wheels, one with each hand. One wheel moves a line up or down, and the other moves it left or right. Five- and six-year-olds have great trouble with this toy, possibly because their corpus callosum is not mature enough to integrate the actions of the two hands. In contrast, consider the task of tapping keys with one hand or two whenever a stimulus appears on the screen. Adults and older children are slower to respond with two hands than with one, presumably because the message to one hand interferes with the message to the other hand. Children younger than 6 years respond just as fast with two hands as with one, again suggesting that they do not yet have a mature corpus callosum (Franz & Fahey, 2007).

Etch A Sketch®

Development Without a Corpus Callosum

Rarely, the corpus callosum fails to form, or forms incompletely, possibly for genetic reasons. People born without a corpus callosum are unlike people who have it cut later in life. First, whatever prevented formation of the corpus callosum undoubtedly affects brain development in other ways. Second, the absence or near absence of the corpus callosum induces the remaining brain areas to develop differently.

People born without a corpus callosum can perform many tasks that split-brain people fail. They verbally describe what they feel with either hand and what they see in either visual field. They also feel objects with the two hands and say whether they are the same or different (Paul et al., 2007). How do they do so? They do not use their right hemisphere for speech (Lassonde, Bryden, & Demers, 1990). Rather, each hemisphere develops pathways connecting it to both sides of the body, enabling the left (speaking) hemisphere to feel both the left and right hands. Also, the brain's other commissures become larger than usual, including the **anterior commissure** (see Figures 4.13 on page 93 and 14.4), which connects the anterior parts of the cerebral cortex, and the *hippocampal commissure,* which connects the left and right hippocampi (see Figure 14.4). The extra development of these other commissures partly compensates for the lack of a corpus callosum. However, the amount of information they convey varies from one person to another. Some people lacking a corpus callosum can say whether what they see on the left matches what they see on the right, whereas others cannot. Those differences may depend on how much the anterior commissure has grown in compensation for absence of the corpus callosum (Barr & Corballis, 2002).

STOP & CHECK

6. A child born without a corpus callosum can name something felt with the left hand, but an adult who suffered damage to the corpus callosum cannot. What are two likely explanations?

ANSWER

6. In children born without a corpus callosum, the left hemisphere develops more than the usual connections with the left hand, and the anterior commissure and other commissures grow larger than usual.

Hemispheres, Handedness, and Language Dominance

For more than 95% of right-handed people, the left hemisphere is strongly dominant for speech (McKeever et al., 1995). Left-handers are more variable. Most left-handers have left-hemisphere dominance for speech, but some have right-hemisphere dominance or a mixture of left and right (Basso & Rusconi, 1998). The same is true for people who were left-handed in early childhood but forced to switch to writing right-handed (Siebner et al., 2002). Many left-handers who have partial right-hemisphere control of speech are also partly reversed for spatial perception, showing more than the usual amount of left-hemisphere contribution. A few left-handers have right-hemisphere dominance for both language and spatial perception (Flöel et al., 2001).

Hand preference relates to some other asymmetries in brain and behavior. Suppose you are hiking through the woods when you come to a fork in the path. Other things being equal, which direction do you choose? You might imagine that you choose randomly, but most people show a tendency to pick one direction more than the other. In one study, people wore a device on their belt that counted the number of times they turned left or right over 3 days. On the average, right-handers turned mostly to the left, and left-handers turned mostly to the right (Mohr, Landis, Bracha, & Brugger, 2003).

Avoiding Overstatements

The research on left-brain/right-brain differences is exciting, but it sometimes leads to unscientific assertions. Occasionally, you may hear a person say something like, "I don't do well in science because it is a left-brain subject and I am a right-brain person." That kind of statement is based on two reasonable premises and a doubtful one. The scientific ideas are (a) that the hemispheres are specialized for different functions and (b) that certain tasks evoke greater activity in one hemisphere or the other. The doubtful premise is that any individual habitually relies on one hemisphere more than the other.

What evidence do you suppose someone has for believing, "I am a right-brain person"? Did he or she undergo an MRI or PET scan to determine which hemisphere was larger or more active? Not likely. Generally, when people say, "I am right-brained," their only evidence is that they perform well on creative tasks or poorly on logical tasks. (Saying "I am right-brained" sometimes implies that *because* I do poorly on logical tasks, *therefore*, I am creative. Unfortunately, illogical is not the same as creative.)

In fact, you use both hemispheres for all but the simplest tasks. Most tasks require cooperation by both hemispheres.

MODULE 14.1 IN CLOSING

One Brain, Two Hemispheres

Imagine you are a split-brain person. Someone asks you—that is, your left hemisphere, the talking side of you—a question to which you honestly reply that you do not know. Meanwhile, your left hand points to the correct answer. It must be an unsettling experience.

Now imagine life from the standpoint of that right hemisphere. You sit there mute at all times, while that other hemisphere is jabbering away. Sometimes, you may disagree with what that hemisphere is saying. Sometimes, you probably wish he or she would just shut up for a while. This must be an unsettling experience, too.

Do split-brain people really have two minds, two consciousnesses? At times, they seem to. At least, there are times when one side can answer a question and the other cannot. We cannot get into someone else's head to know what it is like. Indeed, each hemisphere does not know what, if anything, the other hemisphere is experiencing.

SUMMARY

1. The corpus callosum is a set of axons connecting the two hemispheres of the brain. **404**
2. The left hemisphere controls speech in most people, and each hemisphere controls mostly the hand on the opposite side, sees the opposite side of the world, and feels the opposite side of the body. **404**
3. In humans, the left visual field projects onto the right half of each retina, which sends axons to the right hemisphere. The right visual field projects onto the left half of each retina, which sends axons to the left hemisphere. **404**
4. After damage to the corpus callosum, each hemisphere can respond quickly and accurately to questions about the information that reaches it directly. Each can slowly answer a few questions about information on the other side if it crosses the anterior commissure or one of the other small commissures. **405**
5. Although the two hemispheres of a split-brain person are sometimes in conflict, they find ways to cooperate and cue each other. **408**
6. The right hemisphere is dominant for the emotional inflections of speech and for interpreting other people's emotional expressions in either speech or facial expression. In vision, it attends mostly to overall patterns in contrast to the left hemisphere, which is better for details. **409**
7. The left and right hemispheres differ anatomically even during infancy. Young children have some trouble comparing information from the left and right hands because the corpus callosum is not fully mature. **410**
8. A child born without a corpus callosum does not show all the same deficits as an adult who sustains damage to the corpus callosum. **412**
9. The brain of a left-handed person is not simply a mirror image of a right-hander's brain. Most left-handers have left-hemisphere or mixed dominance for speech; few have strong right-hemisphere dominance for speech. **412**

Continued

KEY TERMS

Terms are defined in the module on the page number indicated. They're also presented in alphabetical order with definitions in the book's Subject Index/Glossary. Interactive flashcards, audio reviews, and crossword puzzles are among the online resources available to help you learn these terms and the concepts they represent.

anterior commissure **412**
corpus callosum **404**
epilepsy **405**
focus **405**
lateralization **404**
optic chiasm **405**
planum temporale **411**
split-brain people **405**
visual field **404**

THOUGHT QUESTION

When a person born without a corpus callosum moves the fingers of one hand, he or she also is likely to move the fingers of the other hand involuntarily. What possible explanation can you suggest?

MODULE 14.2

Evolution and Physiology of Language

Nearly all animals communicate through visual, auditory, tactile, or chemical (pheromonal) displays. Human language stands out from other forms of communication because of its **productivity,** its ability to produce new signals to represent new ideas. For example, chickadees (small birds) have one call to warn their neighbors about a hawk flying high overhead and a louder call for a predator perched nearby (Templeton, Greene, & Davis, 2005). Certain monkeys have one call to indicate "eagle or hawk in the air—take cover" and another to indicate "beware—snake on the ground." But they have no way to indicate "snake in the tree above you" or "eagle standing on the ground." Humans, in contrast, constantly devise new expressions for an unlimited variety of new events.

Did we evolve this ability out of nothing or from some precursor already present in other species? Why do we have language, whereas other species have at most a rudimentary hint of it? And what brain specializations make language possible?

Nonhuman Precursors of Language

Evolution rarely creates something totally new. Bat wings are modified arms, and porcupine quills are modified hairs. We would expect human language to be a modification of something we can detect in our closest relatives, chimpanzees.

Common Chimpanzees

After many unsuccessful attempts to teach chimpanzees to speak, researchers achieved better results by teaching them American Sign Language or other visual systems (B. T. Gardner & Gardner, 1975; Premack & Premack, 1972) (Figure 14.9). In one version, chimps learned to press keys bearing symbols to type messages on a computer (Rumbaugh, 1977), such as "Please machine give apple" or to another chimpanzee, "Please share your chocolate."

Is the use of symbols really language? Not everything that we can translate as a series of words is really language. For example, when you insert your ATM card and enter your four-digit PIN, you don't really understand those four digits to mean, "Please machine give money." Similarly, when a chimpanzee presses four symbols on a machine, it may not understand them to mean, "Please machine give apple." The chimps' use of symbols had features that made many people skeptical of calling it language (Rumbaugh, 1990; Terrace, Petitto, Sanders, & Bever, 1979):

- The chimpanzees seldom used symbols in new, original combinations. That is, their symbol use was short on *productivity*.
- The chimpanzees used their symbols mainly to request, seldom to describe.

Nevertheless, the chimpanzees showed indications of at least moderate understanding. For example, the chimp Washoe, trained in sign language, usually answered "Who" questions with names, "What" questions with objects, and "Where" questions with places, even when she sometimes responded with the wrong name, object, or place (Van Cantfort, Gardner, & Gardner, 1989). Although the gap between humans and chimpanzees is large, we do see at least a rudimentary basis for language in the chimpanzees.

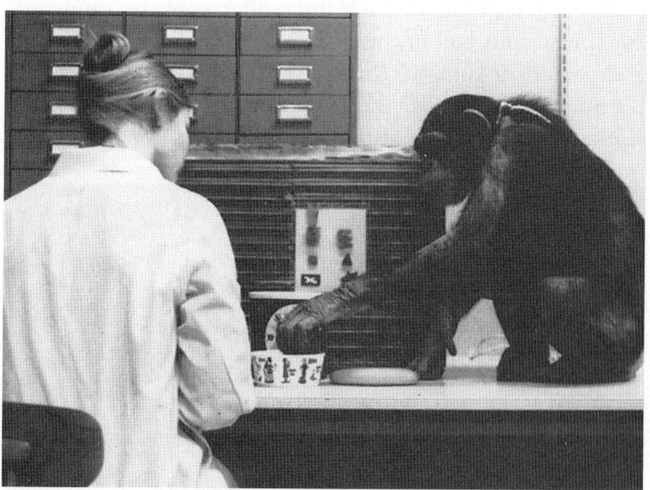

Photo courtesy of Ann Premack

Figure 14.9 One attempt to teach chimpanzees language
One of the Premacks's chimps, Elizabeth, reacts to colored plastic chips that read "Not Elizabeth banana insert—Elizabeth apple wash."

Bonobos

Amid widespread skepticism about chimpanzee language, some surprising results emerged from studies of an endangered species, *Pan paniscus*, known as the bonobo or the pygmy chimpanzee (a misleading name because they are practically the same size as common chimpanzees).

Bonobos' social order resembles humans' in several regards. Males and females form strong, sometimes lasting, personal attachments. They often copulate face to face. The female is sexually responsive on almost any day and not just during her fertile period. The males contribute significantly to infant care. Adults often share food with one another. They stand comfortably on their hind legs. In short, they resemble humans more than other primates do.

Photo courtesy of Duane Rumbaugh

Figure 14.10 Language tests for Kanzi, a bonobo *(Pan paniscus)*
Kanzi listens to questions through the earphones and points to answers on a board. The experimenter with him does not know what the questions are or what answers are expected. *(From Georgia State University's Language Research Center, operated with the Yerkes Primate Center of Emory)*

In the mid-1980s, Sue Savage-Rumbaugh, Duane Rumbaugh, and their associates tried to teach a female bonobo named Matata to press symbols that lit when touched. Each symbol represents a word (Figure 14.10). Although Matata made little progress, her infant son Kanzi learned just by watching her. When given a chance to use the symbol board, he quickly excelled. Later, researchers noticed that Kanzi understood a fair amount of spoken language. For example, whenever anyone said the word "light," Kanzi would flip the light switch. By age 5½, he understood about 150 English words and could respond to such unfamiliar spoken commands as "Throw your ball in the river" and "Go to the refrigerator and get out a tomato" (Savage-Rumbaugh, 1990; Savage-Rumbaugh, Sevcik, Brakke, & Rumbaugh, 1992). Since then, Kanzi and his younger sister Mulika have demonstrated language comprehension comparable to that of a 2- to 2½-year-old child (Savage-Rumbaugh et al., 1993):

- They understand more than they can produce.
- They use symbols to name and describe objects even when they are not requesting them.
- They request items that they do not see, such as "bubbles" (I want to play with the bubble-blower).
- They occasionally use the symbols to describe past events. Kanzi once pressed the symbols "Matata bite" to explain the cut that he had received on his hand an hour earlier.
- They frequently make original, creative requests, such as asking one person to chase another.

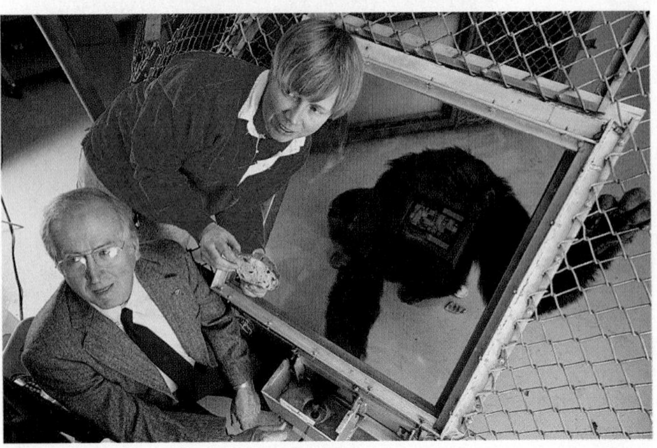

Duane Rumbaugh and Sue Savage-Rumbaugh with chimpanzee Austin

Chimpanzees and bonobos are outstanding teachers of psychology. They never presume that we, as their students, know a damn thing about who they are. And, they certainly aren't impressed with our degrees. Consequently, they are able to teach all manner of important things about what it means to be human and to be ape—that is, if we as students are quiet, listen carefully, and let them tell us as only they can.

Why have Kanzi and Mulika developed more impressive skills than other chimpanzees? Perhaps bonobos have more language potential than common chimpanzees. A second explanation is that Kanzi and Mulika began language training when young, unlike the chimpanzees in most other studies. A third reason pertains to the method of training: Perhaps learning by observation and imitation promotes better understanding than the formal training methods of previous studies (Savage-Rumbaugh et al., 1992).

For more information about bonobos, visit the Block Bonobo Foundation Website at
http://www.blockbonobofoundation.org/

STOP & CHECK

7. What are three likely explanations for why bonobos made more language progress than common chimpanzees?

ANSWER

7. Bonobos may be more predisposed to language than common chimpanzees. The bonobos started training at an earlier age. They learned by imitation instead of formal training techniques.

Nonprimates

What about nonprimate species? Spectacular results have been reported for Alex, an African gray parrot (Figure 14.11). Parrots are, of course, famous for imitating sounds. Irene Pepperberg was the first to argue that parrots can use sounds meaningfully. She kept Alex in a stimulating environment and taught him to say words in conjunction with specific objects. First, she and the other trainers would say a word many times and then offer rewards if Alex approximated the same sound. Here is an excerpt from a conversation with Alex early in training (Pepperberg, 1981, p. 142):

Pepperberg: Pasta! (*Takes pasta.*) Pasta! (*Alex stretches from his perch, appears to reach for pasta.*)
Alex: Pa!
Pepperberg: Better . . . what is it?
Alex: Pah-ah.
Pepperberg: Better!
Alex: Pah-ta.
Pepperberg: Okay, here's the pasta. Good try.

Although pasta was used in this example, Pepperberg generally used toys. For example, if Alex said "paper," "wood," or "key," she would give him what he asked for. In no case did she reward him with food for saying "paper" or "wood."

Alex gradually learned to give spoken answers to spoken questions. He was shown a tray of 12 small objects and then asked such questions as "What color is the key?" (answer: "green") and "What object is gray?" (answer: "circle"). In one test, he correctly answered 39 of 48 questions. Even many of his incorrect answers were almost correct. In one case, he was asked the color of the block and he responded with the color of the rock (Pepperberg, 1993). He also can answer questions of the form "How many blue key?" in which he has to examine objects, count the blue keys among objects of two shapes and two colors, and then say the answer, ranging from one to six (Pepperberg, 1994).

Relying on language is not always helpful. Pepperberg put Alex and three other gray parrots on perches; each had a chain of large plastic links from the perch to an almond on the bottom. (Almonds are favorite foods for parrots.) The parrots untrained in language used their claws to pull up the chain until they reached the almond. Alex and another language-trained parrot repeatedly told the experimenter, "Want nut." When she declined to bring it to them, they gave up (Pepperberg, 2004) (Figure 14.12).

What do we learn from studies of nonhuman language abilities? At a practical level, we gain insights into how best to teach language to those who do not learn it easily, such as people with brain damage or children with autism. At a more theoretical level, these studies indicate that human language evolved from precursors present in other species. These studies also point out the ambiguity of our concept: We cannot decide whether chimpanzees or parrots have language unless we define language more precisely.

Courtesy of Irene Pepperburg/The Alex Foundation

Figure 14.11 Language tests for Alex, an African gray parrot
Alex has apparently learned to converse about objects in simple English—for example, giving the correct answer to "What color is the circle?" He receives no food rewards.

(a)

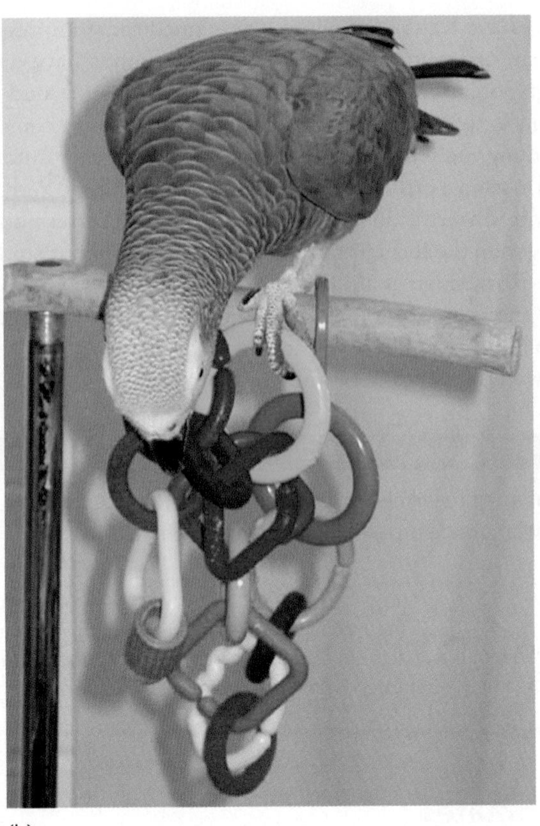
(b)

Figure 14.12 A gray parrot with a reasoning task
Two parrots not trained in language pulled up chain links to reach the treat. Two with language training persisted in saying, "Want nut," without making any effort on their own.

How Did Humans Evolve Language?

How did we evolve the ability to learn language so much more easily than other species? Most theories fall into two categories: (a) we evolved language as a by-product of overall brain development or (b) we evolved it as a brain specialization.

Language as a Product of Overall Intelligence

The simplest view is that humans evolved big brains and therefore great intelligence, and language developed as an accidental by-product of intelligence. In its simplest form, this hypothesis faces serious problems.

First Problem: People With Full-Sized Brains and Impaired Language. If language is a product of overall brain size, then anyone with a full-sized brain and normal overall intelligence should have normal language. However, not all do. In one family, 16 of 30 people over three generations show severe language deficits despite normal intelligence in other regards. Because of a dominant gene, which has been located, the affected people have serious troubles in pronunciation and virtually all other aspects of language (Fisher, Vargha-Khadem, Watkins, Monaco, & Pembrey, 1998; Gopnik & Crago, 1991; Lai, Fisher, Hurst, Vargha-Khadem, & Monaco, 2001). When they speak, their brains show activity in posterior regions instead of the frontal cortex, as in other people (Vargha-Khadem, Gadian, Copp, & Mishkin, 2005).

They have trouble with even simple grammatical rules, as shown in the following dialogue about making plurals:

Experimenter	Respondent
This is a wug; these are . . .	How should I know? *[Later]* These are wug.
This is a zat; these are . . .	These are zacko.
This is a sas; these are . . .	These are sasss. *[Not sasses]*

In another test, experimenters presented sentences and asked whether each sentence was correct and, if not, how to improve it. People in this family accepted many ungrammatical sentences while labeling many correct sentences as incorrect. Evidently, they were just guessing. When they tried to correct a sentence, their results were often odd. For example:

Original Item	Attempted Correction
The boy eats three cookie.	The boys eat four cookie.

In short, a genetic condition can impair language without impairing other aspects of intelligence. Language requires brain specialization, not just brain expansion.

Second Problem: Williams Syndrome. What about the reverse? Could someone with mental retardation have good language? Psychologists long assumed that such a pattern was impossible, until they discovered **Williams syndrome**, affecting about 1 person in 20,000. Despite mental retardation in many regards, many people with Williams syndrome speak grammatically and fluently. The cause is a deletion of several genes from chromosome 7 (Korenberg et al., 2000), leading to decreased gray matter, especially in brain areas relating to visual processing (Kippenhan et al., 2005; Meyer-Lindenberg et al., 2004; Reiss et al., 2004). Affected people are poor at tasks related to numbers, visuospatial skills (e.g., copying a drawing), and spatial perception (e.g., finding their way home). When asked to estimate the length of a bus, three people with Williams syndrome answered "30 inches," "3 inches or 100 inches maybe," and "2 inches, 10 feet" (Bellugi, Lichtenberger, Jones, Lai, & St George, 2000). Throughout life, they require constant supervision and cannot hold even simple jobs.

Nevertheless, they do well in several other regards. One is music, such as the ability to clap a complex rhythm and memorize songs (Levitin & Bellugi, 1998). Another is friendliness and the ability to interpret facial expressions, such as relaxed or worried, serious or playful, flirtatious or uninterested (Tager-Flusberg, Boshart, & Baron-Cohen, 1998). Most people with Williams syndrome show low social anxiety but increased anxiety about inanimate objects (Meyer-Lindenberg et al., 2005), perhaps related to their larger than average amygdala (Reiss et al., 2004).

Their most surprising skill is language. Although their language abilities are generally below average for their age, some individuals have remarkably good language, considering their impairments in other regards. Figure 14.13 shows the result when a young woman with Williams syndrome was asked to draw an elephant and describe it. Contrast her almost poetic description to the unrecognizable drawing.

Let's not overstate the case. People with Williams syndrome do not handle language perfectly (Meyer-Lindenberg, Mervis, & Berman, 2006). They develop language slowly at first, and although many of them make striking gains in later childhood, their grammar continues to be odd, like that of someone who learned a second language late in life (Clahsen & Almazen, 1998; Karmiloff-Smith et al., 1998). If shown a picture of an unfamiliar object and told its name, they are as likely to think the name refers to some part of the object as to the object itself (Stevens & Karmiloff-Smith, 1997). They use fancy words when a common word would work better, such as "I have to evacuate the glass" instead of "empty" or "pour out" the glass (Bellugi et al., 2000). In any case, observations of Williams syndrome indicate that language is not simply a by-product of overall intelligence.

STOP & CHECK

8. What evidence argues against the hypothesis that language evolution depended simply on the overall evolution of brain and intelligence?

9. Describe tasks that people with Williams syndrome do poorly and those that they do well.

ANSWERS

8. Some people have normal brain size but very poor language. Also, some people are mentally retarded but nevertheless develop nearly normal language. **9.** Poor: self-care skills, attention, planning, problem solving, numbers, visual-motor skills, and spatial perception. Relatively good: language, interpretation of facial expressions, social behaviors, some aspects of music.

Language as a Special Module

If language is not a by-product of overall intelligence, perhaps it evolved as a specialized brain mechanism. Noam Chomsky (1980) and Steven Pinker (1994) proposed that humans have a **language acquisition device,** a built-in mechanism for acquiring language. The main supporting evidence is the ease with which most children develop language. For example, deaf children quickly learn sign language, and if no one teaches them a sign language, they invent one of their own and teach it to one another (Goldin-Meadow, McNeill, & Singleton, 1996; Goldin-Meadow & Mylander, 1998).

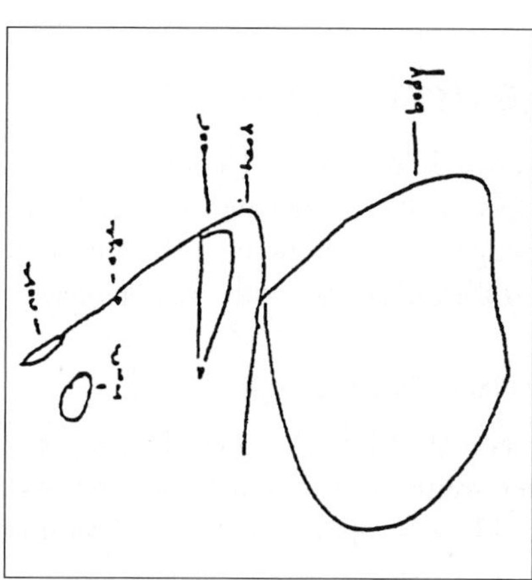

And what an elephant is, it is one of the animals. And what the elephant does, it lives in the jungle. It can also live in the zoo. And what it has, it has long gray ears, fan ears, ears that can blow in the wind. It has a long trunk that can pick up grass, or pick up hay . . . If they're in a bad mood it can be terrible . . . If the elephant gets mad it could stomp; it could charge, like a bull can charge. They have long big tusks. They can damage a car . . . it could be dangerous. When they're in a pinch, when they're in a bad mood it can be terrible. You don't want an elephant as a pet. You want a cat or a dog or a bird . . .

Figure 14.13 **A drawing and a description of an elephant by a young woman with Williams syndrome**
The labels on the drawing were provided by the investigator based on what the woman said she was drawing.
(From "Williams Syndrome: An Unusual Neuropsychological Profile," by U. Bellugi, P. O. Wang, and T. L. Jernigan, S. H. Broman and J. Grafman, Eds., Atypical Cognitive Deficits in Developmental Disorders. *Copyright © 1987 Lawrence Erlbaum. Reprinted by permission.)*

Advocates of the language acquisition device concept sometimes go beyond saying that children learn language readily, claiming that they are born with language; all they have to do is fill in the words and details. Chomsky defends this idea with the **poverty of the stimulus argument:** Children use complex grammar structures that they have seldom heard. For example, even young children will phrase the question

"Is the boy who is unhappy watching Mickey Mouse?"

instead of

"Is the boy who unhappy is watching Mickey Mouse?"

Chomsky and his followers maintain that children have not had enough opportunity to learn that grammatical rule, so they must be born knowing it. However, it is hard to believe that a child is born knowing the grammars of all the possible human languages (Nowak, Komarova, & Niyogi, 2002).

Most researchers agree that humans have specially evolved *something* that enables them to learn language easily. The key question is: What? As we shall see later in this module, certain areas in the left temporal and frontal cortex are essential to human language. Areas in approximately the same location in monkey brains respond to monkey vocalizations (Gil-da-Costa et al., 2006; Petkov et al., 2008), although the anatomy of these areas differs significantly between humans and other primates (Rilling et al., 2008). Evidently, our evolution started with predispositions present in other species and then elaborated upon them greatly.

So back to the original question: How and why did humans evolve language? We don't know, but language is probably not a by-product of overall intelligence. In fact, the opposite is easier to imagine: Selective pressure for social interactions among people, including those between parents and children, favored the evolution of language, and overall intelligence developed as a by-product of language (Deacon, 1992, 1997). Unfortunately, of course, it is difficult to reconstruct the early evolution of human behavior.

STOP & CHECK

10. What is the poverty of the stimulus argument, and what is one observation against it?

ANSWER

10. The poverty of the stimulus argument is the claim that children say complex sentences without adequate opportunity to learn them, so they must be born with an innate grammar. The observation against this idea is that grammatical rules vary among languages, and children could not be born prepared for all the grammars they might have to learn.

A Sensitive Period for Language Learning

If humans are specially adapted to learn language, perhaps we are adapted to learn best during a sensitive period early in life, just as sparrows learn their song best during an early period. One way to test this hypothesis is to see whether people learn a second language best if they start young. The consistent result is that adults are better than children at memorizing the vocabulary of a second language, but children have a great advantage on learning the pronunciation and mastering the grammar. For example, the difference between *a* and *the* is difficult for adult Chinese speakers, whose native language doesn't have articles. A child who overhears a language in the neighborhood, without paying much attention, has an advantage on learning that language later compared to someone not exposed to it at all during childhood (Au, Knightly, Jun, & Oh, 2002). However, there is no sharp cutoff for learning a second language; starting at age 2 is better than 4, 4 is better than 6, and 13 is better than 16 (Hakuta, Bialystok, & Wiley, 2003; Harley & Wang, 1997; Weber-Fox & Neville, 1996).

Another way to test the sensitive-period idea is to study people who were not exposed to any language during early childhood. The clearest data come from studies of deaf children who were unable to learn spoken language and not given an opportunity to learn sign language while they were young. The earlier a child has a chance to learn sign language, the more skilled he or she will become (Harley & Wang, 1997). A child who learns English early can learn sign language later, and a deaf child who learns sign language early can learn English later (except for poor pronunciation), but someone who learns no language while young is permanently impaired at learning language (Mayberry, Lock, & Kazmi, 2002). This observation strongly supports the idea of an early sensitive period for language learning, although it probably does not have a sharp cutoff age.

STOP & CHECK

11. What is the strongest evidence in favor of a sensitive period for language learning?

ANSWER

11. Deaf children who are not exposed to sign language until later in life (and who did not learn spoken language either while they were young) do not become proficient at it.

Brain Damage and Language

Because almost every healthy child develops language, we infer that the human brain is specialized to facilitate language learning. Much of our knowledge about the brain mechanisms of language has come from studies of people with brain damage.

Broca's Aphasia (Nonfluent Aphasia)

In 1861, the French surgeon Paul Broca treated the gangrene of a patient who had been mute for 30 years. When the man died 5 days later, Broca did an autopsy and found a lesion in the left frontal cortex. Over the next few years, Broca examined the brains of additional patients with **aphasia** (language impairment). In nearly all cases, he found damage that included this same area, which is now known as **Broca's area** (Figure 14.14). The usual cause was a stroke (an interruption of blood flow to part of the brain). Broca published his results in 1865, slightly later than papers by other French physicians, Marc and Gustave Dax, who also pointed to the left hemisphere as the seat of language abilities (Finger & Roe, 1996). Broca is given the credit, however, because his description was more detailed and more convincing. This discovery, the first demonstration of a particular function for a particular brain area, paved the way for modern neurology.

We now know that speaking activates much of the brain, mostly in the left hemisphere, and not just Broca's area (Wallesch, Henriksen, Kornhuber, & Paulson, 1985) (Figure 14.15). Damage limited to Broca's area produces only minor or brief language impairment. Serious deficits result from extensive damage that extends into other areas as well. The symptoms vary and are not completely predictable from the location of the damage (Dick et al., 2001).

When people with brain damage suffer impaired language production, we call it **Broca's aphasia,** or **nonfluent aphasia**, regardless of the exact location of the damage. People with Broca's aphasia also have comprehension deficits when the meaning of a sentence depends on prepositions, word endings, or unusual word order—in short, when the sentence structure is complicated.

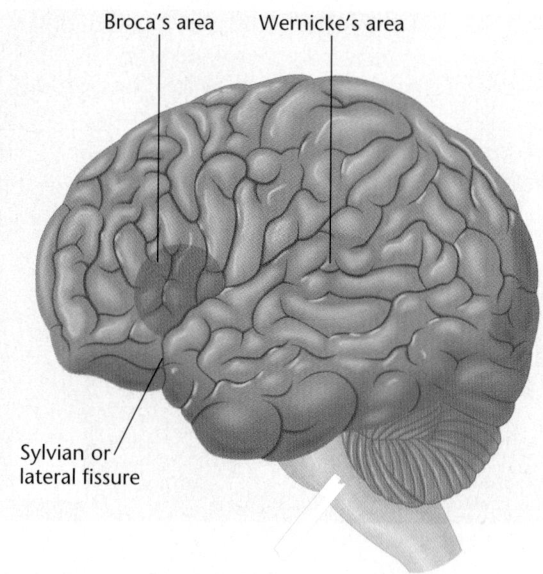

Figure 14.14 Some major language areas of the cerebral cortex
In most people, only the left hemisphere is specialized for language.

Difficulty in Language Production. People with Broca's aphasia are slow and awkward with all forms of expression, including speaking, writing, and gesturing (Cicone, Wapner, Foldi, Zurif, & Gardner, 1979). The frontal cortex is also important for the sign language of the deaf (Neville et al., 1998; Petitto et al., 2000), although the right hemisphere makes more contributions than it does for spoken language (Corina, 1998). So Broca's aphasia relates to language, not just the vocal muscles.

When people with Broca's aphasia speak, they omit most pronouns, prepositions, conjunctions, auxiliary (helping) verbs, quantifiers, and tense and number endings. At least, those are the results for people speaking English. People with aphasia use more word endings if they speak German, Italian, or other languages in which word endings are more important than they are in English (Blackwell & Bates, 1995). Prepositions, conjunctions, helping verbs, and so forth are known as the *closed class* of grammatical forms because a language rarely adds new prepositions, conjunctions, and the like. In contrast, new nouns and verbs (the *open class*) enter a language frequently. People with Broca's aphasia seldom use the closed-class words. They find it difficult to repeat a phrase such as "No ifs, ands, or buts," although they can successfully repeat, "The general commands the army." Furthermore, patients who cannot read aloud "To be or not to be" can read "Two bee oar knot two bee" (H. Gardner & Zurif, 1975). Clearly, the trouble is with the word meanings, not just pronunciation.

Why do people with Broca's aphasia omit the grammatical words and endings? Perhaps they have suffered damage to a "grammar area" in the brain, but here is another possibility: When speaking is a struggle, people leave out the weakest elements. Many people who are in great pain speak as if they have Broca's aphasia (Dick et al., 2001).

Problems in Comprehending Grammatical Words and Devices. People with Broca's aphasia have trouble understanding the same kinds of words that they omit when speaking, such as prepositions and conjunctions. They often misunderstand sentences with complex grammar, such as "The girl that the boy is chasing is tall" (Zurif, 1980). However, most English sentences follow the subject-verb-object order, and their meaning is clear even without the prepositions and conjunctions. You can demonstrate this for yourself by taking a paragraph and deleting its prepositions, conjunctions, articles, helping verbs, pronouns, and word endings to see how it might appear to someone with Broca's aphasia. Here is an example, taken from earlier in this section. Note how understandable it is despite the deletions:

> ~~In~~ 1861, ~~the~~ French surgeon Paul Broca treat~~ed~~ ~~the~~ gangrene ~~of a~~ patient ~~who had~~ been mute ~~for~~ 30 years. ~~When the~~ man die~~d~~ 5 day~~s~~ later, Broca did ~~an~~ autopsy ~~and~~ found ~~a~~ lesion ~~in the~~ left frontal cortex. ~~Over the~~ next few years, Broca examine~~d~~ ~~the~~ brain~~s~~ ~~of~~ addition~~al~~ patient~~s~~ ~~with~~ aphasia (language impairment). ~~In~~ nearly all case~~s~~, ~~he~~ found damage ~~that~~ include~~d~~ ~~this~~ same area, ~~which~~ is now know~~n~~ ~~as~~ Broca's area. ~~The~~ usual cause was ~~a~~ stroke (~~an~~ interruption ~~of~~ blood flow ~~to~~ part ~~of the~~ brain).

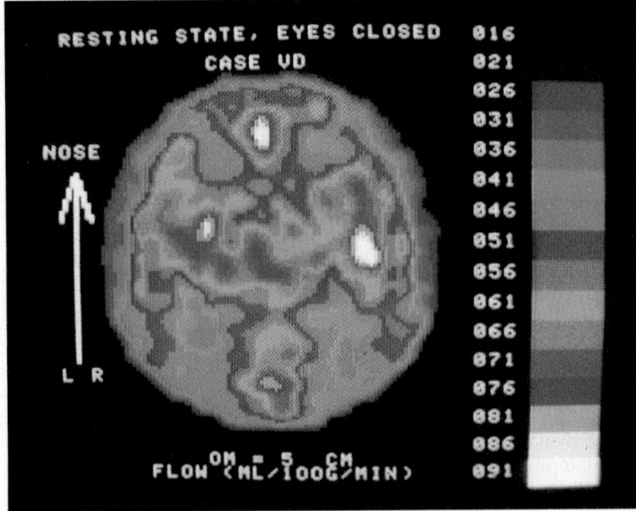

(a)

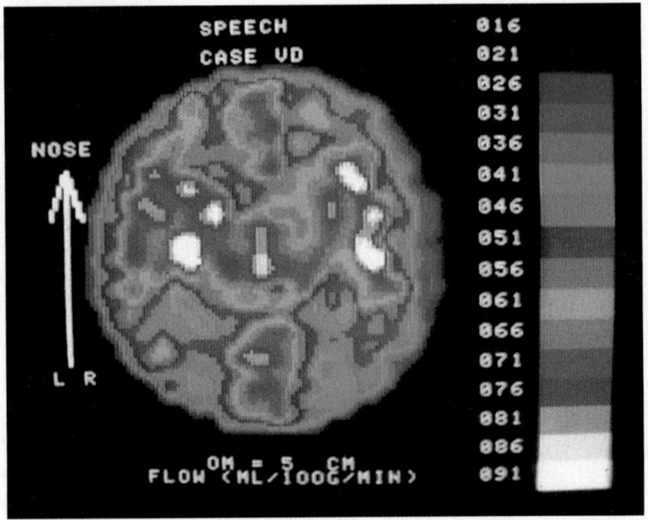

(b)

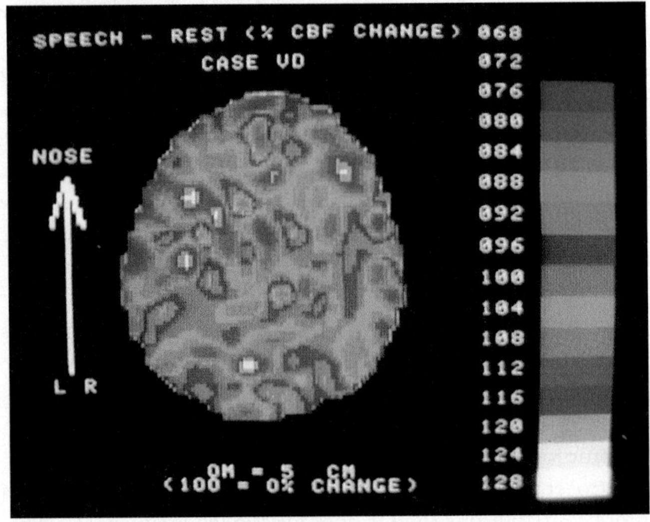

(c)

Figure 14.15 Records showing blood flow for a normal adult Red indicates the highest level of activity, followed by yellow, green, and blue. **(a)** Blood flow to the brain at rest. **(b)** Blood flow while subject describes a magazine story. **(c)** Difference between **(b)** and **(a)**. The results in **(c)** indicate which brain areas increased their activity during language production. Note the increased activity in many areas of the brain, especially on the left side. *(Reprinted from* Brain and Language, 25/2, *Wallesch, Henriksen, Kornhuber, & Paulson, "Observations on regional cerebral blood flow in cortical and subcortical structures during language production in normal man," pp. 224–233, 1985, with permission from Elsevier.)*

Still, people with Broca's aphasia have not totally lost their knowledge of grammar. For example, they generally recognize that something is wrong with the sentence "He written has songs," even if they cannot say how to improve it (Wulfeck & Bates, 1991). In many ways, their comprehension resembles that of normal people who are distracted. If you listen to someone speaking rapidly with a heavy accent in a noisy room, while you are trying to do something else at the same time, you catch bits and pieces of what the speaker says and try to guess the rest (Blackwell & Bates, 1995; Dick et al., 2001). In fact, even when we hear a sentence clearly, we sometimes ignore the grammar. When people hear "The dog was bitten by the man," many of them assume it was the dog that did the biting (Ferreira, Bailey, & Ferraro, 2002). Patients with Broca's aphasia just rely on inferences more often than others do.

STOP & CHECK

12. Is it reasonable to conclude that Broca's patients have lost their grammar?

ANSWER

12. No. They can usually recognize incorrect grammar, even if they cannot state how to correct it. Their speech is like that of someone who finds it painful to speak (leaving out words with the least meaning).

Wernicke's Aphasia (Fluent Aphasia)

In 1874, Carl Wernicke (usually pronounced WER-nih-kee by English speakers, although the German pronunciation is VAYR-nih-keh), a 26-year-old junior assistant in a German hospital, discovered that damage in part of the left temporal cortex produced a different kind of language impairment. Although patients could speak and write, their language comprehension was poor. Damage in and around **Wernicke's area** (see Figure 14.14), located near the auditory cortex, produces **Wernicke's aphasia,** characterized by poor language comprehension and impaired ability to remember the names of objects. It is also known as **fluent aphasia** because the person can still speak smoothly. As with Broca's aphasia, the symptoms and brain damage vary. We use the term Wernicke's aphasia, or fluent aphasia, to describe a certain pattern of behavior, independent of the location of damage.

The typical characteristics of Wernicke's aphasia are as follows:

1. *Articulate speech*. In contrast to people with Broca's aphasia, those with Wernicke's aphasia speak fluently, except for pauses to try to think of the name of something.
2. *Difficulty finding the right word*. People with Wernicke's aphasia have **anomia** (ay-NOME-ee-uh), difficulty recalling the names of objects. They make up names (e.g., "thingamajig"), substitute one name for another, and use roundabout expressions such as "the thing that we used to do with the thing that was like the other one." When they do manage to find some of the right words, they arrange them improperly, such as, "The Astros listened to the radio tonight" (instead of "I listened to the Astros on the radio tonight") (R. C. Martin & Blossom-Stach, 1986).
3. *Poor language comprehension*. People with Wernicke's aphasia have trouble understanding spoken and written speech and—in the case of deaf people—sign language (Petitto et al., 2000). Although many sentences are clear enough without prepositions, word endings, and grammar (which confuse Broca's aphasics), few sentences make sense without nouns and verbs (which trouble Wernicke's patients).

The following conversation is between a woman with Wernicke's aphasia and a speech therapist trying to teach her the names of some objects. (The Duke University Department of Speech Pathology and Audiology provided this dialogue.)

Therapist: *(Holding picture of an apron)* Can you name that one?

Woman: Um . . . you see I can't, I can I can barely do; he would give me sort of umm . . .

T: A clue?

W: That's right . . . just a like, just a . . .

T: You mean, like, "You wear that when you wash dishes or when you cook a meal . . ."?

W: Yeah, something like that.

T: Okay, and what is it? You wear it around your waist, and you cook . . .

W: Cook. Umm, umm, see I can't remember.

T: It's an apron.

W: Apron, apron, that's it, apron.

T: *(Holding another picture)* That you wear when you're getting ready for bed after a shower.

W: Oh, I think that he put under different, something different. We had something, you know, umm, you know.

T: A different way of doing it?

W: No, umm . . . umm . . . *(Pause)*

T: It's actually a bathrobe.

W: Bathrobe. Uh, we didn't call it that, we called it something else.

T: Smoking jacket?

W: No, I think we called it, uh . . .

T: Lounging . . .?

W: No, no, something, in fact, we called it just . . . *(Pause)*

T: Robe?

W: Robe. Or something like that.

The patient still knows the names of objects and recognizes them when she hears them; she just has trouble finding them for herself. In some ways, her speech resembles that of a student called upon to speak in a foreign language class after poorly studying the vocabulary list. As people recover from this type of aphasia, blood flow and brain activity increase in the temporal cortex (Hillis et al., 2006).

Studies with various kinds of brain scans confirm the importance of Wernicke's area and Broca's area for language. When you listen to speech, especially difficult or confusing speech, your brain responds first in the temporal lobe, including Wernicke's area, and then in the frontal lobe, including Broca's area (C.-Y. Tse et al., 2007).

Although Wernicke's area and surrounding areas are important, language comprehension also depends on the connections to other brain areas. For example, reading the word *lick* activates not only Wernicke's area but also the part of the motor cortex responsible for tongue movements. Reading *kick* activates the part of the motor cortex controlling foot movements (Hauk, Johnsrude, & Pulvermüller, 2004). It is as if whenever you think about the meaning of an action word, you imagine doing it.

Table 14.1 contrasts Broca's aphasia and Wernicke's aphasia. For more information about aphasia and its many forms, check The National Aphasia Association (NAA) Website: http://www.aphasia.org/

TABLE 14.1 Broca's Aphasia and Wernicke's Aphasia

Type	Pronunciation	Content of Speech	Comprehension
Broca's aphasia	Poor	Mostly nouns and verbs; omits prepositions and other grammatical connectives	Impaired if the meaning depends on complex grammar
Wernicke's aphasia	Unimpaired	Grammatical but often nonsensical; has trouble finding the right word, especially names of objects	Seriously impaired

STOP & CHECK

13. Describe the speech production of people with Broca's aphasia and those with Wernicke's aphasia.

14. Describe the speech comprehension of people with Broca's aphasia and those with Wernicke's aphasia.

ANSWERS

13. People with Broca's aphasia speak slowly and with poor pronunciation, but their speech includes nouns and verbs and is usually meaningful. They omit prepositions, conjunctions, and other grammatical words that have no meaning out of context. People with Wernicke's aphasia speak fluently and grammatically but omit most nouns and verbs and therefore make little sense. **14.** People with Broca's aphasia understand most speech unless the meaning depends on grammatical devices or complex sentence construction. People with Wernicke's aphasia understand little speech.

Brain Mechanisms for Bilinguals

A bilingual speaker is someone who speaks two languages. Some people are fluent in three or more. How can people keep the languages separate? Do they represent different language in different brain areas?

Part of the answer is that they do not always keep the different languages separate (Thierry & Wu, 2007). To the extent that they do, they don't do it by storing different languages in different areas. The same brain areas process each language (Perani & Abutalebi, 2005). However, in people who are fluent in two or more languages from early childhood onward, the language areas of the temporal and frontal cortex grow thicker than average (Mechelli et al., 2004). In people who are adept at one language and less at the other, the second language takes more effort and therefore activates the language areas and some of the surrounding areas more strongly than the first language does (Perani & Abutalebi, 2005). Shifting from one language to the other strongly activates the frontal cortex, temporal cortex, and basal ganglia (Abutalebi et al., 2007; Crinion et al., 2006). Evidently, the brain works hard to prime one set of word representations and inhibit another.

Music and Language

Language occurs in every human culture, and no other species develops language as we know it. Exactly the same could be said for music. Language and music have many parallels, including the ability of both to evoke strong emotions. Broca's area is strongly activated when orchestral musicians sight-read music, as well as when they perform difficult visuospatial tasks (Sluming, Brooks, Howard, Downes, & Roberts, 2007). The parallels between language and music are sufficient to suggest that they arose together. That is, whatever evolutionary processes helped us develop language also enabled us to develop music.

Consider some of the parallels (Patel, 2008):

- Trained musicians and music students tend to be better than average at learning a second language.
- In both language and music, we alter the timing and volume to add emphasis or to express emotion.
- English speakers average about 0.5 to 0.7 seconds between one stressed syllable and another in speech and prefer music with about 0.5 to 0.7 seconds between beats.
- Greek and Balkan languages have less regular rhythms than English, and much of the music written by speakers of those languages has irregularly spaced beats.
- English usually stresses the first syllable of a word or phrase, whereas French more often stresses the final syllable. Similarly, French composers more often than English composers make the final note of a phrase longer than the others.
- English vowels vary in duration more than French vowels do. For example, compare the vowels in *tourist* or *pirate*. English composers, on the average, have more variation in note length from one note to the next.

These similarities and others suggest that we use the language areas of the brain when we compose music, and we prefer music that resembles our language in rhythms and tones (Ross, Choi, & Purves, 2007). You could think of music as an alternative method of communication.

STOP & CHECK

15. In what way do musical compositions vary depending on the language spoken by the composer?

ANSWER

15. Musical compositions tend to follow the same rhythms that are common in the language spoken by the composer.

Dyslexia

Dyslexia is a specific impairment of reading in someone with adequate vision and adequate skills in other academic areas. It is more common in boys than girls and has been linked to at least four genes that produce deficits in hearing or cognition (Galaburda, LoTurco, Ramus, Fitch, & Rosen, 2006). Dyslexia is an especially big problem among English readers because English has so many words with odd spellings. (Consider the examples *phlegm, bivouac, khaki, yacht, choir, physique,* and *gnat.*) However, dyslexia occurs in all languages and always pertains to a difficulty converting symbols into sounds (Ziegler & Goswami, 2005).

Many people with dyslexia have mild abnormalities in the structure of many brain areas, including microscopic details (Klingberg et al., 2000). They brain abnormalities of English speakers with dyslexia differ from those of Chinese speakers with dyslexia. Chinese is written with symbols that represent words or syllables. Evidently, the nature of the language determines which brain areas will be most important for reading (Siok, Niu, Jin, Perfetti, & Tan, 2008).

As a rule, people with dyslexia are more likely to have a bilaterally symmetrical cerebral cortex, whereas in other people, the planum temporale and certain other areas are larger in the left hemisphere (Galaburda, Sherman, Rosen, Aboitiz, & Geschwind, 1985; Hynd & Semrud-Clikeman, 1989; Jenner, Rosen, & Galaburda, 1999). Furthermore, children with dyslexia show less arousal in the parietal and temporal cortex while reading compared to younger children matched to them for current reading ability (Hoeft et al., 2006). Special education to increase sound awareness increases the activity of these areas during reading (Eden et al., 2004).

Reading is a complicated skill that requires seeing subtle differences as *abode* versus *adobe*, hearing subtle differences as *symphony* versus *sympathy*, and connecting the sound patterns to the visual symbols. In fact, even understanding spoken language requires a combination of vision and hearing. Nondeaf people do far more lip-reading than they realize. Consider your experience when you see a foreign film that is dubbed badly or a film in which the soundtrack is slightly off from the picture.

In the often confusing literature about dyslexia, one point that stands out is that different people have different kinds of reading problems, and no one explanation works for all. Most (but not all) have auditory problems, a smaller number have impaired control of eye movements, and some have both (Judge, Caravolas, & Knox, 2006). Some researchers distinguish between *dysphonetic dyslexics* and *dyseidetic dyslexics* (Flynn & Boder, 1991), although many people with dyslexia do not fit neatly into either category (Farmer & Klein, 1995). Dysphonetic dyslexics have trouble sounding out words, so they try to memorize each word as a whole, and when they don't recognize a word, they guess based on context. For example, they might read the word *laugh* as "funny." Dyseidetic readers sound out words well enough, but they fail to recognize a word as a whole. They read slowly and have particular trouble with irregularly spelled words.

The most severe cases of dyseidetic dyslexia result from brain damage that restricts the field of vision. People who see only one letter at a time have many short eye movements, very slow reading, and particular difficulty with long words. In one study, normal people viewed words on a computer screen while a device monitored their eye movements and blurred every letter on the screen except the one the viewer focused on. The result was very slow reading (Rayner & Johnson, 2005).

Most but not all people with dyslexia have auditory problems (Caccappolo-van Vliet, Miozzo, & Stern, 2004). Brain scans have shown that dyslexics' brains, on the average, show less than normal responses to speech sounds, especially consonants (Helenius, Salmelin, Richardson, Leinonen, & Lyytinen, 2002; McCrory, Frith, Brunswick, & Price, 2000). Many people with dyslexia have particular trouble detecting the temporal order of sounds, such as noticing the difference between beep-click-buzz and beep-buzz-click (Farmer & Klein, 1995; Kujala et al., 2000; Nagarajan et al., 1999). They also have much difficulty making Spoonerisms—that is, trading the first consonants of two words, such as listening to "dear old queen" and saying "queer old dean" or hearing "way of life" and replying "lay of wife" (Paulesu et al., 1996). Doing so, of course, requires close attention to sounds and their order. Many people with dyslexia have trouble with other temporal order tasks as well, such as tapping a regular rhythm with the fingers (Wolff, 1993).

However, the problem cannot be simply impaired hearing. Many deaf or partly deaf people can read, and people with dyslexia have no trouble carrying on a conversation (which would be difficult if their hearing were seriously impaired). The problem must be something more specific, such as paying attention to certain aspects of sound or connecting sound to vision. In one study, dyslexics performed normally at watching nonsense words flashed on the screen and saying whether they were the same or different. (For example, *brap-brap* would be the same and *sond-snod* would be different.) They were also normal at listening to two nonsense words and saying whether they were the same. They were impaired only when they had to look at a nonsense word on the screen and then say whether it was the same as a nonsense word they heard (Snowling, 1980).

Many people with dyslexia also have problems in attention. Suppose a stimulus is going to flash briefly on the screen, and your task is to identify the location of the stimulus or, in another experiment, to identify the direction of tilt of a line (/ vs. \). Sometimes, a fraction of a second before this stimulus, another cue appears on the screen telling you where the stimulus will appear on the screen. For most people, this cue shifts attention in the correct direction and improves performance. For people with dyslexia, it makes no difference, indicating that the cue didn't help them shift attention or that they couldn't shift attention fast enough (Facoetti et al., 2003; Roach & Hogben, 2004). Reading requires shifting attention from one word to another along the line.

Here is another demonstration of attention and reading. Fixate your eyes on the central dot in each display below and, without moving your eyes left or right, try to read the middle letter of each three-letter display:

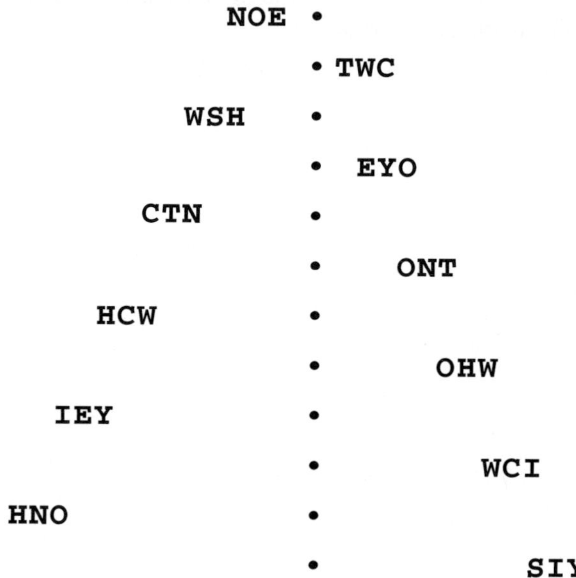

Most people find it easier to read the letters close to the fixation point, but some people with dyslexia are unusually adept at identifying letters well to the right of their fixation point. When they focus on a word, they are worse than average at reading it but better than average at perceiving letters 5 to 10 degrees to the right of it (Geiger, Lettvin, & Zegarra-Moran, 1992; Lorusso et al., 2004). That kind of attentional focus could certainly confuse attempts at reading (De Luca, Di Page, Judica, Spinelli, & Zoccolotti, 1999). Figure 14.16 shows the mean results for normal readers and for people with dyslexia.

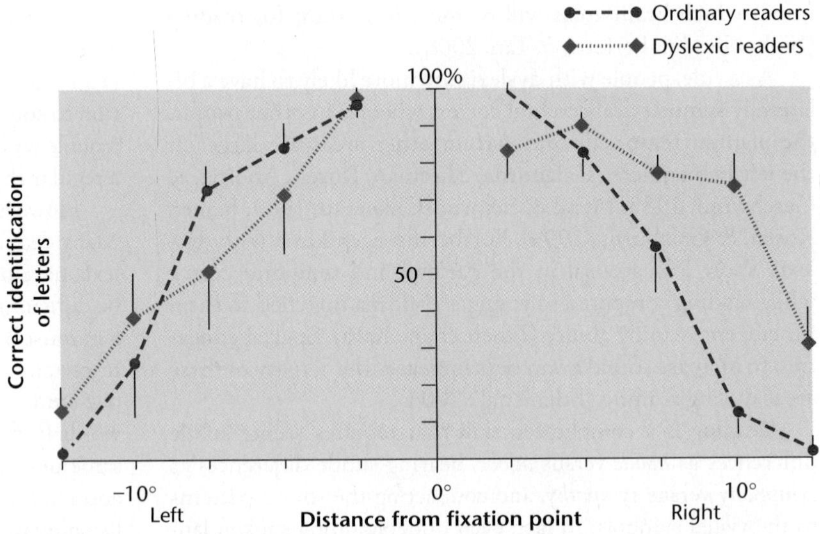

Figure 14.16 Identification of a letter at various distances from the fixation point
Normal readers identify a letter most accurately when it is closest to the fixation point, and their accuracy drops steadily as letters become more remote from that point. Many people with dyslexia show a small impairment for letters just to the right of the fixation point, yet they are substantially more accurate than normal readers are in identifying letters 5 to 10 degrees to the right of fixation. *(Reprinted from "Task-Determined Strategies of Visual Process," by G. Geiger, J. Y. Lettvin, & U. Zagarra-Moran, 1992,* Cognitive Brain Research, *1, pp. 39–52, 1992, with kind permission of Elsevier Science-NL, Sara Burgerhartstraat 25, 1055 KV Amsterdam, The Netherlands.)*

For people with this abnormality, an effective treatment might be to teach them to attend to just one word at a time. Some children and adults with dyslexia have been told to place over the page that they are reading a sheet of paper with a window cut out of it that is large enough to expose just one word. In 3 months, 15 dyslexic children improved their reading skills by 1.22 grade levels (Geiger, Lettvin, & Fahle, 1994). Four dyslexic adults also made spectacular progress; one advanced from a third-grade to a tenth-grade reading level in 4 months (Geiger et al., 1992). After about the first 3 weeks of practice, they no longer needed the special cutout sheet of paper.

One final twist: Of the four adults with dyslexia who went through this process, three decided that they would rather return to being dyslexic! While dyslexic, they could attend to several tasks at once, such as talking to someone, listening to news on the radio, creating a work of art, and so forth. When they learned to read one word at a time, they found themselves able to perform only one task at a time, and they missed their old way of life. In short, their reading skills were tied to their overall attentional strategies.

For more information about dyslexia, visit the British Dyslexia Association Website: http://www.bdadyslexia.org.uk

STOP & CHECK

16. What usually gives the most problems to a person with dyslexia—vision, hearing, or connecting vision to hearing?

ANSWER

16. Generally, the greatest problem arises with connecting visual stimuli to sounds.

MODULE 14.2 IN CLOSING

Language and the Brain

Perhaps the best summary of dyslexia is also the best summary of language impairments in general: Language and reading are sufficiently complicated that people can become impaired in many ways for many reasons. Language is not simply a by-product of overall intelligence, but it is hardly independent of other intellectual functions either.

SUMMARY

1. Chimpanzees can learn to communicate through gestures or nonvocal symbols, although their output does not closely resemble human language. Bonobos have made more language progress than common chimpanzees because of species differences, early onset of training, and different training methods. **415**
2. An African gray parrot has shown surprising language abilities, with a brain organized differently from that of primates. **417**
3. The hypothesis that language emerged as a by-product of overall intelligence or brain size faces major problems: Some people have full-sized brains but impaired language, and people with Williams syndrome have nearly normal language despite mental retardation. **418**
4. People are specialized to learn language easily, but the nature of that specialization is not yet clear. **419**
5. The best evidence for a sensitive period for language development is the observation that deaf children learn sign language much better if they start early than if their first opportunity comes later in life. However, there does not appear to be a sharp loss of language capacity at any particular age. **420**
6. People with Broca's aphasia (nonfluent aphasia) have difficulty speaking and writing. They find prepositions, conjunctions, and other grammatical connectives especially difficult. They also fail to understand speech when its meaning depends on complex grammar. **420**
7. People with Wernicke's aphasia have trouble understanding speech and recalling the names of objects. **422**
8. People who speak several languages use the same brain areas for all. However, those who speak one language better than another activate more of their brain (indicating greater difficulty) when using their less fluent language. **424**
9. Music has many parallels with language. Composers usually write music with rhythm patterns that resemble the rhythm of speech in their own language. **424**
10. Dyslexia (reading impairment) has many forms. The main problem is usually in converting visual signals into auditory information or attending to the right aspects of a visual display. **424**

KEY TERMS

Terms are defined in the module on the page number indicated. They're also presented in alphabetical order with definitions in the book's Subject Index/Glossary. Interactive flashcards, audio reviews, and crossword puzzles are among the online resources available to help you learn these terms and the concepts they represent.

anomia **423**
aphasia **421**
Broca's aphasia (nonfluent aphasia) **421**
Broca's area **421**
dyslexia **424**
language acquisition device **419**
poverty of the stimulus argument **420**
productivity **415**
Wernicke's aphasia (fluent aphasia) **422**
Wernicke's area **422**
Williams syndrome **419**

THOUGHT QUESTIONS

1. Most people with Broca's aphasia suffer from partial paralysis on the right side of the body. Most people with Wernicke's aphasia do not. Why?
2. In a syndrome called *word blindness*, a person loses the ability to read (even single letters), although the person can still see and speak. What is a possible neurological explanation? That is, can you imagine a pattern of brain damage that might produce this result?

MODULE 14.3

Consciousness and Attention

In Chapter 1, we considered the mind–body problem: In a universe composed of matter and energy, why is there such a thing as consciousness? And how does it relate to the brain? These questions may or may not be answerable, and consciousness may or may not turn out to be a scientifically useful concept. However, at this point, let's consider some attempts to study consciousness scientifically. Even if we can't answer the deepest questions, we can at least deal with a few of the subordinate issues.

Consciousness is difficult to define, but for practical purposes, researchers use this operational definition: If a cooperative person reports the presence of one stimulus and cannot report the presence of a second stimulus, then he or she was **conscious** of the first and not of the second. This definition does not apply (one way or the other) to individuals who cannot speak—such as infants, people with Broca's aphasia, or nonhuman animals. We might draw inferences about their consciousness based on other criteria, but we won't use them for research on consciousness.

By this definition, consciousness is almost synonymous with attention. At any moment, a huge number of stimuli reach your brain, but you are conscious of (i.e., able to report) only those to which you direct your attention. Various stimuli compete for your conscious attention (Dehaene & Changeux, 2004). A stimulus can grab your attention by its size, brightness, or movement, but you can also voluntarily direct your attention to one stimulus or another in what is called a "top-down" process—that is, one governed by other cortical areas, principally the prefrontal and parietal cortex (Buschman & Miller, 2007; Rossi, Bichot, Desimone, & Ungerleider, 2007). To illustrate, keep your eyes fixated on the central *x* in the following display. Then attend to the G at the right and step by step shift your attention clockwise around the circle. Notice how you can indeed see different parts of the circle without moving your eyes.

A
Z V
W R
B x G
N K
F P
J

Psychologists have noted the phenomenon of **inattentional blindness** or *change blindness*: Of all that your eyes see at any instant, you are conscious of only those few to which you direct your attention (Huang, Treisman, & Pashler, 2007). If you observe a complex scene, and something in it changes slowly, or changes while you blink your eyes, there is a fairly high chance that you will not notice it (Henderson & Hollingworth, 2003; Rensink, O'Regan, & Clark, 1997). You would notice it, however, if you were paying attention to the particular item that was changing. You can experience this phenomenon with the Online Try It Yourself exercise "Change Blindness."

Brain Activity Associated With Consciousness

Although we don't have even a good hypothesis about *why* brain activity is (sometimes) conscious, we might be able to discover which types of brain activity are conscious (Crick & Koch, 2004). The ideal design is to present a single stimulus, such as a light or sound, that becomes conscious on some occasions but not others. Then determine in what way the brain activity differed between the occasions with and without consciousness.

One clever study used this approach: Researchers flashed a word on a screen for 29 milliseconds (ms). In some cases, it was preceded and followed by a blank screen:

GROVE

In these cases, people identified the word almost 90% of the time. In other cases, however, the researchers flashed a word for the same 29 ms but preceded and followed it with a masking pattern:

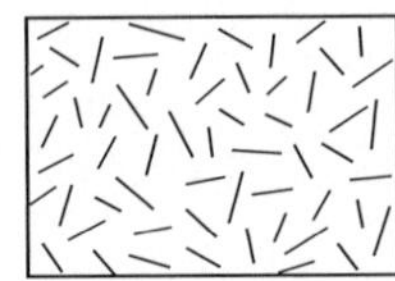

SALTY

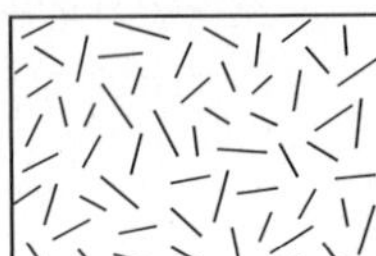

Under these conditions, people almost never identify the word and usually say they didn't see any word at all. Although the physical stimulus was the same in both cases—a word flashed for 29 ms—people were conscious of it in the first case but not the second. Using fMRI and evoked potentials, the researchers found that the stimulus initially activated the primary visual cortex for both the conscious and unconscious conditions but activated it more strongly in the conscious condition (because of less interference). Also, in the conscious condition, the activity spread to several additional areas (Dehaene et al., 2001).

These data imply that consciousness of a stimulus depends on the amount of brain activity. Becoming conscious of something means that its information has taken over more of your brain's activity. What is the current sensation in your left foot? Chances are, before you read this question, you were not conscious of *any* sensation in your left foot. When you directed your attention to your foot, activity increased in the corresponding part of the somatosensory cortex (Lambie & Marcel, 2002). Similarly, when you direct your attention to some visual stimulus, your brain's response to that stimulus increases, while responses to other stimuli decrease (Kamitani & Tong, 2005; Wegener, Freiwald, & Kreiter, 2004). If you are told to pay attention to color or motion, activity increases in the areas of your visual cortex responsible for color or motion perception (Chawla, Rees, & Friston, 1999); in fact, they increase even before the stimulus (Driver & Frith, 2000). Somehow, the instructions prime those areas to magnify their responses.

Further studies found that a conscious stimulus also induces precise synchrony of responses in neurons over various areas of the brain (Eckhorn et al., 1988; Gray, König, Engel, & Singer, 1989; Melloni et al., 2006; Womelsdorf et al., 2007). Synchrony also emerges when people recognize a pattern. When people look at an ambiguous pattern and see a face in it, synchronized patterns occur in widespread areas of the brain. When people look at the same pattern but fail to see the face, that synchrony does not occur (Roelfsema, Engel, König, & Singer, 1997; Roelfsema, Lamme, & Spekreijse, 2004).

STOP & CHECK

17. In the experiment by Dehaene et al., how were the conscious and unconscious stimuli similar? How were they different?

18. In this experiment, how did the brain's responses differ to the conscious and unconscious stimuli?

ANSWERS

17. The conscious and unconscious stimuli were physically the same (a word flashed on the screen for 29 ms). The difference was that a stimulus did not become conscious if it was preceded and followed by an interfering pattern. **18.** If a stimulus became conscious, it activated the same brain areas as an unconscious stimulus but more strongly, and then the activity spread to additional areas. Also, brain responses become synchronized when a pattern is conscious.

Figure 14.17 Binocular rivalry
If possible, look at the two parts through tubes, such as those from the inside of rolls of toilet paper or paper towels. Otherwise, touch your nose to the paper between the two parts so that your left eye sees one pattern while your right eye sees the other. The two views will compete for your consciousness, and your perception will alternate between them.

TRY IT YOURSELF

Here is a second kind of research. Look at Figure 14.17, but hold it so close to your eyes that your nose touches the page, right between the two circles. Better yet, look at the two parts through a pair of tubes, such as the tubes inside rolls of paper towels or toilet paper. You will see red and black vertical lines with your left eye and green and black horizontal lines with your right eye. (Close one eye and then the other to make sure you see completely different patterns with the two eyes.) Seeing something is closely related to seeing *where* it is, and the red vertical lines cannot be in the same place as the green horizontal lines. Because your brain cannot perceive both patterns in the same location, your perception alternates. For a while, you see the red and black lines, and then gradually, the green and black invade your consciousness. Then your perception shifts back to the red and black. For the average person, each perception lasts about 2 seconds before switching to the other, but some people switch faster or slower. Sometimes, you will see red lines in part of the visual field and green lines in the other. These shifts, known as **binocular rivalry,** are slow and gradual, sweeping from one side to another. The stimulus seen by each eye evokes a particular pattern of brain response, which researchers can measure with fMRI or similar methods. As that first perception fades and the stimulus seen by the other eye replaces it, the first pattern of brain activity fades also, and a different pattern of activity replaces it. Each shift in perception is accompanied by a shift in the pattern of activity over a large portion of the brain (Lee, Blake, & Heeger, 2005).

Both the red–black and green–black patterns you just experienced were stationary. To make the brain responses easier to monitor, researchers presented to one eye a stationary stimulus and to the other eye a pattern that pulsated in size and brightness, as shown in Figure 14.18. Then they recorded brain activity in several areas. At times when people reported consciousness of the pulsating stimulus, pulsating activity at the same rhythm was prominent in much of the brain, as

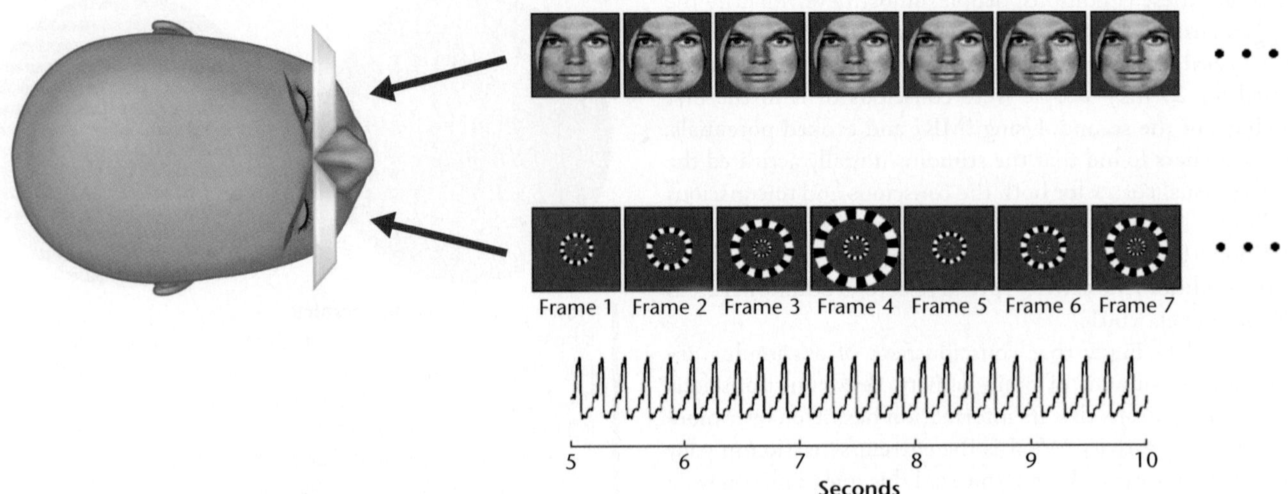

Figure 14.18 Stimuli for a study of binocular rivalry
The pattern in one eye was stationary. The one in the other eye pulsated a few times per second. Researchers could then examine brain activity to find cells that followed the rhythm of the stimulus. *(Reprinted from* NeuroImage, 23/1, *Cosmelli et al. "Waves of consciousness: Ongoing cortical patterns during binocular rivalry," 128–140, 2004, with permission from Elsevier.)*

shown in Figure 14.19. When people reported consciousness of the stationary stimulus, the pulsating activity was weak (Cosmelli et al., 2004). Again, the conclusion is that a conscious stimulus strongly activates much of the brain, virtually taking over brain activity. When the same stimulus is unconscious, it produces weaker and less widespread activity.

STOP & CHECK

19. How could someone use fMRI to determine which of two patterns in binocular rivalry is conscious at a given moment?

ANSWER

19. Make one stimulus pulsate at a given rhythm and look for brain areas showing that rhythm of activity. The rhythm takes over widespread areas of the brain when that pattern is conscious.

Consciousness as a Threshold Phenomenon

In binocular rivalry, you might be aware of one pattern in one part of the visual field and another pattern in another part, but each point in the visual field sees just one or the other. Is that a general principle, or do occasions arise when you are "partly" conscious of one stimulus and partly conscious of another? Does consciousness come in degrees?

This is not an easy question to answer, but one study suggests that consciousness is a yes–no phenomenon. Researchers flashed blurry words on a screen for brief fractions of a second and asked people to identify each word, if possible, and rate *how* conscious they were of the word on a scale from 0 to 100. People almost always rated a word either 0 or 100. They almost never said they were partly conscious of something (Sergent & Dehaene, 2004). These results suggest that consciousness is a threshold phenomenon. When a stimulus

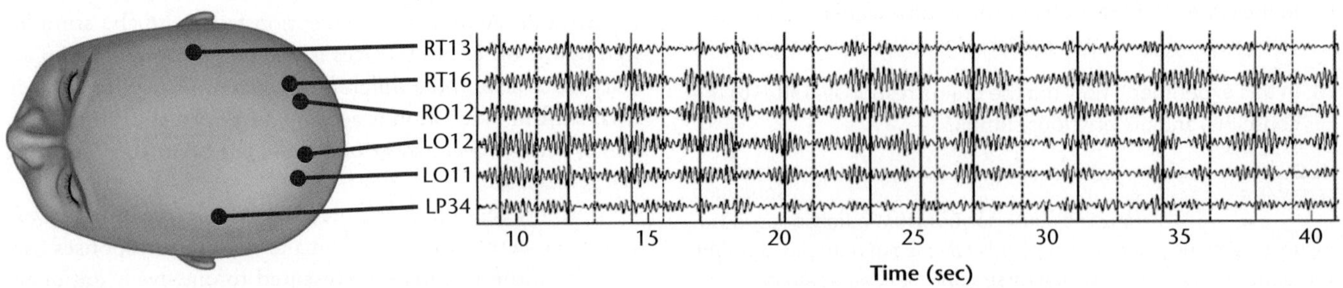

Figure 14.19 Brain activity during binocular rivalry
When the person reported seeing the pulsating stimulus, neurons throughout much of the brain responded vigorously at the same rhythm as the stimulus. When the person reported the stationary stimulus, the rhythmic activity was subdued. *(Reprinted from* NeuroImage, 23/1, *Cosmelli et al., "Waves of consciousness: Ongoing cortical patterns during binocular rivalry," 128–140, 2004, with permission from Elsevier.)*

activates enough neurons to a sufficient extent, the activity reverberates, magnifies, and extends over much of the brain. If a stimulus fails to reach that level, the pattern fades away.

The Fate of an Unattended Stimulus

Consider again the phenomenon of binocular rivalry. While you are attending to, say, the green and black stimulus, your brain does not completely discard information from the red and black stimulus in your other eye. Certainly, if a bright stimulus suddenly flashed in that eye, it would capture your attention. More interestingly, suppose a word fades onto the screen slowly, and you are to report the time at which your attention shifts to the previously unattended eye. The newly appearing word will capture your attention, causing you to shift your attention faster than you would have otherwise. Moreover, if it is a word from your own language, or better yet your own name, it captures your attention faster than if it were a word from some language you do not understand, using some other alphabet (Jiang, Costello, & He, 2007). If a meaningful stimulus captures your attention faster than a meaningless stimulus, somehow your brain had to know it was meaningful *before* it became conscious!

Numerous other studies also show subtle effects on behavior by unconscious stimuli. In one study, a signal flashed on a screen for 50 ms or less, surrounded by interfering stimuli, indicating how much money a person could win by a handgrip response after a second, easily perceived stimulus. Under these conditions, people showed no conscious perception of the stimulus. However, on the average, they made a more vigorous handgrip response after a signal indicating a larger possible payoff (Pessiglione et al., 2007). In another study, people saw one stimulus in one eye and an incompatible stimulus in the other eye (binocular rivalry) for just half a second. With such a brief presentation, people almost always reported conscious perception of just one stimulus or the other. However, if one of the stimuli was a face with an emotional expression, people responded emotionally even on trials when they were not conscious of seeing the face (M. A. Williams, Morris, McGlone, Abbott, & Mattingley, 2004). Figure 14.20 shows the stimuli. The conclusion is that much of brain activity is unconscious, and even unconscious activity can influence behavior in at least subtle ways.

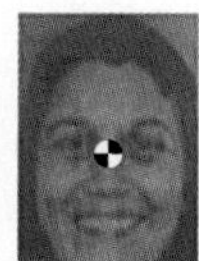

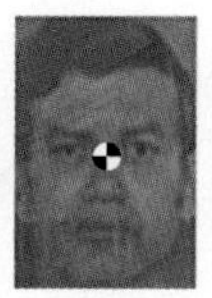
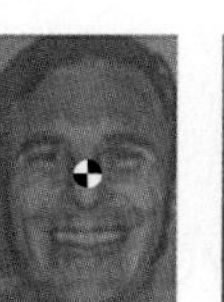

Figure 14.20 Stimuli to test unconscious arousal of the amygdala
People wore filters so that one eye saw the green picture and the other eye saw the red picture. Here the green pictures are houses and the red ones are faces with emotional expressions; in other cases, green and red were reversed. *(Reprinted with permission from "Amygdala responses to fearful and happy facial expressions under conditions of binocular suppression," by M. A. Williams et al.,* Journal of Neuroscience, 24, *2898–2904. Copyright 2004 by the Society for Neuroscience.)*

STOP & CHECK

20. If someone is aware of the stimulus on the right in a case of binocular rivalry, what evidence indicates that the brain is also processing the stimulus on the left?

ANSWER

20. If a stimulus gradually appears on the left side, attention shifts to the left faster if that stimulus is a meaningful word than if it is a word from an unfamiliar language.

The Timing of Consciousness

Are you conscious of events instant by instant as they happen? It certainly seems that way, but if there were a delay between an event and your consciousness of it, how would you know?

Consider the **phi phenomenon**, which perceptual researchers noted long ago: If you see a dot in one position, alternating with a similar dot nearby, it will seem to you that the dot is moving back and forth. Considering just the simplest case, imagine what happens if you see a dot moving from one position to another: • → •. You see a dot in one position, you see it move, and you see it in the second position. Okay, but *when* did you see it move? When you saw it in the first position, you didn't know it was going to appear in the second position. You could not perceive it as moving until *after* it appeared in the second position. Evidently, you perceived it as moving from one position to the second after it appeared in the second position! In other words, the second position caused a change in your perception of what occurred before it.

Another example: Suppose you hear a recorded word that is carefully engineered to sound halfway between *dent* and *tent*. We'll call it **ent*. If you hear it in the phrase "*ent in the fender," it sounds like *dent*. If you hear it in the phrase "*ent in the forest," it sounds like *tent*. That is, later words changed what you heard before them (Connine, Blasko, & Hall, 1991).

STOP & CHECK

21. In what way does the phi phenomenon imply that a new stimulus sometimes changes consciousness of what went before it?

ANSWER

21. Someone who sees a dot on the left and then a dot on the right perceives the dot as moving from left to right. The perceived movement would have occurred before the dot on the right, but the person had no reason to infer that movement until after the dot appeared on the right.

Neglect

People sometimes perceive their body or surroundings inaccurately. These phenomena are interesting in their own right, as well as for their potential relevance to issues of consciousness and attention.

Many people with damage to parts of the right hemisphere show a widespread **spatial neglect**—a tendency to ignore the left side of the body or the left side of objects. (Damage in the left hemisphere seldom produces significant neglect of the right side.) They also generally ignore much of what they hear in the left ear and feel in the left hand, especially if they simultaneously feel something in the right hand. They may put clothes on only the right side of the body. However, all these results vary. Someone might show neglect in one situation and not another or at one time and not another (Buxbaum, 2006). The type of neglect depends on the location of damage. People with damage to the inferior part of the right parietal cortex tend to neglect everything to the left of their own body. People with damage to the superior temporal cortex neglect the left side of objects, regardless of their location (Hillis et al., 2005).

If asked to point "straight ahead," most patients with neglect point to the right of center. If a patient with neglect is shown a long horizontal line and asked to divide it in half, generally the person picks a spot well to the right of center, as if part of the left side wasn't there (Richard, Honoré, Bernati, & Rousseaux, 2004).

People with intact brains generally do not hit the center of the line but veer 2% to 3% to the left of center. Also, if they are asked to indicate a rating of something along a scale from left to right, they show a slight tendency to prefer the left side (Nicholls, Orr, Okubo, & Loftus, 2006). For example, on the questions that follow, most people would rate their political views slightly more conservative on the first question than on the second:

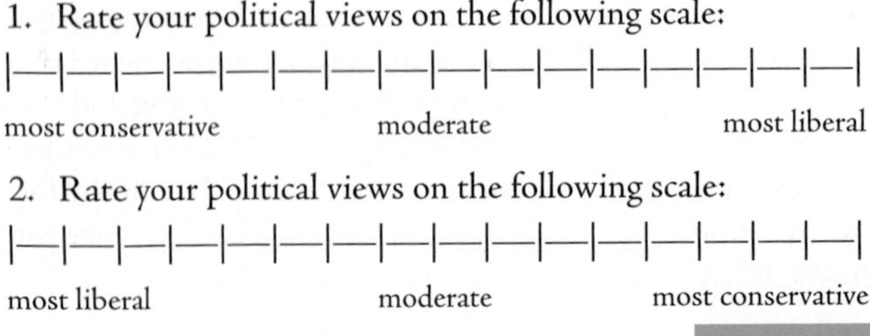

1. Rate your political views on the following scale:
most conservative
moderate
most liberal
2. Rate your political views on the following scale:
most liberal
moderate
most conservative

TRY IT YOURSELF

You might try the following demonstration. Try marking the center of the line below. Then measure it to see how close you came. Most people miss slightly to the left. Curiously, people with extensive musical training usually get within 1% of the exact center (Patston, Corballis, Hogg, & Tippet, 2006).

Some patients with neglect also show deviations in their estimates of the midpoint of a numerical range. For example, what is halfway between 11 and 19? The correct answer is, of course, 15, but some people with neglect say "17." Evidently, they discount the lower numbers as if they were on the left side (Doricchi, Guariglia, Gasparini, & Tomaiuolo, 2005; Zorzi, Priftis, & Umiltà, 2002). At least in Western society, many people visualize the numbers like a line stretching to the right, as in the *x* axis of a graph.

Neglect results from many deficits that vary from one person to another, but in many cases, the main problem is attention rather than impaired sensation. One patient was shown a letter E, composed of small Hs, as in Figure 14.21(c). She identified it as a big E composed of small Hs, indicating that she saw the whole figure. However, when she was then asked to cross off all the Hs, she crossed off only the ones on the right. When she was shown the figures in Figure 14.21(e), she identified them as an O composed of little Os and an X composed of little Xs. Again, she could see both halves of both figures, but when she was asked to cross off all the elements, she crossed off only the ones on the right. The researchers summarized by saying she saw the forest but only half the trees (Marshall & Halligan, 1995).

Several procedures can increase attention to the neglected side. First, simply telling the person to pay attention to the left side helps temporarily. So does having the person look left while at the same time feeling an object with the left hand (Vaishnavi, Calhoun, & Chatterjee, 2001) or hearing a sound from the left side of the world (Frassinetti, Pavani, & Làdavas,

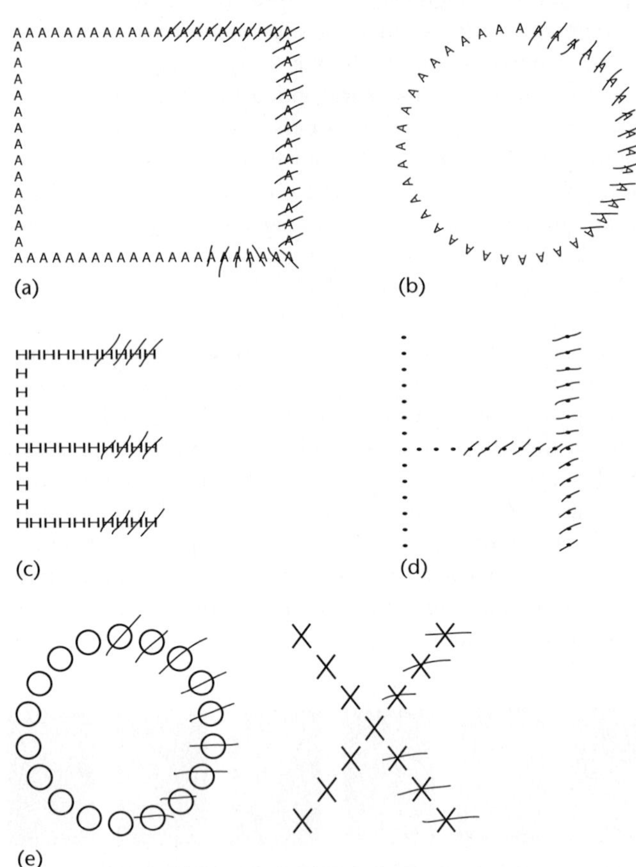

Figure 14.21 Spatial neglect
A patient with neglect of the left side could identify the overall figures as E, O, and X, indicating that she saw the whole figures. However, when asked to cross off the elements that composed them, she crossed off only the parts on the right. *(From J. C. Marshall and P. W. Halligan, "Seeing the forest but only half the trees?"* Nature, 373, *pp. 521–523, Fig. 1 [parts (c) and (e)]. © 1995 Nature.)*

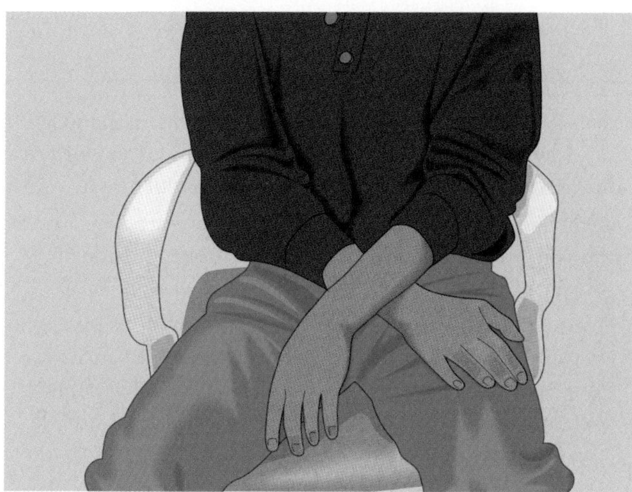

Figure 14.22 A simple way to reduce sensory neglect
Ordinarily, someone with right parietal lobe damage neglects the left arm. However, if the left arm crosses over or under the right, attention to the left arm increases.

2002). Something similar is true for unimpaired people also. Suppose you are staring straight ahead and an experimenter is flashing stimuli on the left and right sides. Your task is to identify something about each stimulus, such as whether it was on the top or bottom half of the screen. If someone touches you just before a visual stimulus, you will respond slightly faster if the touch was on the same side of the body as the visual stimulus (Kennett, Eimer, Spence, & Driver, 2001). That is, a touch stimulus briefly increases attention to one side of the body or the other.

Other manipulations also shift the attention of patients with neglect to their left side. For example, some patients with neglect report feeling nothing with the left hand, especially if the right hand feels something else at the time. However, if you cross one hand over the other as shown in Figure 14.22, the person is more likely to report feeling the left hand, which is now on the right side of the body (Aglioti, Smania, & Peru, 1999). Also, the person ordinarily has trouble pointing to anything in the left visual field but has somewhat better success if the hand was so far to the left that he or she would have to move it to the right to point to the object (Mattingley, Husain, Rorden, Kennard, & Driver, 1998). Again, the conclusion is that neglect is not due to a loss of sensation but a difficulty in directing attention to the left side.

Many patients with neglect also have deficits with spatial working memory (Malhotra et al., 2005) and with shifting attention, even when location is irrelevant. For example, one patient could not listen to two sounds and say which one came first, unless the sounds were very prolonged (Cusack, Carlyon, & Robertson, 2000). In short, the problems associated with neglect extend to many kinds of attention, not just the left–right dimension.

STOP & CHECK

22. What is the evidence that spatial neglect is a problem in attention, not just sensation?

23. What are several procedures that increase attention to the left side in a person with spatial neglect?

ANSWERS

22. When a patient with neglect sees a large letter composed of small letters, he or she can identify the large letter but then neglects part of it when asked to cross off all the small letters. Also, someone who neglects the left hand pays attention to it when it is crossed over the right hand. **23.** Simply telling the person to attend to something on the left sometimes helps temporarily. Having the person look to the left while feeling something on the left side increases attention to the felt object. Crossing the left hand over the right increases attention to the left hand. Moving a hand far to the left makes it easier for the person to point to something in the left visual field because the hand will move toward the right to point at the object.

MODULE 14.3 IN CLOSING

Attending to Attention and Being Conscious of Consciousness

Before the 1970s, many psychological researchers, especially those studying learning in rats, were not convinced that the concept of attention was useful at all. Today, the concept of attention is well established in cognitive psychology, although the concept of consciousness still has a tentative status. Research in this area is difficult because we cannot observe consciousness itself, and we have no access to it beyond what people report. Scientists are justifiably nervous about self-reports. Still, I hope this module convinced you that research on consciousness is neither impossible nor pointless. Technological advances enable us to do research that would have been impossible in the past. Future methods may facilitate still more possibilities.

Continued

SUMMARY

1. Attention to a stimulus is almost synonymous with being conscious of it. Various stimuli compete for attention or consciousness. **428**
2. It is possible to direct attention toward a stimulus deliberately. **428**
3. When someone is conscious of a stimulus, the representation of that stimulus spreads over a large portion of the brain. **428**
4. People almost never say they were partly conscious of something. It may be that consciousness is a threshold phenomenon: We become conscious of anything that exceeds a certain level of brain activity, and we are not conscious of other events. **430**
5. Many stimuli influence our behavior without being conscious. Even before a stimulus becomes conscious, the brain processes the information enough to identify something as meaningful or meaningless. **431**
6. We are not always conscious of events instantaneously as they occur. Sometimes, a later event modifies our conscious perception of a stimulus that went before it. **431**
7. Damage to parts of the right hemisphere produce spatial neglect for the left side of the body or the left side of objects. **431**
8. Neglect results from a deficit in attention, not sensation. For example, someone with neglect can see an entire letter enough to say what it is, even though that same person ignores the left half when asked to cross out all the elements that compose it. **432**
9. People with sensory neglect also have difficulties with working memory and with shifting attention from one stimulus to another, even when the stimuli do not vary from left to right. **433**

KEY TERMS

Terms are defined in the module on the page number indicated. They're also presented in alphabetical order with definitions in the book's Subject Index/Glossary. Interactive flashcards, audio reviews, and crossword puzzles are among the online resources available to help you learn these terms and the concepts they represent.

binocular rivalry **429**
conscious **428**
inattentional blindness **428**
phi phenomenon **431**
spatial neglect **432**

THOUGHT QUESTION

The operational definition of consciousness applies only to people willing and able to report that they are conscious of some events and not others. Research using this definition has determined certain brain correlates of consciousness. Could we now use those brain correlates to infer consciousness or its absence in newborn infants, brain-damaged people, or nonhuman animals?

CHAPTER 14 Exploration and Study

In addition to the study materials provided at the end of each module, you may supplement your review of this chapter by using one or more of the book's electronic resources, which include its companion Website, interactive Cengage Learning eBook, Exploring Biological Psychology CD-ROM, and CengageNOW. Brief descriptions of these resources follow. For more information, visit **www.cengage.com/psychology/kalat.**

The book's companion Website, accessible through the author Web page indicated above, provides a wide range of study resources such as an interactive glossary, flashcards, tutorial quizzes, updated Web links, and Try It Yourself activities, as well as a limited selection of the short videos and animated explanations of concepts available for this chapter.

Exploring Biological Psychology

The Exploring Biological Psychology CD-ROM contains videos, animations, and Try It Yourself activities. These activities—as well as many that are new to this edition—are also available in the text's fully interactive, media-rich

Cengage Learning eBook,* which gives you the opportunity to experience biological psychology in an even greater interactive and multimedia environment. The Cengage Learning eBook also includes highlighting and note-taking features and an audio glossary. For this chapter, the Cengage Learning eBook includes the following interactive explorations:

- Lateralization and Language
- Split Brain
- Hemisphere Control
- Visual-Spatial Processing
- Wernicke-Geschwind Model
- Situated Cognition
- McGurk Effect
- Change Blindness
- Binocular Rivalry
- Capture of Attention by a Meaningful Stimulus
- Phi Phenomenon

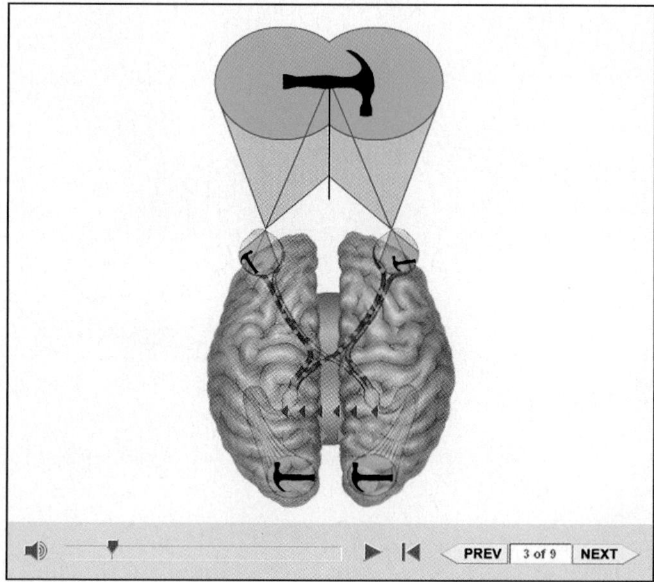

The video *Visual Spatial Processing* illustrates how functional magnetic resonance imaging technology (fMRI) is being used to track visual-spatial processing skills.

CENGAGENOW™ is an easy-to-use resource that helps you study in less time to get the grade you want. An online study system, CengageNOW* gives you the option of taking a diagnostic pretest for each chapter. The system uses the results of each pretest to create personalized chapter study plans for you. The Personalized Study Plans

- help you save study time by identifying areas on which you should concentrate and give you one-click access to corresponding pages of the interactive Cengage Learning eBook;
- provide interactive exercises and study tools to help you fully understand chapter concepts; and
- include a posttest for you to take to confirm that you are ready to move on to the next chapter.

* Requires a Cengage Learning eResources account. Visit **www.cengage.com/login** to register or login.

Suggestions for Further Exploration

The book's companion Website includes a list of suggested articles available through InfoTrac College Edition for this chapter. You may also want to explore some of the following books and Websites. The text's companion Website provides live, updated links to the sites listed below.

Books

Baars, B. J., & Gage, N. M. (Eds.). (2007). *Cognition, brain, and consciousness.* San Diego, CA: Elsevier. Review of research on brain mechanisms of attention and consciousness.

Deacon, T. (1997). *The symbolic species.* New York: Norton. Deep analysis of the evolution of language and intelligence.

Ornstein, R. (1997). *The right mind.* New York: Harcourt Brace. Very readable description of split-brain research and the differences between the left and right hemispheres.

Websites

The National Aphasia Association
http://www.aphasia.org/

The Bonobo Foundation
http://www.blockbonobofoundation.org/

The British Dyslexia Association
http://www.bdadyslexia.org.uk

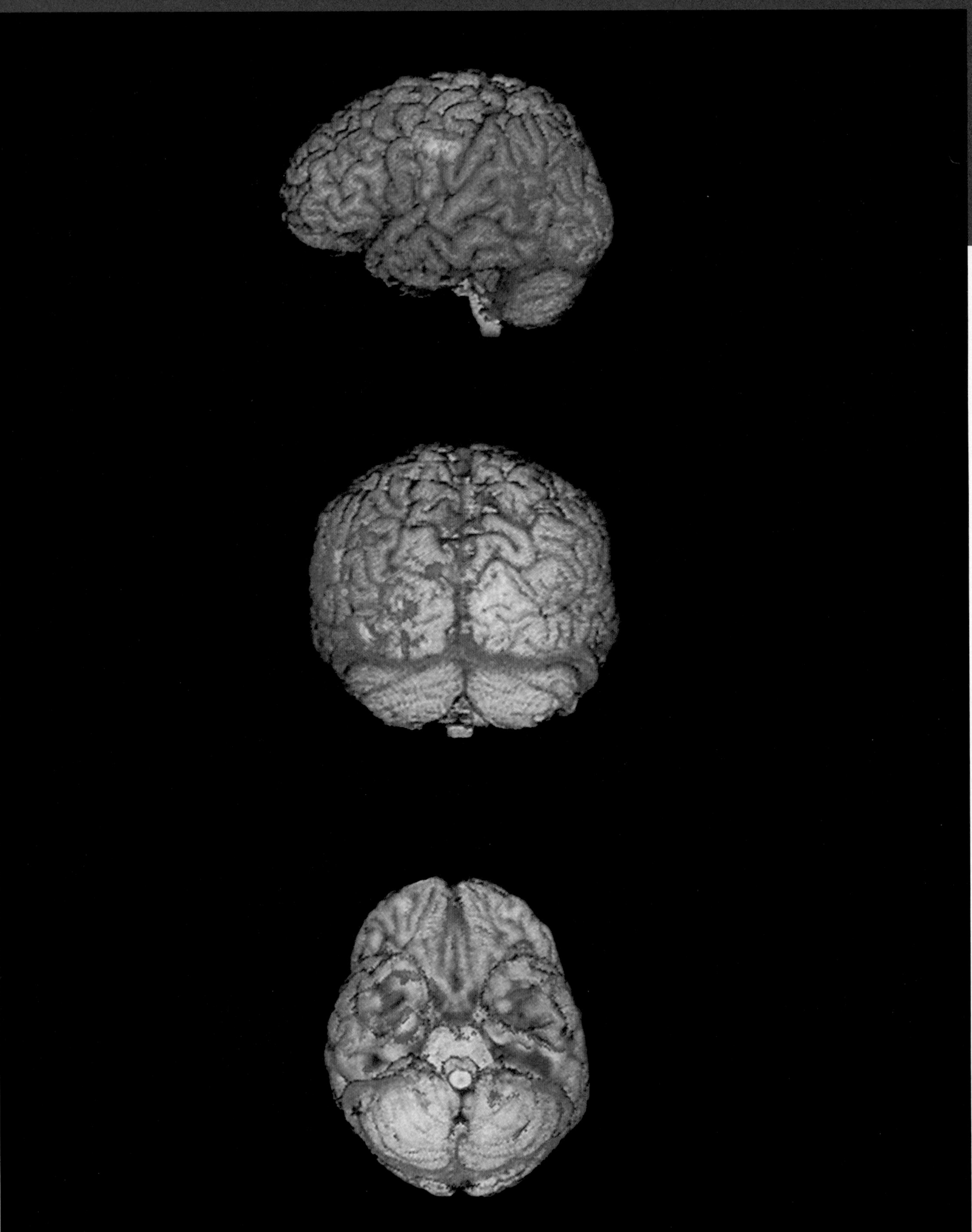

Mood Disorders and Schizophrenia

15

CHAPTER OUTLINE

MAIN IDEAS

1. Psychological disorders result from a combination of environmental and biological influences, including genetics.
2. The effectiveness of certain drugs implies a relationship between neurotransmitter abnormalities and both depression and schizophrenia. However, serious theoretical issues remain.
3. Schizophrenia may be the result of genetic or other problems that impair early development of the brain.

Are mental illnesses really *illnesses,* analogous to tuberculosis or influenza? Or are they normal reactions to abnormal experiences? They are not exactly either. They are outcomes that combine biological predispositions with experiences, and to control them, we need a good understanding of both aspects.

In this chapter, the emphasis is strongly on the biological components of mental illnesses; *Biological Psychology* is, after all, the title of the book. But this emphasis does not imply that other influences are unimportant.

OPPOSITE: PET scans show the brain areas that increase their activation during visual and auditory hallucinations by a patient with schizophrenia.

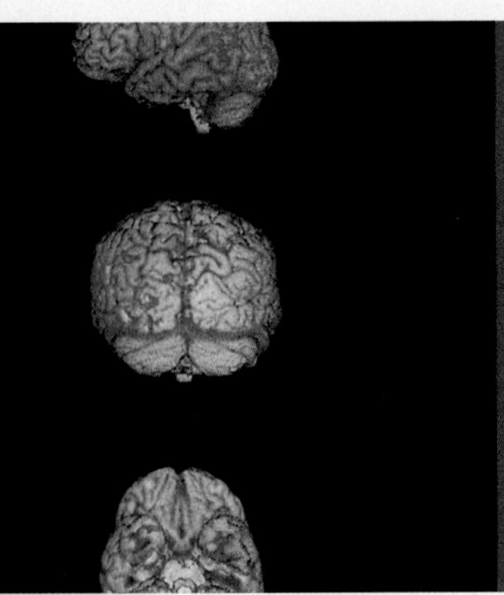

MODULE 15.1

Mood Disorders

Different people can get to the same place by different routes. For example, the people in a room at any moment may have started from different cities or different parts of a city and traveled in different ways, although they all reached the same destination. Similarly, people can become depressed through different routes, including genetics, traumatic experiences, hormonal problems, substance abuse, head injuries, brain tumors, and other illnesses. Despite having different causes, or combinations of causes, these people all look and act depressed (Figure 15.1). In this module, we explore some of the many factors that contribute to depression.

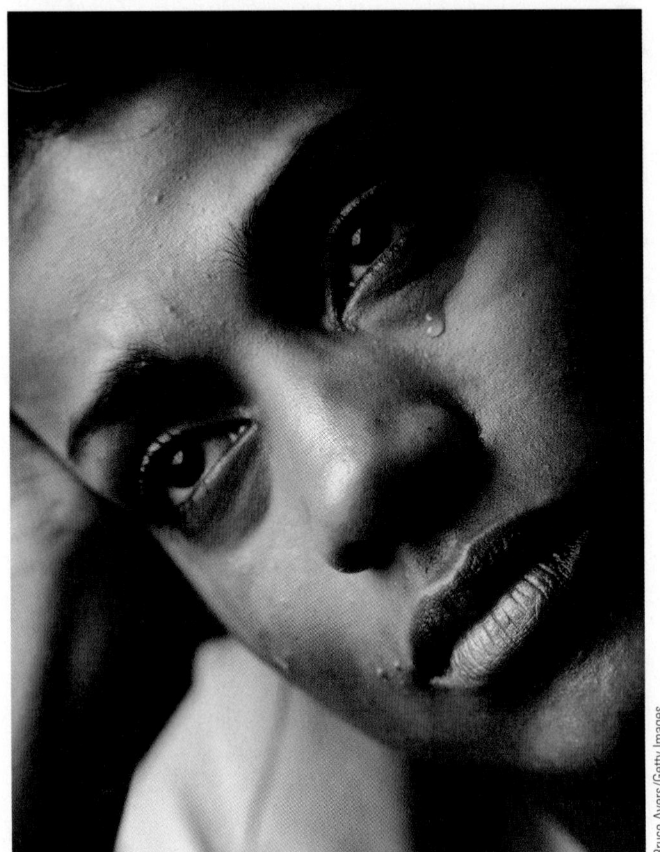

Bruce Ayers/Getty Images

Figure 15.1 The face of depression
Depression shows in people's face, walk, voice, and mannerisms.

Major Depressive Disorder

At times, almost everyone feels sad, discouraged, and listless. Major depression is a more intense and prolonged experience. According to the *DSM-IV* (American Psychiatric Association, 1994), people with a **major depression** feel sad and helpless every day for weeks at a time. They have little energy, feel worthless, contemplate suicide, have trouble sleeping, cannot concentrate, find little pleasure, and can hardly even imagine being happy again.

Indeed, absence of happiness is a more reliable symptom than increased sadness. In one study, people carried a beeper that sounded at unpredictable times to signal them to describe their emotional reactions at the moment. People with depression reported only an average number of unpleasant experiences but far below the average number of pleasant ones (Peters, Nicolson, Berkhof, Delespaul, & deVries, 2003). In two other studies, people examined photographs or films as researchers used brain scans to record their reactions. In both cases, individuals with depression reacted to sad or frightening depictions about the same as anyone else but failed to smile as much at the comedies or pleasant pictures (Rottenberg, Kasch, Gross, & Gotlib, 2002; Sloan, Strauss, & Wisner, 2001). Another study found that people with depression showed an increased response to facial expressions of fear and a decreased response to happy expressions (Monk et al., 2008).

Major depression is diagnosed about twice as often in women as in men. It can occur at any age, although it is uncommon in children. A survey reported that within any given year, about 5% of adults in the United States have a "clinically significant" (i.e., fairly severe) depression (Narrow, Rae, Robins, & Regier, 2002). Over the course of a lifetime, more than 10% suffer from major depression.

Depression occurs in episodes of various durations. That is, almost no one is permanently depressed, and even without treatment, most people eventually feel better. However, new episodes may occur. Most patients can identify a highly stressful event that triggered their first episode of depression. However, later episodes are less and less likely to follow any particular triggering event (Post, 1992). It is as if the brain learns how to be depressed and gets better at it.

Genetics and Life Events

Studies of twins and adopted children indicate a moderate degree of heritability for depression (Q. Fu et al., 2002; Wender et al., 1986). However, the genes are not specific to depression. The close relatives of someone with depression are more likely than other people to suffer not only from depression but also from anxiety disorders, attention-deficit disorder, alcohol or marijuana abuse, obsessive-compulsive disorder, bulimia, migraine headaches, irritable bowel syndrome, and other conditions (Q. Fu et al., 2002; Hudson et al., 2003).

The risk of depression is particularly elevated among relatives of women with early-onset depression—that is, beginning before age 30 (Bierut et al., 1999; Kendler, Gardner, & Prescott, 1999; Lyons et al., 1998). Compare this pattern to alcoholism, where the risk is highest among relatives of men with early-onset alcoholism (as discussed in Chapter 3).

Several genes have been found to increase the risk of depression (Pezawas et al., 2005; X. Zhang, Gainetdinov, et al., 2005). However, the effects of these genes have varied from one study to another. Researchers began testing the possibility that the effects of the genes depend on people's experiences. One gene controls the serotonin transporter protein, which regulates the ability of an axon to reabsorb serotonin after its release, to recycle it for further use. Investigators examined the serotonin transporter genes of 847 people, identifying two types: the "short" type and the "long" type. They also asked each participant to record certain highly stressful events from age 21 until age 26. Those events included financial setbacks, changes of job or housing, divorce, and so forth. Figure 15.2 shows the results. For people with two short forms of the gene, increasing numbers of stressful experiences led to a big increase in the probability of depression. For those with two long forms, stressful events hardly increased the risk of depression at all. Those with one short and one long gene were intermediate. In other words, the short form of the gene by itself does not lead to depression, nor does a series of stressful events, but a combination of both is hazardous (Caspi et al., 2003).

Another study related short and long forms of this gene to early childhood experiences. Researchers asked healthy young adults (not people diagnosed with depression) to fill out a questionnaire concerning symptoms of depression. On the average, those with the short form of the serotonin transporter gene and a history of stressful experiences (either in childhood or more recently) reported more than average symptoms of depression. However, those with the same gene and a consistently supportive environment reported *fewer* than average symptoms (S. E. Taylor et al., 2006). That is, don't think of the short form as a "gene for depression." It is more like a gene for "sensitivity to environmental influences." A person with this gene has trouble dealing with stressful experiences but thrives in a more positive environment.

Other genes have also been found that increase the risk of depression, but mainly among people who were abused or neglected in childhood (Bradley et al., 2008; Haeffel et al., 2008). In mental health, it may be the typical pattern to find that the effects of a gene vary depending on the environment (Moffitt, Caspi, & Rutter, 2006).

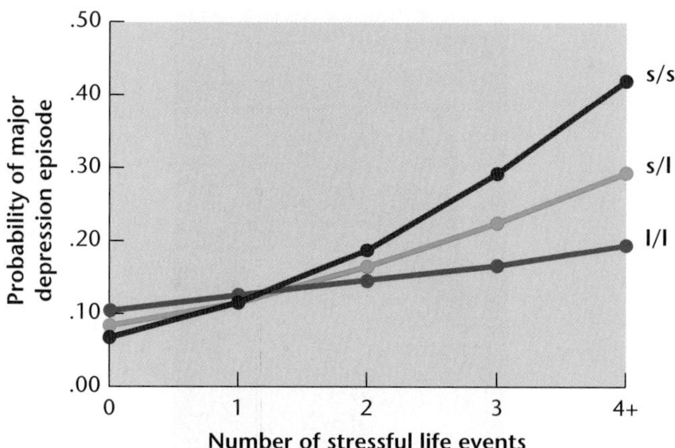

Figure 15.2 Genetics, stress, and depression
The probability of depression increases for people reporting higher numbers of stressful experiences in the previous 5 years; however, the rate of increase depends on their genetics. *(Reprinted with permission from A. Caspi, et al., "Influence of life stress on depression: Moderation by a polymorphism in the 5-HTT gene,"* Science, 301, *pp. 386–389. © 2003 AAAS.)*

STOP & CHECK

1. What is the relationship between depression and the gene controlling the serotonin transporter protein?

ANSWER

1. People with the short form of the gene are more likely than other people to react to stressful experiences by becoming depressed. However, in the absence of stressful experiences, their probability is not increased.

Nongenetic Biological Influences

Genetic differences partly explain why some people are more vulnerable to depression than others are, but other factors contribute also.

A few cases of depression are linked to viral infections. Borna disease, a viral infection of farm animals, produces periods of frantic activity alternating with periods of inactivity (Figure 15.3). In 1985, investigators tested 370 people for possible exposure to this virus (Amsterdam et al., 1985). Only 12 people tested positive for Borna disease virus, but all 12 were suffering from major depression or bipolar disorder. These 12 were a small percentage of the 265 depressed people tested; still, *none* of the 105 nondepressed people had the virus.

Since then, thousands of people have been tested in Europe, Asia, and North America. The Borna virus was found in about 2% of normal people, 30% of people with severe depression, and 13% to 14% of people with chronic brain diseases (Bode, Ferszt, & Czech, 1993; Bode, Riegel, Lange, & Ludwig, 1992; Terayama et al., 2003). Borna virus also occurs in people with psychiatric diseases other than depression (Herzog et al., 1997). This virus is not a common cause of depression, but it illustrates the fact that many different causes can lead to a similar behavioral result.

Figure 15.3 Symptoms of Borna disease
Animals infected with Borna disease have periods of frantic activity alternating with inactivity, much like a person with bipolar disorder. **(top)** Horse with Borna disease. **(bottom)** Same horse after recovery. *(Figure 2, p. 174, from Bode L., and Ludwig H., (1997). "Clinical similarities and close genetic relationship of human and animal Borna disease virus."* Archives of Virology (Supplement 13), *167–182. Springer-Verlag. Photo scan by Kevin J. Nolte.)*

Giving birth also triggers occasional cases of depression. About 20% of women report some degree of **postpartum depression**—that is, depression after giving birth. Most women recover quickly without treatment, but about 0.1% enter a serious, long-lasting depression (Hopkins, Marcus, & Campbell, 1984). Postpartum depression is more common among women who have also suffered major depression at other times (M. Bloch, Rotenberg, Koren, & Klein, 2005).

One study found that after a drug-induced drop in estradiol and progesterone levels, women with a history of postpartum depression suddenly show new symptoms of depression, whereas other women do not (M. Bloch et al., 2000). That is, some women are more vulnerable to depression than others, and hormonal changes can trigger an episode of depression for the vulnerable women. Among older men, a declining level of the hormone testosterone is associated with increased probability of depression (Almeida, Yeap, Hankey, Jamrozik, & Flicker, 2008).

Abnormalities of Hemispheric Dominance

TRY IT YOURSELF

Studies of normal people have found a fairly strong relationship between happy mood and increased activity in the left prefrontal cortex (Jacobs & Snyder, 1996). Most people with depression have decreased activity in the left and increased activity in the right prefrontal cortex (Davidson, 1984; Pizzagalli et al., 2002). Here's something you can try: Ask someone to solve a cognitive problem, such as, "See how many words you can think of that start with *hu-*." Then unobtrusively watch the person's eye movements to see whether they gaze right or left. Most people gaze to the right during verbal tasks, but most individuals with depression gaze to the left, suggesting right-hemisphere dominance (Lenhart & Katkin, 1986).

STOP & CHECK

2. Some people offer to train you to use the right hemisphere of your brain more strongly, allegedly to increase creativity. If they were successful, can you see any disadvantage?

ANSWER

2. Predominant right-hemisphere activity is more common among people who are depressed. We do not know whether increasing someone's use of the right hemisphere would lead to depression, but it is at least a possible risk.

Antidepressant Drugs

You might assume that investigators first determine the causes of a psychological disorder and then develop treatments based on the causes. But the opposite sequence has been more common: First investigators find a drug or other treatment that seems helpful, and then they try to figure out how it works. Like many other psychiatric drugs, the early antidepressants were discovered by accident.

APPLICATIONS AND EXTENSIONS

Accidental Discoveries of Psychiatric Drugs

Nearly all of the earliest psychiatric drugs were discovered by accident. Disulfiram, for example, was originally used in the manufacture of rubber. Someone noticed that workers in a certain rubber factory avoided alcohol and traced the cause to disulfiram, which had altered the workers' metabolism so they became ill after drinking alcohol. Disulfiram became the drug Antabuse, sometimes prescribed for people who are trying to avoid alcohol.

The use of bromides to control epilepsy was originally based on a theory that was all wrong (Friedlander, 1986; Levitt, 1975). Many people in the 1800s believed that masturbation caused epilepsy and that bromides reduced sexual drive. Therefore, they reasoned, bromides should reduce epilepsy. It turns out that bromides do relieve epilepsy but for different reasons.

Iproniazid, the first antidepressant drug, was originally marketed to treat tuberculosis, until physicians noticed that it relieved depression. Similarly, chlorpromazine, the first antipsychotic drug, was originally used for other purposes, until physicians noticed its ability to alleviate schizophrenia. For decades, researchers sought new drugs entirely by trial and error. Today, researchers evaluate new potential drugs in test tubes or tissue samples until they find one with a potential for stronger or more specific effects on neurotransmission. The result is the use of fewer laboratory animals.

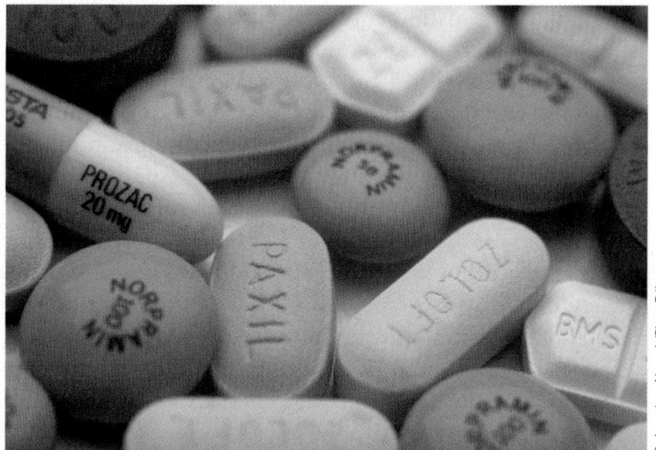

© Jonathan Nourok/PhotoEdit

Figure 15.4 Antidepressant pills
Tricyclic drugs block the reuptake of catecholamines and serotonin by presynaptic terminals. Selective serotonin reuptake inhibitors, such as Prozac, have similar effects but limited to serotonin. MAOIs block an enzyme that breaks down catecholamines and serotonin.

Types of Antidepressants. Antidepressant drugs fall into four major categories: tricyclics, selective serotonin reuptake inhibitors, MAOIs, and atypical antidepressants (Figure 15.4). The **tricyclics** (e.g., imipramine, trade name Tofranil) operate by blocking the transporter proteins that reabsorb serotonin, dopamine, and norepinephrine into the presynaptic neuron after their release. The result is to prolong the presence of the neurotransmitters in the synaptic cleft, where they continue stimulating the postsynaptic cell. However, the tricyclics also block histamine receptors, acetylcholine receptors, and certain sodium channels (Horst & Preskorn, 1998). As mentioned in Chapter 9, blocking histamine produces drowsiness. Blocking acetylcholine leads to dry mouth and difficulty urinating. Blocking sodium channels causes heart irregularities, among other problems. People have to limit their use of tricyclic drugs to minimize these side effects.

The **selective serotonin reuptake inhibitors (SSRIs)** are similar to tricyclics but specific to the neurotransmitter serotonin. For example, fluoxetine (trade name Prozac) blocks the reuptake of serotonin. SSRIs produce milder side effects than the tricyclics, but their effectiveness is about the same. Other common SSRIs include sertraline (Zoloft), fluvoxamine (Luvox), citalopram (Celexa), and paroxetine (Paxil or Seroxat).

The **monoamine oxidase inhibitors (MAOIs)** (e.g., phenelzine, trade name Nardil) block the enzyme monoamine oxidase (MAO), a presynaptic terminal enzyme that metabolizes catecholamines and serotonin into inactive forms. When MAOIs block this enzyme, the presynaptic terminal has more of its transmitter available for release. Generally, physicians prescribe tricyclics or SSRIs first and then try MAOIs with people who did not respond to the other drugs (Thase, Trivedi, & Rush, 1995). People taking MAOIs must avoid foods containing tyramine—including cheese, raisins, and many others—because a combination of tyramine and MAOIs increases blood pressure. Figure 15.5 summarizes the mechanisms of tricyclics, SSRIs, and MAOIs.

The **atypical antidepressants** are a miscellaneous group—everything other than the three types just discussed (Horst & Preskorn, 1998). One example is bupropion (Wellbutrin), which inhibits reuptake of dopamine and to some extent norepinephrine but not serotonin.

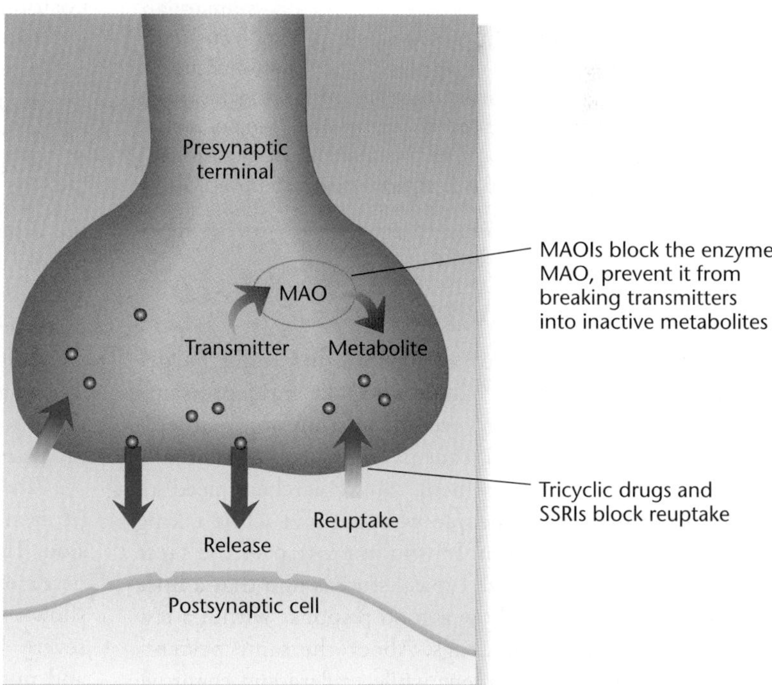

Figure 15.5 Routes of action of antidepressants
Tricyclics block the reuptake of dopamine, norepinephrine, or serotonin. SSRIs specifically block the reuptake of serotonin. MAOIs block the enzyme MAO, which converts dopamine, norepinephrine, or serotonin into inactive chemicals. Atypical antidepressants have varying effects.

In addition, many people use St. John's wort, an herb. Because it is marketed as a nutritional supplement instead of a drug, the U.S. Food and Drug Administration does not regulate it, and its purity varies from one bottle to another. It has the advantage of being less expensive than antidepressant drugs. An advantage or disadvantage, depending on your point of view, is that it is available without prescription. People can get it easily but often take inappropriate amounts. Apparently, it works the same way as the SSRIs. Depending on which study you believe, it is either a little more effective than SSRIs, about equal to them, or much less effective (Linde, Berner, Egger, & Mulrow, 2005). However, it has a potentially dangerous side effect: All mammals have a liver enzyme that breaks down plant toxins. St. John's wort increases the effectiveness of that enzyme. Increasing the breakdown of toxins sounds like a good thing, but the enzyme also breaks down most medicines. Therefore, taking St. John's wort decreases the effectiveness of other drugs you might be taking—including other antidepressant drugs, cancer drugs, AIDS drugs, and even birth-control pills (Moore et al., 2000).

STOP & CHECK

3. What are the effects of tricyclic drugs?

4. What are the effects of SSRIs?

5. What are the effects of MAOIs?

ANSWERS

3. Tricyclic drugs block reuptake of serotonin and catecholamines. They also block histamine receptors, acetylcholine receptors, and certain sodium channels, thereby producing unpleasant side effects. **4.** SSRIs selectively inhibit the reuptake of serotonin. **5.** MAOIs block the enzyme MAO, which breaks down catecholamines and serotonin. The result is increased availability of these transmitters.

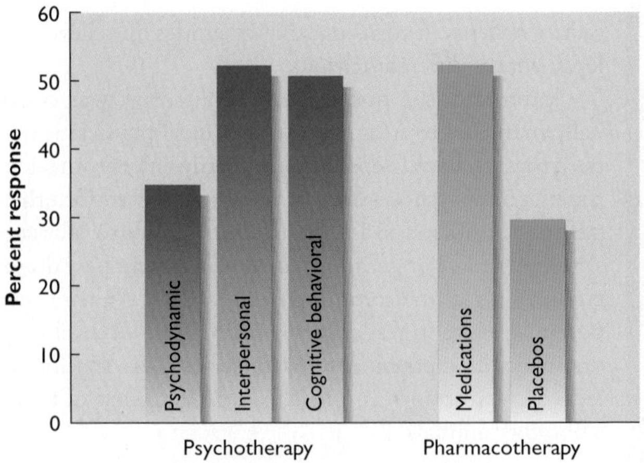

Figure 15.6 Percentage of people responding to various antidepressant treatments
Barely more than half respond well to antidepressants or psychotherapy within a few weeks, and many of those would have improved without treatment.

Effectiveness of Antidepressants

The overall effectiveness of antidepressants could be described as lackluster. Most people who take antidepressants do show improvement. However, depression occurs in episodes of variable duration. That is, most people eventually recover even without treatment. So researchers need to compare the number of people who improve while taking antidepressants to the number who improve over the same time while taking placebos. Typical studies find that a little over half of all patients show a good response within a few weeks on antidepressant drugs. About the same percentage show similar improvement while undergoing cognitive behavioral or interpersonal psychotherapy. However, about 30% improve while taking placebos or while undergoing psychodynamic (Freudian) therapy, which appears hardly better than a placebo (Hollon, Thase, & Markowitz, 2002). Figure 15.6 summarizes these results. A combination of both antidepressants and psychotherapy benefits only a slightly higher percentage of people than either treatment alone (Thase et al., 1997). The effects of antidepressants and those of psychotherapy overlap more than we might have guessed. Brain scans show that antidepressants and psychotherapy increase metabolism in the same brain areas (Brody et al., 2001; S. D. Martin et al., 2001). That similarity should not be terribly surprising if we accept the mind–body monism position. If mental activity is the same thing as brain activity, then changing someone's thoughts should indeed change brain chemistry.

In short, about 30% of people recover from depression within a few weeks with no treatment or only a placebo. Another 20% or so respond to either antidepressants or psychotherapy, a few more respond to a combination of both, and the others do not respond well to either. The percentage of people responding well does not vary significantly from one antidepressant drug to another (Thase et al., 2005). In some cases, people who fail to respond to one drug do improve after an additional few weeks on another drug (Rush et al., 2006; Trivedi et al., 2006). However, we do not know how many of those really responded to the new drug as opposed to the additional time for recovery.

Additional analyses find that antidepressants are barely (if at all) better than placebos for people with mild depression. The benefit of antidepressant drugs relative to placebos becomes greater for people with more severe depression, as shown in Figure 15.7 (Kirsch et al., 2008). Even at the most severe levels, however, antidepressants help some people and not others, possibly because of variations in the drugs' ability to cross the blood-brain barrier (Uhr et al., 2008). Antidepressants are generally ineffective for patients who had suffered abuse, neglect, or other trauma during early childhood. Those patients usually respond better to psychotherapy (Nemeroff et al., 2003).

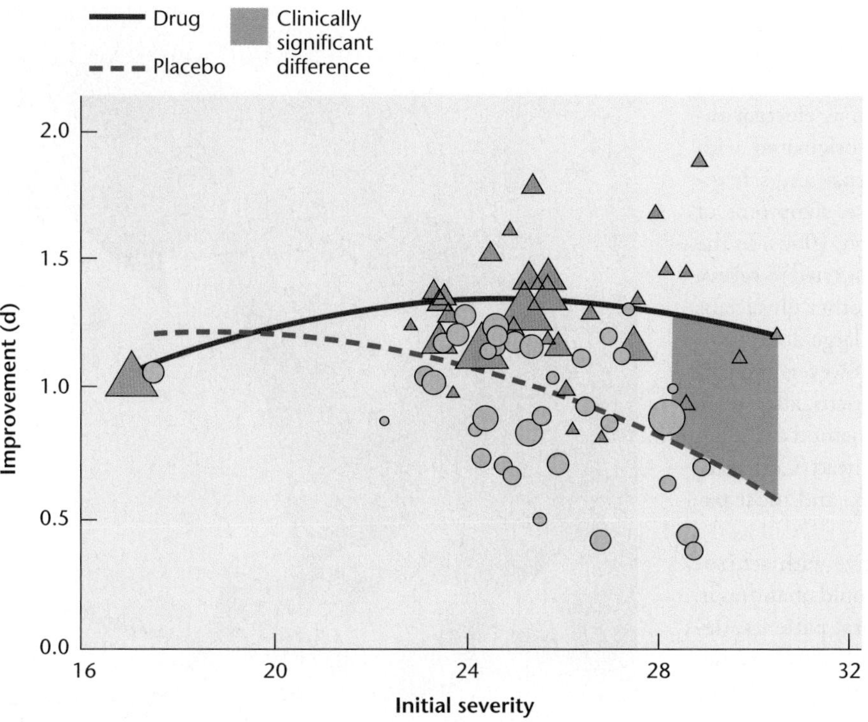

Figure 15.7 Percentage of people experiencing relief from depression while taking either antidepressants or placebos
The difference between antidepressants and placebos is greatest for people with the most severe depression, mainly because they are the least likely to improve by placebos alone. Triangles represent groups on drugs. Circles represent groups on placebos. *(Kirsch, 2008)*

The use of antidepressants for children and adolescents is controversial. Most studies found that antidepressants are generally ineffective for children and adolescents, while sometimes increasing suicidal thoughts (Jureidini et al., 2004; Weisz, McCarty, & Valeri, 2006). In response to these reports, many psychiatrists in the United States and Europe stopped prescribing antidepressants for young people. However, since that decrease, the teenage suicide rate increased, and some believe the increase was due to a failure to treat teenage depression adequately (Gibbons et al., 2007).

STOP & CHECK

6. As depression becomes more severe, what happens to the percentage of patients showing improvement while taking antidepressant drugs or placebos?

ANSWER

6. For more severe cases, the percentage improving remains about the same for patients taking antidepressant drugs, but fewer patients taking placebos show improvement.

Exactly How Do Antidepressants Work? Granted that antidepressants are not highly effective, they are nevertheless somewhat effective, and we would like to understand their mechanism of effect. Understanding how they work should shed some light on the causes of depression. Given that SSRIs relieve depression by blocking reuptake of serotonin, one might assume that depression results from a deficit of serotonin and possibly other neurotransmitters. However, the situation can't be that simple. As discussed in Chapter 12, researchers can measure the metabolite 5-HIAA in cerebrospinal fluid as an indicator of serotonin turnover in the brain. The results vary among studies, but some of them show an *increase* in serotonin turnover for people with depression (Barton et al., 2008). How to interpret that result is uncertain.

Furthermore, it is possible to decrease serotonin levels suddenly by consuming a diet rich in other amino acids but deficient in tryptophan, the precursor to serotonin. Most people with a history of major depression react with a brief bout of depression, but other people tolerate the same decrease in serotonin without feeling depressed (Neumeister et al., 2004, 2006).

The major theoretical problem is the time course: Antidepressant drugs produce their effects on catecholamine and serotonin synapses within hours, but people need to take the drugs for 2 or more weeks before they experience any mood elevation (Stewart et al., 1998). What happens during that time? One possibility relates to the fact that neurons in parts of the hippocampus and cerebral cortex shrink in some people with depression (Cotter, Mackay, Landau, Kerwin, & Everall, 2001). When drugs increase the release of neurotransmitters, the axons also release a neurotrophin called *brain-derived neurotrophic factor* (BDNF) (Guillin et al., 2001). As discussed in Chapter 5, neurotrophins aid in survival, growth, and connections of neurons. BDNF is especially important for synaptic plasticity, and an increase in BDNF improves learning (Martinowich, Manji, & Lu, 2007). Another consequence is to increase the proliferation of new neurons in the hippocampus. Every known antidepressant increases neuron production, and procedures that block neuron production also block the behavioral benefits of antidepressant drugs (Airan et al., 2007).

Still, the honest answer is that we do not fully understand how antidepressant drugs help. The immediate effects on serotonin and other neurotransmitters are clear, but the effects that develop over weeks need further research.

STOP & CHECK

7. In what way does the time course of antidepressants pose a theoretical problem for understanding their mechanism?

ANSWER

7. The antidepressants produce their known effects on the synapses quickly, but their behavioral benefits develop gradually over 2 to 3 weeks.

Electroconvulsive Therapy (ECT). What treatment might help people who respond to neither drugs nor psychotherapy? One possibility, despite its stormy history, is treatment through an electrically induced seizure, known as **electroconvulsive therapy (ECT)** (Fink, 1985). ECT originated with the observation that for people with both epilepsy and schizophrenia, as symptoms of one disorder increase, symptoms of the other often decrease (Trimble & Thompson, 1986). In the 1930s, a Hungarian physician, Ladislas Meduna, tried to relieve schizophrenia by inducing convulsions. Soon, other physicians were doing the same, inducing seizures with a large dose of insulin. Insulin shock is a dreadful experience, however, and difficult to control. An Italian physician, Ugo Cerletti, after years of experimentation with animals, developed a method of inducing seizures with an electric shock through the head (Cerletti & Bini, 1938). Electroconvulsive therapy is quick, and most patients awaken calmly without remembering it.

When ECT proved to be not very effective with schizophrenia, you might guess that psychiatrists would abandon it. Instead, they tried it for other mental hospital patients, despite having no theoretical basis. ECT did indeed relieve depression in many cases. However, its misuse during the 1950s earned it a bad reputation, as some patients were given ECT hundreds of times without their consent.

When antidepressant drugs became available in the late 1950s, the use of ECT declined abruptly. However, it made a partial comeback in the 1970s. ECT today is used only with informed consent, usually for patients who have not responded to antidepressant drugs (Scovern & Kilmann, 1980; Weiner, 1979). It is also sometimes recommended for patients with strong suicidal tendencies because it works faster than antidepressant drugs: Feeling better in 1 week instead of 2 could make the difference between life and death.

ECT is usually applied every other day for about 2 weeks, sometimes more often. Patients are given muscle relaxants or anesthetics to minimize discomfort and the possibility of injury (Figure 15.8). Because the shock is less intense than in earlier years, the risk of provoking a heart attack is low except in elderly patients.

The most common side effect of ECT is memory loss, but if physicians limit the shock to the right hemisphere, the antidepressant effects occur without memory impairment (McElhiney et al., 1995). (Recall that right-hemisphere activity is more associated with unpleasant mood.)

Besides the threat of memory loss, the other serious drawback to ECT is the high risk of relapsing into another episode of depression within a few months (Riddle & Scott, 1995). After ECT has relieved depression, the usual strategy is to try to prevent a relapse by means of drugs, psychotherapy, or periodic ECT treatments (Swoboda, Conca, König, Waanders, & Hansen, 2001).

More than half a century after the introduction of ECT, no one is yet sure how it relieves depression, but like antidepressant drugs, ECT increases the proliferation of new neurons in the hippocampus (Perera et al., 2007). It also alters the expression of at least 120 genes in the hippocampus and frontal cortex alone. Some of the biggest effects pertain to genes related to neurotrophins, arachidonic acid, generation of new neurons, and responsiveness to exercise (Altar et al., 2004). Each of those pathways is known to have strong links to depression.

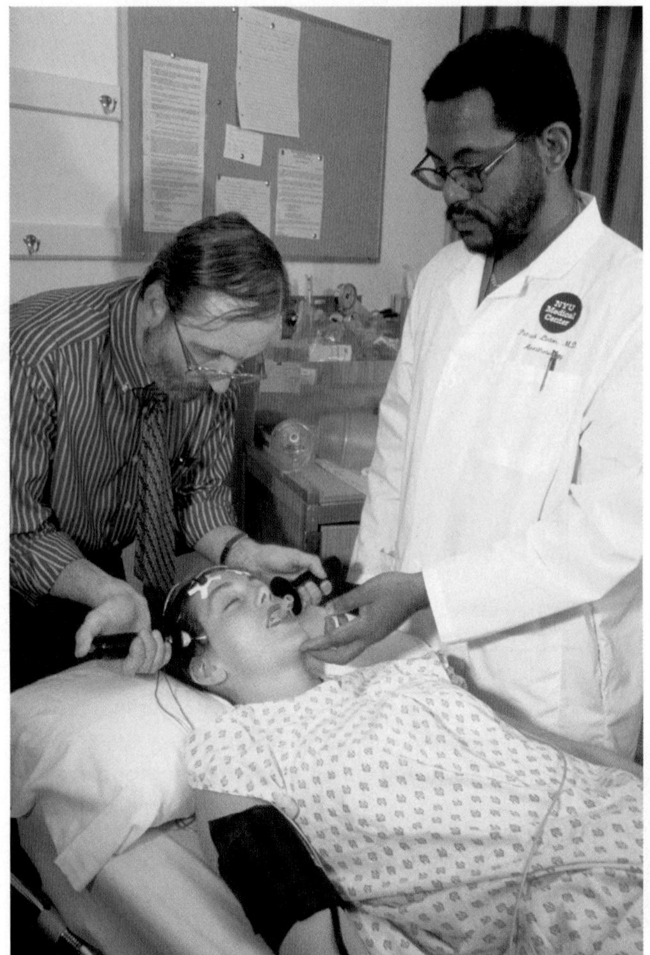

Figure 15.8 Electroconvulsive therapy (ECT)
In contrast to an earlier era, ECT today is administered with muscle relaxants or anesthetics to minimize discomfort and only if the patient gives informed consent.

A similar treatment is repetitive transcranial magnetic stimulation. An intense magnetic field is applied to the scalp, stimulating the axons near the surface of the brain. This procedure is moderately effective against depression, although its mechanism of behavioral effect is not known (Ridding & Rothwell, 2007).

Altered Sleep Patterns. Most people with depression have sleep patterns resembling those of healthy people who went to bed later than usual: They fall asleep but awaken early, unable to get back to sleep, and they enter REM sleep within 45 minutes after going to sleep, as Figure 15.9 illustrates. In addition, people who are depressed have more than the average number of eye movements per minute during REM sleep. Many of their relatives show these same sleep patterns, and the relatives who show these patterns are more likely to become depressed themselves than are relatives who sleep normally (Modell, Ising, Holsboer, & Lauer, 2005). In short, altered sleep is a lifelong trait of people who are predisposed to depression.

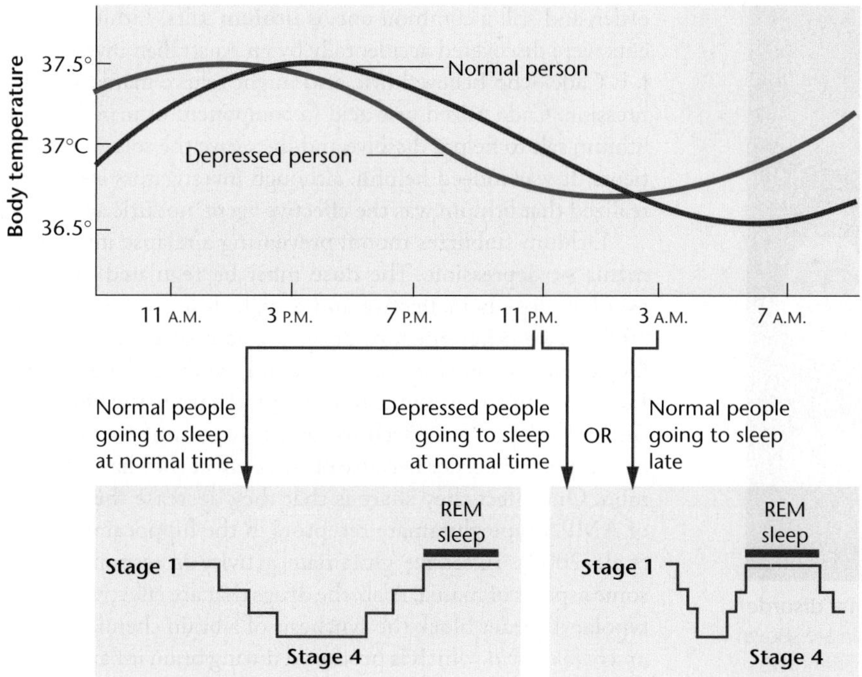

Figure 15.9 Circadian rhythms and depression
Most people with depression have their circadian rhythms advanced by several hours. They sleep as someone else would at a later time. *(Bottom graphs from* Sleep *by J. Allan Hobson, © 1989, 1995 by J. Allan Hobson. Reprinted by permission of Henry Holt and Company, LLC.)*

Surprisingly, although a sleepless night annoys most people, a night of total sleep deprivation is the quickest known method of relieving depression (Ringel & Szuba, 2001). Like other antidepressant treatments, sleep deprivation increases the proliferation of new neurons in the hippocampus (Zucconi, Cipriani, Balgkouranidou, & Scattoni, 2006).

Unfortunately, about half of the people who experience this relief become depressed again after the next night's sleep. It is possible to extend the benefits by altering the sleep schedule on subsequent days. For example, go without sleep altogether for 1 day and then start a schedule of sleeping from 5 P.M. until midnight instead of the usual time. This schedule relieves depression for at least a week in most patients and often longer (Riemann et al., 1999). Combining sleep alteration with drug therapies can provide long-lasting benefits (Wirz-Justice & Van den Hoofdakker, 1999).

Researchers cannot yet explain how sleep deprivation or rescheduling produces mood benefits. A better understanding might lead to other treatments for depression.

STOP & CHECK

8. For what kinds of patients is ECT recommended?

9. What change in sleep habits sometimes relieves depression?

ANSWERS

8. ECT is recommended for people with depression who did not respond to other therapies and for those who are an immediate suicide risk (because ECT acts faster than other therapies). **9.** Getting people with depression to go to bed earlier sometimes relieves depression.

Other Therapies

Each of the currently available treatments for depression has its pros and cons, and some people with depression do not respond well to any of them. The search continues for new and improved treatments. A wide variety of drugs are in various stages of investigation (Berton & Nestler, 2006), and the hormone leptin has shown some promise (Lu, Kim, Frazer, & Zhang, 2006).

The cheapest and simplest antidepressant procedure is a program of regular, nonstrenuous exercise, such as brisk walking for half an hour or more per day (Leppämäki, Partonen, & Lönnqvist, 2002). Moderate exercise increases blood flow to the brain and provides other benefits that are especially helpful to aging people and people with depression (Hillman, Erickson, & Kramer, 2008; Hunsberger et al., 2007). It reduces the effects of stress in laboratory animals as well as people (Greenwood, Strong, Dorey, & Fleshner, 2007). Exercise can be combined with other treatments, such as sleep deprivation, to magnify the benefits (Putilov, Pinchasov, & Poljakova, 2005).

Bipolar Disorder

Depression can be either unipolar or bipolar. People with **unipolar depression** vary between normality and one pole—depression. People with **bipolar disorder**—formerly known as *manic-depressive disorder*—alternate between two poles—depression and its opposite, mania. **Mania** is characterized by restless activity, excitement, laughter, self-confidence, rambling speech, and loss of inhibitions. People with mania become dangerous to themselves and others. Figure 15.10 shows the brain's increase in glucose use during mania and its decrease during depression (Baxter et al., 1985).

People who have full-blown episodes of mania are said to have **bipolar I disorder.** People with **bipolar II disorder** have milder manic phases, called hypomania, which are characterized mostly by agitation or anxiety. In addition to the mood swings, most people with bipolar disorder have attention deficits, poor impulse control, and impairments of verbal memory

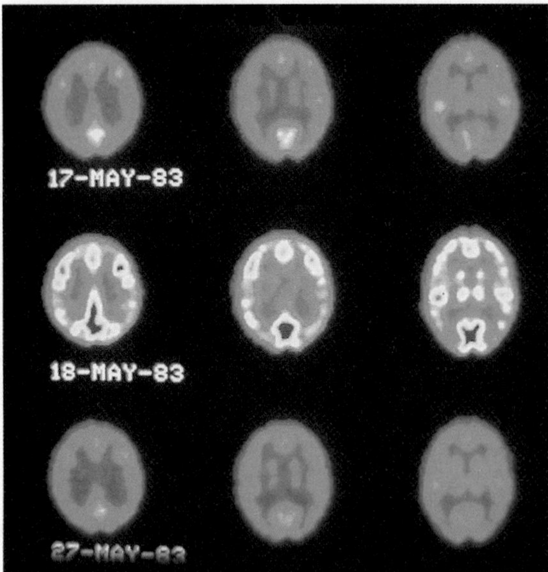

Figure 15.10 PET scans for a patient with bipolar disorder Horizontal planes through three levels of the brain are shown for each day. On May 17 and May 27, when the patient was depressed, brain metabolic rates were low. On May 18, when the patient was in a cheerful, hypomanic mood, the brain metabolic rate was high. Red indicates the highest metabolic rate, followed by yellow, green, and blue. *(Reprinted by permission from Macmillan Publishers Ltd:* Nature, *"A functional neuroanatomy of hallucinations in schizophrenia," Silbersweig et al., 1995.)*

(Quraishi & Frangou, 2002). Diagnoses of bipolar disorder have been increasing since the 1990s, especially among teenagers and young adults (Moreno et al., 2007). It is now estimated that about 1% of people will have bipolar I disorder at some time in life, another 1% will have bipolar II disorder, and 2% to 3% will have "subthreshold" bipolar disorder—a minor case not quite strong enough for a diagnosis of bipolar disorder (Merikangas et al., 2007).

Genetics

Several lines of evidence suggest a hereditary basis for bipolar disorder (Craddock & Jones, 1999). If one monozygotic twin has bipolar disorder, the other has at least a 50% chance of getting it also, whereas dizygotic twins, brothers, sisters, or children have about a 5% to 10% probability. Adopted children who develop bipolar disorder are likely to have biological relatives with mood disorders. Researchers have located two genes that appear to increase the probability of bipolar II disorder (Nwulia et al., 2007). However, the genes merely increase the risk. They by no means guarantee the outcome.

Treatments

Antidepressant drugs are inappropriate for bipolar patients. If they are given to a patient in the depressed phase, the usual result is a swing into mania (Dunner, D'Souza, Kajdasz, Detke, & Russell, 2005). The first successful treatment for bipolar disorder, and still a common one, is **lithium** salts. Lithium's benefits were discovered accidentally by an Australian investigator, J. F. Cade, who believed uric acid might relieve mania and depression. Cade mixed uric acid (a component of urine) with a lithium salt to help it dissolve and then gave the solution to patients. It was indeed helpful, although investigators eventually realized that lithium was the effective agent, not uric acid.

Lithium stabilizes mood, preventing a relapse into either mania or depression. The dose must be regulated carefully, as a low dose is ineffective and a high dose is toxic (Schou, 1997). Two other effective drugs are valproate (trade names Depakene, Depakote, and others) and carbamazepine. Lithium, valproate, and carbamazepine have many effects on the brain. A good research strategy is to assume that they relieve bipolar disorder because of some effect they have in common. One effect they share is that they decrease the number of AMPA type glutamate receptors in the hippocampus (Du et al., 2008). Excessive glutamate activity is responsible for some aspects of mania. Also, the drugs that are effective against bipolar disorder block the synthesis of a brain chemical called *arachidonic acid*, which is produced during brain inflammation (S. I. Rapoport & Bosetti, 2002). Bipolar patients show an increased expression of genes associated with inflammation (Padmos et al., 2008). The effects of arachidonic acid are also counteracted by polyunsaturated fatty acids, such as those in seafood, and epidemiological studies suggest that people who eat at least a pound (0.45 kg) of seafood per week have a decreased risk of bipolar disorder (Noaghiul & Hibbeln, 2003).

Another possible treatment relates to sleep. Patients with bipolar disorder during the depressed phase tend to stay in bed for many hours. During the manic phase, they awaken quickly, sleeping 4 hours or less. A sudden increase in bedrest time predicts that a bipolar patient is about to go into a depressed phase, and a sudden decrease predicts an imminent manic phase (Bauer, Grof, Rasgon, Bschor, Glenn, & Whybrow, 2006). Preliminary studies suggest that getting people to maintain a consistent sleeping schedule in a dark, quiet room could reduce the intensity of mood swings (Wehr et al., 1998). Researchers speculate that the artificial lights, television, and other technology of our society tempt us to stay up late at night and thereby increase the prevalence of bipolar disorder.

STOP & CHECK

10. What are two common treatments for bipolar disorder?

ANSWER

10. The common treatments for bipolar disorder are lithium salts and certain anticonvulsant drugs—valproate and carbamazepine.

Seasonal Affective Disorder

Another form of depression is **seasonal affective disorder (SAD)**, which is depression that recurs during a particular season, such as winter. SAD is most prevalent near the poles,

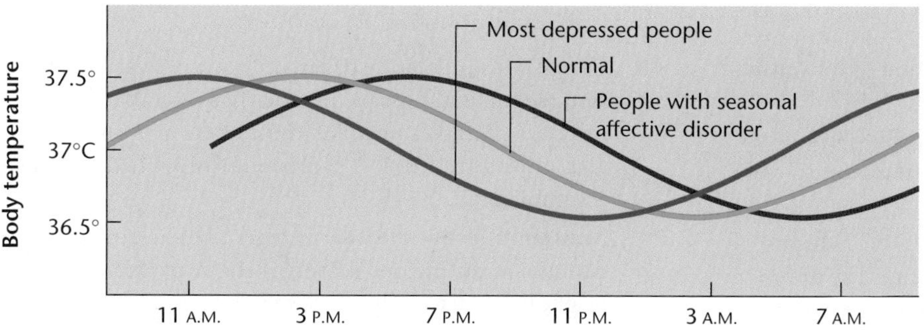

Figure 15.11 Circadian rhythms for major depression and seasonal affective disorder (SAD)
Patients with SAD are phase-delayed while most other patients with depression are phase-advanced.

where the winter nights are long (Haggarty et al., 2002). It is less common in moderate climates and unheard of in the tropics.

SAD differs from other types of depression in many ways; for example, patients with SAD have phase-delayed sleep and temperature rhythms—becoming sleepy and wakeful a bit later than normal—unlike most other patients with depression, whose rhythms are phase-advanced (Teicher et al., 1997) (Figure 15.11). Also, SAD is seldom as severe as major depression.

It is possible to treat SAD with very bright lights (e.g., 2,500 lux) for an hour or more each day. The bright light treatment is effective in morning, afternoon, or evening (Eastman, Young, Fogg, Liu, & Meaden, 1998; Lewy et al., 1998; Terman, Terman, & Ross, 1998). Although its benefits are as yet unexplained, they are substantial. Bright light is less expensive than the other antidepressant therapies and produces its benefits more rapidly, often within 1 week (Kripke, 1998).

The Website of the Society for Light Treatment and Biological Rhythms provides much information about light therapy and biological rhythms: http://www.sltbr.org/

STOP & CHECK

11. What are the advantages of bright light treatment compared to antidepressant drugs?

ANSWER

11. It is cheaper, has no side effects, and produces its benefits more quickly.

MODULE 15.1 IN CLOSING

The Biology of Mood Swings

There is nothing abnormal about feeling very sad or very happy if something unusually bad or good has just happened to you. For people with major depression or bipolar disorder, mood becomes largely independent of events. A traumatic experience might trigger a bout of depression, but once someone has become depressed, the mood persists for months, and even the best of news provides little cheer. A bipolar patient in a manic state has boundless energy and self-confidence that no contradiction can deter. Studying these states has great potential to inform us about the brain states that correspond to moods.

SUMMARY

1. People with major depression find that almost nothing makes them happy. Depression occurs as a series of episodes. **438**
2. Certain genes increase the probability of reacting with depression after stressful or traumatic experiences. Both the genes and the experiences contribute to the onset of depression. **439**
3. Uncommonly, depression can be a reaction to a virus or to hormonal changes. **439**
4. Depression is associated with decreased activity in the left hemisphere of the cortex. **440**
5. Four kinds of antidepressant drugs are in wide use. Tricyclics block reuptake of serotonin and catecholamines but produce strong side effects. SSRIs block reuptake of serotonin. MAOIs block an enzyme that breaks down catecholamines and serotonin. Atypical antidepressants are a miscellaneous group with diverse effects. **440**
6. Antidepressant drugs are not consistently effective. Only slightly more than half of all patients show clear improvement after taking antidepressants, and most of those would have improved on a placebo. Antidepressants show their clearest benefits for people with severe

depression. Many people do not respond well to either psychotherapy or antidepressant drugs. **442**

7. The antidepressants alter synaptic activity quickly, but their effects on behavior require at least 2 weeks. **443**
8. The behavioral effects of antidepressant drugs apparently depend on the release of BDNF, which promotes neuronal growth and plasticity. The drugs also increase the production of new neurons in the hippocampus. **443**
9. Other therapies for depression include electroconvulsive therapy, altered sleep patterns, and nonstrenuous exercise. **444**
10. People with bipolar disorder alternate between depression and mania. Bipolar disorder has a genetic basis. Effective therapies include lithium salts and certain anticonvulsant drugs. A consistent sleep schedule is also recommended. **445**
11. Seasonal affective disorder is marked by recurrent depression during one season of the year. Exposure to bright lights is usually effective in treating it. **446**

KEY TERMS

Terms are defined in the module on the page number indicated. They're also presented in alphabetical order with definitions in the book's Subject Index/Glossary. Interactive flashcards, audio reviews, and crossword puzzles are among the online resources available to help you learn these terms and the concepts they represent.

atypical antidepressants **441**
bipolar disorder **445**
bipolar I disorder **445**
bipolar II disorder **445**
electroconvulsive therapy (ECT) **444**
lithium **446**
major depression **438**
mania **445**
monoamine oxidase inhibitors (MAOIs) **441**
postpartum depression **440**
seasonal affective disorder (SAD) **446**
selective serotonin reuptake inhibitors (SSRIs) **441**
tricyclics **441**
unipolar depression **445**

THOUGHT QUESTION

Some people have suggested that ECT relieves depression by causing people to forget the events that caused it. What evidence opposes this hypothesis?

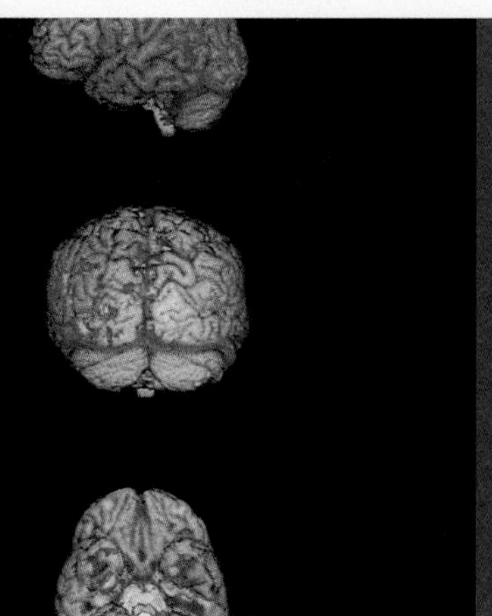

MODULE 15.2

Schizophrenia

Here is a conversation between two people diagnosed with schizophrenia (Haley, 1959, p. 321):

A: Do you work at the air base?

B: You know what I think of work. I'm 33 in June, do you mind?

A: June?

B: 33 years old in June. This stuff goes out the window after I live this, uh—leave this hospital. So I can't get my vocal cords back. So I lay off cigarettes. I'm in a spatial condition, from outer space myself....

A: I'm a real spaceship from across.

B: A lot of people talk that way, like crazy, but "Believe It or Not," by Ripley, take it or leave it—alone—it's in the Examiner, it's in the comic section, "Believe It or Not," by Ripley, Robert E. Ripley, Believe it or not, but we don't have to believe anything, unless I feel like it. Every little rosette—too much alone.

A: Yeah, it could be possible.

B: I'm a civilian seaman.

A: Could be possible. I take my bath in the ocean.

B: Bathing stinks. You know why? 'Cause you can't quit when you feel like it. You're in the service.

People with schizophrenia say and do things that other people (including other people with schizophrenia) find difficult to understand. The causes of the disorder are not well understood, but they include a large biological component.

Characteristics

According to the *DSM-IV*, **schizophrenia** is a disorder characterized by deteriorating ability to function in everyday life and by some combination of hallucinations, delusions, thought disorder, movement disorder, and inappropriate emotional expressions (American Psychiatric Association, 1994). The symptoms vary so greatly that you could easily find several people with the same diagnosis who have almost nothing in common (Andreasen, 1999). Schizophrenia can be either acute or chronic. An **acute** condition has a sudden onset and good prospects for recovery. A **chronic** condition has a gradual onset and a long-term course.

Schizophrenia was originally called *dementia praecox*, which is Latin for "premature mental deterioration." In 1911, Eugen Bleuler introduced the term *schizophrenia*. Although the term is Greek for "split mind," it is *not* related to *dissociative identity disorder* (previously known as *multiple personality disorder*), in which someone alternates among different personalities. What Bleuler meant by *schizophrenia* was a split between the emotional and intellectual aspects of experience: The person's emotional expression or lack of it seems unconnected with current experiences. For example, someone might giggle or cry for no apparent reason or show no reaction to bad news. Not all patients show this detachment of emotion from intellect, but the term lives on.

The Schizophrenia.com Website provides a good source of information on many aspects of schizophrenia: http://www.schizophrenia.com/

Behavioral Symptoms

Schizophrenia is characterized by **positive symptoms** (behaviors that are present that should be absent) and **negative symptoms** (behaviors that are absent that should be present). Negative symptoms include weak social interactions, emotional expression, speech, and working memory. Negative symptoms are usually stable over time and difficult to treat. Positive symptoms fall into two clusters: psychotic and disorganized (Andreasen, Arndt, Alliger, Miller, & Flaum, 1995). The *psychotic* cluster consists of **delusions** (unfounded beliefs, such as the conviction that one is being persecuted or that outer space aliens are trying to control one's behavior) and **hallucinations** (abnormal sensory experiences, such as hearing voices when one is alone). PET scans have shown that hallucinations occur during periods of increased activity in the thalamus, hippocampus, and parts of the cortex, including many of the areas activated by actual hearing (Shergill, Brammer, Williams, Murray, & McGuire, 2000; Silbersweig et al., 1995).

The *disorganized* cluster of positive symptoms consists of inappropriate emotional displays, bizarre behaviors, incoherent speech, and thought disorder. Overall intelligence varies considerably, but on the average, IQ scores are a few points below those of the rest of the population (Woodberry, Giuliano, & Seidman, 2008). The most typical type of thought disorder of schizophrenia is a difficulty understanding and using abstract concepts. Related symptoms include deficits in attention and working memory (Hanlon et al., 2005).

Which of the various symptoms, if any, is the primary problem? According to Nancy Andreasen (1999), a leading investigator of schizophrenia, the main problem is disordered thoughts, which result from abnormal interactions between the cortex and the thalamus and cerebellum. The disordered thinking may lead to the hallucinations, delusions, and other symptoms.

Nancy C. Andreasen
Being a scientist and a clinician is a double privilege. We actually get paid to spend our time asking both scientific and clinical questions that everyone would like to ask and have answered, and people grant us the trust of sharing their most intimate thoughts and experiences with us.

One way to test this idea is to see whether we could make normal, healthy people talk or behave in incoherent ways if we overtaxed their working memory. Imagine yourself in the following study. The researcher shows a series of pictures for 30 seconds each, and you are supposed to tell a short story about each one. If you see the same picture a second time, you are supposed to tell a totally new story about it, unlike your first one. Furthermore, on some trials, you have an additional task to burden your memory while you are trying to tell a story: A series of letters appears on the screen, one at a time. You should pay attention to every second letter. Whenever it is the same as the last letter that you paid attention to, you should press a key. For example,

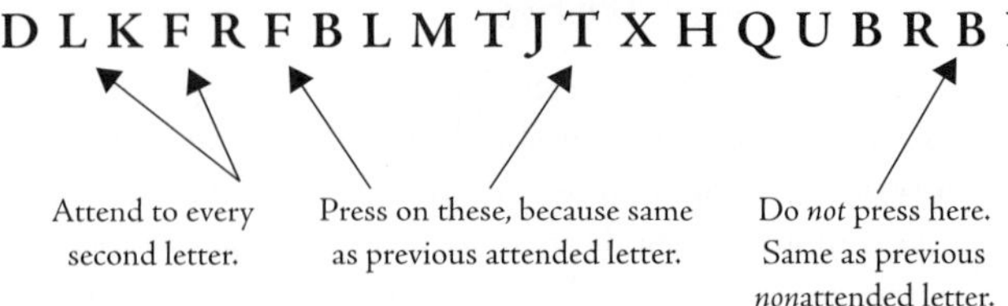
D L K F R F B L M T J T X H Q U B R B N
Attend to every second letter.
Press on these, because same as previous attended letter.
Do *not* press here. Same as previous *non*attended letter.

Most people's speech becomes less clear when they perform this memory task while trying to tell a story. If it is the second presentation of a picture, requiring them to avoid what they said the first time and tell a totally new story, the memory task causes even greater interference, and their speech becomes incoherent, somewhat like schizophrenic speech (Kerns, 2007). The implication is that memory impairment could be the central symptom.

STOP & CHECK

12. Why are hallucinations considered a positive symptom?

ANSWER

12. Hallucinations are considered a positive symptom because they are present when they should be absent. A "positive" symptom is not a "good" symptom.

APPLICATIONS AND EXTENSIONS

Differential Diagnosis of Schizophrenia

Suppose you're a psychiatrist and you meet a patient who has recently deteriorated in everyday functioning and has hallucinations, delusions, thought disorder, and disorganized speech. You are ready to enter a diagnosis of schizophrenia and begin treatment, right?

Not so fast. First you should make a **differential diagnosis,** ruling out other conditions that might produce similar symptoms. Here are a few conditions that sometimes resemble schizophrenia:

- *Mood disorder with psychotic features*: People with depression frequently have delusions, especially delusions of guilt or failure. Some report hallucinations also.
- *Substance abuse*: Many of the positive symptoms of schizophrenia can develop from prolonged use of amphetamine, methamphetamine, cocaine, LSD, or phencyclidine ("angel dust"). Someone who stops taking the drugs is likely, though not certain, to recover from these symptoms. Substance abuse is more likely than schizophrenia to produce visual hallucinations.
- *Brain damage*: Lesions to the temporal or prefrontal cortex, or tumors there, can produce symptoms resembling schizophrenia.
- *Undetected hearing deficits*: Sometimes, someone who is starting to have trouble hearing thinks that everyone else is whispering and starts to worry, "They're whispering about me!" Delusions of persecution can develop.
- *Huntington's disease*: The symptoms of Huntington's disease include hallucinations, delusions, and disordered thinking, as well as motor symptoms. A rare type of schizophrenia, *catatonic schizophrenia,* includes motor abnormalities, so a mixture of psychological and motor symptoms could represent either schizophrenia or Huntington's disease.
- *Nutritional abnormalities*: Niacin deficiency can produce hallucinations and delusions (Hoffer, 1973); so can a deficiency of vitamin C or an allergy to milk proteins (not the same as lactose intolerance). Some people who cannot tolerate wheat gluten or other proteins react with hallucinations and delusions (Reichelt, Seim, & Reichelt, 1996).

Demographic Data

About 1% of people suffer from schizophrenia (Narrow et al., 2002; Perälä et al., 2007). The estimate rises or falls depending on how many mild cases we include. Since the mid-1900s, the reported prevalence of schizophrenia has been declining in many countries (Suvisaari, Haukka, Tanskanen, & Lönnqvist, 1999; Torrey & Miller, 2001). Is schizophrenia actually less common, or are psychiatrists just diagnosing it differently? This is not an easy question to answer. However, even when it is diagnosed today, it appears to be less severe than it often used to be. Perhaps our society is doing something to prevent schizophrenia without knowing what.

Schizophrenia occurs in all ethnic groups and all parts of the world, although it is 10 to 100 times more common in the United States and Europe than in most Third World countries (Torrey, 1986). Part of that discrepancy could be due to differences in recordkeeping, but other possibilities exist, including diet. A diet high in sugar and saturated fat, as is common in prosperous countries, aggravates schizophrenia, whereas a diet rich in fish alleviates it (Peet, 2004).

Lifetime prevalence of schizophrenia is more common for men than women by a ratio of about 7:5. On the average, it is also more severe in men and has an earlier onset—usually in the early 20s for men and the late 20s for women (Aleman, Kahn, & Selten, 2003). The increased prevalence of schizophrenia among men may relate to the fact that men's brains release more dopamine than women's brains do, especially in the basal ganglia (Munro et al., 2006). As we shall see later in this chapter, excess dopamine release has been linked to schizophrenia.

Researchers have documented several unexplained oddities about schizophrenia. The points that follow do not fit neatly into any currently prominent theory. They indicate how many mysteries remain about schizophrenia:

- Schizophrenia is significantly less common than average among people with type 1 (juvenile-onset) diabetes, although it is more common than average in people with type 2 (adult-onset) diabetes (Juvonen et al., 2007).
- People with schizophrenia have an increased risk of colon cancer but below average probability of respiratory cancer or brain cancer (Hippisley-Cox, Vinogradova, Coupland, & Parker, 2007; Roppel, 1978).
- People with schizophrenia seldom develop rheumatoid arthritis or allergies (Goldman, 1999; Rubinstein, 1997).
- Women who have a schizophrenic breakdown during pregnancy usually give birth to daughters. However, those who have a breakdown shortly after giving birth usually gave birth to sons (M. A. Taylor, 1969).
- Many people with schizophrenia have a characteristic body odor, attributed to the chemical *trans*-3-methyl-2-hexenoic acid, and decreased ability to smell that chemical themselves (Brewer et al., 2007; K. Smith, Thompson, & Koster, 1969).

STOP & CHECK

13. Has the reported prevalence of schizophrenia been increasing, decreasing, or staying the same?

ANSWER

13. Schizophrenia has been decreasing in reported prevalence.

Genetics

Huntington's disease (Chapter 8) can be called a genetic disease: Almost everyone with Huntington's disease has an abnormality in the same gene, and anyone with that abnormal gene will get Huntington's disease. At one time, many researchers believed that schizophrenia might be a genetic disease in the same sense. However, accumulating evidence indicates that although schizophrenia has a genetic basis, it does not depend on any single gene.

Twin Studies

The more closely you are biologically related to someone with schizophrenia, the greater your own probability of schizophrenia, as shown in Figure 15.12 (Gottesman, 1991). One of the most important points in Figure 15.12, confirmed by other studies (Cardno et al., 1999), is that monozygotic twins have a much higher **concordance** (agreement) for schizophrenia than do dizygotic twins. Furthermore, twin pairs who are really monozygotic, but thought they weren't, are more concordant than twin pairs who thought they were, but really aren't (Kendler, 1983). That is, *being* monozygotic is more critical than *being treated as* monozygotic.

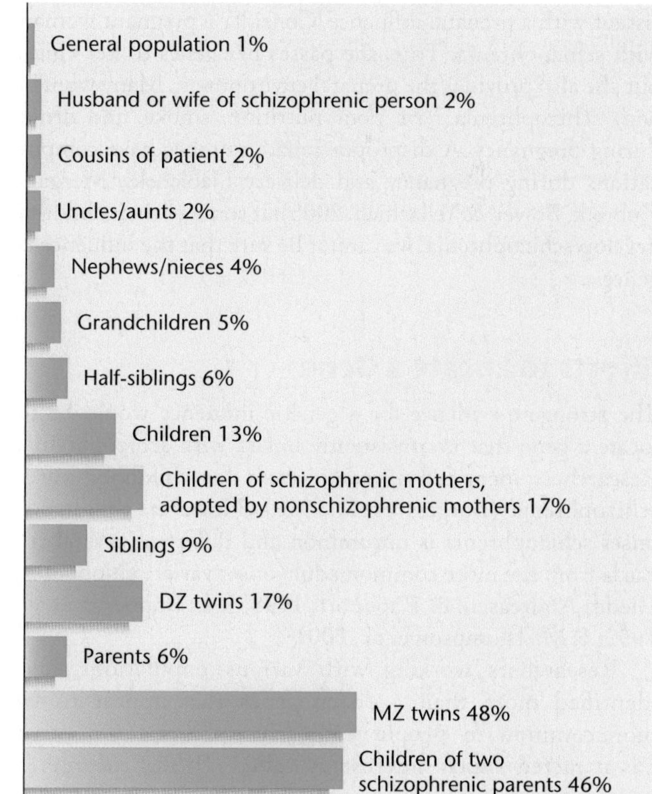

Figure 15.12 Probabilities of developing schizophrenia
People with a closer genetic relationship to someone with schizophrenia have a higher probability of developing it themselves. *(Based on data from Gottesman, 1991)*

The high concordance for monozygotic twins has long been taken as strong evidence for a genetic influence. However, note two limitations:

- Monozygotic twins have only about 50% concordance, not 100%. Monozygotic twins could differ because a gene is activated in one individual and suppressed in another (Tsujita et al., 1998), or they could differ because of some environmental influence.
- In Figure 15.12, note the greater similarity between dizygotic twins than between siblings. Dizygotic twins have the same genetic resemblance as siblings but greater environmental similarity, including that of prenatal and early postnatal life.

Adopted Children Who Develop Schizophrenia

When an adopted child develops schizophrenia, the disorder is more common in the person's biological relatives than adopting relatives. One Danish study found schizophrenia in 12.5% of the immediate biological relatives and none of the adopting relatives (Kety et al., 1994). Note in Figure 15.12 that children of a mother with schizophrenia have a moderately high probability of schizophrenia, even if adopted by mentally healthy parents.

These results suggest a genetic basis, but they are also consistent with a prenatal influence. Consider a pregnant woman with schizophrenia. True, she passes her genes to her child, but she also provides the prenatal environment. Many women with schizophrenia have poor nutrition, smoke, and drink during pregnancy. A disproportionate number have complications during pregnancy and delivery (Jablensky, Morgan, Zubrick, Bower, & Yellachich, 2005). If some of their children develop schizophrenia, we cannot be sure that the influence is genetic.

Efforts to Locate a Gene

The strongest evidence for a genetic influence would be to locate a gene that is consistently linked with schizophrenia. Researchers identified a genetic basis for childhood-onset schizophrenia (Burgess et al., 1998). However, childhood-onset schizophrenia is uncommon and differs in several regards from the more common adult-onset variety (Nopoulos, Giedd, Andreasen, & Rapoport, 1998; J. L. Rapoport et al., 1999; P. M. Thompson et al., 2001).

Researchers working with various populations have identified more than a dozen genes that appear to be more common in people with schizophrenia. One that has attracted much interest is called ***DISC1*** *(disrupted in schizophrenia 1)*, which controls the rate of generation of new neurons in the hippocampus (Duan et al., 2007). Another gene linked to schizophrenia in several studies is important for brain development and plasticity (Hall et al., 2006). However, researchers have not had much success at replicating the results from one population to another. One large study examined nearly 2,000 patients with schizophrenia and a similar number of controls. The researchers found no statistically significant difference between the patients and controls with regard to any of the 14 genes identified as "candidates" by previous studies (Sanders et al., 2008).

In a way, these results should not be surprising. If schizophrenia depended on a single gene, it would be hard for that gene to remain in 1% of the population, given the natural selection pressures against it. People with schizophrenia die younger than other people, on the average (Saha, Chant, & McGrath, 2007), and have fewer than the average number of children. Furthermore, their brothers and sisters do not compensate by having more children than average (Haukka, Suvisaari, & Lönnqvist, 2003). Any gene for schizophrenia should decline rapidly in prevalence, it seems.

Well, if schizophrenia has a genetic basis but we can't find any gene with a consistent link, and any gene that does pertain to schizophrenia can't be passed down through many generations, what is going on? Researchers have suggested that many cases of schizophrenia arise from new mutations. Ordinarily, it would be ridiculous to suggest that a condition affecting 1% of the population could depend on new mutations. Mutations just aren't that common. But suppose—quite realistically—that proper brain development depends on hundreds of genes. A mutation in one gene is a rare event, but a mutation in any of two or three hundred is not so rare. Researchers examined the chromosomes of people with and without schizophrenia and found genetic *microdeletions* and *microduplications* (i.e., elimination or duplication of parts of a gene) in 15% of the people with schizophrenia compared to 5% of the control group (Walsh et al., 2008). Those microdeletions and microduplications were distributed over a great many genes. Thus, the hypothesis is that a new mutation in any of a large number of genes disrupts brain development and increases the probability of schizophrenia. Some of the affected people will pass on their genes, but as fast as natural selection weeds out those genes, new mutations replace them.

One observation supporting this idea is that schizophrenia is somewhat more common among children of older fathers (Byrne, Agerbo, Ewald, Eaton, & Mortensen, 2003; Malaspina et al., 2002). Women are born with all the eggs they will ever have, but men continue making new sperm throughout life, and the possibility of mutations accumulates over time.

We need not assume that all cases of schizophrenia have a genetic basis. Most likely, some cases do, whereas others depend on prenatal environment or other influences on brain development.

STOP & CHECK

14. The fact that adopted children who develop schizophrenia usually have biological relatives with schizophrenia implies a probable genetic basis. What other interpretation is possible?

15. Does the hypothesis of new mutations conflict with the results showing that an aberrant form of the gene *DISC1* is often linked to schizophrenia?

ANSWERS

14. A biological mother can influence her child's development through prenatal environment as well as genetics. **15.** No. Although mutations in many genes can, according to the hypothesis, lead to schizophrenia, the *DISC1* gene could be one where the mutation is more certain to cause schizophrenia.

The Neurodevelopmental Hypothesis

According to the **neurodevelopmental hypothesis** now popular among researchers, schizophrenia is based on abnormalities in the prenatal (before birth) or neonatal (newborn) development of the nervous system, which lead to subtle abnormalities of brain anatomy and major abnormalities in behavior (Weinberger, 1996). The abnormalities could result from genetics or from troubles during prenatal development, birth, or early postnatal development. The hypothesis holds that environmental influences later in life aggravate the symptoms but are not the ultimate cause.

The supporting evidence is that (a) several kinds of prenatal or neonatal difficulties are linked to later schizophrenia; (b) people with schizophrenia have minor brain abnormalities that apparently originate early in life; and (c) it is plausible that abnormalities of early development could impair behavior in adulthood.

Prenatal and Neonatal Environment

The risk of schizophrenia is elevated among people who had problems that could have affected their brain development, including poor nutrition of the mother during pregnancy, premature birth, low birth weight, and complications during delivery (Ballon, Dean, & Cadenhead, 2007). The risk is also elevated if the mother was exposed to extreme stress, such as the sudden death of a close relative, early in her pregnancy (Khashau et al., 2008). None of these influences by itself accounts for many cases of schizophrenia (Cannon, Jones, & Murray, 2002). Schizophrenia has also been linked to head injuries in early childhood (AbdelMalik, Husted, Chow, & Bassett, 2003), although we do not know whether the head injuries led to schizophrenia or early symptoms of schizophrenia increased the risk of head injuries.

If a mother is Rh-negative and her baby is Rh-positive, the baby's Rh-positive blood factor may trigger an immunological rejection by the mother. The response is weak with the woman's first Rh-positive baby but stronger in later pregnancies, and it is more intense with boy than girl babies. Second- and later-born boy babies with Rh incompatibility have an increased risk of hearing deficits, mental retardation, and several other problems, and about twice the usual probability of schizophrenia (Hollister, Laing, & Mednick, 1996).

Another suggestion of prenatal influences comes from the **season-of-birth effect:** the tendency for people born in winter to have a slightly (5% to 8%) greater risk of developing schizophrenia than people born at other times of the year. This tendency is particularly pronounced in latitudes far from the equator (Davies, Welham, Chant, Torrey, & McGrath, 2003; Torrey, Miller, et al., 1997).

What might account for this effect? One possibility is complications of delivery or early nutrition (Jablensky et al., 2005). Another is viral infection. Influenza and other viral epidemics are most common in the fall. Therefore, the reasoning goes, many pregnant women become infected in the fall with a virus that impairs a crucial stage of brain development in a baby who will be born in the winter. A virus that affects the mother does not cross the placenta into the fetus's brain, but the mother's cytokines do cross, and excessive cytokines can impair brain development (Zuckerman, Rehavi, Nachman, & Weiner, 2003). The mother's infection also causes a fever, which can damage the fetal brain. A fever of just 38.5°C (101°F) slows the division of fetal neurons (Laburn, 1996). (Exercise during pregnancy does *not* overheat the abdomen and is not dangerous to the fetus. Hot baths and saunas may be risky, however.) When mice are infected with influenza during pregnancy, their offspring develop a number of behavioral abnormalities, including deficient exploration and deficient social reactions to other mice (Shi, Fatemi, Sidwell, & Patterson, 2003).

Researchers examined the records of tens of thousands of people in Scotland, England, and Denmark over several decades. They found increased schizophrenia rates among people born 2 to 3 months after major influenza epidemics, such as the one in the autumn of 1957 (Adams, Kendell, Hare, & Munk-Jørgensen, 1993). Other studies retrieved blood samples that hospitals had taken from pregnant women and stored for decades. Researchers found increased incidence of influenza virus among the mothers whose children eventually developed schizophrenia (A. S. Brown et al., 2004; Buka et al., 2001). Researchers also found increased rates of schizophrenia in the offspring of mothers who had rubella (German measles), herpes, and other infections during pregnancy (A. S. Brown et al., 2001; Buka et al., 2008).

Certain infections during childhood may also increase the risk of schizophrenia. The parasite *Toxoplasma gondii* (discussed also in Chapter 12 in the context of anxiety and the amygdala) reproduces only in cats, but it can infect humans and other species also. If it infects the brain of an infant or child, it impairs brain development and leads to memory disorder, hallucinations, and delusions (Torrey & Yolken, 2005). People who develop schizophrenia in adulthood are more likely than other people to have had a pet cat in childhood (Torrey, Rawlings, & Yolken, 2000). Blood tests have found antibodies to the Toxoplasma parasite in a higher percentage of people with schizophrenia than in the general population (Leweke et al., 2004; Niebuhr et al., 2008; Yolken et al., 2001). Several of the drugs that relieve schizophrenia block replication of the Toxoplasma parasite (Jones-Brando, Torrey, & Yolken, 2003).

In short, some cases of schizophrenia may develop as a result of infections. This mechanism is an alternative or supplement to genetics and other influences. Evidently, a variety of influences can lead to similar outcomes in schizophrenia.

STOP & CHECK

16. What does the season-of-birth effect suggest about a possible cause of schizophrenia?

ANSWER

16. The season-of-birth effect is the observation that schizophrenia is slightly more common among people who were born in the winter. One interpretation is that influenza or other infections of the mother during the fall lead to impaired brain development of a baby born in the winter.

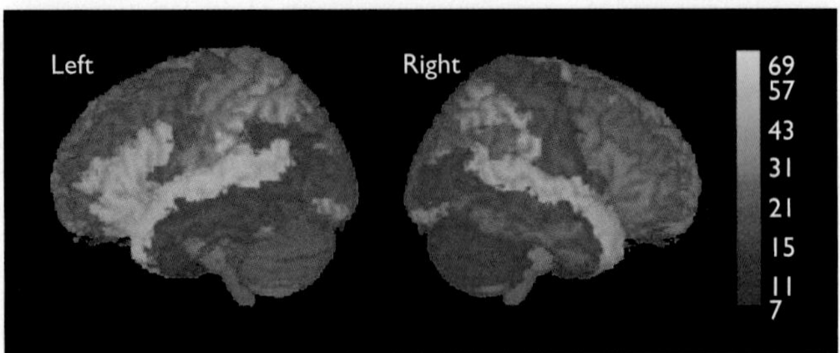

Figure 15.13 Cortical areas showing decreased volume in patients with schizophrenia
Areas marked in yellow showed decreased volume in the largest percentage of studies. Those in various shades of red showed decreases in fewer studies. *(From "Regional deficits in brain volume in schizophrenia: A meta-analysis of voxel based morphometry studies," by R. Honea, T. J. Crow, D. Passingham, and C. E. Mackay,* American Journal of Psychiatry, 162, *2005. Reprinted with permission from the American Journal of Psychiatry, Copyright (2005) American Psychiatric Association.)*

Mild Brain Abnormalities

In accord with the neurodevelopmental hypothesis, some (though not all) people with schizophrenia show mild abnormalities of brain anatomy. The abnormalities are small and variable. Although many studies report brain abnormalities in schizophrenia, they disagree about the location of those abnormalities. Figure 15.13 summarizes 15 studies, including a total of 390 people with schizophrenia. Brain areas marked in yellow showed decreased volume in the most studies, those in various shades of red showed decreases in fewer studies, and those in gray appeared normal in all studies (Honea, Crow, Passingham, & Mackay, 2005). Note that the strongest deficits were in the left temporal and frontal areas of the cortex. Note also that most cortical areas showed mild abnormalities in at least one or two studies. The thalamus, which is in the interior of the brain and therefore not shown in Figure 15.13, is also smaller than average for people with schizophrenia (Harms et al., 2007).

Furthermore, the ventricles (fluid-filled spaces within the brain) are larger than normal in people with schizophrenia (Wolkin et al., 1998; Wright et al., 2000) (Figure 15.14). The increased size of the ventricles implies less space taken by brain cells. Signs of brain damage are especially common in people who had a history of complications during pregnancy or at birth (Stefanis et al., 1999).

The areas with consistent signs of abnormality include some that mature slowly, such as the dorsolateral prefrontal cortex (Berman, Torrey, Daniel, & Weinberger, 1992; Fletcher et al., 1998; Gur, Cowell, et al., 2000). As you might predict, people with schizophrenia perform poorly at working memory tasks, which depend on the prefrontal cortex (Goldberg, Weinberger, Berman, Pliskin, & Podd, 1987; Spindler, Sullivan, Menon, Lim, & Pfefferbaum, 1997). Most patients with schizophrenia show deficits of memory and attention similar to those of people with damage to the temporal or prefrontal cortex (Park, Holzman,

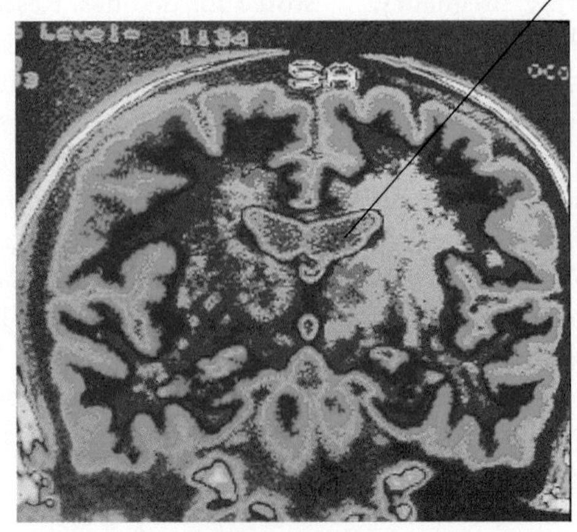

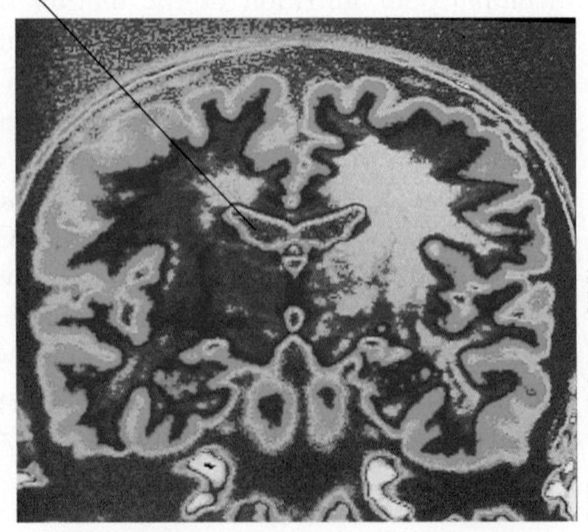

Figure 15.14 Coronal sections for identical twins
The twin on the left has schizophrenia; the twin on the right does not. The ventricles (near the center of each brain) are larger in the twin with schizophrenia.

E. F. Torrey & M. F. Casanova/NIMH

METHODS 15.1

The Wisconsin Card Sorting Task

Neuropsychologists use many behavioral tests to measure the functioning of the prefrontal cortex. One is the Wisconsin Card Sorting Task. A person is handed a shuffled deck of cards that differ in number, color, and shape of objects—for example, three red circles, five blue triangles, four green squares. First the person is asked to sort them by one rule, such as separate them by color. Then the rule changes, and the person is supposed to sort them by a different rule, such as number. Shifting to a new rule requires suppressing the old one and evokes activity in the prefrontal cortex (Konishi et al., 1998). People with damage to the prefrontal cortex can sort by whichever rule is first, but then they have trouble shifting to a new rule. People with schizophrenia have the same difficulty. (So do children.)

& Goldman-Rakic, 1995) (Methods 15.1). At a microscopic level, the most reliable finding is that cell bodies are smaller than normal, especially in the hippocampus and prefrontal cortex (Pierri, Volk, Auh, Sampson, & Lewis, 2001; Rajkowska, Selemon, & Goldman-Rakic, 1998; Selemon, Rajkowska, & Goldman-Rakic, 1995; Weinberger, 1999).

Lateralization also differs from the normal pattern. In most people, the left hemisphere is slightly larger than the right, especially in the planum temporale of the temporal lobe, but in people with schizophrenia, the right planum temporale is equal or larger (Kasai et al., 2003; Kwon et al., 1999). People with schizophrenia have lower than normal overall activity in the left hemisphere (Gur & Chin, 1999) and are more likely than other people to be left-handed (Satz & Green, 1999). All these results suggest a subtle change in brain development.

The reasons behind the brain abnormalities are not certain. Most researchers have been careful to limit their studies to patients with schizophrenia who have never taken, or who have not recently taken, antipsychotic drugs, so the deficits are not a result of treatments for schizophrenia. However, many people with schizophrenia are heavy users of alcohol, marijuana, and other drugs, and it is likely that some of the brain abnormalities are results of excessive drug use (Rais et al., 2008; Sullivan et al., 2000).

The results are inconsistent as to whether the brain damage associated with schizophrenia is *progressive*—that is, whether it increases over time. The brain damage associated with Parkinson's disease, Huntington's disease, and Alzheimer's disease gets worse as the person ages. Brain abnormalities are found in young people shortly after a diagnosis of schizophrenia (Lieberman et al., 2001), and many studies find that the brain abnormalities are no greater in older patients (Andreasen et al., 1990; Censits, Ragland, Gur, & Gur, 1997; Russell, Munro, Jones, Hemsley, & Murray, 1997; Selemon et al., 1995). However, other studies show a moderate degree of increased brain loss as patients age (Cahn et al., 2002; Hulshoff et al., 2001; Mathalon, Sullivan, Lim, & Pfefferbaum, 2001; Rais et al., 2008). Nevertheless, the brains of people with schizophrenia do not show the signs that accompany neuron death—proliferation of glia cells and activation of the genes responsible for repair after injury (Arnold, 2000; Benes, 1995; K. O. Lim et al., 1998). Possibly, the neurons are shrinking without dying. We shall need more research.

Early Development and Later Psychopathology

One question may have struck you. How can we reconcile the idea of abnormalities in early development with the fact that the disorder is usually diagnosed after age 20? The time course may not be so puzzling as it seems at first (Weinberger, 1996). Most of the people who develop schizophrenia in adulthood had shown other problems since childhood, including deficits in attention, memory, and impulse control (Keshavan, Diwadkar, Montrose, Rajarethinam, & Sweeney, 2005). Furthermore, the prefrontal cortex, an area that shows consistent signs of deficit in schizophrenia, matures slowly, not reaching full competence until the late teens (D. A. Lewis, 1997; Sowell, Thompson, Holmes, Jernigan, & Toga, 1999). In one study, researchers damaged this area in infant monkeys and tested the monkeys later. At age 1 year, the monkeys' behavior was nearly normal, but by age 2 years, it had deteriorated markedly (P. S. Goldman, 1971, 1976). That is, the effects of the brain damage actually grew worse over age. Presumably, the effects of brain damage were minimal at age 1 year because the dorsolateral prefrontal cortex doesn't do much at that age anyway. Later, when it should begin assuming important functions, the damage begins to make a difference (Figure 15.15).

Patricia S. Goldman-Rakic
The question of how the brain organizes its subsystems to produce integrated behavior is perhaps the most challenging that can be posed.

The neurodevelopmental hypothesis is plausible but not firmly established. Additional research will be necessary to test the hypothesis more thoroughly.

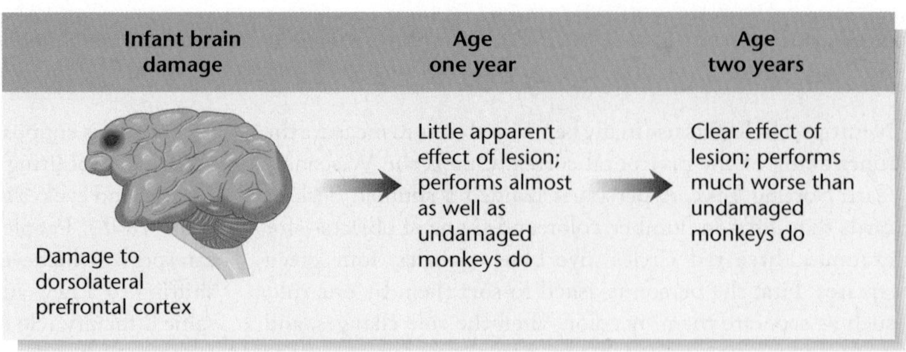

Figure 15.15 Delayed effects of brain damage in infant monkeys After damage to the dorsolateral prefrontal cortex, monkeys are unimpaired at age 1 year but impaired later, when this area ordinarily matures. Researchers speculate that similar damage in humans might produce behavioral deficits not apparent until adulthood. *(Based on P. S. Goldman, 1976)*

STOP & CHECK

17. If schizophrenia is due to abnormal brain development, why do behavioral symptoms not become apparent until later in life?

ANSWER

17. Parts of the prefrontal cortex are very slow to reach maturity; therefore, early disruption of this area's development might not produce any symptoms early in life, when the prefrontal cortex is contributing little anyway.

Treatments

Before antipsychotic drugs became available in the mid-1950s, most people with schizophrenia were confined to mental hospitals, where they deteriorated for the rest of their lives. Today, the mental hospitals are far less crowded because of drugs and outpatient treatment. The nature of those drugs should provide us with some clue about the causes of schizophrenia.

Antipsychotic Drugs and Dopamine

In the 1950s, psychiatrists discovered that **chlorpromazine** (trade name Thorazine) relieves the positive symptoms of schizophrenia for most, though not all, patients. The typical course is that someone begins to experience relief after 2 or 3 weeks on the drug and must continue taking it indefinitely lest the symptoms return. Researchers later discovered other **antipsychotic,** or **neuroleptic, drugs** (drugs that tend to relieve schizophrenia and similar conditions) in two chemical families: the **phenothiazines** (FEE-no-THI-uh-zeens), which include chlorpromazine, and the **butyrophenones** (BYOO-tir-oh-FEE-noans), which include haloperidol (trade name Haldol). As Figure 15.16 illustrates, each of these drugs blocks dopamine synapses. For each drug, researchers determined the mean dose prescribed for patients with schizophrenia (displayed along the horizontal axis) and the amount needed to block dopamine receptors (displayed along the vertical axis). As the figure shows, the drugs that are most effective against schizophrenia (and therefore used in the smallest doses) are the most effective at blocking dopamine receptors (Seeman, Lee, Chau-Wong, & Wong, 1976).

That finding inspired the **dopamine hypothesis of schizophrenia,** which holds that schizophrenia results from excess activity at dopamine synapses in certain brain areas. Although the concentration of dopamine in the brain is no higher than normal, the turnover is elevated, especially in the basal ganglia (Kumakura et al., 2007). That is, neurons release dopamine at a faster than average rate and synthesize more to replace the molecules that cannot be reabsorbed.

Further support for the dopamine hypothesis comes from the fact that large, repeated doses of amphetamine, methamphetamine, and cocaine induce **substance-induced psychotic disorder,** characterized by hallucinations and delusions (positive symptoms of schizophrenia). Each of these drugs increases or prolongs the activity at dopamine synapses. LSD also produces psychotic symptoms. LSD is best known for its effects on serotonin synapses, but it also increases activity at dopamine synapses.

Researchers set out to measure the number of dopamine receptors occupied at a given moment. They used a radioactively labeled drug, IBZM, that binds to dopamine type D_2 receptors. Because IBZM binds only to receptors that dopamine did not already bind, measuring the radioactivity counts the number of vacant dopamine receptors. Then the researchers used a second drug, AMPT, that blocks all synthesis of dopamine and again used IBZM to count the number of vacant D_2 receptors. Because AMPT had prevented production of dopamine, *all* D_2 receptors should be vacant at this time, so the researchers got a count of the total. Then they subtracted the first count from the second count, yielding the number of D_2 receptors occupied by dopamine at the first count:

- First count: IBZM binds to all D_2 receptors not already attached to dopamine.
- Second count: IBZM binds to all D_2 receptors (because AMPT eliminated production of dopamine).
- Second count minus first count equals the number of D_2 receptors bound to dopamine at the first count.

The researchers found that people with schizophrenia had about twice as many D_2 receptors occupied as normal (Abi-Dargham et al., 2000). Another study found that among patients with schizophrenia, the greater the amount of D_2 receptor activation in the prefrontal cortex, the greater the cognitive impairment (Meyer-Lindenberg et al., 2002).

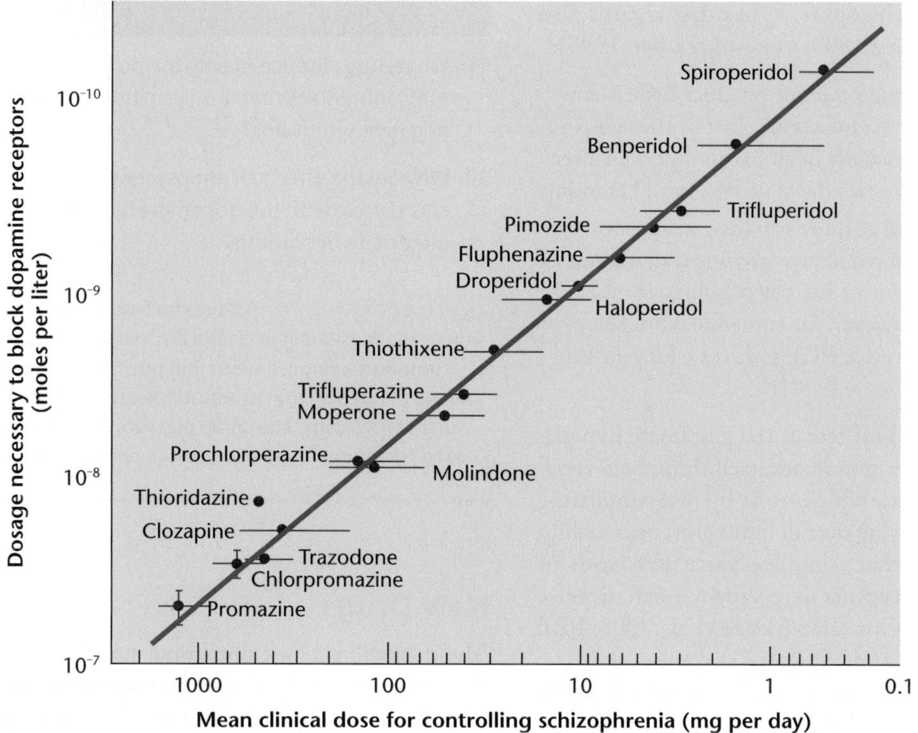

Figure 15.16 Dopamine-blocking effects of antipsychotic drugs
Drugs are arranged along the horizontal axis in terms of the average daily dose prescribed for patients with schizophrenia. (Horizontal lines indicate common ranges.) *Larger* doses are to the left and *smaller* doses are to the right so that *more effective* drugs are to the right. Along the vertical axis is a measurement of the amount of each drug required to achieve a certain degree of blockage of postsynaptic dopamine receptors. Again, *larger* doses are toward the bottom and *smaller* doses are toward the top so that the drugs on top are *more effective. (From "Antipsychotic drug doses and neuroleptic/dopamine receptors," by P. Seeman, T. Lee, M. Chau-Wong, and K. Wong,* Nature, 261, *1976, pp. 717–719. Copyright © 1976 Macmillan Magazines Limited. Reprinted by permission of Nature and Phillip Seeman.)*

However, the dopamine hypothesis has limitations and problems. Recall from the depression module that antidepressant drugs alter the activity at dopamine and serotonin synapses quickly but improve mood only after 2 or 3 weeks of treatment. The same is true for schizophrenia: Antipsychotic drugs block dopamine synapses within minutes, but their effects on behavior build up gradually over 2 or 3 weeks. So blocking dopamine synapses may be an important first step for an antipsychotic drug, but clearly, something else must develop later.

STOP & CHECK

18. How fast do antipsychotic drugs affect dopamine synapses? How fast do they alter behavior?

ANSWER

18. They block dopamine synaptic activity within minutes. They take 2 or more weeks to alter behavior.

Role of Glutamate

According to the **glutamate hypothesis of schizophrenia,** the problem relates in part to deficient activity at glutamate synapses, especially in the prefrontal cortex. In many brain areas, dopamine inhibits glutamate release, or glutamate stimulates neurons that inhibit dopamine release. Therefore, increased dopamine would produce the same effects as decreased glutamate. The antipsychotic effects of drugs that block dopamine are compatible with either the excess-dopamine hypothesis or the deficient-glutamate hypothesis.

Schizophrenia is associated with lower than normal release of glutamate and fewer than normal receptors in the prefrontal cortex and hippocampus (Akbarian et al., 1995; Ibrahim et al., 2000; Tsai et al., 1995). Further support for this hypothesis comes from the effects of **phencyclidine (PCP)** ("angel dust"), a drug that inhibits the NMDA glutamate receptors. At low doses, it produces intoxication and slurred speech. At larger doses, it produces both positive and negative symptoms of schizophrenia, including hallucinations, thought disorder, loss of emotions, and memory loss. PCP is an interesting model for schizophrenia in other regards also (Farber, Newcomer, & Olney, 1999; Olney & Farber, 1995):

- PCP and the related drug *ketamine* produce little if any psychotic response in preadolescents. Just as the symptoms of schizophrenia usually begin to emerge well after puberty, so do the psychotic effects of PCP and ketamine.
- LSD, amphetamine, and cocaine produce temporary schizophrenic symptoms in almost anyone that are not much worse in people with a history of schizophrenia than in anyone else. However, for someone who has recovered from schizophrenia, PCP induces a long-lasting relapse.

It might seem that the best test of the glutamate hypothesis would be to administer glutamate itself. However, recall from Chapter 5 that strokes kill neurons by overstimulating glutamate synapses. Increasing overall brain glutamate would be risky. However, drugs that stimulate particular kinds of metabotropic glutamate receptors have shown much promise in treating schizophrenia (González-Maeso et al., 2008; Patil et al., 2007).

Furthermore, the NMDA glutamate receptor has a primary site that is activated by glutamate and a secondary site that is activated by glycine (Figure 15.17). Glycine by itself does not activate the receptor, but it increases the effectiveness of glutamate. Thus, an increase in glycine can increase the activity at NMDA synapses without overstimulating glutamate throughout the brain. Although glycine is not an effective antipsychotic drug by itself, it increases the effects of other antipsychotic drugs, especially with regard to negative symptoms (Heresco-Levy et al., 1999; Heresco-Levy & Javitt, 2004). Studies on laboratory mice found that extra glycine decreases the behavioral responses to phencyclidine (Yee et al., 2006).

Schizophrenia is a complex disorder. Probably both dopamine and glutamate play important roles, perhaps to different degrees in different individuals.

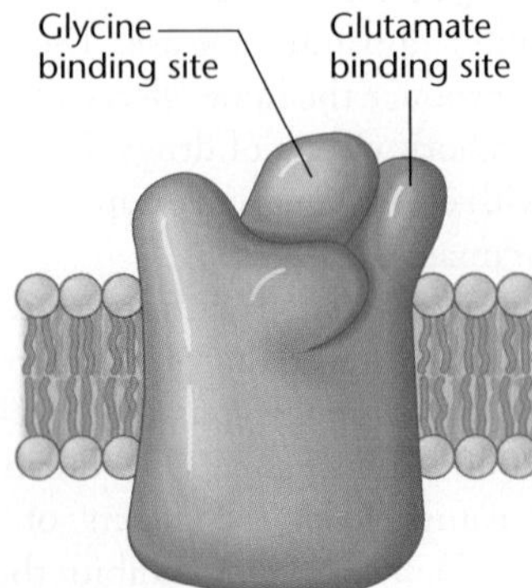

Figure 15.17 An NMDA glutamate receptor
NMDA glutamate receptors have a primary binding site for glutamate and a secondary binding site for glycine. Glycine increases the effect of glutamate.

STOP & CHECK

19. What drugs induce mainly the positive symptoms of schizophrenia? What drug can induce both positive and negative symptoms?

20. Why are the effects of antipsychotic drugs equally compatible with the dopamine hypothesis and the glutamate hypothesis?

ANSWERS

19. Amphetamine, cocaine, and LSD in large doses induce positive symptoms, such as hallucinations and delusions. Phencyclidine induces both positive and negative symptoms. **20.** Dopamine inhibits glutamate cells in many areas, and glutamate stimulates neurons that inhibit dopamine. Therefore, the effects of increasing dopamine are similar to those of decreasing glutamate.

New Drugs

The drugs that block dopamine synapses produce their benefits by acting on neurons in the **mesolimbocortical system,** a set of neurons that project from the midbrain tegmentum to the limbic system. However, the drugs also block dopamine neurons in the *mesostriatal system,* which projects to the basal ganglia (Figure 15.18). The result is **tardive dyskinesia** (TARD-eev dis-kih-NEE-zhee-uh), characterized by tremors and other involuntary movements that develop gradually and to varying degrees among different patients (Kiriakakis, Bhatia, Quinn, & Marsden, 1998).

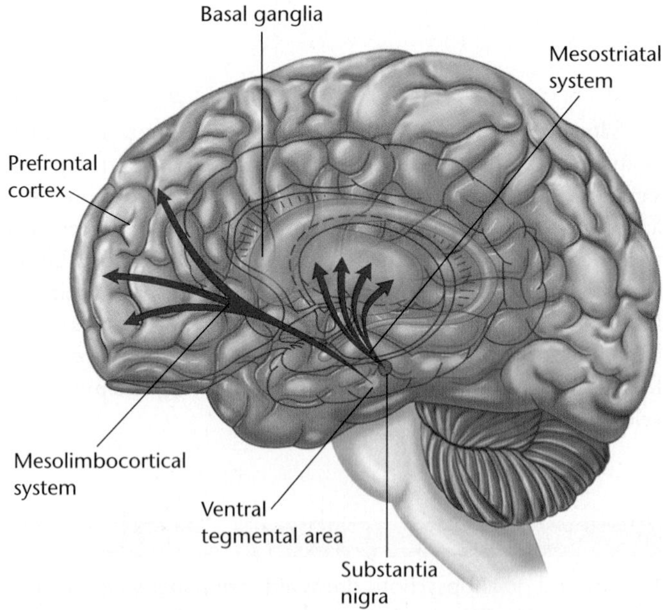

Figure 15.18 Two major dopamine pathways
Overactivity of the mesolimbocortical system is linked to the symptoms of schizophrenia. The path to the basal ganglia is associated with tardive dyskinesia, a movement disorder. *(Adapted from Valzelli, 1980)*

Once tardive dyskinesia emerges, it can last long after someone quits the drug (Kiriakakis et al., 1998). Consequently, the best strategy is to prevent it from starting. Certain new drugs called **second-generation antipsychotics,** or atypical antipsychotics, alleviate schizophrenia without producing movement problems (Figure 15.19). The most common of these drugs are clozapine, amisulpride, risperidone, olanzapine, and aripiprazole. They are more effective than the older drugs at treating the negative symptoms of schizophrenia, and they are now used more widely (J. M. Davis, Chen, & Glick, 2003; Edlinger et al., 2005). Clozapine is generally considered the most effective antipsychotic (McEvoy et al., 2006). Unfortunately, the side effects are serious, including impairment of the immune system. One study found that although the second-generation antipsychotics relieve the symptoms of schizophrenia more effectively than the older drugs, they do not improve overall quality of life more than the older drugs (P. B. Jones, 2006).

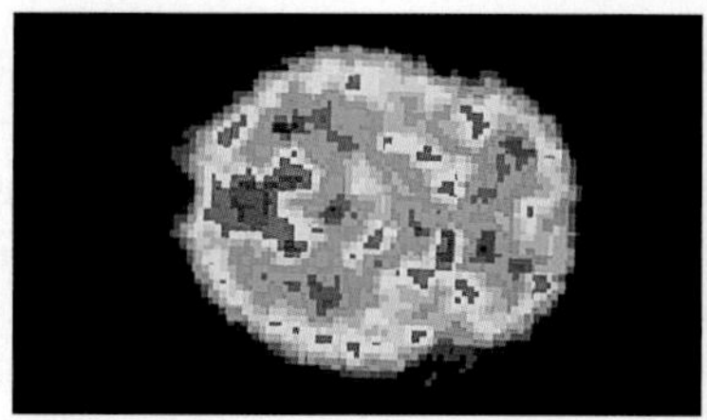
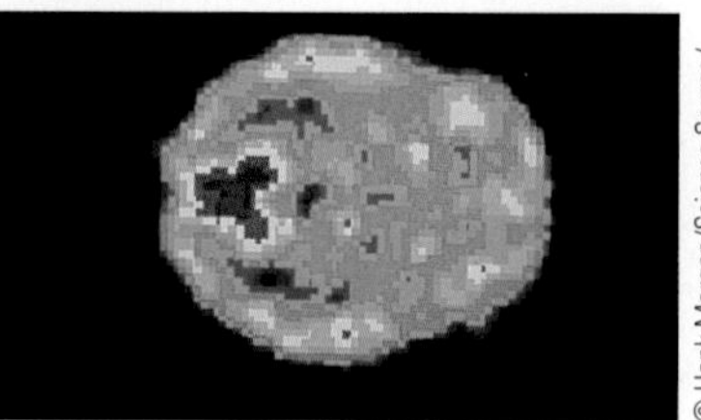
© Hank Morgan/Science Source/Photo Researchers

Figure 15.19 PET scans of a patient with schizophrenia
These PET scans of a patient with schizophrenia **(a)** taking clozapine and **(b)** during a period off the drug demonstrate that clozapine increases brain activity in many brain areas. (Red indicates the highest activity, followed by yellow, green, and blue.)

Compared to drugs like haloperidol, the second-generation antipsychotics have less effect on dopamine type D_2 receptors but more strongly antagonize serotonin type 5-HT_2 receptors (Kapur et al., 2000; Meltzer, Matsubara, & Lee, 1989; Mrzljak et al., 1996; Roth, Willins, Kristiansen, & Kroeze, 1999). They also increase the release of glutamate (Melone et al., 2001). In short, schizophrenia is neither a one-gene disorder nor a one-neurotransmitter disorder.

MODULE 15.2 IN CLOSING

The Fascination of Schizophrenia

A good mystery novel presents an array of clues, mixing important clues with irrelevant information, and the reader's challenge is to figure out who committed the crime. Schizophrenia research is similar, except that we want to know *what* is to blame, not *who*. As with a mystery novel, we have to sort through an enormous number of clues and false leads, looking for a pattern. One difference is that, unlike the reader of a mystery novel, we have the option of collecting new evidence of our own.

I trust it is clear to you that researchers have not yet solved the mystery of schizophrenia. But it should also be clear that they have made progress. The hypotheses of today are not fully satisfactory, but they have much more support than the hypotheses of decades past. The future looks exciting for this area of research.

SUMMARY

1. Positive symptoms of schizophrenia (behaviors that are not present in most other people) include hallucinations, delusions, inappropriate emotions, bizarre behaviors, and thought disorder. 449
2. Negative symptoms (normal behaviors absent that should be present) include deficits of social interaction, emotional expression, and speech. 449
3. Studies of twins and adopted children imply a genetic predisposition to schizophrenia. However, the adoption studies do not distinguish between the roles of genetics and prenatal environment. 451
4. So far, researchers have not located any gene that is strongly linked with schizophrenia in general. A promising hypothesis is that schizophrenia results from new mutations in any of the hundreds of genes that are important for brain development. 452
5. According to the neurodevelopmental hypothesis, either genes or difficulties early in life impair brain development in ways that lead to behavioral abnormalities beginning in early adulthood. 453
6. The probability of schizophrenia is slightly higher than average for those who were subjected to difficulties before or at the time of birth or during early infancy. Childhood infection with a parasite that invades the brain is another possibility. 453

Continued

7. Some people with schizophrenia show mild abnormalities of early brain development, especially in the temporal and frontal lobes. Results have been inconsistent as to whether the brain damage continues to increase after the first diagnosis. **454**
8. Parts of the prefrontal cortex are very slow to mature. It is plausible that early disruption of those areas might produce behavioral symptoms that become manifest as schizophrenia in young adults. **455**
9. According to the dopamine hypothesis, schizophrenia is due to excess dopamine activity. Drugs that block dopamine synapses reduce the positive symptoms of schizophrenia, and drugs that increase dopamine activity induce the positive symptoms. **456**
10. According to the glutamate hypothesis, the problem is deficient glutamate activity. Phencyclidine, which blocks NMDA glutamate synapses, produces both positive and negative symptoms of schizophrenia, especially in people predisposed to schizophrenia. **457**
11. Prolonged use of antipsychotic drugs may produce tardive dyskinesia, a movement disorder. Second-generation antipsychotic drugs relieve both positive and negative symptoms without producing tardive dyskinesia. Most psychiatrists now prescribe second-generation drugs. **458**

KEY TERMS

Terms are defined in the module on the page number indicated. They're also presented in alphabetical order with definitions in the book's Subject Index/Glossary. Interactive flashcards, audio reviews, and crossword puzzles are among the online resources available to help you learn these terms and the concepts they represent.

acute **449**
antipsychotic (neuroleptic) drugs **456**
butyrophenones **456**
chlorpromazine **456**
chronic **449**
concordance **451**
delusions **449**
differential diagnosis **450**
DISC1 **452**
dopamine hypothesis of schizophrenia **456**
glutamate hypothesis of schizophrenia **457**
hallucinations **449**
mesolimbocortical system **458**
negative symptoms **449**
neurodevelopmental hypothesis **453**
phencyclidine (PCP) **457**
phenothiazines **456**
positive symptoms **449**
schizophrenia **449**
season-of-birth effect **453**
second-generation antipsychotics **459**
substance-induced psychotic disorder **456**
tardive dyskinesia **458**

THOUGHT QUESTIONS

1. How might denervation supersensitivity (discussed in Chapter 5) help explain tardive dyskinesia?
2. Why might it be difficult to find effective drugs for someone who suffers from both depression and schizophrenia?

CHAPTER 15 Exploration and Study

In addition to the study materials provided at the end of each module, you may supplement your review of this chapter by using one or more of the book's electronic resources, which include its companion Website, interactive Cengage Learning eBook, Exploring Biological Psychology CD-ROM, and CengageNOW. Brief descriptions of these resources follow. For more information, visit **www.cengage.com/psychology/kalat.**

The book's companion Website, accessible through the author Web page indicated above, provides a wide range of study resources such as an interactive glossary, flashcards, tutorial quizzes, updated Web links, and Try It Yourself activities, as well as a limited selection of the short videos and animated explanations of concepts available for this chapter.

Exploring Biological Psychology

The Exploring Biological Psychology CD-ROM contains videos, animations, and Try It Yourself activities. These activities—as well as many that are new to this edition—are also available in the text's fully interactive, media-rich Cengage Learning eBook,* which gives you the opportunity to experience biological psychology in an even greater interactive and multimedia environment. The Cengage Learning eBook also includes highlighting and note-taking features and an audio glossary. For this chapter, the Cengage Learning eBook includes the following interactive explorations:

Major Depressive Disorder Patient Barbara
Antidepressant Drugs
Magnetic Stimulation of the Brain
Bipolar Disorder Patient Mary
Bipolar Disorder Patient Etta

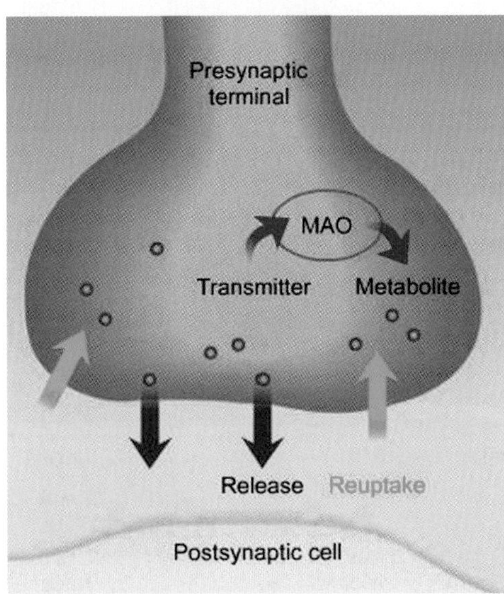

The animation *Antidepressant Drugs* describes mechanisms of MAOIs, tricyclics, and SSRIs.

CENGAGENOW™ is an easy-to-use resource that helps you study in less time to get the grade you want. An online study system, CengageNOW* gives you the option of taking a diagnostic pretest for each chapter. The system uses the results of each pretest to create personalized chapter study plans for you. The Personalized Study Plans

- help you save study time by identifying areas on which you should concentrate and give you one-click access to corresponding pages of the interactive Cengage Learning eBook;
- provide interactive exercises and study tools to help you fully understand chapter concepts; and
- include a posttest for you to take to confirm that you are ready to move on to the next chapter.

Suggestions for Further Exploration

The book's companion Website includes a list of suggested articles available through InfoTrac College Edition for this chapter. You may also want to explore some of the following books and Websites. The text's companion Website provides live, updated links to the sites listed below.

Books

Andreasen, N. C. (2001). *Brave new brain.* New York: Oxford University Press. Excellent discussion of biological research on psychiatric disorders by one of the leading researchers dealing with schizophrenia.

Charney, D. S., & Nestler, E. J. (Eds.). (2004). *Neurobiology of mental illness* (2nd ed.). New York: Oxford University Press. An extensive reference work on all types of psychiatric disorders.

Websites

Society for Light Treatment and Biological Rhythms
http://www.sltbr.org/

Schizophrenia Information and Support
http://www.schizophrenia.com/

* Requires a Cengage Learning eResources account. Visit **www.cengage.com/login** to register or login.

Brief, Basic Chemistry

MAIN IDEAS

1. All matter is composed of a limited number of elements that combine in endless ways.
2. Atoms, the component parts of an element, consist of protons, neutrons, and electrons. Most atoms can gain or lose electrons, or share them with other atoms.
3. The chemistry of life is predominantly the chemistry of carbon compounds.

Introduction

To understand certain aspects of biological psychology, particularly the action potential and the molecular mechanisms of synaptic transmission, you need to know a little about chemistry. If you have taken a high school or college course and remember the material reasonably well, you should have no trouble with the chemistry in this text. If your knowledge of chemistry is pretty hazy, this appendix will help. (If you plan to take other courses in biological psychology, you should study as much biology and chemistry as possible.)

Elements and Compounds

If you look around, you will see an enormous variety of materials—dirt, water, wood, plastic, metal, cloth, glass, your own body. Every object is composed of a small number of basic building blocks. If a piece of wood catches fire, it breaks down into ashes, gases, and water vapor. The same is true of your body. An investigator could take those ashes, gases, and water and break them down by chemical and electrical means into carbon, oxygen, hydrogen, nitrogen, and a few other materials. Eventually, however, the investigator arrives at a set of materials that cannot be broken down further: Pure carbon or pure oxygen, for example, cannot be converted into anything simpler, at least not by ordinary chemical means. (High-power bombardment with subatomic particles is another story.) The matter we see is composed of **elements** (materials that cannot be broken down into other materials) and **compounds** (materials made up by combining elements).

Chemists have found 92 elements in nature, and they have constructed more in the laboratory. (Actually, one of the 92—technetium—is so rare as to be virtually unknown in nature.) Figure A.1, the periodic table, lists each of these elements. Of these, only a few are important for life on Earth. Table A.1 shows the elements commonly found in the human body.

Note that each element has a one- or two-letter abbreviation, such as O for oxygen, H for hydrogen, and Ca for calcium. These are internationally accepted symbols that facilitate communication among chemists who speak different languages. For example, element number 19 is called potassium in English, potassio in Italian, kālijs in Latvian, and draslík in Czech. But chemists in all countries use the symbol K (from *kalium,* the Latin word for "potassium"). Similarly, the symbol for sodium is Na (from *natrium,* the Latin word for "sodium"), and the symbol for iron is Fe (from the Latin word *ferrum*).

A compound is represented by the symbols for the elements that compose it. For example, NaCl stands for sodium chloride (common table salt). H_2O, the symbol for water, in-

TABLE A.1 The Elements That Compose Almost All of the Human Body

Element	Symbol	Percentage by Weight in Human Body
Oxygen	O	65
Carbon	C	18
Hydrogen	H	10
Nitrogen	N	3
Calcium	Ca	2
Phosphorus	P	1.1
Potassium	K	0.35
Sulfur	S	0.25
Sodium	Na	0.15
Chlorine	Cl	0.15
Magnesium	Mg	0.05
Iron	Fe	Trace
Copper	Cu	Trace
Iodine	I	Trace
Fluorine	F	Trace
Manganese	Mn	Trace
Zinc	Zn	Trace
Selenium	Se	Trace
Molybdenum	Mo	Trace

Periodic Table of the Elements

Alkali Metals (group 1) · Alkaline Earth Metals (group 2) · Transition Elements (groups 3–12) · Halogens (group 17) · Noble Gases (group 18)

Period	1 IA	2 IIA	3 IIIB	4 IVB	5 VB	6 VIB	7 VIIB	8 VIIIB	9 VIIIB	10 VIIIB	11 IB	12 IIB	13 IIIA	14 IVA	15 VA	16 VIA	17 VIIA	18 VIIA
1	1 **H** hydrogen 1.008																	2 **He** helium 4.003
2	3 **Li** lithium 6.941	4 **Be** beryllium 9.012											5 **B** boron 10.81	6 **C** carbon 12.011	7 **N** nitrogen 14.007	8 **O** oxygen 16.0	9 **F** fluorine 18.999	10 **Ne** neon 20.179
3	11 **Na** sodium 22.99	12 **Mg** magnesium 24.305											13 **Al** aluminum 26.982	14 **Si** silicon 28.085	15 **P** phosphorous 30.974	16 **S** sulfur 32.060	17 **Cl** chlorine 35.453	18 **Ar** argon 39.948
4	19 **K** potassium 39.098	20 **Ca** calcium 40.08	21 **Sc** scandium 44.955	22 **Ti** titanium 47.90	23 **V** vanadium 50.941	24 **Cr** chromium 51.996	25 **Mn** manganese 54.938	26 **Fe** iron 55.847	27 **Co** cobalt 58.933	28 **Ni** nickel 58.70	29 **Cu** copper 63.546	30 **Zn** zinc 65.38	31 **Ga** gallium 69.72	32 **Ge** germanium 72.59	33 **As** arsenic 74.922	34 **Se** selenium 78.96	35 **Br** bromine 79.904	36 **Kr** krypton 83.80
5	37 **Rb** rubidium 85.468	38 **Sr** strontium 87.62	39 **Y** yttrium 88.906	40 **Zr** zirconium 91.22	41 **Nb** niobium 92.906	42 **Mo** molybdenum 95.940	43 **Tc** technetium (97)	44 **Ru** ruthenium 101.07	45 **Rh** rhodium 102.905	46 **Pd** palladium 106.40	47 **Ag** silver 107.868	48 **Cd** cadmium 112.41	49 **In** indium 114.82	50 **Sn** tin 118.69	51 **Sb** antimony 121.75	52 **Te** tellurium 127.60	53 **I** iodine 126.904	54 **Xe** xenon 131.30
6	55 **Cs** cesium 132.905	56 **Ba** barium 137.33	57 **La** lanthanum 138.906 †	72 **Hf** hafnium 178.49	73 **Ta** tantalum 180.948	74 **W** tungsten 183.85	75 **Re** rhenium 186.207	76 **Os** osmium 190.20	77 **Ir** iridum 192.22	78 **Pt** platinum 195.09	79 **Au** gold 196.967	80 **Hg** mercury 200.59	81 **Tl** thallium 204.37	82 **Pb** lead 207.20	83 **Bi** bismuth 208.980	84 **Po** polonium (209)	85 **At** astatine (210)	86 **Rn** radon (222)
7	87 **Fr** francium (223)	88 **Ra** radium 226.025	89 **Ac** actinium (227) ‡	104 **Rf** rutherfordium (261)	105 **Db** dubnium (262)	106 **Sg** seaborgium (266)	107 **Bh** bohrium (264)	108 **Hs** hassium (269)	109 **Mt** meitnerium (268)	110 **Ds** darmstadtium (271)	111 **Rg** roentgenium (272)	112 **Uub** ununbium (285)	113 **Uut** ununtrium (284)	114 **Uuq** ununquadium (289)	115 **Uup** ununpentium (288)	116 **Uuh** ununhexium (292)	117 **Uus** ununseptium (?)	118 **Uuo** ununoctium (?)

Inner Transition Elements

† Lanthanides 6	58 **Ce** cerium 140.12	59 **Pr** praseodymium 140.908	60 **Nd** neodymium 144.24	61 **Pm** prometheum (145)	62 **Sm** samarium 150.40	63 **Eu** europium 151.96	64 **Gd** gadolinium 157.25	65 **Tb** terbium 158.925	66 **Dy** dysprosium 162.50	67 **Ho** holmium 164.93	68 **Er** erbium 167.26	69 **Tm** thulium 168.934	70 **Yb** ytterbium 173.04	71 **Lu** lutetium 174.97
‡ Actinides 7	90 **Th** thorium 232.038	91 **Pa** protactinium 231.036	92 **U** uranium 238.029	93 **Np** neptunium (237)	94 **Pu** plutonium (244)	95 **Am** americium (243)	96 **Cm** curium (247)	97 **Bk** berkelium (247)	98 **Cf** californium (251)	99 **Es** einsteinium (254)	100 **Fm** fermium (257)	101 **Md** mendelevium (258)	102 **No** nobelium (255)	103 **Lr** lawrencium (260)

Key

- atomic number — 1
- symbol of element — H
- element name — hydrogen
- atomic weight — 1.008

Figure A.1 The periodic table of chemistry
It is called "periodic" because certain properties show up at periodic intervals. For example, the column from lithium down consists of metals that readily form salts. The column at the far right consists of gases that do not readily form compounds. Elements 112–118 have only tentative names and symbols.

dicates that water consists of two parts of hydrogen and one part of oxygen.

Atoms and Molecules

A block of iron can be chopped finer and finer until it is divided into tiny pieces that cannot be broken down any further. These pieces are called **atoms.** Every element is composed of atoms. A compound, such as water, can also be divided into tinier and tinier pieces. The smallest possible piece of a compound is called a **molecule.** A molecule of water can be further decomposed into two atoms of hydrogen and one atom of oxygen, but when that happens the compound is broken and is no longer water. A molecule is the smallest piece of a compound that retains the properties of the compound.

An atom is composed of subatomic particles, including protons, neutrons, and electrons. A proton has a positive electrical charge, a neutron has a neutral charge, and an electron has a negative charge. The nucleus of an atom—its center—contains one or more protons plus a number of neutrons. Electrons are found in the space around the nucleus. Because an atom has the same number of protons as electrons, the electrical charges balance out. (Ions, which we will soon consider, have an imbalance of positive and negative charges.)

The difference between one element and another is in the number of protons in the nucleus of the atom. Hydrogen has just one proton, for example, and oxygen has eight. The number of protons is the **atomic number** of the element; in the periodic table it is recorded at the top of the square for each element. The number at the bottom is the element's **atomic weight,** which indicates the weight of an atom relative to the weight of one proton. A proton has a weight of one unit, a neutron has a weight just trivially greater than one, and an electron has a weight just trivially greater than zero. The atomic weight of the element is the number of protons in the atom plus the average number of neutrons. For example, most hydrogen atoms have one proton and no neutrons; a few atoms per thousand have one or two neutrons, giving an average atomic weight of 1.008. Sodium ions have 11 protons; most also have 12 neutrons, and the atomic weight is slightly less than 23. (Can you figure out the number of neutrons in the average potassium atom? Refer to Figure A.1.)

Ions and Chemical Bonds

An atom that has gained or lost one or more electrons is called an **ion.** For example, if sodium and chloride come together, the sodium atoms readily lose one electron each and the chloride atoms gain one each. The result is a set of positively charged sodium ions (indicated Na^+) and negatively charged chloride ions (Cl^-). Potassium atoms, like sodium atoms, tend to lose an electron and to become positively charged ions (K^+); calcium ions tend to lose two electrons and gain a double positive charge (Ca^{++}).

Because positive charges attract negative charges, sodium ions attract chloride ions. When dry, sodium and chloride form a crystal structure, as Figure A.2 shows. (In water solution, the two kinds of ions move about haphazardly, occasionally attracting one another but then pulling apart.) The attraction of positive ions for negative ions forms an **ionic bond.** In other cases, instead of transferring an electron from one atom to another, some pairs of atoms share electrons with each other, forming a **covalent bond.** For example, two hydrogen atoms bind, as shown in Figure A.3, and two hydrogen atoms bind with an oxygen atom, as shown in Figure A.4. Atoms that are attached by a covalent bond cannot move independently of one another.

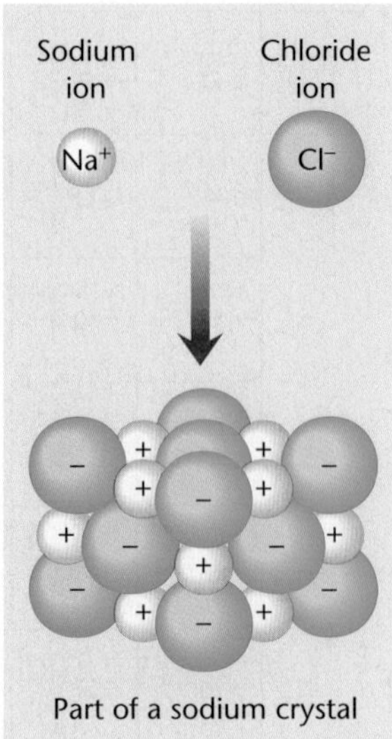

Figure A.2 The crystal structure of sodium chloride
Each sodium ion is surrounded by chloride ions, and each chloride ion is surrounded by sodium ions; no ion is bound to any other single ion in particular.

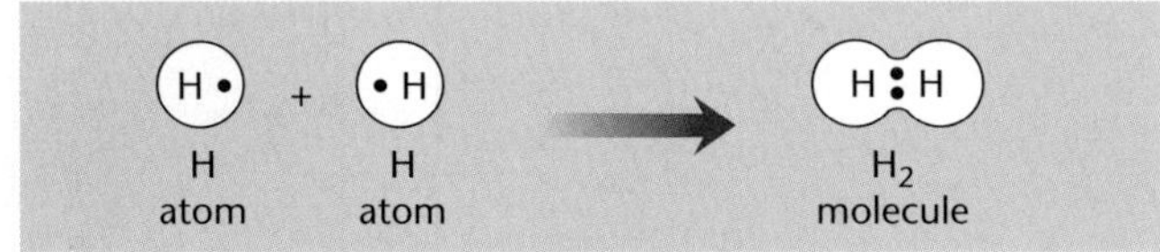

Figure A.3 Structure of a hydrogen molecule
A hydrogen atom has one electron; in the compound the two atoms share the two electrons equally.

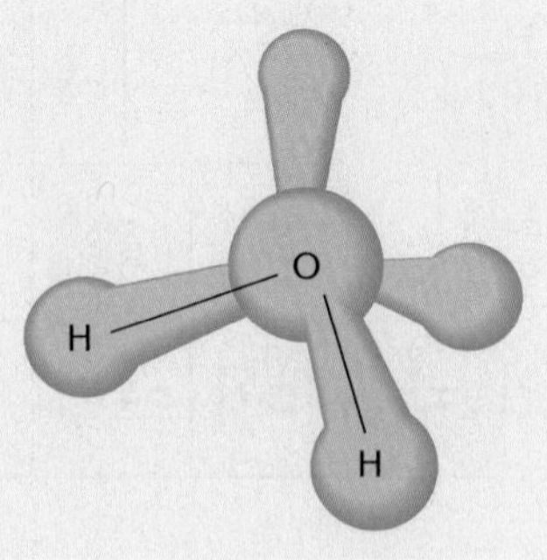

Figure A.4 Structure of a water molecule
The oxygen atom shares a pair of electrons with each hydrogen atom. Oxygen holds the electrons more tightly, making the oxygen part of the molecule more negatively charged than the hydrogen part of the molecule.

Reactions of Carbon Atoms

Living organisms depend on the enormously versatile compounds of carbon. Because of the importance of these compounds for life, the chemistry of carbon is known as organic chemistry.

Carbon atoms form covalent bonds with hydrogen, oxygen, and a number of other elements. They also form covalent bonds with other carbon atoms. Two carbon atoms may share from one to three pairs of electrons. Such bonds can be indicated as follows:

C—C Two atoms share one pair of electrons.
C=C Two atoms share two pairs of electrons.
C≡C Two atoms share three pairs of electrons.

Each carbon atom ordinarily forms four covalent bonds, either with other carbon atoms, with hydrogen atoms, or with other atoms. Many biologically important compounds include long chains of carbon compounds linked to one another, such as:

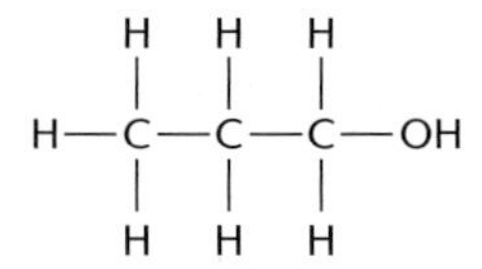

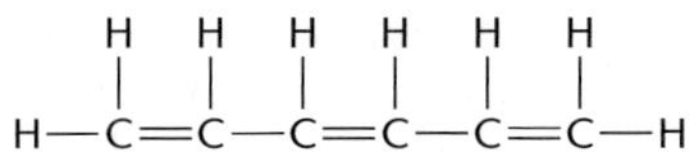

```
   H  H  H              H  H  H  H  H  H
   |  |  |              |  |  |  |  |  |
H—C—C—C—OH         H—C=C—C=C—C=C—H
   |  |  |
   H  H  H
```

Note that each carbon atom has a total of four bonds, counting each double bond as two. In some molecules, the carbon chain loops around to form a ring:

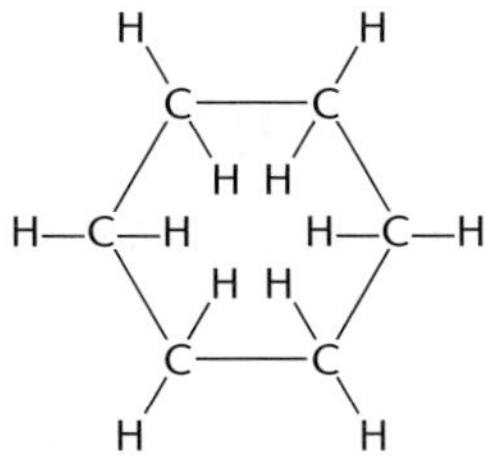

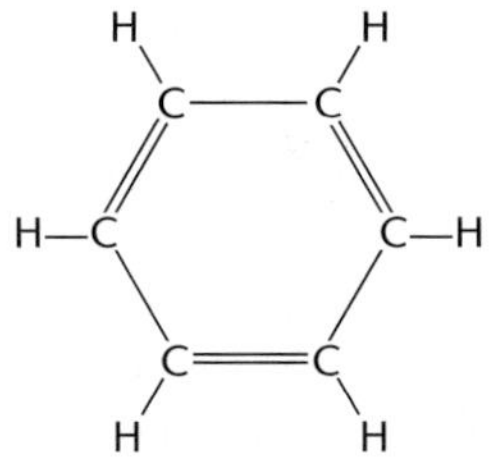

Ringed structures are common in organic chemistry. To simplify the diagrams chemists often omit the hydrogen atoms. You can simply assume that each carbon atom in the diagram has four covalent bonds and that all the bonds not shown are with hydrogen atoms. To further simplify the diagrams, chemists often omit the carbon atoms themselves, showing only the carbon-to-carbon bonds. For example, the two molecules shown in the previous diagram might be rendered as follows:

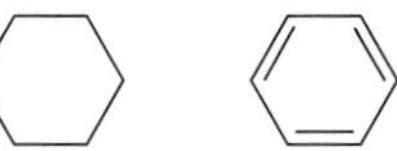

If a particular carbon atom has a bond with some atom other than hydrogen, the diagram shows the exception. For example, in each of the two molecules diagrammed below, one carbon has a bond with an oxygen atom, which in turn has a bond with a hydrogen atom. All the bonds that are not shown are carbon–hydrogen bonds.

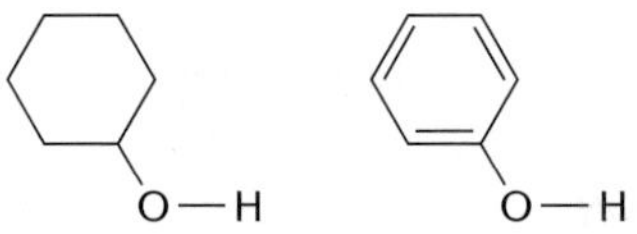

Figure A.5 illustrates some carbon compounds that are critical for animal life. Purines and pyrimidines form the central structure of DNA and RNA, the chemicals responsible for heredity. Proteins, fats, and carbohydrates are the primary types of fuel that the body uses. Figure A.6 displays the chemical structures of seven neurotransmitters that are extensively discussed in this text.

Chemical Reactions in the Body

A living organism is an immensely complicated, coordinated set of chemical reactions. Life requires that the rate of each reaction be carefully regulated. In many cases one reaction

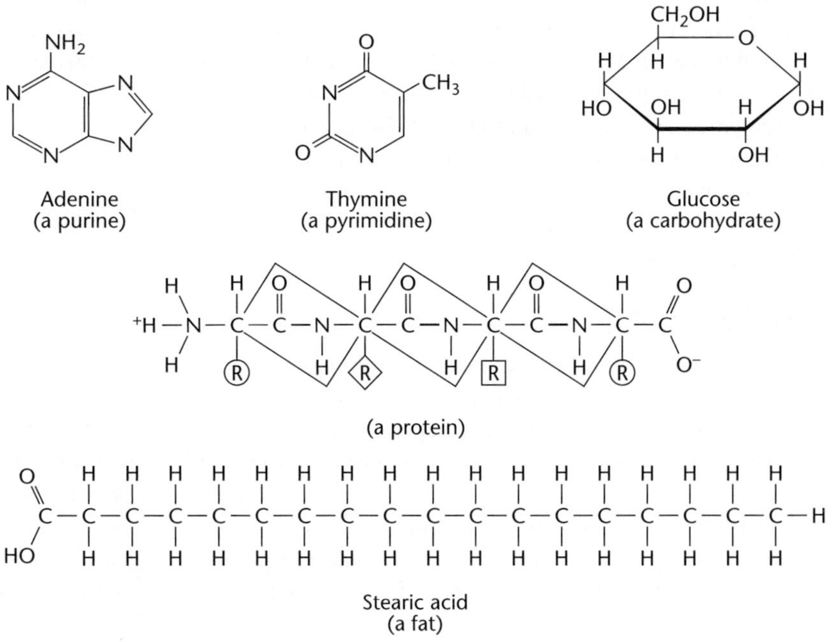

Figure A.5 Structures of some important biological molecules
The R in the protein represents a point of attachment for various chains that differ from one amino acid to another. Actual proteins are much longer than the chemical shown here.

Adenine (a purine)

Thymine (a pyrimidine)

Glucose (a carbohydrate)

(a protein)

Stearic acid (a fat)

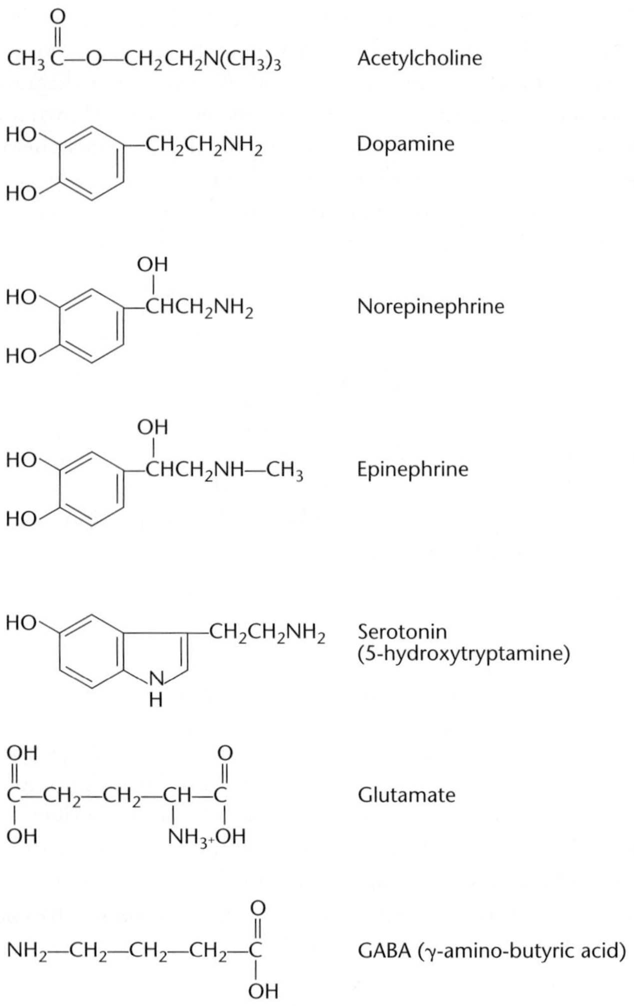

Acetylcholine

Dopamine

Norepinephrine

Epinephrine

Serotonin (5-hydroxytryptamine)

Glutamate

GABA (γ-amino-butyric acid)

Figure A.6 Chemical structures of seven abundant neurotransmitters

produces a chemical that enters into another reaction, which produces another chemical that enters into another reaction, and so forth. If any one of those reactions is too rapid compared to the others, the chemical it produces will accumulate to possibly harmful levels. If a reaction is too slow, it will not produce enough product and the next reaction will be stalled.

Enzymes are proteins that control the rate of chemical reactions. Each reaction is controlled by a particular enzyme. Enzymes are a type of catalyst. A catalyst is any chemical that facilitates a reaction among other chemicals, without being altered itself in the process.

The Role of ATP

The body relies on **ATP (adenosine triphosphate)** as its main way of sending energy where it is needed (Figure A.7). Much of the energy derived from food goes into forming ATP molecules that eventually provide energy for the muscles and other body parts.

ATP consists of adenosine bound to ribose and three phosphate groups (PO_3). Phosphates form high-energy covalent bonds. That is, a large amount of energy is required to form the bonds and a large amount of energy is released when they break. ATP can break off one or two of its three phosphates to provide energy.

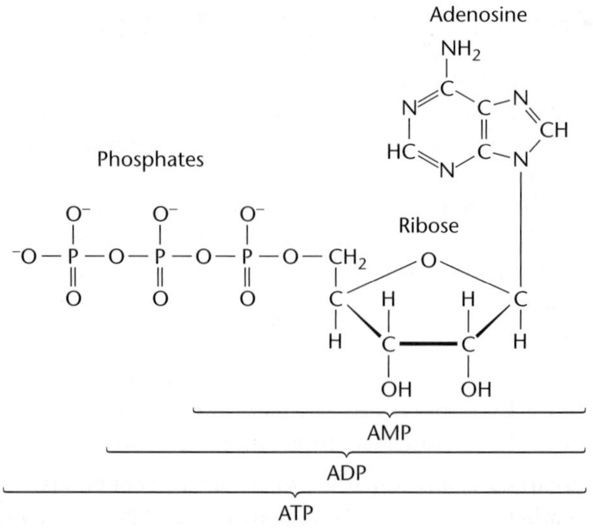

Adenosine

Phosphates

Ribose

AMP

ADP

ATP

Figure A.7 ATP, composed of adenosine, ribose, and three phosphates

ATP can lose one phosphate group to form ADP (adenosine diphosphate) and then lose another one to form AMP (adenosine monophosphate). Each time it breaks off a phosphate group, it releases energy.

Summary

1. Matter is composed of 92 elements that combine to form an endless variety of compounds. **462**
2. An atom is the smallest piece of an element. A molecule is the smallest piece of a compound that maintains the properties of the compound. **464**
3. The atoms of some elements can gain or lose an electron, thus becoming ions. Positively charged ions attract negatively charged ions, forming an ionic bond. In some cases two or more atoms may share electrons, thus forming a covalent bond. **464**
4. The principal carrier of energy in the body is a chemical called ATP. **466**

Terms

atom 464
atomic number 464
atomic weight 464
ATP (adenosine triphosphate) 466
compound 462
covalent bond 464
element 462
enzyme 466
ion 464
ionic bond 464
molecule 464

Society for Neuroscience Policies on the Use of Animals and Human Subjects in Neuroscience Research

Policy on the Use of Animals in Neuroscience Research

The Policy on the Use of Animals in Neuroscience Research affects a number of the Society's functions that involve making decisions about animal research conducted by individual members. These include the scheduling of scientific presentations at the Annual Meeting, the review and publication of original research papers in *The Journal of Neuroscience*, and the defense of members whose ethical use of animals in research is questioned by antivivisectionists. The responsibility for implementing the policy in each of these areas will rest with the relevant administrative body (Program Committee, Publications Committee, Editorial Board, and Committee on Animals in Research, respectively), in consultation with Council.

Introduction

The Society for Neuroscience, as a professional society for basic and clinical researchers in neuroscience, endorses and supports the appropriate and responsible use of animals as experimental subjects. Knowledge generated by neuroscience research on animals has led to important advances in the understanding of diseases and disorders that affect the nervous system and in the development of better treatments that reduce suffering in humans and animals. This knowledge also makes a critical contribution to our understanding of ourselves, the complexities of our brains, and what makes us human. Continued progress in understanding how the brain works and further advances in treating and curing disorders of the nervous system require investigation of complex functions at all levels in the living nervous system. Because no adequate alternatives exist, much of this research must be done on animal subjects. The Society takes the position that neuroscientists have an obligation to contribute to this progress through responsible and humane research on animals.

Several functions of the Society are related to the use of animals in research. A number of these involve decisions about research conducted by individual members of the Society, including the scheduling of scientific presentations at the Annual Meeting, the review and publication of original research papers in *The Journal of Neuroscience*, and the defense of members whose ethical use of animals in research is questioned by antivivisectionists. Each of these functions, by establishing explicit support of the Society for the research of individual members, defines a relationship between the Society and its members. The purpose of this document is to outline the policy that guides that relationship. Compliance with the following policy will be an important factor in determining the suitability of research for presentation at the Annual Meeting or for publication in *The Journal of Neuroscience*, and in situations where the Society is asked to provide public and active support for a member whose use of animals in research has been questioned.

General Policy

Neuroscience research uses complicated, often invasive methods, each of which is associated with different problems, risks, and specific technical considerations. An experimental method that would be deemed inappropriate for one kind of research may be the method of choice for another kind of research. It is therefore impossible for the Society to define specific policies and procedures for the care and use of all research animals and for the design and conduct of every neuroscience experiment.

The U.S. *Public Health Service Policy on Humane Care and Use of Laboratory Animals* (PHS Policy) and the *Guide for the Care and Use of Laboratory Animals* (the Guide) describe a set of general policies and procedures designed to ensure the humane and appropriate use of live vertebrate animals in all forms of biomedical research. The Society finds the policies and procedures set forth in the PHS Policy and the Guide to be both necessary and sufficient to ensure a high standard of animal care and use and adopts them as its official "Policy on the Use of Animals in Neuroscience Research" (Society Policy). All Society members are expected to conduct their animal research in compliance with the Society Policy and are required to verify that they have done so when submitting abstracts for presentation at the Annual Meeting or manuscripts for publication in *The Journal of Neuroscience*. Adherence to the Society Policy is also an important step toward receiving help from the Society in responding to questions about a member's use of animals in research. A complete description of the Society's policy and procedures for defending members whose research comes under attack is given in the Society's *Handbook for the Use of Animals in Neuroscience Research*.

Local Committee Review

An important element of the Society Policy is the establishment of a local committee that is charged with reviewing and approving all proposed animal care and use procedures. In addition to scientists experienced in research involving animals and a veterinarian, the membership of this local committee should include an individual who is not affiliated with the member's institution in any other way. In reviewing a proposed use of animals, the committee should evaluate the adequacy of institutional policies, animal husbandry, veterinary care, and the physical plant. Specific attention should be paid to proposed procedures for animal procurement, quarantine and stabilization, separation by species, disease diagnosis and treatment, anesthesia and analgesia, surgery and postsurgical care, and euthanasia. The review committee also should ensure that procedures involving live vertebrate animals are designed and performed with due consideration of their relevance to human or animal health, the advancement of knowledge, or the good of society. This review and approval of a member's use of live vertebrate animals in research by a local committee is an essential component of the Society Policy. Assistance in developing appropriate animal care and use procedures and establishing a local review committee can be obtained from the documents listed here and from the Society.

Other Laws, Regulations, and Policies

In addition to complying with the policy described above, Regular Members (i.e., North American residents) of the Society must also adhere to all relevant national, state, or local laws and/or regulations that govern their use of animals in neuroscience research. Thus, U.S. members must observe the U.S. Animal Welfare Act (as amended in 1985) and its implementing regulations from the U.S. Department of Agriculture. Canadian members must abide by the *Guide to the Care and Use of Experimental Animals*, and members in Mexico must comply with the *Reglamento de la Ley General de Salud en Materia de Investigacion para la Salud* of the Secretaria de Salud (published on Jan. 6, 1987). Similarly, in addition to complying with the laws and regulations of their home countries, Foreign Members of the Society should adhere to the official Society Policy outlined here.

Recommended References

"Anesthesia and paralysis in experimental animals." *Visual Neuroscience*, 1:421–426. 1984.

The Biomedical Investigator's Handbook for Researchers Using Animal Models. 1987. Foundation for Biomedical Research, 818 Connecticut Ave., N.W., Suite 303, Washington, D.C. 20006.

Guide for the Care and Use of Laboratory Animals, 7th edition. 1996. NRC (National Research Council), Institute of Laboratory Animal Resources, National Academy of Sciences, 2101 Constitution Ave., N.W., Washington, D.C. 20418.

Guide to the Care and Use of Experimental Animals, 2nd edition, vol. 1. 1993. Canadian Council on Animal Care, 350 Albert St., Suite 315, Ottawa, Ontario, Canada K1R 1B1.

Handbook for the Use of Animals in Neuroscience Research. 1991. Society for Neuroscience, 11 Dupont Circle, N.W., Suite 500, Washington, D.C. 20036.

OPRR Public Health Service Policy on Humane Care and Use of Laboratory Animals (revised Sept. 1986). Office for Protection from Research Risks, NIH, 6100 Executive Blvd., Suite 3B01-MSC 7507, Rockville, MD 20892-7507.

Preparation and Maintenance of Higher Mammals During Neuroscience Experiments. Report of a National Institutes of Health Workshop. NIH Publication No. 91-3207, March 1991. National Eye Institute, Bldg. 31, Rm. 6A47, Bethesda, MD 20892.

Seventh Title of the Regulations of the General Law of Health, Regarding Health Research. In: *Laws and Codes of Mexico*. Published in the Porrua Collection, 12th updated edition, pp. 430–431. Porrua Publishers, Mexico, 1995.

The following principles, based largely on the PHS *Policy on Humane Care and Use of Laboratory Animals*, can be a useful guide in the design and implementation of experimental procedures involving laboratory animals.

Animals selected for a procedure should be of an appropriate species and quality and the minimum number required to obtain valid results.

Proper use of animals, including the avoidance or minimization of discomfort, distress, and pain, when consistent with sound scientific practices, is imperative.

Procedures with animals that may cause more than momentary or slight pain or distress should be performed with appropriate sedation, analgesia, or anesthesia. Surgical or other painful procedures should not be performed on unanesthetized animals paralyzed by chemical agents.

Postoperative care of animals shall be such as to minimize discomfort and pain and, in any case, shall be equivalent to accepted practices in schools of veterinary medicine.

Animals that would otherwise suffer severe or chronic pain or distress that cannot be relieved should be painlessly killed at the end of the procedure or, if appropriate, during the procedure. If the study requires the death of the animal, the animal must be killed in a humane manner.

Living conditions should be appropriate for the species and contribute to the animals' health and comfort. Normally, the housing, feeding, and care of all animals used for biomedical purposes must be directed by a veterinarian or other scientist trained and experienced in the proper care, handling, and use of the species being maintained or studied. In any case, appropriate veterinary care shall be provided.

Exceptions to these principles require careful consideration and should only be made by an appropriate review group such as an institutional animal care and use committee.

Policy on the Use of Human Subjects in Neuroscience Research

Experimental procedures involving human subjects must have been conducted in conformance with the policies and principles contained in the Federal Policy for the Protection of Human Subjects (United States Office of Science and Technology Policy) and in the Declaration of Helsinki. When publishing a paper in *The Journal of Neuroscience* or submitting an abstract for presentation at the Annual Meeting, authors must sign a statement of compliance with this policy.

Recommended References

Declaration of Helsinki. (Adopted in 1964 by the 18th World Medical Assembly in Helsinki, Finland, and revised by the 29th World Medical Assembly in Tokyo in 1975.) In: *The Main Issue in Bioethics Revised Edition.* Andrew C. Varga, Ed. New York: Paulist Press, 1984.

Federal Policy for the Protection of Human Subjects; Notices and Rules. *Federal Register.* Vol. 56, No. 117 (June 18, 1991), pp. 28002–28007.

http://www.apa.org/science/anguide.html
This Website presents the ethical guidelines adopted by the Anerican Psychological Association. They are largely similar to those of the Neuroscience Society.

References

Numbers in parentheses following entries indicate the chapter in which a reference is cited.

Abbar, M., Couret, P., Bellivier, F., Leboyer, M., Boulenger, J. P., Castelhau, D., et al. (2001). Suicide attempts and the tryptophan hydroxylase gene. *Molecular Psychiatry, 6,* 268–273. (12)

Abbott, N. J., Rönnback, L., & Hansson, E. (2006). Astrocyte-endothelial interactions at the blood-brain barrier. *Nature Reviews Neuroscience, 7,* 41–53. (2)

AbdelMalik, P., Husted, J, Chow, E. W. C., & Bassett, A. S. (2003). Childhood head injury and expression of schizophrenia in multiply affected families. *Archives of General Psychiatry, 60,* 231–236. (15)

Abercrombie, H. C., Kalin, N. H., Thurow, M. E., Rosenkranz, M. A., & Davidson, R. J. (2003). Cortisol variation in humans affects memory for emotionally laden and neutral information. *Behavioral Neuroscience, 117,* 505–516. (12)

Abi-Dargham, A., Rodenhiser, J., Printz, D., Zea-Ponce, Y., Gil, R., Kegeles, L. S., et al. (2000). Increased baseline occupancy of D_2 receptors by dopamine in schizophrenia. *Proceedings of the National Academy of Sciences, USA, 97,* 8104–8109. (15)

Abraham, N. M., Spors, H., Carleton, A., Margrie, T. W., Kuner, T., & Schaefer, A. T. (2004). Maintaining accuracy at the expense of speed: Stimulus similarity defines odor discrimination time in mice. *Neuron, 44,* 865–876. (7)

Abutalebi, J., Brambati, S. M., Annoni, J.-M., Moro, A., Cappa, S. F., & Perani, D. (2007). The neural cost of the auditory perception of language switches: An event-related functional magnetic resonance imaging study in bilinguals. *Journal of Neuroscience, 27,* 13762–13769. (14)

Accolla, A., Bathellier, B., Petersen, C. C. H., & Carleton, A. (2007). Differential spatial representation of taste modalities in the rat gustatory cortex. *Journal of Neuroscience, 27,* 1396–1404. (7)

Adamec, R. E., Stark-Adamec, C., & Livingston, K. E. (1980). The development of predatory aggression and defense in the domestic cat (*Felis catus*): 3. Effects on development of hunger between 180 and 365 days of age. *Behavioral and Neural Biology, 30,* 435–447. (12)

Adams, D. B., Gold, A. R., & Burt, A. D. (1978). Rise in female-initiated sexual activity at ovulation and its suppression by oral contraceptives. *New England Journal of Medicine, 299,* 1145–1150. (11)

Adams, R. B., Jr., Gordon, H. L., Baird, A. A., Ambady, N., & Kleck, R. E. (2003). Effects of gaze on amygdala sensitivity to anger and fear faces. *Science, 300,* 1536. (12)

Adams, R. B., Jr., & Kleck, R. E. (2005). Effects of direct and averted gaze on the perception of facially communicated emotion. *Emotion, 5,* 3–11. (12)

Adams, W., Kendell, R. E., Hare, E. H., & Munk-Jørgensen, P. (1993). Epidemiological evidence that maternal influenza contributes to the aetiology of schizophrenia. *British Journal of Psychiatry, 163,* 522–534. (15)

Addis, D. R., Wong, A. T., & Schacter, D. L. (2007). Remembering the past and imagining the future: Common and distinct neural substrates during event construction and elaboration. *Neuropsychologia, 45,* 1363–1377. (13)

Ader, R. (2001). Psychoneuroimmunology. *Current Directions in Psychological Science, 10,* 94–98. (12)

Adkins, E. K., & Adler, N. T. (1972). Hormonal control of behavior in the Japanese quail. *Journal of Comparative and Physiological Psychology, 81,* 27–36. (11)

Adler, E., Hoon, M. A., Mueller, K. L., Chandrashekar, J., Ryba, N. J. P., & Zuker, C. S. (2000). A novel family of mammalian taste receptors. *Cell, 100,* 693–702. (7)

Adolphs, R., Baron-Cohen, S., & Tranel, D. (2002). Impaired recognition of social emotions following amygdala damage. *Journal of Cognitive Neuroscience, 14,* 1264–1274. (12)

Adolphs, R., Damasio, H., & Tranel, D. (2002). Neural systems for recognition of emotional prosody: A 3-D lesion study. *Emotion, 2,* 23–51. (14)

Adolphs, R., Denburg, N. L., & Tranel, D. (2001). The amygdala's role in long-term declarative memory for gist and detail. *Behavioral Neuroscience, 115,* 983–992. (12)

Adolphs, R., Tranel, D., & Buchanan, T. W. (2005). Amygdala damage impairs emotional memory for gist but not details of complex stimuli. *Nature Neuroscience, 8,* 512–518. (12)

Adolphs, R., Tranel, D., & Damasio, A. R. (1998). The human amygdala in social judgment. *Nature, 393,* 470–474. (12)

Adolphs, R., Tranel, D., Damasio, H., & Damasio, A. (1994). Impaired recognition of emotion in facial expressions following bilateral damage to the human amygdala. *Nature, 372,* 669–672. (12)

Adolphs, R., Tranel, D., Damasio, H., & Damasio, A. (1995). Fear and the human amygdala. *Journal of Neuroscience, 15,* 5879–5891. (12)

Agarwal, N., Pacher, P., Tegeder, I., Amaya, F., Constantin, C. E., Brenner, G. J., et al. (2007). Cannabinoids mediate analgesia largely via peripheral type 1 cannabinoid receptors in nociceptors. *Nature Neuroscience, 10,* 870–879. (7)

Aggleton, J. P., Blindt, H. S., & Rawlins, J. N. P. (1989). Effects of amygdaloid and amygdaloid-hippocampal lesions on object recognition and spatial working memory in rats. *Behavioral Neuroscience, 103,* 962–974. (13)

Aglioti, S., Smania, N., Atzei, A., & Berlucchi, G. (1997). Spatio-temporal properties of the pattern of evoked phantom sensations in a left index amputee patient. *Behavioral Neuroscience, 111,* 867–872. (5)

Aglioti, S., Smania, N., & Peru, A. (1999). Frames of reference for mapping tactile stimuli in brain-damaged patients. *Journal of Cognitive Neuroscience, 11,* 67–79. (14)

Aglioti, S., Tassinari, G., Corballis, M. C., & Berlucchi, G. (2000). Incomplete gustatory localization as shown by analysis of taste discrimination after callosotomy. *Journal of Cognitive Neuroscience, 12,* 238–245. (7, 14)

Ahlskog, J. E., & Hoebel, B. G. (1973). Overeating and obesity from damage to a noradrenergic system in the brain. *Science, 182,* 166–169. (10)

Ahlskog, J. E., Randall, P. K., & Hoebel, B. G. (1975). Hypothalamic hyperphagia: Dissociation from hyperphagia following destruction of noradrenergic neurons. *Science, 190,* 399–401. (10)

Ahmed, I. I., Shryne, J. E., Gorski, R. A., Branch, B. J., & Taylor, A. N. (1991). Prenatal ethanol and the prepubertal sexually dimorphic nucleus of the preoptic area. *Physiology & Behavior, 49,* 427–432. (11)

Aimone, J. B., Wiles, J., & Gage, F. H. (2006). Potential role for adult neurogenesis in the encoding of time in new memories. *Nature Neuroscience, 9,* 723–727. (5)

Airaksinen, M. S., & Saarma, M. (2002). The GDNF family: Signalling, biological functions and therapeutic value. *Nature Reviews Neuroscience, 3,* 383–394. (5)

Airan, R. D., Meltzer, L. A., Roy, M., Gong, Y., Chen, H., & Deisseroth, K. (2007). High-speed imaging reveals neurophysiological links to behavior in an animal model of depression. *Science, 317,* 819–823. (15)

Akbarian, S., Kim, J. J., Potkin, S. G., Hagman, J. O., Tafazzoli, A., Bunney, W. E., Jr., et al. (1995). Gene expression for glutamic acid decarboxylase is reduced without loss of neurons in prefrontal cortex of schizophrenics. *Archives of General Psychiatry, 52,* 258–266. (15)

Åkerstedt, T. (2007). Altered sleep/wake patterns and mental performance. *Physiology & Behavior, 90,* 209–218. (9)

Albanese, M.-C., Duerden, E. G., Rainville, P., & Duncan, G. H. (2007). Memory traces of pain in human cortex. *Journal of Neuroscience, 27,* 4612–4620. (7)

Albouy, G., Sterpenich, V., Balteau, E., Vandewalle, G., Desseilles, M., Dang-Vu, T., et al. (2008). Both the hippocampus and striatum are involved in consolidation of motor sequence memory. *Neuron, 58,* 261–272. (13)

Albright, T. D., Jessell, T. M., Kandel, E. R., & Posner, M. I. (2001). Progress in the neural sciences in the century after Cajal (and the mysteries that remain). *Annals of the New York Academy of Sciences, 929,* 11–40. (2)

Aldrich, M. S. (1998). Diagnostic aspects of narcolepsy. *Neurology, 50*(Suppl. 1), S2–S7. (9)

Aleman, A., Kahn, R. S., & Selten, J. P. (2003). Sex differences in the risk of schizophrenia. *Archives of General Psychiatry, 60,* 565–571. (15)

Allen, J. S., Damasio, H., Grabowski, T. J., Bruss, J., & Zhang, W. (2003). Sexual dimorphism and asymmetries in the gray-white composition of the human cerebrum. *NeuroImage, 18,* 880–894. (4)

Allison, T., & Cicchetti, D. V. (1976). Sleep in mammals: Ecological and constitutional correlates. *Science, 194,* 732–734. (9)

Almeida, O. P., Yeap, B. B., Hankey, G. J., Jamrozik, K., & Flicker, L. (2008). Low free testosterone concentration as a potentially treatable cause of depressive symptoms in older men. *Archives of General Psychiatry, 65,* 283–289. (15)

Almli, C. R., Fisher, R. S., & Hill, D. L. (1979). Lateral hypothalamus destruction in infant rats produces consummatory deficits without sensory neglect or attenuated arousal. *Experimental Neurology, 66,* 146–157. (10)

Al-Rashid, R. A. (1971). Hypothalamic syndrome in acute childhood leukemia. *Clinical Pediatrics, 10,* 53–54. (10)

Altar, C. A., Laeng, P., Jurata, L. W., Brockman, J. A., Lemire, A., Bullard, J., et al. (2004). Electroconvulsive seizures regulate gene expression of distinct neurotrophic signaling pathways. *Journal of Neuroscience, 24,* 2667–2677. (15)

Altemus, M., & Debiec, J. (2007). Toward a new treatment for traumatic memories. In C. A. Read (Ed.), *Cerebrum 2007: Emerging ideas in brain science* (pp. 125–135). New York: Dana Press. (13)

Alves, E., Summavielle, T., Alves, C. J., Comesda-Silva, J., Barata, J. C., Fernandes, E., et al. (2007). Monoamine oxidase-B mediates ecstasy-induced neurotoxic effects to adolescent rat brain mitochondria. *Journal of Neuroscience, 27,* 10203–10210. (3)

Amateau, S. K., & McCarthy, M. M. (2004). Induction of PGE_2 by estradiol mediates developmental masculinization of sex behavior. *Nature Neuroscience, 7,* 643–650. (11)

Amedi, A., Floel, A., Knecht, S., Zohary, E., & Cohen, L. G. (2004). Transcranial magnetic stimulation of the occipital pole interferes with verbal processing in blind subjects. *Nature Neuroscience, 7,* 1266–1270. (5)

Amedi, A., Raz, N., Pianka, P., Malach, R., & Zohary, E. (2003). Early "visual" cortex activation correlates with superior verbal memory performance in the blind. *Nature Neuroscience, 6,* 758–766. (5)

American Psychiatric Association. (1994). *Diagnostic and statistical manual of mental disorders* (4th ed.). Washington, DC: Author. (15)

Amiry-Moghaddam, M., & Ottersen, O. P. (2003). The molecular basis of water transport in the brain. *Nature Reviews Neuroscience, 4,* 991–1001. (2)

Amsterdam, J. D., Winokur, A., Dyson, W., Herzog, S., Gonzalez, F., Rott, R., et al. (1985). Borna disease virus. *Archives of General Psychiatry, 42,* 1093–1096. (15)

Amunts, K., Armstrong, E., Malikovic, A., Hömke, L., Mohlberg, H., Schleicher, A., et al. (2007). Gender-specific left–right asymmetries in human visual cortex. *Journal of Neuroscience, 27,* 1356–1364. (4)

Andersen, J. L., Klitgaard, H., & Saltin, B. (1994). Myosin heavy chain isoforms in single fibres from m. vastus lateralis of sprinters: Influence of training. *Acta Physiologica Scandinavica, 151,* 135–142. (8)

Andersen, S. L., Arvanitogiannis, A., Pliakas, A. M., LeBlanc, C., & Carlezon, W. A., Jr. (2002). Altered responsiveness to cocaine in rats exposed to methylphenidate during development. *Nature Neuroscience, 5,* 13–14. (3)

Andersen, T. S., Tiippana, K., & Sams, M. (2004). Factors influencing audiovisual fission and fusion illusions. *Cognitive Brain Research, 21,* 301–308. (4)

Anderson, A. K., & Phelps, E. A. (2001). Lesions of the human amygdala impair enhanced perception of emotionally salient events. *Nature, 411,* 305–309. (12)

Anderson, A. K., & Phelps, E. A. (2002). Is the human amygdala critical for the subjective experience of emotion? Evidence of intact dispositional affect in patients with amygdala lesions. *Journal of Cognitive Neuroscience, 14,* 709–720. (12)

Anderson, S. W., Bechara, A., Damasio, H., Tranel, D., & Damasio, A. R. (1999). Impairment of social and moral behavior related to early damage in human prefrontal cortex. *Nature Neuroscience, 2,* 1032–1037. (12)

Andersson, K.-E. (2001). Pharmacology of penile erection. *Pharmacological Reviews, 53,* 417–450. (11)

Andreasen, N. C. (1988). Brain imaging: Applications in psychiatry. *Science, 239,* 1381–1388. (4)

Andreasen, N. C. (1999). A unitary model of schizophrenia. *Archives of General Psychiatry, 56,* 781–787. (15)

Andreasen, N. C., Arndt, S., Alliger, R., Miller, D., & Flaum, M. (1995). Symptoms of schizophrenia: Methods, meanings, and mechanisms. *Archives of General Psychiatry, 52,* 341–351. (15)

Andreasen, N. C., Swayze, V. W., II, Flaum, M., Yates, W. R., Arndt, S., & McChesney, C. (1990). Ventricular enlargement in schizophrenia evaluated with computed tomographic scanning. *Archives of General Psychiatry, 47,* 1008–1015. (15)

Andresen, J. M., Gayán, J., Cherny, S. S., Brocklebank, D., Alkorta-Aranburu, G., Addis, E. A., et al. (2007). Replication of twelve association studies for Huntington's disease residual age of onset in large Venezuelan kindreds. *Journal of Medical Genetics, 44,* 44–50. (8)

Andrew, D., & Craig, A. D. (2001). Spinothalamic lamina I neurons selectively sensitive to histamine: A central neural pathway for itch. *Nature Neuroscience, 4,* 72–77. (7)

Andrews, T. J., Halpern, S. D., & Purves, D. (1997). Correlated size variations in human visual cortex, lateral geniculate nucleus, and optic tract. *Journal of Neuroscience, 17,* 2859–2868. (4)

Angulo, M. C., Kozlov, A. S., Charpak, S., & Audinat, E. (2004). Glutamate released from glial cells synchronizes neuronal activity in the hippocampus. *Journal of Neuroscience, 24,* 6920–6927. (2)

Ankney, C. D. (1992). Sex differences in relative brain size: The mismeasure of women, too? *Intelligence, 16,* 329–336. (4)

Antanitus, D. S. (1998). A theory of cortical neuron-astrocyte interaction. *Neuroscientist, 4,* 154–159. (2)

Antoniadis, E. A., Winslow, J. T., Davis, M., & Amaral, D. G. (2007). Role of the primate amygdala in fear-potentiated startle. *Journal of Neuroscience, 27,* 7386–7396. (12)

Apostolakis, E. M., Garai, J., Fox, C., Smith, C. L., Watson, S. J., Clark, J. H., et al. (1996). Dopaminergic regulation of progesterone receptors: Brain D_5 dopamine receptors mediate induction of lordosis by D_1-like agonists in rats. *Journal of Neuroscience, 16,* 4823–4834. (11)

Appolinario, J. C., Bacaltchuk, J., Sichieri, R., Claudino, A. M., Godoy-Matos, A., Morgan, C., et al. (2003). A randomized, double-blind, placebo-controlled study of sibutramine in the treatment of binge-eating disorder. *Archives of General Psychiatry, 60,* 1109–1116. (10)

Araneda, R. C., Kini, A. D., & Firestein, S. (2000). The molecular receptive range of an odorant receptor. *Nature Neuroscience, 3,* 1248–1255. (7)

Archer, J. (2000). Sex differences in aggression between heterosexual partners: A meta-analytic review. *Psychological Bulletin, 126,* 651–680. (12)

Archer, J., Birring, S. S., & Wu, F. C. W. (1998). The association between testosterone and aggression in young men: Empirical findings and a meta-analysis. *Aggressive Behavior, 24,* 411–420. (12)

Archer, J., Graham-Kevan, N., & Davies, M. (2005). Testosterone and aggression: A reanalysis of Book, Starzyk, and Quinsey's (2001) study. *Aggression and Violent Behavior, 10,* 241–261. (12)

Arendt, J. (1997). Safety of melatonin in long-term use(?). *Journal of Biological Rhythms, 12,* 673–681. (9)

Arkin, A. M., Toth, M. F., Baker, J., & Hastey, J. M. (1970). The frequency of sleep talking in the laboratory among chronic sleep talkers and good dream recallers. *Journal of Nervous and Mental Disease, 151,* 369–374. (9)

Armstead, W. M., Nassar, T., Akkawi, S., Smith, D. H., Chen, X.-H., Cines, D. B., et al. (2006). Neutralizing the neurotoxic effects of exogenous and endogenous tPA. *Nature Neuroscience, 9,* 1150–1155. (5)

Arnold, A. P. (2004). Sex chromosomes and brain gender. *Nature Reviews Neuroscience, 5,* 701–708. (11)

Arnold, A. P., & Breedlove, S. M. (1985). Organizational and activational effects of sex steroids on brain and behavior: A reanalysis. *Hormones and Behavior, 19,* 469–498. (11)

Arnold, S. E. (2000). Cellular and molecular neuropathology of the parahippocampal region in schizophrenics. *Annals of the New York Academy of Sciences, 911,* 275–292. (15)

Arvidson, K., & Friberg, U. (1980). Human taste: Response and taste bud number in fungiform papillae. *Science, 209,* 807–808. (7)

Ascherio, A., Weisskopf, M. G., O'Reilly, E. J., McCullough, M., Calle, E. E., Rodriguez, C., et al. (2004). Coffee consumption, gender, and Parkinson's disease mortality in the cancer prevention study II cohort: The modifying effects of estrogen. *American Journal of Epidemiology, 160,* 977–984. (8)

Aserinsky, E., & Kleitman, N. (1955). Two types of ocular motility occurring in sleep. *Journal of Applied Physiology, 8,* 1–10. (9)

Aston-Jones, G., Chen, S., Zhu, Y., & Oshinsky, M. L. (2001). A neural circuit for circadian regulation of arousal. *Nature Neuroscience, 4,* 732–738. (9)

Athos, E. A., Levinson, B., Kistler, A., Zemansky, J., Bostrom, A., Freimer, N., et al. (2007). Dichotomy and perceptual distortions in absolute pitch ability. *Proceedings of the National Academy of Sciences, USA, 104,* 14795–14800. (7)

Au, T. K., Knightly, L. M., Jun, S.-A., & Oh, J. S. (2002). Overhearing a language during childhood. *Psychological Science, 13,* 238–243. (14)

Avissar, M., Furman, A. C., Saunders, J. C., & Parsons, T. D. (2007). Adaptation reduces spike-count reliability, but not spike-timing precision, of auditory nerve responses. *Journal of Neuroscience, 27,* 6461–6472. (7)

Azrin, N. H., Sisson, R. W., Meyers, R., & Godley, M. (1982). Alcoholism treatment by disulfiram and community reinforcement therapy. *Journal of Behavior Therapy and Experimental Psychiatry, 13,* 105–112. (3)

Babich, F. R., Jacobson, A. L., Bubash, S., & Jacobson, A. (1965). Transfer of a response to naive rats by injection of ribonucleic acid extracted from trained rats. *Science, 149,* 656–657. (13)

Babiloni, C., Brancucci, A., Pizzella, V., Romani, G. L., Tecchio, F., Torquati, K., et al. (2005). Contingent negative variation in the parasylvian cortex increases during expectancy of painful sensorimotor events: A magnetoencephalographic study. *Behavioral Neuroscience, 119,* 491–502. (7)

Babkoff, H., Caspy, T., Mikulincer, M., & Sing, H. C. (1991). Monotonic and rhythmic influences: A challenge for sleep deprivation research. *Psychological Bulletin, 109,* 411–428. (9)

Backlund, E.-O., Granberg, P.-O., Hamberger, B., Sedvall, G., Seiger, A., & Olson, L. (1985). Transplantation of adrenal medullary tissue to striatum in Parkinsonism. In A. Björklund & U. Stenevi (Eds.), *Neural grafting in the mammalian CNS* (pp. 551–556). Amsterdam: Elsevier. (8)

Bäckman, J., & Alerstam, T. (2001). Confronting the winds: Orientation and flight behavior of roosting swifts, *Apus apus. Proceedings of the Royal Society of London. Series B—Biological Sciences, 268,* 1081–1087. (9)

Baddeley, A. D., & Hitch, G. J. (1994). Developments in the concept of working memory. *Neuropsychology, 8,* 485–493. (13)

Baer, J. S., Sampson, P. D., Barr, H. M., Connor, P. D., & Streissguth, A. P. (2003). A 21-year longitudinal analysis of the effects of prenatal alcohol exposure on young adult drinking. *Archives of General Psychiatry, 60,* 377–385. (3)

Bagemihl, B. (1999). *Biological exuberance.* New York: St. Martin's Press. (11)

Baghdoyan, H. A., Spotts, J. L., & Snyder, S. G. (1993). Simultaneous pontine and basal forebrain microinjections of carbachol suppress REM sleep. *Journal of Neuroscience, 13,* 229–242. (9)

Bailey, C. H., Giustetto, M., Huang, Y.-Y., Hawkins, R. D., & Kandel, E. R. (2000). Is heterosynaptic modulation essential for stabilizing Hebbian plasticity and memory? *Nature Reviews Neuroscience, 1,* 11–20. (13)

Bailey, J. M., & Pillard, R. C. (1991). A genetic study of male sexual orientation. *Archives of General Psychiatry, 48,* 1089–1096. (11)

Bailey, J. M., Pillard, R. C., Dawood, K., Miller, M. B., Farrer, L. A., Trivedi, S., et al. (1999). A family history study of male sexual orientation using three independent samples. *Behavior Genetics, 29,* 79–86. (11)

Bailey, J. M., Pillard, R. C., Neale, M. C., & Agyei, Y. (1993). Heritable factors influence sexual orientation in women. *Archives of General Psychiatry, 50,* 217–223. (11)

Bailey, J. M., Willerman, L., & Parks, C. (1991). A test of the maternal stress theory of human male homosexuality. *Archives of Sexual Behavior, 20,* 277–293. (11)

Bakker, J., De Mees, C., Douhard, Q., Balthazart, J., Gabant, P., Szpirer, J., et al. (2006). Alpha-fetoprotein protects the developing female mouse brain from masculinization and defeminization by estrogens. *Nature Neuroscience, 9,* 220–226. (11)

Bakker, J., Honda, S.-I., Harada, N., & Balthazart, J. (2002). The aromatase knock-out mouse provides new evidence that estradiol is required during development in the female for the expression of sociosexual behaviors in adulthood. *Journal of Neuroscience, 22,* 9104–9112. (11)

Ballard, P. A., Tetrud, J. W., & Langston, J. W. (1985). Permanent human Parkinsonism due to 1-methyl-4-phenyl-1,2,3,6-tetrahydropyridine (MPTP). *Neurology, 35,* 949–956. (8)

Ballon, J. S., Dean, K. A., & Cadenhead, K. S. (2007). Obstetrical complications in people at risk for developing schizophrenia. *Schizophrenia Research, 98,* 307–311. (15)

Balthasar, N., Dalgaard, L. T., Lee, C. E., Yu, J., Funahashi, H., Williams, T., et al. (2005). Divergence of melanocortin pathways in the control of food intake and energy expenditure. *Cell, 123,* 493–505. (10)

Baquet, Z. C., Gorski, J. A., & Jones, K. R. (2004). Early striatal dendrite deficits followed by neuron loss with advanced age in the absence of anterograde cortical brain-derived neurotrophic factor. *Journal of Neuroscience, 24,* 4250–4258. (5)

Barbour, D. L., & Wang, X. (2003). Contrast tuning in auditory cortex. *Science, 299,* 1073–1075. (7)

Barinaga, M. (1996). Finding new drugs to treat stroke. *Science, 272,* 664–666. (5)

Barnea, G., O'Donnell, S., Mancia, F., Sun, X., Nemes, A., Mendelsohn, M., et al. (2004). Odorant receptors on axon termini in the brain. *Science, 304,* 1468. (7)

Barnes, B. M. (1996, September/October). Sang froid. *The Sciences, 36*(5), 13–14. (9)

Barr, M. S., & Corballis, M. C. (2002). The role of the anterior commissure in callosal agenesis. *Neuropsychology, 16,* 459–471. (14)

Barton, D. A., Esler, M. D., Dawood, T., Lambert, E. A., Haikerwal, D., Brenchley, C., et al. (2008). Elevated brain serotonin turnover in patients with depression. *Archives of General Psychiatry, 65,* 38–46. (15)

Barton, R. A., & Harvey, P. H. (2000). Mosaic evolution of brain structure in mammals. *Nature, 405,* 1055–1058. (4)

Bartoshuk, L. M. (1991). Taste, smell, and pleasure. In R. C. Bolles (Ed.), *The hedonics of taste* (pp. 15–28). Hillsdale, NJ: Erlbaum. (7)

Bartoshuk, L. M., Gentile, R. L., Moskowitz, H. R., & Meiselman, H. L. (1974). Sweet taste induced by miracle fruit (*Synsephalum dulcificum*). *Physiology & Behavior, 12,* 449–456. (7)

Basil, J. A., Kamil, A. C., Balda, R. P., & Fite, K. V. (1996). Differences in hippocampal volume among food storing corvids. *Brain, Behavior and Evolution, 47,* 156–164. (13)

Basso, A., & Rusconi, M. L. (1998). Aphasia in left-handers. In P. Coppens, Y. Lebrun, & A. Basso (Eds.), *Aphasia in atypical populations* (pp. 1–34). Mahwah, NJ: Erlbaum. (14)

Bastien, C., & Campbell, K. (1992). The evoked K-complex: All-or-none phenomenon? *Sleep, 15,* 236–245. (9)

Battersby, S. (1997). Plus c'est le même chews. *Nature, 385,* 679. (10)

Bauer, M., Grof, P., Rasgon, N., Bschor, T., Glenn, T., & Whybrow, P. C. (2006). Temporal relation between sleep and mood in patients with bipolar disorder. *Bipolar Disorders, 8,* 160–167. (15)

Baulac, S., Huberfeld, G., Gourfinkel-An, I., Mitropoulou, G., Beranger, A., Prud'homme, J.-F., et al. (2001). First genetic evidence of GABAA receptor dysfunction in epilepsy: A mutation in the γ2-subunit gene. *Nature Genetics, 28,* 46–48. (14)

Baum, A., Gatchel, R. J., & Schaeffer, M. A. (1983). Emotional, behavioral, and physiological effects of chronic stresss at Three Mile Island. *Journal of Consulting and Clinical Psychology, 51,* 565–582. (12)

Baum, M. J., & Vreeburg, J. T. M. (1973). Copulation in castrated male rats following combined treatment with estradiol and dihydrotestosterone. *Science, 182,* 283–285. (11)

Bauman, M. D., Toscano, J. E., Mason, W. A., Lavenex, P., & Amaral, D. G. (2006). The expression of social dominance following neonatal lesions of the amygdala or hippocampus in rhesus monkeys (*Macaca mulatta*). *Behavioral Neuroscience, 120,* 749–760. (12)

Bautista, D. M., Siemens, J., Glazer, J. M., Tsuruda, P. R., Basbaum, A. I., Stucky, C. L., et al. (2007). The menthol receptor TRPM8 is the principal detector of environmental cold. *Nature, 448,* 204–208. (7)

Baxter, L. R., Phelps, M. E., Mazziotta, J. C., Schwartz, J. M., Gerner, R. H., Selin, C. E., et al. (1985). Cerebral metabolic rates for glucose in mood disorders. *Archives of General Psychiatry, 42,* 441–447. (15)

Baxter, M. G., & Murray, E. A. (2002). The amygdala and reward. *Nature Reviews Neuroscience, 3,* 563–573. (12)

Bayley, P. J., Frascino, J. C., & Squire, L. R. (2005). Robust habit learning in the absence of awareness and independent of the medial temporal lobe. *Nature, 436,* 550–553. (13)

Bayley, P. J., Hopkins, R. O., & Squire, L. R. (2006). The fate of old memories after medial temporal lobe damage. *Journal of Neuroscience, 26,* 13311–13317. (13)

Baylis, G. C., & Driver, J. (2001). Shape-coding in IT cells generalizes over contrast and mirror reversal but not figure-ground reversal. *Nature Neuroscience, 4,* 937–942. (6)

Bean, B. P. (2007). The action potential in mammalian central neurons. *Nature Reviews Neuroscience, 8,* 451–465. (2)

Bechara, A., Damasio, H., Damasio, A. R., & Lee, G. P. (1999). Different contributions of the human amygdala and ventromedial prefrontal cortex to decision-making. *Journal of Neuroscience, 19,* 5473–5481. (12)

Becker, C., Thiébot, M.-H., Touitou, Y., Hamon, M., Cesselin, F., & Benoliel, J.-J. (2001). Enhanced cortical extracellular levels of cholecystokinin-like material in a model of anticipation of social defeat in the rat. *Journal of Neuroscience, 21,* 262–269. (12)

Becker, H. C. (1988). Effects of the imidazobenzodiazepine Ro15-4513 on the stimulant and depressant actions of ethanol on spontaneous locomotor activity. *Life Sciences, 43,* 643–650. (12)

Beckner, V. E., Tucker, D. M., Delville, Y., & Mohr, D. C. (2006). Stress facilitates consolidation of verbal memory for a film but does not affect retrieval. *Behavioral Neuroscience, 120,* 518–527. (12)

Beebe, D. W., & Gozal, D. (2002). Obstructive sleep apnea and the prefrontal cortex: Towards a comprehensive model linking nocturnal upper airway obstruction to daytime cognitive and behavioral deficits. *Journal of Sleep Research, 11,* 1–16. (9)

Beeman, M. J., & Chiarello, C. (1998). Complementary right- and left-hemisphere language comprehension. *Current Directions in Psychological Science, 7,* 2–8. (14)

Behl, C. (2002). Oestrogen as a neuroprotective hormone. *Nature Reviews Neuroscience, 3,* 433–442. (11)

Behrens, M., Foerster, S., Staehler, F., Raguse, J.-D., & Meyerhof, W. (2007). Gustatory expression pattern of the human TAS2R bitter receptor gene family reveals a heterogenous population of bitter responsive taste receptor cells. *Journal of Neuroscience, 27,* 12630–12640. (7)

Békésy, G.—*See* von Békésy, G.

Bellugi, U., Lichtenberger, L., Jones, W., Lai, Z., & St George, M. (2000). I. The neurocognitive profile of Williams syndrome: A complex pattern of strengths and weaknesses. *Journal of Cognitive Neuroscience, 12*(Suppl.), 7–29. (14)

Belova, M. A., Paton, J. J., Morrison, S. E., & Salzman, C. D. (2007). Expectation modulates neural responses to pleasant and aversive stimuli in primate amygdala. *Neuron, 55,* 970–984. (12)

Benedetti, F., Amanzio, M., Vighetti, S., & Asteggiano, G. (2006). The biochemical and neuroendocrine bases of the hyperalgesic nocebo effect. *Journal of Neuroscience, 26,* 12014–12022. (7)

Benedetti, F., Arduino, C., & Amanzio, M. (1999). Somatotopic activation of opioid systems by target-directed expectations of analgesia. *Journal of Neuroscience, 19,* 3639–3648. (7)

Benes, F. M. (1995). Is there a neuroanatomic basis for schizophrenia? An old question revisited. *The Neuroscientist, 1,* 104–115. (15)

Benes, F. M., Turtle, M., Khan, Y., & Farol, P. (1994). Myelination of a key relay zone in the hippocampal formation occurs in the human brain during childhood, adolescence, and adulthood. *Archives of General Psychiatry, 51,* 477–484. (5)

Benn, S. C., & Woolf, C. J. (2004). Adult neuron survival strategies—Slamming on the brakes. *Nature Reviews Neuroscience, 5,* 686–700. (5)

Benoit, S. C., Air, E. L., Coolen, L. M., Strauss, R., Jackman, A., Clegg, D. J., et al. (2002). The catabolic action of insulin in the brain is mediated by melanocortins. *Journal of Neuroscience, 22,* 9048–9052. (10)

Benschop, R. J., Godaert, G. L. R., Geenen, R., Brosschot, J. F., DeSmet, M. B. M., Olff, M., et al. (1995). Relationships between cardiovascular and immunologic changes in an experimental stress model. *Psychological Medicine, 25,* 323–327. (12)

Benuzzi, F., Lui, F., Duzzi, D., Nichelli, P. F., & Porro, C. A. (2008). Does it look painful or disgusting? Ask your parietal and cingulate cortex. *Journal of Neuroscience, 28,* 923–931. (12)

Berdoy, M., Webster, J. P., & Macdonald, D. W. (2000). Fatal attraction in rats infected with *Toxoplasma gondii. Proceedings of the Royal Society of London, B, 267,* 1591–1594. (12)

Berenbaum, S. A. (1999). Effects of early androgens on sex-typed activities and interests in adolescents with congenital adrenal hyperplasia. *Hormones and Behavior, 35,* 102–110. (11)

Berenbaum, S. A., Duck, S. C., & Bryk, K. (2002). Behavioral effects of prenatal versus postnatal androgen excess in children with 21-hydroxylase-deficient congenital adrenal hyperplasia. *Journal of Clinical Endocrinology & Metabolism, 85,* 727–733. (11)

Berger, R. J., & Phillips, N. H. (1995). Energy conservation and sleep. *Behavioural Brain Research, 69,* 65–73. (9)

Berger-Sweeney, J., & Hohmann, C. F. (1997). Behavioral consequences of abnormal cortical development: Insights into developmental disabilities. *Behavioural Brain Research, 86,* 121–142. (5)

Berlin, H. A., Rolls, E. T., & Kischka, U. (2004). Impulsivity, time perception, emotion and reinforcement sensitivity in patients with orbitofrontal cortex lesions. *Brain, 127,* 1108–1126. (12)

Berlucchi, G., Mangun, G. R., & Gazzaniga, M. S. (1997). Visuospatial attention and the split brain. *News in Physiological Sciences, 12,* 226–231. (14)

Berman, K. F., Torrey, E. F., Daniel, D. G., & Weinberger, D. R. (1992). Regional cerebral blood flow in monozygotic twins discordant and concordant for schizophrenia. *Archives of General Psychiatry, 49,* 927–934. (15)

Bernstein, J. J., & Gelderd, J. B. (1970). Regeneration of the long spinal tracts in the goldfish. *Brain Research, 20,* 33–38. (5)

Berntsen, D., & Rubin, D. C. (2002). Emotionally charged autobiographical memories across the life span: The recall of happy, sad, traumatic, and involuntary memories. *Psychology and Aging, 17,* 636–652. (13)

Berridge, C. W., Stellick, R. L., & Schmeichel, B. E. (2005). Wake-promoting actions of medial basal forebrain β_2 receptor stimulation. *Behavioral Neuroscience, 119,* 743–751. (9)

Berridge, K. C., & Robinson, T. E. (1995). The mind of an addicted brain: Neural sensitization of wanting versus liking. *Current Directions in Psychological Science, 4,* 71–76. (3)

Berridge, K. C., & Robinson, T. E. (1998). What is the role of dopamine in reward: Hedonic impact, reward learning, or incentive salience? *Brain Research Reviews, 28,* 309–369. (3)

Berryhill, M. E., Phuong, L., Picasso, L., Cabeza, R., & Olson, I. R. (2007). Parietal lobe and episodic memory: Bilateral damage causes impaired free recall of autobiographical memory. *Journal of Neuroscience, 27,* 14415–14423. (13)

Berson, D. M., Dunn, F. A., & Takao, M. (2002). Phototransduction by retinal ganglion cells that set the circadian clock. *Science, 295,* 1070–1073. (9)

Berton, O., & Nestler, E. J. (2006). New approaches to antidepressant drug discovery: Beyond monoamines. *Nature Reviews Neuroscience, 7,* 137–151. (15)

Betarbet, R., Sherer, T. B., MacKenzie, G., Garcia-Osuna, M., Panov, A. V., & Greenamyre, J. T. (2000). Chronic systemic pesticide exposure reproduces features of Parkinson's disease. *Nature Neuroscience, 3,* 1301–1306. (8)

Biben, M. (1979). Predation and predatory play behaviour of domestic cats. *Animal Behaviour, 27,* 81–94. (12)

Biernaskie, J., Chernenko, G., & Corbett, D. (2004). Efficacy of rehabilitative experience declines with time after focal ischemic brain injury. *Journal of Neuroscience, 24,* 1245–1254. (5)

Bierut, L. J., Heath, A. C., Bucholz, K. K., Dinwiddie, S. H., Madden, P. A. F., Statham, D. J., et al. (1999). Major depressive disorder in a community-based twin sample. *Archives of General Psychiatry, 56,* 557–563. (15)

Billington, C. J., & Levine, A. S. (1992). Hypothalamic neuropeptide Y regulation of feeding and energy metabolism. *Current Opinion in Neurobiology, 2,* 847–851. (10)

Binder, G. K., & Griffin, D. E. (2001). Interferon-g-mediated site-specific clearance of alphavirus from CNS neurons. *Science, 293,* 303–306. (2)

Bird, A. (2007). Perceptions of epigenetics. *Nature, 447,* 396–398. (1)

Blackless, M., Charuvastra, A., Derryck, A., Fausto-Sterling, A., Lauzanne, K., & Lee, E. (2000). How sexually dimorphic are we? Review and synthesis. *American Journal of Human Biology, 12,* 151–166. (11)

Blackwell, A., & Bates, E. (1995). Inducing agrammatic profiles in normals: Evidence for the selective vulnerability of morphology under cognitive resource limitation. *Journal of Cognitive Neuroscience, 7,* 228–257. (14)

Blake, R., & Hirsch, H. V. B. (1975). Deficits in binocular depth perception in cats after alternating monocular deprivation. *Science, 190,* 1114–1116. (6)

Blake, R., Palmeri, T. J., Marois, R., & Kim,C.-Y. (2005). On the perceptual reality of synesthetic color. In L. C. Robertson & N. Sagiv (Eds.), *Synesthesia* (pp. 47–73). Oxford, England: Oxford University Press. (7)

Blakemore, S.-J., Wolpert, D. M., & Frith, C. D. (1998). Central cancellation of self-produced tickle sensation. *Nature Neuroscience, 1,* 635–640. (7)

Blankenburg, F., Ruff, C. C., Deichmann, R., Rees, G., & Driver, J. (2006). The cutaneous rabbit illusion affects human primary sensory cortex somatotopically. *PloS Biology, 4,* 459–466. (7)

Bliss, T. V. P., & Lømo, T. (1973). Long-lasting potentiation of synaptic transmission in the dentate area of the anaesthetized rabbit following stimulation of the perforant path. *Journal of Physiology (London), 232,* 331–356. (13)

Bloch, G. J., Butler, P. C., & Kohlert, J. G. (1996). Galanin microinjected into the medial preoptic nucleus facilitates female- and male-typical sexual behaviors in the female rat. *Physiology & Behavior, 59,* 1147–1154. (11)

Bloch, G. J., & Mills, R. (1995). Prepubertal testosterone treatment of neonatally gonadectomized male rats: Defeminization and masculinization of behavioral and endocrine function in adulthood. *Neuroscience and Biobehavioral Reviews, 19,* 187–200. (11)

Bloch, G. J., Mills, R., & Gale, S. (1995). Prepubertal testosterone treatment of female rats: Defeminization of behavioral and endocrine function in adulthood. *Neuroscience and Biobehavioral Reviews, 19,* 177–186. (11)

Bloch, M., Rotenberg, N., Koren, D., & Klein, E. (2005). Risk factors associated with the development of postpartum mood disorders. *Journal of Affective Disorders, 88,* 9–18. (15)

Bloch, M., Schmidt, P. J., Danaceau, M., Murphy, J., Nieman, L., & Rubinow, D. R. (2000). Effects of gonadal steroids in women with a history of postpartum depression. *American Journal of Psychiatry, 157,* 924–930. (15)

Blonder, L. X., Smith, C. D., Davis, C. E., Kesler/West, M. L., Garrity, T. F., Avison, M. J., et al. (2004). Regional brain response to faces of humans and dogs. *Cognitive Brain Research, 20,* 384–394. (6)

Bobrow, D., & Bailey, J. M. (2001). Is male homosexuality maintained via kin selection? *Evolution and Human Behavior, 22,* 361–368. (11)

Bocklandt, S., Horvath, S., Vilain, E., & Hamer, D. H. (2006). Extreme skewing of X chromosome inactivation in mothers of homosexual men. *Human Genetics, 118,* 691–694. (11)

Bode, L., Ferszt, R., & Czech, G. (1993). Borna disease virus infection and affective disorders in man. *Archives of Virology* (Suppl. 7), 159–167. (15)

Bode, L., & Ludwig, H. (1997). Clinical similarities and close genetic relationship of human and animal Borna disease virus. *Archives of Virology* (Suppl. 13), 167–182. (15)

Bode, L., Riegel, S., Lange, W., & Ludwig, H. (1992). Human infections with Borna disease virus: Seroprevalence in patients with chronic diseases and healthy individuals. *Journal of Medical Virology, 36,* 309–315. (15)

Boettiger, C. A., Mitchell, J. M., Tavares, V. C., Robertson, M., Joslyn, G., D'Esposito, M., et al. (2007). Immediate reward bias in humans: Fronto-parietal networks and a role for the catechol-O-methyltransferase $158^{val/val}$ genotype. *Journal of Neuroscience, 27,* 14383–14391. (3)

Bogaert, A. F. (2003a). The interaction of fraternal birth order and body size in male sexual orientation. *Behavioral Neuroscience, 117,* 381–384. (11)

Bogaert, A. F. (2003b). Number of older brothers and sexual orientation: New tests and the attraction/behavior distinction in two national probability samples. *Journal of Personality and Social Psychology, 84,* 644–652. (11)

Bogaert, A. F. (2006). Biological versus nonbiological older brothers and men's sexual orientation. *Proceedings of the National Academy of Sciences, USA, 103,* 10771–10774. (11)

Bogaert, A. F., Blanchard, R., & Crosthwait, L. E. (2007). Interaction of birth order, handedness, and sexual orientation in the Kinsey interview data. *Behavioral Neuroscience, 121,* 845–853. (11)

Boivin, D. B., Duffy, J. F., Kronauer, R. E., & Czeisler, C. A. (1996). Dose-response relationships for resetting of human circadian clock by light. *Nature, 379,* 540–542. (9)

Bolaños,C.A.,Barrot,M.,Berton,O.,Wallace-Black, D., & Nestler, E. J. (2003). Methylphenidate treatment during pre- and periadolescence alters behavioral responses to emotional stimuli at adulthood. *Biological Psychiatry, 54,* 1317–1329. (3)

Bonifati, V., Rizzu, P., van Baren, M. J., Schaap, O., Breedlove, G. J., Krieger, E., et al. (2003). Mutations in the *DJ-1* gene associated with autosomal recessive early-onset Parkinsonism. *Science, 299,* 256–259. (8)

Booth, F. W., & Neufer, P. D. (2005, January/February). Exercise controls gene expression. *American Scientist, 93,* 28–35. (8)

Borodinsky, L. N., Root, C. M., Cronin, J. A., Sann, S. B., Gu, X., & Spitzer, N. C. (2004). Activity-dependent homeostatic specification of transmitter expression in embryonic neurons. *Nature, 429,* 523–530. (3)

Bouchard, T. J., Jr., & McGue, M. (2003). Genetic and environmental influences on human psychological differences. *Journal of Neurobiology, 54,* 4–45. (1)

Boucsein, K., Weniger, G., Mursch, K., Steinhoff, B. J., & Irle, E. (2001). Amygdala lesion in temporal lobe epilepsy subjects impairs associative learning of emotional facial expressions. *Neuropsychologia, 39,* 231–236. (12)

Boutrel, B., Franc, B., Hen, R., Hamon, M., & Adrien, J. (1999). Key role of 5-HT1B receptors in the regulation of paradoxical sleep as evidenced in 5-HT1B knock-out mice. *Journal of Neuroscience, 19,* 3204–3212. (9)

Bowles, S. (2006). Group competition, reproductive leveling, and the evolution of human altruism. *Science, 314,* 1569–1572. (1)

Bowles, S., & Posel, B. (2005). Genetic relatedness predicts South African migrant workers' remittances to their families. *Nature, 434,* 380–383. (1)

Bowmaker, J. K. (1998). Visual pigments and molecular genetics of color blindness. *News in Physiological Sciences, 13,* 63–69. (6)

Bowmaker, J. K., & Dartnall, H. J. A. (1980). Visual pigments of rods and cones in a human retina. *Journal of Physiology (London), 298,* 501–511. (6)

Bradley, R. G., Binder, E. B., Epstein, M. P., Tang, Y., Nair, H. P., Liu, W., et al. (2008). Influence of child abuse on adult depression. *Archives of General Psychiatry, 65,* 190–200. (15)

Bramble, D. M., & Lieberman, D. E. (2004). Endurance running and the evolution of *Homo. Nature, 432,* 345–352. (8)

Brandt, T. (1991). Man in motion: Historical and clinical aspects of vestibular function. *Brain, 114,* 2159–2174. (7)

Brasted, P. J., Watts, C., Robbins, T. W., & Dunnett, S. B. (1999). Associative plasticity in striatal transplants. *Proceedings of the National Academy of Sciences, USA, 96,* 10524–10529. (8)

Braun, A. R., Balkin, T. J., Wesensten, N. J., Guadry, F., Carson, R. E., Varga, M., et al. (1998). Dissociated pattern of activity in visual cortices and their projections during human rapid eye movement sleep. *Science, 279,* 91–95. (8, 9)

Braus, H. (1960). Anatomie des Menschen, 3. Band: Periphere Leistungsbahnen II. Centrales Nervensystem, Sinnesorgane. 2. Auflage [Human anatomy: Vol. 3. Peripheral pathways II. Central nervous system, sensory organs (2nd ed.)]. Berlin: Springer-Verlag. (4)

Bredesen, D. E., Rao, R. V., & Mehlen, P. (2006). Cell death in the nervous system. *Nature, 443,* 796–802. (8)

Breiter, H. C., Aharon, I., Kahneman, D., Dale, A., & Shizgal, P. (2001). Functional imaging of neural responses to expectancy and experience of monetary gains and losses. *Neuron, 30,* 619–639. (3)

Brennan, P. A., Grekin, E. R., & Mednick, S. A. (1999). Maternal smoking during pregnancy and adult male criminal outcomes. *Archives of General Psychiatry, 56,* 215–219. (12)

Brewer, W. J., Wood, S. J., Pantelis, C., Berger, G. E., Copolov, D. L., & McGorry, P. D. (2007). Olfactory sensitivity through the course of psychosis: Relationships to olfactory identification, symptomatology and the schizophrenia odour. *Psychiatry Research, 149,* 97–104. (15)

Breysse, N., Carlsson, T., Winkler, C., Björklund, A., & Kirik, D. (2007). The functional impact of the intrastriatal dopamine neuron grafts in Parkinsonian rats is reduced with advancing disease. *Journal of Neuroscience, 27,* 5849–5856. (8)

Bridgeman, B., & Staggs, D. (1982). Plasticity in human blindsight. *Vision Research, 22,* 1199–1203. (6)

Brisbare-Roch, C., Dingemanse, J., Koberstein, R., Hoever, P., Aissoui, H., Flores, S., et al. (2007).

Promotion of sleep by targeting the orexin system in rats, dogs and humans. *Nature Medicine, 13,* 150–155. (9)

Brody, A. L., Saxena, S., Stoesssel, P., Gillies, L. A., Fairbanks, L. A., Alborzian, S., et al. (2001). Regional brain metabolic changes in patients with major depression treated with either paroxetine or interpersonal therapy. *Archives of General Psychiatry, 58,* 631–640. (15)

Brooks, D. C., & Bizzi, E. (1963). Brain stem electrical activity during deep sleep. *Archives Italiennes de Biologie, 101,* 648–665. (9)

Broughton, R., Billlings, R., Cartwright, R., Doucette, D., Edmeads, J., Edwardh, M., et al. (1994). Homicidal somnambulism: A case report. *Sleep, 17,* 253–264. (9)

Brown, A. S., Begg, M. D., Gravenstein, S., Schaefer, C. A., Wyatt, R. J., Bresnahan, M., et al. (2004). Serologic evidence of prenatal influenza in the etiology of schizophrenia. *Archives of General Psychiatry, 61,* 774–780. (15)

Brown, A. S., Cohen, P., Harkavy-Friedman, J., Babulas, V., Malaspina, D., Gorman, J. M., et al. (2001). Prenatal rubella, premorbid abnormalities, and adult schizophrenia. *Biological Psychiatry, 49,* 473–486. (15)

Brown, C. E., Li, P., Boyd, J. D., Delaney, K. R., & Murphy, T. H. (2007). Extensive turnover of dendritic spines and vascular remodeling in cortical tissues recovering from stroke. *Journal of Neuroscience, 27,* 4101–4109. (5)

Brown, G. L., Ebert, M. H., Goyer, P. F., Jimerson, D. C., Klein, W. J., Bunney, W. E., et al. (1982). Aggression, suicide, and serotonin: Relationships of CSF amine metabolites. *American Journal of Psychiatry, 139,* 741–746. (12)

Brown, J., Babor, T. F., Litt, M. D., & Kranzler, H. R. (1994). The type A/type B distinction. *Annals of the New York Academy of Sciences, 708,* 23–33. (3)

Brown, J. R., Ye, H., Bronson, R. T., Dikkes, P., & Greenberg, M. E. (1996). A defect in nurturing in mice lacking the immediate early gene *fos B. Cell, 86,* 297–309. (11)

Brown, T. P., Rumsby, P. C., Capleton, A. C., Rushton, L., & Levy, L. S. (2006). Pesticides and Parkinson's disease—Is there a link? *Environmental Health Perspectives, 114,* 156–164. (8)

Bruno, R. M., & Sakmann, B. (2006). Cortex is driven by weak but synchronously active thalamocortical synapses. *Science, 312,* 1622–1627. (3)

Brunson, K. L., Kramár, E., Lin, B., Chen, Y., Colgin, L. L., Yanagihara, T. K., et al. (2005). Mechanisms of late-onset cognitive decline after early-life stress. *Journal of Neuroscience, 25,* 9328–9338. (12)

Buchert, R., Thomasius, R., Nebeling, B., Petersen, K., Obrocki, J., Jenicke, L., et al. (2003). Long-term effects of "ecstasy" use on serotonin transporters of the brain investigated by PET. *Journal of Nuclear Medicine, 44,* 375–384. (3)

Buck, L., & Axel, R. (1991). A novel multigene family may encode odorant receptors: A molecular basis for odor recognition. *Cell, 65,* 175–187. (7)

Buck, R., & Duffy, R. J. (1980). Nonverbal communication of affect in brain-damaged patients. *Cortex, 16,* 351–362. (14)

Buell, S. J., & Coleman, P. D. (1981). Quantitative evidence for selective dendritic growth in normal human aging but not in senile dementia. *Brain Research, 214,* 23–41. (5)

Buka, S. L., Cannon, T. D., Torrey, E. F., Yolken, R. H., & Collaborative Study Group on the Prenatal Origins of Severe Psychiatric Disorders. (2008). Maternal exposure to herpes simplex virus and risk of psychosis among adult offspring. *Biological Psychiatry, 63,* 809–815. (15)

Buka, S. L., Tsuang, M. T., Torrey, E. F., Klebanoff, M. A., Bernstein, D., & Yolken, R. H. (2001). Maternal infections and subsequent psychosis among offspring. *Archives of General Psychiatry, 58,* 1032–1037. (15)

Bundgaard, M. (1986). Pathways across the vertebrate blood-brain barrier: Morphological viewpoints. *Annals of the New York Academy of Sciences, 481,* 7–19. (2)

Burgess, C. E., Lindblad, K., Sigransky, E., Yuan, Q. P., Long, R. T., Breschel, T., et al. (1998). Large CAG/CTG repeats are associated with childhood-onset schizophrenia. *Molecular Psychiatry, 3,* 321–327. (15)

Burr, D. C., Morrone, M. C., & Ross, J. (1994). Selective suppression of the magnocellular visual pathway during saccadic eye movements. *Nature, 371,* 511–513. (6)

Burrell, B. (2004). *Postcards from the brain museum.* New York: Broadway Books. (4)

Burton, H., Snyder, A. Z., Conturo, T. E., Akbudak, E., Ollinger, J. M., & Raichle, M. E. (2002). Adaptive changes in early and late blind: A fMRI study of Braille reading. *Journal of Neurophysiology, 87,* 589–607. (5)

Burton, R. F. (1994). *Physiology by numbers.* Cambridge, England: Cambridge University Press. (10)

Buschman, T. J., & Miller, E. K. (2007). Top-down versus bottom-up control of attention in the prefrontal and posterior parietal cortices. *Science, 315,* 1860–1862. (14)

Buss, D. M. (1994). The strategies of human mating. *American Scientist, 82,* 238–249. (1)

Buss, D. M. (2000). Desires in human mating. *Annals of the New York Academy of Sciences, 907,* 39–49. (11)

Buss, D. M. (2001). Cognitive biases and emotional wisdom in the evolution of conflict between the sexes. *Current Directions in Psychological Science, 10,* 219–223. (11)

Bussiere, J. R., Beer, T. M., Neiss, M. B., & Janowsky, J. S. (2005). Androgen deprivation impairs memory in older men. *Behavioral Neuroscience, 119,* 1429–1437. (11)

Button, T. M. M., Maughan, B., & McGuffin, P. (2007). The relationship of maternal smoking to psychological problems in the offspring. *Early Human Development, 83,* 727–732. (12)

Buxbaum, L. J. (2006). On the right (and left) track: Twenty years of progress in studying hemispatial neglect. *Cognitive Neuropsychology, 23,* 184–201. (14)

Byl, N. N., McKenzie, A., & Nagarajan, S. S. (2000). Differences in somatosensory hand organization in a healthy flutist and a flutist with focal hand dystonia: A case report. *Journal of Hand Therapy, 13,* 302–309. (5)

Byne, W., Tobet, S., Mattiace, L. A., Lasco, M. S., Kemether, E., Edgar, M. A., et al. (2001). The interstitial nuclei of the human anterior hypothalamus: An investigation of variation with sex, sexual orientation, and HIV status. *Hormones and Behavior, 40,* 86–92. (11)

Byrne, M., Agerbo, E., Ewald, H., Eaton, W. W., & Mortensen, P. B. (2003). Parental age and risk of schizophrenia. *Archives of General Psychiatry, 60,* 673–678. (15)

Caccappolo-van Vliet, E., Miozzo, M., & Stern, Y. (2004). Phonological dyslexia: A test case for reading models. *Psychological Science, 15,* 583–590. (14)

Cadoret, R. J., Yates, W. R., Troughton, E., Woodworth, G., & Stewart, M. A. (1995). Genetic-environmental interaction in the genesis of aggressivity and conduct disorders. *Archives of General Psychiatry, 52,* 916–924. (12)

Cahill, L. (2006). Why sex matters for neuroscience. *Nature Reviews Neuroscience, 7,* 477–484. (4)

Cahill, L., & McGaugh, J. L. (1998). Mechanisms of emotional arousal and lasting declarative memory. *Trends in Neurosciences, 21,* 294–299. (13)

Cahn, W., Hulshoff, H. E., Lems, E. B. T. E., van Haren, N. E. M., Schnack, H. G., van der Linden, J. A., et al. (2002). Brain volume changes in first-episode schizophrenia. *Archives of General Psychiatry, 59,* 1002–1010. (15)

Caine, S. B., Thomsen, M., Gabriel, K. I., Berkowitz, J. S., Gold, L. H., Koob, G. F., et al. (2007). Lack of self-administration of cocaine in dopamine D_1 receptor knock-out mice. *Journal of Neuroscience, 27,* 13140–13150. (3, 4)

Cajal, S. R. (1937). Recollections of my life. *Memoirs of the American Philosophical Society, 8.* (Original work published 1901–1917) (2)

Calder, A. J., Keane, J., Manes, F., Antoun, N., & Young, A. W. (2000). Impaired recognition and experience of disgust following brain injury. *Nature Neuroscience, 3,* 1077–1078. (12)

Caldwell, J. A., Mu, Q., Smith, J. K., Mishory, A., Caldwell, J. L., Peters, G., et al. (2005). Are individual differences in fatigue vulnerability related to baseline differences in cortical activation? *Behavioral Neuroscience, 119,* 694–707. (9)

Calignano, A., LaRana, G., Giuffrida, A., & Piomelli, D. (1998). Control of pain initiation by endogenous cannabinoids. *Nature, 394,* 277–281. (3)

Cameron, H. A., & McKay, R. D. G. (1999). Restoring production of hippocampal neurons in old age. *Nature Neuroscience, 2,* 894–897. (12)

Cameron, N. M., Champagne, F. A., Parent, C., Fish, E. W., Ozaki-Kuroda, K., & Meaney, M. J. (2005). The programming of individual differences in defensive responses and reproductive strategies in the rat through variations in maternal care. *Neuroscience and Biobehavioral Reviews, 29,* 843–865. (5)

Campbell, S. S., & Tobler, I. (1984). Animal sleep: A review of sleep duration across phylogeny. *Neuroscience and Biobehavioral Reviews, 8,* 269–300. (9)

Camperio-Ciani, A., Corna, F., & Capiluppi, C. (2004). Evidence for maternally inherited factors favouring male homosexuality and promoting female fecundity. *Proceedings of the Royal Society of London, B, 271,* 2217–2221. (11)

Campfield, L. A., Smith, F. J., Guisez, Y., Devos, R., & Burn, P. (1995). Recombinant mouse OB protein: Evidence for a peripheral signal linking adiposity and central neural networks. *Science, 269,* 546–552. (10)

Canal, C. E., & Gold, P. E. (2007). Different temporal profiles of amnesia after intra-hippocampus and intra-amygdala infusions of anisomycin. *Behavioral Neuroscience, 121,* 732–741. (13)

Canepari, M., Rossi, R., Pellegrino, M. A., Orell, R. W., Cobbold, M., Harridge, S., et al. (2005). Effects of resistance training on myosin function studies by the in vitro motility assay in young and older men. *Journal of Applied Physiology, 98,* 2390–2395. (8)

Cannon, M., Jones, P. B., & Murray, R. M. (2002). Obstetric complications and schizophrenia: Historical and meta-analytic review. *American Journal of Psychiatry, 159,* 1080–1092. (15)

Cannon, W. B. (1929). Organization for physiological homeostasis. *Physiological Reviews, 9,* 399–431. (10)

Cannon, W. B. (1945). *The way of an investigator.* New York: Norton. (10)

Cao, Y. Q., Mantyh, P. W., Carlson, E. J., Gillespie, A.-M., Epstein, C. J., & Basbaum, A. I. (1998). Primary afferent tachykinins are required to experience moderate to intense pain. *Nature, 392,* 390–394. (7)

Cardno, A. G., Marshall, E. J., Coid, B., Macdonald, A. M., Ribchester, T. R., Davies, N. J., et al. (1999). Heritability estimates for psychotic disorders. *Archives of General Psychiatry, 56,* 162–168. (15)

Carlezon, W. A., Jr., Mague, S. D., & Andersen, S. L. (2003). Enduring behavioral effects of early exposure to methylphenidate in rats. *Biological Psychiatry, 54,* 1330–1337. (3)

Carlsson, A. (2001). A paradigm shift in brain research. *Science, 294,* 1021–1024. (3)

Carpenter, G. A., & Grossberg, S. (1984). A neural theory of circadian rhythms: Aschoff's rule in diurnal and nocturnal mammals. *American Journal of Physiology, 247,* R1067–R1082. (9)

Carreiras, M., Lopez, J., Rivero, F., & Corina, D. (2005). Neural processing of a whistled language. *Nature, 433,* 31–32. (14)

Carruth, L. L., Reisert, I., & Arnold, A. P. (2002). Sex chromosome genes directly affect brain sexual differentiation. *Nature Neuroscience, 5,* 933–934. (11)

Carter, C. S. (1992). Hormonal influences on human sexual behavior. In J. B. Becker, S. M. Breedlove, & D. Crews (Eds.), *Behavioral endocrinology* (pp. 131–142). Cambridge, MA: MIT Press. (11)

Caspi, A., McClay, J., Moffitt, T. E., Mill, J., Martin, J., Craig, I. W., et al. (2002). Role of genotype in the cycle of violence in maltreated children. *Science, 297,* 851–854. (12)

Caspi, A., Sugden, K., Moffitt, T. E., Taylor, A., Craig, I. W., Harrington, H., et al. (2003). Influence of life stress on depression: Moderation by a polymorphism in the 5-HTT gene. *Science, 301,* 386–389. (15)

Cassia, V. M., Turati, C., & Simion, F. (2004). Can a nonspecific bias toward top-heavy patterns explain newborns' face preference? *Psychological Science, 15,* 379–383. (6)

Castellucci, V. F., Pinsker, H., Kupfermann, I., & Kandel, E. (1970). Neuronal mechanisms of habituation and dishabituation of the gill-withdrawal reflex in *Aplysia. Science, 167,* 1745–1748. (13)

Castner, S. A., & Goldman-Rakic, P. S. (2004). Enhancement of working memory in aged monkeys by a sensitizing regimen of dopamine D_1 receptor stimulation. *Journal of Neuroscience, 24,* 1446–1450. (13)

Catalano, S. M., & Shatz, C. J. (1998). Activity-dependent cortical target selection by thalamic axons. *Science, 281,* 559–562. (5)

Catania, K. C. (2006). Underwater "sniffing" by semi-aquatic mammals. *Nature, 444,* 1024–1025. (7)

Catchpole, C. K., & Slater, P. J. B. (1995). *Bird song: Biological themes and variations.* Cambridge, England: Cambridge University Press. (1)

Catmur, C., Walsh, V., & Heyes, C. (2007). Sensorimotor learning configures the human mirror system. *Current Biology, 17,* 1527–1531. (8)

Catterall, W. A. (1984). The molecular basis of neuronal excitability. *Science, 223,* 653–661. (2)

Censits, D. M., Ragland, J. D., Gur, R. C., & Gur, R. E. (1997). Neuropsychological evidence supporting a neurodevelopmental model of schizophrenia: A longitudinal study. *Schizophrenia Research, 24,* 289–298. (15)

Cerletti, U., & Bini, L. (1938). L'Elettro-shock. *Archivio Generale di Neurologia e Psichiatria e Psicoanalisi, 19,* 266–268. (15)

Chabris, C. F., & Glickman, M. E. (2006). Sex differences in intellectual performance: Analysis of a large cohort of competitive chess players. *Psychological Science, 17,* 1040–1046. (4)

Chalmers, D. J. (1995). Facing up to the problem of consciousness. *Journal of Consciousness Studies, 2,* 200–219. (1)

Chalmers, D. L. (2004). How can we construct a science of consciousness? In M. S. Gazzaniga (Ed.), *The cognitive neurosciences* (3rd ed.) (pp. 1111–1119). Cambridge, MA: MIT Press. (1)

Chan, C. S., Guzman, J. N., Ilijic, E., Mercer, J. N., Rick, C., Tkatch, T., et al. (2007). "Rejuvenation" protects neurons in mouse models of Parkinson's disease. *Nature, 447,* 1081–1086. (8)

Chang, E. F., & Merzenich, M. M. (2003). Environmental noise retards auditory cortical development. *Science, 300,* 498–502. (7)

Chaudhari, N., Landin, A. M., & Roper, S. D. (2000). A metabotropic glutamate receptor variant functions as a taste receptor. *Nature Neuroscience, 3,* 113–119. (7)

Chawla, D., Rees, G., & Friston, K. J. (1999). The physiological basis of attentional modulation in extrastriate visual areas. *Nature Neuroscience, 2,* 671–676. (14)

Chee, M. W. L., Tan, J. C., Zheng, H., Parimal, S., Weissman, D. H., Zagorodnov, V., et al. (2008). Lapsing during sleep deprivation is associated with distributed changes in brain activation. *Journal of Neuroscience, 28,* 5519–5528. (9)

Cheer, J. F., Wassum, K. M., Heien, M. L. A. V., Phillips, P. E. M., & Wightman, R. M. (2004). Cannabinoids enhance subsecond dopamine release in the nucleus accumbens of awake rats. *Journal of Neuroscience, 24,* 4393–4400. (3)

Chen, L. M., Friedman, R. M., & Roe, A. W. (2003). Optical imaging of a tactile illusion in area 3b of the primary somatosensory cortex. *Science, 302,* 881–885. (7)

Chen, Z.-Y., Jing, D., Bath, K. G., Ieraci, A., Khan, T., Siao, C.-J., et al. (2006). Genetic variant BDNF (Val66Met) polymorphism alters anxiety-related behavior. *Science, 314,* 140–143. (12)

Cheng, D. T., Knight, D. C., Smith, C. N., & Helmstetter, F. (2006). Human amygdala activity during the expression of fear responses. *Behavioral Neuroscience, 120,* 1187–1195. (12)

Cheour-Luhtanen, M., Alho, K., Sainio, K., Rinne, T., Reinikainen, K., Pohjavuoir, M., et al. (1996). The ontogenetically earliest discriminative response of the human brain. *Psychophysiology, 33,* 478–481. (14)

Chiueh, C. C. (1988). Dopamine in the extrapyramidal motor function: A study based upon the MPTP-induced primate model of Parkinsonism. *Annals of the New York Academy of Sciences, 515,* 226–248. (8)

Chivers, M. L., Rieger, G., Latty, E., & Bailey, J. M. (2004). A sex difference in the specificity of sexual arousal. *Psychological Science, 15,* 736–744. (11)

Cho, K. (2001). Chronic "jet lag" produces temporal lobe atrophy and spatial cognitive deficits. *Nature Neuroscience, 4,* 567–568. (9)

Choi, D.-S., Cascini, M.-G., Mailliard, W., Young, H., Paredes, P., McMahon, T., et al. (2004). The type I equilibrative nucleoside transporter regulates ethanol intoxication and preference. *Nature Neuroscience, 7,* 855–861. (3)

Chomsky, N. (1980). *Rules and representations.* New York: Columbia University Press. (14)

Christian, K. M., & Thompson, R. F. (2005). Long-term storage of an associative memory trace in the cerebellum. *Behavioral Neuroscience, 119,* 526–537. (13)

Chuang, H., Prescott, E. D., Kong, H., Shields, S., Jordt, S.-E., Basbaum, A. I., et al. (2001). Bradykinin and nerve growth factor release the capsaicin receptor from Ptdlns(4,5)P2-mediated inhibition. *Nature, 411,* 957–962. (7)

Ciccocioppo, R., Martin-Fardon, R., & Weiss, F. (2004). Stimuli associated with a single cocaine experience elicit long-lasting cocaine-seeking. *Nature Neuroscience, 7,* 495-498. (3)

Cicone, N., Wapner, W., Foldi, N. S., Zurif, E., & Gardner, H. (1979). The relation between gesture and language in aphasic communication. *Brain and Language, 8,* 324–349. (14)

Clahsen, H., & Almazen, M. (1998). Syntax and morphology in Williams syndrome. *Cognition, 68,* 167–198. (14)

Clark, D. A., Mitra, P. P., & Wang, S. S.-H. (2001). Scalable architecture in mammalian brains. *Nature, 411,* 189–193. (4)

Clark, R. E., Broadbent, N. J., & Squire, L. R. (2007). The hippocampus and spatial memory: Findings with a novel modification of the water maze. *Journal of Neuroscience, 27,* 6647–6654. (13)

Clark, R. E., & Lavond, D. G. (1993). Reversible lesions of the red nucleus during acquisition and retention of a classically conditioned behavior in rabbits. *Behavioral Neuroscience, 107,* 264–270. (13)

Clark, W. S. (2004). Is the zone-tailed hawk a mimic? *Birding, 36,* 494–498. (1)

Clarke, S., Assal, G., & deTribolet, N. (1993). Left hemisphere strategies in visual recognition, topographical orientation and time planning. *Neuropsychologia, 31,* 99–113. (14)

Clayton, E. C., & Williams, C. L. (2000). Glutamatergic influences on the nucleus paragigantocellularis: Contribution to performance in avoidance and spatial memory tasks. *Behavioral Neuroscience, 114,* 707–712. (9)

Cleary, L. J., Hammer, M., & Byrne, J. H. (1989). Insights into the cellular mechanisms of short-term sensitization in *Aplysia*. In T. J. Carew & D. B. Kelley (Eds.), *Perspectives in neural systems and behavior* (pp. 105–119). New York: Liss. (13)

Clem, R. L., Celikel, T., & Barth, A. L. (2008). Ongoing *in vivo* experience triggers synaptic metaplasticity in the neocortex. *Science, 319,* 101–104. (13)

Clutton-Brock, T. H., O'Riain, M. J., Brotherton, P. N. M., Gaynor, D., Kansky, R., Griffin, A. S., et al. (1999). Selfish sentinels in cooperative mammals. *Science, 284,* 1640–1644. (1)

Coan, J. A., Schaefer, H. S., & Davidson, R. J. (2006). Lending a hand: Social regulation of the neural response to threat. *Psychological Science, 17,* 1032–1039. (12)

Cobos, P., Sánchez, M., Pérez, N., & Vila, J. (2004). Effects of spinal cord injuries on the subjective component of emotions. *Cognition and Emotion, 18,* 281–287. (12)

Coderre, T. J., Katz, J., Vaccarino, A. L., & Melzack, R. (1993). Contribution of central neuroplasticity to pathological pain: Review of clinical and experimental evidence. *Pain, 52,* 259–285. (7)

Cohen, B., Novick, D., & Rubinstein, M. (1996). Modulation of insulin activities by leptin. *Science, 274,* 1185–1188. (10)

Cohen, D., & Nicolelis, M. A. L. (2004). Reduction of single-neuron firing uncertainty by cortical ensembles during motor skill learning. *Journal of Neuroscience, 24,* 3574–3582. (8)

Cohen, L. G., Celnik, P., Pascual-Leone, A., Corwell, B., Faiz, L., Dambrosia, J., et al. (1997). Functional relevance of cross-modal plasticity in blind humans. *Nature, 389,* 180–183. (5)

Cohen, S., Frank, E., Doyle, W. J., Skoner, D. P., Rabin, B. S., & Swaltney, J. M., Jr. (1998). Types of stressors that increase susceptibility to the common cold in healthy adults. *Health Psychology, 17,* 214–223. (12)

Cohen-Kettenis, P. T. (2005). Gender change in 46,XY persons with 5α-reductase-2 deficiency and 17β-hydroxysteroid dehydrogenase-3 deficiency. *Archives of Sexual Behavior, 34,* 399–410. (11)

Cohen-Tannoudji, M., Babinet, C., & Wassef, M. (1994). Early determination of a mouse somatosensory cortex marker. *Nature, 368,* 460–463. (5)

Colantuoni, C., Rada, P., McCarthy, J., Patten, C., Avena, N. M., Chadeayne, A., et al. (2002). Evidence that intermittent, excessive sugar intake causes endogenous opioid dependence. *Obesity Research, 10,* 478–488. (10)

Colantuoni, C., Schwenker, J., McCarthy, J., Rada, P., Ladenheim, B., Cadet, J.-L., et al. (2001). Excessive sugar intake alters binding to dopamine and mu-opioid receptors in the brain. *NeuroReport, 12,* 3549–3552. (10)

Colapinto, J. (1997, December 11). The true story of John/Joan. *Rolling Stone,* pp. 54–97. (11)

Colcombe, S. J., Erickson, K. I., Raz, N., Webb, A. G., Cohen, N. J., McAuley, E., et al. (2003). Aerobic fitness reduces brain tissue loss in aging humans. *Journal of Gerontology: Medical Sciences, 58A,* 176–180. (5)

Colcombe, S. J., Erickson, K. I., Scalf, P. E., Kim, J. S., Prakash, R., McAuley, E., et al. (2006). Aerobic exercise training increases brain volume in aging humans. *Journals of Gerontology Series A: Biological Sciences and Medical Sciences, 61,* 1166–1170. (5)

Colgreave, N. (2002). Sex releases the speed limit on evolution. *Nature, 420,* 664–666. (11)

Colom, R., Jung, R. E., & Haier, R. J. (2006). Distributed brain sites for the *g*-factor of intelligence. *NeuroImage, 31,* 1359–1365. (4)

Conn, P. M., & Parker, J. V. (2008). Winners and losers in the animal-research war. *American Scientist, 96,* 184–186. (1)

Connine, C. M., Blasko, D. G., & Hall, M. (1991). Effects of subsequent sentence context in auditory word recognition: Temporal and linguistic constraints. *Journal of Memory and Language, 30,* 234–250. (14)

Considine, R. V., Sinha, M. K., Heiman, M. L., Kriauciunas, A., Stephens, T. W., Nyce, M. R., et al. (1996). Serum immunoreactive-leptin concentrations in normal-weight and obese humans. *New England Journal of Medicine, 334,* 292–295. (10)

Conti, B., Sanchez-Alavez, M., Winsky-Sommerer, R., Morale, M. C., Lucero, J., Brownell, S., et al. (2006). Transgenic mice with a reduced core body temperature have an increased life span. *Science, 314,* 825–828. (10)

Cooke, B. M., Tabibnia, G., & Breedlove, S. M. (1999). A brain sexual dimorphism controlled by adult circulating androgens. *Proceedings of the National Academy of Sciences, USA, 96,* 7538–7540. (11)

Coppola, D. M., Purves, H. R., McCoy, A. N., & Purves, D. (1998). The distribution of oriented contours in the real world. *Proceedings of the National Academy of Sciences, USA, 95,* 4002–4006. (6)

Corder, R., Mullen, W., Khan, N. Q., Marks, S. C., Wood, E. G., Carrier, M. J., et al. (2006). Red wine procyanidins and vascular health. *Nature, 444,* 566. (3)

Corina, D. P. (1998). Studies of neural processing in deaf signers: Toward a neurocognitive model of language processing in the deaf. *Journal of Deaf Studies and Idea Education, 3,* 35–48. (14)

Corkin, S. (1984). Lasting consequences of bilateral medial temporal lobectomy: Clinical course and experimental findings in H. M. *Seminars in Neurology, 4,* 249–259. (13)

Corkin, S. (2002). What's new with the amnesic patient H. M.? *Nature Reviews Neuroscience, 3,* 153–159. (13)

Corkin, S., Rosen, T. J., Sullivan, E. V., & Clegg, R. A. (1989). Penetrating head injury in young adulthood exacerbates cognitive decline in later years. *Journal of Neuroscience, 9,* 3876–3883. (5)

Cosmelli, D., David, O., Lachaux, J.-P., Martinerie, J., Garnero, L., Renault, B., et al. (2004). Waves of consciousness: Ongoing cortical patterns during binocular rivalry. *NeuroImage, 23,* 128–140. (14)

Coss, R. G., Brandon, J. G., & Globus, A. (1980). Changes in morphology of dendritic spines on honeybee calycal interneurons associated with cumulative nursing and foraging experiences. *Brain Research, 192,* 49–59. (5)

Costa, M., Braun, C., & Birbaumer, N. (2003). Gender differences in response to pictures of nudes: A magnetoencephalography study. *Biological Psychology, 63,* 129–147. (4)

Cotter, D., Mackay, D., Landau, S., Kerwin, R., & Everall, I. (2001). Reduced glial cell density and neuronal size in the anterior cingulate cortex in major depressive disorder. *Archives of General Psychiatry, 58,* 545–553. (15)

Courchesne, E., Townsend, J., Akshoomoff, N. A., Saitoh, O., Yeung-Courchesne, R., Lincoln, A. J., et al. (1994). Impairment in shifting attention in autistic and cerebellar patients. *Behavioral Neuroscience, 108,* 848–865. (4)

Cowan, R. L. (2006). Neuroimaging research in human MDMA users: A review. *Psychopharmacology, 189,* 539–556. (3)

Cowart, B. J. (2005, Spring). Taste, our body's gustatory gatekeeper. *Cerebrum, 7*(2), 7–22. (7)

Cowey, A., & Stoerig, P. (1995). Blindsight in monkeys. *Nature, 373,* 247–249. (6)

Cox, D., Meyers, E., & Sinha, P. (2004). Contextually evoked object-specific responses in human visual cortex. *Science, 304,* 115–117. (6)

Cox, J. J., Reimann, F., Nicholas, A. K., Thornton, G., Roberts, E., Springell, K., et al. (2006). An *SCN9A* channelopathy causes congenital inability to experience pain. *Nature, 444,* 894–898. (7)

Craddock, N., & Jones, I. (1999). Genetics of bipolar disorder. *Journal of Medical Genetics, 36,* 585–594. (15)

Craig, A. D., Krout, K., & Andrew, D. (2001). Quantitative response characteristics of thermoreceptive and nociceptive lamina I spinothalamic neurons in the cat. *Journal of Neurophysiology, 86,* 1459–1480. (7)

Craig, A. M., & Boudin, H. (2001). Molecular heterogeneity of central synapses: Afferent and target regulation. *Nature Neuroscience, 4,* 569–578. (3)

Crair, M. C., Gillespie, D. C., & Stryker, M. P. (1998). The role of visual experience in the development of columns in cat visual cortex. *Science, 279,* 566–570. (6)

Crair, M. C., & Malenka, R. C. (1995). A critical period for long-term potentiation at thalamocortical synapses. *Nature, 375,* 325–328. (6)

Cravchik, A., & Goldman, D. (2000). Neurochemical individuality. *Archives of General Psychiatry, 57,* 1105–1114. (3)

Cremers, C. W. R. J., & van Rijn, P. M. (1991). Acquired causes of deafness in childhood. *Annals of the New York Academy of Sciences, 630,* 197–202. (7)

Crick, F. C., & Koch, C. (2004). A framework for consciousness. In M. S. Gazzaniga (Ed.), *The cognitive neurosciences* (3rd ed., pp. 1133–1143). Cambridge, MA: MIT Press. (1, 14)

Crick, F., & Mitchison, G. (1983). The function of dream sleep. *Nature, 304,* 111–114. (9)

Crinion, J., Turner, R., Grogan, A., Hanakawa, T., Noppeney, U., Devlin, J. T., et al. (2006). Language control in the bilingual brain. *Science, 312,* 1537–1540. (14)

Critchley, H. D., Mathias, C. J., & Dolan, R. J. (2001). Neuroanatomical basis for first- and second-order representations of bodily states. *Nature Neuroscience, 4,* 207–212. (12)

Critchley, H. D., & Rolls, E. T. (1996). Hunger and satiety modify the responses of olfactory and visual neurons in the primate orbito-frontal cortex. *Journal of Neurophysiology, 75,* 1673–1686. (10)

Crossin, K. L., & Krushel, L. A. (2000). Cellular signaling by neural cell adhesion molecules of the immunoglobulin family. *Developmental Dynamics, 218,* 260–279. (5)

Cummings, D. E., Clement, K., Purnell, J. Q., Vaisse, C., Foster, K. E., Frayo, R. S., et al. (2002). Elevated plasma ghrelin levels in Prader-Willi syndrome. *Nature Medicine, 8,* 643–644. (10)

Cummings, D. E., & Overduin, J. (2007). Gastrointestinal regulation of food intake. *Journal of Clinical Investigation, 117,* 13–23. (10)

Cunningham, W. A., Van Bavel, J. J., & Johnsen, I. R. (2008). Adaptive flexibility: Evaluative processing goals shape amygdala activity. *Psychological Science, 19,* 152–160. (12)

Cunnington, R., Windischberger, C., & Moser, E. (2005). Premovement activity of the pre-supplementary motor area and the readiness for action: Studies of time-resolved event-related functional MRI. *Human Movement Science, 24,* 644–656. (8)

Cusack, R., Carlyon, R. P., & Robertson, I. H. (2000). Neglect between but not within auditory objects. *Journal of Cognitive Neuroscience, 12,* 1056–1065. (14)

Cutler, W. B., Preti, G., Krieger, A., Huggins, G. R., Garcia, C. R., & Lawley, H. J. (1986). Human axillary secretions influence women's menstrual cycles: The role of donor extract from men. *Hormones and Behavior, 20,* 463–473. (7)

Cynader, M., & Chernenko, G. (1976). Abolition of direction selectivity in the visual cortex of the cat. *Science, 193,* 504–505. (6)

Czeisler, C. A., Johnson, M. P., Duffy, J. F., Brown, E. N., Ronda, J. M., & Kronauer, R. E. (1990). Exposure to bright light and darkness to treat physiologic maladaptation to night work. *New England Journal of Medicine, 322,* 1253–1259. (9)

Czeisler, C. A., Weitzman, E. D., Moore-Ede, M. C., Zimmerman, J. C., & Knauer, R. S. (1980). Human sleep: Its duration and organization depend on its circadian phase. *Science, 210,* 1264–1267. (9)

Dabbs, J. M., Jr., Carr, T. S., Frady, R. L., & Riad, J. K. (1995). Testosterone, crime, and misbehavior among 692 male prison inmates. *Personality and Individual Differences, 18,* 627–633. (12)

Dale, N., Schacher, S., & Kandel, E. R. (1988). Long-term facilitation in *Aplysia* involves increase in transmitter release. *Science, 239,* 282–285. (13)

Dalley, J. W., Fryer, T. D., Brichard, L., Robinson, E. S. J., Theobald, D. E. H., Lääne, K., et al. (2007). Nucleus accumbens D2/3 receptors predict trait impulsivity and cocaine reinforcement. *Science, 315,* 1267–1270. (3)

Dalterio, S., & Bartke, A. (1979). Perinatal exposure to cannabinoids alters male reproductive function in mice. *Science, 205,* 1420–1422. (11)

Dalton, K. (1968). Ante-natal progesterone and intelligence. *British Journal of Psychiatry, 114,* 1377–1382. (11)

Dalton, P., Doolittle, N., & Breslin, P. A. (2002). Gender-specific induction of enhanced sensitivity to odors. *Nature Neuroscience, 5,* 199–200. (7)

Damasio, A. R. (1994). *Descartes' error.* New York: Putnam's Sons. (12)

Damasio, A. (1999). *The feeling of what happens.* New York: Harcourt Brace. (12)

Damsma, G., Pfaus, J. G., Wenkstern, D., Phillips, A. G., & Fibiger, H. C. (1992). Sexual behavior increases dopamine transmission in the nucleus accumbens and striatum of male rats: A comparison with novelty and locomotion. *Behavioral Neuroscience, 106,* 181–191. (3)

Dantzer, R., O'Connor, J. C., Freund, G. G., Johnson, R. W., & Kelley, K. W. (2008). From inflammation to sickness and depression: When the immune system subjugates the brain. *Nature Reviews Neuroscience, 9,* 46–57. (12)

Darwin, C. (1859). *The origin of species.* New York: D. Appleton. (1)

Davalos, D., Grutzendler, J., Yang, G., Kim, J. V., Zuo, Y., Jung, S., et al. (2005). ATP mediates rapid microglial response to local brain injury *in vivo. Nature Neuroscience, 8,* 752–758. (2)

Davidson, R. J. (1984). Affect, cognition, and hemispheric specialization. In C. E. Izard, J. Kagan, & R. B. Zajonc (Eds.), *Emotions, cognition, & behavior* (pp. 320–365). Cambridge, England: Cambridge University Press. (15)

Davidson, R. J., & Fox, N. A. (1982). Asymmetrical brain activity discriminates between positive and negative affective stimuli in human infants. *Science, 218,* 1235–1237. (12)

Davidson, R. J., & Henriques, J. (2000). Regional brain function in sadness and depression. In J. C. Borod (Ed.), *The neuropsychology of emotion* (pp. 269–297). London: Oxford University Press. (12)

Davidson, S., Zhang, X., Yoon, C. H., Khasabov, S. G., Simone, D. A., & Giesler, G. J., Jr. (2007). The itch-producing agents histamine and cowhage activate separate populations of primate spinothalamic tract neurons. *Journal of Neuroscience, 27,* 10007–10014. (7)

Davies, G., Welham, J., Chant, D., Torrey, E. F., & McGrath, J. (2003). A systematic review and meta-analysis of Northern hemisphere season of birth effects in schizophrenia. *Schizophrenia Bulletin, 29,* 587–593. (15)

Davies, P. (2000). A very incomplete comprehensive theory of Alzheimer's disease. *Annals of the New York Academy of Sciences, 924,* 8–16. (13)

Davis, E. C., Shryne, J. E., & Gorski, R. A. (1995). A revised critical period for the sexual differentiation of the sexually dimorphic nucleus of the preoptic area in the rat. *Neuroendocrinology, 62,* 579–585. (11)

Davis, J. M., Chen, N., & Glick, I. D. (2003). A meta-analysis of the efficacy of second-generation antipsychotics. *Archives of General Psychiatry, 60,* 553–564. (15)

Davis, K. D., Kiss, Z. H. T., Luo, L., Tasker, R. R., Lozano, A. M., & Dostrovsky, J. O. (1998). Phantom sensations generated by thalamic microstimulation. *Nature, 391,* 385–387. (5)

d'Avossa, G., Tossetti, M., Crespi, S., Biagi, L., Burr, D. C., & Morrone, M. C. (2007). Spatiotopic selectivity of BOLD responses to visual motion in human area MT. *Nature Neuroscience, 10,* 249–255. (6)

Dawkins, R. (1989). *The selfish gene* (new ed.). Oxford, England: Oxford University Press. (1)

Dawson, T. M., & Dawson, V. L. (2003). Molecular pathways of neurodegeneration in Parkinson's disease. *Science, 302,* 819–822. (8)

Dawson, T. M., Gonzalez-Zulueta, M., Kusel, J., & Dawson, V. L. (1998). Nitric oxide: Diverse actions in the central and peripheral nervous system. *The Neuroscientist, 4,* 96–112. (3)

Day, S. (2005). Some demographic and socio-cultural aspects of synesthesia. In L. C. Robertson & N. Sagiv (Eds.), *Synesthesis* (pp. 11–33). Oxford, England: Oxford University Press. (7)

de Castro, J. M. (2000). Eating behavior: Lessons from the real world of humans. *Nutrition, 16,* 800–813. (10)

de Jong, W. W., Hendriks, W., Sanyal, S., & Nevo, E. (1990). The eye of the blind mole rat (*Spalax ehrenbergi*): Regressive evolution at the molecular level. In E. Nevo & O. A. Reig (Eds.), *Evolution of subterranean mammals at the organismal and molecular levels* (pp. 383–395). New York: Liss. (9)

de Jonge, F. H., Louwerse, A. L., Ooms, M. P., Evers, P., Endert, E., & Van De Poll, N. E. (1989). Lesions of the SDN-POA inhibit sexual behavior of male Wistar rats. *Brain Research Bulletin, 23,* 483–492. (11)

De Luca, M., Di Page, E., Judica, A., Spinelli, D., & Zoccolotti, P. (1999). Eye movement patterns in linguistic and non-linguistic tasks in developmental surface dyslexia. *Neuropsychologia, 37,* 1407–1420. (14)

de Quervain, D. J.-F., & Papassotiropoulos, A. (2006). Identification of a genetic cluster influencing memory performance and hippocampal activity in humans. *Proceedings of the National*

Academy of Sciences, USA, 103, 4270–4274. (13)

Deacon, T. W. (1990). Problems of ontogeny and phylogeny in brain-size evolution. *International Journal of Primatology, 11,* 237–282. (4)

Deacon, T. W. (1992). Brain-language coevolution. In J. A. Hawkins & M. Gell-Mann (Eds.), *The evolution of human languages* (pp. 49–83). Reading, MA: Addison-Wesley. (14)

Deacon, T. W. (1997). *The symbolic species.* New York: Norton (4, 14)

Deadwyler, S. A., Porrino, L., Siegel, J. M., & Hampson, R. E. (2007). Systemic and nasal delivery of orexin-A (hypocretin-1) reduces the effects of sleep deprivation on cognitive performance in nonhuman primates. *Journal of Neuroscience, 27,* 14239–14247. (9)

DeArmond, S. J., Fusco, M. M., & Dewey, M. M. (1974). *Structure of the human brain.* New York: Oxford University Press. (10)

DeCoursey, P. (1960). Phase control of activity in a rodent. *Cold Spring Harbor symposia on quantitative biology, 25,* 49–55. (9)

DeFelipe, C., Herrero, J. F., O'Brien, J. A., Palmer, J. A., Doyle, C. A., Smith, A. J. H., et al. (1998). Altered nociception, analgesia and aggression in mice lacking the receptor for substance P. *Nature, 392,* 394–397. (7)

Dehaene, S., & Changeux, J.-P. (2004). Neural mechanisms for access to consciousness. In M. S. Gazzaniga (Ed.), *The cognitive neurosciences* (3rd ed., pp. 1145–1157). Cambridge, MA: MIT Press. (14)

Dehaene, S., Naccache, L., Cohen, L., LeBihan, D., Mangin, J.-F., Poline, J.-B., et al. (2001). Cerebral mechanisms of word masking and unconscious repetition priming. *Nature Neuroscience, 4,* 752–758. (14)

Del Cerro, M. C. R., Perez Izquierdo, M. A., Rosenblatt, J. S., Johnson, B. M., Pacheco, P., & Komisaruk, B. R. (1995). Brain 2- deoxyglucose levels related to maternal behavior-inducing stimuli in the rat. *Brain Research, 696,* 213–220. (11)

Delahanty, D. L., Raimonde, A. J., & Spoonster, E. (2000). Initial posttraumatic urinary cortisol levels predict subsequent PTSD symptoms in motor vehicle accident victims. *Biological Psychiatry, 48,* 940–947. (12)

Deliagina, T. G., Orlovsky, G. N., & Pavlova, G. A. (1983). The capacity for generation of rhythmic oscillations is distributed in the lumbosacral spinal cord of the cat. *Experimental Brain Research, 53,* 81–90. (8)

Dement, W. (1972). *Some must watch while some must sleep.* San Francisco: Freeman. (9)

Dement, W. C. (1990). A personal history of sleep disorders medicine. *Journal of Clinical Neurophysiology, 7,* 17–47. (9)

Dement, W., & Kleitman, N. (1957a). Cyclic variations in EEG during sleep and their relation to eye movements, body motility, and dreaming. *Electroencephalography and Clinical Neurophysiology, 9,* 673–690. (9)

Dement, W., & Kleitman, N. (1957b). The relation of eye movements during sleep to dream activity: An objective method for the study of dreaming. *Journal of Experimental Psychology, 53,* 339–346. (9)

Dennett, D. C. (1991). *Consciousness explained.* Boston: Little, Brown. (1)

Denys, K., Vanduffel, W., Fize, D., Nelissen, K., Peuskens, H., Van Essen, D., et al. (2004). The processing of visual shape in the cerebral cortex of human and nonhuman primates: A functional magnetic resonance imaging study. *Journal of Neuroscience, 24,* 2551–2565. (6)

deQuervain, D. J.-F., Roozendaal, B., & McGaugh, J. L. (1998). Stress and glucocorticoids impair retrieval of long-term spatial memory. *Nature, 394,* 787–790. (13)

Derégnaucourt, S., Mitra, P. P., Fehér, O., Pytte, C., & Tchernichovski, O. (2005). How sleep affects the developmental learning of bird song. *Nature, 433,* 710–716. (9)

DeSimone, J. A., Heck, G. L., & Bartoshuk, L. M. (1980). Surface active taste modifiers: A comparison of the physical and psycho-physical properties of gymnemic acid and sodium lauryl sulfate. *Chemical Senses, 5,* 317–330. (7)

DeSimone, J. A., Heck, G. L., Mierson, S., & DeSimone, S. K. (1984). The active ion transport properties of canine lingual epithelia in vitro. *Journal of General Physiology, 83,* 633–656. (7)

Detre, J. A., & Floyd, T. F. (2001). Functional MRI and its applications to the clinical neurosciences. *Neuroscientist, 7,* 64–79. (4)

Deutsch, D., Henthorn, T., Marvin, E., & Xu, H. S. (2006). Absolute pitch among American and Chinese conservatory students: Prevalence differences, and evidence for a speech-related critical period. *Journal of the Acoustical Society of America, 119,* 719–722. (7)

Deutsch, J. A., & Ahn, S. J. (1986). The splanchnic nerve and food intake regulation. *Behavioral and Neural Biology, 45,* 43–47. (10)

Deutsch, J. A., Young, W. G., & Kalogeris, T. J. (1978). The stomach signals satiety. *Science, 201,* 165–167. (10)

DeValois, R. L., Albrecht, D. G., & Thorell, L. G. (1982). Spatial frequency selectivity of cells in macaque visual cortex. *Vision Research, 22,* 545–559. (6)

Devane, W. A., Dysarz, F. A., III, Johnson, M. R., Melvin, L. S., & Howlett, A. C. (1988). Determination and characterization of a cannabinoid receptor in rat brain. *Molecular Pharmacology, 34,* 605–613. (3)

Devor, E. J., Abell, C. W., Hoffman, P. L., Tabakoff, B., & Cloninger, C. R. (1994). Platelet MAO activity in Type I and Type II alcoholism. *Annals of the New York Academy of Sciences, 708,* 119–128. (3)

Devor, M. (1996). Pain mechanisms. *The Neuroscientist, 2,* 233–244. (7)

DeYoe, E. A., Felleman, D. J., Van Essen, D. C., & McClendon, E. (1994). Multiple processing streams in occipitotemporal visual cortex. *Nature, 371,* 151–154. (6)

Dhingra, R., Sullivan, L., Jacques, P. F., Wang, T. J., Fox, C. S., Meigs, J. B., et al. (2007). Soft drink consumption and risk of developing cardiometabolic risk factors and the metabolic syndrome in middle-aged adults in the community. *Circulation, 116,* 480–488. (10)

Di Lorenzo, P. M., Hallock, R. M., & Kennedy, D. P. (2003). Temporal coding of sensation: Mimicking taste quality with electrical stimulation of the brain. *Behavioral Neuroscience, 117,* 1423–1433. (2, 7)

Diamond, L. M. (2007). A dynamical systems approach to the development and expression of female same-sex sexuality. *Perspectives on Psychological Science, 2,* 142–161. (11)

Diamond, M., & Sigmundson, H. K. (1997). Management of intersexuality: Guidelines for dealing with persons with ambiguous genitalia. *Archives of Pediatrics and Adolescent Medicine, 151,* 1046–1050. (11)

Diamond, M. C., Scheibel, A. B., Murphy, G. M., & Harvey, T. (1985). On the brain of a scientist: Albert Einstein. *Experimental Neurology, 88,* 198–204. (4)

Diano, S., Farr, S. A., Benoit, S. C., McNay, E. C., da Silva, I., Horvath, B., et al. (2006). Ghrelin controls hippocampal spine synapse density and memory performance. *Nature Neuroscience, 9,* 381–388. (10)

Dichgans, J. (1984). Clinical symptoms of cerebellar dysfunction and their topodiagnostic significance. *Human Neurobiology, 2,* 269–279. (8)

Dick, D. M., Johnson, J. K., Viken, R. J., & Rose, R. J. (2000). Testing between-family associations in within-family comparisons. *Psychological Science, 11,* 409–413. (3)

Dick, F., Bates, E., Wulfeck, B., Utman, J. A., Dronkers, N., & Gernsbacher, M. A. (2001). Language deficits, localization, and grammar: Evidence for a distributive model of language breakdown in aphasic patients and neurologically intact individuals. *Psychological Review, 108,* 759–788. (14)

Dickens, W. T., & Flynn, J. R. (2001). Heritability estimates versus large environmental effects: The IQ paradox resolved. *Psychological Review, 108,* 346–369. (1)

Dierks, T., Linden, D. E. J., Jandl, M., Formisano, E., Goebel, R., Lanfermann, H., et al. (1999). Activation of Heschl's gyrus during auditory hallucinations. *Neuron, 22,* 615–621. (4)

Dijk, D.-J., & Cajochen, C. (1997). Melatonin and the circadian regulation of sleep initiation, consolidation, structure, and the sleep EEG. *Journal of Biological Rhythms, 12,* 627–635. (9)

Dilks, D. D., Serences, J. T., Rosenau, B. J., Yantis, S., & McCloskey, M. (2007). Human adult cortical reorganization and consequent visual distortion. *Journal of Neuroscience, 27,* 9585–9594. (5)

Diller, L., Packer, O. S., Verweij, J., McMahon, M. J., Williams, D. R., & Dacey, D. M. (2004). L and M cone contributions to the midget and parasol ganglion cell receptive fields of macaque monkey retina. *Journal of Neuroscience, 24,* 1079–1088. (6)

DiMarzo, V., Fontana, A., Cadas, H., Schinelli, S., Cimino, G., Schwartz, J.-C., et al. (1994). Formation and inactivation of endogenous cannabinoid anandamide in central neurons. *Nature, 372,* 686–691. (3)

DiMarzo, V., Goparaju, S. K., Wang, L., Liu, J., Bátkai, S., Járai, Z., et al. (2001). Leptin-regulated endocannabinoids are involved in maintaining food intake. *Nature, 410,* 822–825. (3)

Dimond, S. J. (1979). Symmetry and asymmetry in the vertebrate brain. In D. A. Oakley & H. C. Plotkin (Eds.), *Brain, behaviour, and evolution* (pp. 189–218). London: Methuen. (14)

Dinstein, I., Hasson, U., Rubin, N., & Heeger, D. J. (2007). Brain areas selective for both observed and executed movements. *Journal of Neurophysiology, 98,* 1415–1427. (8)

Dominguez, J. M., Brann, J. H., Gil, M., & Hull, E. M. (2006). Sexual experience increases nitric oxide synthase in the medial preoptic area of male rats. *Behavioral Neuroscience, 120,* 1389–1394. (11)

Doricchi, F., Guariglia, P., Gasparini, M., & Tomaiuolo, F. (2005). Dissociation between physical and mental number line bisection in right hemisphere brain damage. *Nature Neuroscience, 8,* 1663–1665. (14)

Doty, R. L., Applebaum, S., Zusho, H., & Settle, R. G. (1985). Sex differences in odor identification ability: A cross-cultural analysis. *Neuropsychologia, 23,* 667–672. (7)

Dowling, J. E. (1987). *The retina.* Cambridge, MA: Harvard University Press. (6)

Dowling, J. E., & Boycott, B. B. (1966). Organization of the primate retina. *Proceedings of the Royal Society of London, B, 166,* 80–111. (6)

Downar, J., Mikulis, D. J., & Davis, K. D. (2003). Neural correlates of the prolonged salience of painful stimulation. *NeuroImage, 20,* 1540–1551. (7)

Drachman, D. B. (1978). Myasthenia gravis. *New England Journal of Medicine, 298,* 136–142, 186–193. (8)

Draganski, B., Gaser, C., Busch, V., Schuierer, G., Bogdahn, U., & May, A. (2004). Changes in grey matter induced by training. *Nature, 427,* 311–312. (5)

Dreger, A. D. (1998). *Hermaphrodites and the medical invention of sex.* Cambridge, MA: Harvard University Press. (11)

Drewnowski, A., Henderson, S. A., Shore, A. B., & Barratt-Fornell, A. (1998). Sensory responses to 6-*n*-propylthiouracil (PROP) or sucrose solutions and food preferences in young women. *Annals of the New York Academy of Sciences, 855,* 797–801. (7)

Driver, J., & Frith, C. (2000). Shifting baselines in attention research. *Nature Reviews Neuroscience, 1,* 147–148. (14)

Du, J., Creson, T. K., Wu, L.-J., Ren, M., Gray, N. A., Falke, C., et al. (2008). The role of hippocampal GluR1 and GluR2 receptors in manic-like behavior. *Journal of Neuroscience, 28,* 68–79. (15)

Duan, X., Chang, J. H., Ge, S., Faulkner, R. L., Kim, J. Y., Kitabatake, Y., et al. (2007). Disrupted-in-schizophrenia 1 regulated integration of newly generated neurons in the adult brain. *Cell, 130,* 1146–1158. (15)

Ducommun, C. Y., Michel, C. M., Clarke, S., Adriani, M., Seeck, M., Landis, T., et al. (2004). Cortical motion deafness. *Neuron, 43,* 765–777. (7)

Dudchenko, P. A., & Taube, J. S. (1997). Correlation between head direction cell activity and spatial behavior on a radial arm maze. *Behavioral Neuroscience, 111,* 3–19. (13)

Duelli, R., & Kuschinsky, W. (2001). Brain glucose transporters: Relationship to local energy demand. *News in Physiological Sciences, 16,* 71–76. (2)

Duff, M. C., Hengst, J., Tranel, D., & Cohen, N. J. (2006). Development of shared information in communication despite hippocampal amnesia. *Nature Neuroscience, 9,* 140–146. (13)

Duffy, C. J., Tetewsky, S. J., & O'Brien, H. (2000). Cortical motion blindness in visuospatial AD. *Neurobiology of Aging, 21,* 867–869. (6)

Dunner, D. L., D'Souza, D. N., Kajdasz, D. K., Detke, M. J., & Russell, J. M. (2005). Is treatment-associated hypomania rare with duloxetine: Secondary analysis of controlled trials in non-bipolar depression. *Journal of Affective Disorders, 87,* 115–119. (15)

During, M. J., Ryder, K. M., & Spencer, D. D. (1995). Hippocampal GABA transporter function in temporal-lobe epilepsy. *Nature, 376,* 174–177. (14)

Dyal, J. A. (1971). Transfer of behavioral bias: Reality and specificity. In E. J. Fjerdingstad (Ed.), *Chemical transfer of learned information* (pp. 219–263). New York: American Elsevier. (13)

Earnest, D. J., Liang, F.-Q., Ratcliff, M., & Cassone, V. M. (1999). Immortal time: Circadian clock properties of rat suprachiasmatic cell lines. *Science, 283,* 693–695. (9)

Eastgate, R. M., Griffiths, G. D., Waddingham, P. E., Moody, A. D., Butler, T. K. H., Cobb, S. V., et al. (2006). Modified virtual reality technology for treatment of amblyopia. *Eye, 20,* 370–374. (6)

Eastman, C. I., Hoese, E. K., Youngstedt, S. D., & Liu, L. (1995). Phase-shifting human circadian rhythms with exercise during the night shift. *Physiology & Behavior, 58,* 1287–1291. (9)

Eastman, C. I., Young, M. A., Fogg, L. F., Liu, L., & Meaden, P. M. (1998). Bright light treatment of winter depression. *Archives of General Psychiatry, 55,* 883–889. (15)

Eaves, L. J., Martin, N. G., & Heath, A. C. (1990). Religious affiliation in twins and their parents: Testing a model of cultural inheritance. *Behavior Genetics, 20,* 1–22. (1)

Eccles, J. C. (1964). *The physiology of synapses.* Berlin: Springer-Verlag. (3)

Eckhorn, R., Bauer, R., Jordan, W., Brosch, M., Kruse, W., Munk, M., et al. (1988). Coherent oscillations: A mechanism of feature linking in the visual cortex? *Biological Cybernetics, 60,* 121–130. (14)

Edelman, G. M. (1987). *Neural Darwinism.* New York: Basic Books. (5)

Eden, G. F., Jones, K. M., Cappell, K., Gareau, L., Wood, F. B., Zeffiro, T. A., et al. (2004). Neural changes following remediation in adult developmental dyslexia. *Neuron, 44,* 411–422. (14)

Edgley, S. A., Jankowska, E., & Hammar, I. (2004). Ipsilateral actions of feline corticospinal tract neurons on limb motoneurons. *Journal of Neuroscience, 24,* 7804–7813. (8)

Edinger, J. D., McCall, W. V., Marsh, G. R., Radtke, R. A., Erwin, C. W., & Lininger, A. (1992). Periodic limb movement variability in older DIMS patients across consecutive nights of home monitoring. *Sleep, 15,* 156–161. (9)

Edinger, K. L., & Frye, C. A. (2004). Testosterone's analgesic, anxiolytic, and cognitive-enhancing effects may be due in part to actions of its 5α-reduced metabolites in the hippocampus. *Behavioral Neuroscience, 118,* 1352–1364. (11)

Edlinger, M., Hausmann, A., Kemmler, G., Kurz, M., Kurzhaler, I., Walch, T., et al. (2005). Trends in the pharmacological treatment of patients with schizophrenia over a 12 year observation period. *Schizophrenia Research, 77,* 25–34. (15)

Edman, G., Åsberg, M., Levander, S., & Schalling, D. (1986). Skin conductance habituation and cerebrospinal fluid 5-hydroxy-indoleacetic acid in suicidal patients. *Archives of General Psychiatry, 43,* 586–592. (12)

Ehrhardt, A. A., & Money, J. (1967). Progestin-induced hermaphroditism: IQ and psychosexual identity in a study of ten girls. *Journal of Sex Research, 3,* 83–100. (11)

Ehrlich, P. R., Dobkin, D. S., & Wheye, D. (1988). *The birder's handbook.* New York: Simon & Schuster. (10)

Eichenbaum, H. (2000). A cortical-hippocampal system for declarative memory. *Nature Reviews Neuroscience, 1,* 41–50. (13)

Eichenbaum, H. (2002). *The cognitive neuroscience of memory.* New York: Oxford University Press. (13)

Eidelberg, E., & Stein, D. G. (1974). Functional recovery after lesions of the nervous system. *Neurosciences Research Program Bulletin, 12,* 191–303. (5)

Eimer, M., & Holmes, A. (2007). Event-related brain potential correlates of emotional face processing. *Neuropsychologia, 45,* 15–31. (12)

Eisenstein, E. M., & Cohen, M. J. (1965). Learning in an isolated prothoracic insect ganglion. *Animal Behaviour, 13,* 104–108. (13)

Ek, M., Engblom, D., Saha, S., Blomqvist, A., Jakobsson, P.-J., & Ericsson-Dahlstrand, A. (2001). Pathway across the blood-brain barrier. *Nature, 410,* 430–431. (10)

Elbert, T., Candia, V., Altenmüller, E., Rau, H., Sterr, A., Rockstroh, B., et al. (1998). Alteration of digital representations in somatosensory cortex in focal hand dystonia. *Neuroreport, 9,* 3571–3575. (5)

Elbert, T., Pantev, C., Wienbruch, C., Rockstroh, B., & Taub, E. (1995). Increased cortical representation of the fingers of the left hand in string players. *Science, 270,* 305–307. (5)

Eldridge, L. L., Engel, S. A., Zeineh, M. M., Bookheimer, S. Y., & Knowlton, B. J. (2005). A dissociation of encoding and retrieval processes in the human hippocampus. *Journal of Neuroscience, 25,* 3280–3286. (13)

Elias, C. F., Lee, C., Kelly, J., Aschkenazi, C., Ahima, R. S., Couceyro, P. R., et al. (1998). Leptin activates hypothalamic CART neurons projecting to the spinal cord. *Neuron, 21,* 1375–1385. (10)

Ellacott, K. L. J., & Cone, R. D. (2004). The central melanocortin system and the integration of short- and long-term regulators of energy homeostasis. *Recent Progress in Hormone Research, 59,* 395–408. (10)

Elliott, T. R. (1905). The action of adrenalin. *Journal of Physiology (London), 32,* 401–467. (3)

Ellis, L., & Ames, M. A. (1987). Neurohormonal functioning and sexual orientation: A theory of homosexuality–heterosexuality. *Psychological Bulletin, 101,* 233–258. (11)

Ellis, L., Ames, M. A., Peckham, W., & Burke, D. (1988). Sexual orientation of human offspring may be altered by severe maternal stress during pregnancy. *Journal of Sex Research, 25,* 152–157. (11)

Ellis, L., & Cole-Harding, S. (2001). The effects of prenatal stress, and of prenatal alcohol and nicotine exposure, on human sexual orientation. *Physiology & Behavior, 74,* 213–226. (11)

Ellis-Behnke, R. G., Liang, Y.-X., You, S.-W., Tay, D. K. C., Zhang, S., So, K.-F., et al. (2006). Nano neuro knitting: Peptide nanofiber scaffold for brain repair and axon regeneration with functional return of vision. *Proceedings of the National Academy of Sciences, USA, 103,* 5054–5059. (5)

Elston, G. N. (2000). Pyramidal cells of the frontal lobe: All the more spinous to think with. *Journal of Neuroscience, 20,* RC95: 1–4. (4)

Emery, N. J., Capitanio, J. P., Mason, W. A., Machado, C. J., Mendoza, S. P., & Amaral, D. G. (2001). The effects of bilateral lesions of the amygdala on dyadic social interactions in rhesus monkeys (*Macaca mulatta*). *Behavioral Neuroscience, 115,* 515–544. (12)

Emmorey, K., Allen, J. S., Bruss, J., Schenker, N., & Damasio, H. (2003). A morphometric analysis of auditory brain regions in congenitally deaf adults. *Proceedings of the National Academy of Sciences, USA, 100,* 10049–10054. (7)

Engert, F., & Bonhoeffer, T. (1999). Dendritic spine changes associated with hippocampal long-term synaptic plasticity. *Nature, 399,* 66–70. (13)

Epping-Jordan, M. P., Watkins, S. S., Koob, G. F., & Markou, A. (1998). Dramatic decreases in brain reward function during nicotine withdrawal. *Nature, 393,* 76–79. (3)

Erickson, C., & Lehrman, D. (1964). Effect of castration of male ring doves upon ovarian activity of females. *Journal of Comparative and Physiological Psychology, 58,* 164–166. (11)

Erickson, R. P. (1982). The across-fiber pattern theory: An organizing principle for molar neural function. *Contributions to Sensory Physiology, 6,* 79–110. (7)

Erickson, R. P., DiLorenzo, P. M., & Woodbury, M. A. (1994). Classification of taste responses in brain stem: Membership in fuzzy sets. *Journal of Neurophysiology, 71,* 2139–2150. (7)

Ericsson, K. A., & Charness, N. (1994). Expert performance: Its structure and acquisition. *American Psychologist, 49,* 725–747. (5)

Eschenko, O., Mölle, M., Born, J., & Sara, S. J. (2006). Elevated sleep spindle density after learning or after retrieval in rats. *Journal of Neurophysiology, 26,* 12914–12920. (9)

Etcoff, N. L., Ekman, P., Magee, J. J., & Frank, M. G. (2000). Lie detection and language comprehension. *Nature, 405,* 139. (12, 14)

Etgen, A. M., Chu, H.-P., Fiber, J. M., Karkanias, G. B., & Morales, J. M. (1999). Hormonal integration of neurochemical and sensory signals governing female reproductive behavior. *Behavioural Brain Research, 105,* 93–103. (11)

Euston, D. R., Tatsuno, M., & McNaughton, B. L. (2007). Fast-forward playback of recent memory sequences in prefrontal cortex during sleep. *Science, 318,* 1147–1150. (9)

Evans, D. A., Funkenstein, H. H., Albert, M. S., Scherr, P. A., Cook, N. R., Chown, M. J., et al. (1989). Prevalence of Alzheimer's disease in a community population of older persons. *Journal of the American Medical Association, 262,* 2551–2556. (13)

Evarts, E. V. (1979). Brain mechanisms of movement. *Scientific American, 241*(3), 164–179. (8)

Eyre, J. A., Taylor, J. P., Villagra, F., Smith, M., & Miller, S. (2001). Evidence of activity-dependent withdrawal of corticospinal projections during human development. *Neurology, 57,* 1543–1554. (8)

Facoetti, A., Lorusso, M. L., Paganoni, P., Cattaneo, C., Galli, R., Umiltà, C., et al. (2003). Auditory and visual automatic attention deficits in developmental dyslexia. *Cognitive Brain Research, 16,* 185–191. (14)

Fadda, F. (2000). Tryptophan-free diets: A physiological tool to study brain serotonin function. *News in Physiological Sciences, 15,* 260–264. (3)

Fadool, D. A., Tucker, K., Perkins, R., Fasciani, G., Thompson, R. N., Parsons, A. D.. et al. (2004). Kv1.3 channel gene-targeted deletion produces "super-smeller mice" with altered glomeruli, interacting scaffolding proteins, and biophysics. *Neuron, 41,* 389–404. (7)

Fagen, Z. M., Mitchum, R., Vezina, P., & McGehee, D. S. (2007). Enhanced nicotinic receptor function and drug abuse vulnerability. *Journal of Neuroscience, 27,* 8771–8778. (3)

Falleti, M. G., Maruff, P., Collie, A., Darby, D. G., & McStephen, M. (2003). Qualitative similarities in cognitive impairment associated with 24 h of sustained wakefulness and a blood alcohol concentration of 0.05%. *Journal of Sleep Research, 12,* 265–274. (9)

Famy, C., Streissguth, A. P., & Unis, A. S. (1998). Mental illness in adults with fetal alcohol syndrome or fetal alcohol effects. *American Journal of Psychiatry, 155,* 552–554. (5)

Fan, P. (1995). Cannabinoid agonists inhibit the activation of 5-HT3 receptors in rat nodose ganglion neurons. *Journal of Neurophysiology, 73,* 907–910. (3)

Fan, W., Ellacott, K. L. J., Halatchev, I. G., Takahashi, K., Yu, P., & Cone, R. D. (2004). Cholecystokinin-mediated suppression of feeding involves the brainstem melanocortin system. *Nature Neuroscience, 7,* 335–336. (10)

Fang, F., & He, S. (2005). Cortical responses to invisible objects in the human dorsal and ventral pathways. *Nature Neuroscience, 8,* 1380–1385. (6)

Fantz, R. L. (1963). Pattern vision in newborn infants. *Science, 140,* 296–297. (6)

Farah, M. J. (1990). *Visual agnosia.* Cambridge, MA: MIT Press. (6)

Farah, M. J., Illes, J., Cook-Deegan, R., Gardner, H., Kandel, E., King, P., et al. (2004). Neurocognitive enhancement: What can we do and what should we do? *Nature Reviews Neuroscience, 5,* 421–425. (13)

Farah, M. J., Wilson, K. D., Drain, M., & Tanaka, J. N. (1998). What is "special" about face perception? *Psychological Review, 105,* 482–498. (6)

Farber, N. B., Newcomer, J. W., & Olney, J. W. (1999). Glycine agonists: What can they teach us about schizophrenia? *Archives of General Psychiatry, 56,* 13–17. (15)

Farmer, M. E., & Klein, R. M. (1995). The evidence for a temporal processing deficit linked to dyslexia: A review. *Psychonomic Bulletin & Review, 2,* 460–493. (14)

Farooqi, I. S., Keogh, J. M., Kamath, S., Jones, S., Gibson, W. T., Trussell, R., et al. (2001). Partial leptin deficiency and human adiposity. *Nature, 414,* 34–35. (10)

Featherstone, R. E., Fleming, A. S., & Ivy, G. O. (2000). Plasticity in the maternal circuit: Effects of experience and partum condition on brain astrocyte number in female rats. *Behavioral Neuroscience, 114,* 158–172. (11)

Fedulov, V., Rex, C. S., Simmons, D. A., Palmer, L., Gall, C. M., & Lynch, G. (2007). Evidence that long-term potentiation occurs within individual hippocampal synapses during learning. *Journal of Neuroscience, 27,* 8031–8039. (13)

Feeney, D. M., & Sutton, R. L. (1988). Catecholamines and recovery of function after brain damage. In D. G. Stein & B. A. Sabel (Eds.), *Pharmacological approaches to the treatment of brain and spinal cord injury* (pp. 121–142). New York: Plenum Press. (5)

Feeney, D. M., Sutton, R. L., Boyeson, M. G., Hovda, D. A., & Dail, W. G. (1985). The locus coeruleus and cerebral metabolism: Recovery of function after cerebral injury. *Physiological Psychology, 13,* 197–203. (5)

Feldman, R., Weller, A., Zagoory-Sharon, O., & Levine, A. (2007). Evidence for a neuroendocrinological foundation of human affiliation. *Psychological Science, 18,* 965–970. (11)

Fendrich, R., Wessinger, C. M., & Gazzaniga, M. S. (1992). Residual vision in a scotoma: Implications for blindsight. *Science, 258,* 1489–1491. (6)

Feng, J., Spence, I., & Pratt, J. (2007). Playing an action video game reduces gender differences in spatial cognition. *Psychological Science, 18,* 850–855. (4)

Fentress, J. C. (1973). Development of grooming in mice with amputated forelimbs. *Science, 179,* 704–705. (8)

Ferguson, C. P., & Pigott, T. A. (2000). Anorexia and bulimia nervosa: Neurobiology and pharmacotherapy. *Behavior Therapy, 31,* 237–263. (10)

Fergusson, D. M., Woodward, L. J., & Horwood, J. (1998). Maternal smoking during pregnancy and psychiatric adjustment in late adolescence. *Archives of General Psychiatry, 55,* 721–727. (12)

Ferreira, F., Bailey, K. G. D., & Ferraro, V. (2002). Good-enough representations in language comprehension. *Current Directions in Psychological Science, 11,* 11–15. (14)

Fettiplace, R. (1990). Transduction and tuning in auditory hair cells. *Seminars in the Neurosciences, 2,* 33–40. (7)

Field, E. F., Whishaw, I. Q., Forgie, M. L., & Pellis, S. M. (2004). Neonatal and pubertal, but not adult, ovarian steroids are necessary for the development of female-typical patterns of dodging to protect a food item. *Behavioral Neuroscience, 118*, 1293–1304. (11)

Filosa, J. A., Bonev, A. D., Straub, S. V., Meredith, A. L., Wilkerson, M. K., Aldrich, R. W., et al. (2006). Local potassium signaling couples neuronal activity to vasodilation in the brain. *Nature Neuroscience, 9*, 1397–1403. (2)

Fils-Aime, M.-L., Eckardt, M. J., George, D. T., Brown, G. L., Mefford, I., & Linnoila, M. (1996). Early-onset alcoholics have lower cerebrospinal fluid 5-hydroxyindoleacetic acid levels than late-onset alcoholics. *Archives of General Psychiatry, 53*, 211–216. (3)

Fine, I., Smallman, H. S., Doyle, P., & MacLeod, D. I. A. (2002). Visual function before and after the removal of bilateral congenital cataracts in adulthood. *Vision Research, 42*, 191–210. (6)

Fine, I. Wade, A. R., Brewer, A. A., May, M. G., Goodman, D. F., Boynton, G. M., et al. (2003). Long-term deprivation affects visual perception and cortex. *Nature Neuroscience, 6*, 915–916. (6)

Finger, S., & Roe, D. (1996). Gustave Dax and the early history of cerebral dominance. *Archives of Neurology, 53*, 806–813. (14)

Fink, G., Sumner, B. E. H., Rosie, R., Grace, O., & Quinn, J. P. (1996). Estrogen control of central neurotransmission: Effect on mood, mental state, and memory. *Cellular and Molecular Neurobiology, 16*, 325–344. (11)

Fink, G. R., Halligan, P. W., Marshall, J. C., Frith, C. D., Frackowiak, R. S. J., & Dolan, R. J. (1996). Where in the brain does visual attention select the forest and the trees? *Nature, 382*, 626–628. (14)

Fink, M. (1985). Convulsive therapy: Fifty years of progress. *Convulsive Therapy, 1*, 204–216. (15)

Finlay, B. L., & Darlington, R. B. (1995). Linked regularities in the development and evolution of mammalian brains. *Science, 268*, 1578–1584. (4)

Finlay, B. L., & Pallas, S. L. (1989). Control of cell number in the developing mammalian visual system. *Progress in Neurobiology, 32*, 207–234. (5)

Fisher, S. E., Vargha-Khadem, F., Watkins, K. E., Monaco, A. P., & Pembrey, M. E. (1998). Localisation of a gene implicated in a severe speech and language disorder. *Nature Genetics, 18*, 168–170. (14)

Fitts, D. A., Starbuck, E. M., & Ruhf, A. (2000). Circumventricular organs and ANGII-induced salt appetite: Blood pressure and connectivity. *American Journal of Physiology, 279*, R2277–R2286. (10)

Fitzgerald, P. B., Brown, T. L., & Daskalakis, Z. J. (2002). The application of transcranial magnetic stimulation in psychiatry and neurosciences research. *Acta Psychiatrica Scandinavica, 105*, 324–340. (4)

Fjerdingstad, E. J. (1973). Transfer of learning in rodents and fish. In W. B. Essman & S. Nakajima (Eds.), *Current biochemical approaches to learning and memory* (pp. 73–98). Flushing, NY: Spectrum. (13)

Flatz, G. (1987). Genetics of lactose digestion in humans. *Advances in Human Genetics, 16*, 1–77. (10)

Fleet, W. S., & Heilman, K. M. (1986). The fatigue effect in hemispatial neglect. *Neurology, 36*(Suppl. 1), 258. (5)

Fletcher, P. C., McKenna, P. J., Frith, C. D., Grasby, P. M., Friston, K. J., & Dolan, R. J. (1998). Brain activations in schizophrenia during a graded memory task studied with functional neuroimaging. *Archives of General Psychiatry, 55*, 1001–1008. (15)

Fletcher, R., & Voke, J. (1985). *Defective colour vision*. Bristol, England: Hilger. (6)

Flöel, A., Knecht, S., Lohmann, H., Deppe, M., Sommer, J., Dräger, B., et al. (2001). Language and spatial attention can lateralize to the same hemisphere in healthy humans. *Neurology, 57*, 1018–1024. (14)

Flor, H., Elbert, T., Knecht, S., Wienbruch, C., Pantev, C., Birbaumer, N., et al. (1995). Phantom-limb pain as a perceptual correlate of cortical reorganization following arm amputation. *Nature, 375*, 482–484. (5)

Florence, S. L., & Kaas, J. H. (1995). Large-scale reorganization at multiple levels of the somatosensory pathway follows therapeutic amputation of the hand in monkeys. *Journal of Neuroscience, 15*, 8083–8095. (5)

Flynn, J. M., & Boder, E. (1991). Clinical and electrophysiological correlates of dysphonetic and dyseidetic dyslexia. In J. F. Stein (Ed.), *Vision and visual dyslexia* (pp. 121–131). Vol. 13 of J. R. Cronly-Dillon (Ed.), *Vision and visual dysfunction*. Boca Raton, FL: CRC Press. (14)

Foerde, K., Knowlton, B. J., & Poldrack, R. A. (2006). Modulation of competing memory systems by distraction. *Proceedings of the National Academy of Sciences, USA, 103*, 11778–11783. (13)

Fogel, S. M., Nader, R., Cote, K. A., & Smith, C. T. (2007). Sleep spindles and learning potential. *Behavioral Neuroscience, 121*, 1–10. (9)

Földy, C., Neu, A., Jones, M. V., & Soltesz, I. (2006). Presynaptic activity-dependent modulation of cannabinoid type 1 receptor-mediated inhibition of GABA release. *Journal of Neuroscience, 26*, 1465–1469. (3)

Forger, N. G., & Breedlove, S. M. (1987). Motoneuronal death during human fetal development. *Journal of Comparative Neurology, 264*, 118–122. (5)

Forger, N. G., Rosen, G. J., Waters, E. M., Jacob, D., Simerly, R. B., & de Vries, G. J. (2004). Deletion of *Bax* eliminates sex differences in the mouse forebrain. *Proceedings of the National Academy of Sciences, USA, 101*, 13666–13671. (11)

Forster, B., & Corballis, M. C. (2000). Interhemispheric transfer of colour and shape information in the presence and absence of the corpus callosum. *Neuropsychologia, 38*, 32–45. (14)

Fortin, N. J., Agster, K. L., & Eichenbaum, H. B. (2002). Critical role of the hippocampus in memory for sequences of events. *Nature Neuroscience, 5*, 458–462. (13)

Foster, D. J., & Wilson, M. A. (2006). Reverse replay of behavioural sequences in hippocampal place cells during the awake state. *Nature, 440*, 680–683. (13)

Fotopoulou, A., Solms, M., & Turnbull, O. (2004). Wishful reality distortions in confabulation: A case report. *Neuropsychologia, 47*, 727–744. (13)

Foundas, A. L., Leonard, C. M., & Hanna-Pladdy, B. (2002). Variability in the anatomy of the planum temporale and posterior ascending ramus: Do right- and left-handers differ? *Brain and Language, 83*, 403–424. (14)

Fox, P. T., Ingham, R. J., Ingham, J. C., Zamarripa, F., Xiong, J.-H., & Lancaster, J. L. (2000). Brain correlates of stuttering and syllable production: A PET performance-correlation analysis. *Brain, 123*, 1985–2004. (14)

Frank, M. J., Samanta, J., Moustafa, A. A., & Sherman, S. J. (2007). Hold your horses: Impulsivity, deep brain stimulation, and medication in Parkinsonism. *Science, 318*, 1309–1312. (8)

Frank, R. A., Mize, S. J. S., Kennedy, L. M., de los Santos, H. C., & Green, S. J. (1992). The effect of *Gymnema sylvestre* extracts on the sweetness of eight sweeteners. *Chemical Senses, 17*, 461–479. (7)

Frankland, P. W., Josselyn, S. A., Bradwejn, J., Vaccarino, F. J., & Yeomans, J. S. (1997). Activation of amygdala cholecystokinin B receptors potentiates the acoustic startle response in the rat. *Journal of Neuroscience, 17*, 1838–1847. (12)

Franz, E. A., & Fahey, S. (2007). Developmental change in interhemispheric communication. *Psychological Science, 18*, 1030–1031. (14)

Franz, E. A., Waldie, K. E., & Smith, M. J. (2000). The effect of callosotomy on novel versus familiar bimanual actions: A neural dissociation between controlled and automatic processes? *Psychological Science, 11*, 82–85. (14)

Frassinetti, F., Pavani, F., & Làdavas, E. (2002). Acoustical vision of neglected stimuli: Interaction among spatially converging audiovisual inputs in neglect patients. *Journal of Cognitive Neuroscience, 14*, 62–69. (14)

Frayling, T. M., Timpson, N. J., Weedon, M. N., Zeggini, E., Freathy, R. M., Lindgren, C. M., et al. (2007). A common variant in the *FTO* gene is associated with body mass index and predisposes to childhood and adult obesity. *Science, 316*, 889–894. (10)

Freed, C. R., Greene, P. E., Breeze, R. E., Tsai, W.-Y., DuMouchel, W., Kao, R., et al. (2001). Transplantation of embryonic dopamine neurons for severe Parkinson's disease. *New England Journal of Medicine, 344*, 710–719. (8)

Freedman, M. S., Lucas, R. J., Soni, B., von Schantz, M., Muñoz, M., David-Gray, Z., et al. (1999). Regulation of mammalian circadian behavior by non-rod, non-cone, ocular photoreceptors. *Science, 284*, 502–504. (9)

Frese, M., & Harwich, C. (1984). Shiftwork and the length and quality of sleep. *Journal of Occupational Medicine, 26*, 561–566. (9)

Fridberger, A., Boutet de Monvel, J., Zheng, J., Hu, N., Zou, Y., Ren, T., et al. (2004). Organ of Corti potentials and the motion of the basilar membrane. *Journal of Neuroscience, 24*, 10057–10063. (7)

Fried, I., Katz, A., McCarthy, G., Sass, K. J., Williamson, P., Spencer, S. S., et al. (1991). Functional organization of human supplementary motor cortex studied by electrical stimulation. *Journal of Neuroscience, 11,* 3656–3666. (8)

Fried, P. A., Watkinson, B., & Gray, R. (2003). Differential effects on cognitive functioning in 13- to 16-year-olds prenatally exposed to cigarettes and marihuana. *Neurotoxicology and Teratology, 25,* 427–436. (5)

Fried, S., Münch, T. A., & Werblin, F. S. (2002). Mechanisms and circuitry underlying directional selectivity in the retina. *Nature, 420,* 411–414. (6)

Friedlander, W. J. (1986). Who was "the father of bromide treatment of epilepsy"? *Archives of Neurology, 43,* 505–507. (15)

Friedman, M. I., & Stricker, E. M. (1976). The physiological psychology of hunger: A physiological perspective. *Psychological Review, 83,* 409–431. (10)

Fritsch, G., & Hitzig, E. (1870). Über die elektrische Erregbarkeit des Grosshirns [Concerning the electrical stimulability of the cerebrum]. *Archiv für Anatomie Physiologie und Wissenschaftliche Medicin,* 300–332. (8)

Fritz, J., Shamma, S., Elhilali, M., & Klein, D. (2003). Rapid task-related plasticity of spectrotemporal receptive fields in primary auditory cortex. *Nature Neuroscience, 6,* 1216–1223. (5)

Fu, L.-Y., Acuna-Goycolea, C., & van den Pol, A. N. (2004). Neuropeptide Y inhibits hypocretin/orexin neurons by multiple presynaptic and postsynaptic mechanisms: Tonic depression of the hypothalamic arousal system. *Journal of Neuroscience, 24,* 8741–8751. (10)

Fu, Q., Heath, A. C., Bucholz, K. K., Nelson, E., Goldberg, J., Lyons, M. J., et al. (2002). Shared genetic risk of major depression, alcohol dependence, and marijuana dependence. *Archives of General Psychiatry, 59,* 1125–1132. (15)

Fu, W., Sugai, T., Yoshimura, H., & Onoda, N. (2004). Convergence of olfactory and gustatory connections onto the endopiriform nucleus in the rat. *Neuroscience, 126,* 1033–1041. (7)

Fuchs, T., Haney, A., Jechura, T. J., Moore, F. R., & Bingman, V. P. (2006). Daytime naps in night-migrating birds: Behavioural adaptation to seasonal sleep deprivation in the Swainson's thrush, *Catharus ustulatus. Animal Behaviour, 72,* 951–958. (9)

Fuller, R. K., & Roth, H. P. (1979). Disulfiram for the treatment of alcoholism: An evaluation in 128 men. *Annals of Internal Medicine, 90,* 901–904. (3)

Fuster, J. M. (1989). *The prefrontal cortex* (2nd ed.). New York: Raven Press. (4)

Gabrieli, J. D. E., Corkin, S., Mickel, S. F., & Growdon, J. H. (1993). Intact acquisition of mirror-tracing skill in Alzheimer's disease and in global amnesia. *Behavioral Neuroscience, 107,* 899–910. (13)

Gage, F. H. (2000). Mammalian neural stem cells. *Science, 287,* 1433–1438. (5)

Gais, S., Plihal, W., Wagner, U., & Born, J. (2000). Early sleep triggers memory for early visual discrimination skills. *Nature Neuroscience, 3,* 1335–1339. (9)

Galaburda, A. M., LoTurco, J., Ramus, F., Fitch, R. H., & Rosen, G. D. (2006). From genes to behavior in developmental dyslexia. *Nature Neuroscience, 9,* 1213–1217. (14)

Galaburda, A. M., Sherman, G. F., Rosen, G. D., Aboitiz, F., & Geschwind, N. (1985). Developmental dyslexia: Four consecutive patients with cortical anomalies. *Annals of Neurology, 18,* 222–233. (14)

Galef, B. G., Jr. (1992). Weaning from mother's milk to solid foods: The developmental psychobiology of self-selection of foods by rats. *Annals of the New York Academy of Sciences, 662,* 37–52. (10)

Galin, D., Johnstone, J., Nakell, L., & Herron, J. (1979). Development of the capacity for tactile information transfer between hemispheres in normal children. *Science, 204,* 1330–1332. (14)

Gallese, V., Fadiga, L., Fogassi, L., & Rizzolatti, G. (1996). Action recognition in the premotor cortex. *Brain, 119,* 593–609. (8)

Gan, W.-B., Kwon, E., Feng, G., Sanes, J. R., & Lichtman, J. W. (2003). Synaptic dynamism measured over minutes to months: Age-dependent decline in an autonomic ganglion. *Nature Neuroscience, 6,* 956–960. (5)

Gangestad, S. W., & Simpson, J. A. (2000). The evolution of human mating: Trade-offs and strategic pluralism. *Behavioral and Brain Sciences, 23,* 573–644. (11)

Gangestad, S. W., Simpson, J. A., Cousins, A. J., Garver-Apgar, C. E., & Christensen, P. N. (2004). Women's preferences for male behavioral displays change across the menstrual cycle. *Psychological Science, 15,* 203–207. (11)

Ganguly, K., Kiss, L., & Poo, M. (2000). Enhancement of presynaptic neuronal excitability by correlated presynaptic and postsynaptic spiking. *Nature Neuroscience, 3,* 1018–1026. (13)

Gao, J.-H., Parsons, L. M., Bower, J. M., Xiong, J., Li, J., & Fox, P. T. (1996). Cerebellum implicated in sensory acquisition and discrimination rather than motor control. *Science, 272,* 545–547. (8)

Garcia, R., Vouimba, R.-M., Baudry, M., & Thompson, R. F. (1999). The amygdala modulates prefrontal cortex activity relative to conditioned fear. *Nature, 402,* 294–296. (12)

García-Pérez, M. A., & Peli, E. (2001). Intrasaccadic perception. *Journal of Neuroscience, 21,* 7313–7322. (6)

Gardner, B. T., & Gardner, R. A. (1975). Evidence for sentence constituents in the early utterances of child and chimpanzee. *Journal of Experimental Psychology: General, 104,* 244–267. (14)

Gardner, E. P., Ro, J. Y., Debowy, D., & Ghosh, S. (1999). Facilitation of neuronal activity in somatosensory and posterior parietal cortex during prehension. *Experimental Brain Research, 127,* 329–354. (8)

Gardner, H., & Zurif, E. B. (1975). Bee but not be: Oral reading of single words in aphasia and alexia. *Neuropsychologia, 13,* 181–190. (14)

Garver-Apgar, C. E., Gangestad, S. W., Thornhill, R., Miller, R. D., & Olp, J. J. (2006). Major histocompatibility complex alleles, sexual responsivity, and unfaithfulness in romantic couples. *Psychological Science, 17,* 830–835. (11)

Gaser, C., & Schlaug, G. (2003). Brain structures differ between musicians and non-musicians. *Journal of Neuroscience, 23,* 9240–9245. (5)

Gavrilets, S., & Rice, W. R. (2006). Genetic models of homosexuality: Generating testable predictions. *Proceedings of the Royal Society, B, 273,* 3031–3038. (11)

Ge, S., Yang, C.-h., Hsu, K.-s., Ming, G.-l., & Song, H. (2007). A critical period for enhanced synaptic plasticity in newly generated neurons of the adult brain. *Neuron, 54,* 559–566. (5)

Geiger, G., Lettvin, J. Y., & Fahle, M. (1994). Dyslexic children learn a new visual strategy for reading: A controlled experiment. *Vision Research, 34,* 1223–1233. (14)

Geiger, G., Lettvin, J. Y., & Zegarra-Moran, O. (1992). Task-determined strategies of visual process. *Cognitive Brain Research, 1,* 39–52. (14)

Gerardin, D. C. C., & Pereira, O. C. M. (2002). Reproductive changes in male rats treated perinatally with an aromatase inhibitor. *Pharmacology Biochemistry and Behavior, 71,* 309–313. (11)

Gerwig, M., Hajjar, K., Dimitrova, A., Maschke, M., Kolb, F. P., Frings, M., et al. (2005). Timing of conditioned eyeblink responses is impaired in cerebellar patients. *Journal of Neuroscience, 25,* 3919–3931. (13)

Geschwind, N., & Levitsky, W. (1968). Human brain: Left–right asymmetries in temporal speech region. *Science, 161,* 186–187. (14)

Ghashghaei, H. T., Lai, C., & Anton, E. S. (2007). Neuronal migration in the adult brain: Are we there yet? *Nature Reviews Neuroscience, 8,* 141–151. (5)

Ghitza, U. E., Fabbricatore, A. T., Prokopenko, V., Pawlak, A. P., & West, M. O. (2003). Persistent cue-evoked activity of accumbens neurons after prolonged abstinence from self-administered cocaine. *Journal of Neuroscience, 23,* 7239–7245. (3)

Gibbons, R. D., Brown, C. H., Hur, K., Marcus, S. M., Bhaumik, D. K., Erkens, J. A., et al. (2007). Early evidence on the effects of regulators' suicidality warnings on SSRI prescriptions and suicide in children and adolescents. *American Journal of Psychiatry, 164,* 1356–1363. (15)

Gibbs, F. P. (1983). Temperature dependence of the hamster circadian pacemaker. *American Journal of Physiology, 244,* R607–R610. (9)

Gibbs, J., Young, R. C., & Smith, G. P. (1973). Cholecystokinin decreases food intake in rats. *Journal of Comparative and Physiological Psychology, 84,* 488–495. (10)

Gifkins, A., Greba, Q., & Kokkinidis, L. (2002). Ventral tegmental area dopamine neurons mediate the shock sensitization of acoustic startle: A potential site of action for benzodiazepine anxiolytics. *Behavioral Neuroscience, 116,* 785–794. (12)

Gigi, A., Babai, R., Katzav, E., Atkins, S., & Hendler, T. (2007). Prefrontal and parietal regions are involved in naming of objects seen from unusual viewpoints. *Behavioral Neuroscience, 121,* 836–844. (4)

Gilbertson, M. W., Shenton, M. E., Ciszewski, A., Kasai, K., Lasko, N. B., Orr, S. P., et al. (2002).

Smaller hippocampal volume predicts pathological vulnerability to psychological trauma. *Nature Neuroscience, 5,* 1242–1247. (12)

Gil-da-Costa, R., Martin, A., Lopes, M. A., Muñoz, M., Fritz, J. B., & Braun, A. R. (2006). Species-specific calls activate homologs of Broca's and Wernicke's areas in the macaque. *Nature Neuroscience, 9,* 1064–1070. (14)

Gilman, J. M., Ramchandani, V. A., Davis, M. B., Bjork, J. M., & Hommer, D. W. (2008). Why we like to drink: A functional magnetic resonance imaging study of the rewarding and anxiolytic effects of alcohol. *Journal of Neuroscience, 28,* 4583–4591. (3)

Gilmore, J. H., Lin, W., Prastawa, M. W., Looney, C. B., Vetsa, Y. S. K., Knickmeyer, R. C., et al. (2007). Regional gray matter growth, sexual dimorphism, and cerebral asymmetry in the neonatal brain. *Journal of Neuroscience, 27,* 1255–1260. (4)

Gilmour, D., Knaut, H., Maischein, H.-M., & Nüsslein-Volhard, C. (2004). Towing of sensory axons by their migrating target cells *in vivo*. *Nature Neuroscience, 7,* 491–492. (5)

Gillette, M. U., & McArthur, A. J. (1996). Circadian actions of melatonin at the suprachiasmatic nucleus. *Behavioural Brain Research, 73,* 135–139. (9)

Giraux, P., Sirigu, A., Schneider, F., & Dubernard, J.-M. (2001). Cortical reorganization in motor cortex after graft of both hands. *Nature Neuroscience, 4,* 691–692. (5)

Giros, B., Jaber, M., Jones, S. R., Wightman, R. M., & Caron, M. G. (1996). Hyperlocomotion and indifference to cocaine and amphetamine in mice lacking the dopamine transporter. *Nature, 379,* 606–612. (3)

Giuliani, D., & Ferrari, F. (1996). Differential behavioral response to dopamine D2 agonists by sexually naive, sexually active, and sexually inactive male rats. *Behavioral Neuroscience, 110,* 802–808. (11)

Gläscher, J., & Adolphs, R. (2003). Processing of the arousal of subliminal and supraliminal emotional stimuli by the human amygdala. *Journal of Neuroscience, 23,* 10274–10282. (12)

Glass, M. (2001). The role of cannabinoids in neurodegenerative diseases. *Progress in Neuro-Psychopharmacology & Biological Psychiatry, 25,* 743–765. (8)

Glendenning, K. K., Baker, B. N., Hutson, K. A., & Masterton, R. B. (1992). Acoustic chiasm V: Inhibition and excitation in the ipsilateral and contralateral projections of LSO. *Journal of Comparative Neurology, 319,* 100–122. (7)

Glick, S. D. (1974). Changes in drug sensitivity and mechanisms of functional recovery following brain damage. In D. G. Stein, J. J. Rosen, & N. Butters (Eds.), *Plasticity and recovery of function in the central nervous system* (pp. 339–372). New York: Academic Press. (5)

Glykys, J., Peng, Z., Chandra, D., Homanics, G. E., Houser, C. R., & Mody, I. (2007). A new naturally occurring $GABA_A$ receptor subunit partnership with high sensitivity to ethanol. *Nature Neuroscience, 10,* 40–48. (12)

Goate, A., Chartier-Harlin, M. C., Mullan, M., Brown, J., Crawford, F., Fidani, L., et al. (1991). Segregation of a missense mutation in the amyloid precursor protein gene with familial Alzheimer's disease. *Nature, 349,* 704–706. (13)

Goddard, M. R., Godfray, H. C. J., & Burt, A. (2005). Sex increases the efficacy of natural selection in experimental yeast populations. *Nature, 434,* 636–640. (11)

Gogos, J. A., Osborne, J., Nemes, A., Mendelsohn, M., & Axel, R. (2000). Genetic ablation and restoration of the olfactory topographic map. *Cell, 103,* 609–620. (5)

Gold, P. E., Cahill, L., & Wenk, G. L. (2002). Gingko biloba: A cognitive enhancer? *Psychological Science in the Public Interest, 3,* 2–11. (13)

Gold, R. M. (1973). Hypothalamic obesity: The myth of the ventromedial hypothalamus. *Science, 182,* 488–490. (10)

Goldberg, T. E., Weinberger, D. R., Berman, K. F., Pliskin, N. H., & Podd, M. H. (1987). Further evidence for dementia of the prefrontal type in schizophrenia? *Archives of General Psychiatry, 44,* 1008–1014. (15)

Goldenberg, G., & Karnath, H.-O. (2006). The neural basis of imitation is body part specific. *Journal of Neuroscience, 26,* 6282–6287. (8)

Goldin-Meadow, S., McNeill, D., & Singleton, J. (1996). Silence is liberating: Removing the handcuffs on grammatical expression in the manual modality. *Psychological Review, 103,* 34–55. (14)

Goldin-Meadow, S., & Mylander, C. (1998). Spontaneous sign systems created by deaf children in two cultures. *Nature, 391,* 279–281. (14)

Goldman, L. S. (1999). Medical illness in patients with schizophrenia. *Journal of Clinical Psychiatry, 60*(Suppl 21), 10–15. (15)

Goldman, P. S. (1971). Functional development of the prefrontal cortex in early life and the problem of neuronal plasticity. *Experimental Neurology, 32,* 366–387. (15)

Goldman, P. S. (1976). The role of experience in recovery of function following orbital prefrontal lesions in infant monkeys. *Neuropsychologia, 14,* 401–412. (15)

Goldman-Rakic, P. S. (1988). Topography of cognition: Parallel distributed networks in primate association cortex. *Annual Review of Neuroscience, 11,* 137–156. (4)

Goldstein, A. (1980). Thrills in response to music and other stimuli. *Physiological Psychology, 8,* 126–129. (7)

Goldstein, J. M., Seidman, L. J., Horton, N. J., Makris, N., Kennedy, D. N., Caviness, V. S., Jr., et al. (2001). Normal sexual dimorphism of the adult human brain assessed by in vivo magnetic resonance imaging. *Cerebral Cortex, 11,* 490–497. (4)

Goldstein, L. B. (1993). Basic and clinical studies of pharmacologic effects on recovery from brain injury. *Journal of Neural Transplantation & Plasticity, 4,* 175–192. (5)

González, B., Rodríguez, M., Ramirez, C., & Sabate, M. (2005). Disturbance of motor imagery after cerebellar stroke. *Behavioral Neuroscience, 199,* 622–626. (8)

González-Maeso, J., Ang, R. L., Yuen, T., Chan, P., Weisstaub, N. V., López-Giménez, J. F., et al. (2008). Identification of a serotonin/glutamate receptor complex implicated in psychosis. *Nature, 452,* 93–97. (15)

Good, C. D., Johnsrude, I., Ashburner, I., Henson, R. N. A., Friston, K. J., & Frackowiak, R. S. J. (2001). Cerebral asymmetry and the effects of sex and handedness on brain structure: A voxel-based morphometric analysis of 465 normal adult human brains. *NeuroImage, 14,* 685–700. (4)

Goodale, M. A. (1996). Visuomotor modules in the vertebrate brain. *Canadian Journal of Physiology and Pharmacology, 74,* 390–400. (6, 8)

Goodale, M. A., Milner, A. D., Jakobson, L. S., & Carey, D. P. (1991). A neurological dissociation between perceiving objects and grasping them. *Nature, 349,* 154–156. (6, 8)

Gopnik, M., & Crago, M. B. (1991). Familial aggregation of a developmental language disorder. *Cognition, 39,* 1–50. (14)

Gorski, J. A., Zeiler, S. R., Tamowski, S., & Jones, K. R. (2003). Brain-derived neurotrophic factor is required for the maintenance of cortical dendrites. *Journal of Neuroscience, 23,* 6856–6865. (5)

Gorski, R. A. (1980). Sexual differentiation of the brain. In D. T. Krieger & J. C. Hughes (Eds.), *Neuroendocrinology* (pp. 215–222). Sunderland, MA: Sinauer. (11)

Gorski, R. A. (1985). The 13th J. A. F. Stevenson memorial lecture. Sexual differentiation of the brain: Possible mechanisms and implications. *Canadian Journal of Physiology and Pharmacology, 63,* 577–594. (11)

Gorski, R. A., & Allen, L. S. (1992). Sexual orientation and the size of the anterior commissure in the human brain. *Proceedings of the National Academy of Sciences, USA, 89,* 7199–7202. (11)

Gothe, J., Brandt, S. A., Irlbacher, K., Röricht, S., Sabel, B. A., & Meyer, B.-U. (2002). Changes in visual cortex excitability in blind subjects as demonstrated by transcranial magnetic stimulation. *Brain, 125,* 479–490. (5)

Gottesman, I. I. (1991). *Schizophrenia genesis.* New York: Freeman. (15)

Gottesmann, C. (2004). Brain inhibitory mechanisms involved in basic and higher integrated sleep processes. *Brain Research Reviews, 45,* 230–249. (9)

Granados-Fuentes, D., Tseng, A., & Herzog, E. D. (2006). A circadian clock in the olfactory bulb controls olfactory responsivity. *Journal of Neuroscience, 26,* 12219–12225. (9)

Graves, J. A. M. (1994). Mammalian sex-determining genes. In R. V. Short & E. Balaban (Eds.), *The differences between the sexes* (pp. 397–418). Cambridge, England: Cambridge University Press. (11)

Gray, C. M., König, P., Engel, A. K., & Singer, W. (1989). Oscillatory responses in cat visual cortex exhibit inter-columnar synchronization which reflects global stimulus properties. *Nature, 338,* 334–337. (14)

Gray, J. A. (1970). The psychophysiological basis of introversion–extraversion. *Behavioural Research Therapy, 8,* 249–266. (12)

Graybiel, A. M., Aosaki, T., Flaherty, A. W., & Kimura, M. (1994). The basal ganglia and adaptive motor control. *Science, 265,* 1826–1831. (4)

Graziadei, P. P. C., & deHan, R. S. (1973). Neuronal regeneration in frog olfactory system. *Journal of Cell Biology, 59,* 525–530. (5)

Graziano, M. S. A., Taylor, C. S. R., & Moore, T. (2002). Complex movements evoked by microstimulation of precentral cortex. *Neuron, 34,* 841–851. (4, 8)

Greene, J. D., Sommerville, R. B., Nystrom, L. E., Darley, J. M., & Cohen, J. D. (2001). An fMRI investigation of emotional engagement in moral judgment. *Science, 293,* 2105–2108. (12)

Greengard, P. (2001). The neurobiology of slow synaptic transmission. *Science, 294,* 1024–1030. (3)

Greenough, W. T. (1975). Experiential modification of the developing brain. *American Scientist, 63,* 37–46. (5)

Greenwood, B. N., Strong, P. V., Dorey, A. A., & Fleshner, M. (2007). Therapeutic effects of exercise: Wheel running reverses stress-induced interference with shuttle box escape. *Behavioral Neuroscience, 121,* 992–1000. (15)

Griffin, D. R. (2001). *Animal minds: Beyond cognition to consciousness.* Chicago: University of Chicago Press. (1)

Griffin, D. R., Webster, F. A., & Michael, C. R. (1960). The echolocation of flying insects by bats. *Animal Behaviour, 8,* 141–154. (7)

Griffiths, T. D., Uppenkamp, S., Johnsrude, I., Josephs, O., & Patterson, R. D. (2001). Encoding of the temporal regularity of sound in the human brainstem. *Nature Neuroscience, 4,* 633–637. (7)

Grillon, C., Morgan, C. A., III, Davis, M., & Southwick, S. M. (1998). Effect of darkness on acoustic startle in Vietnam veterans with PTSD. *American Journal of Psychiatry, 155,* 812–817. (12)

Grill-Spector, K., Knouf, N., & Kanwisher, N. (2004). The fusiform face area subserves face perception, not generic within category identification. *Nature Neuroscience, 7,* 555–562. (6)

Gronfier, C., Wright, K. P., Jr., Kronauer, R. E., & Czeisler, C. A. (2007). Entrainment of the human circadian pacemaker to longer-than-24-h days. *Proceedings of the National Academy of Sciences, USA, 104,* 9081–9086. (9)

Gross, C. G. (1999). The fire that comes from the eye. *The Neuroscientist, 5,* 58–64. (6)

Gross, C. G., & Graziano, M. S. A. (1995). Multiple representations of space in the brain. *The Neuroscientist, 1,* 43–50. (4)

Grosshans, D. R., Clayton, D. A., Coultrap, S. J., & Browning, M. D. (2002). LTP leads to rapid surface expression of NMDA but not AMPA receptors in adult rat CA1. *Nature Neuroscience, 5,* 27–33. (13)

Grossman, E. D., & Blake, R. (2001). Brain activity evoked by inverted and imagined biological motion. *Vision Research, 41,* 1475–1482. (6)

Grossman, E., Donnelly, M., Price, R., Pickens, D., Morgan, V., Neighbor, G., et al. (2000). Brain areas involved in perception of biological motion. *Journal of Cognitive Neuroscience, 12,* 711–720. (6)

Grossman, S. P., Dacey, D., Halaris, A. E., Collier, T., & Routtenberg, A. (1978). Aphagia and adipsia after preferential destruction of nerve cell bodies in hypothalamus. *Science, 202,* 537–539. (10)

Grutzendler, J., Kasthuri, N., & Gan, W.-B. (2002). Long-term dendritic spine stability in the adult cortex. *Nature, 420,* 812–816. (5)

Gubernick, D. J., & Alberts, J. R. (1983). Maternal licking of young: Resource exchange and proximate controls. *Physiology & Behavior, 31,* 593–601. (11)

Guérit, J.-M. (2005). Neurophysiological patterns of vegetative and minimally conscious states. *Neuropsychological Rehabilitation, 15,* 357–371. (9)

Guidotti, A., Ferrero, P., Fujimoto, M., Santi, R. M., & Costa, E. (1986). Studies on endogenous ligands (endocoids) for the benzodiazepine/beta carboline binding sites. *Advances in Biochemical Pharmacology, 41,* 137–148. (12)

Guidotti, A., Forchetti, C. M., Corda, M. G., Konkel, D., Bennett, C. D., & Costa, E. (1983). Isolation, characterization, and purification to homogeneity of an endogenous polypeptide with agonistic action on benzodiazepine receptors. *Proceedings of the National Academy of Sciences, USA, 80,* 3531–3535. (12)

Guillery, R. W., Feig, S. L., & Lozsádi, D. A. (1998). Paying attention to the thalamic reticular nucleus. *Trends in Neurosciences, 21,* 28–32. (4)

Guillery, R. W., Feig, S. L., & van Lieshout, D. P. (2001). Connections of higher order visual relays in the thalamus: A study of corticothalamic pathways in cats. *Journal of Comparative Neurology, 438,* 66–85. (6)

Guillin, O., Diaz, J., Carroll, P., Griffon, N., Schwartz, J-C., & Sokoloff, P. (2001). BDNF controls dopamine D_3 receptor expression and triggers behavioural sensitization. *Nature, 412,* 86–89. (15)

Guisinger, S. (2003). Adapted to flee famine: Adding an evolutionary perspective to anorexia nervosa. *Psychological Review, 110,* 745–761. (10)

Güler, A. D., Ecker, J. L., Lall, G. S., Haq, S., Altimus, C. M., Liao, H.-W., et al. (2008). Melanopsin cells are the principal conduits for rod-cone input to non-image-forming vision. *Nature, 453,* 102–105. (9)

Gunn, S. R., & Gunn, W. S. (2007). Are we in the dark about sleepwalking's dangers? In C. A. Read (Ed.), *Cerebrum 2007: Emerging ideas in brain science* (pp. 71–84). New York: Dana Press. (9)

Guo, S.-W., & Reed, D. R. (2001). The genetics of phenylthiocarbamide perception. *Annals of Human Biology, 28,* 111–142. (7)

Gur, R. E., & Chin, S. (1999). Laterality in functional brain imaging studies of schizophrenia. *Schizophrenia Bulletin, 25,* 141–156. (15)

Gur, R. E., Cowell, P. E., Latshaw, A., Turetsky, B. I., Grossman, R. I., Arnold, S. E., et al. (2000). Reduced dorsal and orbital prefrontal gray matter volumes in schizophrenia. *Archives of General Psychiatry, 57,* 761–768. (15)

Gusella, J. F., & MacDonald, M. E. (2000). Molecular genetics: Unmasking polyglutamine triggers in neurodegenerative disease. *Nature Reviews Neuroscience, 1,* 109–115. (8)

Gustafsson, B., & Wigström, H. (1990). Basic features of long-term potentiation in the hippocampus. *Seminars in the Neurosciences, 2,* 321–333. (13)

Gutschalk, A., Patterson, R. D., Scherg, M., Uppenkamp, S., & Rupp, A. (2004). Temporal dynamics of pitch in human auditory cortex. *NeuroImage, 22,* 755–766. (7)

Gvilia, I., Turner, A., McGinty, D., & Szymusiak, R. (2006). Preoptic area neurons and the homeostatic regulation of rapid eye movement sleep. *Journal of Neuroscience, 26,* 3037–3044. (9)

Gvilia, I., Xu, F., McGinty, D., & Szymusiak, R. (2006). Homeostatic regulation of sleep: A role for preoptic area neurons. *Journal of Neuroscience, 26,* 9426–9433. (9)

Gwinner, E. (1986). Circannual rhythms in the control of avian rhythms. *Advances in the Study of Behavior, 16,* 191–228. (9)

Haas, H., & Panula, P. (2003). The role of histamine and the tuberomamillary nucleus in the nervous system. *Nature Reviews Neuroscience, 4,* 121–130. (9)

Hadjikhani, N., Liu, A. K., Dale, A. M., Cavanagh, P., & Tootell, R. B. H. (1998). Retinotopy and color sensitivity in human visual cortical area V8. *Nature Neuroscience, 1,* 235–241. (6)

Haeffel, G. J., Getchell, M., Koposov, R. A., Yrigollen, C. M., DeYoung, C. G., Klinteberg, B., et al. (2008). Association between polymorphisms in the dopamine transporter gene and depression. *Psychological Science, 19,* 62–69. (15)

Hagenbuch, B., Gao, B., & Meier, P. J. (2002). Transport of xenobiotics across the blood-brain barrier. *News in Physiological Sciences, 17,* 231–234. (2)

Haggarty, J. M., Cernovsky, Z., Husni, M., Minor, K., Kermean, P., & Merskey, H. (2002). Seasonal affective disorder in an Arctic community. *Acta Psychiatrica Scandinavica, 105,* 378–384. (15)

Haidt, J. (2001). The emotional dog and its rational tail: A social intuitionist approach to moral judgment. *Psychological Review, 108,* 814–834. (12)

Haier, R. J., Jung, R. E., Yeo, R. A., Head, K., & Alkire, M. T. (2004). Structural brain variation and general intelligence. *NeuroImage, 23,* 425–433. (4)

Haimov, I., & Arendt, J. (1999). The prevention and treatment of jet lag. *Sleep Medicine Reviews, 3,* 229–240. (9)

Haimov, I., & Lavie, P. (1996). Melatonin—A soporific hormone. *Current Directions in Psychological Science, 5,* 106–111. (9)

Hains, B. C., Everhart, A. W., Fullwood, S. D., & Hulsebosch, C. E. (2002). Changes in serotonin, serotonin transporter expression and serotonin denervation supersensitivity: Involvement in chronic central pain after spinal hemisection in the rat. *Experimental Neurology, 175,* 347–362. (5)

Haist, F., Gore, J. B., & Mao, H. (2001). Consolidation of human memory over decades revealed by functional magnetic resonance imaging. *Nature Neuroscience, 4,* 1139–1145. (13)

Hakuta, K., Bialystok, E., & Wiley, E. (2003). Critical evidence: A test of the critical-period hypothesis for second-language acquisition. *Psychological Science, 14,* 31–38. (14)

Halaas, J. L, Gajiwala, K. S., Maffei, M., Cohen, S. L., Chait, B. T., Rabinowitz, D., et al. (1995). Weight-reducing effects of the plasma protein encoded by the obese gene. *Science, 269,* 543–546. (10)

Haley, J. (1959). An interactional description of schizophrenia. *Psychiatry, 22,* 321–332. (15)

Hall, J., Whalley, H. C., Job, D. E., Baig, B. J., McIntosh, A. M., Evans, K. L., et al. (2006). A neuregulin 1 variant associated with abnormal cortical function and psychotic symptoms. *Nature Neuroscience, 9,* 1477–1478. (15)

Hallem, E. A., Fox, A. N., Zwiebel, L. J., & Carlson, J. R. (2004). Mosquito receptor for human-sweat odorant. *Nature, 427,* 212–213. (7)

Halpern, D. F. (2004). A cognitive-process taxonomy for sex differences in cognitive abilities. *Current Directions in Psychological Science, 13,* 135–139. (4)

Halpern, S. D., Andrews, T. J., & Purves, D. (1999). Interindividual variation in human visual performance. *Journal of Cognitive Neuroscience, 11,* 521–534. (4)

Hamani, C., Schwalb, J. M., Rezai, A. R., Dostrovsky, J. O., Davis, K. D., & Lozano, A. M. (2006). Deep brain stimulation for chronic neuropathic pain: Long-term outcome and the incidence of insertional effect. *Pain, 125,* 188–196. (7)

Hamann, S. B., & Squire, L. R. (1995). On the acquisition of new declarative knowledge in amnesia. *Behavioral Neuroscience, 109,* 1027–1044. (13)

Hamer, D. H., Hu, S., Magnuson, V. L., Hu, N., & Pattatucci, A. M. L. (1993). A linkage between DNA markers on the X chromosome and male sexual orientation. *Science, 261,* 321–327. (11)

Hamilton, W. D. (1964). The genetical evolution of social behavior (I and II). *Journal of Theoretical Biology, 7,* 1–16, 17–52. (1)

Han, C. J., & Robinson, J. K. (2001). Cannabinoid modulation of time estimation in the rat. *Behavioral Neuroscience, 115,* 243–246. (3)

Han, J.-H., Kushner, S. A., Yiu, A. P., Cole, C. J., Matynia, A., Brown, R. A., et al. (2007). Neuronal competition and selection during memory formation. *Science, 316,* 457–460. (13)

Hanaway, J., Woolsey, T. A., Gado, M. H., & Roberts, M. P., Jr. (1998). *The brain atlas.* Bethesda, MD: Fitzgerald Science Press. (12)

Hanlon, F. M., Weisend, M. P., Yeo, R. A., Huang, M., Lee, R. R., Thoma, R. J., et al. (2005). A specific test of hippocampal deficit in schizophrenia. *Behavioral Neuroscience, 119,* 863–875. (15)

Hannibal, J., Hindersson, P., Knudsen, S. M., Georg, B., & Fahrenkrug, J. (2001). The photopigment melanopsin is exclusively present in pituitary adenylate cyclase-activating polypeptide-containing retinal ganglion cells of the retinohypothalamic tract. *Journal of Neuroscience, 21,* RC191: 1–7. (9)

Hanson, K. A., Kay, K. N., & Gallant, J. L. (2007). Topographic organization in and near human visual area V4. *Journal of Neuroscience, 27,* 11896–11911. (6)

Hansson, B., Bensch, S., & Hasselquist, D. (1997). Infanticide in great reed warblers: Secondary females destroy eggs of primary females. *Animal Behaviour, 54,* 297–304. (11)

Haqq, C. M., & Donahoe, P. K. (1998). Regulation of sexual dimorphism in mammals. *Physiological Reviews, 78,* 1–33. (11)

Hara, J., Beuckmann, C. T., Nambu, T., Willie, J. T., Chemelli, R. M., Sinton, C. M., et al. (2001). Genetic ablation of orexin neurons in mice results in narcolepsy, hypophagia, and obesity. *Neuron, 30,* 345–354. (9)

Hargreaves, R. (2007). New migraine and pain research. *Headache, 47*(Suppl 1), S26–S43. (4)

Hari, R. (1994). Human cortical functions revealed by magnetoencephalography. *Progress in Brain Research, 100,* 163–168. (4)

Hariri, A. R., Mattay, V. S., Tessitore, A., Kolachana, B., Fera, F., Goldman, D., et al. (2002). Serotonin transporter genetic variation and the response of the human amygdala. *Science, 297,* 400–403. (12)

Harley, B., & Wang, W. (1997). The critical period hypothesis: Where are we now? In A. M. B. deGroot & J. F. Knoll (Eds.), *Tutorials in bilingualism* (pp. 19–51). Mahwah, NJ: Erlbaum. (14)

Harms, M. P., Wang, L., Mamah, D., Barch, D. M., Thompson, P. A., & Csernansky, J. G. (2007). Thalamic shape abnormalities in individuals with schizophrenia and their nonpsychotic siblings. *Journal of Neuroscience, 27,* 13835–13842. (15)

Harper, L. V. (2005). Epigenetic inheritance and the intergenerational transfer of experience. *Psychological Bulletin, 131,* 340–360. (1)

Harper, S. Q., Staber, P. D., He, X., Eliason, S. L., Martino, I. H., Mao, Q., et al. (2005). RNA interference improves motor and neuropathological abnormalities in a Huntington's disease mouse model. *Proceedings of the National Academy of Sciences, USA, 102,* 5820–5825. (8)

Harris, C. H. (2002). Sexual and romantic jealousy in heterosexual and homosexual adults. *Psychological Science, 13,* 7–12. (11)

Harris, C. R. (1999, July/August). The mystery of ticklish laughter. *American Scientist, 87*(4), 344–351. (7)

Harris, K. M., & Stevens, J. K. (1989). Dendritic spines of CA1 pyramidal cells in the rat hippocampus: Serial electron microscopy with reference to their biophysical characteristics. *Journal of Neuroscience, 9,* 2982–2997. (2)

Harrison, G. H. (2008, January). How chickadees weather winter. *National Wildlife, 46*(1), 14–15. (10)

Hart, B. L. (Ed.). (1976). *Experimental psychobiology.* San Francisco: Freeman. (10)

Hartline, H. K. (1949). Inhibition of activity of visual receptors by illuminating nearby retinal areas in the limulus eye. *Federation Proceedings, 8,* 69. (6)

Harvey, A. G., & Bryant, R. A. (2002). Acute stress disorder: A synthesis and critique. *Psychological Bulletin, 128,* 886–902. (12)

Harvey, C. D., & Svoboda, K. (2007). Locally dynamic synaptic learning rules in pyramidal neuron dendrites. *Science, 450,* 1195–1200. (13)

Hassabis, D., Kumaran, D., Vann, S. D., & Maguire, E. A. (2007). Patients with hippocampal amnesia cannot imagine new experiences. *Proceedings of the National Academy of Sciences, USA, 104,* 1726–1731. (13)

Hassan, B., & Rahman, Q. (2007). Selective sexual orientation-related differences in object location memory. *Behavioral Neuroscience, 121,* 625–633. (11)

Haueisen, J., & Knösche, T. R. (2001). Involuntary motor activity in pianists evoked by music perception. *Journal of Cognitive Neuroscience, 13,* 786–792. (8)

Hauk, O., Johnsrude, I., & Pulvermüller, F. (2004). Somatatopic representation of action words in human motor and premotor cortex. *Neuron, 41,* 301–307. (14)

Haukka, J., Suvisaara, J., & Lönnqvist, J. (2003). Fertility of patients with schizophrenia, their siblings, and the general population: A cohort study from 1950 to 1959 in Finland. *American Journal of Psychiatry, 160,* 460–463. (15)

Häusser, M., Spruston, N., & Stuart, G. J. (2000). Diversity and dynamics of dendritic signaling. *Science, 290,* 739–744. (2)

Haydon, P. G. (2001). Glia: Listening and talking to the synapse. *Nature Reviews Neuroscience, 2,* 185–193. (2)

He, H.-Y., Ray, B., Dennis, K., & Quinlan, E. M. (2007). Experience-dependent recovery of vision following chronic deprivation amblyopia. *Nature Neuroscience, 10,* 1134–1136. (6)

He, W., Yasumatsu, K., Varadarajan, V., Yamada, A., Lem, J., Ninomiya, Y., et al. (2004). Umami taste receptors are mediated by α-transducin and α-gustducin. *Journal of Neuroscience, 24,* 7674–7680. (7)

Healy, S. D., & Rowe, C. (2007). A critique of comparative studies of brain size. *Proceedings of the Royal Society, B, 274,* 453–464. (4)

Hebb, D. O. (1949). *Organization of behavior.* New York: Wiley. (13)

Hegdé, J., & Van Essen, D. C. (2000). Selectivity for complex shapes in primate visual area V2. *Journal of Neuroscience, 20,* RC61: 1–6. (6)

Heimer, G., Rivlin-Etzion, M., Bar-Gad, I., Goldberg, J. A., Haber, S. N., & Bergman, H. (2006). Dopamine replacement therapy does not restore the full spectrum of normal pallidal activity in the 1-methyl-4-phenyl-1, 2, 3, 6-tetrahydropyridine primate model of Parkinsonism. *Journal of Neuroscience, 26,* 8101–8114. (8)

Heims, H. C., Critchley, H. D., Dolan, R., Mathias, C. J., & Cipolotti, L. (2004). Social and motivational functioning is not critically dependent on feedback of autonomic responses: Neuropsychological evidence from patients with pure autonomic failure. *Neuropsychologia, 42,* 1979–1988. (12)

Heisler, L. K., Cowley, M. A., Tecott, L. H., Fan, W., Low, M. J., Smart, J. L., et al. (2002). Activation of central melanocortin pathways by fenfluramine. *Science, 297,* 609–611. (10)

Helenius, P., Salmelin, R., Richardson, U., Leinonen, S., & Lyytinen, H. (2002). Abnormal auditory cortical activation in dyslexia 100 msec after speech onset. *Journal of Cognitive Neuroscience, 14,* 603–617. (14)

Heller, W., & Levy, J. (1981). Perception and expression of emotion in right-handers and left-handers. *Neuropsychologia, 19,* 263–272. (14)

Henderson, J. M., & Hollingworth, A. (2003). Global transsaccadic change blindness during scene perception. *Psychological Science, 14,* 493–497. (14)

Hendry, S. H. C., & Reid, R. C. (2000). The koniocellular pathway in primate vision. *Annual Review of Neuroscience, 23,* 127–153. (6)

Hennig, J., Reuter, M., Netter, P., Burk, C., & Landt, O. (2005). Two types of aggression are differentially related to serotonergic activity and the A779C *TPH* polymorphism. *Behavioral Neuroscience, 119,* 16–25. (12)

Hennig, R., & Lømo, T. (1985). Firing patterns of motor units in normal rats. *Nature, 314,* 164–166. (8)

Herculano-Houzel, S., Collins, C. E., Wong, P., & Kaas, J. H. (2007). Cellular scaling rules for primate brains. *Proceedings of the National Academy of Science, USA, 104,* 3562–3567. (4)

Heresco-Levy, U., & Javitt, D. C. (2004). Comparative effects of glycine and D-cycloserine on persistent negative symptoms in schizophrenia: A retrospective analysis. *Schizophrenia Research, 66,* 89–96. (15)

Heresco-Levy, U., Javitt, D. C., Ermilov, M., Mordel, C., Silipo, G., & Lichtenstein, M. (1999). Efficacy of high-dose glycine in the treatment of enduring negative symptoms of schizophrenia. *Archives of General Psychiatry, 56,* 29–36. (15)

Herkenham, M. (1992). Cannabinoid receptor localization in brain: Relationship to motor and reward systems. *Annals of the New York Academy of Sciences, 654,* 19–32. (3)

Herkenham, M., Lynn, A. B., de Costa, B. R., & Richfield, E. K. (1991). Neuronal localization of cannabinoid receptors in the basal ganglia of the rat. *Brain Research, 547,* 267–274. (3)

Hermans, E. J., Ramsey, N. F., & van Honk, J. (2008). Exogenous testosterone enhances responsiveness to social threat in the neural circuitry of social aggression in humans. *Biological Psychiatry, 63,* 263–270. (12)

Hernandez, G., Hamdani, S., Rajabi, H., Conover, K., Stewart, J., Arvanitogiannis, A., et al. (2006). Prolonged rewarding stimulation of the rat medial forebrain bundle: Neurochemical and behavioral consequences. *Behavioral Neuroscience, 120,* 888–904. (3)

Herrero, S. (1985). *Bear attacks: Their causes and avoidance.* Piscataway, NJ: Winchester. (7)

Herz, R. S., & Inzlicht, M. (2002). Sex differences in response to physical and social factors involved in human mate selection: The importance of smell for women. *Evolution and Human Behavior, 23,* 359–364. (7, 11)

Herz, R. S., McCall, C., & Cahill, L. (1999). Hemispheric lateralization in the processing of odor pleasantness versus odor names. *Chemical Senses, 24,* 691–695. (14)

Herzog, S., Pfeuffer, I., Haberzettl, K., Feldmann, H., Frese, K., Bechter, K., et al. (1997). Molecular characterization of Borna disease virus from naturally infected animals and possible links to human disorders. *Archives of Virology* (Suppl. 13), 183–190. (15)

Hess, B. J. M. (2001). Vestibular signals in self-orientation and eye movement control. *News in Physiological Sciences, 16,* 234–238. (7)

Hesse, M. D., Thiel, C. M., Stephan, K. E., & Fink, G. R. (2006). The left parietal cortex and motor intention: An event-related functional magnetic resonance imaging study. *Neuroscience, 140,* 1209–1221. (8)

Higley, J. D., Mehlman, P. T., Higley, S. B., Fernald, B., Vickers, J., Lindell, S. G., et al. (1996). Excessive mortality in young free-ranging male nonhuman primates with low cerebrospinal fluid 5-hydroxyindoleacetic acid concentrations. *Archives of General Psychiatry, 53,* 537–543. (12)

Hill, S. Y., De Bellis, M. D., Keshavan, M. S., Lowers, L., Shen, S., Hall, J., et al. (2001). Right amygdala volume in adolescents and young adult offspring from families at high risk for developing alcoholism. *Biological Psychiatry, 49,* 894–905. (3)

Hillis, A. E., Kleinman, J. T., Newhart, M., Heidler-Gary, J., Gottesman, R., Barker, P. B., et al. (2006). Restoring cerebral blood flow reveals neural regions critical for naming. *Journal of Neuroscience, 26,* 8069–8073. (14)

Hillis, A. E., Newhart, M., Heidler, J., Barker, P. B., Herskovits, E. H., & Degaonkar, M. (2005). Anatomy of spatial attention: Insights from perfusion imaging and hemispatial neglect in acute stroke. *Journal of Neuroscience, 25,* 3161–3167. (14)

Hillman, C. H., Erickson, K. I., & Kramer, A. F. (2008). Be smart, exercise your heart: Exercise effects on brain and cognition. *Nature Reviews Neuroscience, 9,* 58–65. (15)

Hines, M., Golombok, S., Rust, J., Johnston, K. J., Golding, J., & the Avon Longitudinal Study of Parents and Children Study Team. (2002). Testosterone during pregnancy and gender role behavior of preschool children: A longitudinal, population study. *Child Development, 73,* 1678–1687. (11)

Hippisley-Cox, J., Vinogradova, Y., Coupland, C., & Parker, C. (2007). Risk of malignancy in patients with schizophrenia or bipolar disorder. *Archives of General Psychiatry, 64,* 1368–1376. (15)

Hitchcock, J. M., & Davis, M. (1991). Efferent pathway of the amygdala involved in conditioned fear as measured with the fear-potentiated startle paradigm. *Behavioral Neuroscience, 105,* 826–842. (12)

Hiyama, T. Y., Watanabe, E., Okado, H., & Noda, M. (2004). The subfornical organ is the primary locus of sodium-level sensing by Na_x sodium channels for the control of salt-intake behavior. *Journal of Neuroscience, 24,* 9276–9281. (10)

Hnasko, T. S., Sotak, B. N., & Palmiter, R. D. (2005). Morphine reward in dopamine-deficient mice. *Nature, 438,* 854–857. (3)

Hobson, J. A. (1989). *Sleep.* New York: Scientific American Library. (15)

Hobson, J. A., & McCarley, R. W. (1977). The brain as a dream state generator: An activation-synthesis hypothesis of the dream process. *American Journal of Psychiatry, 134,* 1335–1348. (9)

Hobson, J. A., Pace-Schott, E. F., & Stickgold, R. (2000). Dreaming and the brain: Toward a cognitive neuroscience of conscious states. *Behavioral and Brain Sciences, 23,* 793–1121. (9)

Hochberg, L. R., Serruya, M. D., Friehs, G. M., Mukand, J. A., Saleh, M., Caplan, A. H., et al. (2006). Neuronal ensemble control of prosthetic devices by a human with tetraplegia. *Nature, 442,* 164–171. (8)

Hoebel, B. G., & Hernandez, L. (1993). Basic neural mechanisms of feeding and weight regulation. In A. J. Stunkard & T. A. Wadden (Eds.), *Obesity: Theory and therapy* (2nd ed., pp. 43–62). New York: Raven Press. (10)

Hoebel, B. G., Rada, P. V., Mark, G. P., & Pothos, E. (1999). Neural systems for reinforcement and inhibition of behavior: Relevance to eating, addiction, and depression. In D. Kahneman, E. Diener, & N. Schwartz (Eds.), *Well-being: Foundations of hedonic psychology* (pp. 560–574). New York: Russell Sage Foundation. (10)

Hoeft, F., Hernandez, A., McMillon, G., Taylor-Hill, H., Martindale, J. L., Meyler, A., et al. (2006). Neural basis of dyslexia: A comparison between dyslexic and nondyslexic children equated for reading ability. *Journal of Neuroscience, 26,* 10700–10708. (14)

Hoffer, A. (1973). Mechanism of action of nicotinic acid and nicotinamide in the treatment of schizophrenia. In D. Hawkins & L. Pauling (Eds.), *Orthomolecular psychiatry* (pp. 202–262). San Francisco: Freeman. (15)

Hoffman, P. L., Tabakoff, B., Szabó, G., Suzdak, P. D., & Paul, S. M. (1987). Effect of an imidazobenzodiazepine, Ro15-4513, on the incoordination and hypothermia produced by ethanol and pento-barbital. *Life Sciences, 41,* 611–619. (12)

Hoffman, R. (2001). Thermophiles in Kamchatka. *American Scientist, 89,* 20–23. (10)

Hoffmann, F., & Curio, G. (2003). REM-Schlaf und rezidivierende Erosio corneae—eine Hypothese. [REM sleep and recurrent corneal erosion—A hypothesis.] *Klinische Monatsblatter für Augenheilkunde, 220,* 51–53. (9)

Hökfelt, T., Johansson, O., & Goldstein, M. (1984). Chemical anatomy of the brain. *Science, 225,* 1326–1334. (3)

Holahan, M. R., Taverna, F. A., Emrich, S. M., Louis, M., Muller, R. U., Roder, J. C., et al. (2005). Impairment in long-term retention but not short-term performance on a water maze reversal task following hippocampal or mediodorsal striatal *N*-methyl-D-aspartate receptor blockade. *Behavioral Neuroscience, 119,* 1563–1571. (13)

Holcombe, A. O., & Cavanagh, P. (2001). Early binding of feature pairs for visual perception. *Nature Neuroscience, 4,* 127–128. (4)

Hollister, J. M., Laing, P., & Mednick, S. A. (1996). Rhesus incompatibility as a risk factor for schizophrenia in male adults. *Archives of General Psychiatry, 53,* 19–24. (15)

Hollon, S. D., Thase, M. E., & Markowitz, J. C. (2002). Treatment and prevention of depression. *Psychological Science in the Public Interest, 3,* 39–77. (15)

Holstege, G., Georgiadis, J. R., Paans, A. M. J., Meiners, L. C., van der Graaf, F. H. C. E.,

& Reinders, A. A. T. S. (2003). Brain activation during human male ejaculation. *Journal of Neuroscience, 23,* 9185–9193. (11)

Holy, T. E., Dulac, C., & Meister, M. (2000). Responses of vomeronasal neurons to natural stimuli. *Science, 289,* 1569–1572. (7)

Homewood, J., & Stevenson, R. J. (2001). Differences in naming accuracy of odors presented to the left and right nostrils. *Biological Psychology, 58,* 65–73. (14)

Honea, R., Crow, T. J., Passingham, D., & Mackay, C. E. (2005). Regional deficits in brain volume in schizophrenia: A meta-analysis of voxel-based morphometry studies. *American Journal of Psychiatry, 162,* 2233–2245. (15)

Hoover, J. E., & Strick, P. L. (1993). Multiple output channels in the basal ganglia. *Science, 259,* 819–821. (8)

Hopkins, J., Marcus, M., & Campbell, S. B. (1984). Postpartum depression: A critical review. *Psychological Bulletin, 95,* 498–515. (15)

Hopkins, W. D. (2006). Comparative and familial analysis of handedness in great apes. *Psychological Bulletin, 132,* 538–559. (14)

Hopkins, W. D., Russell, J. L., & Cantalupo, C. (2007). Neuroanatomical correlates of handedness for tool use in chimpanzees (*Pan troglodytes*). *Psychological Science, 18,* 971–977. (14)

Hoptman, M. J., & Levy, J. (1988). Perceptual asymmetries in left- and right-handers for cartoon and real faces. *Brain and Cognition, 8,* 178–188. (14)

Horne, J. A. (1992). Sleep and its disorders in children. *Journal of Child Psychology & Psychiatry & Allied Disciplines, 33,* 473–487. (9)

Horne, J. A., & Minard, A. (1985). Sleep and sleepiness following a behaviourally "active" day. *Ergonomics, 28,* 567–575. (9)

Horridge, G. A. (1962). Learning of leg position by the ventral nerve cord in headless insects. *Proceedings of the Royal Society of London, B, 157,* 33–52. (13)

Horst, W. D., & Preskorn, S. H. (1998). Mechanisms of action and clinical characteristics of three atypical antidepressants: Venlafaxine, nefazodone, bupropion. *Journal of Affective Disorders, 51,* 237–254. (15)

Horvath, T. L. (2005). The hardship of obesity: A soft-wired hypothalamus. *Nature Neuroscience, 8,* 561–565. (10)

Hoshi, E., & Tanji, J. (2000). Integration of target and body-part information in the premotor cortex when planning action. *Nature, 408,* 466–470. (8)

Hovda, D. A., & Feeney, D. M. (1989). Amphetamine-induced recovery of visual cliff performance after bilateral visual cortex ablation in cats: Measurements of depth perception thresholds. *Behavioral Neuroscience, 103,* 574–584. (5)

Howell, S., Westergaard, G., Hoos, B., Chavanne, T. J., Shoaf, S. E., Cleveland, A., et al. (2007). Serotonergic influences on life-history outcomes in free-ranging male rhesus macaques. *American Journal of Primatology, 69,* 851–865. (12)

Hoyte, L., Barber, P. A., Buchan, A. M., & Hill, M. D. (2004). The rise and fall of NMDA antagonists for ischemic stroke. *Current Molecular Medicine, 4,* 131–136. (5)

Hrdy, S. B. (2000). The optimal number of fathers. *Annals of the New York Academy of Sciences, 907,* 75–96. (11)

Hróbjartsson, A., & Gøtzsche, P. C. (2001). Is the placebo powerless? *New England Journal of Medicine, 344,* 1594–1602. (7)

Hsu, M., Sik, A., Gallyas, F., Horváth, Z., & Buzsáki, G. (1994). Short-term and long-term changes in the postischemic hippocampus. *Annals of the New York Academy of Sciences, 743,* 121–140. (5)

Hu, P., Stylos-Allan, M., & Walker, M. P. (2006). Sleep facilitates consolidation of emotional declarative memory. *Psychological Science, 17,* 891–898. (9)

Hua, J. Y., & Smith, S. J. (2004). Neural activity and the dynamics of central nervous system development. *Nature Neuroscience, 7,* 327–332. (5)

Huang, A. L., Chen, X., Hoon, M. A., Chandrashekar, J., Guo, W., Tränker, D., et al. (2006). The cells and logic for mammalian sour taste detection. *Nature, 442,* 934-938. (7)

Huang, L., Treisman, A., & Pashler, H. (2007). Characterizing the limits of human visual awareness. *Science, 317,* 823–825. (14)

Huang, L. Z., Liu, X., Griffith, W. H., & Winzer-Serhan, U. H. (2007). Chronic neonatal nicotine increases anxiety but does not impair cognition in adult rats. *Behavioral Neuroscience, 121,* 1342–1352. (5)

Huang, Y.-J., Maruyama, Y., Lu, K.-S., Pereira, E., Plonsky, I., Baur, J. E., et al. (2005). Mouse taste buds use serotonin as a neurotransmitter. *Journal of Neuroscience, 25,* 843–847. (3)

Hubbard, E. M., Arman, A. C., Ramachandran, V. S., & Boynton, G. M. (2005). Individual differences among grapheme-color synesthetes: Brain-behavior correlations. *Neuron, 45,* 975–985. (7)

Hubbard, E. M., Piazza, M., Pinel, P., & Dehaene, S. (2005). Interactions between number and space in parietal cortex. *Nature Reviews Neuroscience, 6,* 435–448. (4)

Hubel, D. H. (1963, November). The visual cortex of the brain. *Scientific American, 209*(5), 54–62. (6)

Hubel, D. H., & Wiesel, T. N. (1959). Receptive fields of single neurons in the cat's striate cortex. *Journal of Physiology, 148,* 574–591. (6)

Hubel, D. H., & Wiesel, T. N. (1965). Binocular interaction in striate cortex of kittens reared with artificial squint. *Journal of Neurophysiology, 28,* 1041–1059. (6)

Hubel, D. H., & Wiesel, T. N. (1977). Functional architecture of macaque monkey visual cortex. *Proceedings of the Royal Society of London, B, 198,* 1–59. (6)

Hubel, D. H., & Wiesel, T. N. (1998). Early exploration of the visual cortex. *Neuron, 20,* 401–412. (6)

Huber, R., Ghilardi, M. F., Massimini, M., & Tononi, G. (2004). Local sleep and learning. *Nature, 430,* 78–81. (9)

Hudson, J. I., Hiripi, E., Pope, H. G., Jr., & Kessler, R. C. (2007). The prevalence and correlates of eating disorders in the National Comorbidity Survey Replication. *Biological Psychiatry, 61,* 348–358. (10)

Hudson, J. I., Mangweth, B., Pope, H. G., Jr., De Col, C., Hausmann, A., Gutweniger, S., et al. (2003). Family study of affective spectrum disorder. *Archives of General Psychiatry, 60,* 170–177. (15)

Hudspeth, A. J. (1985). The cellular basis of hearing: The biophysics of hair cells. *Science, 230,* 745–752. (7)

Hugdahl, K. (1996). Brain laterality—Beyond the basics. *European Psychologist, 1,* 206–220. (14)

Hughes, J. C., & Cook, C. C. H. (1997). The efficacy of disulfiram: A review of outcome studies. *Addiction, 92,* 381–395. (3)

Hughes, J. R. (2007). Review of medical reports on pedophilia. *Clinical Pediatrics, 46,* 667–682. (11)

Huizink, A. C., & Mulder, E. J. H. (2005). Maternal smoking, drinking or cannabis use during pregnancy and neurobehavioral and cognitive functioning in human offspring. *Neuroscience & Biobehavioral Reviews, 30,* 24–41. (5)

Hull, E. M., Du, J., Lorrain, D. S., & Matuszewich, L. (1997). Testosterone, preoptic dopamine, and copulation in male rats. *Brain Research Bulletin, 44,* 327–333. (11)

Hull, E. M., Eaton, R. C., Markowski, V. P., Moses, J., Lumley, L. A., & Loucks, J. A. (1992). Opposite influence of medial preoptic D_1 and D_2 receptors on genital reflexes: Implications for copulation. *Life Sciences, 51,* 1705–1713. (11)

Hull, E. M., Lorrain, D. S., Du, J., Matuszewich, L., Lumley, L. A., Putnam, S. K., et al. (1999). Hormone-neurotransmitter interactions in the control of sexual behavior. *Behavioural Brain Research, 105,* 105–116. (11)

Hull, E. M., Nishita, J. K., Bitran, D., & Dalterio, S. (1984). Perinatal dopamine-related drugs demasculinize rats. *Science, 224,* 1011–1013. (11)

Hulshoff, H. E., Schnack, H. G., Mandl, R. C. W., van Haren, N. E. M., Koning, H., Collins, L., et al. (2001). Focal gray matter density changes in schizophrenia. *Archives of General Psychiatry, 58,* 1118–1125. (15)

Hunsberger, J. G., Newton, S. S., Bennett, A. H., Duman, C. H., Russell, D. S., Salton, S. R., et al. (2007). Antidepressant actions of the exercise-regulated gene VGF. *Nature Medicine, 13,* 1476–1482. (15)

Hunt, S. P., & Mantyh, P. W. (2001). The molecular dynamics of pain control. *Nature Reviews Neuroscience, 2,* 83–91. (7)

Hunter, W. S. (1923). *General psychology* (Rev. ed.). Chicago: University of Chicago Press. (4)

Huntington's Disease Collaborative Research Group. (1993). A novel gene containing a trinucleotide repeat that is expanded and unstable on Huntington's disease chromosomes. *Cell, 72,* 971–983. (8)

Hurovitz, C. S., Dunn, S., Domhoff, G. W., & Fiss, H. (1999). The dreams of blind men and women: A replication and extension of previous findings. *Dreaming, 9,* 183–193. (6)

Hurvich, L. M., & Jameson, D. (1957). An opponent-process theory of color vision. *Psychological Review, 64,* 384–404. (6)

Hutcheson, D. M., Everitt, B. J., Robbins, T. W., & Dickinson, A. (2001). The role of withdrawal in heroin addiction: Enhances reward or promotes avoidance? *Nature Neuroscience, 4,* 943–947. (15)

Hutchison, K. E., LaChance, H., Niaura, R., Bryan, A., & Smolen, A. (2002). The DRD4 VNTR polymorphism influences reactivity to smoking cues. *Journal of Abnormal Psychology, 111,* 134–143. (3)

Hutchison, K. E., McGeary, J., Smolen, A., & Bryan, A. (2002). The DRD4 VNTR polymorphism moderates craving after alcohol consumption. *Health Psychology, 21,* 139–146. (3)

Hyde, J. (2005). The gender similarities hypothesis. *American Psychologist, 60,* 581–592. (4)

Hyde, K. L., Lerch, J. P., Zatorre, R. J., Griffiths, T. D., Evans, A. C., & Peretz, I. (2007). Cortical thickness in congenital amusia: When less is better than more. *Journal of Neuroscience, 27,* 13028–13032. (7)

Hyde, K. L., & Peretz, I. (2004). Brains that are out of tune but in time. *Psychological Science, 15,* 356–360. (7)

Hynd, G. W., & Semrud-Clikeman, M. (1989). Dyslexia and brain morphology. *Psychological Bulletin, 106,* 447–482. (14)

Hypericum Depression Trial Study Group. (2002). Effect of *Hypericum perforatum* (St John's wort) in major depressive disorder. *Journal of the American Medical Association, 287,* 1807–1814. (15)

Iacoboni, M., & Dapretto, M. (2006). The mirror neuron system and the consequences of its dysfunction. *Nature Reviews Neuroscience, 7,* 942–951. (8)

Ibrahim, H. M., Hogg, A. J., Jr., Healy, D. J., Haroutunian, V., Davis, K. L., & Meador-Woodruff, J. H. (2000). Ionotropic glutamate receptor binding and subunit mRNA expression in thalamic nuclei in schizophrenia. *American Journal of Psychiatry, 157,* 1811–1823. (15)

Iggo, A., & Andres, K. H. (1982). Morphology of cutaneous receptors. *Annual Review of Neuroscience, 5,* 1–31. (7)

Ikeda, H., Stark, J., Fischer, H., Wagner, M., Drdla, R., Jäger, T., et al. (2006). Synaptic amplifier of inflammatory pain in the spinal dorsal horn. *Science, 312,* 1659–1662. (7)

Ikegaya, Y., Aaron, G., Cossart, R., Aronov, D., Lampl, I., Ferster, D., et al. (2004). Synfire chains and cortical songs: Temporal modules of cortical activity. *Science, 304,* 559–564. (2)

Ikonomidou, C., Bittigau, P. Ishimaru, M. J., Wozniak, D. F., Koch, C., Genz, K., et al. (2000). Ethanol-induced apoptotic neurodegeneration and fetal alcohol syndrome. *Science, 287,* 1056–1060. (5)

Imamura, K., Mataga, N., & Mori, K. (1992). Coding of odor molecules by mitral/tufted cells in rabbit olfactory bulb: I. Aliphatic compounds. *Journal of Neurophysiology, 68,* 1986–2002. (7)

Imperato-McGinley, J., Guerrero, L., Gautier, T., & Peterson, R. E. (1974). Steroid 5 alpha-reductase deficiency in man: An inherited form of male pseudohermaphroditism. *Science, 186,* 1213–1215. (11)

Innocenti, G. M. (1980). The primary visual pathway through the corpus callosum: Morphological and functional aspects in the cat. *Archives Italiennes de Biologie, 118,* 124–188. (14)

Innocenti, G. M., & Caminiti, R. (1980). Postnatal shaping of callosal connections from sensory areas. *Experimental Brain Research, 38,* 381–394. (14)

Inouye, S. T., & Kawamura, H. (1979). Persistence of circadian rhythmicity in a mammalian hypothalamic "island" containing the suprachiasmatic nucleus. *Proceedings of the National Academy of Sciences, USA, 76,* 5962–5966. (9)

Irvine, R. J., Keane, M., Felgate, P., McCann, U. D., Callaghan, P. D., & White, J. M. (2006). Plasma drug concentrations and physiological measures in "dance party" participants. *Neuropsychopharmacology, 31,* 424–430. (3)

Irwin, D. E., & Brockmole, J. R. (2004). Suppressing *where* but not *what*: The effect of saccades on dorsal- and ventral-stream visual processing. *Psychological Science, 15,* 467–473. (6)

Isoda, M., & Hikosaka, O. (2007). Switching from automatic to controlled action by monkey medial frontal cortex. *Nature Neuroscience, 10,* 240–248. (8)

Ito, M. (1984). *The cerebellum and neural control.* New York: Raven Press. (8)

Ito, M. (1989). Long-term depression. *Annual Review of Neuroscience, 12,* 85–102. (13)

Ito, M. (2002). The molecular organization of cerebellar long-term depression. *Nature Reviews Neuroscience, 3,* 896–902. (13)

Ivry, R. B., & Diener, H. C. (1991). Impaired velocity perception in patients with lesions of the cerebellum. *Journal of Cognitive Neuroscience, 3,* 355–366. (8)

Ivy, G. O., & Killackey, H. P. (1981). The ontogeny of the distribution of callosal projection neurons in the rat parietal cortex. *Journal of Comparative Neurology, 195,* 367–389. (14)

Iwema, C. L., Fang, H., Kurtz, D. B., Youngentob, S. L., & Schwob, J. E. (2004). Odorant receptor expression patterns are restored in lesion-recovered rat olfactory epithelium. *Journal of Neuroscience, 24,* 356–369. (7)

Jablensky, A. V., Morgan, V., Zubrick, S. R., Bower, C., & Yellachich, L.-A. (2005). Pregnancy, delivery, and neonatal complications in a population cohort of women with schizophrenia and major affective disorders. *American Journal of Psychiatry, 162,* 79–91. (15)

Jacob, S., McClintock, M. K., Zelano, B., & Ober, C. (2002). Paternally inherited HLA alleles are associated with women's choice of male odor. *Nature Genetics, 30,* 175–179. (7)

Jacobs, B., & Scheibel, A. B. (1993). A quantitative dendritic analysis of Wernicke's area in humans: I. Lifespan changes. *Journal of Comparative Neurology, 327,* 83–96. (5)

Jacobs, G. D., & Snyder, D. (1996). Frontal brain asymmetry predicts affective style in men. *Behavioral Neuroscience, 110,* 3–6. (15)

Jacobs, G. H., Williams, G. A., Cahill, H., & Nathans, J. (2007). Emergence of novel color vision in mice engineered to express a human cone photopigment. *Science, 315,* 1723–1725. (6)

James, W. (1884). What is an emotion? *Mind, 9,* 188–205. (12)

James, W. (1894). The physical basis of emotion. *Psychological Review, 1,* 516–529. (12)

James, W. (1961). *Psychology: The briefer course.* New York: Harper. (Original work published 1892) (12)

Jameson, K. A., Highnote, S. M., & Wasserman, L. M. (2001). Richer color experience in observers with multiple photopigment opsin genes. *Psychonomic Bulletin & Review, 8,* 244–261. (6)

Jarrard, L. E., Okaichi, H., Steward, O., & Goldschmidt, R. B. (1984). On the role of hippocampal connections in the performance of place and cue tasks: Comparisons with damage to hippocampus. *Behavioral Neuroscience, 98,* 946–954. (13)

Jenner, A. R., Rosen, G. D., & Galaburda, A. M. (1999). Neuronal asymmetries in primary visual cortex of dyslexic and nondyslexic brains. *Annals of Neurology, 46,* 189–196. (14)

Jerison, H. J. (1985). Animal intelligence as encephalization. *Philosophical Transactions of the Royal Society of London, B, 308,* 21–35. (4)

Ji, D., & Wilson, M. A. (2007). Coordinated memory replay in the visual cortex and hippocampus during sleep. *Nature Neuroscience, 10,* 100–107. (9)

Jiang, Y., Costello, P., & He, S. (2007). Processing of invisible stimuli. *Psychological Science, 18,* 349–355. (14)

Jimerson, D. C., & Wolfe, B. E. (2004). Neuropeptides in eating disorders. *CNS Spectrums, 9,* 516–522. (10)

Johanek, L. M., Meyer, R. A., Hartke, T., Hobelmann, J. G., Maine, D. N., LaMotte, R. H., et al. (2007). Psychophysical and physiological evidence for parallel afferent pathways mediating the sensation of itch. *Journal of Neuroscience, 27,* 7490–7497. (7)

Johns, T. R., & Thesleff, S. (1961). Effects of motor inactivation on the chemical sensitivity of skeletal muscle. *Acta Physiologica Scandinavica, 51,* 136–141. (5)

Johnson, E. N., Hawken, M. J., & Shapley, R. (2001). The spatial transformation of color in the primary visual cortex of the macaque monkey. *Nature Neuroscience, 4,* 409–416. (6)

Johnson, L. C. (1969). Physiological and psychological changes following total sleep deprivation. In A. Kales (Ed.), *Sleep: Physiology & pathology* (pp. 206–220). Philadelphia: Lippincott. (9)

Johnson, M. T. V., Kipnis, A. N., Coltz, J. D., Gupta, A., Silverstein, P., Zwiebel, F., et al. (1996). Effects of levodopa and viscosity on the velocity and accuracy of visually guided tracking in Parkinson's disease. *Brain, 119,* 801–813. (8)

Jonas, P., Bischofberger, J., & Sandkühler, J. (1998). Corelease of two fast neurotransmitters at a central synapse. *Science, 281,* 419–424. (3)

Jonas, S. (1995). Prophylactic pharmacologic neuroprotection against focal cerebral ischemia. *Annals of the New York Academy of Sciences, 765,* 21–25. (5)

Jones, A. R., & Shusta, E. V. (2007). Blood-brain barrier transport of therapeutics via receptor-mediation. *Pharmaceutical Research, 24,* 1759–1771. (2)

Jones, C. R., Campbell, S. S., Zone, S. E., Cooper, F., DeSano, A., Murphy, P. J., et al. (1999). Familial advanced sleep-phase syndrome: A short-period circadian rhythm variant in humans. *Nature Medicine, 5,* 1062–1065. (9)

Jones, E. G., & Pons, T. P. (1998). Thalamic and brainstem contributions to large-scale plasticity of primate somatosensory cortex. *Science, 282,* 1121–1125. (5)

Jones, H. S., & Oswald, I. (1968). Two cases of healthy insomnia. *Electroencephalography and Clinical Neurophysiology, 24,* 378–380. (9)

Jones, P. B., Barnes, T. R. E., Davies, L., Dunn, G., Lloyd, H., Hayhurst, K. P., et al. (2006). Randomized controlled trial of the effect on quality of life of second- vs. first-generation antipsychotic drugs in schizophrenia. *Archives of General Psychiatry, 63,* 1079–1087. (15)

Jones-Brando, L., Torrey, E. F., & Yolken, R. (2003). Drugs used in the treatment of schizophrenia and bipolar disorder inhibit the replication of *Toxoplasma gondii. Schizophrenia Research, 62,* 237–244. (15)

Jordan, H. A. (1969). Voluntary intragastric feeding. *Journal of Comparative and Physiological Psychology, 68,* 498–506. (10)

Joseph, J. A., Shukitt-Hale, B., Denisova, N. A., Prior, R. L., Cao, G., Martin, A., et al. (1998). Long-term dietary strawberry, spinach, or vitamin E supplementation retards the onset of age-related neuronal signal-transduction and cognitive behavioral deficits. *Journal of Neuroscience, 18,* 8047–8055. (13)

Jouvet, M. (1960). Telencephalic and rhombencephalic sleep in the cat. In G. E. W. Wolstenholme & M. O'Connor (Eds.), *CIBA Foundation symposium on the nature of sleep* (pp. 188–208). Boston: Little, Brown. (9)

Joyner, A. L., & Guillemot, F. (1994). Gene targeting and development of the nervous system. *Current Opinion in Neurobiology, 4,* 37–42. (4)

Judge, J., Caravolas, M., & Knox, P. C. (2006). Smooth pursuit eye movements and phonological processing in adults with dyslexia. *Cognitive Neuropsychology, 23,* 1174–1189. (14)

Jueptner, M., & Weiller, C. (1998). A review of differences between basal ganglia and cerebellar control of movements as revealed by functional imaging studies. *Brain, 121,* 1437–1449. (8)

Jureidini, J. N., Doecke, C. J., Mansfield, P. R., Haby, M. M., Menkes, D. B., & Tonkin, A. L. (2004). Efficacy and safety of antidepressants for children and adolescents. *British Medical Journal, 328,* 879–883. (15)

Juvonen, H., Reunanen, A., Haukka, J., Muhonen, M., Suvisari, J., Arajärvi, R., et al. (2007). Incidence of schizophrenia in a nationwide cohort of patients with type 1 diabetes mellitus. *Archives of General Psychiatry, 64,* 894–899. (15)

Kaas, J. H. (1983). What, if anything, is SI? Organization of first somatosensory area of cortex. *Physiological Reviews, 63,* 206–231. (7)

Kaas, J. H., Merzenich, M. M., & Killackey, H. P. (1983). The reorganization of somatosensory cortex following peripheral nerve damage in adult and developing mammals. *Annual Review of Neuroscience, 6,* 325–356. (5)

Kaas, J. H., Nelson, R. J., Sur, M., Lin, C.-S., & Merzenich, M. M. (1979). Multiple representations of the body within the primary somatosensory cortex of primates. *Science, 204,* 521–523. (4)

Kales, A., Scharf, M. B., & Kales, J. D. (1978). Rebound insomnia: A new clinical syndrome. *Science, 201,* 1039–1041. (9)

Kalin, N. H., Shelton, S. E., & Davidson, R. J. (2004). The role of the central nucleus of the amygdala in mediating fear and anxiety in the primate. *Journal of Neuroscience, 24,* 5506–5515. (12)

Kalin, N. H., Shelton, S. E., Davidson, R. J., & Kelley, A. E. (2001). The primate amygdala mediates acute fear but not the behavioral and physiological components of anxious temperament. *Journal of Neuroscience, 21,* 2067–2074. (12)

Kalivas, P. W., Volkow, N., & Seamans, J. (2005). Unmanageable motivation in addiction: A pathology in prefrontal-accumbens glutamate transmission. *Neuron, 45,* 647–650. (3)

Kamitani, Y., & Tong, F. (2005). Decoding the visual and subjective contents of the human brain. *Nature Neuroscience, 8,* 679–685. (14)

Kandel, E. R., & Schwartz, J. H. (1982). Molecular biology of learning: Modulation of transmitter release. *Science, 218,* 433–443. (13)

Kanwisher, N. (2000). Domain specificity in face perception. *Nature Neuroscience, 3,* 759–763. (6)

Kaplan, J. R., Muldoon, M. F., Manuck, S. B., & Mann, J. J. (1997). Assessing the observed relationship between low cholesterol and violence-related mortality. *Annals of the New York Academy of Sciences, 836,* 57–80. (12)

Kapur, S., Zipusky, R., Jones, C., Shammi, C. S., Remington, G., & Seeman, P. (2000). A positron emission tomography study of quetiapine in schizophrenia. *Archives of General Psychiatry, 57,* 553–559. (15)

Kargo, W. J., & Nitz, D. A. (2004). Improvements in the signal-to-noise ratio of motor cortex cells distinguish early versus late phases of motor skill learning. *Journal of Neuroscience, 24,* 5560–5569. (8)

Karmiloff-Smith, A., Tyler, L. K., Voice, K., Sims, K., Udwin, O., Howlin, P., et al. (1998). Linguistic dissociations in Williams syndrome: Evaluating receptive syntax in on-line and off-line tasks. *Neuropsychologia, 36,* 343–351. (14)

Karrer, T., & Bartoshuk, L. (1991). Capsaicin desensitization and recovery on the human tongue. *Physiology & Behavior, 49,* 757–764. (7)

Kas, M. J. H., Tiesjema, B., van Dijk, G., Garner, K. M., Barsh, G. S., Ter Brake, O., et al. (2004). Induction of brain region-specific forms of obesity by agouti. *Journal of Neuroscience, 24,* 10176–10181. (10)

Kasai, K., Shenton, M. E., Salisbury, D. F., Hirayasu, Y., Onitsuka, T., Spencer, M. H., et al. (2003). Progressive decrease of left Heschl gyrus and planum temporale gray matter volume in first-episode schizophrenia. *Archives of General Psychiatry, 60,* 766–775. (15)

Katkin, E. S., Wiens, S., & Öhman, A. (2001). Nonconscious fear conditioning, visceral perception, and the development of gut feelings. *Psychological Science, 12,* 366–370. (12)

Katusic, S. K., Barbaresi, W. J., Colligan, R. C., Weaver, A. L., Leibson, C. L., & Jacobsen, S. J. (2005). Psychostimulant treatment and risk for substance abuse among young adults with a history of attention-deficit/hyperactivity disorder: A population-based, birth cohort study. *Journal of Child and Adolescent Psychopharmacology, 15,* 764–776. (3)

Kauer, J. A., & Malenko, R. C. (2007). Synaptic plasticity and addiction. *Nature Reviews Neuroscience, 8,* 844–858. (13)

Kawasaki, H., Adolphs, R., Kaufman, O., Damasio, H., Damasio, A. R., Granner, M., et al. (2001). Single-neuron responses to emotional visual stimuli recorded in human ventral prefrontal cortex. *Nature Neuroscience, 4,* 15–16. (12)

Kawasaki, H., Adolphs, R., Oya, H., Kovach, C., Damasio, H., Kaufman, O., et al. (2005). Analysis of single-unit responses to emotional scenes in human ventromedial prefrontal cortex. *Journal of Cognitive Neuroscience, 17,* 1509–1518. (12)

Kay, K. N., Naselaris, T., Prenger, R. J., & Gallant, J. L. (2008). Identifying natural images from human brain activity. *Nature, 452,* 352–355. (4)

Kee, N., Teixeira, C. M., Wang, A. H., & Frankland, P. W. (2007). Preferential incorporation of adult-generated granule cells into spatial memory networks in the dentate gyrus. *Nature Neuroscience, 10,* 355–362. (5)

Keele, S. W., & Ivry, R. (1990). Does the cerebellum provide a common computation for diverse tasks? *Annals of the New York Academy of Sciences, 608,* 179–207. (8)

Keller, A., Zhuang, H., Chi, Q., Vosshall, L. B., & Matsunami, H. (2007). Genetic variation in a human odorant receptor alters odour perception. *Nature, 449,* 468–472. (7)

Kelly, T. L., Neri, D. F., Grill, J. T., Ryman, D., Hunt, P. D., Dijk, D.-J., et al. (1999). Nonentrained circadian rhythms of melatonin in submariners scheduled to an 18-hour day. *Journal of Biological Rhythms, 14,* 190–196. (9)

Kendler, K. S. (1983). Overview: A current perspective on twin studies of schizophrenia. *American Journal of Psychiatry, 140,* 1413–1425. (15)

Kendler, K. S. (2001). Twin studies of psychiatric illness. *Archives of General Psychiatry, 58,* 1005–1014. (1)

Kendler, K. S., Gardner, C. O., & Prescott, C. A. (1999). Clinical characteristics of major depression that predict risk of depression in relatives. *Archives of General Psychiatry, 56,* 322–327. (15)

Kendler, K. S., Thornton, L. M., Gilman, S. E., & Kessler, R. C. (2000). Sexual orientation in a U.S. national sample of twin and nontwin sibling pairs. *American Journal of Psychiatry, 157,* 1843–1846. (11)

Kennard, C., Lawden, M., Morland, A. B., & Ruddock, K. H. (1995). Colour identification and colour constancy are impaired in a patient with incomplete achromatopsia associated with prestriate cortical lesions. *Proceedings of the Royal Society of London, B, 260,* 169–175. (6)

Kennaway, D. J., & Van Dorp, C. F. (1991). Free-running rhythms of melatonin, cortisol, electrolytes, and sleep in humans in Antarctica. *American Journal of Physiology, 260,* R1137–R1144. (9)

Kennerley, S. W., Diedrichsen, J., Hazeltine, E., Semjen, A., & Ivry, R. B. (2002). Callosotomy patients exhibit temporal uncoupling during continuous bimanual movements. *Nature Neuroscience, 5,* 376–381. (14)

Kennett, S., Eimer, M., Spence, C., & Driver, J. (2001). Tactile-visual links in exogenous spatial attention under different postures: Convergent evidence from psychophysics and ERPs. *Journal of Cognitive Neuroscience, 13,* 462–478. (14)

Kenny, P. J., Chen, S. A., Kitamura, O., Markou, A., & Koob, G. F. (2006). Conditioned withdrawal drives heroin consumption and decreases reward sensitivity. *Journal of Neuroscience, 26,* 5894–5900. (3)

Kerns, J. G. (2007). Experimental manipulation of cognitive control processes causes an increase in communication disturbances in healthy volunteers. *Psychological Medicine, 37,* 995–1004. (15)

Kerr, D. S., & Abraham, W. C. (1995). Cooperative interactions among afferents govern the induction of homosynaptic long-term depression in the hippocampus. *Proceedings of the National Academy of Sciences, USA, 92,* 11637–11641. (13)

Keshavan, M. S., Diwadkar, V. A., Montrose, D. M., Rajarethinam, R., & Sweeney, J. A. (2005). Premorbid indicators and risk for schizophrenia: A selective review and update. *Schizophrenia Research, 79,* 45–57. (15)

Keskin, O., Kalemoglu, M., & Ulusoy, R. E. (2005). A clinic investigation into prehospital and emergency department delays in acute stroke care. *Medical Principles and Practice, 14,* 408–412. (5)

Kesner, R. P., Gilbert, P. E., & Barua, L. A. (2002). The role of the hippocampus in meaning for the temporal order of a sequence of odors. *Behavioral Neuroscience, 116,* 286–290. (13)

Kesslak, J. P., So, V., Choi, J., Cotman, C. W., & Gomez-Pinilla, F. (1998). Learning upregulates brain-derived neurotrophic factor messenger ribonucleic acid: A mechanism to facilitate encoding and circuit maintenance? *Behavioral Neuroscience, 112,* 1012–1019. (5)

Kety, S. S., Wender, P. H., Jacobson, B., Ingraham, L. J., Jansson, L., Faber, B., et al. (1994). Mental illness in the biological and adoptive relatives of schizophrenic adoptees. *Archives of General Psychiatry, 51,* 442–455. (15)

Keverne, E. B. (1999). The vomeronasal organ. *Science, 286,* 716–720. (7)

Khashau, A. S., Abel, K. M., McNamee, R., Pedersen, M. G., Webb, R. T., Baker, P. N., et al. (2008). Higher risk of offspring schizophrenia following antenatal maternal exposure to severe adverse life events. *Archives of General Psychiatry, 65,* 146–152. (15)

Kiecolt-Glaser, J. K., & Glaser, R. (1993). Mind and immunity. In D. Goleman & J. Gurin (Eds.), *Mind/body medicine* (pp. 39–61). Yonkers, NY: Consumer Reports Books. (12)

Kikuchi-Yorioka, Y., & Sawaguchi, T. (2000). Parallel visuospatial and audiospatial working memory processes in the monkey dorsolateral prefrontal cortex. *Nature Neuroscience, 3,* 1075–1076. (13)

Kilgour, A. R., de Gelder, B., & Lederman, S. J. (2004). Haptic face recognition and prosopagnosia. *Neuropsychologia, 42,* 707–712. (6)

Killackey, H. P., & Chalupa, L. M. (1986). Ontogenetic change in the distribution of callosal projection neurons in the postcentral gyrus of the fetal rhesus monkey. *Journal of Comparative Neurology, 244,* 331–348. (14)

Killeffer, F. A., & Stern, W. E. (1970). Chronic effects of hypothalamic injury. *Archives of Neurology, 22,* 419–429. (10)

Kim, U., Jorgenson, E., Coon, H., Leppert, M., Risch, N., & Drayna, D. (2003). Positional cloning of the human quantitative trait locus underlying taste sensitivity to phenylthiocarbamide. *Science, 299,* 1221–1225. (7)

King, B. M. (2006). The rise, fall, and resurrection of the ventromedial hypothalamus in the regulation of feeding behavior and body weight. *Physiology & Behavior, 87,* 221–244. (10)

King, B. M., Smith, R. L., & Frohman, L. A. (1984). Hyperinsulinemia in rats with ventromedial hypothalamic lesions: Role of hyperphagia. *Behavioral Neuroscience, 98,* 152–155. (10)

King, V. R., Huang, W. L., Dyall, S. C., Curran, O. E., Priestley, J. V., & Michael-Titus, A. T. (2006). Omega-3 fatty acids improve recovery, whereas omega-6 fatty acids worsen outcome after spinal cord injury in the adult rat. *Journal of Neuroscience, 26,* 4672–4680. (5)

Kingstone, A., & Gazzaniga, M. S. (1995). Subcortical transfer of higher order information: More illusory than real? *Neuropsychology, 9,* 321–328. (14)

Kinnamon, J. C. (1987). Organization and innervation of taste buds. In T. E. Finger & W. L. Silver (Eds.), *Neurobiology of taste and smell* (pp. 277–297). New York: Wiley. (7)

Kinomura, S., Larsson, J., Gulyás, B., & Roland, P. E. (1996). Activation by attention of the human reticular formation and thalamic intralaminar nuclei. *Science, 271,* 512–515. (9)

Kinsbourne, M., & McMurray, J. (1975). The effect of cerebral dominance on time sharing between speaking and tapping by preschool children. *Child Development, 46,* 240–242. (14)

Kinsey, A. C., Pomeroy, W. B., & Martin, C. E. (1948). *Sexual behavior in the human male.* Philadelphia: Saunders. (11)

Kinsey, A. C., Pomeroy, W. B., Martin, C. E., & Gebhard, P. H. (1953). *Sexual behavior in the human female.* Philadelphia: Saunders. (11)

Kippenhan, J. S., Olsen, R. K., Mervis, C. B., Morris, C. A., Kohn, P., Meyer-Lindenberg, A., et al. (2005). Genetic contributions to human gyrification: Sulcal morphometry in Williams syndrome. *Journal of Neuroscience, 25,* 7840–7846. (14)

Kiriakakis, V., Bhatia, K. P., Quinn, N. P., & Marsden, C. D. (1998). The natural history of tardive dyskinesia: A long-term follow-up study of 107 cases. *Brain, 121,* 2053–2066. (15)

Kirkpatrick, P. J., Smielewski, P., Czosnyka, M., Menon, D. K., & Pickard, J. D. (1995). Near-infrared spectroscopy in patients with head injury. *Journal of Neurosurgery, 83,* 963–970. (5)

Kirkwood, A., Lee, H.-K., & Bear, M. F. (1995). Co-regulation of long-term potentiation and experience-dependent synaptic plasticity in visual cortex by age and experience. *Nature, 375,* 328–331. (6)

Kirsch, I., Deacon, B. J., Huedo-Medina, T. B., Scoboria, A., Moore, T. J., & Johnson, B. T. (2008). Initial severity and antidepressant benefits: A meta-analysis of data submitted to the Food and Drug Administration. *PLoS Medicine, 5,* e45. (15)

Kleen, J. K., Sitomer, M. T., Killeen, P. R., & Conrad, C. D. (2006). Chronic stress impairs spatial memory and motivation for reward without disrupting motor ability and motivation to explore. *Behavioral Neuroscience, 120,* 842–851. (12)

Klein, D. F. (1993). False suffocation alarms, spontaneous panics, and related conditions. *Archives of General Psychiatry, 50,* 306–317. (12)

Kleiser, R., Seitz, R. J., & Krekelberg, B. (2004). Neural correlates of saccadic suppression in humans. *Current Biology, 14,* 386–390. (6)

Kleitman, N. (1963). *Sleep and wakefulness* (Rev. ed.). Chicago: University of Chicago Press. (9)

Klingberg, T., Forssberg, H., & Westerberg, H. (2002). Increased brain activity in frontal and parietal cortex underlies the development of visuospatial working memory capacity during childhood. *Journal of Cognitive Neuroscience, 14,* 1–10. (13)

Klingberg, T., Hedehus, M., Temple, E., Salz, T., Gabrielli, J. D. E., Moseley, M. E., et al. (2000). Microstructure of temporo-parietal white matter as a basis for reading ability: Evidence from diffusion tensor magnetic resonance imaging. *Neuron, 25,* 493–500. (14)

Kluger, M. J. (1991). Fever: Role of pyrogens and cryogens. *Physiological Reviews, 71,* 93–127. (10)

Klüver, H., & Bucy, P. C. (1939). Preliminary analysis of functions of the temporal lobes in monkeys. *Archives of Neurology and Psychiatry, 42,* 979–1000. (4)

Knoll, J. (1993). The pharmacological basis of the beneficial effects of (2) deprenyl (selegiline) in Parkinson's and Alzheimer's diseases. *Journal of Neural Transmission* (Suppl. 40), 69–91. (8)

Knyazev, G. G., Slobodskaya, H. R., & Wilson, G. D. (2002). Psychophysiological correlates of behavioural inhibition and activation. *Personality and Individual Differences, 33,* 647–660. (12)

Kobayakawa, K., Kobayakawa, R., Matsumoto, H., Oka, Y., Imai, T., Ikawa, M., et al. (2007). Innate versus learned odour processing in the mouse olfactory bulb. *Nature, 450,* 503–508. (7)

Kobett, P., Paulitsch, S., Goebel, M., Stengel, A., Schmidtmann, M., van der Voort, I. R., et al. (2006). Peripheral injection of CCK-8S induces Fos expression in the dorsomedial hypothalamic nucleus in rats. *Brain Research, 1117,* 109–117. (10)

Kodituwakku, P. W. (2007). Defining the behavioral phenotype in children with fetal alcohol spectrum disorders: A review. *Neuroscience & Biobehavioral Reviews, 31,* 192–201. (5)

Koenigs, M., Huey, E. D., Raymont, V., Cheon, B., Solomon, J., Wassermann, E. M., et al. (2008). Focal brain damage protects against post-traumatic stress disorder in combat veterans. *Nature Neuroscience, 11,* 232–237. (12)

Koenigs, M., Young, L., Adolphs, R., Tranel, D., Cushman, F., Hauser, M., et al. (2007). Damage to the prefrontal cortex increases utilitarian moral judgments. *Nature, 446,* 908–911. (12)

Koepp, M. J., Gunn, R. N., Lawrence, A. D., Cunningham, V. J., Dagher, A., Jones, T., et al. (1998). Evidence for striatal dopamine release during a video game. *Nature, 393,* 266–268. (3)

Kohler, E., Keysers, C., Umiltà, M. A., Fogassi, L., Gallese, V., & Rizzolatti, G. (2002). Hearing sounds, understanding actions: Action representation in mirror neurons. *Science, 297,* 846–848. (8)

Kolb, B., Côté, S., Ribeiro-da-Silva, A., & Cuello, A. C. (1997). Nerve growth factor treatment prevents dendritic atrophy and promotes recovery of function after cortical injury. *Neuroscience, 76,* 1139–1151. (8)

Komisaruk, B. R., Adler, N. T., & Hutchison, J. (1972). Genital sensory field: Enlargement by estrogen treatment in female rats. *Science, 178,* 1295–1298. (11)

Komura, Y., Tamura, R., Uwano, T., Nishijo, H., Kaga, K., & Ono, T. (2001). Retrospective and prospective coding for predicted reward in the sensory thalamus. *Nature, 412,* 546–549. (4)

Kondo, I., Marvizon, J. C. G., Song, B., Salgado, F., Codeluppi, S., Hua, X.-Y., et al. (2005). Inhibition by spinal μ- and δ-opioid agonists of afferent-evoked substance P release. *Journal of Neuroscience, 25,* 3651–3660. (7)

Kong, J., Shepel, P. N., Holden, C. P., Mackiewicz, M., Pack, A. I., & Geiger, J. D. (2002). Brain glycogen decreases with increased periods of wakefulness: Implications for homeostatic drive to sleep. *Journal of Neuroscience, 22,* 5581–5587. (9)

Konishi, S., Nakajima, K., Uchida, I., Kameyama, M., Nakahara, K., Sekihara, K., et al. (1998). Transient activation of inferior prefrontal cortex during cognitive set shifting. *Nature Neuroscience, 1,* 80–84. (15)

Kopp, C., Longordo, F., Nicholson, J. R., & Lüthi, A. (2006). Insufficient sleep reversibly alters bidirectional synaptic plasticity and NMDA receptor function. *Journal of Neuroscience, 26,* 12456–12465. (9)

Korenberg, J. R., Chen, X.-N., Hirota, H., Lai, Z., Bellugi, U., Burian, D., et al. (2000). VI. Genome structure and cognitive map of Williams syndrome. *Journal of Cognitive Neuroscience, 12*(Suppl.), 89–107. (14)

Korman, M., Doyon, J., Doljansky, J., Carrier, J., Dagan, Y., & Karni, A. (2007). Daytime sleep condenses the time course of motor memory consolidation. *Nature Neuroscience, 10,* 1206–1213. (9)

Kornhuber, H. H. (1974). Cerebral cortex, cerebellum, and basal ganglia: An introduction to their motor functions. In F. O. Schmitt & F. G. Worden (Eds.), *The neurosciences: Third study program* (pp. 267–280). Cambridge, MA: MIT Press. (8)

Korpi, E. R., & Sinkkonen, S. T. (2006). $GABA_A$ receptor subtypes as targets for neuropsychiatric drug development. *Pharmacology & Therapeutics, 109,* 12–32. (12)

Kosfeld, M., Heinrichs, M., Zak, P. J., Fischbacher, U., & Fehr, E. (2005). Oxytocin increases trust in humans. *Nature, 435,* 673–676. (11)

Kosslyn, S. M., Ganis, G., & Thompson, W. L. (2001). Neural foundations of imagery. *Nature Reviews Neuroscience, 2,* 635–642. (6)

Kosslyn, S. M., & Thompson, W. L. (2003). When is early visual cortex activated during visual mental imagery? *Psychological Bulletin, 129,* 723–746. (6)

Kostrzewa, R. M. (1995). Dopamine receptor supersensitivity. *Neuroscience and Biobehavioral Reviews, 19,* 1–17. (5)

Kotowicz, Z. (2007). The strange case of Phineas Gage. *History of the Human Sciences, 20,* 115–131. (12)

Kourtzi, Z., & Kanwisher, N. (2000). Activation in human MT/MST by static images with implied motion. *Journal of Cognitive Neuroscience, 12,* 48–55. (6)

Kozloski, J., Hamzei-Sichani, F., & Yuste, R. (2001). Stereotyped position of local synaptic targets in neocortex. *Science, 293,* 868–872. (5)

Kozorovitskiy, Y., Hughes, M., Lee, K., & Gould, E. (2006). Fatherhood affects dendritic spines and vasopressin V1a receptors in the primate prefrontal cortex. *Nature Neuroscience, 9,* 1094–1095. (11)

Kraemer, D. J. M., Macrae, C. N., Green, A. E., & Kelley, W. M. (2005). Sound of silence activates auditory cortex. *Nature, 434,* 158. (7)

Krakauer, A. H. (2005). Kin selection and cooperative courtship in wild turkeys. *Nature, 434,* 69–72. (1)

Kraly, F. S., Kim, Y.-M., Dunham, L. M., & Tribuzio, R. A. (1995). Drinking after intragastric NaCl without increase in systemic plasma osmolality in rats. *American Journal of Physiology, 269,* R1085–R1092. (10)

Krause, E. G., & Sakal, R. R. (2007). Richter and sodium appetite: From adrenalectomy to molecular biology. *Appetite, 49,* 353–367. (10)

Kreek, M. J., Nielsen, D. A., Butelman, H. R., & LaForge, K. S. (2005). Genetic influences on impulsivity, risk taking, stress responsivity and vulnerability to drug abuse and addiction. *Nature Neuroscience, 8,* 1450–1457. (15)

Kreitzer, A. C., & Malenka, R. C. (2007). Endocannabinoid-mediated rescue of striatal LTD and motor deficits in Parkinson's disease models. *Nature, 445,* 643–647. (8)

Kreitzer, A. C., & Regehr, W. G. (2001). Retrograde inhibition of presynaptic calcium influx by endogenous cannabinoids at excitatory synapses onto Purkinje cells. *Neuron, 29,* 717–727. (3)

Kringelbach, M. L. (2005). The human orbitofrontal cortex: Linking reward to hedonic experience. *Nature Reviews Neuroscience, 6,* 691–702. (12)

Kripke, D. F. (1998). Light treatment for nonseasonal depression: Speed, efficacy, and combined treatment. *Journal of Affective Disorders, 49,* 109–117. (15)

Krishnan-Sarin, S., Krystal, J. H., Shi, J., Pittman, B., & O'Malley, S. S. (2007). Family history of alcoholism influences naloxone-induced reduction in alcohol drinking. *Biological Psychiatry, 62,* 694–697. (3)

Krupa, D. J., Thompson, J. K., & Thompson, R. F. (1993). Localization of a memory trace in the mammalian brain. *Science, 260,* 989–991. (13)

Kruzich, P. J., Congleton, K. M., & See, R. E. (2001). Conditioned reinstatement of drug-seeking behavior with a discrete compound stimulus classically conditioned with intravenous cocaine. *Behavioral Neuroscience, 115,* 1086–1092. (3)

Kuba, H., Ishii, T. M., & Ohmori, H. (2006). Axonal site of spike initiation enhances auditory coincidence detection. *Nature, 444,* 1069–1072. (2)

Kubista, H., & Boehm, S. (2006). Molecular mechanisms underlying the modulation of exocytotic noradrenaline release via presynaptic receptors. *Pharmacology & Therapeutics, 112,* 213–242. (3)

Kubota, Y., Sato, W., Murai, T., Toichi, M., Ikeda, A., & Sengoku, A. (2000). Emotional cognition without awareness after unilateral temporal lobectomy in humans. *Journal of Neuroscience, 20,* RC97, 1–5. (12)

Kuhlman, S. J., Silver, R., LeSauter, J., Bult-Ito, A., & McMahon, D. G. (2003). Phase resetting light pulses induce *Per1* and persistent spike activity in a subpopulation of biological clock neurons. *Journal of Neuroscience, 23,* 1441–1450. (9)

Kujala, T., Myllyviita, K., Tervaniemi, M., Alho, K., Kallio, J., & Näätänen, R. (2000). Basic auditory dysfunction in dyslexia as demonstrated by brain activity measurements. *Psychophysiology, 37,* 262–266. (14)

Kullmann, D. M., & Lamsa, K. P. (2007). Long-term synaptic plasticity in hippocampal interneurons. *Nature Reviews Neuroscience, 8,* 687–699. (3)

Kumakura, Y., Cumming, P., Vernaleken, I., Buchholz, H.-G., Siessmeier, T., Heinz, A., et al. (2007). Elevated $[^{18}F]$fluorodopamine turnover in brains of patients with schizophrenia. *Journal of Neuroscience, 27,* 8080–8087. (15)

Kumaran, D., & Maguire, E. A. (2005). The human hippocampus: Cognitive maps or relational memory? *Journal of Neuroscience, 25,* 7254–7259. (13)

Kupfermann, I., Castellucci, V., Pinsker, H., & Kandel, E. (1970). Neuronal correlates of habituation and dishabituation of the gill withdrawal reflex in *Aplysia*. *Science, 167,* 1743–1745. (13)

Kurahashi, T., Lowe, G., & Gold, G. H. (1994). Suppression of odorant responses by odorants in olfactory receptor cells. *Science, 265,* 118–120. (7)

Kusunoki, M., Moutoussis, K., & Zeki, S. (2006). Effect of background colors on the tuning of color-selective cells in monkey area V4. *Journal of Neurophysiology, 95,* 3047–3059. (6)

Kuypers, H. G. J. M. (1989). Motor system organization. In G. Adelman (Ed.), *Neuroscience year* (pp. 107–110). Boston: Birkhäuser. (8)

Kwon, J. S., McCarley, R. W., Hirayasu, Y., Anderson, J. E., Fischer, I. A., Kikinis, R., et al. (1999). Left planum temporale volume reduction in schizophrenia. *Archives of General Psychiatry, 56,* 142–148. (15)

Laburn, H. P. (1996). How does the fetus cope with thermal challenges? *News in Physiological Sciences, 11,* 96–100. (5)

Lacroix, L., Spinelli, S., Heidbreder, C. A., & Feldon, J. (2000). Differential role of the medial and lateral prefrontal cortices in fear and anxiety. *Behavioral Neuroscience, 114,* 1119–1130. (12)

Laeng, B., & Caviness, V. S. (2001). Prosopagnosia as a deficit in encoding curved surfaces. *Journal of Cognitive Neuroscience, 13,* 556–576. (6)

Laeng, B., Svartdal, F., & Oelmann, H. (2004). Does color synesthesia pose a paradox for early-selection theories of attention? *Psychological Science, 15,* 277–281. (7)

LaFerla, F. M., Green, K. N., & Oddo, S. (2007). Intracellular amyloid-β in Alzheimer's disease. *Nature Reviews Neuroscience, 8,* 499–509. (13)

Lagoda, G., Muschamp, J. W., Vigdorchik, A., & Hull, E. (2004). A nitric oxide synthesis inhibitor in the medial preoptic area inhibits copulation and stimulus sensitization in male rats. *Behavioral Neuroscience, 118,* 1317–1323. (11)

Lahti, T. A., Leppamäki, S., Ojanen, S.-M., Haukka, J., Tuulio-Henriksson, A., Lönnqvist, J., et al. (2006). Transition into daylight saving time influences the fragmentation of the rest–activity cycle. *Journal of Circadian Rhythms, 4,* 1. (9)

Lai, C. S. L., Fisher, S. E., Hurst, J. A., Vargha-Khadem, F., & Monaco, A. P. (2001). A forkhead-domain gene is mutated in a severe speech and language disorder. *Nature, 413,* 519–523. (14)

Lai, J., Luo, M.-C., Chen, Q., Ma, S., Gardell, L. R., Ossipov, M. H., et al. (2006). Dynorphin A activates bradykinin receptors to maintain neuropathic pain. *Nature Neuroscience, 9,* 1534–1540. (7)

Lake, R. I. E., Eaves, L. J., Maes, H. H. M., Heath, A. C., & Martin, N. G. (2000). Further evidence against the environmental transmission of individual differences in neuroticism from a collaborative study of 45,850 twins and relatives on two continents. *Behavior Genetics, 30,* 223–233. (1)

Lalancette-Hébert, M., Gowing, G., Simard, A., Weng, Y. C., & Kriz, J. (2007). Selective ablation of proliferating microglial cells exacerbates ischemic injury in the brain. *Journal of Neuroscience, 27,* 2596–2605. (5)

Lambie, J. A., & Marcel, A. J. (2002). Consciousness and the varieties of emotion experience: A theoretical framework. *Psychological Review, 109,* 219–259. (1)

Land, E. H., Hubel, D. H., Livingstone, M. S., Perry, S. H., & Burns, M. M. (1983). Colour-generating interactions across the corpus callosum. *Nature, 303,* 616–618. (6)

Landis, D. M. D. (1987). Initial junctions between developing parallel fibers and Purkinje cells are different from mature synaptic junctions. *Journal of Comparative Neurology, 260,* 513–525. (3)

Lang, R. A., Flor-Henry, P., & Frenzel, R. R. (1990). Sex hormone profiles in pedophilic and incestuous men. *Annals of Sex Research, 3,* 59–74. (11)

Larsen, R. J., Kasimatis, M., & Frey, K. (1992). Facilitating the furrowed brow—An unobtrusive test of the facial feedback hypothesis applied to unpleasant affect. *Cognition & Emotion, 6,* 321–338. (12)

Lashley, K. S. (1929). *Brain mechanisms and intelligence.* Chicago: University of Chicago Press. (13)

Lashley, K. S. (1930). Basic neural mechanisms in behavior. *Psychological Review, 37,* 1–24. (13)

Lashley, K. S. (1950). In search of the engram. *Symposia of the Society for Experimental Biology, 4,* 454–482. (13)

Lassonde, M., Bryden, M. P., & Demers, P. (1990). The corpus callosum and cerebral speech lateralization. *Brain and Language, 38,* 195–206. (14)

Lastres-Becker, I., Molina-Holgado, F., Ramos, J. A., Mechoulam, R., & Fernández-Ruiz, J. (2005). Cannabinoids provide neuroprotection against 6-hydroxydopamine toxicity in vivo and in vitro: Relevance to Parkinson's disease. *Neurobiology of Disease, 19,* 96–107. (5)

Lau, H. C., Rogers, R. D., Haggard, P., & Passingham, R. E. (2004). Attention to intention. *Science, 303,* 1208–1210. (8)

Lau, H. C., Rogers, R. D., & Passingham, R. E. (2006). On measuring the perceived onsets of spontaneous actions. *Journal of Neuroscience, 26,* 7265–7271. (8)

Laugerette, F., Gaillard, D., Passilly-Degrace, P., Niot, I., & Besnard, P. (2007). Do we taste fat? *Biochimie, 89,* 265–269. (7)

Laurent, J.-P., Cespuglio, R., & Jouvet, M. (1974). Dèlimitation des voies ascendantes de l'activité ponto-géniculo-occipitale chez le chat [Demarcation of the ascending paths of ponto-geniculo-occipital activity in the cat]. *Brain Research, 65,* 29–52. (9)

Lavidor, M., & Walsh, V. (2004). The nature of foveal representation. *Nature Reviews Neuroscience, 5,* 729–735. (14)

Lazarus, M., Yoshida, K., Coppair, R., Bass, C. E., Mochizuki, T., Lowell, B. B., et al. (2007). EP3 prostaglandin receptors in the median preoptic nucleus are critical for fever responses. *Nature Neuroscience, 10,* 1131–1133. (10)

Lè, A. D., Li, Z., Funk, D., Shram, M., Li, T. K., & Shaham, Y. (2006). Increased vulnerability to nicotine self-administration and relapse in alcohol-naïve offspring of rats selectively bred for high alcohol intake. *Journal of Neuroscience, 26,* 1872–1879. (3)

Le Grand, R., Mondloch, C. J., Maurer, D., & Brent, H. P. (2001). Early visual experience and face processing. *Nature, 410,* 890. (6)

Le Grand, R., Mondloch, C. J., Maurer, D., & Brent, H. P. (2003). Expert face processing requires visual input to the right hemisphere during infancy. *Nature Neuroscience, 6,* 1108–1112. (6)

LeDoux, J. (1996). *The emotional brain.* New York: Simon & Schuster. (12)

LeDoux, J. E., Iwata, J., Cicchetti, P., & Reis, D. J. (1988). Different projections of the central amygdaloid nucleus mediate autonomic and behavioral correlates of conditioned fear. *Journal of Neuroscience, 8,* 2517–2529. (12)

Lee, H. L., Devlin, J. T., Shakeshaft, C., Brennan, A., Glensman, J., Pitcher, K., et al. (2007). Anatomical traces of vocabulary acquisition in the adolescent brain. *Journal of Neuroscience, 27,* 1184–1189. (4)

Lee, M. G., Hassani, O. K., & Jones, B. E. (2005). Discharge of identified orexin/hypocretin neurons across the sleep-waking cycle. *Journal of Neuroscience, 25,* 6716–6720. (9)

Lee, S.-H., Blake, R., & Heeger, D. J. (2005). Traveling waves of activity in primary visual cortex during binocular rivalry. *Nature Neuroscience, 8,* 22–23. (14)

Legrand, L. N., Iacono, W. G., & McGue, M. (2005, March/April). Predicting addiction. *American Scientist, 93,* 140–147. (3)

Lehky, S. R. (2000). Deficits in visual feature binding under isoluminant conditions. *Journal of Cognitive Neuroscience, 12,* 383–392. (4)

Lehrman, D. S. (1964). The reproductive behavior of ring doves. *Scientific American, 211*(5), 48–54. (11)

Leibowitz, S. F., & Alexander, J. T. (1991). Analysis of neuropeptide Y-induced feeding: Dissociation of Y_1 and Y_2 receptor effects on natural meal patterns. *Peptides, 12,* 1251–1260. (10)

Leibowitz, S. F., Hammer, N. J., & Chang, K. (1981). Hypothalamic paraventricular nucleus lesions produce overeating and obesity in the rat. *Physiology & Behavior, 27,* 1031–1040. (10)

Leibowitz, S. F., & Hoebel, B. G. (1998). Behavioral neuroscience of obesity. In G. A. Bray, C. Bouchard, & P. T. James (Eds.), *Handbook of obesity* (pp. 313–358). New York: Dekker. (10)

Lein, E. S., & Shatz, C. J. (2001). Neurotrophins and refinement of visual circuitry. In W. M. Cowan, T. C. Südhof, & C. F. Stevens (Eds.), *Synapses* (pp. 613–649). Baltimore: Johns Hopkins University Press. (6)

Leinders-Zufall, T., Lane, A. P., Puche, A. C., Ma, W., Novotny, M. V., Shipley, M. T., et al. (2000). Ultrasensitive pheromone detection by mammalian vomeronasal neurons. *Nature, 405,* 792–796. (7)

Lemos, B., Araripe, L. O., & Hartl, D. L. (2008). Polymorphic Y chromosomes harbor cryptic variation with manifold functional consequences. *Science, 319,* 91–93. (11)

Lenggenhager, B., Tadi, T., Metzinger, T., & Blanke, O. (2007). Video ergo sum: Manipulating bodily self-consciousness. *Science, 317,* 1096–1099. (4)

Lenhart, R. E., & Katkin, E. S. (1986). Psychophysiological evidence for cerebral laterality effects in a high-risk sample of students with subsyndromal bipolar depressive disorder. *American Journal of Psychiatry, 143,* 602–607. (15)

Lennie, P. (1998). Single units and visual cortical organization. *Perception, 27,* 889–935. (6)

Lenz, F. A., & Byl, N. N. (1999). Reorganization in the cutaneous core of the human thalamic principal somatic sensory nucleus (ventral caudal) in patients with dystonia. *Journal of Neurophysiology, 82,* 3204–3212. (5)

Leon, L. R. (2002). Invited review: Cytokine regulation of fever: Studies using gene knockout mice.

Journal of Applied Physiology, 92, 2648–2655. (10)

Leonard, C. M., Lombardino, L. J., Mercado, L. R., Browd, S. R., Breier, J. I., & Agee, O. F. (1996). Cerebral asymmetry and cognitive development in children: A magnetic resonance imaging study. *Psychological Science, 7,* 89–95. (14)

Leopold, D. A., Bondar, I. V., & Giese, M. A. (2006). Norm-based face encoding by single neurons in the monkey inferotemporal cortex. *Nature, 442,* 572–575. (6)

Leopold, D. A., & Logothetis, N. K. (1996). Activity changes in early visual cortex reflect monkeys' percepts during binocular rivalry. *Nature, 379,* 549–553. (6)

Leppämäki, S., Partonen, T., & Lönnqvist, J. (2002). Bright-light exposure combined with physical exercise elevates mood. *Journal of Affective Disorders, 72,* 139–144. (15)

Lester, B. M., LaGasse, L. L., & Seifer, R. (1998). Cocaine exposure and children: The meaning of subtle effects. *Science, 282,* 633–634. (5)

Leung, H.-C., Gore, J. C., & Goldman-Rakic, P. S. (2002). Sustained mnemonic response in the human middle frontal gyrus during on-line storage of spatial memoranda. *Journal of Cognitive Neuroscience, 14,* 659–671. (13)

Leutgeb, S., Leutgeb, J. K., Barnes, C. A., Moser, E. I., McNaughton, B. L., & Moser, M.-B. (2005). Independent codes for spatial and episodic memory in hippocampal neuronal ensembles. *Science, 309,* 619–623. (13)

LeVay, S. (1991). A difference in hypothalamic structure between heterosexual and homosexual men. *Science, 253,* 1034–1037. (11)

LeVay, S. (1993). *The sexual brain.* Cambridge, MA: MIT Press. (11)

Levenson, R. W., Oyama, O. N., & Meek, P. S. (1987). Greater reinforcement from alcohol for those at risk: Parental risk, personality risk, and sex. *Journal of Abnormal Psychology, 96,* 242–253. (15)

LeVere, T. E. (1975). Neural stability, sparing and behavioral recovery following brain damage. *Psychological Review, 82,* 344–358. (5)

LeVere, T. E., & Morlock, G. W. (1973). Nature of visual recovery following posterior neodecortication in the hooded rat. *Journal of Comparative and Physiological Psychology, 83,* 62–67. (5)

Levi-Montalcini, R. (1987). The nerve growth factor 35 years later. *Science, 237,* 1154–1162. (5)

Levi-Montalcini, R. (1988). *In praise of imperfection.* New York: Basic Books. (5)

Levin, E. D., & Rose, J. E. (1995). Acute and chronic nicotine interactions with dopamine systems and working memory performance. *Annals of the New York Academy of Sciences, 757,* 245–252. (3)

Levine, J. A., Lannngham-Foster, L. M., McCrady, S. K., Krizan, A. C., Olson, L. R., Kane, P. H., et al. (2005). Interindividual variation in posture allocation: Possible role in human obesity. *Science, 307,* 584–586. (10)

Levine, J. D., Fields, H. L., & Basbaum, A. I. (1993). Peptides and the primary afferent nociceptor. *Journal of Neuroscience, 13,* 2273–2286. (3)

Levitin, D. J., & Bellugi, U. (1998). Musical abilities in individuals with Williams syndrome. *Music Perception, 15,* 357–389. (14)

Levitt, R. A. (1975). *Psychopharmacology.* Washington, DC: Hemisphere. (15)

Levitt-Gilmour, T. A., & Salpeter, M. M. (1986). Gradient of extrajunctional acetylcholine receptors early after denervation of mammalian muscle. *Journal of Neuroscience, 6,* 1606–1612. (5)

Levitzki, A. (1988). From epinephrine to cyclic AMP. *Science, 241,* 800–806. (3)

Levy, J., Heller, W., Banich, M. T., & Burton, L. A. (1983). Asymmetry of perception in free viewing of chimeric faces. *Brain and Cognition, 2,* 404–419. (14)

Levy-Lahad, E., Wijsman, E. M., Nemens, E., Anderson, L., Goddard, K. A. B., Weber, J. L., et al. (1995). A familial Alzheimer's disease locus on chromosome 1. *Science, 269,* 970–973. (13)

Leweke, F. M., Gerth, C. W., Koethe, D., Klosterkötter, J., Ruslanova, I., Krivogorsky, B., et al. (2004). Antibodies to infectious agents in individuals with recent onset schizophrenia. *European Archives of Psychiatry and Clinical Neuroscience, 254,* 4–8. (15)

Lewis, D. A. (1997). Development of the prefrontal cortex during adolescence: Insights into vulnerable neural circuits in schizophrenia. *Neuropsychopharmacology, 16,* 385–398. (5, 15)

Lewis, E. R., Everhart, T. E., & Zeevi, Y. Y. (1969). Studying neural organization in *Aplysia* with the scanning electron microscope. *Science, 165,* 1140–1143. (3)

Lewis, T. L., & Maurer, D. (2005). Multiple sensitive periods in human visual development: Evidence from visually deprived children. *Developmental Psychobiology, 46,* 163–183. (6)

Lewis, V. G., Money, J., & Epstein, R. (1968). Concordance of verbal and nonverbal ability in the adrenogenital syndrome. *Johns Hopkins Medical Journal, 122,* 192–195. (11)

Lewy, A. J., Bauer, V. K., Cutler, N. L., Sack, R. L., Ahmed, S., Thomas, K. H., et al. (1998). Morning vs. evening light treatment of patients with winter depression. *Archives of General Psychiatry, 55,* 890–896. (15)

Li, H., Chen, A., Xing, G., Wei, M.-L., & Rogawski, M. A. (2001). Kainate receptor-mediated heterosynaptic facilitation in the amygdala. *Nature Neuroscience, 4,* 612–620. (13)

Li, W., Luxenberg, E., Parrish, T., & Gottfried, J. A. (2006). Learning to smell the roses: Experience-dependent neural plasticity in human piriform and orbitofrontal cortices. *Neuron, 52,* 1097–1108. (7)

Liberles, S. D., & Buck, L. B. (2006). A second class of chemosensory receptors in the olfactory epithelium. *Nature, 442,* 645–650. (7)

Libet, B., Gleason, C. A., Wright, E. W., & Pearl, D. K. (1983). Time of conscious intention to act in relation to onset of cerebral activities (readiness potential): The unconscious initiation of a freely voluntary act. *Brain, 106,* 623–642. (8)

Lieberman, J., Chakos, M., Wu, H., Alvir, J., Hoffman, E., Robinson, D., et al. (2001). Longitudinal study of brain morphology in first episode schizophrenia. *Biological Psychiatry, 49,* 487–499. (15)

Liebman, M., Pelican, S., Moore, S. A., Holmes, B., Wardlaw, M. K., Melcher, L. M., et al. (2006). Dietary intake-, eating behavior-, and physical activity-related determinants of high body mass index in the 2003 Wellness IN the Rockies cross-sectional study. *Nutrition Research, 26,* 111–117. (10)

Lim, K. O., Adalsteinsson, E., Spielman, D., Sullivan, E. V., Rosenbloom, M. J., & Pfefferbaum, A. (1998). Proton magnetic resonance spectroscopic imaging of cortical gray and white matter in schizophrenia. *Archives of General Psychiatry, 55,* 346–352. (15)

Lim, M. M., Wang, Z., Olazábal, D. E., Ren, X., Terwilliger, E. F., & Young, L. J. (2004). Enhanced partner preference in a promiscuous species by manipulating the expression of a single gene. *Nature, 429,* 754–757. (11)

Lin, D. Y., Shea, S. D., & Katz, L. C. (2006). Representation of natural stimuli in the rodent main olfactory bulb. *Neuron, 50,* 937–949. (7)

Lin, J.-S., Hou, Y., Sakai, K., & Jouvet, M. (1996). Histaminergic descending inputs to the mesopontine tegmentum and their role in the control of cortical activation and wakefulness in the cat. *Journal of Neuroscience, 16,* 1523–1537. (9)

Lin, L., Faraco, J., Li, R., Kadotani, H., Rogers, W., Lin, X., et al. (1999). The sleep disorder canine narcolepsy is caused by a mutation in the hypocretin (orexin) receptor 2 gene. *Cell, 98,* 365–376. (9)

Lincoln, G. A., Clarke, I. J., Hut, R. A., & Hazlerigg, D. G. (2006). Characterizing a mammalian circadian pacemaker. *Science, 314,* 1941–1944. (9)

Lindberg, N. O., Coburn, C., & Stricker, E. M. (1984). Increased feeding by rats after subdiabetogenic streptozotocin treatment: A role for insulin in satiety. *Behavioral Neuroscience, 98,* 138–145. (10)

Linde, K., Berner, M., Egger, M., & Mulrow, C. (2005). St. John's wort for depression. *British Journal of Psychiatry, 186,* 99–107. (15)

Lindemann, B. (1996). Taste reception. *Physiological Reviews, 76,* 719–766. (7)

Lindholm, P., Voutilainen, M. H., Laurén, J., Peränen, V.-M., Leppänen, V.-M., Andressoo, J.-O., et al. (2007). Novel neurotrophic factor CDNF protects and rescues midbrain dopamine neurons *in vivo. Nature, 448,* 73–77. (8)

Lindsay, P. H., & Norman, D. A. (1972). *Human information processing.* New York: Academic Press. (7)

Lindvall, O., Kokaia, Z., & Martinez-Serrano, A. (2004). Stem cell therapy for human neurodegenerative disorders—How to make it work. *Nature Medicine, 10,* S42–S50. (8)

Liou, Y.-C., Tocilj, A., Davies, P. L., & Jia, Z. (2000). Mimicry of ice structure by surface hydroxyls and water of a β-helix antifreeze protein. *Nature, 406,* 322–324. (10)

Lippa, R. A. (2006). Is high sex drive associated with increased sexual attraction to both sexes? *Psychological Science, 17,* 46–52. (11)

Lisman, J. E., Raghavachari, S., & Tsien, R. W. (2007). The sequence of events that underlie quantal transmission at central glutamatergic synapses. *Nature Reviews Neuroscience, 8,* 597–609. (3)

Lisman, J., Schulman, H., & Cline, H. (2002). The molecular basis of CaMKII function in synaptic and behavioural memory. *Nature Reviews Neuroscience, 3,* 175–190. (13)

Liu, G., & Tsien, R. W. (1995). Properties of synaptic transmission at single hippocampal synaptic boutons. *Nature, 375,* 404–408. (3)

Liu, L. Y., Coe, C. L., Swenson, C. A., Kelly, E. A., Kita, H., & Busse, W. W. (2002). School examinations enhance airway inflammation to antigen challenge. *American Journal of Respiratory and Critical Care Medicine, 165,* 1062–1067. (12)

Liu, P., & Bilkey, D. K. (2001). The effect of excitotoxic lesions centered on the hippocampus or perirhinal cortex in object recognition and spatial memory tasks. *Behavioral Neuroscience, 115,* 94–111. (13)

Liu, X., Zwiebel, L. J., Hinton, D., Benzer, S., Hall, J. C., & Rosbash, M. (1992). The period gene encodes a predominantly nuclear protein in adult Drosophila. *Journal of Neuroscience, 12,* 2735–2744. (9)

Livingstone, M. S. (1988, January). Art, illusion and the visual system. *Scientific American, 258*(1), 78–85. (6)

Livingstone, M. S., & Hubel, D. (1988). Segregation of form, color, movement, and depth: Anatomy, physiology, and perception. *Science, 240,* 740–749. (6)

Ljungberg, M. C., Stern, G., & Wilkin, G. P. (1999). Survival of genetically engineered, adult-derived rat astrocytes grafted into the 6-hydroxydopamine lesioned adult rat striatum. *Brain Research, 816,* 29–37. (8)

Lockwood, A. H., Salvi, R. J., Coad, M. L., Towsley, M. L., Wack, D. S., & Murphy, B. W. (1998). The functional neuroanatomy of tinnitus: Evidence for limbic system links and neural plasticity. *Neurology, 50,* 114–120. (7)

Loewenstein, W. R. (1960, August). Biological transducers. *Scientific American, 203*(2), 98–108. (7)

Loewi, O. (1960). An autobiographic sketch. *Perspectives in Biology, 4,* 3–25. (3)

Logan, C. G., & Grafton, S. T. (1995). Functional anatomy of human eyeblink conditioning determined with regional cerebral glucose metabolism and positron-emission tomography. *Proceedings of the National Academy of Sciences, USA, 92,* 7500–7504. (13)

Lomber, S. G., & Malhotra, S. (2008). Double dissociation of "what" and "where" processing in auditory cortex. *Nature Neuroscience, 11,* 609–617. (7)

Long, M. A., Jutras, M. J., Connors, B. W., & Burwell, R. D. (2005). Electrical synapses coordinate activity in the suprachiasmatic nucleus. *Nature Neuroscience, 8,* 61–66. (9)

Lord, G. M., Matarese, G., Howard, J. K., Baker, R. J., Bloom, S. R., & Lechler, R. I. (1998). Leptin modulates the T-cell immune response and reverses starvation-induced immunosuppression. *Nature, 394,* 897–901. (10)

Lorrain, D. S., Riolo, J. V., Matuszewich, L., & Hull, E. M. (1999). Lateral hypothalamic serotonin inhibits nucleus accumbens dopamine: Implications for sexual refractoriness. *Journal of Neuroscience, 19,* 7648–7652. (3)

Lorusso, M. L., Facoetti, A., Pesenti, S., Cattaneo, C., Molteni, M., & Geiger, G. (2004). Wider recognition in peripheral vision common to different subtypes of dyslexia. *Vision Research, 44,* 2413–2424. (14)

Lott, I. T. (1982). Down's syndrome, aging, and Alzheimer's disease: A clinical review. *Annals of the New York Academy of Sciences, 396,* 15–27. (13)

Lotto, R. B., & Purves, D. (1999). The effects of color on brightness. *Nature Neuroscience, 2,* 1010–1014. (6)

Lotto, R. B., & Purves, D. (2002). The empirical basis of color perception. *Consciousness and Cognition, 11,* 609–629. (6)

Lotze, M., Grodd, W., Birbaumer, N., Erb, M., Huse, E., & Flor, H. (1999). Does use of a myoelectric prosthesis prevent cortical reorganization and phantom limb pain? *Nature Neuroscience, 2,* 501–502. (5)

Lu, X.-Y., Kim, C. S., Frazer, A., & Zhang, W. (2006). Leptin: A potential novel antidepressant. *Proceedings of the National Academy of Sciences, USA, 103,* 1593–1598. (15)

Lucas, B. K., Ormandy, C. J., Binart, N., Bridges, R. S. & Kelly, P. A. (1998). Null mutation of the prolactin receptor gene produces a defect in maternal behavior. *Endocrinology, 139,* 4102–4107. (11)

Lucas, R. J., Douglas, R. H., & Foster, R. G. (2001). Characterization of an ocular photopigment capable of driving pupillary constriction in mice. *Nature Neuroscience, 4,* 621–626. (9)

Lucas, R. J., Freedman, M. S., Muñoz, M., Garcia-Fernández, J.-M., & Foster, R. G. (1999). Regulation of the mammalian pineal by non-rod, non-cone ocular photoreceptors. *Science, 284,* 505–507. (9)

Luczak, S. E., Glatt, S. J., & Wall, T. L. (2006). Meta-analysis of *ALDH2* and *ADHIB* with alcohol dependence in Asians. *Psychological Bulletin, 132,* 607–621. (3)

Luders, E., Narr, K. L., Thompson, P. M., Rex, D. E., Jancke, L., Steinmetz, H., et al. (2004). Gender differences in cortical complexity. *Nature Neuroscience, 7,* 799–800. (4)

Ludwig, M., & Leng, G. (2006). Dendritic peptides release and peptide-dependent behaviours. *Nature Reviews Neuroscience, 7,* 126–136. (3)

Lund, R. D., Lund, J. S., & Wise, R. P. (1974). The organization of the retinal projection to the dorsal lateral geniculate nucleus in pigmented and albino rats. *Journal of Comparative Neurology, 158,* 383–404. (6)

Lupien, S. J., de Leon, M., de Santi, S., Convit, A., Tarshish, C., Nair, N. P. V., et al. (1998). Cortisol levels during human aging predict hippocampal atrophy and memory deficits. *Nature Neuroscience, 1,* 69–73. (12)

Lyman, C. P., O'Brien, R. C., Greene, G. C., & Papafrangos, E. D. (1981). Hibernation and longevity in the Turkish hamster *Mesocricetus brandti. Science, 212,* 668–670. (9)

Lyons, M. J., Eisen, S. A., Goldberg, J., True, W., Lin, N., Meyer, J. M., et al. (1998). A registry-based twin study of depression in men. *Archives of General Psychiatry, 55,* 468–472. (15)

Lytle, L. D., Messing, R. B., Fisher, L., & Phebus, L. (1975). Effects of long-term corn consumption on brain serotonin and the response to electric shock. *Science, 190,* 692–694. (12)

Macdonald, R. L., Weddle, M. G., & Gross, R. A. (1986). Benzodiazepine, ß-carboline, and barbiturate actions on GABA responses. *Advances in Biochemical Psychopharmacology, 41,* 67–78. (12)

Macey, P. M., Henderson, L. A., Macey, K. E., Alger, J. R., Frysinger, R. C., Woo, M. A., et al. (2002). Brain morphology associated with obstructive sleep apnea. *American Journal of Respiratory & Critical Care Medicine, 166,* 1382–1387. (9)

MacFarlane, J. G., Cleghorn, J. M., & Brown, G. M. (1985a, September). *Circadian rhythms in chronic insomnia.* Paper presented at the World Congress of Biological Psychiatry, Philadelphia. (9)

MacFarlane, J. G., Cleghorn, J. M., & Brown, G. M. (1985b). Melatonin and core temperature rhythms in chronic insomnia. In G. M. Brown & S. D. Wainwright (Eds.), *The pineal gland: Endocrine aspects* (pp. 301–306). New York: Pergamon Press. (9)

Machado, C. J., Emery, N. J., Capitanio, J. P., Mason, W. A., Mendoza, S. P., & Amaral, D. G. (2008). Bilateral neurotoxic amygdala lesions in rhesus monkeys (*Macaca mulatta*): Consistent pattern of behavior across different social contexts. *Behavioral Neuroscience, 122,* 251–266. (12)

MacLean, P. D. (1949). Psychosomatic disease and the "visceral brain": Recent developments bearing on the Papez theory of emotion. *Psychosomatic Medicine, 11,* 338–353. (12)

MacLusky, N. J., & Naftolin, F. (1981). Sexual differentiation of the central nervous system. *Science, 211,* 1294–1303. (11)

Macphail, E. M. (1985). Vertebrate intelligence: The null hypothesis. *Philosophical Transactions of the Royal Society of London, B, 308,* 37–51. (4)

Macrae, C. N., Alnwick, K. A., Milne, A. B., & Schloerscheidt, A. M. (2002). Person perception across the menstrual cycle. *Psychological Science, 13,* 532–536. (11)

Maffei, A., Nataraj, K., Nelson, S. B., & Turrigiano, G. G. (2006). Potentiation of cortical inhibition by visual deprivation. *Nature, 443,* 81–84. (6)

Mague, S. D., Andersen, S. L., & Carlezon, W. A., Jr. (2005). Early developmental exposure to methylphenidate reduces cocaine-induced potentiation of brain stimulation rewards in rats. *Biological Psychiatry, 57,* 120–125. (3)

Maguire, E. A., & Frith, C. D. (2003). Lateral asymmetry in the hippocampal response to the remoteness of autobiographical memories. *Journal of Neuroscience, 23,* 5302–5307. (13)

Maguire, E. A., Gadian, D. G., Johnsrude, I. S., Good, C. D., Ashburner, J., Frackowiak, R. S. J., et al. (2000). Navigation-related structural change in the hippocampi of taxi drivers. *Proceedings of the National Academy of Sciences, USA, 97,* 4398–4403. (13)

Maier, S. F., & Watkins, L. R. (1998). Cytokines for psychologists: Implications of bidirectional immune-to-brain communication for understanding behavior, mood, and cognition. *Psychological Review, 105,* 83–107. (12)

Mair, R. G., Burk, J. A., & Porter, M. C. (2003). Impairment of radial maze delayed nonmatching after lesions of anterior thalamus and parahippocampal cortex. *Behavioral Neuroscience, 117,* 596–605. (13)

Malaspina, D., Corcoran, C., Fahim, C., Berman, A., Harkavy-Friedman, J., Yale, S., et al. (2002). Paternal age and sporadic schizophrenia: Evidence for de novo mutations. *American Journal of Medical Genetics, 114,* 299–303. (15)

Malaspina, D., Harlap, S., Fennig, S., Heiman, D., Nahon, D., Feldman, D., et al. (2001). Advancing paternal age and the risk of schizophrenia. *Archives of General Psychiatry, 58,* 361–367. (15)

Malhotra, P., Jäger, H. R., Parton, A., Greenwood, R., Playford, E. D., Brown, M. M., et al. (2005). Spatial working memory capacity in unilateral neglect. *Brain, 128,* 424–435. (14)

Mallis, M. M., & DeRoshia, C. W. (2005). Circadian rhythms, sleep, and performance in space. *Aviation, Space, and Environmental Medicine,* 76(Suppl. 6), B94–B107. (9)

Malmberg, A. B., Chen, C., Tonegawa, S., & Basbaum, A. I. (1997). Preserved acute pain and reduced neuropathic pain in mice lacking PKCγ. *Science, 278,* 179–283. (7)

Manfredi, M., Stocchi, F., & Vacca, L. (1995). Differential diagnosis of Parkinsonism. *Journal of Neural Transmission* (Suppl. 45), 1–9. (8)

Mangan, M. A. (2004). A phenomenology of problematic sexual behavior. *Archives of Sexual Behavior, 33,* 287–293. (9)

Mangiapane, M. L., & Simpson, J. B. (1980). Subfornical organ: Forebrain site of pressor and dipsogenic action of angiotensin II. *American Journal of Physiology, 239,* R382–R389. (10)

Mann, J. J., Arango, V., & Underwood, M. D. (1990). Serotonin and suicidal behavior. *Annals of the New York Academy of Sciences, 600,* 476–485. (12)

Mann, T., Tomiyama, A. J., Westling, E., Lew, A.-M., Samuels, B., & Chatman, J. (2007). Medicare's search for effective obesity treatments. *American Psychologist, 62,* 220–233. (10)

Maquet, P., Laureys, S., Peigneux, P., Fuchs, S., Petiau, C., Phillips, C., et al. (2000). Experience-dependent changes in cerebral activation during human REM sleep. *Nature Neuroscience, 3,* 831–836. (9)

Maquet, P., Peters, J.-M., Aerts, J., Delfiore, G., Degueldre, C., Luxen, A., et al. (1996). Functional neuroanatomy of human rapid-eye-movement sleep and dreaming. *Nature, 383,* 163–166. (8, 9)

Maraganore, D. M., deAndrade, M., Lesnick, T. G., Strain, K. J., Farrer, M. J., Rocca, W. A., et al. (2005). High-resolution whole-genome association study of Parkinson disease. *American Journal of Human Genetics, 77,* 685–693. (8)

Marcar, V. L., Zihl, J., & Cowey, A. (1997). Comparing the visual deficits of a motion blind patient with the visual deficits of monkeys with area MT removed. *Neuropsychologia, 35,* 1459–1465. (6)

Marin, O., Smeets, W. J. A. J., & González, A. (1998). Evolution of the basal ganglia in tetrapods: A new perspective based on recent studies in amphibians. *Trends in Neurosciences, 21,* 487–494. (4)

Marris, E. (2006). Grey matters. *Nature, 444,* 808–810. (1)

Marshall, J. C., & Halligan, P. W. (1995). Seeing the forest but only half the trees? *Nature, 373,* 521–523. (14)

Marshall, J. F. (1985). Neural plasticity and recovery of function after brain injury. *International Review of Neurobiology, 26,* 201–247. (5)

Martin, E. R., Scott, W. K., Nance, M. A., Watts, R. L., Hubble, J. P., Koller, W. C., et al. (2001). Association of single-nucleotide polymorphisms of the tau gene with late-onset Parkinson disease. *Journal of the American Medical Association, 286,* 2245–2250. (8)

Martin, G., Rojas, L. M., Ramírez, Y., & McNeil, R. (2004). The eyes of oilbirds (*Steatornis caripensis*): Pushing at the limits of sensitivity. *Naturwissenschaften, 91,* 26–29. (6)

Martin, J. T., & Nguyen, D. H. (2004). Anthropometric analysis of homosexuals and heterosexuals: Implications for early hormone exposure. *Hormones and Behavior, 45,* 31–39. (11)

Martin, P. R., Lee, B. B., White, A. J. R., Solomon, S. G., & Rütiger, L. (2001). Chromatic sensitivity of ganglion cells in the peripheral primate retina. *Nature, 410,* 933–936. (6)

Martin, R. C., & Blossom-Stach, C. (1986). Evidence of syntactic deficits in a fluent aphasic. *Brain and Language, 28,* 196–234. (14)

Martin, S. D., Martin, E., Rai, S. S., Richardson, M. A., Royall, R., & Eng, C. (2001). Brain blood flow changes in depressed patients treated with interpersonal psychotherapy or venlafaxine hydrochloride. *Archives of General Psychiatry, 58,* 641–648. (15)

Martindale, C. (2001). Oscillations and analogies: Thomas Young, MD, FRS, genius. *American Psychologist, 56,* 342–345. (6)

Martinez-Vargas, M. C., & Erickson, C. J. (1973). Some social and hormonal determinants of nest-building behaviour in the ring dove (*Streptopelia risoria*). *Behaviour, 45,* 12–37. (11)

Martinowich, K., Manji, H., & Lu, B. (2007). New insights into BDNF function in depression and anxiety. *Nature Neuroscience, 10,* 1089–1093. (15)

Masland, R. H. (2001). The fundamental plan of the retina. *Nature Neuroscience, 4,* 877–886. (6)

Mason, B. J., Goodman, A. M., Chabac, S., & Lehert, P. (2006). Effect of oral acamprosate on abstinence in patients with alcohol dependence in a double-blind, placebo-controlled trial: The role of patient motivation. *Journal of Psychiatric Research, 40,* 383–393. (3)

Mason, M. F., Norton, M. I., Van Horn, J. D., Wegner, D. M., Grafton, S. T., & Macrae, C. N. (2007). Wandering minds: The default network and stimulus-independent thought. *Science, 315,* 393–395. (4)

Massimini, M., Ferrarelli, F., Huber, R., Esser, S. K., Singh, H., & Tononi, G. (2005). Breakdown of cortical effective connectivity during sleep. *Science, 309,* 2228–2232. (9)

Mathalon, D. H., Sullivan, E. V., Lim, K. O., & Pfefferbaum, A. (2001). Progressive brain volume changes and the clinical course of schizophrenia in men. *Archives of General Psychiatry, 58,* 148–157. (15)

Matsumoto, Y., Mishima, K., Satoh, K., Tozawa, T., Mishima, Y., Shimizu, T., et al. (2001). Total sleep deprivation induces an acute and transient increase in NK cell activity in healthy young volunteers. *Sleep, 24,* 804–809. (9)

Matsunami, H., Montmayeur, J.-P., & Buck, L. B. (2000). A family of candidate taste receptors in human and mouse. *Nature, 404,* 601–604. (7)

Mattingley, J. B., Husain, M., Rorden, C., Kennard, C., & Driver, J. (1998). Motor role of human inferior parietal lobe revealed in unilateral neglect patients. *Nature, 392,* 179–182. (14)

Matuszewich, L., Lorrain, D. S., & Hull, E. M. (2000). Dopamine release in the medial preoptic area of female rats in response to hormonal manipulation and sexual activity. *Behavioral Neuroscience, 114,* 772–782. (11)

Maurice, D. M. (1998). The Von Sallmann lecture of 1996: An ophthalmological explanation of REM sleep. *Experimental Eye Research, 66,* 139–145. (9)

May, P. R. A., Fuster, J. M., Haber, J., & Hirschman, A. (1979). Woodpecker drilling behavior: An endorsement of the rotational theory of impact brain injury. *Archives of Neurology, 36,* 370–373. (5)

Mayberry, R. I., Lock, E., & Kazmi, H. (2002). Linguistic ability and early language exposure. *Nature, 417,* 38. (14)

Mayer, A. D., & Rosenblatt, J. S. (1979). Hormonal influences during the ontogeny of maternal behavior in female rats. *Journal of Comparative and Physiological Psychology, 93,* 879–898. (11)

Mayne, T. J. (1999). Negative affect and health: The importance of being earnest. *Cognition and Emotion, 13,* 601–635. (12)

Mazzoni, P., Hristrova, A., & Krakauer, J. W. (2007). Why don't we move faster? Parkinson's disease, movement vigor, and implicit motivation. *Journal of Neuroscience, 27,* 7105–7116. (8)

McBurney, D. H., & Bartoshuk, L. M. (1973). Interactions between stimuli with different taste qualities. *Physiology & Behavior,* 10, 1101–1106. (7)

McCarley, R. W., & Hoffman, E. (1981). REM sleep, dreams, and the activation-synthesis hypothesis. *American Journal of Psychiatry, 138,* 904–912. (9)

McCarthy, G., Puce, A., Gore, J. C., & Allison, T. (1997). Face-specific processing in the human fusiform gyrus. *Journal of Cognitive Neuroscience,* 9, 605–610. (6)

McClintock, M. K. (1971). Menstrual synchrony and suppression. *Nature, 229,* 244–245. (7)

McConnell, J. V. (1962). Memory transfer through cannibalism in planarians. *Journal of Neuropsychiatry,* 3(Suppl. 1), 42–48. (13)

McConnell, S. K. (1992). The genesis of neuronal diversity during development of cerebral cortex. *Seminars in the Neurosciences, 4,* 347–356. (5)

McCrory, E., Frith, U., Brunswick, N., & Price, C. (2000). Abnormal functional activation during a simple word repetition task: A PET study of adult dyslexics. *Journal of Cognitive Neuroscience, 12,* 753–762. (14)

McDaniel, M. A. (2005). Big-brained people are smarter: A meta-analysis of the relationship between *in vivo* brain volume and intelligence. *Intelligence, 33,* 337–346. (4)

McDaniel, M. A., Maier, S. F., & Einstein, G. O. (2002). "Brain-specific" nutrients: A memory cure? *Psychological Science in the Public Interest, 3,* 12–38. (13)

McElhiney, M. C., Moody, B. J., Steif, B. L., Prudic, J., Devanand, D. P., Nobler, M. S., et al. (1995). Autobiographical memory and mood: Effects of electroconvulsive therapy. *Neuropsychology, 9,* 501–517. (15)

McEvoy, J. P., Lieberman, J. A., Stroup, T. S., Davis, S. M., Meltzer, H. Y., Rosenheck, R. A., et al. (2006). Effectiveness of clozapine versus olanzapine, quetiapine, and risperidone in patients with chronic schizphrenia who did not respond to prior atypical antipsychotic treatment. *American Journal of Psychiatry, 163,* 600–610. (15)

McEwen, B. S. (2000). The neurobiology of stress: From serendipity to clinical relevance. *Brain Research, 886,* 172–189. (10, 12)

McEwen, B. S. (2001). Invited review: Estrogen effects on the brain: Multiple sites and molecular mechanisms. *Journal of Applied Physiology, 91,* 2785–2801. (11)

McGregor, I. S., Hargreaves, G. A., Apfelbach, R., & Hunt, G. E. (2004). Neural correlates of cat odor-induced anxiety in rats: Region-specific effects of the benzodiazepine midazolam. *Journal of Neuroscience, 24,* 4134–4144. (12)

McGuire, S., & Clifford, J. (2000). Genetic and environmental contributions to loneliness in children. *Psychological Science, 11,* 487–491. (1)

McHugh, P. R., & Moran, T. H. (1985). The stomach: A conception of its dynamic role in satiety. *Progress in Psychobiology and Physiological Psychology, 11,* 197–232. (10)

McIntyre, M., Gangestad, S. W., Gray, P. B., Chapman, J. F., Burnham, T. C., O'Rourke, M. T., et al. (2006). Romantic involvement often reduces men's testosterone levels—But not always: The moderating effect of extrapair sexual interest. *Journal of Personality and Social Psychology, 91,* 642–651. (11)

McIntyre, R. S., Konarski, J. Z., Wilkins, K., Soczynska, J. K., & Kennedy, S. H. (2006). Obesity in bipolar disorder and major depressive disorder: Results from a National Community Health Survey on Mental Health and Well-Being. *Canadian Journal of Psychiatry, 51,* 274–280. (10)

McKeever, W. F., Seitz, K. S., Krutsch, A. J., & Van Eys, P. L. (1995). On language laterality in normal dextrals and sinistrals: Results from the bilateral object naming latency task. *Neuropsychologia, 33,* 1627–1635. (14)

McKemy, D. D., Neuhausser, W. M., & Julius, D. (2002). Identification of a cold receptor reveals a general role for TRP channels in thermosensation. *Nature, 416,* 52–58. (7)

McKinnon, W., Weisse, C. S., Reynolds, C. P., Bowles, C. A., & Baum, A. (1989). Chronic stress, leukocyte-subpopulations, and humoral response to latent viruses. *Health Psychology, 8,* 389–402. (12)

Mechelli, A., Crinion, J. T., Noppeney, U., O'Doherty, J., Ashburner, J., Frackowiak, R. S., et al. (2004). Structural plasticity in the bilingual brain. *Nature, 431,* 757. (14)

Meddis, R., Pearson, A. J. D., & Langford, G. (1973). An extreme case of healthy insomnia. *EEG and Clinical Neurophysiology, 35,* 213–214. (9)

Mehl, M. R., Vazire, S., Ramirez-Esparza, M., Slatcher, R. B., & Pennebaker, J. W. (2007). Are women really more talkative than men? *Science, 317,* 82. (4)

Meister, M., Wong, R. O. L., Baylor, D. A., & Shatz, C. J. (1991). Synchronous bursts of action potentials in ganglion cells of the developing mammalian retina. *Science, 252,* 939–943. (5)

Melloni, L., Molina, C., Pena, M., Torres, D., Singer, W., & Rodriguez, E. (2007). Synchronization of neural activity across cortical areas correlates with conscious perception. *Journal of Neuroscience, 27,* 2858–2865. (14)

Mellor, J., & Nicoll, R. A. (2001). Hippocampal mossy fiber LTP is independent of postsynaptic calcium. *Nature Neuroscience, 4,* 125–126. (13)

Melone, M., Vitellaro-Zuccarello, L., Vallejo-Illarramendi, A., Pérez-Samartin, A., Matute, C., Cozzi, A., et al. (2001). The expression of glutamate transporter GLT-1 in the rat cerebral cortex is down-regulated by the antipsychotic drug clozapine. *Molecular Psychiatry, 6,* 380–386. (15)

Meltzer, H. Y., Matsubara, S., & Lee, J.-C. (1989). Classification of typical and atypical antipsychotic drugs on the basis of dopamine D-1, D-2 and serotonin$_2$ pKi values. *Journal of Pharmacology and Experimental Therapeutics, 251,* 238–246. (15)

Meltzoff, A. N., & Moore, M. K. (1977). Imitation of facial and manual gestures by human neonates. *Science, 198,* 75–78. (8)

Melzack, R., & Wall, P. D. (1965). Pain mechanisms: A new theory. *Science, 150,* 971–979. (7)

Mendieta-Zéron, H., López, M., & Diéguez, C. (2008). Gastrointestinal peptides controlling body weight homeostasis. *General and Comparative Endocrinology, 155,* 481–495. (10)

Mergen, M., Mergen, H., Ozata, M., Oner, R., & Oner, C. (2001). A novel melanocortin 4 receptor (MC4R) gene mutation associated with morbid obesity. *Journal of Clinical Endocrinology & Metabolism, 86,* 3448–3451. (10)

Merikangas, K. R., Akiskal, H. S., Angst, J., Greenberg, P. E., Hirschfeld, R. M. A., Petukhova, M., et al. (2007). Lifetime and 12-month prevalence of bipolar spectrum disorder in the National Comorbidity Survey Replication. *Archives of General Psychiatry, 64,* 543–552. (15)

Merton, P. A. (1972). How we control the contraction of our muscles. *Scientific American, 226*(5), 30–37. (8)

Merzenich, M. M., Nelson, R. J., Stryker, M. P., Cynader, M. S., Schoppman, A., & Zook, J. M. (1984). Somatosensory cortical map changes following digit amputation in adult monkeys. *Journal of Comparative Neurology, 224,* 591–605. (5)

Meshi, D., Drew, M. R., Saxe, M., Ansorge, M. S., David, D., Santarelli, L., et al. (2006). Hippocampal neurogenesis is not required for behavioral effects of environmental enrichment. *Nature Neuroscience, 9,* 729–731. (5)

Mesulam, M.-M. (1995). Cholinergic pathways and the ascending reticular activating system of the human brain. *Annals of the New York Academy of Sciences, 757,* 169–179. (4, 9)

Meyer-Bahlburg, H. F. L., Dolezal, C., Baker, S. W., & New, M. I. (2008). Sexual orientation in women with classical or non-classical congenital adrenal hyperplasia as a function of degree of prenatal androgen excess. *Archives of Sexual Behavior, 37,* 85–99. (11)

Meyer-Lindenberg, A., Hariri, A. R., Munoz, K. E., Mervis, C. B., Mattay, V. S., Morris, C. A., et al. (2005). Neural correlates of genetically abnormal social cognition in Williams syndrome. *Nature Neuroscience, 8,* 991–993. (14)

Meyer-Lindenberg, A., Kohn, P., Mervis, C. B., Kippenhan, J. S., Olsen, R. K., Morris, C. A., et al. (2004). Neural basis of genetically determined visuospatial construction deficit in Williams syndrome. *Neuron, 43,* 623–631. (14)

Meyer-Lindenberg, A., Mervis, C. B., & Berman, K. F. (2006). Neural mechanisms in Williams syndrome: A unique window to genetic influences on cognition and behaviour. *Nature Reviews Neuroscience, 7,* 380–393. (14)

Meyer-Lindenberg, A., Miletich, R. S., Kohn, P. D., Esposito, G., Carson, R. E., Quarantelli, M., et al. (2002). Reduced prefrontal activity predicts exaggerated striatal dopaminergic function in schizophrenia. *Nature Neuroscience, 5,* 267–271. (15)

Mezzanotte, W. S., Tangel, D. J., & White, D. P. (1992). Waking genioglossal electromyogram in sleep apnea patients versus normal controls (a neuromuscular compensatory mechanism). *Journal of Clinical Investigation, 89,* 1571–1579. (9)

Mihalcescu, I., Hsing, W., & Leibler, S. (2004). Resilient circadian oscillator revealed in individual cyanobacteria. *Nature, 430,* 81–85. (9)

Miles, F. A., & Evarts, E. V. (1979). Concepts of motor organization. *Annual Review of Psychology, 30,* 327–362. (8)

Millán, J. del R., Renkens, F., Mouriño, J., & Gerstner, W. (2004). Brain-actuated interaction. *Artificial Intelligence, 159,* 241–259. (8)

Miller, E. (2000). The prefrontal cortex and cognitive control. *Nature Reviews Neuroscience, 1,* 59–65. (4)

Miller, G. (2007a). Animal extremists get personal. *Science, 318,* 1856–1858. (1)

Miller, G. (2007b). The mystery of the missing smile. *Science, 316,* 826–827. (12)

Miller, G., Tybur, J. M., & Jordan, B. D. (2007). Ovulatory cycle effects on tip earnings by lap dancers: Economic evidence for human estrus? *Evolution and Human Behavior, 28,* 375–381. (11)

Milner, B. (1959). The memory defect in bilateral hippocampal lesions. *Psychiatric Research Reports, 11,* 43–58. (13)

Minokoshi, Y., Alquier, T., Furukawa, N., Kim, Y.-B., Lee, A., Xue, B., et al. (2004). AMP-kinase regulates food intake by responding to hormonal and nutrient signals in the hypothalamus. *Nature, 428,* 569–574. (10)

Minto, C. L., Liao, L.-M., Woodhouse, C. R. J., Ransley, P. G., & Creighton, S. M. (2003). The effect of clitoral surgery in individuals who have intersex conditions with ambiguous genitalia: A cross-sectional study. *Lancet, 361,* 1252–1257. (11)

Mirescu, C., Peters, J. D., & Gould, E. (2004). Early life experience alters response of adult neurogenesis to stress. *Nature Neuroscience, 7,* 841–846. (12)

Misrahi, M., Meduri, G., Pissard, S., Bouvattier, C., Beau, I., Loosfelt, H., et al. (1997). Comparison of immunocytochemical and molecular features with the phenotype in a case of incomplete male pseudohermaphroditism associated with a mutation of the luteinizing hormone receptor. *Journal of Clinical Endocrinology & Metabolism, 82,* 2159–2165. (11)

Mitchell, D. E. (1980). The influence of early visual experience on visual perception. In C. S. Harris (Ed.), *Visual coding and adaptability* (pp. 1–50). Hillsdale, NJ: Erlbaum. (6)

Miyazawa, A., Fujiyoshi, Y., & Unwin, N. (2003). Structure and gating mechanism of the acetylcholine receptor pore. *Nature, 423,* 949–955. (3)

Mochizuki, T., Crocker, A., McCormack, S., Yanagisawa, M., Sakurai, T., & Scammell, T. E. (2004). Behavioral state instability in orexin knock-out mice. *Journal of Neuroscience, 24,* 6291–6300. (9)

Modell, S., Ising, M., Holsboer, F., & Lauer, C. J. (2005). The Munich vulnerability study on affective disorders: Premorbid polysomnographic profile of affected high-risk probands. *Biological Psychiatry, 58,* 694–699. (15)

Moeller, F. G., Dougherty, D. M., Swann, A. C., Collins, D., Davis, C. M., & Cherek, D. R. (1996). Tryptophan depletion and aggressive responding in healthy males. *Psychopharmacology, 126,* 97–103. (12)

Moffitt, T. E., Caspi, A., & Rutter, M. (2006). Measured gene-environment interactions in psychopathology. *Perspectives on Psychological Science, 1,* 5–27. (15)

Mohr, C., Landis, T., Bracha, H. S., & Brugger, P. (2003). Opposite turning behavior in right-handers and non-right-handers suggests a link between handedness and cerebral dopamine asymmetries. *Behavioral Neuroscience, 117,* 1448–1452. (14)

Moita, M. A. P., Rosis, S., Zhou, Y., LeDoux, J. E., & Blair, H. T. (2004). Putting fear in its place: Remapping of hippocampus place cells during fear conditioning. *Journal of Neuroscience, 24,* 7015–7023. (13)

Mondloch, C. J., Maurer, D., & Ahola, S. (2006). Becoming a face expert. *Psychological Science, 17,* 930–934. (6)

Money, J. (1967). Sexual problems of the chronically ill. In C. W. Wahl (Ed.), *Sexual problems: Diagnosis and treatment in medical practice* (pp. 266–287). New York: Free Press. (8)

Money, J., & Ehrhardt, A. A. (1972). *Man & woman, boy & girl.* Baltimore: Johns Hopkins University Press. (11)

Money, J., & Lewis, V. (1966). IQ, genetics and accelerated growth: Adrenogenital syndrome. *Bulletin of the Johns Hopkins Hospital, 118,* 365–373. (11)

Money, J., & Schwartz, M. (1978). Biosocial determinants of gender identity differentiation and development. In J. B. Hutchison (Ed.), *Biological determinants of sexual behaviour* (pp. 765–784). Chichester, England: Wiley. (11)

Mongillo, G., Barak, O., & Tsodyks, M. (2008). Synaptic theory of working memory. *Science, 319,* 1543–1546. (13)

Monk, C. S., Klein, R. G., Telzer, E. H., Schroth, E. A., Mannuzza, S., Moulton, J. L., III, et al. (2008). Amygdala and nucleus accumbens activation to emotional facial expressions in children and adolescents at risk for major depression. *American Journal of Psychiatry, 165,* 90–98. (15)

Monk, T. H., & Aplin, L. C. (1980). Spring and autumn daylight time changes: Studies of adjustment in sleep timings, mood, and efficiency. *Ergonomics, 23,* 167–178. (9)

Monti-Bloch, L., Jennings-White, C., & Berliner, D. L. (1998). The human vomeronasal system: A review. *Annals of the New York Academy of Sciences, 855,* 373–389. (7)

Monti-Bloch, L., Jennings-White, C., Dolberg, D. S., & Berliner, D. L. (1994). The human vomeronasal system. *Psychoneuroendocrinology, 19,* 673–686. (7)

Moore, L. B., Goodwin, B., Jones, S. A., Wisely, G. B., Serabjit-Singh, C. J., Willson, T. M., et al. (2000). St. John's wort induces hepatic drug metabolism through activation of the pregnane X receptor. *Proceedings of the National Academy of Sciences, USA, 97,* 7500–7502. (15)

Moore, T., Rodman, H. R., Repp, A. B., & Gross, C. G. (1995). Localization of visual stimuli after striate cortex damage in monkeys: Parallels with human blindsight. *Proceedings of the National Academy of Sciences, USA, 92,* 8215–8218. (6)

Moore-Ede, M. C., Czeisler, C. A., & Richardson, G. S. (1983). Circadian timekeeping in health and disease. *New England Journal of Medicine, 309,* 469–476. (9)

Moreno, C., Laje, G., Blanco, C., Jiang, H., Schmidt, A. B., & Olfson, M. (2007). National trends in the outpatient diagnosis and treatment of bipolar disorder in youth. *Archives of General Psychiatry, 64,* 1032–1039. (15)

Mori, K., Mataga, N., & Imamura, K. (1992). Differential specificities of single mitral cells in rabbit olfactory bulb for a homologous series of fatty acid odor molecules. *Journal of Neurophysiology, 67,* 786–789. (7)

Morland, A. B., Lê, S., Carroll, E., Hoffmann, M. B., & Pambakian, A. (2004). The role of spared calcarine cortex and lateral occipital cortex in the responses of human hemianopes to visual motion. *Journal of Cognitive Neuroscience, 16,* 204–218. (6)

Morley, J. E., Levine, A. S., Grace, M., & Kneip, J. (1985). Peptide YY (PYY), a potent orexigenic agent. *Brain Research, 341,* 200–203. (10)

Morris, J. A., Jordan, C. L., & Breedlove, S. M. (2004). Sexual differentiation of the vertebrate nervous system. *Nature Neuroscience, 7,* 1034–1039. (11)

Morris, J. S., deBonis, M., & Dolan, R. J. (2002). Human amygdala responses to fearful eyes. *NeuroImage, 17,* 214–222. (12)

Morris, M., Lack, L., & Dawson, D. (1990). Sleep-onset insomniacs have delayed temperature rhythms. *Sleep, 13,* 1–14. (9)

Morrison, A. R., Sanford, L. D., Ball, W. A., Mann, G. L., & Ross, R. J. (1995). Stimulus-elicited behavior in rapid eye movement sleep without atonia. *Behavioral Neuroscience, 109,* 972–979. (9)

Morrone, M. C., Ross, J., & Burr, D. (2005). Saccadic eye movements cause compression of time as well as space. *Nature Neuroscience, 8,* 950–954. (6)

Morton, A. J., Wood, N. I., Hastings, M. H., Hurelbink, C., Barker, R. A., & Maywood, E. S. (2005). Disintegration of the sleep–wake cycle and circadian timing in Huntington's disease. *Journal of Neuroscience, 25,* 157–163. (9)

Morton, G. J., Cummings, D. E., Baskin, D. G., Barsh, G. S., & Schwartz, M. W. (2006). Central nervous system control of food intake and body weight. *Nature, 443,* 289–295. (10)

Moruzzi, G., & Magoun, H. W. (1949). Brain stem reticular formation and activation of the EEG. *Electroencephalography and Clinical Neurophysiology, 1,* 455–473. (9)

Moscovitch, M. (1992). Memory and working-with-memory: A component process model based on modules and central systems. *Journal of Cognitive Neuroscience, 4,* 257–267. (13)

Moss, C. F., & Simmons, A. M. (1986). Frequency selectivity of hearing in the green treefrog, *Hyla cinerea. Journal of Comparative Physiology, A, 159,* 257–266. (7)

Moss, S. J., & Smart, T. G. (2001). Constructing inhibitory synapses. *Nature Reviews Neuroscience, 2,* 240–250. (3)

Mrosovsky, N. (1990). *Rheostasis: The physiology of change.* New York: Oxford University Press. (10)

Mrzljak, L., Bergson, C., Pappy, M., Huff, R., Levenson, R., & Goldman-Rakic, P. S. (1996). Localization of dopamine D4 receptors in GABAergic neurons of the primate brain. *Nature, 381,* 245–248. (15)

Mukamel, R., Gelbard, H., Arieli, A., Hasson, U., Fried, I., & Malach, R. (2005). Coupling between neuronal firing, field potentials, and fMRI in human auditory cortex. *Science, 309,* 951–954. (4)

Muller, M. N., Thompson, M. E., & Wrangham, R. W. (2006). Male chimpanzees prefer mating with old females. *Current Biology, 16,* 2234–2238. (11)

Mulligan, S. J., & MacVicar, B. A. (2004). Calcium transients in astrocyte end feet cause cerebrovascular constrictions. *Nature, 431,* 195–199. (2)

Munk, M. H. J., Roelfsema, P. R., König, P., Engel, A. K., & Singer, W. (1996). Role of reticular activation in the modulation of intracortical synchronization. *Science, 272,* 271–274. (9)

Munoz, D. P., & Everling, S. (2004). Look away: The anti-saccade task and the voluntary control of eye movement. *Nature Reviews Neuroscience, 5,* 218–228. (8)

Munro, C. A., McCaul, M. E., Wong, D. F., Oswald, L. M., Zhou, Y., Brasic, J., et al. (2006). Sex differences in striatal dopamine release in healthy adults. *Biological Psychiatry, 59,* 966–974. (15)

Münzberg, H., & Myers, M. G., Jr. (2005). Molecular and anatomical determinants of central leptin resistance. *Nature Neuroscience, 8,* 566–570. (10)

Murphy, F. C., Nimmo-Smith, I., & Lawrence, A. D. (2003). Functional neuroanatomy of emotions: A meta-analysis. *Cognitive, Affective, & Behavioral Neuroscience, 3,* 207–233. (12)

Murphy, M. R., Checkley, S. A., Seckl, J. R., & Lightman, S. L. (1990). Naloxone inhibits oxytocin release at orgasm in man. *Journal of Clinical Endocrinology & Metabolism, 71,* 1056–1058. (11)

Murrell, J., Farlow, M., Ghetti, B., & Benson, M. D. (1991). A mutation in the amyloid precursor protein associated with hereditary Alzheimer's disease. *Science, 254,* 97–99. (13)

Musacchia, G., Sams, M., Skoe, E., & Kraus, N. (2007). Musicians have enhanced subcortical auditory and audiovisual processing of speech and music. *Proceedings of the National Academy of Sciences, USA, 104,* 15894–15898. (5)

Mustanski, B. S., DuPree, M. G., Nievergelt, C. M., Bocklandt, S., Schork, N. J., & Hamer, D. H. (2005). A genomewide scan of male sexual orientation. *Human Genetics, 116,* 272–278. (11)

Mutch, D. M., & Clément, K. (2006). Unraveling the genetics of human obesity. *PLoS Genetics, 2,* e188. (10)

Myers, J. J., & Sperry, R. W. (1985). Interhemispheric communication after section of the forebrain commissures. *Cortex, 21,* 249–260. (14)

Nadal, A., Díaz, M., & Valverde, M. A. (2001). The estrogen trinity: Membrane, cytosolic, and nuclear effects. *News in Physiological Sciences, 16,* 251–255. (11)

Nadarajah, B., & Parnavelas, J. G. (2002). Modes of neuronal migration in the developing cerebral cortex. *Nature Reviews Neuroscience, 3,* 423–432. (5)

Nadkarni, S., & Jung, P. (2003). Spontaneous oscillations of dressed neurons: A new mechanism for epilepsy? *Physical Review Letters, 91,* 268101. (2)

Nagarajan, S., Mahncke, H., Salz, T., Tallal, P., Roberts, T., & Merzenich, M. M. (1999). Cortical auditory signal processing in poor readers. *Proceedings of the National Academy of Sciences, USA, 96,* 6483–6488. (14)

Nagayama, T., Sinor, A. D., Simon, R. P., Chen, J., Graham, S. H., Jin, K., et al. (1999). Cannabinoids and neuroprotection in global and focal cerebral ischemia and in neuronal cultures. *Journal of Neuroscience, 19,* 2987–2995. (5)

Naggert, J. K., Fricker, L. D., Varlamov, O., Nishina, P. M., Rouille, Y., Steiner, D. F., et al. (1995). Hyperproinsulinaemia in obese fat/fat mice associated with a carboxypeptidase E mutation which reduces enzyme activity. *Nature Genetics, 10,* 135–142. (10)

Nakashima, Y., Kuwamura, T., & Yogo, Y. (1995). Why be a both-ways sex changer? *Ethology, 101,* 301–307. (11)

Narr, K. L., Woods, R. P., Thompson, P. M., Szeszko, P., Robinson, D., Dimtcheva, T., et al. (2007). Relationships between IQ and regional cortical gray matter thickness in healthy adults. *Cerebral Cortex, 17,* 2163–2171. (4)

Narrow, W. E., Rae, D. S., Robins, L. N., & Regier, D. A. (2002). Revised prevalence estimates of mental disorders in the United States. *Archives of General Psychiatry, 59,* 115–123. (15)

Narumoto, J., Okada, T., Sadato, N., Fukui, K., & Yonekura, Y. (2001). Attention to emotion modulates fMRI activity in human right superior temporal sulcus. *Cognitive Brain Research, 12,* 225–231. (12, 14)

Nassi, J. J., & Callaway, E. M. (2006). Multiple circuits relaying primate parallel visual pathways to the middle temporal cortex. *Journal of Neuroscience, 26,* 12789–12798. (6)

Nathans, J., Davenport, C. M., Maumenee, I. H., Lewis, R. A., Hejtmancik, J. F., Litt, M., et al. (1989). Molecular genetics of human blue cone monochromacy. *Science, 245,* 831–838. (6)

Naylor, E., Bergmann, B. M., Krauski, K., Zee, P. C., Takahashi, J. S., Vitaterna, M. H., et al. (2000). The circadian clock mutation alters sleep homeostasis in the mouse. *Journal of Neuroscience, 20,* 8138–8143. (9)

Nebes, R. D. (1974). Hemispheric specialization in commissurotomized man. *Psychological Bulletin, 81,* 1–14. (14)

Nef, P. (1998). How we smell: The molecular and cellular bases of olfaction. *News in Physiological Sciences, 13,* 1–5. (7)

Neitz, M., Kraft, T. W., & Neitz, J. (1998). Expression of L cone pigment gene subtypes in females. *Vision Research, 38,* 3221–3225. (6)

Nelson, C. A., Wewerka, S., Thomas, K. M., Tribby-Walbridge, S., deRegnier, R., & Georgieff, M. (2000). Neurocognitive sequelae of infants of diabetic mothers. *Behavioral Neuroscience, 114,* 950–956. (5)

Nelson, D. O., & Prosser, C. L. (1981). Intracellular recordings from thermosensitive preoptic neurons. *Science, 213,* 787–789. (10)

Nelson, R. J., & Trainor, B. C. (2007). Neural mechanisms of aggression. *Nature Reviews Neuroscience, 8,* 536–546. (12)

Nemeroff, C. B., Heim, C. M., Thase, M. E., Klein, D. N., Rush, J., Shatzberg, A. F., et al. (2003). Differential responses to psychotherapy versus pharmacotherapy in patients with chronic forms of major depression and childhood trauma. *Proceedings of the National Academy of Sciences, USA, 100,* 14293–14296. (15)

Netter, F. H. (1983). *CIBA collection of medical illustrations: Vol. 1. Nervous system.* New York: CIBA. (11)

Nettle, D. (2006). The evolution of personality variation in humans and other animals. *American Psychologist, 61,* 622–631. (12)

Neumeister, A., Hu, X.-Z., Luckenbaugh, D. A., Schwarz, M., Nugent, A. C., Bonne, O., et al. (2006). Differential effects of 5-*HTTLPR* genotypes on the behavioral and neural responses to tryptophan depletion in patients with major depression and controls. *Archives of General Psychiatry, 63,* 978–986. (15)

Neumeister, A., Nugent, A. C., Waldeck, T., Geraci, M., Schwarz, M., Bonne, O., et al. (2004). Neural and behavioral responses to tryptophan depletion in unmedicated patients with remitted major depressive disorder and controls. *Archives of General Psychiatry, 61,* 765–773. (15)

Neville, H. J., Bavelier, D., Corina, D., Rauschecker, J., Karni, A., Lalwani, A., et al. (1998). Cerebral organization for language in deaf and hearing subjects: Biological constraints and effects of experience. *Proceedings of the National Academy of Sciences, USA,* 95, 922–929. (14)

Nevin, R. (2007). Understanding international crime trends: The legacy of preschool lead exposure. *Environmental Research, 104,* 315–336. (12)

Newcomer, J. W., Selke, G., Melson, A. K., Hershey, T., Craft, S., Richards, K., et al. (1999). Decreased memory performance in healthy humans induced by stress-level cortisol treatment. *Archives of General Psychiatry, 56,* 527–533. (13)

Nicholas, M. K., & Arnason, B. G. W. (1992). Immunologic responses in central nervous system transplantation. *Seminars in the Neurosciences, 4,* 273–283. (8)

Nicholls, M. E. R., Orr, C. A., Okubo, M., & Loftus, A. (2006). Satisfaction guaranteed: The effect of spatial biases on responses to Likert scales. *Psychological Science, 17,* 1027–1028. (14)

Nicklas, W. J., Saporito, M., Basma, A., Geller, H. M., & Heikkila, R. E. (1992). Mitochondrial mechanisms of neurotoxicity. *Annals of the New York Academy of Sciences, 648,* 28–36. (8)

Nicolelis, M. A. L., Ghazanfar, A. A., Stambaugh, C. R., Oliveira, L. M. O., Laubach, M., Chapin, J. K., et al. (1998). Simultaneous encoding of tactile information by three primate cortical areas. *Nature Neuroscience, 1,* 621–630. (4)

Niebuhr, D. W., Millikan, A. M., Cowan, D. N., Yolken, R., Li, Y., & Weber, N. S. (2008). Selected infectious agents and risk of schizophrenia among U.S. military personnel. *American Journal of Psychiatry, 165,* 99–106. (15)

Nieuwenhuys, R., Voogd, J., & vanHuijzen, C. (1988). *The human central nervous system* (3rd Rev. ed.). Berlin: Springer-Verlag. (4, 10, 12, 14)

Niki, K., & Luo, J. (2002). An fMRI study on the time-limited role of the medial temporal lobe in long-term topographical autobiographic memory. *Journal of Cognitive Neuroscience, 14,* 500–507. (13)

Nilsson, G. E. (1999, December). The cost of a brain. *Natural History, 108,* 66–73. (4)

Nishimaru, H., Restrepo, C. E., Ryge, J., Yanagawa, Y., & Kiehn, O. (2005). Mammalian motor neurons corelease glutamate and acetylcholine at central synapses. *Proceedings of the National Academy of Sciences, USA, 102,* 5245–5249. (3)

Nishimura, Y., Onoe, H., Morichika, Y., Perfiliev, S., Tsukada, H., & Isa, T. (2007). Time-dependent central compensatory mechanisms of finger dexterity after spinal cord injury. *Science, 318,* 1150–1155. (5)

Noaghiul, S., & Hibbeln, J. R. (2003). Cross-national comparisons of seafood consumption and rates of bipolar disorders. *American Journal of Psychiatry, 160,* 2222–2227. (15)

Nopoulos, P. C., Giedd, J. N., Andreasen, N. C., & Rapoport, J. L. (1998). Frequency and severity of enlarged cavum septi pellucidi in childhood-onset schizophrenia. *American Journal of Psychiatry, 155,* 1074–1079. (15)

Nordenström, A., Servin, A., Bohlin, G., Larsson, A., & Wedell, A. (2002). Sex-typed toy play behavior correlates with the degree of prenatal androgen exposure assessed by *CYP21* genotype in girls with congenital adrenal hyperplasia. *Journal of Clinical Endocrinology & Metabolism, 87,* 5119–5124. (11)

Norman, R. A., Tataranni, P. A., Pratley, R., Thompson, D. B., Hanson, R. L., Prochazka, M., et al. (1998). Autosomal genomic scan for loci linked to obesity and energy metabolism in Pima Indians. *American Journal of Human Genetics, 62,* 659–668. (10)

North, R. A. (1989). Neurotransmitters and their receptors: From the clone to the clinic. *Seminars in the Neurosciences, 1,* 81–90. (2)

North, R. A. (1992). Cellular actions of opiates and cocaine. *Annals of the New York Academy of Sciences, 654,* 1–6. (3)

Norton, A., Winner, E., Cronin, K., Overy, K., Lee, D. J., & Schlaug, G. (2005). Are there pre-existing neural, cognitive, or motoric markers for musical ability? *Brain and Cognition, 59,* 124–134. (5)

Nosenko, N. D., & Reznikov, A. G. (2001). Prenatal stress and sexual differentiation of monoaminergic brain systems. *Neurophysiology, 33,* 197–206. (11)

Nottebohm, F. (2002). Why are some neurons replaced in adult brain? *Journal of Neuroscience, 22,* 624–628. (5)

Nowak, M. A., Komarova, N. L., & Niyogi, P. (2002). Computational and evolutionary aspects of language. *Nature, 417,* 611–617. (14)

Nowak, M. A., & Sigmund, K. (2005). Evolution of indirect reciprocity. *Science, 437,* 1291–1298. (1)

Nugent, F. S., Penick, S. C., & Kauer, J. A. (2007). Opioids block long-term potentiation of inhibitory synapses. *Nature, 446,* 1086–1090. (13)

Nwulia, E. A., Miao, K., Zandi, P. P., Mackinnon, D. F., DePaulo, J. R., Jr., & McInnis, M. G. (2007). Genome-wide scan of bipolar II disorder. *Bipolar Disorders, 9,* 580–588. (15)

Ó Scalaidhe, S. P., Wilson, F. A. W., & Goldman-Rakic, P. S. (1997). Areal segregation of face-processing neurons in prefrontal cortex. *Science, 278,* 1135–1138. (6)

O'Dowd, B. F., Lefkowitz, R. J., & Caron, M. G. (1989). Structure of the adrenergic and related receptors. *Annual Review of Neuroscience, 12,* 67–83. (3)

Oka, Y., Omura, M., Kataoka, H., & Touhara, K. (2004). Olfactory receptor antagonism between odorants. *The EMBO Journal, 23,* 120–126. (7)

O'Kane, G., Kensinger, E. A., & Corkin, S. (2004). Evidence for semantic learning in profound amnesia: An investigation with patient H. M. *Hippocampus, 14,* 417–425. (13)

O'Keefe, J., & Burgess, N. (1996). Geometric determinants of the place fields of hippocampal neurons. *Nature, 381,* 425–434. (13)

Olanow, C. W., Goetz, C. G., Kordower, J. H., Stoessl, A. J., Sossi, V., Brin, M. F., et al. (2003). A double-blind controlled trial of bilateral fetal nigral transplantation in Parkinson's disease. *Annals of Neurology, 54,* 403–414. (8)

Olausson, H., Lamarre, Y., Backlund, H., Morin, C., Wallin, B. G., Starck, G., et al. (2002). Unmyelinated tactile afferents signal touch and project to insular cortex. *Nature Neuroscience, 5,* 900–904. (7)

Olds, J. (1958). Satiation effects in self-stimulation of the brain. *Journal of Comparative and Physiological Psychology, 51,* 675–678. (3)

Olds, J., & Milner, P. (1954). Positive reinforcement produced by electrical stimulation of the septal area and other regions of the rat brain. *Journal of Comparative and Physiological Psychology, 47,* 419–428. (3)

O'Leary, A. (1990). Stress, emotion, and human immune function. *Psychological Bulletin, 108,* 363–382. (12)

Oliet, S. H. R., Baimouknametova, D. V., Piet, R., & Bains, J. S. (2007). Retrograde regulation of GABA transmission by the tonic release of oxytocin and endocannabinoids governs postsynaptic firing. *Journal of Neuroscience, 27,* 1325–1333. (3)

Olney, J. W., & Farber, N. B. (1995). Glutamate receptor dysfunction and schizophrenia. *Archives of General Psychiatry, 52,* 998–1007. (15)

Olson, D. J., Kamil, A. C., Balda, R. P., & Nims, P. J. (1995). Performance of four seed-caching corvid species in operant tests of nonspatial and spatial memory. *Journal of Comparative Psychology, 109,* 173–181. (13)

Olson, E. J., Boeve, B. F., & Silber, M. H. (2000). Rapid eye movement sleep behaviour disorder: Demographic, clinical and laboratory findings in 93 cases. *Brain, 123,* 331–339. (9)

Olsson, G. L., Meyerson, B. A., & Linderoth, B. (2008). Spinal cord stimulation in adolescents with complex regional pain syndrome type 1 (CRPS-1). *European Journal of Pain, 12,* 53–59. (7)

Olton, D. S., & Papas, B. C. (1979). Spatial memory and hippocampal function. *Neuropsychologia, 17,* 669–682. (13)

Olton, D. S., Walker, J. A., & Gage, F. H. (1978). Hippocampal connections and spatial discrimination. *Brain Research, 139,* 295–308. (13)

Ornstein, R. (1997). *The right mind.* New York: Harcourt Brace. (14)

Osborne, L. C., Bialek, W., & Lisberger, S. G. (2004). Time course of information about motion direction in visual area MT of macaque monkeys. *Journal of Neuroscience, 24,* 3210–3222. (6)

Ostrovsky, Y., Andalman, A., & Sinha, P. (2006). Vision following extended congenital blindness. *Psychological Science, 17,* 1009–1014. (6)

Oswald, A.-M., Chacron, M. J., Doiron, B., Bastian, J., & Maler, L. (2004). Parallel processing of sensory input by bursts and isolated spikes. *Journal of Neuroscience, 24,* 4351–4362. (2)

Otmakhov, N., Tao-Cheng, J.-H., Carpenter, S., Asrican, B., Dosemici, A., & Reese, T. S. (2004). Persistent accumulation of calcium/calmodulin-dependent protein kinase II in dendritic spines after induction of NMDA receptor-dependent chemical long-term potentiation. *Journal of Neuroscience, 25,* 9324–9331. (13)

Ouchi, Y., Yoshikawa, E., Okada, H., Futatsubashi, M., Sekine, Y., Iyo, M., et al. (1999). Alterations in binding site density of dopamine transporter in the striatum, orbitofrontal cortex, and amygdala in early Parkinson's disease: Compartment analysis for ß-CFT binding with positron emission tomography. *Annals of Neurology, 45,* 601–610. (8)

Owen, A. M., Coleman, M. R., Boly, M., Davis, M. H., Laureys, S., & Pickard, J. D. (2006). Detecting awareness in the vegetative state. *Science, 313,* 1402. (4)

Padmos, R. C., Hillegers, M. H. J., Knijff, E. M., Vonk, R., Bouvy, A., Staal, F. J. T., et al. (2008). A discriminating messenger RNA signature for bipolar disorder formed by an aberrant expression of inflammatory genes in monocytes. *Archives of General Psychiatry, 65,* 395–407. (15)

Palinkas, L. A. (2003). The psychology of isolated and confined environments. *American Psychologist, 58,* 353–363. (9)

Pallier, P. N., Maywood, E. S., Zheng, Z., Chesham, J. E., Inyushkin, A. N., Dyball, R., et al. (2007). Pharmacological imposition of sleep slows cognitive decline and reverses dysregulation of circadian gene expression in a transgenic mouse model of Huntington's disease. *Journal of Neuroscience, 27,* 7869–7878. (8)

Palop, J. J., Chin, J., & Mucke, L. (2006). A network dysfunction perspective on neurodegenerative diseases. *Nature, 443,* 768–773. (13)

Palva, S., Linkenkaer-Hansen, K., Näätänen, R., & Palva, J. M. (2005). Early neural correlates of conscious somatosensory perception. *Journal of Neuroscience, 25,* 5248–5258. (7)

Panda, S., Sato, T. K., Castrucci, A. M., Rollag, M. D., DeGrip, W. J., Hogenesch, J. B., et al. (2002). Melanopsin (*Opn4*) requirement for normal light-induced circadian phase shifting. *Science, 298,* 2213–2216. (9)

Pandey, G. N., Pandey, S. C., Dwivedi, Y., Sharma, R. P., Janicak, P. G., & Davis, J. M. (1995). Platelet serotonin-2A receptors: A potential biological marker for suicidal behavior. *American Journal of Psychiatry, 152,* 850–855. (12)

Panov, A. V., Gutekunst, C.-A., Leavitt, B. R., Hayden, M. R, Burke, J. R., Strittmatter, W. J., et al. (2002). Early mitochondrial calcium defects in Huntington's disease are a direct effect of polyglutamines. *Nature Neuroscience, 5,* 731–736. (8)

Pappone, P. A., & Cahalan, M. D. (1987). Pandinus imperator scorpion venom blocks voltage-gated potassium channels in nerve fibers. *Journal of Neuroscience, 7,* 3300–3305. (2)

Pardal, R., & López-Barneo, J. (2002). Low glucose-sensing cells in the carotid body. *Nature Neuroscience, 5,* 197–198. (10)

Paré, M., Smith, A. M., & Rice, F. L. (2002). Distribution and terminal arborizations of cutaneous mechanoreceptors in the glabrous finger pads of the monkey. *Journal of Comparative Neurology, 445,* 347–359. (7)

Paredes, R. G., & Vazquez, B. (1999). What do female rats like about sex? Paced mating. *Behavioural Brain Research, 105,* 117–127. (11)

Parent, M. B., Habib, M. K., & Baker, G. B. (1999). Task-dependent effects of the antidepressant/antipanic drug phenelzine on memory. *Psychopharmacology, 142,* 280–288. (9)

Park, I.-H., Zhao, R., West, J. A., Yabuuchi, A., Huo, H., Ince, T. A., et al. (2008). Reprogramming of human somatic cells to pluripotency with defined factors. *Nature, 451,* 141–146. (8)

Park, S., Holzman, P. S., & Goldman-Rakic, P. S. (1995). Spatial working memory deficits in the relatives of schizophrenic patients. *Archives of General Psychiatry, 52,* 821–828. (15)

Parker, G. H. (1922). *Smell, taste, and allied senses in the vertebrates.* Philadelphia: Lippincott. (7)

Parkes, L., Lund, J., Angelucci, A., Solomon, J. A., & Morgan, M. (2001). Compulsory averaging of crowded orientation signals in human vision. *Nature Neuroscience, 4,* 739–744. (6)

Parr-Brownlie, L. C., & Hyland, B. I. (2005). Bradykinesia induced by dopamine D_2 receptor blockade is associated with reduced motor cortex activity in the rat. *Journal of Neuroscience, 25,* 5700–5709. (8)

Parrott, A. C. (2001). Human psychopharmacology of Ecstasy (MDMA): A review of 15 years of empirical research. *Human Psychopharmacology: Clinical and Experimental, 16,* 557–577. (3)

Parton, L. E., Ye, C. P., Coppari, R., Enriori, P. J., Choi, B., Zhang, C.-Y., et al. (2007). Glucose sensing by POMC neurons regulates glucose homeostasis and is impaired in obesity. *Nature, 449,* 228–232. (10)

Pascalis, O., Scott, L. S., Kelly, D. J., Shannon, R. W., Nicholson, E., Coleman, M., et al. (2005). Plasticity of face processing in infancy. *Proceedings of the National Academy of Sciences, USA, 102,* 5297–5300. (6)

Pasterski, V. L., Geffner, M. E., Brain, C., Hindmarsh, P., Brook, C., & Hines, M. (2005). Prenatal hormones and postnatal socialization by parents as determinants of male-typical toy play in girls with congenital adrenal hyperplasia. *Child Development, 76,* 264–278. (11)

Patel, A. D. (2008). *Music, language, and the brain.* New York: Oxford University Press. (14)

Patil, S. T., Zhang, L., Martenyi, F., Lowe, S. L., Jackson, K. A., Andreev, B. V., et al. (2007). Activation of mGlu 2/3 receptors as a new approach to treat schizophrenia: A randomized phase 2 clinical trial. *Nature Medicine,* 1102–1107. (15)

Patston, L L. M., Corballis, M. C., Hogg, S. L., & Tippet, L. J. (2006). The neglect of musicians: Line bisection reveals an opposite bias. *Psychological Science, 17,* 1029–1031. (14)

Patte, C., Gandolfo, P., Leprince, J., Thoumas, J. L., Fontaine, M., Vaudry, H., et al. (1999). GABA inhibits endozepine release from cultured rat astrocytes. *Glia, 25,* 404–411. (12)

Patterson, K., Nestor, P. J., & Rogers, T. T. (2007). Where do you know what you know? The representation of semantic knowledge in the human brain. *Nature Reviews Neuroscience, 8,* 976–987. (13)

Paul, L. K., Brown, W. S., Adolphs, R., Tyszka, J. M., Richards, L. J., Mukherjee, P., et al. (2007). Agenesis of the corpus callosum: Genetic, developmental and functional aspects of connectivity. *Nature Reviews Neuroscience, 8,* 287–299. (14)

Paulesu, E., Frith, U., Snowling, M., Gallagher, A., Morton, J., Frackowiak, R. S. J., et al. (1996). Is developmental dyslexia a disconnection syndrome? *Brain, 119,* 143–157. (14)

Paus, T., Marrett, S., Worsley, K. J., & Evans, A. C. (1995). Extraretinal modulation of cerebral blood flow in the human visual cortex: Implications for saccadic suppression. *Journal of Neurophysiology, 74,* 2179–2183. (6)

Pause, B. M., Krauel, K., Schrader, C., Sojka, B., Westphal, E., Müller-Ruchholtz, W., et al. (2006). The human brain is a detector of chemosensorily transmitted HLA-class 1-similarity in same- and opposite-sex relations. *Proceedings of the Royal Society, B, 273,* 471–478. (7)

Pavlov, I. P. (1927). *Conditioned reflexes.* Oxford, England: Oxford University Press. (13)

Pearson, H. (2006). Freaks of nature? *Nature, 444,* 1000–1001. (8)

Pedersen,, C. A., Caldwell, J. D., Walker, C., Ayers, G., & Mason, G. A. (1994). Oxytocin activates the postpartum onset of rat maternal behavior in the ventral tegmentum and medial preoptic areas. *Behavioral Neuroscience, 108,* 1163–1171. (11)

Peet, M. (2004). Nutrition and schizophrenia: Beyond omega-3 fatty acids. *Prostaglandins, Leukotrienes and Essential Fatty Acids, 70,* 417–422. (15)

Pegna, A. J., Khateb, A., Lazeyrus, F., & Seghier, M. L. (2004). Discriminating emotional faces without primary visual cortices involves the right amygdala. *Nature Neuroscience, 8,* 24–25. (12)

Peigneux, P., Laureys, S., Fuchs, S., Collette, F., Perrin, F., Reggers, J., et al. (2004). Are spatial memories strengthened in the human hippocampus during slow wave sleep? *Neuron, 44,* 535–545. (9)

Peleg, G., Katzir, G., Peleg, O., Kamara, M., Brodsky, L., Hel-or, H., et al. (2006). Hereditary family signature of facial expressions. *Proceedings of the National Academy of Sciences, USA, 103,* 15921–15926. (1)

Pellis, S. M., O'Brien, D. P., Pellis, V. C., Teitelbaum, P., Wolgin, D. L., & Kennedy, S. (1988). Escalation of feline predation along a gradient from avoidance through "play" to killing. *Behavioral Neuroscience, 102,* 760–777. (12)

Pellymounter, M. A., Cullen, M. J., Baker, M. B., Hecht, R., Winters, D., Boone, T., et al. (1995). Effects of the obese gene product on body weight regulation in *ob/ob* mice. *Science, 269,* 540–543. (10)

Penagos, H., Melcher, J. R., & Oxenham, A. J. (2004). A neural representation of pitch salience in nonprimary human auditory cortex revealed with functional magnetic resonance imaging. *Journal of Neuroscience, 24,* 6810–6815. (7)

Penfield, W. (1955). The permanent record of the stream of consciousness. *Acta Psychologica, 11,* 47–69. (13)

Penfield, W., & Milner, B. (1958). Memory deficit produced by bilateral lesions in the hippocampal zone. *Archives of Neurology and Psychiatry, 79,* 475–497. (13)

Penfield, W., & Perot, P. (1963). The brain's record of auditory and visual experience. *Brain, 86,* 595–696. (13)

Penfield, W., & Rasmussen, T. (1950). *The cerebral cortex of man.* New York: Macmillan. (4, 8)

Peng, J., Peng, L., Stevenson, F. F., Doctrow, S. R., & Andersen, J. K. (2007). Iron and paraquat as synergistic environmental risk factors in sporadic Parkinson's disease accelerate age-related neurodegeneration. *Journal of Neuroscience, 27,* 6914–6922. (8)

Pennington, B. F., Filipek, P. A., Lefly, D., Chhabildas, N., Kennedy, D. N., Simon, J. H., et al. (2000). A twin MRI study of size variations in the human brain. *Journal of Cognitive Neuroscience, 12,* 223–232. (4)

Penton-Voak, I. S., Perrett, D. I., Castles, D. L., Kobayashi, T., Burt, D. M., Murray, L. K., et al. (1999). Menstrual cycle alters face preference. *Nature, 399,* 741–742. (11)

Peper, J. S., Brouwer, R. M., Boomsma, D. I., Kahn, R. S., & Hulshoff, H. E. (2007). Genetic influences on human brain structure: A review of brain imaging studies in twins. *Human Brain Mapping, 28,* 464–473. (4)

Pepperberg, I. M. (1981). Functional vocalizations by an African grey parrot. *Zeitschrift für Tierpsychologie, 55,* 139–160. (14)

Pepperberg, I. M. (1993). Cognition and communication in an African grey parrot (*Psittacus erithacus*): Studies on a nonhuman, nonprimate, nonmammalian subject. In H. L. Roitblat, L. M. Herman, & P. E. Nachtigall (Eds.), *Language and communication: Comparative perspectives* (pp. 221–248). Hillsdale, NJ: Erlbaum. (14)

Pepperberg, I. M. (1994). Numerical competence in an African gray parrot (*Psittacus erithacus*). *Journal of Comparative Psychology, 108,* 36–44. (14)

Pepperberg, I. M. (2004). "Insightful" string-pulling in grey parrots (*Psittacus erithacus*) is affected by vocal competence. *Animal Cognition, 7,* 263–266. (14)

Perälä, J., Suvisaari, J., Saarni, S. I., Kuoppasalmi, K., Isometsä, E., Pirkola, S., et al. (2007). Lifetime prevalence of psychotic and bipolar I disorders in a general population. *Archives of General Psychiatry, 64,* 19–28. (15)

Perani, D., & Abutalebi, J. (2005). The neural basis of first and second language processing. *Current Opinion in Neurobiology, 15,* 202–206. (14)

Perea, G., & Araque, A. (2007). Astrocytes potentiate transmitter release at single hippocampal synapses. *Science, 317,* 1083–1087. (2)

Perera, T. D., Coplan, J. D., Lisanby, S. H., Lipira, C. M., Arif, M., Carpio, C., et al. (2007). Antidepressant-induced neurogenesis in the hippocampus of adult nonhuman primates. *Journal of Neuroscience, 27,* 4894–4901. (15)

Peretz, I., Cummings, S., & Dube, M. P. (2007). The genetics of congenital amusia (tone deafness): A family-aggregation study. *American Journal of Human Genetics, 81,* 582–588. (7)

Perlow, M. J., Freed, W. J., Hoffer, B. J., Seiger, A., Olson, L., & Wyatt, R. J. (1979). Brain grafts reduce motor abnormalities produced by destruction of nigrostriatal dopamine system. *Science, 204,* 643–647. (8)

Perrone, J. A., & Thiele, A. (2001). Speed skills: Measuring the visual speed analyzing properties of primate MT neurons. *Nature Neuroscience, 4,* 526–532. (6)

Pert, C. B. (1997). *Molecules of emotion.* New York: Touchstone. (2)

Pert, C. B., & Snyder, S. H. (1973). The opiate receptor: Demonstration in nervous tissue. *Science, 179,* 1011–1014. (3, 7)

Pesold, C., & Treit, D. (1995). The central and basolateral amygdala differentially mediate the anxiolytic effect of benzodiazepines. *Brain Research, 671,* 213–221. (12)

Pessiglione, M., Schmidt, L., Draganski, B., Kalisch, R., Lau, H., Dolan, R. J., et al. (2007). How the brain translates money into force: A neuroimaging study of subliminal motivation. *Science, 316,* 904–906. (14)

Peters, F., Nicolson, N. A., Berkhof, J., Delespaul, P., & deVries, M. (2003). Effects of daily events on mood states in major depressive disorder. *Journal of Abnormal Psychology, 112,* 203–211. (15)

Peters, R. H., Sensenig, L. D., & Reich, M. J. (1973). Fixed-ratio performance following ventromedial hypothalamic lesions in rats. *Physiological Psychology, 1,* 136–138. (10)

Peterson, L. R., & Peterson, M. J. (1959). Short-term retention of individual verbal items. *Journal of Experimental Psychology, 58,* 193–198. (13)

Petitto, L. A., Zatorre, R. J., Gauna, K., Nikelski, E. J., Dostie, D., & Evans, A. C. (2000). Speech-like cerebral activity in profoundly deaf people processing signed languages: Implications for the neural basis of human language. *Proceedings of the National Academy of Sciences, USA, 97,* 13961–13966. (14)

Petkov, C. I., Kayser, C., Steudel, T., Whittingstall, K., Augath, M., & Logothetis, N. K. (2008). A voice region in the monkey brain. *Nature Neuroscience, 11,* 367–374. (14)

Petrovic, P., Kalso, E., Petersson, K. M., & Ingvar, M. (2002). Placebo and opioid analgesia—Imaging a shared neuronal network. *Science, 295,* 1737–1740. (7)

Pexman, P. M., Hargreaves, I. S., Edwards, J. D., Henry, L. C., & Goodyear, B. G. (2007). The neural consequences of semantic richness. *Psychological Science, 18,* 401–406. (4)

Pezawas, L., Meyer-Lindenberg, A., Drabant, E. M., Verchinski, B. A., Munoz, K. E., Kolachana, B. S., et al. (2005). 5-HTTLPR polymorphism impacts human cingulate-amygdala interactions: A genetic susceptibility mechanism for depression. *Nature Neuroscience, 8,* 828–834. (15)

Pfaff, D. W. (2007). *The neuropsychology of fair play.* New York: Dana Press. (12)

Phan, K. L., Wager, T., Taylor, S. F., & Liberzon, I. (2002). Functional neuroanatomy of emotion: A meta-analysis of emotion activation studies in PET and fMRI. *NeuroImage, 16,* 331–348. (12)

Phelps, M. E., & Mazziotta, J. C. (1985). Positron emission tomography: Human brain function and biochemistry. *Science, 228,* 799–809. (4)

Phillips, M. L., Young, A. W., Senior, C., Brammer, M., Andrew, C., Calder, A. J., et al. (1997). A specific neural substrate for perceiving facial expressions of disgust. *Nature, 389,* 495–498. (12)

Piccini, P., Burn, D. J., Ceravolo, R., Maraganore, D., & Brooks, D. J. (1999). The role of inheritance in sporadic Parkinson's disease: Evidence from a longitudinal study of dopaminergic function in twins. *Annals of Neurology, 45,* 577–582. (8)

Pich, E. M., Pagliusi, S. R., Tessari, M., Talabot-Ayer, D., van Huijsduijnen, R. H., & Chiamulera, C. (1997). Common neural substrates for the addictive properties of nicotine and cocaine. *Science, 275,* 83–86. (3)

Pierri, J. N., Volk, C. L. E., Auh, S., Sampson, A., & Lewis, D. A. (2001). Decreased somal size of deep layer 3 pyramidal neurons in the prefrontal cortex of subjects with schizophrenia. *Archives of General Psychiatry, 58,* 466–473. (15)

Pietropaolo, S., Feldon, J., Alleva, E., Cirulli, F., & Yee, B. K. (2006). The role of voluntary exercise in enriched rearing: A behavioral analysis. *Behavioral Neuroscience, 120,* 787–803. (5)

Pillon, B., Ertle, S., Deweer, B., Sarazin, M., Agid, Y., & Dubois, B. (1996). Memory for spatial location is affected in Parkinson's disease. *Neuropsychologia, 34,* 77–85. (8)

Pinker, S. (1994). *The language instinct.* New York: HarperCollins. (14)

Pinto, L., & Götz, M. (2007). Radial glial cell heterogeneity: The source of diverse progeny in the CNS. *Progress in Neurobiology, 83,* 2–23. (2)

Pizzagalli, D. A., Nitschke, J. B., Oakes, T. R., Hendrick, A. M., Horras, K. A., Larson, C. L., et al. (2002). Brain electrical tomography in depression: The importance of symptom severity, anxiety, and melancholic features. *Biological Psychiatry, 52,* 73–85. (15)

Pizzorusso, T., Medini, P., Berardi, N., Chierzi, S., Fawcett, J. W., & Maffei, L. (2002). Reactivation of ocular dominance plasticity in the adult visual cortex. *Science, 298,* 1248–1251. (6)

Plassman, H., O'Doherty, J., & Rangel, A. (2007). Orbitofrontal cortex encodes willingness to pay in everyday economic transactions. *Journal of Neuroscience, 27,* 9984–9988. (13)

Plihal, W., & Born, J. (1997). Effects of early and late nocturnal sleep on declarative and procedural memory. *Journal of Cognitive Neuroscience, 9,* 534–547. (9)

Plomin, R., Corley, R., DeFries, J. C., & Fulker, D. (1990). Individual differences in television viewing in early childhood: Nature as well as nurture. *Psychological Science, 1,* 371–377. (1)

Ploner, M., Gross, J., Timmerman, L., & Schnitzler, A. (2006). Pain processing is faster than tactile processing in the human brain. *Journal of Neuroscience, 26,* 10879–10882. (7)

Pol, H. E. H., Schnack, H. G., Posthuma, D., Mandl, R. C. W., Baaré, W. F., van Oel, C., et al. (2006). Genetic contributions to human brain morphology and intelligence. *Journal of Neuroscience, 26,* 10235–10242. (4)

Poldrack, R. A., Sabb, F. W., Foerde, K., Tom, S. M., Asarnow, R. F., Bookheimer, S. Y., et al. (2005). The neural correlates of motor skill automaticity. *Journal of Neuroscience, 25,* 5356–5364. (8)

Poling, A., Schlinger, H., & Blakely, E. (1988). Failure of the partial inverse benzodiazepine agonist Ro15-4513 to block the lethal effects of ethanol in rats. *Pharmacology, 31,* 945–947. (12)

Polley, D. B., Kvašňák, E., & Frostig, R. D. (2004). Naturalistic experience transforms sensory maps in the adult cortex of caged animals. *Nature, 429,* 67–71. (5)

Poltorak, M., Wright, R., Hemperly, J. J., Torrey, E. F., Issa, F., Wyatt, R. J., et al. (1997). Monozygotic twins discordant for schizophrenia are discordant for N-CAM and L1 in CSF. *Brain Research, 751,* 152–154. (5)

Poncer, J. C., & Malinow, R. (2001). Postsynaptic conversion of silent synapses during LTP affects synaptic gain and transmission dynamics. *Nature Neuroscience, 4,* 989–996. (13)

Pons, T. P., Garraghty, P. E., Ommaya, A. K., Kaas, J. H., Taub, E., & Mishkin, M. (1991). Massive cortical reorganization after sensory deafferentation in adult macaques. *Science, 252,* 1857–1860. (5)

Pontieri, F. E., Tanda, G., Orzi, F., & DiChiara, G. (1996). Effects of nicotine on the nucleus accumbens and similarity to those of addictive drugs. *Nature, 382,* 255–257. (3)

Poo, M.-m. (2001). Neurotrophins as synaptic modulators. *Nature Reviews Neuroscience, 2,* 24–32. (5)

Pope, H. G., Jr., Gruber, A. J., Hudson, J. I., Huestis, M. A., & Yurgelun-Todd, D. (2001). Neuropsychological performance in long-term cannabis users. *Archives of General Psychiatry, 58,* 909–915. (3)

Poremba, A., Saunders, R. C., Crane, A. M., Cook, M., Sokoloff, L., & Mishkin, M. (2003). Functional mapping of the primate auditory system. *Science, 299,* 568–572. (7)

Porter, J., Craven, B., Khan, R. M., Chang, S.-J., Kang, I., Judkewicz, B., et al. (2007). Mechanisms of scent-tracking in humans. *Nature Neuroscience, 10,* 27–29. (7)

Posner, S. F., Baker, L., Heath, A., & Martin, N. G. (1996). Social contact, social attitudes, and twin similarity. *Behavior Genetics, 26,* 123–133. (1)

Post, R. M. (1992). Transduction of psychological stress into the neurobiology of recurrent affective disorder. *American Journal of Psychiatry, 149,* 999–1010. (15)

Posthuma, D., De Geus, E. J. C., Baaré, W. F. C., Pol, H. E. H., Kahn, R. S., & Boomsma, D. I. (2002). The association between brain volume and intelligence is of genetic origin. *Nature Neuroscience, 5,* 83–84. (4)

Potegal, M. (1994). Aggressive arousal: The amygdala connection. In M. Potegal & J. F. Knutson (Eds.), *The dynamics of aggression* (pp. 73–111). Hillsdale, NJ: Erlbaum. (12)

Potegal, M., Ferris, C., Hebert, M., Meyerhoff, J. M., & Skaredoff, L. (1996). Attack priming in female Syrian golden hamsters is associated with a *c-fos* coupled process within the corticomedial amygdala. *Neuroscience, 75,* 869–880. (12)

Potegal, M., Hebert, M., DeCoster, M., & Meyerhoff, J. L. (1996). Brief, high-frequency stimulation of the corticomedial amygdala induces a delayed and prolonged increase of aggressiveness in male Syrian golden hamsters. *Behavioral Neuroscience, 110,* 401–412. (12)

Powell, L. H., Calvin, J. E., III, & Calvin, J. E., Jr. (2007). Effective obesity treatments. *American Psychologist, 62,* 234–246. (10)

Premack, A. J., & Premack, D. (1972). Teaching language to an ape. *Scientific American, 227*(4), 92–99. (14)

Preti, G., Cutler, W. B., Garcia, C. R., Huggins, G. R., & Lawley, H. J. (1986). Human axillary secretions influence women's menstrual cycles: The role of donor extract of females. *Hormones and Behavior, 20,* 474–482. (7)

Price, C. J., Warburton, E. A., Moore, C. J., Frackowiak, R. S. J., & Friston, K. J. (2001). Dynamic diaschisis: Anatomically remote and context-sensitive human brain lesions. *Journal of Cognitive Neuroscience, 13,* 419–429. (5)

Price, M. P., Lewin, G. R., McIlwrath, S. L., Cheng, C., Xie, J., Heppenstall, P. A., et al. (2000). The mammalian sodium channel BNC1 is required for normal touch sensation. *Nature, 407,* 1007–1011. (7)

Prichard, Z., Mackinnon, A., Jorm, A. F., & Easteal, S. (2008). No evidence for interaction between MAOA and childhood adversity for antisocial behavior. *American Journal of Medical Genetics Part B—Neuropsychiatric Genetics, 147B,* 228–232. (12)

Pritchard, T. C., Hamilton, R. B., Morse, J. R., & Norgren, R. (1986). Projections of thalamic gustatory and lingual areas in the monkey, *Macaca fascicularis. Journal of Comparative Neurology, 244,* 213–228. (7)

Pritchard, T. C., Macaluso, D. A., & Eslinger, P. J. (1999). Taste perception in patients with insular cortex lesions. *Behavioral Neuroscience, 113,* 663–671. (7, 14)

Prober, D. A., Rihel, J., Onah, A. A., Sung, R.-J., & Schier, A. F. (2006). Hypocretin/orexin overexpression induces an insomnia-like phenotype in zebrafish. *Journal of Neuroscience, 26,* 13400–13410. (9)

Provine, R. R. (1979). "Wing-flapping" develops in wingless chicks. *Behavioral and Neural Biology, 27,* 233–237. (8)

Provine, R. R. (1981). Wing-flapping develops in chickens made flightless by feather mutations. *Developmental Psychobiology, 14,* 48 B 1–486. (8)

Provine, R. R. (1984). Wing-flapping during development and evolution. *American Scientist, 72,* 448–455. (8)

Provine, R. R. (1986). Yawning as a stereotyped action pattern and releasing stimulus. *Ethology, 72,* 109–122. (8)

Prutkin, J., Duffy, V. B., Etter, L., Fast, K., Gardner, E., Lucchina, L. A., et al. (2000). Genetic variation and inferences about perceived taste intensity in mice and men. *Physiology & Behavior, 69,* 161–173. (7)

Purcell, D. W., Blanchard, R., & Zucker, K. J. (2000). Birth order in a contemporary sample of gay men. *Archives of Sexual Behavior, 29,* 349–356. (11)

Purves, D., & Hadley, R. D. (1985). Changes in the dendritic branching of adult mammalian neurones revealed by repeated imaging *in situ. Nature, 315,* 404–406. (5)

Purves, D., & Lotto, R. B. (2003). *Why we see what we do: An empirical theory of vision.* Sunderland, MA: Sinauer Associates. (6)

Purves, D., Shimpi, A., & Lotto, R. B. (1999). An empirical explanation of the Cornsweet effect. *Journal of Neuroscience, 19,* 8542–8551. (6)

Putilov, A. A., Pinchasov, B. B., & Poljakova, E. Y. (2005). Antidepressant effects of mono- and combined non-drug treatments of seasonal and non-seasonal depression. *Biological Rhythm Research, 36,* 405–421. (15)

Putnam, S. K., Du, J., Sato, S., & Hull, E. M. (2001). Testosterone restoration of copulatory behavior correlates with medial preoptic dopamine release in castrated male rats. *Hormones and Behavior, 39,* 216–224. (11)

Putzar, L., Goerendt, I., Lange, K., Rösler, F., & Röder, B. (2007). Early visual deprivation impairs multisensory interactions in humans. *Nature Neuroscience, 10,* 1243–1245. (6)

Quraishi, S., & Frangou, S. (2002). Neuropsychology of bipolar disorder: A review. *Journal of Affective Disorders, 72,* 209–226. (15)

Rada, P. V., & Hoebel, B. G. (2000). Supraadditive effect of Δ-fenfluramine plus phentermine on extracellular acetylcholine in the nucleus accumbens: Possible mechanism for inhibition of excessive feeding and drug abuse. *Pharmacology Biochemistry and Behavior, 65,* 369–373. (10)

Ragsdale, D. S., McPhee, J. C., Scheuer, T., & Catterall, W. A. (1994). Molecular determinants of state-dependent block of Na^+ channels by local anesthetics. *Science, 265,* 1724–1728. (2)

Rahman, Q., Andersson, D., & Govier, E. (2005). A specific sexual orientation-related difference in navigation strategy. *Behavioral Neuroscience, 119,* 311–316. (4)

Rahman, Q., Kumari, V., & Wilson, G. D. (2003). Sexual orientation-related differences in prepulse inhibition of the human startle response. *Behavioral Neuroscience, 117,* 1096–1102. (11)

Rahman, Q., & Wilson, G. D. (2003). Born gay? The psychobiology of human sexual orientation. *Personality and Individual Differences, 34,* 1337–1382. (11)

Rainnie, D. G., Grunze, H. C. R., McCarley, R. W., & Greene, R. W. (1994). Adenosine inhibition of mesopontine cholinergic neurons: Implications for EEG arousal. *Science, 263,* 689–692. (9)

Rainville, P., Duncan, G. H., Price, D. D., Carrier, B., & Bushnell, M. C. (1997). Pain affect encoded in human anterior cingulate but not somatosensory cortex. *Science, 277,* 968–971. (7)

Rais, M., Cahn, W., Van Haren, N., Schnack, H., Caspers, E., Hulshoff, H., et al. (2008). Excessive brain volume loss over time in cannabis-using first-episode schizophrenia patients. *American Journal of Psychiatry, 165,* 490–496. (15)

Rajkowska, G., Selemon, L. D., & Goldman-Rakic, P. S. (1998). Neuronal and glial somal size in the prefrontal cortex. *Archives of General Psychiatry, 55,* 215–224. (15)

Rakic, P. (1998). Cortical development and evolution. In M. S. Gazzaniga & J. S. Altman (Eds.), *Brain and mind: Evolutionary perspectives* (pp. 34–40). Strasbourg, France: Human Frontier Science Program. (5)

Rakic, P., & Lidow, M. S. (1995). Distribution and density of monoamine receptors in the primate visual cortex devoid of retinal input from early embryonic stages. *Journal of Neuroscience, 15,* 2561–2574. (6)

Ralph, M. R., Foster, R. G., Davis, F. C., & Menaker, M. (1990). Transplanted suprachiasmatic nucleus determines circadian period. *Science, 247,* 975–978. (9)

Ralph, M. R., & Menaker, M. (1988). A mutation of the circadian system in golden hamsters. *Science, 241,* 1225–1227. (9)

Ramachandran, V. S. (2003, May). Hearing colors, tasting shapes. *Scientific American, 288*(5), 52–59. (7)

Ramachandran, V. S., & Blakeslee, S. (1998). *Phantoms in the brain.* New York: Morrow. (5)

Ramachandran, V. S., & Hirstein, W. (1998). The perception of phantom limbs: The D. O. Hebb lecture. *Brain, 121,* 1603–1630. (5)

Ramirez, J. J. (2001). The role of axonal sprouting in functional reorganization after CNS injury: Lessons from the hippocampal formation. *Restorative Neurology and Neuroscience, 19,* 237–262. (5)

Ramirez, J. J., Bulsara, K. R., Moore, S. C., Ruch, K., & Abrams, W. (1999). Progressive unilateral damage of the entorhinal cortex enhances synaptic efficacy of the crossed entorhinal afferent to dentate granule cells. *Journal of Neuroscience, 19*: RC42, 1–6. (5)

Ramirez, J. J., McQuilkin, M., Carrigan, T., MacDonald, K., & Kelley, M. S. (1996). Progressive entorhinal cortex lesions accelerate hippocampal sprouting and spare spatial memory in rats. *Proceedings of the National Academy of Sciences, USA, 93,* 15512–15517. (5)

Ramirez-Amaya, V., Marrone, D. F., Gage, F. H., Worley, P. F., & Barnes, C. A. (2006). Integration of new neurons into functional neural networks. *Journal of Neuroscience, 26,* 12237–12241. (5)

Ramón y Cajal, S. (1937). Recollections of my life. *Memoirs of the American Philosophical Society, 8,* Pts. 1 and 2. (2)

Ranson, S. W., & Clark, S. L. (1959). *The anatomy of the nervous system: Its development and function* (10th ed.). Philadelphia: Saunders. (4)

Rapoport, J. L., Giedd, J. N., Blumenthal, J., Hamburger, S., Jeffries, N., Fernandez, T., et al. (1999). Progressive cortical change during adolescence in childhood-onset schizophrenia. *Archives of General Psychiatry, 56,* 649–654. (15)

Rapoport, S. I., & Bosetti, F. (2002). Do lithium and anticonvulsants target the brain arachidonic acid cascade in bipolar patients? *Archives of General Psychiatry, 59,* 592–596. (15)

Rapoport, S. I., & Robinson, P. J. (1986). Tight-junctional modification as the basis of osmotic opening of the blood-brain barrier. *Annals of the New York Academy of Sciences, 481,* 250–267. (2)

Rasch, B., Büchel, C., Gais, S., & Born, J. (2007). Odor cues during slow-wave sleep prompt declarative memory consolidation. *Science, 315,* 1426–1429. (9)

Rattenborg, N. C., Amlaner, C. J., & Lima, S. L. (2000). Behavioral, neurophysiological and evolutionary perspectives on unihemispheric sleep. *Neuroscience and Biobehavioral Reviews, 24,* 817–842. (9)

Rattenborg, N. C., Mandt, B. H., Obermeyer, W. H., Winsauer, P. J., Huber, R., Wikelski, M., et al. (2004). Migratory sleeplessness in the white-crowned sparrow (*Zonotrichia leucophrys gambelii*). *PLOS Biology, 2,* 924–936. (9)

Raum, W. J., McGivern, R. F., Peterson, M. A., Shryne, J. H., & Gorski, R. A. (1990). Prenatal inhibition of hypothalamic sex steroid uptake by cocaine: Effects on neurobehavioral sexual differentiation in male rats. *Developmental Brain Research, 53,* 230–236. (11)

Rawashdeh, O., Hernandez de Borsetti, N., & Cahill, G. M. (2007). Melatonin suppresses nighttime memory formation in zebrafish. *Science, 218,* 1144–1146. (9)

Rayner, K., & Johnson, R. L. (2005). Letter-by-letter acquired dyslexia is due to the serial encoding of letters. *Psychological Science, 16,* 530–534. (14)

Redmond, D. E., Jr., Bjugstad, K. B., Teng, Y. D., Ourednik, V., Ourednik, J., Wakeman, D. R., et al. (2007). Behavioral improvement in a primate Parkinson's model is associated with multiple homeostatic effects of human neural stem cells. *Proceedings of the National Academy of Sciences, USA, 104,* 12175–12180. (8)

Reeves, A. G., & Plum, F. (1969). Hyperphagia, rage, and dementia accompanying a ventromedial hypothalamic neoplasm. *Archives of Neurology, 20,* 616–624. (10)

Refinetti, R. (2000). *Circadian physiology.* Boca Raton, FL: CRC Press. (9)

Refinetti, R., & Carlisle, H. J. (1986). Complementary nature of heat production and heat intake during behavioral thermoregulation in the rat. *Behavioral and Neural Biology, 46,* 64–70. (10)

Refinetti, R., & Menaker, M. (1992). The circadian rhythm of body temperature. *Physiology & Behavior, 51,* 613–637. (9)

Regan, T. (1986). The rights of humans and other animals. *Acta Physiologica Scandinavica, 128*(Suppl. 554), 33–40. (1)

Reichelt, K. L., Seim, A. R., & Reichelt, W. H. (1996). Could schizophrenia be reasonably explained by Dohan's hypothesis on genetic interaction with a dietary peptide overload? *Progress in Neuro-Psychopharmacology & Biological Psychiatry, 20,* 1083–1114. (15)

Reichling, D. B., Kwiat, G. C., & Basbaum, A. I. (1988). Anatomy, physiology, and pharmacology of the periaqueductal gray contribution to antinociceptive controls. In H. L. Fields & J.-M. Besson (Eds.), *Progress in brain research* (Vol. 77, pp. 31–46). Amsterdam: Elsevier. (7)

Reick, M., Garcia, J. A., Dudley, C., & McKnight, S. L. (2001). NPAS2: An analog of clock operative in the mammalian forebrain. *Science, 293,* 506–509. (9)

Reid, C. A., Dixon, D. B., Takahashi, M., Bliss, T. V. P., & Fine, A. (2004). Optical quantal analysis indicates that long-term potentiation at single hippocampal mossy fiber synapses is expressed through increased release probability, recruitment of new release sites, and activation of silent synapses. *Journal of Neuroscience, 24,* 3618–3626. (13)

Reijmers, L. G., Perkins, B. L., Matsuo, N., & Mayford, M. (2007). Localization of a stable neural correlate of associative memory. *Science, 317,* 1230–1233. (13)

Reiner, W. G., & Gearhart, J. P. (2004). Discordant sexual identity in some genetic males with cloacal exstrophy assigned to female sex at birth. *New England Journal of Medicine, 350,* 333–341. (11)

Reiss, A. L., Eckert, M. A., Rose, F. E., Karchemskiy, A., Kesler, S., Chang, M., et al. (2004). An experiment of nature: Brain anatomy parallels cognition and behavior in Williams syndrome. *Journal of Neuroscience, 24,* 5009–5015. (14)

Reiter, R. J. (2000). Melatonin: Lowering the high price of free radicals. *News in Physiological Sciences, 15,* 246–250. (9)

Remondes, M., & Schuman, E. M. (2004). Role for a cortical input to hippocampal area CA1 in the consolidation of a long-term memory. *Nature, 41,* 699–703. (13)

Reneman, L., de Win, M. M. L., van den Brink, W., Booij, J., & den Heeten, G. J. (2006). Neuroimaging findings with MDMA/ecstasy: Technical aspects, conceptual issues and future prospects. *Journal of Psychopharmacology, 20,* 164–175. (3)

Rennaker, R. L., Chen, C.-F. F., Ruyle, A. M., Sloan, A. M., & Wilson, D. A. (2007). Spatial and temporal distribution of odorant-evoked activity in the piriform cortex. *Journal of Neuroscience, 27,* 1534–1542. (7)

Rensink, R. A., O'Regan, J. K., & Clark, J. J. (1997). To see or not to see: The need for attention to perceive changes in scenes. *Psychological Science, 8,* 368–373. (14)

Rétey, J. V., Adam, M., Gottselig, J. M., Khatami, R., Dürr, R., Achermann, P., et al. (2006). Adenosinergic mechanisms contribute to individual differences in sleep deprivation-induced changes in neurobehavioral function and brain rhythmic activity. *Journal of Neuroscience, 26,* 10472–10479. (9)

Reuter-Lorenz, P., & Davidson, R. J. (1981). Differential contributions of the two cerebral hemispheres to the perception of happy and sad faces. *Neuropsychologia, 19,* 609–613. (12)

Reuter-Lorenz, P. A., & Miller, A. C. (1998). The cognitive neuroscience of human laterality: Lessons from the bisected brain. *Current Directions in Psychological Science, 7,* 15–20. (14)

Reynolds, S. M., & Berridge, K. C. (2008). Emotional environments retune the valence of appetitive versus fearful functions in nucleus accumbens. *Nature Neuroscience, 11,* 423–425. (12)

Rhee, S. H., & Waldman, I. D. (2002). Genetic and environmental influences on antisocial behavior: A meta-analysis of twin and adoption studies. *Psychological Bulletin, 128,* 490–529. (12)

Rhees, R. W., Shryne, J. E., & Gorski, R. A. (1990). Onset of the hormone-sensitive perinatal period for sexual differentiation of the sexually dimorphic nucleus of the preoptic area in female rats. *Journal of Neurobiology, 21,* 781–786. (11)

Rhodes, J. S., van Praag, H., Jeffrey, S., Girard, I., Mitchell, G. S., Garland, T., Jr., et al. (2003). Exercise increases hippocampal neurogenesis to high levels but does not improve spatial learning in mice bred for increased voluntary wheel running. *Behavioral Neuroscience, 117,* 1006–1016. (5)

Rhodes, R. A., Murthy, N. V., Dresner, M. A., Selvaraj, S., Stavrakakis, N., Babar, S., et al. (2007). Human 5-HT transporter availability predicts amygdala reactivity *in vivo*. *Journal of Neuroscience, 27,* 9233–9237. (12)

Rice, G., Anderson, C., Risch, N., & Ebers, G. (1999). Male homosexuality: Absence of linkage to microsatellite markers at Xq28. *Science, 284,* 665–667. (11)

Richard, C., Honoré, J., Bernati, T., & Rousseaux, M. (2004). Straight-ahead pointing correlates with long-line bisection in neglect patients. *Cortex, 40,* 75–83. (14)

Richter, C. P. (1922). A behavioristic study of the activity of the rat. *Comparative Psychology Monographs, 1,* 1–55. (9)

Richter, C. P. (1936). Increased salt appetite in adrenalectomized rats. *American Journal of Physiology, 115,* 155–161. (10)

Richter, C. P. (1950). Taste and solubility of toxic compounds in poisoning of rats and humans. *Journal of Comparative and Physiological Psychology, 43,* 358–374. (7)

Richter, C. P. (1967). Psychopathology of periodic behavior in animals and man. In J. Zubin & H. F. Hunt (Eds.), *Comparative psychopathology* (pp. 205–227). New York: Grune & Stratton. (9)

Richter, C. P. (1975). Deep hypothermia and its effect on the 24-hour clock of rats and hamsters. *Johns Hopkins Medical Journal, 136,* 1–10. (9)

Richter, C. P., & Langworthy, O. R. (1933). The quill mechanism of the porcupine. *Journal für Psychologie und Neurologie, 45,* 143–153. (4)

Ridding, M. C., & Rothwell, J. C. (2007). Is there a future for therapeutic use of transcranial magnetic stimulation? *Nature Reviews Neuroscience, 8,* 559–567. (15)

Riddle, W. J. R., & Scott, A. I. F. (1995). Relapse after successful electroconvulsive therapy: The use and impact of continuation antidepressant drug treatment. *Human Psychopharmacology, 10,* 201–205. (15)

Riemann, D., König, A., Hohagen, F., Kiemen, A., Voderholzer, U., Backhaus, J., et al. (1999). How to preserve the antidepressive effect of sleep deprivation: A comparison of sleep phase advance and sleep phase delay. *European Archives of Psychiatry and Clinical Neuroscience, 249,* 231–237. (15)

Rilling, J. K., Glasser, M. F., Preuss, T. M., Ma, X., Zhao, T., Hu, X., et al. (2008). The evolution of the arcuate fasciculus revealed with comparative DTI. *Nature Neuroscience, 11,* 426–428. (14)

Ringel, B. L., & Szuba, M. P. (2001). Potential mechanisms of the sleep therapies for depression. *Depression and Anxiety, 14,* 29–36. (15)

Rinn, W. E. (1984). The neuropsychology of facial expression: A review of the neurological and psychological mechanisms for producing facial expressions. *Psychological Bulletin, 95,* 52–77. (8)

Rittenhouse, C. D., Shouval, H. Z., Paradiso, M. A., & Bear, M. F. (1999). Monocular deprivation induces homosynaptic long-term depression in visual cortex. *Nature, 397,* 347–350. (6)

Ritz, B., Ascherio, A., Checkoway, H., Marder, K. S., Nelson, L. M., Rocca, W. A., et al. (2007). Pooled analysis of tobacco use and risk of Parkinson's disease. *Archives of Neurology, 64,* 990–997. (8)

Ro, T., Shelton, D., Lee, O.L., & Chang, E. (2004). Extrageniculate mediation of unconscious vision in transcranial magnetic stimulation-induced blindsight. *Proceedings of the National Academy of Sciences, USA, 101,* 9933–9935. (6)

Roach, N. W., & Hogben, J. H. (2004). Attentional modulation of visual processing in adult dyslexia. *Psychological Science, 15,* 650–654. (14)

Robbins, T. W., & Everitt, B. J. (1995). Arousal systems and attention. In M. S. Gazzaniga (Ed.), *The cognitive neurosciences* (pp. 703–720). Cambridge, MA: MIT Press. (9)

Roberson, E. D., & Mucke, E. (2006). 100 years and counting: Prospects for defeating Alzheimer's disease. *Science, 314,* 781–784. (13)

Roberson, E. D., Scearce-Levie, K., Palop, J. J., Yan, F., Cheng, I. H., Wu, T., et al. (2007). Reducing endogenous tau ameliorates amyloid-β-induced deficits in an Alzheimer's disease mouse model. *Science, 316,* 750–754. (13)

Robertson, I. H. (2005, Winter). The deceptive world of subjective awareness. *Cerebrum, 7*(1), 74–83. (4)

Robertson, L. C. (2003). Binding, spatial attention and perceptual awareness. *Nature Reviews Neuroscience, 4,* 93–102. (4)

Robertson, L., Treisman, A., Friedman-Hill, S., & Grabowecky, M. (1997). The interaction of spatial and object pathways: Evidence from Balint's syndrome. *Journal of Cognitive Neuropsychology, 9,* 295–317. (4)

Robillard, T. A. J., & Gersdorff, M. C. H. (1986). Prevention of pre- and perinatal acquired hearing defects: Part I. Study of causes. *Journal of Auditory Research, 26,* 207–237. (7)

Robinson, T. E., & Berridge, K. C. (2001). Incentive-sensitization and addiction. *Addiction, 96,* 103–114. (3)

Robleto, K., & Thompson, R. F. (2008). Extinction of a classically conditioned response: Red nucleus and interpositus. *Journal of Neuroscience, 28,* 2651–2658. (13)

Rocha, B. A., Fumagalli, F., Gainetdinov, R. R., Jones, S. R., Ator, R., Giros, B., et al. (1998). Cocaine self-administration in dopamine-transporter knockout mice. *Nature Neuroscience, 1,* 132–137. (3)

Rochira, V., Balestrieri, A., Madeo, B., Baraldi, E., Faustini-Fustini, M., Granata, A. R. M., et al. (2001). Congenital estrogen deficiency: In search of the estrogen role in human male reproduction. *Molecular and Cellular Endocrinology, 178,* 107–115. (11)

Rodriguez, I., Greer, C. A., Mok, M. Y., & Mombaerts, P. A. (2000). A putative pheromone receptor gene expressed in human olfactory mucosa. *Nature Genetics, 26,* 18–19. (7)

Roelfsema, P. R., Engel, A. K., König, P., & Singer, W. (1997). Visuomotor integration is associated with zero time-lag synchronization among cortical areas. *Nature, 385,* 157–161. (14)

Roelfsema, P. R., Lamme, V. A. F., & Spekreijse, H. (2004). Synchrony and variation of firing rates in the primary visual cortex during contour grouping. *Nature Neuroscience, 7,* 982–991. (14)

Roenneberg, T., Kuehnle, T., Pramstaller, P. P., Ricken, J., Havel, M., Ricken, J., et al. (2004). A marker for the end of adolescence. *Current Biology, 14,* R1038–R1039. (9)

Roenneberg, T., Kumar, C. J., & Merrow, M. (2007). The human circadian clock entrains to sun time. *Current Biology, 17,* R44–R45. (9)

Roesch, M. R., & Olson, C. R. (2004). Neuronal activity related to reward value and motivation in primate frontal cortex. *Science, 304,* 307–310. (13)

Roffwarg, H. P., Muzio, J. N., & Dement, W. C. (1966). Ontogenetic development of human sleep-dream cycle. *Science, 152,* 604–609. (9)

Rolls, E. T. (1995). Central taste anatomy and neurophysiology. In R. L. Doty (Ed.), *Handbook of olfaction and gustation* (pp. 549–573). New York: Dekker. (7)

Rolls, E. T. (1996) The representation of space in the primate hippocampus, and its relation to memory. In K. Ishikawa, J. L. McGaugh, & H. Sakata (Eds.), *Brain processes and memory* (pp. 203–227). Amsterdam: Elsevier. (13)

Rome, L. C., Loughna, P. T., & Goldspink, G. (1984). Muscle fiber activity in carp as a function of swimming speed and muscle temperature. *American Journal of Psychiatry, 247,* R272–R279. (8)

Romer, A. S. (1962). *The vertebrate body.* Philadelphia: Saunders. (5)

Romero, E., Cha, G.-H., Verstreken, P., Ly, C. V., Hughes, R. E., Bellen, H. J., et al. (2007). Suppression of neurodegeneration and increased neurotransmission caused by expanded full-length huntingtin accumulating in the cytoplasm. *Neuron, 57,* 27–40. (8)

Rommel, S. A., Pabst, D. A., & McLellan, W. A. (1998). Reproductive thermoregulation in marine mammals. *American Scientist, 86,* 440–448. (10)

Roorda, A., & Williams, D. R. (1999). The arrangement of the three cone classes in the living human eye. *Nature, 397,* 520–522. (6)

Roppel, R. M. (1978). Cancer and mental illness. *Science, 201,* 398. (15)

Rose, J. E., Brugge, J. F., Anderson, D. J., & Hind, J. E. (1967). Phase-locked response to low-frequency tones in single auditory nerve fibers of the squirrel monkey. *Journal of Neurophysiology, 30,* 769–793. (7)

Roselli, C. E., Larkin, K., Resko, J. A., Stellflug, J. N., & Stormshak, F. (2004). The volume of a sexually dimorphic nucleus in the ovine medial preoptic area/anterior hypothalamus varies with sexual partner preference. *Endocrinology, 145,* 478–483. (11)

Roselli, C. E., Stadelman, H., Reeve, R., Bishop, C. V., & Stormshak, F. (2007). The ovine sexually dimorphic nucleus of the medial preoptic area is organized prenatally by testosterone. *Endocrinology, 148,* 4450–4457. (11)

Rosen, A. C., Prull, M. W., O-Hara, R., Race, E. A., Desmond, J. E., Glover, G. H., et al. (2002). Variable effects of aging on frontal lobe contributions to memory. *NeuroReport, 13,* 2425–2428. (13)

Rosen, H. J., Perry, R. J., Murphy, J., Kramer, J. H., Mychack, P., Schuff, N., et al. (2002). Emotion comprehension in the temporal variant of frontotemporal dementia. *Brain, 125,* 2286–2295. (12)

Rosenbaum, R. S., Köhler, S., Schacter, D. L., Moscovitch, M., Westmacott, R., Black, S. E., et al. (2005). The case of K. C.: Contributions of a memory-impaired person to memory theory. *Neuropsychologia, 43,* 989–1021. (13)

Rosenblatt, J. S. (1967). Nonhormonal basis of maternal behavior in the rat. *Science, 156,* 1512–1514. (11)

Rosenblatt, J. S. (1970). Views on the onset and maintenance of maternal behavior in the rat. In L. R. Aronson, E. Tobach, D. S. Lehrman, & J. S. Rosenblatt (Eds.), *Development and evolution of behavior* (pp. 489–515). San Francisco: Freeman. (11)

Rosenblatt, J. S., Olufowobi, A., & Siegel, H. I. (1998). Effects of pregnancy hormones on maternal responsiveness, responsiveness to estrogen stimulation of maternal behavior, and the lordosis response to estrogen stimulation. *Hormones and Behavior, 33,* 104–114. (11)

Rosenzweig, E. S., Redish, A. D., McNaughton, B. L., & Barnes, C. A. (2003). Hippocampal map realignment and spatial learning. *Nature Neuroscience, 6,* 609–615. (13)

Rosenzweig, M. R., & Bennett, E. L. (1996). Psychobiology of plasticity: Effects of training and experience on brain and behavior. *Behavioural Brain Research, 78,* 57–65. (5)

Rösler, A., & Witztum, E. (1998). Treatment of men with paraphilia with a long-acting analogue of gonadotropin-releasing hormone. *New England Journal of Medicine, 338,* 416–422. (11)

Ross, D., Choi, J., & Purves, D. (2007). Musical intervals in speech. *Proceedings of the National Academy of Sciences, USA, 104,* 9852–9857. (14)

Ross, E. D., Homan, R. W., & Buck, R. (1994). Differential hemispheric lateralization of primary and social emotions. *Neuropsychiatry, Neuropsychology, and Behavioral Neurology, 7,* 1–19. (12)

Rossi, A. F., Bichot, N. P., Desimone, R., & Ungerleider, L. G. (2007). Top-down attentional deficits in macaques with lesions of lateral prefrontal cortex. *Journal of Neuroscience, 27,* 11306–11314. (14)

Rossi, D. J., Brady, J. D., & Mohr, C. (2007). Astrocyte metabolism and signaling during brain ischemia. *Nature Neuroscience, 11,* 1377–1386. (5)

Rossi, D. J., Oshima, T., & Attwell, D. (2000). Glutamate release in severe brain ischaemia is mainly by reversed uptake. *Nature, 403,* 316–321. (5)

Rossi, S., Miniussi, C., Pasqualetti, P., Babiloni, C., Rossini, P. M., & Cappa, S. F. (2004). Age-related functional changes of prefrontal cortex in long-term memory: A repetitive transcranial magnetic stimulation study. *Journal of Neuroscience, 24,* 7939–7944. (13)

Rosvold, H. E., Mirsky, A. F., & Pribram, K. H. (1954). Influence of amygdalectomy on social behavior in monkeys. *Journal of Comparative and Physiological Psychology, 47,* 173–178. (12)

Roth, B. L., Willins, D. L., Kristiansen, K., & Kroeze, W. K. (1999). Activation is hallucinogenic and antagonism is therapeutic: Role of 5-HT_{2A} receptors in atypical antipsychotic drug actions. *Neuroscientist, 5,* 254–262. (15)

Rottenberg, J., Kasch, K. L., Gross, J. J., & Gotlib, I. H. (2002). Sadness and amusement reactivity differentially predict concurrent and prospective functioning in major depressive disorder. *Emotion, 2,* 135–146. (15)

Routtenberg, A., Cantallops, I., Zaffuto, S., Serrano, P., & Namgung, U. (2000). Enhanced learning after genetic overexpression of a brain growth protein. *Proceedings of the National Academy of Sciences, USA, 97,* 7657–7662. (13)

Rouw, R., & Scholte, H. S. (2007). Increased structural connectivity in grapheme-color synesthesia. *Nature Neuroscience, 10,* 792–797. (7)

Rovainen, C. M. (1976). Regeneration of Müller and Mauthner axons after spinal transection in larval lampreys. *Journal of Comparative Neurology, 168,* 545–554. (5)

Rowland, D. L., & Burnett, A. L. (2000). Pharmacotherapy in the treatment of male sexual dysfunction. *Journal of Sex Research, 37,* 226–243. (11)

Roy, A., DeJong, J., & Linnoila, M. (1989). Cerebrospinal fluid monoamine metabolites and suicidal behavior in depressed patients. *Archives of General Psychiatry, 46,* 609–612. (12)

Royer, S., & Paré, D. (2003). Conservation of total synaptic weight through balanced synaptic depression and potentiation. *Nature, 422,* 518–522. (13)

Rozin, P. (1990). Getting to like the burn of chili pepper. In B. G. Green, J. R. Mason, & M. R. Kare (Eds.), *Chemical senses* (Vol. 2, pp. 231–269). New York: Dekker. (10)

Rozin, P., Dow, S., Moscovitch, M., & Rajaram, S. (1998). What causes humans to begin and end a meal? A role for memory for what has been eaten, as evidenced by a study of multiple meal eating in amnesic patients. *Psychological Science, 9,* 392–396. (13)

Rozin, P., & Kalat, J. W. (1971). Specific hungers and poison avoidance as adaptive specializations of learning. *Psychological Review, 78,* 459–486. (10, 13)

Rozin, P., & Pelchat, M. L. (1988). Memories of mammaries: Adaptations to weaning from milk. *Progress in Psychobiology and Physiological Psychology, 13,* 1–29. (10)

Rozin, P., & Schull, J. (1988). The adaptive-evolutionary point of view in experimental psychology. In R. C. Atkinson, R. J. Herrnstein, G. Lindzey, & R. D. Luce (Eds.), *Stevens' handbook of experimental psychology* (2nd ed.): Vol. 1. *Perception and motivation* (pp. 503–546). New York: Wiley (13)

Rozin, P., & Vollmecke, T. A. (1986). Food likes and dislikes. *Annual Review of Nutrition, 6,* 433–456. (10)

Rozin, P., & Zellner, D. (1985). The role of Pavlovian conditioning in the acquisition of food likes and dislikes. *Annals of the New York Academy of Sciences, 443,* 189–202. (10)

Rubens, A. B., & Benson, D. F. (1971). Associative visual agnosia. *Archives of Neurology, 24,* 305–316. (6)

Rubin, B. D., & Katz, L. C. (2001). Spatial coding of enantiomers in the rat olfactory bulb. *Nature Neuroscience, 4,* 355–356. (7)

Rubinow, M. J., Arseneau, L. M., Beverly, J. L., & Juraska, J. M. (2004). Effect of the estrous cycle on water maze acquisition depends on the temperature of the water. *Behavioral Neuroscience, 118,* 863–868. (10)

Rubinstein, G. (1997). Schizophrenia, rheumatoid arthritis and natural resistance genes. *Schizophrenia Research, 25,* 177–181. (15)

Ruby, N. F., Brennan, T. J., Xie, X., Cao, V., Franken, P., Heller, H. C., et al. (2002). Role of melanopsin in circadian responses to light. *Science, 298,* 2211–2213. (9)

Rudolph, U., Crestani, F., Benke, D., Brünig, I., Benson, J. A., Fritschy, J.-M., et al. (1999). Benzodiazepine actions mediated by specific γ-aminobutyric acidA receptor subtypes. *Nature, 401,* 796–800. (12)

Rujescu, D., Giegling, I., Bondy, B., Gietl, A., Zill, P., & Möller, H.-J. (2002). Association of anger-related traits with SNPs in the TPH gene. *Molecular Psychiatry, 7,* 1023–1029. (12)

Rumbaugh, D. M. (Ed.). (1977). *Language learning by a chimpanzee: The Lana Project.* New York: Academic Press. (14)

Rumbaugh, D. M. (1990). Comparative psychology and the great apes: Their competency in learning, language, and numbers. *Psychological Record, 40,* 15–39. (14)

Rupprecht, R., di Michele, F., Hermann, B., Ströhle, A., Lancel, M., Romeo, E., et al. (2001). Neuroactive steroids: Molecular mechanisms of action and implications for neuropsychopharmacology. *Brain Research Reviews, 37,* 59–67. (11)

Rusak, B., & Zucker, I. (1979). Neural regulation of circadian rhythms. *Physiological Reviews, 59,* 449–526. (9)

Rush, A. J., Trivedi, M. H., Wisniewski, S. R., Stewart, J. W., Nierenberg, A. A., Thase, M. E., et al. (2006). Bupropion-SR, sertraline, or venlaxine-XR after failure of SSRIs for depression. *New England Journal of Medicine, 354,* 1231–1242. (15)

Rushworth, M. F. S., & Behrens, T. E. J. (2008). Choice, uncertainty and value in prefrontal and cingulate cortex. *Nature Neuroscience, 11,* 389–397. (13)

Russell, A. J., Munro, J. C., Jones, P. B., Hemsley, D. R., & Murray, R. M. (1997). Schizophrenia and the myth of intellectual decline. *American Journal of Psychiatry, 154,* 635–639. (15)

Russell, M. J., Switz, G. M., & Thompson, K. (1980). Olfactory influences on the human menstrual cycle. *Pharmacology, Biochemistry, and Behavior, 13,* 737–738. (7)

Rutter, M., Pickles, A., Murray, R., & Eaves, L. (2001). Testing hypotheses on specific environmental causal effects on behavior. *Psychological Bulletin, 127,* 291–324. (1)

Rüttiger, L., Braun, D. I., Gegenfurtner, K. R., Petersen, D., Schönle, P., & Sharpe, L. T. (1999). Selective color constancy deficits after circumscribed unilateral brain lesions. *Journal of Neuroscience, 19,* 3094–3106. (6)

Saad, W. A., Luiz, A. C., Camargo, L. A. A., Renzi, A., & Manani, J. V. (1996). The lateral preoptic area plays a dual role in the regulation of thirst in the rat. *Brain Research Bulletin, 39,* 171–176. (10)

Sabel, B. A. (1997). Unrecognized potential of surviving neurons: Within-systems plasticity, recovery of function, and the hypothesis of minimal residual structure. *The Neuroscientist, 3,* 366–370. (5)

Sabo, K. T., & Kirtley, D. D. (1982). Objects and activities in the dreams of the blind. *International Journal of Rehabilitation Research, 5,* 241–242. (4)

Sack, R. L., & Lewy, A. J. (2001). Circadian rhythm sleep disorders: Lessons from the blind. *Sleep Medicine Reviews, 5,* 189–206. (9)

Sackeim, H. A., Putz, E., Vingiano, W., Coleman, E., & McElhiney, M. (1988). Lateralization in the processing of emotionally laden information: I. Normal functioning. *Neuropsychiatry, Neuropsychology, and Behavioral Neurology, 1,* 97–110. (14)

Sadato, N., Pascual-Leone, A., Grafman, J., Deiber, M.-P., Ibañez, V., & Hallett, M. (1998). Neural networks for Braille reading by the blind. *Brain, 121,* 1213–1229. (5)

Sadato, N., Pascual-Leone, A., Grafman, J., Ibañez, V., Deiber, M.-P., Dold, G., et al. (1996). Activation of the primary visual cortex by Braille reading in blind subjects. *Nature, 380,* 526–528. (5)

Saha, S., Chant, D., & McGrath, J. (2007). A systematic review of mortality in schizophrenia. *Archives of General Psychiatry, 64,* 1123–1131. (15)

Sakai, K., Rowe, J. B., & Passingham, R. E. (2002). Active maintenance in prefrontal area 46 creates distractor-resistant memory. *Nature Neuroscience, 5,* 479–484. (13)

Sakurai, T. (2007). The neural circuit of orexin (hypocretin): Maintaining sleep and wakefulness. *Nature Reviews Neuroscience, 8,* 171–181. (9)

Sale, A., Vetencourt, J. F. M., Medini, P., Cenni, M. C., Baroncelli, L., DePasquale, R., et al. (2007). Environmental enrichment in adulthood promotes amblyopia recovery through a reduction of intracortical inhibition. *Nature Neuroscience, 10,* 679–681. (6)

Salmelin, R., Hari, R., Lounasmaa, O. V., & Sams, M. (1994). Dynamics of brain activation during picture naming. *Nature, 368,* 463–465. (4)

Sánchez, I., Mahlke, C., & Yuan, J. (2003). Pivotal role of oligomerization in expanded polyglutamine neurodegenerative disorders. *Nature, 421,* 373–379. (8)

Sander, K., & Scheich, H. (2001). Auditory perception of laughing and crying activates human amygdala regardless of attentional state. *Cognitive Brain Research, 12,* 181–198. (12)

Sanders, A. R., Duan, J., Levinson, D. F., Shi, J., He, D., Hou, C., et al. (2008). No significant association of 14 candidate genes with schizophrenia in a large European ancestry sample: Implications for psychiatric genetics. *American Journal of Psychiatry, 165,* 497–506. (15)

Sanders, S. K., & Shekhar, A. (1995). Anxiolytic effects of chlordiazepoxide blocked by injection of $GABA_A$ and benzodiazepine receptor antagonists in the region of the anterior basolateral amygdala of rats. *Biological Psychiatry, 37,* 473–476. (12)

Sanes, J. N., Donoghue, J. P., Thangaraj, V., Edelman, R. R., & Warach, S. (1995). Shared neural substrates controlling hand movements in human motor cortex. *Science, 268,* 1775–1777. (8)

Sanes, J. R. (1993). Topographic maps and molecular gradients. *Current Opinion in Neurobiology, 3,* 67–74. (5)

Sanger, T. D., Pascual-Leone, A., Tarsy, D., & Schlaug, G. (2001). Nonlinear sensory cortex response to simultaneous tactile stimuli in writer's cramp. *Movement Disorders, 17,* 105–111. (5)

Sanger, T. D., Tarsy, D., & Pascual-Leone, A. (2001). Abnormalities of spatial and temporal sensory discrimination in writer's cramp. *Movement Disorders, 16,* 94–99. (5)

SantaCruz, K., Lewis, J., Spires, T., Paulson, J., Kotilinek, L., Ingelsson, M., et al. (2005). Tau suppression in a neurodegenerative mouse model improves memory function. *Science, 309,* 476–481. (13)

Sapolsky, R. M. (1992). *Stress, the aging brain, and the mechanisms of neuron death.* Cambridge, MA: MIT Press. (12)

Sapolsky, R. M. (1998). *Why zebras don't get ulcers.* New York: Freeman. (12)

Sáry, G., Vogels, R., & Orban, G. A. (1993). Cue-invariant shape selectivity of macaque inferior temporal neurons. *Science, 260,* 995–997. (6)

Satinoff, E. (1964). Behavioral thermoregulation in response to local cooling of the rat brain. *American Journal of Physiology, 206,* 1389–1394. (10)

Satinoff, E. (1991). Developmental aspects of behavioral and reflexive thermoregulation. In H. N. Shanir, G. A. Barr, & M. A. Hofer (Eds.), *Developmental psychobiology: New methods and changing concepts* (pp. 169–188). New York: Oxford University Press. (10)

Satinoff, E., McEwen, G. N., Jr., & Williams, B. A. (1976). Behavioral fever in newborn rabbits. *Science, 193,* 1139–1140. (10)

Satinoff, E., & Rutstein, J. (1970). Behavioral thermoregulation in rats with anterior hypothalamic lesions. *Journal of Comparative and Physiological Psychology, 71,* 77–82. (10)

Sato, W., Yoshikawa, S., Kochiyama, T., & Matsumura, M. (2004). The amygdala processes the emotional significance of facial expressions: An fMRI investigation using the interaction between expression and face direction. *NeuroImage, 22,* 1006–1013. (12)

Satz, P., & Green, M. F. (1999). Atypical handedness in schizophrenia: Some methodological and theoretical issues. *Schizophrenia Bulletin, 25,* 63–78. (15)

Savage-Rumbaugh, E. S. (1990). Language acquisition in a nonhuman species: Implications for the innateness debate. *Developmental Psychobiology, 23,* 599–620. (14)

Savage-Rumbaugh, E. S., Murphy, J., Sevcik, R. A., Brakke, K. E., Williams, S. L., & Rumbaugh, D. M. (1993). Language comprehension in ape and child. *Monographs of the Society for Research in Child Development, 58*(Serial no. 233). (14)

Savage-Rumbaugh, E. S., Sevcik, R. A., Brakke, K. E., & Rumbaugh, D. M. (1992). Symbols: Their communicative use, communication, and combination by bonobos (*Pan paniscus*). In L. P. Lipsitt & C. Rovee-Collier (Eds.), *Advances in infancy research* (Vol. 7, pp. 221–278). Norwood, NJ: Ablex. (14)

Savic, I., Berglund, H., Gulyas, B., & Roland, P. (2001). Smelling of odorous sex hormone-like compounds causes sex-differentiated hypothalamic activations in humans. *Neuron, 31,* 661–668. (7)

Savic, I., & Lindström, P. (2008). PET and MRI show differences in cerebral asymmetry and functional connectivity between homo- and heterosexual subjects. *Proceedings of the National Academy of Sciences, USA, 105,* 9403–9408. (11)

Sawamoto, N., Honda, M., Hanakawa, T., Fukuyama, H., & Shibasaki, H. (2002). Cognitive slowing in Parkinson's disease: A behavioral evaluation independent of motor slowing. *Journal of Neuroscience, 22,* 5198–5203. (8)

Schacter, D. L. (1983). Amnesia observed: Remembering and forgetting in a natural environment. *Journal of Abnormal Psychology, 92,* 236–242. (13)

Schärli, H., Harman, A. M., & Hogben, J. H. (1999). Blindsight in subjects with homonymous visual field defects. *Journal of Cognitive Neuroscience, 11,* 52–66. (6)

Scheibel, A. B. (1983). Dendritic changes. In B. Reisberg (Ed.), *Alzheimer's disease* (pp. 69–73). New York: Free Press. (13)

Schellenberg, G. D., Bird, T. D., Wijsman, E. M., Orr, H. T., Anderson, L., Nemens, E., et al. (1992). Genetic linkage evidence for a familial Alzheimer's disease locus on chromosome 14. *Science, 258,* 668–671. (13)

Schenck, C. H., & Mahowald, M. W. (1996). Long-term, nightly benzodiazepine treatment of injurious parasomnias and other disorders of disrupted nocturnal sleep in 170 adults. *American Journal of Medicine, 100,* 333–337. (9)

Schenk, T. (2006). An allocentric rather than perceptual deficit in patient D. F. *Nature Neuroscience, 9,* 1369–1370. (6)

Schenk, T., Mai, N., Ditterich, J., & Zihl, J. (2000). Can a motion-blind patient reach for moving objects? *European Journal of Neuroscience, 12,* 3351–3360. (6)

Scherer, S. S. (1986). Reinnervation of the extraocular muscles in goldfish is nonselective. *Journal of Neuroscience, 6,* 764–773. (5)

Schienle, A., Stark, R., Walter, B., Blecker, C., Ott, U., Kirsch, P., et al. (2002). The insula is not specifically involved in disgust processing: An fMRI study. *NeuroReport, 13,* 2023–2026. (12)

Schiff, N. D., Giacino, J. T., Kalmar, K., Victor, J. D., Baker, K., Gerber, M., et al. (2007). Behavioural improvements with thalamic stimulation after severe traumatic brain injury. *Nature, 448,* 600–603. (5)

Schiffman, S. S. (1983). Taste and smell in disease. *New England Journal of Medicine, 308,* 1275–1279, 1337–1343. (7)

Schiffman, S. S., & Erickson, R. P. (1971). A psychophysical model for gustatory quality. *Physiology & Behavior, 7,* 617–633. (7)

Schiffman, S. S., & Erickson, R. P. (1980). The issue of primary tastes versus a taste continuum. *Neuroscience and Biobehavioral Reviews, 4,* 109–117. (7)

Schiffman, S. S., Lockhead, E., & Maes, F. W. (1983). Amiloride reduces the taste intensity of Na^+ and Li^+ salts and sweeteners. *Proceedings of the National Academy of Sciences, USA, 80,* 6136–6140. (7)

Schiffman, S. S., McElroy, A. E., & Erickson, R. P. (1980). The range of taste quality of sodium salts. *Physiology & Behavior, 24,* 217–224. (7)

Schlack, A., Krekelberg, B., & Albright, T. D. (2007). Recent history of stimulus speeds affects the speed tuning of neurons in area MT. *Journal of Neuroscience, 27,* 11009–11018. (6)

Schlinger, H. D., Jr. (1996). How the human got its spots. *Skeptic, 4,* 68–76. (1)

Schmid, A., Koch, M., & Schnitzler, H.-U. (1995). Conditioned pleasure attenuates the startle response in rats. *Neurobiology of Learning and Memory, 64,* 1–3. (12)

Schmidt, L. A. (1999). Frontal brain electrical activity in shyness and sociability. *Psychological Science, 10,* 316–320. (12)

Schmidt-Hieber, C, Jonas, P., & Bischofberger, J. (2004). Enhanced synaptic plasticity in newly generated granule cells of the adult hippocampus. *Nature, 429,* 184–187. (5)

Schneider, B. A., Trehub, S. E., Morrongiello, B. A., & Thorpe, L. A. (1986). Auditory sensitivity in preschool children. *Journal of the Acoustical Society of America, 79,* 447–452. (7)

Schneider, P., Scherg, M., Dosch, G., Specht, H. J., Gutschalk, A., & Rupp, A. (2002). Morphology of Heschl's gyrus reflects enhanced activation in the auditory cortex of musicians. *Nature Neuroscience, 5,* 688–694. (5)

Schnider, A. (2003). Spontaneous confabulation and the adaptation of thought to ongoing reality. *Nature Reviews Neuroscience, 4,* 662–671. (13)

Schooler, C. (2007). Use it—and keep it, longer, probably: A reply to Salthouse (2007). *Perspectives on Psychological Science, 2,* 24–29. (5)

Schou, M. (1997). Forty years of lithium treatment. *Archives of General Psychiatry, 54,* 9–13. (15)

Schroeder, J. A., & Flannery-Schroeder, E. (2005). Use of herb *Gymnema sylvestre* to illustrate the principles of gustatory sensation: An undergraduate neuroscience laboratory exercise. *Journal* of *Undergraduate Neuroscience Education, 3,* A59–A62. (7)

Schuckit, M. A., & Smith, T. L. (1996). An 8-year follow-up of 450 sons of alcoholic and control subjects. *Archives of General Psychiatry, 53,* 202–210. (3)

Schuckit, M. C., & Smith, T. L. (1997). Assessing the risk for alcoholism among sons of alcoholics. *Journal of Studies on Alcohol, 58,* 141–145. (3)

Schulkin, J. (1991). *Sodium hunger: The search for a salty taste.* Cambridge, England: Cambridge University Press. (10)

Schwab, M. E. (1998). Regenerative nerve fiber growth in the adult central nervous system. *News in Physiological Sciences, 13,* 294–298. (5)

Schwartz, C. E., Wright, C. I., Shin, L. M., Kagan, J., & Rauch, S. L. (2003). Inhibited and uninhibited infants "grown up": Adult amygdalar response to novelty. *Science, 300,* 1952–1953. (12)

Schwartz, G. J. (2000). The role of gastrointestinal vagal afferents in the control of food intake: Current prospects. *Nutrition, 16,* 866–873. (10)

Schwartz, L., & Tulipan, L. (1933). An outbreak of dermatitis among workers in a rubber manufacturing plant. *Public Health Reports, 48,* 809–814. (3)

Schwartz, M. F. (1995). Re-examining the role of executive functions in routine action production. *Annals of the New York Academy of Sciences, 769,* 321–335. (8)

Schwartz, W. J., & Gainer, H. (1977). Suprachiasmatic nucleus: Use of 14C-labeled deoxyglucose uptake as a functional marker. *Science, 197,* 1089–1091. (9)

Scott, L. J., Figgitt, D. P., Keam, S. J., & Waugh, J. (2005). Acamprosate: A review of its use in the maintenance of abstinence in patients with alcohol dependence. *CNS Drugs, 19,* 445–464. (3)

Scott, S. H. (2004). Optimal feedback control and the neural basis of volitional motor control. *Nature Reviews Neuroscience, 5,* 532–544. (8)

Scott, T. R., & Verhagen, J. V. (2000). Taste as a factor in the management of nutrition. *Nutrition, 16,* 874–885. (10)

Scott, W. K., Nance, M. A., Watts, R. L., Hubble, J. P., Koller, W. C., Lyons, K., et al. (2001). Complete genomic screen in Parkinson disease. *Journal of the American Medical Association, 286,* 2239–2244. (8)

Scovern, A. W., & Kilmann, P. R. (1980). Status of electroconvulsive therapy: Review of the outcome literature. *Psychological Bulletin, 87,* 260–303. (15)

Scoville, W. B., & Milner, B. (1957). Loss of recent memory after bilateral hippocampal lesions. *Journal of Neurology, Neurosurgery, and Psychiatry, 20,* 11–21. (13)

Searle, J. R. (1992). *The rediscovery of the mind.* Cambridge, MA: MIT Press. (1)

Seeley, R. J., Kaplan, J. M., & Grill, H. J. (1995). Effect of occluding the pylorus on intraoral intake: A test of the gastric hypothesis of meal termination. *Physiology & Behavior, 58,* 245–249. (10)

Seeman, P., Lee, T., Chau-Wong, M., & Wong, K. (1976). Antipsychotic drug doses and neuroleptic/dopamine receptors. *Nature, 261,* 717–719. (15)

Segerstrom, S. C., & Miller, G. E. (2004). Psychological stress and the human immune system: A meta-analytic study of 30 years of inquiry. *Psychological Bulletin, 130,* 601–630. (12)

Sehgal, A., Ousley, A., Yang, Z., Chen, Y., & Schotland, P. (1999). What makes the circadian clock tick: Genes that keep time? *Recent Progress in Hormone Research, 54,* 61–85. (9)

Seifritz, E., Esposito, F., Hennel, F., Mustovic, H., Neuhoff, J. G., Bilecen, D., et al. (2002). Spatiotemporal pattern of neural processing in the human auditory cortex. *Science, 297,* 1706–1708. (7)

Sejnowski, T. J., & Destexhe, A. (2000). Why do we sleep? *Brain Research, 886,* 208–223. (9)

Selemon, L. D., Rajkowska, G., & Goldman-Rakic, P. S. (1995). Abnormally high neuronal density in the schizophrenic cortex. *Archives of General Psychiatry, 52,* 805–818. (15)

Selkoe, D. J. (2000). Toward a comprehensive theory for Alzheimer's disease. *Annals of the New York Academy of Sciences, 924,* 17–25. (13)

Selye, H. (1979). Stress, cancer, and the mind. In J. Taché, H. Selye, & S. B. Day (Eds.), *Cancer, stress, and death* (pp. 11–27). New York: Plenum Press. (12)

Selzer, M. E. (1978). Mechanisms of functional recovery and regeneration after spinal cord transection in larval sea lamprey. *Journal of Physiology, 277,* 395–408. (5)

Semendeferi, K., Lu, A., Schenker, N., & Damasio, H. (2002). Humans and great apes share a large frontal cortex. *Nature Neuroscience, 5,* 272–276. (4)

Sergent, C., & Dehaene, S. (2004). Is consciousness a gradual phenomenon? *Psychological Science, 15,* 720–728. (14)

Shah, A., & Lisak, R. P. (1993). Immunopharmacologic therapy in myasthenia gravis. *Clinical Neuropharmacology, 16,* 97–103. (8)

Shah, B., Shine, R., Hudson, S., & Kearney, M. (2003). Sociality in lizards: Why do thick-tailed geckos (*Nephrurus milii*) aggregate? *Behaviour, 140,* 1039–1052. (10)

Shah, N. M., Pisapia, D. J., Maniatis, S., Mendelsohn, M. M., Nemes, A., & Axel, R. (2004). Visualizing sexual dimorphism in the brain. *Neuron, 43,* 313–319. (11)

Shakelford, T. K., Buss, D. M., & Bennett, K. (2002). Forgiveness or breakup: Sex differences in responses to a partner's infidelity. *Cognition and Emotion, 16,* 299–307. (11)

Shalev, A. Y., Peri, T., Brandes, D., Freedman, S., Orr, S. P., & Pitman, R. K. (2000). Auditory startle response in trauma survivors with post-traumatic stress disorder: A prospective study. *American Journal of Psychiatry, 157,* 255–261. (12)

Shapiro, C. M., Bortz, R., Mitchell, D., Bartel, P., & Jooste, P. (1981). Slow-wave sleep: A recovery period after exercise. *Science, 214,* 1253–1254. (9)

Shapley, R. (1995). Parallel neural pathways and visual function. In M. S. Gazzaniga (Ed.), *The cognitive neurosciences* (pp. 315–324). Cambridge, MA: MIT Press. (6)

Sharbaugh, S. M. (2001). Seasonal acclimatization to extreme climatic conditions by black-capped chickadees (*Poecile atricapilla*) in interior Alaska (64° N). *Physiological and Biochemical Zoology, 74,* 568–575. (10)

Sharma, J., Angelucci, A., & Sur, M. (2000). Induction of visual orientation modules in auditory cortex. *Nature, 404,* 841–847. (5)

Shatz, C. J. (1992, September). The developing brain. *Scientific American, 267*(9), 60–67. (5)

Shatz, C. J. (1996). Emergence of order in visual-system development. *Proceedings of the National Academy of Sciences, USA, 93,* 602–608. (6)

Sheehan, T. P., Cirrito, J., Numan, M. J., & Numan, M. (2000). Using *c-Fos* immunocytochemistry to identify forebrain regions that may inhibit maternal behavior in rats. *Behavioral Neuroscience, 114,* 337–352. (11)

Shema, R., Sacktor, T. C., & Dudai, Y. (2007). Rapid erasure of long-term memory associations in the cortex by an inhibitor of PKMζ. *Science, 317,* 951–953. (13)

Sher, L., Carballo, J. J., Grunebaum, M. F., Burke, A. K., Zalsman, G., Huang, Y.-Y., et al. (2006). A prospective study of the association of cerebrospinal fluid monoamine metabolite levels with lethality of suicide attempts in patients with bipolar disorder. *Bipolar Disorder, 8,* 543–550. (12)

Shergill, S. S., Brammer, M. J., Williams, S. C. R., Murray, R. M., & McGuire, P. K. (2000). Mapping auditory hallucinations in schizophrenia using functional magnetic resonance imaging. *Archives of General Psychiatry, 57,* 1033–1038. (15)

Sherrington, C. S. (1906). *The integrative action of the nervous system* (2nd ed.). New York: Scribner's. New Haven, CT: Yale University Press, 1947. (3)

Sherrington, C. S. (1941). *Man on his nature.* New York: Macmillan. (3)

Sherrington, R., Rogaev, E. I., Liang, Y., Rogaeva, E. A., Levesque, G., Ikeda, M., et al. (1995). Cloning of a gene bearing missense mutations in early-onset familial Alzheimer's disease. *Nature, 375,* 754–760. (13)

Shi, L., Fatemi, S. H., Sidwell, R. W., & Patterson, P. H. (2003). Maternal influenza infection causes marked behavioral and pharmacological changes in the offspring. *Journal of Neuroscience, 23,* 297–302. (15)

Shima, K., Isoda, M., Mushiake, H., & Tanji, J. (2007). Categorization of behavioural sequences in the prefrontal cortex. *Nature, 445,* 315–318. (8)

Shimojo, S., Kamitani, Y., & Nishida, S. (2001). Afterimage of perceptually filled-in surface. *Science, 293,* 1677–1680. (6)

Shimura, H., Schlossmacher, M. G., Hattori, N., Frosch, M. P., Trockenbacher, A., Schneider, R., et al. (2001). Ubiquitination of a new form of a-synuclein by parkin from human brain: Implications for Parkinson's disease. *Science, 293,* 263–269. (8)

Shine, R., Phillips, B., Waye, H., LeMaster, M., & Mason, R. T. (2001). Benefits of female mimicry in snakes. *Nature, 414,* 267. (10)

Shirasaki, R., Katsumata, R., & Murakami, F. (1998). Change in chemoattractant responsiveness of developing axons at an intermediate target. *Science, 279,* 105–107. (5)

Shiv, B., Loewenstein, G., Bechara, A., Damasio, H., & Damasio, A. R. (2005). Investment behavior and the negative side of emotion. *Psychological Science, 16,* 435–439. (12)

Shoulson, I. (1990). Huntington's disease: Cognitive and psychiatric features. *Neuropsychiatry, Neuropsychology, and Behavioral Neurology, 3,* 15–22. (8)

Shrager, Y., Levy, D. A., Hopkins, R. O., & Squire, L. R. (2008). Working memory and the organization of brain systems. *Journal of Neuroscience, 28,* 4818–4822. (13)

Shutts, D. (1982). *Lobotomy: Resort to the knife.* New York: Van Nostrand Reinhold. (4)

Siderowf, A., & Stern, M. (2003). Update on Parkinson disease. *Annals of Internal Medicine, 138,* 651–658. (8)

Siebner, H. R., Limmer, C., Peinemann, A., Drzezga, A., Bloom, B. R., Schwaiger, M., et al. (2002). Long-term consequences of switching handedness: A positron emission tomography study on handwriting in "converted" left-handers. *Journal of Neuroscience, 22,* 2816–2825. (14)

Siegel, J. M. (1995). Phylogeny and the function of REM sleep. *Behavioural Brain Research, 69,* 29–34. (9)

Siegel, S. (1987). Alcohol and opiate dependence: Reevaluation of the Victorian perspective. *Research Advances in Alcohol and Drug Problems, 9,* 279–314. (3)

Siepka, S. M., Yoo, S. H., Park, J., Song, W. M., Kumar, V., Hu, Y. N., et al. (2007). Circadian mutant overtime reveals F-box protein FBXL3 regulation of cryptochrome and period gene expression. *Cell, 129,* 1011–1023. (9)

Silbersweig, D. A., Stern, E., Frith, C., Cahill, C., Holmes, A., Grootoonk, S., et al. (1995). A functional neuroanatomy of hallucinations in schizophrenia. *Nature, 378,* 176–179. (15)

Silk, J. B., Brosnan, S. F., Vonk, J., Henrich, J., Povinelli, D. J., Richardson, A. S., et al. (2005). Chimpanzees are indifferent to the welfare of unrelated group members. *Nature, 437,* 1357–1359. (1)

Simner, J., & Ward, J. (2006). The taste of words on the tip of the tongue. *Nature, 444,* 438. (7)

Simon, E. (2000). Interface properties of circumventricular organs in salt and fluid balance. *News in Physiological Sciences, 15,* 61–67. (10)

Simon, N. W., Mendez, I. A., & Setlow, B. (2007). Cocaine exposure causes long-term increases in impulsive choice. *Behavioral Neuroscience, 121,* 543–549. (3)

Sincich, L. C., Park, K. F., Wohlgemuth, M. J., & Horton, J. C. (2004). Bypassing V1: A direct geniculate input to area MT. *Nature Neuroscience, 7,* 1123–1128. (6)

Sinclair, J. R., Jacobs, A. L., & Nirenberg, S. (2004). Selective ablations of a class of amacrine cells alters spatial processing in the retina. *Journal of Neuroscience, 24,* 1459–1467. (6)

Singer, T., Seymour, B., O'Doherty, J., Kaube, H., Dolan, R. J., & Frith, C. D. (2004). Empathy for pain involves the affective but not sensory components of pain. *Science, 303,* 1157–1162. (7)

Singer, W. (1986). Neuronal activity as a shaping factor in postnatal development of visual cortex. In W. T. Greenough & J. M. Jusaska (Eds.), *Developmental neuropsychobiology* (pp. 271–293). Orlando, FL: Academic Press. (6)

Singh, S., & Mallic, B. N. (1996). Mild electrical stimulation of pontine tegmentum around locus coeruleus reduces rapid eye movement sleep in rats. *Neuroscience Research, 24,* 227–235. (9)

Singleton, A. B., Farrer, M., Johnson, J., Singleton, A., Hague, S., Kachergus, J., et al. (2003). α-synuclein locus triplication causes Parkinson's disease. *Science, 302,* 841. (8)

Siok, W. T., Niu, Z., Jin, Z., Perfetti, C. A., & Tan, L. H. (2008). A structural-functional basis for dyslexia in the cortex of Chinese readers. *Proceedings of the National Academy of Sciences, USA, 105,* 5561–5566. (14)

Sirigu, A., Daprati, E., Ciancia, S., Giraux, P., Nighoghossian, N., Posda, A., et al. (2004). Altered awareness of voluntary action after damage to the parietal corex. *Nature Neuroscience, 7,* 80–84. (8)

Sirigu, A., Grafman, J., Bressler, K., & Sunderland, T. (1991). Multiple representations contribute to body knowledge processing. Evidence from a case of autopagnosia. *Brain, 114,* 629–642. (7)

Sjöström, M., Friden, J., & Ekblom, B. (1987). Endurance, what is it? Muscle morphology after an extremely long distance run. *Acta Physiologica Scandinavica, 130,* 513–520. (8)

Skitzki, J. J., Chen, Q., Wang, W. C., & Evans, S. S. (2007). Primary immune surveillance: Some like it hot. *Journal of Molecular Medicine, 85,* 1361–1367. (10)

Sloan, D. M., Strauss, M. E., & Wisner, K. L. (2001). Diminished response to pleasant stimuli by depressed women. *Journal of Abnormal Psychology, 110,* 488–493. (15)

Slob, A. K., Bax, C. M., Hop, W. C. J., Rowland, D. L., & van der Werff ten Bosch, J. J. (1996). Sexual arousability and the menstrual cycle. *Psychoineuroendocrinology, 21,* 545–558. (11)

Sluming, V., Brooks, J., Howard, M., Downes, J. J., & Roberts, N. (2007). Broca's area supports enhanced visuospatial cognition in orchestral musicians. *Journal of Neuroscience, 27,* 3799–3806. (14)

Smith, D. E., Rapp, P. R., McKay, H. M., Roberts, J. A., & Tuszynski, M. H. (2004). Memory impairment in aged primates is associated with focal death of cortical neurons and atrophy of subcortical neurons. *Journal of Neuroscience, 24,* 4373–4381. (13)

Smith, G. P. (1998). Pregastric and gastric satiety. In G. P. Smith (Ed.), *Satiation: From gut to brain* (pp. 10–39). New York: Oxford University Press. (10)

Smith, G. P., & Gibbs, J. (1998). The satiating effects of cholecystokinin and bombesin-like peptides. In G. P. Smith (Ed.), *Satiation: From gut to brain* (pp. 97–125). New York: Oxford University Press. (10)

Smith, K. (2007). Looking for hidden signs of consciousness. *Nature, 446,* 355. (4)

Smith, K., Thompson, G. F., & Koster, H. D. (1969). Sweat in schizophrenic patients: Identification of the odorous substance. *Science, 166,* 398–399. (15)

Smith, L. T. (1975). The interanimal transfer phenomenon: A review. *Psychological Bulletin, 81,* 1078–1095. (13)

Smith, M. A., Brandt, J., & Shadmehr, R. (2000). Motor disorder in Huntington's disease begins as a dysfunction in error feedback control. *Nature, 403,* 544–549. (8)

Smith, S. L., & Trachtenberg, J. T. (2007). Experience-dependent binocular competition in the visual cortex begins at eye opening. *Nature Neuroscience, 10,* 370–375. (6)

Smith, Y. R., Stohler, C. S., Nichols, T. E., Bueller, J. A., Koeppe, R. A., & Zubieta, J.-K. (2006). Pronociceptive and antinociceptive effects of estradiol through endogenous opioid neurotransmission in women. *Journal of Neuroscience, 26,* 5777–5785. (7)

Smulders, T. V., Shiflett, M. W., Sperling, A. J., & DeVoogd, T. J. (2000). Seasonal changes in neuron numbers in the hippocampal formation of a food-hoarding bird: The black-capped chickadee. *Journal of Neurobiology, 44,* 414–422. (5)

Snowling, M. J. (1980). The development of grapheme-phoneme correspondence in normal and dyslexic readers. *Journal of Experimental Child Psychology, 29,* 294–305. (14)

Snyder, L. H., Grieve, K. L., Brotchie, P., & Andersen, R. A. (1998). Separate body- and world-referenced representations of visual space in parietal cortex. *Nature, 394,* 887–891. (8)

Solanto, M. V., Abikoff, H., Sonuga-Barke, E., Schachar, R., Logan, G. D., Wigal, T., et al. (2001). The ecological validity of delay aversion and response inhibition as measures of impulsivity in AD/HD: A supplement to the NIMH multimodal treatment study of AD/HD. *Journal of Abnormal Child Psychology, 29,* 215–228. (14)

Solms, M. (1997). *The neuropsychology of dreams.* Mahwah, NJ: Erlbaum. (9)

Solms, M. (2000). Dreaming and REM sleep are controlled by different brain mechanisms. *Behavioral and Brain Sciences, 23,* 843–850. (9)

Solomon, S. G., & Lennie, P. (2007). The machinery of colour vision. *Nature Reviews Neuroscience, 8,* 276–286. (6)

Somero, G. N. (1996). Temperature and proteins: Little things can mean a lot. *News in Physiological Sciences, 11,* 72–77. (10)

Somjen, G. G. (1988). Nervenkitt: Notes on the history of the concept of neuroglia. *Glia, 1,* 2–9. (2)

Son, G. H., Geum, D., Chung, S., Kim, E. J., Jo, J.-H., Kim, C.-H., et al. (2006). Maternal stress produces learning deficits associated with impairment of NMDA receptor-mediated synaptic plasticity. *Journal of Neuroscience, 26,* 3309–3318. (12)

Song, H., Stevens, C. F., & Gage, F. H. (2002). Neural stem cells from adult hippocampus develop essential properties of functional CNS neurons. *Nature Neuroscience, 5,* 438–445. (5)

Soon, C. S., Brass, M., Heinze, H.-J., & Haynes, J.-D. (2008). Unconscious determinants of free decisions in the human brain. *Nature Neuroscience, 11,* 543–545. (8)

Sowell, E. R., Peterson, B. S., Thompson, P. M., Welcome, S. E., Henkenius, A. L., & Toga, A. W. (2003). Mapping cortical change across the human life span. *Nature Neuroscience, 6,* 309–315. (5)

Sowell, E. R., Thompson, P. M., Holmes, C. J., Jernigan, T. L., & Toga, A. W. (1999). In vivo evidence for post-adolescent brain maturation in frontal and striatal regions. *Nature Neuroscience, 2,* 859–861. (5, 15)

Spalding, K. L., Bhardwaj, R. D., Buchholz, B. A., Druid, H., & Frisén, J. (2005). Retrospective birth dating of cells in humans. *Cell, 122,* 133–143. (5)

Spangler, R., Wittkowski, K. M., Goddard, N. L., Avena, N. M., Hoebel, B. G., & Leibowitz, S. F. (2004). Opiate-like effects of sugar on gene expression in reward areas of the rat brain. *Molecular Brain Research, 124,* 134–142. (10)

Spencer, R. M. C., Zelaznik, H. N., Diedrichsen, J., & Ivry, R. B. (2003). Disrupted timing of discontinuous but not continuous movements by cerebellar lesions. *Science, 300,* 1437–1439. (8)

Sperry, R. W. (1943). Visuomotor coordination in the newt (*Triturus viridescens*) after regeneration of the optic nerve. *Journal of Comparative Neurology, 79,* 33–55. (5)

Sperry, R. W. (1975). In search of psyche. In F. G. Worden, J. P. Swazey, & G. Adelman (Eds.), *The neurosciences: Paths of discovery* (pp. 425–434). Cambridge, MA: MIT Press. (14)

Spezio, M. L., Huang, P.-Y. S., Castelli, F., & Adolphs, R. (2007). Amygdala damage impairs eye contact during conversations with real people. *Journal of Neuroscience, 27,* 3994–3997. (12)

Spiegel, T. A. (1973). Caloric regulation of food intake in man. *Journal of Comparative and Physiological Psychology, 84,* 24–37. (10)

Spindler, K. A., Sullivan, E. V., Menon, V., Lim, K. O., & Pfefferbaum, A. (1997). Deficits in multiple systems of working memory in schizophrenia. *Schizophrenia Research, 27,* 1–10. (15)

Spreux-Varoquaux, O., Alvarez, J.-C., Berlin, I., Batista, G., Despierre, P.-G., Gilton, A., et al. (2001). Differential abnormalities in plasma 5-HIAA and platelet serotonin concentrations in violent suicide attempters. *Life Sciences, 69,* 647–657. (12)

Spurzheim, J. G. (1908). *Phrenology* (Rev. ed.) Philadelphia: Lippincott. (4)

Squire, L. R. (1992). Memory and the hippocampus: A synthesis from findings with rats, monkeys, and humans. *Psychological Review, 99,* 195–231. (13)

Squire, L. R., Amaral, D. G., & Press, G. A. (1990). Magnetic resonance imaging of the hippocampal formation and mammillary nuclei distinguish medial temporal lobe and diencephalic amnesia. *Journal of Neuroscience, 10,* 3106–3117. (13)

Squire, L. R., Amaral, D. G., Zola-Morgan, S., Kritchevsky, M., & Press, G. (1989). Description of brain injury in the amnesic patient N. A. based on magnetic resonance imaging. *Experimental Neurology, 105,* 23–35. (13)

Squires, T. M. (2004). Optimizing the vertebrate vestibular semicircular canal: Could we balance any better? *Physical Review Letters, 93,* 198106. (7)

St George-Hyslop, P. H. (2000). Genetic factors in the genesis of Alzheimer's disease. *Annals of the New York Academy of Sciences, 924,* 1–7. (13)

Stahl, J. E., Furie, K. L., Gleason, S., & Gazelle, G. S. (2003). Stroke: Effect of implementing an evaluation and treatment protocol compliant with NINDS recommendations. *Radiology, 228,* 659–668. (5)

Stalnaker, T. A., Roesch, M. R., Franz, T. M., Calu, D. J., Singh, T., & Schoenbaum, G. (2007). Cocaine-induced decision-making deficits are mediated by miscoding in basolateral amygdala. *Nature Neuroscience, 10,* 949–951. (3)

Stanford, L. R. (1987). Conduction velocity variations minimize conduction time differences among retinal ganglion cell axons. *Science, 238,* 358–360. (2)

Stanley, B. G., Schwartz, D. H., Hernandez, L., Leibowitz, S. F., & Hoebel, B. G. (1989). Patterns of extracellular 5-hydroxyindole-acetic acid (5-HIAA) in the paraventricular hypothalamus (PVN): Relation to circadian rhythm and deprivation-induced eating behavior. *Pharmacology, Biochemistry, & Behavior, 33,* 257–260. (12)

Stark, R. E., & McGregor, K. K. (1997). Follow-up study of a right- and a left-hemispherectomized child: Implications for localization and impairment of language in children. *Brain and Language, 60,* 222–242. (14)

Starr, C., & Taggart, R. (1989). *Biology: The unity and diversity of life.* Pacific Grove, CA: Brooks/Cole. (3, 4, 7, 8, 11)

Stefanis, N., Frangou, S., Yakeley, J., Sharma, T., O'Connell, P., Morgan, K., et al. (1999). Hippocampal volume reduction in schizophrenia: Effects of genetic risk and pregnancy and birth complications. *Biological Psychiatry, 46,* 689–696. (15)

Stein, M. B., Hanna, C., Koverola, C., Torchia, M., & McClarty, B. (1997). Structural brain changes in PTSD. *Annals of the New York Academy of Sciences, 821,* 76–82. (12)

Steiner, T., Ringleb, P., & Hacke, W. (2001). Treatment options for large hemispheric stroke. *Neurology, 57*(Suppl. 2), S61–S68. (5)

Stella, N., Schweitzer, P., & Piomelli, D. (1997). A second endogenous cannabinoid that modulates long-term potentiation. *Nature, 382,* 677–678. (3)

Stephens, T. W., Basinski, M., Bristow, P. K., Bue-Valleskey, J. M., Burgett, S. G., Craft, L., et al. (1995). The role of neuropeptide Y in the anti-obesity action of the obese gene product. *Nature, 377,* 530–532. (10)

Sterpenich, V., D'Argembeau, A., Desseiles, M., Balteau, E., Albouy, G., Vandewalle, G., et al. (2006). The locus coeruleus is involved in the successful retrieval of emotional memories in humans. *Journal of Neuroscience, 26,* 7416–7423. (9)

Stevens, C. F. (2001). An evolutionary scaling law for the primate visual system and its basis in cortical function. *Nature, 411,* 193–195. (4)

Stevens, M., & Cuthill, I. C. (2007). Hidden messages: Are ultraviolet signals a special channel in avian communication? *Bioscience, 57,* 501–507. (6)

Stevens, T., & Karmiloff-Smith, A. (1997). Word learning in a special population: Do individuals with Williams syndrome obey lexical constraints? *Journal of Child Language, 24,* 737–765. (14)

Stewart, J. W., Quitkin, F. M., McGrath, P. J., Amsterdam, J., Fava, M., Fawcett, J., et al. (1998). Use of pattern analysis to predict differential relapse of remitted patients with major depression during 1 year of treatment with fluoxetine or placebo. *Archives of General Psychiatry, 55,* 334–343. (15)

Stickgold, R., James, L., & Hobson, J. A. (2000). Visual discrimination learning requires sleep after training. *Nature Neuroscience, 3,* 1237–1238. (9)

Stickgold, R., Malia, A., Maguire, D., Roddenberry, D., & O'Connor, M. (2000). Replaying the game: Hypnagogic images in normals and amnesics. *Science, 290,* 350–353. (13)

Stickgold, R., Whidbee, D., Schirmer, B., Patel, V., & Hobson, J. (2000). Visual discrimination task improvement: A multi-step process occurring during sleep. *Journal of Cognitive Neuroscience, 12,* 246–254. (9)

Stockman, A., & Sharpe, L. T. (1998). Human cone spectral sensitivities: A progress report. *Vision Research, 38,* 3193–3206. (6)

Stone, V. E., Nisenson, L., Eliassen, J. C., & Gazzaniga, M. S. (1996). Left hemisphere representations of emotional facial expressions. *Neuropsychologia, 34,* 23–29. (14)

Storey, K. B., & Storey, J. M. (1999, May/June). Lifestyles of the cold and frozen. *The Sciences, 39*(3), 33–37. (10)

Stout, A. K., Raphael, H. M., Kanterewicz, B. I., Klann, E., & Reynolds, I. J. (1998). Glutamate-induced neuron death requires mitochondrial calcium uptake. *Nature Neuroscience, 1,* 366–373. (5)

Strack, F., Martin, L. L., & Stepper, S. (1988). Inhibiting and facilitating conditions of the human smile: A nonobtrusive test of the facial feedback hypothesis. *Journal of Personality and Social Psychology, 54,* 768–777. (12)

Strichartz, G., Rando, T., & Wang, G. K. (1987). An integrated view of the molecular toxinology of sodium channel gating in excitable cells. *Annual Review of Neuroscience, 10,* 237–267. (2)

Stricker, E. M. (1969). Osmoregulation and volume regulation in rats: Inhibition of hypovolemic thirst by water. *American Journal of Physiology, 217,* 98–105. (10)

Stricker, E. M., & Hoffmann, M. L. (2007). Presystemic signals in the control of thirst, salt appetite, and vasopressin secretion. *Physiology & Behavior, 91,* 404–412. (10)

Stricker, E. M., Swerdloff, A. F., & Zigmond, M. J. (1978). Intrahypothalamic injections of kainic acid produce feeding and drinking deficits in rats. *Brain Research, 158,* 470–473. (10)

Strickland, T. L., Miller, B. L., Kowell, A., & Stein, R. (1998). Neurobiology of cocaine-induced organic brain impairment: Contributions from functional neuroimaging. *Neuropsychology Review, 8,* 1–9. (3)

Strotmann, J., Levai, O., Fleischer, J., Schwarzenbacher, K., & Breer, H. (2004). Olfactory receptor proteins in axonal processes of chemosensory neurons. *Journal of Neuroscience, 224,* 7754–7761. (7)

Stryker, M. P., & Sherk, H. (1975). Modification of cortical orientation selectivity in the cat by restricted visual experience: A reexamination. *Science, 190,* 904–906. (6)

Stryker, M. P., Sherk, H., Leventhal, A. G., & Hirsch, H. V. B. (1978). Physiological consequences for the cat's visual cortex of effectively restricting early visual experience with oriented contours. *Journal of Neurophysiology, 41,* 896–909. (6)

Strzelczuk, M., & Romaniuk, A. (1995). Fear induced by the blockade of $GABA_A$-ergic transmission in the hypothalamus of the cat: Behavioral and neurochemical study. *Behavioural Brain Research, 72,* 63–71. (12)

Studer, L., Tabar, V., & McKay, R. D. G. (1998). Transplantation of expanded mesencephalic precursors leads to recovery in Parkinsonian rats. *Nature Neuroscience, 1,* 290–295. (8)

Stunkard, A. J., Sorensen, T. I. A., Hanis, C., Teasdale, T. W., Chakraborty, R., Schull, W. J., et al. (1986). An adoption study of human obesity. *New England Journal of Medicine, 314,* 193–198. (10)

Stuss, D. T., & Benson, D. F. (1984). Neuropsychological studies of the frontal lobes. *Psychological Bulletin, 95,* 3–28. (4)

Sullivan, E. V., Deshmukh, A., Desmond, J. E., Mathalon, D. H., Rosenbloom, M. J., Lim, K. O., et al. (2000). Contribution of alcohol abuse to cerebellar volume deficits in men with schizophrenia. *Archives of General Psychiatry, 57,* 894–902. (15)

Sun, Y.-G., & Chen, Z.-F. (2007). A gastrin-releasing peptide receptor mediates the itch sensation in the spinal cord. *Nature, 448,* 700–703. (7)

Sunaert, S., Van Hecke, P., Marchal, G., & Orban, G. A. (1999). Motion-responsive regions of the human brain. *Experimental Brain Research, 127,* 355–370. (6)

Sunaert, S., Van Hecke, P., Marchal, G., & Orban, G. A. (2000). Attention to speed of motion, speed discrimination, and task difficulty: An fMRI study. *NeuroImage, 11,* 612–623. (6)

Sur, M., & Leamey, C. A. (2001). Development and plasticity of cortical areas and networks. *Nature Reviews Neuroscience, 2,* 251–262. (4)

Sutton, L. C., Lea, E., Will, M. J., Schwartz, B. A., Hartley, C. E., Poole, J. C., et al. (1997). Inescapable shock-induced potentiation of morphine analgesia. *Behavioral Neuroscience, 111,* 1105–1113. (7)

Sutton, R. L., Hovda, D. A., & Feeney, D. M. (1989). Amphetamine accelerates recovery of locomotor function following bilateral frontal cortex ablation in rats. *Behavioral Neuroscience, 103,* 837–841. (5)

Suvisaari, J. M., Haukka, J. K., Tanskanen, A. J., & Lönnqvist, J. K. (1999). Decline in the incidence of schizophrenia in Finnish cohorts born from 1954 to 1965. *Archives of General Psychiatry, 56,* 733–740. (15)

Suzdak, P. D., Glowa, J. R., Crawley, J. N., Schwartz, R. D., Skolnick, P., & Paul, S. M. (1986). A selective imidazobenzodiazepine antagonist of ethanol in the rat. *Science, 234,* 1243–1247. (12)

Swaab, D. F., & Hofman, M. A. (1990). An enlarged suprachiasmatic nucleus in homosexual men. *Brain Research, 537,* 141–148. (11)

Swaab, D. F., Slob, A. K., Houtsmuller, E. J., Brand, T., & Zhou, J. N. (1995). Increased number of vasopressin neurons in the suprachiasmatic nucleus (SCN) of "bisexual" adult male rats following perinatal treatment with the aromatase blocker ATD. *Developmental Brain Research, 85,* 273–279. (11)

Swithers, S. E., & Davidson, T. L. (2008). A role for sweet taste: Calorie predictive relations in energy regulation by rats. *Behavioral Neuroscience, 122,* 161–173. (10)

Swoboda, E., Conca, A., König, P., Waanders, R., & Hansen, M. (2001). Maintenance electroconvulsive therapy in affective and schizoaffective disorders. *Neuropsychobiology, 43,* 23–28. (15)

Syken, J., GrandPre, T., Kanold, P. O., & Shatz, C. J. (2006). PirB restricts ocular-dominance plasticity in visual cortex. *Science, 313,* 1795–1800. (6)

Szymusiak, R. (1995). Magnocellular nuclei of the basal forebrain: Substrates of sleep and arousal regulation. *Sleep, 18,* 478–500. (9)

Tabrizi, S. J., Cleeter, M. W. J., Xuereb, J., Taanman, J.-W., Cooper, J. M., & Schapira, A. H. V. (1999). Biochemical abnormalities and excitotoxicity in Huntington's disease brain. *Annals of Neurology, 45,* 25–32. (8)

Taddese, A., Nah, S. Y., & McCleskey, E. W. (1995). Selective opioid inhibition of small nociceptive neurons. *Science, 270,* 1366–1369. (7)

Tagawa, Y., Kanold, P. O., Majdan, M., & Shatz, C. J. (2005). Multiple periods of functional ocular dominance plasticity in mouse visual cortex. *Nature Neuroscience, 8,* 380–388. (6)

Tager-Flusberg, H., Boshart, J., & Baron-Cohen, S. (1998). Reading the windows to the soul: Evidence of domain-specific sparing in Williams syndrome. *Journal of Cognitive Neuroscience, 10,* 631–639. (14)

Taillard, J., Philip, P., Coste, O., Sagaspe, P., & Bioulac, B. (2003). The circadian and homeostatic modulation of sleep pressure during wakefulness differs between morning and evening chronotypes. *Journal of Sleep Research, 12,* 275–282. (9)

Takahashi, K., Lin, J.-S., & Sakai, K. (2006). Neuronal activity of histaminergic tuberomammillary neurons during wake–sleep states in the mouse. *Journal of Neuroscience, 26,* 10292–10298. (9)

Takahashi, T., Svoboda, K., & Malinow, R. (2003). Experience strengthening transmission by driving AMPA receptors into synapses. *Science, 299,* 1585–1588. (13)

Takano, T., Tian, G.-F., Peng, W., Lou, N., Libionka, W., Han, X., et al. (2006). Astrocyte-mediated control of cerebral blood flow. *Nature Neuroscience, 9,* 260–267. (2)

Tanaka, J., Hayashi, Y., Nomura, S., Miyakubo, H., Okumura, T., & Sakamaki, K. (2001). Angiotensinergic and noradrenergic mechanisms in the hypothalamic paraventricular nucleus participate in the drinking response induced by activation of the subfornical organ in rats. *Behavioural Brain Research, 118,* 117–122. (10)

Tanaka, J., Hori, K., & Nomura, M. (2001). Dipsogenic response induced by angiotensinergic pathways from the lateral hypothalamic area to the subfornical organ in rats. *Behavioural Brain Research, 118,* 111–116. (10)

Tanaka, K., Sugita, Y., Moriya, M., & Saito, H.-A. (1993). Analysis of object motion in the ventral part of the medial superior temporal area of the macaque visual cortex. *Journal of Neurophysiology, 69,* 128–142. (6)

Tanaka, Y., Kamo, T., Yoshida, M., & Yamadori, A. (1991). "So-called" cortical deafness. *Brain, 114,* 2385–2401. (7)

Tanji, J., & Shima, K. (1994). Role for supplementary motor area cells in planning several movements ahead. *Nature, 371,* 413–416. (8)

Tanner, C. M., Ottman, R., Goldman, S. M., Ellenberg, J., Chan, P., Mayeux, R., et al. (1999). Parkinson disease in twins: An etiologic study. *Journal of the American Medical Association, 281,* 341–346. (8)

Taravosh-Lahn, K., Bastida, C., & Delville, Y. (2006). Differential responsiveness to fluoxetine during puberty. *Behavioral Neuroscience, 120,* 1084–1092. (12)

Tarr, M. J., & Gauthier, I. (2000). FFA: A flexible fusiform area for subordinate-level visual processing automatized by experience. *Nature Neuroscience, 3,* 764–769. (6)

Tashiro, A., Makino, H., & Gage, F. H. (2007). Experience-specific functional modification of the dentate gyrus through adult neurogenesis: A critical period during an immature stage. *Journal of Neuroscience, 27,* 3252–3259. (5)

Taub, E., & Berman, A. J. (1968). Movement and learning in the absence of sensory feedback. In S. J. Freedman (Ed.), *The neuropsychology of spatially oriented behavior* (pp. 173–192). Homewood, IL: Dorsey. (5)

Taylor, J. P., Hardy, J., & Fischbeck, K H. (2002). Toxic proteins in neurodegenerative disease. *Science, 296,* 1991–1995. (13)

Taylor, M. A. (1969). Sex ratios of newborns: Associated with prepartum and postpartum schizophrenia. *Science, 164,* 723–724. (15)

Taylor, S. E., Way, B. M., Welch, W. T., Hilmert, C. J., Lehman, B. J., & Eisenberger, N. I. (2006). Early family environment, current adversity, the serotonin transporter promoter polymorphism, and depressive symptomatology. *Biological Psychiatry, 60,* 671–676. (15)

Taziaux, M., Keller, M., Bakker, J., & Balthazart, J. (2007). Sexual behavior activity tracks rapid changes in brain estrogen concentrations. *Journal of Neuroscience, 27,* 6563–6572. (11)

Teff, K. L., Elliott, S. S., Tschöp, M., Kieffer, T. J., Rader, D., Heiman, M., et al. (2004). Dietary fructose reduces circulating insulin and leptin, attenuates postprandial suppression of ghrelin, and increases triglycerides in women. *Journal of Clinical Endocrinology & Metabolism, 89,* 2963–2972. (10)

Teicher, M. H., Glod, C. A., Magnus, E., Harper, D., Benson, G., Krueger, K., et al. (1997). Circadian rest–activity disturbances in seasonal affective disorder. *Archives of General Psychiatry, 54,* 124–130. (15)

Teitelbaum, P. (1955). Sensory control of hypothalamic hyperphagia. *Journal of Comparative and Physiological Psychology, 48,* 156–163. (10)

Teitelbaum, P. (1961). Disturbances in feeding and drinking behavior after hypothalamic lesions. In M. R. Jones (Ed.), *Nebraska Symposia on Motivation 1961* (pp. 39–69). Lincoln: University of Nebraska Press. (10)

Teitelbaum, P., & Epstein, A. N. (1962). The lateral hypothalamic syndrome. *Psychological Review, 69,* 74–90. (10)

Teitelbaum, P., Pellis, V. C., & Pellis, S. M. (1991). Can allied reflexes promote the integration of a robot's behavior? In J. A. Meyer & S. W. Wilson (Eds.), *From animals to animats: Simulation of animal behavior* (pp. 97–104). Cambridge, MA: MIT Press/Bradford Books. (8)

Temel, Y., Boothman, L. J., Blokland, A., Magill, P. J., Steinbusch, H. W. M., Visser-Vandewalle, V., et al. (2007). Inhibition of 5-HT neuron activity and induction of depressive-like behavior by high-frequency stimulation of the subthalamic nucleus. *Proceedings of the National Academy of Sciences, USA, 104,* 17087–17092. (8)

Templeton, C. N., Greene, E., & Davis, K. (2005). Allometry of alarm calls: Black-capped chickadees encode information about predator size. *Science, 308,* 1934–1937. (14)

Terayama, H., Nishino, Y., Kishi, M., Ikuta, K., Itoh, M., & Iwahashi, K. (2003). Detection of anti-Borna virus (BDV) antibodies from patients with schizophrenia and mood disorders in Japan. *Psychiatry Research, 120,* 201–206. (15)

Terman, M., Terman, J. S., & Ross, D. C. (1998). A controlled trial of timed bright light and negative air ionization for treatment of winter depression. *Archives of General Psychiatry, 55,* 875–882. (15)

Terrace, H. S., Petitto, L. A., Sanders, R. J., & Bever, T. G. (1979). Can an ape create a sentence? *Science, 206,* 891–902. (14)

Tetrud, J. W., Langston, J. W., Garbe, P. L., & Ruttenber, A. J. (1989). Mild Parkinsonism in persons exposed to 1-methyl-4-phenyl-1,2,3,6-tetrahydropyridine (MPTP). *Neurology, 39,* 1483–1487. (8)

Thalemann, R., Wölfling, K., & Grüsser, S. M. (2007). Specific cue reactivity on computer game-related cues in excessive gamers. *Behavioral Neuroscience, 121,* 614–618. (3)

Thanickal, T. C., Moore, R. Y., Nienhuis, R., Ramanathan, L., Gulyani, S., Aldrich, M., et al. (2000). Reduced number of hypocretin neurons in human narcolepsy. *Neuron, 27,* 469–474. (9)

Thapar, A., Fowler, T., Rice, F., Scourfield, J., van den Bree, M., Thomas, H., et al. (2003). Maternal smoking during pregnancy and attention deficit hyperactivity disorder symptoms in offspring. *American Journal of Psychiatry, 160,* 1985–1989. (5)

Thase, M. E., Greenhouse, J. B., Frank, E., Reynolds, C. F., III, Pilkonis, P. A., Hurley, K., et al. (1997). Treatment of major depression with psychotherapy or psychotherapy-psychopharmacology combinations. *Archives of General Psychiatry, 54,* 1009–1015. (15)

Thase, M. E., Haight, B. R., Richard, N., Rockett, C. B., Mitton, M., Modell, J. G., et al. (2005). Remission rates following antidepressant therapy with bupropion or selective serotonin reuptake inhibitors: A meta-analysis of original data from 7 randomized controlled trials. *Journal of Clinical Psychiatry, 66,* 974–981. (15)

Thase, M. E., Trivedi, M. H., & Rush, A. J. (1995). MAOIs in the contemporary treatment of depression. *Neuropsychopharmacology, 12,* 185–219. (15)

Thiele, A., Henning, P., Kubischik, K.-P., & Hoffman, K.-P. (2002). Neural mechanisms of saccadic suppression. *Science, 295,* 2460–2462. (6)

Thier, P., Dicke, P. W., Haas, R., & Barash, S. (2000). Encoding of movement time by populations of cerebellar Purkinje cells. *Nature, 405,* 72–76. (8)

Thierry, G., & Wu, Y. J. (2007). Brain potentials reveal unconscious translation during foreign-language comprehension. *Proceedings of the National Academy of Sciences, USA, 104,* 12530–12535. (14)

Thoeringer, C. K., Binder, E. B., Salyakina, D., Erhardt, A., Ising, M., Unschuld, P. G., et al. (2007). Association of a Met88Valdiazepam binding inhibitor (DBI) gene polymorphism and anxiety disorders with panic attacks. *Journal of Psychiatric Research, 41,* 579–584. (12)

Thomas, P. K. (1988). Clinical aspects of PNS regeneration. In S. G. Waxman (Ed.), *Advances in neurology* (Vol. 47, pp. 9–29). New York: Raven Press. (5)

Thompson, P. M., Vidal, C., Giedd, J. N., Gochman, P., Blumenthal, J., Nicolson, R., et al. (2001). Mapping adolescent brain change reveals dynamic wave of accelerated gray matter loss in very early-onset schizophrenia. *Proceedings of the National Academy of Sciences, USA, 98,* 11650–11655. (15)

Thompson, R. F. (1986). The neurobiology of learning and memory. *Science, 233,* 941–947. (13)

Ticku, M. K., & Kulkarni, S. K. (1988). Molecular interactions of ethanol with GABAergic system and potential of Ro15-4513 as an ethanol antagonist. *Pharmacology Biochemistry and Behavior, 30,* 501–510. (12)

Timms, B. G., Howdeshell, K. L., Barton, L., Richter, C. A., & vom Saal, F. S. (2005). Estrogenic chemicals in plastic and oral contraceptives disrupt development of the fetal mouse prostate and urethra. *Proceedings of the National Academy of Sciences, USA, 102,* 7014–7019. (11)

Tinbergen, N. (1951). *The study of instinct.* Oxford, England: Oxford University Press. (1)

Tinbergen, N. (1973). The search for animal roots of human behavior. In N. Tinbergen (Ed.), *The animal in its world* (Vol. 2, pp. 161–174). Cambridge, MA: Harvard University Press. (1)

Tingate, T. R., Lugg, D. J., Muller, H. K., Stowe, R. P., & Pierson, D. L. (1997). Antarctic isolation: Immune and viral studies. *Immunology and Cell Biology, 75,* 275–283. (12)

Tishkoff, S. A., Reed, F. A., Ranciaro, A., Voight, B. F., Babbitt, C. C., Silverman, J. S., et al. (2006). Convergent adaptation of human lactase persistence in Africa and Europe. *Nature Genetics, 39,* 31–40. (10)

Toh, K. L., Jones, C. R., He, Y., Eide, E. J., Hinz, W. A., Virshup, D. M., et al. (2001). An h*Per2* phosphorylation site mutation in familial advanced sleep phase syndrome. *Science, 291,* 1040–1043. (9)

Tom, S. M., Fox, C. R., Trepel, C., & Poldrack, R. A. (2007). The neural basis of loss aversion in decision-making under risk. *Science, 315,* 515–518. (13)

Tomchik, S. M., Berg, S., Kim, J. W., Chaudhari, N., & Roper, S. D. (2007). Breadth of tuning and taste coding in mammalian taste buds. *Journal of Neuroscience, 27,* 10840–10848. (7)

Tominaga, M., Caterina, M. J., Malmberg, A. B., Rosen, T. A., Gilbert, H., Skinner, K., et al. (1998). The cloned capsaicin receptor integrates multiple pain-producing stimuli. *Neuron, 21,* 531–543. (7)

Toni, N., Buchs, P.-A., Nikonenko, I., Bron, C. R., & Muller, D. (1999). LTP promotes formation of multiple spine synapses between a single axon terminal and a dendrite. *Nature, 402,* 421–425. (13)

Toomey, R., Lyons, M. J., Eisen, S. A., Xian, H., Chantarujikapong, S., Seidman, L. J., et al. (2003). A twin study of the neuropsychological consequences of stimulant abuse. *Archives of General Psychiatry, 60,* 303–310. (3)

Torrey, E. F. (1986). Geographic variations in schizophrenia. In C. Shagass, R. C. Josiassen, W. H. Bridger, K. J. Weiss, D. Stoff, & G. M. Simpson (Eds.), *Biological psychiatry 1985* (pp. 1080–1082). New York: Elsevier. (15)

Torrey, E. F., & Miller, J. (2001). *The invisible plague: The rise of mental illness from 1750 to the present.* New Brunswick, NJ: Rutgers University Press. (15)

Torrey, E. F., Miller, J., Rawlings, R., & Yolken, R. H. (1997). Seasonality of births in schizophrenia and bipolar disorder: A review of the literature. *Schizophrenia Research, 28,* 1–38. (15)

Torrey, E. F., Rawlings, R., & Yolken, R. H. (2000). The antecedents of psychosis: A case-control study of selected risk factors. *Schizophrenia Research, 46,* 17–23. (15)

Torrey, E. F., & Yolken, R. H. (2005). *Toxoplasma gondii* as a possible cause of schizophrenia. *Biological Psychiatry, 57,* 128S. (15)

Townsend, J., Courchesne, E., Covington, J., Westerfield, M., Harris, N. S., Lyden, P., et al. (1999). Spatial attention deficits in patients with acquired or developmental cerebellar abnormality. *Journal of Neuroscience, 19,* 5632–5643. (8)

Tran, P. B., & Miller, R. J. (2003). Chemokine receptors: Signposts to brain development and disease. *Nature Reviews Neuroscience, 4,* 444–455. (5)

Tranel, D., & Damasio, A. (1993). The covert learning of affective valence does not require structures in hippocampal system or amygdala. *Journal of Cognitive Neuroscience, 5,* 79–88. (13)

Travers, S. P., Pfaffmann, C., & Norgren, R. (1986). Convergence of lingual and palatal gustatory neural activity in the nucleus of the solitary tract. *Brain Research, 365,* 305–320. (7)

Trefilov, A., Berard, J., Krawczak, M., & Schmidtke, J. (2000). Natal dispersal in rhesus macaques is related to serotonin transporter gene promoter variation. *Behavior Genetics, 30,* 295–301. (12)

Treisman, A. (1999). Feature binding, attention and object perception. In G. W. Humphreys, J. Duncan, & A. Treisman (Eds.), *Attention, space, and action* (pp. 91–111). Oxford, England: Oxford University Press. (4)

Trevena, J. A., & Miller, J. (2002). Cortical movement preparation before and after a conscious decision to move. *Consciousness and Cognition, 11,* 162–190. (8)

Trevarthen, C. (1974). Cerebral embryology and the split brain. In M. Kinsbourne & W. L. Smith (Eds.), *Hemispheric disconnection and cerebral function* (pp. 208–236). Springfield, IL: Thomas. (14)

Trimble, M. R., & Thompson, P. J. (1986). Neuropsychological and behavioral sequelae of spontaneous seizures. *Annals of the New York Academy of Sciences, 462,* 284–292. (15)

Trivedi, M. H., Fava, M., Wisniewski, S. R., Thase, M. E., Quitlein, F., Warden, D., et al. (2006). Medication augmentation after failure of SSRIs for depression. *New England Journal of Medicine, 354,* 1243–1252. (15)

Trivers, R. L. (1985). *Social evolution.* Menlo Park, CA: Benjamin/Cummings. (1)

Truccolo, W., Friehs, G. M., Donoghue, J. P., & Hochberg, L. R. (2008). Primary motor cortex tuning to intended movement kinematics in humans with tetraplegia. *Journal of Neuroscience, 28,* 1163–1178. (8)

Tsai, G., Passani, L. A., Slusher, B. S., Carter, R., Baer, L., Kleinman, J. E., et al. (1995). Abnormal excitatory neurotransmitter metabolism in schizophrenic brains. *Archives of General Psychiatry, 52,* 829–836. (15)

Tsai, G. E., Ragan, P., Chang, R., Chen, S., Linnoila, M. I., & Coyle, J. T. (1998). Increased glutamatergic neurotransmission and oxidative stress after alcohol withdrawal. *American Journal of Psychiatry, 155,* 726–732. (3)

Tsankova, N., Renthal, W., Kumar, A., & Nestler, E. J. (2007). Epigenetic regulation in psychiatric disorders. *Nature Reviews Neuroscience, 8,* 355–367. (1)

Tsao, D. Y., Freiwald, W. A., Tootell, R. B. H., & Livingstone, M. S. (2006). A cortical region consisting entirely of face-selective cells. *Science, 311,* 670–674. (6)

Tse, C.-Y., Lee, C.-L., Sullivan, J., Garnsey, S. M., Dell, G. S., Fabiani, M., et al. (2007). Imaging cortical dynamics of language processing with the event-related optical signal. *Proceedings of the National Academy of Sciences, USA, 104,* 17157–17162. (14)

Tse, D., Langston, R. F., Kakeyama, M., Bethus, I., Spooner, P. A., Wood, E. R., et al. (2007). Schemas and memory consolidation. *Science, 316,* 76–82. (13)

Ts'o, D. Y., & Roe, A. W. (1995). Functional compartments in visual cortex: Segregation and interaction. In M. S. Gazzaniga (Ed.), *The cognitive neurosciences* (pp. 325–337). Cambridge, MA: MIT Press. (6)

Tsujita, T., Niikawa, N., Yamashita, H., Imamura, A., Hamada, A., Nakane, Y., et al. (1998). Genomic discordance between monozygotic twins discordant for schizophrenia. *American Journal of Psychiatry, 155,* 422–424. (15)

Tu, Y., Kroener, S., Abernathy, K., Lapish, C., Seamans, J., Chandler, L. J., et al. (2007). Ethanol inhibits persistent activity in prefrontal cortical neurons. *Journal of Neuroscience, 27,* 4765–4775. (3)

Tucker, D. M., Luu, P., & Pribram, K. H. (1995). Social and emotional self-regulation. *Annals of the New York Academy of Sciences, 769,* 213–239. (8)

Turk, D. J., Heatherton, T. F., Kelley, W. M., Funnell, M. G., Gazzaniga, M. S., & Macrae, C. N. (2002). Mike or me? Self-recognition in a split-brain patient. *Nature Neuroscience, 5,* 841–842. (14)

Turner, R. S., & Anderson, M. E. (2005). Context-dependent modulation of movement-related discharge in the primate globus pallidus. *Journal of Neuroscience, 25,* 2965–2976. (8)

Uchida, N., Takahashi, Y. K., Tanifuji, M., & Mori, K., (2000). Odor maps in the mammalian olfactory bulb: Domain organization and odorant structural features. *Nature Neuroscience, 3,* 1035–1043. (7)

Udry, J. R., & Chantala, K. (2006). Masculinity–femininity predicts sexual orientation in men but not in women. *Journal of Biosocial Science, 38,* 797–809. (11)

Udry, J. R., & Morris, N. M. (1968). Distribution of coitus in the menstrual cycle. *Nature, 220,* 593–596. (11)

Uekita, T., & Okaichi, H. (2005). NMDA antagonist MK-801 does not interfere with the use of spatial representation in a familiar environment. *Behavioral Neuroscience, 119,* 548–556. (13)

Uhr, M., Tontsch, A., Namendorf, C., Ripke, S., Lucae, S., Ising, M., et al. (2008). Polymorphisms in the drug transporter gene *ABCB1* predict antidepressant treatment response in depression. *Neuron, 57,* 203–209. (15)

Unterberg, A. W., Stover, J., Kress, B., & Kiening, K. L. (2004). Edema and brain trauma. *Neuroscience, 129,* 1021–1029. (5)

Urry, H. L., Nitschke, J. B., Dolski, I., Jackson, D. C., Dalton, K. M., Mueller, C. J., et al. (2004). Making a life worth living: Neural correlates of well-being. *Psychological Science, 15,* 367–372. (12)

U.S.–Venezuela Collaborative Research Project. (2004). Venezuelan kindreds reveal that genetic and environmental factors modulate Huntington's disease age of onset. *Proceedings of the National Academy of Sciences, USA, 101,* 3498–3503. (8)

Uwano, T., Nishijo, H., Ono, T., & Tamura, R. (1995). Neuronal responsiveness to various sensory stimuli, and associative learning in the rat amygdala. *Neuroscience, 68,* 339–361. (12)

Vaidya, J. G., Paradiso, S., Ponto, L. L. B., McCormick, L. M., & Robinson, R. G. (2007). Aging, grey matter, and blood flow in the anterior cingulate cortex. *NeuroImage, 37,* 1346–1353. (5)

Vaishnavi, S., Calhoun, J., & Chatterjee, A. (2001). Binding personal and peripersonal space: Evidence from tactile extinction. *Journal of Cognitive Neuroscience, 13,* 181–189. (14)

Valente, E. M., Abou-Sleiman, P. M., Caputo, V., Muquit, M. M. K., Harvey, K., Gispert, S., et al. (2004). Hereditary early-onset Parkinson's disease caused by mutations in *PINK1*. *Science, 304,* 1158–1160. (8)

Vallines, I., & Greenlee, M. W. (2006). Saccadic suppression of retinotopically localized blood oxygen level-dependent responses in human primary visual area V1. *Journal of Neuroscience, 26,* 5965–5969. (6)

Valzelli, L. (1973). The "isolation syndrome" in mice. *Psychopharmacologia, 31,* 305–320. (12)

Valzelli, L. (1980). *An approach to neuroanatomical and neurochemical psychophysiology.* Torino, Italy: C. G. Edizioni Medico Scientifiche. (10, 15)

Valzelli, L., & Bernasconi, S. (1979). Aggressiveness by isolation and brain serotonin turnover changes in different strains of mice. *Neuropsychobiology, 5,* 129–135. (12)

van Anders, S. M., & Watson, N. V. (2006). Relationship status and testosterone in North American heterosexual and non-heterosexual men and women: Cross-sectional and longitudinal data. *Psychoneuroendocrinology, 31,* 715–723. (11)

Van Cantfort, T. E., Gardner, B. T., & Gardner, R. A. (1989). Developmental trends in replies to Wh- questions by children and chimpanzees. In R. A. Gardner, B. T. Gardner, & T. E. Van Cantfort (Eds.), *Teaching sign language to chimpanzees* (pp. 198–239). Albany: State University of New York Press. (14)

van den Pol, A. N. (1999). Hypothalamic hypocretin (orexin): Robust innervation of the spinal cord. *Journal of Neuroscience, 19,* 3171–3182. (10)

Van der Borght, K., Havekes, R., Bos, T., Eggen, B. J. L., & Van der Zee, E. A. (2007). Exercise improves memory acquisition and retrieval in the Y-maze task: Relationship with hippocampal neurogenesis. *Behavioral Neuroscience, 121,* 324–334. (5)

Van der Does, A. J. W. (2001). The effects of tryptophan depletion on mood and psychiatric symptoms. *Journal of Affective Disorders, 64,* 107–119. (12)

van der Stelt, M., Veldhuis, W. B., Maccarrone, M., Bär, P., Nicolay, K., Veldink, G. A., et al. (2002). Acute neuronal injury, excitotoxicity, and the endocannabinoid system. *Molecular Neurobiology, 26,* 317–346. (5)

van der Vegt, B. J., Lieuwes, N., van de Wall, E. H. E. M., Kato, K., Moya-Albiol, L., Martínez-Sanchis, W., et al. (2003). Activation of serotonergic neurotransmission during the performance of aggressive behavior in rats. *Behavioral Neuroscience, 117,* 667–674. (12)

Van Essen, D. C., & DeYoe, E. A. (1995). Concurrent processing in the primate visual cortex. In M. S. Gazzaniga (Ed.), *The cognitive neurosciences* (pp. 383–400). Cambridge, MA: MIT Press. (6)

van Honk, J., & Schutter, D. J. L. G. (2007). Testosterone reduces conscious detection of signals serving social correction. *Psychological Science, 18,* 663–667. (12)

Van Horn, J. D., Grafton, S. T., Rockmore, D., & Gazzaniga, M. S. (2004). Sharing neuroimaging studies of human cognition. *Nature Neuroscience, 7,* 473–481. (4)

van Praag, H., Kempermann, G., & Gage, F. H. (1999). Running increases cell proliferation and neurogenesis in the adult mouse dentate gyrus. *Nature Neuroscience, 2,* 266–270. (5)

van Praag, H., Schinder, A. F., Christie, B. R., Toni, N., Palmer, T. D., & Gage, F. H. (2002). Functional neurogenesis in the adult hippocampus. *Nature, 415,* 1030–1034. (5)

Van Wanrooij, M. M., & Van Opstal, A. J. (2004). Contribution of head shadow and pinna cues to chronic monaural sound localization. *Journal of Neuroscience, 24,* 4163–4171. (4)

Van Wanrooij, M. M., & Van Opstal, A. J. (2005). Relearning sound localization with a new ear. *Journal of Neuroscience, 25,* 5413–5424. (7)

Van Zoeren, J. G., & Stricker, E. M. (1977). Effects of preoptic, lateral hypothalamic, or dopamine-depleting lesions on behavioral thermoregulation in rats exposed to the cold. *Journal of Comparative and Physiological Psychology, 91,* 989–999. (10)

van Zutphen, B. (2001). European researchers encourage improvement in lab animal welfare. *Nature, 409,* 452. (1)

Vandenbulcke, M., Peeters, R., Fannes, K., & Vandenberghe, R. (2006). Knowledge of visual attributes in the right hemisphere. *Nature Neuroscience, 9,* 964–970. (14)

Vanderschuren, L. J. M. J., & Everitt, B. J. (2004). Drug seeking becomes compulsive after prolonged cocaine self-administration. *Science, 305,* 1017–1019. (3)

Vanduffel, W., Fize, D., Mandeville, J. B., Nelissen, K., Van Hecke, P., Rosen, B. R., et al. (2001). Visual motion processing investigated using contrast agent-enhanced fMRI in awake behaving monkeys. *Neuron, 32,* 565–577. (6)

Varela, F., Lachaux, J.-P., Rodriguez, E., & Martinerie, J. (2001). The brainweb: Phase synchronization and large-scale integration. *Nature Reviews Neuroscience, 2,* 229–239. (4)

Vargha-Khadem, F., Gadian, D. G., Copp, A., & Mishkin, M. (2005). *FOXP2* and the neuroanatomy of speech and language. *Nature Reviews Neuroscience, 6,* 131–138. (14)

Vawter, M. P., Evans, S., Choudary, P., Tomita, H., Meador-Woodruff, J., Molnar, M., et al. (2004). Gender-specific gene expression in post-mortem human brain. Localization to sex chromosomes. *Neuropsychopharmacology, 29,* 373–384. (11)

Verhage, M., Maia, A. S., Plomp, J. J., Brussard, A. B., Heeroma, J. H., Vermeer, H., et al. (2000). Synaptic assembly of the brain in the absence of neurotransmitter secretion. *Science, 287,* 864–869. (5)

Verrey, F., & Beron, J. (1996). Activation and supply of channels and pumps by aldosterone. *News in Physiological Sciences, 11,* 126–133. (10)

Victor, M., Adams, R. D., & Collins, G. H. (1971). *The Wernicke-Korsakoff syndrome.* Philadelphia: Davis. (13)

Virkkunen, M., DeJong, J., Bartko, J., Goodwin, F. K., & Linnoila, M. (1989). Relationship of psychobiological variables to recidivism in violent offenders and impulsive fire setters. *Archives of General Psychiatry, 46,* 600–603. (12)

Virkkunen, M., Eggert, M., Rawlings, R., & Linnoila, M. (1996). A prospective follow-up study of alcoholic violent offenders and fire setters. *Archives of General Psychiatry, 53,* 523–529. (12)

Virkkunen, M., Nuutila, A., Goodwin, F. K., & Linnoila, M. (1987). Cerebrospinal fluid monoamine metabolite levels in male arsonists. *Archives of General Psychiatry, 44,* 241–247. (12)

Virkkunen, M., Rawlings, R., Tokola, R., Poland, R. E., Guidotti, A., Nemeroff, C., et al. (1994). CSF biochemistries, glucose metabolism, and diurnal activity rhythms in alcoholic, violent offenders, fire setters, and healthy volunteers. *Archives of General Psychiatry, 51,* 20–27. (3)

Visser, E. K., Beersma, G. M., & Daan, S. (1999). Melatonin suppression by light in humans is maximal when the nasal part of the retina is illuminated. *Journal of Biological Rhythms, 14,* 116–121. (9)

Viswanathan, A., & Freeman, R. D. (2007). Neurometabolic coupling in cerebral cortex reflects synaptic more than spiking activity. *Nature Neuroscience, 10,* 1308–1312. (4)

Vliegen, J., Van Grootel, T. J., & Van Opstal, A. J. (2004). Dynamic sound localization during rapid eye–head gaze shifts. *Journal of Neuroscience, 24,* 9291–9302. (7)

Vocci, F. J., Acri, J., & Elkashef, A. (2005). Medication development for addictive disorders: The state of the science. *American Journal of Psychiatry, 162,* 1432-1440. (3)

Vogels, R., Biederman, I., Bar, M., & Lorincz, A. (2001). Inferior temporal neurons show greater sensitivity to nonaccidental than to metric shape differences. *Journal of Cognitive Neuroscience, 13,* 444–453. (6)

Volavka, J., Czobor, P., Goodwin, D. W., Gabrielli, W. F., Penick, E. C., Mednick, S. A., et al. (1996). The electroencephalogram after alcohol administration in high-risk men and the development of alcohol use disorders 10 years later. *Archives of General Psychiatry, 53,* 258–263. (3)

Volkow, N. D., Wang, G.-J., Fischman, M. W., Foltin, R. W., Fowler, J. S., Abumrad, N. N., et al. (1997). Relationship between subjective effects of cocaine and dopamine transporter occupancy. *Nature, 386,* 827–830. (3)

Volkow, N. D., Wang, G.-J., & Fowler, J. S. (1997). Imaging studies of cocaine in the human brain and studies of the cocaine addict. *Annals of the New York Academy of Sciences, 820,* 41–55. (3)

Volkow, N. D., Wang, G.-J., Fowler, J. S., Gatley, S. J., Logan, J., Ding, Y.-S., et al. (1998). Dopamine transporter occupancies in the human brain induced by therapeutic doses of oral methylphenidate. *American Journal of Psychiatry, 155,* 1325–1331. (3)

Volkow, N. D., Wang, G.-J., Fowler, J. S., Logan, J., Gatley, S. J., Hitzemann, R., et al. (1997). Decreased striatal dopaminergic responsiveness in detoxified cocaine-dependent subjects. *Nature, 386,* 830–833. (3)

Volkow, N. D., Wang, G.-J., Ma, Y., Fowler, J. S., Wong, C., Ding, Y.-S., et al. (2005). Activation of orbital and medial prefrontal cortex by methylphenidate in cocaine-addicted subjects but not in controls: Relevance to addiction. *Journal of Neuroscience, 25,* 3932–3939. (3)

Volkow, N. D., Wang, G.-J., Telang, F., Fowler, J. S., Jayne, M., Ma, Y., et al. (2007). Profound decreases in dopamine release in striatum in detoxified alcoholics: Possible orbitofrontal involvement. *Journal of Neuroscience, 27,* 12700–12706. (3)

Volkow, N. D., Wang, G.-J., Telang, F., Fowler, J. S., Logan, J., Childress, A.-R., et al. (2006). Cocaine cues and dopamine in dorsal striatum: Mechanism of craving in cocaine addiction. *Journal of Neuroscience, 26,* 6583–6588. (3)

Volterra, A., & Meldolesi, J. (2005). Astrocytes, from brain glue to communication elements: The revolution continues. *Nature Reviews Neuroscience, 6,* 626–640. (2)

von Békésy, G. (1956). Current status of theories of hearing. *Science, 123,* 779–783. (7)

von der Ohe, C. G., Darian-Smith, C., Garner, C. C., & Heller, H. C. (2006). Ubiquitous and temperature-dependent neural plasticity in hibernators. *Journal of Neuroscience, 26,* 10590–10598. (9)

von Gall, C., Garabette, M. L., Kell, C. A., Frenzel, S., Dehghani, F., Schumm-Draeger, P. M., et al. (2002). Rhythmic gene expression in pituitary depends on heterologous sensitization by the neurohormone melatonin. *Nature Neuroscience, 5,* 234–238. (9)

von Melchner, L., Pallas, S. L., & Sur, M. (2000). Visual behaviour mediated by retinal projections directed to the visual pathway. *Nature, 404,* 871–876. (5)

Vrba, E. S. (1998). Multiphasic growth models and the evolution of prolonged growth exemplified by human brain evolution. *Journal of Theoretical Biology, 190,* 227–239. (5)

Vuilleumier, P. (2005). Cognitive science: Staring fear in the face. *Nature, 433,* 22–23. (12)

Vuilleumier, P., Armony, J. L., Driver, J., & Dolan, R. J. (2001). Effects of attention and emotion on face processing in the human brain: An event-related fMRI study. *Neuron, 30,* 829–841. (12)

Vyazovskiy, V. V., Cirelli, C., Pfister-Genskow, M., Faraguna, U., & Tononi, G. (2008). Molecular and electrophysiological evidence for net synaptic potentiation in wake and depression in sleep. *Nature Neuroscience, 11,* 200–208. (9)

Wager, T. D., Rilling, J. K., Smith, E. E., Sokolik, A., Casey, K. L., Davidson, R. J., et al. (2004). Placebo-induced changes in fMRI in the anticipation and experience of pain. *Science, 303,* 1162–1167. (7)

Wager, T. D., Scott, D. J., & Zubieta, J.-K. (2007). Placebo effects on human μ-opioid activity during pain. *Proceedings of the National Academy of Sciences, USA, 104,* 11056–11061. (7)

Wagner, A. D., Schacter, D. L., Rotte, M., Koutstaal, W., Maril, A., Dale, A. M., et al. (1998). Building memories: Remembering and forgetting of verbal experiences as predicted by brain activity. *Science, 281,* 1188–1191. (4)

Wagner, E. L., & Gleeson, T. T. (1997). Postexercise thermoregulatory behavior and recovery from exercise in desert iguanas. *Physiology & Behavior, 61,* 175–180. (10)

Wagner, U., Gais, S., Haider, H., Verleger, R., & Born, J. (2004). Sleep inspires insight. *Nature, 427,* 352–355. (9)

Waisbren, S. R., Brown, M. J., de Sonneville, L. M. J., & Levy, H. L. (1994). Review of neuropsychological functioning in treated phenylketonuria: An information-processing approach. *Acta Paediatrica, 83*(Suppl. 407), 98–103. (1)

Waldherr, M., & Neumann, I. D. (2007). Centrally released oxytocin mediates mating-induced anxiolysis in male rats. *Proceedings of the National Academy of Sciences, USA, 104,* 16681–16684. (11)

Waldvogel, J. A. (1990). The bird's eye view. *American Scientist, 78,* 342–353. (6)

Wallesch, C.-W., Henriksen, L., Kornhuber, H. H., & Paulson, O. B. (1985). Observations on regional cerebral blood flow in cortical and subcortical structures during language production in normal man. *Brain and Language, 25,* 224–233. (14)

Wallman, J., & Pettigrew, J. D. (1985). Conjugate and disjunctive saccades in two avian species with contrasting oculomotor strategies. *Journal of Neuroscience, 5,* 1418–1428. (6)

Walsh, G. S., Orike, N., Kaplan, D. R., & Miller, F. D. (2004). The invulnerability of adult neurons: A critical role of p73. *Journal of Neuroscience, 24,* 9638–9647. (5)

Walsh, T., McClellan, J. M., McCarthy, S. E., Addington, A. M., Pierce, S. B., & Cooper, G. M. (2008). Rare structural variants disrupt multiple genes in neurodevelopmental pathways in schizophrenia. *Science, 320,* 539–543. (15)

Walsh, V., & Cowey, A. (2000). Transcranial magnetic stimulation and cognitive neuroscience. *Nature Reviews Neuroscience, 1,* 73–79. (4)

Wang, A., Liang, Y., Fridell, R. A., Probst, F. J., Wilcox, E. R., Touchman, J. W., et al. (1998). Associations of unconventional myosin *MYO15* mutations with human nonsyndromic deafness *DFNB3. Science, 280,* 1447–1451. (7)

Wang, H., & Tessier-Lavigne, M. (1999). En passant neurotrophic action of an intermediate axonal target in the developing mammalian CNS. *Nature, 401,* 765–769. (5)

Wang, Q., Schoenlein, R. W., Peteanu, L. A., Mathies, R. A., & Shank, C. V. (1994). Vibrationally coherent photochemistry in the femtosecond primary event of vision. *Science, 266,* 422–424. (6)

Wang, T., Okano, Y., Eisensmith, R., Huang, S. Z., Zeng, Y. T., Wilson, H. Y. L., et al. (1989). Molecular genetics of phenylketonuria in Orientals: Linkage disequilibrium between a termination mutation and haplotype 4 of the phenylalanine hydroxylase gene. *American Journal of Human Genetics, 45,* 675–680. (1)

Wang, X., Lu, T., Snider, R. K., & Liang, L. (2005). Sustained firing in auditory cortex evoked by preferred stimuli. *Nature, 435,* 341–346. (7)

Wang, Z., Faith, M., Patterson, F., Tang, K., Kerrin, K., Wileyto, E. P., et al. (2007). Neural substrates of abstinence-induced cigarette cravings in chronic smokers. *Journal of Neuroscience, 27,* 14035–14040. (3)

Warach, S. (1995). Mapping brain pathophysiology and higher cortical function with magnetic resonance imaging. *The Neuroscientist, 1,* 221–235. (4)

Ward, I. L., Bennett, A. L., Ward, O. B., Hendricks, S. E., & French, J. A. (1999). Androgen threshold to activate copulation differs in male rats prenatally exposed to alcohol, stress, or both factors. *Hormones and Behavior, 36,* 129–140. (11)

Ward, I. L., Romeo, R. D., Denning, J. H., & Ward, O. B. (1999). Fetal alcohol exposure blocks full masculinization of the dorsolateral nucleus in rat spinal cord. *Physiology & Behavior, 66,* 571–575. (11)

Ward, I. L., Ward, B., Winn, R. J., & Bielawski, D. (1994). Male and female sexual behavior potential of male rats prenatally exposed to the influence of alcohol, stress, or both factors. *Behavioral Neuroscience, 108,* 1188–1195. (11)

Ward, I. L., & Ward, O. B. (1985). Sexual behavior differentiation: Effects of prenatal manipulations in rats. In N. Adler, D. Pfaff, & R. W. Goy (Eds.), *Handbook of behavioral neurobiology* (Vol. 7, pp. 77–98). New York: Plenum Press. (11)

Ward, O. B., Monaghan, E. P., & Ward, I. L. (1986). Naltrexone blocks the effects of prenatal stress on sexual behavior differentiation in male rats. *Pharmacology Biochemistry and Behavior, 25,* 573–576. (11)

Ward, O. B., Ward, I. L., Denning, J. H., French, J. A., & Hendricks, S. E. (2002). Postparturitional testosterone surge in male offspring of rats stressed and/or fed ethanol during late pregnancy. *Hormones and Behavior, 41,* 229–235. (11)

Ward, R., Danziger, S., Owen, V., & Rafal, R. (2002). Deficits in spatial coding and feature binding following damage to spatiotopic maps in the human pulvinar. *Nature Neuroscience, 5,* 99–100. (4)

Warren, R. M. (1999). *Auditory perception.* Cambridge, England: Cambridge University Press. (7)

Wässle, H. (2004). Parallel processing in the mammalian retina. *Nature Neuroscience, 5,* 747–757. (6)

Watanabe, D., Savion-Lemieux, T., & Penhune, V. B. (2007). The effect of early musical training on adult motor performance: Evidence for a sensitive period in motor learning. *Experimental Brain Research, 176,* 332–340. (5)

Waxman, S. G., & Ritchie, J. M. (1985). Organization of ion channels in the myelinated nerve fiber. *Science, 228,* 1502–1507. (2)

Weaver, D. R. (1997). Reproductive safety of melatonin: A "wonder drug" to wonder about. *Journal of Biological Rhythms, 12,* 682–689. (9)

Webb, W. B. (1974). Sleep as an adaptive response. *Perceptual and Motor Skills, 38,* 1023–1027. (9)

Weber-Fox, C. M., & Neville, H. J. (1996). Maturational constraints on functional specializations for language processing: ERP and behavioral evidence in bilingual speakers. *Journal of Cognitive Neuroscience, 8,* 231–256. (14)

Wegener, D., Freiwald, W. A., & Kreiter, A. K. (2004). The influence of sustained selective attention on stimulus selectivity in macaque visual area MT. *Journal of Neuroscience, 24,* 6106–6114. (14)

Wehr, T. A., Turner, E. H., Shimada, J. M., Lowe, C. H., Barker, C., & Leinbenluft, E. (1998). Treatment of a rapidly cycling bipolar patient by using extended bed rest and darkness to stabilize the timing and duration of sleep. *Biological Psychiatry, 43,* 822–828. (15)

Weidensaul, S. (1999). *Living on the wind.* New York: North Point Press. (10)

Weinberger, D. R. (1996). On the plausibility of "the neurodevelopmental hypothesis" of schizophrenia. *Neuropsychopharmacology, 14,* 1S–11S. (15)

Weinberger, D. R. (1999). Cell biology of the hippocampal formation in schizophrenia. *Biological Psychiatry, 45,* 395–402. (15)

Weindl, A. (1973). Neuroendocrine aspects of circumventricular organs. In W. F. Ganong & L. Martini (Eds.), *Frontiers in neuroendocrinology 1973* (pp. 3–32). New York: Oxford University Press. (10)

Weiner, R. D. (1979). The psychiatric use of electrically induced seizures. *American Journal of Psychiatry, 136,* 1507–1517. (15)

Weinshenker, D., & Schroeder, J. P. (2007). There and back again: A tale of norepinephrine and drug addiction. *Neuropsychopharmacology, 32,* 1433–1451. (3)

Weiskrantz, L., Warrington, E. K., Sanders, M. D., & Marshall, J. (1974). Visual capacity in the hemianopic field following a restricted occipital ablation. *Brain, 97,* 709–728. (6)

Weiss, P. (1924). Die funktion transplantierter amphibienextremitäten. Aufstellung einer resonanztheorie der motorischen nerventätigkeit auf grund abstimmter endorgane [The function of transplanted amphibian limbs. Presentation of a resonance theory of motor nerve action upon tuned end organs]. *Archiv für Mikroskopische Anatomie und Entwicklungsmechanik, 102,* 635–672. (5)

Weiss, P. H., Zilles, K., & Fink, G. R. (2005). When visual perception causes feeling: Enhanced cross-modal processing in grapheme-color synesthesia. *NeuroImage, 28,* 859–868. (7)

Weissman, D. H., Roberts, K. C., Visscher, K. M., & Woldorff, M. G. (2006). The neural bases of momentary lapses in attention. *Nature Neuroscience, 9,* 971–978. (4)

Weisstaub, N. V., Zhou, M., Lira, A., Lambe, E., González-Maeso, J., Hornung, J.-P., et al. (2006). Cortical 5-HT_{2A} receptor signaling modulates anxiety-like behaviors in mice. *Science, 313,* 536–540. (12)

Weisz, J. R., McCarty, C. A., & Valeri, S. M. (2006). Effects of psychotherapy for depression in children and adolescents: A meta-analysis. *Psychological Bulletin, 132,* 132–149. (15)

Welch, J. M., Lu, J., Rodriguiz, R. M., Trotta, N. C., Peca, J., J, Ding, J.-D., et al. (2007). Cortico-striatal synaptic defects and OCD-like behaviours in *Sapap-3*-mutant mice. *Nature, 448,* 894–900. (3)

Weller, L., Weller, A., Koresh-Kamin, H., & Ben-Shoshan, R. (1999). Menstrual synchrony in a sample of working women. *Psychoneuroendocrinology, 24,* 449–459. (7)

Weller, L., Weller, A., & Roizman, S. (1999). Human menstrual synchrony in families and among close friends: Examining the importance of mutual exposure. *Journal of Comparative Psychology, 113,* 261–268. (7)

Wender, P. H., Kety, S. S., Rosenthal, D., Schulsinger, F., Ortmann, J., & Lunde, I. (1986). Psychiatric disorders in the biological and adoptive families of adopted individuals with affective disorders. *Archives of General Psychiatry, 43,* 923–929. (15)

Wessinger, C. M., Fendrich, R., & Gazzaniga, M. S. (1997). Islands of residual vision in hemianopic patients. *Journal of Cognitive Neuropsychology, 9,* 203–221. (6)

Wessinger, C. M., VanMeter, J., Tian, B., Van Lare, J., Pekar, J., & Rauschecker, J. P. (2001). Hierarchical organization of the human auditory cortex revealed by functional magnetic resonance imaging. *Journal of Cognitive Neuroscience, 13,* 1–7. (7)

Westbrook, G. L., & Jahr, C. E. (1989). Glutamate receptors in excitatory neurotransmission. *Seminars in the Neurosciences, 1,* 103–114. (3)

Westergaard, G. C., Cleveland, A., Trenkle, M. K., Lussier, I. D., & Higley, J. D. (2003). CSF 5-HIAA concentration as an early screening tool for predicting significant life history outcomes in female specific-pathogen-free (SPF) rhesus macaques (*Macaca mulatta*) maintained in captive breeding groups. *Journal of Medical Primatology, 32,* 95–104. (12)

Whalen, P. J. (1998). Fear, vigilance, and ambiguity: Initial neuroimaging studies of the human amygdala. *Current Directions in Psychological Science, 7,* 177–188. (12)

Whalen, P. J., Kagan, J., Cook, R. G., Davis, F. C., Kim, H., Polis, S., et al. (2004). Human amygdala responsivity to masked fearful eye whites. *Science, 306,* 2061. (12)

Wheeler, M. E., & Treisman, A. (2002). Binding in short-term visual memory. *Journal of Experimental Psychology: General, 131,* 48–64. (4)

White, L. E., Coppola, D. M., & Fitzpatrick, D. (2001). The contribution of sensory experience to the maturation of orientation selectivity in ferret visual cortex. *Nature, 411,* 1049–1052. (6)

Whitman, B. W., & Packer, R. J. (1993). The photic sneeze reflex: Literature review and discussion. *Neurology, 43,* 868–871. (8)

Whitwell, J. L., Sampson, E. L., Loy, C. T., Warren, J. E., Rossor, M. N., Fox, N. C., et al. (2007). VBM signatures of abnormal eating behaviours in frontotemporal lobar degeneration. *NeuroImage, 35,* 207–213. (10)

Whyte, J., Katz, D., Long, D., DiPasquale, M. C., Polansky, M., Kalmar, K., et al. (2005). Predictors of outcome in prolonged posttraumatic disorders of consciousness and assessment of medication effects: A multicenter study. *Archives of Physical Medicine and Rehabilitation, 86,* 453–462. (5)

Wichmann, T., Vitek, J. L., & DeLong, M. R. (1995). Parkinson's disease and the basal ganglia: Lessons from the laboratory and from neurosurgery. *The Neuroscientist, 1,* 236–244. (8)

Wicker, B., Keysers, C., Plailly, J., Royet, J.-P., Gallese, V., & Rizzolatti, G. (2003). Both of us disgusted in *my* insula: The common neural basis of seeing and feeling disgust. *Neuron, 40,* 655–664. (8, 12)

Widom, C. S., & Brzustowicz, L. M. (2006). MAOI and the "cycle of violence": Childhood abuse and neglect, MAOA genotype, and risk of violent and antisocial behavior. *Biological Psychiatry, 60,* 684–689. (12)

Wiesel, T. N. (1982). Postnatal development of the visual cortex and the influence of environment. *Nature, 299,* 583–591. (6)

Wiesel, T. N., & Hubel, D. H. (1963). Single-cell responses in striate cortex of kittens deprived of vision in one eye. *Journal of Neurophysiology, 26,* 1003–1017. (6)

Wild, H. M., Butler, S. R., Carden, D., & Kulikowski, J. J. (1985). Primate cortical area V4 important for colour constancy but not wavelength discrimination. *Nature, 313,* 133–135. (6)

Wilens, T. E., Faraone, S. V., Biederman, J., & Gunawardene, S. (2003). Does stimulant therapy of attention-deficit/hyperactivity disorder beget later substance abuse? A meta-analytic review of the literature. *Pediatrics, 111,* 179–185. (3)

Wilensky, A. E., Schafe, G. E., Kristensen, M. P., & LeDoux, J. E. (2006). Rethinking the fear circuit. *Journal of Neuroscience, 26,* 12387–12396. (12)

Willerman, L., Schultz, R., Rutledge, J. N., & Bigler, E. D. (1991). In vivo brain size and intelligence. *Intelligence, 15,* 223–228. (4)

Williams, C. L. (1986). A reevaluation of the concept of separable periods of organizational and activational actions of estrogens in development of brain and behavior. *Annals of the New York Academy of Sciences, 474,* 282–292. (11)

Williams, G., Cai, X. J., Elliott, J. C., & Harrold, J. A. (2004). Anabolic neuropeptides. *Physiology & Behavior, 81,* 211–222. (10)

Williams, J. H. G., Walter, G. D., Gilchrist, A., Perrett, D. I., Murray, A. D., & Whiten, A. (2006). Neural mechanisms of imitation and "mirror neuron" functioning in autistic spectrum disorder. *Neuropsychologia, 44,* 610–621. (8)

Williams, M. A., Morris, A. P., McGlone, F., Abbott, D. F., & Mattingley, J. B. (2004). Amygdala responses to fearful and happy facial expressions under conditions of binocular suppression. *Journal of Neuroscience, 24,* 2898–2904. (14)

Williams, M. T., Davis, H. N., McCrea, A. E., Long, S. J., & Hennessy, M. B. (1999). Changes in the hormonal concentrations of pregnant rats and their fetuses following multiple exposures to a stressor during the third trimester. *Neurotoxicology and Teratology, 21,* 403–414. (11)

Williams, R. W., & Herrup, K. (1988). The control of neuron number. *Annual Review of Neuroscience, 11,* 423–453. (2, 8)

Williamson, D. A., Ravussin, E., Wong, M.-L., Wagner, A., DiPaoli, A., Caglayan, S., et al. (2005). Microanalysis of eating behavior of three leptin deficient adults treated with leptin therapy. *Appetite, 45,* 75–80. (10)

Willingham, D. B., Koroshetz, W. J., & Peterson, E. W. (1996). Motor skills have diverse neural bases: Spared and impaired skill acquisition in Huntington's disease. *Neuropsychology, 10,* 315–321. (8)

Wilson, B. A., Baddeley, A. D., & Kapur, N. (1995). Dense amnesia in a professional musician following herpes simplex virus encephalitis. *Journal of Clinical and Experimental Neuropsychology, 17,* 668–681. (13)

Wilson, J. D., George, F. W., & Griffin, J. E. (1981). The hormonal control of sexual development. *Science, 211,* 1278–1284. (11)

Wilson, R. I., & Nicoll, R. A. (2002). Endocannabinoid signaling in the brain. *Science, 296,* 678–682. (3)

Winer, G. A., Cottrell, J. F., Gregg, V., Fournier, J. S., & Bica. L. A. (2002). Fundamentally misunderstanding visual perception: Adults' belief in visual emissions. *American Psychologist, 57,* 417–424. (6)

Winfree, A. T. (1983). Impact of a circadian clock on the timing of human sleep. *American Journal of Physiology, 245,* R497–R504. (9)

Winocur, G., & Hasher, L. (1999). Aging and time-of-day effects on cognition in rats. *Behavioral Neuroscience, 113,* 991–997. (9)

Winocur, G., & Hasher, L. (2004). Age and time-of-day effects on learning and memory in a non-matching-to-sample test. *Neurobiology of Aging, 25,* 1107–1115. (9)

Winocur, G., Moscovitch, M., & Sekeres, M. (2007). Memory consolidation or transformation: Context manipulation and hippocampal representations of memory. *Nature Neuroscience, 10,* 555–557. (13)

Winston, J. S., Strange, B. A., O'Doherty, J., & Dolan, R. J. (2002). Automatic and intentional brain responses during evaluation of trustworthiness of faces. *Nature Neuroscience, 5,* 277–283. (12)

Wirdefeldt, K., Gatz, M., Pawitan, Y., & Pedersen, N. L. (2005). Risk and protective factors for Parkinson's disease: A study in Swedish twins. *Annals of Neurology, 57,* 27–33. (8)

Wirz-Justice, A., & Van den Hoofdakker, R. H. (1999). Sleep deprivation in depression: What do we know, where do we go? *Biological Psychiatry, 46,* 445–453. (15)

Wirz-Justice, A., Werth, E., Renz, C., Müller, S., & Kräuchi, K. (2002). No evidence for a phase delay in human circadian rhythms after a single morning melatonin administration. *Journal of Pineal Research, 32,* 1–5. (9)

Wise, R. A. (1996). Addictive drugs and brain stimulation reward. *Annual Review of Neuroscience, 19,* 319–340. (3)

Witelson, S. F., Glezer, I. I., & Kigar, D. L. (1995). Women have greater density of neurons in posterior temporal cortex. *Journal of Neuroscience, 15,* 3418–3428. (4)

Witelson, S. F., Kigar, D. L., & Harvey, T. (1999). The exceptional brain of Albert Einstein. *Lancet, 353,* 2149–2153. (4)

Witelson, S. F., & Pallie, W. (1973). Left hemisphere specialization for language in the newborn: Neuroanatomical evidence of asymmetry. *Brain, 96,* 641–646. (14)

Wolf, S. (1995). Dogmas that have hindered understanding. *Integrative Physiological and Behavioral Science, 30,* 3–4. (12)

Wolff, P. H. (1993). Impaired temporal resolution in developmental dyslexia. *Annals of the New York Academy of Sciences, 682,* 87–103. (14)

Wolkin, A., Rusinek, H., Vaid, G., Arena, L., Lafargue, T., Sanfilipo, M., et al. (1998). Structural magnetic resonance image averaging in schizophrenia. *American Journal of Psychiatry, 155,* 1064–1073. (15)

Wolpaw, J. R., & McFarland, D. J. (2004). Control of a two-dimensional movement signal by a noninvasive brain-computer interface in humans. *Proceedings of the National Academy of Sciences, USA, 101,* 17849–17854. (8)

Wolpert, L. (1991). *The triumph of the embryo.* Oxford, England: Oxford University Press. (5)

Womelsdorf, T., Schoffelen, J.-M., Oostenveld, R., Singer, W., Desimone, R., Engel, A. K., et al. (2007). Modulation of neuronal interactions through neuronal synchronization. *Science, 316,* 1609–1612. (14)

Wong, P. C. M., Skoe, E., Russo, N. M., Dees, T., & Kraus, N. (2007). Musical experience shapes human brainstem encoding of linguistic pitch perception. *Nature Neuroscience, 10,* 420–422. (5)

Wong-Riley, M. T. T. (1989). Cytochrome oxidase: An endogenous metabolic marker for neuronal activity. *Trends in Neurosciences, 12,* 94–101. (2)

Woodberry, K. A., Giuliano, A. J., & Seidman, L. J. (2008). Premorbid IQ in schizophrenia: A meta-analytic review. *American Journal of Psychiatry, 165,* 579–587. (15)

Wooding, S., Kim, U., Bamshad, M J., Larsen, J., Jorde, L. B., & Drayna, D. (2004). Natural selection and molecular evolution in *PTC,* a bitter-taste receptor gene. *American Journal of Human Genetics, 74,* 637–646. (1)

Woodson, J. C., & Balleine, B. W. (2002). An assessment of factors contributing to instrumental performance for sexual reward in the rat. *Quarterly Journal of Experimental Psychology, 55B,* 75–88. (11)

Woodson, J. C., & Gorski, R. A. (2000). Structural sex differences in the mammalian brain: Reconsidering the male/female dichotomy. In A. Matsumoto (Ed.), *Sexual differentiation of the brain* (pp. 229–255). Boca Raton, FL: CRC Press. (4)

Woodworth, R. S. (1934). *Psychology* (3rd ed.). New York: Holt. (2)

Woolf, N. J. (1991). Cholinergic systems in mammalian brain and spinal cord. *Progress in Neurobiology, 37,* 475–524. (4)

Woolf, N. J. (1996). Global and serial neurons form a hierarchically arranged interface proposed to underlie memory and cognition. *Neuroscience, 74,* 625–651. (9)

Wright, I. C., Rabe-Hesketh, S., Woodruff, P. W. R., David, A. S., Murray, R. M., & Bullmore, E. T. (2000). Meta-analysis of regional brain volumes in schizophrenia. *American Journal of Psychiatry, 157,* 16–25. (15)

Wu, S. S., & Frucht, S. J. (2005). Treatment of Parkinson's disease: What's on the horizon? *CNS Drugs, 19,* 723–743. (8)

Wulfeck, B., & Bates, E. (1991). Differential sensitivity to errors of agreement and word order in Broca's aphasia. *Journal of Cognitive Neuroscience, 3,* 258–272. (14)

Wurtman, J. J. (1985). Neurotransmitter control of carbohydrate consumption. *Annals of the New York Academy of Sciences, 443,* 145–151. (3)

Wüst, S., Kasten, E., & Sabel, B. A. (2002). Blindsight after optic nerve injury indicates functionality of spared fibers. *Journal of Cognitive Neuroscience, 14,* 243–253. (6)

Wyart, C., Webster, W. W., Chen, J. H., Wilson, S. R., McClary, A., Khan, R. M., et al. (2007). Smelling a single component of male sweat alters levels of cortisol in women. *Journal of Neuroscience, 27,* 1261–1265. (7)

Wynne, C. D. L. (2004). The perils of anthropomorphism. *Nature, 428,* 606. (1)

Xu, H.-T., Pan, F., Yang, G., & Gan, W.-B. (2007). Choice of cranial window type for *in vivo* imaging affects dendritic spine turnover in the cortex. *Nature Neuroscience, 10,* 549–551. (5)

Xu, Y., Padiath, Q. S., Shapiro, R. E., Jones, C. R., Wu, S. C., Saigoh, N., et al. (2005). Functional consequences of a *CK1δ* mutation causing familial advanced sleep phase syndrome. *Nature, 434,* 640–644. (9)

Yamaguchi, S., Isejima, H., Matsuo, T., Okura, R., Yagita, K., Kobayashi, M., et al. (2003). Synchronization of cellular clocks in the suprachiasmatic nucleus. *Science, 302,* 1408–1412. (9)

Yamamoto, S., & Kitazawa, S. (2001). Reversal of subjective temporal order due to arm crossing. *Nature Neuroscience, 4,* 759–765. (2)

Yamamoto, T. (1984). Taste responses of cortical neurons. *Progress in Neurobiology, 23,* 273–315. (7)

Yanagisawa, K., Bartoshuk, L. M., Catalanotto, F. A., Karrer, T. A., & Kveton, J. F. (1998). Anesthesia of the chorda tympani nerve and taste phantoms. *Physiology & Behavior, 63,* 329–335. (7)

Yang, F., Lim, G. P., Begum, A. N., Ubeda, O. J., Simmons, M. R., Ambegaokar, S. S., et al. (2005). Curcumin inhibits formation of amyloid β oligomers and fibrils, binds plaques, and reduces amyloid *in vivo. Journal of Biological Chemistry, 280,* 5892–5901. (13)

Yavich, L., Forsberg, M. M., Karayiorgou, M., Gogos, J. A., & Männistö, P. T. (2007). Site-specific role of catechol-o-methyltransferase in dopamine overflow within prefrontal cortex and dorsal striatum. *Journal of Neuroscience, 27,* 10196–10202. (3)

Yee, B. K., Balic, E., Singer, P., Schwerdel, C., Grampp, T., Gabernet, L., et al. (2006). Disruption of glycine transporter 1 restricted to forebrain neurons is associated with a precognitive and antipsychotic phenotypic profile. *Journal of Neuroscience, 26,* 3169–3181. (15)

Yehuda, R. (1997). Sensitization of the hypothalamic-pituitary-adrenal axis in posttraumatic stress disorder. *Annals of the New York Academy of Sciences, 821,* 57–75. (12)

Yehuda, R. (2002). Post-traumatic stress disorder. *New England Journal of Medicine, 346,* 108–114. (12)

Yeomans, J. S., & Frankland, P. W. (1996). The acoustic startle reflex: Neurons and connections. *Brain Research Reviews,* 21, 301–314. (12)

Yin, H. H., & Knowlton, B. J. (2006). The role of the basal ganglia in habit formation. *Nature Reviews Neuroscience, 7,* 464–476. (8)

Yiu, G., & He, Z. (2006). Glial inhibition of CNS axon regeneration. *Nature Reviews Neuroscience, 7,* 617–627. (5)

Yolken, R. H., Bachmann, S., Rouslanova, I., Lillehoj, E., Ford, G., Torrey, E. F., et al. (2001). Antibodies to *Toxoplasma gondii* in individuals with first-episode schizophrenia. *Clinical Infectious Diseases, 32,* 842–844. (15)

Yoo, S.-S., Hu, P. T., Gujar, N., Jolesz, F. A., & Walker, M. P. (2007). A deficit in the ability to form new human memories without sleep. *Nature Neuroscience, 10,* 385–392. (9)

Yoshida, J., & Mori, K. (2007). Odorant category profile selectivity of olfactory cortex neurons. *Journal of Neuroscience, 27,* 9105–9114. (7)

Young, A. B. (1995). Huntington's disease: Lessons from and for molecular neuroscience. *The Neuroscientist, 1,* 51–58. (8)

Young, S. N., & Leyton, M. (2002). The role of serotonin in human mood and social interaction: Insight from altered tryptophan levels. *Pharmacology, Biochemistry and Behavior, 71,* 857–865. (12)

Yousem, D. M., Maldjian, J. A., Siddiqi, F., Hummel, T., Alsop, D. C., Geckle, R. J., et al. (1999). Gender effects on odor-stimulated functional magnetic resonance imaging. *Brain Research, 818,* 480–487. (7)

Yu, T. W., & Bargmann, C. I. (2001). Dynamic regulation of axon guidance. *Nature Neuroscience Supplement, 4,* 1169–1176. (5)

Zakharenko, S. S., Zablow, L., & Siegelbaum, S. A. (2001). Visualization of changes in presynaptic function during long-term synaptic plasticity. *Nature Neuroscience, 4,* 711–717. (13)

Zatorre, R. J., Bouffard, M., & Belin, P. (2004). Sensitivity to auditory object features in human temporal neocortex. *Journal of Neuroscience, 24,* 3637–3642. (7)

Zeevalk, G. D., Manzino, L., Hoppe, J., & Sonsalla, P. (1997). In vivo vulnerability of dopamine neurons to inhibition of energy metabolism. *European Journal of Pharmacology, 320,* 111–119. (8)

Zeitzer, J. M., Buckmaster, C. L., Parker, K. J., Hauck, C. M., Lyons, D. M., & Mignot, E. (2003). Circadian and homeostatic regulation of hypocretin in a primate model: Implications for the consolidation of wakefulness. *Journal of Neuroscience, 23,* 3555–3560. (9)

Zeki, S. (1980). The representation of colours in the cerebral cortex. *Nature, 284,* 412–418. (6)

Zeki, S. (1983). Colour coding in the cerebral cortex: The responses of wavelength-selective and colour-coded cells in monkey visual cortex to changes in wavelength composition. *Neuroscience, 9,* 767–781. (6)

Zeki, S., McKeefry, D. J., Bartels, A., & Frackowiak, R. S. J. (1998). Has a new color area been discovered? *Nature Neuroscience, 1,* 335. (6)

Zeki, S., & Shipp, S. (1988). The functional logic of cortical connections. *Nature, 335,* 311–317. (6)

Zhang, L. I., Bao, S., & Merzenich, M. M. (2001). Persistent and specific influences of early acoustic environments on primary auditory cortex. *Nature Neuroscience, 4,* 1123–1130. (5)

Zhang, X., & Firestein, S. (2002). The olfactory receptor gene superfamily of the mouse. *Nature Neuroscience, 5,* 124–133. (7)

Zhang, X., Gainetdinov, R. R., Beaulieu, J.-M., Sotnikova, T. D., Burch, L. H., Williams, R. B., et al. (2005). Loss-of-function mutation in tryptophan hydroxylase-2 identified in unipolar major depression. *Neuron, 45,* 11–16. (15)

Zhang, X., Smith, D. L., Meriin, A. B., Engemann, S., Russel, D. E., Roark, M., et al. (2005). A potent small molecule inhibits polyglutamine aggregation in Huntington's disease neurons and suppresses neurodegeneration *in vivo. Proceedings of the National Academy of Sciences, USA, 102,* 892–897. (8)

Zhang, Y., Proenca, R., Maffei, M., Barone, M., Leopold, L., & Friedman, J. M. (1994). Positional cloning of the mouse obese gene and its human homologue. *Nature, 372,* 425–432. (10)

Zhao, Z., & Davis, M. (2004). Fear-potentiated startle in rats is mediated by neurons in the deep layers of the superior colliculus/deep mesencephalic nucleus of the rostral midbrain through the glutamate non-NMDA receptors. *Journal of Neuroscience, 24,* 10326–10334. (12)

Zheng, B., Larkin, D. W., Albrecht, U., Sun, Z. S., Sage, M., Eichele, G., et al. (1999). The *mPer2* gene encodes a functional component of the mammalian circadian clock. *Nature, 400,* 169–173. (9)

Zheng, H., Patterson, L. M., & Berthoud, H.-R. (2007). Orexin signaling in the ventral tegmental area is required for high-fat appetite induced by opioid stimulation of the nucleus accumbens. *Journal of Neuroscience, 27,* 11075–11082. (10)

Zhou, F., Zhu, X., Castellani, R. J., Stimmelmayr, R., Perry, G., Smith, M. A., et al. (2001). Hibernation, a model of neuroprotection. *American Journal of Pathology, 158,* 2145–2151. (9)

Zhou, Q., Homma, K. J., & Poo, M. (2004). Shrinkage of dendritic spines associated with long-term depression of hippocampal synapses. *Neuron, 44,* 749–757. (13)

Zhu, Y., Fenik, P., Zhen, G., Mazza, E., Kelz, M., Aston-Jones, G., et al. (2007). Selective loss of catecholaminergic wake-active neurons in a murine sleep apnea model. *Journal of Neuroscience, 27,* 10060–10071. (9)

Ziegler, J. C., & Goswami, U. (2005). Reading acquisition, developmental dyslexia, and skilled reading across languages: A psycholinguistic grain size theory. *Psychological Bulletin, 131,* 3–29. (14)

Zihl, J., von Cramon, D., & Mai, N. (1983). Selective disturbance of movement vision after bilateral brain damage. *Brain, 106,* 313–340. (6)

Zipser, B. D., Johanson, C. E., Gonzalez, L., Berzin, T. M., Tavares, R., Hulette, C. M., et al. (2006). Microvascular injury and blood-brain barrier leakage in Alzheimer's disease. *Neurobiology of Aging, 28,* 977–986. (2)

Zola, S. M., Squire, L. R., Teng, E., Stefanacci, L., Buffalo, E. A., & Clark, R. E. (2000). Impaired recognition memory in monkeys after damage limited to the hippocampal region. *Journal of Neuroscience, 20,* 451–463. (13)

Zorrilla, E. P., Luborsky, L., McKay, J. R., Rosenthal, R., Houldin, A., Tax, A., et al. (2001). The relationship of depression and stressors to immunological assays: A meta-analytic review. *Brain, Behavior, and Immunity, 15,* 199–226. (12)

Zorzi, M., Priftis, K., & Umiltà, C. (2002). Neglect disrupts the mental number line. *Nature, 417,* 138. (14)

Zou, Z., Horowitz, L. F., Montmayeur, J.-P., Snapper, S., & Buck, L. B. (2001). Genetic tracing reveals a stereotyped sensory map in the olfactory cortex. *Nature, 414,* 173–179. (7)

Zubieta, J.-K., Ketter, T. A., Bueller, J. A., Xu, Y., Kilbourn, M. R., Young, E. A., et al. (2003). Regulation of human affective responses by anterior cingulate and limbic μ-opioid neurotransmission. *Archives of General Psychiatry, 60,* 1145–1153. (7)

Zuccato, C., Ciammola, A., Rigamonti, D., Leavitt, B. R., Goffredo, D., Conti, L., et al. (2001). Loss of huntingtin-mediated BDNF gene transcription in Huntington's disease. *Science, 293,* 493–498. (8)

Zucconi, G. G., Cipriani, S., Balgkouranidou, I., & Scattoni, R. (2006). "One night" sleep deprivation stimulates hippocampal neurogenesis. *Brain Research Bulletin, 69,* 375–381. (15)

Zucker, K. J., Bradley, S. J., Oliver, G., Blake, J., Fleming, S., & Hood, J. (1996). Psychosexual development of women with congenital adrenal hyperplasia. *Hormones and Behavior, 30,* 300–318. (11)

Zuckerman, L, Rehavi, M., Nachman, R., & Weiner, I. (2003). Immune activation during pregnancy in rats leads to a post-pubertal emergence of disrupted latent inhibition, dopaminergic hyperfunction, and altered limbic morphology in the offspring: A novel neurodevelopmental model of schizophrenia. *Neuropsychopharmacology, 28,* 1778–1789. (15)

Zurif, E. B. (1980). Language mechanisms: A neuropsychological perspective. *American Scientist, 68,* 305–311. (14)

Name Index

Subject Index/Glossary

Note: Italicized page numbers refer to figures, illustrations, and tables.